Starting IX:

A Franchise-by-Franchise Breakdown of Baseball's Best Players

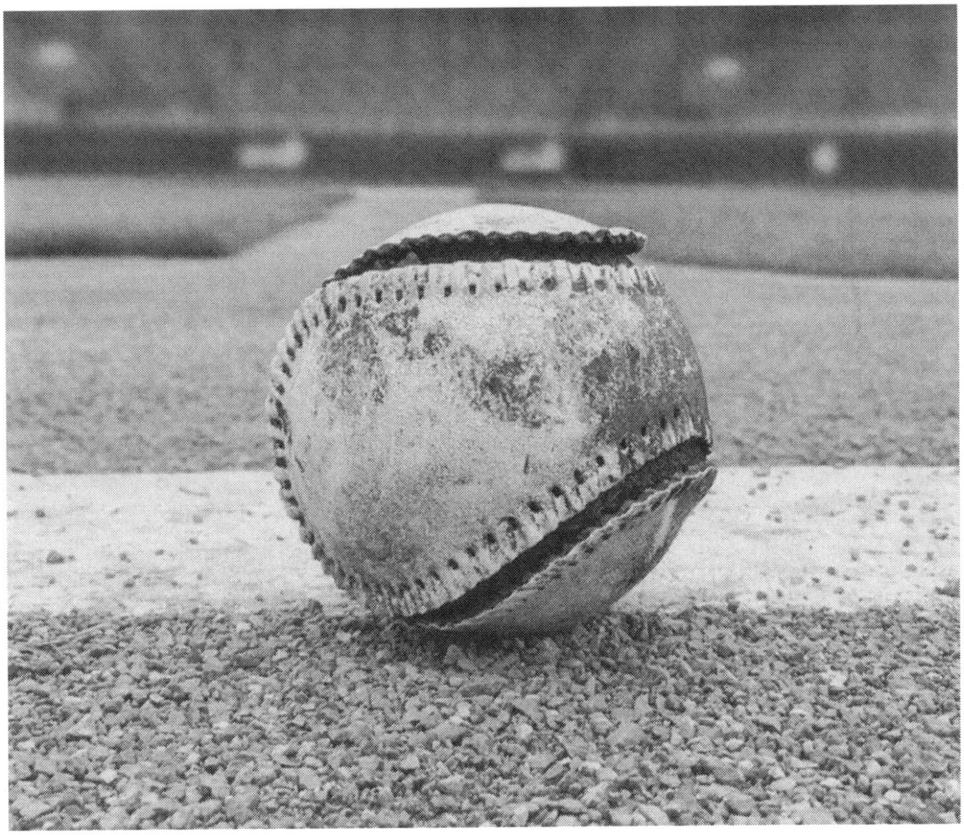

Jim Turvey

Cover illustration by David Dyke

Inside cover photo from Creative Commons; "The Franchise Starting IX's" page photo and "A final note" page photos from Baseball Hall of Fame.

The author gratefully acknowledges the Baseball Hall of Fame, Supah Fans, Baseball Reference, Creative Commons, and Detroit Athletic for permission to use their photos in this book.

All other photos as credited.

A CIP record is available from the Library of Congress

403 pages

ISBN: 978-0-9996454-0-6

Table of Contents

Introduction

The main question this book is answering is: if every team in baseball could create a starting lineup of the best players in their franchise history, what would that team look like?

The process of writing this behemoth began when I was just out of college and had just moved away from my home state of Vermont for the first time.

That's not really true.

It really began in 1996, when I was six years old, and nearly broke my ankle hopping on the "Core Four" Yankees' bandwagon. I would later say that the reason I chose the Yankees as my preferred team was that my father is a Yankee fan (true), but let's be honest, six-year-olds are hard-core bandwagoners. How many six-year-olds do you know that like the trendy underdog team? Zero, that's how many. To be fair, I grew up in Vermont where nearly everyone is either a Yankee fan or a Red Sox fan (probably 70-30 Red Sox), and I did display an early predisposition for hating the Red Sox, as even my punk-ass three-year-old self was furious that the Red Sox beat the Mariners when I went to a Boston-Seattle game in Fenway. I was three years old! Given that my mother is a Red Sox fan, that didn't go over well. However, she couldn't complain, because as an avid baseball lover herself (my mother is where I draw my love of baseball from, more so than my father from whom I gained a love of all sports), she was just happy to see another true lover of the game. I always joke that my first love was baseball, but that's probably a little unfair to my family. Baseball was, however, my first true hobby, and that hobby grew quickly into a love, and watching the sport on TV was no longer enough.

I began to devour baseball card packs and scour garage sales for cheap cards, even if they were those waste of space Fleer sets from the `80s. When my dad showed me his old collection (pretty much every card from 1966-1973 and some great ones from his older siblings dating back to the previous decade), I don't think I left my room, except to attend school, for about a month.

It wasn't the front of the cards that entranced me; it was the backs of the cards.

I would lay the cards out on my bedroom floor and sort them by any means possible. I would make stacks of hitters with 30-home run seasons; stacks of pitchers who reached 200 strikeouts in a year; rookies I thought would be good (damn you, Eric Munson), and rookies I thought wouldn't pan out (at least Josh Beckett kind of sucked by the end of his career). A few years later, I discovered *MLB Showdown*, a baseball card game based on dice rolling, and I pretty much kissed every dollar of allowance or lawn-mowing money good-bye for a three-to-four-year stretch. I played incessantly, and I just couldn't have enough of this vastly underrated Strat-O-Matic knock-off. The next obsession to come along was fantasy baseball; I'll save you the details there because nothing is worse than someone recounting her/his fantasy baseball history. The underlying constant to all these forms of baseball with which I had dalliances were the numbers, the statistics.[1] Baseball has a unique history with statistics, one so intertwined that there will be a brief introductory section on baseball's history with statistics complete with a mini-glossary in just a few pages.

However, as I grew older, I began to slow down with my all-day baseball card dalliances, venturing out to see the big, bad world in my baseball version of Rumspringa. As a result, baseball went on the back burner for the time being. To say the sport was totally out of my consciousness is not fair, and I think I have had a girlfriend or two that would scoff at the fact that I consider my late high school and college-level of interest in baseball as "being put on the back burner," but in comparison to other times in my life, it certainly wasn't the be-all and end-all it sometimes has been.

After college, I managed to find a nice equilibrium (thanks to a great girlfriend and steady job) and my "first love" found itself in my life again. I started picking up old baseball books, books I hadn't looked at in a decade and found myself once again getting lost in their pages. Around this time, I got the idea that would later become this book. I was surprised no one had created a player-by-player breakdown of each team's history, and so I began the research that would become the foundation of this book. Of course, after having done a good deal of the research, being the novice researcher I was at the time, I finally stumbled on *Rob Neyer's Big Book of Lineups*. For those who haven't read it, Neyer selects first and second all-time teams for each franchise along with a few other select lineups, such as the "All-Bust Team," the "Gold Glove Team," and the "All-Rookie Team."

Here I was, looking at what looked an awful lot like "my" idea, and it was already written by one of baseball's most famous writers – well, no wonder no one else had written about it. I decided to push on through because more than a decade has passed, and there are a lot of great players in this book that don't appear in Neyer's book. Also, because so much is written on all aspects of baseball, a lot of the time what is written doesn't matter as much as who writes it and the tone in which they are able to contribute to the illustrious anthology of baseball writing. So, in the following pages, I'm going to try my best to bring my own tone (the Icarus of humor) and voice (~~mildly~~ incredibly schizophrenic) to one of baseball's oldest traditions – comparing old vs. new, righty vs. lefty, and Mantle vs. DiMaggio.

The metaphor of standing on the shoulders of giants dates back to Isaac Newton but is a truly timeless sentiment.

---

[1] I even once posited that my own personal version of heaven was just a database of information on my life. Like how many times I watched the "I like turtles" video on YouTube, or when I first starting liking tomatoes, or whom I texted with most, cumulatively, in my life.

For a history major such as myself, the process of building off of what those in your field have accomplished is paramount. That's how writing this book felt. The origins of "standing on the shoulders of giants" paints the picture of a dwarf perched atop the giant's shoulders. In the case of this book, the metaphor may have to be a dwarf just hoping to be invited to the party of giants and get to be in the presence of said giants. Giants like Bill James, Rob Neyer, Tom Tango (maybe even getting to learn Tango's real name at said party of giants), and countless others. There were numerous times during my writing and research when I thought I had come up with something incredibly clever or possibly eye-opening to the field of baseball statistics. However, nearly every time that happened, a few weeks would pass, and I would stumble upon research from Ben Lindbergh of *The Ringer* or Scott Lindholm of *Beyond the Box Score* that had already solved the same issue I thought I had been the first to solve. This simply speaks to the incredible talent of baseball writers today (and throughout history), a guild in which I would be honored to be able to claim membership.

* * *

Baseball history is filled to the brim with stories. Tall tales and legends alike, told about men who seem bigger than history itself. Ruthian has entered not just the baseball vernacular but also the nation's vernacular to describe a tremendous feat, and if someone at the office tells you your latest presentation was a real home run, you know that you did a good job. (While simultaneously wondering what 1950s movie they stepped out of.)

Why is it that baseball has this place in our hearts?

For many, it is because of our association of baseball with childhood. "As children we were not only allowed to play baseball every day, we were expected to. It made us laugh and cry, win and lose; it broke our hearts and made us feel like champions. And it brought us together. Baseball was life in those wonderful days," author John Grisham has reminisced. Little League is practically a rite of passage in our nation, and the sport's association with summers, at an age when summers meant not a care in the world, is undeniable.

For others, it is either a real, or in some cases adopted, sense of nostalgia for a *simpler time*. Leave it to James Earl Jones in *Field of Dreams* to sum it up perfectly: "The one constant through all the years has been baseball. America has rolled by like an army of steamrollers. It's been erased like a blackboard, rebuilt, and erased again. But baseball has marked the time. This field, this game, is a part of our past. It reminds us of all that once was good, and what could be again." Former president Herbert Hoover once said that the sport had a bigger impact on American life than any institution outside of religion. This may have been closer to the truth in Hoover's time, but the sport does have a unique relationship with this country.

To steal an observation from the excellent book *Baseball & Philosophy*, home plate is the shape of, and named after, home. This doesn't seem coincidental so much as symbolic, and *getting home safe* is a feeling to which any of us can relate. The point of baseball is to make it around the bases more often than the other team, a journey made often by the Cobbs and Hendersons in baseball history, but it is still one that intrigues the sport's fans. As Joe Kraus went on to say in *Baseball & Philosophy*, "Put differently, home doesn't become meaningful until you have experienced the risk that lies in front of it." Karus compared the journey to the idea of the monomyth, a trope as old as *The Odyssey* itself.

Part of what has kept my love of baseball going strong is the allure of going to a baseball game in person. Live baseball has a certain feel to it like no other sport or even event. Maybe it's the fact that even though the Yankees are trying their best to say otherwise, tickets in the bleachers are still reasonable enough for most people to afford if they so wish. Maybe it's the fact that baseball is played during the summer, meaning not only is the weather typically nice, but we also all have the positive connotation of school vacation mixed in with our memories of going to baseball games. Maybe it's the magical aroma of hot dogs, or the singsong calls from vendors walking up and down the aisles offering refreshments from the warm weather. Maybe it's that the game's pace allows time for some thought. Whether it's thoughts of strategy, statistics, or the girl wearing the sundress two sections over, there's something for everybody.

One of the most telling factors about attending a baseball game is "The Rick Turvey Test." Unlike myself, my brother did not inherit any interest of sports from my mother and father. In fact, I think I doubled up on all the sports interest leaving him with absolutely none. There are, however, three sporting events that can grab his attention: the Super Bowl (although this is mostly because of the commercials, so that doesn't really count), the end of televised basketball games (for intense sports drama it really doesn't get much better than that, plus my barbaric yawps made it difficult to focus on anything else when we were on growing up), and baseball games in person.

It was quite the struggle getting him to go to my football or basketball games when we were kids, but if it was a baseball game he was there. This may have been because he could read on the bleachers at them,[2] but I think that this actually is part of the draw. Baseball games have an unbelievably calming effect on people. At football or basketball games, there is so much tension in the crowd that it is palpable, and although it can lead to great moments of celebration it also can be a stressful environment; baseball games seem to have the opposite effect.

My friends and I have spent the last few summers going around on an extended tour of all 30 baseball stadiums. Obviously, there are certain stadiums that stand out architecturally or aesthetically, but one of the main factors we discussed

[2] (Insert "baseball is so boring people have to read during it" joke here.)

after each game (and the thing that seems to stick out the most when remembering the stadiums) is the environment. U.S. Cellular Field where the White Sox play is not an egregiously ugly stadium, but it ranks near the bottom of all of our rankings because of their bizarre prejudice against certain sections of the stadium and the fan base that surrounded us.[3] On the other hand, the Oakland Coliseum is not known as a nice stadium, but it was one of my favorites to think back on, because even though the A's lost, the environment was one of the most satisfying and friendly and just plain entertaining of any stadium we attended. And isn't the real point of baseball, and sports as a whole, to entertain us? It's hard not to get lost in the fact that our team winning is important, and tightly-contested games are fun to watch, but baseball often allows us a constant entertainment that just no other sport can provide. This is really just a long drawn out, and – now that I re-read it – hippy-sounding way of saying that baseball is an awesome and unique sport to be able to see in person.[4]

It is likely because of the sport's approachability, as well as its long history, that the sport has as steeped a history of myths as it does. It seems like, as a nation, we know more about the 1950s Dodgers than the 1950s presidents. It's easier to find a biography of Mickey Mantle than Walter Cronkite, and all these texts are filled with stories and stories of baseball legends and the feats they accomplished – a seemingly endless well of baseball stories from which to draw.

* * *

Baseball's history is also filled with numbers. Numbers so famous they don't even need context: 56; 714; 1.12; 511; 2,130; and later 2,632. When it comes to whether or not to give a player baseball's highest honor and induct him into the Hall of Fame, numbers like 3,000 or 300 are once again so prevalent that context need not apply.

In the book *Baseball & Philosophy*, Jay Bennett and Aryn Martin point out that it may not be a coincidence that baseball's history is so steeped in statistics. The exact origin of the sport has been debated and debated, and the only consensus is that there is no exact date or creator to which we can point (sorry, General Doubleday). However, it is clear that the sport grew in popularity in the post-Civil War United States, an era in which the country was undergoing a "second scientific revolution… in which quantification was a central feature." As such, men like Henry Chadwick created a relationship between baseball and statistics that would only grow stronger as the sport grew. Chadwick created the first box score and helped to popularize not only the sport, but the primal statistics he created alongside the sport, namely: batting average, ERA, and fielding range.

Whatever it is about the sport – maybe it's the fact that its origins came during the quantification revolution; maybe it's the fact that baseball's 162-game season offers a grander sample size for statistics to show their true colors; hell, if you're a cynic the case could be made that baseball is such a slow game that fans needed something to do during the game, thus the popularization of fans keeping score in the stands,[5] regardless – baseball and statistics go together like cocaine and waffles.[6] As Robert S. Wieder put it in 1981, "Baseball fans are junkies, and their heroin is the statistic."

Although the current revolution of statistics, often referred to as the "Moneyball" era of statistics,[7] has brought the sport to an entirely different sphere of statistics, baseball's relationship with statistics has always been robust. That relationship has arguably never been stronger, as some might say baseball appears to be reaching what Bill James referred to as a "Chernobyl of statistics."

"Lies, damned lies, and statistics" is a phrase popularized by Mark Twain, but the far more accurate phrase would be "Statistics don't lie. People do." Statistics can be manipulated into just about any form the statistician wants, which means that keen fans have to have their wits about them, and they need their analytical hats fitted snuggly atop their baseball crowns when parsing the information available to baseball fans today. If you want to be a bit condescending about it, you could repeat what Bill James once said: "Information is not to be held accountable for every misleading claim that somebody can derive from it." In most cases, though, the "Rob Base and D.J. EZ Rock Rule" can be implemented – It Takes Two. The statistician presenting the skewed statistic and the fan absorbing the skewed statistic both play a part in the crime. In my original notes, there was a quote I enjoyed relating to this phenomenon: "Statistics are actually life's most dangerous double-sided sword. If statisticians abuse their powers, and inquisitive minds misinterpret them, there can be almost nothing deadlier." I probably shouldn't be using this quote because I have no idea whom give credit to, but it seemed too pertinent to leave out.[8] And it's true. For statistics to be used to their full potential, they need both disseminators and receptors who are unbiased, and do not have an agenda that could lead to false conclusions. True objectivity is difficult when involving sports, an arena basically created for fanhood, but essential to truly understanding the game. With great statistics comes great

---

[3] This is not to say all White Sox fans are bad, in fact, one of my best friends will probably be quite annoyed by that comment (sorry, DSP), but the people we were near that day were pretty miserable.

[4] Groundbreaking work, I know.

[5] Unsurprisingly, this aspect is part of the beauty of the game in my humble opinion.

[6] This is the first of what will be many, many, probably-too-many strange movie references in this book. If there is ever a sentence that looks like I had a stroke while writing it, just google it and there's a good chance it's from a sitcom, a Will Ferrell movie, or *Kiss Kiss Bang Bang*. Case in point, this bad boy is from *Talladega Nights*. By the way, *Kiss Kiss Bang Bang* is criminally underrated; I'm going to prove that point by slipping nine references to *KKBB* into this book. Challenge accepted. Let's start by saying, "My name is [Jim Turvey], I'll be your narrator… Welcome to the party." [*KKBB* no. 1]

[7] I have my qualms about this name, as the folks at *Baseball Prospectus* and *FanGraphs* were far more responsible for the public's consumption of more advanced analytics than Billy Beane and Michael Lewis, but "Moneyball" does roll off the tongue quite nicely.

[8] There's about a one in a thousand chance I made it up, seeing as I couldn't find a source in a brief query, but that sounds too poetic for this jabroni.

responsibility.

That being said, this book will not simply be a book of statistics. If you wanted to look at each team's franchise leaders in wins above replacement (WAR), a statistic that will indeed be used frequently in this book, Baseball-Reference has that page for you; you don't need this book.

This book will also not simply be a book of baseball stories. What this book is hoping to do, and I believe is able to achieve, is a symbiosis of the two. Narrative and metric. Ruth's called shot and weighted runs created plus. FIP and Pipp, if you will. These will all be entangled in the aforementioned smorgasbord of baseball information.

That being said, there will be numerous statistics used throughout this book, and although these statistics are great, I've been reading a lot of Chuck Klosterman lately, so let's dive down the rabbit hole a bit.

Stats, man

This section was originally a 4-5 page explanation of all the baseball statistics in existence. They were broken down into four categories: the "Back of the baseball card" category, e.g. games played, home runs, etc.; the "OK, you should know these, but here's a friendly reminder" category, e.g. isolated power, strikeouts per nine, etc.; the "We're going to need a bigger baseball card" category e.g. home run rate, BABIP, FIP, etc.; and the "Cellar Door" category, e.g. OPS+, win probability added, and WAR.

A few things became obvious as more of the book was written, however.

Only a handful of the non-obvious statistics are used more than once or twice in the book (we will cover those in a second), and it was just tedious as hell to read through an explanation of games played. If you don't know the difference between at bats and plate appearances, A) You're probably only reading this because you are a friend of mine, curious as to how I spend my free time, and B) It really doesn't matter that much.

Certainly not enough to waste 4-5 pages on definitions of stats that almost assuredly would turn off 70 percent of readers who just started the book. Hell, my mother, who (bless her heart) will read *anything* I write, couldn't get through the section, and, when I was proofreading my own work, my eyes glazed over about a half dozen times. I don't think there will be any stats to really confuse even borderline baseball fans, but if there are, they should have an explanation with them when used the first time in the book. Also, there's this thing called Google you have on your electronic device of choice. It can help you.

With that being said, let's take a brief look at (just a few, I promise) stats that may need clearing up:

The Plus/Minus Crew: OPS+, ERA+: These are statistics you know, but adjusted for context. (Brief reminder, just in case: OPS is on-base percentage plus slugging percentage.) They put the raw statistic (ERA, OPS) on a 100-point scale, with 100 being league average. **For the + statistics, every integer above 100 means one percent better than league average**. For example, when Ryan Howard had an OPS+ 167 in his 2006 MVP season, OPS+ judged that he hit 67 percent better than a league-average hitter in 2006. In the same vein, when Howard's teammate, Cliff Lee, posted an ERA+ of 167 in 2008, his ERA was 67 percent better than league average at run prevention (ERA) that season. The statistic also adjusts for the ballparks played in by the player, as well as opponents faced, which can lead to players on the San Diego Padres and Colorado Rockies seeing big differences from their raw numbers due to the nature of their home stadiums.

The Above Replacement Crew: wins above replacement (WAR), offensive wins above replacement (oWAR), defensive wins above replacement (dWAR):

The modern idea of valuing a player in terms of "wins," or WAR (wins above replacement), is one that has its origins very much in Bill James' writing. This idea of a player being worth "wins" is very different than the typical Wins that we think of in connection with baseball players. Typically, Wins (in the old-school and now somewhat pejorative sense) meant how many times a pitcher went at least five innings with a lead and the team held on to win the actual game. WAR (or "wins") is looking more to judge a player's value to his team over the course of an entire season (and then, cumulatively, a career). This player can certainly be a pitcher, but it is not limited to the Kings of the Mound. When you think about it, it makes sense to question the fact that Justin Verlander was worth 24 of his team's 95 wins in 2011. Verlander is great, but an MLB roster is made up of 25 players, 14-16 of whom are significant contributors. Plus, there was never any way to compare how much a pitcher, like Verlander, was worth compared to a hitter, like his teammate, 2011 Miguel Cabrera. Cabrera had 0 Wins in 2011, but he was worth 7.5 "wins." Verlander, on the other hand, was great, but instead of being worth 24 Wins, he was worth 8.4 "wins." And because "wins" are actually far more valuable to baseball fans than Wins, we will start referring to "wins," from Wins Above Replacement, as wins – no more quotation marks.

There are different ways of measuring a player in terms of wins, but they all feed into a bigger pool of value statistics (along with batting and fielding wins) that are the ingredients to creating overall value statistics like WAR. This idea will be discussed often throughout the book, so eventually it should become second nature to you if it isn't already.

Wins above average (WAA): The main principle of WAR and WAA is that those wins are not in a vacuum, but rather in comparison to the league. WAR tries to measure a player in comparison to their replacement. As *FanGraphs* puts it: "If this player got injured and their team had to replace them with a freely available minor leaguer or a AAAA player from their bench,[9] how much value would the team be losing?" WAA simply asks the same question, but instead of being replaced by an available minor leaguer, the player is being replaced by a league-average major league player, so the wins are deflated. In 2011, Verlander was worth 6.1 WAA, or 6.1 wins over the average MLB pitcher; Cabrera was worth 5.1 wins over the average MLB first baseman. These WAR and WAA totals are also dependent on the position the player plays. But we'll cover that in more detail later in the book. This is the introductory part. Just dip your toes in for now.

Time to address the boogeyman in the room. Yes, WAR is a flawed statistic that can be abused when used as a simple end-of-argument statement. Any metric that would potentially be this powerful couldn't have two different renditions that vary as much as the two main versions (Baseball-Reference and *FanGraphs*[10]) do. For example, in 2013, Baseball-Reference had Mike Trout worth 9.3 wins, whereas *FanGraphs* had Trout worth 10.5 wins. The biggest differential at this point in calculating WAR for position players is the fielding aspects of WAR.[11] There is even more variance in pitcher WAR, as the base of the formula is different for Baseball-Reference (which strictly uses runs allowed) and *FanGraphs* (which uses defense-independent metrics instead). But like I said, this is the nitty-gritty.

I would say, with 100 percent certainty, that by the year 2025, the calculation for WAR (especially in the defensive portion) will be noticeably different than as of when this is published (post-2017 season). And by the year 2035 or maybe even earlier, there's a very good chance that smart baseball minds will be using another metric instead of WAR entirely.[12] That's the nature of statistical progress. But for now, WAR is indeed the best metric to compare players across generations and leagues. Don't believe the troglodytes who say otherwise. It won't be the sole comparison factor, but it's a nice one to have.

Ugghhh, PED's

Look, I hate that this has to be a section in the introduction as much as the next guy, in fact probably 100 times more than the next guy, but it is such a hot button topic that it simply has to be talked about before we start.

The story of baseball and performance-enhancing drugs goes back further than most would think. As far back as the early 1970s[13] Major League Baseball had to implement strategies to limit anabolic steroid use after Congress passed the Comprehensive Drug Abuse Prevention and Control Act of 1970. However, MLB's policy was poorly policed and very ineffective. Even when Congress got stricter with the Anabolic Steroid Control Act of 1990, Major League Baseball still didn't have a strict set of laws regarding anabolic steroid use. Sure, MLB aligned itself with Congress, but with no legitimate system testing players and no recourse should players be caught using, possessing, or distributing steroids,[14] the policy was the moral equivalent of Jack Sparrow's interpretation of the Pirate Code – it was more like a guideline, anyway.

Like many phenomena, anabolic steroids were not completely understood in their nascent years. Whether certain steroids should be legal, over-the-counter drugs was a matter of debate among scientists, throwing yet another wrench into the whole policing-of-steroids dilemma. Major League Baseball took the first real step towards combating the problem in the 2002 Collective Bargaining Agreement when the Player's Association finally agreed to allow a more comprehensive response from MLB to anabolic drug testing. The reader should note that 2002 is after infamous steroid users Mark McGwire and Barry Bonds had broken their "tainted" single-season home run records.

Of course, it was right around this time that baseball started to catch heat for their players looking like bodybuilders, and commissioner Bud Selig acted quickly. Yes, these transgressions probably deserved the punishments they eventually received, but only if those potential punishments had been set before the incidences occurred. Bonds, McGwire, and the several other pre-2002 PED users were dragged in front of judges and made the fall men for a faulty MLB steroid policy system that was the real problem.

Seeing as this is not my field of study, however, if the reader is interested in a true history of baseball and anabolic steroids, they should go to *Game of Shadows* or *Blood Sport*, far superior accounts of baseball's history with steroids.

For the context of this book, all that has to be parsed is: "How much did steroids help the players that were using them?" and, "Should the morality of enhancing one's performance be held against a player when that player is being judged from a historical perspective?" Let's tackle these questions one at a time.

---

[9] Basically the worst player on the 25-man roster.

[10] And to a lesser (read: have to pay for) extent, *Baseball Prospectus'* WARP, a third version of wins above replacement.

[11] For a comprehensive breakdown of the differences simply go to http://www.Baseball-Reference.com/about/war_explained_comparison.shtml.

[12] I've always thought it is interesting to wonder what would happen if a brilliant baseball mind came up with a truly remarkable value metric, one that was indeed better than WAR or anything else we've ever seen, but it said that Coco Crisp was better than Mike Trout. Would it simply be scrapped because of that? Is "common knowledge" our biggest kryptonite? Do we simply need to open our minds more? How can I re up on this weed?

[13] And that's ignoring the legendary Pud Galvin, who drank an "elixir of Brown-Sequard," which consisted of testosterone drained from animal gonads – all in an at attempt to gain an extra advantage. That was in the year of our Lord, 1889!

[14] Commissioner Fay Vincent tried to ban Steve Howe from MLB in 1991 after his seventh failed drug test, but the Players Association appealed and overturned his decision.

"How much did steroids help the players that were using them?"

Unfortunately, for such an important question the answer is decidedly undecided. One might think that with the emphasis that the game's historians have placed on PED use there would be conclusive evidence as to just how much PED use helps players, but once again, the waters are murky. There are simply too many variables for any baseball researcher to wade through in order to get an accurate result. There's the matter of how difficult it is to project what a player would have done had he not taken any PEDs; which PEDs what players were using at what time; the small sample size attached to an individual player in an individual season; and how much the simple placebo effect of confidence gained from taking PEDs changes the player. It's all too much to account for entirely.

The most complete study on the effect of steroids on baseball players' statistics was Nate Silver's "What Do Statistics Tell Us About Steroids?" chapter in *Baseball Between the Numbers*, a thorough study of weighted average change in statistics (before and after) of pitchers and hitters who were caught using steroids. Silver found that there were no significant statistical gains from the players in his survey, and he ended up with the sentiment that "perhaps more than any other issue we've explored in this book, the effect of steroids is a subject that we should understand far better in 10 years' time than we do now." Well, 10 years have passed since Silver wrote that, and there is still very little known about the statistical effects of PEDs.

One way in which baseball researchers could learn much more on the subject is if MLB and the players who have tested positive for PEDs would come forward with more information. Peter Keating of *ESPN the Magazine* put forward what I think is a great idea. He wants MLB to give amnesty to any player willing to disclose exactly what PEDs he was using during an exact timeframe. As Keating says, tests that measure PED performance increases are unreliable because companies (understandably) don't want to put patients at risk with their experiments. However, the players who have used PEDs offer a perfect set of data if only we could have access to their usage patterns, etc. As Keating puts it, this would allow some redemption for players who did cheat, and it would allow baseball fans to get a feel for just how adjusted those tainted numbers from the PED era need to be.

Of course, there would still be plenty of issues with this data (for instance, trusting the players to be 100 percent truthful and/or remember perfectly what drugs were used at what exact time), but it would certainly be a step in the right direction. For now, however, there really isn't great data to determine how much of an impact PEDs make on a player, and as such, it is unfair to make assumptions. With that in mind, although it is not ideal, players who tested positive for PEDs will not have their statistics lessened in this book outside of the use of era-adjusting statistics that make McGwire's and Bonds' home run totals slightly depreciated due to the home-run-heavy era in which they played.

"Should the morality of enhancing one's performance be held against a player when that player is being judged from a historical perspective?"

That answer is a little more controversial.

Athletes, throughout history, have always looked for any advantage possible. And this isn't just athletes. It is human nature to use any edge available to us to our advantage. I could make a silly comparison like the express lane checkout at the grocery store as a SEA (shopping-enhancing advantage), but that clearly isn't in the same realm as taking performance-enhancing drugs. However, is it such a stretch to make the comparison between PEDs and fudging a bit of one's resume? Sure, we would never tell our kids to do it, and it makes us feel a bit guilty, but if rounding a 2.87 GPA up to an even 3.0, or saying that you "managed food distribution" instead of "roller-skated burgers out to folks' cars" helps the resume look a bit better, why not do it?

That "why not?" question is essential. With such an unclear policy for so long, it's hard to blame many of the baseball players who used steroids in the 1990s. (Even if that is the default setting for the general population right now.) There was a poor system testing them, and although there was a vague idea of "drugs that promote muscle growth in a manner similar to testosterone" being disallowed in baseball, there was also no real punishment for using PEDs. The line gets a bit blurrier with the 21st-century enhancers, but the precedent for baseball players toeing the line when it came to advantages they could get is as old as the game itself.

That's the irony of so many of these "old-school" baseball writers having such a hissy fit about PED users. These same writers laud players like Ty Cobb who embodied the true spirit of the game so much that he sharpened his cleats to put the fear of God into shortstops trying to turn two on him. These same writers then vilify Bonds and McGwire for taking one advantage they thought they could get away with.

Express this sentiment to the "old-school"[15] writers, and they may come back with something along the lines of how the Bondses and McGwires of baseball tainted the game by breaking baseball's most hallowed records, and that those numbers mean nothing now. How about the fact that Bob Gibson's record 1.12 ERA came in a year that pitching was so dominant they lowered the mound from 15 inches to 10 inches after the season? Or how about the fact that Hank Aaron played the latter half of his career in his era's equivalent of Coors Field?

Of course, those players didn't break any rules to enhance their statistics, but if the argument is strictly about the

[15] And I put this in quotes because not every writer who considers her/himself "old school" agrees with this sentiment, and therefore shouldn't be lumped in with the asinine ones that do.

hallowed nature of those memorable numbers, the fact remains that those records were partly the result of an enhanced environment for the player.

All of this doesn't even mention the fact that the "PED era" is far from the only era in which performance-enhancing drugs were used. Amphetamines, more commonly referred to as "greenies," are often mentioned as the first true PEDs in baseball history, and they were popped more frequently than sunflower seeds in 1970s MLB locker rooms. Greenies date back to well before the PED era, and without knowing just how much these performance enhancers impacted the players using them, it is once again nearly impossible to dole out arbitrary scorn and statistical punishment.

Really, the PED era opened the eyes of the public to the prevalence of drugs in professional sport, and hopefully increased awareness of just how damaging these supposed enhancers can be to the human body. To attempt any sort of retroactive judgment on the players seems naïve and petty. The best solution is simply to move forward and hope that players in the future use this era as a warning for how to take care of their own bodies.

In this book, PED users will not be punished (with one exception), since most of the metrics that will be used can account for era adjustment, and if as many hitters were juicing as baseball writers would have you believe, then it's just as challenging to outperform the other juicers across the league.[16]

The Process

At this point, the reader probably has a very rough idea of what the book will look like. Unless, of course, you simply flipped to the franchise you support, skimmed through each player's bio, and jumped to the conclusion: "How on earth was (insert childhood hero) not the (insert favorite franchise)'s (insert position)?!!?!" In that case, you may have some understanding of how the book is set up. For the good people who *didn't* do that, here's a brief rundown.

Each Starting IX is divided by franchise, with the franchises appearing in tiers as rated by the accumulated nature of each team's roster. This was no easy task in and of itself, as there are multiple ways to define "franchise" as the word applies to baseball history. Rob Neyer, for example, separated the Philadelphia and Oakland versions of the Athletics in his *Big Book of Baseball Lineups*. However, for my purposes, I used each of the 30 modern franchise's entire history, meaning that the Oakland and Philadelphia (and even Kansas City) Athletics' players were all put into the same pool. This is how Baseball-Reference lists each franchise, and since that site was an essential source for franchise leaders, etc., that is how this book will be set up. It does mean things get a little funky when it comes to teams like the Atlanta Braves, who have about 20 iterations of their name throughout team history, or the Washington Senators who actually make appearances in two different modern franchises. (Don't worry, it will all makes sense.)

Within each franchise section, there is a brief team introduction with a topic spinning off from there, typically revolving around the club's history. There is a retro game diary or two sprinkled in (Minnesota Twins and Seattle Mariners), as well as rundowns on the best stadiums in baseball (Kansas City Royals), and a completely off-topic story about a middle-school Halloween party (Arizona Diamondbacks). Next up comes a player *bio* or *write-up* for each position on the diamond, starting with catcher and moving around the infield left to right. Then it's the same in the outfield. There is one utility hitter (which will be used in different ways throughout the book), and finally one starting pitcher and one closer. At the end of each team section, there is a chart with the statistics each Starting IX player accumulated *as a member of that specific franchise*.

And yes, Smart-Ass Reader, that means that there are 11 players on each franchise "Starting IX." I know how Roman numerals work, but nine is a magical baseball number; 11 isn't. Eleven is a magical soccer number, and maybe someday someone will write an excellent Starting XI book filled with the Premier League's best players in each club's history, but this is baseball; it's Starting IX. Sorry if that's confusing.

Getting back on track, the lengths of the aforementioned bios will vary in length from one word (second base in San Diego) to over 6,000 (center field in New York). In the event that two players are similarly qualified (more on qualifications in a second), there will be a tool-by-tool (power, speed, team success, etc.) breakdown of which player is more deserving. These battles can take place between legends of the game (third base in Atlanta/Milwaukee) or simply two similarly qualified dudes (closers in Seattle).

Let's circle back to those qualifications. In judging these teams, what a player contributed while in that franchise's uniform is all that matters. For instance, Babe Ruth may be the greatest player of all time, but he isn't going to be the Atlanta Braves' starting right fielder just because he made a 28-game pit stop with the franchise at the end of his career. In a less extreme example, Carlton Fisk split time almost directly between the Chicago White Sox and Boston Red Sox during his career. Although this shouldn't tarnish his legacy as a player, it definitely hurt his case to be either team's starting catcher in this book. Players are, however, allowed to appear on more than one franchise Starting IX, a feat a surprising number of players achieve. (One player makes it onto three different franchise Starting IX's, can you guess who?)

---

[16] The most vehement and well-written argument against PED users comes, not surprisingly, from *Sports Illustrated*'s Tom Verducci. Verducci is on record as not voting for any PED-related player because of the clean players he saw who perpetually lost out on roster spots to players who were willing to use PEDs. I agree with him on this insidious side of the PED era, I just don't agree with him on writing off baseball superstars from that PED era. I think Bonds would have been Bonds regardless, and those guys who were clean wouldn't be making appearances in this book even if they did juice up. Now, like many of the men I will quote in this book, Verducci has forgotten more about baseball than I will ever know, but this is my book so I'm setting the rules.

Therefore, the only statistics taken into account when deciding who would get the start at each position were the statistics from that one franchise. The only exception to that rule is if a player made the All-Star Game or won the MVP in season in which he was traded, that acknowledgement counted for both teams. For example, in 2011 Hunter Pence was a National League All-Star. He also was traded from Houston to Philadelphia on July 29, just a few weeks after the All-Star Game. In my process, however, that 2011 All-Star Game appearance counted for him when considering him for both franchises.

* * *

The hardest step in a project like this is often getting started. The task can seem so monumental that to actually start the process can seem more intimidating than facing Randy Johnson during the 1993 All-Star Game. What I ended up doing was using Baseball-Reference's "Franchise Encyclopedia" tool to look at the top 50 players in a few different categories (hits, home runs, WAR, wins, saves, games finished, ERA+) to create a matrix of eligible players at each position for the franchise. The matrix looked somewhat like a football "two-deep" where players were ranked by position with vital information next to each player. In many cases, the most qualified player at each position was obvious, but in the close cases, each player's Baseball-Reference page and SABR biography were analyzed side-by-side until a winner was decided based on statistics, as well as story. When even that couldn't break the tie, the matchup was deemed worthy of a me-stealing-from-Bill-Simmons-stealing-from-Dr.-Jack-style breakdown, which ended up in the book. I made my own decisions first, and then consulted outside sources, such as books that ranked individual franchise's best players of all time (or simply the best players of all time) to make sure players weren't missed somehow, or in case the numbers didn't paint a full portrait of the players that I knew less about coming into this project.

Sprinkled throughout the book, I will include bonus Starting IX lists, baseball and otherwise. These lists will be top nine lists, and will either be related to baseball directly (e.g. Starting IX of players who played in the wrong era), tangentially (e.g. Starting IX of baseball players' names that sound like movie characters), or not related to baseball at all (e.g. Starting IX of best TV characters of all time). The vast majority will be baseball-related, though. I promise.

* * *

As I worked on this project, I had a lot of different goals for this book. By the end, I think I came to the conclusion that while I'd love for this book to be the perfect mix between old-school baseball narrative-telling and new-school sabermetrics, what I really want is simply for this book to give readers some good ideas for lists they can make themselves. I want the reader to disagree with what I have decided so that if you're bored in English class, or bored waiting in line at the DMV, or bored during sex, you can start creating your own Starting IX of the best players to hail from our neighbors to the North, eh? That's what this book started as, and that's what I hope it becomes – a way to get so lost in your baseball thoughts that you forget all about your English teacher droning on about Macbeth, or the fact that there are 50 people in front of you in line to get your new license photo, or…. Well, let's just get started.

The Franchise Starting IX's

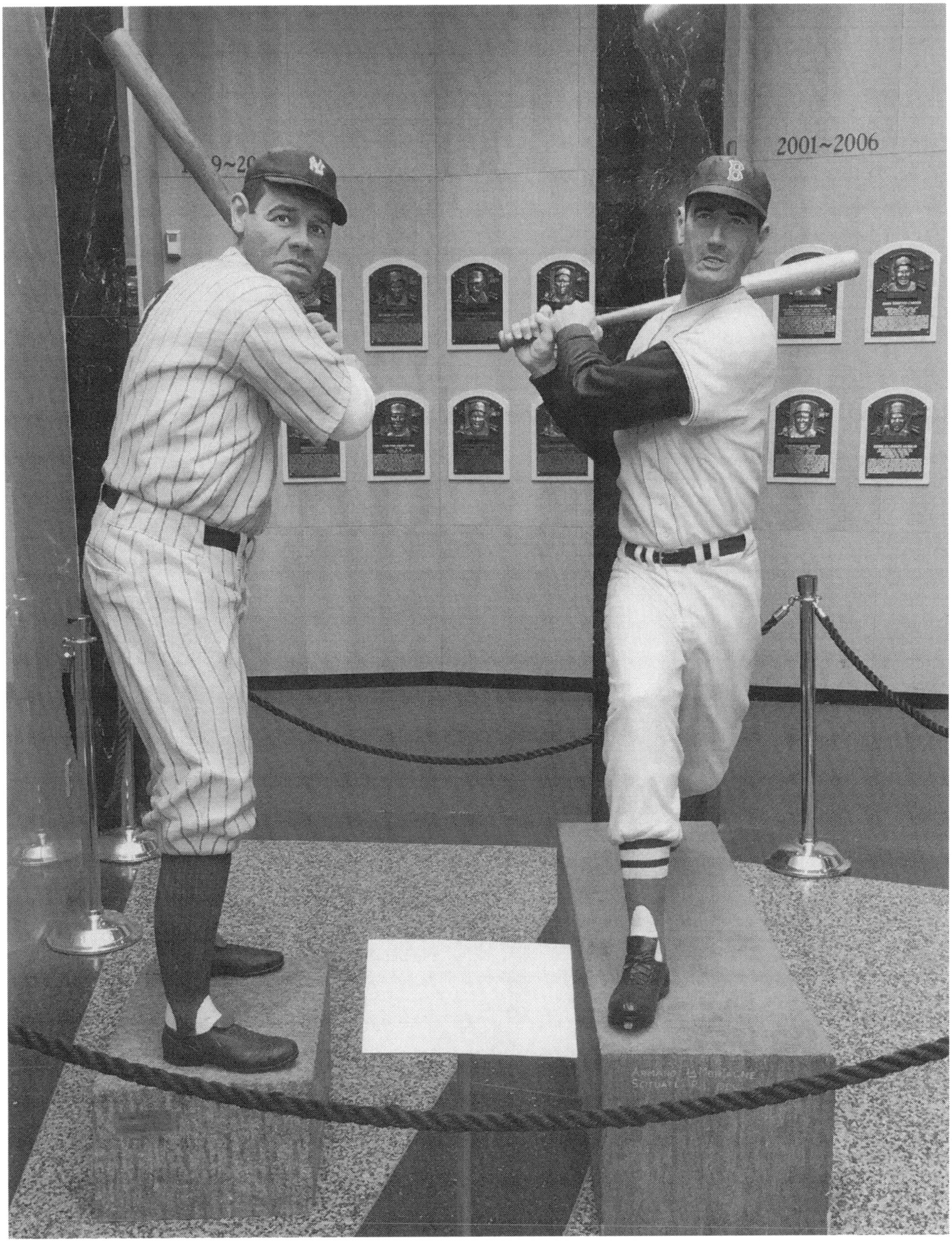

Tier One: Just not enough time

The four teams in the lowest tier have only been Major League Baseball teams a collective 90 years, less than each of the respective ages of the 16 franchises that have been around since the initiation of the American League in 1901. There are definitely some great players among these teams, but there are also some positions that are incredibly weak. Even the Yankees and Cardinals of the baseball world have gone 20 years without a great shortstop or left fielder from time to time throughout the course of their histories. These are also franchises likely to see the most turnover when someone undoubtedly takes a new look at the best players in each franchise's history in 2035. Let's do this thing.

#30 Colorado Rockies (1993-pres.)

(Photo by Paul L Dineen/Creative Commons)

Team Background

Playoff appearances: 4 **Pennants: 1** **World Series titles: 0**
Collective team WAR: 275.0
Strengths: Team chemistry isn't something that has been statistically quantified yet, but it certainly can't hurt to have a group of great guys in the locker room, and the Rockies Starting IX is a great group of guys.
Weaknesses: The battery for the Rockies Starting IX is very weak… Like "third grade me" weak.
What to expect from the next 10 pages: This is the first team, so I wanted to show off a bit of what to expect throughout the book: a bunch of Starting IX lists, some halfway decent baseball research, and a lot of tangents.

The Rockies came into the league in 1993, at the same time as the Marlins; however, they haven't had the chance to bring a ring back to the city like the Marlins have done, twice. Attendance-wise, however, the Rockies are far superior to the Marlins. The Marlins are at a constant struggle to not finish last in the league in attendance. The Rockies, on the other hand, set the all-time record for MLB season attendance in their first season, and were on pace to break that in their second season before switching stadiums. The highlight of their brief time as a franchise, so far, was their run in 2007 that coined the phrase "Rocktober," as they won 14 of their last 15 regular season games to grab a spot in the playoffs. Once in the playoffs, they swept the Phillies in the first round, and the Diamondbacks in the second round, before being swept by the Red Sox in the World Series.

The other thing the Rockies are well known for is their home stadium, Coors Field. Coors is located in Denver, and there are numerous factors leading to its famous reputation. Here are a few snippets from the Rockies official ballpark description from the team's website. The opening line, "1999: Coors Fields firmly founded itself as the most prolific offensive ballpark ever created. The Rockies and their opponents combined for 303 home runs, the most ever in a season at one venue." However, as the Rockies officials point out, "Coors was only a small cog in baseball's shift to a hitter's game." That is not to say that the Coors effect is not real, however, as "the ball travels 9 percent farther at 5,280 feet than at sea level. It is estimated that a home run hit 400 feet in sea level Yankee Stadium... [would travel] as far as 440 feet in the Mile High City." Once again on the flip side, however, "The same 400-foot shot, with a 10-mph wind at the hitter's back, can turn into a 430-foot blast." So, although the altitude does have an impact on the offensive numbers, there are other factors besides the altitude that play just as large a factor, like the wind in Chicago, but are mentioned far less frequently. The Rockies are caught between a rock and a hard place on this front, as they can't simply move the fences back, because that would lead to an insane amount of line drives to drop in the gaps of the suddenly much bigger outfield, and the runs would still come around, just via multiple extra-base hits instead of home runs.

Whatever the cause, however, there is most certainly an effect. The Rockies have scored over 3,000 runs more than the Marlins have. The Marlins entered the league at the same time as the Rockies, meaning the Rockies have scored well over 100 runs a season more than the Marlins, every season. Their team batting average (.275) is the highest of any franchise in baseball history, and on the flip side of that, so is their ERA (4.98). Coors is notably where pitchers have gone to die, and their franchise ERA speaks to that.[17] ESPN's Park Factors has ranked Coors as the most offensive stadium in the league every year since 2009, with the lone exception of 2011, when the stadium ranked second. In 2014, Coors Field earned the distinction by a large margin. In 2014, the difference between Coors and Chase Field, the second-place stadium (1.501 vs. 1.154), in terms of additional runs produced, was more than the difference between the second and last place stadiums in the league (1.154 vs. Safeco's 0.825)!

The difference can be seen in individual player's performances, as well. Dante Bichette has some of the strongest home/road splits of all time. From 1993-1998, the *smallest* difference in his home and road OPS splits in a single season was 279 points, and he hit more than twice as many home runs at home (106) as he did on the road (52) for his entire time in Colorado. Once Bichette really learned how to cater his swing to Coors Field, those splits became even more pronounced, as he hit 90 home runs in Coors compared to just 29 on the road from 1995-1998. As far as pitchers are concerned, outside of a remake of *Magic Mike* with John Malkovich in the lead role, there's just about nothing they'd like to see less than Coors Field. Case in point: Mike Hampton. His two years before Coors he was 37-14 with a 3.02 ERA; his two seasons in Coors, 21-28 with a 5.75 ERA; his two seasons after Coors, 27-17 with a 4.05 ERA. Now this is obviously an incomplete look at outside factors, as well advanced statistics,[18] but Hampton is part of a pattern of disrespect and inappropriate behavior shown by Coors Field to pitchers. The carcasses of pitchers who dared move to the Rockies can be found littered throughout Colorado's brief history already. Want another example? Pedro Astacio had a 3.68 ERA his first six years in Los Angeles, then he came to Colorado and posted a 5.43 ERA in his five seasons there.

Coors has derailed many possibly-talented young starters. The Rockies have used several top draft picks[19] on pitchers who didn't pan out, and although that isn't too uncommon in baseball, there were a few who made it to the big leagues and showed promise, but whose careers were derailed thanks, at least in part, to Coors. Coors is far from the first park to have a drastic effect on the game, as we'll learn quite a bit about Chuck Klein and the Philadelphia Phillies of the Baker Bowl era, as well as cavernous Dodger Stadium – which is thought to be at least part of what launched Sandy Koufax into the discussion for greatest pitcher of all time – later in the book. Even to a lesser extent, the Green Monster in Fenway has made and broken plenty of left fielders' careers. Of the current stadiums, however, Coors has the (deserved) reputation of being the stadium with the biggest impact on pitchers and hitters. However, some day, either the Coors' effect will minimize, or a new stadium with even crazier park effects will come around, and Coors will no longer be thought of this way; it's just the way history works – in waves. For now, though, Rockies fans should enjoy their beautiful stadium that helps put a few extra runs on the board.

---

[17] The second worst franchise ERA is far better, with the Rays at 4.40. In fact, 20 teams have an ERA over a whole run better than the Rockies. Now this footnote almost needs a footnote, because that is a little biased since the Rockies entire franchise history has been in a more offensive part of baseball history, but as a point of comparison, the Marlins ERA is 70 points lower despite existing at the exact same time.

[18] Including the fact that he actually gave up more home runs on the road than at home in his two years at Coors.

[19] Jason Jennings at 16th overall and Jeff Francis at 9th overall, in particular.

* * *

A freeze-frame of the current Rockies doesn't leave a whole lot to be excited about for their fans. However, one of the issues with writing a book is the author-reader time disconnect. For a sports writer at a newspaper or blog, the author-reader time-lapse is a few hours, and maybe a day or two at most if the material takes some time to be stumbled upon. As such, commentary on a franchise's present is useful, and their future still (in theory) predictive. When writing a book, though, there is a fairly good chance that a comment on the Rockies current problems with the front office will be completely eliminated by the time the reader is able to read this, even if that reader buys the very first copy of the book, and this were the final section written. As such, these present/future sections will hopefully trend away from in-the-moment analysis, and look to somewhat bigger picture baseball discussions. As much as I would love to use the space to make predictions about baseball (the DH will be in both leagues by 2025), or even pop culture (Justin Bieber is going to reinvent himself in a Justin Timberlake fashion and actually have the majority of folks who hate him now on his side by 2030), those predictions may either be null and void because they happen earlier than expected, or because a certain Canadian pop star goes full-on Mike Tyson by the time this goes to press.

(I wrote this final paragraph after the 2016 season, and I'm going to leave it entirely unchanged since it perfectly proves its own point after the Rockies made the playoffs in 2017 and now appear to be on the right track.)

Random cool things about the franchise:

- The Rockies mascot was based on the fact that a 66-million-year-old dinosaur bone was found during the construction of the stadium, and I honestly can't determine whether it was a PR stunt or not.
- Their nickname is the "Blake Street Bombers."
- Coors Field is the best stadium for craft beers, despite owning the name of one of the least-drinkable and decidedly-un-craft beers in the world.
- The club topped the 70,000-fan attendance mark 21 separate games in their first two seasons, with more than 80,000 coming to the club's first-ever game in 1993 – the largest Opening Day crowd in baseball history.
- The franchise has 10 batting titles in their 25-year history, more than three times as many as the White Sox have had in their 116-year history.

Starting IX

C Chris Iannetta (2006-2011)

Well, he didn't make an error all of 2008, and he led the National League in double plays turned as a catcher in 2009… In other news, Jim Rice isn't appearing in this book.

1B Todd Helton (1997-2013)

Helton is the most famous Rockie of all time and is not surprisingly the franchise's all-time leader in WAR (61.2),[20] games (2,247), runs (1,401), hits (2,519), total bases (4,292), home runs (369), RBI (1,406), and walks (1,335); for the most part he trails only Larry Walker in the percentage categories (batting average, slugging percentage, etc.), as well. Throughout his career, Helton had to deal with people putting an imaginary asterisk next to his name because he played 81 games a season at Coors. While his career home/road splits are certainly noticeable, Helton would still be a very good, All-Star-level player even with his road splits. If his career was played entirely outside Coors[21] he would be a .287/.386/.469[22] hitter with over 1,000 runs and RBI each and nearly 300 home runs. That's certainly a drop off from the .316/.414/.539 hitter with over 350 home runs that he is in real life, but even on the road, he is about equivalent to Matt Holliday, another player who had to prove his worth outside of Coors after gaining fame with the Rockies.

Putting aside any Coors discussion for a second, though, Helton has some of the most impressive numbers of this century. He became the first player in big league history to collect at least 100 extra-base hits in two consecutive seasons when he did so in 2000-2001. He also tallied over 400 total bases in those seasons, the first player to have back-to-back 400-total base seasons since Jimmie Foxx (1932-1933). Despite his incredible production, and because of the Coors stigma and limited team success, Helton never took home an MVP award, with his best finish coming in 2000 when he came in fifth. This makes "The Toddfather" one of the best players in baseball history to never win MVP.

---

[20] Quick reference point for WAR: somewhere around 50 WAR puts you in the Hall of Fame conversation. For specific reference here, Yogi Berra was worth 59.5 WAR in his career.

[21] Using his career road splits and multiplying by two.

[22] These "slash lines" will be used reguarly throughout the book. The first number is batting average (strong typically being around .300), the second number is on-base percentage (strong typically being around .360), the third number is slugging percentage (strong typically being around .475). The latter two can be combined for OPS, one of the best non-sabermetric stats around because it combnies a player's ability to both get on base as well as hit for power.

Alright, this is the perfect chance for the first bonus Starting IX, the best players to never win MVP:

C) Gary Carter 1B) Todd Helton 2B) Bobby Grich 3B) Eddie Mathews SS) Derek Jeter[23] LF) Tim Raines CF) Al Simmons RF) Al Kaline[24] DH) Johnny Mize/Jim Thome Utility) George Brett/Paul Molitor SP1) Tom Seaver SP2) Pedro Martínez SP3) Pete Alexander SP4) Randy Johnson SP5) Warren Spahn

That's such an unbelievably stacked field that I had to cheat with the normal parameters of a Starting IX, and sneak in a bunch more names. It speaks to just how much talent baseball has seen through the years that none of those guys ever was the best in the league (at least through the lens of the voters) in a single season.

2B Eric Young, Sr. (1993-1997)

Young was in Colorado for only five years, and played only 613 games with the team, but he managed to steal 180 bases in his brief time there. He made his only All-Star appearance while with the club in 1996 and won a Silver Slugger that same year with a slugging percentage of .421 and eight home runs. Ah, the beauty of second base. On June 30, 1996, Young stole six bases in a game, one of only six men to do that in baseball history, joining a man we'll see in just a few pages (Carl Crawford) as the two most recent players to do so. He also achieved the rare and extremely impressive feat of stealing second, third, and home in one time around the bases. Talk about manufacturing a run.

Young's son (Eric Young Jr.) also played for the Rockies for a bit, and, like his father, was most useful on the base paths. Eric Young Jr. stole 144 bases in 557 career games and is currently in the Brewers minor league system. There have been numerous baseball families, and this seems like a good time to pick out a Starting IX of baseball families. This can be fathers and sons or brothers alike, no judgment here, but someone like Hank Aaron whose brother, Tommie, played in only 437 games won't count. No riding your brother's coattails this time, Tommie:

C) Yogi Berra > Son, Dale Berra

1B) Ed Delahanty > Brothers: Frank, Jim, Joe and Tom Delahanty[25]

2B) Roberto Alomar > Father/Brother, Sandy Alomar[26]

SS) Cal Ripken Jr. > Father, Cal Ripken; Brother, Billy Ripken

3B) George Brett > ~~Twin, Woody Harrelson~~[27] Brother, Ken Brett

LF) Barry Bonds > Father, Bobby Bonds

CF) Joe DiMaggio > Brothers: Vince and Dom DiMaggio

RF) Paul Waner[28] > Brother, Lloyd Waner

DH) Ken Griffey Jr. > Father, Ken Griffey

SP1) Dizzy Dean > Brother Paul Dean

SP2) Greg Maddux > Brother, Mike Maddux

SP3) Pedro Martínez > Brother, Ramon Martínez

SP4) Gaylord Perry > Brother, Jim Perry

RP) Darren Oliver > Father, Bob Oliver

(Honorable mention just for his name: Dad Clarkson > Actually had two brothers play professional ball, but surprisingly was surprisingly neither a baseball "Dad" nor "son." He also has possibly the grainiest Baseball-Reference photo of all time; the Zapruder film is easier to see than this thing.)

(Photo from Baseball-Reference)

[23] Although Honus Wagner never won one, he was only eligible four years, and they were in the latter part of his career, and Jeter just tops Arky Vaughan.

[24] I'm actually not the biggest Kaline guy, but too many of Mel Ott's home runs came because of his home park. (Irony of this statement being made in Todd Helton's section, noted.)

[25] The Delahantys were the Molinas of their time.

[26] They have the same name; they are not the same person... This isn't West Virginia, where "father/brother" is a viable title. (Sorry to pick on all the good folks of West Virginia, but you did just help to elect Donald Trump.)

[27] Seriously, look them up side-by-side.

[28] If Tony Gwynn Jr. sticks around a few more years this may be his dad's spot.

I mean why even bother with that picture…

In case modern Rockies fans are wondering, D.J. LeMahieu needs to show me one or two more seasons like 2016-2017 before he gets this spot.

3B Nolan Arenado (2013-pres.)

For all the modern Rockies fans who were upset that LeMahieu didn't make the cut, here's a bone (a dinosaur bone, perhaps?). This spot originally belonged to Vinny Castilla, but given what Arenado has turned into in the past two seasons, he gets the spot over the less-than-memorable Castilla.

In the past three seasons, he has *averaged* 40 home runs, 131 RBI, 104 runs and a .297 batting average per season. Those are some eye-popping numbers, and when combined with his defensive prowess (four straight Gold Gloves; 12.3 defensive wins above replacement in his career), make Arenado one of the best and underappreciated young stars of baseball right now. The 26-year-old has seen his WAR total improve in each of his five major league seasons, and the future is only getting brighter for this young man.

According to almost every profile you can find of the man, he is one of the hardest-working and routine-driven players in the sport, as well. Although I find some of that type of post hoc narrative to be baloney, the results speak for themselves with the season-by-season growth that the SoCal native has shown.

Arenado also seems like a good dude, a typical laid-back Cali kid who used to wear a Star Wars storm trooper helmet when he played video games, according to a profile of Arenado in the *Denver Post*. According to the same profile, Arenado is extremely close with his parents, especially his mother, who was a natural athlete herself, a stud pitcher and shortstop back in her day. You've got a good one, Rockies fans.

SS Troy Tulowitzki (2006-2015)

Tulo spent his first decade in baseball with the Rockies, making quite a name for himself in both Colorado and around the league. While in Colorado, he was arguably the game's top shortstop when healthy, although health was a bit of a bugaboo he just never could ditch. He missed over 10 games every season except for one in his 10 seasons in Colorado, and missed extended periods of time in 2008, 2010, 2012, 2013, 2014 and 2015 with his games played totals for those years reading: 101, 122, 47, 126, 91 and 128.[29] The thing is, even with all that time missed, Tulowitzki still put up strong numbers. In 2010, for instance, he put together maybe his best season to date, finishing fifth in the MVP race while posting 27 home runs and 95 RBI with a .315 BA, a 138 OPS+, and a career high 4.6 oWAR – all in 122 games. In 2014, the story was much the same, with Tulowitzki eating planets for the first couple months, inspiring heaps of praise that this would be the year he finally won an MVP, only to sustain an injury that ended his season on July 19, playing just 91 games that year. In the games he did play, Tulo totaled 71 runs, 21 home runs, slashed .340/.432/.603 with a career high OPS+ of 171, and 5.5 WAR – again in just 91 games. By *FanGraphs* WAR, only Jhonny Peralta was worth more among shortstops during the entire season, and no shortstop was worth more with his bat that season than Tulowitski. In 2013, despite missing 36 games, he was the highest-rated shortstop by *FanGraphs* WAR, and the story was the same except that Tulo missed 40 games, and had an even bigger lead on the second-place shortstop.

Not only is Tulowitski a monster with the bat, but he's a magician in the field. He is the active leader in Range Factor/Game among shortstops (yes, above Andrelon Simmons) and is second all-time to only Omar Vizquel in fielding percentage for the position. His rare combination of being able to get to a ball in the hole and make the accurate throw to first required to get the out made him the best defensive shortstop in baseball in his prime, which, when considering the damage Tulo did with his bat during those years, is like giving Robert De Niro the voice of Andrea Bocelli.

That Tulowitski was able to retain so much value despite missing games year-in and year-out is a two-sided blade. On the one hand, his talent level was so high that even with the games he missed, he was the best shortstop in baseball, per *FanGraphs* WAR, from his first full season in 2007 through the end of his time in Colorado. On the other hand, Tulo was a player that simply could not be counted on for the whole season, a trait that clearly has its drawbacks. The Rockies so often saw their fortunes go as Tulo went, and if that type of player can't be counted on for a whole season, neither can the team. This was not lost on Rockies management who realized that blowing up the team and building around a player who can play 162 games was the best route to go, dealing Tulo to Toronto for Jeff Hoffman (ERA+ of 88 in 130.2 IP with Colorado), Jesus Tinoco (MLB debut TBD), Miguel Castro (7.20 ERA in 24 games with Colorado) and José Reyes (cut by the organization due to myriad factors) at the trade deadline in 2015.

LF Matt Holliday (2004-2008)

A similar player to Helton, Holliday only started his career hitting in Coors before leaving the club via trade. The trade was a successful one for the Rockies, who lost one year of Holliday and in return received Carlos González, Greg

[29] In 2015, he spent 87 games with Colorado before being traded to Toronto and playing in 41 games for the Jays.

Smith, and Huston Street. Smith hasn't had any real impact on the club, but Street and González both have been excellent. Street closed for three years for the team netting 84 saves with a 3.50 ERA before being traded to division rivals San Diego, pretty serviceable for a pitcher in Coors. CarGo has been the real gem of the deal, and, spoiler, there's more to come on him in a bit. From the other side of the trade, the A's gave up a ton to get Holliday, who only spent half a season there before the A's flipped him for a package highlighted by Brett Wallace. Yeah, it wasn't a great deal for the A's. The move is reminiscent of the post-2014 teardown of the A's in which Billy Beane dealt his half-year acquisitions, Jeff Samardzija (for whom he gave up his top prospect, Addison Russell), for a package highlighted by Marcus Semien, who, while a decent player, is not likely to provide the bang-for-the-buck that Russell is currently providing for the Cubs.

Holliday's numbers, however, suggested that although the A's were giving up a lot, it would have been a good idea. In fact, his numbers in Oakland were not bad at all, and flipping him had more to do with the team not seeing him in their future plans, since they were not competing at that time and didn't want to shell out the money that he was due to receive at season's end. They figured better to lose him for a couple of prospects than nothing at all. Holliday has proven himself a more than capable hitter after leaving Coors, and his numbers with the Rockies are quite similar to his numbers for the rest of his career, making him a bit of the anti-Dante Bichette. His .319/.386/.552 slash line while in Colorado is imperceptibly different than his .303/.382/.515 career line, and that line has been dragged down in his late-career seasons. In fact, his career OPS+ (132) is higher than his Colorado OPS+ (131), and his WAR/season has been just about the same after Colorado as well, helping to destigmatize the Coors Effect[30] a bit.

Considering Holliday's move from Colorado to Oakland to St. Louis, it's impressive how smooth Holliday's career arc has been. Outside of the rare player, the typical bell curve shape to a player's career that is typically true of Large N analysis (a large sample size) is not usually true of N=1 (single-player) analysis. Although the "typical player" gets to the majors, adjusts to the pitching, peaks at age 27, holds a three-to-four-year peak, and then slowly regresses from there, it's rare that an actual living, breathing player follows a career arc that smooth. Holliday reached the majors at 24, had his best season at age 27, and saw his WAR slowly go down each season in his 30s. Again, although that is typical when looking at baseball players at the macro level, it is rare to see a player fit so neatly into that bell-shaped curve to his career. However, that was the type of player Holliday was. This is, after all, a player who Ben Lindbergh described as "a sunny sky in San Diego, a pleasant scent we can't smell because it has surrounded us for so long," when writing of Holliday for *Grantland* in 2015.

CF Ellis Burks (1994-1998)

Burks had one particularly strong year (1996) with the Rockies, not coincidentally the year the ball was absolutely flying out of Coors. The Rockies scored 961 runs that season (remarkably, the Seattle Mariners scored 32 runs more, albeit with the help of the best designated hitter of all time, Edgar Martínez), good for nearly six runs of offense a game. For his part, Burks contributed a .344/.408/.639 triple slash line (again, batting average/on-base percentage/slugging percentage) with 142 runs, 40 home runs, 128 RBI, to go with 32 steals and a league-leading 392 total bases. He finished third in the MVP, and it represented the only time in his career he topped 100 runs or RBI, and his total bases were more than 100 higher than his next highest single-season total.

Burks had a strong career despite being a bit of a journeyman, a career in which he played for five different teams. He collected over 350 home runs, 1200 runs and RBI each, 180 steals, and 2,000 hits. In fact, Burks totaled more WAR in his career than Sandy Koufax! Bust that stat out at your next family gathering.

Because I am a stats junkie and love thinking in terms of numbers, I like to carry over these lines of thought into more than just sports. In its current state, society seems primed for an emphasis of statistics in all aspects of life. Say you're a 19-year-old male looking for a college roommate for your sophomore year of college. Your roommate freshman year was decent, but you're on the free agent list and looking for a guy who can bring the one thing every guy wants in his college roommate: WAR (women above replacement). How great would it be to have a database that listed how many girls each potential roommate would bring to a party at your dorm. We all know there's more to a roommate than how many girls he is friends with, but we could figure that stuff out too. We could have VG%, or how much of his day he is willing to commit to playing video games, or even how many GDP (gross, dirty parties) he'll drag you down with. Just like grounded into double plays you want to avoid GDPs, but you just happen to find yourself with around 10 a year regardless.

For females looking for roommates, we could have XBT (extraordinary ability to marathon TV), Clutch (ability to get rid of creepy dudes at the last second), QS (quaint souvenir spotting ability), and MMS (margarita making skills). Imagine how much easier life would be if everything had a database.

These last two paragraphs sponsored by the National Men's Trade Union League circa 1903 and the Foundation for Gender Stereotypes.

[30] The Coors Effect being the impact on baseball offense, not the similarly titled impact when, after drinking a few Coors Lights, a man/woman who started the night as a 5 begins to look like an 8.

RF Larry Walker (1995-2004)

The pride of British Columbia, Walker is arguably Canada's most famous baseball player. Here's your next bonus Starting IX, Canada's Starting IX:

C) Russell Martin 1B) Joey Votto 2B) Pop Smith SS) Arthur Irwin 3B) Corey Koskie LF) Jason Bay CF) Tip O'Neill – Slightly out of position, but his speed would have given him good range in center. RF) Larry Walker DH) Justin Morneau Utility) Matt Stairs – One of this author's favorite players and favorite YouTube clips[31] SP) Fergie Jenkins RP) John Hiller

Not nearly as stout as the family Starting IX, but a lot of countries[32] could do a lot worse. Because they don't have Matt Stairs.

Walker was a solid player before and after his time in Colorado, but he timed his prime perfectly for Colorado. In his decade with the team, he had five particularly strong seasons, the strongest being his 1997 campaign. He totaled 409 total bases, tied for 18th all-time, and deservedly won the league MVP. He totaled 9.8 WAR, and had quite an impressive 143 runs, 49 home runs, and 130 RBI with .366/.452/.720 slashes (one more time, BA/OBP/SLG) to boot. He also won a Gold Glove based on his reputation as having a great arm in addition to solid range in right field. From 1997-1999, he became the first player to hit .363 in three straight seasons since Al Simmons did so from 1929-1931. Walker definitely had some Colorado boosts to his numbers, but the monotonous nature of that qualifier seems a bit much at this point.

Walker was also responsible for one of the most memorable All-Star Game moments in league history. Unlike Ted Williams' or Stan Musial's walk-offs, however, this wasn't the most flattering display of hitting ability from Walker. Instead it came as the result of another player's dominance, one Randy Johnson. In 1997, Randy Johnson's pitching intimidation level was equivalent to coming back from a date with your first girlfriend and seeing her dad sitting on the front porch cleaning his shotgun. Walker was no slouch himself, coming into the All-Star Game hitting .398, but after the left-handed Johnson let the first pitch fly over similarly left-handed Walker's head, Walker flipped around his batting helmet and jaunted over to the right side of the plate – he was not a switch-hitter. The moment perfectly summed up Johnson's dominance in baseball at the time, and was an amusing reminder that the All-Star Game is meant to be fun.

Walker was also a Class-A locker room prankster throughout his career, and further proof that Canada is actually pretty awesome. Check out this excerpt from Jonah Keri's *Up, Up & Away* and try not to name Walker as one of your favorite players of all time afterwards: "Walker was also one of the most fun-loving Expos of all time. The man they called 'Booger' never took baseball – or himself – too seriously. He used a wide array of jokester gear: red clown shoes in his locker, plus diapers and a ballerina outfit that he'd make teammates wear (even when it wasn't officially hazing time)."

Or this story from teammate Darrin Fletcher from the same book: "'There used to be a hot tub in the visitor's locker room. Larry would get in after the game and coax a few players into a bet: how long could he hold his breath under water. Younger players would say 45 seconds, tops. The veterans, we knew, so we'd put money on it. It'd be three, four minutes every time. Larry would duck his head under the water, then put his mouth on one of the jets that had an air pump, and breathe the air. Thinking of all the players who'd been in that hot tub after games, and I'm guessing how rarely they cleaned it… there's no way I would try it, let's put it that way. Didn't bother him one bit.'"

Considering that's a trick that my friends and I used to use to freak our parents out as nine-year-olds, I respect the hell out of Walker doing the same. As a grown-ass man.

Utility Carlos González (2009-pres.)

Previously mentioned as coming over as part of the Holliday trade, Cargo has established himself as a top presence in the Rockies lineup since he came to the squad in 2009. González also has the honor of having been in more trade rumors than he has had hot meals.[33] Despite the near-constant distraction of his name being swirled around in the MLB trade rumors hotbox, González has managed to produce a .292/.351/.521 slash line in his eight years with the club, a mark that is good enough for an OPS+ of 118, a stat in which the Coors effect actually hurts him, as a neutralized stat that accounts for the high run supply in Colorado. For a while, the knock on González was that he couldn't stay healthy, as he played fewer than 130 games in four of his first six seasons with the Rockies, but he has aged well in that regard: his three most recent seasons (2015-2017) saw González play at least 136 games each. As a result of those trade rumors never actually being consummated, and Cargo starting to play a higher percentage of his team's games, González is up to fifth on the Rockies franchise WAR leaderboard (as of the 2017 season). In fact, his name is scattered across the franchise leaderboard, as he has quietly put together a solid career for a franchise that is rather lacking in consistent, long-term success from its players.

---

[31] Out of context quote of the millennium (scratch that, of all millennia): "You're getting your ass hammered by guys. There's no better feeling than to have that done." Welcome to the book, Matt Stairs.

[32] And since Canada is going to be the butt of numerous jokes throughout this book, here's a bone for all you Canadians, because I actually do secretly love our neighbors to the north. Here's a Starting IX (with SP equaling the no. 1 rank and following how you would score baseball C = 2, 1B = 3, etc. from there) of just straight-up Canadians: SP) Ryan Gosling C) Justin Trudeau 1B) Celine Dion 2B) Will Arnett 3B) Matt Stairs SS) Jim Carrey LF) Carrie-Anne Moss CF) Seth Rogen RF) Feist

[33] "Yeah, I heard about that. It was neck-and-neck and then [he] skipped lunch." [*KKBB* no. 2]

SP Ubaldo Jiménez (2006-2011)

Jiménez was signed as a 17-year-old out of the Dominican Republic by the Rockies in 2001. He made it to the big leagues for a cup of tea in 2006 but didn't really make an impact until 2008. Starting that year, Ubaldo (one of the best names in baseball) posted three straight solid seasons, including a near-Cy Young season in 2010. In 2010, he was the owner of one of the most dominant first halves from any pitcher in history. He collected 15 wins (not WAR) before the All-Star break with a 2.20 ERA and an opponent batting average under .200, all the while pitching half his games in Coors. Through his first 14 starts, he was 13-1 with a 1.15 ERA. He got roughed up a bit going forward but still finished the year solidly, posting a 2.83 ERA in August.

Jiménez suffered a precipitous fall after that year and hasn't been the same since. It seems that Colorado may have known something the rest of baseball didn't, as they quickly dealt him for 70 cents on the dollar to Cleveland, in a deal that at the time in 2011 seemed to see Cleveland give up quite a small return for a pitcher who was less than 18 months removed from having been 13-1 with a 1.15 ERA and the National League starting pitcher at the All-Star Game. However, as stated before, Colorado may have noticed something seriously flawed in Ubaldo's mechanics, and since leaving Colorado (usually good news for pitchers), Jiménez has been borderline replacement level, posting 1.8 WAR over three seasons in Cleveland (4.45 ERA), before posting 0.9 WAR in four seasons in Baltimore so far (5.22 ERA).

The prospects that came to Colorado never really amounted to much for the Rockies, but even still, Colorado clearly pulled the trigger at the right time on Ubaldo. The main reason for his productivity drop seems to be a severe decrease in fastball velocity, but the cause of that drop has never been fully explained.

After Jiménez made the move to Cleveland, he made 11 starts for the final two months of the 2011 season. Over that time, he had an ERA of 5.10 and was labeled a bust rather quickly. However, this was based on only 11 starts, one of which was a 3.1 IP, 8 ER fiasco against the power-laden Tigers. If this game had been eliminated, his ERA would have been a far more respectable 4.21, and he may have gone into the 2012 campaign with more confidence (for whatever that is worth). On the other hand, the start before that blowup against the Tigers had seen Jiménez go 8 IP, 0 ER, a result that if eliminated would have seen his ERA rise to 5.81, an ERA that would have been the worst among qualified pitchers in 2011. This variance was obviously extreme in Jiménez's case because of the two-month sample size, but due to the fact that pitchers only get around 33 starts at most in a season, there is far more variance in their statistics than a hitter who gets the opportunity for 162 games in a season. As such, it would be interesting to see a new statistic (say, "ERAST" for *ERA stabilized*) that eliminated a pitcher's best and worst effort of the year in an attempt to find a more accurate depiction of the pitcher's typical outing. For many pitchers, this number would mirror their ERA, as they may have a couple great outings and a couple awful outings. However, sometimes the effect can be much larger. Take Clayton Kershaw in 2014. Although Kershaw finished the season with an outstanding 1.77 ERA, he had a miserable start (1.2 IP, 7 ER) against the Diamondbacks in May. If that start, along with his best start (which was either of his shutouts) were taken away, Kershaw's ERAST would be 1.53, the third-best single-season ERA in MLB since 1920.

This effect is even more pronounced among relievers, seeing as they have an even more pronounced small sample size. Doing a quick check to see which reliever's ERA may be inflated from one bad outing is a useful tool before any fantasy draft. If you looked before your 2015 draft, you would see that Koji Uehara had his ERA jump from 1.75 in 2012 and 1.09 in 2013, all the way to 2.52 in 2014. However, once his 0.2 IP, 5 ER implosion against Seattle is removed, his ERAST looks much more in line with previous seasons, at 1.84. Of course, part of a great reliever is being able to avoid those blow ups, but considering it was the first time he had given up more than two runs in an appearance since 2010, it's clear that it was an anomaly.

Back to Jiménez to finish: he had his best day as a Rockie on April 17, 2010 when he threw the franchise's first-ever no-hitter. Jiménez struck out seven, and even though he walked six and needed 128 pitches, the day was still historic. Of course, if we measured his ERAST, that start would have been eliminated as his top start of 2010...

CP Brian Fuentes (2002-2008)

I'd have to imagine that Rockies fans seeing Fuentes as their franchise closer are having that stomach-dropping feeling that happens when your friend borrows your computer and sees your recent search history come up as "Taylor Swift goat," "Dog Butt + Jesus Christ," and "Jennifer Connelly boobs." Fuentes sported a 3.38 ERA for his time in Colorado, but he offered a not-always-wanted entertainment level whenever he entered to close out the game.

One would think that this isn't entirely on Fuentes, as being a pitcher in Coors is difficult enough, and being a closer with the added pressure of Coors Field is too much for many pitchers. In many ways, closing is all about confidence. The job of the modern closer is pretty simple, as it has become strictly a three-out task. What can become difficult, however, is maintaining the confidence to get those final three outs. This is why closing at Coors can be a real bitch; who would be able to pitch confidently in that environment?

One would think wrong,[34] however, as Fuentes was not all that impacted by closing in Coors. Fuentes pitched for

---

[34] I don't love setting up straw man arguments just to knock them down in the next paragraph, but when the sentiment is as commonplace as a closer needing

the Rockies from 2002-2008. Let's look at the numbers:

Fuentes home/road splits while with the Rockies

Year	Home ERA	Road ERA	Home Blown Saves	Road Blown Saves
2002	3.31	6.97	0	0
2003	2.40	3.18	1	1
2004	8.10	2.95	1	0
2005	2.91	2.90	0	3
2006	3.63	3.23	2	4
2007	1.72	4.50	2	5
2008	3.51	1.84	2	2
Total	3.27	3.33	8	15

Now part of this has to do with the extreme small sample size that comes with the territory of analyzing relief pitchers, but over a seven-year span, some of that noise should start to smooth out. Fuentes totaled 410.1 innings, which is about two full seasons of work for a starting pitcher, definitely a sample size worth its salt. While the road blown save totals are a bit skewed by a four-game stretch in 2007 in which Fuentes blew four consecutive road save opportunities and cost himself the ninth inning job, when combined with the near identical home/road ERA, it would appear the Coors Effect really didn't hit Fuentes too hard.

It is interesting to note that in this book's closest relative (*Rob Neyer's Big Book of Lineups*) Rob Neyer has a section on the 1995 Rockies bullpen where he says, "I'd argue that their [the Rockies top four relievers] collective performance ranks as one of the all-time great seasons by a bullpen," based on their numbers and the era and stadium in which they pitched. In addition, Neyer, as he is wont to do, asks a great brain-teasing question: "Is the bullpen more important for the Rockies, because their starters get knocked out early so often? Or is it less important, because the Rockies don't play as many close games as a typical team?"

Now Neyer didn't try to answer his own question, which likely means that I am unqualified to, but let's take a quick look at the numbers. As has been mentioned previously, 1996 was the season in which the Rockies, and baseball as a whole, went bonkers on the offensive end. Since the season was such an extreme it will be one of our data points. In 1996, the Rockies played 42 games that were defined as a blowout (decided by five or more runs) by Baseball-Reference.[35] This total ranked right in the middle of the pack in the National League, with seven teams playing in more blowout games, two playing in the same amount, and five playing in fewer. That same season, the Rockies starting pitchers averaged 5.7 innings per start, second-worst in the National League, but only 0.6 innings (basically two outs) fewer than the league-leading Atlanta Braves. The answer would seem to be neither factor really matters all that much, but let's double-check by using a season on the other end of the spectrum: the low-offense 2014 season. The Rockies were once again near the cellar in innings pitched by their starters, this time finishing last in the NL, but, once again, the difference was less than an inning (0.7 IP/GS). That's not nothing,[36] but doesn't seem like enough to swing the scale in favor of the bullpen being more important than for any other team. In terms of blowout games, the 2014 Rockies played 52 of these lopsided affairs, six more than any other team in the NL and way above average. Considering the small difference between teams at the top and bottom of the league in innings pitched by a team's starters, it would appear the answer to Neyer's question is likely that the bullpen is slightly less important because of the number of blowout games the Rockies play.

Back to Fuentes, and ending on a rather unfortunate note for Fuentes: it must be noted that Matthew Berry (also known as The Talented Mr. Roto, ESPN's fantasy sports guru) coined the term "Dirty Fuentes" as a blown save, or messy save, that makes fantasy owners feel like someone just gave their team a Dirty Fuentes.

confidence, and a pitcher in Coors lacking confidence, it feels more like a brick man argument.

[35] They were 21-21 in those games.

[36] A double negative even Dan Dierdorf could be proud of!

Starting IX Franchise Roster Stats

Lineup	Yrs	G	R	H	HR	RBI	SB	BB	SO	BA	OBP	SLG	OPS+	dWAR	WAR
Carlos González	9	1115	698	1202	211	685	113	380	994	0.292	0.351	0.511	118	-3.2	22.9
Troy Tulowitski	10	1048	660	1165	188	657	55	435	713	0.299	0.371	0.513	123	**13.4**	39.1
Todd Helton	**17**	**2247**	**1401**	**2519**	**369**	**1406**	37	**1335**	**1175**	0.316	0.414	0.539	133	-5.9	**61.2**
Matt Holliday	5	698	479	848	128	483	66	251	505	0.319	0.386	0.552	131	-4.4	18.4
Larry Walker	10	1170	892	1361	258	848	126	584	659	**0.334**	**0.426**	**0.618**	**147**	0.3	48.2
Ellis Burks	5	520	361	558	115	337	52	202	380	0.306	0.378	0.579	128	-2.6	11.9
Nolan Arenado	5	720	420	800	148	506	11	212	449	0.290	0.340	0.534	118	12.3	27.4
Chris Iannetta	6	458	196	336	63	236	7	241	379	0.235	0.357	0.430	99	3.1	8.2
Eric Young	5	613	378	626	30	227	**180**	254	155	0.295	0.378	0.412	93	3.1	9.4
Pitchers	Yrs	W	W%	ERA	G	CG	SHO	SV	IP	SO	ERA+	WHIP	SO/9	SO/BB	WAR
Ubaldo Jiménez	6	56	0.554	**3.66**	138	8	**3**	0	851.0	773	**128**	**1.284**	**8.2**	2.08	**18.6**
Brian Fuentes	7	16	0.381	3.38	428	0	0	**115**	410.1	470	144	1.238	10.3	2.75	9.7

29 Tampa Bay Rays (2008-pres.); Tampa Bay Devil Rays (1998-2007)

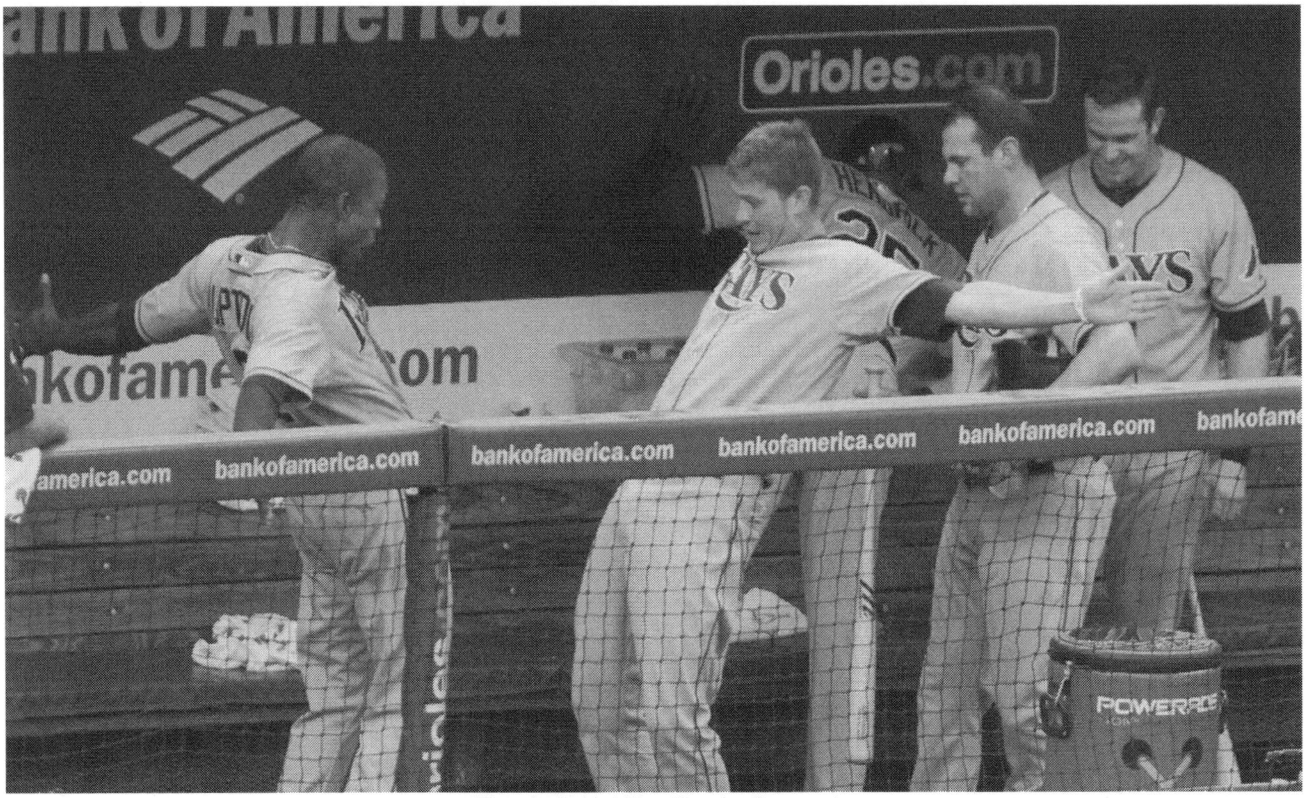

(Photo by Keith Allison/Creative Commons)

Team Background

Playoff appearances: 4 **Pennants: 1** **World Series titles: 0**
Collective team WAR: 230.7
Strengths: A beautiful stadium, a devoted fanbase, hot-but-not-too-hot summers... Wait, what's that?
Weaknesses: Significant lack of depth leading to some serious weak spots in the lineup, including the utility spot, which should be an elite spot usually.
What to expect from the next 10 pages: A franchise that has been around for 20 years in what has been the hardest division in baseball for many of those years. This is the expected results of that. Also, the best managers for each franchise.

The Rays, along with the Arizona Diamondbacks, have the shortest history of any of the franchises being represented in this book. As such, it is unsurprising that they have the fewest wins of any current franchise and bring up the rear in just about every cumulative franchise metric. They do, however, have one pennant, which is more than the Mariners or Nationals can say. They won that pennant in 2008, which was also their most successful regular season, one in which they won 97 games. Although they were cellar-dwellers nine of their first 10 seasons of existence, they were transformed into a contender on a yearly basis thanks to clever spending by the front office and the managing of the inscrutable[37] Joe Maddon.

A book of Maddon's tricks and tactics could, and one day very well may, be written, as he seems to have a different maneuver to stay one step ahead of the rest of the league at all times. He has drills that others don't have (i.e. pitching large baseballs underhand from half the distance of the normal mound for BP), his motivational tactics of individual players can be quirky, encouraging players be themselves and keep spirits high during the long season (e.g. creating the themed road trips like the Nerd Trip in 2012), and his team goals almost always have some great overarching theme (e.g. bringing a 20-foot python into the Rays clubhouse in honor of the Chinese year of the snake). His in-game tactics (e.g. walking Josh Hamilton

---

[37] I'm making a push for inscrutable to make a comeback into the current vernacular, and not just as a racist way to refer to clever Asian people.

with the bases loaded) are as unique as his lineup cards (e.g. setting his lineup as 8-6-7-5-3-0-9[38] in honor of Tommy Tutone), and his quirkiness is genuine, not forced. All of these tactics do seem to work, as Maddon transformed the perennial doormats of the American League East into a team that won 90 or more games in five of six seasons from 2008-2013. (And, of course, brought the first title to Chicago in 108 years after he left Tampa.) Maddon's success with the Rays is made even more impressive by the fact that they lost 90 or more games every single one of their first 10 seasons.

In fact, when choosing managers for each franchise's team, Maddon was the easiest pick, I know it's popular to pump the brakes on the Maddon hype lately, but no one else in Rays history is close to Maddon in terms of managerial success. Here are the chosen managers for each franchise,[39] ranked 1-30:

1) Earl Weaver – Orioles
2) Joe Torre – Yankees: This choice demands a discussion. You honestly couldn't go wrong with any of the top six managers in Yankees history (that includes Joe Girardi who was an absolute wizard to keep the Yankees relevant after the Core Four and before their new motley crew), but the modern game is more nuanced than the era in which Joe McCarthy and Casey Stengel managed, and that's why Torre gets the nod.
3) John McGraw – Giants
4) Bobby Cox – Braves
5) Walter Alston –Dodgers
6) Connie Mack – Athletics
7) Tony La Russa – Cardinals
8) Mike Scioscia – Angels
9) Sparky Anderson – Reds
10) Joe Maddon – Rays
11) Terry Francona – Red Sox
12) Sparky Anderson – Tigers: Jim Leyland's ability to turn the team around completely in the mid-2000s should not go unnoticed, however, and he very nearly stole this spot from Anderson.
13) Cito Gaston – Blue Jays
14) Whitey Herzog – Royals
15) Fred Clarke – Pirates
16) Tom Kelly – Twins
17) Jim Leyland – Marlins
18) Cap Anson – Cubs
19) Lou Piniella – Mariners
20) Al Lopez – White Sox
21) Mike Hargrove – Cleveland: He had to deal with Manny Ramírez and Albert Belle.
22) Dick Williams – Nationals (when they were the Expos)
23) Charlie Manuel – Phillies
24) Davey Johnson – Mets: If Gil Hodges hadn't passed away so young, the beloved Mets manager might have been here.
25) Bob Brenly – Diamondbacks
26) Ron Washington – Rangers: Not always the best game manager, but an extremely popular manager with the players.
27) Harvey Kuenn – Brewers
28) Bruce Bochy – Padres
29) Larry Dierker – Astros
30) Clint Hurdle – Rockies

There's a couple of greats left out because of the limit of one per team (notably: those aforementioned Yankee managers), but this method gives each all-franchise team its skipper.

Back to the Rays: somewhat like their ex-manager, the Rays are always trying to find ways to pick up pieces from the scrap heap in order to get a winning team for cheap. The team has focused on defense and guys who get on base, and their turnaround was well documented in Jonah Keri's *The Extra 2%* (a must-read). As Keri points out in his prologue, this was a franchise about whom no player had qualms taking digs in their early days. Torii Hunter said he'd rather be hit in the head with a fastball than play for Tampa Bay; Roger Clemens listed "Tell a teammate they're traded to the Devil Rays" as the fourth-best prank he could pull on a teammate during a David Letterman "Top Ten." However, the Rays brought on three former Wall Street analysts into their front office (owner Stuart Sternberg, GM Andrew Friedman, and president Matthew Silverman), and the results came quicker than many would have thought. This, in part, began a rush of baseball teams beginning to bring in "non-baseball" minds to hold high positions in the front offices, something that hadn't happened often

---

[38] With each number equaling their position, and 0 being the DH.

[39] One of the hardest tasks in baseball is distinguishing a manager's effect on the team. Many of these all-franchise managers come from the team's most successful era, which enforces the old trope that "good players make a good manager." I have tried to distinguish when there a close comparison, but these managers had to be doing something well to get their teams to succeed, right?

throughout baseball history.

Along the same lines as the "Moneyball" A's, the Rays[40] created a blueprint for success as a small market team. The Rays leaned on smart men, men who didn't necessarily have a history playing the sport but knew how to run a business. This is hugely important in a sport that struggles with salary cap equality more than any other sport by a large margin. This idea is beginning to spread, as noted, and as long as some smaller market teams can stay "One jump ahead of the breadline," baseball will be able to keep the competitive balance that has seen 12 different World Series winners this millennium. That's getting more and more difficult, but as we all know, pressure makes diamonds.

This is getting more difficult because the league has already started to see the beginning of a (depending on your outlook) troublesome trend that has seen the smartest minds in baseball departing for the biggest markets, a brain drain of sorts. The Rays lost aforementioned GM Andrew Friedman to the Dodgers, who gave him the largest contract of any front-office executive in MLB. They then lost manager Joe Maddon to the Cubs just 10 days after Friedman left. The fact that the big brains are starting to get their recognition is good, but if the best teams can already afford the best players and will now be shelling out for the best minds in baseball as well, the competitive balance just noted could be lost. Only time will tell.

Random cool things about the franchise:

- The franchise started a "Turn Back the Clock Night" in 2006 that has become an annual tradition during which the Rays, who have a very limited history, use the day to honor local baseball teams from before the Rays existed, teams that played in leagues such as the Florida State League and the Florida International League.
- The Rays have also created "faux-backs," fake throwback jerseys created in the design of how the team's jerseys would have looked if the franchise had existed in the 1970s, etc.
- The Rays fanbase calls itself the Rays Republic and has some truly unique characters like "The Happy Heckler," Hulk Hogan, and Dick Vitale.
- Tropicana Field has a couple of unique quirks to it as well, such as the fact that the stadium has an aquatic tank in right-center field called the "Touch Tank," which is filled with live cownose rays. The fans can feed the rays with food purchased from the organization, with the proceeds going to the Florida Aquarium.
- In 2006, Rays owner Stu Sternberg created the tradition of Rays fans incorporating "more cowbell," with the franchise handing out cowbells once a year to their fans in honor of Will Ferrell's legendary SNL sketch.

Starting IX

C Toby Hall (2000-2006)

Because the team has such a brief history (and an even briefer history of winning), some positions are definitely going to be ugly; this is one of them. Always tough to strike out and a plus defender… that's about all you can say about Hall. He was a pretty average catcher across the board outside of that. He brought the team only 3.1 WAR with his bat in his time with the team, but he was worth over 6.0 dWAR with his glove and positional value. He actually led the American League in dWAR in 2005, his last full season with the club. He didn't win the Gold Glove despite leading all AL position players in dWAR, because he also led all catchers in errors for the year, which historically have been weighed more heavily by Gold Glove voters than newer metrics. How much an error really costs a team is an interesting question, though.

At the All-Star break in 2014, I did a study based on one of Bill James' arbitration cases. Back in 1985, James was George Bell's arbitration lawyer, and James built a strong case for his client. From his *Historical Abstract* (which will be quoted often in this book), James explains:

"I helped prepare arbitration cases for George three straight years in the 1980s… George had led the AL in errors the first year that we prepared a case for him. We were wondering what to do about that, so I drew up an exhibit entitled 'What Was the Cost of George Bell's Errors?' The exhibit showed that although Bell had led the league in errors with 11, none of the errors had actually cost his team anything. Of the 11 errors, only about three led to unearned runs, all had occurred in games which Toronto had won anyway, and in those three games, Bell had driven in something like seven runs."

So, what I did was look at the 20 players who had committed at least 10 errors by the 2014 All-Star break, and then looked at how much their errors really cost their team. Building on what James had said, I created a new part of the study that would measure how many games it could be argued each player had cost his team. I created a metric called "true losses" which were the measure of how many games the team lost by equal or fewer runs than the player's error cost the team. For example, if Pedro Alvarez made an error that cost his team three runs, and they then lost 4-3, that would be a true loss. If Derek Dietrich made an error that cost his team one run, and they lost 3-2, that would also be a true loss. Finally, if the game went to extra innings and was a loss, any error worth one run or more was counted as a true loss. Therefore, if Josh Donaldson committed an error, which cost his team only one run, and then they lost 10-8, but that final score came in extra innings, then that would still count as a true loss because the extra innings would have never occurred (hypothetically).

---

[40] By the way it is funny to note that their success came immediately after dropping the "Devil" from their team name. Who said there's not a higher being?

The results showed exactly what I was hoping for, which was that errors really don't cost a player's team that much. Of the 20 case studies, only two players had more than two true losses to their name – Pedro Alvarez, who was leading the league with 20 errors, and an incredibly unlucky Starlin Castro, whose Cubs had lost six games in which he had committed an error, five of them true losses. Seven of the players had only had one true loss, and another seven didn't even have one to their name. These results were coming from a study looking at only the ills of these players' fielding and none of the positive impact they brought with their glove. For example, Josh Donaldson was second in the league in errors, but his incredible range meant that he often got to the ball, but this range put himself in hard positions to finish the play and thus was more likely to make an error on that difficult play.

There definitely are some downsides to committing an error: increased pitch count for your pitcher, lack of trust from that player's pitcher and surrounding defense, and if there are enough errors made, a potential benching, but as a whole, errors are a really silly defensive metric.

Back to Hall to finish: it is crazy (and sad) that he made about as much in his final year in Tampa as Roy Campanella made in his entire time in MLB, even after accounting for inflation – woof.

1B Carlos Peña (2007-2010; 2012)

The franchise leader in home runs (163) and walks (460) when he left town (Evan Longoria has since passed him in both categories), that is quite appropriate because those are the two things Peña did well. A journeyman for the first part of his career, Peña found a niche in Tampa, breaking onto the scene with 46 home runs in 2007 while sporting a career-high .282 batting average. Both numbers would drop over the next few years, and Peña bottomed out with two sub-.200 batting average seasons in 2010 and 2012 with the Rays. Because of his batting eye, he still had a decent on-base percentage each year, but the Rays decided to let Peña go and pivoted 180 degrees to the power-lacking but contact-friendly James Loney.

Despite his success in Tampa, Peña still totaled more than a strikeout per game in his 726 games with the club. Of course, there has been plenty of sabermetric work in the last decade or so that shows that batter strikeouts are not really as bad as we had previously thought,[41] but even accounting for the limited harm of strikeouts, Peña is still among the lesser players in this book. This is especially true when considering first base is a position from which big hitting numbers are expected since the defensive input isn't as high. Even though it's early, let's take a look at the worst players who appear at each position in the book. This Starting IX isn't much of a spoiler because most of the players will be coming from these low-ranking teams. Plus, these players kinda suck, so it shouldn't matter that much:

SP) Ubaldo Jiménez C) Brad Ausmus 1B) Carlos Peña 2B) Bret Boone 3B) Kelly Gruber SS) Jason Bartlett LF) Gene Richards CF) B.J. Upton RF) Matt Joyce Utility) Aubrey Huff, aka Huff Daddy CP) José Valverde.

2B Ben Zobrist (2006-2014)

"Zorilla" has become the face of the "New Moneyball" tactic that the Maddon-era Rays used to achieve success. He is a plus defender, has an excellent on-base percentage, offers unique positional flexibility (something that almost no other star player does, as Neil Weinberg pointed out in an excellent piece for *The Hardball Times* called, "Positional Versatility and The Zobrist Fallacy"), and seems to do everything advanced metrics love.

Time for a small refresher on the different levels of wins above replacement (WAR): 0 WAR is the value of a replacement-level player (last man on the bench, first man called up from the minors), 0-2 WAR is what a major league substitute is worth to his team, 2-5 WAR is what a solid starter is worth to his team, 5-8 WAR is an All-Star, and 8+ WAR is an MVP-caliber season. These are obviously guidelines not set rules, but by these standards, Zobrist had two MVP-caliber seasons with the Rays. In 2009, he was worth 8.6 WAR, and in 2011 he was worth 8.7 WAR; he led AL position players in WAR both seasons. He ran into pretty good seasons from Joe Mauer (2009) and Justin Verlander (2011), so even though he had higher WAR than both the MVP winners from each year, the winners seem justified. However, he certainly deserved to be higher than eighth (2009) and 16th (2011), which is where he finished in the MVP those two seasons.

Wins above replacement are obviously a great tool, especially in that WAR allows us to compare cross-generation, cross-position talents in a more apples-to-apples type of comparison, instead of apples-to-oranges like it was for most of baseball history. However, when Miguel Cabrera (38.5 WAR) is only worth 1.0 more win from 2009-2014 than Mr. Zobrist (37.5) here, there does seem to be a little bit of the formula that needs to be tweaked.

By the way, for those still a bit confused on WAR and its principles, there is a good chunk in the introduction set aside for its definition. However, what wasn't discussed in the introduction was a pros and cons list of the most divisive metric in baseball today. Take out your yellow legal pads, and get ready to pay homage to the great Ted Mosby – it's a pros and cons list in regards to WAR:

---

[41] While somewhat paradoxically learning that pitcher strikeouts are more important than we once thought. Figure that one out.

Pros	Cons
* All-inclusive statistic that helps to compare across generations	* Can be an overused crutch that oversimplifies the nuances of baseball if used ad nauseam
* Can help uncover hidden gems in terms of under-the-radar players and seasons	* The formula is still in the process of being perfected and still has its flaws
* The correlation between WAR and team wins in 2012 was 0.86; the correlation between batting average and team wins was 0.27	* WAR (and other advanced metrics) tear down some of baseball's oldest facades (although this could be considered a good thing by some as well)
* WAR adjusts for position (even across pitchers and hitters) and stadium, as well as several other factors that can complicate matters when comparing players	* It can't be calculated with a simple formula like batting average or ERA can, which can raise the level of distrust
* With its abbreviation of WAR, this leads to all types of punny headlines, like, "WAR, huh, what is it good for?"	* With its abbreviation of WAR, this leads to all types of punny headlines, like, "WAR, huh, what is it good for?"
* Includes offensive and defensive contributions	* Because of the imperfect formula, each rendition of WAR (*FanGraphs*, Baseball-Reference, *Baseball Prospectus*) can vary greatly for the same player in the same year

A few words on this chart. The main argument of the anti-WAR crowd is that first point: "Can be an overused crutch that oversimplifies the nuances of baseball if used ad nauseam." Here's the thing, though: that is the biggest straw man argument since the off-set troubles during the filming of *The Wizard of Oz*. The old-school baseball types are inventing these "new-schoolers" – who rely on WAR and WAR only – in their minds. No sabermetrician worth her/his salt (and really just no sabermetrician at all) has tried to compare players using WAR as the only metric. It's a great starting point, but to say that there are sabermetricians out there settling each and every argument by simply pointing to WAR is patently false.

There are still faults of WAR (see rest of the cons), but the fact that the number one complaint about the metric is the result of a straw man argument created by the anti-WAR contingent tells you all you need to know about the stat's value.

Of course, as something of a postscript to his Rays career, Zobrist followed manager Joe Maddon to Chicago, and starred in his role for the 2016 curse-breaking Chicago Cubs, winning World Series MVP in a decision that, hopefully, began to bring some more attention to one of this generation's best players.

3B Evan Longoria (2008-pres.)

In the fall of 2013, I wrote an article for *The Baseball Research Journal* that focused on the future of baseball contracts, and Evan Longoria was one of my case studies (along with Elvis Andrus). Baseball (along with every other sport, it seems) has prospered in recent years from a generous windfall from massive TV contracts being signed by both individual teams, and the league as a whole. Major League Baseball has seen a lot of teams, even in smaller markets, look to lock up their young superstars earlier and earlier. It has taken a bite out of free agency and in theory, it levels the playing field, since big market teams can't just scoop up the best young talent on the market every offseason. However, if one of these contracts goes awry, and a player either severely underperforms for the length of the contract or can't stay healthy, this can be a far bigger blow to a small market team.

The premise of my study was to find a historical comparison to Longoria, and use this player to attempt to predict Longoria's future with the Rays. Using Baseball-Reference's most similar player score, the best model for Longoria after his 2013 season was Scott Rolen. (Alan Trammell was the best fit for Elvis Andrus.) Then, using the current market value of a win (per WAR), which was about $5.5 million dollars at the time, I overlaid Rolen's season-by-season WAR (having retired in 2012, Rolen had already played those "future seasons" that were upcoming for Longoria, having retired in 2012) with the entirety of Longoria's contract.

Year	rWAR	Salary (Millions)	$/WAR Spent by Rays	Projected Lg. Avg. $/WAR	Verdict
2013	6.2	6	967,741	5,200,000	Big Bargain
2014	4.4	7.5	1,704,545	5,400,000	Definite Bargain
2015	8.9	11	1,235,955	5,500,000	Big Bargain
2016	1.5	11.5	7,666,666	5,700,000	Overpaid
2017	5.6	13	2,321,428	5,900,000	Definite Bargain
2018	1.6	13.5	8,437,500	6,100,000	Overpaid
2019	3.2	14.5	4,531,250	6,200,000	Underpaid
2020	3.7	15	4,045,045	6,400,000	Underpaid
2021	1.2	18.5	15,416,666	6,600,000	Hugely Overpaid
2022	3.9	19.5	5,000,000	6,800,000	Underpaid
2023	1.5	13	8,666,666	7,000,000	Slightly Overpaid
Total	41.7	143	3,429,256	6,100,000	Definite Bargain

*Note that Baseball-Reference has updated their WAR formula since this chart was made, so some of the WAR totals aren't the same on Rolen's player card now.

Longoria's contract runs until 2022 with a team option and buyout clause for 2023, so using Scott Rolen's corresponding seasons, this above chart helped to see what the Rays might expect from Longoria. It is not at all surprising that the contract is best for the Rays at the beginning of the deal and fades towards the end. That is the typical nature of these long-term deals, and it's part of the risk.

But now that it has been five seasons since I wrote that piece, it's interesting to compare the route Longoria's career arc was "supposed" to take versus what he has actually done. For the Scott Rolen model, Longoria tallied 26.6 WAR in those five seasons, with two "Big Bargain" seasons, two "Definite Bargain" seasons and one "Overpaid" season. In reality, Longoria tallied a total of 20.2 WAR, but was more consistent than Rolen, with his past four seasons all falling between 3.2 and 3.9 WAR – a solid, above-average starter and well worth his price tag. The deal has most certainly been a boon for the Rays, as Longoria was worth more than $160 million dollars from 2013-2017 alone, according to *FanGraphs* win values tool. Over those four seasons, the Rays actually paid Longoria $49.6 million. "I call that a bargain, the best I evahhhh had."

(Photo from Wikimedia Commons)

Back to Longoria: interestingly enough, it wasn't the Rays contract extension that made news as much as Longoria's first contract. Longoria was inked to a long-term deal just six games into his major league career, one of the many cost-cutting attempts (most of them successful) by Friedman and the Rays front office. As Keri points out in *The Extra 2%*, Longoria was the "single most valuable commodity in the game in *each* of his first three seasons," according to Dave Cameron's "MLB Trade Value" Column for *FanGraphs*. As shown above, Longoria has slowed down a bit, but he is still posting seasons like he did in 2016 in which he hit .273 with 36 home runs, which the Rays will undoubtedly take from their 32-year-old defender of the hot corner.

SS Jason Bartlett (2008-2010)

Bartlett had the most successful time of his career in Tampa Bay. Always a punch hitter and good base runner, Bartlett had somewhat of a power surge in 2009, making the All-Star Game while hitting 14 home runs with a 132 OPS+.[42] That power, along with his typical solid fielding and baserunning allowed him to finish in the top 10 in WAR (6.2) in the American League for the season. Bartlett is the perfect player to have his best seasons in Tampa: he's the type of player who, when he has success under Maddon, has pro-Maddon people screaming "genius," although his detractors point to an inflated BABIP and claim it was merely a fluke year. Either way, Tampa seems to find a few of these players every year, much to the chagrin of the rest of the AL East.

Also helping his case is the fact that Bartlett holds the distinct (dis)honor of being one of eight players in baseball history to hit into the last out of two different no-hitters. So, he's got that going for him, which is nice.

LF Carl Crawford (2002-2010)

Crawford was the first real star of the Rays franchise, and as such, holds several of the team's cumulative records, including hits (1,480), triples (105), and steals (409), as well as batting average (.296). Crawford was first and foremost a speed demon in his time with the Rays. He led the league in triples and steals four times each, while stealing over 400 bases in his 1,235 games with the club. On May 3, 2009, against his soon-to-be teammates in Boston, Crawford stole six bases becoming only the sixth player in MLB history to do so. There are two record holders with seven, one of whom is Billy Hamilton, but not the Billy Hamilton of whom you're thinking. Although modern era Hamilton could one day join "Sliding Billy" Hamilton with seven steals in a game, many of these stolen base records are from before the turn of the 20th century, making Crawford's six steal game even more impressive.[43]

A plus defender, Crawford was healthy for almost all of his Tampa career, and had one of his strongest years in 2010 (his final year with the Rays), which makes his tailspin since leaving the Sunshine State even more intriguing. Crawford openly admitted that he was all about the contract in 2010, and that he played through injury for far too long in his time in Boston. He had Tommy John surgery in August in 2012, but his time as a legitimate starting outfield seemed to end once he left Tampa, as the left side of his body began to just fall apart. Per Eno Sarris (on *Just a Bit Outside*), here are his injuries and days missed after leaving Tampa Bay: 2011 – Left hamstring strain – 30 days; 2012 – Left wrist surgery – Spring Training; 2012 – Left elbow strain – 116 days; 2012 – Left Tommy John surgery – 42 days; 2013 – Left hamstring strain – 33 days; 2014 – Left ankle sprain – 43 days. It's a sad story for a player that was consistently one of the top 15 American League players by WAR for a whole decade (2000-2009).

CF Melvin Upton (2004; 2006-2012)

"Bossman Junior" never quite lived up to his top prospect billing (second overall pick in 2002 draft), or his first full season in 2007 (86 runs, 24 home runs, and 82 RBI, .300/.386/.508 slashes), but he was a productive center fielder for the Rays in his eight years with the franchise, which most folks forget these days because of his atrocious post-Rays numbers. He never topped any of those slashes or RBI in a year after 2007, and he only topped his runs and home run totals one time apiece. The public perception of Upton also suffers a bit because his brother was also so highly touted, meaning their names were brought up what seemed like twice as often, but Melvin (going by B.J. when with the Rays) was definitely a solid power/speed option for the Rays, narrowly missing 30/30 home runs/steals in his final Rays season of 2012 (28 HR/31 SB).

Not to beat a dead horse on the start Upton made to his career, but during the 2008 postseason, it appeared as though Upton had found the lifting off point in his career, as he posted 16 runs, seven home runs, and 16 RBI with six steals in 16 playoff games, and along with Evan Longoria was the Rays best hitter. In the first two rounds of the 2008 playoffs alone, he hit a record-tying seven home runs to help lead the Rays to their first pennant. The breakthrough never really came, however, and although he did provide a solid power/speed duo, the Rays clearly thought his low average and high strikeouts were not worth the price they would have to pay for him and let the Braves signed him in the 2012 offseason. This was just further proof as to why baseball fans should not trust what seem like breakouts in the postseason (see also: David Freese). As far as how Upton fared post-Rays, he can take solace in the fact that he and his brother set the MLB-record for a pair of brothers, as teammates, homering in the same game, when they did so for the fifth time on August 9, 2014, while both were members of the Braves – but not much else.

RF Kevin Kiermaier (2013-pres.)

Yes, Kiermaier is actually a center fielder. Yes, Kiermaier has played less than 500 career games for the Rays. But.

---

[42] It didn't hurt that he was hitting .347 at the halfway point.

[43] Of course, Eric Young, in just the previous team section, was another one of the six, with Otis Nixon joining Crawford and Young as the only post-1912 players to steal at least six bases in a game.

Try to deny these eyes…

(Photo from Wikimedia Commons)

Also, the only other option was legit Matt Joyce. Matt Joyce does not have eyes that pretty. Sorry, Matt Joyce.

Incredibly, KK is actually already up to fourth in Rays history by WAR, and if he can ever put together a fully healthy season, he could be a legitimate MVP candidate thanks to his incredible defensive talent (first in Rays history with 12.1 dWAR already) and a surprisingly competent bat (108 career OPS+).

Utility Aubrey Huff (2000-2006)

Huff was a solid hitter, but a poor fielder, who played for the Rays in their Devil days. Huff's 2003-2004 seasons were excellent from a hitting standpoint, sporting a nice shiny 183/63/211 R/HR/RBI while hitting over .300 for the two seasons combined. Despite the solid offensive numbers, Huff was worth exactly 0.0 WAA in his time with the Devil Rays, and was not the type of player who fit into Joe Maddon's vision of the Rays. As such, he was sent out of town in 2006 – empty home runs and poor defense just aren't going to cut it for Maddon. In return the Rays got Zobrist, who as we covered earlier was a key part of the Rays organizational success and a highly-underrated player. Typical Maddon.

SP David Price (2008-2014)

Price is one of the Rays draft picks who really lived up to his potential. The first overall pick in the 2007 draft, he made it up to the big leagues by September call-ups of 2008. He pitched well in his brief stint and even came in for a few relief appearances in the playoffs. His 2009 campaign was a bit of a letdown, since expectations were set so high after his short stint the previous season. Price bounced back quickly though, finishing second in the Cy Young in 2010 and winning it in 2012, while leading the league in wins[44] and ERA. From there, Price established himself as one of the top pitchers in all of baseball, one who has an electric arm with that natural left-handed fastball fade and great control. Price relied heavily on his velocity when with the Rays, falling just a tenth of a mile hour short of the fastest fastball among pitchers with at least 1,000 innings pitched in his time with the Rays (94.2 mph compared to 94.3 from Justin Verlander).

Of course, Price was traded by the Rays to the Tigers in 2014 as part of a three-team deal that netted the Rays Nick Franklin, Drew Smyly, and Willy Adames. When he left, the rest of the American League East was happier than George Bailey at the end of *It's a Wonderful Life*, as Price always pitched very well against the AL East. Of course, that joy was short-lived, as Price found his way back to the division in the form of a trade from Detroit to Toronto and then a seven-year, $217 million contract with the Red Sox. At this point, Price just needs stints with the Yanks and Orioles to complete his AL East bingo card.

James Shields would seem to be another good candidate at this starting spot, seeing as he is the team leader in decent amount of the cumulative statistics for the Rays franchise, but Price beats him in almost every percentage category, and Price only trails Shields slightly in the cumulative ones. When the two are compared in terms of individual seasons, the comparison becomes even more one-sided. Price owns the top two seasons by wins in Rays history, the top two seasons by

[44] When he won his 20th game of the 2012 season, he was welcomed to the "Black Aces" club, a group of black pitchers who have won 20 games in a season. Price says he was welcomed by texts from C.C. Sabathia and Fergie Jenkins. This kind of feels like Price is majorly trolling everybody, but if he isn't, that's pretty awesome. There have only been 15 members of the club in baseball history, which speaks to the fact that baseball really needs a bit diversity at what is considered one of the most important positions (if not the most important position) on the diamond.

ERA, and the top season by WAR. Shields was certainly a horse for the Rays, and as a result his cumulative stats are impressive, but Price gets the nod going away.

Price was well known in Tampa Bay for being one of the most well-liked teammates, basically a big kid who would challenge teammates to contests such as who could fit the most pieces of gum in their mouth at once. He also has one of the best "From the files of silly abused stats that still manage to impress" – he is one of three left-handed pitchers in American League history to have at least 20 wins, 205 strikeouts, and an ERA 2.56 or lower in a season. I got that stat from my fireworks guy, Donny Eyebrow.

CP Fernando Rodney (2012-2013)

Rodney only pitched in Tampa for two seasons, but one of those seasons was one of the best seasons a closer has had in this millennium. He set the record (since broken) for lowest ERA in season with at least 50 innings (0.60 ERA), and his 641 ERA+ was out of this world. (Yes, that does indeed mean that his ERA was 541 percent better than league average.) Although his numbers slipped in 2013, they were far from catastrophic. His combined numbers still far outpaced what the Rays could have hoped for from a pitcher coming off of five straight seasons with an ERA over 4.00 before he came to town. Rodney is a good way to close out the Rays team, because he is just one more example of seemingly random players coming to Tampa and having complete career rejuvenations within the last five years. Must be something in the water… Or Joe Maddon… Or maybe Jim Hickey.

The Rays success has long been attributed to Maddon and their progressive front office, but the Rays pitching coach from 2007-2017, Jim Hickey, undoubtedly played a huge role in the team's success. When successful, the Rays main strength has been their pitching. In 2012 (their most recent postseason appearance), they posted the best ERA in the American League in 22 years, the lowest opponent batting average since the DH was implemented, and the most strikeouts of any team in AL history (since broken). The Rays emphasized not just getting strike one but also the all-important swing pitch, the 1-1 count, after Hickey and the staff noticed the major difference in opponent on-base percentage on a 2-1 count vs. a 1-2 count. The Rays also increased the use of changeups in their pitchers' repertoires and were among the first teams to implement regular shifting. The team made their players students of the game and had them attend seminars on advanced statistics. The results showed, and their success per dollar has been as strong as any team east of O.co. In fact, for Hickey's reign, the Rays posted the lowest ERA in the AL.

All Hickey's pupils say that his communication and patience were two of the biggest elements of his success as a coach. Hickey would often wait at least six starts before giving any advice, as, ideally, he wanted his pitchers to work through trouble on their own. As a teacher who loves to implement strategies similar to this when students are working through tough math problems, this struck a particular chord with me. His protégés also say that because he wasn't a big-time successful pitcher in the big leagues, Hickey was not set in his ways, yet another ideal asset for both coaches and teachers. Hickey's results were not just intangible stories from admiring peers, however, as there are numerical examples of his strong tutelage. When Chris Archer was called up by the Rays, Hickey noticed that he had an inconsistent release point that came as the result of a short stride. He let the young pitcher struggle through a few starts before finally pulling him aside before a big game against the Yankees. Archer immediately went undefeated in his next eight starts with two shutouts and far superior control.

Before 2014, the Rays pitching staff had an incredible run of health under Hickey, unrivaled by any other team in baseball. Their pitchers avoided Tommy John in an era when that was becoming an impressive feat. The Rays shoulder strengthening program has received a large amount of the credit, and is beginning to spread around the league, as ex-Rays pitchers take the regime to their new teams.

The Rays did well to scoop up Hickey from the Astros, but Houston was just as dumb to let him go. After stalling his progress in Triple-A for numerous years – because ownership believed a good pitching coach had to have been a good pitcher in his own time – Hickey was finally brought up to coach in the big leagues in 2004. In 2005, his first full season in the big leagues, the Astros finished with the second-best ERA in MLB, and went to their first World Series in franchise history. Of course, he was out of town by November 2006. In the emo words of Passenger, "Only know you love her when you let her go."

Starting IX Franchise Roster Stats

Lineup	Yrs	G	R	H	HR	RBI	SB	BB	SO	BA	OBP	SLG	OPS+	dWAR	WAR
B.J. Upton	8	966	539	910	118	447	232	430	1020	0.255	0.336	0.422	105	-3.2	15.4
Carl Crawford	9	1235	765	**1480**	104	592	**409**	293	768	**0.296**	0.337	0.444	107	3.8	35.5
Evan Longoria	**10**	**1435**	**780**	1471	**261**	**892**	51	**569**	**1220**	0.270	0.341	0.483	125	10.7	**50.0**
Aubrey Huff	7	799	400	870	128	449	20	247	412	0.287	0.343	0.477	116	-5.8	11.7
Carlos Peña	5	726	402	559	163	468	12	460	811	0.230	0.360	0.483	**126**	-1.9	18.1
Ben Zobrist	9	1064	565	1016	114	511	102	542	701	0.264	0.354	0.429	117	9.0	36.7
Kevin Kiermaier	5	463	208	415	47	151	60	118	339	0.262	0.319	0.431	108	**12.1**	21.5
Toby Hall	7	586	194	538	44	251	2	93	180	0.262	0.298	0.382	81	6.2	5.8
Jason Bartlett	3	400	209	409	19	150	61	121	241	0.288	0.349	0.403	102	2.4	10.4
Pitchers	Yrs	W	W%	ERA	G	CG	SHO	SV	IP	SO	ERA+	WHIP	SO/9	SO/BB	WAR
David Price	7	82	**0.636**	**3.18**	175	10	2	0	1143.2	1065	**122**	**1.142**	8.4	3.45	**21.3**
Fernando Rodney	2	7	0.538	1.91	144	0	0	85	141.1	158	202	1.04	10.1	3.10	4.3

#28 Miami Marlins (2012-pres.); Florida Marlins (1993-2011)

(Photo from Wikimedia Commons)

Team Background

Playoff appearances: 2 **Pennants: 2** **World Series titles: 2**
Collective team WAR: 180.1
Strengths: Well, they have never lost a series in the MLB playoffs, so maybe in some hypothetical tournament to determine the best franchise Starting IX some of that magic would help them make a run.
Weaknesses: ∞, but especially their starting pitching.
What to expect from the next 13 pages: A team tailor-made for younger fans of baseball. No grainy black and white photos in this section.

The Marlins have had one of the most intriguing histories of any franchise in baseball history. As almost all baseball fans know they twice won the World Series, both times as a wild card, but have never made the playoffs outside of those two seasons. After each championship, they decided to tear down the team that got them there and rebuild with new, young, *cheap*, homegrown players. After their first title in 1997, their teardown led to a 38-game drop-off in the win-loss record, and the team didn't finish above .500 again until 2003, when, of course, they won their second title. Their second teardown did not have as much of an impact on their subsequent 2004 campaign, as the team only won eight fewer games, but the team was not able to rebuild with the success previously seen by the previous Marlins World Series iteration.

One part of the Marlins championships that doesn't often get mentioned is that the Marlins World Series championships are, in the bigger picture, a perfect embodiment of the fact that we are currently in the Golden Age of competitive balance. From 1926-1965, 10 different teams won championships, and the Yankees alone won 19 championships. In the last 17 years, there have been 12 different champions, and no team has won more than three titles. There were an additional eight teams to win pennants during the 17 most recent years, and although part of that has to do with MLB expansion, there is undoubtedly a more level playing field today than in the olden days. Even with the uneven payrolls baseball sees, teams like the A's and Rays have done an incredible job of using analytics and market inefficiencies to compete with the big dogs.

The question of whether or not baseball will stay competitively balanced is an interesting one. On the one hand, it seems like there are so many brilliant minds in baseball, that the times of five truly dominant teams is likely over. On the other hand, MLB needs to only look across the pond at the British Premier League to see a league more steeped in history than MLB, and one that up until their new, shiny TV deal had little to no competitive balance. Some of the brightest minds in Britain ply their trade in the Premier League, but the financial gap was just too much until the little dogs started to get the influx of cash from their NBC TV rights, and a team like Leicester City was able to pull off a miracle. This was despite the best efforts of FIFA to implement a financial fair play rule that was treated somewhat similarly to how Hollywood stars treat the Seventh Commandment. With the windfall of television money coming their way, Major League Baseball could well see the top teams begin to make Godfather offers to the brightest minds in baseball and try to lock down the best players as well as the best personnel, but it will also need to make sure that revenue makes it to the smallest fish. Although not every fan would agree that a competitive balance is essential for Major League Baseball, it should be enjoyed while it lasts, because it may not always be this way.

* * *

Presently, the Marlins seem to be headed in about a million different directions. The team moved into a new stadium for the 2012 season, and with the new stadium came a supposed new dedication to leaving their cheapskate days in the past. The Marlins brought in José Reyes for six years and $106 million, Mark Buehrle for four years and $58 million, and Heath Bell for three years and $27 million. They even made a strong push for Albert Pujols, supposedly offering him a contract worth over $200 million. However, just a year later the Marlins once again stripped down all its parts, but this time without a championship, or even a playoff appearance to show for it. This angered all three people who still considered themselves Marlins fans, and rubbed many of their players the wrong way.

Their owner, Jeff Loria, is not new to this treatment of a city either. Loria first slithered into baseball in 1999 when he purchased the still Montreal-based Expos franchise. He bought in at just a 24-percent stake ($12 million), but quickly began to control more and more as he "triggered a series of cash calls, heard crickets each time, and steadily increased his stake in the Expos," as Jonah Keri describes in his portrait of Loria for *Grantland* after Loria's most recent clearance sale. Loria quickly saw that the franchise was doomed in Montreal, and although this was not Loria's fault *per se* (Right Field, Washington Nationals – Page 72), Loria showed no remorse flipping the Expos to the league for $120 million, which he now had a far greater stake in than the 24 percent he had started off with, thus sealing the Expos fate.

Keri does an outstanding job detailing all the nefarious ways in which Loria has gamed the system in his time around baseball, including threatening relocation to ensure Miami-Dade County financed a new stadium, receiving multiple league handouts, misleading fans about the team's true revenues, and, of course, disengaging yet another fanbase. If I hadn't seen a picture of Loria, I would be 99 percent sure he looked exactly like the villain from Rocky and Bullwinkle. And I still haven't heard him talk, so there's a 95 percent chance that he sounds less genuine than Mike Damone in *Fast Times at Ridgemont High*.

And really, it's a shame that as big a potential baseball market as Miami has been so poorly managed, and that more and more fans have abandoned them ever since Loria sleazed his way into Miami in 2002. As of now, the future of the Marlins is very much up in the air, which seems to be a recurring theme in their history. The most recent move from Loria has been to award Giancarlo Stanton with the longest (13 years) and biggest ($325 million) contract in MLB history, a move that seems to make no sense on several levels. First of all, Stanton was one of the players most vocal about his frustration with Loria's most recent fire sale. There's also the fact that the now-longest contract in MLB history was just handed out by the man who reneged on his last big move in less than a calendar year; and it comes with a full no-trade clause. Granted, it does have an early player opt-out clause for just after Stanton turns 30, but the move as a whole had most of the baseball shaking their heads in confusion. However, considering this is Loria, maybe we should just follow Keri's advice from the last crazy move Loria made: "I don't blame him for any of this. I'm just impressed by how well he worked everything to his advantage, taking advantage of elected officials, short-sighted businessmen, and a system that rewards the kind of behavior that might seem despicable but is impossibly profitable. When it comes to Jeffrey Loria, I'm just in awe." I suddenly just got a little nervous for Giancarlo Stanton…

Random cool things about the franchise:

- The Marlins original CEO, Wayne Huizenga, is best known as the CEO of Blockbuster – hey, maybe Reed Hastings can buy the team if new owner Derek Jeter has buyer's remorse in a few years.
- Among the names considered for the franchise before its inception was the Florida Flamingos.
- The franchise has infinitely more World Series titles than division titles.
- Both World Series titles came out of the wild card spot, the 1997 title making them the first team to win the World Series from the wild card spot and the 2003 title just the third time the feat happened (2002 Angels), making the Marlins the only team to win two titles from the wild card spot, a distinction they still hold today.
- Marlins Park, which opened in 2012, has a pair of bullet-proof aquariums that acts as the backstop, and a home run structure in left-center that may just be the most Miami piece of architecture of all time.
- They also have dancers – the dancers are a big deal.

Starting IX

C Charles Johnson (1994-1998; 2001-2002)

Charles Johnson was the Marlins first-ever first-round pick, and started his career in Florida with great potential before fading out a bit. In his first three seasons with the club he received the following accolades: seventh in Rookie of the Year in 1995; National League All-Star and 11th in MVP in the Marlins World Series-winning 1997 season; caught two no-hitters; and added a Gold Glove each of the three seasons. The Gold Glove win as a rookie put him in the elite company of Johnny Bench, Carlton Fisk, and Sandy Alomar Jr. as the only rookie catchers to win a Gold Glove.

However, because the Marlins decide to have a full-blown fire sale after every championship, Johnson was shipped out of town less than a third of the way through the 1998 season, in a deal that brought Mike Piazza to Florida – for all of eight days before he was flipped to Mets.

Johnson added most of his value to the team on the defensive side of things. He was the National League's dWAR leader in 1997, with 2.6 dWAR compared to his 2.4 oWAR. This was actually his highest oWAR total while with the club, and, as his 96 OPS+ with the franchise can attest to, he was a slightly-below-average hitter in his time in Florida. Johnson was almost exactly the same for the seven seasons after he left Florida, but he never landed in one spot for more than a hot minute. Here are his numbers from Florida vs. the rest of his career, just because of the eerie similarity:

	G	AB	H	R	HR	RBI	BB	SO	BA	OBP	SLG	OPS+	WAR
FLA	587	1936	467	204	75	277	232	499	.241	.324	.418	96	11.7
Others	601	1900	473	261	92	293	243	498	.249	.337	.448	98	10.9

One sad statement on the Marlins as a whole is that, despite netting the team only 11.7 WAR in his time with the Marlins, Charles Johnson is 12th all-time among their position players. Whether this is due to a dearth of quality players, a short franchise history, or the fact that no one seems to stay with the Marlins more than half a decade, it is certainly a damning statistic.

1B Derrek Lee (1998-2003)

Lee didn't really hit his stride until after his days in Florida, but he was a solid performer while with the Marlins, nonetheless. Lee would actually play a pretty good foil to Johnson on this team, as he brought most of his value to the team in his offensive skills. He hit 129 home runs in his time with the team, topping 25 home runs three of his final four years in Miami. However, due to his sieve-like defense, Lee was worth exactly nothing by wins above average (0.0 WAA) in his six years with the team. Lee was there for the team's championship run but did very little in support of it. Honestly, he is here as a placeholder until the team gets their head on straight and plays a legitimate first baseman for a half-decade. I have a yacht purchased in Justin Bour Bay, so I'm really hoping that property can pay off sooner than later, and he can take this spot by something like 2020.

2B Luis Castillo (1996-2005) vs. Dan Uggla (2006-2010)

Time for our first breakdown. For those that didn't read the introduction,[45] these breakdowns will occur sporadically throughout the book, and they are a 100 percent rip-off of Bill Simmons and Dr. Jack Ramsay before him.

In this case, there's the added bonus that Castillo and Uggla personify opposite sides of the spectrum when it comes to ballplayers. Luis Castillo relied on his speed and ability to slap the ball around for singles and steals. Uggla just tried to mash the hell out of the ball every time he came up to the plate.

(Since this is the first breakdown, each chart will have a brief key defining the statistics used that might not be common knowledge. For all career-high slash stats – batting average, slugging percentage, etc. – in all breakdowns, it will be a 300-plate appearance minimum in a season to qualify. In certain categories, the Misc. column will be used to show how many times a player led the league [LL] in a certain statistical category.)

Contact

	BA	lgBA	Seasons ≥ .300*	Career high/low	Seasons ≥ 80 SO	SO%	lgSO%	BABIP
Castillo	.293	.264	5	.334/.263	0	12.7	17.0	.338
Uggla	.263	.263	0	.287/.243	All	22.5	18.1	.302

[45] So, for all of you.

SO% = strikeouts/plate appearances, any stat with % after it just means that stat divided by plate appearances; lg = league rate of whatever stat it is in front of; BABIP = batting average on balls in play

Not surprisingly, Castillo has the edge here. Castillo was able to beat out infield singles, and since he was not trying to drive the ball out as Uggla was, his average was consistently higher than Uggla's. Castillo also got to hit without the defense shifting which is becoming more and more important in today's game. Uggla suffers in this category due to an extremely high strikeout rate in every year with the team. He nearly averaged a strikeout a game (.98) in his five years with the team. Castillo, on the other hand, struck out well below the league average. This is going to be a common theme in this breakdown, but BIG advantage here.

EDGE: Castillo by a lot.

Power

	HR	Seasons ≥ 20 HR	Career high HR	XBH	SLG%	lgSLG%	ISO	HR%	XBH%
Castillo	20	0	6	192	.356	.425	.063	0.4	3.9
Uggla	154	5	33	336	.488	.427	.224	4.6	10.0

XBH = extra-base hits; ISO = isolated power (SLG minus BA)

You can probably see where this is going. Uggla thrived on his power game, whereas Castillo couldn't have cared less. Castillo truly focused on getting on base, and nothing else, as he only once topped 30 extra-base hits in a season (31 in 2003). In contrast, Uggla hit at least 31 *home runs* in four of his five years in Florida. One point that needs to be mentioned is that, in 2000, Castillo hit .334 with 180 hits and 101 runs, and he did all this while totaling 17 RBI for the *entire* season. This means he had a H:RBI ratio of over 10.0; remarkable. Uggla's highest H:RBI ratio was his rookie year, and it wasn't even 2.0. These two are wildly different ball players.

EDGE: Uggla by a country mile.

Batting eye

	BB	Seasons ≥ 70 BB	OBP	lgOBP	OPS+	BB%	SO/BB
Castillo	533	2	.370	.336	94	10.7	1.18
Uggla	363	3	.349	.338	117	10.8	2.09

Reminder: OPS+ = all-encompassing offensive stat scaled so that 100 is league average, and each number above 100 is a percent above-average, while each number below is a percent below league-average. In the example here, Luis Castillo was six percent worse than league average with the bat in Florida, while Uggla was 17 percent better than league average. This stat will be used plenty, so it's a good one to know.

Having a good eye at the plate could potentially be a tiebreaker category for two players of such different skill sets as these two. Often times power hitters are thought of as drawing more walks, but this is usually due more to their waiting for a perfect pitch to drive instead of really having all that good of an eye. This is one case where that seems particularly true. Although their walk rates are nearly identical, the fact that Uggla struck out nearly twice as much as Castillo needs to be considered. Overall, I think the ability to draw walks is more important than the ability to avoid strikeouts, but when the two walk rates are as close as these two, a look at strikeout rate can be the difference.

EDGE: Castillo, in what was finally a close category.

Speed

	SB	Seasons ≥ 20 SB	Career high SB	Rbaser	SB%	XBT%	GDP%	Misc.
Castillo	281	6	62	17	71	48	10	LL 2x SB, 1x CS
Uggla	19	0	6	2	58	43	7	

Rbaser = Baseball-Reference's calculation for how much a player was worth with his baserunning skills. 10 Rbaser runs equal 1.0 WAR; XBT% = Extra Base Taken percentage which is the percent of times the runner advanced more than one base on a single or more than two bases on a double; GDP% = rate of double plays grounded into; CS = caught stealing.

Again, an obvious category so I'll use this space to try to comment on how much speed contributes to the game of baseball. This is something that will be discussed throughout this book, but we can do a point/counterpoint here to look at base stealing in particular. One way to look at it is that even with all of Castillo's speed on the basepaths, he netted his team only 1.7 wins with his baserunning in his entire 10 years with the Marlins.

Of course, this point could be countered by saying that although Castillo had such a small number of extra-base hits in his time with Florida (something that was held against him in the power category), he really had 281 extra bases thanks to his steals; his singles often became doubles and sometimes even triples. Also, when fast runners are on base, they make pitchers have to throw more fastballs to the ensuing batters, a point that doesn't often get mentioned in favor of having speed on the bases. However, it's hard to argue with the advanced metrics, which tend to say baserunning is overrated, especially when Castillo's caught-stealing rate was relatively high for such a prolific base stealer.

One final note against Castillo's edge here being worth as much: despite the vast gap in their base-stealing ability, Uggla, because he got under the ball so often, had a significantly lower grounded-into-double-play percentage than Castillo, a factor that can change the outcome of the game even more than a stolen base.

EDGE (but how much is it really worth): Castillo

Defense

	Fld%	lgFld%	dWAR	RF/9 high/low	lgRF/9	DPs	DP/G	GG	Misc.
Castillo	.983	.983	3.6	5.31/4.72	4.96	747	.662	3	LL 1x GP (2B), PO (2B), E (2B), TZR (2B)
Uggla	.980	.983	-2.0	5.09/4.43	4.84	484	.624	0	LL 2x GP (2B), 1x Assists (2B, E (2B)

RF/9 = just a fancy way of calculating a player's range in the field; DPs = not what you think... double plays; GG = Gold Gloves; TZR = Total Zone Runs is just another measurement of player value from the defensive side of things.

Uggla's reputation as a black hole at second base was a little overstated, at least according to the advanced metrics. He was never a great defender, but he never really killed his team, as many made it sound during his career. Uggla's double plays turned and fielding percentage were not far off of Castillo's (although the myth of fielding percentage has been debunked by numerous baseball writers, even dating back to Henry Chadwick, who favored fielding range over fielding percentage), and the only distinct edge Castillo holds is in his range. This is certainly an advantage, but this category isn't the type of blowout that was seen in power or speed.

EDGE: Castillo

Intangibles

This is a very broad category and one that historically has been number-proof, one that has to do more with the eye test, or what a player brings to the clubhouse. Baseball has such an interesting dynamic – due to the length and day-to-day nature of the game – that a large part of your role with the team is what you bring off the field as well as on it. Some of the things that will be covered in this section throughout the book include injuries, leadership, performance in important moments, clubhouse dynamic, adaptability, personality, and random minutiae that can swing the category either way.

In terms of these two, Uggla was a remarkably consistent presence on the field, playing at least 146 games in each of his seasons with the Marlins and never missing significant time while with the franchise. There's also the fact that Dan Uggla's last name translates to "owl" in Swedish (and I even read his full name translates to "pesky owl" somewhere), so he clearly gets the edge here.

EDGE: Uggla

Team Success

	W	L	W-L%	Seasons $\geq$ 90 W	Division titles	Pennants	WS
Castillo	558	570	.495	2	0	2	2
Uggla	382	394	.492	0	0	0	0

Despite this being a close matchup in terms of win/loss percentage, Castillo cruises to victory on the strength of two World Series victories. Although Castillo didn't actually play in the 1997 World Series, he contributed during the regular season and was a definite contributor by 2003.

EDGE: Castillo

Dominance

Castillo was in the top 10 in the league in steals five of his 10 years in Florida, but each and every one of those years he was also in the top 10 in caught stealing. Surprisingly, the only categories besides steals in which he ever led the league were some defensive metrics, and he was certainly not a dominant defensive player by any stretch of the imagination. Uggla's power wasn't dominant on a league-wide basis – he never finished higher than fourth in the National League in home runs – but he was certainly dominant in power at his position, and power from a second baseman is clearly a valuable commodity.

EDGE: Uggla

Impact on the Franchise

As noted, Castillo was around for the Marlins 2003 championship (and was on the roster, but didn't play, for the 1997 World Series), and he stayed with the club after its lesser fire sale. In fact, thanks to his 10 years in Florida, he is the franchise's leader in games played (1,128), at bats (4,347), runs (675), hits (1,273), triples (42), walks (533), and stolen bases (281). Uggla, on the other hand, used to be the franchise leader in home runs and strikeouts (since surpassed by Giancarlo Stanton), and he never played on a Marlin playoff team. In fact, the image of him crushing home runs into the completely empty bleachers of Dolphin Stadium is the first image that comes to mind when the average fan thinks of Dan Uggla.

EDGE: Castillo

Verdict[46]

During the introduction to this breakdown, I mentioned that it would serve as a breakdown for a larger comparison: the power hitter vs. the slap-and-speed player. This wasn't entirely fair. Castillo simply had more games with the Marlins, and with these positions being determined by their cumulative careers with the Marlins, **Luis Castillo** has to take the position for the Marlins. That doesn't necessarily mean that the slap-and-speed guys have won, however.

Over 1,128 games in his Marlins career, Castillo was worth 22.3 WAR; in 352 fewer games with the Marlins, Uggla was worth 15.6 WAR, not too far off. The advantage given to the power hitter is a common one with the advances in baseball metrics. Although slap-and-speed players have their place on an MLB roster (there has yet to be an MLB owner who has tried to create a roster of power hitters one through nine in the lineup,[47] and that's not because of a lack of power guys), it is generally agreed upon that the drawbacks of the stereotypical power hitter (strikeouts, generally poor defensive play) are outweighed by the benefits (home runs being worth far more than singles, speed being overrated). So, although power hitters are the more valuable players in baseball, consider this (along with the Royals 2014-2015 success) a minor victory for the slap-and-speed guys.

3B Miguel Cabrera (2003-2007)

In his very first game in the big leagues on June 20, 2003, Cabrera set the tone for his career to come. The newly-promoted 20-year-old took Al Levine deep in the bottom of the 11th inning for a walk-off in his first professional game. Later in his rookie season, Cabrera got his first (and to date, only) World Series ring, after leading the Marlins with three home runs and a near team-leading 1.027 OPS in the Marlins NLCS win – a win now most infamous for one Mr. Steve Bartman.

Miggy posted an OPS+ of 106 in his 87-game rookie season, has increased in each of his first four seasons in the majors, and only dropped below 130 this most recent season. Cabrera owns the honor of being one of the few active players to appear multiple times in this book, and one would be hard-pressed to find a player who deserved it more. Cabrera began being talked about in a historical sense after his move to Detroit, but he laid the foundation of his superstardom in Florida.

Cabrera is thought of as one of baseball's most pure hitters; not just of his era, but of all time. Al Kaline called him the best hitter he's ever seen besides Ted Williams, and although I sometimes question this type of sentiment (it often feels like the ex-star is just making the statement to see their name appear in the headlines again), when it is qualified by "besides Player X," the sentiment weirdly feels more genuine. Especially when "Player X" is Ted Williams.

A.J. Pierzynski said of Miggy's hitting, "Miguel Cabrera's bat makes the loudest sound. That's easy. He hit a ball last year that went so far – about 520 feet to dead center field – my ears are still ringing from that. After the inning, I had to

---

[46] Please note that Ben Lindbergh wrote a similar piece comparing the speed vs. power tropes of Juan Pierre and Adam Dunn for *Grantland* in 2015 entitled, "Adam Dunn, Juan Pierre, and why we need WAR." It was one of the biggest cases of, "Goddamnit why have I not published this book yet, this article is exactly what I'm writing that no one can see on my laptop." At least the two players being compared were different.

[47] Outside of my buddy Jon in our *MLB: The Show* franchise. Prince Fielder at shortstop? Yeah, why not?

go get my ears checked to see if they were bleeding."

Despite Cabrera's immense talent, he has never really taken off as "the face of baseball," a term some baseball writers like to throw out when talking about what the modern game is lacking, usually in support of their notions that the sport is in decline. This topic will be covered in greater depth at the Angels center field position, but if Miggy is not the face of baseball, that's more by his choice than because the sport can't generate a visible star. For his part, Cabrera hates interviews and never opens up because he feels that people can't be trusted. In fact, in a rare interview with *ESPN the Mag*, Sam Alipour asked Cabrera, "What's your biggest fear?" Miggy's response: "People. You can't trust people." This makes sense, since he is almost certainly bothered by people asking him for things constantly, here and in his native Venezuela. Of course, there's also the fact he is extremely guarded about his off-field issues. Many baseball fans know about his off-field struggles, and given the way Cabrera treats the subject in Alipour's piece, I think it's fair to leave that part of his life out of his write-up here. There will certainly be some airing out of the dirty laundry in this book for certain players, but we'll try to keep it to those who played eight decades ago instead of those whose legacy is still being built.

With Cabrera, there's enough to talk about with his on-field contributions to the book to fill this section, along with his inclusion on the Detroit Starting IX.

SS Hanley Ramírez (2006-2012)

Hanley has provided baseball its definitive enigma since being traded from the Red Sox to the Marlins as part of a package (with Anibal Sanchez) for Josh Beckett and Mike Lowell in late 2005. (There were other pieces involved, but that was the gist of it.) Hanley made it to the big leagues right away with the Marlins, and he showcased the talent that had made him the centerpiece of the aforementioned deal. Hanley won the league's Rookie of the Year, played 158 games, and netted the Marlins nearly five wins (4.9 WAR) mostly on the strength of his bat (116 OPS+ from the shortstop position).

However, Han-Ram, or El Niño, has spent his entire career with an Eeyore-esque cloud of question marks hovering above him. Questions of his maturity have been so consistent that, when researching for this book, I found an article from *Sports Illustrated* with the byline: "Florida's shortstop is a maddening player, for pitchers who face him and teammates who suffer his lapses in maturity. How good might Hanley Ramírez be if he just grew up?" and when I couldn't find the date of the article for a second, honestly had no clue what year the article was from, as it could have been any season between 2006 and 2011 (it ended up being from 2010), and the only reason it couldn't have been more recent is because it said Florida, and not Miami, Los Angeles, or Boston.

This is a player so talented that he is the only player in MLB history to post at least 180 hits, 45 doubles, 10 triples, 100 runs, and 50 stolen bases in his rookie season. And even if those parameters are bent specifically towards his totals, his rookie season stands up in history, especially considering he played shortstop. However, this is also a player who noticeably failed to hustle on numerous occasions – and not just the stupid not hustling out routine ground balls, which I can give a pass for from time to time, but in the field, when it really cost his team – and often seems to not bring 100 percent on the field. This can be a dangerous game to play, as some players simply have a more fluid feel to their game (àla Ken Griffey Jr.), but when so many teammates, coaches, and ex-players all share the same sentiment about a lack of maturity, it's hard to ignore. At this point, it's probably just best to take him as he is, warts and all.

LF Cliff Floyd (1997-2002)

Floyd was a man of many teams, but he spent six (not all complete) seasons in Florida, more than any of the six other teams he played on during his career. In his time with the Marlins, he posted very solid slashes[48] (.294/.374/.523) and probably is one of the more underrated players of his generation. Anyway, since not too much of note happened during his time in Florida, this space will be used to do the first of several self-indulgent lists! Since this book focuses on baseball, it's abundantly clear that I am a baseball fan, but let's look at which sports would have been the most interesting in each decade throughout the last century-plus. What does this have to do with Cliff Floyd? Nothing.

1900s

1) Baseball: The beginning of the modern era, with stars like Nap Lajoie and Ty Cobb, who weren't necessarily likable guys, but the sport was in a blossoming phase.
2) Horse Racing: Certainly not the sport today that it used to be, my "inherited nostalgia" from movies set in this era makes me think I would love to go down to the tracks to see some races. Definitely not to gamble…
3) Boxing: If it weren't for the increased awareness about concussions, boxing would definitely be the number one sport I wish was still mainstream. It's a sport that was more progressive than many others of its time, having its first black champion within this decade. Of course, the health risks of the sport quickly became abundantly clear, and the sport was dominated by mostly lower-class fighters who were either unaware of the risks or simply needed it as a way of making money. It will be

---

48 Friendly reminder: This simply means batting average/on-base percentage/slugging percentage, but doesn't take a half hour to type out each time. Plus, it sounds cool. These reminders will start fading the further we get into the book.

interesting to see if football suffers a similar fate in the not-too-distant future.
4) Golf: Would have been my favorite sport to play, and it was just starting to get interesting to follow as well.
5) College Football: Was organized and established enough to have All-Americans. Any sport that regularly makes lists as early as 1900 is deserving of a spot in this collection of lists.

1910s

1) Horse Racing: Not the most exciting decade for baseball; also, I love to gamble.
2) College Football: The Notre Dame era, and although this might have turned me off a bit since I'm not a huge fan of the Fighting Irish (sorry, Tim), it was a time when the game was very well established in America's culture.
3) Boxing: Similar to college football, boxing was just too ingrained in American culture to ignore in the early 20th century.
4) Baseball: Still in the top five despite a really strong case not to be. As Bill James put it in his *Abstract*, the players of the 1910s were "shysters, con men, drunks, and outright thieves." The decade ended with the Black Sox scandal and a legitimate fear that the game might not survive a few more years down the same path.
5) Hockey: The NHL was founded towards the end of the decade, and the fact that I can't skate would have made it so that I would have been too impressed with these men flying around the ice not to like the sport. Plus, the hipster gene in me would have wanted to like this sport before it became "popular." And yes, the quotation marks mean "in Canada."

1920s

1) Baseball: Boy, oh boy, did baseball come back strong, though. While Babe Ruth and Lou Gehrig made the Yankees likable (to many, although I'm sure Ruth turned off his fair share), the game evolved towards slugfests with hitting records set that would stand for decades.
2) Boxing: Outside of Ruth, it could be argued Jack Dempsey was the most recognizable athlete to pre-Depression era Americans.
3) Football: The onset of the NFL brings professional football into the top five for the first time and certainly not the last.
4) Soccer: The two first official World Championships kick off a great run of one of the best sporting events every four years – the World Cup.
5) Hockey: With the Original Six now in the mix, hockey just tops college football because, well, I like hockey more than college football now, and don't see why it wouldn't be the same then.

1930s

1) Baseball: Ruth, Gehrig, Foxx, Dean, Gehringer, Greenberg, Medwick, DiMaggio, Ott, Grove, and a brief introduction to Ted Williams; this was a Golden Age.
2) Boxing: If it hadn't been for the men listed above, boxing could easily have been number one with the big boxing scene in New York, and Joe Louis headlining the decade. Part of my love for boxing comes from my obsession with *The Twilight Zone*, a show which Rod Serling's love of boxing regularly permeated.
3) Summer Olympics: I'm not the biggest Olympic person, but Jesse Owens winning his four gold medals and single-handedly destroying Hitler's Aryan supremacy myth is pretty effing awesome.
4) College Basketball: The first NIT tournament means the movement towards March Madness, and the greatest four-day stretch (Opening Weekend) of the year.
5) College Football: With the creation of the Orange, Cotton, and Sugar Bowls to go along with the first AP poll, it was a big decade for the sport.

1940s

1) Baseball: Still on top, even with the drop in play during WWII. Stan Musial, Ted Williams, Warren Spahn, etc. along with the sport's desegregation are enough to keep it number one.
2) Boxing: Still going strong, and my favorite boxer of all time (thanks entirely to Robert De Niro), Jake LaMotta, was reaching relevance as the sport thrived through the war years.
3) Basketball: The NBA is founded, and the sport will find a spot on my top five for the rest of eternity.
4) Football: It seems like we're getting closer and closer to what will be on my top five for the most recent decades.
5) Golf: I may have spoken too soon. Seeing Babe Didrikson play would be too fun not to see.

1950s

1) College Basketball: Bill Russell and Wilt Chamberlain begin their rivalry and begin the journey that would end with the two topping the charts as the most intriguing rivalry of all time. (Outside of LeBron vs. idiot Boston fans.)
2) Football: "The Greatest Game of All Time" happened, and although my team lost in the game (screw you, Alan Ameche), the presence of Johnny Unitas and Jim Brown help football to its highest spot yet… in my made-up, fucking fairy-tale rankings.
3) Soccer: The emergence of Pelé, and the great Brazilian teams that were among the most fun to watch of all time, help to propel soccer to this spot.

4) Golf: Arnold Palmer, Gary Player, Ben Hogan, Didrikson, and even Jack Nicklaus as an amateur.
5) Baseball/Basketball: I refuse to leave either MLB or the NBA off, so I will cheat.

1960s

1) Basketball: Russell vs. Chamberlain moves to the NBA along with Elgin Baylor, Bob Cousy, John Havlicek, the "Big O," and Jerry West to make one of the best eras of the NBA.
2) Baseball: Between the race for 61, Sandy Koufax in his prime, Bob Gibson's magical 1968 season, and the Miracle Mets, the `60s were a pretty cool time for baseball.
3) Boxing: Cassius Clay becomes Muhammad Ali becomes one of the five most famous athletes of all time.
4) Football: The first Super Bowl – and Joe Namath's famous guarantee – highlight a great building block of a decade.
5) Soccer: Pelé still reigns supreme, and England won their last World Cup which appeals to the Anglophile in me. Plus, my two favorite old school players were in their primes as Garrincha and Lev Yashin marched to the beat of their own drums out on the pitch.

1970s

1) Basketball: The ABA/NBA merger occurs, and although Russell vs. Chamberlain was mostly over, Dr. J, Pistol Pete, and The Iceman were just coming into their primes. It was also the last time my beloved Knicks won a championship.
2) Soccer: Total Football, the Dutch brand of soccer (yes, I refuse to call it football) was one of the most appetizing of all time.
3) Boxing: Still highlighted by Ali and Frazier, to go along with George Foreman, this represents the last time for boxing in the top five, as only Mike Tyson spiked my interests among post-Ali boxers. The interest in Tyson was often for reasons not having to do with the sport itself, anyway.
4) Football: Monday Night Football started the revolution toward having as many nights during the week to be filled with football as possible, which is always a good thing. (For Goodell and the money-driven owners, that is.)
5) Baseball: Not one of baseball's best decades from my point of view, with the inception of free agency, stadiums introducing turf, and a dearth of players about whom I feel strongly.[49] However, this is not to say this is the be-all and end-all of opinions on the era (go figure!), as Bill James has it as one of the most entertaining eras in his sometimes-humble opinion. I really wanted to slot Billie Jean King and tennis (particularly the women's brand) in here, but I just can't quit you, baseball.

1980s

1) College Basketball: A good decade for basketball in general. Magic vs. Bird increased popularity for the sport, which then thrived with Bob Knight winning two titles in the decade; one going to Michael Jordan; N.C. State and Georgetown completing two of the greatest runs to championships of all time; and Coach K planting the seeds for his dynasty to come.
2) Basketball: The new rivalry of Magic vs. Bird took to the forefront for the decade, and although the sport faced a serious problem with substance abuse, the sport was too entertaining to leave off the top two spots. Jordan's rise even occurred at the end of the decade.
3) Hockey: Beginning with the Islanders streak of Cups at the start of the decade, and continuing with Gretzky's presence throughout the era, this was one of the most fun times to be a hockey fan. The decade also spurred approximately 9,341 Sean McIndoe (of *Down Goes Brown*) articles in 2014 alone.
4) Football: Joe Montana, Jerry Rice, Walter Payton, the real and original LT, the mighty Bears defense, and a title for my Giants lock down a top five spot.
5) Baseball: Another decade of which I was not a huge fan. Baseball struggled with issues of substance abuse (sensing a theme, you 1980s folks?), and players like Mike Schmidt and Gary Carter weren't enough to bring the sport above this ranking.

1990s

1) Baseball: Finally, a decade for which I was alive, so I can say beyond any doubt that baseball would have been my favorite sport of the `90s because, well, it was. It was my first love, and the "Core Four" Yankees made rooting for my favorite team fun.[50] As for the sport itself, it sank almost as low as it could in 1994 with the strike, but it really made up for that in the second half of the decade with the arms race (no pun intended) that took over the sport. It might not have been the purest quality of baseball, but it was surely entertaining and helped bring baseball back to its fans.
2) College Basketball: If baseball was my first love, college basketball was the girlfriend you fall absolutely head over heels for just after. The players all just seemed so cool (see: *Sports Illustrated* cover with Chris Porter), and reenacting scenes from March Madness in my driveway became how I spent 5-50 hours a week.
3) Basketball: Solid Knicks teams, along with peak MJ and a passionate hatred for Reggie Miller, made for some great early memories of the NBA and what it means to be a Knicks fan.

---

[49] I honestly think part of that is how ugly the baseball cards from the 1970s are.
[50] Something I would learn later is definitely not always true. Thanks, 2004-and-2013-and-2014-and-2016-and-2017-and-really-every-year Knicks teams.

4) College Football: Between bowl season, my man-crush on Kirk Herbstreit, the line of NCAA Football PS2 games (specifically Dynasty Mode), and having games to watch all day Saturday, college football ate up a lot of my first decade.
5) Football: I was a little late to the NFL bandwagon, but my dad helped me along the way to grow and love the sport.

2000s

1) Baseball: The sport still reigned supreme for the awkward stages of my life, despite the fact that all sports took a bit of a back seat to growing up at times.
2) College Basketball: Sean Singletary helped keep the University of Virginia relevant, and March Madness ensured at least three weeks of complete devotion to the sport every year.
3) Football: The Giants started to fill more and more of my time in my teen years, as Eli arrived and, much to my chagrin (at first), replaced the immortal Kurt Warner but later helped bring the Giants to the promised land.
4) College Football: Strangely enough, college sports dominated my interest until I went to college, at which point I made the change to almost exclusively professional sports.
5) Basketball: Not the strongest decade for the sport. AI was incredible on many levels, but as a Kobe-hater waiting for LeBron to make "the jump," I thought the sport, and maybe more precisely the coverage of the sport, was aggravating.

2010s

1) Basketball: Yes, the decade is young, and since I'm writing a book on baseball it would seem that baseball should be number one, but the arrival of LeBron as the best player since MJ (and I think with a chance to top him) and the revival (somewhat) of the Knicks (hey, they made the playoffs that one time…), basketball has been a mainstay throughout.
2) Baseball: Today's young stars represent a great forthcoming generation of baseball that very well may take the number-one spot by the end of the decade. Throw in a few more World Series the quality of Rangers vs. Cardinals or Chicago vs. Cleveland, and the top spot will be hard to deny to my first love.
3) Soccer: In a typical college move, I got very into soccer during my "sophisticated" college years, and have loved delving into the sport's rich history and beginning to follow the leagues all around the world ever since. It also helps that the games are usually on in the morning or early afternoon, meaning that sports can be on all day every day!
4) Football: Another title for the Giants (even sweeter to top the hated Patriots yet again) and countless Sundays at "B-Dubs" watching every fantasy player at once make this probably the best fourth-ranked sport in a single decade.
5) College Basketball: A tight race for fifth against hockey, but March Madness still tops the NHL playoffs. At least until people start gambling more openly on the hockey playoffs.

If each sport is given a total score by giving five points for a first-place finish, four for a second-place finish, etc. the total rankings would look as such:

1) Baseball – 43; 2) Basketball – 27; 3) Boxing – 24; 4) College Basketball – 21; Football – 21

And just to complete the ways in which you can waste time with lists, each decade by how much I feel I would have enjoyed sports, as a whole, in that decade:

1) 1960s 2) 1980s 3) 1940s 4) 2010s 5) 1990s 6) 1930s 7) 1950s 8) 1920s 9) 2000s 10) 1970s 11) 1910s 12) 1900s

It should be noted that these lists were mostly compiled during slow-moving college courses. Who said that my history degree wouldn't do me any good?! Now go make your own.

CF Juan Pierre (2003-2005; 2013)

Pierre came to Florida from Colorado in 2003 as an established presence on the basepaths and solid leadoff man. Pierre played four years total with the team, having played with them for three years immediately after the Colorado move, and then returning to the squad nearly a decade later for his final season. Pierre was a constant among the league leaders in steals, finishing in the top 10 of his league in steals in every single season of his career sans 2011 and his 51-game rookie season. He had nearly 100 more steals than anyone else in the twenty-aughts, or whatever we call that decade from 2000-2009, tallying 97 more steals than the second-place Carl Crawford. Pierre's speed also aged well, with Pierre tallying a league-leading 68 steals in 2010 in his age-32 season.[51] Removing his first and last season, Pierre stole at least 27 bases each year, and his 614 career steals rank 18th all-time.

Like Castillo, however, Pierre was also regularly among the league leaders in caught stealing. In fact, he led his league in caught stealing (seven times) far more times than actual stolen bases (three times). For his career, he stole 614 bases

[51] Since this is the first time using the term "Age-X" season, just know that the cut off is if you have turned that Age X before June 30 of that season. E.g. Juan Pierre turned 32 before June 30 of 2010.

but was caught 203 times, coming in at a 75 percent clip that barely made all the stolen bases worth any true value.

For more on Pierre, check out the excellent *Before the Glory* by Bill Staples and Rich Herschlag. There are stories of Pierre's exploits with holy water while playing Little League; his brother who gave up his job for the Marlins 2003 playoff run; and the importance of other black baseball players to his love of baseball. Overall, Pierre seems like a good dude, and he even got a Jay Z name drop in the track "Déjà Vu" off Beyoncé's *B'Day*.

RF Giancarlo Stanton (2010-pres.)

Stanton has made a name for himself with raw power on par with the Harmon Killebrews and Jimmie Foxxes of baseball history. He posted a slugging percentage over .500 as a 20-year-old rookie despite an on-base percentage of just .326. Stanton's power numbers improved each of the next two seasons, and in his age-22 season, Stanton fell one plate appearance shy of qualifying for the slugging percentage, posting a .608 slugging percentage that would have led MLB.

After an off year in 2013 during which Stanton dealt with nagging injuries for the entirety of the year, Stanton bounced back in 2014 with a league-leading 37 home runs and 299 total bases. He did this despite missing the final few weeks after taking a beanball to the face from the Brewers Mike Fiers. The season earned him the biggest contract in the history of the league, an interesting move touched on briefly in this team's introduction. Only time will tell if the contract really resets the course of Marlins history, but after it was signed, the Marlins President of Baseball Operations, Michael Hill, said that if Stanton hadn't signed the deal, the Marlins would have moved in a far different direction from the busy offseason that followed Stanton's signing. The expectations were high for Stanton, with team president David Samson saying his goal for the contract was to make Stanton "the first face of this franchise – the first player to be drafted, signed, play his entire career and go to the Hall of Fame as a Marlin."

Although that's a lot to put on the precocious power hitter, the fear Stanton puts into opposing pitchers has become clear in recent seasons. Stanton led the league with 24 intentional walks in 2014, and although part of that was due to the weak lineup surrounding him, the (limited) amount of pitches he sees in the strike zone makes it all the more evident. In 2013, Stanton's down season, only Pablo Sandoval saw fewer pitches in the strike zone than Stanton, and that was due more to pitchers knowing they could get Sandoval to swing at pitches anywhere within a five-foot radius of the strike zone than anything else. In 2014, only Sandoval (once again) and Jay Bruce (yeah, I'm not sure either) saw fewer pitches in the strike zone than Stanton, and that's not a coincidence. With the displays that Stanton puts on during batting practice, I think I would pull an intentional "50 Cent first pitch" imitation and just fire the ball into the dugout if I had to pitch to Stanton. Of course, all of this was before his record-chasing 2017 season in which he became the first player in about a decade to make a true run for 61 home runs – a title some still hold as the true home run record (those people are wrong, but oh well). Stanton ended up just short with 59 homers, but 2017 was undoubtedly the Stanton season many of us had long been waiting for.

Stanton has also stolen my heart as my favorite player in the game of baseball right now. It started with a couple of on-field interviews during which he came across as a laid-back and funny guy, but he really sealed the deal with Tim Keown's profile of Stanton in *ESPN the Mag's* 2014 MLB preview issue. In the article, Stanton is portrayed as exactly that same chill dude, the guy who sets up team trips to Europe in the offseason, goes along with it when he's mistaken for The Rock, and shops at Walmart. But what really sold me was when Keown described Stanton as an "old soul in a young man's body." He's the guy who sets up a board game night to get his teammates to hang out without their phones getting in the way, listens to Sinatra, and whose lone vice is grilled cheese sandwiches. I'm so in. Stanton, welcome to the top of the "Players Jim Turvey would want to hang out with" list – an honor that really can't be overstated in its importance. It's funny, though: most of the time, as fans, we really don't know if we would get along with these professional athletes, or even what kind of guys they really are. The best solution may well be to build a persona for our favorite players in our minds[52] and just let our imaginations run with it.

Utility Jeff Conine (1993-1997; 2003-2005)

Conine came to Florida as the 22nd pick in their expansion draft before the 1993 season. In 1993, Conine would go on to finish third in the Rookie of the Year, playing every game and totaling 240 bases during the year. He played with the team through its 1997 title and was brought back during the stretch run of the 2003 season, once again helping the team on its way to its only other title. In fact, he is the only Marlins player to play in both World Series victories, which goes to show how much turnover there has been in the organization. This is even more damning considering he wasn't even there for the entire time between the two titles. In his 32 playoff games with the Marlins, Conine slashed .304/.365/.382 and reminds me very much of the Craig Counsell-type use of the utility spot on these franchise Starting IX's, which we'll get to in a second.

SP José Fernández (2013-2016)

Wow. This one hurts. I was honestly moved to tears when I heard the news of Fernández passing in the fall of 2016,

[52] I truly believe that Brett Gardner, Curtis Granderson, and myself would be the three best friends that anybody has ever had.

one of just two non-friends and family who have drawn that reaction in my adult life (Robin Williams being the other). Fernández was seemingly on every baseball fan's list of favorite players to watch, and more, way more, than that, he seemed like one of the most genuinely happy-to-be-there guys. The stories came pouring in after his passing, with Casey McGehee telling reporters that the hardest part would be telling his son the news. McGehee's son has cerebral palsy, and had become very close with Fernández when McGehee played for the Marlins. McGehee explained that his son's disease made it difficult for many to connect with him, but it was never an issue for Fernández who would always volunteer to hang out with him.

The stories off the field are what built the man, but the lens through which many of us knew Fernández was on the diamond. And honestly, it's hard to truly sum up Fernández with just words. Of all the players who I have seen in my lifetime, Fernández was the one who most needed moving images to truly encapsulate his full persona. Whether it was his borderline delirious reaction to a Giancarlo Stanton home run in the midst of a lost Marlins season; his face after his own home run caused the tight-butthole Braves to clear the benches; or, my personal favorite, his catch of a Troy Tulowitzki line drive that led to an exchange that belongs in the Smithsonian – the man needed to be shown in moving images.

Fernández had gone through so much just for a chance to play the game of baseball, as well. He has one of, if not the, most intriguing origin stories of anyone in baseball. Fernández grew up in Cuba and didn't even think of coming to the U.S. until his stepfather was denied a medical mission out of the control and deemed a threat to defect. His stepfather then did defect, trying 13 times to leave the country before finally learning the tricks of the trade and making it onto the shores of Florida in 2005. José and his mother attempted to follow in his stepfather's path, but their first three attempts came up empty, each attempt landing the teenage Fernández in prison.

On their fourth attempt, they took a different route, one less policed, but disaster struck. Here's a passage from Jordan Ritter Conn's incredible *Grantland* piece on Fernández, "From Cuba with Heat," which was (rightfully) quoted with great regularity after Fernández passed:

"And then he remembers the splash. He heard it one night while he was making small talk with the captain. After the splash, he heard the screams. A wave had crashed over the boat's deck and swept Fernández's mother out to sea. He saw her body and before he had time to think, he jumped in. A spotlight shone on the water, and Fernández could make out his mother thrashing in the waves about 60 feet from the boat. She could swim, but just barely, and as Fernández pushed his way toward her, he spat out salty water with almost every stroke. Waves — 'stupid big,' he says — lifted him to the sky, then dropped him back down. When he reached his mother, he told her, 'Grab my back, but don't push me down. Let's go slow, and we'll make it.' She held his left shoulder. With his right arm — his pitching arm — he paddled. Fifteen minutes later, they reached the boat. A rope dropped, and they climbed aboard. For now, at least, they were going to be OK."

After Fernández passed, Conn penned another piece, this time for *The Ringer*, in which he said that Fernández always liked to play down his past. Fernández "was bored by the story of his own life because he was so deeply thrilled by living it." This *joie de vivre* that Fernández possessed came up in every piece about him, with Grant Brisbee of *SBNation* summing it up best: "[Fernández] was so radiant that when he's ripped away, you almost have to force yourself to remember the talent. How well he played the sport is the afterthought because all you can think about at first is the joy."

Fernández will never be forgotten by those that saw him pitch, and thanks to the era in which he lived, his legacy will live on in the form of those incredible gifs and videos he so easily produced in his all-too-short time on earth. His loss is unprecedented, a tragedy of which noted baseball historian Jay Jaffe said in *Sports Illustrated*, "defies memory to find a precedent that combines youth with accomplishment on par with Fernández." Jaffe had to go back to 1862 for a possible comparison for a player of Fernández's ilk who was lost similarly. To call it a tragedy for baseball misses the bigger picture, where Fernández's girlfriend will now be raising the unborn child they had just announced a week prior to Fernández's death, without the benefit of this supernova of a man. Fernández's passing is one of the most truly unfair moments that has happened to the world of sports in my lifetime, and one that I will not soon forget.

Rest in peace, José.

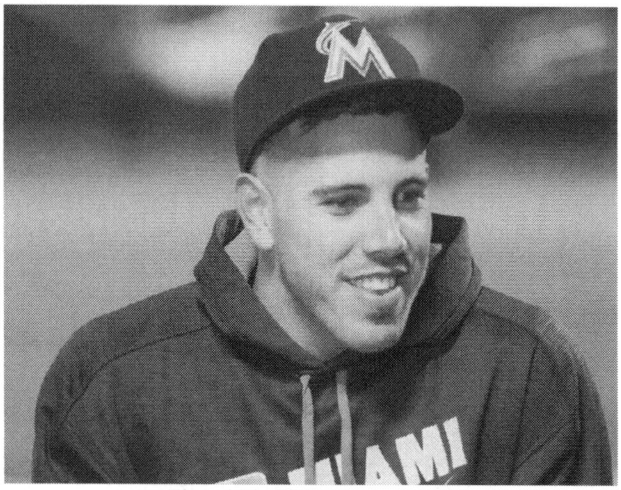

(Photo from Wikimedia Commons)

CP Robb Nen (1993-1997)

In his first full year in Florida, Nen finished 28 games, and he took over the full-time closer's job the next season. He held the job the rest of his time in Florida and was the closer for the 1997 World Series Champion Marlins team and, despite a couple of road bumps in the series, tossed 1.2 innings of essential shutout ball in Game 7. He was sent packing before the next season (where have I heard that before?) and ended up having five more solid years as the Giants closer.

When looking at Nen's numbers it becomes clear that WAR is definitely not the best way to assess a closer's impact on the team, one of the flaws of the stat. For his five years in Florida, Baseball-Reference has Nen as being worth 5.0 WAR, or, on average, one win a season. The true worth of a closer has, and will continue to be, debated until everybody is blue in the face, but even the staunchest closer antagonist would likely admit that the top minor league replacement for Nen (the hypothetical baseline for WAR) would cost the Marlins more than one win a season. Therefore, statistics like save percentage or win probability added are far superior when looking at the merits of a closer.

Finally, from the "random anecdote read and enjoyed" file: Nen went up against Dave Otto in 1994 and made some very random baseball history. It was the first time two pitchers with palindromic names faced each other in baseball history.

Starting IX Franchise Roster Stats

Lineup	Yrs	G	R	H	HR	RBI	SB	BB	SO	BA	OBP	SLG	OPS+	dWAR	WAR
Hanley Ramírez	7	943	666	1103	148	482	230	406	677	0.300	0.374	0.499	129	-3.6	26.8
Luis Castillo	**10**	**1128**	**675**	**1273**	20	271	**281**	**533**	629	0.293	0.37	0.356	94	3.6	22.3
Cliff Floyd	6	637	392	661	110	409	90	268	443	0.294	0.374	0.523	135	-2.2	16.8
Miguel Cabrera	5	720	449	842	138	523	17	322	592	**0.313**	0.388	0.542	143	-5.0	18.2
Giancarlo Stanton	8	986	576	960	**267**	**672**	36	487	**1140**	0.268	0.360	**0.554**	146	0.6	**35.1**
Derek Lee	6	844	422	746	129	417	51	363	734	0.264	0.353	0.469	115	-6.7	9.8
Jeff Conine	8	1014	447	1005	120	553	15	376	677	0.290	0.358	0.455	114	-3.3	13.6
Juan Pierre	4	599	332	682	7	145	190	154	142	0.295	0.345	0.368	91	0.0	7.6
Charles Johnson	7	587	204	467	75	277	1	232	499	0.241	0.324	0.418	96	**8.5**	11.7
Pitchers	Yrs	W	W%	ERA	G	CG	SHO	SV	IP	SO	ERA+	WHIP	SO/9	SO/BB	WAR
José Fernández	4	38	**0.691**	2.58	76	0	0	0	471.1	589	151	1.054	11.2	4.21	13.2
Robb Nen	5	20	0.556	3.41	269	0	0	**108**	314.0	328	122	1.283	9.4	2.71	5.0

#27 Arizona Diamondbacks (1998-pres)

(Photo from Wikimedia Commons)

Team Background

Playoff appearances: 6 **Pennants: 1** **World Series titles: 1**
Collective team WAR: 212.0
Strengths: Starting pitching. Unfortunately for the Diamondbacks, there's only the one spot to fill. The team also has a number of players with good power/speed combinations.
Weaknesses: Hitting for contact would definitely be a weak point, and that decent amount of pop mentioned earlier is only in comparison to their poor contact skills; it can't even come close to compare with the power on the majority of the Starting IX rosters in baseball history.
What to expect from the next 10 pages: Between a Big Unit joke and tales of my middle school love life, this is probably my least mature section. Which is saying a lot…

The Diamondbacks came into the league via expansion in 1998 and achieved success rather quickly due to the signing of Randy Johnson and a trade for Curt Schilling.[53] They won the National League West in their second season in the league and managed to establish themselves as a legitimate contender in the National League as fast as any expansion team has done. They had four All-Stars in 1999, just their second season of existence, a feat matched in the NL by only the Houston Astros. Just two years later, the Diamondbacks reached the promised land and won one of the most memorable World Series ever, ending the Yankees dynasty by walking off against arguably (although who on earth would argue against it) the best playoff closer of all time, Mariano Rivera. It was a series that even the losing manager, Joe Torre, has called the most exciting playoff series he has ever been in – and he's been in his fair share of playoff series.

Game 4 of the series is one of the most distinct memories of my Yankee fanhood as a child. Showing up at a friend's Halloween party, I immediately ditched my tweenage friends to watch the game with the dads in the basement. (Although in all fairness to my fifth-grade self, the fact that there were girls upstairs may have been a leading cause as well.) Most remember this game for Tino's clutch home run in the ninth, or Jeter ringing in November baseball with a typically Jeter-esque walk-off; I remember it, however, for recovering from my general fear of girls to go back upstairs and play a few glorious rounds of spin the bottle.

---

[53] Curt Schilling mandates our first footnote Starting IX, as he will be locking down the starting pitcher spot on my personal most-hated players list. I will use the footnote Starting IX to make top nine lists that are less consequential and more subjective: SP) Curt Schilling – His post-playing days have only hurt him further. C) A.J. Pierzynski 1B) Cap Anson 2B) Jeff Kent 3B) Mike Moustakas SS) Hanley Ramírez LF) Les Mann – BE MORE OF A MAN! CF) Jacoby Ellsbury RF) Dave Roberts – The player; Dave Roberts the manager is one of my absolute favorites. Yes, there are an exorbitant number of Red Sox.

Now that I've gone insanely off-topic, back to the actual facts about the team at hand: that World Series, while remembered by me as a stepping stone towards manhood, actually represented one of the biggest upsets in baseball history, and the end of one of the most dominant stretches a team has ever had.

The case for the 1998-2000 Yankees as the most dominant team over a three-year stretch is a pretty easy one. They won three straight World Series while losing only one game in those three series and gave off the same vibe as the "Fo' Fo' Fo'" Sixers – when it got to the postseason, you might as well just get out of the way. The Diamondbacks went into the series as a team that had only even been in existence for four years, and they seemed over-reliant on two pitchers and one big bat (Schilling, Johnson, and Luis Gonzalez, respectively). As far as the managerial matchup went, it was surefire Hall-of-Fame manager Joe Torre against a man who, at that time the previous year, was in the Diamondbacks broadcast booth.

The Dbacks were fortunate in the sense that they were able to set up their rotation to get the first two games started by Schilling and Johnson and they cruised to victories in Games 1 and 2 by a score of 13-1. Whether or not this helped to give them some confidence against the mighty Yankees is a matter of where one stands in the whole momentum/confidence debate, but the wins were wins regardless. Diamondback manager Bob Brenly is also on the record as saying that they got some help from some unexpected areas: "... We were getting calls from people in baseball almost every day about their pitchers, I got calls from others managers and coaches, players got calls from other players, and our coaches got calls from other coaches. We had great advanced scouting, but this really filled out the report. There were so many people in baseball who were sick of the Yankees winning that they wanted to help us."

This "advanced" scouting could only do so much, though: the Yankees won Games 3, 4, and 5 by one run each, thanks to a shaky Dbacks bullpen and some timely hitting from the Yankees. However, Arizona went back home for Game 6 with Schilling and Johnson giving them a legitimate shot at a title. Johnson and the Dbacks blew the Yanks out of the water in Game 6, setting up an epic Game 7. Established dynasty vs. new kids, Roger Clemens vs. Curt Schilling, the most famous city in the world... vs. New York,[54] and it did not disappoint.

The Diamondbacks drew first blood and held the lead until the seventh inning, when the Yankees tied it at one. Then Alfonso Soriano (my favorite Yankee at the time) looked to be the hero of the World Series as he took Schilling deep to give the Yankees a one-run lead going into the eighth. As a kid, I remember thinking nothing was going to top my favorite player hitting the home run to win Game 7 of the World Series... I was in for a treat.[55] The rest you already know, as every journeyman infielder of the '90s managed to reach base in different obscure ways to somehow defeat the best closer in history. (That last sentence is the least-biased sentence I have ever written.)

* * *

As far as the current state of the team, things have been up and down: Kevin Towers had a hot minute as the GM, making personnel decisions basically stating that players should have grit more than anything else, and at one point (probably) threatened to cut the entire team and replace them with 15 Robot David Ecksteins and 10 Robot Marco Scutaros. The Dbacks did manage to make the playoffs once in Towers' reign, but he made several questionable moves that drove analytical fans of Arizona to the near breaking point. In September of 2014, Towers was fired as the GM, and there was great rejoicing in Arizona. With the way the 2017 season turned out (top wild card spot, legitimate contender for most of the season), the rejoicing makes sense.

---

[54] ** Sad trombone **

[55] Yet another footnote list because it doesn't deserve an actual spot in the book, here are the Starting IX of moments of my extremely privileged sports life:
SP) Super Bowl XLII – My father somehow got his coworker, Joe Kowalski, to sell us his tickets for Super Bowl XLII because Joe didn't want to travel to Arizona, so I was able to see my favorite team win maybe the best Super Bowl ever played over the previously undefeated team that I hated so passionately. (Yeah I don't see this one leaving the top spot for a looooong time.) Shout out to Joe for being such a generous man over the years selling us those tickets (among others) at reasonable prices and allowing me to have the sports memory of a lifetime.
C) Alfonso Soriano's 2001 ALCS Game 4 walk-off home run – Another event boosted due to my attendance, and by the fact that Soriano, like I said, was my favorite Yankee at the time.
1B) Super Bowl XLVI – Another Giants victory over the hated Patriots – almost as satisfying as the first, but I had to watch from the couch. (What a tough life.)
2B) 1996 World Series Game 4 – The beginning of a dynasty looked in trouble when the Braves were up 6-0 in the fifth and were looking to go up 3-1 in the series. Jim Leyritz's epic home run in the tenth saved the day and officially had me hooked on October baseball.
3B) February 20th, 2010, T-Mac becomes a Knick – Another one that I was prvileged enough to have tickets for (props to my Uncle Sam) and turned into an epic affair. McGrady's "resurgence" resulted in one of the best atmospheres in which I've ever been. Also, getting to see Kevin Durant and Russell Westbrook just as they were hitting their stride was really cool.
SS) 2007 NFC Championship – Giants over Packers in an overtime, back-and-forth thriller that set up the number one sports moment of my life.
LF) Manchester City vs. QPR Match Day 38, 2012 – As far as drama is concerned, it's hard to top two goals in stoppage time to win a club their first title in over four decades. Plus, who could deny how cool the moment with Noel Gallagher and the fans was after they won it? If this had been my beloved Tottenham who pulled it off, it would have been a top two or three moment.
CF) 2003 ALCS Game 7 – This one is only a bit lower because it was almost too cruel to Red Sox fans, and it feels bad to even rub it in. Of course, next year all those Red Sox fans felt no remorse rubbing the Yankees blown 3-0 series lead in my face, so it only drops so far.
RF) Virginia 68 Duke 66, February 1, 2007 – Seeing as University of Virginia was my favorite team, Duke was my most hated team, and Sean Singletary was my favorite non-Jason Cain college basketball player ever, seeing him hit a fadeaway to beat Duke was about as good as it got. Alright, moving on.

Random cool things about the franchise:

- Chase Field was the first MLB stadium to sport a swimming pool; it is located in right-center and has a hot tub to boot.
- Their most famous fan is Senator John McCain.
- Conor Jackson, a promising first baseman for the franchise, had his career derailed in part by falling victim to Valley Fever, a disease of the lungs that is on the rise in the nation's southwestern states.
- Since Chase Field has real grass, the roof needs to be opened regularly throughout the season, and with temperatures averaging right around 100 degrees in the middle of the season, the 8,000-ton heating system needs three hours prior to first pitch to cool off to the usual 78 degrees inside Chase Field.
- At one point, on the Diamondbacks Subreddit, a link to the article announcing Towers getting the axe was among the top three posts all-time.
- In 2007, the Diamondbacks changed colors to "Sedona Red and Sonoran Sand," ditching their previous purple and teal colors – why do teams blessed with teal as a core color always feel the need to abandon the most aesthetically pleasing uniform color?

Starting IX

C Miguel Montero (2006-2014)

Montero played the first nine seasons of his career in Arizona before being moved to Chicago during the Cubs "all-in" offseason of 2014. Montero was very solid in his time with the Diamondbacks, posting an OPS+ of 103 to go along with his top-notch defense.[56] Montero was known as a strong defensive catcher before the mini-revolution of pitch-framing statistics that has occurred in the past few years. His reputation was mostly built on the strength of his caught-stealing percentage, a category in which he led the league in 2011 and in which he was above league average in each of his final five seasons in Arizona. Once pitch-framing statistics (Catcher, Brewers – Page 77) had their legitimate origins, it became clear that Montero was even more of a boon behind the plate, coming in as the top-rated framer of 2014 and generally finishing in the top tier in the league each season. With pitch-framing value not solidified yet, it's not entirely possible to know just how much more Montero was worth to the Diamondbacks than his 12.6 WAR, but it is certainly not insignificant.

It's no surprise that the analytically inclined Cubs latched onto Montero. However, it isn't just his ability behind the plate that made him an important part of the Diamondbacks for nearly 10 years. Here's some high praise from the team website: "The first thing people say about Diamondbacks catcher Miguel Montero – especially if they know him well – is that he has an infectious personality. They will say he's a high-energy, colorful character who brings enthusiasm and comic relief to the clubhouse on a daily basis. Former Diamondbacks third baseman Mark Reynolds used to refer to him as a walking reality show waiting to happen. 'All he needs is a microphone and a TV camera to follow him around everywhere and he'd have a hit show,' Reynolds, who now plays for the Orioles, said last season. Predictably, the first thing Diamondbacks manager Kirk Gibson said Wednesday when asked about his starting catcher was more of the same. What does he like most about Montero? 'He's enthusiastic, No. 1, and he brings a good attitude all the time,' Gibson said. 'Miggy always has energy.'"

Oh, and he has been known to lick his bats to determine which one to take to the plate.

1B Paul Goldschmidt (2011-pres.)

Goldy has emerged as the top contributor in the current generation of Diamondbacks. Goldschmidt broke into the major leagues in August of 2011, hit a home run in his second professional game, and had 54 RuBIns (Runs + RBI) in the 48 games of his rookie season. He had an OPS+ of 117 and flashed an above-average power/speed combination with eight home runs and four steals. Goldschmidt built on his strong rookie season in 2012, improving each of his slashes (batting average, on-base percentage, and slugging percentage) and falling just two stolen bases shot of a 20/20 (HR/SB) season.

Goldschmidt's 2013 season was his true breakout season, however. Goldy improved on each of those slash totals once again, becoming a member of the elite .300+ batting average, .400+ on-base percentage, .550+ slugging percentage crew that had just three qualified hitters in 2013 (Miguel Cabrera and Mike Trout were the other two). Goldschmidt was in line to have just as good a season in 2014 but was forced to miss the final two months of the season after being hit on the hand by a pitch from Pirate reliever Ernesto Frieri. The injury spurred one of the most archaic exchanges of the 2014 season when the Diamondbacks organization went full-on Neanderthal and responded by hitting Andrew McCutchen the next night, knocking him out for a several weeks, even though Goldschmidt's injury was an accident.

The saddest part of the whole incident was that people were predicting that McCutchen should watch out the next day before he even got hit due to the Diamondback organization's out-of-date views of the way baseball should be played

[56] And a unique predilection for two-strike home runs.

(Kevin Towers and Kirk Gibson being the main culprits). The eye-for-an-eye, you-hit-our-best-player-we-hit-your-best-player mentality has been snuffed out of baseball for the most part (thankfully), but the Towers/Gibson-era Diamondbacks held onto it like a drowning man in the Pacific holding onto a rotting log with the last vestiges of hope. Partially because of McCutchen's lovability, and partially because the sanest organizations moved out of this mentality over a generation ago, there was a strong pushback to the incident throughout baseball, and with Towers and Gibson out in Arizona, one has to hope that these types of incidents won't rear their ugly heads again.

To end on a better note: Goldschmidt has only continued to wow in his early career. Just seven seasons and 934 games into his career, Goldy is already the all-time leader in WAR (34.8) among Diamondback position players, and deservedly so. He's one of the best and most complete players in the game today.

2B Jay Bell (1998-2002)

A key member of the 2001 Arizona team that went on to win the World Series (although he contributed only one hit in that World Series), Bell played mostly at second base for the team. His best season in Arizona was two seasons prior, his 1999 season, when he hit 38 home runs and drove in 112. This was particularly interesting because of his career before Arizona. While playing for the Pirates from 1989-1996, Bell was much more of a prototypical second basemen, including laying down a combined 69 sacrifice bunts in the 1990 and 1991 seasons (leading the league each year). In fact, Bell was such a prolific bunter that his 39 sac bunts in 1990 were the most in the NL since Pie Traynor's 42 in 1928. Somehow, within the same decade, Bell remade his style of play to produce the aforementioned power-driven 1999 season in which he laid down only four sacrifice bunts all year. Careers rarely change to the extreme of Bell's, and what is even less common is seeing the change go from a sacrifice-heavy hitter to a power-heavy hitter. In fact, Bell is the only player to have played after WWII to have at least 150 home runs and 150 sacrifice hits. Unfortunately, given the time in which he played, there were plenty of questions about that type of transformation.

On July 11, 1999, Jay Bell made one lucky fan's day when he hit a grand slam. It wasn't just that the fan, Gylene Hoyle, loved the Dbacks: she had predicted as part of a million-dollar promotion that Bell would hit a grand slam. Hoyle had only won the tickets to the game through a radio show contest and was put into the Shamrock Farms promotion as a result. When she showed up to the ballpark, she was asked to name a Diamondbacks player who would hit a grand slam that day and an inning in which it would occur. Her nieces and nephews gave her the ideas for Jay Bell, and Hoyle threw out the sixth as a random guess. Making the event even more special, the crowd was aware of the contest, which made for quite a moment. Well known as a good guy in baseball circles, Jay Bell called it his career highlight.

SS Stephen Drew (2006-2012)

The younger brother of J.D., Stephen was drafted by the Diamondbacks and stayed in their system until being traded to the Oakland A's in 2012. Highly touted out of college, Drew seemed to be on the right track in 2008 when he hit .291 with 21 home runs and received MVP votes. He then struggled with injuries and general development problems for a few years before being shipped out of Arizona, as the team (correctly) didn't believe he would develop any further.

Drew did, however, have a very strong 2007 postseason with the Dbacks, and although baseball currently doesn't give out an MVP for the Divisional Series, he would have won the 2007 NLDS MVP, when he led Arizona with a .500 batting average, two home runs, and 16 total bases in a sweep of the Cubs. He has always been a strong defender and has good speed, finishing second in the National League in triples in 2008, 2009, and 2010. That's about it, though.

3B Matt Williams (1998-2003)

Williams was traded to the Diamondbacks from Cleveland in Arizona's inaugural year and settled in nicely during his first two years with the team. This included a very strong 1999 campaign, in which Williams totaled 142 RBI, thanks in part to the team's strong offense. Nicknamed the "Carson Crusher," Williams was a legitimate power threat his whole career. He was a little past his prime upon his arrival in Arizona but provided a veteran example for the expansion Diamondbacks, leading the team in hits in their first playoff series in 1999 and tying for the team lead in RBI in their World Series win. Oh, and his wife is an International Model of the Year.

LF Luis Gonzalez (1999-2006)

The owner of the blooper up the middle that is the sole evidence that Mariano Rivera may actually be a human, Gonzalez enjoyed several strong seasons for the Diamondbacks after coming over from Detroit before the 1999 season. Gonzalez hit a career-high 57 home runs in 2001, which exceeded his next highest season total by 26. He also totaled 419 total bases that season, which is good for a tie for 10th all-time – tied with none other than Lou Gehrig. A power surge like this is certainly not an unprecedented occurrence in baseball history, but sadly for a guy like Gonzo, when the power surge comes at age 33 and took place during an era when everyone was under scrutiny for steroid use, it meant that Gonzalez found himself at center of steroid allegations.

Gonzalez is one of many in this book who were accused of having used performance-enhancing drugs, some of whom later tested positive, but some of whom faced those allegations despite no evidence ever appearing. There are certainly many debates that the steroid era brings up (which will only begin to be covered in this book), but one side of the story that often gets ignored is how these allegations affect the players on a personal level. When Melky Cabrera was suspended 50 games for a positive PED test in 2012, Gonzalez, who is now a member of the Diamondbacks front office, said that it was a shame because now people will go back to saying a player is using PEDs whenever they have breakout seasons. This quote from Gonzalez came from a place of frustration for a player who was never on any official lists of players who tested positive and was never suspended, but whose name was smeared as a result of his standout 2001 season plus the era in which he played. Gonzalez has advocated the release of names on the first drug tests that Major League Baseball took, but knows that the union won't allow this because of all the names that would come out if such a decision were made. I'm not saying anyone other than Luis Gonzalez is in a position to say Gonzo *didn't* use performance enhancers, but no one other than Luis Gonzalez is in a position to say Gonzo *did* use performance enhancers. All I'm trying to say here is imagine the frustration you would feel if you were accused of something as serious as cheating simply because you were successful and had no way of disproving it. As Based God Dean Strang says in *Making a Murderer*, "All due respect to counsel, the state is *supposed* to start every criminal case 'swimming upstream.' And the strong current against which the state is supposed to be swimming is the presumption of innocence. That presumption of innocence has been eroded—if not *eliminated*—here by the *specter* of Brendan Dassey, and that's why the court needs to take further curative action." Now Gonzalez hasn't been punished to the level of Dassey obviously (and may no one ever have to), but Strang's point about presumption of innocence applies to Gonzo, as well.

There is, however, plenty of evidence that Gonzo was one of the best guys in baseball. A *Sports Illustrated* profile from 1999 focused not on his incredible baseball ability but on his genial nature. Just listen to his manager, Buck Showalter: "My father used to say the true test of a man is how he treats people who can be of no benefit to him. You want to know what kind of guy Luis is, you talk to clubbies, doormen, bellmen, cabbies. By that measure, he's one of the best." Arizona's PR director tells the story of a time when Gonzo spotted some of those clubhouse/equipment guys at a Japanese restaurant and picked up their tab after chatting for a bit – he hadn't even eaten with them. The article goes on and on with examples of Gonzalez's good will, which only makes the allegations – which clearly disturb Gonzalez – even more frustrating for a man who seems like one of the good ones.

On a different note: throughout the book, there are some facts that the reader will just scratch their head and say, "Who found this stat?" Well, here's our first entry into that contest: Gonzalez became the first Major League hitter in baseball history to hit a home run into two different bodies of water when he hit a home run into McCovey Cove in 2000. Previously that season, he had found the pool in right-center at Chase Field with a home run.

CF Steve Finley (1999-2004)

Yet another player from the championship 2001 Diamondbacks team, Finley provided a steady glove and a good power/speed combination for the squad. In his first year with the club, despite hitting for his lowest batting average of any season in Arizona, he posted 100 runs, 34 home runs, 103 RBI, and won a Gold Glove. He also posted a .351 batting average in the postseason for the Diamondbacks, and more specifically, a .368 batting average in their 2001 World Series victory.

Not in his Diamondback days, but still worth noting: Finley was included in what was one of the most one-sided trades in baseball history. Finley, along with Curt Schilling and Pete Harnisch (who won 45 games with a 3.41 ERA in four years with the Astros), were sent by the Orioles to Houston in exchange for Glenn Davis who hit .247 with 24 home runs in three washed-up years for the O's. Finley was no stranger to being trade bait: he was traded four times and played for eight different teams to his name in his 19-year career.

RF Justin Upton (2007-2012)

After his brother Melvin was drafted second overall in 2002, Justin was taken first overall by Arizona in the 2005 draft. He managed to make it to the majors just two years later and debuted as a 19-year-old in 2007, playing well in the postseason for them that year. The hype train seemed to have finally arrived at the station in 2011 when he came in fourth in the MVP and helped lead the Dbacks to their fifth NL West crown.[57] However, Upton's numbers regressed in 2012, particularly in the power categories, with rumors that nagging injuries played a role. He was mentioned in trade discussions, which made fans wonder, considering he was only 25 and coming off such a strong 2011 campaign. Those rumors were consummated on January 24, 2013 when Upton and Chris Johnson were shipped to Atlanta in exchange for Martin Prado and three prospects (the only familiar name being Randall Delgado). The move reunited the brothers Upton and led to the single greatest meme of all time (the Braves outfield with the words: "Y'all gonna make me lose my mind" and Justin's and

[57] By the way, the Diamondbacks five division titles are more than twice the combined division titles for the three other teams in this tier (Rockies, Rays, and Marlins).

Melvin's faces along with the words "Upton here" "Upton here" above their heads.)

The trade was deservedly questioned at the time, and it still should be – at least in the sense that Towers seemed to make the move as part of his quest for grit – but as Upton has failed to live up to the lofty standards he set in 6.1-WAR 2011 season, the trade at least won't join the list of the John Smoltz-esque worst trades in baseball history. (Look it up, kids.) The main reason Upton hasn't produced as much value as that 2011 season has been a falling off in his defensive value. The only times Upton rated positively per dWAR was in that 2011 season and his 2015 and 2017 seasons, and despite plus defensive tools, he has regularly cost his team in the field.

Both Justin and his brother Melvin have a reputation of not living up to their potential, particularly in the field, due to a lack of focus and dedication. A look at some of Bill James' advanced defensive metrics actually backs this claim – for Justin, at least. From 2009-2012, no players made more "Out of Zone" plays. This is another way of saying he has the best range and read off the bat. This shows that Justin has a ton of natural talent. Where Upton is lacking is in his ability to keep runners from taking an extra base and in his number of misplayed balls. The most common misplays by Justin were letting the ball bounce off his glove and mishandling the ball after fielding a hit; ESPN Stats & Info has the numbers at 32 of the former and 31 of the latter for that four-year span. He also averaged 2.2 misplays per "good play," which was higher than any right fielder in baseball other than the immortal J.D. Drew. This is even worse considering how many good plays Upton does make. These statistics alone are not enough evidence to say that the accusations of poor focus are true, but they do offer an interesting piece of the puzzle that is Justin Upton.

Utility Craig Counsell (2000-2003; 2005-2006)

Counsell is a utility-type who played multiple positions for the team and was a utility player in the most baseball sense of the word. This utility spot on each franchise's Starting IX will not always be used for players in the (previously-seen) Jeff Conine or Craig Counsell mold: there will be DH's, players who happen to play the same position as a top player in the franchise, or even personalities that simply have to be mentioned – but Counsell fits the classic definition of utility player to a tee.

Counsell played third base, second base, and shortstop for Arizona and was a plus defender at all three positions. Craig's numbers were never off the charts – in fact, they were sub-pedestrian most years – but one of the things many big spenders ignore is the use of having a utility man to whom the numbers just don't do justice. These utility players are vastly underrated but are part of most winning teams.

It's something that real dynasties get, but the ones who struggle to get over the hump don't understand. The Joe Torre-era Yankees dynasty had players like Luis Sojo, Scott Brosius, and Jim Leyritz, who filled in when players needed off days and were generally great clubhouse guys. It's not surprising that Counsell won the NLCS MVP in 2001 because guys like that seem to produce when it matters (ignore his .083 batting average in the World Series, please) and are an essential part of a winning team.

Before he was with the Diamondbacks, Counsell was also on the World Series-winning Marlins team in 1997. In fact, he was the winning run of the Series when Edgar Renteria hit his walk-off single off of Charles Nagy[58] and Cleveland. This relates to Counsell's Diamondbacks days because despite his .083 batting average in the 2001 World Series, he was on base (having reached on an error) when Gonzalez hit his walk-off against Rivera to win the Series.

Now those last two paragraphs go against some statistical beliefs today, mostly the notions that some players are clutch, or that "clubhouse guys" can bring value that there is no metric for currently. Although there has been a lot of statistical research into the idea of "clutch," there have been no real results suggesting the phenomenon is a repeatable trait. However, the idea that certain players can perform better in limited/utility roles is certainly one that has played out over the course of baseball history, and one that we can apply to Counsell.

One of the most entertaining baseball interviews of all time is an exchange between noted sabermetrician Brian Kenny and noted anti-sabermetric hound Ken "Hawk" Harrelson. Harrelson was a player in the 1960s who now provides color commentary – with more color than 18 trillion rainbows – for the Chicago White Sox. Harrelson is the archetype of the old-school baseball fan, denying the place of these newfangled statistics in baseball, proclaiming that until the metrics are better they distract from what really matters in baseball. According to Harrelson, there's only one metric that matters – TWTW. Don't remember seeing that one in the *FanGraphs* statistical glossary? Well, that's because it stands for The Will To Win and is about as quantitative as Jell-O. What Harrelson and others seem to be most worried about is that this game – "a kid's game," as it is described by so many – will be corrupted by a superfluous amount of data surrounding the game. This is hardly a new worry. One *USA Today* article worried that "the next Hall of Fame skipper will be the Apple II." That's not a recent headline, it was three decades ago.

While there are certainly more metrics available than ever before, the sole purpose of these metrics is to allow the players and coaches to be better informed. The goal isn't to reinvent the wheel, but rather to ask whether the wheel is the most efficient mode of transportation. In the interview, Harrelson seems to contradict himself over and over and not really grasp what Kenny is trying to show him using baseball's newer metrics. I mention this not to poke fun at Harrelson, or

[58] Most people think of José Mesa as the goat for blowing the save, but the game went to extra innings where Nagy gave up the winning hit.

question his intelligence, but rather to make the point that most of the baseball folks who argue against sabermetrics do so out of ignorance of the field.[59] Harrelson saw the movie *Moneyball*, but he didn't read the book and refers to imaginary statistics (not including TWTW) like OBPS. Kenny ends the interview with a plea that Harrelson simply check out some of the newer metrics, as he feels a true baseball lover like Harrelson would enjoy delving into the field. This is a plea that I will extend to some of those old-school fans who feel the same way as Hawk. You don't have to become the next Bill James; just make sure you aren't completely ignoring the field out of blind contempt. Baseball fans love knowing as much as they possibly can (just look at some of the bright minds that make up the fanbase), and all sabermetrics hope to do is allow all of us fans to be a little smarter about our favorite sport.

Back to Counsell, however: he earned his status in baseball clubhouses as one of the smartest players in baseball when he was in the majors. One former teammate described Counsell as a sort of *council* for his teammates: "We tease Craig by calling him Uncle Couns because he's kind of like the uncle we all go to for advice. Obviously the guy is book smart – he's got a degree from Notre Dame – but we don't necessarily see that side of him all that much. I think he tries to dumb it down for us. What we do see is his common-sense side." Counsell certainly wouldn't be a bad addition to any all-franchise team, and who knows: maybe there will be a metric that shows just how much Counsell brought to the team through his off-field presence someday.

There will never be a metric that shows how uncomfortable his batting stance must have been, though.

SP Randy Johnson (1999-2004; 2007-2008)

Wow. What a stretch Johnson had with the Diamondbacks. Over eight seasons in Arizona, he managed to have what many would have considered a strong career. After establishing himself as an excellent starter in Seattle in the early `90s, he switched over to the National League and completely obliterated the competition in the senior circuit. In half a season in Houston, he compiled a 10-1 record with 1.28 ERA and didn't slow off that pace too much when he moved west to Arizona that offseason. He won four Cy Young awards in the six years of his first stay in Phoenix. He also finished second in the Cy Young once and led the league in strikeouts five of those seasons. Always having been a power strikeout pitcher, Johnson figured out how to control his walks and jumped his game up another level, becoming an all-time great in the process. He also delivered when it mattered most, posting excellent numbers in the Diamondbacks 2001 championship run and winning co-MVP with Curt Schilling in the World Series thanks to three wins, including Game 7, in relief.

Johnson's numbers really jump off the page at you, and it could be argued that he had the strongest four-year stretch a pitcher has had… so let's find out! This is an exercise that every baseball writer worth her/his salt has at least scribbled in the margins of their college notebooks, and many have published on *Baseball Prospectus*, the *Baseball Research Journal*, etc. That being said, this will be the best of that bunch. Guaranteed.

In Johnson's first four years in Arizona, he won 81 games with a .750 win percentage.[60] But many pitchers have compiled that many wins over a four-year stretch and wins can be more of a team stat than individual stat. He made the All-Star team all four years and won the Cy Young all four years. However, as we'll go into later in the book, not all Cy Young awards are created equal. A Cy Young is based on the competition from pitchers around the league, so although four straight is an impressive feat (the only other to have accomplished it is Greg Maddux),[61] it is not enough to hand him the crown yet. The Cy Young is a good place to start to look for other candidates, however, because dominance over other pitchers in your league is definitely a factor in deciding who had the best four-year stretch for a pitcher.

So, let's meet the candidates.[62] Among the players to just miss the cut: Addie Joss (1906-1909), Bob Feller (1940-1946),[63] Bob Gibson (1968-1971), Roger Clemens (1989-1992), Robin Roberts (1951-1954), Mordecai "Three Finger" Brown (1906-1909), Dazzy Vance (1927-1930), Ed Walsh (1907-1910), Tom Seaver (1970-1973), Cy Young (1901-1904), Christy Mathewson (1908-1911), Lefty Grove (1928-1931) – final cut, Clayton Kershaw (2011-2014), and Pete Alexander (1914-1917).

Now on to the top 5 in chronological order: Walter Johnson (1912-15), Sandy Koufax (1963-66), Greg Maddux (1992-95), Pedro Martínez (1997-2000), and Randy Johnson (1999-2002). There are four charts that will act as a preview/guide for the upcoming breakdowns. The categories are Surface Statistics, Advanced Metrics, League Comparison and Team Success.

(Since this is the first real pitcher breakdown, here's a brief key similar to the key that appeared in the first hitter breakdown. FIP = Fielding Independent Pitching, a stat that simply looks at how a pitcher does in terms of the three true outcomes [strikeouts, walks, home runs]. It is based on a scale similar to ERA; ERA+ = similar to OPS+, it is an all-encompassing run prevention stat scaled so that 100 is league average, and each number above 100 is a percent above-

---

[59] If sabermetric ignorance is bliss, Hawk would be the happiest man on earth.

[60] For fans of the advanced metrics, he also managed an 8.5-WAR season in 2004, while the rest of the team combined for -2.8 WAR. That's absurd.

[61] Maddux did it with two different teams, making Johnson the only one to win four straight with one team.

[62] Although Cy Young awards were a good place to start they definitely weren't the only factor in looking for nominees, especially since the award didn't come into existence until 1956.

[63] Feller went to serve our country right in his prime and probably only missed the final cut because he came back part way through the 1945 season, skewing his numbers somewhat for the four-year period… I kind of feel like a communist for excluding him from the final list.

average, while each number below is a percent below league-average. In the example below, Sandy Koufax had an ERA+ of 172, meaning his ERA was 72 percent better than league average. Walter Johnson at 209 does indeed mean he was 109 percent better than league average. This is another stat that will be used plenty, so it's a good one to know. WAA = wins above average, similar to WAR but with the baseline being a league-average player instead of a replacement-level player.)

Surface Statistics

Name	W	W-L%	ERA	K	WHIP	SO/BB
Walter Johnson	**124**	.713	**1.45**	974	**0.899**	3.99
Sandy Koufax	97	**.782**	1.86	1228	0.909	4.74
Greg Maddux	75	.721	1.98	733	0.953	4.16
Pedro Martínez	77	.755	2.16	1153	0.925	**5.68**
Randy Johnson	81	.750	2.48	**1417**	1.044	4.92

Advanced Metrics

Name	FIP	ERA+	WAR	WAA
Walter Johnson	**1.97**	209	**51.2**	**38.1**
Sandy Koufax	**1.97**	172	36.5	25.2
Greg Maddux	2.54	202	33.2	26.0
Pedro Martínez	2.36	**219**	37.6	29.5
Randy Johnson	2.53	187	38.3	30.2

League Comparison

Name	4x League Leader	3x LL	2x LL	1x LL
Walter Johnson	K, SO/BB, WAR	W, CG, SHO, IP, ERA+, WHIP, FIP	ERA	W-L%, MVP
Sandy Koufax	ERA, All-Star, FIP	W, SHO, K, WHIP, CY	W-L%, IP, ERA+, SO/BB, CG	MVP, WAR
Greg Maddux	IP, ERA+, GG, CY, FIP	W, ERA, WHIP, CG, WAR, All-Star	SHO	W-L%, SO/BB
Pedro Martínez	All-Star	ERA, ERA+, FIP, WHIP, CY	K, SO/BB, WAR	W, W-L%, CG, SHO
Randy Johnson	K, ERA+, All-Star, CY	ERA, FIP, CG	IP, W-L%	W, SHO, WHIP, WAR

Team Success

Name	Playoffs	Division winner	Pennants	World Series	WS MVP
Walter Johnson	0	0	0	0	0
Sandy Koufax	**3**	**3**	**3**	**2**	**2**
Greg Maddux	2	2	1	1	0
Pedro Martínez	2	0	0	0	0
Randy Johnson	**3**	**3**	1	1	1

Now the question becomes how heavily to weigh each of these categories. Team success is probably the hardest to rate because a transcendent pitcher can carry a team to only so much success. In basketball, if you have LeBron James or Kobe Bryant, you know you're making the playoffs at least, but in baseball, a pitcher who pitches every fifth day (or every fourth day in the case of Koufax and sometimes every third day in the case of Walter Johnson) can only take a bad team so far. Also, Walter Johnson is at a disadvantage because the only teams to make the playoffs in his era were the two pennant winners, and he and Koufax both played when there was no Division Series to pad playoff stats. So, this category will probably act as more of a tiebreaker.

Although the surface statistics don't tell us as much as the advanced metrics, there is something to be said for being able to lead your team to victories.[64] The league comparison, and advanced stats, are definitely the most important for making

[64] Wins were such an overrated statistic for so long that it seems new-school statisticians seem to actually undervalue pitchers who are able to get wins. Hopefully we can find a middle ground.

this decision. They allow us to see real dominance over the league in a four-year stretch. When looking at the most inclusive of metrics (WAR) Walter Johnson has the lead by a decent margin. This comes with a grain of salt, though. Pitchers of Walter's era pitched more frequently and longer into games than our other four pitchers. You might be saying, "But why should that hurt his case for most dominant stretch?" Well, what we're looking for here is dominance; if all the other pitchers of this time are also pitching more often and deeper into games, it doesn't take away from the feat, but it hurts your case of standing out from the pack. By this same idea, strikeouts were not nearly as common in Walter Johnson's era, which make his 974 all the more impressive. So, what we're seeing already is that comparing across generations is very tricky. Statistics such as ERA+, which account for ballpark and generational factors, make it a little easier, but the task is still daunting.

The process has to start somewhere, though, and the best way to do this is Agatha Christie-style. Maddux wasn't a huge strikeout guy, and despite having impeccable control later in his career, his strikeout-to-walk ratio wasn't off the charts at this point yet.[65] I'm going to eliminate him for another reason along with that, though. Maddux was an outstanding pitcher, but given the opportunity to face any of these pitchers in their prime, wouldn't you want to face Maddux? Maybe it's because the regular fan has no chance of catching up to any of these other pitchers' fastballs, and they can kind of talk themselves into thinking they could at least make contact off Maddux, but I think that most people would take their chances against Maddux. I don't think this is just speculation. Think about Larry Walker in the 1997 All-Star Game. He abandoned batting from his natural left-handed side because he was straight up terrified of Randy Johnson – and he was one of the best hitters of all time. You think any batter would have done that against Maddux? I certainly don't. Johnson was a bad dude. He is one of only two pitchers (Pedro is the other) to have a season in which he tallied more than twice as many strikeouts as hits allowed. Think about that. In 2001, Johnson became just the second player ever (after Koufax) to strike out greater than 300 more batters than he walked. This came after struggling with control early in his career. This stat might be the most telling: against members of the 3,000-hit club, Johnson allowed a career .157/.272/.254 slash line.[66] Having impeccable control is an excellent trait, but the fear that Johnson, along with the other four pitchers who remain, put in their opposition can't be calculated. One down, four left.

Another way to eliminate a pitcher is through consistency. In order for one to say he had the best four-year stretch as a pitcher, each year should be at the top of his game. This is where Pedro kinda gets screwed. Pedro would probably be the favorite if this was a two-year stretch, and maybe even if you could take the five best non-consecutive seasons from one career, but his 1998 campaign (2.89 ERA, 163 ERA+) is the weakest of the remaining pitchers. Not a bad season by any stretch of the imagination – in fact, quite impressive considering the switch from the pitcher-friendly National League to the hitter-friendly American League and the era in which he was pitching, but it's the weak link of the remaining four. Two down, three still in play.

Only one remaining pitcher missed games due to injury during their four-year stretches; that was Koufax. Now the question becomes how much to punish for injury. Injury alone, especially considering it only caused Sandy to miss around 10 starts, probably wouldn't do it, but injury mixed with the fact Koufax has the worst advanced statistics of the three remaining is enough. Although both Johnsons led pitchers in their league in WAR all four years, Koufax missed the league lead not only the year he was injured but the next year as well. He also trailed both by over 5 WAA, and his ERA+ is the lowest as well (and, remember, ERA+, unlike ERA, should be high), thanks to the fact that Dodger Stadium was one of the friendliest pitcher's parks of all time. Having a friendly home stadium shouldn't hurt you normally, but in a contest as close as this, it does. Three down, two to go.

So, we're down to the two Johnsons, which, believe or not, is not a name of a porno as far as my extensive research could find.[67] These two come from vastly different eras, so a strictly by-the-numbers comparison is very tricky. Randy had the most consistently dominant stretch (lowest ERA+: 181) while Walter had two years where he decided to eat planets (ERA+ of 243 and 259 in 1912-1913).

For my money, I'm taking Randy. The league in 1999-2002 was at the prime of not only PEDs (which should hypothetically be accounted for by league-wide scoring adjustments of ERA+, WAR, etc.), but baseball was openly trying to promote offense after the strike (remember "Chicks dig the long ball"?). So, for Randy to put up his numbers in an era of exceptionally corny slogans is even more impressive than numbers can quantify. Also, he wins the tiebreaker of team success, as well as having the better nickname by a hair. As great of a nickname as "The Big Train" is for Walter Johnson, what man wouldn't have killed to have the nickname "The Big Unit" in college?

CP José Valverde (2003-2007)

Valverde is the franchise's leader in saves, which isn't saying a ton because he was the full-time closer for them in only one season. Valverde is one of the (strangely quite numerous) players who seem to alternate good years and bad years. He had strong 2003, 2005, and 2007 campaigns with weak years between. This phenomenon has always been around, but with the emergence of fantasy baseball, it's even more infuriating than ever. As soon as it seems safe to draft a player

[65] Which is why I considered putting in Maddux for his 1994-1997 stretch instead.
[66] That gem came from @theaceofspaeder via a Jonah Keri article making the case for Johnson as the greatest lefty of all time.
[67] Like I said, least-mature chapter.

because he has turned the corner, he screws the pooch the year you have him, only to bounce back the next year and be a steal for your buddy in the 16th round… not that I'm bitter about Alex Rios or anything. Pablo Sandoval also suffers from this disease, but I'm going to go ahead and take the initiative to name this "Alex Rios disease,"[68] so I can move on and bury the hatchet.

Starting IX Franchise Roster Stats

Lineup	Yrs	G	R	H	HR	RBI	SB	BB	SO	BA	OBP	SLG	OPS+	dWAR	WAR
Stephen Drew	7	773	393	776	72	333	33	275	563	0.266	0.328	0.436	96	4.6	13.1
Steve Finley	6	849	491	847	153	479	70	337	467	0.278	0.351	0.500	111	3.4	18.0
Luis Gonzalez	8	**1194**	**780**	**1337**	**224**	**774**	32	**650**	580	0.298	0.391	0.529	130	-3.9	30.0
Paul Goldschmidt	7	934	614	1010	176	627	117	565	**886**	**0.299**	**0.399**	**0.532**	**146**	-1.3	**34.8**
Justin Upton	6	731	438	739	108	363	80	306	694	0.278	0.357	0.475	118	-1.4	14.3
Miguel Montero	**9**	906	365	795	97	448	2	334	670	0.264	0.342	0.421	103	3.0	12.6
Jay Bell	5	616	360	573	91	304	17	303	437	0.263	0.355	0.458	104	0.8	9.7
Matt Williams	6	595	317	629	99	381	12	163	383	0.278	0.327	0.471	100	2.1	8.2
Craig Counsell	6	664	343	611	24	193	68	276	294	0.266	0.348	0.357	80	**10.6**	12.7
Pitchers	Yrs	W	W%	ERA	G	CG	SHO	SV	IP	SO	ERA+	WHIP	SO/9	SO/BB	WAR
Randy Johnson	8	**118**	0.656	**2.83**	233	**38**	**14**	0	**1630.1**	**2077**	**164**	1.068	**11.5**	4.99	**53.0**
José Valverde	5	9	0.391	3.29	253	0	0	**98**	260.0	331	141	1.173	11.5	2.98	5.6

[68] And I am aware that it has already been called "The Saberhagen Syndrome," which is both catchier and more pronounced in its occurrence, but I really need this, guys.

Tier two: The sad group of '69[69]

Major League Baseball expanded from 20 teams to 24 teams in 1969, less than a decade removed from expanding from 16 to 18 in 1961 and again from 18 to 20 in 1962. The league added the San Diego Padres, Montreal Expos, Seattle Pilots (soon to be the Milwaukee Brewers), and Kansas City Royals. Although no expansion team has ever truly flourished in Major League Baseball, the group that originated in 1969 have had a particularly tough time. The four franchises have combined for just two World Series championships, seven pennants, and 23 playoff appearances compared to 117 losing seasons and 14 seasons of 100+ losses in their 192 combined seasons. Let's meet these lovable losers.

#26 San Diego Padres (1969-pres.)

(Photo by SD Dirk/Creative Commons)

Team Background

Playoff appearances: 5 **Pennants: 2** **World Series titles: 0**
Collective team WAR: 258.4
Strengths: If the 30 Starting IX's were to play games of pickup basketball, the Padres would be pretty solid thanks to a pair of players on their Starting IX who were also drafted into the NBA. Outside of that, the weather, I guess?
Weaknesses: The middle infield. Oh dear lord, the middle infield.
What to expect from the next eight pages: A lot of cool Tony Gwynn stats ripped off from Jayson Stark.

A little bit more on the 1969 crew and MLB expansion as a whole. The San Diego Padres came into the league the same year as the Seattle Pilots (who became the Milwaukee Brewers after one season), the Kansas City Royals, and the Montreal Expos (now the Washington Nationals). As noted, the teams have combined for a remarkably low seven pennants,

[69] "One more, I got 69 touchdowns, if you know what I mean… Only you know what I mean baby." Long live Gronk

and their lone World Series wins have come from the Royals in 1985 and 2015. Of these teams, the Padres have the second most division titles with five, and while the Royals are the most successful (their seven division titles and two rings pace this group), it's fair to say this is not the strongest group of teams. In fact, it's interesting to note the rather limited success that the 14 teams that have come into the league through expansion (starting in 1961) have had.

The first two teams to come into MLB through expansion were the Los Angeles Angels and Washington Senators (now Texas Rangers). These two teams have combined for only one World Series victory and have only three pennants in their over 45 years of history apiece. The next year the New York Mets and Houston Colt .45s (now Astros) joined the National League, and although those two have a slightly better seven combined pennants, they still only have two World Series titles. Given that there have been over 90 years of combined history for the two, seven pennants are still a low number. The next expansion was the four teams just mentioned above, whose lackluster performance has been covered. Eight years later, the Toronto Blue Jays and Seattle Mariners joined the league, and although the Blue Jays have a pair of titles to their name, those back-to-back World Series wins in 1992-93 represent the only pennants those two franchises have to date.

Major League Baseball then waited 16 years before adding any more teams, but in the comparative light of the other expansion teams, the Rockies and Marlins have practically been the Yankees and Cardinals. The Rockies rode a September in which they won 21 of 22 games in 2007 to make the playoffs, eventually sweeping their way to the World Series before losing to the Red Sox. The Marlins have won as many World Series as any other expansion team (2), despite their brief and wacky history that was covered in their team write-up. Finally, the most recent expansion to date took place in 1998, as the Diamondbacks and (Devil) Rays have combined for two pennants and one title (the Dbacks walk-off in 2001).

To recap, that's 24 pennants and 10 World Series titles from *all* expansion teams, ever. Baseball is a sport steeped in history, and it would appear that the playoffs have followed suit. Part of this has to do with the historic teams (Yankees, Cardinals, etc.) continuing to dominate even in the modern era, but it also speaks to how hard it is to establish a new franchise and fanbase, even over an extended period of time.

Not surprisingly, the Padres have a bit of a checkered history themselves. When new owner Ray Kroc took over in 1974, during the season opener he took the PA microphone and announced to the crowd, "Ladies and gentlemen, I suffer with you… I've never seen such stupid baseball playing in my life." This seemed like as good a sign as any to many Padres fans that they were rooting for a troubled franchise. The Padres, like many franchises in their situation, seem stuck in one of the most difficult, and common, ruts that professional franchises deal with. The vicious cycle of having trouble winning, having few fans show up for games because of it, and therefore having less money to go buy players to help you win. One benefit that the Padres have is that they play in the ideal environment for a baseball team. Their stadium is in a gorgeous location, and the team once went over 1,000 home games without a rainout. If the Padres can put together a few solid seasons and are able to land a Trout-like superstar, the crowds should flock to Petco and the club should find itself in a much better situation. Obviously, if it were that easy, the club would have found their own Trout decades ago.

Random cool things about the franchise:

- Ray Kroc, the founder of McDonald's, was the team owner from 1974-1984.
- Although not technically the mascot, the San Diego Chicken (a `70s phenom on par with the pet rock) entertained Padre fans for many of the grooviest times in Padres history.
- The team's actual mascot, The Swinging Friar, looks like a cross between Friar Tuck from the Disney version of *Robin Hood* and Chris Farley.
- The franchise has a unique connection with military, as it became the first professional sports team to establish a department within the organization for military affairs, which organizes an annual event to honor the military.
- The Padres often sport their camouflage uniforms, and the location of a great number of our nation's naval fleets being ported in San Diego only strengthens the connection between the two. The Padres have become the first pro sports team to fly the POW/MIA flag at every home game.
- The 1980 Padres became the first team to have three 50-stolen base players on the same squad (Gene Richards, Ozzie Smith, and Jerry Mumphrey).
- Ginny Baker is awesome and, hopefully someday, real.

Starting IX

C Gene Tenace (1977-1980)

Tenace is often considered one of the most underrated catchers of all time. This is because of his ability to draw walks and his play during an offense-depleted era. There's something about walks, maybe it's because I consider myself a baseball stat nerd, or maybe it's the fact that drawing walks was the only thing I could do successfully back when I played ball, but I tend to adore players with inflated walk totals. To call Tenace a walk master would still be doing his ability to draw free passes a disservice. He owns the second highest on-base percentage minus batting average of any player all-time,[70] and he led the league in walks twice.

Tenace also earned a reputation as a particularly clutch player, especially during his time with the A's. In the 1972 ALCS, his only hit of the series drove in the Series-winning run in Game 5. In that year's World Series, Tenace hit four home runs and became the first player to hit a home run in his first two at bats of World Series play.

Tenace played with the Padres for only four years, but he was worth an average of nearly 5.0 wins a season and had an on-base percentage over .400 during his time there. This was made even more surprising given his .237 batting average while with the team.

It is no surprise that given the nature of his game, he was barely looked at for the Hall of Fame, but he almost certainly belongs there. JAWS has him ranked as the 13th-best catcher of all time, ahead of catchers like Buck Ewing, Ernie Lombardi, and Roy Campanella who are all enshrined in Cooperstown. (Granted, Campy's time in the Negro Leagues isn't counted by JAWS, and the fact that his career was cut short by injury is ignored as well.)

What's JAWS you may ask?

Besides the greatest Bond villain of all time, JAWS is a statistical measurement of a player that weighs both career and peak value and is most often used to help determine if a player is worthy of a place in the baseball Hall of Fame (by fans, not the voters, mind you). Longevity and dominance are two traits commonly measured when assessing a candidate for the Hall of Fame, and by combining a player's career WAR and their peak WAR (their seven-year prime), JAWS (created by Jay Jaffe of *Baseball Prospectus* and now *Sports Illustrated*) allows baseball fans to see where players rank at their position all-time. Each position has a typical JAWS average for Hall of Famers (43.9 for catchers, 58.1 for right fielders, and on down the line), which allows us to compare players pining for entrance into the Hall and see how they stack up from both a longevity and dominance perspective against their historical peers, specifically at their position. It's an incredibly useful tool when comparing baseball legacies.

A final note on Tenace: he gets a shoutout from David Koechner (as Champ Kind, the sports guy) in *Anchorman*: "Gene Tenace at the plate, and Whammmmy!" Given that Tenace played in San Diego[71] in the '70s, the reference isn't totally random.

1B Adrián González (2006-2010)

González established himself as a Padre after a cup of tea in Texas. He was a rare power threat in PETCO and reached 40 home runs in 2009. He also led the league in walks (119) and had his best overall season in San Diego (6.9 WAR). González had one comparable season in Boston and parlayed it into the cover of the preeminent baseball video game franchise of the day, *MLB The Show*.

Now the *Sports Illustrated* jinx and the *Madden* curse are both well-known phenomena, but so far *MLB The Show's* cover players have done anything but struggle.

Year	Player	GP Year Before	OPS+ Year Before	GP Year After	OPS+ Year After
2006	David Ortiz	159	158	151	161
2007	David Wright	154	133	160	149
2008	Ryan Howard	144	144	162	125
2009	Dustin Pedroia	157	123	154	110
2010	Joe Mauer	138	171	137	140
2011	Joe Mauer	137	140	102	102
2012	Adrián González	159	155	159	117
2013	Andrew McCutchen	157	162	157	157
2014	Miguel Cabrera	148	190	159	146
2015	Yasiel Puig	148	145	79	110
2016	Josh Donaldson	158	151	155	152

The difference between the two previously mentioned "curses" and *MLB The Show* likely has nothing to do with actual voodoo. *Sports Illustrated* and *Madden* simply chose players that had passed their peak, while *MLB The Show* chose players just reaching the peak, and thus, have less regression to deal with than older athletes. The only two players who graced the cover of *The Show* at 30 years or older were Ortiz and Cabrera, two freaks of nature who were each exactly 30 the season the game came out. The others were all in their 20s, with Puig the youngest at age 23, and interestingly enough, the one who actually did see some drop-off. By contrast, *Madden* notoriously chose quarterbacks and running backs – two fragile positions, with running backs especially short-lived in their success.

But screw that, the *Madden* curse reigns supreme!

---

[70] Max Bishop is first.

[71] "Discovered by the Germans in 1904, they named it San Diego, which of course, in German, means 'a whale's vagina.'"

Final note on González: he has embraced his Mexican heritage (while born in the U.S., both his parents are native Mexicans) while playing the majority of his career in Southern California. He frequently uses "El Mariachi Loco" as his walk-up song and told ESPN, "I wanted something that can be Mexican and people can enjoy. You want to let people know what you're about and where you're from." Good stuff.

2B Mark Loretta (2003-2005)

Yikes.

3B Chase Headley (2007-2014)

Headley earns the spot at third base here for two reasons. First, he truly is the best third baseman in the limited history at the hot corner in San Diego. But he also is here thanks to the fact that he won me a $1,000 fantasy baseball league in 2012. I bought into the Headley stock when he started to heat up in early June, and his great end to the year (19 home runs and 63 RBI in the final two months), at a position of low fantasy production no less, captured me the title.

It's interesting to think about the impact that fantasy baseball (along with fantasy football, basketball, and even bass fishing[72]) has on modern sports fans. Whether it's that fans are more aware of which players' names can be turned into puns, or whether fans are basing their loyalties on players instead of teams with increasing frequency ("back in my day…"), fantasy sports undoubtedly have a large impact of the modern generation's fanhood.

Fantasy baseball (or rotisserie baseball) famously came into existence in 1980 with Dan Okrent and his crew. Nearly every one of ESPN's 30 for 30 documentaries is excellent, but the one entitled "Silly Little Game" is among the best. It tells the story of a group of friends who created the first rotisserie fantasy baseball leagues (named after the New York City restaurant La Rotisserie Francaise in which the founders would meet). Of course, the days of Okrent and his crew calculating all statistics by hand – and showering the champion with Yoo-Hoo chocolate milk – have now grown into the multi-billion-dollar industry that is fantasy sports. Although the game's creators didn't see any money off of the eventual explosion of fantasy sports – and there is a natural bitterness that accompanies that fact – the documentary is light-hearted with an only-slightly-acidic tone coming across from the game's apostles.

Back to the first point in Headley's favor (the fact that he truly is the best third baseman in the limited third-baseman history of the San Diego Padres): in 2012, he became just the second Padres hitter in franchise history to lead the league in RBI. The only other Padre to do so was a man who will be discussed here shortly.

SS Khalil Greene (2003-2008)

Given the fact that Khalil Greene is somehow getting a start in this book, this seems like around the right time to go over the best players who were not able to make any of the all-franchise teams: (*Mild spoilers for teams and breakdowns yet to come, if you're trying to guess your team's Starting IX before you read it.*)

C) Bill Dickey 1B) Dan Brouthers 2B) Lou Whitaker 3B) Scott Rolen SS) George Davis LF) Joe Medwick CF) Billy Hamilton RF) Dwight Evans SP1) Cy Young SP2) Roger Clemens SP3) Greg Maddux SP4) Kid Nichols SP 5) Juan Marichal RP) Goose Gossage CP) Billy Wagner.

One thing Greene does have going for him is the fact that he is the only Padres first-round draft pick from 1995-2009 to be worth more than 6.0 WAR in his entire career. Six of those picks were in the top ten, and four were in the top five, including a no. 1 overall pick who never made the big leagues (Matt Bush in 2004). Want to know the reason for the Padres' futility over the last couple decades? That's a good place to start.

LF Gene Richards (1977-1983)

Besides sharing a name with my college landlord, Gene Richards was best known for patrolling left field for the Padres in the late `70s and early `80s. Richards came to the team as the first overall selection in the 1975 amateur draft, and his 18.8 career WAR is very close to the average value of the first overall pick (as determined by the numerous studies that have looked at the average output of each pick in the MLB draft). What is interesting about these studies is just how quickly the value plummets, considering baseball is not a sport in which the draft is really given much thought – we hear stories about players like Albert Pujols who come from the 13th round rather regularly. That being said, it's still best to have the top pick, and it's not even close. By the end of the first round, the average career WAR drops to almost 0.0, and those tales of 13th-round success stories are not as common as we remember them to be. Given that fact, it's interesting that the MLB draft doesn't get any real coverage, at least in the first round, where there is a decent chance these guys will show up in the big leagues, at least for a time being. The NFL and NBA do have the added advantage (at least in this case) of not having a minor-league system, so the players drafted will either be up at the top level of play, or cut, by the time the season starts.

---

[72] Yes, fantasy bass fishing is a real thing. Yes, I was in a league once – finished in second place, too. I had a lot of free time on my hands in high school…

Given the amount of hype (and therefore $$) that currently comes with the NFL – and to a lesser extent NBA – draft, it seems like it would be in the best interest of MLB to somehow begin to hype their draft as much as the NFL and NBA, something I'm sure they are trying, but have failed to do, so far.

Back to Richards: he relied on his speed for his value, finishing in the top 10 in the National League in triples six times and leading the league in 1981. He racked up significant steal totals while with the team, but given the era in which he played and the frequency with which he was caught stealing, it is fair to ask how much value was truly attained from his 242 steals as a Padre (Rbaser says 1.4 wins).

Even though he had minimal pop in his bat, he was still a solid hitter whose .357 on-base percentage while in America's finest city was underlined by an OPS+ of 113. He was nothing if not consistently above average in his time with the club, posting six straight seasons with a positive value per wins above average, which, although it may not seem like a ringing endorsement, is more difficult than it sounds. In fact, it is a feat that Alfonso Soriano and Ryan Howard were never been able to achieve.

CF Steve Finley (1995-1998)

Finley is the first guy in the book to show up twice. Already having been on the Arizona Starting IX, Finley also had a big impact in his four years with San Diego. His OPS+ of 112 with the Padres was as high as he had with any of the eight teams he played for in his career, and the 602 games he played with the team was second only to Arizona. Finley was with the Padres during their successful late `90s, and his 1996 campaign was by far his strongest: he hit 30 home runs and stole 22 bases to go along with a .298 average, 136 OPS+, and 5.7 WAR. There could have been a few Padre right fielders moved over to center field given that Finley ranks a mere 28th among position players in franchise WAR, but none of them seemed to be even quasi-legitimate center fielders, and moving to center from right field is far more difficult than the reverse.

For a man with plenty of stops in his career, Finley managed quite the career as a whole, totaling 44.0 WAR and being one of just eight players in history in the 300/300 HR/SB club.

RF Tony Gwynn (1982-2001)

Far and away the Face of the Franchise, Gwynn "is" the Padres as much as any one player has ever signified an entire franchise. His career wins above replacement are more than double any other Padre and more than triple any non-Dave Winfield Padre. Although his on-field value was immense, his attitude towards being Mr. Padre was just as important. He embraced being in San Diego, which is what makes him truly stand out among players who have ever gone by "Face of the Franchise." Gwynn went to college at San Diego State (where he also coached after his retirement) and, in a way, limiting Gwynn to "Mr. Padre" undersells a man better described as "Mr. San Diego."[73] In his Hall of Fame acceptance speech, he made numerous references to how he was only ever a Padre and thanked the fans of San Diego, telling them that they were the inspiration for his play. His relationship with San Diego was as symbiotic as any athlete has ever had with his/her city.

When most fans think of Gwynn, they don't think of him looking like the typical athlete (he as a bit rotund in his later years), but Gwynn was, in fact, an incredible athlete. In addition to being an amazing baseball player, Gwynn was drafted in the 10th round of the NBA draft by the Los Angeles Clippers on June 10, 1981, the same day that the Padres drafted him in the third round of the MLB draft. It's fair to say Gwynn made the right decision in choosing baseball, as he was one of the most natural hitters of all time. He used to say, "I love to hit. I can't wait until it's my turn. Sometimes, I think that's all that baseball is. I root for the other team to go down 1-2-3 so I can hit again." His eight batting titles are second only to Ty Cobb in the history of baseball, and he is the only man to have won four batting titles in two different decades. If I were that good at something, it's all I would think about as well. Keep in mind there were far fewer teams (and therefore players) in Cobb's era, and Cobb only played against white players, making Gwynn's batting titles all the more impressive.

The man who *SI* called "The Best Hitter since Ted Williams" in a 1997 cover feature, Gwynn has hitting numbers that are so remarkable that they often hearken back to eras past, when batting averages were much higher. His 1994 batting average of .394 was the highest average in the National League since "Memphis Bill" Terry in 1930. His average was never below .300 the entire 1994 season, and after April 23, the 13th game of the year, he didn't end a single game with his average below .376; it was an incredible season from an incredible player. However, Gwynn missed a chance at history when the 1994 strike canceled the final 45 games of Gwynn's season, which would have given him a chance to catch his idol, and good friend, Ted Williams' record .400 season. Williams, a San Diego native, grew close to Gwynn throughout his life, and the two shared many great memories, including the 1999 MLB All-Star Game in Fenway Park. This spine-tingling moment was a tribute to two of baseball's most "pure" hitters of all time, as the two threw out the first pitch together.

When Cal Ripken Jr. and Tony Gwynn were inducted into Cooperstown, the two beloved one-team, one-city stars drew an attendance of 75,000, which is the all-time record for an induction ceremony. One has to wonder if even a Jeter-led induction ceremony in 2019 will be able to top that figure.

Back to Gwynn's hitting: he has some of the most outstanding hitting numbers of all time, and since his passing was

[73] When the Padre organization released a statement after Gwynn's death, this exact turn of phrase was used.

relatively recent and he was so beloved by every baseball writer he met, a glut of statistics appeared across the vast array of articles on Gwynn's legacy after his passing in June of 2014. Let's check out some of the best:

* Gwynn faced Greg Maddux (arguably the best pitcher of Gwynn's era) 107 times in his career (more than any other pitcher Gwynn faced). Gwynn hit .415 and never struck out a single time. In case you thought that was just because Maddux wasn't a big strikeout guy; Gwynn faced Pedro Martínez 35 times in his career, striking out a grand total of zero times against Pedro, as well.
* Gwynn had 297 three-hit games compared to just one three-strikeout game.
* His 19 straight .300+ batting average seasons are second to only Ty Cobb.
* His best five-year period for batting average was .368, better than Ted Williams ever did over a five-year stretch. Over that stretch, he hit over .350 with two strikes.
* Speaking of success with two strikes, Gwynn hit .302 with two strikes for his career. Among players for whom Baseball-Reference has data available, that average is not only first, but it is first by *40 points* (second is Wade Boggs at .262).
* In 1997, Gwynn became one of four players to hit .350 or higher five straight seasons, and the first since Al Simmons (1925-1931).
* Roy Halladay struck out more times in 18 at bats in 2013 (17) than Gwynn did in 535 at bats in 1995 (15).
* Of the members of the 3,000-hit club born after 1900, he has the highest batting average.
* Gwynn had over 300 steals to go along with his .330+ batting average. The four other members of that 300+ steals, .330+ batting average: Ty Cobb, Tris Speaker, George Sisler, and Eddie Collins. None played past 1930.
* The 5.5 on his cleats referred to the spot between shortstop and third base that he would pepper with opposite field pokes game-in and game-out. When he passed, the Padres were playing in Seattle, and the Mariners grounds crew honored Gwynn by putting Gwynn's number (19) in the 5.5 hole of their infield.
* Gwynn called his bat "Seven Grains of Pain." It was a very small bat due to his small hands.
* Gwynn would often read where the fielders were moving as the pitcher was in his windup to figure out what pitch was coming.

Gwynn wasn't just a hitter, however: he was also a five-time Gold Glove winner and, as noted, stole over 300 bases for his career. He set numerous Padres records, including becoming the first Padre to top 200 hits in a season and the first to win a batting title – he did both in his third season in the majors (1984). He is one of only 17 players to play at least 20 years and have each season be with the same team, a nice boost for loyalty in a book that rewards team loyalty.

In the end, Larry Bowa may have summed it up best. When Bowa was manager of the Padres, he was upset after one game and told the media he only had 10 good players. Gwynn came up to him after and asked if he was one of those 10. Bowa's response: "Tony, you're one through ten."

Utility Dave Winfield (1973-1980)

Probably the second-best player in Padres history, Winfield is relegated to the utility spot thanks to sharing a position (right field) with Mr. San Diego. The Padres drafted Winfield in 1973, but the Padres weren't the only ones with their eye on him. In fact, he was drafted in the MLB, NFL, ABA, and NBA drafts, making him the only athlete in history drafted into four different leagues. He came with incredible expectations, making the major-league roster before even playing a single game in the Padres minor-league system.[74] He also didn't get off to an entirely great start when, after being drafted by the Padres, he said, "To be honest, I'd never heard of them."

These expectations led to a bit of disappointment from fan bases throughout his career when Winfield seemingly failed to live up to his potential over and over again. Outside of leading the league in RBI, total bases, intentional walks, and OPS+ in 1979, Winfield never truly dominated the league leaderboards, despite his prodigious talent. He never had more than 193 hits in a season, and he only hit above .308 once.

However, what Winfield lacked in dominance, he made up for with his consistency. He is one of only three players to have a hit in seven consecutive All-Star Games, along with Mickey Mantle and Joe Morgan. More impressively, however, along with Hank Aaron and Willie Mays, Winfield is one of only three men to have 3,000 hits, 450 home runs, and 200 steals in his career. He is also one of only three players to play 1,000 games in both the American and National League and, despite not doing so while with the Padres, aged particularly well. He became the oldest player to hit for cycle when he did so in 1991 at the age of 39, and the next year, while over the age of 40, he knocked in the winning run in the top of 11th inning to win Game 6 of the World Series for the Blue Jays – this despite being given the nickname "Mr. May" by Yankees owner George Steinbrenner earlier in his career for his supposed lack of clutch ability.

Clutch ability and the general lack of evidence that it exists as a repeatable skill among MLB hitters is something that will be covered in greater detail throughout the book, but here's one interesting theory put forth by Leonard Newman in *The Baseball Research Journal* (Vol. 42, No.2): every hitter at the big-league level is clutch because the ones who choke in

---

[74] According to Baseball-Reference, he never appeared in a single minor league game his whole career.

the clutch have been weeded out on their way to *the show*. As he puts it, "unmotivated, highly self-conscious men with trouble controlling anxiety are unlikely to be found on the rosters of teams in the American and National Leagues." For someone like myself who has covered sports at the high school and college level, this is a very compelling argument. When covering sports at those levels, high school in particular, you definitely see players who crumble under pressure and generally fall short of the psychological traits shared by major leaguers. But this makes sense. There is *very* limited weeding out of players at the high school level, but by the time a player has established himself as one of the 750 or so best players in the world at his craft, he's highly unlikely to have the traits associated with folding under pressure repeatedly. For me, that's one of the best arguments against certain players being "extra clutch."

Winfield spent the first eight years of his career in San Diego, a total topped by only his nine years in the Bronx. His 31.9 WAR with San Diego are the highest of any team for Winfield, and his 8.3-WAR 1979 campaign was his best shot at an MVP (finishing third behind Keith Hernandez and Willie Stargell, who tied for first).

Finally: it is somewhat surprising that Winfield ended up in Toronto, given his history with the city. As a member of the Yankees in 1983, while warming up between innings, Winfield threw a ball that hit and killed a seagull. He was booed throughout the rest of the game, and after the game was arrested and later released on $500 bail. His court date was canceled and charges of animal cruelty were eventually dropped. They must really love their seagulls in Canada.

SP Jake Peavy (2002-2009)

Jake Peavy burst on the scene in 2004 after two middling seasons in the Padres rotation. He won the ERA title and finished 15-6 but didn't make the All-Star team or receive a single vote for the Cy Young. Three of the next four years would be strong campaigns for Peavy, and he was rewarded with a Cy Young in 2007, just the 12th unanimous selection in the trophy's history. Because of his early debut age (21), and his early success, when he won his ERA title in 2004, he became the youngest pitcher to do so since Dwight Gooden more than 20 years earlier. He also became the youngest Padres pitcher to make the All-Star Game when he did so the next season. Although he was almost certainly boosted by pitching in PETCO Park (neither of his ERA titles were accompanied by ERA+ titles) in his eight years with San Diego, he proved himself a reliable option, which he continues to be around the rest of the league, even as he ages.

Peavy is a pretty mild-mannered guy off the field, but he's about as competitive as it gets on the field. In his words, "I try not to yell; I try not to swear. But at 7 o'clock every night, I turn into someone different. I'm out there trying to focus. I'm competing. I can't control myself. But I have three little boys. I want them to be able to watch their daddy pitch without hearing all the yelling… But I wear my emotions on a sleeve. I'm conscious of it. I love to compete. I am not a crazy animal. But it's been 11 or 12 years of this. I don't think I'm going to change. And I'm not going to apologize."

I can respect that.

CP Trevor Hoffman (1993-2008)

If Gwynn is the franchise's most famous hitter (and he certainly is), Hoffman is the Padres most famous pitcher. The MLB all-time leader in saves for nearly five years (until Mariano Rivera topped him), Hoffman spent 16 seasons in San Diego. He took over the closer's role in his first full season with the club and retained that position his entire time there. That is no easy feat for a reliever, but it was well deserved, with Hoffman never posting an ERA+ below 100 in any season with the Padres. Despite being a reliever, he is the franchise's all-time leader in WAR among pitchers, and he is among the top 10 in innings pitched in franchise history.

Hoffman was best known for two things: his entrance music (AC/DC's "Hell's Bells") and a killer changeup that acted as his "Rivera cutter" – the one pitch he could consistently go to for results. Both were just as awesome as you can possibly imagine.

Most folks may not be jealous of a MLB closer who never won a World Series and played in the relative obscurity of San Diego for his whole career,[75] but check out this excerpt from an excellent 2002 *SI* feature from Tom Verducci on Hoffman and try not to feel a bit of jealousy creep up:

"Hoffman has a home three miles away, in Rancho Santa Fe, the 16th-most-expensive town in America if you judge by average house price ($1.65 million) as estimated by *Worth* magazine; a beach house 2 ½ miles down the road in idyllic Del Mar; a former NFL cheerleader for a wife; three sons who wrestle Dad on the clubhouse carpet when he's done with work; two years remaining on a four-year, $32 million contract; the coolest entrance in baseball; and a reputation for having as much fun – everywhere but on the mound – as the law allows. In short, at 34, the dude has pretty much scored the whole damn burrito."

---

[75] With so much of the media located on the East Coast, Hoffman, who typically came into games around 1:00 a.m. EST to finish off Padres victories, definitely flew under-the-radar.

Starting IX Franchise Roster Stats

Lineup	Yrs	G	R	H	HR	RBI	SB	BB	SO	BA	OBP	SLG	OPS+	dWAR	WAR
Gene Richards	7	939	484	994	26	251	242	338	408	0.291	0.357	0.383	113	-3.4	18.8
Tony Gwynn	**20**	**2440**	**1383**	**3141**	135	**1138**	**319**	**790**	434	**0.338**	0.388	0.459	132	-8.3	**68.8**
Adrián González	5	799	464	856	161	501	1	403	618	0.288	0.374	0.514	141	-4.3	20.3
Dave Winfield	8	1117	599	1134	154	626	133	463	585	0.284	0.357	0.464	134	-3.4	31.9
Chase Headley	8	908	398	873	87	401	73	377	**844**	0.266	0.346	0.410	113	1.1	19.1
Gene Tenace	4	573	233	384	68	239	17	423	386	0.237	**0.403**	0.422	136	2.6	19.7
Steve Finley	4	602	423	662	82	298	85	203	344	0.276	0.334	0.458	112	-4.9	8.6
Mark Loretta	3	413	236	506	32	186	18	157	141	0.314	0.377	0.438	121	0.5	11.3
Khalil Greene	6	659	301	594	84	328	23	175	521	0.248	0.304	0.427	96	3.7	9.3
Pitchers	Yrs	W	W%	ERA	G	CG	SHO	SV	IP	SO	ERA+	WHIP	SO/9	SO/BB	WAR
Jake Peavy	8	92	0.575	3.29	212	7	3	0	1342.2	**1348**	119	1.186	9.0	3.10	24.7
Trevor Hoffman	16	54	0.458	**2.76**	**902**	0	0	**552**	952.1	1029	**146**	**1.043**	**9.7**	**4.04**	**25.9**

#25 Washington Nationals (2005-pres.); Montreal Expos (1969-2004)

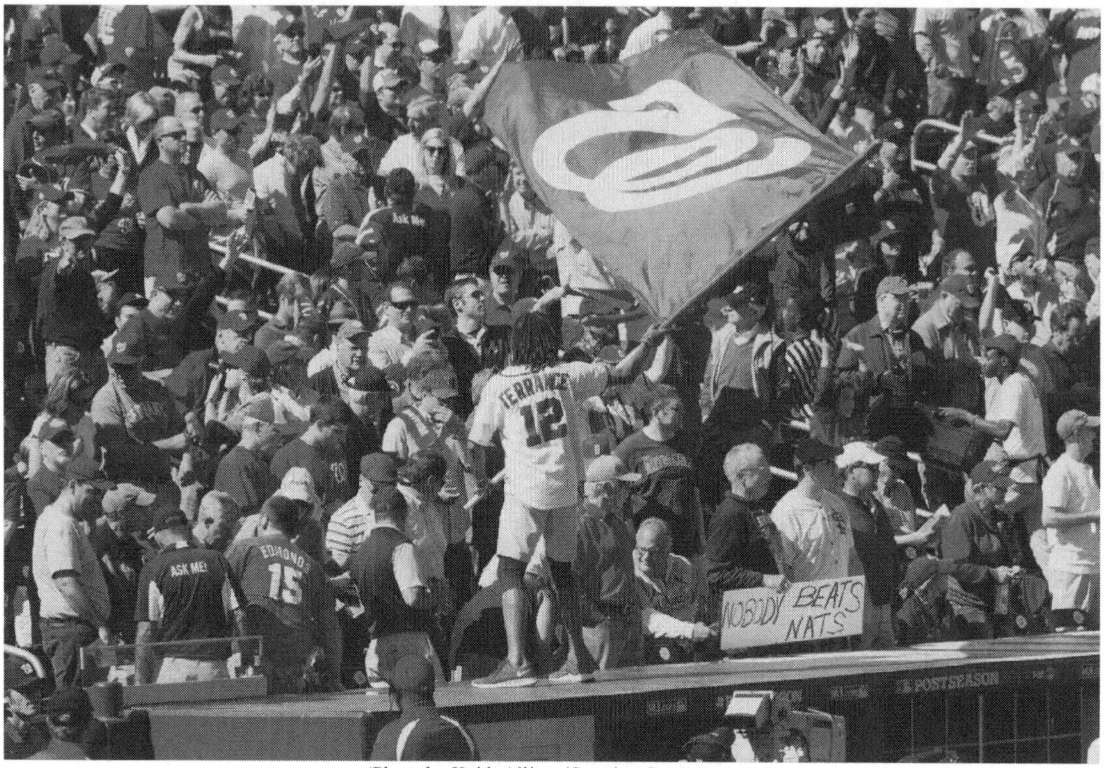

(Photo by Keith Allison/Creative Commons)

Team Background

Playoff appearances: 5 **Pennants: 0** **World Series titles: 0**
Collective team WAR: 361.2
Strengths: There's a ton of talented players here…
Weaknesses: Sadly, none of them stuck around as long as they could have.
What to expect from the next nine pages: The name Jonah Keri. Like a million times. Also, a Lindsay Lohan nod.

As noted under the team's strengths and weaknesses section, the Expos/Nationals franchise has had a lot of talented players pass through the team's history, but they have had very few talented "lifers." Some of the top names to pass through but not make the franchise Starting IX: Pedro Martínez, Randy Johnson, Alfonso Soriano, Larry Walker, Moises Alou, Adam Dunn, Orlando Cabrera, Andrés Galarraga, and Livan Hernandez. These guys didn't make the Starting IX because they simply weren't with the franchise long enough. Of the players who actually made the Starting IX, only one played for the franchise his entire career.

Along those lines, my natural inclination was to turn this team intro into a study that looked at which teams drafted the most talent in the 1990s, under the assumption that the Expos would be at the top of the list or right near it. However, this intro is going to be a little less about the Expos and more about sports research (and really any research in general). Anyone who has done any significant research knows what's coming. When I did my study – looking at the top 25 hitters and top 25 pitchers of the 1990s by fWAR and seeing which team drafted them – my conclusion did not at all match my hypothesis. My hypothesis was that the Expos would be one of the teams that drafted the best talent of the `90s, and that it was simply their inability to hold onto these players that in part led to their eventual folding. What I actually found was something much different. First, it was actually the White Sox who drafted the most elite talent of the `90s, but no team actually stood out that much. Sure, the White Sox led the way with four players drafted that were among the top 25 pitchers and top 25 hitters (Frank Thomas, Robin Ventura, Jack McDowell, and Alex Fernandez), but there were eight teams right behind them at three players apiece, and there were only three teams that failed to draft one such player (Phillies, Mets, Brewers). Where were the Expos? Right in the middle with two players (Randy Johnson and Larry Walker). I couldn't make the case that the Expos got screwed because their small market nature meant they couldn't hold onto these players (at least with this study). Sure, they ranked 19th in the league in terms of average years they kept their top-25 players, but right below them were such "small-market misers" as the Red Sox, Yankees, and Tigers.

Although small sample size would seem the first explanation, when I did the same study on a year-by-year basis from 2011-2015, there was no real definite conclusion there, either (other than that the A's really hate building their team through the draft).

So why waste half a page for a study that didn't really tell the reader anything? Well for one, I can say that what we *weren't* able to see can be informative... But really, it's because of something every baseball writer goes through: when you spend multiple hours doing something like this it just kills you to completely throw it away. It's like spending an entire afternoon cooking an awesome meal for a dinner party you're hosting – complete with four courses, all your food groups, tons of healthy ingredients – and then just dumping it in the trash can right before the first guest shows up. It's brutal. So yeah, maybe it's a bit narcissistic to include this page in the final cut of this book, but that's part of the reason I chose to self-publish. Plus, now you know the Expos can't claim to have drafted more talent than the rest of the league in the `90s despite what it may have seemed like at the time.

Random cool things about the franchise:

- Montreal became the first city outside of the United States to have a Major League Baseball team when the city got the team in 1969.
- Before the Expos, the city of Montreal hosted the minor-league Royals, where Jackie Robinson played before joining the Dodgers and breaking the color barrier at the professional level.
- The Expos were known as "Nos Amours," or "The Ones We Love" to the native French speakers of Montreal.
- The Expos' logo, one of the best in baseball's history, can be read as "eb" for Expos Baseball, or "M" for the city of Montreal. The logo was italicized to emphasize forward movement of the sport in the city.
- The Expos relationship with strike-shortened seasons is a love-hate affair. In 1981, the team benefited from the strike-shortened season, making the only playoff appearance in team (not franchise) history, benefiting from the strange half-season standings that came as a result of the strike. Of course, they were much more famously hard done by the 1994 strike that canceled the World Series the year that the Expos were 74-40, had the best record in the National League by eight games, and had the talent to make a serious run at the pennant.
- Pete Rose had a cup of tea with the Expos in 1984 and actually collected his 4,000th hit as a part of the team.
- The Nationals became the third different team – after the franchises that became the current Texas Rangers and Minnesota Twins – to play in the city of Washington D.C. when the club moved there in 2004.

Starting IX

C Gary Carter (1974-1984; 1992)

Carter played 12 seasons in Montreal, his first 11 seasons and later – because of how beloved he was north of the border – he returned for his final year to retire with the Expos. He is first in franchise history in WAR (55.6), third in games (1,506), fourth in home runs (220), fourth in RBI (823), as well as fifth in runs (707) and hits (1,427). Carter was an outstanding defensive catcher for the Expos and, despite playing a position that is difficult to quantify statistically (Catcher, Angels – Page 120), put up a dWAR of 21.1 in his time there. During the 1983 season alone, he won the team 4.0 games with his mitt. He also had a great postseason in his one trip there with Montreal, sporting a batting average over .400 and an on-base percentage a hair below .500 to go with a pair of home runs in 10 games. The Expos enjoyed most of their team success with Carter in town, which is part of the reason he was so beloved by the city.

There was more to it, though: Jonah Keri wrote an excellent piece for *Grantland* after Carter's death in February of 2012 that gave perspective on Carter as a player and person. Keri mentions that in his final game Carter (fittingly) hit a walk-off double in front of nearly 42,000 fans. Two years before (when Carter had not been in town) in the Expos final game of the season there were barely over 4,000 fans in attendance. Carter's farewell drew tenfold a normal season finale in Montreal. Granted, the team was better and the crowd knew that it was Carter's last game, but to give some more perspective, the crowd was just above 30,000 for the last game the Expos ever played in Montreal. By that logic, Carter retiring meant 33 percent more to Montreal than the entire franchise leaving town.

Carter's childhood had a huge effect on his life, as he lost his mother – who had molded Gary into a mature young man at a precocious age – when he was just 12 years old. Carter was one of the most natural athletes baseball has ever seen, dominating every sport he played as a kid,[76] and he was forced to become an adult at an early age because of the

---

[76] When he won the Punt, Pass, and Kick competition as a seven-year-old, Carter was flown to D.C., given a personal tour of the White House, and handed a signed letter from JFK telling him that he was a future leader of the U.S. The next year he got a sculpted bust put into the Football Hall of Fame, and he even got into a commercial.

aforementioned tragedy that struck his family in his pre-teen years.

Perhaps it was because of these formative years that he was able to handle all the pressure that was put on him when he came up with the team. As Keri puts it, "[Carter] was the savior of the Expos before he even set foot in the major leagues." The club told their scout to scare other teams away from Carter before the 1972 draft, spreading lies and misinformation to hurt Carter's stock and ensure that Carter was there for the Expos to draft.[77] Granted, this may well not have been what actually let him drop to the Expos, but either way it shows how much the club wanted the Culver City prospect. The expectations heaped on Carter, however, meant that he was sometimes resented by his teammates for being the so-called "Golden Boy" of the franchise. Carter personified what every franchise would want from their "Golden Boy," though, as he was so pure that some believed it be an act. But Carter truly was a good man and is deservedly an Expos legend.

1B Ryan Zimmerman (2005-pres.)

This pick is a bit of a stipulated pick on two fronts. First of all, Zimmerman was a third baseman for much of his career in Washington (his rookie season was the first year the team played in the nation's capital), but he thrived at first base in 2017 and is too old to move back across the diamond, so the working assumption is that he will stay at first base for upcoming seasons. There also was far superior competition at third base, as the only competition at first base was Ron Fairly, a mediocre first baseman for the Expos in the `70s who had a few clever quips in his post-playing days.

This pick is also based on Zimmerman keeping up this production during his first base days in Washington. Zimmerman quietly snuck into the top five in most franchise statistics by this point in his career, but he needs at least one full, dominant season at first to qualify for the position. For people reading this in 2015 thanks to their time machine kindles that are yet to be produced, Zimmerman's recent success might be a bit of a surprise. It looked like Zimmerman was dead in the water on several occasions in his career, most notably in 2016 when he hit .218 and no longer had the defensive value of a third baseman. However, the 2017 seasons did wonders to rejuvenate his levels of production. The most straight-forward explanation for his late-career bounceback is the emphasis he began to put on elevating his swing. This "elevation revolution" is just about the buzziest catchphrase in baseball writing these days, and Zimmerman has been just one of many who have seen their production spike with a simple tweak to elevating their swing more.

(Whether baseball historians will look back on paragraphs like the last one and chuckle with how naive we were not to mention the league juicing the baseball is a whole nother matter entirely.)

2B José Vidro (1997-2006)

Vidro played with the franchise for 10 years and was part of the team when they moved from Montreal to Washington. Always a slap hitter, Vidro hit over .300 as an Expo and added power to his repertoire during his best seasons. His BABIP (batting average on balls in play) with the team was .314 (compared to a league average of .298 over that span), which supports the idea that some hitters can maintain a higher BABIP if they are good at finding gaps and are good slap hitters, not just if they are lucky. Jeff Wiser phrased it wonderfully in an article on *Beyond the Box Score*: "We often equate BABIP to luck, but there's a saying around sports, and life in general, that one often makes his or her own luck. BABIP falls in this category." There are certain players whose style of hitting lends itself to a higher BABIP, especially speedy players who mash the ball into the ground and players who can find gaps in the defense. Therefore, implying that Vidro was lucky during his time with the Expos may well be an inaccurate statement, especially given the large sample size.

Vidro was also a tough strikeout during his career, and of players with at least 1,000 at bats with the franchise, he ranks second in batting average (.301), as well as currently residing among the top six in games played (1,186) and hits (1,280) with the franchise.

Also working for Vidro is the fact that second base was a historically awful position for the Expos. It was a position that may have cost them dearly in their heyday of the early 1980s, as the club's primary second baseman hit a total of zero home runs from 1980-1984 (Rodney Scott in 1980-1981 and Doug Flynn 1982-1984). Read that sentence again. Seriously. As Jonah Keri (whom that nugget is from) noted, for a club that was always in contention throughout the early `80s, Vidro likely could have put them over the top if only he had been on the club a couple decades prior.

3B Tim Wallach (1980-1992)

Wallach was a steady presence with the team for 13 years and is the franchise leader in games (1,767) and hits (1,694), with Zimmerman only recently passing him in doubles (360) and RBI (905). His batting average (.259) and on-base percentage (.317) with the team were dragged down by a few quite poor seasons sprinkled into his time in Montreal, and although he was never a stud, it would seem harsh to leave off the franchise leader in two categories as essential as games played and hits. Wallach was also a five-time All-Star, three-time Gold Glove winner, and two-time Silver Slugger winner in Montreal.

---

[77] A knee injury, the possibility he might choose football over baseball, and a high price to sign him eventually helped him fall all the way to the 53rd pick.

A key point in Wallach's legacy was when he was moved across the diamond to first base by his manager Tom Runnels. Many Expos fans considered this move the last in a series of questionable decisions that got Runnels fired. The move led to a near full-scale mutiny from the team, per Keri's Expos expose, and the sentiments spilled over to the fans and media.

The decision was not actually a poor one, as Rob Neyer points out: "Wallach was thirty-three and it certainly looked like his good years were mostly (and perhaps completely) behind him." However, fans ignored the fact that Wallach put up almost the exact same offensive line in 1992 (split time at first and third) as he did in 1991 (solely at third base), and it was just age catching up with him instead of the switch made by Runnels. For most, it was the principle of the move that hurt Runnels' stock, so the numerical argument regarding his inevitable decline wouldn't have mattered regardless.

"Fans ignoring the fact" is hardly an issue that relates strictly to Wallach's statistics, and it is hardly an issue that relates to only sports. One of the most interesting ideas in social science is the study that people actually become more entrenched in their beliefs when faced with statistical proof opposing their position. (Both liberals and conservatives are nodding vigorously right now.) It seems that the strategy that most social scientists believe will yield the greatest reward is to build a narrative bridge for those you are trying to convince. Christie Aschwanden sums it up well in her article "Your brain is primed to reach false conclusions" on *FiveThirtyEight*: "If you want someone to accept information that contradicts what they already know, you have to find a story they can buy into. That requires bridging the narrative they've already constructed to a new one that is both true and allows them to remain the kind of person they believe themselves to be."

Once baseball front offices become more adept at this strategy, appeasing fanbases will be a lot easier.

SS Hubie Brooks (1985-1989)

Brooks had five successful years at shortstop in Montreal after coming over from New York in the trade that sent Gary Carter to the Mets. Brooks played for the Expos in some pretty lean years, with the club never finishing higher than third in the division.

In 1986, Brooks was off to his best season start – a possibly an MVP campaign – when he suffered a thumb injury. Through the half year he played, he posted a .340 batting average with an OPS+ of 161, to go with 4.7 WAR and 3.5 WAA, despite playing in only 80 games. He even managed to win the Silver Slugger despite playing only half the season, and it was by far his most productive season in the majors even though he missed half of it. Remarkably, this was one of only four times that a player was worth more than 3.0 wins above average over the course of a season that constituted 80 or fewer games for that player. Here are the other three cases:

1949 Joe DiMaggio – Joltin' Joe missed the first half of the 1949 campaign with a heel injury, one that had many wondering if his career would be over. Joe quickly dispelled those ideas with a home run in his first game back and four home runs in his first three games returning from injury. In almost exactly half a season, DiMaggio totaled a triple slash of .346/.459/.596 with an OPS+ of 178 to go along with 58 runs, 14 home runs, and 67 RBI and 4.4 WAR, which if extrapolated over a full season would have been among Joe's best seasons in the big leagues (of course, that's a dangerous game with all of these examples). He managed to finish 12th in the MVP and helped lead the Yankees charge past the Red Sox for yet another pennant and World Series.

1995 Matt Williams – The year after hitting 46 home runs during the strike-shortened season of 1994, Williams continued to pummel the ball to start 1995. In fact, in the 162 games from the beginning of the 1994 season to midway through 1995, Williams hit 62 home runs, which would have been the home run record at the time. However, a foul ball off his foot took a big chunk out of his 1995 campaign, and he had to settle for a very similar line to DiMaggio's 1949 season: triple slash of .336/.399/.647 with an OPS+ of 177 with 53 runs, 23 home runs, and 65 RBI and 4.6 WAR. Williams is an oft-forgotten part of baseball history in the 1990s, but he was one of the best power hitters in an era of great power hitters.

1999 Jason Kendall – Kendall was just starting to establish himself as a perennial All-Star when he had his breakout season in the first half of 1999. Unfortunately, he dislocated his ankle trying for a bunt hit (somewhere Matt Garza rejoiced), and his season ended far too early. Due to the type of player Kendall was, his line was quite different from DiMaggio's and Williams'. He had only eight home runs, but his 22 steals (out of 25 attempts) were outstanding for a catcher, and his .332 average, 62 runs, and 4.1 WAR underline how strong a season he was having. After the injury, Kendall's speed (and thus his baserunning efficiency) would never be quite the same.

Of all these seasons, none totaled more than Brooks' 4.7 WAR, proving, as will be said numerous times throughout this book: injuries suck.

LF Tim Raines (1979-1990; 2001)

Raines was a speed demon/on-base extraordinaire for the Expos during the 1980s. He ranks first in franchise history in runs (947), triples (82), and stolen bases (635), and is in the top five for almost every offensive category. In his first four full seasons, he led the league in steals each year with an incredible 314 steals while only being caught 51 times. In his first six seasons, he tallied at least 70 steals in each season, making him the only player in MLB history to have six consecutive 70-steal seasons. Raines was a successful base runner throughout his career and is fifth all-time in career stolen bases. His total with the Expos alone would put him 15th on that list. Raines was an efficient base stealer as well, with the highest stolen base percentage (84.7 percent) of any player with at least 500 attempts in baseball history.

Raines was no slouch with the stick, either, winning the batting title in 1986 and posting a .301 batting average in his time with the Expos. It wasn't his average that stands out historically, however; it was his ability to get on base. In his career, he got on base more times (3,977) than such luminaries as Tony Gwynn (3,955) and Roberto Clemente (3,656).

Despite his great speed, Raines had below-average defensive range in left field and posted a negative dWAR most years with the Expos. However, his slightly below average defense was not nearly enough to keep him from becoming one of, if not the, best players of the 1980s. At the beginning of the decade, the Expos were offered numerous trade packages for Raines. Eighteen teams supposedly inquired about Raines' availability, with the Cubs offer centered around Hall-of-Fame pitcher Bruce Sutter, but the Expos declined them all. By the end of the decade, Raines completed a 10-year stretch (the "hidden decade" of 1981-1990) in which he accumulated more fWAR[78] than any other player in the National League.

Raines' early days were not without struggle, though. For many players, their growing pains take the form of adjusting to major-league breaking balls or pitchers figuring them out, but for Raines, his biggest struggle was off the field. What at first seemed to be a run-of-the-mill sophomore slump ended up being much more. Raines came out to *Sports Illustrated* with the story of his rampant cocaine use. He used before games, after games, and occasionally even during games. The most famous Raines story is how would make a point to slide into second base headfirst every time, due to the vial of cocaine he had in his back pocket. However, Andre Dawson, "The Hawk," took Raines under his wing and became a mentor and older brother to the young (Raines made his MLB debut at the age of 19) and impressionable Raines.

Despite all the success Raines had in his first decade in the big leagues, he had what he likely held as his personal career highlight in 2001 as a 41-year-old. On October 4, 2001, Raines and his son Tim Jr. became the second father-son combination in baseball history (after Ken Griffey Jr. and Sr.) to play for the same team in a major league game, a truly unique and historic achievement.

After a long and painful wait, Raines was finally granted admission to the hallowed halls of Cooperstown in 2017. The result was in large part thanks to the work of the advanced stats coalition of baseball writers. Jonah Keri, in particular, spearheaded this movement and is said to have taken Hall of Fame voters out to dinners at which Keri would pitch the "Raines as a Hall of Famer" argument. As a result of this effort (as well as, you know, Raines putting together a very Hall of Fame-worthy career), in his 10th and final year on the ballot Raines joined the elite of baseball history with a plaque of his own in the Baseball Hall of Fame.

CF Andre Dawson (1976-1986)

"The Hawk" was an excellent power/speed dual threat who won Rookie of the Year with the Expos in 1977 and went on to live up to the potential he showed in that first season. It's interesting how often players who win RoY don't pan out, though. There have been 140 winners of the award since its inception, and Dawson's success is not as common as one might think. If the 140 are split into five groups: Hall of Famers, multiple-time All-Stars, role players, complete busts, or injury-ravaged players, the results are surprising. Let's take a trip down Memory Lane and assign each and every RoY winner (pre-2007) into one of the aforementioned categories:

Well, before we start, here are a pair of special cases: Sam Jethroe – His rookie season occurred when he was 32 years old, not 28, as he was believed to be when he joined the Boston Braves in 1950. He came to the majors via the Negro Leagues after Robinson broke the color barrier. He posted two solid seasons in Boston before things got interesting. Jethroe played in an era in which black players were not allowed to get hurt, and so even though his skills were not actually fading, Boston used his injury as an excuse to cut him and avoid paying him pension. Stay classy, Boston.[79]

Ken Hubbs – Hubbs passed away after the 1963 season (his second full season) in a plane crash. He had completed only two full seasons in the big leagues and was a top-notch fielder but a below-average hitter.

Injury plagued (8): Herb Score – I won't go into detail about every player's injuries, but I could have also listed Score under Special Cases. Score was a dominant pitcher for his first two years in the league, until fellow Rookie of the Year winner Gil McDougald hit a line drive that struck him in the face. The incident was so severe that McDougald said he would retire if Score was blinded as a result. Score was able to recover, but, sadly, he later suffered arm injuries that ended his career for good. This was a career most likely headed towards greatness as well. Mickey Mantle said Score was the toughest American League southpaw he ever faced, and Yogi Berra selected him for his own "Greatest Team of All Time."

Others: Ron Hansen, Mark Fidrych, John Castino, Sandy Alomar Jr., Marty Cordova, Kerry Wood, and Scott Williamson.

Bust (20): Harry Byrd, Joe Black,[80] Don Schwall, Walt Dropo, Bob Grim, John Montefusco, Pat Zachry, Butch

[78] The "f" before WAR there simply means the FanGraphs version of wins above replacement.

[79] Boston is easy to pick on when it comes to race relations, but it was really the entire AL that struggled with integrating black players in this era. The NL was far more progressive.

[80] Borderline special case, Black was 28 when he came over from the Negro Leagues. Unlike Jethroe, however, he was actually 28, not 32, and the Dodgers

Metzger, Alfredo Griffin, Joe Charboneau, Ron Kittle, Jerome Walton, Pat Listach, Bob Hamelin, Todd Hollandsworth, Ben Grieve, Jason Jennings, Eric Hinske, Angel Berroa, and Bobby Crosby.

Role Player (37): Wally Moon,[81] Bill Virdon, Jack Sanford, Tony Kubek, Albie Pearson, Tom Tresh, Gary Peters, Curt Blefary, Tommie Agee, Tommy Helms, Stan Bahnsen, Ted Sizemore, Lou Piniella, Carl Morton, Earl Williams, Chris Chambliss, Gary Matthews, Al Bumbry, Mike Hargrove, Bake McBride, Bob Horner, Steve Howe, Dave Righetti, Steve Sax, Alvin Davis, Ozzie Guillen, Vince Coleman, Todd Worrell, Benito Santiago, Walt Weiss, Chris Sabo, Gregg Olson, Eric Karros, Hideo Nomo, Kazuhiro Sasaki, Jason Bay, and Huston Street.

All-Star (28): Alvin Dark, Don Newcombe, Roy Sievers, Gil McDougald, Harvey Kuenn, Jim Gilliam, Bob Allison, Tony Oliva, Dick Allen, Thurman Munson,[82] Jon Matlack, Fred Lynn, Lou Whitaker,[83] Rick Sutcliffe, Fernando Valenzuela, Darryl Strawberry, Dwight Gooden, José Canseco, Mark McGwire, David Justice, Chuck Knoblauch, Tim Salmon,[84] Raul Mondesi, Nomar Garciaparra, Scott Rolen, Rafael Furcal, Justin Verlander, and Ryan Howard.

Hall of Fame (21): Jackie Robinson, Willie Mays, Luis Aparicio, Frank Robinson, Orlando Cepeda, Willie McCovey, Billy Williams, Pete Rose,[85] Tom Seaver, Rod Carew, Johnny Bench, Carlton Fisk, Andre Dawson, Eddie Murray, Cal Ripken Jr., Mike Piazza, Jeff Bagwell, Derek Jeter,* Ichiro Suzuki,* Albert Pujols,* and Carlos Beltrán.*
* Players likely to be inducted into the Hall sooner or later

Dontrelle Willis (2): Dontrelle Willis and Hanley Ramírez

There are quite a few players labeled as busts here who may not have been considered busts under different circumstances. Part of the bust label is because many people would think of those players as decent role players if they hadn't set such high expectations for their careers by winning Rookie of the Year. One thing that stuck out during the research for this section was how many interesting stories went along with these players. Believe it or not, the number of footnotes with little tidbits was actually cut down significantly from the first draft.

A similar comparison seems to be Child-Star Syndrome, a disease from which so many famous child actors suffer. Many child stars go on to be messed up (Shia LeBeouf) or just never thought of again (Bradley Pierce, *Jumanji*). This would be a great chart in and of itself, and here's a shout-out to one famous child star from each category.

Injury plagued: Lindsay Lohan – Nose injuries… too much of a cheap shot? Maybe I'm just bitter because she was my absolute favorite when she was in her prime, with *Parent Trap* and *Mean Girls* being two of my straight-up favorite movies of all time.

Bust: The Olsen twins – Although I'm not entirely giving up on them making one more Minnie Miñoso-like comeback; probably with similar results.

Role Player: Neil Patrick Harris – NPH's name came up frequently as a possible replacement for David Letterman on CBS Late Night before Stephen Colbert eventually got the gig, and if he were to make that sort of jump, he would certainly outrank this role-player ranking. As is, he was excellent as the womanizing Barney Stinson in *How I Met Your Mother* and was also at the forefront of famous actors to come out, a trend that can hopefully make its way into the machismo-filled world of sports sooner than later.

All-Star: Jason Bateman – For *Arrested Development* alone, Bateman could be considered an All-Star, but with *Horrible Bosses* and being in a movie seemingly every two months, Bateman has established himself as a top-notch post-child-star actor.

Hall of Fame: Natalie Portman – Seemingly every guy's celebrity crush, she has the perfect amount of girl-next-door charisma and acting chops to be one of Hollywood's most popular actresses. She has two Oscar nominations and won for her role in *Black Swan*.

Willie Mays: Ron Howard – one of the best directors of all time and in the hearts of the current generation as the voiceover in *Arrested Development*.

---

probably hoped for more than they ended up getting from him.

[81] Do yourself a favor and check out the unibrow; Anthony Davis may have some competition.

[82] Munson also passed away prematurely in a plane crash.

[83] With over 70 WAR, Whitaker should be in the Hall of Fame, but he still isn't, sadly.

[84] Salmon is on par with all the other All-Star players but somehow never made an All-Star Game.

[85] Yes, he's not technically in the Hall of Fame, but check out his write-up (Utility, Reds – Page 277) for why that's just silly.

Back to baseball: the RoY process was a little difficult because the bust and injury-plagued tiers usually overlapped, as so many times injuries lead to players becoming busts. There were also players who were solid players or even All-Star caliber players who had careers dampened by injury as well. I also stopped with the year 2006 because the jury is still out on the newer Rookie-of-the-Year winners, as even established guys like Ryan Braun and Evan Longoria could fall victim to injury, or declining skills. They are locks for the All-Star tier, but will they make it into the Hall of Fame tier as well? So this is not a perfect list, but it is interesting to note the numbers in each different tier.

The only tier that really needs further explanation is the "Dontrelle Willis" tier. He received his own tier because he really could have been in any one of the tiers at different points of his career. His first few years, people regarded him as a true ace and seemingly a lock to win over 200 games. He was even thought to be a threat for 300 wins because of how young he was when he started winning in the majors. He then became a bit of a bust as he struggled through 2006 and 2007. He then suffered injuries that cost him several years, and most recently tried to rebuild himself into a solid role player for different teams. His Marlin teammate Hanley Ramírez makes this tier as well, although he could move into the All-Star tier with a few consistent, productive, healthy seasons in a row.

Dawson himself turned into a Hall of Fame player, who combined speed[86] and power throughout his career. He is also the first player to win a MVP award from a last place team, beating A-Rod and his 2003 Rangers to the punch. Dawson's MVP season came the year after he left Montreal and was unusual in that it was right after he joined a new team. It is often said that players perform best before a big contract, and in a sense this was true of Dawson as well. When Dawson signed with Chicago in 1987, it was a blank-contract signing. He told the Cubs to pay him what he was worth and proceeded to put up his incredible MVP season and got a fat contract as a result.

RF Vladimir Guerrero (1996-2003)[87]

"Vlad the Impaler" was one of my personal favorite players of all time[88] and was basically the only reason to see the Expos play for their final years in Montreal. He was an unbelievably exciting player who played the way he wanted, famously getting a hit off a pitch that bounced before it reached home plate. He never studied tape of opposing pitchers, instead choosing to play baseball video games to get his scouting reports. He had one of the most amazing arms in baseball, frequently making SportsCenter's Top 10 on throws from the outfield. He was coming into his prime just around the time my childhood baseball fandom was coming into its prime, and there's definitely something to be said for seeing players live and how it can change your opinion of them beyond the numbers. Whether this is for better or worse (likely better if you can use the numbers *and* what you see for yourself), it certainly helps explain some of the journalistic porn written about players of the past like Joe DiMaggio and Sandy Koufax.

Vlad was born in the Dominican Republic and grew up in abject poverty, drinking from puddles because of a lack of running water and working full-time starting in fifth grade (he'd been cutting class to work part-time for years before that). When he reached the majors, he was nicknamed "El Mudo" (The Mute) because of his relative silence with the media, a silence that came out of a fear of coming across stupid in his second language.

The whole explosion of sports media that has taken over the country is a topic that I wrote about regularly when writing for the *Crookston Daily Times*, a lovely newspaper in northwest Minnesota. As a sports reporter, I was torn about the future of the industry. As a young professional hoping to make sports writing a career, cutting down on the number of sports-reporter jobs obviously wasn't ideal. At the same time, the empathetic bone in my body felt for these athletes who have dozens of reporters shoving mics in their face day-after-day. The more uncomfortable and standoff-ish the player (àla Marshawn Lynch or Russell Westbrook), the more the media seem to swarm. The conclusion I came to was that the best path for the industry to take would be to rely on the technology available to lessen the stress for players. Get one or two beat reporters who can become close with the athletes and simply have all the other reporters live tweet questions into the interview. That way the athlete isn't overwhelmed and may actually give the reporter some interesting quotes if that trust can be built. The delay would be minimal for the other reporters and everyone would benefit. There's no reason to keep relying on the out-of-date practice of sending every reporter into the locker room after the game. That originated when there weren't means of disseminating information as efficiently as today. And sports reporters wouldn't have to worry that they were being cut out entirely like at *The Player's Tribune* (Derek Jeter's brainchild), a site where athletes write the stories themselves (and I'm less cynical than those who say none of the writing done there is actually by the athletes), and everyone comes away a

---

[86] This will simply be a footnote because the point will be discussed ad nauseam with our next player, but the turf at Olympic Stadium really cost Dawson some of his elite speed. He had 12 knee surgeries, and after stealing 208 bases through his first seven full seasons (he had one steal in 24 games in 1976), he had only 105 stolen bases the remaining 13 seasons of his career. Part of that decline is natural aging, and part of that had to do with a hellacious knee injury in high school, but a whole lot of it is the result of what the Olympic Stadium turf did to his knees. Bill Lee said of Dawson's knees, "I mean his knees looked like fucking Frankenstein's face." The fact that Dawson made it into the exclusive 400 home run/300 steals club (there are only three other members – Barry Bonds, Alex Rodriguez, and Willie Mays) is even more impressive with that in mind. Without the turf killing his knees he easily could have joined Bonds as the only member of the 400-400 club.

[87] Expos expert Jonah Keri has a great piece on Guerrero on *Grantland* for any Vlad fans. Probably should have put this footnote at the end, as y'all are bound to stop reading this write-up and head over there now.

[88] Vlad is one of only two players I have ever painted my chest for, as four friends and I in middle school spelled out V-L-A-D-Y on our chests and B-O-N-D-S on our backs when we went to see the Expos play the Giants for a class field trip to Montreal.

winner.[89]

Back to Guerrero, however: he started his career as a decent fielder and a solid base runner as well, stealing 77 bases from 2001-2002,[90] but thanks to the turf at the Olympic Stadium, Vlad's knees were ruined, which robbed him not only of a few end-of-career seasons, but also took away some of his speed and fielding tools.

Jonah Keri sums up the issues with the field well in his history of the club, *Up, Up & Away*:

"Ron McClain, the Expos head trainer for 25 seasons, repeatedly warned the team about the wall and the damage it could do to the players. Management estimated the cost of replacing it at around $250,000, a pittance given the team's revenue stream, especially when the health of its core assets was involved. Still, nothing happened. Instead, several Expos outfielders got hurt smashing into it, including Andre Dawson, who suffered a broken bone in his knee.

"More concerning for the players was the playing surface itself, a paper-thin layer of turf laid over another paper-thin layer of padding, perched on top of a thick layer of concrete. Here again, McClain warned his bosses what could happen. He was told the cost of replacing the turf would be around $1 million, a tougher financial burden to handle, but still a move that could save the team multiple times that, given the likelihood of games lost to injury. Again, no dice… If there were ever a baseball field custom-designed to destroy the health of its players – especially its outfielders – this was that field."

Unfortunately, that cavalier attitude toward the bigger picture is part of what made the whole franchise crumble. Maybe Vlad's knees are the perfect metaphor for the Expos franchise? Maybe I'm just a little drunker than my typical Thursday morning?[91]

Utility Rusty Staub (1969-1971; 1979)

"Le Grand Orange" was the club's first ambassador to the city and loved his role as such, going as far as taking French lessons to truly be able to engage the community. He was a strong hitter but a bit of an interesting fielder, making him a perfect fit for this utility spot if we think of the utility spot as a DH (which of course he couldn't actually be when playing for the Expos in the NL). Manager Gene Mauch once said: "[Staub] led the league in fantastic catches of routine fly balls."

Staub played two stints for the Expos, first from 1969-1971, and then he later made a cameo in the latter half of the 1979 season. Staub returned to the Expos in 1979, and, according to Serge Touchette, an Expos beat reporter from 1976 until the team moved to Washington, Staub received the loudest ovation he ever heard in his life. The noise was so loud that from the moment he got into the on-deck circle the PA man was drowned out.

This pick is very much an off-field selection, as he played only 518 gams with the club (although he was worth an impressive 18.5 wins during those 518 games), but you're not going to find many Expos fans arguing with this one.

Nationals fans, on the other hand, may be griping that Bryce Harper should lock down this spot as a tribute of days to come (as well as his 7+ WAR advantage on Staub), but for now, Le Grand Orange holds down the spot.

SP Steve Rogers (1973-1985)

Captain America's doppelnamer,[92] Rogers spent all 13 years of his career in Montreal and is the franchise leader in wins (the old-school version, not wins above replacement) by over 50. His career winning percentage was barely over .500, but that was more the result of the teams on which he played, as he boasted a 3.17 career ERA and led the league in ERA in 1982. He was often a tough-luck loser; throughout his career he had only 19 "cheap wins" compared to 72 "tough losses," per Baseball-Reference.

Rogers often acted like a man who had been bitten by the bad-luck snake one too many times, often failing to hide his disgust with fielders who made mistakes behind him. His ostentatious displays, along with his more-than-occasional dust-ups with his managers[93] led the Montreal media to nickname him "Sigh," first as a reference to his predilection for showing up teammates, but also as a reference to his dominance on the mound; spelled "Cy" when not being used as a pejorative.

In addition to being a bit prickly at times, many Expos fans remember Rogers for his ill-fated role in the Expos' only playoff appearance in their time in Montreal. In Game 5 of the 1981 NLCS, a series in which Rogers had already started and won Game 3, he entered the game in the ninth inning and surrendered a home run to Rick Monday, allowing the Dodgers to move on to the World Series and forever cementing the day as "Blue Monday" for Expos fans.

Ironically, Rogers' playoff pitching was excellent that season, going 3-1 (with the one loss being "Blue Monday") with an ERA of 0.98. He had even out-dueled Steve Carlton in both games of that year's NLDS. The event also wasn't enough to keep Keri from stating: "If we're dealing only with what pitchers did while playing with the Expos, Rogers was

---

[89] "Win-Win-Win. I win for having successfully mediated a conflict at work."
[90] Although he was not quite as good a base runner as the steals make it seem, as he was caught stealing 36 times in those two years.
[91] For the record, Keri (who should be deferred to on all subjects Expos-related) said, "In the end, the Expos needed a champion, someone with money and power who could run the team through the harsh 1990s, then reap the benefits in the next decade when an explosion in national and local TV deals and a vastly expanded revenue-sharing program made even the poorest teams prosperous and relatively secure. No one ever showed up. That, more than anything, is why baseball didn't work in Montreal."
[92] My friend Dan's made up word when I asked him if there was a German word for two people who share the same name.
[93] Rogers' relationship with Dick Williams (Expos manager from 1977-1981) could have supplied enough material for its own *Real Life: Montreal* spin off.

clearly the greatest pitcher the team ever had."

It will be interesting to see if Stephen Strasburg or Max Scherzer stick around Washington long enough to topple Rogers. They both have the talent to do pass him if they have the patience to stick around the seemingly-cursed franchise for a decade-plus.

CP Jeff Reardon (1981-1986), Chad Cordero (2003-2008), Mel Rojas (1990-1996; 1999), John Wetteland (1992-1994), Tim Burke (1985-1991), Mike Marshall (1970-1973)

It seems like every season there are about five teams who tinker with a closer-by-committee system, so why not give it a shot here? Yes, it's slightly cheating, but none of these guys inspire much confidence with their Expos/Nationals resumes, so a committee might be needed anyways.

As smart baseball minds have pointed out, though, to truly implement a successful closer-by-committee, the collection of pitchers need to complement each other well; each guy with his own specialty that covers for a different teammate's weaknesses. So, here's the breakdown:

Tim Burke: The most prolific closer in the team's history, Burke also had the starkest RHB/LHB splits, making him pretty much a righty specialist in this imaginary bullpen.

Chad Cordero: The Nationals have fewer left-handed closers than CBS has quality comedies, and Cordero actually had reverse RHB/LHB splits in his career, making the right-handed Cordero the lefty specialist in this pen.

Mike Marshall: If the team needs a multi-inning save, Marshall's the man. As his website (drmikemarshall.com) proclaims, he owns the single-season closer records for most appearances (106), most innings pitched (208), most consecutive appearances (13), and most games finished (84). It should be noted that on the site Marshall has a Q&A section that has an introduction that states:

"In 2000, I came online. Immediately, readers sent me questions. Since then, I receive questions every day. I cannot wait to wake up and get to my computer. I love the questions, the challenges to my theories and everything about my Question/Answer files. I lose myself and time with your questions. I want to thank everybody who has sent me a question. You make my day."

If that didn't make you smile, you may not have a heart.

Jeff Reardon: Known as "The Terminator," he's their go-to guy for kind of obscure games. Why do I say that? Well he's one of the more obscure record holders in MLB history, having held the MLB career saves record for less than a year between the 1992 and 1993 seasons.

Mel Rojas: He's the guy for a bases-loaded, nobody-out situation. Yes, that scenario is a bit specific, but he's the man for the job, having completed one of the rarest feats in baseball, the nine-pitch, three-strikeout inning (May, 1994).

John Wetteland: The dude when you need a guy to just spit heat. Or wear a really effing dirty baseball cap.

Starting IX Franchise Roster Stats

Lineup	Yrs	G	R	H	HR	RBI	SB	BB	SO	BA	OBP	SLG	OPS+	dWAR	WAR
Tim Raines	**13**	1452	**947**	1622	96	556	**635**	**793**	569	0.301	0.391	0.437	131	-4.8	48.9
José Vidro	10	1186	614	1280	115	550	21	397	463	0.301	0.363	0.459	111	-4.1	16.2
Andre Dawson	11	1443	828	1575	225	838	253	354	896	0.280	0.326	0.476	122	8.1	48.1
Vladimir Guerrero	8	1004	641	1215	234	702	123	381	484	**0.323**	0.390	**0.588**	148	-1.6	34.6
Gary Carter	12	1503	707	1427	220	823	34	582	691	0.269	0.342	0.454	121	**21.2**	**55.6**
Tim Wallach	**13**	**1767**	737	**1694**	204	905	50	514	1009	0.259	0.317	0.418	105	11.2	36.8
Rusty Staub	4	518	290	531	81	284	24	310	206	0.295	0.402	0.497	**149**	-1.5	18.5
Ryan Zimmerman	**13**	1552	883	1664	**251**	**937**	42	582	**1213**	0.280	0.344	0.476	117	2.9	36.5
Hubie Brooks	5	647	291	689	75	390	27	157	427	0.279	0.322	0.441	111	-2.2	8.7
Pitchers	Yrs	W	W%	ERA	G	CG	SHO	SV	IP	SO	ERA+	WHIP	SO/9	SO/BB	WAR
Steve Rogers	**13**	**158**	0.510	3.17	399	**129**	**37**	2	**2837.2**	**1621**	116	1.232	5.1	1.85	**45.3**
Best of each CP	8	43	0.623	**2.61**	**425**	0	0	**152**	600.1	419	142	1.173	7.4	2.32	12.0

#24 Milwaukee Brewers (1970-pres.); Seattle Pilots (1969)

(Photo from Wikimedia Commons)

Team Background

Playoff appearances: 4 **Pennants: 1** **World Series titles: 0**
Collective team WAR: 341.2
Strengths: Lots of power in the lineup.
Weaknesses: Not much contact; also, the starting pitcher isn't too hot.
What to expect from the next 12 pages: A haunted hotel; the art of framing; a brief father/son comparison; a reference to Tim Blake Nelson; a tangle with the PED monster; a BrewBreakdown; THE handlebar mustache; and a mediocre starting pitcher. This is a surprisingly fun Starting IX.

The Brewers began their career in Seattle in 1969 as the Pilots. The Pilots have the rather embarrassing claim to fame of being the most recent franchise, and the only since 1901, to have their inaugural season in one city, only to immediately move to another city the next season.[94] The move itself has gone down in baseball lore with a classic baseball history narrative surrounding it. When the Pilots were breaking camp from Spring Training in 1970, the team equipment trucks were told to head north from Tempe, where the team had been playing their preseason games, and await further word on whether to head to Seattle or Milwaukee. By the time the trucks got to Utah, the Pilots were officially ruled bankrupt, sealing the Pilots one-season fate in Seattle. They were subsequently sold to (future commissioner) Bud Selig and his group of investors in Milwaukee.

Selig and the Brewers have an intertwined history thanks to Selig cutting his teeth as the Brewers owner and president for over two decades before being chosen as baseball's commissioner in 1992. Even after Selig became commissioner, he transferred ownership to his daughter, and some believed he still had a hand in the club's decisions. As such, the Brewers team section makes sense as a place to discuss Selig's legacy as commissioner.

Given that Selig was baseball's commissioner for over two decades, it's unsurprising that his legacy is a vast and, at times, controversial one. There was his expansion from 26 teams to 30; his threat of contraction (Minnesota); interleague play as a special occasion, and then the subsequent year-round interleague play; giving World Series' home-field advantage to the league that wins the Midsummer Classic (now defunct); his ability to have labor peace in baseball since 1995; as well as

[94] The best part of that: the fact that it was a team named the Milwaukee Brewers (different franchise, though) who were the original team to be around for only one year in 1901 before becoming the St. Louis Browns. Revenge!

numerous less flashy, but significant nonetheless, moves that made waves across the sport as well as the world of sports as a whole.

However, when students in the year 3670 are studying the commissioners of baseball like we currently study the emperors of Rome (I assume this is what the year 3670 will be like…), Selig's legacy will be defined most by two things: PEDs and parity.

PEDs are a can of worms the size of Texas that were discussed briefly in the introduction and will be discussed throughout the book. Just about everything surrounding their effect on the game of baseball is shrouded in controversy and uncertainty. The fact is that although Selig *may* have turned a bit of a blind eye on steroids during the `90s when baseball was benefiting from the McGwires, Sosas, and Bondses of baseball, no league has a stricter policy on PEDs than baseball in today's world. Major League Baseball was the first league to crack down on steroids, and there's a decent chance the NFL, NBA, and even NHL may someday look back on the current eras of their leagues as foolheartedly lax on the PED use going on in those leagues right now (again, that's only speculation and uncertainty, though). Baseball has gotten itself just about as clean as possible right now, and although it was a bit sketchy there for a bit, the league is where it needs to be today.

The other narrative most commonly tied to Selig has been his devotion to an increase in league-wide parity. This has been a far less controversial stance, as, unless you are a Yankees or Cardinals fan whose singular interest in the sport is when his/her team is winning, what Selig has done to level the MLB playing field has been excellent. Selig added the wild card in 1994 (although it wasn't used until 1995 because of the work stoppage that canceled the 1994 postseason) and recently added a second wild card, bringing the total number of participants in the league's playoffs to 10. (Although many still think of there being eight *true* playoff teams, as the loser of the one-game wild card playoff doesn't get more than one game in the postseason.)

The transformation to the sport has been incredible, with every single MLB franchise making a playoff appearance this century. Over half the league's teams (19) have won a pennant since 2000, and from 2001-2010, only the Red Sox won multiple championships. It wasn't just the addition of the wild cards that brought parity to the league. Selig's emphasis on revenue sharing was another cornerstone of his tenure, and the smaller market teams have been able to succeed at a far greater pace thanks to Selig. MLB teams' records are less consistent year-to-year now than they ever have been before, and that is thanks in large part to Selig and the way he helped give the little guys a chance.

* * *

The Brewers, one of those "little guys," have never reached 100 wins in a season, but they have had stretches of punctuated success like from 1981-1982, when they reached the NLCS one season and won the pennant the next year. They have also been a relevant team in (relatively) recent years, making the playoffs in 2008 and reaching the NLCS in 2011.

The Brewers began their time in Major League Baseball in the American League, in the AL West due to their location in Seattle. However, once they moved to Milwaukee, it took only two seasons for the league to correct and move the Brewers to the East Division, which required less travel and placed them in a division with Cleveland and Detroit (although not with Kansas City, Minnesota and Chicago). Then, in 1998, with the addition of the Arizona Diamondbacks and Tampa Bay Devil Rays, Major League Baseball reached 30 teams, and interleague play was introduced. The American and National League had previously met only in exhibitions, spring training, the All-Star Game, and the World Series. The new meetings were limited and specialized, and they started with each division playing its locational mirror in the other league (e.g. the Yankees and Mets played because the AL and NL East played each other). Since baseball had to have an even number in each league, the Brewers were moved to the NL Central, giving the division six teams (compared to four teams in the AL West) and 16 teams in the NL (compared to 14 teams in the AL). Of course, in recent memory, MLB decided to make interleague play a season-long event, and move one team from the NL to the AL to even out the leagues (and divisions). Instead of moving the Brewers back to the AL – given that they had previously played in the AL and currently resided in the six-team NL Central – MLB instead moved the Astros. The reasoning was that the Texas Rangers and Houston Astros would make for natural rivals, and the additional travel cost of adding another Texas team to the division was less than adding the far-more-removed Milwaukee Brewers – probably a good decision.

Random cool things about ~~the franchise~~ a hotel...

The Brewers have one of the best secret home field advantages in baseball – the local Pfister Hotel, where opposing players are sometimes forced to stay. The hotel was featured in *ESPN the Mag*, with players' opinions on the hotel ranging from mild ("I was so flustered. I honestly thought there might be someone in my room," Bryce Harper said) to distracting ("I have to sleep with the blinds open and the lights on," Justin Upton said) to strangely xenophobic ("It almost feels like you're in Prague or something," C.J. Wilson said) to curiously specific about which ghosts he doesn't like ("I don't like the ghosts *there* [emphasis added]," Pablo Sandoval said) to terrified ("It's freaky as shit. The less time I'm there, the better," Giancarlo Stanton said) and finally just downright hateful ("Oh f--- that place," Michael Young said). The players told stories of wonky electronics, clothes being moved, loud noises, etc. basically the stuff that one might scoff at when reading about but become terrifying when actually inhabiting the room by oneself in the middle of the night. Brewers opponents have suffered many sleepless nights before heading to Miller Park thanks to the Pfister Hotel.

Starting IX

C Jonathan Lucroy (2010-2016)

When this position was originally picked, it was B.J. Surhoff who had the spot, but Lucroy flew past Surhoff, surpassing Surhoff's Brewer WAR total before being traded out of Milwaukee. That WAR total for Lucroy isn't even including a secret weapon of Lucroy's that isn't yet taken into account in Baseball-Reference WAR: Lucroy's pitch framing.

Although the idea that pitch framing – the art of the catcher receiving the ball in a way that is most convincing to the umpire to call it a strike – can be quantified statistically is new, the idea as a whole is as old as baseball itself. However, as Ben Lindbergh pointed out in his *Grantland* article "The Art of Pitch Framing," when a skill does not have any numbers attached to it, it's a lot easier to slip under the radar.

The art of pitch framing is one based on limited body movement, the ability to let the ball catch the glove, and allowing the umpire a clear view of the pitch as long as possible. For catchers like Lucroy, it's a science. As part of a profile of Lucroy for *ESPN the Mag's* 2015 MLB preview, Robert Sanchez noted how Lucroy honed his art by catching 1,000 balls a week from a pitching machine that fired even more intense pitches (100+ mph fastballs, 94 mph sliders, etc.) than he would typically face, practicing his receiving skills the whole time. His pitch framing is undoubtedly a talent but it is one that came with a lot of work. From that same article, Lucroy said of his framing: "I've had several umpires tell me, 'You make it look so good'... And you know, I'm not trying to trick an umpire. I'm not a magician. What I do is not smoke and mirrors. My job is to make the pitcher look as good as possible." And Lucroy does that job well.

According to StatCorner, here are Lucroy's ranks, across all of baseball, in pitch framing since his rookie season: 3rd (2010), 1st (2011), 5th (2012), 1st (2013), 3rd (2014), 15th (2015), and 16th (2016). Before a recent "slide" (to still within the top 20), Lucroy was a top five framer each and every year for half a decade.[95] For those seven years combined, Lucroy was worth 15.3 wins according to the best calculations we have out there now, none of which are accounted for in his 18.1 Brewers WAR. Basically, he has been worth nearly the exact same amount with his framing skills as the rest of his game combined. That may seem crazy, and the stat is indeed in its nascent stages so there is some fine-tuning to be expected in the next few years, but the point remains the same: Lucroy's value in Milwaukee, via his ability to frame pitches, was through the roof.

1B Cecil Cooper (1977-1987)

If I were cleverer,[96] I could have had fun with this position. It very nearly was a breakdown between a Cecil (Cooper) and a son of a Cecil (Prince Fielder), but it wasn't close enough because of the fielding of the Fielder...[97] Just to clarify, despite the fact that Prince Fielder hit more home runs than Cecil Cooper in nearly 500 fewer at bats, the -13.9 dWAR he cost the team from the field was just too much to start him over Cooper, especially when Cooper was with the Brewers an extra four seasons, helping his loyalty as well as his ability to accumulate counting statistics.

Cooper, a black man from Texas, played in an era in which black players had established themselves in the league and represented about a fifth of the league. Although Jackie Robinson had broken the color barrier decades before, as will be discussed later in the book, the true desegregation of baseball wouldn't really occur until about 20 years after that. Because of Robinson and Larry Doby (who broke the color barrier in the American League) and others, baseball in black neighborhoods was immensely popular in the middle of the 20th century, and kids were growing up with dreams of playing Major League Baseball. Unfortunately, that has been a trend on the decline in recent years. Howard Bryant of ESPN wrote an interesting piece on the diminishing number of black players in MLB in a piece called "Going, Going, Gone" in the February 17, 2014 issue of *ESPN the Mag*. In this piece, Bryant notes that despite baseball's rich history of being at the forefront for civil rights for black men – there were black owners of Negro League teams in a time when many black citizens couldn't own nearly anything – today's baseball is noticeably lacking black players. In 2014, black players made up less than 10 percent of big leaguers (around eight percent), way down from the 20 percent figure in the 1970s given above. Bryant notes several reasons for this, including MLB's increased population from foreign countries (from Japan and the Dominican Republic, especially) and two-sport athletes leaning away from baseball these days. However, he also notes a few more disturbing trends, such as the incredible lack of college scholarships given to D1 black athletes, and, as Jimmy Rollins hypothesized, the lack of fathers in many young black men's lives, eliminating a vast majority from a historically father-son game. Likely all these factors are playing a role in the decrease of black athletes in baseball and are things that need to be looked into further. To the league's credit, they started the RBI program in 1989 to revive baseball in inner cities and, more recently, appointed Dave Dombrowski (the President of Baseball Operations for the Red Sox as of 2016[98]) to lead a committee looking into the matter

---

[95] Lucroy fell off a cliff in terms of framing in 2017, and it will be interesting to see if that is part of a downward trend, or if it was a one-year fluke.

[96] I still think "more clever" sounds better than "cleverer," but Microsoft Word keeps correcting it, so I'll let it stay; I, for one, welcome our new Mac overlords.

[97] Instead, I kinda felt like Michael Scott, racking his brain for "something about pudding."

[98] And one of the most fascinating and successful general managers of our era. Check out Rany Jazayerli's profile on *Grantland* called, "Trust in Dave Dombrowski," or "The Tigers Wouldn't Trade Dave Dombrowski" from Dustin Nosler over at *The Hardball Times*.

further. However, these measures haven't been able to produce results yet, and given the phenomenal symbiotic relationship between baseball and black history in America, it would be a travesty if the numbers continue to trend downwards.

As far as Cooper, he was a man described by Dan Okrent in *Nine Innings* as "professorial" who possessed an "unrelenting analytical approach" to hitting.[99] After trying out "as many batting stances as times at bat" early in his career, Cooper finally found a stance that worked and later drew comparisons to Rod Carew for his ability to put the ball in play effectively.

2B Rickie Weeks (2003; 2005-2014)

Pop quiz: What do you get when you combine a position that is historically among the shallowest in terms of talent, and a franchise that has only made the playoffs four times in 49 seasons?

Answer: Rickie Weeks, of course!

3B Don Money (1973-1983)

Blessed with a name straight out of *The Godfather*, Don Money served as the inspiration behind (but not the starting third baseman for) easily one of the most fun Starting IX's to compile – the Starting IX of baseball names that sound like movie character names, along with their character description, and the actor that would play them. These are based on the player's name, not their real-life personalities (for the most part):

C) King Kelly: The protagonist of any great silent film, he wouldn't even have to act, seeing as his life was basically a movie (a lot more on him at the Cubs utility spot).
Played by: Goosebumps Walkaway.

1B) Harry Heilmann: The bad guy in an Indiana Jones movie, or a season of *24*.
Played by: Mads Mikkelsen (better known as the guy with the cool eye in *Casino Royale*, or Caecilius in *Dr. Strange*).

2B) Cupid Childs: The short, pudgy, suspiciously-powerful man in a bad romantic comedy.
Played by: Jack Black.

3B) Deacon White: The religious man whose sermons are more bluster than anything else.
Played by: Isiah Whitlock Jr. (better known as the "Ah sheeeeeet" guy from *The Wire*).

SS) Rabbit Maranville: Another who wouldn't have to act, but if he did, he could easily fill a character with his name alone. He could be the person who leads our group of misfits through the forest with his outdoor skills and witty banter.
Played by: Tim Blake Nelson.

LF) Chet Lemon (only played one career game in left field, but center fielders can play anywhere in the outfield): He would fit into a 1980s buddy cop movie on the merits of his name, as well as his style and look.
Played by: Richard Pryor.

CF) Duke Snider: He would be a jazz saxophone player in a film noir flick. The type of guy who knew everything about the seedy underground of the city.
Played by: Denzel Washington once – sorry, if – he ever ages.

RF) Dixie Walker: We need a female lead in what is a sausage fest so far, so we'll give it to Dixie Walker and hope he isn't too offended.[100] She would be a southern belle, and the love interest for all.
Played by: Jennifer Lawrence (because what can't she do?).

DH) JD Drew: Toby from *The Office*.
Played by: Paul Lieberstein (Toby from *The Office*).
SP1) Pud Gavin: The pudgy kid next door in a *Stand By Me* coming-of-age movie.
Played by: Young Sean Astin.

SP2) Burleigh Grimes: Oil man àla Daniel Day Lewis in *There Will Be Blood*.

---

[99] Okrent also described Cooper's skin tone as coffee ice cream colored… Personally, I like to describe my own skin tone as "three-month old Vanilla Bean, covered with freezer burn."
[100] And if he was offended, he was a racist, so who cares? Also, he died in 1982. Also, this is a book that, like, five people will read.

Played by: Daniel Day Lewis in *There Will Be Blood.*

SP3) Silver King: Monarch in a mystic, far-off land in a *Never-Ending-Story*-type in-your-face parable.
Played by: David Bowie.

SP4/LHP1) Kenny Rogers: Based on name recognition alone, Rogers has to be a southern cowboy/card shark.
Played by: A John Wayne-type. Or, if we're going a little more outside the box, Brad Pitt. I could see it working.

SP5) Ned Garver:[101] Pud's annoying dad, the type who always goes out to get the mail in his boxers.
Played by: Stephen Tobolowsky.

Long relief) Dizzy Trout: An extra on the *Deliverance* set.
Played by: The older brother of Billy Redden (the Banjo Kid).

Middle relief) Smoky Joe Wood: The wise old man in the neighborhood, who spends time on his patio giving life lessons to the youngsters.
Played by: Morgan Freeman, of course.

CP) Joakim Soria: Although it's true that Soria hates the nickname "The Mexicutioner" – and it is indeed insensitive, behind the times, and certainly not a politically correct nickname – Hollywood has more discreet racism than any other institution in America, so it'll fit right in.
Played by: If we're going with the questionable selection of "The Mexicutioner," we might as well go fully questionable and assign Danny Trejo to play him.

I'd watch the hell out of that movie.

As far as actual baseball is concerned, Money was a solid, but never elite, player. He was a man described by Dan Okrent as playing baseball "with surpassing professionalism. He was a great sign-stealer, a still-powerful hitter, a useful, if slow-footed, man afield," in *Nine Innings*, an excellent account of a Brewers-Orioles game late in Money's career that was an excellent source for this Brewers chapter.

Money's cumulative numbers are lower than their actual value because of the era in which he played. He made four All-Star games while being a power hitter who never topped 90 runs or RBI in a season. Due to the era in which he played, his style of play, and his above average defense, he is one of the players whom WAR favors the most over raw numbers in the book.

Money's name came up on Opening Day 2013, when Bryce Harper broke his record as the youngest player to hit multiple home runs on the first day of the baseball season. Money had been two months shy of 21 when he accomplished the feat in 1969, and Harper beat that by over a year on Opening Day 2013. Interestingly enough, Money hit those home runs off of another man in this book, Fergie Jenkins. Finally: Money also holds the record for fewest errors in a season by a third baseman, having committed just five in 1974 for Milwaukee.

SS Robin Yount (1974-1993)

Yount holds just about every cumulative record for the Brewers, and among the captains assigned to each team, he and Tony Gwynn were the easiest to choose. He became the first homegrown Brewer to make the Hall of Fame in 1999, when he made it on the first ballot. Yount was said to be one of the most well-balanced players in the sport's history, and the numbers back it up. Of all the outstanding players in the history of baseball, only Willie Mays, George Brett, and Yount have over 3,000 hits, 250 home runs, 200 steals, and 100 triples. He also was the seventh member of the 250/250 HR/SB club.

Yount also played two of the most important positions according to the old baseball adage that the best players should be put up the middle (catcher, second base/shortstop, and center field). He embodies this mantra more than any other player in history, as he is the only player to win an MVP at shortstop as well as center field in league history. In 1980, Yount also won the Silver Slugger for American League shortstops in the award's inaugural year, and he went on to win two more for his career.

Yount made his Major League debut at the age of 18, and initially his dedication to the sport at which he excelled was questioned. No less an authority than Bill James says in his *Baseball Abstract* that he questioned Yount's dedication to the game when it was reported that he might want to retire from baseball to pursue golf. As James notes,[102] however, Yount recovered in style, going on to have one of the most consistent careers, playing less than 120 games in a season only in his

---

[101] I had this guy in here before Ben and Sam's infamous phone call with Garver on the *Effectively Wild* podcast for those who listen to *EW*. I did a double-take when doing a first edit.

[102] Right before going off on a bit of a tangent about Watergate… And yes, I realize people in glass houses shouldn't throw stones, especially when that person literally just dedicated a page and a half to a fake movie with names from across baseball's history.

rookie year and the lockout season of 1981. Because of his early debut, only Cobb and Aaron reached 3,000 hits at a younger age, and Yount retired at the relatively young age of 38. If he had really stretched out the end of his career, he could have certainly signed with other teams and played out the string collecting more and more hits, probably ending up among the top five in hits all-time. Instead, he chose to spend his whole career with Milwaukee, one of the few legends to be able to stick with one team through and through.

Maybe in part because of his lack of college education, Yount was not always thought of as the brightest crayon in the box. He had a high Baseball IQ, but he was so focused on the sport at such a young age that it seemed to be all he knew. Kind of like Congressman Murray, for whom Ben Wyatt runs a congressional campaign in *Parks and Recreation*, Yount "had a great capacity to sit on a four-hour plane ride, staring blankly into space, never examining so much as an in-flight magazine." He turned it on when he had to, and when he didn't he just sat there; there were no surprises, it was perfect…

LF Ryan Braun (2007-pres.)

There is a player who will come up in about 25 pages who is the only player left off of his team's Starting IX because of a steroid-related incident. He's the only player in the book who received that "punishment," because, as has been noted time and time again, I just don't feel we know enough about PEDs and their effect on a player to dole out the right punishment in a statistical sense. That being said, Braun came real close to being the only other player left off. Similar to the player to come, it wasn't the use of steroids that turned me off, but the situation surrounding. In Braun's case, the biggest knock on him is that once he was caught, during the 2011 playoffs, he tried to squirm his way out of it, blaming the urine sample collector who took his case and going down swinging in nearly every sense of the word. Of course, less than two years later, MLB showed they were not going to let Braun, and the rest of the arbitration cases they had to face from the Biogenesis Report, walk all over them. Braun took his medicine, accepting a larger-than-normal 65-game ban for his first-time offense, which canceled his 2013 campaign after just 61 games played.

When Braun went down, he really went down, and the media let him have it. Whether it was Jerry Crasnick of ESPN saying, "His baseball legacy will never recover," or Jeff Passan of Yahoo, who absolutely firebombed Braun:

"[Braun] is the guy who takes performance-enhancing drugs, gets caught, lies about it, wins and still feels it necessary to smear a completely innocent man who did his job exactly how protocol said he should. He is someone willing to lie to teammates, to fans, to everyone, building this tower of propaganda that Monday toppled all over him. He is a cockroach. And on Monday, he went splat."

Braun was getting it from all angles. His teammates were none too pleased, he heard boos at every opposing stadium for many years, and he still does in some of his division rivals' stadiums. And it was deserved. Braun made hefty allegations about Dino Laurenzi Jr., the urine sample collector, implying that he had a motive to taint Braun's sample, and Braun never mentioned Laurenzi when he made his eventual public apology.

Here's where it gets tricky, though: to this point, Braun is clearly the villain. A man who cheated, got caught, lied, slandered, and eventually non-apologized. But that was 2013. Since then he has been nominated for a 2014 Roberto Clemente Award for his work in the community, and he supposedly called individual fans apologizing for his behavior. I have given, and will continue to give, many players a break throughout this book, because I believe we never know the full story. Even ex-ball players can never really know what their teammates are going through. Now I'm not going to turn all the way around and say that just because Braun was nominated for a Roberto Clemente Award I guarantee he's a great guy. I think it helps to fill out our picture of him, but it's not the be-all and end-all. Just like his 2011-2013 debacle isn't his be-all and end-all.

Braun is a player who already ranks third all-time in WAR in Brewers franchise history, and he is back to hitting the ball all around the park, presumably without any help from any foreign substances. Maybe that's all he needs to be.

CF Gorman Thomas (1973-1976; 1978-1983; 1986)

"Stormin' Gorman" was a go-big-or-go-home player of the late `70s and early `80s who stole the show in the aforementioned *Nine Innings* by Dan Okrent. The book is a phenomenal one and tells the story of a game played on June 10, 1982, while weaving a narrative that covers the players, and Brewers franchise as a whole, into the game story. It's a seminal work, and Gorman Thomas jumps off the pages as a character more befitting a work of fiction than a real-life. Here are some samples: "[Thomas] was rarely clean-shaven; his shirttails were forever hanging out; he drank his beer and smoked his Marlboros and walked and talked and behaved the tough guy." He was a popular guy who "knew the fans loved him. He knew the clubhouse, in some way, revolved around him." He led the league in home runs in two seasons and "loved talking about 'dialing 8' – long distance in every road hotel – when he came to the plate. He lived for the home run…"

After four unsuccessful seasons of trying to establish himself with the club from 1973-1976, when Thomas came up in 1978 he came up with one goal for each at bat – to leave the yard. From 1978-1982, he finished in the top five in the league in home runs every year. He said of his approach: "[Fans] come to see me strike out, hit a home run, or run into a fence." Given his approach at the plate, it is unsurprising that among the top 100 outfielders ranked by Bill James in his *Abstract*, Thomas owns the highest ratio of R+RBI per hit, as well as lowest batting average (by over 10 points). That low batting average, again, wasn't a mistake. "I might be able to hit .280 or .290, but not with 35 bumps. I'm here for the bumps," Gorman used to say.

Thomas wasn't Joe DiMaggio or Andruw Jones in center, but he was serviceable, and a bit tricky. Okrent noted that Thomas used a trick in the outfield where he would pretend a ball was going to drop in front of him, but make the shoestring catch at the last second, allowing him to double up the runner. Thomas also certainly gave it his all, with Okrent saying of his fielding style: "He used outfield walls as if they were blocking sleds." Possibly because of all those collisions with the fence, Luis Tiant said, "[Thomas] was so ugly he could be anything in the jungle he wanted to be, but not the hunter."

Thomas was a man's man in the Ron Swanson-iest way possible, one who drank beers with the fans tailgating in the parking lot, and one who would often "strut around" the grounds "half dressed" before the stadium was opened up to the public, "luxuriating in the life of a ballplayer." This type of lifestyle rubbed some folks the wrong way (as funny as it is to read about, imagine having this goon as a co-worker), and he occasionally butted heads with teammates and managers. The fans sure as hell loved him, though.

RF Corey Hart (2004-2012) vs. Jeromy Burnitz (1996-2001)

Time for a BrewBreakdown. It may be a bit of an ugly breakdown, but in the words of Tracy Jordan: "Freaky deakies need love too." Also, this seems like a decent way to boost sales in the elusive Midwest.

Contact

	BA	lgBA	Seasons ≥ .280	Career high/low	Seasons ≥ 120 SO	SO %	lgSO%	BABIP
Hart	.276	.266	3	.295/.260	2	20.4	17.7	.313
Burnitz	.258	.270	1	.281/.232	5	20.8	16.6	.281

Corey Hart managed a higher average in his time with the Brewers than Burnitz, which is made more impressive by the fact that the league as a whole was hitting a few points lower at the time. Burnitz also struck out marginally more often, despite Hart playing in an era in which strikeouts were more frequent. And while Hart's batting average on balls in play was much higher than Jeromy's, over such a large sample size it's fair to surmise that Hart was more successful at finding gaps – dropping balls behind infielders and in front of outfielders (like a seasoned slow-pitch softball pro) – rather than just getting lucky.

EDGE: Hart

Power

	HR	Seasons ≥ 30 HR	Career high HR	XBH	SLG%	lgSLG%	ISO	HR%	XBH %
Hart	154	2	31	398	.491	.422	.215	4.1	10.5
Burnitz	165	4	38	345	.508	.434	.250	5.0	10.6

The power battle between these two is really close. Burnitz had slightly elevated home run totals, but compared to league rates the two are nearly even. Hart was also nearly Burnitz's equal in terms of extra-base hits, as Hart had significantly higher doubles totals with Milwaukee. In terms of strictly *power*, however, Burnitz has a slight edge over Hart.

EDGE: Burnitz by a bit

Batting eye

	BB	Seasons ≥ 70 BB	OBP	lgOBP	OPS+	BB%	SO/BB
Hart	269	0	.334	.336	116	7.1	2.88
Burnitz	423	5	.362	.343	123	11.2	1.86

Corey Hart attacked the pitcher early in the count and often made him pay. As such, he was never a man with a high walk total. Partially due to his strong power numbers, Burnitz did have significant walk totals throughout his career, and his on-base percentage reflected his patience at the plate.

EDGE: Burnitz

Speed

	SB	Seasons ≥ 20 SB	Career high SB	Rbaser	SB%	XBT%	GDP%	Misc.
Hart	83	2	23	1	67	49	12	2x 20/20 HR/SB
Burnitz	42	1	20	-13	56	38	7	1x 20/20 HR/SB

Neither Brewer was much of a blazer on the basepaths, but Hart did have three seasons as a relevant base runner (two 20/20 HR/SB seasons; 57:20 SB:CS); whereas, Burnitz only had one year with 20 steals, and he got caught stealing 13 times that season alone. Hart was also more aggressive on the bases, regularly taking the extra base. Although Hart grounded into more double plays than Burnitz, this was due in large part to Burnitz being more of a flyball hitter.

EDGE: Hart

Defense

	Fld%	lgFld%	dWAR	RF/9	lgRF/9	Assists	GG	Misc.
Hart	.987	.985	-4.5	2.12	2.20	29	0	LL 1x GP (RF), RF/9 (RF), Fld% (RF)
Burnitz	.978	.981	-1.2	2.04	2.13	57	0	LL 1x GP (OF)

Similar to their contributions on the basepaths, neither Burnitz nor Hart were particularly strong fielders, relying much more on their bats to bring value to the Brewers. Hart began his career as a solid fielder, but he quickly deteriorated into a below-average right fielder. Burnitz followed a similar pattern, but he had already had a few years on his odometer before Milwaukee. Honestly, neither player was of much value, positive *or* negative, in the field, and this hypothetical Brewers outfield as a whole would be pretty weak on the defensive side of things, so why get picky now?

EDGE: Draw

Intangibles

Both players were extremely injury-susceptible for most of their careers, but they seemed to find a magical elixir during their times in Milwaukee that kept them on the field. No Ryan Braun jokes, guys. Hart did miss his final year in Milwaukee to injury, however.

EDGE: Burnitz

Team Success

	W	L	W-L%	Seasons ≥ 90 W	Division titles	Pennants	WS
Hart	473	472	.501	2	1	0	0
Burnitz	360	421	.461	0	0	0	0

While Corey Hart was a Brewer, the team enjoyed their second-most successful stretch. Burnitz's Brewers were far less successful, never finishing above third in their division (the AL as well as NL Central) and never topping .500.

EDGE: Hart

Dominance

Jeromy Burnitz never led the league in any significant statistical categories while in Milwaukee, but he did receive MVP votes in 1997 and 1998. The only time Hart led the league in any statistical categories was in a couple of fielding categories early in his career, but as noted earlier defense wasn't his strong suit for most of his time in Milwaukee. He did, however, receive (minimal) MVP votes in 2010 and was a two-time All-Star compared to just one All-Star season for Burnitz. Neither player would have ever been considered a dominant force, but in their primes, Hart stuck out from the pack a tiny bit more than Burnitz.

EDGE: Hart by the smallest of margins

Ability to have the same name as an `80s pop star

It's times like these that I wish I spoke German because they almost certainly have a single word that represents the small sentence I had to write to name this category (Duranduranameskrieg, perhaps). Corey Hart obviously had to withstand numerous references to his name throughout his career, and Burnitz almost certainly didn't have to endure numerous taunts about wearing sunglasses at night, which is a positive in my book.

EDGE: Burnitz

Verdict

This is a pretty close one – two similar players with similar production (separated by 0.1 WAR for their Milwaukee careers, as well as in their top season with the club) for their time in Milwaukee. In fact, if I wanted to make myself feel bad I would point out that this breakdown was probably an abuse of breakdown power, a comparison of two players who, while similarly skilled, just don't really matter enough for a full breakdown. I'd have to imagine even Brewer fans might not have a strong preference between these two.

But I'm not in the game of making myself look bad, and plus we already made it this far, right?

In the end, **Corey Hart** played with the club about a season's worth more of games (163 to be exact), so Hart takes a real close one. Well done, freaky deakies.

Utility Paul Molitor (1978-1992)

Molitor played the first 15 years of his career in Milwaukee and was one of the most versatile players in baseball. The strange thing about Molitor is that while he was indeed very versatile, he still played more games as a designated hitter than any other position for his career.[103] This was a man who played every position in the game sans catcher and was a solid fielder at all these positions. He netted only -0.4 dWAR in his time in Milwaukee, and this number would be positive if it were not for all the games he was slotted at the DH position (a position that draws a large dWAR penalty). As such, it's quite surprising that such a versatile defender was often resigned to the DH slot that is thought of (with good reason) as the "Elba" which slow-footed, poor defenders are sent to as a punishment for their lack of versatility. One has to imagine if he were to play in the modern era, his positional versatility would be used to far more value, especially on a club like the Tampa Bay Rays or Chicago Cubs.

As far as the bat was concerned, Molitor certainly hit as well as many other DHs. He lacked the power typical of the position but more than made up for it with his ability to reach base. Tenth all-time in career hits (3,319), his Brewer total alone (2,281) is higher than DH Supreme Edgar Martínez (2,247) had in his whole career. Like a fine wine, Molitor seemed to get better as time went on, hitting 20 points higher in the second eight seasons (.312) with the club than his first seven (.291). In 1987, he accomplished his most famous feat as a Brewer, hitting for the fifth-longest hit streak in baseball history (39 straight games). The game in which he lost the streak was memorable as well, as the Brewers won 1-0 in 10 innings over Cleveland. This is not what most people remember, however, as they recall that Molitor was on deck when pinch-hitter Rick Manning drove in the winning run, meaning that Molitor would not get one more chance to extend his streak to 40 games. Poor Manning has to be the only man to win a game for his team with a walk-off only to feel bad about it afterwards.

Molitor's magnum opus was his 1982 season. During the regular season, Molitor slashed .302/.366/.450, leading the league with 136 runs and topping the 200-hit mark. He finished 12th in the MVP, and the team won its first (and to date only) pennant, defeating the California Angels in the ALCS. Molitor had an OPS of 1.065 for the series and was the team's most valuable contributor with the bat. Molitor kept the ball rolling in the World Series, becoming the first player in World Series history to get five hits in a game when he did so in Game 1 of the 1982 Fall Classic. The Brewers eventually fell in seven games to the Cardinals, but it was the height of both the Brewers and Molitor's success.

Flash forward a decade, and the Brewers should have felt all right about letting Molitor go when he hit free agency after the 1992 season. He was 36 years old and DHing for them, but as fate would have it, Molitor would go on to net over 1,000 more hits while hitting .313 (15.8 WAR) and winning a title in his new home (Toronto). In fact, Molitor's first season in Toronto was his first season with 100 RBI, making him the oldest player to have his first 100 RBI season. However, that's nothing compared to his 1996 season. He became the first player to end the season at 40 years old and collect 200 hits since Sam Rice in 1930, hitting .341 and driving in over 100 runs for only the second time in his career. With hindsight being 20/20, it's easy to say the Brewers were being penny-pinchers with the low-ball offer that ended with Molitor leaving town, but given the frequency with which contracts given to players in their late 30s eventually become albatrosses, it's hard to truly blame the Brewers.

Ending on his legacy as a whole: given that Molitor made his debut at such a young age (21 years old) and was a total stud throughout his career, it's no surprise that his cumulative statistics are very impressive. When he retired, he was

---

[103] Looking at just his time in Milwaukee, he played 395 games as the DH, 400 games at second base, and 791 games at third base.

only the fifth player in history to have amassed 3,000 hits and 500 stolen bases. He is also still one of only three players in MLB history to collect 3,000 hits, 600 doubles, and 500 stolen bases. The only other two are Honus Wagner and Ty Cobb.

SP Teddy Higuera (1985-1991; 1993-1994)

The Brewers don't necessarily have a history of outstanding pitching. Even in their pennant-winning 1982 season, their ace went 17-13 with a 3.91 ERA and 97 ERA+. In fact, they had only one starter with an ERA+ over 100[104] for the season, and even the bullpen only had one pitcher with an ERA+ over 120. In the World Series itself, only one of the four Brewer pitchers to start a game had an ERA under 4.50 (Mike Caldwell) for the series, and he struck out a measly six batters through over 17 innings of work in the World Series.

With all that said, Higuera does get the spot thanks in large part to three seasons from 1986-1988. During this stretch, he posted the following numbers for his average season:
18-10, 3.06 ERA, 213 strikeouts, 141 ERA+, 1.153 WHIP, 2.90 SO/BB, 7.8 WAR

The number that really jumps out there is the WAR total. Higuera led the league in WAR in 1986 (which means he had a reasonable claim to MVP), finished seventh in 1987, and was sixth in 1988. In comparison, an in-his-prime Roger Clemens was worth 25.4 WAR over those same seasons – only 2.1 wins more than Teddy. Obviously, Clemens aged a bit better than Higuera, but for those three years, Higuera was nearly as valuable as anybody in baseball. However, as with pitchers throughout baseball history, injuries derailed a promising career.

Higuera managed a combined 20-16 record with a 3.63 ERA (107 ERA+) over the next two seasons, but the ship was showing signs of leaks. Higuera missed about 20 combined starts over the two seasons, and he had injuries to both his ankles and back that started to wear his body down on both fronts. Then Higuera suffered a torn rotator cuff in 1991, which demanded numerous surgeries and acted as the Muhammad Ali to the Sonny Liston of his pitching career. Higuera only made 20 more starts after 1991, posting a 7.11 ERA in those rough, post-surgery innings.

One final point needs to be made under the umbrella of the Brewers starting pitcher spot: one of the greatest (and most frustrating) things about sports writing in this day and age is how narratives and opinions change in the blink of an eye. When I selected Higuera for this spot it was before the 2013 season. I thought I could comment on how Yovani Gallardo was being pumped up to be a possible Player of the Future for this spot, but I wasn't sold on it. I had good points on how his WHIP was not that good, and how people fall in love with the K and fail to see other flaws in a pitcher's game. Now Gallardo is no longer in Milwaukee and is working to cement his role as an aggressively mediocre middle of the rotation guy.

And who knows, maybe a few years down the road Gallardo will have figured out some flaws in his mechanics, and he will become the pitcher many thought he could be, completely negating the prior paragraph, while at the same time completely justifying the point it is making. That's part of the beauty of the history of baseball. We have the ability to be a step removed so that we can look at the players and the numbers from a "calm" perspective instead of the reactionary perspective sports writers must have in the moment.

CP Rollie Fingers (1981-1982; 1984-1985)

Dan Plesac actually beats Fingers in most Brewers relief pitcher cumulative statistics including saves and WAR, but Fingers was definitely the more dominant closer, and he could almost make the case for the closer's role based on his 1981 season alone. In the strike-shortened 1981 season, Fingers went 6-3 with a league-leading 28 saves, a 1.04 ERA, a 333 ERA+, and a 0.872 WHIP. He also became the first relief pitcher to win MVP and Cy Young in the same season. This brings us to an interesting question, should a relief pitcher ever win an MVP?

No.

That's the right answer, but let's take a look at why. For one, Fingers was only on the field for a total of 78 innings the entire season. That's the equivalent of a position player who played less than nine full games all season, or a clutch pinch-hitter used only at the end of games. Now the argument that relief pitchers enter for the most important part of the game is true, but it is also a little skewed, especially in Fingers' case. First, Fingers blew six saves for the season, meaning that although his numbers look great on the surface, his save percentage of 82 percent was rather pedestrian in comparison to a normal closer. It is true that closers often end up near the league lead in win probability added,[105] but they are also never among the league leaders in WAR. True, they suffer from lack of playing time, but that's exactly the point, a player who's on the field for only 78 innings in a season cannot be the league's most valuable player. And although Fingers was able to throw more innings than any of the starters on the team in the 1973 World Series with the A's, over the course of a full season a closer will never achieve that feat.

Time to change the narrative to a more positive one for Fingers, though. First, and foremost – the mustache. It came around as a result of Fingers and several other teammates growing out mustaches to try to make Reggie Jackson shave his,

[104] Remember ERA+ is set on a scale where 100 is league average, with an ERA+ of 120 meaning the pitcher's ERA (adjusted for opponent and park) was 20 percent better than the league average and an ERA+ of 80 meaning that the pitcher was 20 percent worse than the league average.

[105] Fingers was second in the league in 1981.

but instead, A's owner Charlie Finley loved the publicity the 'staches were getting, and it became a thing, with every player who had a stache on "Mustache Day" getting $300 from Finley. As Fingers put it, "guys would have grown mustaches down on their ass to get three hundred dollars out of Charlie!" Fingers' mustache was the stuff of legends as well. One time Fingers entered a game with his classic waxed mustache drooping because, when he had fallen asleep in the bullpen, teammate Darold Knowles melted Fingers' wax job while the Brewers closer caught a few zzzs. Fingers' dedication to the stache was not to be doubted, either. When it came to the end of his playing days, Fingers could have played with Cincinnati in 1986, but owner Marge Schott said that he needed to shave to play for the Reds, and he refused, choosing retirement instead. A true man of morals.

In terms of his merits as a player, Fingers also became the second relief pitcher to enter the Hall of Fame in 1992, and I promise we won't go into the merits of a man who was on the field for the innings-equivalent of 189 games in his entire career being in the Hall of Fame.[106]

Fingers thought of his closing duties in simple terms: you either get the job done or you don't. Rollie Fingers called the phenomenon "Shithouse or Castle," and he was in the castle far more often than he was in the shithouse. It wasn't always a guarantee that Fingers would make it to the castle, however, or even have full use of his sight for that matter. While in the minor leagues, Fingers was struck with a line drive and as a result had to have his jaw wired shut. This may seem rough enough, but it took the doctors a while to realize he was allergic to the medicine, and so he spent a while throwing up constantly with his jaw wired shut. He lost 40 pounds in that time and was lucky to regain sight in both eyes.

Let's end Fingers' write-up, and the Brewers section as a whole, by noting that there are numerous great t-shirts available online with Fingers' likeness and famous moustache that can (and should be) purchased for a reasonable price. (The one pictured below was found on a now-defunct website, though.)

If you don't want that shirt, you might be the police.

[106] Yes, I did just passive-aggressively go into the merits of whether a man who was on the field for the innings equivalent of 189 games in his entire career should be in the Hall of Fame. For the record, I actually do believe Fingers should be in the Hall because although he may never have been the league's true Most Valuable Player, he was an important part of it's history, and that's what the Hall of Fame really should be seen as.

Starting IX Franchise Roster Stats

Lineup	Yrs	G	R	H	HR	RBI	SB	BB	SO	BA	OBP	SLG	OPS+	dWAR	WAR
Paul Molitor	15	1856	1275	2281	160	790	**412**	755	882	0.303	0.367	0.444	125	-0.4	59.6
Rickie Weeks	11	1142	684	1009	148	430	126	492	1102	0.249	0.347	0.424	105	-9.9	12.3
Robin Yount	**20**	**2856**	**1632**	**3142**	251	**1406**	271	**966**	**1350**	0.285	0.342	0.430	115	5.8	**77.0**
Ryan Braun	11	1458	937	1699	**302**	989	193	511	1146	0.302	0.364	**0.540**	139	-7.3	45.6
Gorman Thomas	11	1102	524	815	208	605	38	501	1033	0.230	0.325	0.461	119	-2.4	18.4
Cecil Cooper	11	1490	821	1815	201	944	77	367	721	0.302	0.339	0.470	123	-8.4	30.5
Corey Hart	9	945	529	950	154	508	83	269	775	0.276	0.334	0.491	116	-4.5	15.7
Don Money	11	1196	596	1168	134	529	66	440	539	0.270	0.338	0.421	114	1.7	28.2
B.J. Surhoff	9	1102	472	1064	57	524	102	294	323	0.274	0.323	0.380	92	5.9	15.4
Pitchers	Yrs	W	W%	ERA	G	CG	SHO	SV	IP	SO	ERA+	WHIP	SO/9	SO/BB	WAR
Teddy Higuera	9	94	0.595	3.61	213	50	12	0	1380.0	1081	117	1.236	7.1	2.44	**30.6**
Rollie Fingers	4	13	0.433	2.54	177	0	0	97	259.0	196	150	1.081	6.8	3.02	7.9

#23 Kansas City Royals (1969-pres.)

(Photo from Wikimedia Blog)

Team Background

Playoff appearances: 9 **Pennants: 4** **World Series titles: 2**
Collective team WAR: 368.1
Strengths: Balance. There really isn't a position far weaker than all the others on this Royals Starting IX. Something tells me this team would be a pesky out if the Starting IX's were to have a tournament against each other.
Weaknesses: Although balance is great, outside of third base (and possibly their closer), there really aren't any truly dominant players.
What to expect from the next 13 pages: A lot of references to some of the best minds in baseball, and a Starting IX that was the most fun to research.

The Royals were the whipping boys of baseball in the post-1994-strike baseball scene for nearly two decades. From 1995-2012, they failed to record a single winning season, and they went 28 years without a playoff appearance. Their period of greatest success revolved mostly around the career of George Brett, as they made the playoffs seven times in a 10-year stretch from 1976-1985. In more than half of those playoff seasons, Brett was the team leader in WAR. After that, they quickly became a despondent franchise, one whose fans, though loyal, were brought to loyalty tests akin to a married George Clooney attending the Playboy Mansion.

Of course, those who remained loyal were rewarded in recent seasons with one of the most magical playoff runs in recent years. First, a wild card win for the ages in 2014, and then a surreal World Series victory the next season. But enough ink has been spilled about that run, and all of it coming recently. For this franchise, the highlights really come down to that 2014 playoff run, the 1985 and 2015 World Series wins, George Brett, and a really nice stadium – one of the nicest in baseball.

Because I love baseball, and because I am blessed to be privileged enough to do something as time-consuming and pricey as this, my friends and I have started a pilgrimage to all the baseball stadiums across the country. So far, we've been to 25 of the 30 current stadiums, and within a couple summers will have hopefully hit them all. The five missing are Coors Field, Marlins Park, Minute Maid Park, Tropicana Field, and Turner Field. Of the stadiums attended, Kauffman Stadium is one of my absolute favorites, so I figured I'd do a Starting IX of the best stadiums that I've been to. This is not a list based on anything other than how much I enjoyed the stadium so it will take into account the fans, the food, the beer, and the history of the ballpark all rolled into one complete (and very subjective) ranking.

First, for honorable mention, the stadium I am most looking forward to: Coors Field. This is my sneaky guess for number one when I make it there. Now onto the real deal. Remember, the positions line up with their number in a baseball box score (SP = 1, C = 2, 1B = 3, SS = 6, etc.):

RF) Citi Field (Mets) – This one might get a boost because it was the drunkest I've ever been at a baseball game, but I do remember having a great time. Plus, the fans were really into the game despite the Mets fielding an awful team at the time.

CF) Oakland-Alameda County Coliseum (A's) – Probably not on a lot of people's favorite stadium lists, but the fans were so nice, and there was something about that huge open field that really appealed to me.

LF) PETCO Park (San Diego) – Another weak team, but a game I thoroughly enjoyed thanks to a slight mistake in the ticket purchase. We bought the cheapest tickets possible (naturally) and ended up in center field behind a big sandpit where kids were playing the whole time. It was a slightly obstructed view, but we got to have our feet in the grass, and we moved into actual seats halfway through the game. I must say I liked the first seats even more, though, thanks to the cool perspective of watching from ground level in straight away center field.

SS) Dodger Stadium (Dodgers) – Similar to the Coliseum, Dodger Stadium might not be on a lot of favorite stadium lists, but I thoroughly enjoyed it. My friends disliked the outdated feel of it, but I loved the Sega Genesis-style scoreboard, and the retro feel the stadium (perhaps unintentionally) had.

3B) PNC Park (Pirates) – One of the highest-rated stadiums, generally, and with good reason. It was actually the first stadium on our first trip, and it set the bar quite high in terms of all other stadiums after. The Roberto Clemente Bridge as the backdrop might be the most beautiful backdrop of any stadium in baseball (only the next stadium can challenge in that regard).

2B) Oriole Park at Camden Yards (Orioles) – Universally praised with great reason. The area surrounding the stadium is as nice as any in baseball, and the old-school/new-school balance is better than anywhere else I have been, stadium or otherwise.

1B) Wrigley Field (Cubs) – One of the most recent to be attended, Wrigley lived up to the hype. I'm glad that I waited (not on purpose, mind you) until the Cubs got good, as I managed to see them during their magical 2016 summer in which the city had as much hope as ever. The crowd was ablaze the entire game, and it was quite the experience.

C) Kauffman Stadium (Royals) – The Water Spectacular in center field alone gets it into the top ten, but the stadium as a whole was gorgeous, and the big screen in center was one of the best and easiest to read. To top it all off, the experience came for a very reasonable price.

SP) Yankee Stadium (Yankees) – I'm a bit biased, having grown up a Yankee fan, but the new stadium is pretty incredible. Obviously the monuments in center are great, but I'm not sure there's another stadium out there (with the possible exception of Wrigley) that has the same awe-inspiring feel to it when you walk through the gates out to your seat.

Also, in line with the above stadium listing, it must be said that the Midwest has by far the most entertaining fans, just ridiculous hecklers that really provide an extra level of enjoyment to every game.

* * *

Changing tacks, this is an appropriate time to pay homage to *Rob Neyer's Big Book of Baseball Lineups* once again. This book was already discussed in the introduction, but in case the reader skipped the intro, or it's not fresh in the reader's mind, Neyer's book is the closest thing in the field of baseball writing to this endeavor. The book was published in 2003, and although Neyer addresses many of the same criteria for choosing lineups, the lineups differ significantly – for the most part. The one team lineup that doesn't differ significantly is this Kansas City squad. Unfortunately for Royals fans, this makes sense as the team fielded very little talent from 2003 up until very recently. Even some of the baseball teams with the longest histories have seen some roster turnover from when Neyer wrote until now, but the Royals just didn't manage to develop any great talent for a long stretch there.

Neyer's inclusion in Royals section also makes sense given that the Royals are the team he has supported through thick and thin. In fact, the Royals, despite their generation-long ineptitude, have quite a few impressive baseball minds among their fan base. In addition to Neyer, Bill James aka the "father of sabermetrics" grew up a Royals fan, although he is now employed by the Red Sox, so that may have changed. Since this was James' team of interest for a long time, though, each player's write-up will have a brief quote or statistical nugget from James.[107] They will be brief enough that you're not simply re-reading his thoughts, but long enough to honor his connection to the team. That's not it, though, as Rany Jazayerli, one of the founders of *Baseball Prospectus*, and a current contributor to *The Ringer* and *FiveThirtyEight*, also supports the Royal Blue.

The Royals inability to find/develop talent has been a long confounding topic for these great baseball minds, as if the irony of these brilliant baseball minds rooting for such a clueless organization was too strong to not come to be. One of the best exchanges on the team came between Jazayerli and Jonah Keri (who knows pain considering he is *still* a Montreal Expos fan) on *Grantland* in the spring of 2013, when Royals frustration was near its peak. In the piece, Rany points out that the Royals had nine of the top 100 prospects according to Baseball America in 2011,[108] and that only two had reached the majors, and those two were Eric Hosmer and Mike Moustakas, two players who were hardly considered success stories at

---

[107] I hate to be a slave to a page in Bill James' rhyme book, but the dude is a legend for a reason.

[108] The most any team has had since the ranking's inception in 1990.

this time of Rany and Keri's chat.

Jazayerli made mention of each and every one of the talents the Royals developed in the last decade (Alex Gordon, Billy Butler, Zack Greinke, Mike Sweeney, Mark Quinn, Bob Hamelin, Angel Berroa, Carlos Beltrán), and to a T, each and every one of them scuffled in their first few years. And these were the prospects *who made it to the big leagues*. Rany and Jonah threw around a couple of theories as to the failure of the Royals to develop talent, but by far the most interesting take away was the anti-Beane epidemic of a complete disregard for plate discipline on an organizational level for decades. Check out this nugget.

"Oh, Jonah. You really had to bring up the Royals and plate discipline, didn't you? In 1980, George Brett hit .390 and the Royals went to their first World Series. They finished a respectable sixth in the AL in walks that year. In the 32 seasons since, the Royals have been in the top half of the AL in walks ONCE. That was in 1989, when — not coincidentally — they won 92 games, their highest win total since 1980… Not only have the Royals been worse than average in walks drawn for 23 YEARS IN A ROW, but in the past 23 years not a single player — not one player — has drawn even 90 walks in a season. At this point, the people of Kansas City have no concept of what it means to have a lineup that grinds out at-bats — you might as well ask them if they want to go to the beach after the ballgame.

And although the organization now pays lip service to the concept that walks are important, they're showing no signs of turning things around. Last year they finished dead last in the AL in walks for the eighth time in 30 years, and dead last in the majors for the fifth time (even though NL teams don't have the benefit of the DH). As I'm writing this, the Royals are, guess what, dead last in the AL in walks. Since starting the season 17-10, the Royals have drawn just 28 walks in their last 14 games, which is probably why they've won just three of them.

Wednesday night, they somehow took three walks in the top of the third against the Angels — and wound up scoring seven runs in the inning. You'd think someone in the organization would take notice. But they never do. They never do."

You can taste the pain of a brilliant baseball mind who has watched his team do everything wrong for nearly the entirety of his fanhood, and there's nothing he can do about it. Personally, I always find myself rooting for the Royals. Their awesome jerseys, great stadium, and the lovable loser nature they carried for the majority of their existence make for an easy second team to pick up and root for.

Random cool things about the franchise:

- Lou Piniella had the first hit in franchise history.
- Although they have adopted the crown as part of their logo, the team was not named for royalty, in that sense, originally. Instead, they were named after the American Royal all-Midwestern event that takes place annually in K.C. It is a part-rodeo, part-livestock, part-Barbecue contest extravaganza.
- The Royals Wikipedia page contains a section entitled, "Rock Bottom: 2004-2012" – yes, that is indeed nine years of rock bottom.
- Current manager Ned Yost is buddies with Dale Earnhardt Jr., and he served as part of Junior's pit crew during the 1994 strike-shortened season.
- Two final alcohol-related anecdotes from the Royals 2014 postseason run: 1) after the Royals swept the Angels in the ALDS, Eric Hosmer picked up a supposed $3,000 bar tab at a local bar where the Royals and their fans were celebrating, and 2) after the Royals won the 2014 ALCS, Paul Rudd (a big-time Royals fan) invited everyone (via an interview on the field) back to his mom's house for a kegger, can you imagine what that place would've been like if that offer came after their 2015 World Series victory?

Starting IX

C Salvador Pérez (2011-pres.)

Doesn't it feel like just yesterday that Pérez broke into the league? Well, 2017 was Pérez's seventh season behind the dish for the Royals, and he has already proven himself to be the top catcher in franchise history. Pérez broke into the league in 2011, as a rather middling prospect, no. 17 in the Royals system and not to be found on any of the top 100 lists around baseball. Despite hitting .331 in 39 games at the end of the 2011 season, Pérez was sent back to the minors to start 2012, but it wasn't too long before he got another chance at the big league level. Pérez made the most of it again, hitting .301 with 11 home runs in what amounted to about a half season in 2012. The next season (2013) was the true breakout for the fun-loving Venezuelan. Pérez hit .292 with 13 home runs and 79 RBI in a full season (138 games), made the All-Star Game, won a Gold Glove, and even drew MVP votes. Well he actually drew *an* MVP vote, and although this vote didn't come from Dave Fleming, Fleming did make an interesting case for Pérez as MVP on Bill James website, which will have to be good enough for what James thinks of Pérez. One of the key points Fleming makes is that Pérez was a beast in key situations for the Royals all season, and although Fleming doesn't go as far as to say Pérez saved his best for those "clutch" situations, I might just cross that bridge for him.

The position of catcher is one of the most unique in the sport; it's (arguably) the one position in baseball that takes a real definitive physical toll on the player. (I do think the mental toll of playing 162 games in 180-ish days gets glossed over very often.) Bending down and getting up over and over, getting slammed by foul tips, having to knock down 100 mph heat from the closer – catcher is a brutal position. As such, if there was one position that could be excused for taking a random at bat in the eighth inning of an 8-2 blowout loss for granted, it would be catcher. The numbers back this with Pérez as well. In his career, he has hit .297 with a .477 slugging percentage with runners in scoring position versus.258 with a .415 slugging percentage with the bases empty. In "late & close" plate appearances, Pérez has hit .308 with a .504 slugging percentage compared to his career totals of .272 and .442, respectively. When Fleming wrote about Pérez the next season, he went out of his way to point out that "Salvador Pérez continues to prove that 'clutchiness,' like Bigfoot, totally exists."

It would also make sense that Pérez might experience this phenomenon more than other catchers as, throughout his Royals career, he has been "ridden hard and put away wet," as Ben and Sam pointed out in an episode of *Effectively Wild*. What that means for the non-horse-riding crowd among us is that the Royals have used and abused Mr. Pérez. Pérez set an MLB record for innings caught behind the plate over the course of two seasons during the Royals magical 2014-15 run. He spent 2,298 innings squatting behind home during the regular season of those two years, and he chipped in another 400+ innings during those two pennant-winning playoff runs. That's a hell of a lot of wear-and-tear, and maybe it's not surprising that Pérez never saw his batting average go up in any of his first six MLB seasons. What *is* surprising is that Pérez has been able to increase his home run total in all seven of his MLB seasons, and, when added to his excellent defense, he has been one of the more valuable catchers in baseball since his debut. Only four catchers (Russell Martin, Jonathan Lucroy, Yadier Molina, and Buster Posey) have been more valuable (by WAR) since 2011, and Pérez played only 115 games in 2011-2012.

Pérez's WAR (19.3) might not even due him total justice, either. One aspect of catcher WAR that isn't included in the current Baseball-Reference formula is game-calling. Calling a game is something that has always been linked to catchers, but often more in the abstract than the material. That's because it's a hell of a hard aspect of the game to quantify. As Ben Lindbergh has said, game-calling is kind of like dark matter, as in we can't really figure out the effect, but if everything else is quantified, game calling is whatever value is left. When Harry Pavlidis came out with his original game-calling stats for ESPN in April of 2015, Pérez ranked among the best in the game, coming in a tie for sixth over the three-year stretch from 2012-2014. Pavlidis' analysis had Pérez game-calling worth about 1.5 wins over the three seasons. Not a total game-changer, but, considering how close the Royals came to missing the playoffs in 2014, the impact was undoubtedly felt.

1B John Mayberry (1972-1977)

Mayberry and Mike Sweeney had very similar numbers with the Royals and were the two top candidates for this position. Sweeney played more than twice as many years in Kansas City than Mayberry did, but he really had only one season more of productivity than Mayberry. Despite the extra years, Sweeney was worth only 2.0 more WAR than Mayberry because of the fact that Mayberry was playing in a much harder era for hitters. Another factor in the decision to go with Mayberry instead of Sweeney at first base was because the team had more success in Mayberry's time (two playoff appearances) than in Sweeney's time, when the club was consistently at the bottom of the American League. Mayberry enjoyed almost all of his success while in Kansas City and didn't do too much outside of his six years in the City of Fountains. In fact, in his six years with the Royals, he was worth six times more (per WAR) than the 10 years he spent with the Blue Jays, Astros, and Yankees combined.

We'll leave the description of his acrimonious departure from the team to Bill James: "Mayberry, suffering from an all-night party with his brothers, in from Detroit, played as bad a game as one could possibly play, dropping pop ups and striking out twice with men in scoring position. Herzog finally pulled him aside and asked what the hell was wrong, 'The man couldn't even talk,' wrote Herzog, 'and I knew what was wrong… God only know the kind of stuff they did. It must have been a hell of a party.' Mayberry single-handedly cost the Royals the playoffs [this came in Game 4 of the ALCS], and Herzog insisted that the Royals get rid of him. He was never the same player again."

The previous numbers certainly back up said fall from grace.

(And don't even come at me with your "Eric Hosmer should be in this spot" nonsense.)

2B Frank White (1973-1990)

White was a lifelong Royal, playing all 18 seasons of his career with the club and accumulating over 2,000 hits, good for second in Royals history. He is also second in games played (2,324), and he is near the top in numerous cumulative statistics thanks to those 18 years of service to the team. White was an excellent fielder who won the Royals nearly as many games with his defense as he did with his bat according to Baseball-Reference's dWAR. In fact, only three second basemen in baseball history have won more games with their glove than White (21.4 dWAR). He was a generally average postseason performer, but he did have an outstanding 1980 ALCS and managed to win the first Championship Series MVP ever handed out. Baseball-Reference has Bill Mazeroski as his most similar comparison, and that seems to be a pretty fair one, while perhaps slightly flattering to White. Bill James also compares the two, and he rates Bill Mazeroski two spots higher than White in his *Historical Abstract*. James doesn't think there was much separating the two, though. When discussing White, James wrote,

"Taking his career as a whole, [White] was interchangeable with Bill Mazeroski; easily distinguishable, but interchangeable. Both White and Mazeroski were right-handed hitters who hit around .260 with somewhere around 160 home runs. Neither player would take a walk, so both had terrible on-base percentages, below .300. Each player won eight Gold Gloves. Both players had long careers with one team. Both players played on many outstanding teams; each was a regular on one World Championship team. Mazeroski was the best ever at turning the double play; White was faster and probably covered more ground."

The most interesting part of White's legacy with the Royals, however, is that he was a product of the now defunct Royals Academy. The Royals Academy was a great idea that will probably come back somewhere down the line, and it was groundbreaking (at least in terms of baseball in the U.S.) in its time. The Royals Academy was a multifaceted "industry" that, while it stayed open, allowed the Royals to gather young players of elite athleticism who hadn't necessarily played baseball before and turn them into ballplayers. It also allowed them to work with the players they currently had, as the team created a 121-acre, five-diamond complex to be used for training and instruction in Sarasota, Florida. The fields were built to be exact replicas of the Royals home stadium, and the complex had dorms for the players. More than anything else, the Royals Academy pushed the boundaries of what was "common knowledge" in baseball, which is always a great thing.

Among its notable achievements, the Academy was among the first in baseball to actually test player's eyesight. George Brett, for example, had a slight case of double vision right after he blinked, but he worked with a noted eye doctor to fix the problem, which helped him hit better at night. The Academy was even studied by NASA because of their use of resistance training. The Academy's motto was "experimentation without expectation," and it almost sounds like the way one might hear Daryl Morey describe his current G League team, the Rio Grande Valley Vipers.[109] The team tried all kinds of different training techniques to see what worked. One time they brought in a pair of trampolines and split the team into two groups: players who had tried to do back flips on a trampoline before, and those that hadn't. For a few days, the group that had already tried back flips were allowed to jump around on their own and practice. Those that had not previously attempted one had to sit and watch a professional gymnast, thus learning the gymnast's technique. After the two days, each group was tested, and the group that had observed the professional gymnast had far more success completing their back flips. The point of the exercise was to preach visualization as well as quality of practice. Many of the players who graduated from the Academy – including those that didn't even go on to professional baseball careers – cite incredible life lessons from their time in the Academy. For those interested in learning more about the Royals Academy, check out Richard Peurzer's excellent piece in *The National Pastime*, "The Kansas City Royals' Baseball Academy."

Not only was White part of the Royals Academy, he hailed from Kansas City and was even part of the construction crew that built Kauffman Stadium way back in the early `70s. His return to the franchise was just another great part of the Royals 2014 playoff run. White had written off the franchise in 2011 when he was passed over for the manager position, a position he felt he had the right to after decades of service to the franchise. After retiring from playing, White stayed with the organization wearing many different hats (minor league manager, broadcast member, front office member), but hadn't made any contact with the team since being passed over for manager, not even attending games again until the 2014 playoffs. Although the two sides didn't officially bury the hatchet, it was great to see one of the franchise's most important players in the stands, supporting the latest iteration of the club. Although White is no longer affiliated with the Royals, he still shares a strong connection with the city, recently announcing a plan to run for office in Jackson County.

3B George Brett (1973-1993)

Easily the most famous Royal, Brett holds pretty much every Royals record and was an integral part of the team's greatest period of success. In fact, in terms of WAR (88.4), Brett is very nearly worth twice as much as any other Royal in team history and is worth more than the no. 2 and no. 3 Royals in history put together. Brett is a great enough player that he transcends being looked at in a Royals sense and can be put into better perspective when looked at in a MLB sense. He is one of only four players in MLB history to have 3,000 hits, 300 home runs, and a .300 batting average (Hank Aaron, Willie Mays, and Stan Musial being the other three). With the exception of the strike-shortened 1981 season and his 13-game cup of tea in 1973, he never played less than 100 games in a season. In 1976, he had six straight three-hit games, the first time that had been accomplished in MLB history, and he finished the season with a .333 average and his first batting title.

Brett's most famous season, however, was his 1980 season, which included his famous run at .400. He finished the year with a .390 batting average and was hitting .400 as late as September 19 before slipping just a bit, coming up just shy of the magical .400 figure. During the season, he had 118 RBI in 117 games, making him the first player to average more than one RBI per game since 1950. During the same season, he also came one double away from 300 total bases despite missing 45 games to injury. His OPS+ of 203 meant he was 103 percent more productive than the typical hitter – he was basically George George Brett Brett. Interestingly, despite being such a great hitter, it was Brett who supposedly coined the term

---

[109] Or it sounds a bit like Manchurian Global, if you're a bit more cynical.

"Mendoza Line" when he started the 1980 season a bit slow, saying that he always checks the box scores to see who is below the dreaded .200 batting average cut off. Of course, poor Mario Mendoza, whose name now lives in infamy, was hitting over .300 as late as June 27 of the 1980 season.

Brett was also one of the best big-game players in baseball history, for what that's worth.[110] His career .337/.397/.627 slash line in 43 playoff games is remarkable, as are his 104 total bases in those games. If his playoff numbers were translated into a full, 162-game season, they would total 113 runs, 38 home runs, and 87 RBI with 392 total bases and the aforementioned slashes. In his nine career playoff series, he had more series with an OPS over 1.000 than below (five to four).

He was a first ballot Hall of Famer who received 98.2 percent of the vote, an incredibly high percentage that is good for sixth all-time. His 88.4 career WAR is good for fifth all-time for third basemen, which, if possible, may actually underrate him. He is the only third baseman in baseball history with 5,000 total bases in his career, and he is the only third baseman to ever complete a 20/20/20 season with doubles, triples, and home runs. There have been only seven players to join that club.[111] According to Bill James, Brett had the "most balanced offensive skills" of any player in the 3,000-hit club. He got this by looking at every player's hits, secondary bases, and R+RBI, and then seeing who had the lowest variance between those three numbers. Bill James is the best. Brett managed to grab the no. 2 all-time third baseman rank in James' book, and only Adrián Beltré has made a possible case to pass him since.

Baseball fans in passing – or fans without as much historical context to their knowledge – likely know Brett for his infamous blow up during the Pine Tar Game against the Yankees during the 1983 season. After Brett hit a two-run home run in the top of the ninth to put the Royals up 4-3, Yankee head coach Billy Martin requested that home plate umpire Tim McClelland look at Brett's bat for an illegal amount of pine tar. McClelland did so, and he ruled that Brett had more pine tar on his bat than the MLB rulebook permitted, thus ruling Brett out and the game over. At this point, Brett fired out of the dugout like a starved Rottweiler cut loose to attack the medium rare porterhouse that was rookie umpire Tim McClelland. The photo of Brett tearing out of the dugout was about 30 years too early for the meme era, but the blogosphere would have had a heyday with the photo/gif to almost Lance-Stephenson-blowing-into-Lebron's-ear levels had the Pine Tar Incident happened in 2017. McClelland's ruling was eventually protested and overturned, and the Royals ended up getting the win.

SS Freddie Patek (1971-1979)

Appropriately nicknamed "The Flea," Patek was one of the shortest players of all time.[112] Measuring at 5'5" and weighing less than 150 lb., Patek still managed to have a positive impact on the Royals for nearly a decade. A plus fielder (especially in 1972 when he led all of baseball in assists and Total Zone Runs and led all shortstops in double plays turned, Range Factor/Game, and dWAR), Patek also was an excellent base stealer, which made up for his light bat. A career .309 on-base percentage meant that Patek needed every one of his 336 steals as a Royal. In fact, there were three years with the Royals in which Patek had more steals than RBI, and his OPS+ never reached 100 in any season during his career. He did post two solid postseason series with the club (1976 and 1977), reaching base 15 times in the two series and driving in nine. Patek can also stake his claim as Bill James' first interviewee.

According to James, Freddie tried to hit for more power than he had. James' analysis of Patek may be the only example I could find of Bill James possibly analyzing a player with his heart instead of his normal cold, hard facts. James comments on how "[Patek] did, I am certain, hit more MF8s and MF7s than anybody in the history of baseball." Given that James is a Royals fan, this sounds exactly what a fan of the Royals in the `70s would exasperatedly say about Patek. It sounds like a Red Sox fan bemoaning J.D. Drew's innumerable backward K's, even though it likely just seemed that way.

LF Alex Gordon (2007-pres.)

Joining Sal Pérez as the only two current Royals on the squad, Gordon has had an interesting career arc. Gordon came up as a super prospect in 2007, having been the second pick of the 2005 draft, and he had a respectable first year: 60 runs, 15 home runs, and 60 RBI with .247/.314/.411 slashes (just your friendly reminder that those slashes are batting average/on-base percentage/slugging percentage). His second year he made minor improvements, mostly in his batting eye, such that his on-base percentage went up almost 40 points, his walks went up 50 percent, and he struck out less, but his other numbers stayed similar. This was not enough for the player expected to turn the franchise around, and the pressure mounted. Gordon had his worst two years in 2009 and 2010, and he ended up playing nearly as many games in the minors as he did with the Royals during those two years. Amazingly, Gordon re-found his form in 2011, and he established himself as one of the AL Central's top all-around players for a good half a decade. Interestingly, Gordon also moved from third base to left field during those troublesome years, and his naturally strong third baseman's arm has been a huge boon in the outfield, where he is regularly among the league leaders in outfield assists. Gordon is currently one of the most underrated players in

---

[110] And I don't mean that in a snide way, but *literally* for however much stock you, the reader, puts into big-game performances.

[111] Incredibly, two of them (Curtis Granderson and Jimmy Rollins) did so in 2007. And maybe even more impressively, they both also had at least 20 steals, making them two of the four such players all-time to be part of the 20/20/20/20 club (along with Willie Mays and Frank Schulte).

[112] Although as Bill James said of Patek, "Freddie was very short, but not accurately described as small; he had shoulders and arms."

the game, not earning the respect he should for his solid contributions both in the field and at the plate. There were even a few weeks in 2014 when the sabermetric crowd began wondering if he might be a legitimate MVP candidate. His lack of recognition is due in part to the fact that he plays in Kansas City; in part to the fact that he was considered a bust for so long; and in part because his game is the type that flies under the radar. He is a doubles hitter, with a good eye, a good glove, and an outstanding arm who deserved more attention, especially during his prime.

Since there aren't too many significant contemporary quotes from Bill James on Alex Gordon, instead let's take a look at Bill James, the man, as profiled by Ben McGrath in *The New Yorker*.

"James is a man of many seeming contradictions. He is an English major who has made a name for himself as a math whiz. He has been called the Sultan of Stats, despite arguing that you should 'never use a number when you can avoid it.' He is a self-described 'scientist' who frequently reveals little concern for precision, a relentless counter who can't be bothered with individual sums. James is a rigorously organized thinker who is hopelessly disorganized when negotiating mundane daily responsibilities. He is, he says, a 'completely ethical person,' and yet he is obsessed with crime. ('Why the justice system doesn't work better than it does is to me a topic of great fascination.') He has long been revered by rationalists for promoting the virtues of objective analysis, and yet, after an extended hibernation from writing about contemporary baseball – during the nineties, he focused mainly on the history of the game – he remerged on the statistical scene with a new metric to define the overall contribution of each player, whose formula has a built-in 'subjective element,' allowing him to adjust the numbers more or less as he pleases. And, after so many years of presenting himself as the consummate outsider, he has now, in middle age, gone inside."

McGrath's profile was written just after James got a job working as an advisor for the Boston Red Sox in 2003. A year later the Red Sox broke their 86-year World Series drought and have won three titles in the relative short time since his hiring. James would be the first to tell you correlation does not equal causation, but let's just say it doesn't hurt to have one of the most unique minds in baseball on your payroll.

CF Amos Otis (1970-1983) vs. Willie Wilson (1976-1990)

Time for arguably the closest breakdown of the book:

Contact

	BA	lgBA	Seasons ≥ .300	Career high/low	Seasons ≥ 80 SO	SO %	lgSO%	BABIP	Misc.
Otis	.280	.261	2	.301/.247	3	12.0	13.7	.297	
Wilson	.289	.264	5	.332/.253	7	13.6	14.1	.332	LL 1x BA

Both players had similar numbers in their time with the Royals. Wilson enjoyed a better stretch than Otis did at any point in his career when he topped .300 every year from 1979-1982. He finished that stretch with a batting title[113] and a BA nearly 60 points above league average. On the other hand, Otis was a superior contact hitter in the sense that he made contact more often than Wilson, posting lower strikeout totals on a yearly basis while with the Royals. In the end, though, Otis' ability to avoid the "K" is not enough to give him the edge over Wilson's superior batting averages.

EDGE: Wilson

Power

	HR	Seasons ≥ 20 HR	Career high HR	XBH	SLG%	lgSLG%	ISO	HR%	XBH%	Misc.
Otis	193	2	26	623	.433	.387	.152	2.4	7.8	LL 2x 2B
Wilson	40	0	9	414	.382	.400	.092	0.6	5.7	LL 4x 3B

This one seems pretty evident from the numbers, and it doesn't need too much of a deeper look. Wilson couldn't even ride his propensity for triples and a high batting average to a league-average slugging percentage. Wilson's 0.6 home run percentage was less than half that of Warren Spahn's career home run rate. (Yes, *that* Warren Spahn, the Braves pitcher.)

Large EDGE: Otis

---

113 Unfortunately, Wilson pulled a José Reyes and sat out Game 162 with a four-point lead in the batting title. Robin Yount, the man chasing Wilson, went four-for-five (with two home runs), but fell one point behind Wilson for Wilson's 1982 batting title "victory." Boooooooo! (Yes, this is a hot take, but it's one I agree with, so I'm rocking it.)

Batting eye

	BB	Seasons ≥ 40 BB	OBP	lgOBP	OPS+	BB%	SO/BB
Otis	739	10	.347	.328	118	9.3	1.29
Wilson	360	0	.329	.329	95	4.9	2.75

Another category quite obvious from the numbers, Wilson topped out at 39 walks in 1984 (yes, that 40-walk cut off in the chart is perfectly selected to screw Wilson over, thanks for noticing) and did not see the advantage of working the count.[114] More telling is the fact that even in his best years it was never a trait of his. For example, the year he won his batting title, Wilson finished well below the top 10 in AL on-base percentage, a "feat" not accomplished by many. In fact, since Wilson did it in 1982, only two other AL players have won a batting title and not finished in the top 10 in on-base percentage. Otis, on the other hand, while not dominant in terms of plate discipline, did manage to consistently top 40 walks a season, peaking with 71 freebies in 1977.

EDGE: Otis

Speed

	SB	Seasons ≥ 30 SB	Career high SB	Rbaser	SB%	XBT%	GDP%	Misc.
Otis	340	5	52	43	79	54	10	LL 2x SB%, 1x SB, 1x 20/20
Wilson	612	11	83	111	84	59	6	LL 5x 3B, 2x SB%, 1x SB

Both Otis and Wilson were speedy players who led their league in steals once apiece. Wilson, however, was a much more consistent base stealer. The total steals for each player makes this obvious, as well as the fact that Wilson had more than twice as many 30-steal seasons as Otis. What really separates Wilson from other fast players is that he had his speed affect all parts of his game. The advanced stats show this with his extra base taken percentage markedly higher than Otis, as well as the fact that he grounded into fewer double plays. Players like Lou Brock, who will be discussed later, weren't able to have their speed translate to aspects of their game other than steals, which brings to question the true value of that type of speed guy. I think the best comparison is a power hitter who only hits home runs but no doubles or solid line drives. Sure, they can swing for the fences, but there's always the feeling that that power is a bit empty. Wilson's speed wasn't empty.

Wilson also had the edge in pure speed. As Bill James put it, "I suppose it is the Royals fan in me speaking, but I still believe that Wilson may have been the fastest man to ever play major league baseball." Considering James saw *plenty* of both players, it's fair to assume Wilson has the edge here.

EDGE: Wilson

Defense

	Fld%	lgFld%	dWAR	RF/9	lgRF/9	Assists	GG	Misc.
Otis	.991	.980	-4.2	2.78	2.83	116	3	LL 2x OF Fld%, 1x OF assists, OF TZR, OF RF/9
Wilson	.988	.981	8.9	2.94*	2.86	71	1	LL 3x OF TZR, 2x OF RF/9 1x OF assists, OF Fld%

* This number represents Wilson's RF/9 as a center fielder throughout his career because the Royal-specific data is not available at this time

Otis and Wilson have very similar fielding percentages so we don't have to worry too much about that, but the difference in the two players' range goes along with what we saw in the previous chart – Wilson is able to use his speed better than Otis. Although Otis had more outfield assists than Wilson, this can be a dangerous statistic. Sometimes outfielders can rely on their reputation of having a big arm to the point that runners don't test them taking extra bases. This is not the case for Wilson, however, as his held runner percentage is right in line with league averages for his career.

What surprises me here, at first, is that Wilson's dWAR is so much better than Otis'. His range is certainly better, but the edge Otis enjoys in assists would seem to begin cancel that out, especially since he also had a slightly better fielding

[114] Maybe that makes him more of a "true Royal"...

percentage. However, under closer inspection this difference does make sense. Even if Wilson only got to only six percent more of the batted balls to reach the outfield than Otis (Wilson's range divide by Otis' range), that means in an average season (300 chances), Wilson got to 18 more batted balls. Now granted these might not all be fly balls that guaranteed an out for the Royals, but it could also have been a ball in the gap that Wilson got to, saving an extra base that Otis couldn't have. Therefore, those 18 opportunities multiplied by 14 seasons makes about 250 total, a lot more of a difference than 45 assists.

EDGE: Wilson

Intangibles

As mentioned in previous breakdowns, intangibles are very open to interpretation. In terms of health, Wilson was quite durable for a speedy player, playing in over 100 games each and every season after he became an established big leaguer in 1978. However, this is not really a way to separate him from Otis, because the only time in Otis' prime that he didn't play 100 games in a season was the strike-shortened 1981 season, in which he played 99 games.

Another intangible that has been looked at is a player's success in the playoffs. Otis had solid playoff numbers, with a .295 batting average, eight steals, and three home runs in 22 playoff games. Those are a little skewed, however, based on his huge 1980 World Series in which he had 11 of his career 23 postseason hits, and all three of those home runs (sadly in a losing effort). Wilson was more consistent in the playoffs, never posting a series batting average as low as two of Otis', and posting a solid .273 batting average in the postseason overall.

Both players are in the Royals Hall of Fame, but both also have a few black marks on their name. For Otis, it is the fact that he used a corked bat for his entire AL career. He has said it helped him a lot, and he regrets it now, saying, "I'm also in the hall of shame. That's when you cheat in the big leagues." On the flip side, he pulled off an excellent Good Samaritan impression in 1977 when he picked up eight local high school baseball players who were stranded in a flash flood. He drove them to his place and let them stay the night saying only, "If it was my kids sitting there, I would've wanted someone to do something for them, too." He drove each and every one of the kids home the next day, as well. According to Bill James, this was not a rare occurrence either: "About once a year or so it would break into the letters to the editor that [Otis] had been caught secretly performing some unusual act of good citizenship – stopping on the interstate to pick up a fan having car trouble or something."

The black mark on Wilson's name was the result of off-field issues. In 1983, Wilson was arrested along with two other Royals on charges of attempted cocaine possession to which he pleaded guilty. He was originally suspended for the whole 1984 season, but he was reinstated by Commissioner Kuhn and was playing again by May 15. However, as many have noted (including Bill Simmons when discussing Tim Raines Hall of Fame candidacy), cocaine was not really thought of then in the same way it is now, as it was widely popular in the early `80s. It is mostly in hindsight that society has become aware of just how devastating the drug can be. There's also the fact that Wilson was the only one of the three Royals busted whom the Royals thought of highly enough to keep on the team. After this incident, Wilson seemed to clean up his act with no further incidents to his name. This is not to excuse the arrest, but rather to put it in perspective. Considering these two were so even in terms of health and playoff performance, the positives attached to AO trump Wilson and his cocaine suspension.

EDGE: Otis

Team Success

	W	L	W-L%	Seasons $\geq$ 90 W	Division titles	Pennants	WS
Otis	1,011	879	.535	6	5	1	0
Wilson	957	829	.536	5	5	2	1

Both players played on the Royals for the franchise's most successful seasons and were actually teammates from 1976-1983. It is interesting to note that Wilson was consistently the leadoff hitter; whereas, Otis was moved all around the lineup never really settling into his own spot in the lineup. Wilson was there for the Royals lone World Series victory and contributed 11 hits to the cause; Otis had retired by that point.

EDGE: Wilson

Dominance

So, we have previously seen all the categories in which each player led the league, and it is not surprising that the most relevant area of dominance for each player is speed. Wilson was certainly more dominant when it came to speed, but Otis was a more complete player adding in more power and a better eye – but this isn't a weak-ass "complete player" category, this is DOMINANCE.[115] Therefore, Wilson's dominance is his specialty area gives him the edge.

EDGE: Wilson

Who was better at being stuck on a desert island with Tom Hanks for four years?

(Photo from Wikimedia Commons)

EDGE: Wilson

Impact on the Franchise

Although both players were solid in their own right, neither had an extremely long-lasting impact on the franchise in the sense as some others in this book. As previously mentioned, both are members of the Royals Hall of Fame, and Otis came to the team in only their second year of existence. He was one of the team's most popular players in the club's early years and remained so for his whole stint in Kansas City. The two are second and third in team history in WAR, but this being the Royals, neither player is even sniffing big-time star status. One way to think about impact on a franchise is who the club would engrave onto their Mount Rushmore? For the Royals, it very well might just be a huge George Brett, but if they had to add others, they would likely go with Bret Saberhagen and Kevin Appier – leaving one last spot. It would almost certainly go to one of these players, and the fact that "AO" was so popular with the fans, came to Kansas City first, and didn't have quite the black mark on his name that Wilson had, the Royals would likely go with Otis.

EDGE: Otis

Verdict

This is about as tight a match-up as we're going to see, and one of these men could certainly be moved to left or right field (as was done when they played in the same outfield in real life, along with third outfielder Al Cowens, who was also a true center fielder[116]) and grabbed a starting spot, but this breakdown was too juicy to pass up. This comparison also brings to the fore the age-old debate of whether you would rather have a player dominant in one ability, or consistently above-average in a number of abilities? For my money, I would tend to lean towards the player who is dominant in his trait, in this case Willie Wilson. It may, in part, be the impact fantasy baseball has had on me, but I am very partial to building a team with a number of players who specialize in one area and letting each of their weaknesses be picked up by their teammates. However, the Royals are Bill James team, and as such, the verdict has to go to him... And it's **Amos Otis**. Not only is Otis James' favorite Royal, but he is also 32 spots higher than Wilson in James' center field rankings. Both players' value came basically entirely from their time in Kansas City. Since Wilson's career was just covered in detail, the utility spot, while deservedly Wilson's, will be filled by a different Royal so that more of their history can be covered.

RF Danny Tartabull (1987-1991)

Tartabull was in Kansas City for only five years; he racked up nearly a strikeout a game; he cost the team nearly 10.0 wins by dWAR; and he missed over 150 games in his five years with the team. However, he had enough positives in his game that the Yankees made him the highest paid player in the AL when he left Kansas City in 1992. As you probably guessed from all the parts of the game he lacked, Tartabull was an excellent hitter, posting .290/.376/.518 slashes with an OPS+ of 144 while with the Royals. This may not have been enough to warrant the top contract in the American League, but

---

[115] U-S-A! U-S-A!

[116] For a team that has often struggled to develop talent, center field has been a gold mine for the Royals over the years. In addition to Otis and Wilson, Carlos Beltrán, David DeJesus, Lorenzo Cain and Johnny Damon also patrolled the grass in front of Kauffman's grand Water Spectacular.

hey, it's the Yankees. That hitting was also enough to get him the starting right field spot for the Royals franchise, although he's arguably the worst player to appear on this Starting IX.

Tartabull and his father José were polar opposites about whom Bill James said: "There has never been a father/son combination in the majors in which the son so little resembled the father as a player except possibly Yogi and Dale Berra. José was among the fastest players in baseball in his era, a good outfielder and a decent singles hitter, but not a strong enough hitter to be a regular. Danny was a power hitter but a brutal outfielder and an indifferent base runner. José was a friendly little guy with a sense of humor, but a man who kind of melted into the woodwork. Danny had a big smile, was articulate and had a sense of style, but he was hyper-sensitive, moody, and never well-liked."

Utility Hal McRae (1973-1987) (but really Willie Wilson) (but we're talking about McRae) (so really, McRae)

McCrae came to the Royals in 1973 and found his niche, going on to stay with the team for the final 15 years of his career. A middling hitter who had neither plus contact nor power while in Cincinnati, McRae found a penchant for both in Kansas City. After a poor first season, McRae went on to post .296/.359/.462 slashes for the rest of his Royals career. He would lead the league in doubles twice, which, much like Billy Butler (who was among the toughest competition for this spot), seems to have been the result of playing half his games in spacious Kauffman Stadium. For his career, McRae hit 104 home runs on the road to just 87 at home, and he hit just 216 doubles on the road in comparison to 268 at home.

One noticeable flaw in McCrae's game is the fact that he may not have had as much speed as he thought he had. His career 59 percent stolen base rate, and the fact that his career range factor was far below league average, implies that McRae may have been a bit too cavalier with his 5'11" frame. However, as Bill James points out, McRae's aggressive tendencies on the basepaths were not surprising, or even out of place. In fact, he was one of the fastest players in the minors before breaking his leg severely while playing in Puerto Rico. The break was so intense that James says it cost him his shot at Cooperstown for a number of reasons: "It delayed the start of McRae's major league career by several years; it kept him from being a part of the Big Red Machine; and it cost him his speed."

However, McRae was still one of the most well-respected players to ever don the Royal Blues, and he brought with him to Kansas City the lessons he learned as a role player on the Big Red Machine. He eventually went on to manage the club after his playing days were over.

SP Bret Saberhagen (1984-1991)

Saberhagen came up with the Royals in 1984 and won two Cy Youngs over a stretch of eight years with the team. Saberhagen's rise coincided with the peak of the Royals, and his performance in the 1985 playoffs was a large reason the Royals won their first title. He won Games 3 and 7 of the World Series, and even though neither game was particularly close, his two victories landed him MVP for the series. He did this at the ripe age of 21.

Although 1985 was the year he broke onto the scene,[117] 1989 was the crowning achievement of his career. He won the Cy Young, and quite deservedly so. He led the league in wins (23), winning percentage (.793), ERA (2.16), complete games (12), innings pitched (262.1), ERA+ (180), WHIP (0.961), and strikeout to walk ratio (4.49), while also capturing his lone Gold Glove. His 9.7 WAR are topped only by Zack Greinke's 2009 season in terms of production for any Royal in a single season – pitcher or otherwise – in team history. At the end of the season he was 25 and looked primed to become baseball's next sure thing. But injuries, along with inconsistencies, began to crop up for "Sabes." While with the Royals, he had a bit of the "Alex Rios disease"[118] posting WAR totals of: 1.5, 7.3, 2.0, 8.0, 3.8, 9.7, 3.6, and 5.1. This inability to put together two straight excellent seasons made it so that the Royals felt they could trade him after the 1991 season (after one of his "up" seasons). The trade didn't bring in too much for the Royals, but Saberhagen posted only one more season with more than 4.0 WAR and only two seasons with more than 3.0 WAR, so the move didn't really burn them either.

CP Dan Quisenberry (1979-1988)

For what it's worth (which is very little) Quisenberry takes the prize for my favorite player of the `80s.[119] He was a dominant closer mixed with a self-proclaimed humorist. He looked like Wade Boggs mixed with Billy Mays, which only added to his extreme likeability. From an on-field perspective, once he established himself as the Royals closer, he led the league in saves five of his first six seasons in the role, and he led the league in games finished four of those six seasons. In the

[117] Along with the rest of the Royals rotation which was, according to you-know-who, the best rotation of the 1980s. "The best starting rotation of the 1980s belonged to the 1985 Kansas City Royals: Saberhagen, Charlie Leibrandt, Mark Gubicza, and Danny Jackson. The second best rotation of the 1980s belonged to the 1987 Royals, and consisted of the same four pitchers," James wrote in his *Historical Abstract*.

[118] Look at me boldly ignoring that Saberhagen's name has already been tied to this phenomenon – "Alex Rios disease" forever!

[119] Since it's not really baseball analysis, we'll relegate this list to a footnote, but here are my favorite players in each decade: 1870s: Any non-Cap Anson player. 1880s: King Kelly. 1890s: Ed Delahanty. 1900s: Christy Mathewson. 1910s: Walter Johnson. 1920s: Mickey Cochrane. 1930s: Jimmie Foxx. 1940s: Stan Musial. 1950s: Stan Musial. 1960s: Warren Spahn – True, he was 39 years old in 1960, but I think his two no-hitters in the 1960s make him eligible. 1970s: Tom Seaver. 1980s: Dan Quisenberry. 1990s: Ken Griffey Jr. 2000s: Vladimir Guerrero. 2010s: Andrew McCutchen. Last place in every single decade: Curt Schilling. By the way, I'm hoping/guessing it will be Aaron Judge for the 2020s.

five years he led the league in saves, he finished no worse than fifth in the Cy Young and 11th in the MVP. In 1983, his 45 saves set a major league record. He was also used in the ideal "reliever" role instead of current "closer" position. He pitched well over 100 innings each year he was healthy and totaled a much higher WAR total than today's closers – because, well, he was worth a lot more than today's closers. He was often brought in to pitch more than two innings, and he pitched up to four innings on five separate occasions during his 1980 campaign. His ERA+ for his 10 years in Kansas City was 160, which would be good for second all-time to Mariano Rivera, and for his career as a whole it is 146, still good for eighth all-time. That figure tops such luminaries as Roger Clemens, Cy Young, Christy Mathewson, and Greg Maddux (who are obviously starters, and faced with a far greater challenge than relief pitchers, but still). He had phenomenal control, and despite the fact that the rest of the write-up will look past his performance on the field, don't walk away from this write-up thinking that Quisenberry was anything less than one of the five preeminent relief pitchers of all time.

Where "Q" really made his name, though, was with his personality. It was a personality which often times shone through most in his post-game interviews. Always willing to give a quote, and a funny one at that, he provided endless entertainment both off and on the field for his fans. Here are some of his top gems:

His quip when he saw the Minnesota Metrodome: "I don't think there are any good uses for nuclear weapons, but then, this may be one."

After one of his rare career at bats, which ended with a groundout: "I thought they were in a zone, but they were playing man-to-man."

When asked what happens when his sinker isn't working, "The batter still hits a grounder. But in this case the first bounce is 360 feet away."

Now for a few great Quiz stories from the always great *Baseball Anecdotes*:

"In the bullpen, [Quisenberry] would pass the time by playing teammate Renie Martin's protuberant teeth as if they were xylophone keys while Martin sang about the game in process."

"After he gave up a game-winning pinch-hit… someone asked if that was the worst possible way to lose a game. He proceeded to rattle off 20 worse ways, including balking a runner all the way from first and an earthquake causing the center fielder to miss the last out."

"Reporter: 'Did you know your records this year are actually better than they were last year?' Quisenberry: 'How do you know? I'm into classical this year instead of pop.'"

And one more from Bill James *Abstract* for good measure,

"Quiz used to play a game with Denny Matthews, Royals broadcaster, which tells you something about him. 'Your word for today is 'homily' he would tell Matthews, or 'xenophobic' or 'divaricate.' "Your word is 'penumbra'" Matthews would respond, or 'triumvirate,' or something. Denny would have to figure out some way to work the word 'homily' into his broadcast without the listeners realizing anything was going on, and Quiz would have to figure out some way to work the word 'penumbra' into his post-game interview."

When you think about it, it's not really surprising that such a quirky dude would be in the bullpen. There have been numerous bullpen personalities over the years, ranging from the truly quirky (Mitch Williams) to the probably-faking-it (Brian Wilson), all of them entertaining in their own way (well, maybe not Wilson). This leads to the question of which came first the chicken or the egg? Do naturally quirky dudes flock to the bullpen as if it were a physical manifestation of a year-round Insane Clown Posse concert, or does the bullpen bring out the quirkiness of these normally average guys?

I think there are two factors here. First of all, even though the bullpen is not always thought of as an essential part of a team, most teams roster at least seven bullpen arms at a time, nearly a third of their active roster. That's a lot of people to find one or two quirky guys on each team. Second, the ways they kill time in the bullpen is awesome, but it definitely points to the fact that they often pitch less than 100 innings a year, meaning they are actively participating in their profession for approximately 11 hours in an entire season.[120] (And I do realize that a ton of time is given to training, warm ups, etc., meaning that relievers don't "work" for only 11 hours in a year, I'm just saying there is a lot of dead time out there in the pen.) Some of the things relievers have been known to do: flick pumpkin seeds at targets such as fans or security guards; try to hit their chewed-up gum onto the field or into the stands; and make mini-airplanes out of gum wrappers. All these point towards a great time being had in the bullpen.[121]

Finally, once a team gets one of these guys in the bullpen, the chemistry out there is such that all the relievers start to join in these quirky games, and suddenly everyone in the bullpen is doing this stuff. Eventually it just spills over from bullpen-to-bullpen as guys move around the league.

Who knows if any of these theories are correct, but all I know is that if I had to live an alternate life, I would hope for it to be as a reliever in the Royals bullpen in the 1980s.

Of course, the Royals section has to be brought to conclusion by Mr. Bill James, so let's let him describe Quisenberry: "He was a skinny man with a long nose and small teeth and a pencil mustache, and he was a beautiful man." Aaaand scene.

---

[120] Rough estimates: an average baseball game is 180 minutes, take away 40 minutes of commercials, divide the remaining 140 up into 18 half innings means each half inning is approximately 8 minutes, and a typical reliever will throw around 80 innings in a season, thus 640 minutes, or 10 hours and 40 minutes.

[121] Best fit for a TV character at an MLB position: Andy Dwyer from *Parks and Rec* as a MLB closer. Of course, Chris Pratt is better known as first baseman Scott Hatteberg when it comes to the big screen.

Starting IX Franchise Roster Stats

Lineup	Yrs	G	R	H	HR	RBI	SB	BB	SO	BA	OBP	SLG	OPS+	dWAR	WAR
Alex Gordon	11	1412	719	1337	160	608	96	565	**1274**	0.259	0.340	0.419	105	7.6	32.7
Amos Otis	14	1891	1074	1977	193	992	340	739	953	0.280	0.347	0.433	118	-4.2	44.6
George Brett	**21**	**2707**	**1583**	**3154**	**317**	**1596**	201	**1096**	908	0.305	0.369	0.487	135	1.2	**88.4**
John Mayberry	6	897	459	816	143	552	16	561	457	0.261	0.374	0.448	132	-5.0	21.2
Hal McRae	15	1837	873	1924	169	1012	105	616	697	0.293	0.356	0.458	125	-16.3	27.7
Salvador Pérez	7	813	329	822	114	423	3	114	491	0.272	0.301	0.442	99	10.9	19.3
Danny Tartabull	5	657	348	674	124	425	28	325	592	0.290	0.376	**0.518**	**144**	-9.6	12.7
Freddie Patek	9	1245	571	1036	28	382	336	413	586	0.241	0.309	0.321	78	11.2	20.4
Frank White	18	2324	912	2006	160	886	178	412	1035	0.255	0.293	0.383	85	**21.4**	34.7
Pitchers	Yrs	W	W%	ERA	G	CG	SHO	SV	IP	SO	ERA+	WHIP	SO/9	SO/BB	WAR
Bret Saberhagen	8	110	0.585	3.21	252	64	14	1	1660.1	1093	128	**1.134**	5.9	3.30	40.8
Dan Quisenberry	10	51	0.537	**2.55**	573	0	0	238	920.1	321	**160**	1.150	3.1	2.31	25.6

Tier three: Don't zone out…

The third tier of franchises is a collection of teams who fly under the radar a bit, either because they are always second banana in their own city (Mets and Angels), are located outside the U.S. (Blue Jays), haven't had any real success to speak of (Mariners and Rangers), or only recently did anything that would register in the long history of baseball (Astros). That doesn't mean these Starting IX's won't be filled with their share of entertaining anecdotes and self-indulgent lists, however. In fact, given that these teams are typically the ones fans read least about, there's much to be learned in these upcoming pages.

#22 Toronto Blue Jays (1977-pres.)

(Photo by Keith Allison/Creative Commons)

Team Background

Playoff appearances: 7 **Pennants: 2** **World Series titles: 2**
Collective team WAR: 270.8
Strengths: Excellent defense around the infield and a pitcher who gets a lot of ground balls is a good duo. With the power they have from the outfield and first base, this could be a potential tough matchup for a lot of other Starting IX's.
Weaknesses: Lack of any real all-timers keeps the Jays a tier below some of the top franchises.
What to expect from the next nine pages: A cameo from a much wiser man than myself, and a fair amount of Canada jokes, don'cha know?

For the Blue Jays team intro, I'm going to hand the reigns over to a good friend, Will Begley. Mr. Begley and I went to high school together, and he is without question the cleverest man I have ever met. A few years back, he made a cameo on the Bay Area Sports blog for which I was writing, contributing a piece in which he created anagrams for all of the Oakland A's players for an incredibly entertaining piece for the website. I got such a kick out of his work that I asked Will if he would do me the honor of repeating his excellent bit for the Toronto Blue Jays Starting IX. Being the gentleman that he is, Mr. Begley obliged and delivered (as well as lending a big helping hand in the editing process of the book) and the result is surely the funniest part in my entire book. Which, of course, was not even written by me… Enjoy!

Canada is once again aflame with delight at the success of their own hometown baseball team. I refer, of course, to the Montreal Expos, who have started making semi-regular playoff appearances – triumphs that are diminished only slightly by the fact that they now play in a new stadium in a new country under a different name with better players and no bilingual introductions. But attendance figures at Expos games at Olympic Stadium – the finest example of what I believe is called the "crashed-spaceship" school of architecture – have stayed roughly steady for the last 20 years, plus or minus 500 people.

But forgive my foray down Memory Lane (Rue de Remembrance?): I grew up in northern Vermont, where my big league baseball options were the Red Sox (four-hour drive, ninety-dollar tickets) and the Expos (two-hour drive, one-dollar tickets on select Sundays – one Canadian dollar, mind you), and so I have never fully overcome my youthful fondness for a ballgame with fewer runs during it than national anthems before it. Farewell, Expos; je me souviens (that's French for "Go Habs!").

The true Canadian team now is the again-proud Toronto Blue Jays, who made the playoffs in 2015 for the first time since Joe Carter homered, simultaneously ending the 1993 World Series and becoming an impossible-to-remember bar trivia answer ("Bill Mazeroski and…screw it, let's just put Bill Mazeroski twice"). Toronto was a great deal further from my home growing up, and so to properly introduce the greatest Blue Jays of all time, I've had to shy away from traditional modes of baseball analysis, like the "eye test," baseball "know-how," "gut" intuition, and "twinges in my arthritic elbow." Unfortunately, I'm still not clear on how to determine WAR without a graphing calculator and an animal sacrifice, so I'm trying a third way.

Both grizzled scouts and twenty-something Ivy-League assistant GM's can agree with the immortal Branch Rickey (1881-1965): "I don't want a player who hasn't got the guts to fight back. I want a player whose [name can be rearranged to spell COBRAS JOIN NIKE]." Rickey's strange anagrammatic predilections paved the way, of course, for Jackie Robinson to break the color barrier. In similar fashion, I find that you can learn a lot about the all-time greatest Blue Jays players by going beyond the numbers and into the letters. Here's information on the best Jays gleaned from the rearrangement of the letters in their names.

For example, we all know that Roy Halladay and Tom Henke were excellent pitchers, but without checking their anagrams, we might not have known that they were also excellent people. It's never been about chasing big contracts for Thomas Anthony Henke (THE MONEY? HA! NO THANKS), and the even the most despicable players receive good-natured congratulations from Roy Halladay (A-ROD? HALL? YAY!). Less supportive players were left off the all-Toronto roster, as you can tell from the arrogant sneering at unsuccessful bullpens by Dave Stieb (BET I'D SAVE).

The battery-mate for these starters is harder to pick, but amid such luminaries on the ballot as Alberto Castillo, Rod Barajas, and Gregg Zaun, the winner was Ernie Whitt (THE WRITE-IN). Around the infield, we have the financially careless Carlos Delgado (LOSE A GOLD CARD) at first base; at the hot corner, opinionated Court TV fan Kelly Wayne Gruber (KEY LAWYER: BUNGLER); and a double-play combo of store-design guru Tony Fernández (NEED ZANY FRONT) and the Hall of Famer who won't shut up about his own fantasy stats, Roberto Alomar (ROTO BORE ALARM).

In the outfield, there's George Bell (EEL BLOGGER), who apparently works in the offseason as a freshwater-fishing critic. There's center fielder Vernon Wells, who played in the American League his entire career despite a fondness for the senior circuit (NL'S NEW LOVER) and throwing problems from a nagging injury (SWOLL'N NERVE). Splitting time between outfield and the abominable DH "position" is Joseph Carter, best known for his World Series homer, his preferred mode of transportation (OPRAH'S REC JET), and the emails he sends to the team in his capacity as clubhouse fashion police (RE: PEACH JORTS).

In right field is my personal favorite, José Bautista. From his full name, we can find the underpinnings of a number of his most famous moments, whether his fight with the cantankerous Rougned "RUN, DO-GOODER" Odor or his unforgiving bat-flip in the 2015 ALDS: it's all because José Bautista Santos IS SO NOT A JESUS AT BAT. From his even fuller name, we can understand the mixed reaction to said bat-flip south of the border: someone should have warned José Antonio Bautista Santos that USA IS NOT A BAT-TOSS NATION, JOE.

I don't know who the best Blue Jays manager is, but I do know Cito Gaston GOTS ACTION. I'm similarly ignorant about the front office, but I do know why Alex Anthopoulos was always loathe to hire training staff from Boston and Chicago (NO SOX HEAL UP A LOT).

In summary, I assume you've learned as much from this analysis about the Toronto Blue Jays as I have (to wit, nothing). But don't worry, I haven't wasted all of your time. If you should ever make it up to Toronto, Ontario (ROTO-ROOT NATION) to take in a game, your anagramming expertise will help you through an inevitable cultural confusion when you arrive at the stadium. The letters in "Rogers Centre" can be rearranged to spell – fittingly, somehow – ROGERS CENTER.

I mean that's just too good. Thanks Will!

Random cool things about the franchise:

- The team held a "Name The Team" contest, and the leading vote-getter was simply "The Blues," but since the University of Toronto already had that name, "Blues" was vetoed, and they became the Blue Jays.
- The Jays are one of only three teams (along with the Braves and Mariners) to be under corporate ownership; fans of

"sticking it to THE MAN" will have to look elsewhere for their baseball fandom.

- Tom Cheek, the team's long-time play-by-play guy on the radio, once called a stretch of 4,306 consecutive games until the death of his father, when he took two days off.
- The Jays have their own song, "OK Blue Jays," which specifically references the Jays history and is played during each home game before the seventh inning stretch.
- José Bautista's FOH bat flip.

Starting IX

C Ernie Whitt (1977-1978; 1980-1989)

Whitt was a reliable backstop for the Jays right before their championship years. Whitt had a positive dWAR every year for the Blue Jays, which, although it may not sound very difficult, actually is because of the volatile nature of fielding metrics as they are currently calculated. Although best known for his glove work, you should know that Whitt also did some damage with the bat. He was part of history on September 14, 1987, when the Blue Jays hit a record 10 home runs against the Baltimore Orioles. Whitt played a large role in that history, totaling three home runs just by himself. Of course, he also made history from the other perspective when he flew out for the final out of one of the more obscure perfect games in MLB history. This piece of history took place on May 15, 1981 and belonged to Len Barker, a right-handed pitcher for Cleveland who had two good seasons his entire career. Barker finished his career 74-76 in 248 career starts but will always be remembered in baseball history thanks to his perfecto.

The list of pitchers to throw perfect games in MLB history flies a bit in the face of the idea that a pitcher has to be one of the game's elite to join the record books with such an achievement. There are 23 perfect games in MLB history (sorry, Armando Galarraga), and splitting the 23 men who threw them into four categories (Meh, All-Star, Veterans Committee Hall of Famer, and True Hall of Famer) reveals how questionable some of these guys are. Here's the breakdown with their career WAR in parenthesis:

Meh: Lee Richmond (12.2), Charlie Robertson (6.7), Don Larsen (12.2), Len Barker (11.1), Dallas Braden (5.3), Philip Humber (1.0)

All-Star: Mike Witt (21.8), Tom Browning (19.7), Dennis Martínez (49.5), Kenny Rogers (51.1), David Wells (53.5), Matt Cain (31.0)

Veterans Committee Hall of Famer: Monte Ward (28.4),[122] Addie Joss (45.9),[123] Jim Bunning (60.3), David Cone (61.7), Mark Buehrle (59.2),[124] Félix Hernández (52.2 and counting)

True Hall of Famer: Cy Young (170.3), Sandy Koufax (53.2), Catfish Hunter (36.6), Randy Johnson (104.3), Roy Halladay (65.6)

I was even a little generous with my tiers, counting Cone and Buehrle as Hall of Fame-esque talents, counting on King Félix to keep going, and slotting Halladay in with the True Hall of Famers. But check out that first tier. Those six guys wouldn't even be baseball afterthoughts if it wasn't for a single, 27-out performance that has them etched forever in our memory.

1B Carlos Delgado (1993-2004)

Delgado played for the Jays for 12 years beginning in 1993. He had only two plate appearances that first year and didn't play in the playoffs at all, but he was awarded a World Series ring nonetheless.[125] He went on to earn that ring, however, and ranks first in team history in runs (889), doubles (343), home runs (336), RBI (1,058), total bases (2,786), oWAR (39.1), and walks (827). Among players with at least 1,000 at bats for Toronto, he ranks first in OPS (.949).

The Player A vs. Player B blind resume comparison is a classic way to surprise people about certain players, so we'll give it a shot here:

	BA	OBP	SLG	R	H	HR	RBI	BB	OPS+	dWAR	WAR	MVP
Player A	.280	.383	.546	1241	2038	473	1512	1109	138	-17.9	44.3	0
Player B	.282	.360	.529	1194	2232	475	1540	937	147	-19.7	57.5	1

Here are the two players' playoff numbers:

[122] Ward is an interesting case because he became a shortstop and accrued another 22.4 as a hitter at the end of his career.
[123] Joss is a pretty legit Hall of Famer, and we'll talk about his HoF case later, but he was technically elected by the Veteran's Committee.
[124] True, David Cone and Mark Buehrle are not in the Hall of Fame, but their numbers are on par with the rest of the guys in this tier. Same thing will apply to one player in the "True Hall of Fame" tier.
[125] Token reminder that Barry Bonds never won a ring in his career. Gotta love RINGZZZZ logic.

	G	R	HR	RBI	BA	OBP	SLG	Series Victories	Rings
Player A	10	8	4	11	.351	.442	.757	1	0
Player B	36	18	7	20	.278	.359	.511	4	2

These two players have very even careers. A discerning eye will notice that Player B probably played in an era with less offense than Player A because, despite a lower on-base percentage and slugging percentage, he has a higher OPS+. Player B also has more playoff success, but Player A has excellent numbers in limited playoff games. Player B is first-ballot Hall-of-Famer Willie Stargell, while, as you probably guessed, Player A is Carlos Delgado. I don't think Delgado should be a first-ballot Hall-of-Famer, but I think he should be in the Hall of Fame, and he certainly didn't deserve the disgusting, first-year-off-the-ballot treatment he got when he received just 21 votes (3.8 percent) in 2014. The fact that he made only two All-Star Games during his career speaks to the fact that he was extremely underappreciated as a player throughout his career, a trait that clearly carried over to the legacy portion of his lifetime. This is even more of a shame because he was also a Roberto Clemente Award winner for his work in the community and an all-around great guy, in addition to being a hell of a ballplayer. Jayson Stark, as Jayson Stark is wont to do, wrote an excellent piece saying the same thing after Delgado fell off the ballot in 2014. The article was chock full of interesting statistical comparisons, just like every Jayson Stark article is.

As far off being a man of morals, Delgado refused to stand for God Bless America during the 2004 season, as a means of protest for the American involvement in the Iraq War. This was far before the time of Colin Kapernick and the NFL protest saga, and it speaks to his being ahead of the times both in terms of his stand of the Iraq War, as well as non-violent forms of protest.

2B Roberto Alomar (1991-1995)

Roberto Alomar didn't quite hit his prime in his time with Toronto, but he was a strong player who finished sixth in the MVP each of his first three years with the team. He also won two World Series with the team and was an excellent player for them in the playoffs, winning the 1992 ALCS MVP, as well as being a top performer in the 1993 World Series. In fact, the 1993 World Series was the dénouement to an excellent season for several Blue Jays, as Alomar, along with teammates Paul Molitor and John Olerud, became the first trio of teammates to take the top three spots in the race for the batting title – even more impressive considering it occurred in an era after MLB expansion. Alomar built one of the most successful careers for a player who played for enough teams to be considered a journeyman. He played for seven different teams and never played for one city for more than five years, however, he tallied 66.8 WAR for his career, good for 126th in baseball history.

After leaving Toronto, while with the Orioles, Alomar infamously spit on umpire John Hirschbeck after Hirschbeck made a third strike call with which Alomar did not agree. The dispute spilled over to the post-game when Alomar disclosed information about Hirschbeck's family, saying that Hirschbeck was angry about his son who had passed away undiagnosed a year before. Hirschbeck followed Alomar into the lock room, but the two were separated. Alomar excused his actions by saying that Hirschbeck had called him in a racial slur, and the situation was one of the nastiest player/umpire disputes in baseball history (probably second to Sherry Magee, Phillies left fielder, who will be discussed later).

I contemplated punishing Alomar by leaving him off this hypothetical team,[126] but I think one mistake like that, in the heat of an intense game, can be forgiven for this context. Let me make sure to clarify, it should not be excused or be seen as acceptable, by no stretch of the imagination – especially his antics after the game – but everyone can make one mistake. For instance, Chris Paul is one of the players seen in the highest regard in the NBA (outside of his whininess), but if you remember when he was in college he made a name for himself by kneeing Julius Hodge in the crotchal region. Also, as noted earlier, Alomar didn't do the spitting while playing as a member of the Blue Jays, in fact it was in a game against the Blue Jays, so it shouldn't affect his standing as a Jay.

To end on a more positive note: baseball author Robert Cohen said of Alomar that he was "perhaps the finest defensive second baseman in baseball history." Now the numbers certainly don't agree with this, and Bill Mazeroski-proponents would certainly scoff at the statement, but Alomar was certainly a very strong fielder in his prime. He was also the first (and as of now, only) player to sport the Toronto Blue Jay hat on his plaque in the Hall of Fame. He was elected to the Hall of Fame in 2011 along with long-time Blue Jays General Manager Pat Gillick.

3B Josh Donaldson

This spot was originally given to Kelly Gruber, but given that he slashed just .259/.307/.431 (102 OPS+) in 921 rather pedestrian games for the Blue Jays in his career, Toronto fans will be fine with a rather quick hook for Gruber, as his replacement is the man who locks down the hot corner for the current iteration of the Jays. There were many times in this book that the historical player was given the tiebreaker over the modern player, and as such, there are some pretty strong current players who might have a right to be upset about missing out on a spot. Here's a Starting IX of the current players with the best cases for inclusion who didn't actually make the cut:

---

[126] A fate worse than death!

SP) Chris Sale, Chicago White Sox CP) Kenley Jansen, Los Angeles Dodgers C) Yadier Molina, St. Louis Cardinals 1B) Joey Votto, Cincinnati Reds 2B) Dustin Pedroia – More on this in actual Red Sox second base spot 3B) Kyle Seager, Seattle Mariners SS) N/A LF) Christian Yelich, Miami Marlins CF) A.J. Pollock RF) Charlie Blackmon, Colorado Rockies – Yes, he plays center, but he's got more of a grudge than any of the right fielders Utility) José Altuve, Houston Astros

As far as Donaldson's case for the spot is concerned, some Blue Jay fans would likely have given him the spot after his debut season. Donaldson slashed .297/.371/.568 for an OPS+ of 151 and 8.8 WAR in his much deserved 2015 MVP season. He helped lead the Blue Jays to their first ALCS since the early 1990s and then went right back out and did it all again in 2016. While 2017 was a down year for both Donaldson and the Jays (Donaldson missed 49 games but still managed an OPS+ of 144 when he was in the lineup), by 2020 there should be no doubt at all as to who is the greatest third baseman in Blue Jays history.

SS Tony Fernández (1983-1990; 1993; 1998-1999; 2001)

Fernández was a serial Jay, so to speak. He started his career there and was part of a big trade in 1990 that sent him and Fred McGriff to San Diego for Roberto Alomar and Joe Carter. Fernández found his way back north of the border halfway through the 1993 season and was a key contributor to the World Series-winning Blue Jays team. He left after the season, but came back to the team via free agency twice, once in 1997 and again in 2001. Fernández managed to make four stints with the club for at least a part of 12 different seasons, and although he played for six other clubs, he was never anywhere else more than two seasons.

As for his actual ability, he was a severely underrated part of Blue Jays history, as he is the franchise leader in both WAR for position players (37.4) and games played (1,450). He was electric in the field, and the love for Fernández runs deep in many parts of Toronto. In 2016, Ari Shapiro penned an excellent retrospective on Fernández for *Jays Journal*, gushing, "For this prince of San Pedro de Macoris found a way to leave an indelible mark in the most unlikely of Northern fantasies… and took his rightful place amongst the titans of his childhood sport, becoming the greatest player to ever wear a Blue Jays uniform." I'm not sure I'm fully on board with final conceit of Shapiro's piece, but Fernández is undoubtedly a severely under-remembered player in Blue Jays history, as well as the history of the sport, as a whole.

LF George Bell (1981; 1983-1990)

I'm a real sucker for just plain dumb nicknames, and George Bell being nicknamed "Liberty" Bell, is about as dumb as it gets – so naturally I love it. Bell was a great power hitter in the years leading up to the Blue Jays Golden Years of 1992-1993. He won the MVP in 1987, with a .308/.352/.605 slash line to go with 111 runs, 47 home runs, and 134 RBI. His poor defense, and his (lack of) positional value dragged down his WAR (5.0 in 1987), but he was definitely a key component of those two Blue Jay playoff teams. Although he made numerous errors in left field, Bell had a strong arm, leading left fielders in assists each season from 1985-1987, and he had decent range, to boot.

As was noted in Toby Hall's section (**Catcher, Rays – Page XX**), Bill James was enlisted to prepare George Bell's arbitration cases three straight seasons and was able to prepare the same case for Bell to receive more money each year. If you're interested in how that case played out, and either can't remember back 100 pages, or skipped ahead to the Blue Jays section, head back to Hall, but I do want to bring up Bell's arbitration case for a separate reason. Although arbitration is a key element of baseball – and franchise building – it is a confusing process, and one about which many fans don't know as much as they should.

The late 1960s and early `70s were a revolutionary time for MLB players and owners in terms of how they could interact. For generations, MLB players had practically no rights contractually, and every player had a reserve clause in his contract. This meant that even when the contract was up, the team owned that player's rights, so the player had no say in where he would play unless his team no longer wanted him. Marvin Miller (an economist who had also worked with the Steelworkers Union) and Curt Flood (an outfielder for the Cardinals) helped spur the movement towards more rights for players; rights that seem commonplace today (free agency and the elimination of the reserve clause), but it was a slow process.

As the process was going on (the original court rulings came back in favor of the owners maintaining the reserve clause), the head of the Player Relations Committee, Ed Fitzgerald, pushed for the inclusion of arbitration hearings for players and teams who could not come to agreements on salary. The idea was worrisome to some owners,[127] even though it was originally seen as an alternative to free agency (instead of in cohesion with free agency as we see today), some owners (the conniving, clever ones with more business savvy) realized that total free agency would flood the market, and thus keep contracts at a lower level, thus eliminating some leverage from the players. However, those owners were overruled, and arbitration hearings (the process of going to an outside source for contract negotiations) became a part of the MLB process.

How the process works in modern baseball is as a last-ditch effort for the two sides to come together. The reason that is, is because the two sides go in, each with a salary in mind, and make their cases to a panel of arbitrators, who then give

[127] Most notably, A's owner Charlie Finley who we will look at in closer detail in the A's Starting IX introduction.

a verdict that comes down directly with one side. There is no more negotiating, which is why the process is called "Final Offer Arbitration," and it can be a big risk for both sides, who ideally could figure out an agreement beforehand.

Players start the process of becoming eligible for arbitration the day they make their team's major league roster, and from that time forward, they begin to collect service time that counts towards when they are eligible. For the most part, players are eligible after three seasons (there are a few "Super Two" cases, but that would take a couple pages to thoroughly explain), and since players are eligible for complete free agency after six seasons, the arbitration zone is typically after a player's third, fourth and fifth seasons. Arbitration can be offered to players past the six-season mark, typically as a sign of the team's interest in retaining that player. The team will also make the arbitration offer so that they can be reimbursed with a compensatory pick in the draft if the player signs elsewhere. A free agent typically won't go to arbitration, as it only guarantees a one-year contract, and the risk of the arbiters siding with the team is an unnecessary evil after those six years of service.

When the process actually does get to arbitration, the hearing takes place in a neutral city, with representatives (such as Bill James for George Bell) from each side making their case (oftentimes using baseball statistics), and the arbiters deciding a winner and a loser of the hearing with the winner's salary going into the books for the next season. Most of this information came from an excellent *Baseball Prospectus* article by Thomas Gorman on the subject entitled, "The Arbitration Process," so hit that up if you want to learn even more on the subject.

CF Vernon Wells (1999-2010)

Wells was a high draft pick for the Jays and seemed to be on the path to stardom early in his career. He slowed down significantly on that path, however, especially after he left Toronto.[128] Wells was the classic player who hit a lot of doubles and people were sure those two-baggers would turn into home runs and make him a certified star, but it never happened. This is a very common misconception among prognosticators (and fantasy players). Very often players who hit a lot of doubles early in their career are expected to make a jump in power (James Loney and Billy Butler were two you always heard about), but often these players disappoint by not making that next step, instead remaining doubles hitters. As for Wells, after he hit 49 doubles and led the league in total bases in 2003, he never topped the 33 home runs that he hit that same year, and he never had a slugging percentage as high as 2003, either.

In terms of how Wells is as a guy, he won the 2010 Branch Rickey Award for his work with youth in the community, and he and his wife have consistently been major contributors to whichever community in which they have lived. He also, like Clayton Kershaw, is famous for his *gosh darnit* approach to cursing, for which his teammates often gave him a hard time.

Of course, when many fans think of Vernon Wells today, they think of arguably one of the most overpaid players of his generation. Wells signed a back-loaded contract for $126 million over seven years after the 2006 season. Wells immediately saw a drop in his production, especially in the surface statistics, and the gripes began immediately. The "Players get paid too much" trope is a tale as old as time, a song as old as rhyme. Henry Chadwick, one of the OG baseball statisticians, said near the turn of the *20th century*, "you must proportionately lower your salaries. One thousand dollars for seven months of such services as a professional ballplayer is called upon to perform, even when he is not indisposed, is amply sufficient." Vernon Wells was making more than 45 times that "amply sufficient" $1,000 sum *every single time he stepped to the plate* by the end of his contract.

RF José Bautista (2008-pres.)

It has been a very strange career path that Bautista has taken to stardom. Bautista broke into the majors in 2004 as a man without a position, and he would soon be a man without a team. In 2004 alone, he managed to play for four different teams, playing multiple positions on every single team. He accomplished that feat while playing no more than 23 games with any single team in that wild season. After that, Bautista played a few poor years for the Pirates, getting playing time only because of how weak the team's roster was at that point, and then he was traded to Toronto for the classic "player to be named later." It took Bautista a little over a year to settle in, but once he did, "Joey Bats" really found his groove, hitting 54 home runs to pace the league in 2010. He was seen as a flash in the pan at first, but he really backed it up with an excellent encore performance in 2011. The next two seasons saw slight dips in production for Bautista, but those were due more to injury as well as the league moving toward a more pitching-dominated era than a slip in actual talent. Bautista made the All-Star Game every year from 2010-2015, and he posted an OPS+ of at least 132 every season from 2010-2015. He even managed to move into the top spot in Blue Jays history for WAR among position players, a crazy thought just a few years ago (of course, after a -1.7 WAR season from Bautista in 2017, Fernández is back to franchise leader). Bautista is an established star at this point and, as noted, has one of the most unique career arcs of any player in the current generation.

Jeff Passan, of *The Post Game*, wrote an excellent profile of Bautista, which portrayed the late-to-breakout star as

[128] Wells was traded away while underperforming on a mammoth contract, and he netted the Blue Jays Mike Napoli in return. This would have been an absolute steal for the Jays if they hadn't gone and swapped Napoli to the Texas Rangers for Frank Francisco four days later.

one of the most unique – and intelligent – minds in the game. Bautista has obviously been asked ad nauseam about his out-of-nowhere success and, instead of taking the easy "I just hard work" approach to answering the question, has a more nuanced response:

"'Sometimes there is a reason,' Bautista says (to whom? Not me). 'It's just not simple.' In his free time, Bautista reads books on exceptionality. 'I'm trying to understand why mediocre people become good at what they do,' he says, 'and why good people become the best.' So he mixes other players' post-career musings on success with real mental protein. He's gotten into Malcolm Gladwell. He recently finished 'Outliers.'"

Outliers is, of course, Malcolm Gladwell's book that famously puts forward the idea that after 10,000 hours honing a skill, a person becomes an expert in that field. There's the possibility that Bautista simply reached that *magical* 10,000-hour mark, but there's also the (much more likely) possibility that the coaching staff in Toronto, the ones that helped him incorporate a leg kick into his swing and a more aggressive approach at the plate, simply unlocked the potential of a player who was once among the highest-rated in the Pirates organization (at a time in which the Pirates were not known for unlocking the potential of their own young players). Either way, MLB is all the better for it, as Bautista is one of baseball's most entertaining (and polarizing) stars, something that seemed unthinkable early in his career. He's even responsible for the coolest moment of my baseball lifetime, with his world-burning bat flip in Game 5 of the 2015 ALDS.

As far as where to come down on Bautista from a fan's perspective, it is just as complicated and full of ups-and-downs as his career arc. On the one hand, he'll do something amazing like his responses to Passan above, or his epic bat flip. Then he'll do something dumb like slide overtly hard into second base and get punched in the face by Rougned Odor. But then after the game, he'll have an incredibly nuanced response to the entire blowup, and, I mean, the dude can take a punch. Then again, he'll start saying dumb things like how the Blue Jays 2016 ALCS series against Cleveland was rigged and that there were "circumstances" going against Toronto. He and his teammates will freeze out the media and look like a bunch of mini-politicians complaining about a rigged system. Then, finally, you'll read about his not-for-profit organization "The Bautista Family Education Fund," and how he went back to get his bachelor's degree in order to set up that fund that helps young players from outside the U.S. learn the benefits of schooling in the States. Really, Bautista is just one of a million examples in this book that people aren't simply TV characters of whom we can say "GOOD" or "BAD," but rather complex characters that require serious refinement when thinking about and discussing their legacy.

Utility Joe Carter (1991-1997)

Every Blue Jays fan, and every baseball fan for that matter, remembers Carter as the man who won the 1993 World Series for Toronto with this walk-off home run off Mitch Williams. Carter's career with the Jays was actually not as impressive as one would imagine, but to leave off the player with the most defining moment in team history seemed wrong. (Also, it's not like Jesse Barfield is a game changer at the utility position.) Carter's home run meant more to the city of Toronto than many championships for other cities because of the city's barren sports landscape surrounding it. The Raptors and Maple Leafs were playoff teams around the same time but suffered heartbreak after heartbreak, and as the recent Raptors and Blue Jays rejuvenations have highlighted, Toronto is one of the best sports cities in North America. If it weren't for the Jays back-to-back World Series, the city wouldn't have a championship (excluding the many titles for the Toronto Argonauts in the Canadian Football League) since 1966-1967 when the Leafs last won.

Back to Carter: if the average baseball fan thinks of Carter as a great clutch performer, it is only fair to point out that in analytic circles he is thought of quite differently. He is often considered the face of the now debunked "RBI man" and "clutch performer." Both RBI and clutch performances have been under attack since the dawn of sabermetrics, and Carter is the poster boy for both, especially on the RBI front. With 10 seasons of 100+ RBI, Carter is in an elite class of 18 players to accomplish this feat; he has the same number of 100-RBI seasons as Willie Mays. However, simply looking at Carter's RBI is a poor way to decipher his true value, as he also had the "distinction" of being the eighth player since 1901 (and the only one with double-digit home runs at the time) to drive in 100 runs with a slugging percentage under .400 in a season (1990). There are numerous factors that led to Carter's high RBI totals, including his strong health, the production of his teammates, and his place in the lineup, all of which point to his RBI totals maybe not being worth as much as Joe Carter fans would care to acknowledge.

SP Roy Halladay (1998-2009)

Believe it or not, this was one of the hardest decisions in the book, and it wasn't even because of the man some of you are thinking of – Dave Stieb (the franchise leader in WAR). Instead, the man I almost put here was Roger Clemens. In his two years in Toronto, Clemens did about as good an impression of Julius Caesar as one can do; he came, he saw, he conquered. In 1997-1998, he won 41 games, lost only 13, while leading the league in strikeouts as well as ERA and ERA+ both years. On top of that, he deservedly won the Cy Young Award both seasons, and he led all pitchers in WAR both times for a combined total of 20.1; pretty heady stuff.

Halladay, however, just had more time with the Jays, while also being a top pitcher in his own regard. Debuting with the club in 1998, Halladay spent his first 12 seasons in Toronto until being traded away to Philadelphia after the 2009 season. He was one of the best control pitchers in the game and a total workhorse. He led the league in complete games five times with Toronto, including his last three years there. He surprisingly never won an ERA title despite a top-five finish five times in Toronto alone. He only had one Cy Young with the team compared to Clemens' two, but in the end, Clemens needed maybe two more dominant years, or three or four solid years, to earn this spot.

There's also the fact that Doc Halladay was beloved by the fans of Toronto, and as such, they saw fit to not hold it against him when he was traded to Philadelphia after the 2009 season, no easy task for a star player to pull off. When in Toronto, Halladay was often called the best pitcher to not have pitched in the playoffs. He proved everyone right when he took the mound on October 6, 2010, and fired the second ever no-hitter in postseason history (Don Larsen's World Series perfect game being the only other) in his first-ever playoff appearance. In fact, 2010 was a pretty special year for Halladay, despite leaving his beloved Blue Jays. On May 29, 2010, Halladay threw the 20th perfect game in MLB history, one of his 21 victories for the season. Halladay threw nine complete games, four shutouts, and had a 7.30 strikeout to walk ratio. All of this resulted in Halladay capturing his second Cy Young of his career (his first came in 2003 as a Blue Jay). Two things facts stood out about this. First, Doc became the second pitcher in MLB history to win the Cy Young the same year that he threw a perfect game – Sandy Koufax was the other – and second, he joined Tom Glavine as the only two pitchers in MLB history to win Cy Young awards seven years apart.

Part of the reason Toronto fans didn't hold it against Halladay that he left for postseason success in Philly was because Halladay was one of the humblest men in baseball. After his perfect game, he bought watches for every guy on the Phillies that said, "We did it together," and after his incredible 2010 campaign, all he talked about was the role his teammates had in his success. This coming from a man who trailed only Randy Johnson and Javier Vasquez[129] in fWAR among pitchers in the 2000s decade.[130]

Speaking of decades, Halladay is a man who might well have been better suited to play in another decade entirely. He was well known for his incredible stamina, having led the league in complete games seven out of nine years from 2003-2011, including five straight years from 2007-2011. Halladay pitched much more like a pitcher from days of yore than any of his peers, which got me thinking: what if we built a Starting IX of players whose style of play didn't necessarily fit in their era? Not that they would have benefited from changing eras, because then they might have lost what made them stand out in their own era, but simply that their style of play was more befitting of another time:

C) Jorge Posada – This is not about the fact that Posada's game might have worked better in the 1950s, but rather the fact that if he was a catcher in New York in the `50s, it would have guaranteed him a couple MVPs.[131]

1B) Roger Connor – The Home Run King before Ruth, Connor would have thrived in a more homer-friendly era.

2B) Jackie Robinson – We could really put every Negro League star on this list as a change in era would have allowed them to actually play in the major leagues for their full careers, but Robinson, in particular, would have fit in with a later-era, high-base-running style, as well.

3B) Brooks Robinson – He would be the GIF god.

SS) Alex Rodriguez – A prodigious talent that simply couldn't handle this generation's extreme pressure that went along with being the megastar that he was.

LF) Al Simmons – One of the game's most underrated players in history. Just wait til you get to the A's section. You'll have a Simmons-gasm.

CF) Michael Bourn – Bourn was made for the high base-stealing era of the 1980s; if he grew out his hair he would even look the part.

RF) Reggie Jackson – He'd be a perfect fit for the media-crazy, me-first, Twitter era that we live in today. Oh boy, Reggie Jackson in his prime on Twitter, that is something I'd pay to read. Plus, he was a Three True Outcomes hitter before his time.

Utility) Pete Rose – If only he'd played in an era when being slightly corrupt was generally acceptable, and players like Hal Chase were constantly gambling on the side. His hair-on-fire style of play would have fit right in then, too.

SP) Roy Halladay

CP) Dizzy Dean – His arm troubles could have been relieved with a move to the bullpen where his blazing fastball and quirky personality would have been perfect for the closing role.

* Sadly, this write-up needed a post script in the final days before publishing. Halladay, 40, passed away when his plane crashed in the Gulf of Mexico. The one bright spot of a tragic death like this is that is brings to the fore all the incredible stories of these men, and Halladay was no exception. The tales of his unreal work ethic (like truly unreal, even when compared to other world-class athletes) and his true kind soul spread like wildfire in the days after his passing, as his loss was one that weighed heavy on the sport as a whole. Rest in peace, Doc.

---

[129] I'm as shocked as you are.

[130] If we change eliminate the nominal arbitrary cut off of "decade" being 2000-2009 and switch to 2001-2010, Halladay's 54.4 WAR blow second-place Roy Oswalt's 48.3 fWAR out of the water.

[131] From 1951-1963, a New York (Yankees or Dodgers) catcher won the MVP seven times.

CP Tom Henke (1985-1992)

A closer throughout his whole career, Henke spent all eight of his seasons in Toronto as the club's closer. He had 217 saves with the team and finished off 150 other games. This is one huge difference in the way closers are handled in baseball today. The games finished-to-saves ratio has been an evolving one throughout baseball history, or at least since relief pitchers started to get regular work. Bill James does a great breakdown of how a relief ace is used most effectively for the team. He states what many have said after him – and is a shared sentiment among everyone except MLB managers it seems – which is that using a team's relief ace strictly in save situations is really silly. Of course, actually turning back the clock to use a team's best reliever in the most important moment is easier said than done, as Ben Lindbergh and Sam Miller learned in their season running the Sonoma Stompers (*The Only Rule Is It Has to Work*).

Back to Henke: in addition to locking down the closer's role his whole time in Toronto, he sported 10.3 strikeouts per nine and a 3.88 strikeout to walk ratio during his time with the club – pretty solid, especially for a reliever in his era. Henke also held hitters to a measly .203 batting average against and converted 85 percent of his saves. He did blow a save in Game 6 of the 1992 World Series, but the Jays were able to come back and win the game in extras, getting him a ring before he left that offseason.

Starting IX Franchise Roster Stats

Lineup	Yrs	G	R	H	HR	RBI	SB	BB	SO	BA	OBP	SLG	OPS+	dWAR	WAR
Paul Molitor	3	405	270	508	51	246	54	193	176	**0.315**	0.387	0.484	128	-4.0	10.6
Josh Donaldson	3	426	309	460	111	300	15	258	363	0.285	0.387	**0.559**	150	2.4	21.1
Roberto Alomar	5	703	451	832	55	342	206	322	291	0.307	0.382	0.451	123	-0.8	22.2
Carlos Delgado	**12**	1423	**889**	1413	**336**	**1058**	9	**827**	**1242**	0.282	0.392	0.556	142	-10.4	36.7
Vernon Wells	**12**	1393	789	1529	223	813	90	406	762	0.280	0.329	0.475	108	1.6	28.7
George Bell	9	1181	641	1294	202	740	59	255	563	0.286	0.325	0.486	119	-6.1	21.1
Tony Fernández	**12**	**1450**	704	**1583**	60	613	172	439	493	0.297	0.353	0.412	106	**11.9**	**37.3**
Joe Carter	7	1039	578	1051	203	736	78	286	696	0.257	0.308	0.473	104	-7.6	8.3
Ernie Whitt	**12**	1218	424	888	131	518	22	403	450	0.253	0.327	0.420	102	8.9	19.3
Pitchers	Yrs	W	W%	ERA	G	CG	SHO	SV	IP	SO	ERA+	WHIP	SO/9	SO/BB	WAR
Roy Halladay	**12**	148	0.661	3.43	313	49	15	1	2046.2	1495	133	1.198	6.6	3.29	48.5
Tom Henke	8	29	0.500	**2.48**	446	0	0	**217**	563	644	**167**	**1.025**	**10.3**	**3.88**	17.0

#21 Texas Rangers (1972-pres.); Washington Senators (1961-1971)

(Photo by Staff Sgt. Alan Garrison/Creative Commons)

Team Background

Playoff appearances: 8 **Pennants: 2** **World Series titles: 0**
Collective team WAR: 316.8
Strengths: As anyone who ever followed baseball would guess – offense. And considering these Starting IX's are skewed towards offense (only two pitchers included) that's a good thing for the Rangers. This is also a surprisingly awesome defensive infield.
Weaknesses: Some of the impressive offensive numbers their players posted were the result of the Steroid Era (as well as the Rangers home stadium), and at times their power numbers have been a bit empty in terms of true production. Also, their pitching is butt.
What to expect from the next eight pages: A decent number of complex personalities. This will be your local psychologist's favorite chapter.

The Rangers franchise started off in Washington in 1961 and struggled mightily in the team's 11 years in our nation's capital. Their best finish was either fourth out of six, or sixth out of 10 – pick your poison really. The club relocated to Texas in 1972 and continued to struggle, but they began putting together some good years starting in 1974. Over the next eight seasons, they finished in the top half of their division six times, with four seasons in second place. The franchise's first real successful period started with the strike-shortened 1994 season. Despite a pretty pitiful record (42-52), they were somehow in first in their division when the lockout robbed fans of the final third of the season, and the Rangers parlayed that into three division crowns in the following five seasons. Nothing serious came of those division titles, however, as the team won just one playoff game in their three postseasons (1996, 1998, and 1999).

Moving forward, the first decade of this millennium kind of shat all over the Rangers. They started the decade with four straight last-place finishes, then moved up to three straight third-place finishes, one more last-place finish, and they ended the decade with slight improvement moving up to second for the last two years of the decade.

Despite these poor records, the Rangers definitely weren't bereft of talent; they just seemingly couldn't find a pitcher to save their lives (or their runs). Part of it was the ballpark, but part of it was the fact that they just plain had bad pitching. Their "ace"[132] in 2007 was Kevin Millwood who rocked a gorgeous line: 5.16 ERA, 89 ERA+, 1.622 WHIP, and netted them exactly 0.2 WAR; needless to say, this was the year they slipped back into last in the division. There has been almost no historical precedent for a franchise struggling this much to find pitching, with the lone exception being the Baker Bowl-era Phillies, but they were even more the result of their home stadium.

However, under Mike Maddux's guidance the team turned the corner about a decade ago, finally becoming a successful pitching team in addition to the great hitting team they've always been. The Rangers saw their team ERA drop nearly a full point (0.99, to be exact) in Maddux's first season (2009), and the club regularly landed in the top tier of ERA leaders during Maddux's tenure, despite their history and offense-friendly ballpark. After never having a team ERA below 4.00 from 1991-2009 (with many of those seasons well over 5.00), Maddux got the team ERA below 4.00 four straight seasons from 2010-2013. In the club's 15 seasons before Maddux that they spent in Globe Life Park in Arlington (built 1994 and originally called The Ballpark in Arlington), their collective ERA was over 5.00. In the seven seasons with Maddux as their pitching coach (2009-2015), the team ERA was 4.07 – basically a whole run better.

The Rangers and Maddux mutually decided to part ways after the 2015 season – their ERA was 4.37 in 2016 and 4.70 in 2017. Not saying they're doomed, but it is certainly surprising that the Rangers decided to let Maddux go. (Maddux moved to the Nationals, who were second in all of baseball with a 3.51 ERA in 2016. Correlation certainly doesn't guarantee causation, but…)

Ending on a better note for the Rangers: the culture surrounding the team right now is among the best in baseball. Manager Jeff Banister is able to combine analytics and player wherewithal as well as any manager in the game, and he isn't afraid to try new things. The future is definitely bright in Texas. Now they just have to shake off their recent playoff struggles (including the 2011 World Series, in which multiple times they were one strike away from what would have been the first title in franchise history) and bring that first World Series victory to the Dallas-Fort Worth metro.

Random cool things about the franchise:

- The Rangers mascot is currently a palomino-style horse, which should ring alarm bells for any Will Ferrell-era SNL fans… "A palomino? They're gorgeous. Beautiful golden fur."
- Bob Short, the man who moved the Rangers from D.C., is the same man who moved the Lakers from Minneapolis.
- The first-ever manager for the franchise was Ted Williams.
- The club was famously owned by George Dubya from 1989-1998.
- Current GM Jon Daniels was the youngest-ever GM when he was hired at the ripe age of 28 back in 2005 – god damn wunderkinds making everyone else feel so inadequate.
- Google Derek Holland's mustache and weatherman debut. Also know that his nickname is Dutch Oven.
- Elvis Andrus learned English by reading the lyrics to Rascal Flatts songs while listening to the music at the same time. On behalf of the English language, Mr. Andrus, I'm so sorry.

Starting IX

C Ivan Rodriguez (1991-2002; 2009)

"Pudge" started his career in Texas, and while playing in the Lone Star State established himself as one of the premier backstops in the game. Rodriguez did so starting at the ripe age of 19, making his debut as the youngest player in the league, a usual sign of a good career to come. Rodriguez, although certainly an excellent hitter, will always be remembered for being one of, if not the, greatest defensive catchers of all time. By dWAR (obviously one statistic out of many), Pudge out-produced Johnny Bench's whole career with his time in Texas alone. In fact, Rodriguez is the all-time leader in dWAR among catchers and tied for eighth all-time among all position players. Rodriguez was infamous for throwing out runners, and he almost single-handedly killed off the running game of the opposition throughout his time with the franchise. Rodriguez led the league in caught stealing percentage nine times in his career, and seven of those came with Texas. You'd think runners would start to learn at some point.

Pudge was also more-than-adept with the bat, as evidenced by his eight consecutive seasons with a .300+ batting average – a feat topped among catchers by only Mike Piazza's nine such consecutive seasons. When he clubbed 47 doubles in 1996, Rodriguez set an MLB record for catchers (since topped by Jonathan Lucroy's 53 doubles in 2014). He was reliable as well, setting the AL catcher record for plate appearances in a season (1996). Rodriguez was among the most respected players in the league, as evidenced by his 10 Gold Gloves and six Silver Slugger Awards during his time in Texas. He even snagged an MVP (1999). It's no surprise then that he is among the top five in most hitting categories in Rangers history and is the franchise leader in All-Star Games (10). Rodriguez was rewarded for this amazing career with a first-ballot Hall of Fame entrance in 2017.

Given the importance of catching, it is necessary to note that Jim Sundberg was also an excellent catcher for the

[132] And I'm going by after-the-season ace, not even cheating by just looking at an Opening Day starter who had a bad year.

Rangers franchise. He is sixth in franchise history in WAR (34.7), and he nearly grabbed the utility spot for the franchise. However, Sundberg's best trait, by far, was his defense behind the plate, which is more than covered by Pudge, and thus he would be a waste at the utility spot.

1B Mark Teixeira (2003-2007)

Teixeira gets the nod here in a bit of a controversial decision. By the numbers, Rafael Palmeiro would seem to be the obvious choice. He has pretty much the same year-by-year numbers as Teixeira, and he played twice as many years in Texas. Teixeira was by far the better fielder, but that was not nearly enough to make him deserve the spot on the numbers alone. In fact, despite the defensive deficiencies, Palmeiro's WAR (44.4) with Texas was still more than twice Teixeira's (21.5). The deciding factor was Palmeiro's 2005 testimonial in front of Congress.

I have said, and will say throughout this book, that I don't believe that every case of steroid use is the same. I don't believe that the cheating from the Steroid Era is all that different from the cheating throughout baseball history – players will always attempt to gain any advantage possible. But Palmeiro is a bit different. Never have I been more turned off by a player than I was by Palmeiro after he pointed to the camera and said, "I have never used steroids," only to test positive a few months later. The move practically defined audacious, and it hurt the game of baseball as much as any moment in the Steroid Era. This is partially an indictment of Palmeiro – who has maintained that he was set up and was unaware of taking whatever caused that positive test – but it is also an indictment of the impact that moment had on the rest of the league. Palmeiro's complete denial made fans unsure about good guys like Luis Gonzalez, who, as noted earlier, also denied steroid use only to have fans not fully believe him because of guys like Palmeiro. Palmeiro's testimony led to the public opinion that if someone like Palmeiro isn't afraid to lie directly into the camera *in front of Congress*, how can we trust any of these guys? Palmeiro is among the franchise leaders in many offensive categories, while Tex is not, but I just can't stand that Palmeiro gave all the baseball haters of the mid-2000s the satisfaction of showing how some players *really were* lying and cheating guys who were ruining the game. So, although Palmeiro deserves the credit of this spot, Teixeira will fill it instead.

As far as Teixeira is concerned, although he faded hard in his late Yankee years, some of his career totals are quite impressive. A powerful switch-hitter, Tex holds the record (along with Nick Swisher) for most games with home run from both sides of the plate (14). He also has more multi-home run games (42) than such luminaries as David Ortiz (41), Ralph Kiner (40), Ted Williams (37) and Stan Musial (37).

2B Ian Kinsler (2006-2013)

Kinsler is the first of a few players from the Rangers most recent era that make this roster. He was a consistent presence at the top of the Rangers lineup for eight years, with well over half of his Ranger at bats coming from the leadoff spot. He delivered a hard-to-come-by combination of power and speed from that spot atop the order. In his eight years with the team, he topped 150 home runs and steals (156 and 172, respectively) and had two 30/30 HR/SB seasons to his name. He was never one to hit for the highest average (especially for a leadoff hitter, and especially in his last few years in Texas), but his solid batting eye more than made up for it, as he sported a .349 on-base percentage in Texas. In a way, he was the actual perfect leadoff hitter, instead of the prototypical speedy singles hitter who can't draw a walk to save his life.

One knock against Kinsler when he was in Texas, was that he had some pretty interesting (and possibly incriminating) home/road splits. For his time in Texas, he was a .305 hitter at home and a .244 hitter on the road. His home run splits were not quite as intense, with 85 coming at home versus 71 on the road, but the rest of his power splits were more noticeable, with over 200 more total bases at home and an OPS nearly 200 points higher. Players play better at home for all sorts of reasons (home cooking; a good night's sleep; no travel; knowing your own ballpark better; more generous umpires), but when the splits are this big and the home park has a reputation as a stadium for hitters, the question of whether Kinsler could produce elsewhere was a fair one for his time in Texas.

Of course, the entire previous paragraph had to be in the past tense because of the trade that sent Kinsler from Texas to Detroit in the 2013 offseason. The trade saw Kinsler flipped for Prince Fielder and seemed to benefit both teams on the surface. With a closer look, however, the money that Texas had to take on for Fielder, a man that was a glorified Richie Sexson (power-hitting defensive sieve at a position filled with those types), made the trade a win for Tigers GM Dave Dombrowski. Of course, when the normally-healthy Fielder – one missed game from 2009-2013 and only 13 missed games from 2006-2014 – went down to a season-ending injury in 2014, and was then subsequently forced into early retirement because of recurring neck issues in 2016, the trade got even more lopsided.[133] This is especially true since Kinsler has been able to put to rest any questions from the previous paragraph with his success in Detroit (19.9 WAR in four seasons in Detroit), making the trade even main painful for Texas.

For his part, Kinsler didn't mind Texas getting done hard in the deal. As he put it in *ESPN the Magazine* just months after being traded from Texas: "I hope [the Texas Rangers] go 0-162." He also gave a little wave to the Rangers bench after a home run against them in June of 2014, one that was far from friendly, and Kinsler very well might decline the hypothetical

[133] Not to put that on Fielder, he is, by all accounts, one of the best men in baseball and had terrible luck with that neck injury.

invitation to join this Rangers Starting IX.

His interview as a whole made me lose a bit of respect for Kinsler, as he did anything but take the high road when discussing Jon Daniels, the Rangers president of baseball operations and GM, and the man who traded Kinsler. Kinsler said of his old boss, "Daniels is a sleazeball. He got in good with the owners and straight pushed [Nolan] Ryan out." Daniels' response was far more professional, saying of Kinsler, "He was a key member of the best teams in the history of the franchise. He's entitled to his opinion." Now this could have been the result of a poorly-timed interview, or even a reporter twisting his words, but from other Kinsler stories floating in the baseball ether, he definitely sounds like a bit of a dick. One of his biggest qualms with Daniels was that he traded Michael Young, which led to a clubhouse leadership void. Then, when Rangers management asked Kinsler to step up and become a leader, his response was classic butt-hurt, over-privileged male: "They wanted me to lead these young players,[134] teach them the way to compete, when the only thing I should be worried about is how I'm performing in the game." Now one bad interview doesn't make a man, but he certainly came across as a teammate I would not have wanted. Now you might say hey nong man, didn't you cut Palmeiro for a bad personality? Well, the Rangers need a few of their actual best players on this hypothetical list of their best players, so Kinsler stays.

3B Adrián Beltré (2011-pres.)

The Legend of Beltré has reached cult hero status in recent seasons. Let's go through some of his greatest moments:

* Multiple (multiple!) home runs from a knee
* His refusal to let anyone touch his head… and everyone subsequently trying to touch his head
* That time Elvis Andrus blew a midge out of his eye
* Beltré's infield fakeouts on pop ups to Elvis Andrus, where Beltré mimes catching the ball at the same time
* The numerous times he has gone 15-20 feet out of the baseline to avoid a tag in a rundown
* When he was ejected from a game for moving the on-deck circle. And it only made him more lovable
* Whenever he catches a runner in a pickle and just stops moving entirely
* In-dugout camera staredowns (and the subsequent smile when he breaks)
* Literally any interaction between him and his good pal Félix Hernández

And really there's so much more. He's the best Little Things player to watch in all of baseball – oh and he's a future Hall of Famer. His past seven seasons have been spent entirely with Texas, and he has been worth over 40.0 WAR, collected MVP votes in all but the most recent season (2017), won three Silver Sluggers, and won three Gold Gloves. He does it with the bat; he does it with the glove; he does it with the smile; he does it in the clubhouse. Simply put: he's one of the best the game has ever seen from a holistic experience. Thankfully for the Rangers (and really all baseball fans), it doesn't look as though Beltré is going anywhere, as the 38-year-old missed some action this most recent season but still managed an OPS+ of 135 in 94 games for Texas in 2017.

SS Alex Rodriguez (2001-2003)

A-Rod came to town via a ludicrous 10-year, $252 million deal that crushed any previous contract signed in MLB history.[135] Although it may seem inconsistent to leave Palmeiro off the all-franchise team for lying about steroid use and then put Rodriguez on despite his being guilty of the same thing, there are a few deciding factors in that decision. First, the point was already made by leaving off Palmeiro,[136] if the decisions in the book were going strictly by the same method throughout, then Rodriguez would have to be left off, but that would leave numerous great players off, along with plenty of blurred lines. Also, although Rodriguez did lie in a televised interview, it is a little different than lying under oath in front of Congress. Granted, lying is lying, and there is no evidence to the fact that A-Rod would not have covered his ass with a lie in front of Congress as well, but still, he never did lie about it while under judicial oath.

There's also the fact that Rodriguez, for all his baggage, is one of the game's all-time legends. He holds the single-season record for most home runs as a shortstop (57), as well as by a third baseman (52). It shouldn't be shocking that no other player in MLB history can stake the claim of holding the single-season home run record for two different positions. He's the only shortstop to have hit 50 home runs in a season, and he has done it twice. Along with Babe Ruth, he is the only hitter in baseball history to hit more than 40 home runs in six straight seasons (Ruth had seven).

---

[134] One of whom was Jurickson Profar, a talented young middle infielder whose presence led to the Rangers asking Kinsler to change positions (something Michael Young had done throughout his career). Kinsler refused, saying, "These kids gotta earn it; that's what I did."

[135] His *annual* salary could have paid the salaries of over 500 Dallas teachers and over 600 Dallas firefighters during the time he was in Arlington. (I know it's considered a #hotsportstake to compare player salaries to other professions and, even though the two aren't really related, in the grand societal scheme they kind of are. It's silly how much athletes are paid. It has more to do with what we as a society place emphasis on, and we shouldn't punish the players by simply lining the pockets of the owners with even more money, but still, that A-Rod salary stat above is really depressing.)

[136] I know deep down Palmeiro really regrets the fact that he lied about steroid use because now he's getting left off this random, increasingly-subjective list of the franchise's best players.

Despite all of these incredible numbers, A-Rod has fallen into the strange category of players whose personalities and off-field transgressions are so great that they eclipse the athlete's on-field abilities. Like Barry Bonds and Pete Rose in the baseball world, or O.J. Simpson and Mike Tyson in the sports world as a whole, Rodriguez may very well see his legacy not be tied to his on-field contributions, despite the incredible nature of those on-field accomplishments. Although the human nature behind these sentiments is understandable, it is frustrating to those who want to look at his legacy as a baseball player and nothing else. Granted removing the man from the numbers turns the national pastime into merely a matrix of numbers, but one has to wonder how much differently Rodriguez would be remembered today with just a few different ripples in the pond of human history. In fact, one of baseball's preeminent writers, Rany Jazayerli, tackled this exact issue in an excellent piece for *Grantland.*

Jazayerli begins his piece on A-Rod stating that Rodriguez had one of the most unique public perceptions of all time. As Rany puts it, "If it's true that 'some are born great, some achieve greatness, and some have greatness thrust upon them,' as Shakespeare wrote, then it stands to reason the same is true of villainy: Some are born villains, some achieve villainy, and some have a bull's-eye tattooed on their backs by fate. Some, however, choose the scenic route, traveling all three roads on their way to everlasting infamy. Like Alex Rodriguez."

He notes that some of the general dislike for A-Rod stemmed from factors outside his control, such as being so good at such a young age; while other factors were completely within his control, such as his vanity, nights out on the town, and dalliance with Madonna. However, the overarching theme of Jazayerli's piece is that the 1995 Collective Bargaining Agreement, in which the Players' Association pushed for players to reach free agency earlier than in the previous CBA, set his career down a path that led to a great deal of the stigma he suffered throughout his days in baseball. It is because of that CBA that A-Rod got the deal he did with the Rangers, and that he began to fill the role of baseball heel. The piece is a must-read for any baseball fan, especially one who feels strongly about Alex Rodriguez. The most interesting part is that Rodriguez had a deal in place in which he took a pay cut to play for the Red Sox right before 2004. Something tells me not only Rodriguez's reputation, but a whole chunk of baseball history would be a lot different if the Players' Association hadn't nixed that deal. The MLBPA nixed the deal because of the possible precedent it would set, allowing teams to mangle this idea and make it so that when teams performed salary dumps, they would demand the savings come from the players. It's a fair point, but it is very interesting to think about the good will A-Rod might have attained (something that mattered more to him than many others) if he had taken a pay cut and been present for the Sox breaking their 100+ year curse. It's one of baseball's great "What If's."

To bring it back to Texas specifically: A-Rod ended up playing for the Rangers for only three years, but what a three years they were. He led the league in home runs each season (totaling 156), slashed a combined .305/.395/.615 with an OPS+ of 155, and won an MVP in 2003, his final year with the team. That MVP was a bit controversial, as it came when the Rangers finished 71-91 in the cellar of the AL West. The award launched a million hot takes on the subject of whether a player should win the MVP from such a poor team. I actually agree with the sentiment that an MVP should come from a team at least competing for a playoff spot, the logic being that each win a player contributes to his team is much more valuable when those wins push the team from just outside of the playoffs to the middle of the playoff picture. Vince Gennaro, the current President of the Society of American Baseball Research, wrote a book *Diamond Dollars* in which he discussed win value and how team wins 86-90 are exponentially more valuable than wins 81-85 of an MLB season. Wins 81-85 are, in turn, exponentially more valuable than wins 76-80 because of their proximity to the tier in which playoff teams reside. So, for a Rangers team that won only 71 games, it's fair to question if Rodriguez was truly the most "valuable," at least by the "moving towards the playoffs" definition of Most Valuable. (By twisting that logic, it also makes sense not to take a player from a runaway team like the 2016 Cubs, as even if Kris Bryant hadn't been there, the team likely would have still made the playoffs, given that they won 103 games.)

One final note on the Rangers shortstop position as a whole: while A-Rod certainly deserves his place here, there are a few other names that deserve recognition. For one, Toby Harrah was one of the most underrated players of his generation. An on-base wizard with an excellent glove, Harrah was the type of player who has popped up numerous times in this book as an under-the-radar type of player – he deserves to be remembered. Elvis Andrus is also still in the midst of putting together a solid resume for the current iteration of the club. He passed Rodriguez in terms of franchise WAR this most recent season (2017), but be honest, would you rather have a decade of solid Andrus, or three years of once-in-a-lifetime Rodriguez. I'm going with the transcendent A-Rod. (This will be the decision that inevitably angers the vast majority of Rangers fans, and for that, please grant me a thousand pardons.)

LF Rusty Greer (1994-2002)

Greer played all nine of his seasons (although he played over 150 games in only two of those seasons) in Texas. His most similar player on Baseball-Reference was at one point Nick Markakis,[137] and that's a pretty solid comparison. Greer has a way more badass nickname (The Red Baron) than Markakis, but outside of that the comparison looks pretty spot-on. Both are left handed outfielders who boast strong batting averages and an ability to draw walks, along with the fact that their pop is

[137] It's now Kevin Youkilis.

more often in the form of double than a homer. Markakis will hope the second half of his career is not similar to Greer's because Greer was out of the league by age 33, and in his last three years, he was a shadow of the once-productive player he had been to start his career. This was thought to be the result of his aggressive style of play, and given the nature of his injuries, this assumption seems to be a fair one.

Greer struggled in his postseason career, gathering only four hits in 10 playoff games, but since this is supposed to be a positive write-up, we can focus instead on the fact that he finished third in the Rookie of the Year in 1994… Yeah, this isn't the Rangers strongest position. It is fun to note that Greer received an MVP vote in 1997, separating him from Nick Markakis, who Sam Miller of *ESPN* considers the best player in baseball history to have never made an All-Star Game or collect an MVP vote – Greer never made an All-Star Game, either.

CF Josh Hamilton (2008-2012; 2015)

Hamilton is one of the most interesting stories in the last 20 years of baseball history. By this point, most people know the story of his unbelievable natural talent, and his subsequent struggles with substance abuse. These troubles seemed to derail his promising career, and Hamilton was labeled a bust for a long time.

For many, Hamilton finally made the breakthrough that had long been given up on when he slashed .292/.368/.554 with an OPS+ of 131 to go along with 52 runs, 19 home runs, and 47 RBI in just 90 games with the Reds in 2007, eight full years after the Devil Rays had made him the first overall draft pick of the 1999 MLB Draft. That offseason, the Reds decided they wanted to sell high on Hamilton, shipping him to the Texas Rangers for Danny Herrera and Edinson Volquez, the Rangers top-rated prospect in 2005 and a hot commodity at the time.

Hamilton rewarded the Rangers faith in him by having a near-MVP season that first year. He led the league in RBI (130) and total bases (331), while putting on what I still believe to be the best home run derby performance at that year's event in Yankee Stadium. However, the next year Hamilton fell off the wagon briefly, and photos of him in a drunken state surfaced. For an athlete who had his career previously derailed by such demons, it was a very big story and worrisome for Hamilton and his health. After that, Hamilton enlisted the help of his strong support from the franchise, having a Rangers coach carry money for his meals when on the road and asking his friends and teammates to help keep him honest. Hamilton's faith in God was also a staple of his ability to stay clean during this time. In addition to his slip in sobriety, Hamilton missed nearly half of the 2009 campaign due to injury and saw a significant drop in his production across the board.

Once again, however, Hamilton showed his resiliency, winning the AL MVP in 2010, a season in which he led the league in batting average (.359) and slugging percentage (.633), while collecting 95 runs, 32 home runs, and 100 RBI in just 133 games. In fact, those games missed were the only argument against Hamilton's distinction as the best hitter in baseball. And although Hamilton did miss some action in his final two seasons in his first Texas go-around (2011 and 2012), he still managed to hit 68 home runs with an OPS+ of 136 over the latter two years. Eventually, Hamilton's age and injury history meant that Texas was all right letting division rival Los Angeles sign Hamilton after the 2012 season, a contract that ended up embroiled in controversy when the Angels tried to back out of it, but that's not a story for the Texas Starting IX.

Hamilton has been very open about his struggles but has seen relapses occur every couple of years. In a piece on Hamilton for *Sports Illustrated*, Tom Verducci wrote, "Somewhere down the rabbit hole, choice surrendered to addiction… one of the most pitiable baseball stories ever told." In that same piece, Verducci highlighted the incredible run Hamilton had in Texas, that included Hamilton's magical home run derby performance in Yankee Stadium, the Rangers near-World Series victory in 2011, and the fact that only Derek Jeter sold more jerseys than Hamilton during Hamilton's time in Texas. He was a beloved fan favorite, and one with whom the fans were able to offer an empathetic response when they heard the news on his 2015 relapse. Not every athlete is given that sort of empathy, but the love of the fans – and the sport of baseball – almost certainly helped Hamilton during his toughest times.

RF Juan González (1989-1999; 2002-2003)

"Juan Gone"[138] played his first 11 seasons in Texas and hit 372 of his 434 career home runs with the club. Despite being a defensive sieve, he was a valuable player for the franchise in his time with them. Due to his poor eye and his brutal defense, his WAR is suspiciously low throughout his career and probably sells a great hitter a little bit short. Another explanation of his low WAR totals is that González's main skill, power, was in abundance at the time he played. His 47 home runs in 1996 were good for only fifth *in the American League* that season, and his 128 RBI in 1999 were once again fifth in the AL. Although González is the franchise leader in home runs and RBI, he played in only two All-Star Games while in Texas. Like many before him on this list, Gonzo's career is considered tainted by the wonderfully antiquated voters for the baseball Hall of Fame. González may not be a Hall of Fame-level player (he certainly had some holes in his game), but he has been entirely written off despite having some of the most impressive offensive seasons of the 1990s, gathering two MVPs

[138] González is better known as "Igor" in his home country of Puerto Rico, where he is one of the nation's biggest and brightest benefactors. So much so that he drew comparisons to Roberto Clemente from Puerto Rican officials that Tom Verducci spoke to for an article entitled, "Puerto Rico's New Patron Saint" for *Sports Illustrated*.

along the way. This post-career judgment is almost certainly a harsh verdict for a man who cleared the fences with ease his entire career.

Let's lighten the mood for Juan Gone a bit, and slap in a quiz along the vein of something you might see on Sporcle, the always-fun quiz website. Can you name the 27 players in MLB history with at least two MVP awards? Answers are in the footnotes. Try to time yourself to do it in under five minutes:

MVPs	Name	Team(s)	Decade(s)		MVPs	Name	Team(s)	Decade(s)
7		Pirates, Giants	1990s, 2000s		2		Rangers	1990s
3		Yankees	1950s		2		Tigers	1930s, 1940s
3		Dodgers	1950s		2		Giants	1930s
3		Yankees	1930s, 1940s		2		Yankees	1960s
3		A's, Red Sox	1930s		2		Giants	1950s, 1960s
3		Yankees	1950s, 1960s		2		Reds	1970s
3		Cardinals	1940s		2		Braves	1980s
3		Rangers, Yankees	2000s		2		Tigers	1940s
3		Phillies	1980s		2		Orioles	1980s, 1990s
3		Cardinals	2000s		2		White Sox	1990s
2		Cubs	1950s		2		Reds, Orioles	1960s
2		Reds	1970s		2		Red Sox	1940s
2		Tigers	2010s		2		Brewers	1980s
2		Yankees	1920s, 1930s		2		Angels	2010s

That 1940s Tigers player is the trickiest one, right?[139]

Utility Michael Young (2000-2012)

Young played his first 13 years in Texas before being dealt away after the 2012 season. A consistent presence on the team throughout his time there, he left the franchise as its leader in games played (1,823), runs (1,085), hits (2,230), doubles (415), and triples (55) – distinctions he still holds as of the end of the 2017 season. It wasn't just in a Rangers sense that he was great: from 2001-2012, only Ichiro, Derek Jeter, and Albert Pujols totaled more hits than Young. In a time when free agency is king and players never seem to stick with one team, Young garnered an immense amount of respect in Texas for sticking with the team through thick and thin. His clubhouse mentality was the stuff of legend, and numerous teammates considered him either a brother figure or a father figure based on what age they were when they had Young as a teammate.

Young got away with a season that only a true clubhouse leader – and unofficial team captain (teammates call him The Face, as in the Face of the Franchise) – could get away with in 2012, however. He was worth -1.7 WAR and posted a negative oWAR (-0.4) as well as a negative dWAR (-2.1). Young was a player whose results never really gelled with WAR as a statistic – his career-high was 3.8 in 2006 – so the -1.7 WAR total may be a bit harsh. But considering that Young was an everyday player in one of the best lineups in baseball and he managed only 67 RBI to go along with a .312 on-base percentage, he clearly wasn't the player he used to be. Young was such an instrumental part of the clubhouse, and had been with the team for so long, that the team stuck with him as long as they could. In the end, when considering the Rangers lost the AL West by only one game and a minor league call up would have hypothetically led them to almost two more victories than Young (now who knows about the clubhouse dynamic), it is hard to blame the Rangers for parting ways with Young after the 2012 season. The drop off was even starker given that Young's 2011 campaign had been his best of his career – at least judging by the surface stats of batting average (.338) and RBI (106) – and he seemed the type of player who could have a long career and slow decline with his bat control abilities.

The utility spot is perfect for Young, who was pushed around the infield a bit by the emergence of Elvis Andrus and the signing of Adrián Beltré in his time with the Rangers. Even though Young was always at home in Texas, he was never really at home in his own infield.

SP Charlie Hough (1980-1990)

There's not a lot of pitching depth in Rangers history, so while this knuckleballer gets the call over Kenny Rogers and Fergie Jenkins, it is due more to the lack of anyone else than incredible numbers. Hough was an innings-eater for the

[139] Starting at the top of the first column and working our way down: Barry Bonds, Yogi Berra, Roy Campanella, Joe DiMaggio, Jimmie Foxx, Mickey Mantle, Stan Musial, Alex Rodriguez, Mike Schmidt, Albert Pujols, Ernie Banks, Johnny Bench, Miguel Cabrera, Lou Gehrig, Juan González, Hank Greenberg, Carl Hubbell, Roger Maris, Willie Mays (how on earth he has only two is beyond me), Joe Morgan, Dale Murphy, Hale Newhouser, Cal Ripken Jr., Frank Robinson, Frank Thomas, Ted Williams, Robin Yount. Also, yes: Barry Bonds has more than twice as many MVPs as anyone else in MLB history. Again, G.O.A.T.

Rangers in their not-so-salad days of the 1980s. He recorded at least 10 wins and at least 10 losses in nine straight years with the club, a truly impressive accomplishment of mediocrity.[140] His ERA was always good, and considering the ballpark in which he pitched, Hough could have expected a few more wins some of those seasons even though the team struggled. He did have over 30.0 WAR (the most of any Ranger pitcher) in his 11 years with the team and is the franchise leader in wins (139), games started (313), innings pitched (2,308), strikeouts (1,452) and complete games (98).

On a semi-related note: he managed to pull off one of the most impressive injuries of all time when he broke his pinky while pinky-shaking… can't make that up. Maybe it's the nature of the game, but baseball tends to lend itself really well to bizarre injuries like Hough's. Time to bust out a rather silly Starting IX and look at the most ridiculous injuries in baseball history – this will be a ranked list, not a list by position:

SP) Glenallen Hill – Cut himself on a glass table that he smashed "while dreaming he was being attacked by spiders." C) José Cardenal – Missed a game because he couldn't blink. 1B) John Smoltz – Burned himself trying to iron his shirt while the shirt was still on. 2B) Kevin Mitchell – The king of bizarre injuries, he injured himself eating a donut. 3B) Charlie Hough SS) Joel Zumaya – My kind of injury, Zumaya suffered arm inflammation after playing too much "Guitar Hero." LF) Vince Coleman – One of the most famous injuries, he missed the World Series after getting rolled up in the stadium tarp. CF) Ryan Klesko – Pulled a muscle while picking up his lunch tray. RF) Moises Alou – Tore his recovering ACL after running over his own kid with a bike.

Finally, it is interesting to note that Hough was moved from the bullpen to the rotation as the result of one of baseball's earliest sabermetric studies. Statistician Craig Wright did a study that showed the Hough would be much more successful in the rotation, and the club decided to go with the information presented. They ended up with the starter who now represents their all-franchise team – not bad.

CP John Wetteland (1997-2000)

Wetteland beats out Francisco Cordero because he was steadier as a closer. Wetteland came over to Texas after closing out the World Series for the Yankees in 1996 and posted two excellent seasons (1997-1998) and one solid one (1999) in which Wetteland somehow finished sixth in the Cy Young; maybe the voters thought it was a lifetime achievement award that year… for a career reliever with less than 300 saves at that point…

Wetteland flamed out to an early retirement, however, and was out of the game of baseball just after his 34th birthday. The only case for Cordero over Wetteland is that Cordero was able to net the Rangers Carlos Lee (for half a season) and Nelson Cruz (who combined for over 18.0 WAR in total for the Rangers) when he was traded out of town.

Starting IX Franchise Roster Stats

Lineup	Yrs	G	R	H	HR	RBI	SB	BB	SO	BA	OBP	SLG	OPS+	dWAR	WAR
Ian Kinsler	8	1066	748	1145	156	539	172	462	568	0.273	0.349	0.454	111	8.0	35.1
Alex Rodriguez	3	485	382	569	156	395	44	249	379	0.305	0.395	**0.615**	**155**	2.6	25.5
Josh Hamilton	6	697	441	814	150	531	40	240	607	0.302	0.359	0.542	134	-1.6	22.7
Juan González	**13**	1400	878	1595	**372**	**1180**	24	375	1076	0.293	0.342	0.565	133	-10.9	31.7
Mark Teixeira	5	693	426	746	153	499	11	318	555	0.283	0.368	0.533	128	0.5	21.5
Ivan Rodriguez	**13**	1507	866	1747	217	842	81	309	781	0.304	0.341	0.488	112	**20.8**	**49.9**
Adrián Beltré	7	979	563	1159	184	634	7	296	470	0.308	0.360	0.517	132	8.6	41.6
Rusty Greer	9	1027	643	1166	119	614	31	519	555	0.305	0.387	0.478	119	-7.2	22.3
Michael Young	**13**	**1823**	**1085**	**2230**	177	984	89	532	**1152**	0.301	0.347	0.444	104	-8.7	25.5
Pitchers	Yrs	W	W%	ERA	G	CG	SHO	SV	IP	SO	ERA+	WHIP	SO/9	SO/BB	WAR
Charlie Hough	11	**139**	0.531	3.68	344	**98**	11	1	**2308.0**	**1452**	111	1.282	5.7	1.50	**33.1**
John Wetteland	4	20	0.625	2.95	248	0	0	**150**	253.0	248	167	1.194	8.8	3.18	7.9

[140] Quite appropriately, Hough finished his career with 216 wins and 216 losses.

#20 Los Angeles Angels of Anaheim (2005-pres.); Anaheim Angels (1997-2004); California Angels (1965-2003); Los Angeles Angels (1961-1964)

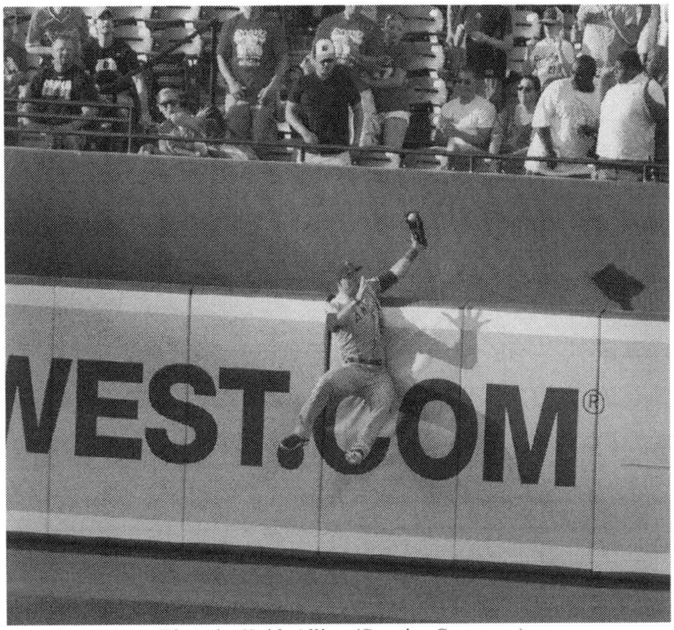

(Photo by Keith Allison/Creative Commons)

Team Background

Playoff appearances: 10 **Pennants: 1** **World Series titles: 1**
Collective team WAR: 345.5
Strengths: A lot of seriously underrated players, depth across the board, and the possible G.O.A.T.
Weaknesses: Underrated players can typically only be so great. If you're truly great – as many of the names that are going to start popping up soon are – you start to get your due eventually.
What to expect from the next 11 pages: Mike Trout. Don't worry folks, he's here.

The Angels have existed with the same nickname since their arrival in 1961, but they have gone through quite a few changes, both nominal and locational, to their host city. The team has actually been playing in the same stadium since 1966, but they have gone through a bevy of different ways to let people know that they play in the 92806. The team has managed to include the state, city, and larger metropolitan area all within their name and have currently settled for two out of the three. Maybe one day we'll see the Los Angeles Angels of Anaheim California on the sports ticker.

Regardless of their name, with Mike Trout locked in as an Angel for the foreseeable future, the team is quite relevant for fans of the game. Baseball is a sport in which one player can only be so much of a drawing card – since a batter only gets to the plate around four times in a game, starting pitchers go only once every five days, and relief pitchers have unreliable schedules – but Trout is as close to a true calling card as there is in baseball today. With that in mind, in honor of stealing good ideas from other sports writers, here are the 2017 MLB At Bat power rankings. Every year, NBA writer Zach Lowe releases his League Pass power rankings, a list which orders all 30 NBA teams by how much fun they are to watch. Teams are ranked based upon the quality of the players on the team, the quality of "characters" on the team (big boosts for someone like a Boogie Cousins or when-he-was-actually-watchable Andray Blatche), the quality of the announcers, the aesthetic of the court and uniforms, and general likeability of the team. Brief notes before we start with the MLB version. The total is out of 100 with the breakdown as such: Quality of current players – 30 points; entertainment value of current coach – 5 points; announcing crew – 20 points; stadium aesthetic – 10 points; minutiae – 5 points; crowd – 10 points; team history – 5 points; gif-ability of team – 10 points. With that in mind, here are the 2017 MLB At Bat rankings:[141]

---

[141] Yes, the Angels do come in second-to-last in the rankings. Sorry guys.

Team	Players	Coaches	Announcers	Stadium	Minutiae	Crowd/ relevance	Team history	Gif-ability	Total	Rank
Red Sox	29	4	20	8	0	14	5	9	89	1
Cubs	30	5	12	6	4	14	4	8	83	2
Giants	26	5	19	7	2	10	5	5	79	3
Royals	18	4	16	8	4	13	2	8	73	4
Rangers	25	5	13	4	4	11	2	9	73	4
Yankees	21	4	12	7	5	11	5	7	72	6
Nationals	28	2	14	4	2	12	2	7	71	7
Orioles	19	5	15	9	1	13	3	3	68	8
Dodgers	15	2	19	3	4	11	5	9	68	8
Tigers	24	2	14	6	3	9	4	5	67	10
Astros	27	3	11	7	4	7	2	6	67	10
Pirates	16	4	12	10	5	8	3	8	66	12
Marlins	22	3	10	3	5	7	1	9	60	13
Cleveland	23	4	6	5	2	8	3	6	57	14
Mariners	20	2	8	6	4	9	2	6	57	14
Mets	12	2	9	5	4	13	3	8	56	16
Rockies	17	2	7	9	4	6	1	7	53	17
Blue Jays	14	0	3	3	3	14	3	10	50	18
Brewers	11	2	18	5	4	5	1	4	50	18
Dbacks	8	2	14	5	5	6	1	7	48	20
Cardinals	9	1	8	3	2	10	4	4	41	21
Rays	13	3	13	1	1	3	1	3	38	22
A's	6	3	13	3	4	5	3	1	38	22
Phillies	4	2	10	6	3	4	3	5	37	24
Reds	3	1	13	4	2	5	3	5	36	25
White Sox	10	2	0	4	2	7	3	6	34	26
Padres	1	1	17	7	2	3	1	2	34	26
Twins	5	3	9	5	2	7	3	2	34	28
Angels	7	4	6	2	4	4	2	4	33	29
Braves	2	1	2	2	1	4	2	2	16	30

Here are some scattered thoughts on the rankings.

Player notes: It's incredible how wasted Trout is. Yes, the Brewers have more fun players than the Cardinals, come at me, BFIB. The Dodgers are the ultimate stars and scrubs (in terms of enjoyment to watch), so it's fitting that they settle in

15th. If Giancarlo Stanton can stay healthy and not get traded out of town, the Marlins have the highest ceiling among the middle ranks. I'm a little surprised the Mets ended up so low, but go ahead and look at their lineup these days. Congratulations, Padres fans. The Phillies, and their young arms in particular, have some great upside as well. The Red Sox outfield alone guarantees a top five spot. If Aaron Judge is truly our Lord and Savior, the Yankees will once again be atop these rankings soon.

Manager notes: I'm still a Scioscia believer. Congratulations, Blue Jays fans. I am not a Mike Matheny believer. Trying to decipher Joe Maddon's moves and intentions is always fun. I can't wait for the autopsy that proves Buck Showalter is actually Dumbledore. Quick, name the Padres manager. Trying to keep up with Jeff Bannister's lineup changes is awesome. Ned Yost is highly-rated for just so many reasons.

Announcer notes: Friend-of-a-friend connection to the Diamondbacks booth, so that gives them a little boost. If Vin Scully was still around, this is a runaway category for the Dodgers; they are still up there. Seattle's Dave Sims sounds like you left your podcast on 1.5 speed – slow down, man. The Mets lose a lot of points for currently employing Keith Hernandez – like a lot of points (I know a lot of folks love him, but man do I hate him). One commenter on Carson Cistulli's 2016 Broadcaster Rankings on *FanGraphs* (a good source for helping out with these rankings) said of Rangers play-by-play guy Steve Busby, "Busby's main entertainment value comes from his apparent lack of awareness of obvious double entendre. He has provided many superb sound bites since taking over in the booth, such as the time he described David Murphy's run of success in the second spot of the lineup as 'eating that number two hole up.' A favorite of his is the term 'fisted;' when L.J. Hoes fouled a ball off the handle of the bat one day, he said, incredibly, 'And Hoes got fisted.'" I participated in a SABR ranking of all 30 broadcasts a couple years back and drew the Padres and Rays – I really liked both team's broadcasts. Those two are not broadcasts you'd normally stumble upon, but they were both pleasant surprises. I still live in a world where I have refused to admit that Don Orsillo and Jerry Remy are no longer a duo, and moments like the "pizza toss" and "boob grab" happen on a yearly basis, so this rank is a bit skewed. I'm a sucker for any announcer who randomly voiced a baseball video game at some point in my childhood. How many Tiger fans out there are living the Johnny Kane Lyf? If Jim Peterson were interested in baseball instead of basketball, the Twins would be a lot higher. I can't even sarcastically say "Congratulations, White Sox fans," because I'm truly sorry for you.

Stadium notes: Hold your horses, Cubs fans. A good chunk of what makes Wrigley great is the fans. That's a different category. There are a lot of stadiums that I enjoyed in person but just don't translate that well on TV. Nothing is prettier on TV than the Roberto Clemente Bridge, though. Although the waterfalls in Kauffman are close. Congratulations, Rays fans. The Citgo sign > Monument Park, at least in this category because it is so much more visible on TV.

Minutiae notes: This category *definitely* includes little things like how the stadium grass is cut, how fun the trivia questions are during the broadcast, and the team mascots. And it is *definitely not* an excuse for me to give the Red Sox a 0 and the Yankees a 5. Ok, maybe it's some of both. But seriously, Balfour Rage in Oakland, King's Court in Seattle, and Carlos Gomez attacking swarms of flies all played roles in this category.

Crowd/relevance notes: Any team can have a great crowd when they're winning, so this category tries to balance those two. I was really tempted to give the Blue Jays the lone top spot, but Cubs fans are still having their moment, ok? The Twins/Braves avoided the bottom spot because in their heydays the fans were glorious. The Royals lost two points because of how quickly they went from lovable losers to insufferable asshats. The Yankees were docked points for their "No poor people can sit next to me" policy.

Gif-ability notes: That Angels number is entirely thanks to Mike Trout. And Albert Pujols' march towards historic milestones, I suppose. Congratulations, A's fans. The José Bautista bat flip single-handedly wins this category. And it wasn't even in 2017. That's how glorious it was. Kershaw curveballs; Corey Seager godliness; Yasiel Puig doing whatever he does, wherever he does it; the Dodgers have it all. Giancarlo Stanton + Ichiro Suzuki + old clips of José Fernández (RIP) = 9. Manny Machado is great, but other than him, who are we really gif-ing in Baltimore? Can the Pirate, Marlin, and Red Sox outfields just combine for one super (fun) team?

Final note: I am off to commit ritualized seppuku due to the fact that the Red Sox came out on top of these rankings.

Random cool things about the franchise:

- The rally monkey. Also: the fact that the idiotic "Rally Monkey" probably could have been elected mayor of Anaheim if there had been an election at the time.[142]
- The fact that the guy who thought of the idea for the rally monkey couldn't keep his job with the Angels past 2007.
- Both José and Bengie Molina played over 300 games at backstop for the Angels.
- Gene Autry (better known as the singing cowboy) was the first owner of the franchise. The franchise was later owned by the Walt Disney Company, and they are now owned by Arturo Moreno, the first Latin American owner in any of the four major sports leagues in the U.S.
- Their inaugural season winning percentage of .435 is the best ever in MLB expansion history.
- Their name fully translated is just The Angels Angels of Anaheim.
- "California Spectacular," the name of the cool rock formation in center field, is the most likely name for a yet-to-be-

[142] There actually was an election for mayor at that time, but sadly some dude named Pringle won.

released Red Hot Chili Peppers album.
- They supposedly popularized thundersticks in the U.S., which means I supposedly want to murder them.
- On the flip side, they play "Build Me Up Buttercup" during the seventh-inning stretch, so they're back to being all good with me.

Starting IX

C Bob Boone (1982-1988); Mike Napoli (2006-2010)

This matchup doesn't need a full breakdown, but it is an interesting look at the difference between offense and defense at the catcher position. As will be noted often in this book, fielding is the last facet of the game that seems to be primed for another statistical revolution. And if fielding remains a bit of a mystery, catcher fielding is the sport's *Dr. Who* – its longest running mystery. Throughout baseball history, baseball enthusiasts have posed their thoughts on the position's value. How a catcher can handle a pitching staff (Catcher, Royals – Page 89), and how he can frame a pitch (Catcher, Brewers – Page 77) are two parts of being a catcher that are just being discovered statistically, and there's plenty more work to be done.

The dichotomy of Boone and Napoli fits right into the mystery of a catcher's value. If you are on the side that thinks a catcher can influence the game more than any other position player while in the field – Boone is your man. If you think catchers just relay what the manager calls to the pitcher and rarely have to make their own decision making (meaning their offensive output is far more important) – Napoli is your man. Personally, I lean towards the Boone end of the spectrum and think that when the statistical fielding revolution takes place, catcher is going to be its George Washington, the one who comes out of the revolution looking the best.

By that logic, let's take a look at Napoli's and Boone's respective values if brought to this type of "level playing field" perspective. If you are still a bit confused about WAR, you may want to skip ahead. Also, if you are a stats major, this is not going to be up to your standards. It's for the middle class: people who love playing with baseball stats but don't mind if the process is a little less than perfect.

Basically, we're trying to find how much more value Boone would have if the current baseball metrics said that defense was as valuable as offense is. If we take Boone's dWAR totals (remember, this is a statistic measuring a player's value in the field by "wins") in comparison to the other catchers of his time, and then we bring them up to league oWAR (the offensive part of the WAR calculation) totals, we can get a better feel for his worth from this perspective.

For example, in 1982 Boone's 3.1 dWAR total was not only good enough to lead all catchers, he actually led *all* AL position players by a solid margin. The second-highest dWAR total for a catcher in 1982 was Gary Carter who posted 2.7 dWAR in the NL. Therefore, Boone's dWAR total was 15 percent higher than any other catcher, and since the highest *oWAR* for a catcher in 1982 was 6.8 (also posted by Gary Carter), if we bring the dWAR value up to oWAR's level, we have Boone worth 7.8 wins above replacement just from the defensive side (15 percent higher than Carter's league-leading 6.8 oWAR). In addition to his 1.4 oWAR in 1982, this would have him worth around 9.0 wins in 1982 alone (and yes, oWAR and dWAR are not simply added together to create WAR, but this isn't meant to be exact anyway), only 2.0 less than Napoli was worth, by standard WAR, to the Angels in his five years there. Like I said, the process isn't perfect but hopefully it's fun and you'll get the gist by the end.

If we apply this principle to the rest of Boone's time with the club, his adjusted WAR totals look as such:[143]

	1982	1983	1984	1985	1986	1987	1988
dWAR	3.1	1.8	1.5	2.4	2.6	1.7	1.5
Adjusted dWAR	7.6	2.2	3.8	5.6	2.9	2.7	1.7
oWAR	1.4	1.0	-1.5	0.4	-0.1	0.1	2.4
WAR	3.5	1.8	-0.9	1.8	1.7	1.1	3.1
Adjusted WAR	9.0	3.2	2.3	6.0	2.8	2.8	4.1

If these totals are all added up, Boone is worth 30.2 nWAR (new wins above replacement), a far greater total than Napoli's 11.1 nWAR.

Obviously, this is a flawed system for a couple reasons. First, it makes the assumption that a dominant, top-of-the-league catcher can impact a game as much from the defensive side as the offensive side, which, as discussed, may not be true. It also may be influenced too heavily by a few of Gary Carter's top offensive years which are among the best offensive years from a catcher in baseball history. It also eliminates some of the nitty-gritty of the WAR calculations, as oWAR and dWAR

[143] The exact formula to find the adjusted dWAR was: (Boone's dWAR/top catcher's dWAR) multiplied by (top catcher's oWAR). Sure, some of the fancy *FanGraphs* writers would do this in a more statistically sound manner, but the end result is so clear that this way is efficient enough, as well as slightly easier to understand. (I hope.)

are not simply added together in the regular formula. It does, however, provide a little more context as to how much value a catcher could have if defense was weighed as heavily as offense.

Those who are skeptical of how much a catcher can truly influence a game from behind the plate, take into account to Keith Woolner's tally of the 10 ways in which a catcher can influence a pitcher's performance, from *Baseball Between the Lines*:

"1) He can study the opposing batters and call for the right pitches in the right sequence.
2) He can use his glove and body to frame incoming pitches to subtly influence the umpire to call more strikes.
3) He can be attuned to what a pitcher wants to throw, or what pitches he is throwing well, and keep his pitcher comfortable.
4) He can control the tempo of the games, calling pitches quickly when a pitcher is in a groove or slowing things down by heading out to the mound for a quick meeting.
5) He can monitor a pitcher's emotional side and use leadership and psychological skills to help a pitcher maintain his focus.
6) He can be skilled at blocking balls in the dirt so that the pitcher is not afraid to throw a low pitch with runners on base.
7) He can watch for signs of fatigue and work with the manager to decide to make a pitching change before the game gets out of hand.
8) He can engage in conversation or actions to distract the batter while staying within the rules of the game. A distracted batter is less likely to get a hit.
9) He can remain aware of the game situation and call for an unexpected pitch for the situation, gaining the element of surprise.
10) He can prevent opposing base runners from stealing, either by throwing them out or keeping them from trying to steal at all."

Now, there are a couple of qualms I have with this list: there seems to be some overlap in a few of these; managers may have a bigger impact on a couple of these than is being credited; and a few other positions could stake a claim to being able to do some of these. Even with that said, what other position (non-pitcher, who goes every five days), wields that much power over the game?

As far as looking at Boone's numbers themselves: he never topped 10 home runs in a season with the Angels and his on-base percentage with the team was below .300, but his Baseball-Reference page is littered with black ink on the defensive side of things – four Gold Gloves with the Angels (seven overall); five-time leader among catchers in games caught, assists, and Total Zone Runs; three times in double plays and caught stealing percentage; two times in dWAR; and once each in putouts and caught stealing. It is because Boone was so much more dominant than Napoli at what he did well that I'm giving him the advantage here. Plus, he's got baseball flowing through his veins. He was the son of a big league ballplayer (Ray Boone) and the father to both Aaron and Bret Boone – that's a baseball family legacy right there. The Angels will have to find some bats to make up for Boone in their hypothetical lineup, but this seems like the way to go.

1B Rod Carew (1979-1985)

Let's start by saying that Rod Carew is not usually thought of as either 1) an Angel, or 2) a first baseman. Carew was most productive during his days at second base for the Minnesota Twins, and he is often remembered as such. However, in his 12 years in Minnesota, Carew posted a .393 on-base percentage; in his seven years in California, he posted a .393 on-base percentage – doesn't get closer than that. Essentially, four things changed when he moved to Anaheim:

1. He struggled much more with injuries.
2. He lost some of the limited power he previously had possessed.
3. He lost a lot of his base-stealing prowess.
4. He moved positions.

After missing no more than 20 games in a season for his final eight years in Minnesota, Carew missed that many games in five of his seven years in Cali, and the only two years he didn't miss 20 games, he missed 16 (1980) and 17 (in the strike-shortened 1981) in two of his first three seasons with the Angels. Because he was injury-prone with the Angels, most of Carew's cumulative totals with the Twins are more than double those with the Angels despite a relatively-similar slash line – .334/.393/.448 in Minnesota compared to .314/.393/.392 in California. The most notable difference is the slip in slugging. This makes sense because he was 33 years old upon his arrival in the Golden State, an age when power skills can begin to wane. Carew never topped three home runs in a season for the Angels, and he didn't even manage to drive in 60 runs in a single year. Again, part of this was due to missed games, but his best slugging percentage season in California (.437 in 1980) wasn't even as high as his slugging percentage for his cumulative time in Minnesota. This was also due in part to the change in ballpark to the less hitter-friendly Angels Stadium, but his OPS+ also dropped nearly 20 points (137 to 119) between the two franchises. Please note: that 119 OPS+ with the Angels was still quite strong.

As to be expected, Carew also saw a slip in his base running production as he aged in California – especially in regards to his stolen base frequency. In Minnesota, Carew stole 271 bases in 1,635 games, a rate of one steal every 6.03 games. In California, he stole 82 bases in 834 games, a rate of one steal every 10.17 games. He was also not nearly as efficient in his base stealing, with his stolen base success rate slipping from 69 percent with the Twins (which, honestly, already was not great) to 56 percent (downright awful) with the Angels. Despite his drop in speed, he was still well above replacement level as a player, tallying 17.3 WAR in his seven seasons with the Halos.

Carew was the best first baseman in Angels history in part because the Angels don't have a legacy of strong first basemen (even Albert Pujols hasn't been *Albert Pujols* in Anaheim). Carew still hit well in an Angel uniform, despite the injuries, giving him the advantage over the type of player who was never that good and just played there for a while. (I'm looking at you, Wally Joyner.)

Similar to his time in Minnesota, Carew had two ALCS appearances in California, but he had no World Series appearances for either club. His club was the underdog in all four series, and he lost to the Orioles in each of his first three ALCS appearances before losing to the Brewers in his final playoff appearance. Carew knew when to hang 'em up. When he retired in 1985, it was the year he topped 3,000 hits and the only year of his professional career that he didn't make the All-Star Game. He was one of the game's best hitters of all time, a man of whom fellow ballplayer Alan Barrister said, "He's the only guy I know who can go 4-for-3."

2B Bobby Grich (1977-1986)

Grich came to the Angels in 1977 from the Orioles and was already a strong defensive second baseman. Upon his arrival, Grich increased his power but saw a slip in some of his some of his other production. Similar to Carew, Grich aged in California (Carew came over two years later than Grich), but unlike Carew, Grich's improved power stroke helped make up for his other fading skills. In 1979, he became one of two second basemen in 20th century to top 30 home runs and 100 RBI in a season. Two years later, he led the league with 22 home runs in the strike-shortened 1981 season. His triple slashes were almost the antithesis of Carew's: .262/.372/.405 in Baltimore compared to .269/.370/.436 with the Angels.

The slight uptick in power was a little bit of an illusion, however, because the years he was in Baltimore were less offensive years around the league, and his OPS+ was actually three points higher with the Orioles (127 to 124). This explains why his five full seasons in Baltimore were each worth 6.0 WAR or higher, but he never reached that level again while with the Angels. Grich also played much better defense in his time in Baltimore racking up over 11.0 dWAR in his 5+ years in the Old Line State, compared to 4.9 dWAR with the Angels. Grich did, however, set a Major League record.997 fielding percentage with the Angels in 1985, breaking his own record from 1973, showing he still had some definite skill in the field.

Grich has become somewhat of a Tim-Curry-in *Rocky-Horror-Picture-Show*-like obsession for the sabermetric-minded baseball fans of recent years. Underrated in his day, Grich now has the statistical backing to show that he belongs in the discussion with not just the best second basemen of his generation but in the discussion with the best second basemen of all time. Hallofstats.com is a website that "shows us what the Hall of Fame would look like if we removed all 211 inductees and replaced them with the top 211 eligible players in history, according to a mathematical formula." It's basically Jim Turvey catnip. Barry Bonds is considered the top player of all time by Hall of Stats, so this will certainly be ignoring all controversies, etc. and simply looking at the numbers. And boy does Hall of Stats love Grich. Not only does Grich easily make the cut for the Hall (Hall Rating of 139, with 100 being the cut off), but he also got his very own article stating his case on the site. Adam Darowski wrote the piece, and, within it, he points out several pro-Grich arguments. Without stealing too much from Mr. Darowski, the most convincing points are that only four second basemen in history (8,000 plate appearance minimum) have a higher OPS+ than Grich, and they're a veritable Who's Who of legends (Rogers Hornsby, Nap Lajoie, Eddie Collins, and Joe Morgan). Darowski also points out that Grich is in the top 10 among second basemen all-time in both oWAR *and* dWAR. Considering there are 18 second basemen in the Hall of Fame, it's hard to argue he belongs on the outside looking in. Now, as has been pointed out previously and will undoubtedly be pointed out again, stats – WAR specifically – are not the be-all and end-all of baseball discussions, but when the numbers are *that* evident, it's hard to disagree. Put Bobby in the Hall.

3B Troy Glaus (1998-2004)

The first player from the Anaheim-name days to appear on this Starting IX, Glaus played for the team from 1998-2004. Glaus was a highly-touted pick for the club in 1997 and, despite an injury-plagued career, found pretty solid success. His 2000 season was his best and should have earned him more than the zero MVP votes that it garnered him. He led the league with 47 home runs, walked over 100 times, and was worth nearly 2.0 dWAR. He did strike out more than once a game, but his ability to draw a walk, and his .284 average, more than made up for it.

Glaus also played a huge role in the Angels lone championship. In the 2002 ALDS, Glaus hit three home runs in the first two games of the series against the Yankees, and he hit .318 for the series as a whole. Glaus excelled the very next series, this time against the Twins in the ALCS, hitting over .300 for the second straight series. Glaus hit only one home run, but it was a big one, giving the Angels the lead for good in Game 3 (the series having been previously tied at 1-1). The Angels wouldn't lose another game in the series. No easy feat, Glaus saved the best for last during the 2002 playoffs, and he ended up the 2002 World Series MVP as a result. Even though all three of his series home runs came in losses, his eight RBI and .467 on-base percentage were good enough to win him the award, and he became only the sixth third baseman to win the

World Series MVP award. He joined elite company in doing so, as the other five were all legends: Brooks Robinson, Pete Rose, Mike Schmidt, Ron Cey, and *clears throat* Scott Brosius… well they can't *all* be legends.

SS Jim Fregosi (1961-1971)

Fregosi came up with the club during their inaugural year (1961) and was established as the future shortstop by the time the franchise switched names (1965). With a solid bat and an excellent glove, Fregosi provided several All-Star seasons, and a couple borderline-MVP seasons, while playing for the Angels. A relatively healthy player while in California, when Fregosi was shipped out of town he fell victim to several injuries that never allowed him to play at the same level again.

Fregosi leaving the Angels is actually what he is best known for today, as the Angels traded him for a package highlighted by Nolan Ryan. Fregosi's injuries derailed a trade that was at the time thought to be an even trade. At first blush this doesn't seem possible, considering the Mets gave up *Nolan Ryan*, but when one considers that Fregosi had comparable numbers through his first eight full seasons to Derek Jeter (44.8 WAR for Fregosi to 40.7 WAR for Jeter) and Cal Ripken Jr. (50.5 WAR), along with the fact that Ryan had been worth only 3.0 WAR in his 4+ seasons with the Mets, it's possible to imagine a scenario in which the Mets don't get fleeced. Although, it's the Mets, so of course they had to get fleeced.

One final note on Fregosi: so much of how we look at numbers has changed (mostly for the better) since Fregosi's time, and Fregosi's 1967 season illustrates the point. Fregosi had a solid season in 1967, with 75 runs, nine home runs, and 56 RBI to go along with .290/.349/.395 slashes, but it was nothing spectacular. His 5.4 WAR was an All-Star level, but it was only his fourth-best season total while with the Angels. His 1.2 dWAR was, again, solid, but only his fifth-best total while with the club. However, it was 1967 in which he finished the highest in the MVP vote in his entire career, and he won his only Gold Glove. Why is this? Because he finally hit for a good batting average. Never mind that his on-base percentage was better in four other seasons with the Angels, or that he more than doubled his home run output just three years later. Many sportswriters have pointed out that the best way to win a Gold Glove is actually with your bat, and this certainly seems to be the case for Fregosi. Even though he was always a spectacular glove man, it was only in 1967 that he was rewarded with a Gold Glove. Now, this isn't entirely fair because 1967 was a special year, a year in which batting .290 was much more impressive than normal (Carl Yastrzemski was the only player to hit over .300 in the AL), and pitching dominated the game to such an extreme that the pitching mound was lowered just two seasons later. But even still, the power of the batting average as a statistic in Fregosi's era was out of control. (Of course, folks may well say the same about WAR in today's era. It's all just a little bit of history repeating.)

LF Brian Downing (1978-1990)

Downing takes a close position battle over the Angels franchise leader in almost every cumulative statistical category (Garret Anderson) in what can only be considered a victory for advanced metrics (one of many in this book, I know). On the surface, Anderson should be starting in left field for the team to which he dedicated 15 years and over 2,000 games of his life; however, the numbers tell a more complete story. First of all, Downing is no slouch in terms of dedication to the franchise, he played in over 1,600 games in 13 seasons with the Angels. A quick look at the difference between these two players shows why the edge goes to Downing, though:

* Anderson hit .296 with the Angels but had only a .327 on-base percentage due to his inability to draw walks. Downing hit .271, but his .372 on-base percentage easily trounces Anderson's mark.
* Anderson must have had put on some serious baseball repellent at the beginning of each game, as he managed to be hit by only six pitches total in his 2,013 games with the Angels. Downing was closer to Adam Sandler in *Happy Gilmore*, getting hit by 105 pitches in his time with the club.
* Anderson played in an era during which players routinely hit over 50 home runs a season and power records were being broken left and right. Downing would have fit perfectly into this time, but instead he played in the much more home run-dampening environment of the 1980s.
* Brian Downing was nicknamed "The Incredible Hulk." Garrett Anderson was not.

Anderson and Downing were similar in that neither player was a plus fielder, and although Garrett Anderson's Angels enjoyed far more playoff success,[144] this alone isn't enough to unseat Downing from this spot.

Downing is an interesting player who, according to Bill James, underwent the most incredible transformation of any ballplayer throughout his career. Not even as a player necessarily, but more so his appearance transformed such that 1992 Brian Downing wouldn't even be recognizable when standing next to 1973 Brian Downing. In the words of James: "He went from 'a boyish, Terry Kennedy-type' to 'almost a dead ringer for the actor Christopher Reeve, Superman.'"

A similar thing happened to a guy with whom I went to high school. When I graduated high school, he was probably

[144] Anderson only reached based at a .266 clip over the course of eight different playoff series, but he hit the three-run double in Game 7 of the 2002 World Series that put the Angels ahead for good.

130 pounds soaking wet and was just about the nerdiest-looking dude ever (not in a bad way, mind you). Then my sophomore year of college a buddy of mine found him in an extreme fitness magazine, and the dude was absolutely yoked. I wouldn't be surprised if he weighed twice as much as the last time I had seen him, and he was completely cut. I guess if there's a lesson to draw from this random anecdote, it's that life can be really weird.

CF Mike Trout (2011-pres.)

Trout takes the position over Jim Edmonds and Torii Hunter , two solid players who played a combined 12 seasons with the club , and honestly the decision was made after Trout had played just two seasons in the pros (Trout now has seven seasons , six full , under his belt) . Anyone who doesn't agree that Trout is already an all-time legend is talking moonshine . I'm all in on him *historically* , and although this may not seem as bold now considering his established superstar narrative (and the fact that he is already the franchise leader in WAR) , he was originally given this spot even before he deserved it . Throughout the book , young , promising players will be getting brief mentions as potential heirs to the throne but not actually given the starting spot . Now you may be wondering why in the pluperfect hell[145] I decided to go against that with Trout here , or maybe you wonder why silly putty picks shit up[146] – anyways , the reason is that Trout isn't like those other guys . In fact , he is historically elite , already among singular company with what he has done each and every season . Time for a look at some of the insanely impressive stats from Trout's rookie season :

* Trout's WAR for his rookie year (10.8) was higher than Ted Williams' WAR the year he hit .406 . It's also a full win better than any season Albert Pujols has had in his entire career .
* Those 10.8 WAR were the third-best since 2000 . In fact , only Bonds had a better WAR as a position player in this millennium .
* In 2012 , Trout became the first player *ever* to hit 30 home runs , score 125 runs , and steal 45 bases .
* He was also the first ever to hit at least .320 , with 30 home runs and 45 steals .
* Did we mention that he was a 20-year-old rookie ?
* Only Lloyd Waner , Joe Dimaggio , Vada Pinson , and Ted Williams scored more runs in modern-era rookie seasons .
* He was one steal away from joining Eric Davis[147] and Barry Bonds as only players to hit 30 homers and steal 50 bases in a season , rookie or otherwise (something tells me he would have gotten one steal in the 20 games he missed before being called up) .
* The Angels were 6-14 before calling him up ; they were 83-59 after calling him up . Guess that was a good move .
* Best age-20 season by fWAR for any player in baseball history .
* First 30/30 rookie in baseball history .
* During the course of the 2012 , he robbed four potential home runs at the wall .
* He was still in the womb when *Terminator 2* came out in theaters .
* Barry Bonds is the only player not in the Hall of Fame with a better season by fWAR than Trout's 2012 rookie campaign .
* He was rewarded with the AL Rookie of the Year , making him the youngest ever winner of that honor . (Of course , that same season Bryce Harper became the youngest overall winner of a Rookie of the Year award over in the NL .)

That's just 2012 . Trout's *rookie* campaign was clearly in rarified air , and on the strength of that one season alone he would have always been remembered by Angels fans and baseball fans alike . The sentiment around baseball after Trout's rookie season was similar to those around baseball after Fred Lynn won the MVP in his 1975 rookie season . Lynn famously said he felt like everybody thought , "What's he going to do next year , run for president ?" When the bar is set so high , the pressure only mounts to top the previous expectations set , especially at such a precocious age .

And Trout has done anything but disappoint in his time since . Let's go back to the bullet-point set up for some of his top accomplishments since that incredible freshman campaign :

* Best age-21 season by fWAR in baseball history .
* Joined Willie Mays as the only two players with multiple .320+ BA , 25+ home runs , 30+ stolen base seasons . And he did it in his first two professional seasons .
* Became the youngest player in AL history to hit for the cycle , doing so at the ripe age of 21 years and 287 days old .
* Made less than 1/50th of what Alex Rodriguez made in 2013 and was worth more than 15x as much by fWAR .
* First player in MLB history with 50 home runs and 70 steals before his 22nd birthday .
* By his third season , he had more 7.0+ WAR seasons than : Derek Jeter , Vladimir Guerrero , Reggie Jackson , Ichiro ,

---

145 It had been a while since a forced reference to *Kiss Kiss Bang Bang* [*KKBB* no. 3], so get ready.

146 … And another! [*KKBB* no. 4]

147 Eric Davis is one of baseball's hidden gems and great "What If?" questions. Look at his numbers in his prime. He was diagnosed with colon cancer in 1997, and then came back to hit 28 home runs with a 151 OPS+ in 1998. Davis and Darryl Strawberry grew up in the same part of south central L.A. and were Little League buddies. The two both had incredible career paths, and the documentary *Harvard Yard* offers a unique look at where these two men came from, and why their roots mattered so much to them.

Sammy Sosa , Tony Gwynn and Pete Rose had in their entire respective careers !
* Most fWAR through age-22 season .
* With 2014 MVP , he became the youngest unanimous MVP , the first unanimous AL MVP since 1997 , and the second player to ever win an MVP after a pair of runner up seasons .
* Most fWAR through age-23 season .
* First player in over 50 years to have three 25+ home run seasons before the age of 23 .
* In his first five seasons with the Angels , he owned the first , second , third , fourth , and sixth-best seasons for position players , by WAR , in Angels history .
* As Paul Hembekides pointed out in his "25 facts for Mike Trout's 25th birthday" article for *ESPN* , Trout had more hits homers , runs , and total bases at his age than all of the all-time leaders in each of those categories when they were 25 .

* First multiple-time league leader in walks and runs in the same season since Ted Williams .
* In 2016 , he joined Ty Cobb as only players with a .315 BA , 115 walks , 120 runs , and 30 steals in a season.
* The only players in AL history with 300 total bases , 100 walks , and 25 steals in a season ? Mike Trout (2016) and Mike Trout (2013) .
* Scored 17 percent of his team's runs in 2016 , the highest percentage since Rickey Henderson in 1985 .
* Led the league in WAR his five straight seasons , first to do so since Babe Ruth .
* Most fWAR through age-24 season .
* No Mets hitter has ever had a season with 9.0 WAR ; Trout has four such seasons .
* Already has more career WAR than Enos Slaughter , George Sisler , and innumerable other Hall of Famers .
* Trout through age 25 season : .306/.410/.566 ; Mantle through age 25 season : .316/.427/.574 .

(That last section came from an *Effectively Wild* episode in which Ben and Sam drafted Trout facts from the Angels media guide , with the last three coming from Sam Miller himself on Twitter @SamMillerBB .)

Trout has spent his first six seasons shattering century-old records and establishing himself on the Mount Rushmore of current athletes . The current mountain : NBA – LeBron James ; NFL – Tom Brady ; Wild Card – Jordan Spieth . One interesting thing about Trout's emergence as the best player in baseball is the question of whether he can become "The Face of Baseball ." When I chose the Mount Rushmore of athletes , I included Trout, but in all honesty , the most recognizable baseball players today are the stars of the past : Derek Jeter , David Ortiz , Barry Bonds , and maybe most famously , Babe Ruth . When the highest Q score in your sport played almost a century ago , you might have an issue . Numerous baseball writers have written about whether Trout can take up the mantle from those players to be the face of the sport .

The answer , in all likelihood , is no .

Baseball today has changed immensely . Selig's reign as commissioner leveled baseball's playing field such that one team making the World Series six times in eight years , as the Yankees did in 1996-2003 , is no longer reasonable . That stretch of dominance , especially in a market as big as New York , carved the faces of Jeter and Mariano Rivera onto the sports landscape's Rushmore . But that's unlikely to happen again .

Baseball is trending more and more towards viewership on local broadcasts and away from national broadcasts . More folks are watching their home team , and as such , the Nick Markakis types are likely far better known within their own market , but the Mike Trout types are less well known within the national market . (Please note : this section was written before Aaron Judge emerged as the very-possible Face of Baseball in 2017 , but I'd like to see the sustainability of Judge before completely changing my tack in regards to the sentiment expressed in the last three paragraphs .)

This isn't necessarily a bad thing , just look at how much teams are benefiting from the boost in local ratings . Sure , it may be harder for the sport's stars to be recognized on a national stage , but those things come in waves . Baseball should embrace its connection with the local fans , as this connection can be truly unique . The NFL has homogenized its fanbase with its emphasis on fantasy football and NFL RedZone ; the NBA is a sport that thrives on stars ; what does NHL stand for , again ?[148] Baseball can have its niche as the "local market sport" and still do plenty well for itself . Plus , given that Trout is a man so ~~boring~~ lowkey that his favorite non-baseball activity is following the weather , maybe it's for the best the sport doesn't feel the need to shove Trout down our throats these days .

P . S . If you understood the punctuation gag throughout this write-up , this book is truly for you .

RF Tim Salmon (1992-2006)

Not to be too biased, but it is with great sadness that I have to put Tim Salmon here. Nothing against Salmon at all; in fact, with him in right field and Trout in center, if I were a better writer I would even be able to think of some awesome aquatic-themed joke.[149] The reason I'm sad, however, is because I'd love to be able to put one of my absolute favorite players

---

[148] The NHL is the whipping boy of professional sports leagues, but I actually enjoy the regular season and thoroughly enjoy the playoffs.

[149] "Let's take a little ride. Trout… Am I right? Sturgeon… I don't think so, pal. Salmon… Oh, I'm going to say that again, salmon. Who thought that was a

of all time here – Vladimir Guerrero. Instead, thanks to Olympic Stadium, by the time Guerrero made it to Anaheim his knees were absolutely shot, and he just wasn't the same electrifying player he was when he came into the majors. His career is a definite "What If" candidate, as we touched on briefly before (Right Field, Nationals – Page 72).

Salmon was no slouch, though, as he played all 14 of his MLB seasons with the Angels and, along with Garret Anderson, is the only player in franchise history to play for the team during three different name iterations: California Angels, Anaheim Angels, and Los Angeles Angels of Anaheim. Salmon finished his career with 299 home runs, over 2,000 RuBIns (runs + RBI), and took home the Rookie of the Year award in 1993. He also got a ring with the team in 2002.

Utility Chone Figgins (2002-2009)

Figgins beats out Darin Erstad and a few other possible candidates despite the fact that Erstad totaled more WAR with the team and produced slightly better numbers (especially in the postseason), for one big reason: Figgins fits utility role far better. Throughout the book this utility spot has been used for several different purposes. Figgins fills the utility spot in the actual-utility-player-on-a-baseball-team role. This may seem obvious, but this spot has also been used for roles such as DH, or me subjectively wanting to make note of a certain player. This classic utility role of the "everything guy," or "the glue guy," is one Figgins embodied throughout his career. While with the Angels, Figgins played third base, second base, center field, left field, right field, and shortstop, and he netted the team over 3.0 wins with his glove and positional value.

Figgins had plus speed, even for the prototypical speed/utility type, collecting 280 steals in his time with the club and leading the league with 62 steals in 2005. Unlike many speed/utility guys, Figgins also had a good batting eye, allowing him to post a solid .363 on-base percentage for his time with the Angels. He even led the league in walks in 2009 with 101. Despite the team's success while he was there, Figgins never really had a great playoff series, and his career .172 playoff batting average speaks to that.

As a final note: Chone's name, pronounced "Shawn,"[150] is definitely worth a spot in the "Most Commonly Misspelled Name Team" Starting IX. This one is by position.

C) Mike Scioscia 1B) Jimmie Foxx 2B) Rogers Hornsby 3B) Chone Figgins SS) Jhonny Peralta – Captain. LF) Carl Yastrzemski CF) Maximilian Carnarius RF) Gavvy Cravath Utility) Torii Hunter SP) Bert Blyleven CP) Andy Pettitte (not a closer, but I wouldn't mind him closing out a game for me).

SP ~~Chuck Finley~~ Nolan Ryan (1972-1979)

This was originally going to be a write-up about Chuck Finley, and although it may have been a controversial decision to start Finley over Nolan Ryan, I felt confident in the decision. I was going to point out that although Finley didn't own the prettiest ERA – his biggest two rivals for the spot, Frank Tanana and Ryan, had better ERAs with relatively comparable Angel careers – that was due to the era in which all three pitched more than anything else. I was going to compare each pitcher's ERA+, with Finley and Tanana (ERA+ of 118 each) slightly ahead of Ryan (115). I was going to say that although Ryan's numbers with the club were impressive – especially the strikeouts[151] – his walk totals were too much, and if I were giving the ball to one guy to win me a game, as tempting as the possibility of a no-hitter would be with Ryan, the possibility of all those walks coming back to burn the team would seem to be even greater. I thought my point was even more relevant in these hypothetical franchise vs. franchise match-ups because all the players hitting against Ryan were going to be the best hitters in history (and Toby Hall). These would-be hitters who could work the count and would have the bat speed to catch up to Ryan's heat.

As it turns out, Nolan Ryan seems to have become so overrated that he's now underrated. This is a common phenomenon that occurs as a result of the pendulum nature of how we view players. Throughout his career, Ryan actually was overrated, thanks to his no-hitters and flame-throwing nature, in addition to the awe he inspired in the hitters he faced. Reggie Jackson, maybe the cockiest player in baseball history, said he was afraid to face Ryan. Rickey Henderson said you were nobody unless Nolan Ryan had struck you out. In Nolan Ryan's second no-hitter, Norm Cash came out for his ninth-inning at bat with a table leg to face Ryan. In high school, Ryan supposedly fractured one hitter's arm with a pitch, and then cracked the next batter's helmet. He supposedly did this on back-to-back pitches.

However, after he retired,[152] the pendulum swung the other way, and sabermetricians started tearing down the myth of Ryan. This isn't entirely fair. Ryan was pretty outstanding. Looking at how the top offensive players of 1972-1979 (Ryans' eight seasons with the Angels) fared against Ryan is perfect proof of that. When the idea for this study was conceived, I was convinced that the data would back up my belief that the best players would eat Ryan alive because they had the bat speed and batting eye to eliminate Ryan's strengths. I couldn't have been more wrong. Ryan ran a train on the top hitters in the

---

good idea, right? Bass… This guy over here knows what I'm talking about. Halibut… Thank you, good night."

[150] I will neither confirm nor deny the fact that my friends and I made tons of Chode Figgins jokes back in high school.

[151] Interestingly, it is Finley, not Ryan, who holds the MLB record for most four-strikeout innings, with three separate instances.

[152] Ryan almost retired at the age of 37, as Jonathan Hock told Slate's *Hang Up and Listen* podcast. Ryan tore his UCL in a playoff game in 1986, and James Andrews offered to do the surgery. Ryan declined because of his advanced age, instead simply giving it the offseason to heal. Defying all science, it managed to heal itself and Ryan pitched another seven seasons.

league at this time. By looking at the top 10 players over that eight-year stretch (by the offensive contributions to their *FanGraphs* WAR), it is clear that Ryan's fastball was overpowering for any MLB hitter. For reference, his .718 OPS against the top competition of his era (which you're about to see), is the equivalent of turning these top hitters into Benito Santiago (career OPS of .722, albeit in a slightly friendlier-hitting era). Check out the dominance Ryan had over the top challengers he faced in his prime:

Players	PA vs. Ryan	BA vs. Ryan	OPS vs. Ryan	Walks	Strikeouts
Reggie Jackson	81	.210	.786	18	22
Rod Carew	109	.301	.835	15	29
Ken Singleton	50	.300	.765	10	16
Jim Rice	38	.177	.616	3	16
Bobby Grich	49	.171	.637	12	9
Amos Otis	100	.216	.686	11	24
John Mayberry	110	.200	.717	23	18
Don Baylor	30	.095	.462	7	8
Fred Lynn	33	.304	.863	9	7
Mike Hargrove	52	.300	.812	12	9
Average	65.2	.227	.718	12	15.8

As a result, Finley loses his spot to Ryan, and Ryan continues his trek towards a proper rating of his talent. The pendulum is due to settle somewhere in the middle eventually. Ryan was a pitcher whose greatest strength was also his greatest weakness. Ryan tried to be unhittable every single pitch of every single game. Even down 3-0 to the league's lightest hitter, he'd be bringing his hottest heat. Given this, it's incredible that he was so durable. He was a man who faced both Roger Maris and Mark McGwire during a career that spanned 28 years (27 seasons) and four decades. Although he isn't one of the top 10 pitchers in baseball history, he shouldn't be punished for the fact that some folks think he is.

CP Troy Percival (1995-2004)

Although "K-Rod" may have famously burst onto the scene as the closer when the Angels won their lone title, Troy Percival is actually the best closer in the team's history. Even though it was Rodriguez that impressed the Angels so much that they let Percival go, if Percival were in his prime, that decision would never have been made. Percival was the team's closer for nine consecutive seasons, a remarkable feat given the common turnover at the position. He was a four-time All-Star and hit his prime at the same time as the club. His 47 saves in 51 opportunities in the 2002 regular season, and his 7-for-7 in the playoffs, certainly helped key the Angels lone World Series title.

Starting IX Franchise Roster Stats

Lineup	Yrs	G	R	H	HR	RBI	SB	BB	SO	BA	OBP	SLG	OPS+	dWAR	WAR
Mike Trout	7	925	692	1040	201	569	165	571	874	0.306	**0.410**	**0.566**	**172**	2.4	**55.2**
Rod Carew	7	834	474	968	18	282	82	405	312	0.314	0.393	0.392	119	-4.1	17.3
Tim Salmon	14	1672	986	1674	**299**	1016	48	**970**	**1360**	0.282	0.385	0.498	128	-11.6	40.5
Troy Glaus	7	827	523	748	182	515	49	470	784	0.253	0.357	0.497	120	2.4	22.5
Jim Fregosi	11	1429	691	1408	115	546	71	558	835	0.268	0.340	0.403	116	11.5	45.9
Brian Downing	13	1661	889	1588	222	846	27	866	759	0.271	0.372	0.441	126	-8.1	37.8
Bobby Grich	10	1222	601	1103	154	557	27	630	758	0.269	0.370	0.436	124	4.9	34.9
Bob Boone	7	968	286	742	39	318	11	232	248	0.245	0.297	0.323	71	**14.5**	12.1
Chone Figgins	8	936	596	1045	31	341	**280**	412	613	0.291	0.363	0.388	99	3.5	22.2
Pitchers	Yrs	W	W%	ERA	G	CG	SHO	SV	IP	SO	ERA+	WHIP	SO/9	SO/BB	WAR
Nolan Ryan	8	138	0.533	3.07	291	**156**	**40**	1	2181.1	**2416**	115	1.294	10.0	1.86	40.2
Troy Percival	10	29	0.433	2.99	**579**	0	0	**316**	586.2	680	**157**	**1.101**	**10.4**	2.69	16.9

#19 Houston Astros (1965-pres.); Houston Colt .45's (1962-1964)

(Photo from Wikimedia Commons)

Team Background

Playoff appearances: 11 **Pennants: 2** **World Series titles: 1 (!)**
Collective team WAR: 410.5
Strengths: The Killer BBBBBBBBBB'ssssss.
Weaknesses: Unfortunately, one letter of the alphabet a franchise Starting IX does not make.
What to expect from the next nine pages: The plot to an episode of *Glee*: A transphobic jock, a defensive manager, a lopsided deal, an underrated character being discovered with a magical moment, ball jokes, a cautionary tale, Hunter Pence, and a guy who performed when it mattered most. And let's be honest, the Killer B's definitely sound like a band from *Glee*.

Congratulations to a city, a group of 25 guys, a front office, and an ownership group who thoroughly deserved the championship they just won (2017). By now everyone knows the story: after nearly two decades of relevance, the Astros bottomed out in 2011 and began the rebuilding process by hiring Jeff Luhnow, the vice president of player operations for the Cardinals for nearly a decade. Needless to say, the Cardinals great success during that period helped Luhnow get the job, but so did his 25-page plan that he showed up with to the Astros interview.

The Astros drew some heat league-wide at the start of their rebuild, as many saw the early seasons of Luhnow's version of team building as too callous and/or extreme. The *tanking* strategy is one that always draws the ire of many, so there were always going to be questions as to whether "raising" these players in a losing environment might harm their long-term growth (José Altuve says hello). When this type of tanking is combined with cold, calculated numbers having so much of a say in the team's decisions, the result is often what we saw in Houston – that the *process* is under the microscope from Jump Street. Another drawback players and media pointed out was that the Astros were at one point considered a poor free agent destination thanks in part to the fact that players know that the team had no intention of winning. However, some players also stayed away because of the Astros heavy use of sabermetrics, which has been seen (fairly or not) as dehumanizing to the players. Many people thought that the team relied too heavily on numbers, seeing their players as just that: numbers, instead of human beings.

To delay the inevitable discussion of how this rebuild turned out, let's take one quick detour. We'll touch on the softer (read: more human) side of analytics in the A's team section, but the next wave of hard sabermetrics will likely be the one in which scouts and analytics can come together, and some of those big sweeping studies can be looked at in a N=1 instead of Large-N analysis. What I mean by N=1 and Large-N is being able to establish trends in *one, single player* instead of *league-wide*. Being able to notice a league-wide trend is great; being able to truly know the future outcome of your minor league players is otherworldly. Scouting revolves around N=1 analysis, because you need that *one* player that is being scouting to pan out in this specific case – there is no large sample size to go on. Russell Carleton of *Baseball Prospectus* has said, "The next big thing is understanding how each player works and, instead of strategies that can be applied across entire organizations, understanding the nuances of each player on a case-by-case basis."

Back to the chip the Stros just won: it came at a perfect time, as Luhnow and the Astros would have inevitably seen some pushback begin to happen should they have failed to reach the postseason, even for a year or two. We live in a results-based world, and even if Luhnow had a great process, the world of the fan is all about results. Of course, the fans of the Astros (and the skeptics they had around the league) now have the ultimate result, a championship for the city of Houston, a city just months removed from a devastating hurricane, a city still in the midst of rebuilding itself.

Among the sabermetric community, it is quite in vogue to shed narrative at all costs, but when a team full of top picks (Carlos Correa and George Springer no. 1 overall; Alex Bregman no. 2 overall), out-of-nowhere-superstars (José Altuve), former down-on-their-luck janitors (Evan Gattis), and a collection of others embody the young and diverse city they play for, winning a championship that was (incredibly) predicted by Sports Illustrated's Ben Reiter three years ago in the midst of a 92-loss season, it's hard to not to crack a smile, ignore all the stats and metrics that undoubtedly played a huge role in the team eventual victory, and just watch the sport of baseball with the childlike wonder it often demands.

Random cool things about the franchise:

- The Astros came into the league along with the New York Mets in 1962, just a year after the league's first expansion of the modern era. All told, baseball gained eight new teams in the `60s.
- Google the old Colt .45's logo – it's tight.
- Their retro star and stripes jerseys are also very excellent.
- The Astrodome, built in 1965 and originally called Harris County Domes Stadium, was the world's first domed stadium.
- In their third season as a franchise, pitcher Ken Johnson became the first Major League pitcher to lose a complete game no-hitter, as a pair of errors, one committed by Johnson himself, led to a 1-0 defeat.
- Houston Astro Bob Watson scored the 1,000,000th run in MLB history in 1975.
- The club gives a yearly award to the players who embodies, "a good teammate, a great friend, a fine father and a humble man," named the Darryl Kile Award. Kile was an Astros pitcher from 1991-1997 who died of a coronary disease while still active in the big leagues – the first active player to die in the regular season since Thurman Munson in 1979.
- Shea Serrano's burgeoning fandom.
- Carlos Correa's on-field, post-championship proposal.

Starting IX

C Brad Ausmus (1997-1998; 2001-2008)

Well, this will take the shine off the Astro fans' high for a minute. This is ugly. Ausmus was with the club for two different stints and spent 10 years in Houston total. Ausmus really didn't bring much outside of a good glove to the team, but he was indeed a very good defender. Of those 10 years with the Astros, for only two of them did Ausmus post a greater oWAR than dWAR (once again, oWAR simply means the offensive side of WAR, while dWAR means the defensive side of WAR). This is both impressive and embarrassing, as dWAR is usually a much lower number (Catcher, Los Angeles Angels – Page 120). In fact, in his 10 years total with Houston, Brad posted a barely-positive oWAR (0.5) but a dWAR of 11.1, good for second in Astros history. Given that Ausmus was 8.5 wins *below* average (per WAA) while with the Astros, you would think there is someone to better represent the team, but Ausmus' defense ended up being the key, and I believe that his defense and ability to handle pitching staffs is still a bit underrated by the numbers.

Ausmus was one of the smartest players in baseball when he was in the game. A Dartmouth graduate, he never had any grade below a 'B' while there. He also managed to stay around the big league circuit long enough to be third all-time in putouts among catchers. He is eighth all-time among catchers in games played and didn't hit the disabled list until his 17th season in the big leagues – not bad for a career .251 hitter.

Of course, Brad's name has come back into the headlines lately, during his run as the Detroit Tigers manager (2014-2017). This isn't too surprising considering that during Ausmus' playing days, former Astros manager Phil Garner was asked why he was playing Ausmus so frequently at catcher. "I have to keep him playing, because if he starts managing he'll be better than me," Garner said. Ausmus himself said of baseball: "I always enjoyed the cerebral part. It was much more difficult to hit – that was the part of the game I didn't really enjoy." Fitting on all levels.

1B Jeff Bagwell (1991-2005)

A lifetime Astro, Bagwell had a dominant 10-year stretch (1994-2003) in which he helped the `Stros gain relevancy. Bagwell came to the Astros via one of the most lopsided trades of all time. In 1990, the Red Sox traded Bagwell to Houston for Larry Andersen. Andersen was a middle reliever who the Red Sox were getting for only a few months, and to say his name has gone down in infamy would be putting it lightly. He threw 22.0 innings for the Red Sox and pitched very well, with an ERA of 1.23 and ERA+ of 338, but he became a cautionary tale of giving up top prospects for reliever rentals. Andersen signed with the Padres in the offseason, and Bagwell became, well, *Bagwell*. On the plus side for the Sox, at least Andersen was funny, with notable quotes such as: "Why do you drive on the parkway, and park on the driveway?" "Why do you sing 'Take Me Out to the Ball Game' when you're already there?" and "How does a fly, flying right side up, land on the ceiling upside down?"[153]

Back to Bagwell, during the previously mentioned 10-year stretch, he posted .301/.420/.574 slashes with season averages of 116 runs 37 home runs and 116 RBI. His best season was 1994, as he became the fourth unanimous MVP in the history of the award and posted an incredible line of 104 runs, 39 home runs, and 116 RBI in only 110 games (thanks to the strike-shortened season). If he had kept up this pace (always a dangerous game, I know), he would have posted 153 runs 57 home runs and 171 RBI, to go with a 213 OPS+ and 442 total bases. At that point in time, the 153 runs would have only been topped by nine players in the 20th century and would have been the best total since 1931. The 57 home runs would have been topped by only five players ever, would have been the most since Roger Maris' 61, and the most ever in the NL.[154] The 171 RBI would have been tied for seventh all-time, the best since 1938, and a number that hasn't been reached since. The 442 total bases would have been fifth all-time, only 15 shy of Babe Ruth's record, and a total not topped since. Basically, he had an incredible year, and he was robbed of a chance at one of the all-time seasons because of the stoopy, poopy strike.

Nineteen ninety-four was far from Bagwell's only good season, however. In 1997, he became the 1st first baseman to go 30/30 HR/SB[155] and in 1999 repeated that feat. He ended his career as the only first baseman to have 400 home runs and 200 stolen bases, and he has the sixth most home runs for any player who played his whole career with one franchise. In 2002, Bagwell joined Lou Gehrig as one of only two first baseman to have 12 straight seasons with an OPS+ of 130 or higher. Of course, he did it again the next year, as well. Unfortunately, Bagwell's body began to break down on him late in his career, and he was forced to retire in 2005, never getting to the "accumulating statistics" stage of his career. A glaring wrong was righted when Bagwell was righted when Bagwell was elected to the Hall of Fame in January of 2017. The fact that he had to wait as long as he did is still ridiculous, and it speaks to the voters letting their "Steroid Paranoia" (a great potential Indie Rock album name) get the best of them with regularity.

2B Craig Biggio (1988-2007)

Another one of the "Killer B's," Biggio was also a lifetime Astro. He played 20 seasons for the club and made it into the 3,000-hit club in his final season. This final season goes to show how much respect Biggio had earned with the club because Bernie from *Weekend at Bernie's* would have been worth more to the Astros than Biggio in 2007. He posted -2.1 WAR with 112 strikeouts versus 23 walks, but that 3,000th hit meant as much to the city as it did to Biggio. By achieving all 3,060 hits in Houston, he joins a group of nine other Hall of Fame (or sure-fire Hall of Fame) players with 3,000 hits who played for one franchise their whole career: Stan Musial, Carl Yastrzemski, Derek Jeter, Cal Ripken Jr., George Brett, Robin Yount, Tony Gwynn, Al Kaline, and Roberto Clemente.

Earlier in his career, Biggio was one of the best, most underrated second baseman of all time. Many people know how much of a Biggio proponent Bill James is, which is about the best guy to have in your corner. James' logic is that Biggio does many of the little things that go unnoticed (on-base percentage, getting hit by pitches, and lack of double plays grounded into) but make a great player.

There are numerous facts about Biggio that have gone unnoticed, like the fact that he is one of two players in history with 3,000 hits, 250 home runs, and 400 stolen bases (Rickey Henderson is the other). Or the fact that he became the third player in baseball history to have 3,000 hits and not make it into the Hall of Fame on the first ballot (Rafael Palmeiro and Paul Waner were the other two).

Nothing shows his value more than his 1997 season. It was Bill James' wet dream, as Biggio was hit by 34 pitches and grounded into zero double plays. I'll let James take it from there. "He was the fifth player ever to play a full season without grounding into a double play, and missed the major league record for most plate appearances without grounding into a double play by only four. The 34 HBP was the highest total in the National League in 26 years, the second-highest total of

---

[153] Of course, fans of *Stranger Things* will immediately think of the flea and the acrobat with this quote.

[154] It should be noted that Matt Williams was on pace for 63 home runs that season, and if he had broken Maris' record, Williams would have certainly stolen some votes from Bagwell in the MVP race.

[155] In case you were wondering, Brandon Phillips was the 2nd second baseman to have a 30/30 season, David Wright was the 3rd third baseman, and Jimmy Rollins is the shortest shortstop.

the twentieth century. I have always linked those two stats together, long before Biggio, as 'little stats.'" James goes on to say that Biggio is the best "little stats" player in baseball history. I'm pretty sure Bill James looks at Biggio's 1997 season that way I look at a 16-oz. sirloin served to me on Rihanna's butt. In 1997, Biggio hit "just" .309, but his OBP was .415. He was also a 77 percent career base stealer, and he was a doubles machine, fifth all-time, two more factors in his underrating. In his book *The Stark Truth*, Jayson Stark ranks Biggio the most underrated second basemen of all time and says that arguably no player followed his "ten-step plan for How to Become More Underrated" closer than Biggio. The six steps Biggio hit were: playing in the central time zone, overshadowed by other stars (team and league-wide), lack of height, asked for a pay cut, lack of playoff experience, and intangibles.

In addition to Stark's list, Biggio's career .234/.295/.323 slash line in those limited playoff appearances didn't help the matter, and if it wasn't for Biggio getting to the magical 3,000 hit plateau, he might have been destined to live under the radar of all but baseball purest enthusiasts in his post-playing days.

3B Doug Rader (1967-1975)

Well, a bit of a drop off here. Rader was by no stretch of the imagination a "Killer B," unless the "B" stands for "basically average." In his nine years with the club, he was worth just 2.6 WAA (wins above average). Never much of an on-base threat, Rader did have solid power and run-producing abilities (five seasons with 75+ RBI), as well as an above-average glove (although his five straight gold gloves flatter him). He also struck out too much and didn't draw enough walks to make up for it.

He was, however, quite an interesting man. When he went into managing after his playing career, Peter Gammons wrote an excellent profile of him for *Sports Illustrated*. For most of his career, Rader was thought of as a quirky dude who, as Gammons says, was "the zany, flaky Houston Astro third baseman who sat on a birthday cake in the clubhouse; Doug Rader, the madman in Jim Bouton's book *Ball Four* who advised kids to eat baseball cards to ingest all the information printed on them; Doug Rader, the raging tyrant-manager of the Texas Rangers who was fired after ferocious confrontations with players and writers." However, Gammons goes behind the curtain, looking at Rader's childhood in an adopted family, and although the point of emphasis in the piece in that there is much more to this man than his goofy exterior, the goofy exterior remains pretty awesome. Nowadays, I think we are far more attuned to this "revelation" that players are more than just their exterior, and we know that there is often far more to the player than how they are portrayed to us, the fans. It is because we are so aware that I don't feel bad cherry-picking the crazy stories from the article and skimming over what Gammons would think to be the meat of the story, such as how emotional Rader gets when discussing his parents, as well as his relationship with his own son.

With all that being said, here are a few gems from the Rader profile: "Rader was a much-loved clown. There was the time, for example, when he went to the movies, bought an ice cream bar, ate the paper and tossed the ice cream away. Sometimes after games, he and Astro roommate Roger Metzger would lie on their backs in the clubhouse shower and slither across the floor in what were called 'the upside-down seal races.' One evening when Astro teammate Norm Miller and his wife were coming to his house, Rader decided he wasn't in the mood to entertain, so he greeted them stark naked. His guests quickly departed. Said Rader afterward, 'That works every time.'" Then there's the fact that Rader believes he should have been a Tahitian warlord rather than a ball player. All these stories just prove that baseball's history is scattered with some of the best characters in the history of sports. Whether it's due to the day-to-day nature of the game, or the lengthy history of the game, I'm not complaining.

SS Carlos Correa (2015-pres.)

Correa was officially the last addition to any Starting IX roster in this book. For the majority of this book's existence, the Astros shortstop position was filled by Craig Reynolds, an aggressively mediocre Houston shortstop from the `80s who was worth less than a win per season in his 11 seasons in Houston. It's with no hesitation that Correa is handed this Starting IX spot.[156]

In fact, the only thing that made it take so long is that when this book was first being started, Carlos Correa was only months removed from being the first overall pick of the 2012 MLB draft. He didn't make his MLB debut until partway into the 2015 season (year three of the book; well after rosters were mostly finalized), but it didn't take long for Houston to realize they had made the right decision at the top of the 2012 draft. Correa blitzed out to a Rookie of the Year 2015 season, hitting .279 with an OPS+ of 135 in his 99 games as a rookie. He tallied 22 homers, 14 steals, and 4.1 WAR, even drawing a couple down-ballot MVP votes in his first season.

Correa took somewhat of a lateral step in his sophomore season, still producing at an All-Star level (124 OPS+, 6.0 WAR) but not quite making the leap that many had expected from the young stud. When Correa was slashing just .226./.305/.344 after the first month of the 2017 season, there was a touch of chatter as to whether Correa was merely going

[156] My only regret in cutting out the Reynolds section is that it had a great shoutout to my college friend Lauren and her devastating "K" text messages. Oh well, I guess I semi-gave a shoutout to her in this footnote anyways.

to be good instead of great. (Mind you, his natural talent never led to any true worries about his long-term prognostication. After all, this was a 22-year-old making regular starts in his third season for a World Series contender.)

However, Correa flipped the switch after that, posting an OPS over 1.000 over the course of the next 60 games before an injury once again derailed the potential *full breakout*. This time, Correa came back from injury for a strong September and finally arrived in the postseason. The incredible 2017 run from the Astros shed a bit more light on several Astros (José Altuve stealing the first round, Justin Verlander the ALCS, and George Springer the World Series), but Correa was arguably the most consistent playoff Astro, posting a slugging percentage over .500 in each of the three Houston series, en route to the franchise's first title in club history.

Correa finally got his moment when he proposed to his girlfriend after Game 7 of the World Series, a touching moment that undoubtedly endeared the lovable 23-year-old to any and all baseball fans. Correa has the reputation of being, not just a game changer on the field, but also a potential clubhouse leader for the next few decades. His jovial and bilingual nature, as well as his natural aura, have all been lauded by scouts for years now, and when Ben Lindbergh wrote a piece comparing Carlos Correa and Corey Seager (the Dodgers young stud shortstop), the scouting reviews on Correa were reminiscent of the Jeters and DiMaggios of the world: "Correa has a special leadership quality that you just don't see often," one scout said.

It takes a special player to be a 56-year-old franchise's best shortstop by the age of 23 years old, and Correa is just that kind of special player.

LF José Cruz (1975-1987)

Cruz spent the prime 13 years of his career with the Astros and was a solid hitter throughout his time with the club. He both scored and drove in over 1,000 runs in his career, but he never topped 100 runs or RBI in a single season. He did, however, hit .300 or better six times and was a constant threat on the base paths. Because of the era in which he played, one that was tough on hitters, his WAR (51.2 in Houston) and OPS+ (125 in Houston) are better than his surface numbers look. His offensive numbers were also depreciated because of his home stadium.

For his first decade in Houston, the Astrodome consistently ranked among the hardest stadiums for batters to hit in, with a batting park factor that averaged just over 92 (with 100 being average). Even after that first decade, it never even reached an average hitting stadium, per batting park factors. In 1983, Cruz lost out on the batting title by five points, with a .318 batting average for the season. This was significant because it was the closest a hitter would ever get to a batting title while playing their home games in the Astrodome.

Cruz put together quite a solid career and is third in franchise history in WAR, trailing only Bagwell and Biggio. He was also one of the best fits for his era of any player, all time. His combination of speed and ability to get on base were perfect for the mid-1970s and `80s version of baseball.

Despite the fact that this era was a popular one (most notably a favorite of Bill James), the 1980s, for whatever reason, are my least favorite era of baseball. I'm not sure if that's because: there don't seem to be any "true legends" from this time; that the aforementioned style of play isn't my favorite; that the Yankees were irrelevant; or something as immaterial as not having as many baseball cards from that time. Regardless, it ranks below just about any other decade for me. Having said that, even in the 1980s, players like Cruz made baseball great.

CF César Cedeño (1970-1981)

Another speedy Astro from the `70s, Cedeño and Cruz had very similar careers. As a matter of fact, their slash lines from their time in Houston were remarkably similar – .292/.359/.429 for Cruz and .289/.351/.454 for Cedeño. Cedeño obviously had a little bit more pop and, in fact, had more speed on the basepaths, but their WAR and WAA again show their similar impact on Houston – 26.2 WAA and 51.2 WAR for Cruz against 29.0 and 49.6 for Cedeño.

Cedeño debuted at age 19 and was a pretty great player for his first eight years. He started hot, as he had the second-highest WAR among outfielders through their respective age-22 seasons. At the end of the 1977 season, he was only 26 (one year before hitters supposedly hit their prime) and already had over 1,200 hits, well over 1,100 RuBIns,[157] and a 131 career OPS+ (reminder: this meant he was 31 percent more productive than league average as a hitter). In fact, Baseball-Reference has Carl Yastrzemski as his most similar player at age 27. Cedeño made "The Sporting News" all-decade team for the 1970s and was considered a star in the making. The Astrodome was even being called "Cesar's Palace" in his honor, and he was drawing comparisons to Willie Mays. He really tailed off after this, though, mostly due to the fact he played more than 111 games in a season only three more times in his career, and he never topped 10 home runs in a season ever again.

His career is now used as a cautionary tale, as David Schoenfield did in a 2012 article on Cedeño. The turning point in Cedeño's career, in the opinion of Schoenfield – and many of the people who saw him play – was an incident during the 1973 offseason. He was home in the Dominican Republic with his mistress, and what started as drunken tomfoolery ended with an accidental shooting of the girl and an involuntary manslaughter charge for Cedeño. The incident would be bait for

---

[157] RuBIns = runs + RBI. The term is basically my "fetch." I really want to make it a thing, but Regina George keeps shooting me down.

opposing fans[158] for years to come, and it is one of the supposed reasons for decline in Cedeño's game. For what it's worth, Cedeño said the incident never affected his play (even though he once went into the stands to confront a fan who crossed the line), instead citing injuries that slowed him down. Rob Neyer pointed out, in dispute of Schoenfield and the rest, that Cedeño continued to excel on the field throughout the 1970s as a whole, and it was instead a gruesome ankle injury in the 1980 NLCS which was the true turning point of his career. He was only 29, but he was never the same again. The numbers support Neyer's case, but as we know, correlation does not equal causation. When considering that Cedeño himself said the incident wasn't what slowed him down, and that the numbers do seem to support Neyer's theory (Cedeño tallied 26 home runs and 102 RBI in the 1974 season immediately after the incident), it's fair to assume injuries were indeed the true cause of his downfall.

The most interesting part of Cedeño's tale is that Schoenfield was using it to tamper Mike Trout-mania, a comparison Angels fans will now have nightmares about every single night, forever.

RF Hunter Pence (2007-2011)

Pence was drafted by the Astros in 2004 and made his way up to the bigs by 2007. He spent his first four and a half seasons with the team before being traded to the Phillies for a package highlighted by Jarred Cosart (now in Miami) and Jon Singleton (infamously "addicted to marijuana"). In his time with Houston, Pence was a productive player, very consistently averaging around 25 home runs, with 80 runs and RBI apiece, and a batting average just shy of .300. Never a terror, Pence was nonetheless a consistent producer on some pretty mediocre Astros teams. Pence got out of Houston right as they were truly bottoming out, and he has continued to produce consistent results throughout his career. Ironically, his statistics are about as vanilla as stats come, a complete contradiction to his personality.

Pence is one of the goofiest dudes in baseball today, and he's pretty hard to dislike. Check out any of his ESPN head shots, or his nickname (Captain Underpants) for proof. In the 2012 playoffs, his "Reverend Hunter" speeches fired up the Giants and put Pence on the map as a character all around the league.

Many players have breakout seasons *statistically* in their careers, but for Pence, 2014 was his *personality* breakout season. It started in May when Pence tweeted out that someone had stolen his scooter. Pence was famous in San Francisco for scootering around town, and he offered a bobblehead of himself on the scooter, and no questions asked, if it was returned. The story grabbed the attention of the city as a whole, and a little over a week later the scooter showed back up.

Then, midway through the season, homemade signs started popping up at opposing MLB stadiums trolling Pence.[159] Some referenced baseball tangentially: "Hunter Pence whispers sorry when he catches a fly ball," but the majority were funny for the lack of relevance to baseball. The signs blew up social media and began appearing in every single stadium Pence traveled to; it was the fans in Flushing-Meadows who truly outdid themselves, though. Of all the Hunter Pence signs, about half the truly funny ones were from Pence's trip to New York. A few of the highlights: "Hunter Pence prefers baths;" "Hunter Pence eats sub sandwiches sideways;" and "Hunter Pence eats pizza with a fork."

For his part, Pence was a great sport about the signs, even releasing a joke rap in which he played along with many of the jokes that appeared across the league. He even made a (somewhat corny) sign of his own: "Hunter Pence loves his fans." What a guy.

Pence-mania continued into the Giants 2014 postseason run, with Pence releasing poetry, leading the team in a "Do we have big balls?" chant after their divisional series win, firing up the Giants crowd WWE-style.

Pence is a throwback to another era with his bigger-than-life personality that doesn't feel forced. He's a gem, and we should cherish his time in baseball.

Utility Lance Berkman (1999-2010)

In the 10 seasons defining the decade of the 2000s, Berkman was one of the most productive players in baseball. For the decade, he had over 300 home runs and nearly (15 shy) 2,000 RuBIns. He did this while walking nearly as much as he struck out, maintaining a .300 average, and posting an on-base percentage over .400 for the decade. He was always excellent at getting on base and, as such, is the franchise leader in on-base percentage (.410). Because the decade was so hitter-friendly, and Berkman played mostly first base and outfield (two positions lower on the scale when it comes to value), his WAR isn't as great as it would seem to be given those previous numbers, but he was a perennial All-Star and often a threat in the MVP race. He is almost certainly undersold by the current iteration of WAR.

He was also a strong playoff performer for the Astros, as only once in six series did he post an on-base percentage below .400, and that was his first playoff appearance. Berkman also hit six home runs in his six playoff series as an Astro. His career on-base percentage of over .400 was fourth among active players at the time of his retirement in 2013. Never a strong fielder, the utility spot is perfect for a man who never anything special with the glove in his time with the franchise.

[158] Who had no souls, apparently.

[159] The whole thing started when Pence's girlfriend brought a sign referencing Seinfeld when the team was playing the Mets in New York. The next day there were a couple more signs with Seinfeld references, and the phenomenon caught on.

One key feature of Berkman's game at the plate was the versatility he brought on with his switch-hitting ability. His numbers are good enough to make the all-time Starting IX for switch-hitters (OPS left/right splits included, with left being first because that is the majority of any switch-hitters' at bats; league-average OPS in 2017 was .750):

C) Jorge Posada – .846/.852
1B) Eddie Murray – .860/.785
2B) Frankie Frisch – .803/.676
3B) Chipper Jones – .947/.889
SS) George Davis – Played before they tracked splits… I.e. "he's getting too old for this split"
LF) Tim Raines – .818/.791
CF) Mickey Mantle – .965/.998
RF) Lance Berkman – .995/.777
Utility) Pete Rose – .804/.735
SP) Tony Mullane – Switch-hitter when used as a hitter and actually posted over 7.0 WAR as a hitter in his career.

Interestingly, Berkman has the biggest difference between his production as a left-handed batter versus as a right-handed batter of any of the switch-hitters listed above, and one has to wonder how much of an advantage he really gained by switch-hitting when the splits were as big as Berkman's. This topic has been touched on for years, and opinions are varied.

One study by James Gentile looked at the limited number of players who switch-hit for part of their career but abandoned it because of Berkman-like struggles from one side of the plate. There are not many of these men that qualified, and there are even fewer recognizable names. J.T. Snow is the main name who made the change partway into his career, giving us a chance to see how he fared. Here's a look at his OPS by season centered around when he made the switch from trying to face lefties as a switch-hitter (from the right side) to simply facing them as his natural, left-handed self:

J.T. Snow

Season	AB	OPS vs. LHP
1992	3	.000
1993	87	.651
1994	84	.634
1995	161	.755
1996	186	.523
1997	133	.559
1998**	70	.485
SWITCH	XX	XX
1999	172	.650
2000	129	.747
2001	49	.774
2002	70	.811
2003	48	.616
2004	47	.784
2005	37	.552
2006	6	.833

** Snow made the change at the very end of the 1998 season, so his one double in three at bats as a left-handed batter against left-handed pitching was added to his 1999 total, instead of 1998.

This is far from a perfect study, considering the minuscule sample size of one player. Snow performed better after the switch, although that can't entirely be removed from the fact that he was also further into his career and improving as a hitter, as a whole. However, the bounce back from very poor results against left-handed pitchers in 1996-1998 can be seen, and along with the success Shane Victorino had in his experimental abandonment of switch-hitting, one has to wonder how beneficial it would be for some struggling switch-hitters to simply choose their strong side of the plate and stick with it.

Back to Berkman specifically, though: we're going to end on a negative note. I usually like to end on a positive note, but with Berkman it makes the most sense chronologically, plus I happen to disagree with Berkman as strongly as I disagree with anyone in this book. Lance Berkman retired in 2013, but he made plenty of headlines in 2015 when he became a vocal supporter of the city of Houston's removal of an anti-discrimination law that protected the rights of several classes of citizen, including housing and employment discrimination on account of race, age, sexual orientation and gender identity. Now if this was all, I would say I disagree with Berkman, but he has every right to vote how he votes, and it's even his right to film commercials stating so. I would disagree *vehemently*, and I would encourage athletes with the opposing view to film their own commercials (more on that in a second), but I'd let bygones be bygones and not end his write-up putting him on blast.

But then I saw this quote from Berkman:

"To me, tolerance is the virtue that's killing this country. We're tolerant of everything. You know, everything is okay, and as long as you want to do it and as long as it feels good to you then it's perfectly acceptable do it. Those are the kinds of things that lead you down a slippery slope, and you'll get in trouble in a hurry."

That's goddamn stupid.

Like beyond stupid. That's dangerous. Now Berkman backed off (a little bit) from his comments when there was a massive blowback, and he explained that he meant that this blanket tolerance he is so worried about had to do more with ideas than people, but guess what? His original comments got about 100 times more notice than his follow-up comments. And as an athlete, that's something that needs to be recognized. Sports today often act as a prism for many people in the country to start conversations about a topic they might not otherwise broach with their friends. That's why Michael Sam even being drafted was such a big deal, and it's why Mone Davis' run at the Little League World Series was one of the best moments of the past decade. Lately these types of conversations have centered more around stories in the NFL (domestic abuse, kneeling during the anthem) and NBA (Jason Collins, LeBron's stand after Trayvon), but MLB has historically done the same (Jackie Robinson, Glenn Burke). People deservedly give crap to the fact that ESPN is more powerful than CNN, and the fact that the Super Bowl is the most viewed television event, and that's fair. It is kinda effed up to think about, but the fact is: sports play a major factor in our lives. When they can sneak in a moral lesson, it's almost like Ryan crushing up some Advil in Michael Scott's apple sauce after he grills his foot in *The Office*. People go to sports (or apple sauce) for a release from the real world, so when sports can make a stand it sometimes becomes more effective because people have their guard down. Some people may hate that, but I think the arc of history has shown this phenomenon to be incredibly important. Berkman has to be more aware of that, and he needs to realize that tolerance is a virtue, and he will be on the wrong side of history if he doesn't see that. Moral grandstanding over, back to baseball.

SP Roy Oswalt (2001-2010)

Oswalt was a dominant pitcher during almost the exact same time Berkman was a dominant hitter. Oswalt pitched for the club from 2001 through half of the 2010 season and, during that stretch, posted an ERA above 4.00 only once. He never had an ERA+ below 100 during that run, meaning that, even in his worst year, he pitched better than the league-average pitcher. Oswalt had several brilliant seasons and is one of only a handful of pitchers in baseball history to finish in the top five of the Cy Young in five of his first six seasons in the majors. Even though he didn't always play on the best Astros teams, he managed to post a .636 winning percentage in his time there, and for his first eight seasons, he never posted a winning percentage below .630.

Oswalt had a knack for getting big wins in his time in Houston, and in what can only be considered the strongest praise he has ever been given, none other than Bill James called Oswalt "the best Big Game pitcher in MLB history." James put together a metric that looked at games towards the end of the season in which the team's won-loss outcome would greatly affect their standing in the playoff race, and the winner of his hypothetical-but-statistically-based crown was Mr. Roy Oswalt. As Rob Neyer put it, "Baseball writers say BIG GAMES are important ... but how many baseball writers have defined and counted big games? How many have then filled out their Hall of Fame ballots with a systematic method at hand? I'm going to take a wild guess that the answer is zero. But that's why Bill James is Bill James and everybody else isn't. You can't really blame Hall of Fame voters for not being Bill James, because Bill is *sui generis*." And Neyer is right. For all the old-school folks clamoring about Jack Morris' big game ability, not one of them have done anything to actually prove it.

Oswalt was also great at holding down the running game. He holds the post-WWII record for most consecutive innings pitched among right-handed starting pitchers without an opposing runner even *attempting* to steal a base at an absurd 217.1 innings. Interestingly enough, it's a Yankee lefty we'll see later in this book who holds the top spot on this list. With the stolen base starting to fade a bit in relevancy, this list may soon be topped by a more recent pitcher, and Yordano Ventura made it an impressive 171.2 innings to start his career without allowing a runner to even attempt a steal. But for now, the honor is all Oswalt's.

Oswalt grew up in Weir, Massachusetts and is one the biggest hunters around – baseball player or otherwise. He won the local Big Buck contest so many years in a row that his hometown had to cancel the event because it no longer held any intrigue. He used his flexible schedule that came with being a Major League Baseball player to track the biggest deer, using both old school tracking techniques – hoof prints, patience, etc. – as well as high tech equipment such as motion sensors.

He also suffered one of the most bizarre, superhero-origin-sounding injuries while in the minor leagues that he credits – in a tongue-in-cheek manner – as leading to his success in the big leagues. He calls it "The Spark Plug Story," as he supposedly was jolted the entire length of his garage when he grabbed a bare spark plug. His arm had been hurting, but, when he recovered from the shock, he told his wife, "My truck done shocked the fire out of me, and my arm don't hurt no more."

CP Billy Wagner (1995-2003)

In his prime, Wagner was one of the most dominant closers in history and is definitely at the top of most hitters' list of whom they would least like to face with the game on the line. I think it's also fair to say that, because of the speed of his fastball and movement on his slider, most civilians (as in non-professional baseball players) would have Wagner near the top of the list of scariest pitchers to face if ~~given the chance to~~ forced to face an MLB pitcher. In Rob Neyer's and Bill James' *Guide to Pitchers*, Wagner is given the fourth-best fastball of all time, the highest rank for any left-handed pitcher. Here's the real kicker, though: Wagner is actually right-handed! After breaking his right arm twice as a kid, Wagner taught himself to throw left-handed.

While Wagner very well may have gone on to a career as a Major League pitcher even as a righty, it was undoubtedly an advantage for Wagner to be a lefty coming up through the ranks. In every sport, it seems as though the left-handed "quirk" is advantageous.[160] When Wagner taught himself to be left-handed, he (probably unknowingly at the time) helped his future hopes as a professional ballplayer. Man, some guys get all the breaks...[161]

In his nine years in Houston, Wagner had only one bad season versus several dominant ones. He managed to strike out over 100 hitters in a season three times in those nine years, doing so despite never topping 86.0 innings pitched. He also had more than 14.0 strikeouts per nine innings three separate seasons in Houston and averaged more than 12.0 SO/9 for his nine seasons total. In fact, in 1997, Wagner tallied 14.4 SO/9, which set a Major League record among pitchers with at least 50.0 innings pitched. In 1998, he broke the record he had just set by tallying 14.6 SO/9. For an encore, in 1999, Wagner once more broke his own record, tallying 14.9 SO/9, a record that would stand until Éric Gagné in 2003. (And, of course, has been shattered basically each and every year in the past half-decade by the absurd group of relievers in baseball right now.)

Wagner's biggest struggle while with Houston was his pitching in the playoffs, posting an ERA over 9.00 in his four combined playoff series. The playoffs are a little unfair to relief pitchers, however, as Wagner didn't even manage to throw 5.0 innings combined in his Houston playoff run, so it was really like one bad start for a starting pitcher. Unless a pitcher has thrown as many relief innings as Mariano Rivera, playoff totals for relievers can't come close to passing the small sample size test and probably shouldn't be used to judge a pitcher.

Although Wagner is 97.0 innings short of qualifying for the all-time record for fewest hits allowed per nine innings, his career total of 6.0 hits allowed per nine innings would be far and away the all-time leader. If he were to come back and throw those 97.0 innings to qualify, even if he doubled his career total and gave up 12 hits per nine innings in those additional 97.0 innings needed to qualify, he would still be the all-time leader in fewest hits allowed per nine innings, supplanting Nolan Ryan.

For those still unsure of Wagner's dominance (and somehow either too young or too old to remember him), we'll seal his write-up by noting that he has had several cases made for him to be in the Hall of Fame by those in the media. As a reliever shy of 1,000 innings, he might not get there, but he's still in the "At least people are talking about a chance at the Hall of Fame" category of player.

Starting IX Franchise Roster Stats

Lineup	Yrs	G	R	H	HR	RBI	SB	BB	SO	BA	OBP	SLG	OPS+	dWAR	WAR
Craig Biggio	**20**	**2850**	**1844**	**3060**	291	1175	414	1160	**1753**	0.281	0.363	0.433	112	-3.9	65.1
Cesar Cedeño	12	1512	890	1659	163	778	**487**	534	735	0.289	0.351	0.454	129	-0.8	49.6
Jeff Bagwell	15	2150	1517	2314	**449**	**1529**	202	**1401**	1558	0.297	0.408	0.540	**149**	-7.9	**79.6**
Lance Berkman	12	1592	1008	1648	326	1090	82	1040	1121	0.296	**0.410**	0.549	146	-8.1	48.0
Hunter Pence	5	680	353	768	103	377	61	195	519	0.290	0.339	0.479	117	0.3	16.0
José Cruz	13	1870	871	1937	138	942	288	730	841	0.292	0.359	0.429	125	1.4	51.2
Carlos Correa	3	361	210	399	66	248	29	168	309	0.288	0.366	0.498	138	2.2	16.3
Doug Rader	9	1178	520	1060	128	600	32	402	848	0.250	0.318	0.402	104	1.2	18.3
Brad Ausmus	10	1259	415	970	41	386	51	396	629	0.246	0.318	0.327	69	11.1	4.9
Pitchers	Yrs	W	W%	ERA	G	CG	SHO	SV	IP	SO	ERA+	WHIP	SO/9	SO/BB	WAR
Roy Oswalt	10	143	0.636	3.24	303	19	7	0	1932.1	1593	133	1.196	7.4	3.57	**45.5**
Billy Wagner	9	26	0.473	2.53	464	0	0	**225**	504.1	694	171	**1.039**	**12.4**	3.63	16.0

---

[160] Although the left-handed "quirk" isn't as advantageous in real life, where one study showed left-handed people live around nine years less than right-handed people. I'm a little skeptical of that study, but there are certainly a lot of parts of life that are severely right-hand biased.
[161] I will not apologize for that joke.

#18 Seattle Mariners (1977-pres.)

(Photo by Jim Turvey/Baseball Hall of Fame)

Team Background

Playoff appearances: 4 **Pennants: 0** **World Series titles: 0**
Collective team WAR: 382.2
Strengths: Definite sleeper team among the franchise Starting IX's. Seriously, get ready for some crazy-good names coming at you.
Weaknesses: At the risk of starting to sound like a broken record: the Mariners simply lack depth in top-tier talent and in ability to keep that top-tier talent around. The franchise (and its Nintendo-wielding owners) deserve some blame, but if the franchise had existed before free agency, the roster would look a lot more stacked.
What to expect from the next 12 pages: The first Retro Game Diary. Which I think you'll either love or think is a flaming pile of turd writing. Biggest risk/reward in the book.

In their 40-year history, the Mariners have never won a World Series or even a pennant. They have four playoff appearances to their name, with the two most famous series involving the Yankees – one in a positive light, and one in a negative light. To go out of chronological order, but get the bad out of the way first, the 2001 Mariners lost a five-game ALCS to the Yankees, but what they did before the series is what has earned them a spot in history. Before the playoffs came around, the Mariners tied the MLB record for regular season wins with 116 victories. This, despite losing Randy Johnson, Ken Griffey Jr., and Alex Rodriguez over the course of the previous three seasons. The team embodied "The Ewing Theory" – Bill Simmons' name for when a team starts to perform better after *losing* a star player (be it to trade, free agency, injury, etc.). The Mariners instead embodied the team aspect of baseball, as they had eight hitters top 3.0 WAR in 2011. They were led by a career season from Bret Boone, and a sign-of-things-to-come rookie year from Ichiro Suzuki; this more than made up for their lost star power.

The other famous Mariner playoff team was the 1995 team that took on the Yankees in the ALDS. The series is considered one of the best of all time, and with good reason. The series went all five games, and there were a couple of classics. Due to the legendary nature of these games, it's a perfect time to use the classic Retro Game Diary trope.

The Mariners lost the first two games of the series in New York but captured Game 3 under Randy Johnson's dominance. Game 4 was crazy in its own right, with the Mariners breaking a 6-6 tie in the bottom of the eighth with five runs, almost to give it back in the ninth. That left a winner-take-all Game 5 in Seattle. The Retro Game Diary is an homage to Bill Simmons, who would often bust one out for an important Red Sox game. This version should make sense if you don't read it while watching the game, but it will probably make more sense if you read it while watching the game. Even if you saw the game live (but especially if you didn't), I suggest you fire up YouTube and watch along. Game 5, 1995 ALDS, New York Yankees at Seattle Mariners (YouTube time listed before each comment if you want to follow along):

00:07 We're off and running with a slow-mo introduction to some of the big names for each team. Man, there were some fun guys on these two teams: Griffey, Edgar, Jeter, Tino – names that bring back waves of memories of great `90s baseball.
01:05 I'm watching this just after the 2015 MLB postseason wrapped up, and I'm so sad there isn't any more baseball to watch for another five months.... Well, at least live baseball. This game should suffice for now.
01:25 Brent Musberger and Jim Kaat on the call. Interesting duo.
01:45 Kaat begins the broadcast by saying the Mariners will "win even if they lose" because of their strong season overall. Sure, you try telling that to the sold-out Kingdome crowd.
02:01 Game 5 starter for Seattle, Andy Benes, with a 5.86 ERA in his 12 starts with the club in 1995 – yep we're in the mid-1990s all right.
02:50 "You talk about a 'Seattle heart attack' – just look at the middle, the heart, of the Seattle lineup." Ok Kaat, you're back in my good graces.
07:54 Benes strikes out Wade Boggs to start. That's quite the rarity, Boggs struck out just 198 times in his 601 games with the Yanks. The crowd reacts appropriately, with the first of many roars.
08:50 "Benes the Menace" sign in the bleachers. Pun grade: A-
16:35 More on this later, but man oh man did Ken Griffey Jr. have a gorgeous swing. That being said, both pitchers look good early, as they trade a pair of one-two-three frames in the first inning.
23:30 Edgar Martínez is soooo severely underrated historically. His ovation his first time up is by far the loudest of any of the Mariners, even topping Griffey. In all fairness, Martínez was the Game 4 hero with a grand slam that swung the game, but he was a near-God in Seattle for a decade-plus.
24:06 Damn, David Cone's slider/curve is fillllllthy. Looks like a wiffle ball on steroids.
32:11 Kaat with a pretty cool analogy for Cone's slider, comparing his spin to the late-breaking spin that professional bowlers put on their balls that cut into the middle of the lane at the last second. Would be interesting to get the Statcast spin rate for Cone's breaking ball and see if it was as good as it appears.
33:12 Oh, would you look at that – 20-year-old Alex Rodriguez on the Mariners bench. Isn't that quaint?
37:25 Three big strikeouts from Cone, after Dos Martinez (Edgar and Tino) started the inning with back-to-back singles. We're now headed to the third, and it's still Scoreless in Seattle.
40:57 Maybe it speaks to Musberger and Kaat's collective intelligence, but they haven't really said anything lampoon-worthy yet, at least in terms of "what we know about baseball today." In fact, they've been really impressive with good stats and analysis. (Unlike John Smoltz in the 2017 World Series. Have we somehow gone backwards with our announcers over the last 20 years?)
52:28 "And with all these great players, it's Joey Cora who hits the first home run." Brent Musberger, OG Roast Master.
Mariners 1 Yankees 0 Bottom Three
53:25 Cool to note that the Mariners only got to this game because of an incredible last six weeks of baseball, centered around the slogan "Refuse to Lose," which many people attribute with saving baseball in Seattle.[162] As of August 23, the Mariners were 11 ½ games behind the California Angels in the AL West, and the sport as a whole was on the precipice in the nation's Pacific Northwest. Flash-forward to the current game, and just listen to the crowd now.
56:38 Paul O'Neil absolutely turns on an inside fastball with a man on first, and just like that the crowd at the Kingdome now sounds like the audience at a Yo-Yo Ma concert in Royal Albert Hall. **Yankees 2 Mariners 1 Top Four**
59:49 "No team in the major leagues can boast they have the best pitcher in the league, Randy Johnson, the best hitter in the league, Edgar Martínez, and – when healthy – the best all-around hitter in the league [Griffey]... They have all three right here in Seattle." Remind me again how the Mariners never won a title.
1:05:18 This game is heating up as the Mariners come right back to tie it up. Jay Buhner, who by outside appearances looks to be an A+ level redneck, drives in Martinez to tie it up. **Yankees 2 Mariners 2 Bottom Four**
1:06:58 Fun little aside: when I was little I used to listen to John Sterling and Michael Kay calling Yankee games every night on the radio. Tino Martinez joined the Yankees in 1996, and whenever he did something important, Sterling would say "Constantino Martinez!" because that is Tino's full name. However, being a naïve pre-teen, I always assumed he was saying "Constant Tino Martinez" because of how he constantly came up with big hits. That's how clutch the dude was.
1:33:49 "The Captain" before "*The Captain*," Yankee first baseman Don Mattingly comes through with a one-out, two-run

[162] And Zack Kram notes was part of the inspiration for the epic "Backyard Baseball" computer game, in Kram's excellent piece for *The Ringer* "How 'Backyard Baseball' Became a Cult Classic."

ground-rule double, a big moment in what would be Mattingly's only playoff series of his career. After an intentional walk to Dion James, the Mariners have their backs against the wall. **Yankees 4 Mariners 2 Top Six**
1:35:49 Mike Stanley now at the plate with the bases loaded and one out for the Yankees. During the 1995 season, Stanley was 9-for-11 with a pair of grand slams when batting with the bases loaded. You think Mariners fans are a bit nervous?
1:42:42 Benes goes 3-2 to both hitters, but he escapes the bases-loaded jam without any further damage, thanks to a pop up and a flyout. Every Mariner fan loses only one year off the end of their life instead of two or three.
2:01:26 The whoosh noise to introduce the past showdowns between Norm Charlton and Paul O'Neill reeks of PowerPoint presentations of my youth – and I love it. Benes is finally out for the Mariners after 6.2 innings pitched.
2:09:46 Best moustaches in baseball history Starting IX:
P) Rollie Fingers C) King Kelly 1B) Keith Hernandez 2B) Danny Espinosa SS) Johnnie LeMaster 3B) Gary Gaetti LF) 1984 George Foster CF) Jim O'Rourke RF) Frenchy Bordagaray Dead Last) Scott Spiezio
2:11:40 Mattingly at the plate: "Which will it be? Donny Baseball... or Donny Strikeout… or neither." You can do better than that Musburger.
2:15:43 Broadcast just showed this stat: the Mariners had beaten the Yankees five times in the final inning of games in 1995 before Game 5! Maybe it's the Yankee fans who should be a bit nervous.
2:16:00 Randy Johnson warming in the bullpen… Showalter and Pinella going head-to-head in a playoff chess match… The crowd goes electric… My baseball boner is getting huge here in the bottom of the eighth.
2:18:16 Griffey sends a ball nearly into orbit, just absolutely smashing a high fastball from Cone, and the Kingdome is rocking. **Yankees 4 Mariners 3 Bottom Eight**
2:26:38 A-Rod cameo… as a pinch-runner no less. This game is getting wacky.
2:29:40 David Cone is still in the game even after three Mariners reach to load the bases. The tying run is now on third, the go-ahead run on second, and Mariano Rivera is warming in the bullpen. Let's just say that wouldn't be the case if this were any season after 1995.
2:34:05 That's some Grady Little/Pedro Martínez ish from Buck Showalter/David Cone right there as Cone walked three of the last four batters he faced, the final one bringing in the tying run. **Yankees 4 Mariners 4 Bottom Eight**
2:36:02 Randy Johnson (on one day's rest) and Andy Pettitte warming in their respective bullpens, as Mariano Rivera enters the game for New York. "I PLAY FOR KEEPS" – Buck Showalter and Lou Piniella, October 8, 1995.
2:38:48 Rookie Mariano Rivera enters in a two-out, bases-loaded, elimination-game, crowd-loud-as-hell situation, and he gets the backwards K – because of course he does.
2:39:53 Leadoff double from Yankees' Tony Fernández. That deflated the Kingdome quicker than Controlled Demolition Inc., who *blew up* the Kingdome just 12 years later.
2:44:23 Walking a batter after he tried to lay down a sac bunt twice is about as sacrilegious as Satan tap-dancing on a nun's grave. That gets Mariners pitcher Norm Charlton out of the game, and guess who's coming in – Sir Randy of Johnson. It's go time, mo fo's. The "RAN-DY" chants rain down as soon as Pinella started his walk to the mound.
2:46:06 Kaat just informed viewers that Piniella said Johnson wouldn't pitch more than one inning in this game. Remember that for later.
2:49:42 Just trying to bunt against Johnson is like chugging 17 Coors Lights and then trying to catch a fly out of midair… But a lot scarier. Boggs never had a chance there. One out. Gahhhh, Randy Johnson was so good.
2:53:25 Johnson made that look easier than Paris Hilton after a dozen seven-and-seven's. On to the **bottom of the ninth**. We'll do inning updates now that it's getting into the land of the walk- off.
2:57:12 The shot they keep showing of "The Boss," George Steinbrenner, with his head not visible, half in the shadows of a fancy box seat is the most Steinbrenner shot of all time.
3:08:03 I don't care if you're not watching this – go to this point in the game and watch the snag from the second base umpire as we head to extra innings. That's some ump swag – so damn nonchalant. **Top of the tenth.**
3:14:42 1995 Randy Johnson – this is a promise ring: "I will never b w/ any1 but u." Onto the **bottom of the tenth**.
3:24:05 It's awesome watching these old games, but there really is no substitute for not knowing the outcome of a game. It's why sports are among the last vestiges of what still has to be seen live on television. **On to the eleventh**. "The series that won't end," Musburger.
3:25:39 Mike Stanley may have the most basic-white-guy name and face, but he has a leadoff walk against The Big Unit, soooooo…
3:27:37 You know that thing where the U.S. beat the Soviet Union in the Olympics at some sport on ice? Randy Velarde knocking in a run against The Big Unit is more of a miracle than that. **Yankees 5 Mariners 4 Top Eleven**
3:30:52 The blurred-out-mouth-when-a-player-is-swearing technology apparently didn't exist in 1995, as Jim Leyritz just tears into the home plate umpire after he gets called out on strikes.
3:34:56 Just a reminder that this was the first year the Division Series was in place, meaning that this was an entirely new phenomenon for the league. Think it went over well around baseball? On to the **bottom of the eleventh** with the Yankees leading by one. Cora then Griffey then Edgar.
3:36:22 Holy hell, Cora leadoff bunt single. If "DEEZ NUTS" existed in 1995 it would have been mandated by law for Cora to bust that puppy out upon arriving safely at first base.

3:38:18 Ken Griffey Jr. is good at baseball. First and third, nobody out, Edgar up.
3:39:58 And that's the play you all remember folks. Pandemonium in Seattle. Griffey all the way around from first on Edgar's double. Baseball is effing awesome. **Mariners 6 Yankees 5. Ballgame**
3:42:56 In the words of Ron Burgundy, "I'm not even mad. That's amazing." What a hell of a game. Good starting pitching at the beginning. Fun back-and-forth in the middle innings. Some dominant bullpen work. Extra Innings. A win probability chart that looks like Tom Cruise's mood levels during the course of a week. And finally, a walk-off win in front of a bonkers crowd. 10/10, even if you didn't re-watch it with this game diary, go re-watch it now.
3:46:00 Even as someone who was a Yankee fan right in this era, I can't help but watch every minute of this post-game coverage as the scene is just incredible. Cool to get the home broadcast of the play as well. That's a wrap.

Random cool thing about franchise:

- Just Google, "Mike Blowers Home Run Prediction." That's more than enough.

Starting IX

C Dan Wilson (1994-2005)

Dan Wilson came to the Mariners along with Bobby Ayala in exchange for Bret Boone (who they would later get back) and Erik Hanson in 1994. Wilson went on to play the final 12 years of his career in Seattle, playing on all four of the Mariner playoff teams in franchise history, but he slashed a measly .091/.129/.102 in those 30 playoff games.

Due to Wilson's long tenure with the club, his name is scattered across the top tens of the Mariners record book, and he leads the franchise all-time in dWAR (10.8). Defense (in particular his rapport with the pitching staff) is where Wilson left his mark, with any contributions from his bat coming as a pleasant surprise. His most productive stretch was from 1995-1997, which saw him worth over 5.0 dWAR, while hitting 42 combined home runs. Wilson would seem a likely candidate to give up his spot in the franchise's Starting IX in the future, of course that would require the Mariners to draft and develop a decent catcher, which hasn't exactly been a strength.

1B Alvin Davis (1984-1991)

On the surface, Davis seems similar to Wilson. He appears all over the top 10 of the Mariners record books, seemingly due to his longevity with the team rather than any dominant years. However, Davis actually burst onto the scene in his rookie season (1984), winning Rookie of the Year but saw his stats (while maybe not his profile, he grabbed the nickname Mr. Mariner during his tenure in Seattle) slide a bit from there. In his rookie year, Davis became one of an extremely low number of players to make the All-Star Game after beginning the year in the minor leagues. He posted a .284/.391/.497 triple slash with 80 runs, 27 home runs, and 117 RBI to go along with 5.9 WAR. However, this would be the best season of his career, as his declining defensive ability and god awful 1991 season brought an end to his days with Seattle after just eight seasons. Davis is not alone in his role as a cautionary tale for setting high expectations. We already saw the vast number of Rookie of the Year winners who had varying degrees of success (Center Field, Nationals – Page 70), and Davis himself slotted in as a role player in that breakdown. In Davis' honor let's take a look at the Starting IX of players who never quite panned out, leaving out players already discussed in Dawson's section.

C) Bill Salkeld – Interestingly enough, most catchers that have a good start to their career go on to be successful. Of all the positions, the group of busts is weakest among catchers, but the Pirates backstop of the 1940s nabs the spot thanks to a 3.7-WAR rookie season in an 8.7-WAR career.

1B) Les Fleming – One of the many players to have a war act as an interrupter to his career, Fleming was never the same after returning from WWII in 1945; and who can blame him? In fact, it is remarkable so many players did come back to have successful careers.

2B) Lou Klein – Easily one of the most fascinating stories on this team, Klein had a stellar 1942 rookie campaign for Cleveland in which he drew votes for league MVP. He went to war the next season, and when he came back found himself battling for his spot at second base. Right around this time, a wealthy Mexican customs broker named Jorge Pasqual was trying to start a rival league to MLB in Mexico. He was incredibly rich and attempted to lure MLB players to his Mexican start-up league with large salaries and, in the words of Baseball Almanac, "unique gifts." Klein was one of the over 20 major leaguers to jump ship, and when Happy Chandler came down with a ban for all the players who had joined the Mexican League, Klein didn't find his way back to MLB until 1949. At that point, Klein was not nearly the same player he had been before the war, and his career ended by 1951.

3B) Eric Hinske – Hinske won Rookie of the Year for the Blue Jays in 2002 but never produced nearly the same value over his next 11 seasons. Not to go solely by WAR, but he was worth only 0.3 more WAR in those next 11 seasons than he was worth in his rookie season alone.

SS) Billy Grabarkewitz – "Grabs" played more games at second base than shortstop but was a utility infielder throughout his career. He's also the captain of this Starting IX, having fallen off a cliff harder and faster than arguably any player in history. He hit .289 with 17 home runs and 19 steals for the Dodgers in his first full season. He never played in more than 87 games in a season the rest of his career. He hit .203 the rest of his career and totaled 11 home runs and 13 steals in 276 games. He was out of the league within five years.

LF) Mitchell Page – Page should be best known (in any real baseball fan's mind) for his cameo in *Angels in the Outfield*. As far as his work on the real-life diamond, Page managed just 2.1 WAR in the seven seasons following his 6.0-WAR 1977 rookie season for the Oakland A's.

CF) Dutch Zwilling – Another player who appeared in multiple leagues, Zwilling played in Chicago while playing in the American League, Federal League (his two most successful seasons), and National League. His "decline" had more to do with appearing in different leagues at different times, but he still has one of the stranger Baseball-Reference pages. His last name is also the *last name* listed in baseball history – the anti-Hank Aaron, quite appropriately.

RF) Rich Coggins – Pretty straightforward case of a letdown.

SP) Mark Fidrych – There were innumerable choices for starting pitchers that fell into this category (especially in the early days of baseball) thanks to the complete ambivalence given to taking care of pitcher arms throughout much of baseball history, but Fidrych was unique in the era he fell apart, as well as the scale of his downfall. "The Bird" became a national icon during his rookie 1976 season for the Detroit Tigers but suffered an injury while goofing around in the outfield during spring training that played a large role in his lost career. It's a shame too, because Fidrych was truly a one-of-a-kind personality who would talk to the ball, himself, the mound, and really anything in sight, all while helping league-wide attendance in a way not seen since Sandy Koufax and Satchel Paige.

RP) John Rocker – Never have I been happier that a player was a flash in the pan than in the case of Rocker. For those who don't know about Rocker, he is worth a Wikipedia deep dive, but only if you're in the mood to get angry at life.

Finishing up with a final note on Davis: he was the first player elected to the Mariners Hall of Fame, doing so in 1997, and he is far more beloved in Seattle than many outsiders might realize (and some might assume based on his stats). With Davis, I was able to learn this from both written sources as well as friends and family who have Seattle connections. My one worry with this book is that many teams will have an Alvin Davis-type who will end up being the bee in their bonnet when he doesn't make the Starting IX. Another similar player will be covered at the Red Sox second base spot, and that's why I'd encourage any and all fans to give their feedback to me once their done reading the book. After all, isn't the point of sports to have something to chat about/debate?

2B Bret Boone (1992-1993; 2001-2005)

Bret Boone started his career as a Mariner in 1992 but didn't really leave his mark until his return in 2001. He had a stint with Cincinnati and dalliances with Atlanta and San Diego during his inter-Maregnum (yes, that is a made-up word). After signing as a free agent before the 2001 season, Boone got busy real quick. He had 22 home runs and 84 RBI before the All-Star break in 2001, and he eclipsed career highs in both categories just weeks later. Boone didn't slow down in the second half either, propelling the surprise Mariners with a league-leading 141 RBI for the season. For the year, he finished with 8.8 WAR, trailing only Jason Giambi and finishing behind only the Giambino and teammate Ichiro Suzuki in the MVP race. In fact, Boone's 8.8 WAR total is the only season among the top 10 in franchise position player WAR that isn't from the Big Three of Ichiro, Griffey, and A-Rod.[163]

Boone was the only Mariner hitter to perform well in the Mariners ALCS loss to the Yankees that season, hitting two of the team's five home runs, as well as being the only regular to sport an average above .300.

With solid 2002 and 2003 campaigns, Boone proved he was not a one-year fluke, and his 19.0 career WAR for the Mariners ranks him 10th all-time among position players in team history. It also doesn't hurt that he is the older brother of Yankee hero (or maybe more accurately, Red Sox villain) Aaron Boone. Everyone knows Little Boone for his walk-off homer against Tim Wakefield in the 2003 ALCS, but it was also his injury during that offseason that paved the way for Yankees to become the frontrunners – over the Red Sox – in the chase for A-Rod. A pretty excellent screw job of the Sawks in its own right. Good job by you, Aaron. Pretty soon this will be Robinson Canó's spot.

3B Adrián Beltré (2005-2009)

Beltré's time in Seattle was mostly thought of as a bust, thanks in large part to the massive contract he signed with the Mariners in 2005 after a near-MVP season with the Dodgers in 2004. However, as is so often the case, the prevailing narrative wasn't an accurate one, as, for Beltré's five seasons in Seattle, he topped 3.0 WAR each year – even topping 5.0 in a season twice. Much of that was due to Beltré's defensive prowess, but Beltré was also above average as a hitter in his 715 games in the Pacific Northwest, sporting an OPS+ of 101 and hitting over 100 home runs with the club.

Still, despite some solid numbers, his time in Seattle will be remembered more often in a negative light than positive

---

[163] Although Edgar Martínez ranks just as high as these three in terms of Mariner production, his single-season production never ranks as high because of the limits of his value (according to WAR, at least) as a designated hitter.

one. Expectations were set high after his 2004 world-destroying season, and the contract he was given showed it. Instead, he hit .266 with the team and missed over 50 games in his final season with the club.[164] Of course there's also the fact that, ever since Beltré left Seattle, he has been one of, if not the, best third basemen in the game. His OPS+ has topped 128 every season but one since, and he's averaged 5.9 WAR per season, dropping below 5.6 in a season only once. So when looking at Beltré's career as a whole, most folks point to Seattle as the low point, which although not entirely fair, also says a fair amount about the state of the hot corner in Seattle history that he still gets the spot.

Seattle fans, if they even are still bitter about Beltré, are just about the only baseball fans on the planet who don't love Beltré these days, as the Dominican third baseman has about as big a cult following as any modern player in MLB (as was covered in his Rangers write-up). He's a lock for the Hall of Fame, and he's well deserving of that honor which he will one day achieve. Of course, by the time Beltré is Hall of Fame eligible, Kyle Seager may well have taken this Starting IX spot from him, truly dampening that glorious day for Beltré…

SS Alex Rodriguez (1994-2000)

Rodriguez, before he was A-Rod, came up with the Mariners for a cup of tea in 1994, but the strike meant his rookie season would have to wait until 1995. The Mariners selected Rodriguez with the no. 1 pick of the 1993 draft, so the turnaround was quick for young Alex, who made his MLB debut at the youthful age of 18 years and 346 days old.

In 1995, in what was supposed to be his first full season, Rodriguez struggled. He wavered between Triple-A and the majors, en route to a .232/.264/.408 triple slash, showing bursts of power (see the .176 ISO[165]) but no real control of the strike zone (see the 28.2 percent strikeout rate). However, when Rodriguez broke out in 1996, it was for good. He came in second in the MVP, and if it wasn't for Safeco robbing Rodriguez (and numerous other right-handed power hitters through the years) of precious home runs and RBI (the true voter-pleasing statistics), he likely would have bested Juan González for the American League MVP in just his age-20 season. Rodriguez won the batting title (.358), led the league in total bases (379), runs (141) and doubles (54), while playing excellent defense (1.7 dWAR) at a valuable position. It's no surprise – although it is wildly impressive – that David Schoenfield of *ESPN* ranked Rodriguez's age-20 season the best season of any player under the age of *25*, all-time. All-time! Best! Schoenfield even called the decision "a pretty easy call." This was well before even A-Rod haters would suggest he was taking PEDs, which is part of the reason that the argument against these all-time greats (A-Rod, Barry Bonds, Roger Clemens) not making the Hall because of a few seasons of PED use is ridiculous. These guys were legends before they made a dumb decision (or in A-Rod's case – decisions, plural), and they deserve a spot in Cooperstown.

Back to Seattle: Rodriguez spent his first five full seasons there before moving to Texas, and he was outstanding in each one. He topped 5.0 oWAR every season, reaching 8.5 WAR or higher in three of those seasons. He reached levels of offensive production seemingly unthinkable considering the pitching-friendly confines of Safeco Field in the '90s. It's hard to remember now, but before he was A-Rod, Rodriguez was a likable a young talent, who was overlooked in the Pacific Northwest for half a decade.

LF Raul Ibañez (1996-2000; 2004-2008; 2013)

Ibañez had three different stints with the Mariners during his unique career arc. The Beatles may as well have written "The Long and Winding Road" about Ibañez's career – this is a man who finished his career with more home runs in his 40s than in his 20s.

Ibañez was drafted in the 36th round of the 1992 draft and bounced around from position to position while in the Mariners minor league system. One might have assumed Ibañez was an overtired first-year med student with all the cups of coffee he had with the Mariners major league squad, collecting six plate appearances in August, 1996, six more in August, 1997, and then 20 more after getting a September call up a few weeks later that season. In 1998, Ibañez once again had to wait until August to get a major league plate appearance, but this time he collected 103 plate appearances and slashed .255/.291/.408 for an OPS+ of just 81. Those numbers, along with the fact that he was a 26-year-old who didn't have the pedigree of other prospects, meant Ibañez had to once again start the next season in the minor leagues. In fact, in his final two seasons of his first Seattle stint (1999 and 2000), Ibañez never played in more than 92 games (and never topped 227 plate appearances), meaning that in his first stint with the club, Ibañez made just 518 plate appearances (less than a typical season) over the course of five seasons and nine years. After the 2000 season, the Mariners didn't look to re-sign Ibañez.

It took Ibañez signing with Kansas City in 2001 to establish himself as even a starter-level major leaguer. Ibañez was in K.C. for only three seasons, but in that time, he improved his OPS+ from 73 in Seattle all the way up to 112 in K.C. He established himself as a regular in the every-day lineup, taking the full-time left field position during his final season with the Royals. When his contract in K.C. was up, Seattle came a-knocking once again, despite Ibañez's lack of production

---

[164] As one of the rare players in the infield who didn't wear a cup, a bad bounce sent Beltré to the disabled list with testicular bleeding. When he came back to the lineup, Ken Griffey Jr. had the PA guy play the waltz from *The Nutcracker* for Beltré's walk up music.

[165] Slugging percentage minus batting average as a measure of raw power.

during his first Seattle stint.

This time, Ibañez took the starting job in left field and grabbed a hold of it. In this five-year stint in Seattle (his age-32 through age-37 seasons), Ibañez averaged 85 runs, 23 home runs, and 98 RBI per season with .291/.354/.477 slashes and an OPS+ of 120. In fact, his OPS+ was at least 115 each and every season and, despite some pretty laughable defense at a position where defense shouldn't be that challenging, was worth around 3.0 wins a season.

Ibañez left Seattle once again, this time after the 2008 season at the age of 37. Given his age, one wouldn't blame Mariner fans for thinking they had seen the last of an effective Raul Ibañez. However, Ibañez kept chugging on his career redemption path, making his first All-Star Game at the age of 37 in Philadelphia (2009), hitting a career-high 34 home runs and setting career highs in numerous offensive categories (slugging, OPS, OPS+). After 2009, Ibañez posted two more above-average seasons in Philly, before one solid season (at least hitting-wise) in New York.

However, Ibañez was mostly seen as a stopgap in each of those stops, and as such, he was back on the market before the 2013 season. Seattle decided to bring back RAUUUUUUUUL for much the same reasons as the teams in previous years had: a veteran player to mentor the younger players with a workout routine that had allowed him to have his best years in the second half of his career. Any offense he brought would be an added bonus.

Well, what a bonus they got.

At the ripe age of 41, Ibañez absolutely tore up the league in 2013. He hit 29 home runs (with a home run rate of 5.9 percent and an ISO of .244[166]) and continued to amaze and astound with his late-career success. There are innumerable statistics that show just how unique Ibañez's career arc was: he hit 278 of his 305 career home runs after the age of 30, the highest percent of any player in history; in terms of home runs from a player's age-30 season on, Ibañez ranks 22nd all-time, with more post-30 home runs than Frank Robinson, Harmon Killebrew Carl Yastrzemski, Manny Ramírez, Ernie Banks, Frank Thomas, Ken Griffey Jr., A-Rod and numerous others; only seven players in the history of baseball (Babe Ruth, Barry Bonds, Rafael Palmeiro, Hank Aaron, Dave Winfield, Stan Musial, and David Ortiz) have more RBI after the age of 30 than Ibañez.

Ibañez played one final season split between the Angels and the Royals, but his roots are in Seattle, with his work in the community earning him The Hutch Award during the 2013 season, specifically for his work in the Seattle community. The Hutch Award is an annual award named after Fred Hutchinson and given to the player who "best exemplifies the fighting spirit and competitive desire" of Hutchinson, a former baseball player whose name holds a lot of clout in the Emerald City. Hutchinson was born in Seattle, and there is a Cancer Research Center in Seattle named after the late Fred Hutchinson.

It's only a matter of time before a man of Ibañez's ilk is given a coaching job (he's advising in the Dodgers front office right now), and if he'd prefer to simply hang out with his family and work with his local charities, Ibañez will certainly always have a place in the hearts of the people of Seattle, where Ibañez and his family have their home.

CF Ken Griffey Jr. (1989-1999; 2009-2010)

Griffey was born November 21, 1969 in Donora, Pennsylvania. One might have guessed he was destined for greatness not just because his father was a great ballplayer, but also the fact that a pretty decent outfielder in his own right shares a birth date (November 21) and hometown (Donora, Pennsylvania) with Griffey. That man: Stan "*The* Man" Musial.

Griffey became the Face of the Franchise[167] soon after his debut as a 19-year-old (1989). He ushered in a new era of baseball, and his backward hat and perfect-looking swing became the envy of every young baseball fan across the globe. Even though it has never been stated, I'm convinced Griffey was the inspiration for Benny the Jet Rodriguez in *Sandlot*. True, Rodriguez was Hispanic, but there's no way Griffey's baseball mannerisms didn't impact how David Evans wrote the part and Mike Vitar played the part. He also seemed to spawn half the characters in *Backyard Baseball*, the classic computer game that came out just after his prime (and we now know had Seattle roots).

Griffey managed to have quite an impact on the field as well. He played center field with an awe-inspiring grace, leading to no less a source than Ozzie Smith calling him the second best defensive outfielder all-time. His smooth uppercut swing led to huge home run totals in his prime. In fact, no one had more total bases in the `90s, and no one ever hit 350 home runs faster start a career. Griffey also holds the MLB record with a home run in eight straight games, and from 1996-1999 alone, Griffey hit over 200 home runs, well over 1,000 RuBIns (runs+RBI), had 75 steals, an OPS of .996, and was worth over 30.0 WAR – all for the Mariners. In fact, his WAR and adjusted statistics, including OPS+, are not quite fair.

One thing that is never heard about Griffey, despite the era in which he played, is any accusation of steroid or PED use. For one, he didn't look the part, relying more on a lithe, lean power and a long swing with strong wrists (àla Alfonso Soriano) instead of the (unnaturally) bulging muscles of Mark McGwire and Sammy Sosa. Given the era in which he played, this makes Griffey's numbers even more impressive.[168]

Outside of just his numbers being impressive, it speaks volumes to Griffey's character that he never fell into the steroid trap. It's made even more noteworthy because unfortunately Griffey's career was knocked off track by injuries. Many

---

[166] For comparison: Miguel Cabrera's career home run rate is 4.9 percent and his career ISO is .236.

[167] And likely the face of the poster you had up above your bed.

[168] It would be interesting to come up with an OPS+ that adjusted for those that did and didn't use steroids in the PED Era.

players, including Mark McGwire, said that if it weren't for injuries they never would have used steroids. In fact, here's what McGwire said in an interview with Dan Patrick: "If I never had injuries, I don't think I ever would have even thought of doing what I did. I didn't need to do anything for any more strength. I was already a home run hitter. You do stupid things in your life. You do things that you think might help you at the given time, not knowing what the ramifications are later on. It's something I have to live with every day."

That's a pretty telling quote, and one can see his thought process – especially with MLB doing such a good job of looking the other way. But it only helps to embolden Griffey's character. This was a man who had injuries rob him of becoming one of the five-to-ten greatest players of all time. Griffey staying away from PEDs is all the more impressive with the full context.

Given the impact Griffey had on the sport as a whole, it's only fair that he receives a spot in two Starting IX lists just in his write-up alone. First, he is the captain of the coolest players of all time.

C) Carlton Fisk – How his epic, arms-waiving home run in the 1976 World Series doesn't have a nickname for itself is one of the world's greatest injustices.

1B) David Ortiz – "This is our *fucking* city."

2B) Chase Utley – His hair alone is almost enough to get him on the list, but the clincher was his multiple references on *It's Always Sunny in Philadelphia,* including Mac's incredible letter to him.

3B) Mike Lowell[169] – No one outside of Clooney mastered the silver fox look as well as Lowell did.

SS) Derek Jeter – He and Cristiano Ronaldo will hold spots on lists of this type forever. Or at least until landing gorgeous members of the opposite sex becomes uncool. (It's why Jenny Slate is one of the five coolest women in Hollywood. Along with, you know, her spot-on sense of humor and role as Mona-Lisa Saperstein in *Parks and Rec.*)

LF) Stan Musial – As if I could leave him off of any list, ever.

CF) Ken Griffey Jr.

RF)[170] Vlad Guerrero – My favorite player to watch of all time.

DH) Joe DiMaggio – The baseball-wide crush on DiMaggio was unrivaled.

SP) Tom Seaver – Just read Bill Simmons article on meeting Seaver and revel in the awe of an amazing fan-meets-player story.

RP) Mariano Rivera – The ultimate crunch-time performer.

As noted earlier, Griffey redefined baseball culture, making the sport "cooler" than it had ever been, and there's a strong case to be made that no player will ever reach the height of "Griffey cool" ever again. Part of it was the popularization of backwards hat (when he was a kid he'd wear his father's cap and it slid over his eyes, so he just flipped it around), part of it was video games and Hollywood cameos, part of it was the sleek late-`90s Mariners jerseys, but a whole heck of a lot of it was the swing. Oh, that swing. As such, Junior also deserves his spot on the Starting IX of favorite swings (in my lifetime):[171]

C) Joe Mauer 1B) Albert Pujols 2B) Alfonso Soriano 3B) Chipper Jones SS) Alex Rodriguez LF) Barry Bonds CF) Ken Griffey Jr. RF) Gary Sheffield – I'll defend this til the day I die. DH) Will Clark

Two thoughts on the list above: left-handed batters are just guaranteed to have nicer swings – that's a fact. Also, the reason I chose "of my lifetime" was because I could flash back to imitating the swings of all my favorite players growing up. Is there anything better than being out in your yard as a kid, throwing a wiffle ball around and pretending that you are leading your squad to the World Series? No, no there isn't.

RF Ichiro Suzuki (2001-2012)

Ichiro will go down as one of the best contact hitters[172] of all time, as well as one of the best foreign imports the game has seen. Coming over to Seattle as a 27-year-old, Ichiro had over 1,200 hits in the Japanese professional leagues before his MLB days. Once in the States, he became a cult hero in the Seattle market and was arguably the face of global baseball for over a decade.

While in Japan, Ichiro played in the Nippon League, Japan's top league and the second-best professional baseball league in the world. By most modern research, the league is about on par with – if not slightly above – a Triple A-level of play, and numerous players have successfully made the trip across the Pacific to come play Major League Baseball. Before the path to MLB from the NPB was tried and true, the Nippon League still had some of baseball's most talented players, men who played their whole careers in Japan, and, as such, are not as well known in the U.S. as more current players who made it over to MLB. The all-time MLB home run king may be Barry Bonds, but Sadaharu Oh can stake his claim to over 100 more home runs in his career than Bonds. Oh's career total of 868 home runs is the world record for career home runs, and he had an incredible 15 Central League batting titles (including 13 in a row). He was the Babe Ruth of the NPB, winning Triple Crowns in back-to-back seasons (1973-1974) and leading the league in walks 19 of his 22 seasons. Oh also holds the world record for walks in a career, and his career on-base percentage of .453 would be fifth all-time in MLB history.

---

[169] Why the hell are there so many Red Sox on this list? Is this some sort of sadomasochist list I'm making?!
[170] It should be noted that the outfield positions provided way more "cool depth" than any other position, and it wasn't even close.
[171] Griffey would be on the list regardless of how far back we went.
[172] Although the tales of lore of Ichiro's batting practice power are some of the best in baseball.

Of course, the comparison is a difficult one. Oh had a similar short porch in right field to Ruth (295 feet down the line for Oh compared to 296 for Ruth), but Oh had a bit shallower center field to work with (394 feet compared to 408 in the Bronx). Plus, pitching in the Nippon League in the 1970s was not on par with MLB in the 1920s, even if there were some inflated offensive totals in baseball's "Golden Era" of the Roaring `20s. Oh's accomplishments are impressive nonetheless, and if Oh had made the move to MLB, there's little doubt in my mind that he would have been a regular All-Star.[173] Certain modern studies have shown that power numbers tend to drop a bit when making the move from NPB to MLB (think Hideki Matsui), but a hitter with a good batting eye – a trait the world record holder in walks undoubtedly had – translates well.

In terms of Ichiro's adjustment to MLB pitching: it didn't take Ichiro long to adjust to MLB, as he won not only the Rookie of the Year in 2001, but also the league MVP, as the Mariners raced out to the highest win total in league history. In his first 10 years in the league, Ichiro had 2,244 hits, 170 more hits than the second-most prolific hitter in *any* 10-year stretch (Paul Waner). He topped .300 each of those 10 seasons and averaged over 38 steals a season, despite ending that stretch as a 36-year-old.

During that time, Suzuki endeared himself to the city of Seattle with his excellent play but also as a natural location fit in the Pacific Northwest. The Mariners are the closest possible U.S. team to Japan, and Ichiro was a perfect personality fit, as his dry wit was perfect for the quirky Pacific Northwest. When making the trip from Seattle to Cleveland one time, he dropped this bomb: "To tell the truth, I'm not excited to go to Cleveland, but we have to. If I ever saw myself saying I'm excited going to Cleveland, I'd punch myself in the face, because I'm lying." He also espoused some philosophy with the gem: "I'm told I either look bigger than I do on television or that I look smaller than I look on television. No one seems to think I look the same size." He even showed his confident side when he said, "If I'm in a slump, I ask myself for advice." Finally, he also has an All-Star tradition steeped in the annals of baseball lore.

For nearly a decade, Ichiro would storm into the American League locker room before the midsummer classic and fly into a profanity-laden tirade about how the AL had to show their supremacy over the National League. Each year the American League's first-time All-Stars were shocked and awed as the diminutive, foreign-born Suzuki would unleash a R.-Lee-Ermey-in-*Full-Metal-Jacket*-level rant. The veterans knew what was coming, but they made sure the secret stayed on the down low so that next year's crop could be in just as much shock and awe. The AL didn't lose to the NL from Ichiro's rookie season (2001) until 2009. Coincidence? Doubt it.

Utility Edgar Martínez (1987-2004)

Thanks to his role as a DH, his location on the always forgotten West Coast (the Pacific Northwest, no less), the late bloom to his career, and his soft-spoken demeanor, Martínez has become one of baseball's forgotten superstars. Playing alongside Ken Griffey Jr., Alex Rodriguez, and Randy Johnson also probably hurt his case, but only Griffey was worth more WAR than Martínez in his time as a Mariner (and even that was by only 2.1 WAR, meaning the difference was negligible in reality). In fact, Martínez topped even Griffey in terms of offensive WAR for the franchise, coming in as the franchise leader with 66.4 oWAR.

Need more proof of his unheralded greatness? In 1995, "Gar" became the first right-handed, two-time AL batting champ since Joe DiMaggio, and that season started a run of six straight years during which he hit .320 or better. He is one of 15 players with at least 12 seasons with an on-base percentage of .400 or greater,[174] and we saw what he did in big postseason games during the Game Diary above. Remember, he was just as big in Game 4 of that series. He hit .571 for that series as a whole, with a cool 1.000 slugging percentage. Martínez could even handle Mariano Rivera, with 10 hits in 16 career at bats against arguably the toughest relief pitcher of all time. Martínez had three doubles and two home runs in that sample, which can only be explained by Martínez's ability to go to the opposite field, i.e. going with the cutting movement of Rivera's famous cutter, a point made by Michael Schur on an excellent episode of his podcast with Joe Posnanski, *The Poscast*.

Martínez got a late start his career, as he didn't lock down a full-time job with the Mariners until he was 27 years old (1990) – the age at which most players are in the thick of their prime. From there, Martínez truly peaked in his 30s, going to the All-Star Game five times as a tricenarian after making the midsummer classic only once in his 20s.[175] It is a shame that Martínez is still not enshrined in Cooperstown, especially considering – as many have pointed out – if he had simply been the worst fielding third baseman of all time, he'd be a lock for the Hall given his offensive production. It's only because he played at the highly-stigmatized DH position that he has been kept out.

According to his teammate Jay Buhner, Martínez owed his top-notch hitting ability to the doughnut he always had around his bat. "You want to know why Edgar is so good? It's that doughnut. I wouldn't be shocked if he sleeps with the damn thing," Buhner told *Sports Illustrated* in a feature on Edgar. In that same article from 2000, Jamie Moyer went on to talk about how, when he first came to Seattle, he was amazed by the fact that Martínez would take batting practice with the doughnut on his bat, but Martínez somehow managed to never have the pitch hit the part of the bat with the doughnut on it. It is pretty remarkable, and considering we're about to move into a bunch of player sections from teams with longer histories

[173] A late-career Hank Aaron and mid-career Oh faced off in Japan for a pretty cool Home Run Derby in 1974 that you can find on YouTube.
[174] Including nine consecutive seasons, culminating with his age-40 season.
[175] Between the late-career successes of Martínez and Ibañez, the Mariners Starting IX may have to be sponsored by Cialis.

that have some possible tall tales among their pages, it is an appropriate sequitur.

SP Félix Hernández (2005-pres.)

When I first started working on this book (and calling it a *project* rather than a *book* out of fear of a jinx), Randy Johnson got the nod here. Félix had a section as the Player of the Future, but after a couple additional dominant seasons, a lengthy contract extension, and the fact that I stumbled on Rob Neyer's narrative that Johnson wanted out of Seattle so bad that he didn't pitch up to what he was capable of during the end of his Seattle days, King Félix gets the start with Johnson as a close number two.

Hernández's career got off to a quick start, as he made his debut at the ripe age of 19 years old. At the time of his debut, the recent history of pitchers making debuts in their teenage years was far from impressive. In fact, one had to go back to Doc Gooden in 1984 to find any real success, needing to trudge through plenty of Edwin Jackson/Rick Ankiel-types to get there. Regardless, the hype was high in Seattle, as well as across the baseball world as a whole – just read Jonah Keri's foaming-at-the-mouth game diary of Hernández's second start in the big leagues. In his first season, the precocious Venezuelan did not disappoint, throwing 84.1 innings of 2.67-ERA ball, with a WHIP below 1.00, and over 8.0 strikeouts per nine (back when 8.0 strikeouts per nine was impressive, not a red flag).

In his second season, though, Hernández fell off quite a bit, with his ERA jumping up to 4.52 (his ERA+ of 98 was still far from horrible for a 20-year-old), and his home run rate more than doubling (0.5 to 1.1 per nine). Félix's sophomore slump turned out to be just that, a blip in the radar from which he slowly but surely made his way back to the top of the pitching ladder. His progress culminated with a pair of seasons, 2009 and 2010, that were as strong as anyone in baseball, snagging a Cy Young as well as a Cy Young runner-up, while going a combined 32-17 with a 2.38 ERA (172 ERA+), with over 8.0 strikeouts and just 7.3 hits allowed per nine (leading the AL in H/9 both seasons).

If 2010 was the "94" space in Chutes and Ladders…

(Photo from Make Lemons/Creative Commons)

Félix rolled a one in 2011,[176] slipping down a few notches to around the level he was at in his third season – still above average (109 ERA+) but not nearly the dominant level of the previous two seasons. This led to plenty of (subtlety racist, if we're going to be honest) hot takes on how Hernández didn't have the drive to be an elite pitcher and was content with the heights he had reached already. Hernández continued the metaphor of his career as a game of Chutes and Ladders the next few years, rolling a combined 10 in 2012-13 to get him back solidly in the top-tier of pitchers, before climbing the ladder once again in 2014 to get to the game's peak.

The most satisfying part of it all – for Hernández as well as people who hate hot takes – had to be that Félix had another incredible season in 2014, the season after signing a massive contract extension, which, if he had truly been one to rest of his laurels, would have given him enough money to take a Rip Van Winkle-esque rest on those laurels. Instead, Hernández personified the exact opposite of the hot takes, showing the drive and self-motivation to get to the next level (with another near-Cy Young season) directly after he got seven years and $175 million from the Mariners. His final 2014 stats (15-6, 2.14 ERA, 0.915 WHIP, 6.8 WAR) were absolutely studly.

Hernández also proved his critics wrong by staying in small-market, not-always-competitive Seattle, after another hot take that spread was that he was ready to leave town after he gave even the slightest hint of not being happy with the

[176] If anyone doubted that I actually worked in schools for two years, hopefully using Chutes and Ladders as a reference point for a pitcher's performance eliminates that doubt.

team's failure in the AL West.[177] Especially considering all the talent that we've seen on the previous pages that jumped at the chance to leave Seattle, Félix sticking around, when every pundit and his dog had him moving to the Yankees as soon as he could, made Félix even more popular than he had previously been in Seattle. The fans still show their love for Hernández with a section at Safeco Field called "The King's Court." It's a group of diehard fans at every Félix home start who shower their hero with about as much love as any player in modern baseball gets.

And the Mariner fans love Hernández for good reason. In the second half of the 2014 season, the 6' 3" righty made history by making 16 consecutive starts of at least seven innings pitched while allowing two or fewer runs – a major league record that previously belonged to Tom Seaver at 13 such games.

If there is any justice in the world, Hernández – the most prevalent player to never have made the postseason in the league right now – will help to break the Mariners decade-plus long playoff slump before he retires in the northwest green and silver of Seattle.

CP J.J. Putz (2003-2008) vs. Kaz Sasaki (2000-2003)

It's time for the elusive closer breakdown that you've all been waiting for. Since closers don't have as many stats to track their ability, the categories won't have the charts used in the past, but rather mention the relevant statistics within the text itself.

Power

Putz maintained a strikeout rate of over one K per inning in his time with the Mariners, topping out at 11.9 strikeouts per nine in 2006. Sasaki also relied on the strikeout as a valuable tool, sporting a strikeout per nine rate (9.8) just higher than Putz (9.4) in his four seasons. Although Sasaki relied on his heavy split-fingered fastball to get his strikeouts, Putz was much more typical as a closer, relying on the speed of his fastball. If power is defined as fastball speed Putz has the edge, if power is defined by simply being an overpowering pitcher, then it gets much closer, as Sasaki's splitter was arguably better than any pitch Putz had. We'll go with the heater.

Nomenclature EDGE: Putz

Control

Neither pitcher had particularly-great or particularly-weak walk rates. Sasaki's slightly higher walks per nine rate (3.1 compared to 2.9 for Putz) was countered by his slightly higher strikeout rate, resulting in nearly identical strikeout-to-walk rates for the two (Putz leads 3.24 to 3.14). There is not nearly enough to separate the two, however.

EDGE: Draw

Advanced Statistics

Putz more than doubles Sasaki's WAR total with the club thanks in part to having pitched in 80 more games than Sasaki, but also thanks to his 4.0-WAR 2007 campaign. In terms of ERA+, the two are nearly even again, with Putz holding a slight edge: 143 to 138. Putz's 2007 alone was worth more in terms of WAR than Sasaki's four years. There are certainly plenty of cases for WAR being a slightly misleading stat, but Putz get the edge here.

EDGE: Putz

Reliability

J.J. Putz converted 81 percent of his saves as the Mariners closer and only allowed inherited runners to score 29 percent of the time. As impressive as those numbers are, however, they both trail Sasaki, albeit slightly. Sasaki converted 85 percent of his saves and only allowed inherited runners to score just 25 percent of the time.

EDGE: Sasaki

---

[177] According to a *New York Times* piece on Félix, the deciding factor for him staying in Seattle was pancakes. Well, more so the comfort of staying in a community he knows and feels connected to, but that includes Chace's Pancake Corral, a local eatery where Félix loves to indulge.

Dominance/ Intimidation

Sasaki and Putz both had one season in which they drew votes for the league MVP despite their role in the bullpen. Sasaki edged Putz two-to-one in terms of All-Star appearances and won Rookie of the Year thanks in part to being 32 years old in his "rookie year" (he came over to MLB after a decade in the NPB). Putz, however, led the league in games finished in 2007, the only category in which either man can claim to have led the league in their time with Seattle. Despite the slight edge in plaudits that Sasaki received in his time with the club, he was never as dominant as Putz was in 2007. Putz was lights out that year, only blowing two saves en route to his 4.0 WAR total.

EDGE: Putz by a hair.

Team Success

In the four years with Sasaki as the closer, the Mariners made the playoffs twice, neither time resulting in a pennant (of course). Sasaki was quite respectable in the playoffs, finishing off eight games for the club and only blowing one save. Putz never saw Mariners playoff baseball and was part of only two winning seasons in his six total seasons with the team.

EDGE: Sasaki

Final Verdict

This is a really close matchup that could go either way. Putz has longevity, as well as his 2007 season on his side; Sasaki has the fact that he was the undisputed closer his entire time with the Mariners, as well as the fact that he played with only Seattle to his advantage. However, Sasaki could likely have been with the team even longer had he not left the team under suspicious circumstances in 2003. Sixty-one games into 2003, Sasaki landed on the DL, supposedly due to an injury he suffered while carrying his suitcases upstairs. The Mariners weren't sure about his story, and when the rumor that he had suffered the injury while drinking and practicing wrestling moves came out, the Mariners decided to move on from Sasaki, who ended up back in Japan. If Sasaki hadn't been forced out of Seattle and had stayed even one more season, he would have gotten the spot, but the extra time for **Putz** is enough to give him the edge since the two were so evenly matched outside of tenure with the club.

Starting IX Franchise Roster Stats

Lineup	Yrs	G	R	H	HR	RBI	SB	BB	SO	BA	OBP	SLG	OPS+	dWAR	WAR
Ichiro Suzuki	12	1844	1176	**2533**	99	633	**438**	513	792	**0.322**	0.366	0.418	113	4.8	56.8
Alex Rodriguez	7	790	627	966	189	595	133	310	616	0.309	0.374	**0.561**	138	6.2	38.0
Ken Griffey Jr.	13	1685	1113	1843	**417**	1216	167	819	1081	0.292	0.374	0.553	144	8.5	**70.4**
Edgar Martínez	**18**	**2055**	**1219**	2247	309	**1261**	49	**1283**	1202	0.312	**0.418**	0.515	**147**	-9.7	68.3
Adrián Beltré	5	715	372	751	103	396	49	192	494	0.266	0.317	0.442	101	9.3	21.2
Raul Ibañez	11	1110	540	1077	156	612	21	367	707	0.279	0.341	0.466	115	-7.8	14.5
Bret Boone	7	803	467	863	143	535	50	262	610	0.277	0.336	0.478	116	0.2	19.0
Alvin Davis	8	1166	563	1163	160	667	7	672	549	0.281	0.381	0.453	128	-9.8	19.9
Dan Wilson	12	1251	433	1071	88	508	23	268	739	0.262	0.309	0.384	80	**10.8**	13.5
Pitchers	Yrs	W	W%	ERA	G	CG	SHO	SV	IP	SO	ERA+	WHIP	SO/9	SO/BB	WAR
Félix Hernández	13	**160**	0.584	**3.20**	375	25	11	0	**2502.1**	**2342**	125	1.184	8.4	3.25	**52.2**
J.J. Putz	6	22	0.595	3.07	308	0	0	101	323.0	337	143	1.158	9.4	3.24	8.4

#17 New York Mets (1962-pres.)

(Photo from Wikimedia Commons)

Team Background

Playoff appearances: 9 **Pennants: 5** **World Series titles: 2**
Collective team WAR: 350.9
Strengths: Arguably one of the top five pitchers of all time, in his prime; arguably the best offensive catcher the game has ever seen, in his prime; and one of the most naturally powerful hitters of all time, in his prime.
Weaknesses: Depth of great players. Their utility spot is mediocre at best, and like many expansion teams, they don't have the "lifers" who played with the franchise for their whole career.
What to expect from the next 10 pages: Two of the longer extended pop culture references, and not one, but TWO, three-row charts. Go crazy, folks!

The Mets came into existence after both the Dodgers and the Giants abandoned New York, and, appropriately, the origin of the Mets colors – blue from the Dodgers and orange from the Giants – act a tribute to the New York teams of past, both of whom moved to the West Coast in 1958. The return of a National League baseball franchise to New York was inevitable after the Dodgers and Giants moved from New York to California. The year the Giants and Dodgers both abandoned the East Coast, NL President Warren Giles said, "I feel the way I did about marriage when I was 20 years old… I'm positive [the return of NL baseball to New York] is going to happen, but I don't have any idea when – or with whom."

When the Mets first joined the league, the idea of them replacing the Dodgers and Mets seemed like a slap to the face of New Yorkers. In 1962, the Mets' inaugural season, the team finished 60 ½ games out of first place, or as Dan Okrent put it, two months out of first place. They didn't turn it around quickly either. According to some fancy metrics from Rob Neyer's and Eddie Epstein's *Baseball Dynasties* book, they suffered the worst stretch in baseball history in their opening salvo (321-648 in their first six seasons).

However, they completely flipped the switch in 1969, and the Miracle Mets had the entire city falling in love with them. Just one year after a 73-89 campaign – and only two years removed from a 61-101 campaign – the Mets won 100 games and captured the franchise's first playoff spot. They didn't stop there, getting the franchise's first regular season pennant, first playoff series win (over the Atlanta Braves), and capping their run with a World Series title over the in-their-prime Baltimore Orioles. This was a team that, in addition to all the futility listed above, had finished ninth or 10th in the 10-team NL every season since their admittance to the league seven years earlier. Suddenly they found themselves on top of the baseball world. They did this in the first-ever MLB season to feature a League Championship Series, as, after over 60 years of pennant winners meeting in the World Series, the Mets chose their first-ever season with a regular season pennant to have to take down the West division champions Atlanta Braves, a team who only got into the playoffs due to the playoff expansion that season. The Braves were not able to stop the Miracle Mets, however, and thanks to many of the players on the upcoming pages, the city of New York continued its long history of baseball championships with the first to belong to the borough of Queens.

After a period of success from 1969-1973 that ended with a World Series loss in 1973, the Mets fell back off for a decade or so before another bout of strong play in the mid-to-late `80s. Starting in 1984, the Mets finished first or second in the NL East seven straight seasons, highlighted by another magical World Series title in 1986. Although the 1986 World Series is often remembered for Billy Buckner choking away what would have been the Red Sox first World Series win in 68 years, it *should* be remembered as an incredible comeback from a Mets team that had their last rites read to them on multiple occasions in the series. The World Series victory capped an incredible playoff run that included two of the most famous playoff series of all time, obviously the 1986 World Series, but also the NLCS that preceded it. The six-game series included a 1-0 Game 1; a walk-off win for the Mets in Game 3; a twelve-inning walk-off for the Mets in Game 5; and an incredible Game 6 that deserves a closer look.

With the Mets up 3-2 in the series, Game 6 went back to Houston, and the Astros jumped out to a quick 3-0 lead in the bottom of the first inning. They did so on a collection of hits off Mets starter Bob Ojeda. Ojeda settled down after the first, however, and both pitchers traded zeroes on the board until the top of the ninth. With a 3-0 lead, and a starter (Bob Knepper) who looked to be in complete control (having allowed only two hits through eight innings), the Astros felt comfortable with their chances of forcing a Game 7. The Mets had other ideas, however, and a leadoff triple by pinch-hitter Lenny Dykstra set the tone for the inning. Mookie Wilson followed up with a single, and after a Kevin Mitchell groundout, Keith Hernandez doubled home Wilson, making it a 3-2 game and chasing Knepper (he arguably should have been removed earlier). Dave Smith came into the game and proceeded to walk the first two batters he faced. All Ray Knight had to do was hit a sacrifice fly to tie the game and force extra innings.

In extra innings, the teams traded zeroes for a while until the Mets finally broke through in the top of the 14thinning, taking the lead with a single, a walk, a sacrifice bunt, and a single. In the bottom of the inning, the Mets sent out the immortal Jesse Orosco to attempt to close out the game and send the Mets to their third World Series. This time it was the Astros turn to ruin the opposing closer's night, as Billy Hatcher ensured the Astros wouldn't be going home just yet, with a shot down the left field line that cleared the fence and tied the game back up.

So, on they went, and after a scoreless 15th, the Mets had simply had enough. They dropped three runs on the Astros in the top of the 16th, and with their closer, Orosco, still in the game, they were ready to meet the Red Sox in the World Series (the Sox having won Game 7 of a nearly-as-fun ALCS that same night). Of course, the Astros weren't going to go that easy. After a leadoff strikeout by Astros third baseman Craig Reynolds, the next three hitters reached, and one run came around to make the score 7-5. After inducing a groundout, Orosco now had to get just one more out to clinch the pennant. Glenn Davis had other ideas, and after a single of his brought in yet another run, the Astros had tying run in scoring position and their number five hitter, Kevin Bass (a .311 hitter during the regular season) up to the plate. The count ran full, because of course, but finally Jesse Orosco put the Astros away and the Mets moved on to what would be such a memorable World Series that the incredible 1986 NLCS is often forgotten – it shouldn't be.

In keeping with the roller coaster first 30 or so years of extreme high and lows, the Mets have had an interesting last 20 or so years. They enjoyed two strong seasons in 1999-2000, which included an NL pennant before getting swept by their big-brother New York Yankees in the World Series. They also had a memorable 2006 NLCS highlighted by Adam Wainwright's Hammer of Thor-esque curveball on playoff god Carlos Beltrán to end the series.[178]

However, Mets fans also saw their owners invest in a Ponzi scheme, and they saw a discrimination lawsuit in the front office. Of course, those seem far away now with the glow of yet another pennant in 2015, and a future full of Ks thanks to a squadron of young pitchers. Generation K 2.0 (or literally anything catchier than that) has the Mets headed for seeming contention for the next decade, but if we've learned anything from Mets prior history, something that stable seems unlikely. (Queue the 2017 season.)

Random cool things about the franchise:

- The Mets five pennants are the most among all expansion teams.
- The Mets have about as many famous fans as any team in baseball history: Ben Stiller, Stephen Colbert, Tim Robbins, Robert De Niro, Nas, Adam Sandler, Chris Rock, Jerry Seinfeld, Glenn Close, George Carlin, Julian Casablancas, Susan Sarandon, Jon Stewart, Ray Romano, Jimmy Kimmel, Philip Seymour Hoffman, Viggo Mortensen, Julia Stiles, Matt Dillon, Hilary Swank, and numerous others.
- The Mets were the last baseball team to call the legendary Polo Grounds their home.
- Mr. Met is the best mascot in baseball – this is a fact, not an opinion.
- Chipper Jones owns their soul – this is also a fact.
- Within the first decade of the team's existence they brought Casey Stengel, Gil Hodges, Duke Snider, Yogi Berra, and Willie Mays – all New York baseball legends – into the franchise's embrace as either a player or a manager.

---

[178] The series also featured one of the best catches in MLB playoff history, when Endy Chavez robbed Scott Rolen of a home run earlier in Game 7.

Starting IX

C Mike Piazza (1998-2005)

Piazza came to the Mets in the latter half of his career, playing for the franchise for eight years. He came to the team via one of the most deplorable attempts to break up a team in history. On May 14, 1998, the Dodgers sent a package of Piazza and Todd Zeile to the Marlins, receiving in exchange: Manuel Barrios, Bobby Bonilla, Jim Eisenreich, Charles Johnson, and Gary Sheffield. This seems like a lot to give up given that Bonilla was a six-time All-Star, Johnson was on his way to his fourth straight Gold Glove, and Sheffield would go on to top 500 home runs, but Piazza might have made the trade worth it. Even though he was approaching 30 years old, he had been in the top 10 in the MVP each of the last five years and was considered the top catcher (a vital position) in the game. What made this trade particularly egregious, however, is that less than 10 days later, the Marlins showed what they were really up to by to sending Piazza to the Mets for a package that basically gave them three years of Preston Wilson producing 2.0 WAR/season… and that's it. Wilson may have been a solid prospect, but even in his wildest dreams he wouldn't have become Gary Sheffield, who, remember, was just one of the five Marlins players they gave up to get Wilson (via Piazza). This was one of the most blatant salary dumps in baseball, and it happened less than a year after the Marlins had won the World Series.

Back to Piazza: He played more games with the Mets than any other team, and as such, chose to don a Mets hat when he was voted into the Hall of Fame in 2015. For a little while it seemed like Piazza might be the victim of some good ole-fashioned "guilty by PED association Hall of Fame freeze out," but luckily voters came to their senses. He was basically being punished for hitting a lot of home runs (and having a bit of back acne) in an era suspicious of home run hitters (and back acne). Leaving out the best hitting catcher of all time was just too egregious in the end, as Piazza's credentials against some catchers already enshrined in Cooperstown were bonkers. Let's take a blind look at two players:

	G	BA	OBP	SLG	R	HR	RBI	WAR
Player A	726	.331	.394	.572	443	177	563	31.9
Player B	1884	.273	.378	.363	687	28	734	29.7

Player B got on base almost as frequently as Player A, but that's where the similarities stop. Now, doing this whole breakdown with each player listed as "Player A" and "Player B" is far too confusing,[179] so let's just get to the big reveal now. Player B, as you might expect, is the lowest ranked catcher to get into the Hall of Fame on his catching merits alone, Rick Ferrell. The real twist, however, is that Player A is not just Piazza (as you figured) but only the seven years (two of which he played less than 100 games) in which Piazza played for the Dodgers. Back to the comparison.

Piazza produced nearly as much in the classic counting stats, and actually outpaced Ferrell in WAR, despite the fact the he played in well less than half the games (less than 40 percent of the games in fact) that Ferrell played in his career. Now the attentive reader might say: "but what about the eras in which they played?" In Piazza's era, the league averaged 9,640 runs per season, and this is indeed much higher than Ferrell's era in which the league averaged 5,986 runs per season. That would seem to be the difference *except* there were only eight teams in the American League when Ferrell played. With 14 teams in the league during Piazza's time that means teams averaged 689 runs per season compared to 748 in Ferrell's time. They also played 162 games in Piazza's era compared to 152 games in Ferrell's era, making the average runs/game/team equal to 4.25 in Piazza's era compared to 4.86 for Ferrell.

So not only did Piazza – just while in L.A. – produce nearly as much as Ferrell, but he did it in a less-friendly hitting era in terms of runs scored per game. It is not as if Piazza never went on to be successful after Los Angeles either. Based on standard metrics, he produced more in New York (89 more runs, 43 more homers, 92 more RBI), and even by advanced metrics he was only slightly off his Dodger pace while paying for the Mets. It seems clear that Piazza was about twice the hitter that Ferrell was, but what about defense?

By the most all-inclusive of defensive metrics, dWAR, the difference between Piazza and Ferrell was worth less than 5.0 wins for their entire careers. There are some more damning numbers of Piazza, however. First off, Piazza caught only 23 percent of base runners stealing for his career. That's by far the lowest of any catcher in the Hall, and even his career high of 35 percent caught stealing (1993) barely tops the current lowest career rate of any other catcher in the Hall. Ferrell also holds a huge advantage in reputation. For many positions, it may not be necessary to put a lot of weight into reputation, but with the inability to truly rate catchers on their defense still, catcher is the one position that some weight should be given to rep. A catcher's rep can also help to slow down the opposing running game if the team has a Pudge-esque backstop.

Even with this defensive advantage, however, there is no way that Rick Ferrell was a better ball player than Piazza. With Piazza so clearly better than several of the catchers in the Hall, it was just too hard to keep him out, especially when the basis of his freeze-out was hints and allegations rather than incidents and accidents. Glad the BBWAA got this one right. It does seem like they're starting to get their act together a little bit more.

---

[179] Trust me, I tried it.

1B Keith Hernandez (1983-1989)

Hernandez may be the best argument that defensive metrics are not entirely where they need to be right now. By current dWAR totals, Hernandez netted just 0.5 defensive wins above replacement for his entire career. This is coming from the man who is one of only five non-pitchers to win at least 10 straight gold gloves. He was also the best fielding first basemen that baseball guru Rob Neyer ever saw (which, for what it's worth, I weigh heavier than the 10 straight Gold Gloves). Hernandez was a productive enough hitter to be considered a good ball player, but where he really made his name was with the glove, and yet somehow, according to dWAR, he only won his team half a game in his entire career.

Of course, this is due in heavy part to the fact that he played first base. If you look at the breakdown of his dWAR contributions, he was worth 66 runs (or 6.6 *wins*) to the Mets in his time with the club. However, his positional adjustment for playing first base (one of the easiest positions to play in baseball) meant that nearly all of that value was supposedly taken off the board. Although it is true that players can do the least harm to their team's defense while at first base, it is not fair to assume that first baseman cannot have a big impact with their glove work while manning first base. This is something that needs to be worked on in the sabermetric field, as positional adjustments for WAR still seem a bit hefty at times.

Outside of his glove work, Hernandez is often best remembered for his cameo on *Seinfeld*. As an homage to one of the great episodes of one of the great TV series, let's use Hernandez's write-up to look at the Starting IX of greatest TV characters all-time – According to Jim (and by that I do not mean the terrible TV show, I mean according to yours truly):

SP) Michael Scott, *The Office* (US) – The best character from the best show; what else is there to say? I realize he based his character off of Ricky Gervais' creative genius, but the theft only lasted one season and then Steve Carell just took a hold of that character that he made entirely his own. Who else could be that lovable while making you want to strangle him at the same time?

C) Rod Serling, *The Twilight Zone* – This is cheating a bit because he worked in limited segments at the beginning and end of each anthological episode, but the show is one of the all-time greats, and Serling's introductions and closing comments (in addition to the work he put into the show's creative, off-camera production) were always on point.

1B) Omar Little, *The Wire* – Easily the most badass character in all TV history, Omar took *The Wire* to a whole nother level with his emergence. Omar is also one of those characters the viewer can tell wasn't necessarily supposed to be around long in the original script, but he demanded a consistent role with his breakout performance. HBO showed they were far ahead of their time with a gay, black, scar-faced character as their breakout star in 2002.

2B) Charlie Kelly, *It's Always Sunny in Philadelphia* – Considering my general dislike for nearly every other part of the show (sans Dee), it's incredible that Charlie kept me watching for so long. Besides Michael Scott, Charlie is the most quotable TV character of all time. Some of the best Charlie highlights: "Wild card, bitches!" "Vormhat's wormhat!" "Attica!" "Pepe Silvia!" "Let's chop cats!" the time capsule butt dance, and the entire "Bums: Making a Mess All Over the City" episode. Rafi from *The League* was left off this list because he was too similar to Charlie, but he may have somehow perfected that type of character even more. Charlie just came first.

3B) Rainbow Johnson/Andre Johnson Jr., *Black-ish* – So by this point the reader has figured out that it is not the best TV characters of all time, but rather this author's personal favorites, and it probably should have gone in the footnotes. Feel free to skip ahead to Edgardo Alfonzo starting at second base for the Mets. I won't blame you. P.S. I just couldn't decide between these two absolute gems in what is the funniest show on cable TV right now.

SS) Liz Lemon, *30 Rock* – This could really go to any character on the show, but the fact that the show is her brainchild, and the fact that Lemon is the one "working on her night cheese" gives her the edge.

LF) Eleven, *Stranger Things* – When, in season one, she stops Mike mid-air and comes around the corner to break the arm of that one bully, I legit jumped off my couch and yelled "Hell yes!" Most badass moment on a show in a long time.

CF) Johnny Drama, *Entourage* – Easily lampooned now, but *Entourage* was the best bro show of all time in its prime. It was the guy response to *Sex and the City*, and be honest, what group of guys out there didn't assign each member of their friend group a Vinny, an E, a Turtle, and a Drama? I was Drama.

RF) Rob and Laurie Petrie, *The Dick Van Dyke Show* – They blazed the path for so many comedy couples after them and have yet to be surpassed.

Utility) Bill Hader, *Saturday Night Live* – His ability to do impressions of absolutely anyone makes him a perfect utility guy.

Bench) The entire cast of "Parks and Recreation" – It's a rare show that can have as many as five different comedic actors lead an episode and still have it be one of your favorites. "Parks and Rec" does it better than anyone else. Also, Leslie Knope and Ron Swanson are the best platonic relationship to ever grace the small screen.

2B Edgardo Alfonzo (1995-2002)

Edgardo Alfonzo was an efficient second baseman for the Mets from 1995-2002.[180]

---

[180] I really want to leave that as all for Alfonzo, but the fact that he has the fourth-highest WAR among Mets position players all-time has to be a fact that even most Mets fans probably didn't know until now.

3B David Wright (2004-pres.)

Wright is the Mets all-time leader in WAR among position players, which I guess shouldn't surprise since he has been considered by many to be the Face of the Franchise for the better part of the last decade. His name is scattered across the Mets statistical leaderboard due to the fact that he is a classic five-tool player. In fact, he has six seasons with 20 home runs, 15 stolen bases, and a .350 on-base percentage, are more such seasons than any other third baseman in MLB history.

Wright was drafted by the Mets in the first round of the 2001 amateur draft and came up through their farm system as a highly-touted prospect. While he was still in the minors, the Seattle Mariners offered the Mets a package for Wright that centered around the Mets receiving legendary manager Lou Piniella in return – the Mets declined. When Wright finally arrived in the majors, he had expectations through the roof and even received a standing ovation from the Mets faithful upon stepping into the batter's box for his first professional at bat.

Wright lived up to the hype and, as a result, has a rabid fanbase within the Big Apple. His fans (or maybe "stalkers" is a better word) would find out his daily routine – where he ate and worked out – in order to find their hero and let him feel their support. Wright still has a great attitude, and while he is no longer a regular All-Star, he still has a good personality (arguably even more engaging than the sometimes too-perfect New York baseball legend before him, Derek Jeter) and does good work in the charity sphere. In only his second year in the big leagues, Wright started a foundation to support multiple sclerosis research.

At *Beyond the Box Score*, Steven Martano made an excellent case for David Wright as the Don Mattingly of the Mets, a comparison that works on many levels. (The poor Mets, getting their Face of the Franchise compared to a Yankee in each of the last two paragraphs – such is life for Mets fans.) Their career arcs are very similar, and at the time of this writing, it looks like Wright's playing days might be in jeopardy. Martano noted both Mattingly and Wright's seemingly poor timing in terms of team success – Wright missed all of the 2015 playoffs as well as the 2016 NL wild card game, while Mattingly famously never won a playoff series with the Yankees. Even if Wright does have to settle for riding off into the sunset, it says a lot that he has already made the case to be the Queens' version of one of the most beloved Yankees.

One final note: when it was believed that Wright's spinal stenosis may be career-ending, Bryan Grosnick at *Beyond the Box Score* wrote an excellent piece, highlighted by an awesome reference to "Crane Wife 3," a lovely song by The Decemberists. Grosnick wrote about how we, as fans, follow the careers of athletes. Not a typical *BTBS* article but one of the best. There you go Mets fans, now we have Wright compared to a Japanese parable instead of a Yankee, happy?

SS José Reyes (2003-2011; 2016-pres.)

Unlike the previous two men who were both known for being the complete package, Reyes is mostly known for one thing – his speed. Reyes has led the league in triples four times with the Mets and stolen bases another three times. Despite these numbers, Reyes has often had to battle to be considered at the top at his position – even within his own division. The NL East was stocked with phenomenal shortstops during Reyes' first stint with the Mets, as Jimmy Rollins and Hanley Ramírez plied their trade with Mets divisional rivals – the Phillies and Marlins, respectively. Reyes seemed to make the jump his last year in his first New York stint (2011), when he finally added another element to his game via the batting title he won.

However, there are a few issues with the conclusion that this was truly a seminal event in Reyes making the jump from star to superstar. First off, he was always a very competent hitter, and although his .337 average in 2011 was his single-season best, he was a .286 career hitter before the campaign. Also, he accomplished this feat in only 126 games, the fewest games played for a batting champ since Manny Ramírez in 2002. Finally (*hot take incoming*), the way he won it was hardly how a superstar would win a batting title. He started the final game with a two-point lead in the race for the batting crown and dropped down a bunt hit. Confident that his now three-point lead on Ryan Braun was enough, he asked out of the game to preserve his lead. Sadly, the Baseball Gods (in particular Ted Williams' frozen spirit) didn't intervene, and Reyes won the title. Reyes isn't the only one to do this (Left Field, Twins – Page 220), and players will continue to do it as long as batting titles are relevant, but it never makes it any less weaselly[181] a thing to do.

As far as Reyes' relationship with the Mets, it's clearly very strong, because when he came back to the team in 2016 after having been released by the Colorado Rockies, he was given a standing ovation. This despite the fact that he was less than a year removed from domestic abuse charges. Not saying Mets fans should have booed, but something a bit less than a homecoming fit for a king would have been nice.

LF Kevin McReynolds (1987-1991; 1994)

McReynolds came to New York after establishing himself in San Diego, and he didn't fail to produce. He was remarkably consistent in his main stint with the Mets (1987-1991). He came back to the club for one season in 1994 but was not the same player. During his five main seasons, he averaged 76 runs, 24 home runs, and 87 RBI, his batting average

[181] And that's weaselly, not Weasley, àla Ron and Ginny, who would never do such a thing. Percy might have, though.

ranged from .259 to .288, and his OPS+ was between 108 and 142 every season. In 1988, he set the major-league record by stealing 21 bases in a season without getting caught, a record which wasn't broken until recently by a man whom we will get to in a bit. McReynolds was also known for having a strong arm, and he led the league in assists as well as double plays turned from the outfield multiple times in his career.

McReynolds was a country boy through and through, and although he was hyped up by his agent and city as a superstar in his early playing days, that was not a title McReynolds readily accepted – or accepted at all for that matter. For McReynolds, baseball was simply the way he made money so he could hunt and fish all winter. As such, he hated the media during his career, and he "had the attitude toward publicity of a CIA operative in Moscow," per Jim Murray of the *LA Times*. McReynolds easily could have been one of the famous Mets of the `80s but chose not to be, and as such, there simply aren't that many stories of crazy antics or rants from the Little Rock native.

CF Carlos Beltrán (2005-2011)

Beltrán's baseball career looks a bit like Steve Carell's film career.[182] Both men burst onto the scene around 2000, but both did so in supporting roles. Carell stole the show in *Bruce Almighty*, and even though no one could top Will Ferrell in *Anchorman*, Carell damned near did with Brick Tamland. Meanwhile, Beltrán won Rookie of the Year and flew around the outfield somewhat overshadowed by Johnny Damon, and most certainly overshadowed by the fact that he played baseball in Kansas City.

Both men were meant for stardom, however, and for Carell it came in the form of *The 40-Year-Old Virgin*, and to a lesser extent, *Little Miss Sunshine*.[183] For Beltrán, it was being traded at the deadline of the 2004 season. After arriving in Houston, Beltrán cranked out 23 home runs and 28 steals in just 90 games, but that was just the beginning. That same postseason, Beltrán hit eight home runs in the NLDS and NLCS combined, hitting well over .400 with a slugging percentage over 1.000.

Naturally, this set unbelievably high expectations for both of these men. Carell was given leads in *Evan Almighty*, *Dan in Real Life*, and *Get Smart*. Beltrán was given a seven-year, $119-million contract from the Mets, the biggest contract to which they had ever signed a player. Because of these heightened expectations, despite the fact that both men performed quite comparably to previous levels, they were deemed unsuccessful. In Carell's case, *Evan Almighty* is considered one of the biggest busts of all time, and people began to question whether Carell could take the lead in a great film. Beltrán will always be remembered by Mets fans for watching Wainwright's curve go past him to end the 2006 NLCS. What will be forgotten is the fact that Beltrán was worth 8.2 WAR during the regular season and had hit three home runs in the NLCS already, as good as any other Met. Also, that pitch from Wainwright might have been the nastiest pitch of all time, and the sign of a great, young pitcher announcing his arrival on the scene.

Once these men had been labeled busts, or at least had been knocked off the perch on which they were briefly sat, they began to exceed expectations again. Carell partnered with Tina Fey in *Date Night*, which may have been his best career move. It allowed people to ignore *Dinner for Schmucks* and focus on his better projects like *Despicable Me* and *Crazy, Stupid, Love*.[184] For Beltrán, a move out of New York meant a move out of the spotlight, which was more than all right with him. In his first two seasons removed from New York (2012-2013), he was named an All-Star each year and was regularly tabbed an underrated part of the Cardinals success.

What is ignored about both men is that they really performed the same throughout their careers,[185] it was just the expectations that changed so much. In Kansas City, Beltrán put up 24.7 WAR in 795 games (5.0 WAR/162 games), and in New York he put up 31.3 WAR in 839 games (6.0 WAR/162 games). The same thing is true of Carell. *Dan in Real Life* and *Get Smart* are the same Carell[186] as in *40-Year-Old Virgin*, he's just surrounded by immensely different talent, and he had much higher expectations. Both men underwent the same roller-coaster ride of expectations despite performing consistently above average, they just never reached the true extended pinnacle reserved for the all-time greats. Of course, the parallel goes on with both men having their strong suit – Beltrán's playoff numbers and Carell's TV career – being taken at less than full value. In Beltrán's case, the playoffs are such a small sample size that it is a requirement for every sabermetric baseball fan to chant "small sample size theater" at least 15 times a day while facing the setting sun in the west, which means the worth of Beltrán's incredible postseason output is diminished a bit. For Carell, there is still a stigma to TV work, although, thankfully, it is starting to be worn down. Time will tell how the legacy of each ages (Carell has a bit more flexibility with aging in his profession), but the comparison holds for now.

---

[182] We're going to table Carell's role on *The Office* for now because, as you just learned a few pages back, I am far too in love with the show – and Carell's Michael Scott – to be a fair judge.
[183] Only to a lesser extent because he was not the lead – the movie is brilliant.
[184] One of the most re-watchable movies in existence.
[185] Again, we're ignoring Carell's TV career, in which he clearly makes vast improvements as Michael Scott from Season 1 to Season 2.
[186] *Evan Almighty* is 2005 Carlos Beltrán – let's just pretend it didn't happen.

RF Darryl Strawberry (1983-1990)

While Carlos Beltrán has one of the most interesting baseball paths, Darryl Strawberry has one of the most interesting life paths. In fact, Strawberry is easily a charter member of the Starting IX of players whose lives make for the most interesting biographies (this is a by-position, not ranked Starting IX):

SP) Satchel Paige C) Moe Berg 1B) Hal Chase 2B) Jackie Robinson 3B) Alex Rodriguez SS) Rabbit Maranville LF) Shoeless Joe Jackson CF) Ty Cobb RF) Darryl Strawberry Utility) King Kelly

Strawberry was an uber-prospect while playing high school ball in south-central Los Angeles – not exactly the warmest environment for growing up. He was drafted first overall in the 1980 draft, and the pressure began to mount right off the bat for Straw. He was called the "Black Messiah" and "Black Ted Williams" before he even debuted in the big leagues. He had one of the smoothest swings of all time, using his wiry 6'6" frame to create more raw power than the Great Whites of Shark Week.

Strawberry spent the second half of the 1980 season, all of 1981-1982, and the beginning of 1983 in the minors, putting up massive statistics which only helped to increase the size of his star. Strawberry lived up to the hype, however, collecting the 1983 Rookie of the Year Award, hitting 26 home runs with an OPS+ of 134 while stealing 19 bases in 122 games.

In his prime, Straw was a complete player, but he was best known for his power, and with good reason. In 1988, he hit a home run off the Olympic Stadium roof in Montreal – the only player to do so during the stadium's 28-year run. He did so with a swing so easy it seemed to defy physics that the ball could travel that far with the batter not doing a Prince Fielder-esque spin at the end of it. The 1988 season would end up the height of Strawberry's powers, as he finished second in the MVP thanks to a league-leading 39 home runs, .545 slugging percentage (the only Mets slugging percentage title in team history), .911 OPS, and 165 OPS+ – the only black ink on his Baseball-Reference page in his career.

Straw also established himself as one of the most popular players in baseball at the time, being named to the next eight All-Star Games, leading the Mets to a World Series, and even playing a pivotal role (albeit never on screen) in the deliciously depraved *Bad Lieutenant*. Of course, the New York media, instead of embracing his talent, focused on doubting the nature/severity of his increasingly common injuries as well as highlighting any off-field kerfuffles in which Straw found himself. In reality, Strawberry was just a kid who had grown up without a positive male role model in his house who was thrown into the big city scene of New York (and later his hometown of L.A.) and didn't have the strength to turn down the innumerable bad influences forcing their way into his life.

I feel comfortable making that leap because Strawberry is, to date, the most famous person I have had the honor of interviewing in person. When I talked to him at the University of Minnesota Crookston campus before an event he was hosting, I asked him about what advice he would give to the younger version of himself, and what he believed went wrong in those early days. His response: "Somewhere along the line – it happens to all of us – something happens inside," Strawberry noted. "Then it depends what road we take. Do we take the right road of going this way, or do we take the road of being influenced by others? A lot of times, as a kid, we follow others because we want to fit in. We want to be a part of the crowd." For Strawberry and those wild Mets of the `80s, there were simply too many outside forces pulling them towards eventual downward spirals. Those forces eventually overcame Strawberry's natural talent and left him a shell of his former self.

Considering the heights Strawberry reached, the second half of his career is almost unparalleled in baseball history. Through nine seasons, Strawberry had 748 runs, 280 home runs, and 832 RBI with a 144 OPS+ in 1,248 games played. His final eight seasons, he posted 150 runs, 55 home runs, and 168 RBI with a 111 OPS+ but only 335 games played. In the latter half of his career, Strawberry battled severe depression as well as alcohol and cocaine abuse.

The good news for this write-up is that not only did Strawberry's Mets days end well (he never had an OPS+ below 125 in a single season for the Mets), but so has the off-field version of the man. He married his current wife, Tracy – a powerhouse who truly impressed in the brief meeting I had with the two – in 2006. Strawberry is now an ordained minister who lives a substance-free life and travels the country telling his story in hopes of saving others who are currently where he was when he was at his lowest.

Utility Howard Johnson (1985-1993)

Surprisingly not the hotel mogul, Johnson flies under the radar a bit in Mets history because his peak was only five seasons. However, during that five-year stretch (1987-1991), Johnson was a very productive hitter. Other than Barry Bonds, Johnson is the only National League player with more than two 30/30 HR/SB seasons, having three such seasons during that five-year period. He is also one of just two switch-hitters to lead National League in home runs, and in 1987, he set the NL record for home runs by switch-hitter with 38. That total has since been topped by several different players, with Lance Berkman (2006) and Chipper Jones (1999) the current NL record holders with 45 switch-hit dingers a pop, but Johnson had the record for most of the `90s. The biggest knock on Johnson was that he was never the best in the field (which makes this utility spot fitting). In 1991, he became the first member of the 30/30/30 club, with errors being the third 30… woof. Maybe unsurprisingly, just like the "Rob Schneider Fan Club," the 30/30/30 club still has only one member.

SP Tom Seaver (1967-1977; 1983)

One of the all-time great players – and men – Tom Terrific is the Mets all-time leader in WAR (76.1), as well as nearly every other pitching category in existence. Seaver received 98.8 percent of the Hall of Fame vote in his inaugural year of eligibility, the second-highest such total all-time. That is a slightly skewed honor (Babe Ruth, Ty Cobb and the earliest legends all had to battle against each other in the inaugural vote in 1936), but it is an amazing feat nonetheless. In fact, he long held the highest percentage until Junior Griffey topped him in 2016 (99.3 percent). The story behind the five votes that Seaver didn't receive is just as good, as three ballots were left blank in protest of Pete Rose being banned from the Hall, one voter was recovering from heart surgery and failed to notice Seaver's name, and one (tool) said he refused to vote for players in their first year of eligibility. Considering all the folks Cobb was going up against in his own inaugural election, Cobb's 98.2 percent may be more impressive, but Seaver's percentage remains a feather in his cap, and it could have been even higher if not for a few flukes and one asshole.

Seaver was a popular guy in the media, as well as among his teammates, because he tried his damnedest to win even while mired on some truly awful teams. He was quoted as saying of his time in New York, "I not only wanted to win, but I wanted everybody else to want to win too." As the dude who throughout college not only wanted to get drunk, but also wanted everyone else to want to get drunk too, I can appreciate Seaver's cause.

In his rookie year, Tom Terrific went 16-13 for a team that finished 40 games below .500. Two years later, he would go on to be the (deserved) face of the 1969 "Miracle Mets." Posting a 25-7 record with a 2.21 ERA and 165 ERA+, Seaver was worth 7.2 WAR en route to his first Cy Young, and the young Mets won the franchise's first World Series Championship. Seaver followed that up in 1970 with his first ERA title, first ERA+ title, and first strikeout title. He also set a record by striking out 10 consecutive batters to end a game on April 22, 1970.

Seaver became a bit of an icon, pitching in the biggest city in the world and even being painted by Andy Warhol in Warhol's *Athlete Series*. Seaver, however, remained humble throughout his career and was always one of the more approachable famous athletes of his time. Bill Simmons tells a story of how before he was "Grantland-inventor/TV personality Bill Simmons," his buddy Gus was going into business with Seaver. One thing led to another and Simmons got to stand in the batter's box against one of his all-time heroes, Seaver, who was trying to get back into shape for a final push at the majors in 1987. It's a cool story, and it paints the picture of a stud athlete with the perfect balance of a competitive streak and a sense of humor, even in his post-playing days.

* * *

It should be no surprise that a man nicknamed "The Franchise" would get the start here, but Dwight Gooden might have had the best season ever for any pitcher – Mets or otherwise – in 1985. As a 20-year-old, Gooden posted a 24-4 record with a 1.53 ERA, 16 complete games, 268 strikeouts, a 0.965 WHIP, a 229 ERA+, and 13.2 WAR (even netting 1.1 oWAR). He led the league in every one of these categories except WHIP, won the Cy Young, and probably should have won the MVP. At the time, Gooden's 229 ERA+ was the best since Bob Gibson's 1968 season and the second best since 1914.[187] Gooden's 13.2 WAR was the best of any player since Babe Ruth in 1923, and that total has not been topped since.

Cubs first baseman Leon Durham said, "All these years later, I'm still trying to figure out how Gooden finished *fourth* in the MVP. His pitch does everything. It moves, it sinks, it rises." That was just his fastball. He also threw two different types of curveballs, a hard curve and a slow curve, and hitters struggled with both. Struggled may be an understatement. Hitters only managed to scrape together a .270 *slugging percentage* against Gooden in 1985, and he threw eight shutouts. In addition to the shutouts, there were two other games where he pitched nine innings with no runs allowed and got a no-decision. There were two more eight-inning starts with no runs allowed, and there were three complete games with only one run allowed. He hit double-digit strikeouts in 11 outings. Only two of his starts were not quality starts, and in his four losses he allowed a total of nine runs. Baseball-Reference WAR rates it the fourth-best pitching season since 1901, trailing only two Walter Johnson seasons and one Cy Young year, both of which came back in the day when hitters didn't hit home runs, and the game was entirely different. Gooden threw 276.2 innings in 1985; Johnson averaged 358.0 innings in his two seasons (1912-1913) above Gooden, while Young tallied 371.1 innings in his 12.6-WAR 1901 season.

The sad part is how Doc faded from what could have been a career on par with Seaver, if not better. David Schoenfield summed it up well when ranking his best players under 25 of all time: "What happened? Sure, there were the drugs and maybe hitters learned to lay off the high fastball and maybe he lost the feel for his curveball – as good as Blyleven's they said – and then pitching coach Mel Stottlemyre instructed him not to go for strikeouts all the time and he hurt his shoulder in 1989 and was definitely never the same after that. But in 1985, in that glorious summer, Dr. K was as good as any pitcher ever was." Schoenfield gave Gooden the no. 2 rank among players under 25 all-time. One point that Schoenfield commented on, and Rob Neyer has expounded upon, was the idea that, although Doc's drug habit certainly didn't help, it was the shoulder injury at age 24 that truly derailed Gooden's career.

---

[187] Pedro Martínez and Greg Maddux have since topped Gooden's 1985 ERA+ twice each.

* * *

As far as Seaver is concerned, he may not have had quite the peak that Gooden did, but man did he have himself a career. In his 11+ seasons with the Mets, he won 198 games with a 2.57 ERA and a trio of Cy Young awards. Seaver managed to accumulate 30.2 WAR after his time in New York (clearing the 100.0 career WAR hurdle in the process), but he was never at his peak after he left the Big Apple. His 76.1 WAR (not counting oWAR) with the Mets are topped by only eight pitchers in terms of WAR accumulated for one franchise: Walter Johnson – Senators (152.3), Kid Nichols – Braves (108.5), Christy Mathewson – Giants (95.6), Warren Spahn – Braves (92.0), Phil Niekro – Braves (90.0), Bob Gibson – Cardinals (81.9), Cy Young – Cleveland Spiders (81.6) and Roger Clemens – Red Sox (81.3). The appearance of Phil Niekro among those men may or may not have blown my mind when I was researching this list.

CP John Franco (1990-2004)

John Franco pitched in 1,119 games in his career, third most all-time. Every single one of those outings came out of the bullpen, and he retired with 424 saves, good for second most all-time when he retired. Although that record has been surpassed by Trevor Hoffman and then Mariano Rivera, Franco still sits fifth all-time in saves (K-Rod has also passed him), and fourth in games finished (774). Franco pitched for 21 years, from 1984-2005 (missing the 2002 season), and so he saw first-hand the transformation of the closer role in Major League Baseball. Franco earned the Reds full-time closing role in 1986, and over the next four years, he would throw an average of 87.0 innings a season, with his games finished total nearly double his actual saves total. This was a time in which a closer would often be brought in to get five or six outs, and managers didn't bring their closer in strictly for save situations. In fact, comparing Franco's first and last seasons as a full-time closer is quite informative:

Year	GP	IP	IP/G	GF	SV	GF/SV
1986	74	101.0	1.57	52	29	1.79
1998	61	64.2	1.06	54	38	1.42

In just over a decade, the closer's role completely shifted, and in the decades since, the role has only continued to be specialized. Want more proof? Franco was the first closer to have over half of his appearances begin in the ninth inning. Modern managers use their closers almost strictly for the ninth inning of games in which their team has a lead of three or fewer runs. Although sabermetricians don't necessarily agree with the stringent use of closers in their current roles,[188] the specialization of bullpens as a whole has undoubtedly had a net positive in terms of bullpen success. Jonah Keri and Neil Payne wrote a piece for *FiveThirtyEight*, "How Bullpens Took Over Modern Baseball," in which they used lots of nice charts and fancy stats to prove this success. With lower pitch totals expected, relievers are throwing harder than ever and breaking off nastier breaking pitches than previous generations. Just skip ahead to the discussion at the closer position for the Braves Starting IX for further proof.

In terms of Franco, the Mets didn't have a great deal of success during his time with the team. Franco was, however, able to win the first pennant of his career while with the club at the ripe age of 40. Of course, age was never much of a factor for Franco who threw in the majors until the age of 44.

Even if Franco's numbers weren't the top among Mets relievers (which they are), it would be hard to deny him this spot. He was born in Brooklyn, the son of a NYC sanitation worker and nephew of a NYC firefighter, and an eventual St. John's (Queens) graduate. Franco was an immense contributor to the city throughout his career, especially in the aftermath of the September 11th attacks. Franco won the Lou Gehrig Memorial Award in 2001, in large part thanks to his contributions to the city of New York. He remains a New Yorker through and through, helping to grow the game in the city after his retirement.

[188] Brandon McCarthy: "I've actually had this discussion more in a baseball clubhouse, or plane flights, than I have any other thing that follows sabermetric principles, and that's the misusage of your relief ace. I've never understood it; it makes no sense to me. You don't save your number one starter for Game 7 of the World Series if you can win it in Game 6. It just doesn't make any sense." Backing McCarthy up is the fact that the most critical situation in the game (by win probability) only occurs in the ninth inning about 40 percent of the time. We saw a step in the "right" direction in the 2016 MLB playoffs, especially in the Cleveland bullpen, but it is still to be seen if that will carry over to any regular season. I have my doubts.

Starting IX Franchise Roster Stats

Lineup	Yrs	G	R	H	HR	RBI	SB	BB	SO	BA	OBP	SLG	OPS+	dWAR	WAR
José Reyes	11	1255	855	1491	104	505	**403**	406	637	0.286	0.338	0.438	105	2.1	27.8
Carlos Beltrán	7	839	551	878	149	559	100	449	545	0.280	0.369	0.500	129	4.3	31.3
David Wright	13	1583	**949**	**1777**	242	**970**	196	**761**	**1292**	0.296	0.376	0.491	133	1.0	**49.9**
Daryl Strawberry	8	1109	662	1025	**252**	733	191	580	960	0.263	0.359	0.520	**145**	-3.8	36.5
Mike Piazza	8	972	532	1028	220	655	7	424	546	0.296	0.373	**0.542**	136	-2.0	24.5
Keith Hernandez	7	880	455	939	80	468	17	471	459	0.297	0.387	0.429	129	0.4	26.5
Edgardo Alfonzo	8	1086	614	1136	120	538	45	458	498	0.292	0.367	0.445	113	6.1	29.5
Kevin McReynolds	6	787	405	791	122	456	67	263	341	0.272	0.331	0.460	120	-4.3	15.7
Howard Johnson	9	1154	627	997	192	629	202	556	827	0.251	0.341	0.459	124	-6.1	21.9
Pitchers	Yrs	W	W%	ERA	G	CG	SHO	SV	IP	SO	ERA+	WHIP	SO/9	SO/BB	WAR
Tom Seaver	12	**198**	0.615	**2.57**	401	**171**	**44**	1	**3045.2**	**2541**	**136**	**1.076**	7.5	3.00	**76.1**
John Franco	14	48	0.462	3.10	**695**	0	0	**276**	702.2	592	132	1.365	7.6	2.14	11.2

Tier four: They've just been around so long

This is a collection of teams who have been around since baseball's early days (1901 for the American League; 1876 for the National League) but haven't reached the peaks that some of the teams we'll be seeing in the top 10 have reached. Think of these teams like Robert Duvall's acting career. Not necessarily that great, but the roster is bound to have some gems along the way (*To Kill a Mockingbird* = Ernie Banks, *The Godfather* = Bob Feller, *Sling Blade* = Chase Utley). The main reason they rank higher than the previous teams is mostly because of their length of tenure, as there are still plenty of duds along the way *(The Judge* = Víctor Martínez, *The Apostle* = Fred Tenney).

P.S. Get ready for this to be a lot more focused on baseball's history than its present.

#16 Chicago White Sox (1901-pres.)

(Photo by Geoff Livingston/Creative Commons)

Team Background

Playoff appearances: 9 **Pennants: 6** **World Series titles: 3**
Collective team WAR: 495.5
Strengths: The ultimate example of finding enough good players in a 115-year history.
Weaknesses: If there's a Sox team that can actually claim to be cursed, it's these Sox, not the Red ones. Or maybe it's just Karma coming back around for the 1919 World Series.
What to expect from the next 13 pages: Some names that are so old that some of the Baby Boomers might not even recognize them. Also, all the sports cities in the U.S. ranked from 56 to 1.

Speaking of cursed, between the White Sox 87-year title drought (1917 to 2005), and the recently-broken 107-year-old World Series drought on the north side of the Windy City, Chicago had a pretty solid claim to be the roughest city for a baseball fans before the past decade or so. Taking a step back to the sports scene as a whole, Chi-Town has still had its fair share of success even before getting off the schneid with the Cubbies, though. The top-of-the-line team in Chicago is undoubtedly the Bulls, who have six NBA championships to go along with the man considered by nearly everyone to be the greatest NBA player of all time. The Second City also has the Blackhawks, who have five Stanley Cups (including two in the last decade) and they are one of the Original Six founding members of the NHL. Finally, the city has the Bears, who, although they have been more of a punchline in recent seasons, have nine league championships (granted, only one came when after the creation of the Super Bowl), had a dominant run in the `80s, were a consistent playoff team in the `00s, and have one of the more established histories in the league. Looking at the city's sports history as a whole, things aren't too bad; probably somewhere in the middle of the pack.

However, as you might guess, "somewhere in the middle of the pack" is not a good enough conclusion in this book. Let's take a look at the 56 cities that currently have or have had in the past at least one professional team in the Big Four Professional Sports Leagues[189] and rank each city by the success of their sports teams. Before I actually did the research for this, I had a list of rules/disclaimers as to how this process was going to be assessed, but then I just found a Wikipedia page with a list of all the championships by sport and by city, and since some of the tracking was a real bitch (the Braves and A's have both played in three cities in their franchise history, for example), we're just going to trust Wikipedia. A bit of a dangerous game, sure, but their math will be checked.

A few of those disclaimers still apply: 1) Cities will be counted as a whole, I'm not breaking down Chicago into the north/south side, nor I am even going to split New York into its Burroughs. If the city has more than one team that counts *for* the city not *against* it. Even though those teams are bound to be rivals and putting their success together is not how any rational fan would do it, too bad. Think of it as a reward for giving its citizens a chance to choose between two different teams, a definite boon for any sports fan who knows the pain of having been born a football fan in Detroit. 2) Recent history is going to be weighed a little more heavily than past history. There are probably not too many octogenarians reading this book, and even if there were, I assume they cherish their team's title in 2000 more than the one in 1950, or at least they remember it better. 3) This is not judging the fans on how intense or devoted they are, so don't worry if your city is lower than you think it should be. In a few cases, teams will get a bump for having a particularly avid fan base that could make going to a game extra-fun, but in this era, there really aren't any "dumb" or "bandwagon" fan bases (except Boston). 4) Championships count, but so do fun/entertaining players. Would you rather have rooted for the 2001 title-winning Anaheim Angels, or the 2007 World Series-losing, Colorado Rockies? Don't answer that question. 5) Being able to claim you were/are a suffering fanbase gets a few bonus points. What pre-2004 Red Sox fan or any-era Lions fan doesn't somewhat relish the opportunity to humblebrag about sticking with their team through thick and thin? That's a sports tradition as old as time. 6) No touching of the hair or face. (Las Vegas is not included in the rankings, since they haven't even completed a season with one team at the point this is being written.) Let's begin:

Tier One – Don't currently have a team:

56) Providence, RI – Providence Steam Roller (NFL)
55) Akron, OH – Akron Pros (NFL)
54) Rochester, NY – Rochester Royals (NBA)
53) Syracuse, NY – Syracuse Nationals (NBA)
52) Canton, OH – Canton Bulldogs (NFL)

Providence, Akron, and Canton were all home to NFL teams in the league's earliest days, and they haven't had a professional team within the city limits since 1926 in the case of the two Ohio teams and 1933 in the case of Providence. Why the edge to Akron and Canton? Well, LeBron's championship for the Cavaliers was basically a championship for Akron, and Canton – which, in addition to having two NFL titles compared to just one for the other two teams – has the NFL Hall of Fame, giving it the edge in this lowest tier. The two New York cities both had NBA teams, and they had those teams far more recently than the aforementioned NFL teams. Rochester lost the Royals for Cincinnati (and eventually Sacramento) in 1957 (after winning their lone title in 1951), and the Nationals left Syracuse in 1963. In addition to having their team is little more recently, the Nationals moved only as far as Philadelphia, which gives them the slight edge.

Tier Two – One team*, no championships:

51) Columbus, OH – Columbus Blue Jackets (NHL)
50) Jacksonville, FL – Jacksonville Jaguars (NFL)
49) Winnipeg, MB – Winnipeg Jets (NHL)
48) Nashville, TN – Nashville Predators (NHL)
47) San Diego, CA – San Diego Padres (MLB)
46) Memphis, TN – Memphis Grizzlies (NBA)
45) Oklahoma City – Oklahoma City Thunder (NBA)
44) Orlando, FL – Orlando Magic (NBA)
43) Sacramento, CA – Sacramento Kings (NBA)

[189] Sorry Major League Soccer and all you crazy college towns.

42) San Jose, CA – San Jose Sharks (NHL)
41) Charlotte, NC* – Carolina Panthers (NFL) and Charlotte Hornets (NBA)
40) Salt Lake City, UT – Utah Jazz (NBA)
39) Vancouver, BC – Vancouver Canucks (NHL)

Lots of teams in this tier, but no real standouts among them. Charlotte is notable for being the only city with two professional teams to still be without a championship, but the rest kind of blend together. The Thunder or Grizzlies would seem to have the best chance of moving up a tier with a championship sooner than later. The Jazz, the Magic, and the Canucks stand out from the crowd a bit thanks to having been to multiple finals in their respective sports – the Jazz and Magic having been twice and the Canucks thrice. The Magic are slightly off the pace of the other two because despite their highs, there have been plenty of lows. The (Winnipeg) Jets and Predators get the edge over the Jaguars thanks to their awesome home crowds.

Tier Three – One team, been to the promised land:

38) Raleigh, NC – Carolina Hurricanes (NHL)
37) Ottawa, ON – Ottawa Senators (NHL)
36) Calgary, AB – Calgary Flames (NHL)
35) Portland, OR – Portland Trailblazers (NBA)
34) Edmonton, AB – Edmonton Oilers (NHL)
33) Newark, NJ – New Jersey Devils (NHL)

The Oilers head the way with five titles (all coming in the `80s), but they have had some serious lowlights since. The Devils had a Braves-like run during almost the exact same time as Maddux, Smoltz, and Glavine, which makes Newark the top of the third tier. It's noticeable how many hockey teams we have seen so far. It makes sense, though, given hockey's spread into Canada, and the fact that the Original Six have dominated NHL history even more so than the original MLB teams when it comes to championships.

Tier Four – Couple teams, just the one chip:

32) New Orleans, LA – New Orleans Saints (NFL) and New Orleans Pelicans (NBA)
31) Atlanta, GA – Atlanta Falcons (NFL), Atlanta Hawks (NBA) and Atlanta Braves (MLB)
30) Indianapolis, IN – Indiana Pacers (NBA) and Indianapolis Colts (NFL)

We're starting to get to some teams that would be pretty fun to root for (Saints, Braves, and the Indianapolis teams), but these teams simply haven't gotten enough RINGZ to warrant higher rankings. Each city has had its share of playoff success, however, and they have seen some of the top talent in their respective sports (Drew Brees, Anthony Davis, Julio Jones, the Braves rotation of the `90s, and Peyton Manning, to name a few).

Tier Five – Couple teams, limited rings:

29) Anaheim, CA – Anaheim Ducks (NHL) and Los Angeles Angels of Anaheim (MLB)
28) Buffalo, NY – Buffalo Sabres (NHL) and Buffalo Bills (NFL)
27) Milwaukee, WI – Milwaukee Bucks (NBA) and Milwaukee Brewers (MLB)
26) Tampa Bay, FL – Tampa Bay Lightning (NHL), Tampa Bay Buccaneers (NFL), and Tampa Bay Rays (MLB)
25) Seattle, WA – Seattle Seahawks (NFL) and Seattle Mariners (MLB)
24) Houston, TX – Houston Texans (NFL), Houston Rockets (NBA), and Houston Astros (MLB)

There are some seriously snakebitten franchises here, as well as some franchises that have had some lengthy playoff droughts. Both Buffalo franchises are known to be about as cursed as any, and there are plenty of expansion franchises in this tier. In the current climate, Seattle is about as good a sports town as you'll find, and they have a title from when the Supersonics were in town, but there were some dogged years for the Mariners. Plus, having the Sonics ripped away from them was about as painful a break up between a sports team and its city as we've seen. Houston was already atop this tier before their 2017 World Series win, so their most recent title only emboldened their 24th overall rank.

Tier Six – Four teams, one championship:

23) Phoenix, AZ – Arizona Cardinals (NFL), Arizona Coyotes (NHL), Phoenix Suns (NBA), and Arizona Diamondbacks (MLB)

Phoenix is the lone one-championship city to be able to offer its fans a team in all four major professional sports leagues, a huge benefit for any sports-obsessed American. However, the teams don't have the history that most of the four-sport cities have, and they haven't had that much success either. The Diamondbacks have the city's lone championship, and that came on a Mariano Rivera blown save, so they're nearly shut out. Of course, by the same token, the Cardinals are one crazy Santonio Holmes catch away from having one of their own, but such is the nature of sports. In general, having four teams is awesome, and the D'Antoni-era Suns were about as fun a team to root for as any, making Phoenix a top-25 sports city despite a rather brief history.

Tier Seven – Ohhhhhh Canada :(

22) Montreal, QC – Montreal Canadiens (NHL)

21) Toronto, ON – Toronto Maple Leafs (NHL), Toronto Raptors (NBA), and Toronto Blue Jays (MLB)

While Phoenix is rather new to the game, Toronto and Montreal rely on their history to boost them ahead of Phoenix. Both Canadian cities have had lots of success in their histories (mostly from their hockey teams), but they've been lacking lately. The Maple Leafs haven't won a Stanley Cup since 1967, and the Canadiens haven't won one since 1993. The Canadiens have a Yankees-like history of titles, however, with 24 in total, the second-most of any professional sports franchise, while the Maple Leafs have 13 of their own. Toronto gets the edge because they still have their baseball team (fresh off some invigorating playoff runs) and an NBA team (although the Raptors have never been to the NBA Finals), something the city of Montreal can't say.

Tier Eight – Model franchises:

20) San Antonio, TX – San Antonio Spurs (NBA)

19) Green Bay, WI – Green Bay Packers (NFL)

If these cities had just a few more teams, they would be in the top tier in these rankings, but they both have just the one team. The Spurs and Packers are about as good as it gets if a city can get only one team, though – the Spurs have missed the playoffs exactly once since I was born. Even that season was the year they bottomed out and got Tim Duncan with the top overall pick, so they even handled their lone losing season perfectly. In fact, the Spurs have as many NBA titles (5), as seasons they have missed the playoffs (5) in franchise history – talk about spoiled.

The Packers have 13 NFL titles, with four of them being Super Bowls, and they have made the playoffs 19 of the past 24 seasons. Both teams have arguably the greatest coach in their respective sport's history with the Packers being built on the strength of Vince Lombardi in the 1960s, and Spurs fans still enjoying the benefits of having Gregg Popovich in the huddle.

Tier Nine – How much does one title relieve the pain:

18) Cleveland, OH – Cleveland Browns (NFL), Cleveland Cavaliers (NBA), and Cleveland Professional Baseball Team (MLB)

The Mistake by the Lake were slotted 23rd in a tier named "What have you done for me lately?" before the Cavs 2016 title, but thanks to LeBron and the Cavs, the answer to that question is now a resounding, "Came back from 3-1 down against the team that set the regular-season record for wins in what was one of the most epic comebacks of all time led by our hometown hero who returned to Cleveland something no one supposedly ever does." So how much does that move Cleveland up? About four spots apparently, as the Browns still exist, and there is still plenty of scar tissue from that 64-year title drought across the city before the spring of 2016. A 2016 or 2017 Cleveland Spiders World Series win might have done the trick to push them up around a 13th ranking.

Tier Ten – Success, but not four teams:

17) Cincinnati, OH – Cincinnati Bengals (NFL) and Cincinnati Reds (MLB)

16) Baltimore, MD – Baltimore Ravens (NFL) and Baltimore Orioles (MLB)

15) St. Louis, MO – St. Louis Blues (NHL) and St. Louis Cardinals (MLB)

14) San Francisco, CA – San Francisco 49ers (NFL) and San Francisco Giants (MLB)

13) Oakland, CA – Oakland Raiders (NFL), Golden State Warriors (NBA), and Oakland A's (MLB)

The decision to put Oakland over San Francisco may be a bit controversial, but here are some facts:

1) Although the Warriors fans on any given night may be 95 percent San Fran yuppies, the stadium is still located in Oakland as of the time of press, and therefore, Oak Town gets to stake its claim to what is the most fun superteam ever created. (Even if they are kind of villains of the league now.)

2) The A's have won more World Series titles in Oakland than the Giants have won in San Francisco. Both teams are transplants with long histories, and although the Giants success is far more recent (and therefore more relevant), the A's do have four titles in Oakland compared to three for the Giants in San Francisco. It's easy to forget now, what with the Giants winning a title practically every year that ends in an even digit, but the Giants went their first 52 years in the Bay Area without a title. One could argue that this only makes the most recent three all that much sweeter (and I agree that the Giants have a slight edge over the A's), it's not as big an edge as one might think.

3) Although the Raiders had a heinous decade before their 2016 revival, they were one of the most fun teams to watch for the majority of the franchise's history. They had a wild card owner in Al Davis that put winning before everything else, and they have three Super Bowl victories to show for it (one of which came while they team was in L.A.). Their current team is a fun run-and-gun bunch of goons led by Derek Carr and Khalil Mack, and, man, who can argue with the team colors?! Obviously the Niners are one of the truly elite NFL franchises, with five Super Bowl victories and the *best* big-game quarterback of all time (Joe Montana[190]), but once again, the edge isn't as big as the modern fan might think.

---

[190] Take that, Brady!

In the end, these two cities are very close in terms of who is more blessed with their sports franchises, and with the upcoming moves for both the Raiders and the Warriors, Oakland won't be rated higher much longer, but for now, Oakland is the plucky underdog that I just can't help but support.

Sorry, Cincinnati, Baltimore, and St. Louis, I just spilled way too much ink for that Bay Area breakdown, hope you don't disagree with the ranking.

Tier Eleven – Four teams, but not the monoliths:

12) Minneapolis-St Paul, MN – Minnesota Vikings (NFL), Minnesota Wild (NHL), Minnesota Timberwolves (NBA), and Minnesota Twins (MLB)

11) Miami, FLA – Miami Dolphins (NFL), Florida Panthers (NHL), Miami Heat (NBA), and Miami Marlins (MLB)

10) Washington D.C. – Washington Professional Football Team (NFL), Washington Capitals (NHL), Washington Wizards (NBA), and Washington Nationals (MLB)

9) Denver, CO – Denver Broncos (NFL), Colorado Avalanche (NHL), Denver Nuggets (NBA), and Colorado Rockies (MLB)

8) Dallas, TX – Dallas Cowboys (NFL), Dallas Mavericks (NBA), Dallas Stars (NHL), and Texas Rangers (MLB)

Some folks might think these cities are a bit overrated due to the fact that they simply have four professional teams, but for a sports junkie like myself, being able to follow (or attend) a game the entire year is too big an advantage to slip behind the less-than-four-team cities, as impressive as their resumes may be.... Excluding this city...

Tier Twelve – Just give them an NBA team already:

7) Pittsburgh, PA – Pittsburgh Steelers (NFL), Pittsburgh Penguins (NHL), and Pittsburgh Pirates (MLB)

Pittsburgh has a juggernaut NFL team (the Steelers have the most Super Bowl wins with six); a hockey team that can stake its claim to multiple generational talents (Crosby today and Lemieux in the `90s), as well as five Stanley Cups victories (including the last two); and a baseball team that even when they aren't winning titles is a trendy, fun team with an amazing ballpark and a crazy-nice view of the city. If only they had an NBA team.

Tier Thirteen – Them big boys:

6) Detroit, MI – Detroit Lions (NFL), Detroit Red Wings (NHL), Detroit Pistons (NBA), and Detroit Tigers (MLB)

5) Philadelphia, PA – Philadelphia Eagles (NFL), Philadelphia Flyers (NHL), Philadelphia 76ers (NBA), and Philadelphia Phillies (MLB)

4) Chicago, IL – Chicago Bears (NFL), Chicago Blackhawks (NHL), Chicago Bulls (NBA), Chicago White Sox (MLB), and Chicago Cubs (MLB)

3) Los Angeles, CA – Los Angeles Rams (NFL), Los Angeles Chargers (NFL), Los Angeles Kings (NHL), Los Angeles Clippers (NBA), Los Angeles Lakers (NBA), and Los Angeles Dodgers (MLB)

The top six cities all have multiple championships in each of the four professional sports leagues. Detroit brings up the rear for a couple reasons:

1) Despite having four NFL titles, none of those have come in the last 50+ years.

2) Half of the city's 22 titles are Stanley Cups, and even though I included the NHL among the four professional sports leagues, the league is definitely the ugly stepchild of the bunch. Although hockey is pretty great to watch, most Americans would rank a Stanley Cup as having the lowest value of the four professional titles.

3) The city hasn't really had its share of transcendent athletes. Sure, Barry Sanders was amazing, but he retired early; Isaiah Thomas was far better than many people realize thanks in part to his notorious post-playing career, but he wasn't a top-ten NBA player all-time; Ty Cobb and Gordie Howe are all-timers, but if you saw Cobb play there's a very good chance you're reading this book from your ghost kindle, and Howe played 50 years ago and suffers from the whole "having played hockey thing"[191] – plus he wasn't as flashy as a Wayne Gretzky/Mario Lemieux-type.

Philly is next, as none of the current franchises in the City of Brotherly Love have more than three titles, and the city as a whole went 25 years without a title quite recently (from 1983 to 2008). Chicago, the "cursed city" introducing this whole exercise (remember that, a couple thousand words ago), comes in at a highly-respectable fourth, despite their baseball teams really not picking up the slack. I guess, "somewhere in the middle of the pack," was a wildly inaccurate statement, making this whole ordeal useful in the end.

The city of L.A. is really pissed right now, because...

Tier Fourteen – This millennium's winner:

2) Boston, MA – New England Patriots (NFL), Boston Bruins (NHL), Boston Celtics (NBA), and Boston Red Sox (MLB)

But there's no denying that Boston (Titletown 2K) has topped their West Coast rivals this millennium, and, thanks in part to teams with longer histories, overall. In fact, given the absurdity of counting the entire city of New York as one

---

[191] I don't hate hockey, I swear, it's just clearly a step below the Big Three.

monolith, it can be argued – as much as it pains me – that Boston is the ultimate sports town… But then you turn on the local sports radio, saw your own head off with a plastic knife, and realize that New York is better.

Tier Fifteen – Duh:

1) New York, NY – New York Jets (NFL), New York Giants (NFL), New York Islanders (NHL), New York Rangers (NHL), Brooklyn Nets (NBA), New York Knicks (NBA), New York Mets (MLB), and New York Yankees (MLB)

You know how when you're reading an online listicle, and one answer is just so damn obvious it kind of ruins the surprise (Kim Kardashian is the most annoying celebrity of all time, no way!) – that's what New York's victory is like. The sheer volume of teams in New York make it so that a Ticker Tape Parade is bound to be on the city schedule once every couple years. In fact, with eight pro teams, the city *should* have a title every four years, considering there are an average of 30.5 teams per league. The case could be made that New York actually should be lower given their actual number of titles (the Yankees own over half of their 48 titles) and how much depth from which they have to draw.

It's like Marshall's argument in *How I Met Your Mother*, when he does the math on how many girls Barney hits on every night. The fact that Barney has slept with 200 women, while impressive,[192] is actually an embarrassingly low total. He calculates that Barney's "batting average" with women is .012, or as Marshall puts it, "eight times worse than one-handed pitcher, that's right, pitcher, Jim Abbott."[193] The Knicks are a joke; the Jets are damn near as funny; the Mets were run by a dude who fell for a Ponzi scheme; the Islanders had one good decade; the Rangers had a 54-year title drought stanched in 1994 but are currently working on another 20+ year drought; the Nets have been a New York team for a grand total of five years now; the Giants (and Jets) technically play in Jersey.

[*Stephen A. Smith voice*]: How-ev-ah, each of those teams have titles (the Nets have ABA titles, but whatev), and as we just saw with Chicago, even a couple crummy teams can be overwhelmed by a few dynamite franchises. Although the Giants likely fall just outside that "dynamite franchise" level, the Yankees define it. Their 27 World Championships are the most in North American sports, and their interlocking NY is the most recognizable sports brand in the world. They're so historically mighty that when they miss the playoffs for a couple seasons in a row it's treated as a drought of biblical proportions. So, with the Yankees – and the depth of teams – New York reigns supreme.

Quickly back to the White Sox, since the Yankees just pulled off the biggest incident of scene-stealing since Kevin Hart in *Scary Movie 3*: the White Sox franchise has one of the most intriguing histories of any team in baseball history, despite what baseball fans of the last decade might think. The Black Sox Scandal is of course the most infamous of those, and in some ways, it set the tack for this franchise for a long, long time. The incident saw eight players from the 1919 White Sox throw that year's World Series, taking money from local gangsters who were placing money on the Cincinnati Reds in said World Series, intentionally helping the Reds defeat their own team. The incident rocked not only Chicago, but all of baseball, with the only positive being that the event drew so much attention to the issue the league had with the throwing of games, that the harsh judgement from Commissioner Kenesaw Mountain Landis (the eight players were found guilty not by a court of law, but by Landis, and were subsequently thrown out of baseball forever) really spooked the entire sport into avoiding any future involvement in throwing games. In addition to the Black Sox, there is also the Bill Veeck Sox, as well as the "Hitless Wonders" from just before the scandal that rocked the franchise. There is plenty of great literature on all these eras, which makes me feel a little better about dedicating their team section to other teams and other sports.

Random cool things about the franchise:

- Obama is a fan.
- During the team's 1906 "Hitless Wonders" title run, no regular hitter had an average above .279. The team hit .230 as a whole (worst in the league), but they still managed to win the World Series.
- The eight Black Sox players (who we will actually cover at the Cleveland left field spot) were actually acquitted when tried in the Chicago court system.
- The franchise's most recent mascot, "Southpaw," plays off their South Side tradition.
- The most infamous Veeck promotion (Disco Demolition Night) came when Veeck was in charge of the White Sox, a night that ended with a White Sox forfeit after the Disco Demolition-ing fans got out of control, causing damage to the field.
- The White Sox participated in the longest game, in terms of innings (25), in MLB history on May 8, 1984.

---

[192] Impressive = very STD-y, and a prime example of the gender double standard.

[193] See, it's all baseball related.

Starting IX

C Carlton Fisk (1981-1993)

There was some pretty tight competition for this spot in the form of Sherm Lollar (12 years, 1,358 games played, and 26.1 WAR) and Ray Schalk (17 years, 1,757 games played, and 28.6 WAR), but in the end Fisk gets the spot. It definitely didn't hurt that he is the best baseball player to ever come out The 802 aka my home state aka Vermont. In fact, Fisk is likely the only player born in Vermont that you've heard of,[194] which isn't too surprising given the size of the state, it's limited population, and the even more limited length of time a kid can play outdoor baseball during the year.

Fisk was the type of player who "wouldn't ask out of a game if he had both his legs cut off," according to teammate Bill Lee. Fisk began his career in Boston and established himself in style, becoming the first unanimous Rookie of the Year in MLB history and finishing fourth in the MVP in 1972. He made the All-Star team, won a Gold Glove, and contributed with the bat to the tune of an OPS+ of 162 – a figure he would never again top the rest of his career. Incredibly, for a player who had his best hitting season in his rookie year, Fisk still had a long and stable career. He ended his career with the most games caught, and he played 24 seasons in the major leagues.

The only strike against Fisk as the catcher for the White Sox Starting IX is how much he loved his time in Boston, and the fact that he never really came to grips with leaving the Red Sox. When Fisk returned to Fenway[195] after leaving the Red Sox for the White Sox in 1980, he said of playing in front of the Green Monster: "I feel like I'm turning my back on an old friend."

Fisk had every reason to like Chicago, though, as he had a career revival of sorts on the South Side. Well, maybe revival isn't the right word, but rather *extension*. Despite coming to Chicago as a 33-year-old backstop (a position that ages a lot faster because of the beating they get behind the plate), Fisk managed to play another 13 years after heading to Chicago. He played catcher for the near-entirety of his time with the club and retired as a 45-year-old having made an appearance in four different decades (1960s, `70s, `80s, and `90s). Fisk had his best season (1985), by Triple Crown numbers, as a 37-year-old, when he scored 85 runs, hit 37 home runs, and drove in 107 runs. He even stole 17 bases! He only hit .238, but still, not half bad for a guy celebrating his 20th high school reunion. Fisk continued to play above-average defense behind the plate into his 40s and, partially as a result of that defense, was worth nearly 30.0 WAR for the White Sox.

1B Frank Thomas (1990-2005)

"The Big Hurt" slugged his way to over 400 home runs in the first 16 years of his career, all while playing for the White Sox. Thomas got on base with reckless abandon, sporting a batting average over .300 for his White Sox career, to go with several times leading the league in walks. This led to a .427 on-base percentage in Chicago that would be good for 13th all-time (and behind only Barry Bonds and Joey Votto, post-1950) if we took only his Chicago playing days. Thomas hit 40 or more home runs five times in Chicago but, because of the era in which he played, never led the league in long balls. He did, however, win a batting title and several OPS titles thanks to his patient approach at the plate. During his playing days, White Sox announcer Hawk Harrelson said of Thomas, "Thirty years from now, if you take a poll, they'll say, 'Frank Thomas is the best hitter who ever lived.'" Now, Harrelson is a Tommy Heinsohn-esque homer, so that should be taken with a grain of salt the size of Thomas' biceps, but still.

During Thomas' best consecutive 10-year stretch, he posted average slashes of 104 runs, 34 home runs, and 115 RBI with an OPS over 1.000; pretty incredible numbers for a single season, let alone a 10-year average, especially one that includes the strike-shortened 1994 season. In his first full seasons in the big leagues, Thomas started a streak of seven seasons with a batting average over .300, at least 20 home runs, 20 doubles, 100 RBI, 100 runs, and 100 walks, joining Ted Williams as the lone two to do so in even four straight seasons. Williams did it six straight years, from 1941-1949 (with a few years of service interrupting in the middle), making Thomas the only man in the history of the game with those lofty totals each of his first seven full seasons in the bigs. Don't think this was lost on Thomas, a self-proclaimed stat-o-phile. Thomas told ESPN: "Money is not the thing that motivates me, stats are." His teammates in Chicago called him the Stat King, and he was able to recite historical, as well as current, player's statistics with impressive recall. This was with good reason, as Thomas has some of the most jaw-dropping numbers in history, especially in his prime.

Speaking of his prime, during the aforementioned 1994 season, Thomas was playing at his absolute pinnacle, and when the strike hit, he was on pace for 152 runs, 49 home runs, and 148 RBI to go along with over 150 walks, an average over .350, a Ted-Williams-like .487 on-base percentage, and an OPS+ well over 200. If the strike hadn't canceled the end of the year, and Thomas had kept up this incredible pace, this would rank as one of the best seasons of all time. Thomas deservingly won the MVP. Now projecting out a season to go exactly as it was at around the two-thirds mark of the season is a dangerous thing (so naturally this is the third time we will do so for the 1994 season in this book), as many an "all-time"

---

[194] Daric Barton and Birdie Tebbetts are the only two other names fans have even a chance of recognizing.

[195] Home of his famous "waving it fair" home run in the 1976 World Series.

season has been derailed by a poor final third. Finishing a season this strong can often be a challenge, as many stars can attest to.[196] In fact, Thomas himself was in a bit of a swoon before the season was cut short, hitting only .260 with just six home runs in the 27 post-All-Star Break games. Even with a second half swoon, Thomas almost certainly would have set his career-high in home runs (43), considering he needed only six home runs in the final 49 games to do so.

Thomas finished his career with Oakland and Toronto but will mostly be known for his days in Chicago. He finished his ChiSox days as the franchise leader in oWAR (74.4), on-base percentage (.427), slugging percentage (.568), runs (1,327), doubles (447), home runs (448), and RBI (1,465), all categories which he still leads.

2B Eddie Collins (1915-1926)

An unheralded legend of the game, Collins ranks in the MLB top 20 all time in WAR (123.9), games (2,826), on-base percentage (.424), runs (1,821), hits (3,315), triples (187), walks (1,499), and stolen bases (741). As such, it is no surprise Collins is the second best all-time second baseman according to JAWS, trailing the one and only Rogers Hornsby. According to Bill James, Collins is also the second-best second baseman of all time, this time trailing only Joe Morgan – meaning he is ahead of Rogers Hornsby (Second Base, A's – Page 311).

Collins spent 13 years in Philadelphia to go along with the 12 seasons in Chicago that we will be looking at here. As such, his numbers, though still impressive, don't quite do him justice when looked at on a per-team basis – part of why I felt the need to give his career totals some dap at the beginning of this bio. Although plenty of credit has been given to Collins historically (he has been called "the best" at just about everything by ex-managers), it seems as though his name has been a bit lost in the modern realm. Most of the praise Collins received in his day dealt with his smarts, and his ability to be a team player. Collins was to "team player" praise as Ruth was to praise in just about every other aspect of the sport.

Even just looking at strictly his Chicago numbers, Collins is no slouch. He compiled over 2,000 hits and posted only one season with an on-base percentage lower than .400 while with the White Sox. He was pretty much a singles hitter for his career, but in his era (and even to an extent today) a second baseman could get away with that, especially if he was as good a singles hitter as Collins. Despite never hitting more than six home runs in a season for Chicago, he managed to be worth over 5.0 WAR/season during his White Sox tenure.

In the 1917 World Series, Collins paced the team with a .409 batting average in the series victory, and he then avoided being a part of the Black Sox Scandal two years later. Collins, along with Ray Schalk, acted as the leader of the White Sox faction of players that were considered gentleman, and they were not among those who took bribes in the 1919 World Series. It is unsurprising that some of the players didn't know the fix was in, because the team was so horribly divided that the players from each faction rarely interacted.

After his career was over, Collins had the honor of being a captain (with Honus Wagner as his opposing captain) in the greatest pick-up game the sport has ever seen. It was played after the opening ceremony for the Baseball Hall of Fame in 1939, as representative players from each of the 16 teams in Major League Baseball made up the rosters that Collins and Wagner managed. It was played on Doubleday Field and was the first-ever Baseball Hall of Fame Game. It is also one of the few games in baseball history for which I would sacrifice an actual human being to be able to go back in time and attend.

3B Robin Ventura (1989-1998)

Ventura played his first 10 seasons in Chicago, and like many on these lists, he was a very consistent presence. Discounting his first cup-of-tea season with the club, Ventura was worth over 4.0 WAR/season, making him a borderline All-Star year-in and year-out, despite actually making the Midsummer Classic only once as a member of the White Sox. Ventura, although never outstanding at any one aspect of the game,[197] was a complete player who brought every skill to the diamond – outside of a good set of wheels. Ventura was also a good clubhouse guy and unsurprisingly went back to the organization after his career, eventually being hired as the White Sox manager, a position he held from 2012-2016.

Ventura gained some of this clubhouse clout in one of the more memorable moments in MLB history. In 1993, Ventura was coming off his first All-Star Game, and he was beginning to establish himself as a player in the league; Nolan Ryan was 46 and by this point had solidified his spot as the picture you find in the dictionary when you look up "grizzled veteran."[198] So when Ventura charged the mound after being hit by a Ryan pitch, it was going to be newsworthy anyways. The headlock that Ryan got Ventura into before treating him like his baby brother, is what made the event legendary. Now I feel bad including this in here, because Ventura has spent so much of his lifetime trying to live this down, but it is certainly a career event of note for him, and it also led to the cool story that follows:

Paul Konerko was an established veteran on the White Sox team in Ventura's first few years as the White Sox manager. Even before his professional playing days, however, Konerko's and Ventura's paths crossed. Konerko played on

---

[196] The immortal Ival Goodman – who we'll see in a bit – had an OPS of 1.000 as late as late as August 24 of 1938 but saw his end of season OPS fall to .901. Rod Carew, who was chasing history with a .402 average at the All-Star break in 1983, finished the season with a far more pedestrian .339 average.
[197] One could argue his defense in 1998 was dominant (Gold Glove, 3.4 dWAR, best Total Zone Runs in the league), but it was only one season.
[198] "Look up idiot in the dictionary. You know what you'll find?" "A picture of me?" "No! The definition of the word 'idiot,' which you fucking are." [*KKBB* no. 5]

the U.S. Junior Olympic team in 1993, and as a youngster, he had the honor of meeting ex-Team USA player Robin Ventura. Ventura had been tasked with delivering the Junior Olympic team a speech about sportsmanship and how to act in order to get to the big leagues. The team then got to go to a White Sox game that afternoon. Well, smart readers, have you figured out the connection? That's right, this was the game that Ventura charged Ryan, a day that Ventura says must have had 500,000 fans in attendance because it seems that everyone he meets says he/she was at the game. Ventura himself handles it well because it does come up so often,[199] and he and Ryan seem to have patched up their differences.

SS Luke Appling (1930-1950)

"Old Aches and Pains" played all 20 of his seasons as a White Sock. Appling got his somewhat insulting nickname from how often he complained about nagging injuries. Of course, he rarely missed games, making him like the coworker who every single day exults his ability to never miss work, while simultaneously hacking up a lung and complaining all day. This personality trait led to Appling also being called "The Indestructible Invalid," one of the all-time greatest nicknames.

Appling (2,749 career hits) probably would have reached the 3,000-hit plateau if he hadn't missed all of 1944, and most of 1945, serving his country overseas in WWII. Similar to Collins, Appling was mostly a singles hitter,[200] and as such, it would have been fitting if he had been able to get those 3,000 hits. Even though he was 43 years old at the time of his retirement, something tells me that, if he had been playing in the modern game, he would have switched teams[201] and played out the string, trying to reach 3,000 hits on a different team. It wouldn't have been a hard sell, as he was a player whose on-base percentage was .439 in his penultimate season. Although *3,000* has always been a hallowed number, the media today plays this milestone number up to be a bigger deal than ever – basically a Hall of Fame guarantee – and team loyalties aren't nearly as strong today as they were in Appling's era.

Regardless, he was a key member of the White Sox in his time there (albeit with zero playoff appearances in his career) and is the franchise leader in career WAR (74.5). Appling's two best years by WAR (1936 and 1943) are his two seasons in which he won his batting titles, which isn't surprising, but certainly not always the case.

Maybe nothing shows Appling's prowess as a contact hitter better than a couple of stories about Appling and foul balls. Appling reportedly once fouled off 23 pitches in one game, but the story behind that number is even better. Before the game, Appling wanted to give two baseballs to admiring fans, but he was denied by the team because the balls cost $2.75 a piece, and teams didn't have nearly the cash flow then that they have now. His first time at bat, "The Indestructible Invalid" worked the count full and proceeded to foul off 10 straight pitches, at which point he shouted towards the team secretary who had denied him the baseballs earlier – "That's $27.50, and I'm just getting started." According to legend, he sent another $35.75 worth of foul balls into the stands that day. There were also numerous studies measuring just how much Appling cost the team year-in and year-out in with foul balls into the crowd. One such study said the White Sox saved $1,400 a year when Appling went off to war, with another study suggesting the figure was actually $2,300. These were assuredly an inexact science, but in an era when Appling salary itself was barely five figures ($11,000 in 1943, the year before he left for WWII), even the lower of those figures is quite significant. On the modern pay scale, it would be as if Robinson Canó cost the Mariners $3 million in baseballs in just his first season in Seattle. That's nuts.

The other thing to know about Appling was how well he aged. In all of baseball history, there are only 18 instances of players age 38 or older having 5.0+ WAR seasons, and Appling has two of those. The other players to have two such seasons: Barry Bonds, Babe Ruth, Honus Wagner, and Willie Mays. The latter of those two seasons for Appling (1949) came when Appling was 42 years old, making him the oldest player to ever have a season with 5.0+ WAR. And although it wasn't in a true MLB game, he also managed to hit a home run off Warren Spahn in the 1982 Old Timer's Game at the ripe age of 75. Not bad for a guy who hit only 45 home runs in his whole career.

Appling's talents didn't age as well off the field, as he was a better hitter than manager. When managing the A's in 1967, Appling felt bored, so he went to get a hot dog and a beer from the concession stand… During the middle of a game. Needless to say, he was not hired back in 1968.

LF Orestes "Minnie" Miñoso (1951-1957; 1960-1961; 1964; 1976; 1980)

"The Cuban Comet" may not be the most famous White Sox left fielder (don't worry we'll get to a certain shoe-lacking Joe later), but he was certainly their best. Miñoso was famous for many reasons – among them: his late career comebacks, his hustle, being one of the first black Cuban players in the league, and having a quirky personality. We will go into depth about Miñoso here, because Jackie Robinson (deservedly) gets so much recognition for breaking the league's color barrier that sometimes the other guys who did so much to move the game forward don't get quite enough recognition.

---

[199] Thanks in part to the Rangers having it as part of their pre-game video before every game for almost 20 years. (They removed it before the 2012 season once Ventura was back in the league as a manager. I don't know if this speaks more to how epic the fight was, or the fact that the Rangers really didn't have a lot going on for them in those 20 seasons. Oh, and guess who the Nolan Ryan-owned Rangers opened the 2012 season playing against; you guessed it, the Robin Ventura-led White Sox. Plotlines abound!)

[200] Although, Appling did manage to get more extra-base hits than strikeouts in his career.

[201] The White Sox did not want him anymore, as they were changing the direction of the club.

In many circles, Miñoso is thought of as the Latin Jackie Robinson. Although Miñoso was not the first darker-skinned Latin American player to play in the Major Leagues, he was the first true standout, a player that an entire generation of Cuban ballplayers looked up to. In a documentary that came out on Miñoso in 2011 called "Baseball's Been Very, Very Good To Me,"[202] Latinobaseball.com's Ralph Paniagua says of Miñoso, "Guys like Juan Marichal and Orlando Cepeda, when Minnie comes into a room, they bow down." In fact, it was Cepeda who referred to Miñoso as the Latin Jackie Robinson. The aforementioned documentary is chock-full of excellent Miñoso stories, but let's set those into context.

Saturnino Orestes Armas Miñoso Arrieta, or Minnie, was plucked from the Negro Leagues after the 1948 season by Cleveland. Miñoso was blocked by a couple of talented Cleveland players that we'll see once we get to their Starting IX, making him somewhat expendable, and so the White Sox made their push to land Miñoso in early 1951. The White Sox got the deal done, and when Miñoso took the field on April 17, 1951, he became the first black player to take the field for the White Sox in franchise history.

Miñoso made an immediate impact, finishing second in the Rookie of the Year, while making the All-Star team and finishing fourth in the MVP. He led the league in triples (14), steals (31), and hit by pitches (16). Those 16 times Miñoso was hit were partially thanks to Miñoso's inclination to crowd the plate, but they were also partially due to his skin color. Miñoso chose to fight back with his feet, and he was a mad man on the base paths. He led the league in steals his first three full seasons, as well as times caught stealing in his second and third seasons. He was the face of the "Go, Go White Sox," the first iteration of the club that the city could really get behind since being burned by the 1919 Black Sox.

Miñoso and the city built an incredibly symbiotic relationship during the 1950s, as Miñoso made five All-Star appearances with the club in the decade (he also made one with the White Sox in 1960 and one with Cleveland in 1959) and finished in the top-four of the MVP three of his first four full seasons. Although the White Sox didn't win a pennant while Miñoso played with the club, the team posted a winning percentage over .500 every year Miñoso was with the team, this after going 10 years from 1941-1950 without doing so once.

As such, Miñoso was one of the most beloved players in White Sox history, with Richard Lindberg saying of Miñoso in *The National Pastime*, "[Miñoso was] certainly the most popular player in club history." The fact that Miñoso was given an honorary World Series ring in 1959 (the White Sox won the pennant but lost the World Series to the Dodgers), despite the fact that Miñoso actually played for Cleveland at the time, speaks to his beloved nature in the organization and the massive role he had in the club's revival. Miñoso's beloved nature was due in part to the team's success when he was there, in part to how talented a player he was, and in part to his historical impact, but it also had to do with the fact that he was quite the lovable man.

Miñoso once sent back a preseason paycheck to the White Sox saying, "I am sending this contract you sent to me, because I guess you was wrong about it. It looks like a contract which belong to me for a year of `53 or `54, not for Miñoso after fine 1956 year I have. I can't think this contract belong to me. It belongs to another player of the club. This salary has expired and is no good for me for next season. Contract for me should have more money than one sent by mistake for next season." He once took a pitch to the jaw that required 11 stitches, but he stayed in the game to run the bases. Miñoso once said of his (baseball) hometown, "I love the people of Chicago. They make a gentleman out of Minnie." He kept this joie de vivre into his Golden Years and, as an 89-year-old, would do 150 sit-ups first thing every morning.

Speaking of age, it is a stunt pulled by Bill Veeck for which Miñoso is most often remembered. In 1976, and then again in 1980, Miñoso made appearances on the White Sox,[203] making him one of only two players (Nick "The Clown Prince of Baseball" Altrock being the other) to appear in an MLB game in five different decades. In fact, the Red Sox even tried to get him on the field for a sixth decade in 1990, but the commissioner blocked their attempt for health reasons. Now this may seem like an attention-grabbing stunt on the surface, but for a man who loved baseball as much as Miñoso, that was hardly the case. This was a man who, even after he was cut in 1964, came back to the ballpark to hang out and warm up with the guys, saying, "That's the way I am. I'm going to die this way...wanting to play more baseball."

Some people have (stupidly) used these stunts as a reason that Miñoso shouldn't be in the Hall of Fame, but people are idiots and countering that argument would only imply that it has any leg to stand on, whatsoever. Miñoso likely belongs in the Hall on statistics alone, but when considering his role as an ambassador to the game, the decision becomes a no-brainer. Sadly, he still doesn't have his plaque in Cooperstown, and since he passed in March of 2015, he will not be able to attend his induction should the Veteran's Committee ever get their act together and vote him in. But Miñoso is in a better place now, probably playing his sixth decade of ball in the Good Place and not worrying about Cooperstown and the like.

CF Chet Lemon (1975-1981)

In Bill Simmons' *Book of Basketball*, he mentions in Bob Pettit's bio that he has to punish players from previous generations a bit because he just can't picture them really keeping up with the new guys.[204] I definitely agree with this, and

---

[202] Yes, Garrett Morris stole Miñoso's catch-phrase "baseball has been very, very good to me," for his Latino baseball player character, Chico Escuela, on *Saturday Night Live* in the `70s. It may have been slightly racist, but Miñoso had such a good view on life I like to think he would have seen the humor in the character and found Morris' take entertaining, while maybe rolling his eyes a bit.

[203] As a 54-year-old, Miñoso got a hit off of Frank Tanana as a part of the "over-the-hill-gang" in 1976.

[204] Grumpy Old Editor's note: It was actually the editor of Simmons' book who disagreed most with Pettit's high rank.

although I am trying to go by the numbers for the most part, when there are two similar careers, such as Lemon and Fielder Jones (who played at the turn of the 20th century), the more recent player is typically going to win out.

Jones was a solid player in his own time, and he played for the White Sox in the first eight seasons of the franchise's existence (1901-1908). He outpaces Lemon in runs and hits by a relatively large margin, and he even beats him out in WAR (31.8 to 24.9).

There are a few reasons I'm going with Lemon, though. The first is not a good reason really, but I reserve the right to use strange logic in this book. The time in which Lemon played (the 1980s) is a highly-ignored period of baseball, and it is definitely under-represented throughout this book. It wasn't the prettiest era for baseball, but it does deserve some recognition.

The more reasonable purpose for starting him goes back to the era argument. One thing that goes a bit under the radar is how much improvement has been made in scouting for the sport. The ways in which players are recruited to play baseball, trained, and then brought up to the big leagues today (and even in the `80s when Lemon played) is totally different than in the days of Jones. I think it's fair to say that the league in which Jones played was missing a far greater chunk of the country's potential best players (even before thinking about the fact that Jones didn't have to play against any black players). Many of the best ball players during Jones' day may have either never been properly scouted, and thus gone under the radar, or an even greater number probably had to start supporting their family with other jobs at such a young age they couldn't be worried with something as trivial as training to play baseball. This is not something I will hold against all the players from Jones' era, but I think it is something important to remember when putting these players into a historical perspective. In fact, if we want to look at the flip side of that coin, if Fielder Jones had been born when Lemon was, maybe he would have been born into a situation where he would have been able to spend winters training indoors, and he could have been an even better ballplayer. "What if's" like that can become dangerous, as so many controls have to be put on all possible factors that we'll never truly know.

For instance, look at this Zach Lowe-esque "this, but that," "on-other-hand," "point-counterpoint" style analysis.

Point: In every sport that is measured objectively – i.e. most of the Olympic events – records are broken continuously throughout history, as athletes learn how to train better and hone their bodies with more precision.[205]

Counterpoint: Part of the beauty of baseball is that the main skill is hand-eye coordination, which, although it can be improved, is much more innate than something like speed and strength which are easier to be improved with modern training techniques.

To actually finish by discussing Lemon: he played his first seven (six full) seasons with the White Sox and was a good ball player who went on to have success with division rival Detroit after leaving Chicago. Lemon was a strong defender who holds the American League outfield records for chances (524) and putouts (512) in a season (1977). However, he was also one of the worst base runners of all time, as he is one of three players in MLB history to have less than 60 steals and been caught stealing more than 75 times, with 58 steals compared 76 times caught stealing in his career. To end on a positive, under-the-radar, sabermetric note: Lemon[206] led the league in hit by pitches four out of five years from 1979-1983, which, to go along with his outstanding range in the outfield, made him a valuable and somewhat forgotten part of White Sox history.

RF Magglio Ordóñez (1997-2004)

Ordóñez, like Lemon, played the first half of his career para Los Calcetines Blancos before hopping on 94 East and heading to division rival Detroit to end his career.[207] Ordóñez had his best five-year stretch with the South Siders from 1999-2003, posting an average season of 102 runs, 32 home runs, and 118 RBI with .312/.372/.546 slashes. He was a below-average fielder, and that fact, in addition to the league's offensive mood and (lack of) positional scarcity, made him worth "only" 4.5 WAR/season during those five years, despite posting what look like near-MVP numbers. Before nagging injuries hit Ordoñez, he was a pretty solid base runner for the ChiSox as well, going 31/25 HR/SB in 2001, while being caught stealing only seven times.

After his major league career, Ordóñez moved back to his hometown in Venezuela and was elected Mayor of Sotillo, running as a Socialist after years of public support for Hugo Chavez. Of course, his electoral victory as a Socialist led to plenty of snarky comments about how much Ordóñez had enjoyed the benefits of a free market while collecting over $133 million during his baseball playing days. Whenever politics are involved it means there will be a divide in opinion, and although Ordóñez did win his election, there are certainly Venezuelans who no longer support their local sports hero. This was evidenced by the fact that Ordóñez was booed at the 2009 World Baseball Classic by Venezuelan fans who didn't find his political stances to be satisfactory.

---

[205] Point taken from *The Book of Baseball Literacy* by David Martínez, a very strong book that I highly recommend.
[206] Is it a bad sign that I watch so much TV that, when I hear the name "Lemon" in my head, it's in Jack Donaghy's voice?
[207] Where he most memorably sent the Tigers to the 2006 World Series with an ALCS-winning walk-off home run.

Utility Paul Konerko (1999-2014)

Nellie Fox was originally the choice to fill the utility role for the White Sox. Fox was an incredibly difficult player to strikeout and was the hitter whom Whitey Ford called, "the greatest hitter he ever faced."

But Fox didn't fit the utility spot well. Sure, he may have been way higher than Konerko in WAR (46.9 to 28.8), but he was primarily a singles hitter like so many other hitters on this White Sox team. If this team were to play, they would be putting a lot of pressure on Frank Thomas to be the main power guy, with smaller power contributions from other players (Fisk, Ventura, Miñoso, Ordóñez), but Thomas was going to be the only legit power source if Fox were chosen over Konerko. Konerko gives the team a perfect number four hitter; whereas, Fox would have been best at the top of the order, where Appling and Collins already reside. Fox and Konerko had nearly equal offensive contributions for the White Sox (Konerko: 33.8 oWAR, Fox: 34.5 oWAR), and although Fox would have hypothetically given the White Sox more flexibility from this utility spot (middle infielders can typically move around the diamond easier than corner infielders), he played only eight games anywhere other than second base in his entire 2,303-game career.

Konerko also gets the nod because there will be fewer and fewer modern players as we move into these original 16 franchises. This is due in large part to pre-free agency players often playing far more games with one franchise than current players do because they simply didn't have the autonomy that modern players have.

With that settled, let's focus on Konerko a bit. Konerko retired in 2014 after 18 seasons (16 of which were in Chicago), and on the surface, it would seem he chose a poor year to have his retirement tour. He was going up against Derek Jeter's ~~canonization~~ ~~coronation~~ ~~circle-jerk~~ retirement tour, which was the moral equivalent of releasing a Wes Anderson film the same week as a Michael Bay film; that Anderson film (Paul Konerko) is going to go under-the-radar for a lot of casual observers, with only the true cinema (baseball) fans taking notice. Konerko did, however, receive a Lifetime Achievement Award from CSN Chicago; have his number retired by the White Sox; and even had White Sox chairman Jerry Reinsdorf hint at the possibility of an eventual statue to honor Konerko outside U.S. Cellular.

Konerko was all about his retirement taking a back seat to Jeter's, saying to *USA Today*, "When I saw Jeter's announcement that he was retiring I said, 'Perfect!' I'm not a big fan of being the whole focus of attention."

The Yankees, for their part, made a nice gesture when Konerko played his final game in New York, with Jeter himself presenting Konerko a signed first base bag. I'm sure the two had a chuckle about the whole retirement tour sideshow while the media took their pictures.

Konerko didn't take the normal path to becoming a "Face of the Franchise" player. He took the road less traveled, becoming the only player in MLB history to play less than 100 games for two teams (Dodgers and Reds) at the beginning of a career in which he went on to play 16 or more seasons with one team afterwards. He truly found his place in Chicago and made it his own. As such, he deserves to be honored on his team's Starting IX, a team for which he hit 432 home runs and collected over 2,500 RuBIns.

SP Ed Walsh (1904-1916)

Big Ed is the all-time leader in ERA for all qualified pitchers in MLB history at a ridiculous 1.82. Walsh's ERA record seems a pretty safe one at first glance. The game has certainly moved towards more runs since Walsh's era. However, a quick glance at the top 15 shows a way in which he could be dethroned. Mariano Rivera is 11th all-time, and if his rookie year – in which he did not yet have a defined role – is removed, his ERA drops to 2.02, which would be good for fourth all-time and within sniffing distance of Walsh. Now matching, let alone topping, Rivera's career success would be extremely difficult for even for today's relievers, but because it is plausible I would tend to leave Walsh's 1.82 career ERA off the list of truly unbreakable records.

It is interesting to think about just how much the statistics of Walsh and his contemporaries benefited from the era in which they played. Being able to doctor the baseball, as well as regularly using baseballs that were in poor condition because the league was too cheap to swap out the ball when it was damaged, gave pitchers a huge advantage. That's part of the reason (along with the changing number of pitchers in a rotation and the expanded role of bullpens) that so many of those early-era pitching records are so unattainable in the modern game.

Just think about this: over an eight-day stretch in 1908, Walsh threw 41.1 innings in an attempt to win the White Sox a pennant, a pennant that they came up just shy of winning. His 464.0 innings pitched that season were a modern record. He salary was $3,500[208] that year… How much does Tommy John cost?

Walsh achieved a decent amount of success through his top pitch, his spitball, which he could supposedly make move four different ways. He made the pitch famous and even made a living as one of the top spitballers once the rest of the league caught on. For his first few years using the spitball, he would lick the actual ball. He stopped this tradition quickly when, in 1909, the A's applied some of their own magic to the ball – horse manure. After this, Walsh stopped his licking approach and did some serious head hunting of the A's for a bit as retribution. Not to be denied, Walsh often still went to his spitball after, instead applying the saliva by spitting on it. In fact, he went to his spitter *very* often. "Few outside of the

[208] With a $3,500 bonus for winning 40 games.

players on the team know how much I use the spitball in actual games," Walsh said. "Well, sometimes nine out of 10 balls I throw are of that style of delivery." That quote was from Walsh in 1912, so clearly manure could only do so much to slow this man down.

Final thought: Walsh was a handsome chap and was well aware of it. He would often pimp and pose on the mound, the early-history baseball version a peacock.[209] Sometimes he would strike a pose at the top of his wind up, a pose he would hold for up to a minute. (He was Daisuke Matsuzaka's childhood hero.)

CP Hoyt Wilhelm (1963-1968)

Wilhelm had one of the strangest careers of anybody in baseball history. He played 20 years, which is pretty typical, but he debuted at 30 years old and played until 16 days shy of 50 – not at all typical. He got the delayed start to his career thanks to time in the service[210] (Wilhelm was 18 when the draft was implemented) and a general hesitancy among pro clubs in the late `40s and early `50s to implement a knuckleballer such as Wilhelm. However, Wilhelm eventually did enough in the minors to impress Leo Durocher and the Dodgers, in what has to be considered one of the first stats-over-eye-test victories in early scouting. Wilhelm and his knuckleball burst onto the scene his rookie season, finishing second in the Rookie of the Year and fourth in the MVP. He led the league in games pitched (71), ERA (2.43), ERA+ (152), and winning percentage (.833), going 15-3 out of the bullpen and helping to spearhead the First Reliever Revolution (though many teams were slow to catch on).

Wilhelm spent time with nine different teams during his career, 95 percent of the time coming out of the bullpen, but he was available to make spot starts every now and then. His six-year stint in Chicago was his longest, and best, with any team. His 171 ERA+ with the team is better than any other stop during his career – a career otherwise known as the "Traveling Bullpen Tour of Wilhelm" – and his 1.92 ERA in Chicago was undoubtedly elite. Surprisingly, despite all these travels, the man who helped mainstream the knuckleball played in the playoffs only once in his career, winning a World Series in 1954 with the Giants. Although there are a few names ahead of Wilhelm on the ChiSox saves leaderboard, Wilhelm was the "closer" when closers were used more as relief aces. In fact, Wilhelm was at the forefront of the change to teams thinking that a pitcher out of the bullpen as a real weapon. Thanks to his role as mostly a relief pitcher – as well as a knuckleballer[211] – he was able to play late into his lifetime and accumulated an impressive legacy. Many think of Wilhelm as the Grandfather of Relief Pitching.

Starting IX Franchise Roster Stats

Lineup	Yrs	G	R	H	HR	RBI	SB	BB	SO	BA	OBP	SLG	OPS+	dWAR	WAR
Nellie Fox	14	2115	1187	2470	35	740	73	658	192	0.291	0.349	0.367	95	20.3	46.9
Eddie Collins	12	1670	1065	2007	31	804	**368**	965	205	0.331	0.426	0.424	133	3.0	66.6
Frank Thomas	16	1959	**1327**	2136	**448**	**1465**	32	**1466**	1165	0.307	**0.427**	**0.568**	**161**	-20.2	68.2
Magglio Ordóñez	8	1001	624	1167	187	703	82	333	431	0.307	0.364	0.525	127	-4.2	25.2
Robin Ventura	10	1254	658	1244	171	741	15	668	659	0.274	0.365	0.440	117	12.4	39.3
Luke Appling	**20**	**2422**	1319	**2749**	45	1116	179	1302	528	0.310	0.399	0.398	113	19.0	**74.5**
Minnie Miñoso	12	1373	893	1523	135	808	171	658	427	0.304	0.397	0.468	133	-4.5	41.3
Chet Lemon	7	785	403	804	73	348	45	281	377	0.288	0.363	0.451	126	3.4	24.9
Carlton Fisk	13	1421	649	1259	214	762	67	460	798	0.257	0.329	0.438	109	7.1	28.8
Pitchers	Yrs	W	W%	ERA	G	CG	SHO	SV	IP	SO	ERA+	WHIP	SO/9	SO/BB	WAR
Ed Walsh	13	195	0.609	**1.81**	426	249	**57**	35	2946.1	1732	146	0.995	5.3	2.85	63.4
Hoyt Wilhelm	6	41	0.554	1.92	361	0	0	99	675.2	521	**171**	**0.935**	6.9	3.12	16.4

[209] "I'm black NBC, very proud, like peacocks, right Janet? I think we got it."
[210] Wilhelm was a Purple Heart recipient and pitched his whole career with shrapnel in his back from WWII.
[211] A knuckleball which Rob Neyer ranks as the best of all time.

#15 Baltimore Orioles (1954-pres.); St. Louis Browns (1902-1953); Milwaukee Brewers (1901)

(Photo by Keith Allison/Creative Commons)

Team Background

Playoff appearances: 14 **Pennants: 7** **World Series titles: 3**
Collective team WAR: 522.9
Strengths: The infield is dynamite, especially in terms of defensive abilities, and they have a legitimate ace.
Weaknesses: The outfield isn't quite there, and offensively they lack in the power department outside a few sluggers.
What to expect from the next 14 pages: The Negro League stars, who almost had a chapter unto themselves. Also, the best moment in baseball history determined. Absolutely. With no room for arguing.

The Orioles have over 100 years of history, and three different locations, to their name. Despite that, there will still likely be some names on this team that even an above-average baseball fan might not recognize. That is not to say the franchise has been a failure, in fact, Ripken's Run and the Robinsons' Reign were particularly strong, but there have certainly been multiple weak stretches in franchise history.

One of the weakest stretches came during the team's origins, back when they were known as the Browns. Located in St. Louis, the Browns won one pennant in over 50 years, and they managed to lose 100 games in eight different seasons (despite eight fewer regular season games at the time). Despite their futility, if I had been a baseball fan back in the 1940s and `50s, I would have been a Browns fan for the one simple reason: Bill Veeck. Baseball's most eccentric owner, Veeck came to own the Browns in 1951. Veeck is a legend who was just mentioned briefly in the Chicago White Sox section and will be covered more thoroughly in the Cleveland intro, but he was such a character that it's hardly a surprise to see his name show up so often.

When Bill Veeck was the owner of the Brows, he often came up with promotional stunts to maintain attendance despite the team's poor performance. Once, in 1951, he let the fans manage the game. The fans voted on the starting lineups a few weeks ahead of time, and the fans who filled the stands were given "YES" and "NO" signs when they arrived at the stadium. They were seated behind first base and were able to vote on important decisions in the game, such as whether to hit-and-run or when to pull the starter. A quick estimate was made, and the decision was then carried out while the Browns manager, Zack Taylor, sat in a rocking chair in his slippers, smoking a pipe. The Browns won the game, and maybe it shouldn't be surprising that the fans did better than Taylor, considering he has the lowest winning percentage (.350) for any MLB manager with as many games coached (649).

Back when Veeck first bought the team, he hired Rogers Hornsby (who had been out of baseball 15 years) along with Marty Marion to manage the Browns, and he brought in the indelible Dizzy Dean to announce. He did this as an attempt to undermine the Browns cross-town rivals (the St. Louis Cardinals), as all three were Cardinal legends. Of course, the

Cardinals were the far more entrenched (and successful) St. Louis club, and after a few seasons in St. Louis, Veeck decided to sell his shares in the club to a group that moved the team to Baltimore.

The club was able to turn things around after moving to Baltimore in 1954, and by the late 1960s had actually created quite a nice dynasty. Led by Brooks and Frank Robinson, the O's put up arguably the best two-year and three-year stretches in baseball history. The preeminent source on baseball dynasties is the appropriately named, *Baseball Dynasties* by Rob Neyer and Eddie Epstein, a source that has been, and will be, referenced numerous times throughout this book. In their book, Neyer and Epstein look at 15 of the greatest dynasties over two-year and three-year stretches. They use different analytical ways to determine how dominant each team was, and one of the methods used was to measure runs scored and runs surrendered over multiple seasons to create a Standard Deviation Score. This allowed Neyer and Epstein to rank the teams against each other across different time periods. The 1969-1971 Orioles finished with the top three-year stretch for any Standard Deviation Score in baseball history. This shouldn't be surprising, as for the 1969-1970 seasons, the O's posted a combined .670 win-loss percentage, a percentage that has been topped by only three teams in a single 162-game season, let alone in two combined seasons.

The team continued their success through the late `70s and the first half of the `80s, capturing another title (they won in 1966 and 1970) in 1983, when Cal Ripken Jr. had his breakout MVP season in what was just his second full season. Ripken learned the "don't take this success for granted" trope the hard way, however, as despite Ripken's outstanding career, the O's would go another 13 seasons before returning to the postseason at all, and Ripken would never win another pennant, let alone another title. When Ripken retired in 2001, as a 41-year-old, he had played in only 28 career playoff games, with the most important nine of those coming all the way back in 1983.

As for recent history: the Orioles have been one of baseball's hardest mysteries to solve. Under Buck Showalter the team has continually outperformed projections, as well as in-season metrics like Pythagorean win-loss and third-order winning percentage. With the state of baseball analysis and projections as advanced as it is today[212] that is an impressive feat and speaks not only to Showalter's talent as a manager, but the players' ability to perform above expectations.

Random cool things about the (word) *franchise*: Before the current MLB franchise named the Baltimore Orioles came into existence in 1954, there were a few different iterations of "Baltimore Orioles." While technically part of the Yankees franchise history, the first "Baltimore Orioles" were a charter member of the American League (1901), but Ban Johnson knew he needed a team in the major market of New York, so he moved the team to the Big Apple in 1903. There is some controversy over whom the history of those Orioles "belongs to. "Personally, I'm going with Baseball-Reference and including them with the Yankees, rather than the modern-day Orioles.

There was also a minor league team in the International League called the Baltimore Orioles that were among the best minor league teams in history. They did not have a major league affiliate since the modern system of Triple-A, Double-A, Single-A affiliates did not exist in its modern form (we'll learn about that later in the Dodgers introduction), but they rostered such stars as Babe Ruth and Lefty Grove before they became big time MLB stars. The team was built in large part thanks to the scouting of Jack Dunn who will be discussed in more detail later (Starting Pitcher, A's – Page 315).

- While your brain is hurting from trying to determine just what makes a "franchise," check out Brady Anderson's 1996 Orioles campaign which may just be the most magical, unicorn, quadruple rainbow, flash-in-the-pan season of all time – just go check it out.
- One of my favorite silly sports traditions is when fanbases shout part of the National Anthem louder than the rest, which **O's** fans are able to do thanks to the "**OH** say can you see" section of Francis Scott Key's historic melody.

Starting IX

C Chris Hoiles (1989-1998)

Hoiles played his whole career with the Orioles, even though it was a relatively brief career. He played 10 seasons and was the O's main catcher for eight. He was about average for seven of those, but he had a great 1993 season. He set career highs in runs (80), home runs (29), RBI (82), batting average (.310), and WAR (6.8). He even had his best defensive season, sporting a 1.3 dWAR. By reaching 7.0 *FanGraphs* WAR (remember, the formulas for Baseball-Reference and *FanGraphs* WAR are slightly different) in fewer than 550 plate appearances, he also joined an eight-player list that includes four Hall of Famers (plus Barry Bonds, Chipper Jones, and Mark McGwire) for players to reach such a high value in so few plate appearances in a single season.

For a while, it appeared as though Hoiles was most likely a placeholder in this position for the player of the future, Matt Wieters. Wieters got a lot of buzz during the beginning of his career in Baltimore (making four All-Star appearances), but by the time he left after the 2016 season, a lot of the shine had worn off. Injuries and ineffectiveness led to Wieters

[212] And rapidly advancing just as quickly. A lot of the metrics in the book will seem dated in 3, 2, 1…

dropping from a 12.4-WAR player in his first four seasons with the Orioles to just a 3.9-WAR player in his final four seasons with the club.

1B Eddie Murray (1977-1988; 1996)

"Steady Eddie" played with the Orioles for the first 12 years of his career and made another brief, half-year stint with the O's at the end of his career. In his first year with the club, Murray became the first player ever to win Rookie of the Year while playing DH. Along with Carl Yastrzemski,[213] they are the only two in baseball history to reach 100 hits in their first 100 games in the majors. Murray truly earned his "steady" nickname in Baltimore, never really missing time and always performing at an above-average level. Excluding his final truncated stop in Baltimore, Murray missed more than 10 games in a season only once, and as such, he is the all-time leader in games played at first base. He had at least 110 hits and 20 doubles for 19 consecutive seasons, and he hit under 25 home runs in a season just twice for Baltimore – the season he missed time to injury, and the strike-shortened season of 1981, a season in which he actually led the league in home runs (22). His OPS+ was never below 120 in a single Baltimore season, and his lowest WAR total was 3.2. He led the league once each in games, home runs, RBI, walks, on-base percentage, and OPS+. Murray was also one of baseball's top switch-hitters in history and amassed the second-most home runs by a switch-hitter to date. He is also the only switch-hitter in the elite group of players with 3,000 hits and 500 home runs. The three non-switch-hitters are Hank Aaron, Willie Mays, and Rafael Palmeiro.

Murray didn't establish himself with any one team after leaving the Orioles, but he managed to gather up enough home runs at each stop to make it into the 500-home run club, which at the time had only 14 members. As Bill James put it, "His best year was every year." He is in the top five in many Orioles statistical categories and is second in home runs for the franchise. Nobody had more RBI throughout the 1980s, and Murray defined the old saying (and Ben Golliver favorite) that a player's best ability is availability.

2B Bobby Grich (1970-1976)

Bet you didn't pick up this book figuring to see Bobby Grich in here twice, but Grich is one of the most criminally underrated players of all time. In fact, he is approaching the "so underrated they are now overrated" tier of baseball history along with Ron Santo and Tim Raines.

Grich's main talents – getting on base via walks and hit by pitches, in addition to his strong fielding – are not what draw the attention of regular baseball fans. Much ink has been spilled on baseball's most underrated players of all time, including Jayson Stark's excellent book "The Stark Truth," so without going into too much detail on why each player is underrated, here is the Starting IX for most underrated players of all time.

C) Craig Biggio – Biggio spent most of his career at second base, but he came up to the majors as a catcher and spent his first four years there before moving to second. His case for being underrated was already laid out (Second Base, Astros – Page 130).

1B) Jimmie Foxx – Highly regarded by today's fans, the fact that it took him eight Hall of Fame elections to receive entry into Cooperstown and received only 6.2 percent of the Hall of Fame vote in 1947, show his underrated nature.

2B) Bobby Grich

3B) Edgar Martínez – Spent far more time as a DH, but he spent his first few years at the hot corner and was an average fielder, just another reason it's silly to hold his playing DH against him.

SS) Alan Trammell – Rarely hit into double plays, wasn't afraid to get hit with a pitch, and played excellent shortstop for his entire career – the perfect player to be underrated.

LF) Barry Bonds – Yes, this is crazy, but people punish his numbers because of the PED use more than they should.

CF) Carlos Beltrán – Another player we have covered in depth.

RF) Shoeless Joe Jackson – When people think of him, it's for all the wrong reasons; he was an earlier Bonds in that sense. He was not quite the player Bonds was, but he wasn't *that* far off – Jackson had an OPS+ of 170 for his *career* (ninth all-time).

SP) Lefty Grove – Same reasons as Jimmie Foxx.

In terms of his time with the Orioles in the first half of the 1970s, Grich was a stud second baseman. A great fielder, in seven seasons with the club, he saved them 11.3 wins by dWAR, including 3.9 in 1973 alone, leading the league's position players in total WAR (8.3). From 1973-1975, Grich led the American League in putouts, assists, and range factor for second basemen every year. Later in his career, after he left the Orioles, he remade himself as a power threat, and he actually tied for the league lead in home runs in the strike-shortened season with the man right next to him on this imaginary infield, Eddie Murray. Grich also had an excellent eye throughout his years with the O's, topping 100 walks twice and sporting a .372 on-base percentage as an Oriole despite a rather paltry .262 batting average in Baltimore.

---

[213] Who is actually a pretty good career comp for Murray.

3B Brooks Robinson (1955-1977)

A 23-year career, all with the O's, resulted in Robinson being in the upper echelon of all-time Oriole legends. (He trails only a certain shortstop in the minds of many.) A consistently good hitter (nearly 3,000 hits), and a consistently great fielder (16 straight Gold Gloves), Robinson was the most popular Oriole for fans of his generation and one of the most widely-loved players around the league at the time. His nickname, "The Human Vacuum Cleaner," was quite appropriate for a man who deserved each of those aforementioned 16 Gold Gloves. Robinson's ranks in every fielding category among third basemen all-time shows just how great he was: games played – first; assists – first; putouts – first; fielding percentage – first. Yeah, he was the best defensive third baseman of all time, no debate allowed. Total Zone Runs are a measurement of how many runs above or below average a player is worth at their position based on their range and fielding ability. Robinson not only leads all third basemen in this category historically, but he is first among *all* fielders at *any* position, and it isn't even particularly close. Robinson is worth over 50 runs more than Andruw Jones, who is second all-time (293-242). According to dWAR, Robinson won the Orioles nearly 40 games (38.8) during his career, and this total actually seems low, for a number of reasons.

What people who aren't stat-heads sometimes argue is that statisticians can sometimes overlook anything outside of the numbers. Numbers are an important part of assessing players – especially when they can help to more-objectively compare two players – but Robinson's glove was almost certainly worth more than 2.0 wins a season to the O's over his career. How many times do you think the Orioles had a lead in a game when their opponent started to make their move with a rally, only to have Robinson make a sublime play at third and completely kill their momentum? A play like that might help out his numbers (range factor, fielding percentage, etc.), but the numbers would not do justice to the fact that the play Robinson just made may have just won the mental side of the game.

Another thing statistics sometimes can't account for is some of the subtleties of having a true game-changer. How many opposing batters do you think were trying to lay down bunts for hits when a dude named The Human Vacuum Cleaner was manning the hot corner? Not many. How much more confident do you think his pitching staff had to be knowing Robinson was going to get anything near him? A pitcher pitching with confidence is then able to attack the strike zone (especially low-and-in to right-handed batters) and really control the game. As Robinson himself said, "It's a pretty sure thing that the player's bat is what speaks loudest when it's contract time, but there are moments when the glove has the last word."

Robinson was also a very good postseason performer for the Orioles, winning a World Series MVP in one of his two World Series wins with the club. He posted a career .303 batting average in the playoffs and hit .485 for the 1970 playoffs, as a whole. His teammates almost certainly weren't surprised by his rampant playoff run, as Robinson was the man who showed up for 1970 spring training with luggage that read "1970 World Champions."[214] He also kept up his excellent glove work in the playoffs, leading Johnny Bench to say, "I will become a left-handed hitter to keep the ball away from that guy."

A final story that epitomizes Robinson's fielding ethic: in his early days, when he still felt he had to prove himself, Brooks went face-first into a concrete ledge, chipping five teeth, and basically knocking himself out. When he heard the trainer call for an ambulance, however, he shook it off and went back out to the field to finish what he had started.

Somewhat ironically, "Brooks Robinson, Fielder Extraordinaire" hit into a record four triple plays during his career. In the words of Michael Scott: "How the turn tables."

SS Cal Ripken Jr. (1981-2001)

Undoubtedly the man most people think of when they think of the Orioles, "The Iron Man"[215] certainly deserves the recognition. Ripken played all 21 years of his career for the Orioles and is the team leader in basically every statistical category you can imagine. Due to the extreme length of his career, you get a bit of the good with the bad. Although he is the all-time leader in home runs by a shortstop, he was also baseball's all-time leader in double plays grounded into for more than a decade (Albert Pujols just passed him), and he is fourth all-time in outs made. This makes sense. While Ripken's counting stats were inevitably helped by all his games played, his slashes (and negative counting stats) were hurt by playing through injuries and fatigue to keep his streak going. However, like Brooks Robinson, Ripken was an excellent fielder and brought the Orioles over 30.0 wins via dWAR thanks to a solid glove (18.1 wins via Rfield) and tough position (15.0 wins via his positional adjustment). When we get down to brass tacks, though, what Ripken will always be known for is the fact that he played 2,632 straight games, shattering what was previously believed to be an unbreakable record set by Lou Gehrig. During the middle of his streak, he played five consecutive seasons without missing so much as a single inning.

In 2002, MasterCard set up a vote for baseball fans to determine the Most Memorable Moment in Baseball History. Ripken breaking Gehrig's record for most consecutive games played ended up as the people's choice as the winner. Not that this moment wasn't a great moment in baseball history, but it seems like a good opportunity to do a completely subjective,

---

[214] This is reminiscent of the Jedi mind trick Doc Rivers pulled during the 2008 Ubuntu Boston Celtics season, when he took $100 from each player and staff member and left it in the ceiling of the Staples Center during the Celtics only regular season trip to L.A to face the Lakers. The meaning: the Celtics would have to return to meet the Lakers in the NBA Finals to reclaim that money. Of course, they did.

[215] Still not quite as cool a nickname as his predecessor, "The Iron Horse."

picked by me, mini-bracket to determine the same question. I'll use the top nine moments from the MasterCard vote[216] and add in seven other essential moments in baseball history. With those 16 moments, each will be randomly assigned a number 1-16, and we'll do this March Madness style. LET THE GREAT EXPERIMENT BEGIN!

Round One

1) 2001 – New York's first game after 9/11
vs.
16) 1985 – Pete Rose passes Ty Cobb as the all-time hits leader

As I said before, I randomly assigned these seeds, and not to foreshadow too much, but in terms of "Chill Factor," it's hard to top the goosebumps anyone got who watched the night that baseball returned to New York. This game showed the rest of the country that we may have been down, but we weren't out, and it showed the city's strength as much as a silly game like baseball is able to. Top it off with the fact that it was a great game, and that the Face of the Franchise at the time (Mike Piazza) hit the go-ahead home run in the eighth, and it is a candidate to make a good run. Rose never had a chance.

2) 1941 – Joe DiMaggio's 56-game hit streak
vs.
15) 1941 – Ted Williams posts most recent .400 batting average

Quite appropriately this matchup offers a similar dilemma to the one that 1941 AL MVP voters faced 70+ years ago. Although the MVP should have been given to Williams – that will be discussed later – DiMaggio's streak is maybe the most-discussed event in the baseball lexicon, and with good reason. Sorry Ted, but you're losing to Joltin' Joe again.

3) 1998 – Mark McGwire and Sammy Sosa break Maris' single-season home run record
vs.
14) 1920 – Babe Ruth sold to Yankees

McGwire and Sosa's run towards 61 revitalized the sport in a way that has only really been done a half dozen or so times in baseball history, if that. Sadly, they are up against the man that revitalized the sport the first time it needed it. After the Black Sox Scandal rocked the baseball world in 1919, Ruth moving to baseball's biggest stage and becoming a home run god was exactly what baseball needed. Ruth went on to be the game's biggest star and played a large role in making baseball the national pastime for so long. There has also never been another moment that got the credit for sealing the fate of two franchises for as long as the sale of Ruth did to both Boston and New York. This is not to say that the curse was a real thing, but instead that from that moment on, the Red Sox were the Bobby Brady to the Yankees Greg Brady – at least until 2004.

4) 1939 – Lou Gehrig retires with his "luckiest man" farewell speech
vs.
13) 1995 – Cal Ripken breaks Lou Gehrig's consecutive game streak

These two men will obviously be tied together in history forever, and right around now you're probably thinking I fixed these match-ups because they have been pretty perfect. This is a hard one because without Gehrig, Ripken's moment loses a lot of its meaning. On the flip side, when Ripken made his run at Gehrig it meant that a lot of fans from the younger generation were able to learn more about Gehrig, including digging into the MLB archives to watch his farewell speech. For me, Gehrig's speech – highlighted by the fact that he was suffering from ALS a disease that would later take his name – means that this moment is just a little bit more special, although Ripken got a tough draw to say the least.

5) 1960 – Bill Mazeroski's World Series walk-off
vs.
12) 1999 – Ted Williams at Fenway All-Star Game

These are two completely different events and the first real oddball match-up in the bracket. Mazeroski's home run came in Game 7 of the World Series, the most important game of the year; Williams' came in the All-Star Game, a glorified exhibition game, and one in which Williams wasn't even playing, obviously. Mazeroski's home run capped a series victory in which the Yankees outscored the Mazeroski's Pirates by 28 runs and resulted in a Pirates championship that, if it wasn't lucky, was certainly fluky; Williams being enveloped by every star in the game, in such sheer revelry that it appeared as if Zeus himself had descended from Olympus[217] was far from fluky, it was a brilliant piece of marketing by MLB. So, with this apples and oranges comparison, one of the best ways to settle it is which would be a more memorable event to attend. Although a World Series walk-off is every kid's dream when they're playing baseball growing up, the buzz in Fenway as Williams circled the field and then threw out the first pitch is giving me goosebumps just writing this. Williams moves on.

---

[216] Eliminating the tenth place finisher (Nolan Ryan throws his seventh no-hitter) because, although impressive, it was not one of the 10 best moments in baseball history. I'm sorry.

[217] Seriously, go find the video on YouTube and just look at the players' faces as they surround Williams on the mound. They can't help but smile in awe and admiration.

6) 1951 – Bobby Thomson's shot heard round the world
vs.
11) 1956 – Don Larsen's World Series perfect game

Two Cold War baseball events that took place in New York less than five years apart find themselves head-to-head here. Thomson's blast was a walk-off home run that capped a near-month long charge[218] back from a 13-game deficit to the Dodgers. The home run itself came in Game 3 of a playoff for the pennant before baseball had a League Championship Series, and it capped about as exciting a pennant race as baseball has ever seen. Larsen's perfect game came in Game 5 of the 1956 World Series and was part of a Yankees come back from down 2-0 in the series, en route to winning their 17th World Series. There has been only one other no-hitter in postseason play, and no other perfect game has ever been thrown in the playoffs, let alone in the World Series. However, maybe it's the fact that we saw three perfect games in 2012 alone, or the fact that the history major in me loves the Revolutionary War reference of Thomson's blast, or maybe it's even the classic call from Russ Hodges, but for my money I'm taking Thomson's shot.

7) 1936 – Original Hall of Fame class induction
vs.
10) 1947 – Jackie Robinson breaks the color barrier

Sorry, no breakdown here. Sure, seeing Ty Cobb, Babe Ruth, Honus Wagner, Christy Mathewson, and Walter Johnson enter the "hallowed" Hall would have been amazing, but Robinson breaking the color barrier blows that out of the water.

8) 1974 – Hank Aaron breaks Babe Ruth's all-time home run record
vs.
9) 1988 – Kirk Gibson hits pinch-hit home run to win Game 1 of the World Series

A pair of epic home runs that are pictured as much in the mind's eye for each player rounding the bases as much as the home run itself, makes for another great matchup. In Aaron's case, it was the two fans who decided to escort him on his way around the bases, and in Gibson's case, it was his limping trek around the bases while fist-pumping to a level never seen before Tiger Woods. In the pro-Gibson column, there's the fact that he was injured and watching the game from the clubhouse television before Lasorda called upon him – pretty epic. Although not a walk-off, it did win the game for the Dodgers, and it eventually propelled them to their sixth (and most recent) World Series victory. The game was also called by the man who should voice every baseball moment – Vin Scully.[219]

As much as Gibson's home run benefits from the "Scully Bump," it's just not possible to leave Aaron breaking the most hallowed baseball record out in the first round. As outfielder Bill Buckner (yes, that same *Bill Buckner*) said when explaining why he climbed the wall even though he knew Aaron had hit that 715th home run way out of his reach, "They were offering $30,000 for it."

Round Two (The Quarterfinals)

1) 2001 – New York's first game after 9/11
vs.
8) 1974 – Hank Aaron breaks Babe Ruth's all-time home run record

This is where the match-ups start to get real interesting, and where a bit of bias may come in. As a baseball historian, one always wants to make sure that events are put into their proper historical perspective. Baseball, and its writers, have done a phenomenal job of making sure baseball history is learned by today's generation. That being said, there is something to say for having lived through the moment. When the World Trade Center was attacked, I was in fifth grade, and it had about as big an impact on my childhood as any world event. The amazing thing is what I remember most isn't the fear that we felt following the attack, but rather the feeling of camaraderie that brought our nation together and left us stronger than ever.[220] It seems silly that a baseball game can really be on people's mind after such a horrible attack on humanity, but, often times, sports and entertainment are exactly what is needed to get people's minds off the horrible things in life and focused on the little things that can bring us joy. The Mets game on September 21, 2001 did just that, and for that reason it is moving on.

---

[218] With a little help from their friends... Aka Herman Franks with a telescope in the center field clubhouse. But more to come on that later.

[219] One of the main ways you can tell if someone is at the top of their profession is if someone who knows nothing about the profession can spot them as the best. I have separately had both a family member and a girlfriend, who didn't know who Scully was, comment on how great an announcer he was without any prompting. The man is a legend.

[220] As I write this, it is important to note that I am living in Boston, only three days removed from the Boston Marathon Bombings. That same sense of unity is taking over the city, and it is a feeling I am proud to be a part of.

2) 1941 – Joe DiMaggio's 56-game hit streak
vs.
10) 1947 – Jackie Robinson becomes the first African-American Major Leaguer

Here comes what very well may have been the top two seeds had they not been seeded randomly pre-bracket.[221] No two moments in baseball history have as much written about them as these two. Here's the big difference, though – only one of them truly affected the rest of baseball history. True, whenever a player gets a hit in 25 straight games the clamor about Joltin' Joe's record begins, but it really can't compare to Robinson (and Larry Doby in the far less forward-thinking American League) coming to the big leagues to make the game a better place for all athletes in the future.

14) 1920 – Babe Ruth sold to Yankees
vs.
6) 1951 – Bobby Thomson's shot heard round the world

Another all-New York match-up, this once again pits off-field versus on-field. As mentioned before, Thomson's blast not only won the pennant, but it ended a comeback of epic proportions in the final weeks of the season.[222] It also claimed the Giants-Dodgers, East Coast, OG rivalry in its favor, as well as the fact that both teams would soon move out to California, leaving two fan bases shell-shocked on the Eastern Seaboard. However, when baseball's most famous player is sold within the division, Thomson's shot simply doesn't have enough firepower to compete.

(One fun game to play is wondering just how different "The Shot Heard Round The World" would have been if it occurred in 2016 instead of 1956. Would the moment have been even crazier if it single-handedly made Twitter explode, or would some of the mystique be taken away by everybody sharing his/her pointless opinion on the game via his/her Facebook status immediately after. The best sports moment to play this game with is Willis Reed's Game 7 appearance in the 1970 NBA Finals. Reed came out of the tunnel to play despite a severe leg injury, and the buzz from the crowd seemed to propel the Knicks to their first ever title, despite Reed making only two baskets the entire the game. [They *were* the first two shots of the game.] If that had happened today, wouldn't Adrian Wojnarowski have tweeted out that Reed was playing before the actual game? And since everyone at the game is on their phones the whole time now,[223] the crowd would have known about Reed's big moment before the fact, and the magic of the moment would have been gone. There's a lot of good to be said about all of today's technology, but the aura that comes with not knowing every single detail, and relying on anticipation instead, seems truly lost with the advances in the "right now" generation.)

4) 1939 – Lou Gehrig retires with his "luckiest man" farewell speech
vs.
12) 1999 – Ted Williams at Fenway All-Star Game

Two incredible off-field moments. In case you couldn't tell by now, even though this book usually favors the cold hard numbers of baseball, when it comes to this bracket, I'm a sucker for spine-tingling moments that seem ripe for the movies. Although Williams at Fenway was spine-tingling, Hollywood literally made a movie about Gehrig with the key scene being his speech. A biopic about Williams could easily include a scene with his Fenway farewell, but it wouldn't be the defining scene, as Gary Cooper's speech was in *Pride of the Yankees*.

Round Three (The Semi-Finals)

Before we move on to the match-ups it's interesting to note just how well the random number generator that that Google gave me was at producing a storyline-filled bracket. On one side of the bracket there's Gehrig's farewell speech and New York's first post-9/11 game going in a match-up to decide the winner from the "Most spine-tingling-wish-you-were-there" category. On the other side, there's Robinson breaking the color barrier pitted against Ruth's sale to the Yankees in the "Moment that had the biggest impact on the game" category. Good job, randomness.

1) 2001 – New York's first game after 9/11
vs.
4) 1939 – Lou Gehrig retires with his "luckiest man" farewell speech

Once again, another all-New York match-up. It would be interesting to see a non-Yankee fan do this bracket, huh? Too bad. One of the best things about brackets are the surprises. We see it every March, and it's why we as a nation fill out millions of brackets on ESPN, but every year there's nary a perfect bracket by the end of the first weekend. It's why growing up, whenever I made a bracket of my favorite songs, somehow my *favorite song* never actually won. Brackets are filled out in the moment. One game Florida Gulf Coast can beat Georgetown, and in one bracket "Skinny Love" can knock off "Baba O'Riley." Brackets like this can give us an in-the-moment glimpse of how we were thinking at the exact time they were filled

---

[221] How dumb would that have been, though? Hmmm, he ranked Ripken's consecutive game streak higher than Gibson's pinch-hit homer, I wonder who will win?
[222] Similar to the final day of the 2012 MLB season, which, itself, was on the short list before the final cut down to 16.
[223] Queue "Old Man Yells At Cloud" meme.

out. This is a match-up that will feel that impact. As mentioned in a footnote above, the fact that I am currently living in Boston and attended the 2013 Boston Marathon (thankfully I watched far from the finish line, over in Brookline), I am currently feeling the energy that envelops a city after an attack on its security. The outpour of support from friends, family, neighbors, and the city as a whole has been a remarkable thing to see first-hand, and although the devastation was not nearly on the level of the World Trade Center attack, it has had me thinking about how awe-full it is to be in a city when something like this happens. I spelled awe-full that way on purpose. Obviously the attack was awful; it was thoughtless, spineless, and an act of cowardice that took the lives of three innocent civilians and scarred many more physically as well as emotionally. Since the attack, however, I have also been *full of awe*, seeing the runners who ran that twenty-seventh and twenty-eighth mile to give blood that they were surely lacking after the marathon. Full of awe at the togetherness of this city in helping out the Boston Police Department's investigation with any and all helpful tips they can send their way. Full of awe at how resilient the city is. Maybe I will look back somewhere down the line, and say, "Gehrig probably should have topped the Mets post-9/11 game," but for now – for this bracket – the Mets move on.

10) 1947 – Jackie Robinson becomes the first African-American Major Leaguer
vs.
14) 1920 – Babe Ruth sold to Yankees

If this were a real NCAA bracket, the previous match-up would have been your typical Kentucky versus Louisville showdown. A closely contested battle between two rivals who are in close proximity to each other, somewhat like the 2012 Final Four game between the two aforementioned schools. By that logic, this match-up would be the two teams that you don't realize are on totally different levels until they matchup – think Duke versus West Virginia in 2010. Sure, West Virginia looked good on its trip to the Final Four, but Duke was just too talented. Jackie Robinson is Duke. Ruth's sale may have greatly impacted two franchises, but Robinson's, and – I'll continue to say it – Doby's impact breaking the color barrier affected the league unlike Ruth's sale ever could.

Round Four (The Final)

1) 2001 – New York's first game after 9/11
vs.
10) 1947 – Jackie Robinson becomes the first African-American Major Leaguer

While it has made a fairy-tale run, the buck stops here for the Mets. Robinson's breaking the color barrier not only impacted baseball history, but it was one of the first steps towards the Civil Rights movement that would define much of the latter half of the 20th century.[224]

Now that that has been settled, two quick Ripken anecdotes and the most random stat of all time.

Actually, let's lead off with the random/awesome stat: Ripken homered when his games played streak reached 250 games, 500 games, 750 games, 1,000 games, and 1,500 games. Some have made the case that this is because he always came through in big games (like his final All-Star appearance when he homered and took home the game's MVP award), but this more likely seems like one of the coolest coincidences in baseball history.

On to the anecdotes: in 1998, Ken Rosenthal, who was writing for the *Baltimore Sun*, wrote that Ripken should voluntarily end his consecutive games streak. Ripken "responded"[225] by hitting a foul ball into press row that smashed Rosenthal's computer. Obviously this is a story that stretches the boundaries of what Ripken could or could not purposely do, but who'd doubt it from a man who didn't miss a day of work from the time Paul McCartney and Stevie Wonder had a no. 1 hit single ("Ebony and Ivory") until after *Titanic* was busy breaking box-office records?

Ripken's write-up will conclude the way he wanted to be remembered, an excerpt from his speech at the baseball Hall of Fame during his first-ballot induction:

"Did you ever stop to think about how your life would unfold or imagine how you would like your life to turn out? One of those reflective pauses happened in my life when I was around eighteen years old. I thought I had it all figured out: I would play big league baseball until about forty-five and then worry about the rest of my life after that. It took me a little while, but I did come to realize that baseball was just one part of my life – with the possible exception of this weekend, of course. This was never more clear to me then when we had children. I realized that the secret of life is life."

LF Ken Williams (1918-1927)

Williams is the first player listed on this team who played for the franchise when they were in St. Louis. He played there for 10 years, posting a .326 batting average. Although his career was short, he put up eight strong seasons with the Browns, including an excellent two-year stretch from 1922-1923 in which he had a combined 234 runs, 68 home runs, and

---

[224] And is defining much of the last few years, as well.
[225] Put in quotes because only Roy Hobbs could actually control what happened next.

246 RBI with a .344 batting average, a .425 on-base percentage, and was worth 15.5 WAR. In fact, in 1922, Williams became the first player ever to hit 30 home runs and steal 30 bases in a season, and he was the only one to have done so until 1956 when Willie Mays joined him.

Due to the MVP voting process, however, Williams didn't receive even a single vote for the award that impressive 1922 season. That was because voters could choose to vote for only one player per team. The far more established George Sisler hit .420, while Urban Shocker won 24 games on the mound, both doing so as teammates of Williams. Still, Williams was worth 7.9 WAR and became the first American League player to hit three home runs in a game. He even stole the title of the Home Run King, as Babe Ruth was suspended for the first 33 games of the 1922 season, with a poem showing up in *The Sporting News* that ended: "Who makes the fans forget Babe Ruth? Ken Williams."

Williams also receives this book's honorary award for "Most Grapes of Wrath-looking Baseball-Reference Photo of all time."

(Photo from Baseball-Reference)

I don't think even Henry Fonda looks as much like Tom Joad as Ken Williams does there.

CF Baby Doll Jacobson (1915; 1917; 1919-1926)

There were two real candidates here, Mr. Baby Doll[226] and Paul Blair. When looking at their career totals with the Orioles, their numbers are relatively similar – Blair leads in runs 737 to 711; Jacobson leads hits 1508 to 1426; Blair leads home runs 126 to 76; Jacobson leads RBI 704 to 567; and Jacobson's rather large .316 to .254 lead in batting average could even be canceled out by Blair's excellent fielding. The question then becomes should a player be punished for having the years in which he struggled come as a part of his franchise, or should he be rewarded for being with the team longer and being able to accumulate higher statistical totals? Let me explain.

Between Paul Blair's first and final two seasons in Baltimore, he was cumulatively worth -0.4 WAR, meaning the Orioles would have hypothetically been better off calling up the best player from the minors for those 293 games Blair played in Baltimore. For Jacobson, he had four seasons with a WAR of a decent negative margin during his career, but only one came with the O's and that was in his final Baltimore season and was only 50 games.

The main way a player having his worst years with a franchise hurts his franchise statistics is by dragging down his percentage stats i.e. batting average, on-base percentage, etc., but most cumulative stats are actually helped out by the mere fact that there are more years with the franchise, even if they were bad years. For instance, Blair had a few exceptionally bad years with the Orioles, namely his last year when he posted -1.1 WAR, but he added 74 hits and 15 steals to his Baltimore totals that same season. Jacobson had the same struggles getting used to the league and hanging on too long at the end of his career, but he did it with other teams. So, Jacobson missed out on a couple hundred hits with the club, but he didn't do it at the expense of a sub-Mendoza batting average for multiple seasons for the franchise.

The verdict: it definitely does hurt a player's case to have his weak years with the franchise because this Starting IX is being built not based on one season of a player, but rather their career with the team as a whole. Paul Blair had his struggles in Baltimore, Jacobson had his elsewhere, which is why Jacobson gets the spot despite Blair having the edge in longevity with the franchise.

RF Frank Robinson (1966-1971)

Robinson came to Baltimore before the 1966 season and had an immediate impact, posting one of the best seasons an Oriole has ever had. During the regular season, he won the Triple Crown thanks to 122 runs, 49 home runs, and 122 RBI with a triple slash of .316/.410/.637 – all of which led the league. He was worth 7.7 WAR, which is lower than expected, namely because he cost the team 2.0 wins by dWAR (again, that accounts for his defense as well as his lack of positional

[226] Jacobson got his unique nickname on Opening Day in 1912 when "Oh You Beautiful Doll" was playing and Jacobson hit a home run. Man, it was easy to get a nickname back then.

scarcity, as he was a right fielder). He also became one of only five players[227] to win both the regular season and World Series MVP, as he helped lead the Orioles to the 1966 title, finishing up the most successful inaugural season a player has ever had with a new team. In winning the regular season MVP, he also became the first player to win an MVP in each league.

This should be no surprise given the fact that Robinson had some serious motivation after being traded away from Cincinnati in a less-than-friendly situation. As baseball writer Jim Murray said of Robinson, "He plays the game the way the great ones played it – out of pure hate." The trade, although unfair with our Historical 20/20 Glasses on, seemed relatively fair at the time. Robinson was shipped to Baltimore in exchange for three players (highlighted by Milt Pappas) after he and Reds owner Bill DeWitt exchanged words. This happened both before and after the trade. The two went back and forth over various news formats, with the general gist being that DeWitt thought Robinson was "an old thirty," and Robinson thinking "that was below the belt." Robinson is a man who once said, "Pitchers did me a favor when they knocked me down. It made me more determined. I wouldn't let that pitcher get me out." Clearly this was not a man who you could slight and then live to tell the tale.

In addition to Robinson's "*MLB The Show*-with-the-sliders-all-the-way-down" 1966 season, the team itself had plenty of success during his six years in town, with two titles and four pennants during that time. Robinson had only one poor season with the team, and he was a key part of the O's 1970 championship team, hitting two home runs in the World Series. He was shipped out of town after the 1971 season, but not before he won the 1971 All-Star Game MVP, which made him the first man in baseball history to win Rookie of the Year, MVP, World Series MVP, and All-Star Game MVP. One of the most respected men in baseball, Robinson was made player/manager for Cleveland in 1975, making him the first black manager in MLB history. He also coached the O's for over two years, taking home Manager of the Year in 1989. It is not a coincidence that the franchise enjoyed its greatest success when Robinson was around. As Brooks Robinson said of Frank Robinson's impact, "What changed around here the most and made us the team we are today was the arrival of Frank in 1966... Leadership isn't a matter of color, it's a matter of how much of yourself you're willing to give to another man and how much of you he is willing to accept. Frank gave everything of himself and we accepted everything he gave us."

Utility George Sisler (1915-1927)

A player bio told in two acts:

Part I

Ty Cobb said of Sisler, "[he is] the nearest thing to a perfect ball player."

Most of Sisler's lore is due to a stretch from 1920-1922 which culminated with an MVP in 1922. Over those three seasons, he gathered 719 hits, which is the most hits over a three-year stretch in baseball history. During those three years and 719 hits, Sisler managed to strike out only 60 times for an incredibly impressive hit-to-strike out ratio of nearly 12:1.

While his three-year stretch was impressive, it was his 1922 season that was his best. His 257 hits in the season (.407 BA) were the most in baseball history until Ichiro topped them in 2004. He was one double, two triples, and one home run away from creating a group that he would still be the only member ever of, with 250 hits, 50 doubles, 20 triples, 20 home runs, 40 steals, and a .400 average. As is, no one has reached all the totals he did in the same season anyways, they're just not quite as aesthetically pleasing. Unsurprisingly, Sisler hit safely in 125 of the 142 games in which he played that season and had a 41-game hit streak,[228] which was an MLB record until Joe DiMaggio broke it with his famous streak in 1941.

Sisler timed this year very well, as 1922 was the first year that baseball gave out an MVP award, and Sisler won it, making him an excellent trivia answer for the rest of his life. In 1911, Cobb had won the first Chalmers Award, which was basically an MVP, but the Chalmers was wrapped in an attempted advertising ploy that didn't work, and as such, it was eliminated in 1914. When Sisler won the MVP in 1922, the award was similar to the modern NFL MVP in the sense that there was only one MVP awarded to the entire sport, instead of one per league, as is done in modern baseball. Two years later, baseball adopted the current method of giving an MVP to one player from each league.

Part II

Bill James said of Sisler, "Perhaps the most overrated player in baseball history."

The offseason after 1922 continued to be a defining time for Sisler, as he had a horrible sinus attack that caused him to miss all of the 1923 season and affected him greatly going forward. He still hit .320 after the attack, but his OPS+ was merely 97 in his seven seasons after 1923, a stark drop from his OPS+ of 155 in his eight seasons before 1923. His batting eye was never quite the same.

To Bill James' salvo to open Part II: James certainly has a fair amount of statistical support for his claim that Sisler is among the most overrated of all time, even if some of Sisler's decline came from that sinus attack during the 1922 offseason. As James pointed out, despite Sisler's .340 average, his career on-base percentage (.379) is lower than Gene

---

[227] Sandy Koufax, Reggie Jackson, Willie Stargell, and Mike Schmidt being the other four.

[228] Sisler and Cobb are the only two players in baseball history to have two hit streaks of over 34 games.

Tenace (.388), a man who sported a career .241 batting average. Sisler was also famed for his baserunning, but in the years that caught stealing was a stat, he was among the leaders each year. He was caught stealing 26 times in 1916 alone. His isolated power for his career was .128, or two points worse than Gerardo Parra for his current to date... Now this is not to say he was less than the player Parra is, but Sisler certainly relied on his batting average to carry him into the Hall of Fame with ease. And as Ferdinand Lane said when taking the statistic of batting average down a peg, "Would a system that placed nickels, dimes, quarters, and 50-cent pieces on the same basis be much of a system whereby to compute a man's financial resources." Sisler was a man who collected nickels (singles), while the Babe Ruth's of the world were collecting 50-cent pieces (home runs). This logic is what has made current Major League scouts rely much more on on-base and slugging percentages than batting average in today's scouting reports.

Despite a career in which he never played in the postseason, Sisler was still able to play for some of the great minds in baseball history. In fact, he played for Branch Rickey in minors, as well as in the majors. This seems as good a time as any to mention that Rickey and Bill Veeck are the two names that seem to appear the most, and for the longest span of time, in baseball history. Hollywood has Six Degrees of Kevin Bacon; baseball might have Three Degrees of Branch Rickey.

Finally, since we are in the disparaging act of Sisler's bio, it should be noted that there were rumors that Sisler drove nails (which he then filed down) into his bat to hit the ball harder.

I think it's harsh to call Sisler the most overrated player of all time, especially considering the harsh decline to his numbers after his sinus attack. However, it is fair to point out just how much of his value came from his batting average, a statistic that has seen better days.

SP Jim Palmer (1965-1984)

Palmer played all 19 years of his career with the Orioles, and he was on the team for all three World Series that the Orioles have won in franchise history. Palmer gathered a win in each of these World Series, the only Oriole to do so. A fan favorite,[229] Palmer is the franchise leader in most every pitching category, even games pitched, a category usually led by a reliever. An excellent fielder, as well as post-season performer, Palmer won four Gold Gloves and had an 8-3 record with a 2.61 career ERA in the playoffs.

He almost didn't have any of that, however, as Palmer had one of the strangest career paths baseball has ever seen. Palmer came up in 1965 and worked mostly out of the bullpen (where he managed the impressive feat of hitting a home run in his first career win). In 1966, Palmer joined the rotation and was quite successful, especially given his precocious age of 20 years young. Palmer really burst onto the scene in the 1966 World Series, though, as he became the youngest pitcher to throw a shutout in the World Series, doing so in a victory over Sandy Koufax. This matchup would later be looked at as a turning point in baseball history, as Koufax was on his way out, and Palmer – who grew up idolizing Koufax – was in the midst of building a name for himself. However, right when it seemed like Palmer had his breakout, he then missed most of 1967 and all of 1968 with bicep problems that seemed, at the time, like they could be career-ending.

Palmer was able to overcome these injuries, however, and didn't let them ruin his career, a feat made even more impressive given the state of baseball medicine at the time. Needless to say, these kind of career-saving surgeries weren't nearly as frequent in Palmer's time as they are today. Palmer came back in fashion in 1969, throwing a no-hitter in his first year back and finishing the 1969 season with an ERA of 2.34. The resiliency Palmer showed shouldn't be surprising given that Palmer had to show this kind of resiliency as a child. He was an orphan who grew up with adopted parents – another potentially tough situation that he overcame.

After 1969, he was able to settle down and stay healthy. As a result, Palmer threw more innings and had more wins than any other American League pitcher in the 1970s. In 1971, he was part of the famous rotation that boasted four 20-game winners – Dave McNally (21-5), Pat Dobson (20-8), and Mike Cuellar (20-9) joined Palmer (20-9).[230] Palmer continued to (successfully) battle injuries throughout the decade, and his manager (Earl Weaver) tended to give him a hard time about the constant nagging injuries, leading Palmer to say, "The only thing Weaver knows about pitching is that he couldn't hit it."

From 1972-1975, Palmer put together a stretch that was almost worthy of recognition as a top four-year stretch all-time (Starting Pitcher, Diamondbacks – Page 54), but his 1974 season eliminated him from the running. He won the Cy Young award the other three years, leading the league in ERA and wins two times apiece. His 1974 season was pretty bad though, as he was below average (per wins above average), had a 7-12 record, and missed part of the season (he did still have just a 3.27 ERA, though). He also made a solid start in the postseason, but he even had bad luck there, losing a complete game four-hitter in which he gave up only one run.

During his career, Palmer gained a reputation as one of the best clutch pitchers in baseball, and former manager Jim Frey listed him as the best big-game pitcher in baseball history. The fact that, in 1983, Palmer became the first pitcher to win a World Series game in three different decades certainly doesn't hurt his case as a big-game pitcher either. Palmer also never

[229] Especially among the ladies. A simple Google image search shows the other side of Palmer's fame.
[230] They weren't, however, the only team to do so, as the 1920 White Sox also did so with Ed Cicotte (of Black Sox fame), Red Faber, Dickey Kerr, and Lefty Williams all topping 20 wins the season after the Black Sox World Series.

gave up a grand slam in his career, and he managed to hold hitters to a .233 slugging percentage with the bases loaded. He lived for the big moments.

CP Stu Miller (1963-1967)

Miller came to the Orioles at the end of his career, after having made the transition from starter to closer a few years earlier. He enjoyed five successful seasons as a closer for the O's, leading the league in saves in his first year with the team (1963). His 1965 campaign was even more impressive though, as he gathered 14 wins, as well as 24 saves (and 55 games finished), to go along with a sparkling 1.89 ERA. Miller's best pitch was his changeup, which was not only his best pitch, but, according to Rob Neyer and Bill James, the best changeup in the history of baseball (as of 2004, at least).

What really made Miller's changeup unique was that it was a straight change, one that relied heavily on an arm motion that Miller had perfected in order to throw hitters off – it started off looking just like a fastball. Harmon Killebrew once said, "I faced a lot of tough pitchers in my career, but Stu Miller gave me more trouble than anyone else because of his great motion… If I'd had to face him every day I'd have been back in Payette, Idaho real fast." Dick Hall said of hitters facing the pitch, "They'd sit around waiting for the change-up, but it took so long to get there that they went on and swung anyway." By the time Miller got to Baltimore he had perfected the pitch, and it was a major part of what made him so successful with the Orioles.

Fun story about Miller: while in the 1961 All-Star Game, Miller felt the wrath of Candlestick Park and was knocked off the pitching rubber by a particularly strong gust of wind from the bay.

One of the other options for this position was Satchel Paige. Paige came to Major League Baseball in 1948 at the ripe age of 42 after having been an established Negro League star for over 20 years. Paige put up good numbers for Baltimore, numbers that become even more impressive when you think about his age, but he certainly got robbed of being one of the most recognized stars in MLB history due to the segregation of the sport before 1947.

There were a great number of Negro League stars that deserve recognition for their achievements outside of MLB, and there was consideration at one point of putting together a Starting IX for them in addition to the 30 MLB franchises, but that was decided against for a few reasons. First of all, the statistics for the Negro Leagues are rather rudimentary, as the league was set up much differently than MLB at that time. The Negro League teams would barnstorm across the U.S. with far less structure. So for a book focusing strongly on statistics, this seemed challenging. Also, there are a great number of leagues throughout baseball history that deserve recognition (the Nippon Professional Baseball Organization of Japan, the All-American Girls Professional Baseball League, and the Korean Baseball Organization, to name a few), and including them all would be too great a task. Here's a quick look at some of the best Negro League stars, though:

Satchel Paige: Paige was an incredible, almost mythical, figure. His first few starts after Bill Veeck signed him to an MLB roster (Cleveland) shattered attendance records for the franchise and throughout baseball. His first three starts drew over 200,000 fans – including a night-game record 72,562 in his first start – and Paige finished his first season with the club at 6-1 with a 2.48 ERA; this was as a 42-year-old reliever, a change from his starting pitcher career.

A true showman, some of the best baseball "lore" stories involve Paige. He frequently told his outfielders to grab a seat because he wasn't going to need them. He once walked two players to intentionally load the bases in the ninth and face the other most famous Negro League star of the time, Josh Gibson. Paige promptly struck him out.

Paige certainly had swing-and-miss stuff. When he came to try out for Cleveland, owner Bill Veeck had then manager/superstar Lou Boudreau face Paige to prove that he could hang with the best of them. The performance has almost certainly been aggrandized at this point, but the takeaway was the same regardless – Paige was unhittable.

Certainly not a shy guy, Paige loved to promote his own myth. He claimed to have thrown 55 no-hitters and over 300 shutouts during his time in the Negro Leagues. He claimed to have started 29 games in one month and won 104 of his 105 games pitched in 1934. He also says that he struck out 22 in a barnstorming exhibition against major leaguers, and he kept all of these self-documented records in a notebook that he valued as much as any possession.

It wasn't just Paige who was impressed by Paige, however, as Bill Veeck called him the best pitcher he ever saw and said his presence on the field was rivaled by only Babe Ruth. Even if those previous numbers are exaggerated (and let's be honest, they likely are), he was one of the all-time great pitchers, as well as one of the all-time best personalities.

He once said, "Age is a question of mind over matter. If you don't mind, it doesn't matter." Paige also had six catchphrases that he called Words of Wisdom by Satch. Some were very helpful such as number one: "Avoid fried meats, which angry up the blood," and, well, some weren't, such as number five: "Avoid running at all times" – maybe not the best advice for future athletes. Paige is most well-known for his fastball, but according to Satchel, he also had a looper, a nothing ball, a bat dodger, and a hurry-up ball – what is this *Backyard Baseball*?! I half expect him to say he was facing Achmed Khan and Pete Wheeler in the batter's box. That being said, I am immediately petitioning MLB to have every pitcher name their pitches in this manner.

Josh Gibson: Gibson was the Babe Ruth of the Negro Leagues, with many sources having him credited with over 800 home runs in his career. Of course, as was just mentioned, statistics from Negro League stars are exceptionally iffy, and barnstorming schedules meant far more than the 154-game schedules that were going on in MLB at the time. Plus, the stadiums Gibson homered in were different than their MLB counterparts, and the levels of competition varied from day-to-day.

None of this is to diminish Gibson's legend, however. Gibson had great numbers in the limited action he had against major league players, many of whom he faced while they were barnstorming during the MLB offseason. Legend has it that Gibson hit a home run out of Yankee Stadium during a Negro League game when Gibson was only 18 years old, and although the legend itself may well be exaggerated,[231] it's similar to many legends in this book. The fact that the myth is so readily accepted says nearly as much about the player as the validity of the myth.

Robert Cohen said in *A Team for the Ages*, "The bottom line is this: Johnny Bench was the greatest catcher to ever played in the major leagues, Josh Gibson was the greatest catcher in baseball history." In a cruel twist of fate, Gibson died three months before Jackie Robinson broke the MLB color barrier, despite Gibson being just 35 years of age.

Oscar Charleston: Charleston's historical MLB comparisons tend to be 1) Ty Cobb for his ability to hit for average, and 2) Tris Speaker for his ability to cover so much ground in the outfield – pretty incredible. Here's the kicker: Charleston was also a power hitter. In one scrimmage – against a St. Louis Cardinals team that had finished 20 games over .500 in the MLB regular season and had superstar Rogers Hornsby – Charleston stole the show, hitting four home runs in the game, two of which came off Jesse Haines, a member of the Cardinals Hall of Fame. Right fielder Dave Malarcher, who played next to Charleston, said all he did was catch foul balls because Oscar's range was so unlimited in the outfield.

Rube Foster: Foster was a solid player, but most of his lore comes from his ability to promote the Negro League, a league in desperate need of promotion. As is the case with much of the history of the Negro Leagues, the history of just how much Rube did seems a bit blurry, but he acted in many ways as the league's "Czar," helping to run just about everything under the league's umbrella. Buck O'Neil falls into this category of player/promoter of the league.

Joe Williams: Reportedly once struck out 27 batters in a 12-inning game. The game was played in the dark and Williams was 44 years old. Of course, this shouldn't be surprising given that he reportedly had at least a dozen 20-strikeout games in his career.

Turkey Stearnes: A man truly devoted to his bats, Stearnes kept these bats in special cases, and he would often talk to them. His all-time ranks among Negro Leaguers are quite impressive. He is first in triples, second in home runs and doubles, and fifth in batting average. Cool Papa Bell said of him, "If they don't put [Stearnes] in the Hall of Fame, they shouldn't put anybody in."

Mule Suttles: According to the prolific Negro League historian John Holway, Suttles is the true Negro League record holder for home runs in a career. That's right, more than Josh Gibson.

Monte Irvin: The Newark Negro League Club said of Irvin, "Monte was the choice of all Negro National and American League club owners to serve as the number one player to join a white major league team… He was the best qualified by temperament, and character, ability, sense of loyalty, morals, age, experience, and physique to represent us as the first black player…" Instead he became the fourth when he joined the Giants in 1949.

Buck Leonard: Leonard and Gibson formed the Ruth-Gehrig combo of the Negro Leagues. Monte Irvin said of Leonard, "Satchel Paige and Josh Gibson got more publicity in the Negro League, but Buck Leonard was just as good."

Pop Lloyd: The best shortstop in Negro League history, and one of the best shortstops in all of baseball history, Lloyd was the ultimate leadoff guy. The Honus Wagner comparisons were many-and-closely-bunched (is that the opposite of few-and-far-between? Sure), and his manager called him "Cuchara," which is Spanish for "tablespoon." Why? Because Lloyd was such a good table-setter.

Cool Papa Bell: Another man of myth, and boy there were some great Cool Papa myths. Like how he slapped a single up the middle and ran so fast that his own ball struck him as he got to second base. Or how Paige said of him, "Bell could turn off a light and get in bed before the lights went out." Obviously both of those anecdotes easily transcend the barrier of exaggeration and veer into actual mythology. But they're still awesome.

Moving into the slightly more believable realm, Cool Papa (I refuse to call him Bell when Cool Papa is his nickname) regularly turned bunts into doubles. He supposedly hit .430 in an underrated and competitive Mexican League at the ripe age of 43. Eddie Gottlieb said of Cool Papa, "[He] was the black Willie Keeler with the bat, and the black Tris Speaker in center field."

---

[231] Three guesses who debunked this one. I'll give you a hint, it rhymes with Nob Reyer.

Let's end with an awesome quote from Cool Papa: "They say that I was born too soon. I say the doors were opened too late."

Starting IX Franchise Roster Stats

Lineup	Yrs	G	R	H	HR	RBI	SB	BB	SO	BA	OBP	SLG	OPS+	dWAR	WAR
Bobby Grich	7	786	432	730	70	307	77	457	520	0.262	0.372	0.405	127	11.3	36.0
George Sisler	12	1647	1091	2295	93	962	**351**	385	278	0.344	0.384	0.481	132	-4.4	52.5
Cal Ripken Jr.	21	**3001**	**1647**	**3184**	**431**	**1695**	36	**1129**	**1305**	0.276	0.340	0.447	112	34.6	**95.5**
Eddie Murray	13	1884	1084	2080	343	1224	62	884	969	0.294	0.370	0.498	139	-6.4	56.3
Frank Robinson	6	827	555	882	179	545	35	460	452	0.300	0.401	0.543	**169**	-8.4	32.3
Brooks Robinson	**23**	2896	1232	2848	268	1357	28	860	990	0.267	0.322	0.401	104	38.8	78.4
Bill Jacobson	10	1243	711	1508	76	704	81	317	355	0.317	0.364	0.459	115	-0.9	27.9
Ken Williams	10	1109	757	1308	185	811	144	497	240	0.326	0.403	**0.558**	144	-2.2	40.4
Chris Hoiles	10	894	415	739	151	449	5	435	616	0.262	0.366	0.467	119	5.1	23.4
Pitchers	Yrs	W	W%	ERA	G	CG	SHO	SV	IP	SO	ERA+	WHIP	SO/9	SO/BB	WAR
Jim Palmer	19	**268**	0.638	2.86	**558**	**211**	**53**	4	**3948.0**	**2212**	125	1.18	5.0	1.69	**68.1**
Stu Miller	5	38	0.514	2.37	297	0	0	99	502.0	432	145	1.12	7.7	2.44	12.1

#14 Cleveland Spiders[232] (1915-pres.); Cleveland Naps (1903-1914); Cleveland Bronchos (1902); Cleveland Blues (1901)

(Photo from Wikimedia Commons)

Team Background

Playoff appearances: 13 **Pennants: 6** **World Series titles: 2**
Collective team WAR: 532.4
Strengths: They excel at the marquee positions (shortstop, center field, second base) with the exception of catcher, and they are using the old "starting pitcher in a closing pitcher's clothes" trick in their CP Starting IX spot.
Weaknesses: There are definitely a few players who simply wouldn't show up on the Starting IX for most of the teams moving forward from here.
What to expect from the next 13 pages: Social Justice Warrior Jim Turvey. Some may want to skip. We've already started with the team name. It only spirals from here.

With the Cubs 2016 World Series victory, the longest active World Series drought belongs to Cleveland, who is currently sans a World Series title since 1948. The drought is up to the fifth-longest in baseball history, trailing only the two famous Chicago droughts, the Red Sox 86-year curse, and the Phillies run from 1903-1980. Cleveland also went more than 40 years between pennants (1954-1995), but that 1995 pennant started an excellent seven-year stretch with five straight division titles and six in seven years. They made the World Series twice, losing both times, with one series going seven games and one going six.

Although Cleveland has taken some (deserved) grief in recent years for their mascot (Chief Wahoo), their team name actually has a pretty fascinating origin. The story goes back to the turn of the 20th century, when Louis Sockalexis, a

[232] Not trying to make a scene with this, but I'll be referring to this franchise as Cleveland, The Land, or the Spiders (a defunct National League team that played in the 1880s and 1890s) for this entire chapter, with the exception of one paragraph about the team's name in a second. I'm doing this because not only is the team name racially insensitive and out of touch, but even back when it was acceptable, it was just factually incorrect. Christopher Columbus didn't land in India! I'll never understand the use of "Indians" over "Native Americans;" they were never Indian! The idea to refer to the franchise as the Spiders came from baseball writer Pete Beatty on an episode of the *Effectively Wild* podcast.

talented Native American ball player, came up with the club in 1897. He excelled so much that *Sporting News* said he would completely change the culture of losing in Cleveland, rendering their current name (the Spiders) irrelevant. However, during the season, at a team celebration, Louis was introduced to alcohol for the first time, and his descent began there. He became more and more of a drinker and was almost always in a state of inebriation. He wasn't able to handle "the outside world" and ended up returning to his reservation, a decision that had support from his friends and family. This is a sad story, and one hopes that when the seemingly inevitable renaming of the team happens, Sockalexis will have his story told once again rather than having his image exploited. It is said that Sockalexis, and his heritage, are at least partially responsible for Cleveland being named the Indians in 1915, as a nod to one of the city's first great ball players. Sockalexis was the first recognized minority to have played in the National League.

Maybe appropriately, Cleveland has had their fair share of characters in team history. The most prominent was a man who very well may be the greatest character baseball will ever see – Bill Veeck. Yes, this is indeed the third consecutive team write-up to mention him, but that's not a surprise considering Veeck's name is scattered throughout the legends of baseball's early days. Cleveland was the first major league team Veeck owned, after owning the Milwaukee Brewers (then a minor league outfit). Veeck had previously attempted to buy the Philadelphia Phillies. In honor of this nonconformist genius, we're hijacking the "Random cool things about the franchise" bit and replacing it with a little bit longer "Random cool things about Bill Veeck."

Random cool things about Bill Veeck: Veeck began his baseball career as a fan ambassador at Wrigley Field. He would go around collecting feedback from the Chicago fans during games and was the first of his kind to do this. It was here that he learned the art of fan interaction. Engaging fans became Veeck's calling card across his three different ownership stints in Major League Baseball. The list of Veeck's stunts is nearly endless. Veeck most famously sent three-foot, seven-inch Eddie Gaedel up to bat during a Browns game and later dropped Eddie and two other little people out of a helicopter dressed as Martians. The little people had to try to convince the diminutive Nellie Fox and Luis Aparicio to join their fellow Martians in the battle against the giant Earthlings. Veeck also hired Jackie Price (Baseball's Sad Clown) to do stunts on the field, and as pre-game hype one time, Price hung upside down from a 12-foot high bar and hit baseballs as far as 150 feet. There was also: Ten-Cent Beer Night, Disco Demolition Night, jazz combos wandering the stands, a contortionist who performed on the third base line to distract pitchers, his creation of the first season-ticket plans, the first over-the-phone ticket purchases, and the now-common practice of special days at the ballpark to engage all sorts of fans.

Veeck catered to women and children, two subsets of fans largely ignored by the other owners of his day. He was very proud of the far superior women's restrooms in all of his ballparks, and he had nurseries at the ballparks. Veeck also gave away nylons right after WWII, when they were in high demand. Veeck's creativity with his home ballparks was far from limited to women's restrooms. Veeck was the one to plant the now ballpark-defining ivy on Wrigley's outfield walls, and he created the first exploding scoreboards when he was owner of the crosstown White Sox decades later.

Veeck not only connected with ignored subsets of fans, but he also forged great connections with his players. The man did so much with and for African-American players in baseball that *Sporting News* called him "the Abraham Lincoln of baseball." As noted previously, before Veeck ever got a team of his own, he was interested in buying the Philadelphia Phillies after the 1942 season. What wasn't noted before was that he was hoping to integrate the National League years before Branch Rickey did so (1947). Whether or not the other owners blocked Veeck because of his intent to desegregate the major leagues is a point that has been debated, but the point stands that Veeck easily could have been the one to break baseball's color barrier. Once he did get a team, Veeck made sure to give an equal opportunity to black players, and Larry Doby eventually called Veeck a second father. Doby broke the color barrier in the American League for Veeck in Cleveland, and when Doby was introduced to the team, the players who were not open to being teammates with Doby were not re-signed the next season. If establishments refused service to Doby, Veeck would in turn refuse service to them. Veeck brought 14 African-American players to camp in Cleveland in 1949, decades before the sport was truly integrated, with even the average black player getting a chance in The Land before anywhere else.

Veeck was a hell of a personality, a man who lost his leg to an injury suffered in WWII and was able to see the humorous side of it. He would "tan" his wooden leg as the summer went on, painting it darker as the months went by. He also carved an ash tray into the replacement leg so that he could simply throw his cigarette butts into the wooden leg. Veeck often sat in the bleachers with his hometown fans, frequently shirtless, collecting feedback.

The closest modern comparison for Veeck is Mark Cuban, but even that undersells the audacity of Veeck's proposed changes to the sport. In addition to all of the changes he supported that did go through (introducing "Take Me Out to the Ballgame" during the seventh inning stretch; players' names on the back of their jerseys; supporting the DH rule), Veeck suggested numerous other ideas that baseball didn't go for, including Velcro walls to catch outfielders running into the outfield fence.

First and foremost, though, Veeck was ahead of his times. He was the only owner to testify on Curt Flood's side during the fight against the reserve clause (Left Field, Toronto Blue Jays – Page 104), just one of the many times Veeck proved himself one of the most progressive minds in baseball, if not America. To learn even more about this man/myth/legend, check out Paul Dickson's book *Baseball's Greatest Maverick*, or read any of Veeck's three autobiographical works.

Starting IX

C Víctor Martínez (2002-2009)

Martínez didn't break into the league at the same precocious age as some bigger prospects, and he wasn't an established starter until his third year in the league. That being said, once he was established, he had four excellent seasons before an injury-plagued 2008 campaign. From 2004-2007, Martínez had an average line of 78 runs, 21 home runs, and 99 RBI with .302/.376/.484 slashes. He put in a solid postseason performance for the 2007 Cleveland team that made it to Game 7 of the ALCS against Boston. In fact, the Spiders led the series three games to one before the Red Sox stormed back to take the series on the strength of J.D. Drew's infamous grand slam.

Although he abandoned his full-time post behind the plate shortly after leaving Cleveland, Martínez was mostly a catcher in The Land, playing 684 of his 821 games as the backstop. Martínez was an average defensive catcher, gaining most of his value from his bat, while not costing the team much behind the plate. Martínez made three All-Star appearances in Cleveland, although he didn't make it in 2005. This, despite 2005 being his most valuable season by WAR (5.2) and his second-highest finish in the MVP race while playing in Cleveland.

Of course, Martínez's best season was one of his most recent, as Martínez finished second in the AL MVP in 2014, after posting an incredible offensive season that was on par with anyone in baseball, but he did so as a member of the Tigers. Martínez nearly had more home runs (32) than strikeouts (42) that season, the type of accomplishment that has become exceedingly rare in the modern game.[233] Martínez did so at the age of 35, and given the struggles Cleveland has had behind the plate since Víctor left, seeing Martínez have his best offensive season come after leaving town – as a 35-year-old with a division rival no less – was less than ideal for The Land.

1B Jim Thome (1991-2002; 2011)

Number seven on the all-time home run list, Thome is one of the most under-the-radar players in baseball history. However, I don't necessarily think he is one of the most underrated players of all time. This may seem to be a difference of semantics, but in Thome's case I think it is correct. Thome had three main traits going for him. First, he was obviously one of the best power threats in baseball history. However, his season-high was 52 home runs in an era in which players were shattering home run records, and therefore he went somewhat unnoticed in the field that was his strongest asset. He led the league in home runs only once despite averaging over 40 home runs per season during his nine-year prime. Even in limited plate appearances as a journeyman late in his career, Thome was able to crank out home runs at a high rate. If continued through a full season, his 7.4 home run percentage (simply home runs divided by at bats) over 108 games with Minnesota in 2010 would have been the third-best of his career and good enough to lead the National League that year by a solid margin.[234] He was 40 at the end of the season.

Another strong suit of Thome's was his batting eye and ability to draw walks. Most power hitters draw a greater number of walks than contact hitters, but Thome was particularly strong in this regard, leading the league in walks three times and topping 100 walks in a season nine times in his career. He had 10 seasons with an on-base percentage over .400, and his career on-base percentage is .402 (with a .414 on-base percentage while in The Land).

Finally, Thome is considered one of the true ambassadors to the game and someone every team would like to have in their clubhouse. Basically the anti-Jeff Kent, Thome received numerous glowing reviews from his teammates over the years. When he joined the 600-home run club, Jayson Stark wrote an article that might as well have been Thome's application for sainthood. He talks about how Thome said hello to everyone involved with the organization every step of the way in his career – not just his teammates and coaches, but the stadium vendors, security guards, and season-ticket holders. Even though the article does read a bit flowery, it is quite heartwarming to hear that when Thome "demanded" a trade it was because his father was sick, and he just wanted to move closer to home. It does make you wonder, however, how many of those "headcase" athletes who demanded trades actually had legitimate reasons to leave town, but no one looked into it or listened to their story with the right mindset.

Not to take away from Thome, but it is amazing how much the media can paint the public opinion of certain players. When Tom Brady screams at his teammates during a game, it's because "no one wants it more than Brady; what a winner." When Dez Bryant does the same thing, it's because "he's a clubhouse cancer who never learned to play the right way." That's why it was so awesome when the audio came out from one of Dez Bryant's sideline "blowups" during the 2013 season, and it turned out to be Bryant using positive reinforcement, simply repeating "we're the best in the NFL" over and over. Man, what a cancer…

Although it may be an oversimplification to the say that the way the media[235] paints certain athletes is strictly tied to

---

[233] Among players with at least 10 home runs in a season, only two have had more home runs than strikeouts in a season since 1961: George Brett in 1980 (24:22) and Barry Bonds in 2004 (45:41). Man, Bonds was stupid good.

[234] José Bautista led the AL with a 7.9 home run percentage.

[235] Although this is far from just a media problem. Read "Searching for Racial Earnings Differentials in Major League Baseball" by Matt Swartz on *The*

race, it would be ignorant to say that race (or maybe more accurately, socio-economic status[236]) has nothing to do with it. Dez Bryant is a player who comes from a *tough* background. When he was coming into the league, instead of receiving support to help adjust to a new league, Bryant had to answer questions before the draft from certified jackass, then-VP of Cowboys scouting Jeff Ireland, as whether Bryant's mother was a prostitute. We have come a long way in society, but it often seems that many people see the progress that has been made as final and believe that all is right between black and white and rich and poor in this country.[237] That is ignorant and will actually bring us further back than we have come. If you don't move forward, you begin to move backwards. All right, rant over, back to Thome and his statistics. And just to clarify: ***none of this is to take away from Thome, a man who deserves every ounce of praise heaped on him, full stop.***

Due to the fact that Thome had such a long career, and that he excelled so strongly in a few categories in particular, he is rather high up in several career ranks. As already mentioned, he is eighth all-time in home runs. In addition to that, he is seventh all-time in walks, fifth in AB/HR, and second in strikeouts. He also has the rare distinction of being among the top five youngest players in the league at the beginning of his career, as well as being among the top five oldest players in the league at the end of his career. He also as many 100-run seasons as three significant men in this book combined – Tony Gwynn, Kirby Puckett, and Dave Winfield; not bad names individually, let alone combined. Thome has more walk-off home runs than anyone else in MLB history (13), and he is one of only six players to hit 40 home runs in a season in both leagues. He also holds the bizarre distinction of being the first player to hit a home run off a pitcher with a last name starting with every letter of the alphabet…[238] That's a weapons-grade "Who found this stat?" stat, right there.

2B Nap Lajoie (1902-1914)

Lajoie ended up on Cleveland through a series of strange events. He began his career on the Philadelphia Phillies, but when Ban Johnson created the American League in 1901, Lajoie stayed in Philly but switched teams, joining the newly created Philadelphia A's. Lajoie was key to the American League becoming the league we know it as today. There were numerous leagues trying to get their start at this time, but only the AL was able to gain footing on the national scene, thanks in large part to the number of established stars that joined their ranks. The biggest of these stars was, by far, Lajoie. Lajoie had enjoyed his time in the National League with the Phillies, but he was upset with the team for paying fellow teammate Ed Delahanty $400 more than him.[239] Lajoie would later say that this perceived slight was the reason he joined the upstart AL, even though the actual boost he got in salary from the A's was far greater than the $400 to which he makes reference.

In his first season in the AL, Lajoie won the Triple Crown and set the AL record for batting average (obviously, since it was the inaugural year) at .426 – still the record today. Although impressive, there are certainly a few caveats with that number: it was the American League's inaugural season and foul balls didn't count as strikes, giving an obvious advantage to hitters that would be corrected soon after. However, possibly an even bigger boost came from the expansion factor. League-wide, offensive numbers always skew higher in expansion seasons. In fact, some of the most famous offensive seasons in baseball history have come as the result of expansion (1961 and 1998 being the most famous cases). Considering the entire league was pretty much full of expansion teams, and the level of talent wasn't equal to what Lajoie had seen in previous NL seasons – or would see once the AL grew stronger – it's probably fair to attach a little asterisk next to Lajoie's .426 average. However, let's not take too much away from Lajoie. Because of his immense popularity, the A's were able to outdraw the far more established baseball team in the City of Brotherly Love (Phillies), and the NL responded by forcing an injunction that banned Lajoie from playing professional baseball in the city of Philadelphia unless it was for the Phillies. Lajoie skirted around the ruling by choosing to play for Cleveland the next season (and 13 more seasons after that) and skipping Cleveland's games in Philadelphia for that first year. This was a good idea considering when Cleveland played in Philadelphia, the team bus was greeted by the local sheriff looking for "the Frenchman" – Lajoie's nickname. Eventually the A's would move on, and Lajoie actually ended his career back with the club in Philly in 1916.

Lajoie enjoyed his greatest success with Cleveland, though, despite all the scuttlebutt surrounding his move there. He won batting titles his first two full seasons with the team, and in his 1904 season, he led the league in hits (208), doubles (49), RBI (102), batting average (.376), on-base percentage (.413), slugging percentage (.546), OPS+ (203), total bases (302), and WAR (8.6). If there had been an MVP award at the time, he would have run away with it. Lajoie was so central to the team that they were renamed the Cleveland Naps – that's about as powerful as you can be as a player and about as important to the franchise as one can be. In 13 seasons with the team, he collected over 2,000 hits while hitting .339. He topped out with a 10.0-WAR season in 1906 and tallied 5.0 WAR for his team in 10 different seasons. As far as his rank in team history, he is first in hits (2,047) and WAR (80.0), second in games played (1,614), third in total bases (2,726), RBI (919), and OPS+ (155), and fourth in steals (240).

Hardball Times for an interesting study on salary differential among different races. It's an incredibly nuanced look at the issue.

[236] Although those two are still depressingly intertwined.

[237] And for that matter straight and gay, male and female, and sooooo many other issues, but let's not get too crazy in what is supposed to be a baseball book here.

[238] Except the letter "X" because there has never been a major league pitcher with a last name starting with "X."

[239] Granted, Lajoie was still getting more than the set player salary cap with an extra $400 under the table, but he wanted to be the highest-paid player in the league.

Lajoie had a particularly strong season in 1910. Toward the end of the season, he was engaged in a tight race for the batting title with Ty Cobb. On the final day of the season, Lajoie bunted for seven base hits but still fell short of Cobb. If this sounds suspicious, that's because it was indeed. Cobb was not the most popular guy in the league, and the opposing manager, Jack O'Connor, admitted later that he told his third basemen to play deep, enabling Lajoie to get those hits. As much as Cobb did to earn that league-wide dislike, it's probably best Lajoie didn't win the batting title on the strength of those bunts.

Lajoie was so feared during the 1910 season that one pitcher, Russ Ford, tried to avoid pitching to him altogether by "intentionally walking" him his first three at bats. At the time, the process did not include the catcher standing away from the plate, so when Ford tried to pitch far enough outside to walk him, Nap simply poked the ball the other way and had three hits after his first three at bats.[240] In his fourth trip to the plate, Ford figured out a better way to deal with Lajoie – he threw four straight pitches behind his back. Lajoie was no stranger to getting walked, in fact he was the first man in baseball history to receive one of its biggest honors: a bases loaded *intentional* walk.

Finally, it should be noted that Lajoie was not merely a producer with the bat for his career, he was an all-around stud. He earned the nickname "The D'Artagnan of the Diamond" for his slick fielding.

3B Al Rosen (1947-1956)

Rosen had a brief but successful career, spending all 10 seasons with Cleveland. Rosen's first full year was 1950 (his first three seasons he played only 35 games combined), and he collected at least 100 runs, RBI, and walks, while hitting 37 home runs and tallying over 300 total bases. He was fourth in the AL in WAR and established himself as one of the top third basemen in the league. From 1950-1954, Rosen averaged 95 runs, 31 home runs, and 114 RBI with .298/.396/.528 slashes, and he won an MVP in 1953. In that impressive 1953 campaign, Rosen missed out on the Triple Crown by one batting average point. In fact, in his final at bat of the season, he appeared to beat out an infield hit but missed first base in his hurry to get to the bag. The umpire made the right call, a call which Rosen admitted was the right one. Sadly, this was pretty much it for Rosen's career as he played only two more seasons and wasn't nearly as effective as he had been before injuries started to hamper his production.

Throughout his career, Rosen's RBI totals were exceptionally strong, which should come as no surprise, given that he "wrote the book" on RBI in a *Sport* piece entitled: "They Pay Off On Runs Batted In." In the article, he discusses the importance of RBI, saying, "when your RBI total starts to mount, you can sense the added faith your teammates have in you every time you go to the plate." For all the sabermetricians out there, he also noted that the talent in front of the batter plays a huge role in RBI totals. Despite his limited participation in the second half of the decade, Rosen was still *The Sporting News* choice for AL third baseman of the 1950s.

For this Spiders third base position, Rosen beat out Ken Keltner and Bill Bradley. All three had pretty much the same WAR totals for their time in Cleveland,[241] but the other two had slightly longer careers than Rosen. As such, neither player was as dominant as Rosen, but they put up higher totals in most of the cumulative statistics. Bradley played at the beginning of the 20th century and was a solid defensive third baseman, netting the team 10.7 wins by dWAR in his time there. Keltner was the third baseman whom Rosen sat behind at the beginning of his career, as Keltner blocked Rosen's path to a major league starting spot from 1947-1949. Keltner[242] was also a solid defensive third basemen, netting the team over 7.0 by dWAR in his 11+ seasons with the team.

The first reason that Rosen got the start at third is that, in this case, dominance over a few years was favored over consistency. The other reason is because in the end offense is more irreplaceable than defense. Defense is certainly an essential part of the game and a component of the game that is sadly overlooked by many casual fans. There are certainly positions at which defense is more important than others, and third base is one of those, but even at those positions a bat is worth more than a glove.

Mostly, it is a matter of opportunity. For this example, in 1951, Rosen played all 154 games on the schedule. He had 661 plate appearances versus 453 defensive chances, a significant difference. Fielding is also an area with far less variance between good and bad fielders. Among AL third baseman with at least 100 chances in the field, the difference between the highest and lowest fielding percentage was 50 points (.978 versus .928). A player with 453 chances, such as Rosen had in 1951, would make 10 errors with a .978 fielding percentage; that number would jump to 33 with a .928 fielding percentage. Although 23 errors are quite a difference, it is nowhere near the difference made by the top and bottom third baseman on the offensive side. The difference between the highest batting average (.326) and the lowest (.235) is 60 hits, a far greater difference. And that's just batting average, not on-base percentage or slugging percentage.

Now this is not a perfect comparison by any means. By looking at only fielding percentage, that ignores range, an essential part of fielding. It also ignores the fact that not all errors (or hits) are created equal. However, it does go to show the general idea that a bat is worth more than a glove for the most part. Great fielders are also easier to find than great batters. In

[240] Of course, in 2006, we would see Miguel Cabrera take that a bit further when he took Todd Williams to center to drive in the go-ahead run on a pitch that didn't get far enough away from Cabrera on an attempted intentional walk.
[241] Bradley: 35.1, Keltner: 33.8, and Rosen: 32.6.
[242] Best known as the man who made two excellent plays on Joe DiMaggio in the game that would have been the 57th of Joe DiMaggio's hit streak, thus halting history.

the words of Rob Neyer: "Shake a tree, and a dozen gloves will fall out."[243]

SS Lou Boudreau (1938-1950)

Boudreau was the face of the Spiders in the 1940s and held a starring role on the last Cleveland championship team way back in 1948. He became the player/manager of the squad in 1942 at the ripe age of 24 and, despite sometimes struggling with the job, was the leader of the 1948 World Series team. His 1948 campaign was his best year, and one of the stronger years a shortstop has ever had. He tossed up a .355/.453/.534 triple slash to go with 116 runs, 18 home runs, and 106 RBI and won the MVP. It was the only time in his career that he hit more than 10 home runs in a season, and although he didn't win the batting title that year (as he did in 1944), it was the highest batting average of his career. These numbers are made all the more impressive by the fact that "Handsome Lou" struck out only nine times all season! A difficult man to strike out his whole career, Lou had well more than twice as many walks as strikeouts (766 to 297) in his time in Cleveland.

Back to 1948, "Old Shufflefoot" also led the league in WAR (10.4) by almost two wins, and his dWAR of 3.0 was the fourth and final time he led the league in dWAR in his career. Boudreau's strong defense was built on the strength of his sure hands – he led the league in fielding percentage eight out of nine years from 1940-1948. In 1948, Boudreau led the team to a tie atop the AL, and in the one-game playoff against the Red Sox, he went 4-for-4 with a pair of home runs.

Although Lou was a bit overwhelmed at times as a 24-year-old player/manager (who can really blame him, he was the youngest man to ever take over a team at the beginning of a season), "The Good Kid" is credited with creating the shift to help slow down Ted Williams, when Boudreau was manager in 1946. Some sources say the shift was implemented much earlier, but most at least credit Boudreau with being the first to implement it to slow down Williams. With the shift as prevalent as it is today, that legacy has only become emboldened. It is also not as though he was an unpopular manager. Before the 1948 season, Bill Veeck was contemplating a new manager, but the *Cleveland News* ran a poll, and the over 100,000 fans that voted came back with in a rousing 10-1 ratio in favor of keeping Boudreau as manager. Of course, they were rewarded with the aforementioned 1948 championship. Patience is a virtue.

Boudreau had more hits than anyone else in the 1940s, but one of the best stories about him has little to do with baseball. Jackie Price, one of baseball history's lost gems, played as Boudreau's backup in 1946 and was more of a side show than baseball player. He was kept on the team by Veeck for fan entertainment reasons first and foremost. So when Price decided to release a live snake into a cabin full of women on one road trip (movie sequel idea: Snakes on a Train), it inevitably caused a scene. When the team was questioned, one player – rumored to be Joe Gordon – said it was the manager, Lou Boudreau, who released the snakes. Since Boudreau was not only an established player in the franchise, but also the current manager, it is not surprising that Price didn't play another game for Cleveland after the incident.

Boudreau lasted much longer than Price, and he was so popular in Cleveland that after Bill Veeck chose not to re-sign Boudreau – losing him to the Red Sox before the 1951 season – Veeck felt the need to go from bar-to-bar in Cleveland apologizing in person to the fans. Boudreau played only 86 more games in his career after Cleveland, wrapping up a 15-year career in 1952 with a four-game season in Boston.

LF Albert Belle (1989-1996) vs. Shoeless Joe Jackson (1910-1915)

The left field position in Cleveland has two of baseball's most controversial figures. Naturally, they put up similar statistics and demand a breakdown.

Contact

	BA	lgBA	Seasons ≥ .300	Cleveland high/low	Seasons ≥ 80 SO	SO %	lgSO%	BABIP	Misc.
Belle	.295	.267	3	.357/.260	5	15.9	15.9	.295	
Jackson	.375	.270	6	.408/.327	0	5.0	9.8	.391	LL 2x H

The first thing that really stands out is the league batting average for each of the two. This took me by surprise, as the inflated batting averages atop of the leaderboards in Jackson's era would seem to have implied the league batting average was much higher in his era than Belle's. However, given the similarity in league batting average, Shoeless Joe becomes the clear victor in the contact category. In 1911, Jackson became the only player in MLB history to hit .400 in his first full season. He lost that batting title to Ty Cobb, however – possibly a sign of the bad luck to come for Jackson. There were five times in his career that Jackson hit over .350 but didn't win the batting title. On two separate occasions, Jackson had more triples than strikeouts in a single season, once with The Land (1912) and in his final season with the White Sox (1920).

[243] It should be noted, however, that oftentimes defensive-minded players are cheaper on the open market than offensive-minded players, as Tangotiers, and later Ben Lindbergh, pointed out in a comparison between how much Adam Dunn (a slugger) and Juan Pierre (a defensive-minded speedster) – two nearly identical contemporaries per WAR – made salary-wise in their respective careers. Of course, salary played no role in determining these Starting IX squads.

Although he loses the category handily, it should be noted that unlike many sluggers of his time, Belle did not strike out at an exorbitant rate.

EDGE: Jackson

Power

	HR	Seasons ≥ 25 HR	Career high HR	XBH	SLG%	lgSLG%	ISO	HR%	XBH%	Misc.
Belle	242	6	50	481	.580	.412	.285	6.2	12.3	LL 3x RBI, TB, 2x SLG, 1x OPS, OPS+, HR, 2B
Jackson	24	0	7	281	.542	.354	.167	0.9	10.1	LL 1x TB, SLG, OPS, 2B, 3B

This is clearly Belle's category, but let's cover a few interesting notes. Jackson's home run percentage and extra-base hit percentage, although noticeably lower than Belle's, were each about twice the league average for his era. The two also have about the same difference in slugging percentage above league average (in fact, Jackson was higher above league average than Belle), but this is bloated by Jackson's exceptional batting average, as we see when comparing the two in isolated power. Belle was one of the strongest power threats of the `90s, leading all of baseball in RBI for the decade.

EDGE: Belle

Batting Eye

	BB	Seasons ≥ 70 BB	OBP	lgOBP	OPS+	BB%	SO/BB	Misc.
Belle	396	3	.369	.338	150	10.1	1.57	
Jackson	267	1	.441	.341	182	9.6	0.53	LL 1x OBP

These two were very similar in their ability to draw walks. Belle averaged a walk every 2.3 games, while Jackson drew one every 2.5 games in a slightly less walk-friendly era. Both men had outstanding OPS+ numbers while with Cleveland, with Shoeless Joe's mark of 182 easily leading Cleveland in team history. Jackson's career OPS+ of 170 is good for seventh all-time, but Belle is no slouch himself, with his 144 career mark good for 56th all time.

EDGE: Draw

Speed

	SB	Seasons ≥ 10 SB	Career high SB	Rbaser	SB%	XBT%	GDP%	Misc.
Belle	61	2	23	2	70.9	47	14	LL 1x GDP
Jackson	138	5	41	-1	75.4*	XX	XX	

* Caught stealing data not available in 1910 and 1913

This is another case in which the lack of advanced metrics luckily didn't matter in the end. Jackson holds a distinct advantage over Belle, even though Belle did have a couple of seasons with plus steal totals. Jackson played in a more speed-friendly era, and he tailored his game to match.

Slight EDGE: Jackson

Defense

	Fld%	lgFld %	dWAR	RF/9	lgRF/9	Rfield	GG	Misc.
Belle	.974	.981	-7.2	2.13	2.17	-29		LL 2x E (LF), 1x Assists (LF), PO (LF), DP (OF), RF/G (LF)
Jackson	.974	.962	-3.5	2.22	2.23	2		

Let's be honest, neither guy has a chance to start for the all-time franchise Starting IX because of his defense. Neither was horrible in the field, but Jackson was closer to average than Belle.

EDGE: Jackson

Team Success

	W	L	T	W-L%	Seasons ≥ 90 W	Division titles	Pennants	WS
Belle	493	420	0	.540	2	2	1	0
Jackson	401	462	22	.465*	0	0	0	0

* Because of unavailable win/loss splits for Jackson's era, those totals are not exact

Belle cruises to victory with this one, as the late Belle-era Spiders enjoyed their greatest bout of success since the days of Lou and the boys back in the `40s. Their pennant in 1995 was not only the first pennant for the franchise since 1954 – it was their first *playoff* appearance since 1954. Jackson had incredibly poor timing with the club, as the team posted a winning season in six of the eight seasons before he came to town and was at least .500 in the eight seasons right after he left (including a title in 1920), but the team was just 2-for-6 in terms of winning seasons while Shoeless Joe was there.

EDGE: Belle by a significant margin

Dominance

If OPS+ can be considered a strong indicator of dominance, then these two men were both forces. As noted before, the two men have exceptional OPS+ totals for their career, especially in their time with Cleveland. Both men racked up big total base numbers throughout their careers and were often overlooked offensive threats because of the other men playing in their era. In fact, in 1995, Belle became the first (and to the moment, only) player to hit 50 home runs and 50 doubles in the same season, and he did so in only 143 games.

(This got me thinking. Who, among current players, is the most likely to challenge this feat? In the past five seasons, only four players have tallied even 40 of each: Miguel Cabrera [2012], Chris Davis [2013], Nolan Arenado [2015] and Josh Donaldson [2015]. Of those, the latter two seem much more likely than the first two thanks to their age, with Arenado further benefitting from the amazing Coors Effect, as well as being a bit younger than Donaldson. If I had to set odds for Arenado joining Belle in the 50/50 club, I'd say one in five and feel decent about it.)

Back to the breakdown: one edge for Shoeless Joe, Belle does not hold the distinction of having baseball's most famous player as a protégé. Babe Ruth said of Jackson, "I copied Jackson's batting style because I thought he was the greatest hitter I had ever seen. I still think the same way." This may have been a way of Ruth taking Ty Cobb down a peg,[244] since Cobb and Ruth were usually the two thought of as the two best of all time, but it is impressive nonetheless.

Slight EDGE: Jackson

Level of Controversy

As noted earlier, neither Belle nor Jackson were without their share of off-field distractions, and this is a big category. Let's cover Belle first.

Albert Jojuan Belle grew up a Boy Scout, National Honor Society member, and VP of the Future Business Leaders of America, but this is not the side of Belle that many saw in his time in the major leagues. Belle had a particularly strained relationship with the media,[245] and if there's one lesson every reader should take from this book, it's that the media can pretty much control the public opinion of each and every professional athlete. Belle either never learned the lesson of not messing with the media, or he just didn't care. Either way, there were numerous accounts of Belle's problems with the media, and his subsequent lack of an MVP – and treatment as a total afterthought for Cooperstown – can both be tied to this fact.

Belle's temper was not limited to baseball, as he notoriously once hopped in his car to chase down kids who egged his house one Halloween. He made it "locker room law" that the thermostat must be set at a cool 60 degrees, a perfect metaphor for every baseball writer complaining about the "chilly" Albert Belle. There was also a corked bat incident (to which he still claims innocence, going as far as to claim malfeasance on the part of MLB), and the time he threw a baseball at

[244] Similar to how Larry Bird, and other NBA legends, have said they'd rather have Kobe Bryant as a teammate over LeBron James, even though that would make them stupid people if it were true. Instead, it seems as if they feel more of a threat to their legacy from LeBron than Kobe, so they need to get in front of that by cutting LeBron down.

[245] He once told Michael Bamberger that *Sports Illustrated* could "kiss [his] black ass" when Bamberger went in search of an interview in 1996. The article ("He Thrives on Anger") is still an intriguing portrait of Belle as seen through just about every angle besides a direct sit down.

a fan who was taunting him. From all accounts, he has mellowed in his post-playing days, as many uber-competitors do, but it is likely too late for his reputation in the eyes of many.

Here's the thing though: Belle was immensely popular with the fans in Cleveland. His play demanded it, and the fans didn't care that much about his surly relationship with the media. If you had a camera and microphone shoved in your face 162 days a year, you might be too.

* * *

Shoeless Joe's controversy is better known, but it didn't actually come *while he was with Cleveland*, instead coming in his next stop as a part of the 1919 Black Sox. His level of participation in the incident is one of the most documented events in baseball history. We'll cover a bit more of Jackson's legacy as a whole in just one second.

EDGE: Curveball, neither was really that controversial for the Cleveland Professional Baseball Team.

Final Verdict (just not on what you think)

Neither player was in Cleveland for all that long; Belle played just six full seasons in Cleveland, and Jackson didn't even manage that, playing just four full seasons. Jackson holds the edge in terms of WAR, despite the limited number of years, but this seems like a case in which the era adjustments may be too strong. Jackson was indeed one of the best hitters of all time, but when Belle was in his prime, WAR didn't seem to do an efficient job of judging Belle's value. Replacement level players in Jackson's era were also almost certainly several tiers below the replacement level players in Belle's era, and in the end, **Albert Belle** gets the nod by the slimmest of margins.

That being said, this "Verdict" space is about to get hijacked in an attempt to render a verdict on Shoeless Joe in the Black Sox Scandal. Apologies to strictly-Cleveland fans, you may want to skip ahead. You know I can't help it with the tangents.

Right off the bat, we need to establish the facts:

- Shoeless Joe Jackson was originally offered $10,000 to throw the 1919 World Series but turned away teammate Chick Gandil who was contacting Jackson on behalf of the back-alley gangsters set to make money from the fix.
- When Gandil approached Jackson a second time (Jackson was, after all, the top position player for the 1919 White Sox, making him a key piece in the fix), he offered $20,000 and Jackson accepted.
- Jackson went 12-for-32 in the World Series, with a home run and six RBI, but the White Sox lost to the Reds in eight games (it was a best-of-nine series).
- Late in the next season, the story of the fix broke, and White Sox owner Frank Comiskey suspended the seven players still with the White Sox from the team immediately.
- A Cook County grand jury acquitted the eight players involved in the scandal, but Commissioner Kenesaw Mountain (yes, Mountain) Landis came down hard on the accused, banning them from baseball for life.

Now there are, of course, a few things to parse. Let's start with the most straight-forward: while some of the eight accused tried to push back against the charges, Jackson never took that tack, instead always admitting that he did indeed take the money, although he ended up getting $5,000 instead of $20,000. Although Jackson references his 12 hits (tying a World Series record at the time) as evidence that he still tried in the Series, it has been noted by many that his hits came in the games that the White Sox weren't trying to throw, going 8-for-16 in their wins and 4-for-16 in their losses. He also failed to collect an RBI until Game 6 of the series.

Now come the cavalcade of caveats, most of which paint the portrait of Jackson as baseball's most prominent martyr. First off, the two stacks of high society he was due to receive ($20,000 for those who didn't watch *Rounders* in the past week) was three times more than his annual salary – remember this was a time when ball players often had to have offseason jobs to get by. Now, Jackson came up for a raise in the offseason, but it should be noted that the $5,000 he did end up receiving from the fix went to his sick sister's hospital bills. During the offseason after the scandal (before the story broke), Jackson reportedly went to Comiskey's office to tell his owner about the fix (and possibly return the money, though that's hard to know for sure), but the meeting never happened with Comiskey too busy to meet with Jackson.

There's also the matter of timing on Jackson's part. As will be discussed later in the book (Utility, Cincinnati Reds – Page 277), baseball has a long history with gambling. The sport's integrity was being called into question during this era, with players like Hal Chase (one of baseball's truly underrated villains) supposedly on the perpetual payroll of some real sketchy folk. As such, when the Black Sox Scandal came around, Commissioner Landis saw the perfect opportunity to come down with the hammer, and it worked. Landis' harsh sentence (along with ballplayers starting to make more money) helped eradicate baseball of a disease that had, at one point, threatened to kill the sport.

So, what should the historical verdict on Jackson be? Personally, I think Landis made the right decision in banning

Jackson and the Black Sox.[246] As noted above, the decision helped, in large part, to put baseball on the right track, scourging the league of legitimacy questions and keeping baseball from becoming a WWI-era WWE, where fans couldn't trust the results they saw in front of them. That being said, the lifetime ban from the Hall of Fame seems harsh, and I think it should be removed. Jackson is by far the best player in baseball history missing from the Hall (sorry, Mr. Rose), and his sad legacy makes his case only more sympathetic. Ted Williams penned a piece in *The National Pastime* in which he said that Shoeless Joe should be let into the Hall and finished by saying, "Come on in, Joe, your wait is over. Let's talk hitting."

Jackson has been dead since 1951, so this would obviously be more of a symbolic gesture than anything else, but with game fixing no longer an issue in Major League Baseball,[247] there's no real harm in letting Joe join his pals in Cooperstown.

CF Tris Speaker (1916-1926)

Tris Speaker came to The Land from Boston in 1916 and, like Lajoie, had an excellent first season with the club. He led the league in hits (211), doubles (41), batting average (.386), on-base percentage (.470), slugging percentage (.502), OPS+ (186), and had the highest WAR (8.7) among position players. Speaker's career was split quite evenly between Cleveland and Boston, compiling one of the best careers of all time in those two locales. He is the all-time MLB leader in doubles (796), and he is in the top 10-20 in numerous other categories. After his rookie year, Speaker never had an on-base percentage below .395 until his final season, a season in which he played only 64 games. Speaker was a remarkably consistent player over the course of his career, in his 18 seasons of over 100 games in Cleveland and Boston, a stretch from 1909-1926, he had a WAR of at least 4.6 every season, very often well above that threshold. Remember, 5.0 WAR represents All-Star-level value (he topped 5.0 WAR in an incredible 15 straight seasons, only Hank Aaron had more consecutive such seasons with 17). Speaker won a World Series in 1920 with Cleveland, one of three he won in his career. Speaker was no stranger to winning. In seasons which he appeared in at least half of his team's games, he didn't suffer a losing record until 1924, his 18th season in the majors.

Speaker had good competition for this spot in the form of Earl Averill and Kenny Lofton. Averill was an excellent hitter in the time after Speaker finished patrolling center field in Cleveland. In fact, Averill started in Cleveland just three years after Speaker left. He topped 30 home runs three times and had a .322 batting average for his time in Cleveland. He also reached double-digit triples eight times, leading the league in 1936. He knocked in an average of over 100 RBI per season for his 10 full years with the club, topping out at 143 in 1931. Speaker gets the nod over Averill because even though his numbers are quite comparable – in fact, Averill had more runs, home runs, and RBI by a solid margin – the era in which Averill played produced far more runs than Speaker's era. From 1916-26, Speaker's years in Cleveland, the American League averaged 5,429 runs a year. From 1929-39, Averill's years in Cleveland, the American League averaged 6,427 runs a year. Speaker's production was close to Averill's in an era when that was much harder to do, thus elevating him over Averill.

Lofton was a speed man, a group who tend to be overlooked, and he led the league in steals each of his first five full seasons with Cleveland, producing 31.0 WAR for those years. In fact, both players probably could have started in left or right field for the team if either position had been a little bit weaker. Lofton and Averill rank fourth and fifth, respectively, in franchise WAR.

RF Manny Ramírez (1993-2000)

Manny may be best-remembered for his Red Sox antics and the "Manny being Manny"[248] lifestyle he made famous there, but his time in Cleveland was extremely productive (and quirky), as well. Once established as a full-time player, Manny became a run-producing machine, totaling more than one RBI a game for his last three seasons with the team and hitting better than a home run every fourth game. In fact, the comparison between Manny's eight years in Boston and his eight years in Cleveland is a rather close one. His cumulative stats are slightly skewed towards Boston because he played over 100 more games with them, but his .313/.407/.592/152[249] slashes in Cleveland are remarkably similar to his .312/.411/.588/155 slashes in Boston. His WAR is about 3.0 wins higher in Boston, again, due to having more full seasons there. His final three years in Cleveland and first five in Boston represented an eight-year stretch during which he finished in the top 10 in the MVP each and every year. Say what you will about Manny as a dude, the guy was an all-time great hitter.

Both franchises also enjoyed their highest levels of success in a long time while Ramírez was there. Each reached two World Series with Ramírez in town, the Spiders losing both, the Red Sox winning both. Manny was essential to both

---

[246] That being said, David Shiner, in a 1997 *Baseball Research Journal* article, projected the rest of Joe's career if he hadn't been banned. He projects 1,553 runs, 156 home runs, 1,474 RBI and a .368 average. This is noteworthy because his batting average would then top Ty Cobb's, and Jackson would be the new all-time batting average leader. Shiner comes to this conclusion by noting that Jackson was banned just before the offensive explosion that occurred in baseball in the 1920s. His logic is sound, and he supports it well by showing the career batting average of six Hall of Famers at the time Jackson was banned and then comparing that figure to their final career batting average – all six men saw an increase in their career batting average.

[247] In order to triple A-Rod's salary, gamblers would have to offer him the GDP of a decent-sized country

[248] I'm a fan of almost all of the "This is Sportscenter" commercials, but the "Manny being Manny" spot has to be at the top of the list.

[249] BA/OBP/SLG/OPS+

teams' playoff success, and his 29 postseason home runs are the best all-time, by a significant margin. The difference between Manny and second-place Bernie Williams is the same as the difference between second-place Williams (22) and tenth-place Babe Ruth (15).[250] Although Ramírez is not solely responsible for both teams' success, the results do speak to his ability to play for a winner, which might surprise some given that Manny was trashed later in his career for not being a good clubhouse guy. Ramírez hit safely in every single postseason game of the 2004 playoffs, a measure of just how important he was to the team.

David Ortiz is on the record as calling Manny "a crazy motherf***er," but he did so in an endearing way. Ramírez has been alternately loved and hated by every fanbase for which he played. Julian Tavarez once said, "There's a bunch of humans out here, but to Manny, he's the only human." He's a man who could have three biographies, two *New Yorker* profiles, an autobiography, and another couple biopics about him, and still no one would truly understand him. Many have tried, but no one has succeeded.

The most recent curve in the long and winding road that is Manny's life has seen Ramírez turn to Christianity and become such a changed man that Theo Epstein has entrusted Ramírez with grooming the young talent in the Cubs organization. Manny has been a mentor to the likes of Kris Bryant, Jorge Soler, and Javier Baez.

Utility Kenny Lofton (1992-1996; 1998-2001; 2007)

Lofton is a perfect utility player, as he could fill in at a few positions and is a great threat on the base paths. His 66 steals as a rookie in 1992 set the record for an American League rookie. He would also be the perfect leadoff man for this fake team. Lofton was an excellent on-base man and, with his blazing speed, usually didn't take long to make it to second base after a walk. Lofton helped kick start numerous rallies over the years for Cleveland, including his famous dash home in the 1995 ALCS. In Game 6 of the ALCS, Cleveland had a 1-0 lead into the top of the eighth. Tony Pena led off the inning with a double, and Lofton followed it up with a bunt single. He then proceeded to steal second and eventually came around to score on a passed ball, providing the straw that broke the Mariners back, delivering Cleveland its first pennant since 1954.

With Lofton in the leadoff spot, the lineup could potentially look like this:

1) Lofton 2) Tris Speaker 3) Manny Ramírez 4) Albert Belle 5) Nap Lajoie 6) Al Rosen 7) Jim Thome 8) Lou Boudreau 9) Víctor Martínez

With good starting pitching (upcoming), and a lineup with very few holes, the Spiders Starting IX could be a bit of a sleeper if the teams were to actually play out a season or tournament.

SP Bob Feller (1936-1956)

Feller had strong competition for this starting pitcher spot in the form of the man who will instead fill the closer's role (Addie Joss), as well as Stan Coveleski. Coveleski put up numbers close to Feller for his time with Cleveland, but lost to Feller relatively handily due to two factors. First, Stan was grandfathered into spitball rules; he was one of the last to throw it, and it provided a large portion of his value. Second, Feller missed significant time due to WWII. Many players did, but, along with a few others in this book – Stan Musial and Ted Williams come to mind – Feller missed time in his absolute prime. In 1942, Feller went off to war, fresh off four straight seasons leading the league in strikeouts and three straight seasons in the top three of the MVP. In fact, Feller was the very first Major Leaguer to enlist for WWII. When he went to war at age 23, he had 107 wins and 1,233 strikeouts. He actually could have avoided military duty because his dad was sick, but he decided to serve his country, nonetheless. If he had stayed behind, his numbers would have been through the roof against the meek hitters the war years had to offer. If we simply project him to top the American League in strikeouts by one in each 1942-45 season – which seems a fair bet given that he led the AL in strikeouts every full season he played from 1938-1948 – he would have an additional 507 strikeouts. If he stayed healthy, he would have also had at least another 60 wins. With those totals added to his final career tallies, Feller ends up with 326 wins and 3,088 strikeouts. With over 300 wins and 3,000 strikeouts, he would be in elite company (10 men), and only Walter Johnson, Greg Maddux, Roger Clemens, Steve Carlton, Nolan Ryan, and Don Sutton would have had as many wins among pitchers with 3,000 strikeouts. However, as Rob Neyer has pointed out, Feller's arm gave way at a pretty young age, and he already had thrown 1,448 innings before the war despite not even having turned 23 yet. There's at least a possibility that he would have dominated the hitters during the war but then severely faded after that.

Feller had a start like few other athletes have ever had. His fame started early, and that fact was not lost on his father. His dad built a baseball field in the family's backyard and centered a team around his son on the mound. He then charged people to see games in which his son pitched – *when his son was a 12-year-old.* (In LaVar Ball's high school yearbook, he cited Bob Feller's father as a personal hero.) Half a decade later, as a 17-year-old, while still in high school,

---

[250] Ruth got all those home runs in the World Series, though, as the playoffs only expanded past the two pennant winners playing in the World Series in 1969. As such, Ruth is the all-time leader in World Series home runs. Naturally.

Feller struck out eight of the first nine Cardinals (yes, the MLB St. Louis Cardinals) he faced in an exhibition, a Cardinals team that had won the World Series two years ago. The media coverage got to the point that his high school graduation was broadcast live on NBC Radio to the entire nation. In his first season, as an 18-year-old, he had a 15-strikeout performance, as well as a 17-strikeout performance that came in his second career start. Those 17 strikeouts were an AL record and tied for the MLB record. He was on the cover of *Time Magazine* before he had made even 10 career starts; not even LeBron could stake claim to that sort of early-age hype.

Feller was a flame-thrower whose fastball was the no. 1 fastball throughout the 1940s according to Rob Neyer and Bill James, in their book on pitching. He also had the fastest recorded pitch until Nolan Ryan came along. In 1997, Feller unleashed a nice #OldGuyTake after being asked about a 102-mph radar reading on a Robb Nen fastball, saying, "That was my changeup."[251]

Feller was a bit in the mold of Nolan Ryan, or, maybe more appropriately since Feller came 30 years earlier, Ryan was a bit in the mold of Feller. In his third season, Feller set the record for most walks in a season with 208 free passes. He also threw three no-hitters and 12 one-hitters in his career. Before Nolan Ryan came along, only Walter Johnson had even half the number of combined one-hitters and no-hitters that Feller had. Feller was also an innings horse, leading the league in innings pitched for five straight years from 1939-1947 (with seasons missing due to service). In 1946, his 348 strikeouts broke Rube Waddell's league record, but his strikeout totals from earlier in his career are just as impressive. In 1939, only eight pitchers had 100 strikeouts; Feller had 246, more than 50 above Bobo Newsom in second and well over 100 more than Tommy Bridges in third. The great Stan Musial called him "the toughest he ever faced."

Feller's fastball was the stuff of legend. During one of his no-hitters, one batter, Mike Kreevich, complained to the ump, and the umpire responded by asking what was wrong with the pitch. Kreevich responded, "It sounded a little high."

Finally, Feller was a smart and forward-thinking man (despite his #OldGuyTake from earlier). He made lots of money barnstorming against Negro League teams, and he put his money into investments, eventually building his own corporation. He feels like the type of player who would have done very well in today's game, both because of his before-his-time velocity and strikeout totals, as well as his ability build his social image, which is of the utmost importance in the modern era.

CP Addie Joss (1902-1910)

Joss was not a closer, but he is essential to Cleveland baseball history, especially in comparison to any of the actual relievers in franchise history.[252] Joss passed away very young, and the sickness that eventually took his life cut into his career significantly. Joss played his final game at age 30, and he passed away less than a year later. When he did play, he was excellent, wining two ERA titles and amassing a 1.89 career ERA that is good for second all-time. He is baseball's all-time WHIP leader (0.968), and although his numbers may have been helped by the absence of a late-career swoon, his excellence is still undeniable. His ERA+ (142) is good for 12th all-time. At age 30, his last season as a pro, his most similar player comparison on Baseball-Reference was Ed Walsh. This is a very accurate pitcher for Joss to be compared to, and he is the only man above Joss in terms of all-time ERA.[253]

When Joss passed away, he was so young that he had completed only nine years of major league service, meaning he was ineligible for the Hall of Fame. Eventually, however, his numbers were too good to leave out of the Hall, and he was granted admittance by the Veteran's Committee in 1978. Although the Veteran's Committee has made some pretty egregious decisions over the years, including Joss was the right decision.

In 1908, Joss was involved in a tight pennant race that saw the White Sox and Spiders battling down the stretch. Joss faced off with Big Ed Walsh, who already had 40 wins on the season. Joss was able to step up to the pressure, and he threw the second perfect game in modern baseball history to keep the Spiders in the pennant race.[254] Two years later, on April 20, 1910, Joss no-hit the White Sox for the second time, making him the only pitcher to no-hit the same team twice. It was one of the last starts he ever made, and it was an appropriate way for Joss to wrap up his career.

Joss even had an eye for talent. After Walter Johnson's first start Joss noted, "That young man is another Cy Young." Too bad he never got a chance to become a scout after his playing days, a time-honored profession among ex-ballplayers.

---

[251] He also claims to have been measured by military radar that read a pitch of his at 107.9 mph...

[252] Go ahead and mention any of these names to a Cleveland native: Bob Wickman, Doug Jones, or Chris Pérez. Check out their reaction. Those are the top three closers (by saves) in Spiders history.

[253] Of course, Walsh got the start just a few teams ago on the White Sox Starting IX.

[254] A pennant they would not claim, however.

Starting IX Franchise Roster Stats

Lineup	Yrs	G	R	H	HR	RBI	SB	BB	SO	BA	OBP	SLG	OPS+	dWAR	WAR
Kenny Lofton	10	1276	975	1512	87	518	**452**	611	652	0.300	0.375	0.426	109	12.6	48.5
Lou Boudreau	13	1560	823	1706	63	740	50	766	297	0.296	0.382	0.416	122	**22.7**	61.7
Tris Speaker	11	1519	1079	1965	73	886	155	857	146	0.354	**0.444**	0.520	158	0.0	74.2
Manny Ramírez	8	967	665	1086	236	804	28	541	780	0.313	0.407	**0.592**	152	-7.5	29.9
Nap Lajoie	13	1614	865	**2047**	33	919	240	408	222	0.339	0.389	0.452	155	11.4	**80.0**
Al Rosen	10	1044	603	1063	192	717	39	587	385	0.285	0.384	0.495	137	0.4	32.6
Jim Thome	13	1399	928	1353	**337**	937	18	**1008**	**1400**	0.287	0.414	0.566	152	-8.4	47.9
Albert Belle	8	913	592	1014	242	751	61	396	622	0.295	0.369	0.580	150	-7.2	27.3
Víctor Martínez	8	821	413	900	103	518	1	347	407	0.297	0.369	0.463	120	0.2	19.2
Pitchers	Yrs	W	W%	ERA	G	CG	SHO	SV	IP	SO	ERA+	WHIP	SO/9	SO/BB	WAR
Bob Feller	**18**	**266**	0.621	3.25	570	**279**	44	22	**3827.0**	**2581**	122	1.316	6.1	1.46	**65.2**
Addie Joss	9	160	0.623	**1.89**	286	234	**45**	5	2327.0	920	**142**	**0.968**	3.6	2.53	45.9

#13 Atlanta Braves (1966-pres.); Milwaukee Braves (1953-1965); Boston Braves (1941-1952, 1912-1935); Boston Bees (1936-1940); Boston Rustlers (1911); Boston Doves (1907-1910); Boston Beaneaters (1883-1906); Boston Red Stockings (1876-1882)

(Photo by Keith Allison/Creative Commons)

Team Background

Playoff appearances: 23 **Pennants: 17** **World Series titles: 3**
Collective team WAR: 635.4
Strengths: Power hitting. They have the all-time home run king, the guy with the third-most home runs of any switch-hitter in the history of the game, and neither one even gets the title of the best raw power on the team. That goes to the guy in the utility spot.
Weaknesses: Name recognition. Outside of the BIG names that you'll know right off the bat, try guessing this Starting IX. It's not that easy.
What to expect from the next 15 pages: The realization that time is fleeting (CP) and a really fun breakdown between a pair of franchise legends.

The Braves have quite a long history with several location and name changes, as one can see above. They have won the championship four times (three since the World Series came into play) and have 17 pennants to their name. They reached their 10,000th win as a franchise in 2011[255] despite having some pretty poor teams for the majority of team history; not

[255] One of only eight teams to achieve that feat so far: Braves, Giants, Cubs, Dodgers, Cardinals, Braves, Reds, Pirates, and Yankees.

surprisingly, they were also the second franchise to lose 10,000 games (only the Phillies got there faster). They did enjoy some success in the 1950s with several players who will be on the Starting IX below, but their strongest time as a franchise was undoubtedly from 1991-2005. During that stretch they won 14 of 15 division titles,[256] including a stretch of 11 straight from 1995-2005. Despite this enormous stretch of divisional dominance, they won only one World Series in that time (1995). They did reach the World Series four other times, meaning the team captured five pennants during their dominant decade and a half. Of course, when comparing pennants across generations, the comparison is not a fair one. When the Braves began their stretch of playoff success (1991), only two teams from each league made the playoffs, compared to the four teams that made the playoffs beginning in 1994 after the addition of another division and the wild card. However, 1994 is not the lone split when it comes to baseball playoff history, as 1969 was the inaugural year for the League Championship Series, when the playoffs expanded beyond simply a matchup of each league's pennant winner. Whether it is more impressive to win the regular season pennant or the postseason pennant is an interesting topic of debate in modern baseball, especially as recent World Series matchups have included more and more teams charging through the playoffs from the wild card spot. Most sabermetric types might say that winning the regular season pennant takes more skill, but ask any team, player, or fan and they will undoubtedly take the playoff pennant and spot in the World Series. With that being said, regular season pennant winners often get lost in the mix when looking back historically, so let's take a minute to honor the ghosts of regular season pennant winners past:[257]

Regular Season Pennant Winners (Postseason pennant winners in bold, World Series winners bold and italicized)

1969-1993

Year	AL	NL
1969	**Baltimore Orioles**	***New York Mets***
1970	***Baltimore Orioles***	**Cincinnati Reds**
1971	**Baltimore Orioles**	***Pittsburgh Pirates***
1972	***Oakland A's***	Pittsburgh Pirates
1973	Baltimore Orioles	Cincinnati Reds
1974	Baltimore Orioles	**Los Angeles Dodgers**
1975	Oakland A's	***Cincinnati Reds***
1976	**New York Yankees**	***Cincinnati Reds***
1977	Kansas City Royals	Philadelphia Phillies
1978	***New York Yankees***	**Los Angeles Dodgers**
1979	**Baltimore Orioles**	***Pittsburgh Pirates***
1980	New York Yankees	Houston Astros
1982	**Milwaukee Brewers**	***St. Louis Cardinals***
1983	Chicago White Sox	Los Angeles Dodgers
1984	***Detroit Tigers***	Chicago Cubs
1985	Toronto Blue Jays	**St. Louis Cardinals**
1986	**Boston Red Sox**	***New York Mets***
1987	Detroit Tigers	**St. Louis Cardinals**
1988	**Oakland A's**	New York Mets
1989	***Oakland A's***	Chicago Cubs
1990	**Oakland A's**	Pittsburgh Pirates
1991	***Minnesota Twins***	Pittsburgh Pirates
1992	***Toronto Blue Jays****	**Atlanta Braves**
1993	***Toronto Blue Jays***	Atlanta Braves

* Tied with the Oakland A's at 96-66

[256] The only one they didn't win was the strike-shortened season of 1994.
[257] Not including the strike-influenced 1981 and 1994 seasons.

1995-2016

Year	AL	NL
1995	**Cleveland**	***Atlanta Braves***
1996	Cleveland	**Atlanta Braves**
1997	Baltimore Orioles	Atlanta Braves
1998	***New York Yankees***	Atlanta Braves
1999	***New York Yankees***	**Atlanta Braves**
2000	Chicago White Sox	San Francisco Giants
2001	Seattle Mariners	Houston Astros
2002	New York Yankees	Atlanta Braves
2003	**New York Yankees**	Atlanta Braves
2004	New York Yankees	**St. Louis Cardinals**
2005	***Chicago White Sox***	St. Louis Cardinals
2006	New York Yankees	New York Mets
2007	***Boston Red Sox****	Arizona Diamondbacks
2008	L.A. Angels of Anaheim	Chicago Cubs
2009	***New York Yankees***	Los Angeles Dodgers
2010	Tampa Bay Rays	Philadelphia Phillies
2011	New York Yankees	Philadelphia Phillies
2012	New York Yankees	Washington Nationals
2013	***Boston Red Sox***	**St. Louis Cardinals**
2014	L.A. Angels of Anaheim	Washington Nationals
2015	***Kansas City Royals***	St. Louis Cardinals
2016	Texas Rangers	***Chicago Cubs***
2017	Cleveland	**Los Angeles Dodgers**

* Tied with Cleveland at 96-66

With just a quick glance, it's clear that the wild card has ensured far more chaos in the playoffs, as a far lower percent of regular season pennant winners have taken the official pennant since 1994. Only three NL regular season pennant winners in the past 13 years have won the actual pennant, and only six AL teams have done so in the 18 years this millennium. (Think of those teams as "winning the double" as they refer to it in European soccer leagues.) It is interesting to note that of those relatively rare "doubles" (nine time in 22 divisional era years), three have come in the past five seasons. It is almost certainly a statistical blip in the radar, but if the best teams in baseball are indeed getting smarter about solving the so-called randomness of playoff baseball, it wouldn't be too surprising given how much information baseball front offices have these days.

Looking over the two charts above, it becomes even more amazing that the Braves won only the one title. They were the best regular season team in the NL nine times from 1992-2003 and have only the four pennants and one ring to show for it. The Braves had the best NL record each year from 1992-1999, an amazing run. If this run had come earlier in baseball history, when only the NL and AL regular season pennant winners met in the World Series, they would undoubtedly be thought of as one of the true dynasties in baseball history, instead of falling decidedly behind the late-1990s, early-2000s Yankees in that era.

The fact that the Braves had one lone World Series victory is also somewhat surprising considering the old adage that teams built around pitching often enjoy success in the postseason. And boy did those Braves teams have pitching. One fallacy that was spread during the time the Braves were winning hidden pennants – but failing to win World Series – was the fact that their pitching out of the bullpen collapsed in the postseason, and that the perceived bullpen failures cost their elite starters those precious playoff wins. Over to you Mr. Neyer:

"I'll get right to the product: Atlanta's relievers have not, on the whole, pitched poorly in the postseason… Even when you consider the inherent advantage relievers have in ERA… it's hard to argue that the relievers have been any worse than the starters."

Between those ellipses, Neyer looked at the numbers for both the Atlanta starters and relievers in Atlanta's 49 postseason losses from 1991-2002, with the relievers having the lower ERA: 3.41 to 4.55. Once again, leave it to Rob to debunk the myth. Neyer concluded that actually the rotations performed admirably in the Braves losses, and the Braves postseason failures came down to hitting. I would add a little bit of bad luck played a role as well, which, as Billy Beane knows, can derail plenty of playoff dreams.

The aforementioned `90s and `00s Braves teams had the feel of the Buffalo Bills of the early `90s, or Dr. J's Sixers of the `80s, with Dr. J's Sixers being the best comparison because they each managed to break through for one title, while the Bills lost all four of their Super Bowl appearances. All these teams had the feel of a franchise that could've won multiple championships if they got just a few lucky breaks, but instead they just missed out on being one of their sport's memorable dynasties.

Finally, thanks to being owned by TV magnate Ted Turner, the Braves were televised far more than any other team in baseball's middle ages. Turner bought the team in 1976, a time when there was a lack of easily viewable games outside of a fan's home market. This was well before MLB Extra Innings, or the At Bat app, online streaming, etc. came into play. That meant if fans wanted to watch any game outside of their hometown team (which wasn't even that frequently an option before the expansion of cable) the Braves on TBS were their only option. TBS marketed the Braves as "America's Team," and the impact was certainly profound. Even today, you can find Braves fans all over the country, especially in states without a distinct hometown team.

Random cool things about the franchise:

- In a truly southern move, the Braves became the first stadium to have a Waffle House within their confines when they got one at Turner Field in 2013.
- Those 14 consecutive division titles are a record across all American Major Sports Leagues.
- They are the only MLB franchise to win a World Series while playing in three different cities (Boston, Milwaukee, and Atlanta).
- With roots dating back to 1871, they are the longest contiguous franchise in American Major Sports League history.
- This franchise was once called the Beaneaters – I know that was written above, but I think it deserves a second shoutout.
- The franchise's three World Series wins in 17 tries is by far the worst World Series winning percentage of all time, once again recalling the "Buffalo Bills of MLB" tag, and it makes a good (and often unheard) case for the Braves being the most tortured MLB franchise.
- With "Spahn and Sain and pray for rain," the Braves can stake their claim to the catchiest dynamic duo of pitchers in league history.
- When the team moved to Atlanta, the event was seen as the opening of the floodgates for baseball to the south, but it was a movement that never took off as much as the sport might have hoped.
- Rembert Browne is a fan.

Starting IX

C Joe Torre (1960-1968)

More famous for his post-playing days, Torre gets the call here in a close one over Javy Lopez.[258] A consistent bat with the Braves during the time of their move to Atlanta, Torre was also able to net them Orlando Cepeda when he was traded out of town. The call between Lopez and Torre was close, and Lopez was certainly around for more team success – and he put up good numbers in those postseasons – but one thing always stuck in my craw with Lopez: The Free Agent Year Boost.

The debate of whether or not this is a real phenomenon is one that is a popular topic in modern baseball analytics. On the one side, people will see that Lopez put up by far the best numbers of his career the year he was set to hit free agency. They'll say this is a very common occurrence, which is infuriating because it brings to mind whether or not the player was playing as hard as he possibly could the previous seasons when he wasn't set to receive a new contract. Some will even point out that if some players do save that little bit extra, shouldn't it be saved for time when winning is the incentive instead of a pay day. It's not like you're in a profession that's paying you peanuts.[259]

On the other hand, others will say that this is merely confirmation bias, and fans only notice its perceived regularity because it is far more noticeable when it does happen than when it doesn't.

The answer, as is usually the case, likely lies somewhere in the middle. The answer likely depends on how the question is framed, and there have been many studies that supported each side of the argument. Usually in cases like this, the old-school guys stick to their guns, and the new school guys swoop in and prove them wrong. However, this case isn't as simple. The old-school guys definitely share a strong opinion, as Sparky Anderson said, "Give me 25 guys playing for a contract, and I'll show you a world champion." And as anyone who watched the DVD extras of "The Life and Times of Hank

[258] Despite the fact that Lopez has the record for home runs by a catcher in a single season (42).
[259] For fans of Andrew Sharp, this would make for an excellent #Hotsportstake.

Greenberg"[260] will know, all the players from Greenberg's generation openly admitted to having played harder because the contracts they were on were year-to-year.

The numbers, however, don't back up this theory as much as some would like. There have been studies showing that some players see slight boosts in their numbers during contract years, but the "noise" associated with these studies, in particular the fact that most players head into free agency around the time they are reaching their prime anyway, have stagnated the studies.

Lopez's big season taking place in his contract year could have been entirely a coincidence, but I tend to fall on the side that believes players can deride motivation from a contract year, so sorry Javy Lopez, you're taking a back seat to Torre on this one.

As far as Torre the ballplayer, he was more of an offensive threat than a defensive one, especially during his days as a catcher. Whitey Herzog said of him, "The fans in center field saw his number better than the ones behind the plate." This is similar to Lopez, who derived the majority of his value from his bat. Torre made the All-Star Team five times while with the Braves (and four times after), and he finished second in the Rookie of the Year in 1961.

After his Braves days, Torre played for the Cardinals and eventually the Mets. His standout season was his 1971 MVP season, in which he slashed, or maybe more appropriately *smashed*, .363/.421/.555 with a batting title and the league-lead in RBI (137) and total bases (352).

1B Fred Tenney (1894-1907; 1911)

Tenney played for three different variations of the Braves, all in Boston: The Beaneaters, the Doves, and the Rustlers. At first blush, these franchises would appear to be early versions of the Boston Red Sox franchise, but they are actually early iterations of the Braves instead (Team Introduction, Baltimore Orioles – Page 172). Tenney was a consistent bat throughout his career with the franchise, netting them about 3.0 WAR every year and finishing just shy of 2,000 hits with the team. Although he regularly collected high hit totals with the team, the impact of these hits is a bit disputed, as Tenney is in the top 15 all-time for single percentage.[261] During his career, of his 2,231 total hits, 1,862 were singles, meaning that 83.5 percent of his career hits were of the one-bag variety. That's like bringing your jar of coins to the bank and realizing that 83.5 percent of them are pennies – not a great feeling. (Granted, singles were far more common in the light-hitting days in which Tenney played.)

Tenney became the player/manager of the Braves in 1905 and was nearly an innovator in his time. One of the little-known facts of Jackie Robinson breaking the color barrier is that there was no real "rule" that banned black players from Major League Baseball. Instead it was a "Gentlemen's Agreement," with no word in human history having been used in a less strict sense than how "gentlemen" was used in that pact. Tenney, however, was willing to sign a black shortstop named William Matthews, but he was denied by the higher-ups in the league who could have really hurt Tenney's career going forward. The most remarkable part is that the color line wouldn't be broken for over 40 years, showing just how slow MLB (and society) can be to move sometimes. Clearly there were men in baseball not as ignorant as the sport itself may have been, but as is often the case, the men in power were the ones most behind the times, and the ones who feared change the most.

Finally, two fun facts from Bill James' *Abstract* blurb on Tenney. First, Tenney played a part in the addition of the balk into the baseball rulebook. He and Christy Mathewson worked on a play to eliminate the hit-and-run where Mathewson would fire the ball to first, Tenney would fling it back, and Mathewson would fire to home before the runner could take his lead or the batter even knew what was happening – not a bad idea before it was illegal. A second – and certainly not as flattering – side note about Tenney is that he was chosen as the ugliest player of the 1890s by Susan McCarthy (Bill James' wife) in James' *Abstract*.

2B Rabbit Maranville (1912-1920; 1929-1933; 1935)

Second base wasn't Maranville's primary position, but he did play 323 games at second during his second stint with the franchise at the end of this career. Maranville started his career with the franchise in 1912 as a shortstop, a position where he played seven full seasons from 1913-1920 (he missed most of 1918 to injury). As such, Maranville was part of the 1914 team dubbed "The Miracle Braves," who went from 69-82 in 1913 to 94-59 the next season, winning a pennant and then a four-game World Series in 1914. The turnaround was even more incredible given that, through 67 games of 1914, the team sat at 27-40. They were in last place on July 6, but they finished 68-19 and rode their scorching hot second half to the franchise's first World Series victory.

Maranville himself is about as well known a player as they come in baseball lore, even getting himself an entire book of tales called, *Run, Rabbit, Run: The Hilarious and Mostly True Tales of Rabbit Maranville*. The book is filled with classic turn-of-the-century-type stories of the ballplayer, most of which have been presumably exaggerated a bit over the

---

[260] All one of you.

[261] "Fifty-two percent of the country is single. That's a market that has been dominated by apartment rentals. Let's take some of that market. I call it: Singles City."

years but are at least based on some sort of truth – the truth being that Maranville was a total wild card. He supposedly got his nickname from his oversized ears (I feel ya, brotha), and he was a well-known prankster, one of the first clowns in baseball history. An old-school, Larry Walker-type, pranking his teammates with the type of aplomb that only a beloved teammate can get away with (like dumping water on sleeping teammates).

All things considered (Maranville's alcoholic tendencies, his lifelong commitment to the sport, his tales of mischief) I think it's fair to say no ballplayer checks off more boxes on the "Early History Baseball Player" bingo card than Mr. Maranville.

3B Chipper Jones (1993-2012) vs. Eddie Mathews (1952-1966)

This is one of the best breakdowns in the book, somewhat of an old school vs. new school showdown. This breakdown is one that looks at two faces of the franchise, and two all-time greats, facing off mono a mono.

Contact

	BA	lgBA	Seasons ≥ .300	Career high/low	Seasons ≥ 90 SO	SO %	lgSO%	BABIP	Misc.
Jones	.303	.270	10	.364/.248	4	13.3	17.1	.313	LL 1x BA
Mathews	.273	.261	3	.306/.233	8	14.6	N/A	.275	

By numbers alone, Jones gets a decent advantage here – Mathews was no slouch, he was just more often in the .260–.290 range for his batting average. Batting average on balls in play (BABIP) was included in this chart because over the course of a full career, it becomes clear which hitters actually have the bat control to post a sustainably high BABIP. Jones clearly had the better bat control. Another statistic of note: Jones is the only switch-hitter in baseball history (min. 5,000 AB) to hit at least .300 from both sides of the plate.

EDGE: Jones

Power

	HR	Seasons ≥ 40 HR	Career high HR	XBH	SLG%	lgSLG%	ISO	HR%	XBH%	Misc.
Jones	468	1	45	1055	.529	.430	.226	4.4	9.9	
Mathews	493	4	47	901	.517	.400	.243	5.1	9.3	LL 2x HR

This one is much closer, with both guys having very similar numbers. Mathews is more of a home run guy, with Jones having more of his power numbers come from peppering the gaps with extra-base hits. Three factors are going to play a role into deciding who gets the edge here. First, the era in which each played. This becomes noticeable in the statistics above: while Jones has the higher slugging percentage, it is Mathews who had a higher slugging percentage compared to league average for the years in which he played. Jones played in a time when home runs were much more in vogue, making Mathews' power numbers slightly more impressive. Second, and tied to the last point, is dominance in power. Mathews led the league in home runs twice, and he put up more home runs than Jones as a Brave, despite playing in four fewer seasons with the club. Mathews was also the second-youngest to reach 400 home runs (31 years old). Finally, something that often gets lost beneath all these statistics is perception, or "the one sentence theory." Perception can obviously be flawed, but usually it is based in truth. If you were to ask a baseball fan to describe each player with one sentence, Mathews would almost certainly have his home run prowess mentioned in his one sentence; I think Jones often would not.

EDGE: Mathews by a tiny bit

Batting eye

	BB	Seasons ≥ 100 BB	OBP	lgOBP	OPS+	BB%	SO/BB	Misc.
Jones	1512	3	.401	.341	141	14.3	0.93	LL 1x OBP, OPS+
Mathews	1376	5	.379	.326	145	14.3	1.03	LL 4x BB 1x OBP, OPS+

Well, it doesn't get much closer in terms of batting eye than an exact tie in career walk rate. These two men both excelled at working the count to their favor and knowing that a walk can often be as good as a hit. There is some excellent work being done with statistics for how much batters control the strike zone, with batters' swing rates on pitches both inside and outside the strike zone now able to be tracked. We also have that information for some of Jones' era, and it turns out he was an absolute stud when it came to plate discipline. When researching an article about Joey Votto, I stumbled across just how crazy some of the Chipper Jones stats were. There are three instances this millennium of a hitter swinging at fewer than 12 percent of pitches outside of the strike zone, while simultaneously swinging at more than 70 percent of pitches in the strike zone – basically the ultimate strike zone knowledge. Those three instances: Barry Bonds in 2002 (aka the greatest hitting season of all time by OPS+) and two Chipper Jones' seasons (2002 and 2004). That's incredible. It takes a patient hitter to swing at few pitches outside the strike zone. It takes an all-time legend to both lay off pitches outside the zone and swing at pitches in the zone. That's a true batting eye. And it's enough to topple Mathews' four walk titles.

EDGE: Jones

Speed

	SB	Seasons ≥ 20 SB	Career high SB	Rbaser	SB%	XBT%	GDP%	Misc.
Jones	150	2	25	3	77	45	11	2x 20/20
Mathews	66	0	12	0	64	42	6	

Speed was certainly not a main facet of either of these two players' game, and it is not for many other third basemen, for that matter. Jones had decent speed at the beginning of his career, swiping 25 bases and being caught stealing only three times in 1999, but he quickly lost that speed a few seasons into his career. Mathews never was a base stealer, but he did post impressively low grounded-into-double-play stats for his whole career.[262] At first blush, this would seem to imply that he may have known how to get down the line quickly when it mattered, but it is almost certainly due to the fact that Mathews was much more of a fly ball hitter (sadly groundball to flyball rate isn't available for Mathews) and avoided double plays in that manner rather than using his speed, or lack thereof.

EDGE: Begrudgingly Jones

Defense

	Fld%	lgFld%	dWAR	RF/9*	lgRF/9	Double Plays	GG**	Misc.
Jones	.957	.956	-1.6	2.42	2.65	276	0	LL 1x E at 3B
Mathews	.954	.955	6.3	3.02	3.01	369	0	LL 3x E at 3B, 2x 3B TZR, 1x 3B DP, 3B RF/9

* For RF/9 and league comparison we will use Jones' and Mathews' numbers from their time at third base
** The Gold Glove award only came into play in Mathews sixth season

For one of the most important parts of the game, there are simply not enough defensive statistics throughout most of baseball history. That being said, this matchup isn't close enough to need a deeper dive into the numbers. Mathews was a strong fielder, with better range than Jones[263] and probably should have won a few Gold Gloves in his day (his dWAR was higher than Ken Boyer's in both 1958 and 1963, with Boyer taking the award each year). Jones didn't kill the Braves at the hot corner, but Mathews was certainly a cut above him.

EDGE: Mathews

Intangibles

By all accounts, Jones was the leader of the Braves for his final decade in the league, after most of the Big Three Braves pitchers (Maddux, Glavine, and Smoltz) had moved to other teams or were in lesser roles. Jones was one of the most respected players in baseball, and that was on full display during his farewell tour in 2012. At each stop along the way, Jones received gifts from the opposition, gifts that varied in scope and scale.[264] Also, watch his 2012 All-Star Game clubhouse

---

[262] His career six percent grounded into double play rate is almost half the league average of 11 percent, which was exactly Jones' percentage.
[263] Although it is interesting to note how much better the average range was in Mathews' time. This may due to the fact that there is more of an emphasis on hitting third basemen in the game today. The same may be said of the shortstop position in the future.
[264] The unaffiliated dude who turned his cornfield into Jones' face is pretty cool, too.

speech and tell me those young stars don't respect the hell out of good ole' Larry "Chipper" Jones. So, since we have only stories like these, and not numbers, this is another field that would be interesting to see some sort of statistical analysis, even though it would be very difficult. (And I realize not everyone shares my turn-everything-into-numbers sentiments.)

Could we someday see statistics that could quantify off-field results as well as on-field, or is this getting a little bit too "Big Brother" for everybody? There have been studies, both in front offices and among the baseball writing elite (including Sam Miller) that attempt to calculate chemistry, but there haven't been any definitive conclusions, at least not available for public consumption.

Injuries are another key factor we have tracked in intangibles. If you're not on the field, then you're worth nothing to your team (unless you're Wally Pipp). Jones started his career with excellent health, playing in 150+ games for eight straight seasons, but he struggled with injuries and general end-of-career days off in the second half of his career. Mathews enjoyed great health *throughout* his career with the Braves, and because he left the Braves for his twilight years, never found himself playing less than 134 games in a season as a member of the Braves.

Finally, by being a switch-hitter, Jones made it difficult for managers to play matchups out of the bullpen in late-game scenarios – something modern managers do ad nauseam. Having the edge in two out of three of these factors means Jones taking this category.

EDGE: Jones

Team Success

	W	L	T	W-L%	Seasons ≥ 90 W	Division titles	Pennants	WS
Jones	1,449	1,049	1	.580	12	11	3	1
Mathews	1,218	994	11	.551	4	2	2	1

Both players won one World Series while with the Braves, but Jones played during the Braves Golden Era of the `90s, and he played in a time in which Championship Series and Divisional Series were present to boost playoff numbers by sheer volume of games played. As such, Jones has far more playoff appearances than Mathews, and the statistical comparison between the two heavily favors Jones. It is interesting to note that while the Braves had Warren Spahn, Hank Aaron, *and* Mathews they were able to make only two World Series (one win), thanks in large part to some strong Dodger teams of the same era. In fact, both Braves iterations had similar track records, but with divisions of only five teams, the Braves of the `90s were able to win their division much easier, and thus, they have more playoff appearances for Jones to rack up the stats. It is undeniably impressive that from the moment Chipper took a starting role, the team won 11 straight division titles.

EGDE: Jones

Dominance

	BB	AB/HR	HR	OBP	OPS+	SO	RF/9 3B	Fld% 3B	BA	OPS	MVP
Jones	XX	XX	XX	1	1	XX	XX	XX	1	1	1
Mathews	4	3	2	1	1	1	1	1	XX	XX	XX

Both players relied on consistency more so than dominance throughout the majority of their career, although each did lead their league in a few categories throughout their careers. Jones countered Mathews' two home runs titles with an MVP (a season in which Chipper didn't lead the league in any statistical categories, mind you), but in general, the two put in consistently good years over crazy dominant ones. Since we have to decide as to who had a more dominant stretch, the tiebreaker has to go to Mathews for reaching 400 home runs as fast as he did to start his career, as well as his reputation as one of the most dominant power hitters of his generation.

EDGE: Mathews

Impact on the Franchise

It's hard to top Jones in terms of impact on the Braves franchise, but Mathews remains the only player to play with the franchise while it was in Boston, Milwaukee, *and* Atlanta. In fact, he is the only player in baseball history to play for the same franchise in three different cities. Mathews was also inducted into the Braves Hall of Fame in its inaugural year (1999).

Jones, however, stayed with the franchise for his entire career and became the Face of the Franchise for the latter portion of his playing days. Jones meant enough to the franchise that they never traded him. Even though the trade that sent

Mathews out of town wasn't his own doing, can you honestly picture the Braves ever trading Chipper, even if it got to the point where he was using a walker to get out to third base?[265] This may be skewed slightly by having lived through Jones' final days with the Braves, but the man was a GD legend for the Braves.

EDGE: Jones

Ability to kill the Mets

Not really a fair category since Mathews couldn't do damage to the Mets franchise until the final years of his career (the Mets came into existence in 1962 and Mathews left the team in 1966), but as any Mets fan will tell you, even if they had been around longer in Mathews' era, there's no way Mathews would have killed them as much as Chipper did (although it is pretty hilarious that Mathews still did have a .977 career OPS against the Mets, the highest of any team he faced at least 12 times in his career). And who doesn't love torturing Mets fans? Plus, Jones is the ultimate troll. The dude named his son Shea, and then told the *New York Times* it had nothing to do with his demolition of the Mets during his career.[266]

EDGE: Jones

Verdict

In the end, despite my hyping the matchup at the beginning, **Jones takes the spot with relative ease**. If it came down to only the statistics, it would have been exceptionally close, but since there is more to the picture than just the cold, hard stats, Jones gets the edge. Jones has already returned to the franchise as a special assistant to baseball operations, and if it weren't for a certain player yet to show up, Jones would likely be thought of as Mr. Brave.[267] Plus, who can go against a guy who got his nickname from being called "a chip off the old block," while growing up playing for his dad? In a sport that worships the father-and-son dynamic, Jones has to get some credit for his nickname origin. Don't worry, Mathews is still going to get his due.

SS Herman Long (1890-1902)

Long was part of the franchise in the late 1800s and into the turn of the century. He was an excellent fielder and a plus hitter, usually a high run-scorer, he led the league in home runs in 1900, a very rare feat for a shortstop, especially in that era. Long was strongly tied to his ethnic roots, as he went by both "Germany" and "The Flying Dutchman," although nicknames based on ethnicity were very common in his time. Long's best year was 1896, a year in which he had over 100 runs and RBI each, while posting a .345 batting average and striking out only 16 times all season. He was a plus fielder and, along with Joe Quinn, was Bill James' choice for the best double play combination of the 1890s. He also lit up the base paths, especially early in his career, stealing 89 bases his rookie season. Unsurprisingly, he is the Braves all-time steals leader (434). He's also the epitome of what I meant when I said, at the beginning of this chapter, "Outside of the BIG names that you'll know right off the bat, try guessing this Starting IX. It's not that easy."

LF Hugh Duffy (1892-1900)

Duffy was a true baseball lifer. His career in the sport lasted 68 years, or, sadly, more twice Addie Joss' entire lifetime. A New Englander through and through (remember the Braves spent plenty of their early days in Boston), he scouted for the Red Sox after he retired and hung around long enough that he was called Fenway Park's Mr. Chips, a reference guaranteed to make every reader under the age of 70 queue up a Google search.[268] Among his on-field accomplishments, Duffy can claim to be the first man to reach base three times in one inning, and he is also the only player to hit .300 in four different leagues. He did so in the American League, National League, American Association, and the Players' League. This is obviously a result of the times in which he played, but he was certainly among the best of his time. Back in 1894, as a member of the Braves (then Beaneaters) franchise, Duffy was the second Triple Crown Winner, although it was not referred to as the Triple Crown that time.

In said 1894 season, Duffy had one of the best seasons any player has ever had in baseball history. He led the league with a .440 batting average, had a league-leading 18 home runs and 145 RBI, while also leading the league in hits (237), doubles (51), OPS (1.196), and total bases (374), to go along with 160 runs. His .440 batting average is the second-highest ever, and the highest in NL history. There is a bit of debate over early statistics (First Base, Chicago Cubs – Page 228) and

---

[265] Also known as 2012.

[266] Although plenty of publications just assumed he was named after Shea Stadium and published headlines saying as much. FAKE NEWS!

[267] Which definitely sounds like a character from the sequel to *The Incredibles*. (That joke was written before it was announced that there is actually going to be a sequel to *The Incredibles*, because, Hollywood.)

[268] For the record, despite being under 70, I have actually seen that movie, although it was by force of my father, not by choice. It was all right.

often different sources say different things, but his .440 average is still used on Baseball-Reference. The debate over older baseball book-keeping is a topic broached throughout this book, and it will become a more common theme as we move into the older teams and older players that appear in these pages. Back to Duffy: if an MVP were given out for 1884, he would have certainly received it, and he may be the first example of a breakout 27-year-old, a trope that is now the well-worn mantra of every fantasy baseball player.

Duffy also owns the second highest batting average (.332) among Braves with at least 1,000 at bats for their career, and he was a prolific base stealer as well, trailing only the man starting at shortstop for this Starting IX in terms of steals for the franchise. For his nine years with the team, Duffy averaged over 100 runs and RBI per year and was a frequent league-leader in his time with the franchise. In the Beaneaters' 1892 championship win (pre-World Series), he hit .462 with nine RBI in a six-game series win. He was probably the most valuable player of the series, even though the award wasn't given at that point.

Don't think Duffy's 1894 made him a flash-in-the-pan, as he led the majors in hits, RBI, and home runs throughout the decade of the 1890s. Along with Tommy McCarthy, the two were called the "Heavenly Twins" and were renowned for their strong defensive abilities[269] when they roamed the outfield together from 1892-1895. Duffy is one of the many hidden gems from baseball's earliest days that I so thoroughly enjoyed learning about in the process of writing this book.

CF Andruw Jones (1996-2007)

Jones burst onto the scene in the 1996 postseason as a 19-year-old. He particularly excelled in the Braves World Series loss to the Yankees, hitting .400 with two home runs and some outstanding defense. Those two home runs came in his first World Series game, and they made him the youngest player to ever homer in a World Series game, replacing Mickey Mantle in the record books. He had also homered in his last at bat of the NLCS, making him the second player ever to hit home runs in three straight at bats in October. Defense and power became Jones' calling card for the next decade, as he won 10 straight Gold Gloves (1998-2007) and led the league in home runs in 2005 with 51.[270] He finished second in the MVP that year, and he averaged over 30 home runs a season for his career with the Braves.

All of Jones' defensive metrics with the Braves measure off the charts, which is not surprising if you saw him play. His glove, range, and arm all made him one of the best defensive center fielders of all time. It is due to this that Jones beat out Dale Murphy, another strong candidate for the center field position for the Braves. Murphy had good success with the bat throughout his time with the Braves, but he simply isn't in the same ballpark (or even area code) as Jones on the defensive side of the ball. Even still, despite his over 60.0 WAR with the Braves, there are some fans who think of Jones as a bit of a bust, or a guy who never quite reached his ceiling. Maybe it was because of the Griffey comparisons he demanded with his precocious debut in 1996; maybe it was because he was the "Other Jones" to Chipper, who overshadowed him for so long in Atlanta; maybe it was even because the team never won a title with *this* Jones, but whatever the reason, Andruw Jones gets a bit of a raw deal from some Braves fans. That shouldn't be the case; Jones was one of the best players in franchise history.

RF Henry Aaron (1954-1974)

Appropriately the first name you'll find in *The Baseball Reference*, Aaron is the man who made Muhammad Ali once say, "The only man I idolized more than myself." Aaron is one of baseball's true kings. He is easily the most famous Brave of all time, and deservedly so. The all-time home run king for 33 years until Mr. Bonds came around,[271] Aaron was the face of the Braves for two decades worth of baseball and a true model of consistency. He never hit more than 47 home runs in a season (and that 47-homer season came when he was 37 years old and missed more than 20 games over the course of the year), but he was consistently a top home run threat in the league, leading the league in long balls four times and finishing in the top five an incredible 14 times. He hit 20 or more home runs in 20 straight seasons. He never had a season with more than 10.0 wins above replacement, but he averaged over 6.0 WAR per season in his 21 seasons with the Braves. He has the *incredible* MLB record of 17 straight seasons of 5.0 or more WAR – that's one of my, like, five favorite stats of all time. He won only one MVP award but received votes 19 straight years and made the All-Star game every year but his rookie season (giving him a record 21 All-Star Game appearances). His career batting average with the Braves was .310, but he only hit above .330 once. It is not a stretch to call Aaron the most consistently great player of all time. In fact, it might be crazy not to award him that moniker.

Aaron was a smart player who tailored his game to the ballpark in which he played. During the season in which the Braves moved into Atlanta-Fulton County Stadium, soon to be known as "the launching pad," Aaron led the league in home runs, stating, "The ball really flies out of Atlanta Stadium, and when I swing, I'm swinging to put it out of the park. Nothing thrills the fans like a home run, and it's our first season down here, so I'm trying to give them all the thrills I can."

Aaron was so intent on the opposing pitchers that he would often study them by looking through the tiny holes in his

[269] Duffy is Bill James' second outfielder on his all-Gold Glove team of the 1890s, collecting five Bill James Gold Gloves for his career.

[270] But as Jayson Stark points out, of the 45 seasons in baseball history in which a player hit 50 home runs, Jones owns the lowest slugging percentage (.575), OPS (.922), and OPS+ (136) in said season.

[271] And in the eyes of many, still the real home run king. But that's a debate for later in the book.

cap while sitting on the bench between at bats. By doing so, he was able to isolate just the pitcher out of the whole game surrounding, and the results spoke volumes.

As a team, the Braves never achieved great success in Aaron's career, but in his three playoff appearances, he posted a .362 batting average with six home runs and 16 RBI. It would be interesting to see, if Aaron had played in a later era when the wild card existed, would he have been able to cobble together a far more impressive playoff portfolio? Granted, his actual sample size is small, but he played for a team that often finished in what would now be a wild card position,[272] Aaron could have potentially put up great playoff numbers if he had played in a later era when playoff expansion had occurred.

Of course, what Aaron is best known for is his chase for the home run record. Jackie Robinson may have broken baseball's color barrier with the help of Branch Rickey in 1947, but baseball (and the U.S. of A) was still by no means a welcoming environment for a black man in Aaron's time. The lead-up to Aaron breaking Ruth's all-time home run record was a very clear and chilling reminder of this. Chasing Ruth's record in the Deep South,[273] in the early 1970s, was an immensely challenging task. As Aaron himself said, "Patience is something you pick up pretty naturally when you grow up black in Alabama. When you wait all your life for respect and equality and a seat in the front of the bus, it's nothing to wait a little bit longer for the slider on the inside." I'm sure this patience came in handy when Aaron wanted to press for those final few home runs to pass Ruth.

Chasing Ruth's record, regardless of the environment, would have been a high-pressure situation, but Aaron seemed to ratchet up his production during the time leading up to his record-breaking home run. Aaron broke Ruth's record in Atlanta on April 8, 1974, and in the 31 games leading up to and including the record-breaking game, he posted some unbelievably impressive numbers. The numbers, which we will get to in a second, would be good for any 31-game stretch, but considering the environment, they were even more incredible.[274] Towards the end of his push to break Ruth's record, Aaron was quoted as saying, "I used to love coming to the ballpark. Now I hate it. Every day becomes a little tougher because of all this." Aaron supposedly received nearly a million pieces of mail (both negative and positive) in the lead up to his breaking Ruth's record. Some baseball players go into mini-slumps when approaching a milestone due to the pressure, but during the aforementioned 31-game stretch, Aaron hit well over .400 with 13 home runs, 41 RBI, and 28 runs. He entered as a pinch-hitter in three of those games, so he was basically on pace for 162 runs, 75 home runs, and 237 RBI if he kept that pace for a 162-game season; talk about stepping up in a pressure situation.

When Aaron was approaching Ruth's record, and even now as we look back on the two, there is a natural tendency to compare the two all-time sluggers. One of the main troubles with comparing generations is that there are just so many factors. These two men, who are inevitably always compared, really played baseball in totally different environments. As G. Scott Thomas says in *Leveling the Field*, "Ruth played only in the daytime, Aaron mostly at night. Ruth played only on grass, Aaron sometimes on artificial turf. Ruth played against only whites, Aaron against players of all races, therefore competing against a much larger pool of players. Ruth traveled by train, Aaron by jet. Ruth rarely faced relief pitchers, Aaron often did."

This doesn't even take into account expansion, differing ballpark dimensions, changes made to the rules, the ball itself, or the scouting advancements that have been made as time has gone on. One of the most interesting, and damning, arguments against hitters of the 1930s that I have seen comes from Christina Kahrl of *ESPN*, who points out that many hitters on the top teams of yore beat up on the worst opponents of the time, padding their stats against a bottom half of the league that really had no business being in professional baseball. In 1935, Lou Gehrig slugged .831 against the losing half of the league compared to just .462 against the two other winning teams in the league.

In the end, there's only so much that even statistics such as OPS+, or other "era-neutral statistics," can really do to compare Ruth and Aaron, or any other cross-generational comparison. When those inevitable comparisons are made, the smart baseball fan must know that they come with a grain of salt. Of course that has never stopped baseball writers (including yours truly, in this book, over-and-over again) from endless such comparisons, but it is definitely something that should be on every baseball fan's mind as they read about the sport and its history.

Utility Eddie Mathews (1952-1966)

Mathews may have lost out on the third base spot to Chipper, but that's only because he was going against probably the second-best Brave of all time; Mathews is more than deserving of a spot on the team. Not a utility player in the sense that some of the previous utility spots have been filled, Mathews is a utility player more in the mold of an extra bat for the team. In fact, if the team were actually to step on the field, Mathews would probably start at third, with Chipper at DH based on the defensive section of the breakdown covered above, but Chipper still gets the honorary nod at third for the Starting IX. Since we've covered quite a bit about Mathews already, we'll go just briefly into a few tidbits.

---

[272] The Braves finished second in four of Aaron's first seven years, in addition to two first-place finishes and one third-place finish.

[273] This is not to give the North a pass, race relations in the North were (and are) far from where many Northerners would like to think they were (and are), but the Deep South was indeed home to some of the most vocal racist fans.

[274] One note that always gets mentioned, but with good reason, is the fact that Aaron had to wait an entire offseason in between home run no. 713 and the record-tying home run he hit in the first game of the 1974 season. I wonder if he had some sleepless nights that offseason thinking about going for the record, while he and his family were getting hundreds of death threats a day? There was certainly a huge amount of support for Aaron in his quest for the record, as well, but something tells me it's a little harder to ignore the negative messages being sent to you and your loved ones.

Mathews was highly-touted as a youngster. As a matter of fact, at his high school graduation dance, at 12:01 am, Johnny Moore, a Boston Braves scout, showed up to sign him. This was due to the fact that high school players could not be signed, so Moore outsmarted the system to get his prized prospect, showing up the literal minute he was no longer in high school. After this, Mathews had an interesting start to his career. He became the first rookie to hit three home runs in a game; set the rookie record for home runs in a season; and his total of 47 home runs as a 21-year-old is still the highest total for a player of that age today. He was on the cover of the first-ever issue of *Sports Illustrated* (1954). Despite all these accomplishments, however, he struggled off the field and didn't seem quite ready for all the attention he got at first.

In fact, Mathews became a poster boy for the media thinking that once you are a famous athlete you are never allowed to make another mistake in your life. An actual quote from *Sport Magazine* in 1955 gives a glimpse into how reporters thought of the baseball stars of the time: "The moment [Mathews] hit his 40th home run in 1953 he surrendered his right to privacy." Reporters today would never put it so bluntly, but it is still a prevailing notion in this era that our famous athletes (or actors, musicians, politicians) must be under the microscope 24/7. This seems unfair, but very often it is the juiciest stories that sell, and I can't say I'm doing anything to prevent this phenomenon, as there are many stories about players' lives that appear in this book. One thing that should be remembered, however, is the age of the player. It may seem unfair to bias by age, but I think giving players a few years to mature and learn how to deal with the spotlight would allow more players to avoid negative headlines for the rest of their careers. The incident to which Furman Bisher was referring to in *Sport* occurred when Mathews was only 21 years old, and although it certainly makes Mathews come across as immature (he taunted a police officer after speeding through a red light), that's because he *was* immature – he was only 21. Think about yourself as a 21-year-old… Not a pretty sight, I presume.

Of course, Mathews went on to mature and become one of the more respected players in baseball eventually, and this "black mark" on his name seems even less important than it was in the moment.

A few quick facts about the rest of Mathews' career: although he was not with the Braves at the time, Mathews is one of three Hall of Fame players (along with Joe DiMaggio and Johnny Mize) to end his career with a World Series-winning season. Just goes to show how hard it is to actually "go out on top."

Finally, two Mathews stories that have a distinct "Butterfly Effect" feel to them. One has a legitimate impact on baseball, the other not so much. First, in Mathews' words, when he was a kid, "My mother used to pitch to me and my father would shag balls. If I hit one up the middle, close to my mother, I'd have some extra chores to do. My mother was instrumental in making me a pull hitter." Being a pull hitter is always useful for a power hitter, as the short porches in right and left field can be havens for home run seekers. This swing he adopted maybe wasn't as career-altering as Kurt Warner giving up being a grocer to play quarterback, but it likely helped Mathews reach that historic 500-home run mark. It also led to Ty Cobb saying of Mathews, "I've only known three or four perfect swings in my time. This kid has one of them."

In a less monumental, but still intriguing "Butterfly Effect" story: in the 1952 Topps set, the last card was an Eddie Mathews card. Obviously, this being Mathews' rookie card, it would be valuable regardless, but today it is worth even more than expected because of the fact that many kids in those days kept their card stacks in rubber bands, making the first and last cards of the set more valuable because many of the first and last in sets suffered a large amount of wear and tear, thinning out the market for the Mathews cards that are actually in good condition.

SP Warren Spahn (1942-1964)

This was a tricky one, and a borderline option to do a breakdown, but two full Bill Simmons/Dr. Jack breakdowns for one franchise would be a bit much. However, in Spahn, Kid Nichols, and Greg Maddux,[275] the Braves have three of the top 11 pitchers of all time according to Bill James.[276] Spahn is the franchise leader in wins (356), innings pitched (5,046), shutouts (63), and he has twice as many All-Star Game appearances as any other pitcher in Braves history (14). As such, he narrowly beat out the aforementioned Maddux as well as the old-schooler, Nichols, for the starting spot. Maddux simply wasn't with the team quite long enough, and the two out-of-this-world seasons he did post with the Braves weren't enough to overcome Spahn's consistent, top-of-the-line pitching throughout his time with the Braves.[277] Spahn over Nichols is a little more debatable.

Nichols has some of the best numbers of any pitcher in baseball history. In fact, he is fifth all-time in WAR for pitchers (116.6), but this is where I have a slight bias against pitchers from Nichols' era. These pitchers threw close to twice as many innings as the average starter today, and about 100 more innings per season than the pitchers in Spahn's era. Granted, this is impressive in terms of durability, but it also took away from career longevity.[278] Ballparks in Nichols' time were also much more favorable for pitchers. Ballparks such as the Polo Grounds had dimensions that went as deep as 500 feet to center;[279] Nichols' home stadium had a distance of 440 feet to center field. This not only gave the pitcher home run

[275] And really, you could toss Phil Niekro, John Smoltz, and Tom Glavine into the SP spot for a lot of franchises and have them be happy about it.
[276] With only Maddux really having any value outside of his time with the Braves franchise.
[277] In neither season did Maddux make 30 starts, a number that Spahn surpassed 17 straight seasons from 1947-1963. On the other hand, Maddux was with the club for three or his record four straight Cy Youngs. Like I said, not an easy decision.
[278] Nichols trails Spahn in several cumulative statistics because of this.
[279] Granted left and right field were often shallower than today, but the home run itself wasn't as much a part of the game at this time, regardless.

protection, but allowed pitchers to attack hitters, which as we see in the modern game, is often when pitchers are at their best. In fact, modern fans (or even fans in Spahn's era) would hardly recognize the game of baseball in which Nichols played. Here are just some of the differences – with the year the rule got modernized in parentheses: the ball only had to bounce once in fair territory to be a fair ball (1877); pitchers threw underhand (1883); bats could be flat on one side (1885); The hitter got to choose where the pitcher had to throw it (1887); nine (and later eight) balls were needed for a walk (1889); the pitcher's mound was just 50 feet from home plate (1893); sacrifices counted as an at bat (1893); and balks weren't in the rulebook at all (1898). Players also used to leave their gloves on the field while they were batting – just gloves sitting there, obstructing batted balls. Scuffing the baseball was allowed well into the 20th century, and the strike zone was far different. The game just wasn't the same, which is why cross-generational comparisons are so difficult, a common theme in this book chock-full of cross-generational comparisons...

On the plus side of Nichols' case, he did win 30 or more games a record seven seasons – one of the most unbreakable records – as well as becoming the youngest pitcher to reach 300 wins when he did so at the age of 30. Maybe the most impressive Nichols stat: he started 562 games – and finished 532 of those.

However, Spahn has some pretty impressive accomplishments of his own. In addition to leading the Braves in all the aforementioned categories, Spahn has his place in baseball history with several notable achievements. He was the first left-handed pitcher to ever win the Cy Young, and he holds the record for individual times leading the league in wins (8). That includes a stretch when he led the league in wins an impressive five straight seasons (1957-1961). He even had an impact with his bat. His 35 home runs are tied for second all-time among pitchers, and in 1958, he posted an OPS+ of 131 and was worth 1.9 oWAR in just 41 games and 122 plate appearances. For comparison, Rod Carew has a career OPS+ of 131.

Spahn managed all these accomplishments despite missing three seasons (1943-1945) to serve in WWII, receiving both a Purple Heart and Bronze Star while overseas. Since Spahn won at least 20 games 13 times in his career, projecting him at missing out on 60 wins in those three seasons seems reasonable at first blush. If this was indeed the case, he would have won 423 games in his career, meaning only Cy Young would have won more games in baseball history. Spahn himself knows the danger of that game, however. When asked if his time overseas cost him a chance at 400 wins, he responded, "I matured a lot in those three years, and I think I was better equipped to handle major league hitters at 25 than I was at 22. Also I pitched until I was 44. Maybe I wouldn't have been able to do that otherwise." This is an incredibly calm, level-headed, and nuanced response to a question that is worth asking. For the record, I do agree with Spahn that he wouldn't have been able to pitch until he was 44, but if we say the 13 wins he collected in his final two seasons would have likely been around 45 wins in those first three season he would still be at 395 career victories, good for third all-time and spitting distance from 400.

It is also hard to argue that any non-big-right-handed-Texan pitcher (looking at you Nolan Ryan and Roger Clemens) aged as well as Spahn. Spahn has the most wins of any pitcher of the live-ball era, and the most wins of any lefty, ever. He threw two no hitters after the age of 39 and won 20 or more games in 13 straight seasons, tied for an MLB record. Stan Musial said of him, "I don't think Spahn will ever get into the Hall of Fame. He'll never stop pitching." Part of this has to do with the innings he saved himself early in his career as Spahn duly noted above, but it takes more than a late start to maintain your body at pitching level into your mid-40s.

Spahn was also an excellent quote, and one of many players who I feel as though I would have been good friends with when reading about them. So, although Nichols may have the edge in WAR, Spahn is getting the start here, and while you may be calling, "Erroneous! Erroneous on both accounts!" I don't see another Goddamn narrator, so pipe down.[280] (Please actually read that footnote.)

Finally, and this is completely irrelevant so don't judge me, but there is something about players from the 1950s and `60s that have a special place in my heart. When I was younger, I inherited my father's and my uncle's baseball card collection. So my love for the game, in part, stemmed from scouring over the piles and piles of cards from the era of my father and his siblings. Baseball cards today have much more flash and pizzazz,[281] but there's something about those old cards, especially the 1959 Topps set, that have a distinct aura to them. Among that set is a Warren Spahn card that I believe is part of the reason I like him so much. It was always one of my favorite cards, and it definitely didn't hurt Spahn in this debate, mainly because I love little pieces of baseball irrelevancies that every fan has but, at the same time, are different for each and every one of us.

Now that we have settled that mini-debate, time for a few quick stories about Spahn: in 1952, he was offered a contract that would pay him 10 cents for every ticket sold for admission to a Braves home game. Because the then-Boston Braves had such poor attendance, he turned it down insisting on $25,000 instead. The team moved to Milwaukee the next year, and he would have made more than $150,000 if he had taken the ten-cent-per-ticket offer, as the team drew great crowds in their first year in Milwaukee.

Spahn also pitched in what many consider to be one of, if not the, best-pitched game in baseball history. On July 2, 1963, Spahn went up against the San Francisco Giants ace Juan Marichal. The Giants sported a lineup that included Willie Mays and Willie McCovey, while the Braves sported a lineup with Hank Aaron and Eddie Mathews. However, the hitters

---

280 Little double movie reference there with the first hopefully obvious enough to not need explanation (*Wedding Crashers*, just to be safe). The second is, surprise, surprise, *Kiss Kiss Bang Bang*. [*KKBB* no. 6]

281 And I have to admit the bits of jerseys and bats are pretty awesome.

would have little say for quite some time. In fact, for 15 innings neither team was able to score until Willie Mays (of course) was able to make the breakthrough with a walk-off home run in the 16th inning. The final line for the two pitchers: Spahn went 15.1 innings, allowing nine hits and only one walk, while striking out two in the 1-0 loss; Marichal topped him with a remarkable 16.0 innings, eight hits, four walks, and 10 strikeouts. Their pitching performances are likely never to be repeated again, as pitching counts are (rightfully) under such strict limits in the modern game. There is an entire book written on that one game called *The Greatest Game Ever Pitched*, by Jim Kaplan. Fun side note to the game: the whole game lasted only 4 hours and 10 minutes, more than half an hour shorter than a nine-inning, Yankees-Red Sox game in 2006. (That's not a joke.)

CP Craig Kimbrel (2010-2014)

Kimbrel broke on to the scene as an immediately dominant force late in 2010, and he established himself so quickly that *Baseball Digest* said of him, "The Braves closer has become head and shoulders the best reliever in baseball. He is so much better than the next-best reliever that he is in his own tier, and it really isn't even clear who the next best reliever is." That quote came after just two full seasons. In five seasons with the Braves, Kimbrel sported a spiffy 1.43 ERA and 266 ERA+. He reached the All-Star Game each of his four full seasons with the squad and finished in the top 10 in the Cy Young all four full seasons, as well. He led the NL in saves all four of those seasons.

Kimbrel's entrance into the scene came right as the Great Relief Pitcher Blossoming occurred around the league. Throughout the entirety of baseball history up until 2012, only four closers (at least 20 saves and 50.0 IP) were able to post a season with an ERA+ over 350: John Smoltz in 2003 (385), José Mesa in 1995 (418), Jonathan Papelbon in 2006 (517), and Dennis Eckersley in 1990 (603). In the past six seasons alone, that total has been matched: Koji Uehara in 2013 (379), Craig Kimbrel in 2012 (399), Fernando Rodney in 2015 (641), and Zach Britton in 2016 (827). And remember, ERA+ measures against the rest of the league, meaning that all these recent relievers are not only absolutely killing it, but they're doing so in comparison to all the other relievers who are absolutely killing it. Of the 20 lowest relief pitcher ERAs *in MLB history* (min. 50.0 IP), exactly half have come since 2011. That's absurd.

There are several factors in play here. For one, teams are more likely to keep a potential end-of-the-rotation starting pitcher in the bullpen now that teams see that they can undergo a Wade Davis-like transition from a mediocre starter (4.57 ERA) to lights-out reliever (1.65 ERA). It's why we see Aroldis Chapman locking down the ninth instead of seeing if his 100+ mph heat would translate over the course of 33 starts in a season.

There's also the extreme specialization of relievers. Lefty specialists have been a baseball trope for a while, but it's rare to see any reliever go more than an inning these days, and simply stated: the shorter the outing, the better the numbers will be for the pitcher. Not having to face a single batter more than once in an outing is a huge edge for pitchers and a big reason we're seeing such an extreme jump in production from major league bullpens.

Of course, all of this takes away from the fact that there really are just a lot of amazing relief pitchers in the game right now. Take Craig Kimbrel. He never flirted with the rotation and was never handed easy end-of-game situations. He took over the closer's role in his first full season and never looked back. As Joe Posnanski noted on his excellent *Joe Blogs*, Kimbrel origin story is an excellent one, one that is similar to that of Billy Wagner (Closer, Astros – Page 135). Kimbrel broke his foot while attending Wallace State Community College, and he used his time rehabbing to practice throwing from his knees. The end result was almost 10 extra miles an hour on his fastball, and he never looked back.

As a 24-year-old in 2012, he had a season in which he had a 399 ERA+, a 0.654 WHIP, and he struck out 16.7 batters per nine. In the second half of the season, he had a strikeout to walk ratio of 15:1. He became the first player in baseball history to strike out over half of the batters he faced in a single season (Chapman has since joined him), and he posted the lowest FIP (0.78) in modern baseball, a record that he still holds despite all these relief studs of recent years making a run at the throne. In many ways, Kimbrel was the OG reliever boss for this generation. (Mariano Rivera still gets the previous generation OG boss title, and Hoyt Wilhelm gets the title of first OG reliever boss.) The Braves iteration of Kimbrel may have been a bit of a product of his environment, but who in history wasn't?

Starting IX Franchise Roster Stats

Lineup	Yrs	G	R	H	HR	RBI	SB	BB	SO	BA	OBP	SLG	OPS+	dWAR	WAR
Herman Long	13	1647	1292	1902	88	964	**434**	536	364	0.280	0.337	0.390	95	16.6	35.4
Hugh Duffy	9	1153	998	1545	69	927	331	459	149	0.332	0.394	0.455	121	-1.1	28.6
Chipper Jones	19	2499	1619	2726	468	1623	150	**1512**	1409	0.303	0.401	0.529	141	-1.6	85.0
Hank Aaron	**21**	**3076**	**2107**	**3600**	**733**	**2202**	240	1297	1294	0.310	0.377	**0.567**	**158**	-2.7	**142.1**
Eddie Mathews	15	2223	1452	2201	493	1388	66	1376	1387	0.273	0.379	0.517	145	6.3	94.4
Joe Torre	9	1037	470	1087	142	552	10	334	518	0.294	0.356	0.462	130	4.9	33.3
Andruw Jones	12	1761	1045	1683	368	1117	138	717	1394	0.263	0.342	0.497	113	**26.2**	61.0
Fred Tenney	15	1737	1134	1994	17	609	260	750	414	0.300	0.376	0.367	111	2.7	39.1
Bill Sweeney	7	902	396	902	10	349	153	369	200	0.280	0.356	0.354	106	-2.5	12.3
Pitchers	Yrs	W	W%	ERA	G	CG	SHO	SV	IP	SO	ERA+	WHIP	SO/9	SO/BB	WAR
Warren Spahn	20	**356**	0.609	3.05	714	374	**63**	28	**5046.0**	2493	120	1.189	4.4	1.81	92.0
Craig Kimbrel	5	15	0.600	1.43	294	0	0	**186**	289.0	476	266	0.903	14.8	4.41	12.2

#12 Minnesota Twins (1961-pres.); Washington Senators (1901-1960)

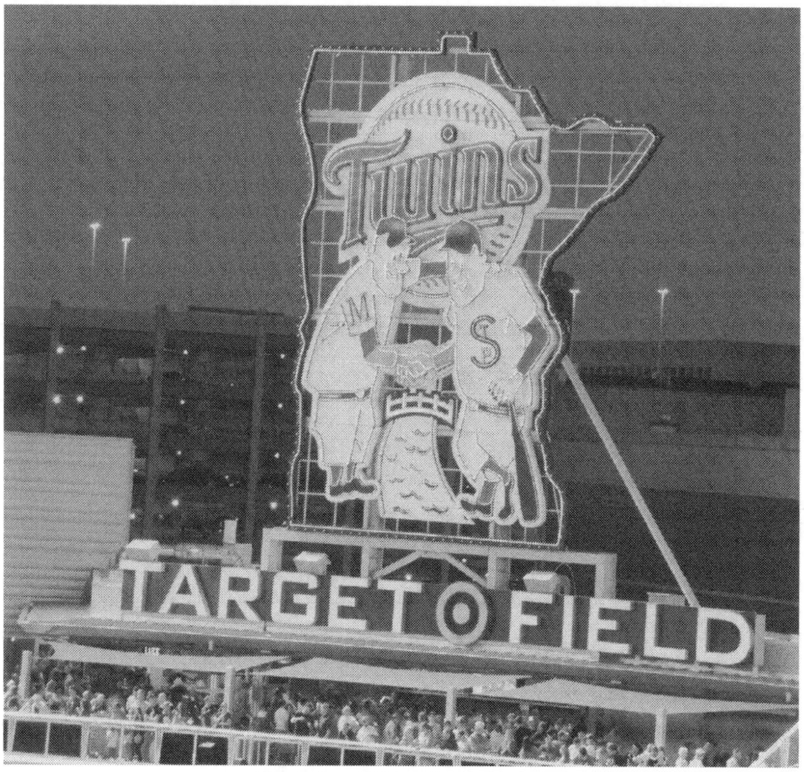

(Photo from Wikimedia Commons)

Team Background

Playoff appearances: 15 **Pennants: 6** **World Series titles: 3**
Collective team WAR: 601.0
Strengths: Their starting pitcher is as strong as any team's starting pitcher in this entire book. If they hypothetically faced off with each team, and could throw this guy every game, there's a good chance they'd go a lot further than their no. 12 ranking suggests.
Weaknesses: They really have only one big power hitter. A lot of the players on this team were good hitters, but there might be a little too much pressure on the lone Big Fly Guy.
What to expect from the next 12 pages: Another Retro Game Diary. No one ever said I wasn't a stubborn son of a bitch. There are also a lot of players that are going to confuse the great people in Crookston who bought this book thinking they were going to get a full roster of Twins players… Sorry everyone, the Senators also had some great players in their day, as well. Finally, not one, but TWO quizzes!

The Twins and Senators have a unique history that, to date, is almost an exact split in terms of the number of years each team has contributed to the franchise. The Senators were in existence for 60 years, and the Twins completed their 57th year in 2017. This gives us an interesting chance to equitably compare the two teams. The comparison might have been a bit more interesting if it was a little more even, though. The Senators were a notoriously bad team, dragged to relevancy by maybe the best pitcher of all time (hold that thought).

The Senators managed to win three pennants and one World Series, but they also finished under .500 in 41 of their 60 seasons, including 11 seasons below .400. Just to give perspective, a team has to lose 98 games in the modern MLB to finish below .400. It was said of the Washington D.C.: "First in peace, first in war, last in the American League." That's a bit of an exaggeration, however, as from 1910-1943, they didn't finish last in the entire American League even once, despite some rough years. Remember, parity in the early days of baseball wasn't what it is today, as the big boys (i.e. the Yankees) often beat up on the rest of the league year-after-year. The Twins, on the other hand, have the same number of pennants (three) as the Senators, but turned two of them into championships. They also (thanks in part to an expanded playoff system) have 11 playoff appearances to the Senators' three, and the Twins have finished below .400 in only four seasons in their time in Minnesota.

Another way to compare the two legacies is to look at how many players each team has on the franchise Starting IX. On the impending Starting IX, there are six Twins[282] and five Senators, with the "tiebreaker" coming down to the closer position, a position that didn't really exist in the Senators' time. In this sense, the Senators are right on par with the Twins. It's worth noting that this may be due in large part to the fact that players stayed with their original franchise much longer before the advent of free agency, and thus players accumulated greater numbers with one team instead of an array of teams. Overall, the Twins have almost certainly been a more productive iteration of the franchise than the Senators were.

* * *

One of the franchise's most memorable moments since their move to Minnesota came in Game 7 of the 1991 World Series. Since I was the ripe age of one year old at the time of this game, I wasn't able to watch when it actually happened. However, thanks to MLB putting up the whole game on YouTube, I can now go back and watch it as if it really is October of 1991. If you didn't read the brief intro to the Mariners retro game diary, go check it out. For the rest of you, let's do this:

00:10 The opening shot alone – a sold-out crowd with every fan waving their towels – sets the mood for an epic Game 7.
01:09 Solid montage/recap of the epic series so far. The close up of Jack Morris' mustache takes the cake for the best clip from the montage.
02:45 Jack Morris and John Smoltz (our two pitchers this evening) by their 1991 season stats:
Morris: 18-12 3.43 ERA 3.66 FIP 125 ERA+ 246.2 IP 163 SO 1.289 WHIP
Smoltz: 14-13 3.80 ERA 3.52 FIP 103 ERA+ 229.2 IP 148 SO 1.232 WHIP
Incredibly, each pitcher led his respective league in wild pitches… How bizarre.
03:01 By the way, Smoltz has a handicap of around two on the golf course. Dude is an athlete.
03:23 Why does announcer Jim Kaat keep winking at the camera? Does he know something I don't know?
04:02 "Feels like we've died and gone to *seven*." Looks like Tim McCarver still had it back in 1991.
06:56 Kent Hrbek looks a bit like a poor man's (poor woman's?) Jason Sudeikis.
09:02 Morris cruises through the first, not allowing a single base runner while overpowering Ron Gant to end the inning.
11:36 Don't know if it's the camera angle or the build of the two men pitching, but the mound seems to be elevated far above home plate. It's the perfect harbinger of doom for the hitters, who will be overmatched all game.
12:30 Cool on-screen stat: the 1987 Twins became the first team to ever win a World Series in which the two teams won every single home game. Not to act as the spoiler to a game that happened over 20 years ago, but *if* the Twins win this game, it would complete another World Series in which every game was won by the home team.
12:31 Terry Pendleton was a part of that St. Louis Cardinals team that lost every game in Minnesota in 1987, as well as this Braves team. I'm guessing he didn't move to Minnesota after retiring.
14:56 As good as Morris looked in the first, Smoltz looked even better, as he induced at least three ugly swings. In fact, let's just agree that we all know the pitchers will look good this game, and instead we can focus on the random crap outside of that fact.
19:13 Brian Hunter comes inches away from driving in David Justice, as he smacks a ball down the line but it is just foul. I wonder if that run would have been important…
19:26 The diamond transitions used by the CBS broadcast make the game feel like a modern-day middle school video project created by a fifth-grader who just learned how to use iMovie.
22:22 I must say I'm somewhat disappointed that MLBClassics didn't upload the game with all the original commercials from the broadcast. I feel as though they would have been a goldmine for unintentional humor.
23:35 I can't tell if the complete lack of a scoreboard on the screen (with the inning, balls and strikes, and men on base) makes the viewing experience feel more organic, or if it's going to really confuse me later in the game. I'm guessing by the seventh inning I'm basically going to be Nicholas Brody when he's rescued by American troops in the *Homeland* premiere.
26:54 Smoltz gives up his first hit with two outs in the second, and Shane Mack makes it two hits right after. The first chance of the night for Minnesota.
31:47 Mike Pagliarulo hits one down the first base line, but Smoltz does well to cover the bag, and the game remains scoreless.
34:55 I feel like I'm in one of those Klondike commercials, and, if I watch this game without the mini box score on the screen for five more seconds, I'll get a Klondike bar. Except instead of five seconds it has lasted 45 minutes, and instead of someone bringing me a Klondike bar, no one is bringing me a Klondike bar.
42:33 Just had to rewind to make sure I heard McCarver correctly when he said Nick Esasky had been on the DL for two years with vertigo. I heard right.
45:40 Finally, a really well-hit ball off Smoltz as Dan Gladden drives one down the line. You can tell the crowd knows how

[282] Looking at where they spent the majority of their career.

few runs are likely to be scored, and they are cheering accordingly.
49:35 Awesome "Kirby" chant by the Minnesota fans. That was one of the best player/city relationships in its prime.
51:45 Smoltz gets Puckett with a man on third and two outs on an excellent slider. End of three innings (I think. Seriously I'm almost at Nick Brody status already)[283] and still no score, but each team has had a chance now.
52:17 Borderline eephus pitch from Morris there, as he bloops two straight pitches in at 63 mph that each catch David Justice off guard.
59:12 A two-out double from Braves left fielder Brian Hunter, and then Greg Olson hits a liner to right… but it's caught by Shane Mack. That's four left on base for Atlanta so far. I haven't seen a group of Minnesotans so relieved since Michele Bachmann finally left office in 2015.
1:08:27 Strange feet-first slide into first on a bunt hit by Lonnie Smith. I feel like that's a phenomenal way for somebody, either the base runner or the first baseman, to break an ankle.
1:16:32 Morris dodges, dips, dives, ducks, and dodges out of another threatening situation. This time Morris gets out of first and third with one out, a near wild pitch, and a 3-1 count to Ron Gant. So far, Smoltz has definitely looked more dominant than Morris.
1:17:34 The broadcast has done a great job of incorporating little facts/stories/opinions on famous World Series moments, particularly about other Game 7s. You really should be watching along (although I know you're not).
1:29:42 Smoltz's slider looks like Johan Santana's slider… in its prime… in a video game. It's pretty unfair.
1:35:02 The fact that Smoltz grew up a Tigers fan – and a Jack Morris admirer – only acts to augment this awesome pitching matchup.
1:37:38 The Minnesota fans are cheering when John Smoltz fails to throw a strike right now. I think they're clued in to the fact that one run will probably win this game.
1:41:35 The sixth and seventh innings just took less than 20 minutes combined, as the two pitchers combined to throw 44 pitches in the two innings. I know we said no more of this, but wow, both pitchers are cruising.
1:41:39 More on that point: this game is now the only World Series Game 7 to go through seven innings scoreless.
1:47:45 Maybe Terry Pendleton shouldn't have won the 1991 MVP over Barry Bonds, but man did he play well in this series. He slashed .367/.424/.667 with a pair of home runs and seemed to come up big time-after-time. This time it was a one-out double for Pendleton after a leadoff single from Lonnie Smith to start the eighth. Smith should have scored on that double, but Chuck Knoblauch and Greg Gagne pulled off an awesome stunt up the middle to fake out Smith and make him slow down at second. This allowed Gladden to get his throw into the infield in time to hold up the speedy Smith. Very poor base running for the Braves, and a very heady play from the Twins. Still, we have second and third with nobody out and the three-four-five hitters coming up for the Braves.
1:51:45 Man, I wish I didn't know how this game ended. (Cut to Braves fans nodding while simultaneously pounding their heads into a concrete wall.)
1:53:41 I feel as though being a therapist in Atlanta on October 28, 1991 would have been a very lucrative move.
1:53:51 Morris is fired up, and deservedly so, after he once again gets out of a massive jam without giving up a run. I'll tell you what, there may not be a lot of evidence pointing towards clutch being a sustainable long-term trait, but re-watching this game, I can sort of empathize with the voters who claim that "clutch" is real and that Morris had it in spades. This time it was groundout, an intentional walk, and a double play to escape the jam.
1:55:30 Maybe it's because the city saw their team win a Game 7 at home just four years ago, but the Twins crowd has never had a nervous vibe to it up until this point of the game. Instead, they seem to have a subtle confidence that has seemingly worn on the Braves.
2:01:57 Now it's Braves fans' turn to get nervous, as Puckett comes up with first and third and one out after Knoblauch completes a successful hit-and-run to move Al Newman to third base in the bottom of the eighth. That'll do it for Smoltz. What an outing: 7.1 IP 6 H 0 R 1 BB 4 K ND
2:03:31 Twins fans miss a chance to love their hero even more, as Kirby is intentionally walked to set up Mike Stanton (one of the toughest left-handed pitchers) versus Kent Hrbek (left-handed batter) with the bases loaded.
2:06:02 Hrbek hits a soft liner that turns into a double play, and the 0-0 duel marches on.
2:10:15 Morris polishes off the ninth and after nine shutout innings I think it's fair to look at the rest of Morris' World Series starts up to this point:

Game 1, 1984: 9.0 IP 8 H 2 ER 3 BB 9 K W
Game 4, 1984: 9.0 IP 5 H 2 ER 0 BB 4 K W
Game 1, 1991: 7.0 IP 5 H 2 ER 4 BB 3 K W
Game 4, 1991: 6.0 IP 6 H 1 ER 3 BB 4 K ND

The Big Game reputation was certainly well-earned.
2:15:45 Another possibly important baserunning gaffe, as Chili Davis (Twins) does a great job of working a nine-pitch at bat before driving one to the right field gap to lead off the bottom of the ninth. He misses first, however, and as such he can't go to second for what would have been a double.

---

[283] And yes, I do realize I could just pull up the play-by-play on Baseball-Reference, but it's more fun to try to relive the experience as the fans did in 1991.

2:17:47 Stanton allows another hit on a perfectly placed bunt by Harper and injures himself twisting back to first to field the bunt. He has now given up two straight hits to start the ninth and will be pulled with the crowd going nuts.
2:20:40 Mark Lemke and Rafael Belliard turn another great double play, and now it is man on third, two outs. P.S. They turned that with Harper sliding halfway to China on his attempt to break up the double play at second base.
2:26:31 Braves dance out of the bottom of the ninth threat, and this is now the third extra-inning game of this 1991 World Series. There were also two other one-run games that narrowly avoided extras earlier in the series. It was a mildly entertaining series.
2:29:00 First extra-inning World Series Game 7 since 1924. Hey, guess what franchise starred in that Game 7? I'll give you a hint, you'll hear more about that Game 7 sooner than later.
2:32:12 Why do I feel as though even if this game went 20 innings, somehow Jack Morris would still be out there? Justin Verlander reminds me a lot of Jack Morris. Both guys maintain their velocity in the late innings with supernatural ability. The term "extra gear" gets thrown around a lot in other sports, but those two guys embody the trait far more than many. On to the bottom of the tenth as Morris now has ten scoreless innings.
2:34:12 Based entirely on this game, I think it's fair to put Dan Gladden in the Hall of Fame. Audacious play from the now-Twins radio broadcaster, as Gladden turns a single into a double thanks to the bouncy Metrodome turf and pure hustle. Sadly, McCarver had to ruin it by trying to start "the bat" as the nickname for Gladden's broken-bat double. That's a force, Tim.
2:36:50 "Little things" MVP Knoblauch moves Gladden over to third with one down. Now the inevitable walks to Puckett and Hrbek thus setting the stage for pinch-hitter Gene Larkin. One out, bases loaded, 0-0, bottom of the tenth, Game 7, World Series.
2:39:21 Gene Larkin's career slash line over parts of seven seasons in MLB: .266/.348/.374.
2:39:59 Oh by the way, Larkin is injured and can't run, so the double play is very possible. You can't write this stuff.
2:41:56 And of course, **Larkin delivers**. Larkin drives the first pitch to the opposite field gap, and the Twins and their fans go straight bonkers. A walkoff win World Series win.
2:42:30 I love when announcers know to just take a back seat to the natural noise of baseball, allowing the sounds of celebration and the bitter silence of defeat show the viewers what is going on, instead of trying to throw themselves in the middle of it. Vin Scully is the king of this.
2:44:22 And thus ends one of the five or so greatest games in MLB history.

A few more things on this incredible series. It pitted the first AL team to go worst-to-first in their division and win a pennant against the first NL team to go worst-to-first and win a pennant. Maybe even more impressively, the Braves had finished in last three straight seasons (1988-1990) before reaching the Promised Land in 1991. They went on to enjoy their most successful stretch in franchise history with 1991 as the jumping off point. In Game 7, the two biggest swings in win probability were the two double plays in the eighth inning. That seems appropriate given the pitcher's duel we just witnessed.

Random cool things about the franchise:

- The 1987 champion Twins were the first team to grace the back of a Wheaties box – if that's not honor, I don't know what is.
- If you look at a map of the U.S. and check out the territory that can be considered *Twins territory*, it's quietly an absurdly large chunk of land, it's just not very densely-populated.
- The team gave out more than 2.3 million "Homer Hankies" in 1987 – remember when those things were a big deal?
- The coldest game in franchise history came in April of 2014, when the game-time temperature was below freezing at a brisk 31 degrees Fahrenheit.

Starting IX

C Joe Mauer (2004-pres.)

Mauer burst onto the professional scene in 2004, when he slashed .308/.369/.570 in 35 games in his debut season. Mauer was already known by die-hard MLB fans, since he was the top pick of the 2001 Draft. As far as Minnesotans were concerned, Mauer was well known even before that, as the handsome St. Paul native was the first-ever athlete to win the U.S.A. Today High School Athlete of the Year in two different sports. He won as a quarterback his junior year and as a catcher his senior year. The multi-talented Minnesota native decided to pursue a career in baseball, and he timed his entrance to the big leagues perfectly, as the Twins made him the no. 1 overall pick in 2001.

Of course, there are plenty of stories that start this way but end in sorrow and misery both for the player and the team, as the heightened expectations can often crush a Hometown Hero like Mauer. Fortunately, the smooth-swinging lefty has somehow exceeded expectations throughout most of his career. Mauer has won three Gold Gloves, five Silver Sluggers, three batting titles, and an MVP in his 14 seasons in the big leagues, most of those accolades coming while playing the most demanding position on the diamond (catcher). Don't believe that catching is the most demanding position? Consider that when Mauer won his first batting title in 2006, he was the first catcher to win a batting title in American League history. He is currently the only catcher with three batting titles, and he's the only catcher to lead the league in each of the triple slash categories (BA, OBP, SLG) in a single season (2009). In a four-year span from 2006-2009, Mauer managed to win as many batting titles behind the dish as all other catchers in MLB history combined! Buster Posey has since won a batting title, but seriously, think about that previous stat for a second.

Speaking of 2009, Mauer's 2009 MVP season was incredibly impressive (and with hindsight, a bit of an outlier), as he hit a career-best 29 home runs, in addition to his typically high batting average (.365). This was no ordinary career-high either; Mauer has not topped 13 home runs in any other season, and he certainly doesn't appear to be headed anywhere near that total again as his career winds down.

More so than his production, however, Mauer was (and still is) beloved in the Twin Cities because of the turn around the franchise made while under Mauer's leadership. Along with Justin Morneau, Johan Santana, and manager Rod Gardenhire, Mauer helped lead the Twins to four division titles in his first seven seasons. Coincidentally or not, since Mauer's numbers took a hit in 2011, the club bottomed out a bit. Now Mauer fills the role of grizzled veteran on a young and exciting Twins team that made the playoffs in 2017.

Back to Mauer's early days, they read like one of those old-timey baseball legends that are beginning to show up with greater regularity as we move along in this book. There's the story of how Mauer was asked to leave tee-ball because he was hitting the ball too hard, or the fact that he only struck out once in his entire high school baseball career. Every statistic from his high school days are remarkable, in fact, and having spent a few years in Minnesota myself, it's even more impressive that he could become such a good baseball player when the spring sports season is typically cut at least in half because the weather is so cold.

Mauer's swing is about as smooth and efficient a swing as there has been in baseball, and he's a scout's wet dream. He looks like a baseball player through and through, and he does everything the scouts love. Mauer may have slid from his lofty spot among baseball's elite hitters at this point, but his prime should not be discounted for the awe it inspired.

Fittingly, it appears as though Mauer is going to play his whole career in one city; his hometown no less. Mauer is the epitome of Minnesota, and he was one of the easiest selections in this book. I mean, how many guys can say fans in their hometown have worn fake versions of their sideburns, as Mauer can claim after the Metrodome starting selling fake versions of Mauer's famous sideburns in his early seasons.

Let's have Cubs manager Joe Maddon end this one: "I think when God made his blueprint for catchers, he stamped Joe out."

1B Player X

Time for a little game ripped from Matthew Berry, ESPN fantasy guru. We'll run down a series of hints as to whom the mystery player at first base for the Senators/Twins Starting IX is and see how long it takes you to guess the player:

* His paternal grandfather was supposedly the strongest man in the Union Army.
* Of all the fun facts I learned researching this book, that one was the single least-surprising of all of them.
* He is the best baseball player to ever hail from Idaho.
* He was called up by the Senators in 1954 as a 17-year-old.
* Player X was almost drafted by the Red Sox. The first time he went to Fenway he said, "the wall seemed so close that I could touch it."
* His lifetime stats at Fenway (averaged over a 162-game season): 117 runs, 47 home runs, and 136 RBI with .316/.419/.619 BA/OBP/SLG. Talk about a missed opportunity.
* He did not become a full-time starter for the team until his sixth season, but when he broke onto the scene it was with 42 home runs in 1959.
* He would top 40 home runs in five of his first six seasons as a regular with the club.
* In his first appearance at Metropolitan Stadium (Minnesota's stadium when the team moved from D.C.), he collected four hits, one of which was a 450-foot home run to dead center.
* In 1967, he hit a home run in Metropolitan Stadium that shattered *two* seats in the UPPER DECK. Think about that. The seats were painted orange and not sold again.
* In 1969, he tied an American League record by homering at least twice in each AL stadium.
* From 1961-1970 (one of those hidden decades), Player X *averaged* over 40 home runs a season.
* Orioles manager Paul Richards said of him, "[He] can knock the ball out of any park, including Yellowstone."
* In 1972, Player X broke Jimmie Foxx's record for most home runs by a right-handed batter in AL history. He held the record until A-Rod came along.
* Senators coach Ossie Bluege said of him, "He hit line drives that put the opposition in jeopardy. And I don't mean infielders. I mean outfielders."
* He is rumored to be the Jerry West of Major League Baseball. According to legend, it is his picture that is the silhouette of a batter in the MLB logo.

So, do you know who it is?[284]

2B Rod Carew (1967-1978)

Carew is the franchise leader in WAR among hitters (63.7). We already saw Carew on the Angels Starting IX, but Minnesota was where Carew really made a name for himself, and where he had his best years. Carew was a hit machine in his 12 years with the Twins, winning seven batting titles, including four in a row (1972-1975). He also topped 5.0 WAR seven times in Minnesota, topped 7.0 WAR four times, and topped out at 9.7 in his 1977 MVP campaign. In 1969, Carew stole home seven times,[285] despite stealing only 19 bases total. In 1972, he became the first player to win a batting title without hitting a home run. And in 1977, he won the batting title by 52 points, the second-largest margin of victory, all-time.

Not a bad list of accomplishments for a man born on a train. (Yes, you read that right.) Carew was a player who received praise from numerous sources. Whether it was Wade Boggs calling him the best pure hitter of all time, Rollie Fingers calling him the best clutch hitter of all time, or, best of all, Mike D of the Beastie Boys saying that he "got mad hits like [he] was Rod Carew," the man was highly respected by his peers, as well as the public.

We already touched on much of Carew's career in his Angels section, so just a few quick tidbits here: Carew had four different batting stances that he supposedly switched based on the type of pitcher he was facing. Before Melky Cabrera did it on August 10, 2014 (in a 19-inning game), Carew was the last player to reach base safely eight times in a game, when he did so in May of 1972.

One final note on Carew that goes to show just how complicated race and sport were in Carew's day: Calvin Griffith, owner of the Twins in 1978, was quoted as saying, in regards to the team's move to Minnesota, "I'll tell you why we came to Minnesota. It was when I found out you only had 15,000 blacks here. Black people don't go to ball games, but they'll fill up a rassling ring and put up such a chant it'll scare you to death. We came here because you've got good, hardworking white people here."

Carew would later note how much Griffith had supported him during his days in Minnesota, but given that Carew publicly (and rightfully) expressed disgust with those comments, it's not too surprising that he was out of town before the beginning of the 1979 season, with one year still left on his contract.

3B Eddie Yost (1944-1958)

Yost was known as "The Walking Man," and with good reason. He led the league in walks six times (four with the Senators) and ranks 11th all-time in walks. Because of these facts, it's even more important to look at his career on-base percentage (.394) than his career batting average (.254). The 140-point gap between the two is greater than noted on-base machines Rickey Henderson, Ted Williams, and Joe Morgan. In his time in Washington, Yost had four seasons in which he walked more than twice as many times as he struck out. Yost was also a solid power hitter, but he suffered from playing half his games in Griffith Stadium. He played 862 games in Griffith Stadium totaling 25 home runs; in just 266 games playing in Detroit's Briggs Stadium, he had 28; and he nearly topped his 25 Griffith Stadium home runs in just 148 games in Fenway Park (19).

SS Joe Cronin (1928-1934)

Joe Cronin was a top-of-the-line infielder who was considered one of the game's first great shortstops. Shortstop was not thought of as an offensive position in Cronin's time, so his offensive prowess and positional scarcity made him one of the most valuable players of his era. In a four-year stretch from 1930-1933, Cronin totaled 28.5 WAR on the basis of his strong defensive (8.9 dWAR) as well as his strong offensive capabilities (.401 on-base percentage with 486 RBI). The final year of that stretch (1933) coincided with the first Midsummer Classic, and seeing as he was the top shortstop in the AL, it was unsurprising to see him selected to start in that affair.

Similar to Yost, Cronin's home run totals also suffered from playing in Griffith Stadium, as he totaled his five highest home run seasons as a member of the Red Sox after leaving Washington. Once again similar to Yost, Cronin had far better power numbers on the road. He totaled more home runs in his 152 games in Comiskey Park than he did in his 558 games in Griffith Stadium. Cronin also rebuilt himself at age 36 as a pinch-hitter, as he went on to set an AL record with five pinch-hit home runs in one season (1943), a record that still stands. He was always a great hitter, though, and Connie Mack once said of Cronin, "With a man on third and one out, I'd rather have Cronin hitting for me than anybody I've ever seen, and that includes Cobb, Simmons and the rest of them." When MLB named their All-Century Team, Cronin was named to the squad. Shortstops of this century now fill most lists of the top offensive shortstops of all time due the explosion of Jeter/A-Rod/Nomar/Tejada-types that have dominated the last 20 years, but Cronin locked down the 20th century.

---

[284] Harmon Killebrew!

[285] And should have had an eighth steal of home (which would have tied the MLB single-season record), as on his eighth attempt he came barreling into home and knocked over both the catcher and umpire. However, in the ensuing chaos, the catcher was able to make it look like he held onto the ball, even though he had originally dropped it. Grain of salt time: this story is from Carew himself.

Cronin reinvented himself numerous times in his life and was a lifetime baseball man who truly loved the sport. He was a player, manager, general manager, AL president, member of the Hall of Fame board of directors, and Veteran's Committee member before his days were over. He also made the bold move of marrying the niece of longtime Washington Senators owner (and stadium namesake), Clark Griffith.

LF Goose Goslin (1921-1930; 1933; 1938)

Another player from the Senators "Golden Age," Goslin was an excellent hitter who contributed in each and every offensive category. His 1924 and 1925 campaigns really announced his presence to the baseball world, as he totaled a combined 37 triples, 30 home runs, and 42 steals while collecting 400 hits and a .339 average. The team also arrived on the scene with back-to-back pennants, the former resulting in a title. In the two World Series, Goslin totaled six home runs and was the breakout offensive star of both series. After the 1924 World Series, W.O. McGeehan of the *Washington Post* wrote: "For the country at large the eagle may remain the national bird, but for the National Capital the greatest bird that flies is the Goose."

Goslin ran like a duck with the palms of his hands facing down, which played a role in his nickname. He also drew the nickname from his large nose, of which he quipped: "I've been hitting .344 as a one-eyed hitter, you know. If I could see around my nose, I'd hit .600." He was a bit of a character, with an open stance that saw him nearly face the pitcher and a hard swing that often resulted in Goslin ending up on his bum. He also liked to have fun after games, which helped to build his reputation (or tarnish it, depending on how closely you adhere to The Good Book).

One black mark on his record was that he tried to take the coward's route to a batting title. Even worse than José Reyes – who sat out the final game of the season to win his batting title – Goslin chose that same path before being taunted by his teammates. He took the bait and went up to bat in the final game of the season knowing he needed a walk, a hit, or to be thrown out of the game to win the batting title. Once he got down two strikes in the at bat, he started arguing strikes and balls, even going as far as stepping on the umpire's toes in an attempt to get thrown out, thus winning the batting title without having to work for it. The umpire realized what he was doing and left him in the game. Sadly, the Baseball Gods were zoning out, as Goslin got a hit and won the batting crown over Heinie Manush.

That season (1928) was an intriguing one, however, and the batting title ended up being just a bullet point in a rather odd season for Goslin. He injured his arm goofing around during the offseason, and as such, he could barely throw the ball 20 feet for much of the season. In fact, the Senators set up a unique type of relay on every ball hit to him, and it was shortstop "Gunner" Reeves, nicknamed for his impressive arm, who met Goslin in the outfield and fired it into the infield for him. This arrangement led to Goslin's manager calling him "the only outfielder in history with a caddie." This almost certainly cost the Senators a few wins along the way and was not popular among the media. One particularly frustrated reporter guessed that it cost the Senators "more than a dozen losses." I'm going to go ahead and dismiss that as too high a number, but he was definitely lucky that he was still able to bring it at the plate. Speaking of which, Goslin actually made the switch to a heavier bat that season, and he had a different swing entirely, which only adds even more allure to his eventual batting title.

Goslin spent three different stints in Washington, including a 38-game stint in his final season (1938). He collected over 43.0 WAR in his time with the franchise and over 66.0 WAR for his career as a whole.

CF Kirby Puckett (1984-1995)

We mentioned Puckett's popularity briefly during the Game 7 retro diary, but his well-deserved popularity in Minnesota cannot be overstated. Due to a battle with glaucoma, he played only 12 seasons in his career, but he played each season for the Twins, and he played each season well. His lowest batting average for a single season was .288, and he averaged 209 hits per 162 games. He remained relatively healthy throughout his career despite his hard play and was able to collect 2,304 hits and 50.9 WAR despite playing basically half as many games as Pete Rose played in his career.

He was also a key member of both Twins championship teams and hit over .300 during their two playoff runs. He especially shined in the 1991 ALCS and was named the series MVP. His most famous moment came in Game 6 of the 1991 World Series, when he made an incredible catch at the wall to preserve an early 2-0 Minnesota lead. Puckett followed that up with a walk-off homer in the 11th inning to set up the epic Smoltz-Morris Game 7 battle that was detailed at the beginning of this chapter. Prior to Game 6, Puckett had exclaimed to his teammates: "Jump on my back. I'll carry you." Boy, was he right.

He even has one of the best random facts about him: his 31 home runs in 1986 are good for the highest single-season total for a player listed at 5'8" in baseball history.

However, it is not all positive for Kirby, and this is where it gets sad. There is an aspect of research for this book that seems like prying into people's lives (because it basically is). For most of his career, Puckett was known as the man who went on to be a member of the Humanitarian Hall of Fame; a man who refused to accept money for signing autographs. This was a man who won the Branch Rickey Award and the Roberto Clemente Award, as well.

His post-playing career became proof that people are truly complex characters. There were multiple allegations of domestic violence against Puckett, including an intense story that had him holding a gun to his wife's head while their daughter was in her arms.

RF Tony Oliva (1962-1976)

Oliva burst onto the scene in 1964, leading the league in hits (217), runs (109), doubles (43), total bases (374), extra-base hits (84), and batting average (.323), to go along with winning Rookie of the Year, starting in the All-Star Game, and a fourth-place finish in the MVP. Those 374 total bases broke Joe DiMaggio's previous MLB rookie record for total bases. Oliva also became the first Rookie of the Year to win the batting title. He followed that up with another batting title the next season, becoming the first player to ever win a batting title in his first two years (obviously). In that season, Oliva continued his strong overall play, finishing second in the MVP this time. Over the next six years, his production would slip a bit, but it was not far off his blazing start. In fact, through his first eight full seasons, Oliva had totaled 1,455 hits, over 700 runs as well as RBI, a .313 batting average, a 140 OPS+, and 42.2 WAR.

Even during this stretch, however, there were signs of a precipitous fall. Oliva suffered knee problems so serious that, after his career, Rod Carew recalled, "I roomed with a guy with bad knees for years and used to listen to him cry like a baby at night. I'd be asleep and sometimes I'd hear Tony moaning and groaning… He'd get up during the middle of the night and go down to get ice, wandering all over the hotel trying to find ice to put on his knee." Oliva also won Rookie of the Year at the age of 26, an old age for someone to break into the big leagues and maintain success for the long term. In many ways, Oliva's career turned out similar to Ryan Howard, another player who won Rookie of the Year at age 26. Howard won an MVP at 27 and had seven great seasons before his sharp decline.

Sadly, Oliva has literally become a cautionary tale. In *A Team for the Ages* (released in 2004), Robert Cohen uses Oliva as an example of why he can't rate Derek Jeter, Alex Rodriguez, and Nomar Garciaparra as high as they may deserve at this point of their career because of the possible injury risk. Of course, Nomar proved Cohen's point and became a bit of a cautionary tale himself. Oliva, however, still finished his career above .300 (while playing his prime in one of the hardest eras to hit for a strong average), and he collected one more batting title (1971).

Oliva also had a huge impact in a historic sense. He was one of the first prominent Cuban players, and he came to the United States just as Fidel Castro came to power and Cuban-American relations began to disintegrate. As such, Oliva was unable to return to Cuba to visit his family, something Cuban players faced for generations. Many of the Cuban players who came to the U.S., before the recent warming of relations, faced a litany of difficulties: the sketchy folks who got them into the country, living without family, language barriers, and the feeling of being an outsider even in their new home.

Dan Le Batard once asked José Fernández a question that sounded silly on the surface: "Which was worse, the time he spent in Cuban prison as a teenager, or the first few months in America?" Fernández's response was telling: "America was worse, by far." The electric Marlins pitcher said he would often just go into the woods near his school and cry.

When he came to the States, José Contreras was so lonely that he would pay for dinner with random Cuban strangers to feel some sort of connection. He could only attend his father's funeral by cell phone. When we watch baseball, fans only see the very surface value of the entertainment. Stories like these provide a fuller picture of what is truly going on in the lives of these humans we see as players.

The transition process for Cuban defectors is currently trying to be changed – by none other than one of Fidel Castro's sons (Tony) who is at the forefront of this movement – but a player who wants to defect from Cuba and come play in the United States still faces a tough road to the country, as well as a lot of obstacles once he gets here. Still, Oliva helped blaze the path for those players to be able to make it to the big leagues at all, a situation where they can eventually make their millions and play the game they love for a living.

Side note: all the online SABR Bios are worth a read, but Oliva's is especially well-researched and interesting. Go check it out. Hours turn to days getting lost in those SABR Bio archives.

Utility Sam Rice (1915-1933)

Sam Rice was one player who slipped through the cracks when I made my initial selections for the Twins Starting IX. In fact, I originally had the far-less-productive (albeit far-more-versatile) Cesar Tovar in the utility spot. Now, because I had Tovar in this spot originally, I collected a solid number of fun tidbits about Tovar, so it's time for another quiz! I'm going to write 10 facts about either Tovar or Rice, and you can check the footnotes to check your answers:

A) This player played every position on the field in a single game. The first batter he pitched against (Bert Campaneris) was the only player who had previously played every position in a single game.
B) This player finished his career just 13 hits shy of 3,000. Do I smell a "Mr. 3000" reboot?! I certainly hope not.
C) This player is the only player to collect 200 hits in his age-40 season.
D) This player has the lone hit in an incredible five one-hitters (which is tied for an MLB record). He was the only thing standing between history for luminaries: Dave McNally Mike Cuellar, Catfish Hunter, Barry Moore, and Dick Bosman.
E) This player is the only player to have tallied at least 300 win shares in Bill James' *Abstract*, while having started his career after the age of 25.
F) This player is best-known for making a controversial catch in the World Series that carried him over the fence but was still ruled an out.

G) This player is the most recent to lead the league in both doubles and triples in the same season.
H) This player's entire family was killed in a tornado while he was in the minor leagues, a fact that he didn't share with anyone during his playing days.
I) This player was the lone player to steal an MVP vote from Carl Yastrzemski in Yaz's near-unanimous 1967 MVP season. The writer who did so came from this player's home town and received a lot of pushback for his decision.

Go check your score![286]

SP Walter Johnson (1907-1927)

This one was pretty close between Johnson and Brad Radke, but in the end Johnson took it by a hair...

In all seriousness, in my opinion (and the opinion of many others) Johnson is the best pitcher of all time. As such, he easily earned the starting pitcher spot for the franchise. Johnson pitched all 21 of his seasons in the nation's capital and, barring an unforeseen future uber-star, will always be remembered as the franchise's best player.

(Again, this is giving current Twins fans credit for truly seeing the Senators as a previous iteration of the club. It may technically be, but ask most Twins fans who the best player in franchise history is, and they're likely not going to say Walter Johnson.)

There are many incredible numbers for Johnson in his career. One set of awe-inspiring numbers deal with his ability to keep the ball in the park.[287] Johnson gave up only 97 home runs in his career. That's just one more than his top competition for this spot (Bert Blyleven) allowed in a two-year span (1986-1987). For his career, Johnson allowed 0.1 home runs per nine innings, and he had three seasons in which he threw over 250.0 innings and didn't allow a single home run all year. The most impressive of these seasons was 1916, in which he threw 369.2 innings without giving up a single long ball (he was also able to hit one home run himself). In fact, there were four seasons in his career in which he *hit* more home runs than he allowed and four other seasons in which he hit the same number as he allowed.

Johnson was also the first big-time strikeout pitcher. He was the first pitcher to reach 3,000 career strikeouts,[288] and he led the league in Ks 12 times in his career, including eight in a row during his prime. He had seven straight seasons with 20 wins, 200 or more strikeouts, and an ERA under 2.00 (1910-1916). Amazingly, he did mostly all of this on the strength of one pitch – his fastball. Johnson's heater is one of the most ballyhooed in the history of the sport, with Rob Neyer and Bill James ranking it as the best fastball among starters of all time. This makes sense since it was basically his only pitch for 15 years. As was pointed out in Neyer's and James' book: "The great pitchers of the Dead Ball Era – and don't get us wrong, they *were* great pitchers – were basically one-pitch pitchers. Walter Johnson didn't worry much about refining his curve ball until he was in his mid-thirties."

One of the other most notable things about Johnson was that although he was a truly dominant pitcher, he was never on a consistently good team throughout his career. During his career, he won 38 complete games by a score of 1-0[289] but lost another 27 games by the reverse scoreline. His team *did* achieve more success later in his career (hold that thought), but for most of his career, Johnson was a star on a scrub team. On the next page is a chart with a comparison of his winning percentage, the team winning percentage, and the difference between the two.

Johnson consistently outperformed the team throughout his career. Only once before his final two years (he was 38 for the 1926 season) did he have a worse winning percentage than his team, and that was in 1920 when he pitched only 21 times (15 starts). Even then, the difference was imperceptible. Even though Johnson's 1913 season represented the biggest difference between his personal winning percentage and the team's winning percentage, his 1911 campaign is the most impressive. Johnson won nearly two-thirds of his games for a team that finished seventh in the AL and had a record of 39-77, "good" for a .319 winning percentage in games when Johnson wasn't the pitcher of record. Now, of course, Johnson was the ace of the squad, so it's expected that he post a better win-loss than the rest of the starters, but the consistency with which he dragged his team toward relevancy is what truly stands out.

Baseball is very much a team sport, but a dominant pitcher is one of the few players who can individually affect the outcome of a game. Still, starting pitchers were out there only once every four-ish games in Johnson's era, and they pitch even less frequently in today's game. One of the most impressive stats on "The Big Train"[290] is that he holds the record for wins in a decade, with 265 wins in the 1910s. He did this despite the club not making the playoffs once during the decade and finishing under .500 just as often as they finished over .500 during those 10 years.

---

[286] A) Tovar B) Rice C) Rice D) Tovar E) Rice F) Rice G) Tovar H) Rice I) Tovar
[287] Now to be fair, since we pointed out how much Griffith Stadium killed home runs in the batter's sections, we would be remiss not to mention it when crediting Johnson, as well.
[288] No other pitcher reached this plateau for another 48 years.
[289] These represent 38 out of his MLB-record 110 shutouts for his career.
[290] As dubbed by no less an authority than Grantland Rice.

Year	Johnson W-L%	Team W-L%	Difference Johnson vs. Team W-L%
1907	5-9 .357	49-102-3 .325	+.032
1908	14-14 .500	67-85-3 .441	+.059
1909	13-25 .342	42-110-4 .276	+.066
1910	25-17 .595	66-85-6 .437	+.158
1911	25-13 .658	64-90 .416	+.242
1912	33-12 .733	91-61-2 .599	+.134
1913	36-7 .837	90-64-1 .584	+.253
1914	28-18 .609	81-73-4 .526	+.083
1915	27-13 .675	85-68-2 .556	+.119
1916	25-20 .556	76-77-6 .497	+.059
1917	23-16 .590	74-79-4 .484	+ 106
1918	23-13 .639	72-56-2 .563	+.076
1919	20-14 .588	56-84-1 .400	+.188
1920	8-10 .444	68-84-1 .447	- .003
1921	17-14 .548	80-73-1 .523	+.025
1922	15-16 .484	69-85 .448	+.036
1923	17-12 .586	75-78-2 .490	+.096
1924	23-7 .767	92-62-2 .597	+.170
1925	20-7 .741	96-55-1 .636	+.105
1926	15-16 .484	81-69-2 .540	- .056
1927	5-6 .455	85-69-3 .552	- .097
Career	417-279 .599	1,559-1609-51 .492	+.107

Another way of looking at how much Johnson meant to the team is to look at the team's WAR leader in each year that Johnson pitched for them. Of the 18 seasons in which he made more than 15 starts, Johnson led the team in WAR a mind-numbing 16 of them. The first 12 seasons of his career, he led the team in WAR each and every season. This is obviously the longest stretch in which one player has led the Senator/Twin franchise in WAR. The second-longest streak, somewhat surprisingly, belongs to Chuck Knoblauch, who led the Twins in WAR five straight seasons from 1993-1997. In 1913, Johnson was worth 16.0 WAR; the next highest total on the team was Clyde Milan who was worth 4.3 WAR.

Johnson not only dominated with his arm, but he was also one of the best hitting pitchers in history. In 1918, he tied for the team lead in home runs… albeit with one long ball that season. He had an OPS+ over 100 in five separate seasons during his career and totaled 24 home runs (23 as a pitcher), which is good for tenth all-time among pitchers. His hitting was strong enough throughout his career that he netted the team 13.3 offensive WAR, and he hurt the team with his bat in only two seasons, per Baseball-Reference oWAR.

Johnson, like many pitchers in his time, was a workhorse. He completed 531 of his 666 career starts, and he led the league in innings pitched five times in his career (including four straight years from 1913-1916). He topped 300.0 innings in nine straight seasons during his prime and, outside of his first and last seasons, threw under 225.0 innings only once. For one four-day stretch in 1908 (September 4-7), he started three straight games, throwing a shutout in each one and allowed only 12 hits combined in the three games. Johnson was clearly not just consistent; he was consistently dominant. His 147 career ERA+ trails only Clayton Kershaw, Pedro Martínez, and Lefty Grove among qualified starters who pitched for more than five years. His ERA+ topped 200 four separate seasons, with his 259 ERA+ in 1913 bested by only four different men in baseball history.[291] On two occasions in his career, after loading the bases, Johnson was able to strike out the side on nine pitches. One of these times was against Tigers Hall of Fame outfield trio of Bobby Veach, Ty Cobb, and Sam Crawford. Johnson is the only pitcher to win the pitching Triple Crown (wins, ERA, strikeouts) on three separate occasions. In fact, when I was contemplating the structure of this book and whether teams that were no longer around should be represented with ties to their current franchise, Johnson was one of the main reasons I decided to include them. There's just no way any baseball book would be complete without giving him his fair shakes.

I think the thing that makes me respect Johnson maybe more than any other athlete, however, is the fact that for as many stories of his dominance as there are, there are just as many stories of Johnson's good nature. There are numerous stories of Johnson easing up on the mound versus rookies and former teammates when he had a big lead. There are also numerous more stories saying how he was always the guy in the clubhouse that the rookies would be seen naturally gravitating towards because of his warm personality.

One story, in particular, shows the approach Johnson had to the game of baseball and life in general. In 1912, Johnson and Boston's Smoky Joe Wood were each having seasons for the ages. Johnson had set the AL record for consecutive wins earlier in the season with 16 straight wins, as the team was finally reaching relevancy. Later in the same

[291] Incredibly, Greg Maddux topped it in back-to-back years (1994-1995).

season, Johnson and Wood met in a showdown hyped as "Johnson defending his record." This was due to the fact that Wood was in the midst of a winning streak of his own that was currently at 13 straight wins. The intensity was taken up a level as Smoky Joe chirped a bit before the game, with Johnson preferring to let his game do the talking.

The game lived up to the hype, and the only run of the game came in the sixth inning when a two-out double by Tris Speaker was followed up with a line drive to right field. Senators right fielder Danny Moeller, try as he might, couldn't quite make the play, as the ball bounced off his glove allowing the only run of the game to cross the plate. Because of the hyped-up nature of the game, and the fact that his play ended up deciding the game, Moeller was devastated after the game, blaming himself for the loss, and Moeller was in tears in the clubhouse. What did Johnson do? He went over to Moeller and consoled him, telling him not to feel bad, and that he (Johnson) should have struck the batter out. Not too hard to see why rookies and new players were drawn to him, huh?

Here's one final story on Johnson, which will seem like an appropriate end to his bio because it came near the end of his career and was a very cathartic experience for him.

The franchise discussion hinted that Johnson was involved in the Senators most memorable moment in the team's history. This is not at all surprising, given that for many years he *was* the franchise, and he never gave up on the team to find greener pastures. By 1924, Johnson had played for the Senators for 17 years, and he had never once been to the playoffs. Before the season's start, he said that it would be his last season, and in true Disney form, the team ended up winning their first pennant. They met the Giants, who had won four straight pennants and were looking to avenge a 1923 World Series loss.

In the current sports scene, sports writers will often invent story lines to sell what they're saying. Suddenly a midseason Brewers game in San Diego is the biggest game ever because Ryan Braun is returning to the city where he had the best cheeseburger of his life. In this case, however, it's almost impossible to deny the story of the Senators coming together behind their leader to bring him to his first World Series in what he said would be his final season. Naturally, Johnson started Game 1, but he gave up two runs in the 12th inning and took the 4-3 series-opening loss. The Senators won two out of the next three games to set up an important Game 5. With the series tied at two, Johnson took the mound again, but he took yet another loss. This time Johnson gave up six runs (four earned) in eight innings.

Now if this were in the present day, even as respected and popular as Johnson was, one has to imagine there would be about a hundred Bill Simmons-esque "LeBrondown" articles questioning Johnson. They would ask whether Johnson was actually what had been holding the team back all these years. They would posit that Christy Mathewson and Cy Young were far better pitchers. The Senators put any such noise aside and were able to focus on the task at hand, winning Game 6 by a score of 2-1. (It should be noted that, in the midst of the crazy 2017 World Series, the 1924 World Series came up on numerous occasions as arguably the best World Series of all time.)

Game 7, however, would go on to become quite the memorable moment in franchise history. The Senators took a 1-0 lead in the fourth inning on the strength of a solo home run by second baseman Bucky Harris. However, a couple of errors quickly erased that lead in the top of the sixth, and the Giants went ahead 3-1. The score stayed this way until the bottom of the eighth when Bucky Harris struck again, this time with a two-out, bases-loaded single to tie up the game. The Senators then brought in their legend, Walter Johnson, to pitch the top of the ninth. To deny Johnson at this point would have meant the Baseball Gods would have to spit in the face of not only the best pitcher of all time but, also, one of the sport's best men. It turned out to be the perfect decision, as Johnson threw four shutout innings before Earl McNeely hit a walk-off double for the Senators in the bottom of the 12th, finally giving Johnson the title of World Champion, a title that he had truly earned. Being able to be on the mound and – thanks to an error in the 12th – on the basepaths as his beloved Senators[292] won their first title made for one of the most satisfying ends to a career for any player ever. **

** *For some reason, Johnson didn't use this opportunity to walk away on top, instead coming back for three more seasons, despite what he had said about retiring. For the sake of hyperbolic narrative and glory, though, I'm going to completely ignore that fact and say that Johnson rode off into the sunset right after the 1924 World Series.*

CP Joe Nathan (2004-2010; 2011)

Pretty tough act to follow, but Nathan truly deserves his spot on this Starting IX for the six seasons of dominance (2004-2009) that he gave the Twins. His best season was an electric 2006 campaign that saw him finish 7-0 with 61 games finished and an ERA of 1.58 (ERA+ of 284). For Nathan's seven years in Minnesota, his line read: 24-13 with 260 saves, 394 games finished, a 2.16 ERA, a 204 ERA+, a 0.956 WHIP, and 10.9 SO/9. As far as modern closers are concerned, given the dominance and duration of tenure (very few modern closers make it more than two or three years in that role), this stretch puts him in the upper echelon of his era.

[292] Johnson is the only pitcher in the 300-win club to get every win with the same team.

Starting IX Franchise Roster Stats

Lineup	Yrs	G	R	H	HR	RBI	SB	BB	SO	BA	OBP	SLG	OPS+	dWAR	WAR
Eddie Yost	14	1690	971	1521	101	550	58	1274	705	0.253	0.389	0.368	108	-9.2	26.3
Rod Carew	12	1635	950	2085	74	733	271	613	716	**0.334**	**0.393**	0.448	137	1.8	**63.7**
Kirby Puckett	12	1783	1071	2304	207	1085	134	450	965	0.318	0.360	0.477	124	-1.0	50.9
Harmon Killebrew	**21**	**2329**	1258	2024	**559**	**1540**	18	**1505**	**1629**	0.258	0.378	**0.514**	**145**	-17.7	60.5
Tony Oliva	15	1676	870	1917	220	947	86	448	645	0.304	0.353	0.476	131	-4.6	43.0
Sam Rice	19	2307	**1466**	**2889**	33	1044	346	680	266	0.323	0.375	0.429	113	-3.5	52.6
Joe Mauer	14	1731	954	1986	137	875	52	888	948	0.308	0.391	0.443	126	2.3	53.4
Joe Cronin	7	940	577	1090	51	673	56	466	274	0.304	0.387	0.455	118	11.8	36.7
Goose Goslin	12	1361	854	1659	127	932	117	488	337	0.323	0.386	0.502	131	-1.4	43.2
Pitchers	Yrs	W	W%	ERA	G	CG	SHO	SV	IP	SO	ERA+	WHIP	SO/9	SO/BB	WAR
Walter Johnson	**21**	**417**	0.599	**2.17**	**802**	**531**	**110**	34	**5914.1**	**3509.0**	**147**	1.061	5.3	2.57	**152.3**
Joe Nathan	7	24	0.649	2.16	460	0	0	**260**	463.1	561.0	204	0.956	10.9	4.19	18.4

#11 Chicago Cubs (1903-pres.); Chicago Orphans (1898-1902); Chicago Colts (1890-1897); Chicago White Stockings (1876-1889)

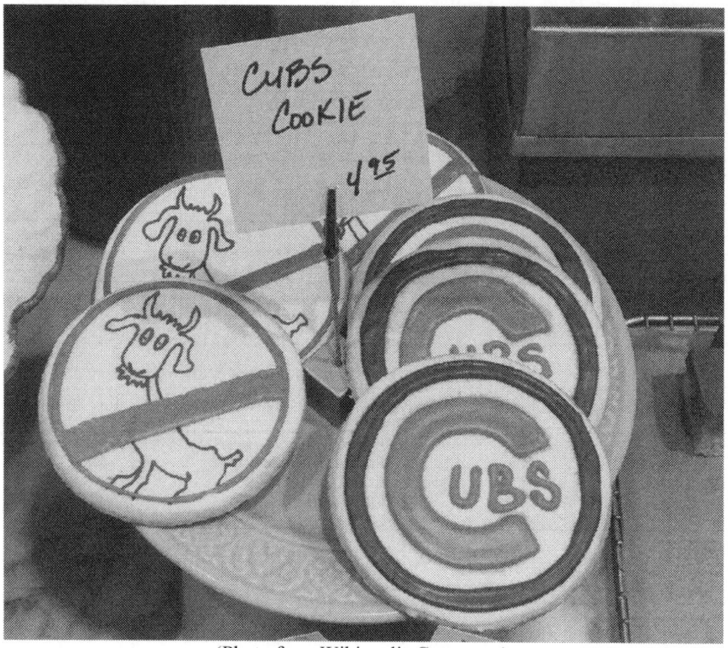

(Photo from Wikimedia Commons)

Team Background

Playoff appearances: 19 **Pennants: 17** **World Series titles: 3**
Collective team WAR: 583.7
Strengths: The infield. The majority of Cubs legends just so happen to have spent the majority of their career residing in the infield. There are some especially strong bats considering the usual production from hitters in the infield.
Weaknesses: There are some good outfielders here, don't get me wrong, but the teams from here on out have absolute legends in the outfield. All-timers. This collection just can't match the long-term production from these older teams.
What to expect from the next 13 pages: A brief discussion of the greatest teams (individual season) in baseball history. Also, maybe the most fun personality in this entire book: King Kelly.

First of all, congratulations! You Cubs fans were the butt of so many jokes for so many years, but you made it through to the other side with arguably the most cathartic sports experience any fan base has ever had. One hundred and eight years of suffering broken by a 3-1 comeback in the World Series – and one of the wildest Game 7s in history – is the kind of stuff no other fan base can relate to (with the possible exception of the Red Sox). The moments in Game 7, and throughout the magical 2016 season, should never be forgotten. Kris Bryant smiling as he fielded the ball for the final out of the Series summed up the moment perfectly – this young Cubs squad was just about the perfect team to root for in the moment.

As far as the Cubs before 2016, they have one of the longest histories for any franchise in baseball, dating back to what is considered, by many, to be the inaugural year of modern baseball history (1876). And although there aren't any current Cubs fans who were around to experience it, from 1906-1910, the franchise had about as excellent a stretch of baseball as any team has ever had.

The five-year period of dominance began in 1906, when the Cubs posted a record of 116-36, good for a ridiculous .763 winning percentage – still the best win-loss percentage in a season in baseball history. To break that record in the modern, 162-game schedule, a team would have to win 124 games. Given that it might be a while before we see a team chase down that record, it seems like as good a time as any to toss in a Starting IX of the best single-season teams in baseball history. Lots of ink has already been spilled on this subject, with numerous books dedicated to this exact question, so this will be brief even though the topic is one of the most fascinating and divisive among baseball friends and enemies:

SP) 1927 New York Yankees – It's trendy to pick otherwise, but man is it hard to defend any other choice.

C) 1970 Baltimore Orioles – The peak of arguably the best modern dynasty.

1B) 1998 New York Yankees – I tend to favor more recent teams over the older teams, as they had to go through more teams to have their success, and the league as a whole is far superior top-to-bottom today.

2B) 1931 Philadelphia A's – In spite of the previous point on earlier eras, this A's team was fricken awesome.

3B) 1906 Chicago Cubs – I'm not typically a RINGZ guy, but as you'll see in a second, this Cubs squad couldn't quite finish the deal, with a loss in the World Series that slightly dings their legacy.

SS) 1939 New York Yankees – Probably should be a little bit higher, but there are just too many damn elite Yankee teams. It gets boring.

LF) 1975 Cincinnati Reds – The good, ole Big Red Machine gets their first ring.

CF/RF) New York tie: 1986 Mets/1961 Yankees – Couldn't leave either of these two off.

In that record-setting 1906 season, the Cubs fell in the World Series to the crosstown "Hitless Wonders," as the White Sox pulled off one of the first big upsets in World Series history. The manager of the White Sox, Fielder Jones, said, "I guess this proves the leather is mightier than the wood." It's interesting to note that he referenced the team's defense, and not the team's pitching, as we probably would have today.

It's pretty incredible that those "Hitless Wonders" were able to get any runs off the Cubs in the series as a whole, as the Cubs pitchers in 1906 allowed a measly 6.6 hits per game, the lowest in modern history. For comparison, the 1930 Phillies allowed 7.7 *runs* per game. Of course, there are some heavy run-scoring environment caveats that need to be attached to that comparison, but even with context, the difference is vast.

The Cubs did end up with World Series titles in 1907 and 1908, but to imply the Cubs had anything other than a tough time for the ensuing century would be a fallacy. George Will once said Cubs fans are "93 percent scar tissue," and whether it was 1984, 2003, or just the year-to-year drudgery of having to deal with the ghosts of failed seasons past, Will's is a pretty fair statement. That's why 2016, and really the couple years leading up to 2016, were so incredible. Fans could start to see the shape of what Theo Epstein and Jed Hoyer were doing, got their reward, and will go down in baseball history.

Random cool things about the franchise:

- The Cubs lead all franchises in runs scored and hits.
- The franchise has won 100 or more games in a single season six times – amazingly going over 100 years between 100-win seasons. They went from the Tinker-to-Evers-to-Chance days of 1910 until 2016 between 100-win seasons.
- Jake Johnson of *New Girl*[293] is a big-time Cubs fan, and he's definitely my favorite Cubs fan (Bill Murray shows his face just a litttttttle too much).
- Steve Bartman can come out of hiding now.
- Theo Epstein ate goat in the Wrigley bleachers after the 2016 win – honest to God.
- The Baseball Almanac entry on the Cubs begins, "If you were to draw up the perfect baseball franchise, chances are you might come up with the Chicago Cubs," which gives you a feel for how even though they had a brutal title drought, Chicago's "North Siders" do have a fair amount going for them (a long history, a gorgeous stadium, loyal fan base, etc.). Now they have "Won before I died."

Starting IX

C Gabby Hartnett (1922-1940)

Hartnett was the backstop for the Cubs for nearly two decades. He was an excellent catcher both offensively and defensively, finishing his career with over 50.0 oWAR and finishing with a positive dWAR each and every season in the bigs. Although he was robbed of a couple hundred games due to playing catcher in an era when catcher's protective gear was still rather rudimentary, Harnett's cumulative statistics are helped by his long career. His slashes are quite excellent, and if he played in the modern game, he probably would have had much stronger numbers. I say this for two reasons.

First, as just noted, he would have had much better protective gear, which would have allowed him to play about 25 more games a year for his whole career. Compare Hartnett's career to the career of Gary Carter. Carter was a much better defensive catcher than Hartnett, but their numbers offensively are quite similar. Carter played 19 years to Hartnett's 20, and their 162 game averages were 71 runs, 19 home runs, and 96 RBI for Hartnett and 72/23/86 for Carter. Hartnett had two top-three MVP finishes, same as Carter, and Hartnett was even able to produce in an era in which runs were harder to come by. In fact, Hartnett was one of the best offensive performers of his era. In 1930, Hartnett hit 37 home runs, while the other seven

[293] Quick side note, power ranking the top six characters in *New Girl*: 1) Winston – Breaks the mold for stereotyped black actors in comedies, as he is the straight up weirdest (in the best way possible) dude on TV. 2) Nick – A nearly perfect character, he has some of the best facial reactions ever. 3) Coach – Basically the opposite of Winston, but he's still awesome. 4) Cece – Whenever she is given anything to work with (which is not nearly as often as it should be), she kills it. 5) Jess – She grew from annoying to meh to downright funny in the latter seasons. 6) Schmidt – Definitely overrated, but still pretty damn funny, which says a lot about the depth of talent among the cast.

starting National League catchers *combined* for 39 long balls. Despite these similarities, Carter played an average of 127 games a season, 26 more than the 101-game average from Hartnett in his career. So, if we take those 26 games a year, we could boost all of Hartnett's numbers by 25 percent, making his career totals with the Cubs 1,059 runs, 289 home runs, and 1,441 RBI (instead of 847 runs, 231 home runs, and 1153 RBI); quite the difference.

The second reason Hartnett could have played more games if he had played in the modern game, is that if a hitter as talented as Hartnett appeared in the Cubs organization in today's game, they probably would have tried to switch his position to a corner outfield/infield spot. Hartnett had excellent range, fielding, and caught stealing percentage, but his dWAR only netted the Cubs 6.5 wins for his career. And although he never had a negative dWAR, he also never won more than a whole game, per dWAR, in a season with his defense. If he played a corner outfield position (or first base àla Joe Mauer), he probably could have played at least an average of 133 games per season, which would have boosted his career totals to: 1,129 runs, 308 home runs, and 1,537 RBI.

From a non-statistical perspective, Hartnett is most often remembered for having hit the "Homer in the Gloaming," a home run that helped win the Cubs the 1938 pennant. The home run took place on the last pitch before the game would have to be called due to darkness. If the game had been postponed, it would have set up a double header the next day in which the score would be reset. Despite falling behind in the count 0-2, and the difficulty of hitting in the twilight (remember this was well before the days during which baseball was played under the lights), Hartnett crushed Mace Brown's delivery into the bleachers. Hartnett only knew he had won them the game because of the crowd's reaction. The home run put the Cubs in first place, where they stayed for the rest of the year, before eventually being swept in the World Series by the mighty Yankees.

As far as his off-field status, Hartnett was one of 14 children, of which the first seven were boys and the final seven were girls. He was also among the first to really push for the lifting of the "ban" on black players from professional baseball, which fits the narrative that he was a generally good man, despite the fact that he was once infamously photographed with Chicago mobster Al Capone before a Cubs game.

1B Cap Anson (1876-1897)

Unlike the Cubs backstop, Anson was a real dirtball. He was also one of the first real stars of baseball – a man who played during the sport's nascent stages. He was around as the NL formed and was signed by William Hulbert, the man who formed the league, in 1876. In that inaugural NL season, Anson hit .356, and the Cubs (then called the Chicago White Stockings, believe it or not) won the National League's first championship.

Despite much shorter schedules (not topping 100 games until 1884), Anson managed to gather the most hits in franchise history (3,012), becoming the first player to reach 3,000 hits, at least according to many sources (more on that in a second). In Anson's time, WAR was a statistic dominated at the top by pitchers because of how many innings they threw,[294] but he led offensive players in WAR twice and was a solid defender. He also led the league in RBI eight times (thanks in part to hitting in one of the most loaded lineups in the league). Anson played to the ripe age of 45, and he played the last 19 seasons as a player/manager. He continued to manage until 1898, one year after he had retired from playing. When Anson retired, he held the Major League records for games (2,524), at bats (10,281), hits (3,435), doubles (582), RBI (2,075), and runs (1,999).

That hits total is where Anson's story gets very interesting, though. What is not disputed is that, when Anson retired, he was the MLB hit king. What *is* disputed is to just how many hits he can stake claim. If you look different places you can get as many as five different answers (ESPN, MLB, Baseball Hall of Fame, *FanGraphs*, and Baseball-Reference). Those different answers actually represent progress, however, as newspapers in the early 20th century were pulling numbers out of the deep crevices of their buttholes, with the *New York Times, Washington Post* and *Washington Times* all citing different career totals within the span of two months, in 1914, when Nap Lajoie and Honus Wagner made their own chases at 3,000 career hits. Although the folks at SABR and the like have now cleared up the issue of lazy scorebook keeping (the original issue among the three different newspaper reports), a couple of confounding factors still remain.

First of all, there's the fact that, as noted above, the National League was formed in 1876, so many outlets will not count the 423 hits Anson collected while playing in the National Association from 1871-1876. Then there's the matter that, in 1877, walks were counted as hits, robbing Anson of another 60 hits, bringing his career total without those two boosts to 2,995, and thus robbing Anson of the title of original member of the 3,000-hit club. It's really even more confusing than that, with differences in box scores and potentially extra helpful scorers in Chicago (Cheryl Wright does a nice job for *Son of Sam Horn* breaking down these differences), but considering that all but one of those outlets give Anson over 3,000 hits, I think it's fair to give him the magical 3,000. As David Hill posited for *Call to the Pen*, when Anson broke the 3,000-hit barrier he did it according to the rules of the game. Just because we realize it is silly to count walks as hits now, it's hard to recall those hits. And since we've been using *Baseball-Reference* for all career stats up to this point, we're giving him credit for 3,435 career hits, with 3,012 of those coming in Chicago, specifically.

However, as a man, we won't be giving Anson any breaks. His personality was as grating as a cackle from Janice on

[294] Of course, WAR wasn't *actually* calculated in Anson's days, but it can be calculated retroactively.

Friends,[295] and he was cited for numerous nasty qualities. For one, he refused to play against black players. The story goes that, when Anson went to Toledo, they knew Anson's dislike for black players, and as such, the team told him that they would be starting their black catcher (even though the catcher was actually injured); Anson forfeited the game rather than play against him. Granted, this was a time in U.S. history when many men, sadly, shared this sentiment, but it still doesn't excuse his behavior. Especially considering this sentiment was coming from a man who loved baseball so much that, for 10 years after his retirement, he would polish his collection of 400 bats every day in case a team called him back into action.

However, this can't deny his place in baseball (and Cubs) history, as he was one of the pioneers of the hit-and-run, as well as implementing the pitching rotation during his numerous years as a player and manager. He was also a good businessman and talented enough to make baseball immensely popular. As such, he helped promote baseball in its earliest days and needs to be discussed, really big warts and all, when talking about the sport's early history.

2B Ryne Sandberg (1982-1997)

"Ryno" was a third-ballot Hall of Famer, who was one of the most well-rounded players in Cubs history. Nearly a member of the 300/300 home run/stolen base club, Sandberg finished just 18 home runs short. Surprisingly, he never had a 30/30 HR/SB season, as his speed and power peaked at different times in his career. In his 1984 MVP season, Sandberg was one triple and one home run away from becoming the first player ever with 200 hits, 20 doubles, 20 triples, 20 homers, and 20 steals in a season.[296] Six years later, Ryno led the NL in home runs (40), becoming the first NL second basemen to do so since Rogers Hornsby in 1925.

Sandberg was an incredible fielder, as well. When he made the switch from third base to second base, he started receiving accolades immediately. Sandberg became the first NL player to win a Gold Glove in his first season at a new position, when he made the switch in 1983. He finished his career with the highest fielding percentage among second basemen, and he had 15 individual streaks of 30 or more errorless games in his career. He also recorded nine consecutive Gold Gloves at second base from 1983-1991.

Sandberg was basically a Cubs lifer, having played only 13 games in Philadelphia before being traded to the Cubs.[297] He extended his career with the Cubs in his post-playing days, managing minor league affiliates of the Cubs, before eventually taking over the managerial position of the Philadelphia Phillies in 2013, a position he held for three seasons. Sandberg really didn't have any holes in his game back when he was a player, which was contrary to the rest of his team, which had more holes than a slice of Swiss. He made the playoffs only twice in his career – and never made it to the World Series – but he posted a .385 batting average in his 10 playoff games. Like Hammerin' Hank, I think that Sandberg would have been an excellent postseason performer if he had been on a more successful team, or if he had asked out of town to get to play for a winning franchise. Santo respected the Cubs too much, though, and he stuck with the club through thick and thin (mostly thin).

There is one game in particular that truly resonates with Cubs fans and Sandberg alike, as it harkened the arrival of this star player and endeared him forever to his Chicago fan base. In 1984, the Cubs were in the midst of a 40-year *playoff* drought and weren't sure what they had in the young, and seemingly talented, Sandberg. The team entered their contest on June 23 against the Cardinals trailing the Cards by only a game and a half in the division. The game wasn't originally a national broadcast, but it was switched to national TV after the scheduled NBC game was rained out. The Cardinals jumped ahead 7-0 in the second inning, but the fans that stayed were rewarded handsomely. The Cubs rallied to draw to within one (9-8) at the end of the eighth inning.

This seemed to be the end of their rally, however, as Bruce Sutter entered the game for St. Louis and was presently in his prime, partway through his 45-save, 1.54 ERA, third-in-the-Cy-Young season. Sandberg, however, had a good scouting report on Sutter, and he hit a blast that cleared the fence, that was, in his words, "like an out-of-body experience… I couldn't feel my hands or my feet as I tried to get around the bases. I was numb." With the game tied up, it went to extra innings, where the Cardinals once again took control with two runs. Now it seemed a lock that Sutter would close it down.

However, the Cubs managed to get Sandberg up to the dish once again, and he managed to hit another home run off Sutter, this time of the two-run variety, rounding the bases to be greeted by a scene that looked – in the words of the Cubs players – like they had won the pennant. The game went on until the next inning when the Cubs Dave Owen hit the walk-off single, but Ryne was still the hero. A *5-for-6 day with seven RBI and two home runs off of the best closer in baseball* will tend to do that. He became the first player to hit two home runs off Sutter and left that day to chants of "MVP, MVP," an award he would indeed win just months later. The Cubs went on to win the division, and Sandberg announced himself, with style, to the franchise he now represents at second base.

---

[295] Of course, we all secretly love Janice's laugh if only because we know it announces the presence of the glorious Maggie Wheeler, so maybe that's not the perfect example.

[296] Jimmy Rollins ended up being the first to do so in 2007.

[297] Sandberg was a throw-in in the deal, but thanks to his incredible career, he ended up making the trade one of the most one-sided trades in history. The Cubs gave up Ivan de Jesus (who was worth only 2.9 WAR in his three years in Philly) for Sandberg and the "main piece of the deal" at the time, Larry Bowa (1.5 WAR with the Cubs).

3B Ron Santo (1960-1973)

Because of the nature of Santo's game (high walk totals and excellent fielding but a total lack of team success), Santo was vastly underrated during his career. He had to be elected into the Hall of Fame by the Veteran's committee in 2012 after never receiving more than half the vote during his eligibility. It also seems that, sadly, it may have taken Santo's passing to stir up some pro-Santo chatter for the Hall. He passed in 2010 and was elected to Cooperstown less than two years later. Correlation doesn't mean causation, but it seems unlikely to be a complete coincidence. Santo was able to live until the rather ripe age of 70, despite the fact that he had diabetes dating back even before his playing days. Once he became comfortable with the fact that he could use his celebrity to increase awareness about the disease, Santo did just that, becoming a face of the fight against the disease.

His career numbers are certainly worthy of the Hall, as his average WAR/season was over 5.0 for his 15-year career (again, 5.0 WAR in a season is right around an All-Star level of production). He should have won the 1967 MVP and had a good argument for 1964 as well. In 1967, Santo led all players in WAR with 9.8; the next highest was Roberto Clemente with 8.9. He didn't lead the league in any offensive categories other than walks,[298] but he was in the top five in runs (107), total bases (300), home runs (31), and was top 10 in hits (176), on-base percentage (.395), and slugging percentage (.512); a pretty complete package. For those who like their judgments old school and by the Eye Test, Santo also won the Gold Glove that year.

In 1964, Santo was second in WAR (8.9) and led the league in on-base percentage (.398), triples (13), and walks (86), as well as multiple defensive metrics. The 1964 leader in WAR was Willie Mays, who probably should have won the award, as his 11.0 WAR were nearly 5.0 wins higher than the actual winner, Ken Boyer, who boasted 6.1 WAR. WAR is not the be-all and end-all of every argument, but when the discrepancy is that high – and Mays had a higher batting average, on-base percentage, slugging percentage than Boyer, with more runs, home runs, and stolen bases – it's pretty clear who was better. Santo, himself, had similar cumulative statistics to Boyer, as well as better slashes, and it was the year he took over the Gold Glove mantle from Boyer at the NL third base position. So, Santo has a good argument that he had a better year than the actual MVP winner in 1964, but he probably still didn't deserve to win the award, as Mays should have won.

Santo was well-liked by the Cubs fans, becoming a fan favorite of the Bleacher Bums at Wrigley during the 1969 pennant race. It started as an accident, when Santo jumped and clicked his heels after one victory, but the crowd loved it, and it became a thing. It didn't go over well with opposing fan bases, though, but it continued to be popular with the home crowd. The Cubs eventually fell shy of the pennant, and the Mets' Tom Seaver eventually did a heel-click of his own after a late-season New York win over Chicago.

Santo was famously pictured in the on-deck circle, as a black cat walked past him, during a game during that same 1969 pennant, and the picture was used as a symbol for Cubs collapse and the bad luck as a franchise, in general. It should be noted that Santo also caught a lot of flak around the league – and even among his teammates – when he was not shy with his criticism of his teammate Don Young after Young made a couple mistakes in the outfield in an important game during that same 1969 season. Between the heel-clicking and the teammate-ripping, Santo's league-wide popularity wasn't very high. This opinion of Santo was relatively common throughout his career, as Santo was not a guy to mince words, and he found himself in random beefs throughout the league during his career. For his part, Ernie Banks still holds Santo at least partly responsible for the Cubs 1969 collapse, saying of Santo, "They say one bad apple can spoil the whole barrel, and I saw that," in reference to the Santo's comments on Young.

Santo never lost any popularity among the Cubs fans, however, and he provided the voice of the Cubs radio for 20 seasons after his retirement.

SS Ernie Banks (1953-1971)

If an educated baseball fan was asked to name the best power-hitting shortstop of all time, a smart response might be Ernie Banks. After all, before Banks hit 44 home runs in 1955, no shortstop had ever topped 39 home runs in a season; Banks topped that number four straight seasons (1957-1960).

There are few things wrong with the previous statement, however. The main fallacy is that "Mr. Cub" actually played more games at first base than at shortstop for his career. The first half of his career was mostly at shortstop (1,125 games), but the second half of his career came mostly at first base (1,259 games). I realize that in saying that I am then breaking my own rule of trying to put players at the position they'd played most frequently for the franchise, but in this case the games were almost equally split, and there was depth at first base, but not at shortstop, in Cubs history.

The second fallacy of the aforementioned statement is that Banks does indeed have excellent numbers, but he also is boosted immensely by his two MVP years (1958-1959). His home run totals in those two years make up 18 percent of his career total; his run and RBI totals from those two years both make up 17 percent of his career; those two seasons were also his only two full seasons with over a .300 batting average; they account for 29 percent of his career WAR. The WAR total is a bit skewed because players can have a negative WAR, but the results across the board are clear, Banks' career totals were

[298] Not exactly the flashiest MVP category.

strongly supported by those two seasons. There's nothing wrong with this per se, but it shows that his career as a whole might not have been as consistent as it looks from the outside. One positive to the Banks as the greatest power-hitting shortstop argument is that these two years did both come while Banks was playing short, and not later at the far-less-taxing first base position.

Riding the strength of those two seasons, Banks had more home runs from 1955-1960 than such luminaries as Willie Mays, Hank Aaron, and Mickey Mantle. He was not only the first shortstop to lead the league in fielding percentage and home runs in the same year (1960) but also the only shortstop of the 20th century to lead his league in home runs.

In the modern era, the left side of the Yankees mid-2000s infield (Derek Jeter and Alex Rodriguez) could each make a good argument for being the best offensive shortstop of all time, so instead let's go for a different superlative, albeit a less flattering one for Banks: Who are the best players to have never played in the playoffs? Here's the Starting IX:

C) Joe Torre – Well, he certainly made up for it in his post-playing career.

1B) Ernie Banks – We'll put him at first base for *this* Starting IX.

2B) Brian Roberts – The only player from the divisional era, injuries robbed Roberts of a playoff appearance in 2012, when the rest of the team made it.

3B) Ron Santo – If Cubs fans weren't on such a high from 2016, they might be banging their heads against a wall seeing both Banks and Santo on this list.

SS) Luke Appling – "Old Aches and Pains" toiled 20 seasons on the Southside of Chicago without a single playoff appearance.

LF) Minnie Miñoso/Ralph Kiner – Two players that have appeared/will appear in these pages.

CF) Cy Williams – Played for the Cubs and Phillies during their respective heydays of poor play.

RF) Harry Heilmann – More to come on Heilmann, as well.

Utility) George Sisler – Already considered one of the all-time greats, he could have been even better if he stayed healthy. A couple playoff appearances wouldn't have hurt his legacy, either.

Pitcher) Fergie Jenkins – Poor Canadians. Poor Cubs.

A few notes on the above list: there were a surprisingly high number of shortstops on the list of players with the most games played without playing in the postseason. There was also an unsurprisingly high number of players from before the divisional era, but that is to be expected given the difficulty of making the playoffs when a team had to win the pennant just to do get a single playoff game.

Despite his team's lack of success, Banks was known as one of the happiest men in the game, his pre-game chatter often showing off his love for the game. He would sing to the audience and is most well-known for saying: "It's a great day for a ballgame, let's play two." Considering his unbelievable talent, who could blame him for wanting to play two?

According to Banks, he wasn't really into sports as a kid, but at his mother's request, he and his father went to a psychic to learn about what was to come of her son. Banks' father asked the psychic whether he would be a baseball player or go into the army,[299] and the psychic responded, "The boy will play baseball." If only she knew how right she'd be. Trelawney-esque vision from that one.

LF Billy Williams (1959-1974)

Playing almost his whole career in Chicago, "Sweet Swingin' Billy from Whistler" certainly deserves a spot in the nickname Hall of Fame, in addition to the spot he rightfully has in baseball's actual Hall of Fame. Despite hitting over 400 home runs for his career[300] (with 392 of them coming in his 16 seasons with the Cubs), Williams never led the league in long balls. He also never made the postseason while with the Cubs (notice a theme here). Both of these factors, as well as the one in the footnote, point to why Williams is usually an underrated player in the annals of history.

Williams was one of the most easy-going, fun players to play the game of baseball. In a manner only he could say, Bill James said of Williams, "He enjoyed playing in Wrigley Field, enjoyed playing day baseball, enjoyed hitting, enjoyed playing the field. But unlike Banks, he wouldn't go out of his way to tell you about it." The sabermetric Godfather went on to call Williams, "Ernie Banks without the PR." Regardless of whether Banks was a bit full of hot air or not, this Cubs all-franchise team would be one of the most fun teams to be a part of. Outside of Anson (and the one story about Santo), there really isn't a guy who isn't considered a good guy, and some of the guys who are about to show up (especially the utility spot) are some of the great characters in baseball.

CF Hack Wilson (1926-1931)

Most famously the single-season RBI record holder (191), Wilson was a stocky player[301] whose career, although impressive, was a little bit of a flash in the pan. Luckily for Cub fans, Chicago acted as the pan in which Wilson flashed. His

---

[299] What diverse options!

[300] A career that took place mostly before baseball lowered the mound in the 1960s, a move made because of how much pitchers were dominating baseball. Williams' two highest home run totals in a season came after this change, despite Williams being 32 and 34 years old, respectively, in those seasons.

[301] With tiny 5 ½ size shoes.

six seasons in Chicago included his five most productive seasons, a stretch during which he led the league in home runs four times. His 1930 season was quite impressive; he led the league in home runs (by 16), RBI (by 21, in his record setting year), walks, slugging percentage, OPS, and oWAR, to go along with a .356 batting average. He was not in the running for MVP, due to the fact that no MVP was awarded that season (the award was transitioning from its old rules to the modern rules for selection), but he almost certainly would have won the award. In lesser seasons he had received votes, and although his defense was always poor and the Cubs didn't make the playoffs, he was clearly the best offensive player in the league.

Wilson's 1930 season was even more impressive given what happened in the 1929 World Series. Wilson was the goat of 1929 World Series, missing two fly balls in same inning, blunders that allowed the A's to come back from an 8-0 deficit in the seventh inning. Because of the times, it's a fair question to ask if fixing had anything to do with the two plays,[302] but given his history of poor defensive play and the sunlight in the outfield that day, it's fair to say Wilson's name shouldn't be muddied with accusations. Wilson was able to have a sense of humor about his errors in World Series, and he would joke later in life with fans about the mishaps. When in the Cubs hotel dining room, he once asked the waiter to dim the lights so he wouldn't misjudge his soup.

RF Sammy Sosa (1992-2004) vs. Bill Nicholson (1939-1948)

All right, we come to the first debate centered around a player linked to performance-enhancing drugs and the inherent drama that surrounds this on-going, hot-button issue. I covered a bit of my opinion on the matter in the introduction, but this will allow us to go a little further in-depth.

Contact

	BA	lgBA	Seasons ≥ .300*	Career high/low	Seasons ≥ 100 SO	SO %	lgSO%	BABIP	Misc.
Sosa	.284	.269	4	.328/.253	11	23.3	16.3	.307	LL 3x SO
Nicholson	.272	.265	1	.309/.220	0	12.9	9.4	.282	LL 1x SO

Even though Sosa was thought of as strictly a power source, he was actually a pretty solid contact hitter, sporting a solid batting average most years. On the surface, Sosa seems to have the higher strikeout rate by a lot, but a context-neutral look shows they are actually pretty close. Sosa struck out at a rate 43 percent higher the average player in his more strikeout-heavy era; whereas, Nicholson, who played in an era with far fewer strikeouts, struck out at a rate 37 percent higher than the average player.

When he hit .328 in 2001, Sosa set the record for the highest batting average in a season of any player in MLB history with at least 150 strikeouts. Sosa did, however, go over 100 strikeouts in 11 out of his 13 years with the Cubs, and the only two years he didn't go over 100, he missed significant time to injury. Sosa also struck out at a rate of more than once a game for his entire Cubs career, and no one right-handed batter in baseball history has ever struck out more. Even still, Sosa's high average, and the fact that each player's strikeout rates in comparison to the league are similar, gives Sosa the slight edge.

EDGE: Sosa

Power

	HR	Seasons ≥ 30 HR	Career high HR	XBH	SLG%	lgSLG%	ISO	HR%	XBH %	Misc.
Sosa	545	11	66	871	.569	.426	.285	6.2	10.4	LL 3x TB 2x HR
Nicholson	205	1	33	503	.471	.374	.199	3.7	9	LL 2x HR 1x TB

It's hard to top Sosa from a power perspective. He has a legitimate case as one of the best five-to-ten power hitters of all time. When Nate Silver took a look at which hitters had the highest percent of their career WAR to come from home runs, Sosa led the way, with an incredible 91.3 percent of his career value coming from home runs. Only Harmon Killebrew even came close. Even outside the fact that he played in an era with inflated home run totals, Sosa was among the best power sources in baseball history. Surprisingly, Sosa didn't lead the league in home runs any of the three times he topped 60 dingers in a season, but he did in his two next-highest season totals (2000 and 2002). From 1998-2002, Sosa hit an incredible 292 home runs (more than many Ryne Sandberg, Roger Maris, Brooks Robinson, and Don Mattingly had in their respective careers, and more than the entirety of baseball in five individual seasons of baseball's Dead Ball Era), as well as hitting for 1,951 total bases – some 175,590 feet when added together. During that stretch, he had the third, fifth, and sixth-highest

[302] Chicago was also a notoriously corrupt city during this time. Anyone who doesn't realize this should read *Capone* by Laurence Bergreen. Actually, really just everyone should read that biography, it's dope.

single-season home run totals in baseball history, and he is still the only player to have hit 60 home runs in three different seasons.

In fact, Sosa owns the record for most home runs over a five-year stretch (1998-2002), six-year stretch (1998-2003), seven-year stretch (1997-2003), eight-year stretch (1996-2003), nine-year stretch (1995-2003), and 10-year stretch (1995-2004) in MLB history. His 103 extra-base hits in 2001 are tied for the single-season record for right-handed batters in MLB history. Steroids or not, the dude was pretty unreal.

Nicholson was a legitimate power threat in his own right; his 1943-1944 seasons were on par with some of Sosa's in terms of comparing to the rest of the league; Sosa simply did it for much longer. Sosa became the first player in National League history to drive in at least 100 runs in nine consecutive years (1995-2003), and he holds the record for most home runs in a month with an incredible 20 round trippers in June of 1998; Nicholson has nothing to match.

The final note, and one we'll cover in more depth later on, is the fact that Nicholson put up his best batting season in the WWII-depleted 1943 season. He was, however, a huge part of the team's offense, becoming the third man to drive in over 20 percent of the team's runs for the year. Still, Sosa cruises to this victory.

EDGE: Sosa

Batting Eye

	BB	Seasons ≥ 70 BB	OBP	lgOBP	OPS+	BB%	SO/BB	Misc.
Sosa	798	5	.358	.340	139	9.4	2.48	LL 1x IBB
Nicholson	696	7	.368	.334	136	12.4	0.98	

This is a close one; both players were solid, but not outstanding, at drawing walks. Most of Sosa's walks came due to pitchers pitching around him after his home run totals went through the roof.[303] Because of his high strikeout totals, Sosa's strikeout/walk ratio is very poor, and that, along with Nicholson's more consistent ability to draw walks, makes the difference here.

EDGE: Nicholson

Speed

	SB	Seasons ≥ 10 SB	Career high SB	Rbaser	SB%	XBT%	GDP%	Misc.
Sosa	181	7	36	-8	70	44	9	2x 30/30
Nicholson	26	0	8	-1	N/A	40*	11*	

*Data only available starting in 1945

Sosa was surprisingly agile for a man whose legacy is tied to his ability to hit the long ball. Sosa actually had a higher stolen base total than home run total his first five years in the league, which included his first two seasons with the Cubs.

EDGE: Sosa

Defense

	Fld%	lgFld%	dWAR	Assists	GG	Misc.
Sosa	.975	.979	1.0	117	0	LL 3X TZR (RF), RF/G (RF) 2X GP (RF), PO (RF), Assists (RF), E (RF) 1X DP (RF)
Nicholson	.978	.975	-5.4	107	N/A	LL 4X PO (RF) 3X RF/G (RF) 2X GP (RF), Assists (RF), Fld% (RF) 1X E (RF)

Defense is yet another category in which Sosa performed better than would be assumed. His defense was actually a positive for the team, per dWAR, despite playing a corner outfield position with the team through his age-35 season. In 1996, his first 40-home run season, he was worth more than 2.0 wins by dWAR for the year, finishing second in the entire league in dWAR. Nicholson rated slightly below average per dWAR, but he was among the league leaders in right field in several

[303] Although Rob Neyer, in his *Big Book of Lineups*, credits hitting coach Jeff Pentland for helping Sosa to improve from walking 115 times in his first 2,006 plate appearances to walking 116 times in his 693 plate appearances in 2001 alone, a trend that continued for the rest of Sosa's career.

defensive metrics throughout his career. His range was stronger than his arm, and besides the dWAR totals, these two men appear very even in the field.

EDGE: Sosa by a hair

Team Success

	W	L	T	W-L%	Seasons $\geq$ 90 W	Division titles	Pennants	WS
Sosa	869	941	1	.480	1	1	0	0*
Nicholson	649	689	11	.485	1	1	1	0*

* Of course…

Because these players were both on the Cubs prior to 2016, team success was never a guarantee. As such, neither player enjoyed too many playoff opportunities while in the Windy City. Nicholson's 1945 Cubs were the best team that either player played on, and although Nicholson had led the team in WAR the previous three years, he did not that year. In the 1945 World Series, Nicholson did have eight RBI, but he got on base at only a .267 clip. In Sosa's limited playoff experience, he didn't perform too well, as his best series came in their losing 2003 NLCS effort. (I promise you Cub fans that's the only time that notorious series will be mentioned in this chapter.) As a whole, Sosa hit .245 in 15 playoff games, and although his on-base percentage was over .400, his only home run came in that 2003 NLCS. In the end, Nicholson was on the best Cubs team of either player, he was the only one to reach a World Series, and his team had the superior winning percentage, so he takes this category.

EDGE: Nicholson

Dominance

	LL in R	LL in HR	LL in RBI	LL in TB	All-Star Appearances	Silver Sluggers	Misc.
Sosa	3	2	2	3	8	6	1x MVP
Nicholson	1	2	2	1	4	N/A	2x top 3 MVP

Both players had similar numbers in terms of dominance over their league, especially in terms of leading the league in certain categories, but Sosa had his above-average stretch for longer than Nicholson (as shown by the eight All-Star appearances). Sosa also managed to reach the pinnacle of dominance by winning an MVP;[304] whereas, Nicholson finished one vote behind Martin Marion in his closest run at MVP. It seems very subjective to punish Nicholson for missing out on an MVP by a single vote, but if you compare the two seasons, ignoring any MVP voting, Sosa had the better season, regardless. Nicholson does have the distinct honor of being intentionally walked with the bases loaded, an honor reserved for someone truly feared.[305] His play leading up to that bases-loaded intentional walk deserved it, to say the least. During one hot streak in late July, 1944, Nicholson set an NL record with four home runs in a double header; set another NL record with home runs in four consecutive at bats; and tied a record with five home runs in three games and six home runs in four games. This all culminated in the aforementioned intentional walk with the bases loaded.

In the end, however, Sosa's five-year Reign of Home Run Terror gives him the advantage here.

EDGE: Sosa

Controversy

There is a certain amount of controversy involved with each of these player's statistics.

With Sosa, you all know the reasons why: the suspicion of steroid use, the corked bat,[306] the Congressional hearing, the forgetting how to speak English, the denial of steroid use through an attorney, the positive steroid test, the whole turning-white thing, and finally the pigeons. Let's take these on one at a time:

The suspicion of Sosa's steroid use is yet another case that deserves nuance. The only official tie from Sosa to PEDs is his inclusion in the New York Times report of over 100 players who tested positive on the anonymous survey tests from

---

[304] Especially impressive since he won it over a man (Mark McGwire) who set the all-time single-season home run record that year.

[305] Abner Dalrymple, Nap Lajoie, Del Bissonette, Barry Bonds, and Josh Hamilton are the others in history to accomplish that feat.

[306] It should be noted that physicist and baseball fanatic (but mostly physicist) Alan Nathan has come to the conclusion that corked bats don't actually add any distance to a fly ball. A corked bat does move faster because it is lighter, but the lesser weight behind the swing counteracts the speed added.

2003 (DH, Red Sox – Page 346). Those tests were in some ways flawed, but regardless: Sosa became one of the martyrs of the "Steroid Era." After the 1994 strike, Major League Baseball's popularity was in the doldrums, and Bud Selig, along with the rest of Major League Baseball, knew that they had to find a way to win back the fans they lost during the strike. In 1993, MLB average game attendance was at 31,337, but, in 1995, that number dropped to 25,260. Baseball needed a *shot in the arm*. Major League Baseball got that *injection* when Sosa and McGwire made their run at history in 1998.

Major League Baseball undeniably benefited from this home run boom. Average game attendance was back up to over 30,000 by 2000, while home run totals went from 4,081 in 1995 to 5,064 in 1998. In fact, baseball's first nine seasons of over 5,000 home runs all took place from 1998-2006. Part of that had to do with the fact that baseball expanded to 30 teams by adding the Arizona Diamondbacks and Tampa Bay Devil Rays in 1998, but the connection between the home run arms race and the revival of the sport's popularity, was undoubtedly a strong one. Historical precedent backs this theory, as a home run boom also followed the biggest black mark in baseball history prior to the 1994 strike – the Black Sox Scandal in 1919. In 1919, there were 447 home runs in Major League Baseball, the next three years saw home runs increase at an incredible rate. There were 630 home runs league-wide in 1920, 937 in 1921, and 1,055 in 1922.

All of this is to say that the powers that be in Major League Baseball were more than alright with turning a blind eye to just how these increased home run totals were occurring. Baseball's apathy towards steroids and their use in the sport was completely flipped on its ear when, less than a decade after their historical obliteration of Roger Maris' home run record, Sosa and McGwire sat in front of Congress with their participation in baseball's "Steroid Era" having blown up more than any of them could have thought possible.

So, although Sosa (and the other scapegoats of the steroid era) are certainly not without fault, the idea that McGwire, Sosa, Palmeiro, etc. were breaking steroid policies similar to what are currently in place, is false. The biggest claim against Sosa and company may be that they duped fans by repeatedly denying their use of steroids. This is certainly a fair argument, but the case for being duped should really be aimed at MLB and Selig. When Sosa used steroids, it had to be kept on the low down, but it was not regarded with the same level of illegality as the current era. Sosa and others quickly were quickly scapegoated when Selig saw the response to steroids in the court of public opinion.

Let's get to the important matters of Sosa's legacy, however – his increasing whiteness and the pigeons. Sosa notoriously seemed to see his pigment fade in his post-playing days, most noticeably at the 2009 Latin Grammy's when he looked like he could have been Kristen Stewart's older brother. Now race, and skin color in particular, is a very sensitive subject, so without poking fun of Sosa's increasing whiteness too much, let's just say it was fascinating to observe.

Then there's the matter of his name being popularized in numerous rap lyrics. Now I am quickly getting in over my head, but we should note that the Chief Keef references (he has a song called "Sammy Sosa" and goes by SOSA) may well be completely smoking-related, or potentially related to the end of *Scarface* when Al Pacino is taken down by a man named Sosa. The Akon reference, however, is certainly to Sammy Sosa. In his song "Cashin' Out," Akon says, "I got big money visions, Sammy Sosa pigeons; What that mean? That mean they jumping out the kitchen."

Now there's a lot to unpack there, and I am by no means an expert, but in the process of Sosa research, I learned that Sammy Sosa may well have owned his own flock of pigeons, which I'm pretty sure trumps any of the other narratives that I could care about in "Cashin' Out." As noted above, Chief Keef has also adopted the nickname Sosa, which you can google to figure out more about before I step on Shea Serrano's toes with all this rap writing.

As for Nicholson, his numbers are not without controversy, either; just in a much different sense. Nicholson's prime was the 1943 and 1944 seasons. Obviously, there was a pretty important event going on in the world at this time that meant many players were drafted to go overseas once the United States became involved in WWII.[307] Some players were ineligible for the draft, but the list of players who left for the draft is incredible. With over 500 players going overseas, here are some of the highlights: Luke Appling, Yogi Berra,[308] Bill Dickey, Dom and Joe DiMaggio, Larry Doby,[309] Bobby Doerr, Bob Feller, Hank Greenberg, Gil Hodges, Charlie Keller, Ralph Kiner, Bob Lemon, Johnny Mize, Stan Musial, Red Ruffing, Johnny Sain, Warren Spahn, and Ted Williams. To deny the major leagues were depleted at this point in time would be insane.

Now let's clarify for a second, I don't mean to imply that Nicholson should be considered controversial for not entering the draft,[310] but rather that his numbers were inflated in the years during which all these sure-fire Hall of Fame players were overseas. The game of baseball obviously took a great dip in quality in these years, and just because Nicholson was the best of that bunch does not mean that he was truly the second-best baseball player in the world in 1944, just that he was the second-best player playing in the majors that year. Nicholson's precipitous drop off after 1944 could certainly be contributed to getting older, or timing his prime for the war years, but either way, it would appear that Sosa's years came when he was competing against the best of the best, and Nicholson's best years did not.

Nicholson himself would not have agreed with the previous assessment, however, and he has said that he believed the quality of play was actually lower after expansion than during the war years. Although that may not be true, Nicholson's numbers are "essentially legit" according to Bill James because of the different ball used during the war, and the fact that

---

[307] Since this isn't a history book we won't go into detail, but the draft changed in 1942, so that the number of men drafted to war increased greatly before the 1943 season.
[308] Before he ever played a game in the bigs.
[309] Also before his career.
[310] Nicholson had dreamed of joining the Navy his whole life, but he was color blind.

Wrigley was a difficult stadium to hit in during Nicholson's time there. The league-wide run totals for the WWII years also support these claims of a depleted league-wide offense in 1943 and 1944.

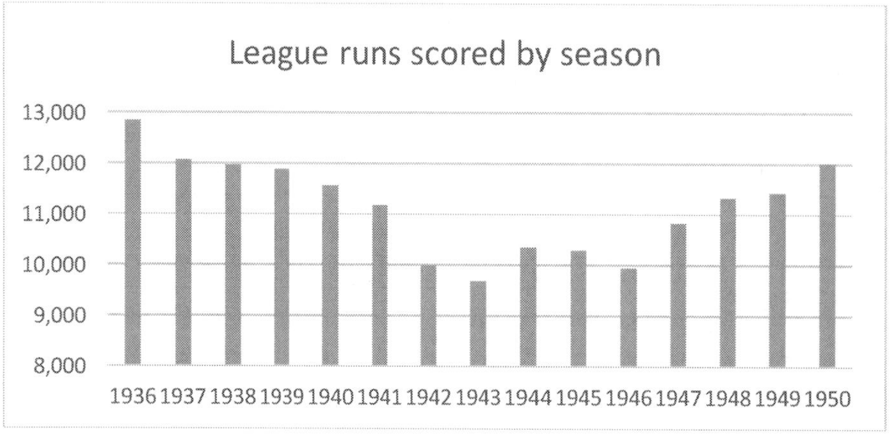

Now, this does nothing to dispel the idea that the talent pool was highly-depleted during the war years, but Nicholson's offensive totals certainly seem as though they might not be as inflated as one might have imagined without context. Given the lower number of runs scored during those 1943 and 1944 seasons, even though Nicholson may have been picking on slightly worse pitchers, I don't think it is fair to trash his numbers entirely.

In the end, the biggest argument against Sosa is not a matter of his character, but rather against his play. Cody Derespina did a series for Newsday in which he profiled many of the players on the edge of making the Hall of Fame in 2012. He sums up the argument against Sosa perfectly and succinctly: "The argument can be made for some of the other suspected steroid cheats – Roger Clemens and Barry Bonds, in particular – that they were Hall of Famers before they ever allegedly injected anything. The same cannot be said for Sosa."

Before 1997, Sosa averaged 23 home runs a season, owned a .257 batting average, and had a OPS+ only slightly above average (107). At the age of 28, Sosa made his explosion into a new player, and while a jump in statistics at this age would not be unexpected, the extreme nature of this jump is what draws attention. The next five years saw Sosa average way more than twice as many home runs (58 per season), hit over .300, and post an OPS+ of 167. The question of just how much steroids help an athlete on an individual level is something we still don't know well enough, but Sosa's numbers are undoubtedly inflated for a longer period of time than Nicholson, who only saw two seasons of possible increase.

EDGE: Sosa (with edge meaning his numbers are more controversial)

Verdict

Although Sosa has the more questionable of the numbers, and is the more questionable of characters, Sosa's extended time with the team, and the fact that he had positive results before his time in question (thanks to his strong defense and smart baserunning, he had WAR totals of 3.8 or higher in four of his five seasons prior to 1997, including 10.7 WAR in 1995-1996 combined) mean that **Sosa gets the edge here**. Baseball and sport "purists" will disagree, but Only the Good Die Young, right Billy?

Utility Mike "King" Kelly (1880-1886)

The first step to realizing why Kelly got this spot is to behold the 'stache this man had:

(Photo from Baseball-Reference)

Granted, mustaches were more common in Kelly's day, but I have to imagine that was still pretty epic even in his time. Kelly was an immensely popular player who, among other notable achievements, helped popularize the steal. He would take off well before the bag and finish in what today would be called a hook slide. This became so famous that he had an entire poem written about it entitled, "Slide, Kelly, Slide." That poem eventually inspired a song (and even a movie!) by the same title. Kelly was famous enough to write the first autobiography to come from an American athlete. His plaque in the baseball Hall of Fame literally says, "[Kelly] was one of the biggest deals of baseball's early history." Mike "King" Kelly was so dope.

Kelly is a perfect fit as the utility man for the Cubs. However, to call him a utility man somewhat undermines his role. He led the league in oWAR twice (once with the Reds) and won two batting titles, while scoring well over one run per game for his time with the Cubs (728 runs in 681 games). The reason I call him a utility man is because he managed to play all nine positions while in Chicago. This is an immensely impressive feat, and if we were building an actual team, it would help to have a second catcher due to the specialized nature of the position. Catchers are also usually the smartest players on the field, with many managers being ex-catchers, including some of the best of all time (Joe Torre, Mike Scioscia, Connie Mack, and Branch Rickey).

Kelly was indeed one of the smartest players of his time. On multiple occasions, he used his smarts to trick players into outs, but my personal favorite trick of his came when he was a player-manager for Boston. He was on the bench, and when a pop up came near him that was out of the reach of his catcher, Kelly yelled, "Kelly now catching for Boston" and proceeded to make the put out. This led to a rule change, which was previously unstated, that said substitutions had to be made at a dead ball.

This story should come without surprise, as Kelly had a penchant for bending/completely obliterating the rules as a player. Nobody took advantage of the fact that there used to be only one umpire more than Kelly. He would trip players by throwing his catcher's helmet in their way, and he would even go from first base to third base via the pitcher's mound, finding second base to be an unnecessary evil.[311] Kelly did have some less "cutesy" stories about him. He would regularly show up to games under the influence, and he had a nasty penchant for blowing paychecks on booze and horses. This was not a fact lost on the Cubs organization, as he had a clause in contract for good behavior.

A self-proclaimed story from Kelly best sums up his mindset and regard for his own self-importance. The story goes that upon being invited to the White House to shake President Grover Cleveland's hand, Kelly said he squeezed the President's hand so hard Cleveland winced.

In *Baseball Anecdotes* by Steve Wulf and Dan Okrent, the portrait the two paint of Kelly is incredible: "His cane a-twirling as though he were the entire population, his Ascot held by a giant jewel, his patent leather shoes as sharply pointed as Italian dirks." Kelly was occasionally accompanied by a black monkey and a Japanese valet, making him just about the most absurd man of all time. Fans showed their support for his unique style by giving him a white horse and beautiful carriage so that he could arrive to the games the way he ought to. Like I said, he was dope.

His game on the field followed suit in its strangeness. Bill James analysis of his fielding numbers is one of the most entertaining analyses in his *Abstract*, go check it out.

There are hitters who posted bigger numbers with the Cubs, but considering the era in which Kelly played, the argument for his inclusion on the all-time roster is much stronger. For instance, Stan Hack was worth north of 50.0 WAR in his time with the Cubs (more than twice as much as Kelly), but he also got to play nearly twice as many games a season as Kelly and played in a far greater era for hitters. He never led the league in oWAR, as Kelly did twice, and his OPS+ of 119 with the Cubs is far inferior to Kelly's OPS+ of 149. Plus, Hack was never accompanied by a monkey, so it was an easy choice really.

SP Mordecai Brown (1904-1912; 1916) vs. Fergie Jenkins (1966-1973; 1982-1982)

Both players spent a short time in the major leagues in other cities before coming to Chicago and making their names as Cubs pitchers. Here we'll do a (mini) breakdown of which man deserves to start for the club. You might say, "Why not let them both on, it's not as if there are an exorbitant number of pitchers in this book?" To which I would respond, "A man with two watches never knows what time it is," while tipping the world's largest fedora.

Both players pitched for the Cubs for 10 years, as well as throwing solid seasons for other franchises during their careers. In fact, both men had quite similar careers not only with the Cubs, but also for their entirety. Strictly on paper, Brown – a man missing the better part of two of his fingers – appears to have the edge due to 21 more victories and an ERA over a run lower, but let's dig deeper. Brown pitched in much more of a pitcher's era than Jenkins, and although Jenkins did pitch partially during the near dead-ball era of the early-to-mid 1960s, he pitched most of his time in Chicago after the mound was lowered and pitchers began to struggle. Although "Three-Finger" Brown still has the edge in ERA+ (153 to 119), Jenkins can counter with the fact that he won the Cubs 8.0 more games than Brown per WAR. Jenkins also has the advantage in highest individual-season WAR (10.3 to 8.7) and had much higher strikeout totals, finishing his career as the only pitcher with over 3,000 strikeouts and under 1,000 walks – a distinction that Greg Maddux, Pedro Martínez, and Curt

---

311 I wonder what Dallas Braden and his grandma would say!

Schilling now also share.

Brown can counter that with the fact that the team had more success when he was there, but as we have mentioned before, baseball is not a sport driven by one player, so if anything, Jenkins could say the fact that he managed to win on worse teams is actually more impressive. Although both men are in the Hall of Fame, Jenkins has the distinct honor of being Canada's first Hall of Famer.[312] "Fly" is a pretty sweet nickname for Jenkins (who played for the Harlem Globetrotters from 1967-1969), but is it really better – or more impressive than – Brown being aptly nicknamed "Three-Finger?" And there's the rub, really you couldn't go wrong with either of these guys, and by WAR you'd be better off with Jenkins, but the fact that Brown had such a successful career with part of two fingers missing[313] is pretty damn impressive and gets him the nod between these two supremely even candidates.[314]

Brown posted seven straight seasons in the top five in the league in ERA and was the first pitcher to have double-digit saves in a season when he did so in 1911. Speaking of 1911, during the season Mr. Three Finger started 20 games and finished 20 different games.

Throughout his career, Brown owned Christy Mathewson, arguably the best pitcher in the game, winning nine straight at a point in time when the two were the two top pitchers in baseball. Imagine that in modern society for a second. Every day would feature millions of spawning Skip Baylesses crawling out of the earth's core with freshly-cooked Christy-Mathewson-is-soft hot takes.

CP Lee Smith (1980-1987)

Smith was the all-time leader in saves (478) before Trevor Hoffman (601) and Mariano Rivera (652) went on to pass him in the new millennium. He began his career with the Cubs and pitched out of the bullpen for the vast majority of the time. Smith embodied the changing role of the closer in baseball in his years with the Cubs. When he began to close full-time in 1982, he saw his innings decrease each year, as the closer's role evolved during the `80s to look more and more like what it is today – with the closer rarely going more than one inning for the save. Smith was very consistent, if never truly dominant, in his eight years with the club, never posting an ERA over 3.65, but having a sub 2.50 ERA only once. Smith became a bit of a journeyman at the end of his career and ended up playing for eight teams in total, but the Cubs were his signature team without a doubt.

Starting IX Franchise Roster Stats

Lineup	Yrs	G	R	H	HR	RBI	SB	BB	SO	BA	OBP	SLG	OPS+	dWAR	WAR
King Kelly	7	681	728	899	33	480	53	229	179	0.316	0.367	0.453	149	-1.6	24.3
Ryne Sandberg	15	2151	1316	2385	282	1061	344	761	1259	0.285	0.344	0.452	115	12.8	67.7
Billy Williams	16	2213	1306	2510	392	1353	86	911	934	0.296	0.364	0.503	135	-15.6	61.6
Ron Santo	14	2126	1109	2171	337	1290	35	1071	1271	0.279	0.366	0.472	128	9.4	72.0
Sammy Sosa	13	1811	1245	1985	**545**	1414	181	798	**1815**	0.284	0.358	0.569	139	1.0	58.5
Ernie Banks	19	**2528**	1305	2583	512	1636	50	763	1236	0.274	0.330	0.500	122	4.9	67.4
Cap Anson	**22**	2277	**1722**	**3012**	97	**1880**	247	953	321	0.331	0.396	0.448	142	4.4	**84.4**
Hack Wilson	6	850	652	1017	190	769	34	463	461	0.322	0.412	**0.590**	**155**	-4.0	31.1
Gabby Hartnett	19	1926	847	1867	231	1153	28	691	683	0.297	0.370	0.490	126	6.5	52.3
Pitchers	Yrs	W	W%	ERA	G	CG	SHO	SV	IP	SO	ERA+	WHIP	SO/9	SO/BB	WAR
Mordecai Brown	10	188	0.686	1.80	346	206	**48**	39	2329.0	1043	153	0.998	4.0	2.34	45.3
Lee Smith	8	40	0.440	2.92	458	0	0	**180**	681.1	644	134	1.255	8.5	2.44	19.1

---

[312] Being from Canada, Jenkins played much more hockey than baseball growing up. He gave up hockey when his mom said to him, "You better consider getting out [of hockey] because the only two black things out there on the ice are you and the puck."

[313] The feed chopper that did the deed was actually saved by his uncle and turned into a local tourist attraction.

[314] And I think it's a ridiculous argument to say that Brown benefited from missing part of two fingers. I understand the logic that maybe it put a different kind of curve on his pitch or something, but to be able to recover from that accident and pitch professionally, I don't think it's something any of us would volunteer to do. That being said, his curve was the second best of all time according to Neyer and James in their book on pitching and was the pitch Ty Cobb called the most devastating he ever faced, so maybe he did have a good thing going…

#10 Philadelphia Phillies (1890-pres.); Philadelphia Quakers (1883-1889)

(Photo from Wikimedia Commons)

Team Background

Playoff appearances: 14 **Pennants: 7** **World Series titles: 2**
Collective team WAR: 616.5
Strengths: At first base, second base, and center field, the Phillies have three of the most underrated players in baseball history.
Weaknesses: If you want to be in the next tier, you simply can't have a hole as big as the Phillies do at the catcher position.
What to expect from the next 15 pages: An inside-joke-ridden Starting IX for fans of the *Effectively Wild* podcast. The complex history of Dick Allen. Mac's letter from *Always Sunny*. A player making an umpire bleed. A nice, meaty breakdown. Pitching drunk. And we haven't even gotten to Crazy Steve Carlton yet. One of the most entertaining Starting IX's, for sure.

For a team that has been around nearly as long as Larry King, the Phillies have a rather sordid history. Much of their early history is filled with fun-but-depressing nuggets, such as how for a 30-year stretch (1920-1949), the franchise didn't have a single 20-game winner in an era chock full of them; or, how in 1930, they scored 944 runs (over six a game) and still finished in the cellar with over 100 losses. That season they scored eight or more runs and lost 21 times; they lost two straight games in which they scored 15 runs; their relief pitchers allowed runs to score in a mind-melting 71 percent of their appearances.

Much of the pitching struggles in this era of Phillies history were due to the absurd home/road splits produced by their home stadium, the Baker Bowl. In 1929, the Phillies hit .340 at home compared to .277 on the road – this type of split was much more the rule than the exception for the Baker Bowl Phillies (1887-1938). The Baker Bowl was only 280 feet to right field and 300 feet to right center. It must be mentioned that the Baker Bowl did have ample foul territory that helped to dilute hitting somewhat, but the giant bump in center field that came from deciding to build an outfield directly above train tracks certainly didn't help fielders at all.

The ballpark had nearly as much personality as it had offense. There used to be a giant advertisement for Lifebuoy soap on the infamous right field wall that said, "The Phillies use Lifebuoy soap." Naturally, this led to a brilliant vandal writing "and they still stink" below. The team used sheep and rams to trim the grass because the owners were too cheap to hire actual groundskeepers, but they were forced to abandon this method when one of the rams attacked an employee, forcing a switch to a more conventional way of mowing the lawns in 1925. On a less embarrassing note for the field, it was the site of the first World Series attended by a U.S. president (Woodrow Wilson), as well as the home of Babe Ruth's final home run in the major leagues.[315]

The Baker Bowl makes one think about the quirkiest things a home team could do to their home stadium and get away with it. In the modern game, Tal's Hill in Houston was a creature too beautiful to live, as the weird in-play hill and pole in center field were removed from Minute Maid Park in 2016. Of course, if Ben Lindbergh and Sam Miller ever get their hands on a major league team (and given the success they had running the Pacific League Sonoma Stompers,[316] they may just get the call one day), the two hosts of *Effectively Wild* (Ben still hosts, Sam is now at *ESPN*), the podcast from *FanGraphs*, and previously *Baseball Prospectus*, may just do some crazy stuff. One of the most entertaining – and truly "Effectively Wild moments" came when Ben and Sam discussed what would happen in groundskeepers were banned. This eventually led to Sam pondering if corn could grow in the infield, if bears would show up, and if locals driving trucks through the field would be inevitable. The podcast is amazing for many reasons, and tangents like this only make it better. Here's an insider Starting IX for listeners of the pod. For those who aren't listeners, you really should be.

SP) The Ned Garver cold call C) Anytime the two break and can't help but laugh for an extended period of time, especially in the Ben and Sam days 1B) Smash Mouth following Ben on Twitter 2B) Burn the ships 3B) Their love of drafts SS) Overgrown infield LF) Ben's exasperation with Sam wanting to play the "Guess the player by the BP Annual Comment" game CF) Ben's burrito eating style RF) "Ben isn't here and we're lacking production, so this is me singing you the introduction. Effectively WILD!"

It should be noted that the excellent spinoff of *Effectively Wild*, *Banished to the Pen*, a website run by listeners of the show, does an annual breakdown of the best Ben and Sam (and later, Jeff) moments, which was quite helpful in remembering some of the best moments in the pod's illustrious career to date.

* * *

Back to the franchise: the most productive time in the Phillies history came in two bursts: the late-1970s-to-early-80s and the late-2000s-to-the-early-2010s.

The first burst of success was powered by a pair of gents who will be highlighted on these upcoming pages, and it saw the team take home a World Series title in 1980. The second bout of success brought another World Series title to the City of Brotherly Love in 2008. It was powered by another dynamic duo on this Starting IX, as well as an excellent pitching staff that all fell short of the one starter/one closer set-up for this book. Although a starting baseball lineup does technically have only one starting pitcher, there are times in this book when going with only one starting pitcher hamstrung some team's true history. There are a couple of teams upcoming where that rule will be danced around a bit, and while I debated adding a full rotation at one point after I started, I'd have to imagine there aren't too many folks disagreeing with the sentiment that this book is already long enough.

Random cool things about the franchise:

- The Philadelphia Phillies have the longest continuous name-and-city partnership in American professional sports (1890).
- The franchise once had an owner who tried to rename them the Blue Jays in 1943 and 1944, but the fans weren't having it.
- In 2007, the franchise became the first American professional sports franchise to reach 10,000 losses.
- In their inaugural season, they had a dude whose nickname was Bob "Death To Flying Things" Ferguson.
- Speaking of legendary Phillies who won't show up on the franchise Starting IX, they also had the man who was the supposed inspiration for the movie *The Natural* – a first baseman named Eddie Waitkus.[317]
- Their Triple A affiliate is the Lehigh Valley IronPigs, and the logo is just as cool as you would hope.

---

[315] Much of the latter half of that Baker Bowl information came from an excellent presentation by George Skornickel at the SABR 43 convention in Philadelphia.
[316] Check out their book chronicling their year with the team *The Only Rule Is It Has to Work*. Seriously, good stuff.
[317] The author of *The Natural*, Bernard Malamud, never said whether Waitkus was actually the inspiration, true to classic, mysterious old-school writer form.

Starting IX

C Jack Clements (1884-1897)

Clements was a left-handed catcher for the Phillies in their earliest days. He is said to have been the first backstop to wear a chest protector. The MLB record holder (by a large margin) for games played as a southpaw backstop, Clements was a short squat man who, as he aged, got significantly rounder and surlier. Never known as the friendliest of chaps, by the end of his time in Philadelphia, he had more than worn out his welcome. He did manage to play exactly 1,000 games for Philadelphia, though. Clements was such a disruptive presence behind the plate that David Nemec, in Clements' SABR Bio, surmised:

"[Clements] was not particularly well liked by many of his teammates and was remembered with loathing by legions of young pitchers who debuted with the Phillies during his later years with the team. By the early 1890s Clements had developed an utter disdain for rookie hurlers and would mock their deliveries by catching them bare handed and deliberately returning the ball at their feet whenever they missed his target or threw a pitch he didn't like… his temperament only got worse as he aged, and it probably is as good a reason as any that the Phillies teams in the mid-1890s had so little luck with young arms and such poor pitching in general to accompany what year after year was the strongest hitting club in the majors."

Knowing how loathe SABR members are to overreact, that is a huge black mark on Clements' record. However, with the skill of the two pitchers throwing to him on this Starting IX, he probably wouldn't be disappointed very often.

A great portion of Clements' value came on the offensive side of the ball, as he was one of baseball's first real power hitters. He is the *only player* in the 19th century to play at least 1,000 games and hit more home runs than triples, and his 17 home runs in 1893 were the MLB record for the catching position until the home run boom of the 1920s. Even more impressive was that he hit those 17 home runs in just 94 games and 420 plate appearances. Clements sported a 118 OPS+ for his Philadelphia career, and although Carlos Ruiz was a solid contributor to the Phillies in recent years, he's not quite on Clements' level.

1B Dick Allen (1963-1969; 1975-1976)

"Bill James once described Allen as someone who 'did more to keep his teams from winning than anybody else who ever played major league baseball.' On the surface, Allen's actions down the stretch in 1976 might appear to at least suggest as much. But beneath it, when focusing on actions that hindered the club's potential, one wonders if anything Allen might have done in '76 could match the organization's long-standing reluctance to embrace and encourage the development of black ballplayers in Philadelphia in the decades leading up to that season. Viewed through this lens, perhaps the succession of events that transpired during the club's '76 stretch run caused the organization to finally confront a demon it mistakenly thought it had slayed through its relocation to the Vet and the transition in ownership from father to son. As such, perhaps it was Dick Allen, more than any other factor, who finally compelled the organization to modernize its approach to black athletes at last."

– Mitchell Nathanson

When a player bio starts out with a quote within a quote, it's probably not too surprising to find out that Dick Allen was one of the most interesting and divisive characters in the history of baseball.

As is noted above, Bill James was famously harsh in his criticism of Allen, but in the years since, there has been a pushback to James' comments, a sentiment that may not go as far as to call Allen the world's best teammate, but is a far cry from the stand that James (and a lot of the media in Allen's time) took. More on that in second, however.

With his appearance on this Starting IX, Allen makes his third stint with the franchise, as he began his career in Philly, playing with the squad from 1963-1969 then leaving for a while before a late-career return (1975-1976). During his two stints with the team, Allen had an OPS over .900 and hit over 200 home runs, despite playing in an offense-depleted era (153 OPS+). Today, the mighty slugger is more well known for his relationship with the city, media, and fans than his on-field achievements, though. When a player has never received more than 20 percent of the vote for the Hall of Fame,[318] but he has an entire *Baseball Research Journal* dedicated to busting the myths around how you are remembered, the on-field stuff tends to fall by the wayside.

The case that James made against Allen was that Allen tore the locker room apart wherever he went and was entirely handicapped by his immaturity. From the modern perspective, there's a lot more evidence against this claim than for it.

For one, the team's winning percentages with and without Allen paint a clear picture of a team that needed Allen a whole lot more than the other way around. From 1964-1967, with Allen playing for the Phillies they had a .542 winning

[318] Allen's potential spot in the Hall of Fame is a whole nother matter that won't be covered in this section but has been laid out in certain spots online, including a strong piece by Christopher Williams on *Older but not Wiser*.

percentage, but without him they had just a .469 winning percentage. In terms of the bigger picture, Philly's winning percentage for the six years before Allen: .433; with Allen: .499; and after Allen: .452. Granted there were other factors, but still, those numbers are hard to deny.

Don't like numbers? How about testimonials from the teammates and coaches that he supposedly tore apart? In the 1995 edition of *Baseball Research Journal*, Craig Wright interviewed several teammates and managers of Allen, all of whom said that not only was Allen never a divisive member of the clubhouse, but he also was a player that they would have traded for in an instant had he not already been on the team, thanks to his incredible talent. The only complaint many had was that he was notoriously tardy, but all those who mentioned that negative also noted that it never affected his on-field performance, with the exception of one game to which he was late because the time of the game was moved up. Chuck Tanner (Allen's manager in Chicago) said of Bill James' take on Allen, "[James] is full of shit, and you be sure to tell him that."

The biggest blemish on Allen's resume came in 1965, when Allen was just establishing himself as a superstar in Philadelphia. Veteran teammate Frank Thomas made a comment that Allen perceived as racist, and when Allen confronted Thomas, the two came to blows. Allen punched Thomas in the face before Thomas hit Allen in the shoulder with a bat. The incident had numerous repercussions. The most immediate was that the Phillies cut the 36-year-old veteran, Thomas, the next day, a casualty that Phillies fans held against Allen for the remainder of his time in Philadelphia. The incident didn't just impact Allen's off-field legacy, however, as the shoulder injury Allen suffered greatly hindered Allen's defensive abilities at third base, and he eventually had to make the move to the far-less-demanding first base spot he fills here. Allen was indeed a volatile man, and Philadelphia was a city in the midst of some incredibly nasty race riots when Allen – a black man – played for the team, so maybe it was only a matter of time until the relationship between this headstrong man and headstrong city crumbled. And boy did it crumble. Allen took to wearing a helmet when playing in the field to protect himself from projectiles from the crowd… in his home stadium. He said of the city: "I can play anywhere, first base, third base, left field, anywhere but Philadelphia."

By the end of his time with the club, it was pretty clear that the fans didn't want him there, and that Allen didn't want to be there either. He would trace, with his cleat, "Boo" and "Oct. 2," the date of his final game under contract with Philadelphia, into the infield dirt in front of his first base position.

Throughout this time, the local media often portrayed Allen in his surliest moments, choosing to focus on the fact that he wanted to leave town[319] instead of the loyal work he did on the field, playing through numerous injuries during his time in our nation's first capital. There was also the fact that Allen was absolutely demolishing NL pitching and helping to single-handedly make the Phillies a respectable offense. In 1968 – the year of the pitcher – Allen drove in 90 runs, while no other Phillie drove in more than 48. Remember, this is when he was supposed to be forcing his way out of town as a malcontent.

Eventually both Allen and the Phillies got what they wanted, and if the two were a newly-divorced couple, Allen was the ex-wife who took up yoga, dropped 15 pounds, and completely won the break up. The Phillies were the didn't-realize-what-he-had-ex-husband who thought he was going to go out and kill it, and then realized he had the same unused condom in his wallet eight months after the break up. Allen won MVP for the White Sox in 1972 with one of the best seasons in MLB history, a near Triple Crown that saw him lead the league in a plethora of offensive categories.

As is almost always the case, it wasn't too long before the ex-husband wanted the ex-wife back, and Phillies announcer Richie Ashburn spearheaded the cause to get Allen back in Philadelphia. It's fair to ask how on earth Allen ended up back in Philadelphia just five years after their acrimonious split, but lo and behold the two were indeed reunited in 1975. Of course, like any relapse, even though it started out alright, it was doomed from the get go. To make a long story[320] short, sooner than later the clubhouse was splintered again and Allen had seemingly worked his "magic" on an up-and-coming team. Some folks went so far as to say that Allen had managed to poison Mike Schmidt, making him the man who could never lead the Phillies to a 1980s dynasty.

Of course, the mere fact that Philadelphia was so willing to take Allen back seems like a pretty succinct argument to the claim that Allen "did more to keep his teams from winning than anybody else who ever played major league baseball." Unless the Phillie owners were really into S&M, why bring a guy like that back? Occam's Razor would certainly seem to say that Allen really wasn't a cancer, and that the idea of him as one was an illusion created by the fans and media about a man who once said one of the saddest and most telling quotes I have ever heard: "I had been hearing I was a bum for so long that I began to think maybe that's just what I was."

Allen eventually retired in 1977 after half a season in Oakland, as injuries wore him down and forced him to step away from baseball at the relatively young age of 35, an under-appreciated and oft-misremembered part of baseball history.

2B Chase Utley (2003-2015)

I'm really tempted to simply post the letter from Mac in *It's Always Sunny In Philadelphia*, written to Utley, along with Utley's response – and we will indeed end his write-up that way – but as a perennially underrated player, it would be

[319] With his own fans throwing stuff at him, could you blame him? If you are the Philadelphia media, the answer is yes.
[320] And it is a very interesting long story, written by Mitchell Nathanson in the 2013 edition of *The National Pastime*.

unfair to completely shaft Utley like that.

Despite the fact that his teammates Ryan Howard and Jimmy Rollins won back-to-back MVPs in 2006 and 2007, Utley actually had better seasons by WAR than each of them both years, and was, in many ways, the true driving force behind the Phillies return to relevance in the early portion of the 21st century. Utley had his full-time break out as a 26-year-old in 2005, and for the next six years, only Albert Pujols produced more WAR. During that same time, Utley never finished higher than seventh in the MVP race. Utley got sneaky value from his position (second base), fielding (11.9 wins from fielding runs on B-Ref), productive base running (77 steals in 87 attempts from 2005-2010[321]), and solid overall offensive production (average of 67 extra-base hits per season for those six seasons). All of which accumulated in an *average* of 7.5 WAR/season during that secretly really-really-really-ridiculously-good-looking stretch from 2005-2010.

Although Utley's production slipped in his final seasons past in Philly, he still had more value than most folks would have guessed. He was worth at least 3.0 WAR each season from 2011-2014, and he never posted an OPS+ below 110 for a full season until 2014, his final full season in Philly – even then he posted an OPS+ of 108. It is quite in vogue to invoke the "peak vs. longevity" argument about Utley's legacy in baseball (and more to the point, his possible induction into baseball's Hall of Fame), but at this point, Utley has proven his longevity, joining the incredibly elite company of just four other second baseman to post 10 consecutive seasons with 3.0 or more WAR. The other four? Eddie Collins, Lou Whitaker, Nap Lajoie, and Rogers Hornsby; some pretty great names. Utley deserves to be in the Hall of Fame with his career to date.

Utley was so good for the Phillies that he somehow managed to conquer the daunting Philly faithful, and as such, he is one of the most beloved Philadelphia athletes in living memory. When Utley returned to Philadelphia for the first time as a Dodger, he hit a solo home run and a grand slam – and got a curtain call *from the Phillies fans* after both. As Claire McNear pointed out for *The Ringer*, part of why he became so beloved was that he embodied the Philadelphia spirit. Or as McNear so perfectly summed up: "He was a real asshole, but to the right people."

Now for the real reason you all came here, though. The letter Mac (aka Ronald McDonald) wrote Utley on *It's Always Sunny in Philadelphia*:

Dear Chase,

I feel like I can call you Chase because you and me are so much alike. I would love to meet you some day. It would be great to have a catch. I know I can't throw as fast as you, but I think you would be impressed with my speed. I love your hair. You run fast. Do you have a good relationship with your father? Me neither. These are all things we can talk about and more. I am sure our relationship would be a real home run!
Rooting for you always,
Mac

And Utley's actual response:

Dear Mac,

I feel like I can call you Mac because you called me Chase. Sorry it took me five years to write you back, but I'm really busy playing a lot of baseball for the Phillies. Thank you for the compliment on my hair, it's my fourth favorite thing after baseball, running fast, and my dad. I'm sorry your dad doesn't like you, maybe you could become a better son. Meeting you and having a game of catch sounds like a lot of fun, but like I said I'm really busy playing a lot of baseball for the Phillies. I hope you have a good life. Fans like you make my life a "grand slam!"
Your good friend,
Chase

3B Mike Schmidt (1972-1989)

Mike Schmidt is by far the best hitter the Phillies franchise has ever seen, but he has always had a bit of a strange relationship with the city of Philadelphia. The fans never really accepted him as one of their own, and as such, they often gave him a much harder time than he deserved. One story that seems like it could be filed under the "needs-a-thorough-double-check" category of baseball lore is that as he was talking to a bus driver before picking up his daughter at school, the children on the bus started chanting, "Choke! Choke! Choke!" at Schmidt. His response said it all: "That's your Philadelphia fan in the making." Schmidt was once quoted as saying, "Philadelphia is the only city in the world where you can experience the thrill of victory and the agony of reading about it the next day."

The strangest part of Schmidt's relationship with Philadelphia is that it's not as though he was inconsistent. For a 14-year stretch (1974-1987), he had only one season in which he did not top 30 home runs with an OPS+ of 140. Even in that season, he had 21 home runs and an OPS+ of 122. In fact, only Hank Aaron has more 30-home run seasons than Schmidt's 13 such seasons. Schmidt is also topped by only one man (Babe Ruth this time) in number of 35-home run seasons, with Schmidt's 11 such seasons ranking second all-time. There are only 25 players, all-time, who totaled more WAR in their

[321] Including a record 23-for-23 in 2009 that is the most steals with a 100 percent stolen base percentage season since 1950, when caught stealing became an official statistic.

careers than Schmidt, and many of those men split their value between teams. Schmidt stayed in Philadelphia his entire career; at least one half of this baseball marriage was faithful.

Schmidt was unlucky in that he had his best season in the strike-shortened season of 1981, with an OPS+ of 198 and an MVP, while leading the league in 10 significant statistical categories. He capped off this season by leading the Phillies to their first World Championship ever, and he took home the series MVP. Given the nature of Schmidt's career, it makes perfect sense that his best season would be a strike-shortened one. All the good graces Schmidt earned in 1981 were somehow forgotten by 1983. When he started slow, the not-always-100-percent-loyal Philadelphia fans turned on him. It is often said that closers need a short memory, well in that case, some teams should start turning to their angry fan bases to close out their games because no one has a shorter memory than an angry sports fan. The way the Phillies fans rode Schmidt throughout the `80s is pretty absurd given that no player hit more home runs in the decade than Schmitty, and only Wade Boggs and Rickey Henderson were worth more, per WAR.

The only possible logic behind the fans' anti-Schmidt sentiments might have been that his traditional statistics were not on par with other superstars in the league. It is somewhat surprising that Schmidt never posted a season with a .300 batting average, 30 home runs, and 100 RBI, but this was mostly due to his poor teammates (hurting his RBI chances), playing in a poor era for hitters, and his preference to on-base percentage over batting average. He led the league in on-base percentage three times, including one season (1983) in which he hit a mere .255 but got on base at a .399 clip.

In many ways, Schmidt ushered in the era of the modern athlete. He was a Three True Outcomes hitter, leading the league in home runs eight seasons, as well as leading the league in strikeouts and walks four times apiece. However, it wasn't his mentality on the field that made him the man that ushered in the modern athlete, but the reaction to him off the field instead. His career coincided with the media boom around sports, which brought 24/7 coverage to sports and the athletes that played the game. In many ways, this "ESPN-ization" of sports thrust athletes into a totally different spotlight than the athletes of previous eras. Suddenly athletes had to watch everything they said, and they began to sound more like politicians.

As our access to athletes increased, the few who didn't hold their tongue, or weren't in the "politician mold" of media interaction, began to be ostracized. In his post-playing days, Schmidt was painfully aware of this. "I think you play with your God-given personality, but if I had it to do all over again, I'd probably figure out a way, in this media age, to realize the value of people's perceptions and what it would mean to me down the road, what it would mean off the field," Schmidt once said. "And maybe I'd do things a little differently." This quote is unbelievably telling in the era of modern sports, and in a greater sense, the current media age in general. It's interesting to see the backlash to this mentality in the modern era, when fans (and even talking heads) are sick of athletes giving us no real view into their true personalities. Obviously the catch-22 to the modern dilemma is that the fans and talking heads are the reason that athletes are so clammed up today.

SS Jimmy Rollins (2000-2014)

The Rollins-Utley up-the-middle duo on this Starting IX is a perfect example of how usually you can tell when certain franchises had their renaissance periods just by looking at their Starting IX. Although Carlos Ruiz and Ryan Howard fell just short of starting spots in the franchise Starting IX, the Phillies very nearly had four-fifths of their all-time best infield all on the field at the same time, during their 2000s mini-dynasty. When combined with an elite rotation, it's not very difficult to see how this team had so much success.

Rollins has some pretty cool nuggets – both statistical and anecdotal – that can be stumbled upon on the world wide web. By far the coolest is that, when he was 13 years old and living in Oakland, he and his brother were chosen to be in an MC Hammer music video. A few years later, when he was in high school, he was in a Mavis Staples music video.

Rollins, a black man in a sport that has seen the number of black players disintegrating in recent years, has been very outspoken about baseball needing to reach out and do their best not to lose the connection. In an interview with *Sports Illustrated*, Rollins said, "The black player today pretty much has to be a superstar. The role player, the guy off the bench, baseball's not looking to black players in those positions. Baseball has to take the blinders off." Sadly, like so many of the race issues nation-wide in recent years, this quote very easily seems like it could have been said back in 1950, yet it still rings very true. This topic doesn't need a full dive into here, especially since it has been noted on a few occasions throughout the book (and the book is a baseball book after all), but just read Ralph Ellison's *Invisible Man*, a seminal work from 1952, and tell me the second half of the book doesn't feel like it could have easily been a CNN story in the post-Ferguson world.

To get back to baseball: Rollins was part of the Great Shortstop Revolution, playing in an era in which the position was not only stacked around the league, but even within his own division. José Reyes, Hanley Ramírez and Rollins all battled for the title of Top Shortstop in the NL East at same time. That helps to explain Rollins' relatively low All-Star total (3), but even that can't explain how Rollins managed to win the Silver Slugger, Gold Glove, and MVP in 2007 without making the All-Star Game that year. Somewhat incredibly, the strange phenomenon of the eventual MVP not making the All-Star Game has happened 13 times in MLB history, as written about for *Baseball Prospectus* by Ben Lindbergh in 2012. Of those 13, only Rollins collected a Silver Slugger, Gold Glove and MVP in a season in which he didn't make the All-Star Game. If Rollins *had* made the Midsummer Classic, he would have joined some pretty elite company in the Super Quad Squad (season winning MVP, Silver Slugger, Gold Glove and making the All-Star Game), a squad led by the man next to him on this diamond, Mike Schmidt, who pulled off the impressive feat three times (tied for an MLB record with Barry Bonds, of course). Rollins' name also brushes shoulders with Bonds in another interesting, if not a bit random, stat. Rollins had 11 seasons with at least 20 doubles, 20 steals, and 10 home runs, which ties him for second-most (with Bonds) such seasons in baseball history, trailing only a somewhat surprising name that we will actually get to quite soon.

Rollins finally packed up his things and left Philadelphia after the 2014 season when – and stop me if this sounds familiar – the relationship between the Phillies star player and the city soured. Phillies aficionado Michael Baumann wrote an excellent article on Rollins for *Grantland* with the key paragraph summing up the city's relationship with oh so many players: "But in spite of all [Rollins] has accomplished and how much he's wanted to play out the string with the organization that drafted him 18 years ago, there's a significant portion of the fan base that very loudly and very persistently insists on Donovan McNabbing the shit out of him." I hate to keep picking on the Philly fans (really all fans in the Northeastern part of the country are this bad), but the amount of literature on Philadelphia's relationship with their star athletes is truly remarkable.

LF Sherry Magee (1904-1914)

Yet another Phillies great who was unpopular with the home crowd, Philadelphia's disapproval of Magee makes much more sense than Schmidt and Rollins. Magee was a bit of a typical early 20th-century player, in that he was an unfortunate stereotype of his nationality – Magee was a fiery Irishman with a penchant for fighting. In fact, in 1911, he was suspended for 29 games after an altercation with an umpire. It is this altercation for which Magee is best remembered in baseball history, but that is an unfair assessment of the man as a whole. A brief look at that incident is needed to round out his character, but having this incident as his entire legacy ignores so much about Magee as a player and man.

The incident occurred on July 10, 1911, with the Phillies in the middle of a pennant race, only a half game out of first. When Magee was called out on what he thought was a high pitch, he threw his bat and the air and started to storm off. At this point rookie umpire Bill Finneran tossed him from the game. Magee wheeled around and charged the umpire, clocking him in the face and knocking him out cold. Blood was everywhere, and the incident was (understandably) considered a black mark on the game. Magee was handed the longest suspension the sport had seen since 1877, and when he was reinstated after 29 games, the Phillies had fallen out of the pennant race.

If one were to look at this event just on the surface, it's clear why Magee's legacy became tainted. However, there are a few historical footnotes to the story that paint a slightly different picture of Magee and are necessary to fill out the portrait of the event. For one, Bill Finneran was a rookie umpire, and it was well known around the league that he was a jackass who constantly bragged about his fighting prowess. It was said that he often told players he wanted to fight them. Magee also pleaded his case that Finneran called him "a vile name," and this is why he had gone after him. Magee's actions were still entirely unacceptable, but these historical footnotes belong in the story itself instead of on the periphery.

The fact that the Phillies fell out of the pennant race is another fact that often gets brought up in concordance with this story, implying that Magee hurt his team by not being able to control his temper. This is not entirely true. In fact, for the first week and a half, the Phillies actually made up games and took the lead in the NL pennant race. It was a 2-10 swoon in August that ruined their chances at a pennant, and as good a player as Magee was, no player can really be worth more than three or four wins over the 29-game stretch that he missed.[322] Although Magee may have helped keep them in the pennant race a bit longer, they ended the season 19.5 games out of first place.

Finally, and this is not historically based, but rather an opinion, so I'll keep it brief: Magee got really unlucky with how his punch landed. He managed to hit Finneran's jaw and nose, and the result was blood everywhere. Of all the places to hit somebody, the nose has to be the worst place in terms of keeping the hit low profile. The amount of blood, mixed with Magee's reputation, was the perfect mix for a big suspension, one that was harsher than it had to be.

Moving on to Magee as a player, he was one of the most well-rounded players of his generation. He could hit for contact and power, had great wheels, and while not a great outfielder, was also not a burden on his team while playing left field. His best season came in 1910, when he led the league in batting average (.331), on-base percentage (.445), slugging percentage (.507), and OPS+ (174), as well as runs (110), total bases (263), RBI (123), and WAR among position players (6.7). Tack on the fact that he stole 49 bases, and that his RBI total was 35 runs higher than the next highest NL player, and Magee would have surely won the MVP if it had existed then. His batting title was even more impressive given that he topped Honus Wagner, a feat no player had achieved since 1905.

As mentioned earlier, Magee was rather unpopular among the players and fans, but his popularity did increase when he was named captain of the club in 1914. This didn't last long, however, as he was traded before the 1915 season. The final nail in the unfortunate coffin for Magee's legacy was that the Phillies won the pennant the following year, leaving many to think that Magee had been what was holding the Phillies back from the pennant for so many years. This is the ultimate case of Magee not being able to win to save himself. When he was suspended and missed 29 games, it was his fault that the team lost the pennant because he wasn't there. Then, when he left town, it was somehow his fault that they hadn't won a pennant previously because he *was* there. Funny how the fans and media can spin it either way.

---

[322] Unless you're Troy Tulowitzki circa April, 2014.

One final, ironic note on Magee is that he ended his career as an umpire, of all trades. Official shouts to Tom Simon for his article, "Sherry Magee," in the 2001 *Baseball Research Journal*, as well as his SABR bio report on Magee, both of which provided great information for this write-up. In fact, a shout out to the Society for American Baseball Research as a whole. They are an awesome society of baseball nerds who were an unbelievably welcoming group when, as a 23-year-old in a sea of Baby Boomers, I attended my first SABR convention in Philadelphia in 2013. It was an incredibly fulfilling few days, and an annual event I would *highly* recommend to any baseball fan. The only problem with SABR is that they spend more time talking about the 1860s than most Civil War professors, but the new generation of SABRites seems to be balancing that out with an aggressive, modern, statistical push.

CF Richie Ashburn (1948-1959)

Richie Ashburn is one of the most underrated players of all time, and one who had to wait far too long to be enshrined in Cooperstown.[323] Ashburn played with the Phillies for the first 12 years of his career and was a staple at the top of the Phillies lineup throughout the 1950s. In fact, no player had more hits in the 1950s than Richie Ashburn, and he collected every single one of them as a Phillie.

Ashburn and the Phillies kicked off the 1950s in style, with the famous Whiz Kid squad of 1950. The 1950 pennant race has been overshadowed in the collective baseball history by The Shot Heard Round The World that won the pennant the next season, but the 1950 pennant race was a humdinger in and of itself. The young (and all-white, which was noticed by many) Phillies shot out to a fast start, leading the National League for most of the season, before a late slip and a push from the Brooklyn Dodgers led to a pennant-deciding final series between the two teams. The entire season came down to the final game, a game in which the two team's aces, Robin Roberts for Philly and Don Newcombe for Brooklyn, squared off. If the Phillies lost, it would mean an additional three-game playoff for the pennant; a win would give Philly the pennant. The two aces pitched like aces for the first five innings, with neither team able to break through. Finally, the Phillies got on the board in the top of the sixth, as Willie Jones drove in Dick Sisler to take the 1-0 lead. The Dodger response was immediate, however, as their captain, Pee Wee Reese, had the most important of his three hits on the day, taking Roberts deep to the opposite field, clearing the right field fence and tying up the game at 1-1. The score remained the same all the way into the 10th inning, but only thanks to the man we're here to talk about, Richie Ashburn. With no one out in the bottom of the ninth, the Dodgers got men on first and second, and when Duke Snider singled to center, it was all but assumed that he had just hit the walkoff single needed to keep the Dodger season going. Ashburn had been cheating in a bit, though, and he had an absolute cannon to boot. He showed off said cannon by hosing down Cal Abrams at home, and allowing Roberts to dance his way out of trouble and get the game into extra innings. Once in extras, Dick Sisler came up with a three-run home run (which he celebrated in a fashion that would make José Bautista blush), sending the Phillies to their first pennant since 1915.

Where Ashburn, himself, made his name[324] was roaming the great plains of Shibe Park; and by roaming, I mean whizzing and flying around like he had a Nimbus 2000 hidden under his uniform. In fact, Ashburn has as many 500-putout seasons (four) as the rest of all outfielders in baseball history combined. Despite this fact, Ashburn is not always remembered in the same vein as Willie Mays or Tris Speaker in baseball history. Jerry Mathers breaks it down well in his piece, "The Greatest Fielding Outfielder of All," though:

"Speaker is usually the Golden Boy of fielding outfielders, but as Mathers notes, 'Ashburn led in putouts nine times, Speaker seven. Both led in assists three times. Speaker led in errors once, Ashburn never. Ashburn led in chances per game 10 times, Speaker seven. Speaker led in double plays six times to Ashburn's three. Speaker led twice in percentage, Ashburn never.'"

So, although the debate for best-fielding outfielder of all time certainly shouldn't begin and end with Ashburn, it should certainly include him. Surprisingly enough, he is not rated as highly by dWAR as would be thought, which only gives further credence to the fact that dWAR, and fielding statistics as a whole, still have some work to be done.

Ashburn was not just a glove; however, he was an excellent hitter, especially in his role as a leadoff man. Every leadoff man should emphasize getting on base, and Ashburn did that as well as any. He was in the top 10 in the National League in times on base every season from 1949-1958, and he led the league in that category five times in his career. He also led the league in walks four times and won two batting titles. In fact, in 1958, he became the second man ever (only Honus Wagner had done it previously) to lead the league in walks while also winning a batting crown.

He was a player of whom Bill James said was Pete Rose before Pete Rose came around. Ashburn went 110 percent in the field and at the plate. He ran out every ground ball as hard as humanly possible and focused more on getting on base via a single or walk than worrying about power.

Bill James has an incredible story on Ashburn that he uses in his *Historical Abstract* that we'll use to wrap up Ashburn's section:

"One time Ashburn hit a line drive into the stands, striking a young woman in the side of the face and knocking her

---

[323] Anyone who has read Tina Fey's *Bossypants* knows that Don Fey agrees with me on this front.
[324] Literally, there is an entertainment area in center field at the current Phillies stadium named Ashburn Alley. This name also spawned the excellent blog run by Michael Baumann named *Crashburn Alley*, which, naturally, covered the Phillies.

unconscious. The stadium gasped, Ashburn stepped out of the box and watched in alarm as medics rushed to her side. In a few minutes the woman revived, the stretcher came, and the ballgame resumed. And Ashburn hit another line drive foul, and struck the poor woman again as she was being carried out of the stadium.

Ashburn visited the woman in the hospital after the game, invited her to come down and meet the players, befriended her and her family, and corresponded with the woman for the rest of his life."

RF Chuck Klein (1928-1933; 1936-1939; 1940-1944) vs. Bobby Abreu (1998-2006)

You know the deal by now.

Contact

	BA	lgBA	Seasons ≥ .300	Career high/low	Seasons ≥ 80 SO	SO %	lgSO%	BABIP	Misc.
Abreu	.303	.270	6	.335/.277	9	18.3	17.3	.352	
Klein	.326	.295	7	.386/.218	0	7.1	8.5	.319	LL 2x H, 1x BA

Both players hit at around 30 points above the league average during their days in Philadelphia. Klein played in an era with far fewer strikeouts in the game but was still able to strike out less than the league average; Abreu came in just higher than the league-average strikeout rate.

Hitting in the Baker Bowl for half his games each season he was in Philadelphia undoubtedly helped Klein's numbers. In fact, for his career, he hit .395 in the Baker Bowl (OPS of 1.153), even with some of his late-career struggles. Abreu, on the other hand, managed to have a borderline insane .352 batting average on balls in play for his nine years in Philly. He had two seasons with a BABIP over .390, and he never had a BABIP below .324 in a season with the Phillies.

Trying to figure out which of these factors benefited each Philly left fielder more is certainly an interesting debate. Both factors could somewhat (emphasis: *somewhat*) be related to skill, in addition to luck. For Klein, he undoubtedly learned the nuances of the Baker Bowl and used them to his utmost advantage. From 1929-1933, Klein posted five consecutive 200-hit seasons, the first NL player ever to do so. Of course, put him in Dodger Stadium in 1968, which you can actually do with Baseball-Reference's Neutralized Batting tool, and those numbers deflate faster than a Tom Brady football. Klein wouldn't have topped 188 hits, 32 home runs, or a .320 batting average in any of those seasons, with that .320 average being the only season in which he would have hit better than .300 in his entire career, *per the B-Ref Neutralized Batting tool*. Of course, this Neutralized Batting tool isn't perfect, but it does shed a light on just how much stadium and era matter when comparing players.

For Abreu's part, there is an increasing feel among baseball analysts that batting average on balls in play is a statistic somewhat in control of the batter (and pitcher). Hitters with incredible bat control, and an ability to hit the ball to all parts of the field, end up among the BABIP leaderboards year-after-year, an accomplishment which would not be achievable if the stat were entirely luck-based. Abreu's line drive rates were consistently above 20 percent, and they were often among the league leaders. Bat control, as an ability, seems a more impressive feat than mastering a home stadium, giving Abreu the advantage.

EDGE: Abreu

Power

	HR	Seasons ≥ 20 HR	Career high HR	XBH	SLG%	lgSLG%	ISO	HR%	XBH%	Misc.
Abreu	195	7	31	585	.513	.435	.209	3.3	9.9	LL 1x 2B
Klein	243	6	43	643	.553	.422	.228	4.2	11.1	LL 4x HR, TB, 3x SLG, R, 2x 2B, RBI, OPS, 1x OPS+

In terms of raw power, Klein would certainly look to have Abreu beat. He was a perpetual threat to lead to league in home runs but, once again, benefited greatly from playing in the Baker Bowl. His career slugging percentage at the Baker Bowl was .705; at no other stadium was it higher than .553. Abreu benefited from the era in which he played, but not as much as Klein benefited from the Baker Bowl. Just like in the contact category, despite the edge Klein got from the Baker Bowl, he did have some outstanding numbers.

During his five-year uber-prime, he led the league in home runs four of five years. In 1929, he set the NL record for home runs in a season, with 43 home runs (only to see that record broken the next season). The only year in that prime that he didn't lead the league in home runs, Klein had to settle for setting the NL record for extra-base hits (107). Klein was able to capture the fifth Triple Crown of the modern era in 1933 and became one of six players ever to win the Triple Crown and lead the league in on-base percentage and slugging percentage as well. Maybe the craziest part of playing in Klein's era is that, in 1930, he posted 40 home runs, 170 RBI, and a .386 batting average – and he didn't even lead the league in any of those categories. In fact, he didn't even really come close in any of them. Hack Wilson hit 56 home runs and drove in 191 runs; while Bill Terry became the most recent NL hitter to post a .400 average, hitting .401 that season. During his second stint in Philadelphia, Klein became the first NL player to hit four home runs in a single game.

(A quick shoutout to Gavvy Cravath, a Phillies left fielder who wasn't quite on par with these two, but deserves a shoutout in the power category, as he was the home run king before Babe Ruth came along. Although that's a bit like being the best ice cream company before Ben & Jerry's.)

All things being equal, Klein had better power in his prime, but Abreu's power lasted longer. Throw in Abreu's home run derby title, showing the power he was capable of, and this one gets even closer, but still not close enough.

EDGE: Klein

Batting eye

	BB	Seasons ≥ 80 BB	OBP	lgOBP	OPS+	BB%	SO/BB	Misc.
Abreu	947	9	.416	.343	139	16.1	1.14	
Klein	471	0	.382	.355	139	8.2	0.87	LL 1x OBP

Abreu both walked and struck out more than Klein in his time with the Phillies. This was due in part to the different eras in which they played, but also due in part to their styles. Abreu was always one of the most patient hitters in all of baseball, almost to a fault at times. Klein, on the other hand, was aggressive, trying to attack the pitcher early in the at bat. Notice the tie in OPS+ that supports just how close these two men were at the plate. Back to the category at hand, however, and this is the first easy category so far.

EDGE: Abreu

Speed

	SB	Seasons ≥ 25 SB	Career high SB	Rbaser	SB%	XBT%	GDP%	Misc.
Abreu	254	6	40	16	76	46	7	LL 2x PwrSpd, 1x 3B, 2x 30/30
Klein	71	0	20	-2	N/A	N/A	N/A	LL 1x SB

A lot of the metrics to measure speed don't date back as far as Klein's era (as we have seen in many of these cross-generational breakdowns), but it seems clear that Abreu's sneaky speed is enough to take this category. Abreu had the best sneaky speed of his generation, never looking like a base runner, while simultaneously putting up strong stolen base totals. It should be noted that in 1932, Klein led the league in home runs and steals, the most recent player to do so, but he totaled only 20 steals, as the game had swung away from the stolen-base-oriented league it had been just a few years before.

EDGE: Abreu

Defense

	Fld%	lgFld%	dWAR	Assists	GG	Misc.
Abreu	.983	.980	-1.9	89	1	LL 3X GP (RF) 2X Assists (RF) 1X PO (RF), DP (RF), TZR (RF), RF/G (RF)
Klein	.966	.971	-10.7	170	N/A	LL 4X E (RF) 3X DP (RF), Assists (RF) 2X GP (RF) 1X PO (RF)

Klein's strengths and weaknesses as an outfielder are shown quite well above. (Even though his fielding stats in Philadelphia specifically were a beast to put together because of the fact that Baseball-Reference doesn't break down fielding stats by team. Therefore, the league fielding numbers include a bit of guesswork, but close enough to tell the story.) Klein had one of the best arms in the game, but he was prone to mistakes. Klein's arm was so good, in fact, that he set a modern-day MLB record (post-1901) with 44 assists in 1930, a record that still stands. Klein attributed this success to his coach simply telling him to not hold on to the ball as long. You'd think he might have figured that one out on his own… As for

Abreu, he was incredibly solid, while never mind-blowing. He was consistent in all aspects, with a plus arm. Basically, he was the opposite of Klein. For my money, when it comes to defense, I want a guy who isn't going to lose me the game, instead of a guy who could win me the game. I'm going safe.

EDGE: Abreu

Team Success

	W	L	T	W-L%	Seasons ≥ 80 W	Division titles	Pennants	WS
Abreu	672	681	0	.497	5	0	0	0
Klein	512	885	7	.366	0	0	0	0

Unfortunately for Abreu, the Phillies long string of success came right *after* he left town. They reached the cusp of success with Bobby, finishing in second in each of his final two and a half seasons with the team, right before rattling off five straight division titles, two pennants, and one World Series victory in the first five years after he left. Adding insult to injury, the Yankees also went on the win a World Series title right after Abreu's departure from New York, and for his career, Abreu never won a pennant. Clearly this is not an indictment of Abreu as a player, but simply a statement to make you feel bad for him.

Klein's Phillies were notoriously dreadful, not even sniffing a pennant in his entire time there. The club finished at least 12 games back every season, often far more than that. They were often in the cellar, and their incredible lack of run prevention was already covered in the team write-up at the beginning of the chapter.

Although Abreu might have had bad luck in terms of timing his exit from Philadelphia, his Phillies teams were vastly superior to Klein's.

EDGE: Abreu-era Phillies

Klein's "De-Klein..."

For Klein, consistency was his downfall, as his career sputtered after his aforementioned dominant five-year stretch (1929-1933). As bright as Klein's star shone those five years, it exploded immediately after. When Klein was traded to Chicago to ply his trade for the Cubs, he would never be worth more than 3.4 wins in a season, after averaging more than 6.0 WAR/season in his Philadelphia prime. Those five prime years ended up being 70 percent of his career value, per WAR. Klein spent only two and a quarter seasons in Chicago before being moved back to Philadelphia, but he was never the same after 1933. Some folks say the reason for Klein's drop-off was the move away from the friendly confines of the Baker Bowl, while others have noted that his health deteriorated, starting in 1934. Although Klein certainly missed more games after 1933, his production also dropped in terms of his averages, not just in terms of accumulation, so one has to wonder whether the stadium change did indeed have a big impact.

One of the proponents of the injury theory was his Chicago teammate, Billy Herman, who said, "Klein got off to a great start with us after we got him from the Phillies, but then he pulled a hamstring muscle. He was a hell of a competitor, but he was just tearing up that leg. The blood started to clog in it, and I swear, the leg turned black." Time to do a little fact-checking. If Klein did indeed start 1934 as productive as his Philadelphia days, it might be fair to say that it was the injuries that did him in, and that he wasn't just a product of his home stadium. And what do you know? In the first half of the 1934 season, Klein slashed .317/.388/.589 and was on pace for 126 runs, 38 home runs, and 130 RBI, numbers right in line with his best seasons in Philadelphia. However, Klein got injured in the second half of the season, and after he returned from injury, he played just 22 games, slashing .176/.256/.230 with just one home run. Now there was some decline between those two events, as he failed to hit a home run in the 16 games in the second half of the season before his injury, but at the same time, he still managed to hit .385 during that stretch. Although the Baker Bowl certainly helped Klein's numbers a bit, it seems like ignoring his leg injury in Chicago would be missing the complete picture.

One final note: the above quote from Herman was taken from *The Man Who Stole First Base*, whose authors agree, adding that Klein was also under enormous pressure in Chicago, having come to town with a huge contract and not wanting to let down his new team by missing time. With all of these factors taken together, referring to Klein as a hitter who simply took advantage of the Baker Bowl seems unfair in retrospect, and his legacy needs to be adjusted likewise.

Verdict

This is a real close matchup. I mean, as was noted, the two had the exact same OPS+ (139) while in Philadelphia. Of course, these two men are also right next to each other as fourth and fifth-most overrated right fielders of all time in *The Stark Truth*, Jayson Stark's book on the most overrated and underrated players of all time, so maybe I know nothing at all. Still, I doubt Phillie fans would be upset with either of these guys manning left field. I'm going with **Bobby Abreu**. We just saw there were layers to Klein's decline, and I typically hate holding a stadium advantage against a player; it's not as if there was anything that player could have done differently to change it. What do we want Klein to have done? Politely asked the team owners to give him a bit more of a challenge by pushing back the walls? C'mon. Still, Abreu was the actual better player, with consistency as his calling card. In fact, with his 12 seasons of 20 doubles, 20 steals, and 10 home runs, Abreu is the mystery man mentioned briefly in Jimmy Rollins write-up with the most such seasons in MLB history. Abreu had seven and a half of those seasons in Philadelphia, and he played more than 150 games in each of his eight non-trade seasons in Philly. No one had more plate appearances in the 2000s than Abreu, and in that same decade, he became just the fourth hitter (Hornsby in the `20s, Gehringer in the `30s and Helton in the `00s) to reach 400 doubles in one decade.

Abreu also played in a more recent era, while Klein played before the sport was even integrated. In a matchup this close, that has to count for something. Plus, as has been noted, these teams are starting to skew towards older players, so getting a player that anyone under the age of 70 has heard of is never a bad idea.

Utility Ed Delahanty (1888-1889; 1891-1901)

Delahanty was one of the larger-than-life figures from the early days of baseball, one whose personality reads like a character out of a book. He was one of five Delahanty brothers to play Major League Baseball and was by far the most successful. Only Mike Schmidt and Chase Utley tallied more wins above replacement among Phillies positional players in a career than "Big Ed." Because of his ability as an all-around hitter, and the fact that he played so early in the history of baseball, Delahanty has a lot of firsts attached to his name. He was the first player to win a batting title in both the American League and National League. He was the first player to hit .400 three times, and he was part of the Philadelphia outfield that all hit at least .400 in 1894. This outfield consisted of Delahanty, "Sliding Billy Hamilton," and Sam Thompson. The team actually had a fourth outfielder, Tuck Turner, who hit over .400 in 82 games that season, giving them four outfielders with an average over .400, a feat that will surely never be matched again. Billy Hamilton was a great player in his own right; nearly missing out on the utility spot Delahanty has filled here. Back to Delahanty, though, he was the second player ever to hit four home runs in a game, and when he arrived at home plate that game, the opposing pitcher was waiting there to shake his hand. Delahanty also once went 9-for-9 in a double-header.

Delahanty is considered the first bad-ball hitter in baseball history, according to SABR's *Baseball First Stars*. This isn't to imply that he couldn't take a walk, but more so that he could hit anything in sight. Remember, batters got to choose where they wanted the pitch during baseball's nascent stages, so a hitter being able to hit balls in the dirt and at the eyes wasn't something too common in Delahanty's day. Delahanty once hit a ball so hard it broke into pieces, although given the quality of baseballs they played with back then, that feat may not be as impressive as it sounds to modern fans.

Unfortunately, the most intriguing story about Delahanty comes off the field and, in fact, deals with his death. Big Ed was one of a great number of early stars who came to a premature demise. His is a rather mysterious story, with all the facts never fully discovered, and the narrative surrounding it sounding like Hitchcock-gone-wrong. At the age of 35, definitely still in his playing years, Delahanty went missing for a week, until his body was discovered at the bottom of Niagara Falls. The story that came out – but was never set in stone due to a lack of facts – was that a man fitting Big Ed's description was kicked off his train for drunkenly waving a knife around. Later that night, at a nearby bridge, another man (possibly the same man, but neither was properly identified) was trying to cross the bridge, but he was turned around by the night watchmen after a brief argument. A week later, Delahanty was found at the bottom of Niagara Falls. One distinct possibility is that the night watchmen knocked Big Ed off of the bridge, but Delahanty's valuables had been taken off his person, so the possibility of him having been mugged and then pushed off the bridge by a stranger were also high. This story, and the hypotheses on his demise, are the work of Eric Nadel and Craig R. Wright in their book, *The Man Who Stole First Base*. A great source for this book and an excellent read for any curious baseball fan.

SP Pete Alexander (1911-1917; 1930)

Another trope that has shown up with many of these older players – who are becoming more and more common in these later pages – is a struggle with alcohol. Pete Alexander was one of many early baseball players who battled alcoholism, particularly at the end of his career. In fact, Bill Veeck once said, "Grover Cleveland Alexander drunk was a better pitcher than Grover Cleveland Alexander sober." In many ways, Alexander best epitomized the early 20th century baseball player, and his struggles with alcohol were an unfortunate part of that.

Alexander started his career with the Phillies, and man what a start to his career he had. As a rookie, he won 28 games, a rookie record that still stands and will likely never be broken. He kept going strong, and in the final three years of his first stint in Philadelphia, he won 94 games, with at least 30 wins in each season. He also won the ERA crown each of those three years, which is extra-impressive considering he pitched his home games in the Baker Bowl. In fact, for the only two years of this first stint that Baseball-Reference has for his splits (1916-1917), Alexander threw better at home than on the road. At first this might not make sense, seeing as the Baker Bowl was known for producing some of the highest home run totals in the league, but remember, Alexander pitched before the "home run boom" of the 1920s and `30s. The Baker Bowl was still a haven for home runs, as Gavvy Cravath can attest to, but those numbers were significantly lower than to be considered devastating to a pitcher. For all his time in Philadelphia, Alexander allowed only 0.2 home runs per nine innings, and he gave up more than 10 home runs in a season only once. That was in 1912, and his 11 home runs allowed led the league that season. Pitchers in Alexander's day had to worry much more about keeping runners off base, and Alexander did this as well as any pitcher in his time. He led the league in fewest hits per nine innings, as well as WHIP, two times apiece, and he worked to improve his walk rates as his career progressed.

One way in which Alexander distinguished himself was as a total workhorse. In an era of pitchers regularly going the distance, Alexander still stood out. He threw over 300.0 innings each of his seven original years in Philadelphia, and he averaged 356.0 innings per season over that time. Unsurprisingly, he led the league in innings pitched six of those seven years, finishing third in 1913. For that same seven-year stretch of time, he threw 219 complete games, or just three less than Nolan Ryan had in his career, and more than five times any active player. The highest amount of complete games that Alexander had in a season was 38 in 1916, more than pitchers get total starts in a season today. That same season, Alexander set the MLB record with 16 shutouts.[325] To put in perspective how different today's game is, those 38 complete games would be equal to the 2013 totals for the entire pitching staff of the Colorado Rockies… and the Braves, and the Marlins, and the entire AL Central, and the league-leading (per complete games) Rays, and the Giants, and the Astros, and the Orioles. *Combined.* Yeah, it's a different world.

On two separate occasions in his career, Pete Alexander threw a complete doubleheader. That is exactly what it sounds like – he threw a complete game in the first game of a doubleheader, and then he went out and threw another complete game that same day. In other words, he had the same number of complete games in one day that Stephen Strasburg has in his career to date. By the way, he won all four of the games in those two complete doubleheaders. The only other pitcher in MLB history to throw more than one complete doubleheader was Joe McGinnity, a man who was literally nicknamed "Iron Man."

Alexander was shipped out of Philadelphia after the 1917 season because the team feared that he would be drafted for WWI (classy). He did serve briefly, but he still managed to have 11 more winning seasons as a pitcher, giving him 19 winning seasons for his career, the most in baseball history. However, he was never quite as dominant after he left Philadelphia. His epilepsy got worse after the war, and his drinking increased the more he suffered from epilepsy. In one of baseball's saddest stories, his life splintered, and along with it, so did Alexander's happiness. He did have a few more stellar moments in his career (the 1926 World Series with the Cardinals was a definite highlight, especially his Game 7 relief appearance[326]), however, even for those moments, his sobriety was usually in question. His sad story culminated at his Hall of Fame induction, at which point he was flat broke and took the moment to comment on the fact that his Hall of Fame plaque didn't feed him. He was a bitter man, particularly at Major League Baseball, an organization which he felt abandoned its players after their playing days, leaving them penniless.[327] He was offered a job with the Hall of Fame, but he declined.

Although Alexander's story is a sad one, he was still one of the greatest pitchers of all time, so let's end on a more positive note: Alexander was actually born Grover Cleveland Alexander, named so after the President at the time of his birth. He was also portrayed by Ronald Reagan in the 1952 film, *The Winning Team.* This makes him the only baseball player to be named after one U.S. President and played by another on film.

CP Steve Carlton (1972-1986)

Despite the team's lack of success for much of franchise history, the Phillies have two of the best front-end starters in baseball history. (We're not even going to get to Robin Roberts, the franchise leader in pitching WAR.) With Alexander taking the starting role, you'd be hard-pressed to find a more devastating pitcher to take the helm at the end of a game than Carlton. Despite being a starter, Carlton would certainly suffice as the closer of this imaginary roster. His fastball/slider combination would be nearly impossible for hitters to figure out when facing him out of the bullpen. According to Rob Neyer and Bill James, Steve Carlton owned the best slider of all time, and they are not alone in that opinion. Willie Stargell said of Sandy Koufax first, and later of Carlton, "Hitting against Steve Carlton is like eating soup with a fork." In fact, when Carlton pitched, his teammates called it "Win Day," which would be perfect for our newly-transformed Phillies closer.

Carlton was a good pitcher before he came to Philadelphia, winning 20 games in his final season in St. Louis, before the Phillies cashed in one of their young pitchers (Rick Wise) for arguably one of the top five left-handed pitchers of all time in Carlton. As the story goes, both the Cardinals and Phillies didn't want to pay their respective starters (Carlton and Wise)

[325] Technically he tied George Bradley's total from 1876, but some dude threw 79 complete games in a season during those early years, and pitchers weren't throwing from the same distance at that point. Alexander's 16 shutouts seem the correct record to honor.

[326] We'll keep it to a footnote since it was during Alexander's time with the Cardinals, but James R. Harrison's epic description of the 39-year-old Alexander entering Game 7 as a reliever deserves to be here:

"The Cardinals were going to try a new pitcher. Forty thousand pairs of eyes peered anxiously through the gray mist toward the bullpen out in deep left. There was a breathless pause, and then around the corner of the stand came a tall figure in a Cardinals sweater. His cap rode rakishly on the corner of his head. He walked like a man who was going nowhere in particular and was in no hurry to get there. He was a trifle knock-kneed and his gait was not a model of grace and rhythm. Any baseball fan would have known him a mile away. It was Grover Cleveland Alexander. Alexander the Great was coming in to pull the Cardinal machine out of the mudhole. The ancient twirler who had gone nine full innings the day before, was shuffling in where younger men feared to tread."

[327] How long until we see a similar speech at a Hall of Fame acceptance speech in Canton?

$65,000, the price each pitcher was asking. However, both teams were willing to pay that figure for the other team's pitcher, so the swap was made, with Wise being the happier of the two at the time. Well, the Phillies would go on to be the far happier team, as they straight fleeced the Cardinals with our historical, 20/20 hindsight glasses on.

Carlton went on to throw three 20-win, 200-strikeout seasons with the Phillies,[328] making him one of four left-handed pitchers to do so in baseball history, along with Rube Waddell (who had four), Sandy Koufax, and Randy Johnson. In the last decade, four southpaws have achieved these numbers at least once – David Price and Gio González in 2012, Dallas Keuchel in 2015 – with Clayton Kershaw the closest to joining the ranks, with two such seasons (2011 and 2014) already. It will be interesting to see if any current left-handers can join the four others in the elite company of the three-time 20-win/200-strikeout lefties. Kershaw would certainly seem to be the prohibitive favorite. A couple long shots that could potentially challenge this mark might be Madison Bumgarner and Jon Lester. One way we know Lester won't be catching Carlton is in pickoffs, where Carlton is the all-time leader dating back to the statistic's origin around WWII. In fact, Carlton (146) has nearly 50 percent more pickoffs in his career than the next highest man, Mark Buehrle (100).

Carlton's best season was undoubtedly his 1972 campaign, his first in Philadelphia. He collected 27 of the Phillies 59 wins, one of the highest percentage of a team's wins by a starting pitcher in MLB history. He also managed to slash .197/.236/.265 as a hitter, meaning that the line he allowed to opposing hitters (.207/.257/.291) was only a hair higher than what he, a full-time pitcher, was able to do at the plate. Carlton won the pitching Triple Crown, leading the league in wins (27), ERA (1.97), and strikeouts (310), as well as games started (41), complete games (30), innings pitched (346.1), ERA+ (182), and strikeout to walk ratio (3.56). It was an incredible year for Carlton's debut in the City of Brotherly Love.

Despite all his success with the franchise, Carlton was yet another Phillie who froze out the local media because of their treatment of his personal life. In fact, he had a 15-year media hiatus. It's easy to pick on Philadelphia (especially the city's sports fans), but to imply it was entirely their fault leaves out a very important part of the equation: Carlton was (and is) a Class-A kook. When Carlton broke his media silence six years after his retirement, the interview (with Pat Jordan of *Philadelphia Magazine*) became maybe the most "must read" athlete profiles of all time. Carlton had always been thought of as a dude who marched to the beat of his own drum – the man had a $15,000 "mood behavior" room built for him in Philadelphia – but this was next level. Here are some quotes with brief analysis from the article, which you should be immediately firing up in your internet browser, by the way:

"I like it here because the people are spiritually tuned in." Ok that's reasonable, maybe a little bit hippy-dippy-ish, but nothing too extraordinary. The fact that he moved to Durango, Colorado, a town 6,506 feet above sea level where the air is so thin that residents are often light-headed, moves to kook factor up a bit, but we're only getting started.

"The Revolution is definitely coming." Even Carlton wasn't exactly sure what he meant by this, as he went on to make a couple of vaguely racist comments right after.

"I don't miss baseball. I never look back. You turn the page. Eternity lies in the here and now. If you live in the past, you accelerate the death process. Your being is your substance." You're losing me a bit here, Steve.

"Fear makes our own prisons. It's instilled in us by our government and the Church. They control fear. It's the Great Lie. But don't get me started on that." Yes, we'd hate for you to come across strange here.

"I'm waiting for the coldness to come out of the walls." Ok, that one kind of made sense in context, but it definitely looks funny out of context, so let's roll with it.

"The mind is the conscious architect of your success. What you hold consciously in your mind becomes your reality." In some cases more than others.

"Do you know if you store guns in PVC pipe, they can last forever underground without rusting?" Ok, maybe not every quote needs commenting on…

"Don't tell me that two plus two equals four. How do you know that two is two? That's the real question." You know, in comparison to some of the other quotes, this one ain't half bad.

"Things creep into your mind. Your mind is always chattering." Aaaaand we're back.

"I never know what time it is, or what day it is. Time is stress. Pressure melts away if you don't deal with time. I don't believe in birthdays, either." Let's tap out there.

Carlton also espoused beliefs that President Clinton was covering up for a black son and lesbian wife; that the government was spreading viruses to kill off "gays and blacks"; that all citizens should be able to walk around fully armed; and that the *Manchurian Candidate* style of hypnotized killing for the government happened in real life. He basically sounded like Tracy Jordan in the "30 Rock" premiere: "Affirmative action was designed to keep women and minorities in competition with each other to distract us while white dudes inject AIDS into our chicken nuggets. That's a metaphor."

Given the history of quirky dudes thriving in the bullpen, putting Carlton as the Phillies closer on their Starting IX looks like the best decision in this book.

---

[328] And he missed by only five strikeouts in 1976 and two strikeouts in 1977. He also would have likely achieved those figures in the strike-shortened 1981 season when he had 13 wins and 179 strikeouts in 14 fewer starts than he was typically getting per season.

Starting IX Franchise Roster Stats

Lineup	Yrs	G	R	H	HR	RBI	SB	BB	SO	BA	OBP	SLG	OPS+	dWAR	WAR
Richie Ashburn	12	1794	1114	2217	22	499	199	946	455	0.311	0.394	0.388	111	7.9	57.4
Ed Delahanty	13	1557	1368	2214	87	1288	411	643	384	0.348	0.414	0.508	153	-3.9	60.9
Chase Utley	13	1551	949	1623	233	916	142	625	958	0.282	0.366	0.481	122	17.0	61.5
Mike Schmidt	**18**	**2404**	**1506**	2234	**548**	**1595**	174	**1507**	**1883**	0.267	0.380	0.527	147	**17.6**	**106.5**
Dick Allen	9	1070	697	1143	204	655	86	517	1023	0.290	0.371	0.530	153	-9.7	35.4
Bobby Abreu	9	1353	891	1474	195	814	254	947	1078	0.303	0.416	0.513	139	-1.9	47.0
Sherry Magee	11	1521	898	1647	75	886	387	546	466	0.299	0.371	0.447	143	-6.8	47.8
Jimmy Rollins	15	2090	1325	**2306**	216	887	453	753	1145	0.267	0.327	0.424	97	13.9	46.1
Jack Clements	14	1000	536	1079	70	636	54	308	304	0.289	0.352	0.426	118	9.1	29.0
Pitchers	Yrs	W	W%	ERA	G	CG	SHO	SV	IP	SO	ERA+	WHIP	SO/9	SO/BB	WAR
Pete Alexander	8	190	**0.676**	2.18	338	219	**61**	15	2513.2	1409	140	1.075	5.0	2.51	60.3
Steve Carlton	15	**241**	0.600	3.09	185	39	0	0	3697.1	**3031**	120	1.211	7.4	2.42	64.6

Tier Five: (Nearly) Best of the Best

We're getting there. Now we're at the teams who have not only been around for a long time, but they've had some serious success within their team history. They have had all-time legends pass through their locker rooms, and they've held onto that talent (for the most part). There are a few weak spots here and there, but those flaws almost add to their loveable nature. These teams are, like, the most real, man.

#9 Pittsburgh Pirates (1891-pres.); Pittsburgh Alleghenys (1882-1890)

(Photo from Good Free Photos)

Team Background

Playoff appearances: 17 **Pennants: 9** **World Series titles: 5**
Collective team WAR: 604.3
Strengths: The outfield depth is among the most even and high-quality in baseball history. In fact, their position players as a whole are incredibly strong.
Weaknesses: So, can you pass the fourth-grade reading comprehension test on what the weakness of the Pirates is? It's their pitching, and their starting pitching in particular. In fact, if they had a starter on par with the other teams in this tier, the Pirates would likely have a top-five Starting IX.
What to expect from the next 16 pages: A completely subjective ranking of the coolest team in baseball. Also, The Great Pittsburgh Outfield Shit Show.

The Pirates have to be one of baseball's coolest teams – both presently and historically. They have one of the coolest team names, some of the best logos in baseball history, numerous talented and entertaining players in their history, an amazing stadium, a great city in which they play, and success but not to the point of gluttony.

This begs the question of whether any baseball team can truly compare to the Pirates' level of cool, so let's do this dance. The easiest team to eliminate has to be the Yankees. They have way too many bandwagon fans, and even the real fans are usually dicks. They've had far too much success to be considered cool anymore, and the whole "no facial hair" thing sucks. The Los Angeles Dodgers joined the Yankees in the least-cool baseball teams with their recent gluttonous payrolls, and plus: any team playing in Los Angeles can be only so cool. (The Clippers were probably the ceiling for an L.A. team, and even they wore out their welcome after a couple good seasons.) The Marlins could be cool thanks to their constant young talent, but the fact that everyone knows the talent won't be there in a few years puts a cap on the coolness of the Miguel Cabrera and Giancarlo Stanton types. Toronto doesn't even play in the United States of America – next. The White Sox will never be Chicago's team, and the years they trotted out those Paul Konerko and Adam Dunn-filled lineups were just too ugly to ignore. Speaking of the Chicago, the Cubs are currently auctioning off the very back row of their bandwagon for approximately the price of one T206 Honus Wagner card. The same goes for the Royals who only recently got their crap together and have spit in the face of analytics for far too long.

The Braves have a large fanbase all around the country thanks to Ted Turner, and their pitching staff of the '90s perfected the win-enough-to-be-cool-but-not-too-much-for-the-public-to-get-sick-of-you model, but their mascot is more than vaguely racist, and that stupid tomahawk chant is the stuff of nightmares. The Rockies play in an incredible stadium in a fun town and have lots of offense to boot, but until they have a team that epitomizes cool as well as the "We Are Family" 1979 Pirates, they'll be just off the pace. The Red Sox actually had a decent case for this honor until they came closer into the spotlight and everyone realized the asshats that compose Red Sox Nation. Have you ever listened to Boston sports talk radio? I'm pretty sure it's what they use for torture at Guantanamo Bay. The Nationals should still be the Expos, and nothing from Texas is really *that* cool – sorry Rangers and Astros. The Mets suffer from the same disease as the White Sox, and the whole Ponzi scheme thing is not exactly a stunt that a fly franchise would pull.

Admit it, you completely forgot about Cleveland, Cincinnati, Minnesota, and San Diego until just now – so did their fans. The Diamondbacks perpetually have a crazy front office, their championship in 2001 was as exciting as it gets, and they even have a swimming pool in center field. However, they lack the history of the Pirates for now. The Cardinals epitomize the way baseball ought to be played – said every Cardinals fan ever. The Phillies don't even stand a chance within their own state. The Angels suffer from the disease of Los Angeles, and although Trout is awesome, those big contracts they handed out for Josh Hamilton and Albert Pujols are big black marks.

That leaves the Pirates, Rays, A's, Giants, Brewers, Orioles, Mariners, and Tigers. Any of these choices would be acceptable, but to find the truly coolest franchise, the quest must continue. Every franchise has its black marks, but Ty Cobb is the likely the most notorious of the bunch, sorry Detroit. The O's have a petulant man-child running the team who can't figure out what he wants to do with the franchise. The Brewers and Mariners were both definite candidates for "you forgot about these teams didn't you," as well as never having won anything. The A's and Rays have made a living on succeeding despite penny-pinching tactics, but their exploits have been covered ad nauseam, and thus they have lost their hipster chic. The A's bay area partners, the Giants, are an awesome team with a great stadium, but people living in the Bay Area already get enough.

So now that I have pissed off the other 29 fanbases, it is decided, the Pirates are the coolest franchise… when the person deciding truly wants them to be.

Random cool things about the franchise that make it the coolest:

- Andrew McCutchen.
- Their old-school logos, seriously, go google their old-school logos.
- While you're on google, look up "Jason Grilli + grilled cheese," I swear it's not a trap.
- They got their "Pirate" name when they supposedly "pirated" a player from the Philadelphia A's in 1891.
- Their Starting IX has a decidedly old-school vibe to it.
- The sport's renaissance among black citizens in Pittsburgh during the 1930s was the baseball equivalent to Harlem for art, and the Homestead Grays were a national treasure.
- We. Are. Fam-a-leeee. The 1979 Pirates took the Sister Sledge classic to its extreme, embodying the classic song on their way to a World Series victory.
- The incredibly aesthetic Roberto Clemente bridge behind PNC Park.
- Andrew McCutchen's mom: National Anthem singer.
- Michael Keaton is a fan? You're right, let's just skip that one.
- Bing Crosby owned the team for a bit? Is that better?
- How about their retro, pillbox hats from the 1970s? There we go, that's a winner.
- They had Barry Bonds when he was cool.
- In 1971, they made history with the first-ever all-minority lineup.
- They were the first MLB team to be owned by a gay owner, although he came out after selling his shares.
- They were the first team to sign an Indian player (from the actual country of India, not the mistaken-identity natives to the U.S.).
- Are you sensing a theme here? They're an incredibly inclusive organization and have been at the forefront of just about every progressive movement in the sport. They are deserving of the coolest franchise label.

Starting IX

C Jason Kendall (1996-2004)

Jason Kendall is a snowflake. A beautifully unique man both on the field and off it. This is a man who redefined what catchers could do, batting over .300 in his nine seasons with Pittsburgh and stealing 140 bases along the way. His statistical profile was that of a second baseman, not a catcher. He had more steals than home runs in every single season of his career except one, and, even that season, he had the same total. He was a catcher who hit leadoff, and he paved the way for catchers like Joe Mauer and Russell Martin. Mauer went on to become the first catcher to win a batting title in the American League, and Martin was a backstop who stole 21 bases in 2007.

Kendall was also a pretty unique dude off the field. He told *Sports Illustrated* that if he wasn't playing baseball, he'd be living the life of Mitch Buchannon, the main character on *Baywatch*. He was also never one to shy away from saying what he thought, often in the most abrasive way possible. When he was told in 1999 that Pittsburgh hoped to be competing for a championship in 2001, the season PNC Park was due to be opened, Kendall responded, "F--- that. F--- 2001. I want to win now. Who cares about 2001? The world could blow up in two years. We could all be dead by then."

Somewhat ironically, Kendall named his book: *Throwback: A Big-League Catcher Tells How the Game Is Really Played.* Ironic in the sense that he was about as much of a throwback catcher as *Orange is the New Black* is a throwback TV show. Of course, his interesting choice in title didn't stop him from keeping up that elite-level abrasive tone. As Miles Wray pointed out in his excellent review of Kendall's book on *Baseball Prospectus* (in fact, just read Wray's review, not the book, unless you're reading the book for some strong unintentional comedy and reinforced baseball stereotypes), Kendall really stuck it to the analytical folks with this gem of a sentence: "There's no such thing as framing; anybody who says there is can go screw himself." Well, that seems uncalled for.

1B Willie Stargell (1962-1982)

"Pops" Stargell was one of the most iconic players in baseball history. First and foremost, he was an outstanding hitter with prodigious power. His home run totals were greatly slowed by the fact that, up until 1971, he played his home games in spacious Forbes Field, and it's not shocking that he led the league in home runs two of the first three years after he escaped Forbes. If he had played his prime in Three Rivers Stadium (where the Pirates moved in 1972), his 475 career home runs would have reached 500, and he may well have approached 600. Heck, put him on the 2000 Rockies each year, and according to Baseball-Reference's Neutralized Batting, he would have hit 627 career home runs. It's no surprise that no player in the 1970s hit more home runs than Stargell (296), though it is certainly impressive given the fact that he reached his 30th birthday before the 1970 season even started.

Stargell didn't let Forbes Field get the best of him, however. In the 62 years that Forbes served as the home of the Pittsburgh Pirates, only 18 balls were ever hit entirely out of the stadium. Incredibly, seven of those home runs belong to Willie Stargell and his immense power. He also hit the first two home runs to ever leave Dodger Stadium, a feat made more impressive given that the Dodgers weren't even in his division. Stargell also hit the first home run out of Jerry Park in Montreal, and he became such a popular player in his visits to Montreal, that the pool became known as "La piscine de Willie (Willie's pool)." Whenever he came to town, he was one of the biggest draws for the fledgling Expos. Think of Stargell as Giancarlo Stanton before Giancarlo Stanton.

Although it may be slightly cheating to include a man who played only 848 of his 2,144 games at first base as the club's starting first baseman, no Pirate fan will complain, especially given the cluster eff that is about to ensue in the Pirates franchise outfield and utility spots, anyways.

In addition to being a star on the field, Stargell was also an icon for his role in the slow-moving desegregation of baseball. Although Jackie Robinson cracked the league in 1947, this did not make baseball truly desegregated, despite the sport's best efforts to appear so. Baseball has long prided itself on the fact that the sport was desegregated before nearly any other facet of life. Although Branch Rickey and Happy Chandler were certainly important pioneers in breaking the color barrier, it was a long time before black players had a true home in Major League Baseball.

Part of this was due to the nature of race relations in the country itself. For example, Stargell's career got off to a terrifying start when a fan with a shotgun threatened him at a minor league game before he even made his MLB debut. Typically, when baseball historians think of black players who had tough times in the big leagues, it is names like Jackie Robinson, Larry Doby, Roy Campanella, and all the other early black players that come to mind. It speaks to the slow-evolving nature of race relations in this country, however, that players like Stargell, who played an entire generation after Robinson, had to endure some of the same struggles that Robinson and others had to.

As noted in the team introduction, Stargell was part of the first all-minority lineup, when manager Danny Murtaugh sent out nine minority regulars to the diamond on September 1, 1971. This was an important moment because one of the biggest obstacles – an obstacle that is still rearing its ugly head across all career fields across the globe today – is minorities not being given a chance to fail. For most of the late `40s, `50s, and `60s, there were black players in baseball, but they were

All-Stars. This may not seem bad at first, but it is obviously a loaded reality. It means that those black players who were merely average – or, god forbid, replacement level – weren't getting roster spots. Fans and ownership were all right with having black players on their roster, but only if they were elite players.

Mark Armour did an excellent study for SABR in which he looked at this exact issue. Armour went through every player in baseball from 1946-1986 and compared the overall percentage of black players (he defined "black" as a player who would not have been able to play before Jackie Robinson) to the percentage of All-Star participants who were black. He also compared what percent of league-wide win shares came from black players. The results were unsurprisingly depressing. Each and every year, black players made up a higher percent of the league-wide win shares than they would have represented if the league were truly desegregated. In all but one year, black players were more represented at the All-Star Game than the limited number of black players in the major leagues would statistically expect. The takeaway is clear: if you were a black superstar, there was room for you on "integrated" rosters; if you were black and a replacement-level player, teams indeed had no issue making you replaceable. (This is the exact issue Jimmy Rollins said still existed just a few seasons ago.)

Stargell embraced his role as one of the faces of the black baseball player during his era, and during the late `70s, Stargell acquired the nickname "Pops" for being the head man for the "We are Family" Pirates team that won the 1979 World Series. Stargell had one of the best seasons in MLB history, winning MVP, League Championship Series MVP, and World Series MVP. Throughout the season, he gave "Stargell Stars" to teammates who made great plays. He became one of the most famous clubhouse leaders the sport has seen.

2B Bill Mazeroski (1956-1972)

Mazeroski is best known for his walkoff home run to win the 1960 World Series, but it is because of his glove that he is in the Hall of Fame.[329] His home run, which ended the 1960 World Series,[330] was the first home run to do so and has been recounted innumerable times, but it doesn't bring up the interesting question: what were the best World Series of all time? Sounds like a perfect Starting IX:

SP) 1924-26 – Sure, this is cheating big time, but this three-year stretch of World Series championships is simply unrivaled in baseball history. The 1924 World Series was covered in Walter Johnson's write-up (Starting Pitcher, Twins – Page 222), as it featured Johnson's crowning achievement as part of a seven-game series between the Washington Senators and the New York Giants. The series featured four one-run games – three of which were decided on the final at bat, and Game 7 went to 12 innings. Johnson should have left on top after 1924 because, in 1925, the Pirates stormed back from down 4-0 and later 6-3 to win Game 7 against Johnson, who followed up his career highlight with an unfortunate sequel. The next year didn't feature The Big Train, but it did offer a possibly intoxicated Pete Alexander closing out Game 7 for the Phillies, as well as a probably drunk Babe Ruth caught stealing to end the series. This was an unprecedented run in World Series history.

C) 1975 – Seven-game barn-burner featuring Carlton Fisk's famous "waving his home run fair" homer in Game 6. Naturally, the Sox lost in seven to the Reds, a common theme in baseball history before 2004.

1B) 1972 – A showdown between the A's and Reds, the 1972 series featured six of the seven games being decided by one run or fewer, with a walk-off in Game 4. There was great pitching abound.

(*** This is where I would slot the 2017 World Series that just ended.)

2B) 1986 – Need it be explained?

3B) 1912 – There have been a few eight-game series in World Series history, but 1912 is unique in that it is the only eight game series that came when the World Series was actually a best-of-seven series. The other eight-game series were as a result of a best-of-nine set up, but a tie in Game 2 forced 1912 to go to eight games. In the deciding Game 8, ace righty Christy Mathewson lost in extras innings, as the Boston Red Sox prevailed over the New York Giants. The series was also notable for numerous catches deemed the greatest of all time by the newspapers covering the series. Granted the World Series tradition was less than a decade old at the time, but still.

SS) 2011 – One of several recent great series, Game 6 was possibly the best World Series game of all time. In fact, by an "excitement per inning" basis – a metric included in an interesting presentation on "Measuring the Excitement of Baseball Games" by Michael Freiman at SABR 43 – this game ranked first among the top 20 most exciting World Series games of all time. (This was before Game 5 of the 2017 World Series, of course.) This pool of games was determined by looking at how certain game events changed each team's probability of winning the World Series the most. Game 6's high ranking makes sense, as numerous times it seemed a lock that the Rangers would bring home the franchise's first title. However, David Freese and the Cardinals had other plans and eventually won the series in Game 7.

LF) 1960 – Easily the most bizarre World Series of all time, although the Pirates won in seven (on Mazeroski's

[329] Well, his glove and John T. Bird. Bird put together a campaign in which he wrote a 300-page argument for Maz's Hall of Fame induction with interviews from old players, some of whom were Hall of Fame players themselves.

[330] After his World Series-winning home run, the 14-year-old boy who ended up with the home run ball came into the Pirates locker room and celebrated with the team. Mazeroski signed the ball and gave it back to the boy (Andy Jerpe), who proceeded to use it and eventually lose it in a game of pick up with his friends just a few months later. As Erik Malinowski pointed out in his piece on Mazeroski's ball and other lost items in baseball history for *Just a Bit Outside*, it was pretty much the plot of *The Sandlot* three decades before the film came out.

home run), they were outscored by 28 runs for the series as a whole. The Yankees won games by scores of 16-3, 10-0, and 12-0, while the Pirates squeaked out wins by scores of 6-4, 3-2, 5-2 and 10-9. The fact that it was the mighty Yankees who were on the losing side of the series made it all the more fascinating.

CF) 1991 – Game 7 was covered in the Twins team introduction and may very well be the best Game 7 of all time. The series as a whole was no let down. Five of the games were decided by one run, and three were decided in extra innings. The Twins ended up winning both Games 6 and 7 in extra innings, and in such heartbreaking fashion that it's no wonder Atlanta fell apart in the `90s. What's that? They won 14 of the next 15 division titles. nvm.

RF) 2001 – Pain. So much pain.

Back to Mazeroski: his standing in historical circles brings up a bigger question. If defense truly is underrated by metrics today, then is Maz actually properly rated after all? Of course, if we do indeed have a firm grasp on how much defense matters to baseball, then Mazeroski is hugely overrated, thanks in large part to his 1960 World Series home run. Yes, he does own the NL record for double plays and earned the nickname, "No Hands"[331] because of how fast he turned the double play, but his 19.0 offensive wins above replacement for his career leave *a lot* to be desired for a Hall of Famer.

Although his place in the Hall of Fame can be questioned, Mazeroski's dedication to the game, and perilous journey to the big leagues, is not in doubt. Mazeroski grew up extremely poor in rural West Virginia. He took his first job at the age of five, as he directed traffic around a dangerous bend on a street near his family's shack. His mom was forced to kick his dad out of the house after his dad showed up one time drunk, with a gun, saying he was going to shoot everybody. One day in the life of five-year-old Mazeroski had more adversity in it than my entire cushy life has had.

The first ever "baseballs" Mazeroski hit were rocks. It was only when the family did their version of "shopping" (going down to the Ohio River to recover items when the flooding receded) that Mazeroski got real baseballs[332] to hit. If the journey is truly greater than the destination, Mazeroski had a hell of a life.

3B Pie Traynor (1920-1935; 1937)

Traynor was a man before his time. In his era, third basemen were thought strictly as glovemen. However, similar to how Ernie Banks helped to show shortstops could produce with the bat, Traynor (along with Home Run Baker, who played just before him) helped to show teams they could get offensive production from their third baseman.

One interesting note about the lack of hitting from the third base position in the early days of baseball, is that while third basemen today are expected to hit, second basemen are usually allowed to get away with being strictly glovemen and are not asked to provide a lot at the plate. In Traynor's day, however, there was Rogers Hornsby, Eddie Collins, and numerous other second basemen who produced great hitting totals. The expectations switch seems to have occurred gradually over time, and if anything, today's expectations are less logical than those of early baseball. Although second base can be a difficult position to field (due to the unnatural pivot on double plays), third base is undoubtedly a more difficult position to field. It is one of the hardest positions in the game and is called the hot corner for a reason. So, if you were to allow some slack on the hitting end from either second or third base, it would make sense to expect more offense from the less-demanding defensive position – second base. However, it seems that more banjo-hitting fielders today are at second base than third. Due to the ebbing nature of baseball history, there is almost certainly going to be a time in the not-too-distant future when second and third base switch offensive expectations again.

Back to Traynor: it is partially due to his success hitting at third base before the position "required" it, that Traynor was a bit overrated by the peers of his time. However, he is hardly a household name these days and may actually be a bit underrated[333] in modern times. He was the only third baseman voted into Hall of Fame in the first four decades of voting, and in his career, he had only 278 strikeouts, also known as two weeks for Adam Dunn.

It seems like a logical time to comment again on how some of these teams are beginning to skew more heavily towards older players. At first blush, this would seem to be illogical, as today's players are almost certainly more talented than in previous eras. They have far better habits, scouting is far superior, the baseball field no longer looks like a Five for Fighting concert;[334] so why is it that there are so many older players on teams with such long histories? Simple. Before free agency, players stayed with their teams for much longer than in today's game. Not by chance, but simply because all but the biggest stars lacked any sort of autonomy as to where they played. Therefore, each player was able to accumulate far greater statistics in his much longer stint with the team. If these teams were based merely on the most talented players to ever put on the franchise jersey, the teams would be heavily representative of the modern game. Instead, since we are taking into account how long the player was with the franchise, the older players gain a large advantage. Also, in the case of the Pirates, there's

[331] As much as I love old-school nicknames, "No Hands" seems like it would be a pretty terrible nickname for a baseball player, even if it was meant as a compliment. Reminds me of in *New Girl* when Winston finally gets a nickname from his cop friends and it ends up being "Toilet." This, of course, leads to the brilliant quip: "Flush, flush, what's the rush?"

[332] They also got their pots and pans in this manner.

[333] For the record, the "Bleacher Report-ification" of sports articles makes it so I cringe every time I use the word overrated/underrated. It immediately triggers visions of 50-slide "articles" in which the rising action is seeing Adam Jones as the no. 15 most overrated player, and the climax is the shocking [*Borat voice*: "not"] conclusion that some San Francisco Giants infielder is the most underrated.

[334] A bunch of white dudes standing in a field with *grass* everywhere.

the fact that before the last half-decade, they sucked for a really long time in the modern era, but they were a strong team in their nascent years.

We'll end Traynor's bio with another one of the great "old-timey" stories about players from his era. After his retirement, Traynor worked in baseball broadcasting, where he would walk 10 miles roundtrip from his home every day; I'm assuming out of love for the game.

SS Honus Wagner (1900-1917)

Wagner's name has lived on through baseball history in no small part thanks to his T206 baseball card of legend, which has been sold for as much as $2.8 million dollars; but he should truly be remembered for much more.

Wagner is arguably one of the five best baseball players of all time, and those that saw him play would say there is no argument. Ed Barrow, who was the manager of no less than Babe Ruth, and a man who saw all the old greats play, said, "If I had a choice of all men who have played baseball, the first man I would select is Honus Wagner." In the original Hall of Fame vote, only Ty Cobb received more votes than Wagner.

Wagner played 21 seasons, playing until the ripe age of 43, with the final 18 seasons coming with the Pirates. He was a strange-looking man, bow-legged with arms so long that Lefty Gomez said, "[Wagner] could tie his shoelaces without bending down." He was nicknamed "The Flying Dutchman," and the way he flew around the bases made the nickname was truly appropriate. Wagner played in an era without many home runs, but he collected nearly as many extra-base hits as anyone in his time, and even if he was held to a single, he usually stole second anyways.

Wagner's Baseball-Reference page is littered with bold and italics, as the man led the league in at least one major category (and usually more) seemingly every year. From 1900-1911, there was only one year in which he failed to lead the league in multiple statistical categories. He won eight batting titles, led the league in steals five times, OPS+ six times, RBI four times, runs and hits two times, and extra-base hits seven times. He led the league in oWAR an incredible nine times during the 'aughts (1900-1909), and led position players in WAR an amazing 11 times in his career. He was a great fielder as well as batter; he hit for average as well as power; he had speed as well as sure hands in the field; simply put: he was one of the most all-around talented players to ever play the game, and he embodied the five-tool player. In the field, it was said that he used his enormous hands to scoop up the ball and whatever else was near it, whipping the mix to first base in a smooth transition. His first baseman, Kitty Bransfield, said of his time with Wagner, that when Wagner fired to first, he (Bransfield) would just catch the largest object flying his way.

All that being said, his "back-up" at the franchise's shortstop position may very well be the second-best shortstop of the 20th century.

Arky Vaughan made the classic case for an underrated player throughout his career. He hit triples instead of home runs; he totaled double-digit triples in each of his first six seasons, as well as eight of his first nine years in the bigs. He drew walks instead of tallying big hit totals; he led the league in walks three times and, despite winning a batting title and hitting .318 for his career, never led the league in hits. He played solid defense in a time before Gold Gloves; he netted 11.0 dWAR in his 10 years with the Pirates. Bill James, not one to allow these statistics to go unnoticed, ranked Vaughan as the second-best shortstop of all time behind only Wagner (before the Jeter-A-Rod-Garciaparra-Tejada explosion, it must be noted). Of course, there are now metrics to support this, and his 64.0 WAR in those 10 years comes out to an impressive 6.4 WAR/season for his entire time in Pittsburgh. However, he had the tough luck of playing the same position as one of the true all-time greats, and as Bill James puts it, the difference between Wagner and Vaughan is about the same as the difference between Vaughan and the 30th-ranked shortstop, so the decision to go with Wagner here is an easy one.

Wagner, like many old ball players, had a tough post-baseball life. Wagner became an alcoholic who used to go from bar to bar drinking all day and night. However, he didn't have the money to do so (remember, players were paid peanuts back in Wagner's day), so instead he would go into Pittsburgh bars and slam a silver dollar onto the bar counter. The noise would cause the patrons to look over and recognize the man they knew as the Flying Dutchman. They would then buy him a drink. He'd go around all day doing this.

Wagner deserves to be done right at the end of his write-up, so let's turn to the legendary sportswriter Arthur Daley to take us home: "There's something almost Lincolnesque about [Wagner], his rugged homeliness, his simplicity, his integrity, and his true nobility of character."

The Great Pittsburgh Outfield Shit Show

The Pirates have one of the longest histories in baseball, and as such, it is only natural that there would be a great number of strong candidates for their all-franchise team. However, there are many teams with great histories, and no part of the diamond is as talented – and so equal in their talent – as the Pirate outfield. There are five strong candidates for the three positions, with a player of the future to boot: Ralph Kiner, Barry Bonds, Max Carey, Roberto Clemente, and Paul Waner, with Andrew McCutchen lingering a few more good years away. Instead of the typical breakdown, these five men are going to get a different treatment. Each player will get his own write-up stating the case for his placement on the team. The categories will be the same as in other breakdowns, but without any comparison… to start. Then the players will be ranked, first through fifth, on each category, and the cumulative ranking for each player will determine who gets to start, with no emphasis on the specific outfield position (left field, right field, etc.). May the best Pirate win.

Ralph Kiner (1946-1953)

Contact

Kiner was never known for his reliance on making contact with the ball, but rather his prodigious power, as the next section will show. He was a career .279 hitter and a man who never hit over .313 in a single season. He led the league in strikeouts his rookie season, but, after that, he was able to cut down on his whiffs and never hurt himself too much with the contact aspect of his game. He just didn't bring home the bacon because of it either.

Power

If there's one thing Kiner was known for, it was his power stroke. He led the league in home runs in his rookie season… and his second season… and third… and fourth… and fifth… and sixth… and seventh.[335] These seven straight seasons are the only time in baseball history a player has led the league in home runs seven straight years, let alone his first seven seasons.

In fact, until back problems derailed his career, Kiner was as close to a sure bet to land among the all-time home runs leaders as there ever was. According to SABR research, in 1951, Kiner had an 85 percent chance of reaching 500 home runs for his career. He finished with 369 home runs, well shy of 500. That 85 percent chance of reaching 500 he had, is the second-highest total for any player to not actually reach 500. The highest was Lou Gehrig who finished with 493, and Gehrig falling short was a totally different set of circumstances.

Kiner was the first NL player to reach 50 home runs in a season twice, and he is one of only four players to hit at least 100 home runs in his first three full seasons. In fact, Kiner is tied with Albert Pujols for the most home runs through his first three full seasons (114). Kiner's home run percentage was second to only Babe Ruth when he retired and has only been passed by four men since (Mark McGwire, Barry Bonds, Jim Thome, and Giancarlo Stanton).

Kiner's power was far from a late-blooming trait, as his childhood ballpark had to be rearranged because Kiner kept breaking the windows of the school beyond his hometown outfield fences.

Batting Eye

Kiner drew a great number of walks in his prime, although like many sluggers, the question of whether this was due to a strong batting eye or the fear of his power is a fair one to ask. He did, however, lead the league in walks three times and was perpetually among the league leaders.

Speed

Kiner was not fast at all. He was slow to start, and then he had back problems.

Defense

Kiner was not a great defender either, as his poor speed and lack of agility hurt him in the field. In fact, his speed and defense limited him such that Branch Rickey said of him: "Kiner has so many other weaknesses that if you had eight Ralph Kiners on an American Association team, it would finish last." This quote needs some context, though. It was part of a smear campaign that Rickey employed when he was attempting to trade Kiner but fearing the fans would be upset if he traded their best player. He felt the need to belittle Kiner's talent because Kiner was so popular with the Pirates fans that Rickey knew he would be crucified if he shipped Kiner out of town without publicly rationalizing the move.

Intangibles

Kiner's injury-plagued second half of his career does him no favors here, even though he does do well in some other manifestations of the term *intangible*.

Kiner was a well-known and popular guy in his era, a man who hung out in famous circles. According to Robert T.

[335] Maybe that's what LeBron and the Heat were talking about after they joined forces in Miami. "How many home run titles did Ralph Kiner win to start his career?!!" "Not one! Not two! Not three…"

Broadwater's biography of Kiner, the Pirate outfield was infamous for his celebrity friends, as he golfed with the likes of Esther Williams, Jack Benny, Randolph Scott, Jack Lemmon, Frank Sinatra, and others. For everyone under the age of 80, just trust me that those are real people. Kiner was a handsome bachelor who had groupies who followed him everywhere. He had a DiMaggio-lite persona about him. Of course, this doesn't matter much when choosing men for a hypothetical baseball team. But it also doesn't hurt…

Kiner was also a long-time announcer after his playing days, calling games for the Mets for over 50 years and doing so in a style that made Kiner a household name as an announcer for the next generation of fans. In fact, to many, Kiner's incredible success on the field was relatively obscured by his status as an announcer. Kiner frequently misspoke or simply got his words twisted around when trying to announce, but he did so in the most congenial and unassuming manner possible. After Kiner's passing, Jayson Stark wrote a piece recalling some of Kiner's malapropisms (which Stark had collected during his time at the *Philadelphia Inquirer*), of which my personal favorite was when, on Father's Day, he wished all the dads watching a happy birthday.

Team Success

Kiner was with the Pirates from 1946-1953 season. During his time there, the Pirates were perpetual cellar dwellers, finishing dead last in the NL three of those seasons and second-to-last another three years. Only once did a Kiner-led Pirates team finish over .500, and not once did they make the playoffs.

Dominance

For those first eight years of Kiner's career (1946-1953), he was as dominant a power hitter as the league has ever seen, hitting 329 home runs. Over that stretch, the next closest hitter by home runs was Stan Musial (221). That's nearly 50 percent more home runs for Kiner over those eight seasons, an unprecedented dominance in the realm of the long ball. If injuries had not derailed his career, he would possibly have been above having to sort through this mess of a Pirate outfield and would instead have a spot all to his own.

Impact on the Franchise

Kiner enjoyed nearly all of his success with the Pirates and, as mentioned earlier, was extremely popular with the hometown fans. However, as Branch Rickey infamously told Kiner during contract disputes: "We finished last with you, we can finish last without you."

Barry Bonds (1986-1992)

Contact

Although Bonds, like Kiner, was better known for his power hitting, he was also an impressive all-around hitter throughout his career. It is surprising, then, that his batting average while with the Pirates was only .275. For the most part, this is due to Bonds' first few seasons in which he was still adjusting to hitting at a major league level. His final three seasons in Pittsburgh he hit .301, topping out at .311 in 1992, his final season with the club.

Power

Similar to his contact numbers, Bonds' power numbers in Pittsburgh were not nearly what they were in San Francisco. He managed 176 home runs in his seven seasons, with his Pittsburgh high coming in 1992 with 34 home runs. Part of this was due to the park in which he played, as he led the league in OPS+ his final three years in Pittsburgh, topping out with a remarkable OPS+ of 204 in 1992. Don't let people fool you, Bonds was incredible far before his San Francisco days.

Batting Eye

If there is one skill that was consistently great in Bonds' game throughout his whole career, it was his batting eye. In his final four years with the Pirates, Bonds averaged over 100 walks a season, boosted by his 127 walks to lead the league in 1992. When the PED discussion comes into play, what can never be disputed about Bonds is that he had the best non-Ted-Williams batting eye in history. Performance-enhancing drugs don't give you that.

Speed

Bonds originally earned his daily bread with his speed and athleticism, both in the field and on the basepaths. Bonds stole nearly as many bases in his seven years with Pittsburgh (251) as he did in his 15 years in San Francisco (263). His career-high came in 1990 when he stole 52 bases, only being caught 13 times.

Defense

Bonds was an incredible defender in his early days, with range, speed, and instincts to spare. He was worth 10.8 dWAR in his seven years with the team, and he won a Gold Glove each of his last three seasons. Bonds had incredible range that allowed him to lead all left fielders in putouts his final four years with the Pirates (1989-1992). He also led left fielders in assists three of those seasons, and the defensive metrics back the strong play that Pirate fans saw from Bonds in his time next to the Monongahela, Allegheny, and Ohio Rivers.

Intangibles

This would seem to be the place to discuss Bonds' well-documented connection to PEDs, but they will be discussed later in the book, as it is not Bonds' seasons with the Pirates that are under suspicion.

As far as his high-leverage production, Bonds was less-than-stellar in his three NLCS appearances with the Pirates, collecting only three RBI in total, and the Pirates suffered first-round exits each time. He was, however, able to score 10 runs, steal six bases, and post a .337 on-base percentage. Given that he finished no worse than second in the MVP those three seasons, though, one would expect him to take more than a complementary role in his team's playoff success. In terms of health, Bonds played no fewer than 140 games in a season after his rookie year and was a lock for 600 plate appearances every season.

Although the merits of his PED use will not be discussed here, it is of note that even this early in his career, Bonds was a bit of a surly fellow. Never one to go out of his way to please reporters, Bonds made the fatal mistake of "wronging" the media, a mistake which can set the course of a player's narrative for his entire career. This is not to say that Bonds didn't bring on some of the media derision that dogged him his entire career, but it was certainly a two-way street.

Team Success

As was mentioned in the last section, Bonds' Pirates made the playoffs his final three seasons with the team but failed to make it on to the next round each time. In the final such series, Bonds' throw home was just a hair too late to nab Sid Bream at the plate, allowing the Braves to make the World Series. Although it may not have been satisfying in the eyes of many Pirate fans, that 1992 League Championship Series represented the Pirates only postseason appearance for over 20 years until the McCutchen-led Pirates made the playoffs in 2013.

Dominance

Bonds' dominance in Pittsburgh was not nearly as flashy as it was in his San Fran days. He did total two of his record seven MVPs while with the Pirates, but outside of a runs-scored title in 1992 and three OBP titles in his final three seasons with the Pirates, most of his black ink comes from his days with the Giants. His final four years with Pittsburgh saw him finish no worse than fourth in WAR among National Leaguers, leading the league in 1990. In 1992, Bonds became the first player to hit .300 with 30 home runs, 100 runs, 100 RBI, 100 walks, and 30 steals in the history of baseball. He won his first three Silver Sluggers and Gold Gloves in his final three years in Pittsburgh, and his career was clearly – and unfortunately for Pirates fans – on the upward track when he left town.

Impact on the Franchise

The last point in the final paragraph is, for many, the narrative Bonds cemented when he left Pittsburgh. Many Pirate fans saw the writing on the wall, as the Pirates were likely not going to be able to afford the contract Bonds would demand in the open market. That's what made the Pirates loss in the 1992 NLCS even tougher, as many Pirates fans believed the only way to lure Bonds back was with a title. Alas, their playoffs ended in failure, and Bonds was out the door before the 1993 season.

Max Carey (1910-1926)

Contact

Maximilian Carnarius (Carey's given name) was first and foremost a devil on the basepaths. He realized this and, as such, tried to rely on his ability to make contact with the ball and turn a single into a double with a steal. Carey topped a .300 average in five seasons of over 100 games, topping out at .343 in 1925. However, Carey topped 200 hits in a season only once, and his career .287 average with the Pirates was only nine points above the league average of .278 in the 17 seasons he spent in Pittsburgh.

Power

N/A... He reached double-digit home runs only once, and that was 10 home runs in 1922 during the league-wide home run explosion. Carey was always among the league leaders in triples, leading the league twice, but that was due far more to his speed than his power.

Batting Eye

Carey posted what seem to be mediocre walk totals for his career, but they were actually strong in comparison to the league. He led the league twice (1918 and 1922), and his career .363 on-base percentage is quite strong given his batting average. Carey's 1,040-to-695 career walk-to-strikeout ratio is an impressive one.

Speed

Carey's speed was undoubtedly his strongest trait on the baseball field, and the numbers back it up. He had the most steals of the 1920s, most impressively with 51 steals in 53 attempts in 1922 (although caught stealing numbers are not perfect for Carey's era). His 688 steals with Pittsburgh are the most in franchise history, and his high triple totals were already noted. Carey led the league in steals 10 times, all as a Pirate, which was a record until Rickey Henderson broke it in 1991. However, Henderson led the league "only" nine times as an Athletic, meaning that no player has led the league in steals for one franchise as many times as Carey did with the Pirates. Carey also used his smarts to get some steals, as he knew that spitballers wouldn't throw to first when they were throwing the saliva-covered pitch, so he got a better jump against them.

Defense

Given his incredible speed, it is surprising that Carey was better known for his arm than his range in the field. His 339 career assists rank fourth all-time among outfielders in the modern era. His range was above average as well, but he was not the most sure-handed outfielder of his day. This brought his defensive metrics down to about league-average. According to his SABR bio, Carey ran into errors trying to make plays that no other players would have tried. On an unrelated note, Carney wore flip-down sunglasses in the field before they were popular around the league. Those things were around in the 1920s?!

Intangible[336]

Carey was the type of player who was always willing to make adjustments. He became a switch-hitter only after making the majors and struggling. He remodeled his swing at the age of 34 to copy Ty Cobb, and he had his most successful year the next season, hitting .343. He noticed a change in Walter Johnson's wind-up in Game 7 of the 1925 World Series which tipped off when he was throwing his curve. Bishop let his team know, resulting in a 9-7 comeback win in the most important game of his career. Carey stayed very healthy throughout his career, topping 100 games in 14 of his 15 full seasons with the Pirates and playing in 140 or more games in 10 of those seasons. High marks all around. 10 points for Gryffindor.

Team Success

The Pirates most successful moment from Carey's era was the aforementioned Game 7 win over Walter Johnson, and although this was an awesome feat, it was the only time in Carey's career that he played in the playoffs.

Dominance

Carey's dominance on the field came almost entirely as a runner, as we have already covered. His best singular performance was in one 18-inning game. In this game, Carey drew three walks in addition to six hits and stole three bases, including a steal of home. Carey was never able to top 5.1 WAR in a season, and although his 52.2 WAR as a Pirate is impressive, he was never a truly dominant player.

Impact on the Franchise

Carey was the Pirates captain in their 1925 World Series victory, which Carey's keen eye helped Pittsburgh to secure. The end of Carey's time in Pittsburgh was a bit rocky, as he was released after he and some of the other Pirates veterans tried to stage a revolt against Fred Clarke, the team's manager, that would eventually be known as The Great Pirate Mutiny. However, the club took him on as a manager just a few years later, and a relationship that had been built on 17 years of play was repaired. The two (Carey and the organization) ended on good terms.

Roberto Clemente (1955-1972)

Contact

Clemente famously ended his career with exactly 3,000 hits, becoming just the 11th player to join the 3,000-hit club. Clemente passed away that offseason (more to come on that), and the question of just how many hits he could have accumulated, although a somewhat callous one, is still an interesting question.[337] As is, his 3,000 hits sit 31st all-time in MLB history. In his final season, Clemente was limited to just 102 games, the lowest total of his career, but he still managed to collect 118 hits en route to a .312 batting average. The three seasons prior to 1972, however, Clemente enjoyed a career revival of sorts, hitting a combined .346 with an OPS+ of 157. Given his career arc, it is reasonable to think that Clemente could have played another three seasons at worst (he was 38 at the time) and collected another 400 hits with relative ease. Those 3,400 hits would place him in the top 10 all-time.

This is almost certainly a low projection given the bizarre career arc of Clemente. In the first half of his career (1955-1963), Clemente posted an OPS+ of 109, not too far above league average. In the second half of his career (1964-1972), that number rose to 151, meaning his production, relative to the league, made a 39 percentage point jump after he hit the age of 29, an incredibly unique career arc (outside of the PED era, where career arcs were more messed up than Jason Pierre-Paul's right hand).

---

336 "Bet you didn't think so I command you to; panoramic view, look I'll make it all manageable."

337 It should be noted that Clemente had spoken to teammates about not returning after the 1972 season, but ballplayers love saying they won't be back next year. Actually walking away is way harder than saying you're going to walk away.

Baseball fans were robbed of a possible Minnie Miñoso-esque career path when Clemente passed away in the 1972 offseason. Clemente was still able to have an incredible career, and focusing on what it could have been, instead of what it was, does injustice to the resume he has. Clemente won four batting titles in his career (three after the age of 30, of course), despite hitting in an offense-depressed stadium, in a pitching-heavy era, bringing his career slash line much lower than his true talent deserved.

Clemente became the first player in 20th century to get back-to-back five-hit days when he did so on August 22-23, 1970. His seven career five-hit games are topped by only Pete Rose and Tony Gwynn.

Power

For as famous as Clemente is, his ability to hit the long ball was never his strength. He was consistent with his power, and he posted solid extra-base hit totals thanks to his doubles and triples, but home runs were never a key component of his game. He never reached 30 long balls in a season, and his 240 career home runs are more a tribute to his 18 years in the league than any real power streak. Plus, he didn't get the same run in the `70s outside of Forbes Field that Stargell got.

Batting Eye

Clemente was a free-swinger, and although he never posted egregious strikeout totals, he was never one to work the count. When asked what pitch Clemente hit off him one time, Don Drysdale responded, "Ball four." Clemente's highest walk total was in 1969 when he drew a grand total of 56 walks. However, given that his career strikeout-to-walk ratio is below two-to-one, calling him reckless at the plate seems wrong. Similar to modern players like Robinson Canó and Vladimir Guerrero, Clemente's ideology was to attack early in the count instead of the Wade Boggs-ian approach of making the pitcher work. In the words of BoJack Horseman's feline agent, Princess Carolyn, "There's more than one way to skin a me."

Speed

Clemente was regarded as one of the most natural athletes the game of baseball has ever seen. The description of an athlete with "graceful speed" may have been invented with regards to Joe DiMaggio, but Clemente seemed to embody the idea of natural athleticism more than any player not named Willie Mays. His career stolen base records do not support this conclusion, but Clemente was one of the most likely players to turn a single into a double, and a double into a triple. Clemente's high doubles and triples totals throughout his career were likely the support that older fans of Clemente used, but with current statistics, a metric like extra base taken percentage comes in handy. Derek Jeter is a player in today's game who is thought to often take an extra base and rely on graceful speed as well. For his career, Jeter had an extra base taken percentage of 45 percent; Clemente blows that out of the water, coming in at 55 percent. Craig Biggio is another player who fits the mold of a smart aggressive base runner; he is at 45 percent, as well. Vlad Guerrero was aggressive to the point of reckless at times; his career extra base taken percentage was 47 percent. Clemente's extra base taken percentage was well above-average throughout his career, and it lends credence to his speed being judged on more than just his mediocre stolen base totals.

Defense

Before his ill-timed passing, Clemente was best known for his defense. His "easy speed" and natural instincts helped, but what he really lived on was the birth defect he had that replaced his right arm with a Howitzer that launched intercontinental ballistic missiles.[338] He led NL right fielders in assists six different seasons, but that number would have been far higher had anyone dared to run on him. His 254 career assists from right field are the most in MLB history, and he totaled nine or more assists in all but one season. These high assists totals do come with the caveat that Clemente was well-known for missing the cut-off man in an attempt to get the out.

Clemente was also prone to high error totals, but don't let that fool you; he was a hell of a defender. His Total Zone Runs speak for themselves. Total Zone Runs (TZR) is a metric used to measure "the number of runs above or below average the player was worth based on the number of plays made." In terms of TZR, Clemente is the best right fielder of all time, second among all outfielders (to Andruw Jones), and fifth among all position players in MLB history. The fact that he did this from right field, a position often thought of as a throwaway spot on the diamond, is remarkable. Assuaging a former note, his high error totals were mostly due to his ability to get to a ball that others would never have reached.

Intangibles

In addition to being one of the most interesting players on the field, Clemente was a mighty interesting man off the field. He was often called a man of many contradictions, and with good reason. Here was a man who throughout his career was thought of as a bit surly but is now remembered for his heroic passing while bringing aid to Central America. He was a poet insomniac who took even perceived slights very hard and held grudges for a long time. It is not surprising that he did not have a strong relationship with the media for most of his career. Clemente said of the media, "When the sportswriters write about a black or Hispanic player, it's always something controversial. When they write about white players, it's usually nice

[338] For all the military heads freaking out about that sentence, I realize it is mixing metaphors, but Clemente's arm deserves the best of all worlds.

– human interest stuff." Although there is a lot to unpack there, he's not entirely wrong, especially in his era. Clemente wasn't afraid to speak his mind and often complained about nagging injuries, something that most major leaguers frown upon, since it implies that they are not all playing through some day-to-day ailments.

Overall, Clemente's reputation should probably be somewhere between boorish – as it was during his career – and gallant – as it has been after his career. A human person requiring nuance, go figure.

Team Success

The Pirates won two of their five World Series with Clemente, and the club was a strong contender for many of his years in Pittsburgh. Compared to many of the Pirates we have seen so far, Clemente has a nice edge.

Dominance

Clemente was dominant in two areas: fielding and batting average. His four batting titles speak for themselves and his dominance in fielding categories such as putouts (two-time league leader in right field), assists (six-time league leader in right field), TZR (10-time league leader in right field), and range factor/game (six-time league leader in right field) paint a deservedly strong picture of Clemente.

On the flip side, Clemente never posted a season with at least a .300 average, 30 home runs, and 100 RBI, and although some of that was due to the era in which he played, there is the possibility that, as taboo as it may be to ask, did Clemente's unfortunate passing lead to his legacy being a bit inflated? As noted before, Clemente's career arc was an exceptional one, seeing Clemente seemingly get stronger as he reached his mid-30s. He peaked in the 1971 World Series, a little over a year before his passing, calling into question numerous "What If's."

It's probably unfair to promote the idea that Clemente's legacy was increased from his passing, but it is something that should not be totally dismissed when reading about him. There are certainly cases of preferential treatment being given to those who passed away early. Kurt Cobain was a visionary, but is his poster hanging in every freshman dorm room today without his early passing? Chris Farley was a hysterical dude – and one of the best physical comedians of all time – but the rest of *SNL* during his time was pretty epic too, and they are far less respected than Farley today (mainly because they put out a whole lot of crap in their post-*SNL* days that Farley never got the chance to make).

It feels very callous to call to front this part of human psychology, but when attempting to take a totally objective stance on Pittsburgh Pirate outfielders, it needs to be at least mentioned.

Impact on the Franchise

Clemente is one of the few players of whom it could be said that he had a bigger impact on the game of baseball as a whole than his franchise in particular. He was a pioneer among Puerto Rican baseball players, and sadly, he had to deal with his fair share of racism along the way.

When Clemente passed away it was on a New Year's Eve flight to Nicaragua. Clemente spent time each offseason doing charity work in Central America, and in the winter of 1972 when disaster struck Nicaragua in the form of an earthquake, Clemente knew his help was needed. As such, he sent over multiple care packages, but when he heard that corrupt government officials had intercepted the first three sets, Clemente decided to go over with the fourth flight. He was well aware of the inherent danger of making the trip – it was an overloaded plane with a history of engine failure. Before he left for his ill-fated flight, he told his wife, "When your time comes, it comes; if you are going to die, you will die."

He took the risk, however, and in an immensely unfair twist of fate, the flight went down off the coast of Isla Verde, Puerto Rico on December 31, 1972. After Clemente's death, hundreds of people went to the beach to look for his body even though they knew he was dead. And even though it was New Year's Day, because this man represented so much more than a ballplayer to the people of Puerto Rico, they appeared in droves on the shores. For this man, impact on his franchise is simply not enough of a measurement.

It should be noted that he *did* indeed have quite an impact on the Pirates, and his presence is felt by anyone who goes to a Pirate game these days. That awesome yellow bridge behind PNC Park is called Clemente Bridge, and the stadium as a whole is a tribute to Clemente. The right field wall is 21 feet high in honor of his uniform number, and it feels very much like the Pirates are (rightfully) promoting his legacy as the Face of the Franchise when attending a game at PNC Park.

Paul Waner (1926-1940)

Contact

Paul Waner was an excellent contact hitter, winning three batting titles during his career and collecting eight 200-hit seasons. Only Ty Cobb, Pete Rose, and Ichiro Suzuki have more seasons with 200 hits, and Waner's 3,152 career hits rank 17th all-time. In his time with the Pirates, Waner had nearly 10 hits for every strikeout, collecting 2,868 hits compared to just 325 strikeouts, an absurd ratio. Paul's brother Lloyd was also an excellent hitter, and he also played for the Pirates. The two brothers have the second most hits for any pair of teammates all-time, and the highest mark for any pair of brothers. The two Waners collected more hits in the majors than any other siblings, even the three Alous and DiMaggios and the whole litter of Delahantys (five of `em). Waner's worst batting average for his first 12 years in Pittsburgh was .309, and for that 12-year stretch, his cumulative average was an impressive .348.

Power

Despite the growing prevalence of the long ball during the time in which Waner played, Paul focused mostly on the contact side of hitting, never putting too much emphasis on the home run. His highest home run total in a single season was 15 in 1929, and he only reached double digits three times in a season. His power often came in the form of other extra-base hits. His triples totals were strong, most notably in his rookie year when he hit 22, and he led the league in doubles twice. As such, only Willie Stargell and Honus Wagner had more extra-base hits as a Pirate than Waner, an impressive feat given that he hit only 109 home runs with the team.

Batting Eye

Waner's batting eye was strong, with almost three times more walks than strikeouts in Pittsburgh and an on-base percentage over .400.

Speed

As noted earlier, Waner had strong triples totals, reaching double-digit triple totals each of his first 10 seasons, by far the best total post-1920. He never had strong stolen base totals, however, topping out at 18 in 1930. He averaged 110 runs/season in his first 12 years, and although some of that was due to a strong lineup surrounding Waner, he was an excellent base runner, especially early in his career.

Defense

Waner was about as average a defender as can be by the more advanced metrics, but the traditional metrics rate him well. He was always among the leaders in right field putouts and range thanks to his strong speed, and he was able to combine that with sure enough hands to lead right fielders in fielding percentage four times in his career. His arm was nothing outstanding, but thanks to the era in which he played, his 236 assists from right field are fourth all-time. Probably because of the nature of his excellence in the standard metrics, Waner had a strong defensive reputation. In reality, Waner is the perfect mix of overrated by some metrics and underrated by others, perfectly canceling out to a solid, above-average fielder.

Intangibles

Like many men in his era, Waner battled alcoholism during his playing days and often came to games hungover. His remedy for hangovers was 15 straight back flips, which almost makes me hungover just thinking about it.

Paul and his brother Lloyd are the all-time leaders in games played as brothers, and the origin of their nicknames can be traced back to their similar DNA. For their careers, Paul was called "Big Poison," while Lloyd went by "Little Poison." The story goes that Brooklyn fans were behind the nickname (they seem to create every nickname), and the fan that christened them was saying, "big person" and "little person," but his heavy Brooklyn accent led to the use of, "poisons" instead of "persons." Apocryphal? Maybe. Awesome anyway? Certainly.

Paul Waner also gets a little Pittsburgh Pirates cred because he timed his career with them perfectly. As soon as Waner left Pittsburgh, his numbers began to drop, and he became a bit of a journeyman.

Team Success

The Pirates won only one pennant while Waner played for them, and that year they ran into the buzz saw that was the 1927 Yankees. Those Yankees have often been called the best team ever (including by yours truly in the Cubs write-up) and had Babe Ruth and Lou Gehrig in their primes. Despite the fact that the Pirates were swept, it should be noted that Paul and Lloyd Waner out hit Ruth and Gehrig in the series, collecting 11 hits to Ruth and Gehrig's 10. However, Ruth and Gehrig's hits were much more productive going for 22 total bases to the Waner's 15. The Pirates were never awful when Waner was there, in fact, they would have made numerous playoff appearances in today's playoff setup of multiple division winners plus wild card teams, but they made only the one actual World Series trip due to the limited nature of playoff participants for most of baseball history.

Dominance

Waner had more than half of his league-leading events occur in his first three seasons, with an especially dominant 1927 season. He was rightfully rewarded with an MVP, even though it was his previous season, his rookie campaign, in which he led all National League hitters in WAR (5.3). Waner became a Hall of Famer in 1952, his sixth season on the ballot, far from first-ballot, but also not gaining entry by the skin of his teeth.

Impact on the Franchise

Paul Waner's name is scattered across the Pirates franchise statistical leaderboard, and he and his little brother were key members of Pirates history. However, as his relatives found out when they visited PNC Park in 2005, his memory is not as sharp in the mind of modern fans as might be expected. As Joseph Wancho writes in his SABR Bio of Waner, when Waner's grandnephew and daughter asked to see some pieces of Waner's lore at PNC, they couldn't find any hint of Waner's impact on the franchise. Unfortunately, this is a curse for many players of that generation, a fate to which Waner was not immune.

POF Andrew McCutchen (2009-pres.)

There have already been about 10 pages of Pirate outfielder reading, so let's keep it simple here. If McCutchen posts two-to-three more All-Star, near-MVP seasons, he'll get his name in the mix, but there is too much talent and depth for him as of the end of the 2017 season, especially given his slight dip in production over the last couple of seasons.

Calculating the results

Time to tally up the results, with a few brief comments if need be.

Contact: 1) Roberto Clemente 2) Paul Waner 3) Max Carey 4) Barry Bonds 5) Ralph Kiner

Pretty straight forward here. Clemente over Waner might throw some folks off, but when the era adjustments are accounted for, the decision becomes clear.

Power: 1) Ralph Kiner 2) Barry Bonds 3) Roberto Clemente 4) Paul Waner 5) Max Carey

Bonds is baseball's home run king, but that transformation came in San Francisco. Plus, Kiner may well have challenged Babe Ruth's record had he stayed healthy.

Batting Eye: 1) Barry Bonds 2) Max Carey 3) Ralph Kiner 4) Paul Waner 5) Roberto Clemente

Kiner had bigger walk totals than Carey, but that was because of the era in which he played and the fear he put in pitchers more than a strong batting eye, per se.

Speed: 1) Max Carey 2) Barry Bonds 3) Roberto Clemente 4) Paul Waner 5) Ralph Kiner

Defense: 1) Roberto Clemente 2) Barry Bonds t-3) Max Carey and Paul Waner 5) Ralph Kiner

Carey and Waner are simply too even to truly distinguish one from the other. I guess that's what a tie implies, but for some reason it seemed to need saying.

Intangibles: 1) Max Carey 2) Ralph Kiner 3) Roberto Clemente 4) Paul Waner 5) Barry Bonds

The vaguest and broadest-reaching category was certainly the hardest to rank, but each "intangible" section was dissected, with points added and subtracted in the least-scientific way possible.

Team Success: 1) Roberto Clemente 2) Max Carey 3) Paul Waner 4) Barry Bonds 5) Ralph Kiner

Dominance: 1) Ralph Kiner 2) Roberto Clemente 3) Barry Bonds 4) Paul Waner 5) Max Carey

Another example of Bonds in Pittsburgh, that's the biggest thing here. If we included his San Francisco days, he would cruise to victory, but we'll get to that part of his career later in the book. Kiner over Clemente may throw some folks off, but those first seven seasons for Kiner were about as dominant as you'll find in baseball history.

Impact on the Franchise: 1) Roberto Clemente 2) Max Carey 3) Paul Waner 4) Ralph Kiner 5) Barry Bonds

This was another tough category. How long each player was in Pittsburgh certainly had an impact on their rank, but so did any large accomplishments attributed to the player (hence Carey over Waner for Carey's supposed help in capturing the 1925 title).

Verdict

1) Roberto Clemente 2) Max Carey 3) Barry Bonds 4) Ralph Kiner 5) Paul Waner

Couple of things stand out. Max Carey is much higher than I would have expected, and Waner is much lower. In terms of WAR, Waner (68.2) is actually second to Clemente (94.5) among this group, and Clemente honestly should have just had his right field position locked down.

I would have been tempted to give the edge to Kiner over Bonds, but in the end Kiner is a better fit for the utility spot (hold that thought) because his train wreck defense wouldn't hurt the team. Waner is almost certainly underrated by this methodology, but he simply didn't have any categories in which he stood out. He was the only Pirate outfielder who failed to win a single category, and he came in second only once. Waner was also the only guy to never come in last in a category, but those five penultimate finishes doomed him. If you include him in your own personal Pirate outfield there will be no hard feelings. This top three also works out nicely with a left fielder (Bonds), center fielder (Carey), and right fielder (Clemente).

Utility) Choose your own adventure: Kiner, Waner, Arky Vaughn (1932-1941)

Another crazy tight matchup, and instead of forcing you to read yet another 10 pages of comparison, it's time to give the reader a little autonomy. Feel free to pick your own Pirate at the utility position, just know that the selection can be viewed as a personality test of sorts.

If you choose **Kiner**: You're a bit lazy, you just chose the first name that popped up; you like power, both in your hitters and in your life; you prefer peak to longevity and dominance over consistency; you like a baseball lifer, someone who stuck around the game after he was done playing; you're a sucker for a charismatic personality – you may be part of a cult and just not realize it.

If you chose **Waner**: You're a middle child who understands the pain of not being first or last; you like a man who can hold his booze (and brings it to the field with him); you felt bad when you read that section about his grandkids not finding any signs of him at PNC Park these days; you prioritize family and respect the fact that Paul and his brother roamed the outfield together for so long.

If you chose **Vaughn**: You're a contrarian and think that because I listed Vaughn last that means I think he is the worst choice, so you're choosing him Goddammit; you live by the WAR and die by the WAR; you believe that shortstops are the most talented defensive players and therefore would be perfect in the utility spot, as they could fill in anywhere on the field; you like the first name Arky.

SP Sam Leever (1898-1910)

Considering the Pirates illustrious history, the catalog of starting pitchers is exceptionally weak. Leever was a solid pitcher for 13 years around the turn of the 20th century, but his 41.8 WAR with the club paints an accurately underwhelming ace of a top-nine Starting IX.[339] Leever won one ERA (and ERA+) title in his time in Pittsburgh and collected a solid number of wins with a Pittsburgh team that was relevant most of his career. He was a versatile pitcher who would often come out of the bullpen for the club, and he specialized in keeping the ball in the ballpark. However, considering the strength at many other positions in the club, the pitching would be the hypothetical downfall of the Pirates Starting IX.

Leever's nickname was "Goshen Schoolmaster" because of the fact that after he graduated Goshen high school, and the fact that he was a teacher for seven years before finally becoming a professional ballplayer – basically the most straightforward-and-literal-while-still-sounding-really-cool nickname of all time. Leever was also a frugal outdoorsman who made his own gunpowder. Of course, he also suffered costly injuries during his in-season trapshooting. Leever could pitch only one inning in his planned Game 2 start of the 1903 World Series and then didn't have his best stuff in Game 6 when he was once again called upon (somewhere Trevor Bauer's drone is nodding). He was torn apart by the press, but he bounced back for several more strong seasons with the Pirates. He never made it back to the World Series, though.

CP Roy Face (1953; 1955-1968)

Full name Elroy Face, Roy is most often remembered for his 1959 season in which he won 17 straight games and finished the season 18-1, good for the best winning percentage in a single season in baseball history. That win streak, when continued back to the previous season, included 22 straight wins overall. Although impressive, four of those wins were the result of blown saves. Face's season highlights the difference in the roles of closers today versus in Face's era. The fact that he blew so many games wasn't as big a deal because he often would be in the game for multiple innings and, as such, giving up a run wasn't the end of the world. Modern closers are usually allotted only one inning; therefore, one run is of far greater importance.

In his career, Face was also involved in a rumor that goes to highlight the difference between the world Face lived in and today's world. Face suffered an injury in 1959 that, although Face claimed was the result of a broken glass, was originally reported to be the result of Roberto Clemente cutting him with a razor blade after a disagreement. Placed in the modern era, this would have spread about a million times faster and been far more damaging for both men's reputation (especially Clemente's). See: Blake Griffin and the Punch That Broke the Camel's Back... And Matias Testi's Face.

Face was a bit of a wild card, once setting fire to Pirate bats in the bullpen in order to break them out of a slump. As a result, he briefly earned the nickname "Elroy the Torch" from Joe Gergen. Staying right in line with his wild card nature, Face relied heavily on a forkball for most of his career, a pitch that is almost never seen today and was never all that common. Face used to say that neither he nor the hitter knew where the pitch was going, but obviously, this was a bit of hyperbole, as his control rates were strong throughout his career.

[339] You have to go back to the no. 20 Angels to find a Starting IX starting pitcher with fewer WAR for his franchise than Leever on these rosters.

Starting IX Franchise Roster Stats

Lineup	Yrs	G	R	H	HR	RBI	SB	BB	SO	BA	OBP	SLG	OPS+	dWAR	WAR
Max Carey	17	2178	1414	2416	67	721	**688**	918	646	0.287	0.363	0.391	111	0.2	52.5
Honus Wagner	18	2433	**1521**	2967	82	1474	639	877	665	0.328	0.394	0.468	154	20.8	**120.3**
Roberto Clemente	18	**2433**	1416	**3000**	240	1305	83	621	1230	0.317	0.359	0.475	130	12.1	94.5
Willie Stargell	**21**	2360	1194	2232	**475**	**1540**	17	**937**	**1936**	0.282	0.360	0.529	147	-19.7	57.5
Barry Bonds	7	1010	672	984	176	556	251	611	590	0.275	0.380	0.503	147	10.8	50.1
Pie Traynor	17	1941	1183	2416	58	1273	158	472	278	0.320	0.362	0.435	107	2.0	36.2
Arky Vaughan	10	1411	936	1709	84	764	86	778	227	0.324	0.415	0.472	141	11.0	64.0
Jason Kendall	9	1252	706	1409	67	471	140	454	403	0.306	0.387	0.418	108	5.1	30.6
Bill Mazeroski	17	2163	769	2016	138	853	27	447	706	0.260	0.299	0.367	84	**19.1**	36.2
Pitchers	Yrs	W	W%	ERA	G	CG	SHO	SV	IP	SO	ERA+	WHIP	SO/9	SO/BB	WAR
Sam Leever	13	194	0.660	2.47	388	241	39	13	2660.2	847	123	1.141	2.9	1.44	41.8
Elroy Face	15	100	0.518	3.46	**802**	6	0	**186**	1314.2	842	110	1.239	5.8	2.43	20.6

#8 Cincinnati Reds (1890-1953, 1960- pres.); Cincinnati Redlegs (1954-1959); Cincinnati Red Stockings (1882-1889)

(Photo by Lee Burchfield/Creative Commons)

Team Background

Playoff appearances: 15 **Pennants: 10** **World Series titles: 5**
Collective team WAR: 556.6
Strengths: The Reds strengths and weaknesses are eerily similar to the Pirates: Stacked lineup…
Weaknesses: Quality of starting pitching just not there.
What to expect from the next 11 pages: A dude named Heinie. Another dude named Noodles.

The period of the Reds greatest success came in the 1970s when they ran the "Big Red Machine" in the Queen City. During the grooviest decade we've seen, the Reds reached four World Series, winning two of them and running out some of the best teams baseball has ever seen. As such, a high number of players from those teams appear on this Reds Starting IX.

The club recently became the sixth team to pass 10,000 wins as a franchise and have done so with more wins than losses in their illustrious history. The Reds have also would make Shakespeare proud, as a Red by any other name is just as winning. That's just a really pretentious way of saying that the Reds have winning records under all three of their different franchise names (listed above, the Reds, the Redlegs, and the Red Stockings).

The franchise got there thanks in part to 34 different 20-game winners, 11 different 25-game winners, and four different 30-game winners (the most recent coming in 1889). That horrible segue was really just to give me an opportunity to bring up Baseball-Reference's Play Index. The Play Index is probably the most valuable tools any baseball writer (or curious fan) can have, giving access to the billions and billions of statistics easily sorted and manipulated with the click of a few buttons.

Wondering which switch-handed second baseman has the most home runs in history? The answer is Roberto Alomar. How many times has a pitcher at least 40 years old struck out at least 150 hitters in a season? Twenty-three times, with Nolan Ryan doing so six (six!) different seasons. It's also useful for team queries, not just players. Bet you didn't know that 1977 Boston Red Sox are the only team in baseball history with five home runs in three straight games, doing so from June 17-19 against the Yankees. There's basically no question the Play Index can't answer, and it's an invaluable tool for any baseball fan who likes to play around with numbers.

As you can probably tell by this point of the Reds team intro, there no real theme here. The Rays had the best managers in baseball history, the Angels got the MLB At Bat rankings, and the Blue Jays, of course, got Mr. Begley's excellent anagrams – the Reds? They're getting a brief Play Index shout out and now a list of bar room baseball argument starters. You win some, you lose some. Anyway, bust these divisive bad boys out and the bar and sit back and enjoy the hours upon hours of circular debate between you and your baseball-loving friends:

* Who had a better moustache – Rollie Fingers or Goose Gossage? For that matter, who had the funnier name of the two?
* Is the shift good or bad for baseball?
* Who is the true single-season home run king?
* What's the best rivalry in baseball?
* Will WAR still be a stat we use in 2050?
* Will we ever see a left-handed catcher again?
* Is Yasiel Puig good for the game or bad for the game?
* Fenway or Wrigley
* Should baseball players "stick to sports" or use their place in the spotlight to comment on society? Do you feel the same way if they express opinions opposite of yours?
* Is it harder to throw a major league level curveball or hit a major league level curveball?
* Could you be a league-average second baseman, strictly from a defensive perspective? (The answer is clearly no, but this is an actual debate that was had by my group of friends.)
* Would you take PEDs if it was the difference between being a career minor leaguer or a replacement-level major leaguer?
* DiMaggio or Mantle (you'll know the correct answer by the end of this book)
* WHAT DOES BASEBALL NEED TO DO TO ATTRACT MORE YOUTH VIEWERS?!?!?
* How many at bats would it take for you to get a hit off an MLB pitcher?
* What would be your first move if you were hired as the Reds GM? (There's a bone for you, Cincy fans.)
* Does anyone in the world have a weirder voice than John Lackey?
* Should there be a hard cap in Major League Baseball?
* Is a four-homer game really more impressive than a perfect game? Remember, there are still fewer four-homer games in MLB history.
* What would Giancarlo Stanton's stats have looked like if you dropped him into the 1970s?
* Is Mike Trout already a top-50 player all-time? How about top 25? Top 10?
* Who is your favorite non-Hall of Fame player all-time, and why isn't it Bernie Williams?
* Which non-baseball professional athlete would have been the best baseball player (John Elway, perhaps?), and just how good would he/she have been?
* What is the best baseball conspiracy you have ever heard?
* To robo-ump or not to robo-ump?
* How can the sport spice up the television viewing experience without turning itself into a real-life version of Blernsball from *Futurama*?
* Who do you enjoy more the scrappy .280 hitter, or the preternaturally talented .330 hitter?
* Is baseball just a metaphor for America?
* Are we living in the Matrix?

Stick with those, and your bar debates will never Go Hungry AGAIN! (Yes, that is indeed a beyond-ridiculously obscure *Lion King* reference, thanks for noticing.)

Random cool things about the (early days of the) franchise:

The Cincinnati Red Stockings, formed in 1869, were baseball's first professional baseball team. That squad was a juggernaut, winning literally every game that season (the exact number of wins in all games is a bit shaky, but their multi-season win streak got to around 80). By the time the National League formed in 1876, they had slipped quite a bit in comparison to the rest of the sport, and they went 9-56 in the inaugural season of the league. Even worse, the Reds were banned from the league for playing games on Sunday and selling beers at their games. (Heathens!)

This is where it gets a bit confusing with team name and how to define an MLB franchise. Technically, those first Reds teams aren't aligned with the modern iteration of the Reds because they joined the American Association in 1882, only coming back to the NL in 1890 after having been banned from the league previously. (The American Association was far more relaxed, as it let teams sell beer and play on Sundays.) However, if you go by Baseball-Almanac, their entire team history is together, and although that may not technically be correct, it seems silly to have the first 10 years of the Cincinnati baseball team (with "Red" right there in the name) just floating without any connection to modern baseball because they were such an impressive unit, so I agree with Baseball-Almanac, personally. Long story short: baseball history is weird and confusing.

Starting IX

C Johnny Bench (1967-1983)

In the discussion for best catchers of all time, Bench combined defensive, offensive, and play-calling ability as well as anyone the game has ever seen. Aptly nicknamed "The Little General," Bench had a positive dWAR each of his first 14 years in the league, which just so happened to be all his years behind the plate. He led the league in caught stealing percentage three times and, if possible, was underrated defensively because of how he was able to control the pitching staff from behind the plate. Bench was a well above-average hitter as well, topping 100 RBI six times for his career. He had a career high 148 in 1970, [his] first MVP year. That same year he also became the first catcher to ever lead the league in both home runs (45) and RBI in the same season, and then he did it again two years later, capturing another MVP.

Bench was a regular contributor to the Reds playoff success during the "Big Red Machine" years. He appeared in 10 playoff series with the Reds and hit 10 home runs. The most impressive part of that, however, is that he hit a home run in nine different series, meaning that there was only one playoff series in which he didn't homer. From a defensive perspective, he absolutely shut down the opponent's running game in the postseason, surrendering only six successful steals in 45 League Championship and World Series games in the Big Red Machine's prime (1970-1979). For comparison, during those 45 games, the Reds stole 54 bases. (That gem was from David Schoenfield of *ESPN*.)

Before his career began, Bench came across to some as a bit over-confident, declaring that he would win Rookie of the Year and become the first $100,000 catcher. Bench proved to be self-confident rather than over-confident, as both claims turned out to be true. The line between confident and cocky is one that many athletes straddle, and a part of the game that the media has never really understood. Young athletes are often portrayed as too brash, or too big for their britches, if they talk a bit before they have quote-unquote *proven it*. A home run/bat flip combo is regarded with the same vitriol as leaving a turd in the middle of the clubhouse. However, what is lost on many writers is that without that inflated sense of self, many of these athletes wouldn't have been able to get as far as the big leagues. Believing in oneself – even to what sometimes seems, to an outside perspective, like an inordinate amount – is one part of sports that seems to have the biggest disconnect between those who played professionally and those who didn't. This makes sense. What doesn't make sense, but still happens all the time, is the fact that the same men who use this (perhaps slightly-inflated) sense of self to drive themselves to success can't recognize this trait in other players, instead getting angry when players do things like the aforementioned bat flips, or slightly arrogant post-game comments. When the pointy-headed media types freak out about it, that makes sense. When it's like looking in a mirror for some athletes, and they still can't recognize it, that's mind-numbing.

Anyway, back to Bench: in his book, *Playing the Field*, Jim Kaplan stated, "Johnny Bench changed catching more than any player influenced any position in baseball history." Although debatable and bold, it isn't as if this statement is complete hyperbole. Chief Bender and Candy Cummings had huge influences on the pitching position, as they are credited with inventing the curveball and slider, respectively. Before Ernie Banks, there weren't shortstops that hit with much power. Nobody in baseball history impacted the game as a whole as much as Babe Ruth. And Jackie Robinson, well, he's kind of important to baseball history. But Bench certainly did have an immense impact on the art of catching. Bench helped to popularize the hinge catcher's mitt, and he helped baseball fans realize that an incredible defensive catcher can also be a massive contributor with the bat. Read any biography of Bench and it will note that he redefined the position. It's no mistake he's thought of by many as the G.O.A.T behind the dish.

1B Tony Pérez (1964-1976; 1984-1986)

Another key contributor to the "Big Red Machine," Pérez was a consistent, although never dominant (the only non-defensive metrics in which he ever led the league were double plays grounded into and oWAR, once a piece), player who suited up for the Reds the first 13 years of his career, later returning for his final three seasons. In 12 full seasons with the Reds, Pérez drove in 100 runs half of those years and, after establishing himself as a full-time player, never dropped drove in fewer than 90 RBI for more than a decade (1967-1977). Pérez put together a strong 1975 playoff run during which he hit .250 but managed to score seven runs, hit four home runs, and have 11 RBI, helping the Reds win their first World Series in 35 years. Pérez is an interesting case of being both underrated and overrated at the same time, and he's a perfect example of how statistics can be manipulated. He's a prime case for why you should always come to your own conclusions and not just follow the flow of conversation about a player.

On the one hand, Pérez is a bit like Joe Carter, a player whose reputation benefited greatly from hitting in the middle of the order for a very strong offense team,[340] and his RBI totals flatter him. One of the biggest cases for Pérez to be in the discussion with the other elite Reds players relies heavily on those RBI. As sabermetricians love to point out, RBI are one of the worst metrics when used as the sole measure of a hitter. Hence, overrated. However, Pérez played in a run-dampening environment for the beginning of his career, and he was a better defender than he is given credit for. Hence, underrated. In

[340] In 1975, the Reds led the NL in runs scored by over 100 runs.

aggregate, Pérez is actually properly-rated historically, but many people you ask would either consider him to be either much worse or much better than he actually was because of the unique nature of his career.

For the Reds franchise, however, the present and future at first base is, and has been, bright. This spot should soon be taken over by one Joey Votto. Votto will be with the franchise for the foreseeable future, as they locked him up through at least 2023 with a mammoth contract in 2011. Votto has all the tools to be a late-career superstar, and even though this contract will pay him $25,000,000 after he has turned 40, it was a deal the Reds had to make to keep their face of the franchise in town; the Yankees would have offered a King's ransom, all the tea in China, and half of Ron Swanson's underground gold if he reached free agency. As mentioned, Votto's skill set and position seem likely to age well, with the only risk being small injuries piling up, but that's like the over-protective grandpa who doesn't want you to drive because he saw an accident on the news last night – injuries happen. Votto's skill set leans heavily on his ability to get on base as well as anybody in baseball, as he has led the league in on-base percentage six of the past eight years (2010-2013 and 2016-2017), as well as leading the league in walks for five of those years (2011-13, 2015, and 2017). Although a dip in home run totals and a lost 2014 season may seem troublesome, his OPS has stayed relatively steady over the years, and one lost season is far from a death knell for one of baseball's most consistent stars.

In order to take over this position, Votto wouldn't have to do a ton, as he has, amazingly, already passed Pérez in WAR with the Reds. One thing Votto still needs to do is have some postseason success. This wouldn't be essential, and Votto could pass him regardless within a few seasons, but Pérez has a massive edge with his playoff appearances and playoff success right now. So far, Votto has struggled, as has the team, with Joey driving in only one run in eight playoff games. The team has struggled in the playoffs as well, and some team success would certainly help bolster Votto's resume. If Votto were able to compile three more 6.0+ WAR seasons, the postseason success may not be a necessity, as he will have established himself as the top first baseman in franchise history anyways.

Herein lies one of the toughest things about this system, however. Projecting careers is one of the most difficult things to do.[341] As the always-entertaining Michael Baumann noted, "Sports is one of the few remaining arenas in which it's still socially acceptable to make guesses and call them predictions." The metaphorical highway of baseball history is lined with the carcasses of once-promising careers that would have "projected" to be Hall of Fame players. Some of these players were derailed because of injury, and some just saw their skills fade faster than expected. Any way it happens, it happens without the prognosticator being able to see it coming (most of the time). Granted some players play a certain way that lends itself to injury, or some outperform their peripheral statistics to the point that it becomes obvious that their numbers will come crashing down to earth, but really the art of baseball projections is still an inexact science when put to an N=1, individual player test. That being said, I do think Votto will have earned a right to this position by 2019 or so and will be worth the contract the Reds gave him.[342] Votto has a near perfect swing – from 2010-2012 there were more perfect games across the big leagues than Joey Votto infield pop-ups(!)[343] – and the kind of contact he makes rarely fades into the sunset. He had an on-base percentage of .394 in plate appearances that reached two strikes in 2012 for Chrissakes.

For now, though, Pérez gets the nod, as his 16 seasons and two rings can't be matched by Votto' 11 ringless seasons just yet. Rings are only used as a tiebreaker in this book, but this matchup is tight enough – and the "Big Red Machine" is a big enough deal in Reds history – that they are the deciding factor for now.

2B Joe Morgan (1972-1979)

Better known by today's generation for being an announcer on ESPN[344] than a two-bagger for the Reds, Morgan was an integral cog of "The Big Red Machine," if not the most important cog. A WAR fiend,[345] Morgan amassed more than 47.0 WAR in his first five years in Cincinnati and led the league in oWAR each of his first six years with the club. He came to the team as an already established second baseman, with two All-Star appearances and a Rookie of the Year runner-up while in Houston, but his game really elevated in Cincinnati. Morgan came to a Reds team that was in the midst of building a winning mentality. Morgan only helped to improve this attitude, and the team enjoyed its period of greatest success while he was there. Morgan was a plus defender in his time in Cincinnati, with his four best dWAR seasons and all five of his Gold Gloves coming as a member of the Reds. His batting stance is also one of the all-time greats, and one that is butchered to hilarious results in almost any video game trying to recreate it.

As is, Morgan is one of the all-time greats, especially at the second base position, but if he could have enjoyed the career success he had in Cincinnati for his whole career, he would have been in the discussion among the top five-to-ten players of all time. When looking at his numbers, they don't appear to be all-world at first glance. His batting average in Cincinnati was a workmanlike .288, and although he hit .327 and then .320 in his MVP seasons, that still doesn't stick out too much. His 1975 MVP set the record for largest margin of victory for an MVP, a surprising fact given that he was more

---

[341] While simultaneously being one of the most fun things to do.
[342] For the record I think Votto ends up with a top-20 all-time on-base percentage, and at least one more MVP to go with at least one ring for his career.
[343] Shoutout to Jeff Sullivan of *Fangraphs* for that gem.
[344] And one who was so bad he spurred Firejoemorgan.com, the brilliant blog from Michael Schur (the creator of *Parks and Rec*, *Brooklyn Nine-Nine* and *The Good Place*), the number one person on earth I most want to meet and have dinner with.
[345] He owns the top four single-season WAR totals in Reds history.

beloved by advanced metrics than traditional metrics. Did the voters that year actually have their heads on straight? It's far more likely that even a broken clock is right twice a day, and that they were drinking the "clubhouse leader on the best team in baseball" Kool-Aid.

Morgan's power numbers were respectable in Cincy, with over 150 home runs in his eight years in the Queen City. He relied more on consistency, though, as he never topped 27 home runs in a season. The numbers that do stand out, however, were his ability to get on base, and what he did once he got on base. His .415 on-base percentage with the club is outstanding – through his first six years with the club, it was .429. This becomes even more impressive given the era in which he played. When Morgan retired, he was the NL all-time leader in base on balls (1,865) and trailed only Babe Ruth in all of baseball history. Once he got on base, he was not afraid to run those bases, stealing over 400 bases with the club (his first five years in Cincy he averaged 62 steals a year) and scoring over a 100 runs a year on average for his time with the Reds. This ability to get on base, and succeed once there, along with his defensive ability and the fact that any offense from a team's second baseman is usually gravy, all made Morgan an essential cog in The Big Red Machine.

A couple more quick tallies in Morgan's achievements column: he's the only second baseman to have won consecutive MVPs, and in fact, the only second baseman to have won even more than one MVP. In 1977, Morgan had only five errors all season which set an NL record for second baseman, and the next season he went 90 games without an error, setting another record for the position. Probably his own personal career highlight was that he knocked in the game-winning runs in Games 3 and 7 of the 1975 World Series. Finally, when Bill James created a statistic to measure the smartest player in baseball history (fielding percentage compared to league average, stolen base percentage, strikeout to walk ratio, and walk frequency), Morgan came out on top.

Finally, two final quotes that, in combination, serve to perfectly sum up Morgan. The first is from Morgan himself. When Morgan was called a troublemaker by his manager, Morgan's response was, "Anyone was a troublemaker who was smarter than Harry Walker, and that didn't take much." The second came from Bill Russell (the baseball one, not the basketball one), who said of Morgan, "Isn't it interesting how good teams seem to follow him around?"

3B Heinie Groh (1913-1921)

A solid, defensive-minded infielder with limited power, Groh's best ability was getting on base. Sound familiar? Groh was not part of The Big Red Machine – and he is no Joe Morgan – but he was a good player for the Reds in their early days. He was a decent run producer and had plus steals totals, but for the years in which caught stealing was tracked, it's clear that he wasn't the best base runner due to the lofty number of times he was cut down on the basepaths, something Morgan almost never did.

Back to his positives, though: Groh drew walks at almost exactly a 2:1 ratio of how much he struck out, and he was in the top five in the league in on-base percentage five of his nine years in Cincinnati. He also finished second in the league in oWAR three straight years (1917-1919), finishing third the season before that. According to Greg Gajus, a respected baseball historian of Groh's era, Groh would have won one MVP for sure (1919), and possibly two others (1916 and 1918), had the award been in place. Groh capped that 1919 season as a member of the first championship-winning Reds team.

Now Heinie Groh has a rather unusual name (and rather entertaining if you still have the maturity level of a five-year-old, as I do), which gives us a perfect opportunity to do a Starting IX of the funniest names in baseball history. There will be no nicknames included, although I reallllly wanted to include "Chicken Wolf." Get ready for a bunch of dick jokes.[346]

SP) Johnny Dickshot C) Rusty Kuntz 1B) Guy Bush 2B) Urban Shocker 3B) Dick Padden SS) Jack Glasscock LF) Coco Crisp CF) Dick Pole RF) Dan Smith, BYU

Back to Groh as a player: he had a truly funky batting stance, standing all the way at the front of the batter's box with both feet facing the pitcher a la Tony Bautista. He was also the first player to use a bottle bat – thicker barrel, tiny handle – which he used to slap the ball all over the field.

SS Barry Larkin (1986-2004)

A Red for life, Larkin is high up on the franchise statistical lists for many a metric. He is top five in both offensive and defensive WAR, third in games played, second in hits, has the top Power/Speed number in team history, and is, at worst, in the top 10 in basically every category in Reds history. Despite playing at a high level for an extended period of time (see his 12 All-Star appearances and his 1995 MVP), Larkin never led the league in any surface statistic in his career. He did lead the leagues in WAR in 1988, and he was frequently in the top five in numerous statistical categories – especially batting average and stolen bases – but his "dominance" came in the form of being so well-rounded.

Larkin struggled a bit with nagging injuries throughout his whole career and, as such, missed at least 35 games in 10 of his 19 years in the league. If it hadn't been for injuries, he likely would have surpassed 3,000 hits and been a member of

[346] After I did this, I saw that Cespedes Family BBQ, one of the best Twitter follows out there, did a bracket of the best names in baseball history, and it's a lot more thorough. C'est la vie.

the 250/250 career home runs/stolen bases club. As is, he was the first shortstop to reach the (admittedly arbitrary) plateaus of 2,000 hits, 170 home runs, and 350 steals (Derek Jeter and Jimmy Rollins have since joined him). Larkin, like many of this team already, had a good batting eye, and for his career, he drew more walks than he had strikeouts. This Reds lineup would be a sneaky choice as a top offensive threat in the hypothetical Starting IX tournament to take place precisely never.

Larkin was the only shortstop in the 1990s to steal 50 bases, doing so in 1995, and he did so at a phenomenal rate throughout his entire career. In fact, his career stolen base percentage (83.1 percent) is third all-time for players with as many career steals as Larkin (379), and he never got caught stealing more than 10 times in a season – not bad for a guy often battling lower body injuries.

Larkin was also a very good postseason player for the Reds, and in four playoff appearances (which included one World Series win), he hit .338 with 11 runs and eight steals in 17 games. Along with the rest of this infield, Larkin was solid defensively, amassing over 13.0 wins, per dWAR, for the Reds over the course of his career. Along with his one MVP, Larkin also has a Roberto Clemente Award for "best exemplifying the game of baseball, sportsmanship, community involvement, and the individual's contribution to the team," and a Lou Gehrig Memorial Award for "exemplary contributions to both his community and philanthropy." These three achievements all came during a pretty successful three-year stretch from 1993-1995.

Larkin's 1995 MVP season wasn't actually Larkin's best season by many measures. His WAR (5.9) was good for fifth among position players (compared to first in 1988 and fourth in 1991) and only the fourth-best total of his career. He more than doubled his home run total the next season (going from 15 to 33) when he became the first shortstop to go 30/30 HR/SB. His .319 batting average was his best average for a season over 100 games, but his career average was .295, so he was never much lower than .300. He played only 131 games (granted it was a 144-game season due to the strike, but still that's about 10 percent of the season missed), and he didn't lead the league in any statistical category. In the end, his career-high stolen base total, along with his team's success, played a large role in him getting the MVP. The biggest reason, however, may have been due to Major League Baseball treating the award as a bit of a lifetime achievement award. This makes sense: Larkin was a well-respected man by the media. He was a man who had, as noted, won both the Roberto Clemente and Lou Gehrig awards in the previous two seasons.

This is done in any award-giving community (NBA and NFL MVPs, Emmy's, Oscars, etc.), and it is not always the worst thing, but it does usually take the award away from a more deserving recipient. Here is a quick list of the MLB MVP awards that are a little hard to explain:

1988 Kirk Gibson (NL): Gibson was awarded the MVP despite not garnering any black ink on his baseball card. It was, however, the best season of his career by WAR, and Gibson went on to prove the voters prescient when he provided one of the best moments in baseball history with his pinch-hit home run in Game 1 of the 1988 World Series. Maybe the baseball writers know what they're doing! Oh, we're just getting started, though.

1979 Willie Stargell (NL): At first glance, this appears to be a case of the baseball writer's pulling a "2006 Academy Awards" and awarding ~~Martin Scorsese~~ Willie Stargell an ~~Oscar~~ MVP for ~~"The Departed"~~ the 1979 baseball season. It was not Stargell's best work,[347] but he sure as hell deserved it at this point. There is an underlying story, however, as was covered in the Pirates Starting IX. Stargell's Pirates enjoyed great success in 1979, and it was under Stargell's "Pops" tutelage that the team really came together. That was what really won McCovey the award, even more so than his lifetime achievements.

1964 Ken Boyer (NL): A possible candidate for a lifetime achievement case? Boyer had never screwed over by the baseball writers before, and he was only in his 10th season in the league. It might have had more to do with team success or possibly a (*gasp*) slightly racist group of old white baseball writers (seriously check out Willie Mays, Dick Allen, or Roberto Clemente that year and tell me they didn't deserve it; although Ron Santo was way better than Boyer too, and he was white as can be) wanted a "nice, respectable" third basemen with "good fundamentals" and "a hard-work attitude" to win the award… Nah, nothing like that has ever happened in *our* national pastime.

1944 Marty Marion (NL): Marion was able to travel overseas and helped to single-handedly take down the German Army while simultaneously finding a cure for polio and playing an MVP-level shortstop for the Cardin… Oh that didn't happen, then I have no idea how he won this award.

1926 Bob O'Farrell (NL): I have no hard evidence, but I'm 95 percent sure sexual favors were involved.

1914 Johnny Evers (NL): The best case to rival Larkin for "lifetime achievement award MVP," Evers had a solid year, but there were certainly more logical choices. It wasn't Evers best season, but he was part of the famous Tinker-to-Evers-to-Chance combination of baseball lore. Of course, there's one big difference between Larkin and Evers, the MVP wasn't around for much of Evers career, meaning that he actually couldn't have won it in many of his best seasons. It is funny, though, that in both cases it was a middle infielder from the Midwest who was given the awarded a bit late – probably because every other year it went to an outfielder/catcher from a team in New York.

An interesting current note on Larkin to end: Larkin gets credit with the current Reds organization for what he

---

[347] For my money, the top five Scorsese films: 1) *Raging Bull* 2) *Goodfellas* 3) *The Departed* 4) *The Last Waltz/ Shine a Light* (cheating I know) 5) *Mean Streets*. Way down the list: *Taxi Driver*. Not for me.

probably thought of as a throw-away comment to Zack Cozart when, in Spring Training in 2015, Larkin asked the young Reds shortstop (who currently starts for the team) if he had ever thought of simply trying to crush the inside of the ball. Cozart was apparently sitting on the roof toilet from *Scrubs*, because the epiphany was immediate, and Cozart became a viable MLB hitter overnight. Cozart's OPS+ before that Larkin comment: 76; afterwards: 115.

LF Frank Robinson (1956-1965)

One of the nice things about setting up a list of teams like this, is that some players are able to compile strong enough statistics with two teams to appear multiple times in this book. This is the sign of a truly gifted player, but at the same time, one who, for whatever reason (either the player wanting to leave the organization or the organization not wanting the player enough), didn't stay with one organization their whole career. Usually the most talented players of all time are valuable enough to their team that the team will do anything within their power to keep them, and as a result, many of the all-time greats stay with one team for the majority of their prime.

This wasn't the case with Robinson. As was mentioned in his Orioles write-up (Page 180), Robinson had a rather nasty divorce from the Reds, with plenty of vitriol spit from both sides. This explains how Robinson ended up on two team's Starting IX's, despite being one of the all-time legends. For Robinson, when his new team (Orioles) topped his old team (Reds) in the 1970 World Series (five years after his acrimonious divorce from the Reds), the victory was even sweeter for Robinson; and the loss was even more bitter for Reds fans.

Since this is the Reds section, however, we will focus on Robinson's time in Cincy. Robinson broke into the league in 1952, and he did so in style. He won Rookie of the Year behind 122 runs, 38 home runs, and 83 RBI, as well as .290/.379/.558 slashes (143 OPS+). Robinson continued at an excellent pace for his time in Cincy, netting the club over 6.0 wins a year on average for his 10 years there. His *average* season with the Reds was 104 runs, 32 home runs, and 101 RBI with .303/.389/.554 slashes (150 OPS+). He even stole over 160 bases in those 10 seasons, topping out at 26 steals in 1963.

Robinson stuck around baseball after his playing days and became a (reluctant) pioneer. He was reluctant only in that he believed he shouldn't have to be pioneering. He became the first black manager when he was hired by Cleveland in 1974, starting the gig as a player/manager at the outset of his tenure. He hit a home run in his managerial debut, but that was far from the highlight of the day for Robinson, as Rachel Robinson, Jackie Robinson' wife, was in attendance, an honor which Robinson truly recognized.

After a while, Cleveland moved on from Robinson, who eventually took the Giants managerial role, adding the title of "First black manager in the National League" to his resume. A fact that, given it was six years after his breakthrough as the first black manager in the American League, bothered Robinson more than anything. While Robinson has been pioneering across the sport at all levels (he is currently the Honorary American League President), Robinson would undoubtedly prefer if he, as a black man, had some company in the front offices of MLB teams. Right now, the NBA has not just stolen the crown as the most progressive sport in terms of hiring practices, they are running away and hiding with it. Baseball, for a sport so steeply tied to the progress in race relations in the U.S., really needs to step up and once again be at the forefront of inclusion in the world of sports ownership and management.

CF Vada Pinson (1958-1968)

Pinson played 18 years in the majors and was a Red for his first 11 seasons. Once he got established, his first nine full seasons in Cincy were his nine highest WAR totals for his career. Like the man to his right, in left field,[348] Pinson was a Red in the 1960s[349] and left the team before their Big Red Run of Success in the next decade. Pinson was actually a childhood friend of Frank Robinson's, and Robinson was one of the reasons Pinson signed in Cincinnati. Pinson had a solid power/speed combo that resulted in five 20/20 HR/SB seasons in his time in Cincinnati. Never a top home run threat, Pinson did have solid total base numbers due to strong doubles and triples totals, leading the league in each category two separate times while with the club. Pinson's greatest strength lay not in his dominance in one particular season, but rather in his consistency for the team, another theme with this Reds Starting IX. For a stretch of nine years, Pinson never missed more than eight games in a season, hit under .287 only once, and scored under 90 runs only one time, as well.

Pinson experienced a phenomenon opposite of what will be covered in the second base spot for the Oakland A's. His best years were early, and his numbers never reached that point again partially due to the fact that his prime years were in a pitching era instead of a hitting era. Although Pinson's supposed early peak is due a bit to the era in which he played, even by advanced metrics, he hit his peak in his age-22 season and then petered off gradually from there. This type of career arc is becoming more and more common in baseball today. Jeff Zimmerman of *FanGraphs* wrote a very interesting piece in which he studied hitters in the post-Steroid era (2006-2013) and looked at several metrics (wOBA, wRC+, as well as home runs and steals) to study new-era aging curves. He found that in nearly all of these metrics, hitters, as a whole, were peaking as they came into the league and then gradually declining the rest of their career. This has been more commonly thought of as the

[348] It's weird how that works, huh?
[349] Better than being a "Red" in the 1950s! Can I get an amen, Senator McCarthy?!

aging curve for pitchers, but hitters (thanks to some extracurricular help) appeared to be peaking nearly a decade into their careers during the 1990s and early 2000s. According to Zimmerman, the modern result is due to the fact that current hitters are more prepared, mentally and physically, for the major leagues at a younger age thanks to advancements made in training, etc. He also attributes the new aging curve to teams now knowing better when a player should be brought up from the minor leagues.

Finally, there was a very interesting story in Bill James' write-up of Pinson in his *Historical Baseball Abstract*, although saying a story from James' *Abstract* is interesting is somewhat redundant, since James' *Abstract* is the moral equivalent to Herodotus' *The Histories*, but for baseball fans. There was a Cincinnati sports writer, Earl Lawson, who seemed to goat Pinson on a daily basis in the local *Cincinnati Seasons*. The two had their issues for a while until one day Lawson came into the clubhouse unaware that Pinson's teammates had been riling him up about what to do with Lawson. Pinson confronted Lawson, and when things escalated, Pinson punched Lawson. The journalist called the cops, pressed charges, and eventually settled out of court. It may have been the way James told the story, or the fact that I'm a bit of a contrarian, but reading James' rendition of it, I actually felt myself taking Pinson's side.

RF Ival Goodman (1935-1942)

Goodman played only eight seasons in Cincinnati, and in two of those he played under 100 games. A solid extra-base hitter, Goodman led the league in triples the first two years of his career. In 1938, he had 27 doubles, 10 triples, 30 home runs, and posted the highest WAR of his career (5.9). Goodman had double-digit triples totals his first five years in the big leagues, one of only three players in Major League Baseball history to do so. He played on two pennant-winning Reds teams (1939 and 1940) and won the World Series in 1940. In that series, he scored and knocked in five runs apiece.

Goodman was a magnet for the baseball, as well. In one four-year stretch, he led the league in hit by pitches three times and finished second the other year. This isn't really a skill per se, but since getting on base is so important, it also isn't a bad stat in which to lead the league (although the bruises may say otherwise). He is yet another player on this team who finished his career with more walks than strikeouts, a growing trend which really has me considering the Reds as a sleeper contender for the best lineup so far. This lineup would be brutal to go deep into a game against.

Utility Pete Rose (1963-1978; 1984-1986)

The natural thing to talk about with Rose is the Hall of Fame controversy. That will be touched upon, but first let's assess his career from a non-tainted perspective. Rose is the Reds career leader in numerous categories: WAR (77.7), games played (2,722), runs (1,741), hits (3,358), total bases (4,645), walks (1,210), and extra-base hits (868). He also has five of the top six single-season hit totals in Reds franchise history. A great number of his accomplishments come from the fact that he had such a long career, and as such, he is the all-time leader in all of baseball history in games (3,562), plate appearances (15,890), at bats (14,053), and hits (4,256). His 1973 MVP and three batting titles show he was more than just a player with a long career, though. Part of Rose's game for which he was most famous was his effort, which garnered him the nickname "Charlie Hustle." He once said, "I'd walk through hell in a gasoline suit to keep playing baseball."

It is no surprise, but is nonetheless impressive, that although he has over 2,500 more plate appearances than the next highest Red, he is only sixth in franchise history in double plays grounded into. Rose went full-blast, 24/7/365 for the Reds. He did take it too far sometimes, most famously separating Ray Fosse's shoulder in an All-Star Game, in part derailing a promising career for Fosse. A simple google image search of "Pete Rose" returns numerous photos of him diving headfirst into bases and just leaving it all on the field. (An image then used hilariously as a sexual metaphor in *Arrested Development*.)

It is fitting that Rose take the utility position, as he was an All-Star at five different positions during his career and was the first player to ever play 500 games at five different positions (first base, second base, third base, left field, and right field). Rose never was a WAR machine like some of the other all-timers – he topped 8.0 WAR in a season only once and that doubled as the only season in which he even topped 7.0 WAR – but don't be fooled, he's deserving of his status as a legend.

In 1978, Rose became the first switch-hitter to hit 50 doubles in a season, and although his hit and run totals garnered him plenty of black ink, there are plenty of les-flattering statistics for baseball's all-time leading hits man. He has the second-lowest slugging percentage (.409) of any member of the 3,000-hit club, and he has the fifth-lowest wins above average of that 31-man group (28.6). His career stolen base success rate was 57.1 percent, far below the threshold at which one should be stealing bases. The point can even be made that Rose really played out the string at the end of his career just for the all-time hits record.[350] Rose's slugging percentage was .315 over his final five years, and how much he was actually helping his team could be called into question. This was a man about whom Johnny Bench said, "I've never seen anyone more statistics conscious than Pete Rose," and although Bench was saying this in a positive light, the man clearly was obsessive about attaining the Holy Grail that was Cobb's hit record. *The Sporting News* went so far as to post the headline, "Pete Rose: Baseball's steadiest out-producer?" late in Rose's career.

---

[350] In the irony of all ironies, near the end of Jimmy Rollins' days in Philadelphia, Rose put Rollins on blast for trying to stay with the Phillies and run up his hit total with the franchise.

Still, while Rose may be a bit overhyped in terms of anyone thinking he's the best hitter of all time because of the hit record, eliminating him from the discussion of great players is wrong. He gave 110 percent all day, which is indeed a skill and can help to set the tone for a ball club. Rose made the playoffs eight different seasons, and his teams were not usually in the cellar for long. His type of play brought out the best in teammates, and although he wasn't the most popular guy, each team needs someone like him to set the intensity for the club. This isn't something that has necessarily been determined yet by statistics, but anyone who has ever played on a team at any level knows it's true. He managed to play at least 148 games every season for a decade-and-a-half prime, and considering the hair-on-fire style he was playing, that was no easy feat. Just look at how many times Bryce Harper (who names Pete Rose as his baseball idol) has been on the DL with his style of play. Health is most certainly a skill.

Pete Rose helped popularize the head-first slide, which in a way acts as a pretty solid metaphor for Rose as a player. The head-first slide (especially into first base) isn't really that helpful in terms of arriving at the base any faster. It does, however, fire up the crowd and sometimes fellow teammates, and the old-school guys love it.[351] Rose took every advantage he thought could help him, worked for every hit he got, and sprinted every inch he had to. While a lot of these "baseball antics" may not have actually done that much (hustling out a routine grounder probably nets an extra one or two times on base in a given season), it didn't matter to Rose, all that mattered was baseball.

This is why it is such a shame that he isn't in the Hall of Fame. It's pretty hard to make the case for anyone loving baseball more than Rose, and on a statistical level, he certainly deserves to have a plaque in Cooperstown. However, Selig made his stance on Rose clear:[352] Rose gambled on baseball, and that's going to keep him out as long as Selig has any say in the matter (and don't think Selig's pull has ended just because he is no longer the commissioner). There have been a lot of comparisons between what Rose did to be left out of the Hall and what PED users did to being on the outside looking in. This is a pretty useless discussion unless you're a baseball writer out of ideas and on a short deadline. Rose put a bit of a black mark on the game, but he gained no advantage whatsoever from the bets that he placed *on his own team* when he was the manager of the Reds. Part of the reason MLB came down so hard on Rose has to do with baseball's complicated history with the fixing of games.

The most famous, non-Pete Rose, non-PED user to be absent in Cooperstown is Shoeless Joe Jackson. He was the most famous member of the Black Sox, and his story was covered earlier: he and his teammates accepted bets to fix the 1919 World Series. Eight players from the team drew lifetime banishments from baseball as a result. Although this was the most famous incident, it came as the culmination of a long-running problem with the fixing of games across Major League Baseball in this era. One notorious player, Hal Chase, was a great player but a heinous man, taking money from any and everyone to throw games left and right. There were also others, but Chase is the most famous, and so when the Black Sox scandal broke, Commissioner Landis brought down the hammer hard because he believed it necessary to root out this insidious problem from baseball. However, in doing so, he also set a precedent for how Major League Baseball would deal with future instances of gambling involved in the sport. Thus, even though there was no evidence that Rose gambled against his own team, he got the book thrown at him.

Whether Rose's ban should be lifted or not is one of baseball's most divisive talking points, and honestly there's no right answer. There's plenty of gray, and although I believe he should be in the Hall, I certainly wouldn't disregard what the Rose-ban proponents have to say. For my money, the winning argument is that the Hall is a baseball museum first and foremost. It's been discussed numerous times in this book, just look at how awful a lot of baseball's best players were. They were clansmen, murderers, wife beaters, and casual racists – and none of them were kept out because of their sins. It seems wrong to keep out Rose.

SP Noodles Hahn (1899-1905)

Good ole Noodles only threw six full seasons with the Reds, but all six seasons were strong ones. He led the league in strikeouts his first three full seasons in the league, topping out at 239 in 1901, when he was responsible for 22 of his team's 52 wins, the second-highest rate of a team's single-season wins total from one pitcher in the modern era (Steve Carlton, 1972). That same season, Hanh set the modern single-game strikeout record with 16 strikeouts, a record that stood until 1933. The previous year (1900) Hahn threw the first no-hitter of the century. Hahn had good control and threw a lot of innings while with the club. After his 1899 season, his rookie campaign, he said, "This year shows me what I can do when I'm not drinking. I'll never again indulge in any kind of strong drink."

Hahn is the franchise leader in WAR (among pitchers), despite not being in the top 10 in games started, thanks to six straight seasons with 6.0+ WAR each. He threw a lot of complete games and shutouts, and his 134 ERA+ is good for fourth in franchise history (behind two relievers and José Rijo). He was in the top three in the league in pitcher WAR each of his

[351] Although Rose's hatred for the unwritten rules of baseball is where he would lose those old school guys. He has spoken in support of Ben Davis bunting to break up Curt Schilling's perfect game.

[352] Commissioner Giamatti was the one to originally send down the ruling, but he died just eight days after his decision to ban Rose for life. One has to wonder if Giamatti had lived longer whether he would have lessened the sentence in time. In fact, an interesting What If: What if Selig and others have felt the need to uphold this decision Giamatti made in his final days as a tribute to one of baseball's most famous commissioners? Would Rose have been better off if Giamatti had lived a while longer? All hypothetical (and a bit callous), but fun to think about.

first six full seasons, but he never managed lead the league. He won over 20 games four times, and his single-season ERA+ never dropped below 112. He was the youngest pitcher to win 100 career games with mound at its modern distance (60 feet, 6 inches).

Despite not playing for the entirety of the decade, he was *The Sporting News*' choice for the NL left-handed pitcher of the decade (1900s). His rookie season was the tenth-best season ever for a 20-year-old according to Bill James, and if it hadn't been for arm trouble (move Hahn to the modern game, and he could be a rich man's C.C. Sabathia), he could have had a far longer and more successful career. After posting 45.8 WAR for his first seven seasons (an *average* of 7.6 per season), Hahn posted a season worth 0.1 WAR in year eight and then 0.0 WAR in year nine before fading off into the sunset. His career is one of the ultimate "What if he had played with modern science and pitch limits?" examples.

CP Aroldis Chapman (2010-2015)

Easily one of the most exciting players in baseball today, this spot was originally filled with fun nuggets on Chapman's dominance in terms of stats and pitch speed, but as you can probably guess, this section took a bit of a turn in the 2015 offseason. As one has probably learned by this point in the book, although this is clearly a baseball book first and foremost, there are most certainly issues that take precedent over baseball, and I am definitely in the group that believes these issues should not be merely swept under the rug for the sake of "sticking to sports."

The fact that Chapman has arguably the liveliest arm in baseball history shouldn't overshadow the allegations of domestic abuse that came up when he was being shopped by the Reds after the 2015 season. Domestic abuse has been a hot-button topic around sports for several years now, but that's not what I'm going to write about here. (It seems pretty straight-forward: domestic abuse is horrendous, and players who are found guilty should lose their jobs.) What I find far more interesting is a question that many have tried to answer over the years and, although simple on the surface, is far more complicated in real life. The question: can you root for a team/player whose morals/actions you do not agree with?

It's very easy to take the high road and say that once a player is charged with a crime on the level of domestic abuse, he should be dead to you. And I like to think that most of us who pay enough attention to these things would indeed feel very slimy whenever we see Chapman on the mound. However, how many of us can actually say that if Chapman were on our favorite team, and he were to take the mound in the ninth inning of Game 7 of the World Series (oh hey Cubs fans), they would be actively rooting against him? And the crazy part is, this is as straight-forward as the question can get. What about if your team has some particularly slimy policies. For example, when it came out that the Raiders were paying their cheerleaders less than $5.00 an hour. Do you have to stop rooting for the team as a whole? Can you become a fan again once they change their archaic views and double the pay for these women?

What about a piece-of-crap owner like Donald Sterling? What if he's just an egomaniac who simply uses money to buy championships like George Steinbrenner? What if it's something as minor as you met your favorite player and he was kind of a dick, do you need to find a new favorite player? A new favorite team? And when it comes to players, can we give them a second chance if they prove remorseful and seemed to have turned over a new leaf? How much should their personal lives seep into how we view them as athletes, and how much should it impact our likes and dislikes?

The answers to these questions are not simply binary, but rather they are layered, nuanced, incredibly vague, and usually dependent on the individual. Personally, a guy like Daniel Murphy is going to be someone I'm simply never going to be able to root for until he changes how he feels about homosexuality. I just have too many friends and relatives that I care about too deeply to support a player who wouldn't support them. However, then I wonder how many other players that I still actively cheer for have the same opinion and simply haven't stated it. Should not stating these views be enough for me to still like them? Even more vague, what if I just haven't read those comments, but a player I love actually *has* made public statements similar to Murphy, he just didn't hit home runs in six consecutive playoff games and thus get thrust into the spotlight? Can I claim ignorance is bliss? To mix metaphors: if a tree falls in the woods and nobody's around to hear it, is it still a homophobe?

In all honesty, I think the most important thing to do is simply to discuss these questions rather than simply saying, "Oh well, those are hard questions to answer, let's just change the subject because I'm kind of uncomfortable." I have no issue if you still cheer for Chapman, as long as you are privy to what he did, have talked with people who have experience in this field, and are aware both as a fan and as a human. People (and organizations) make mistakes, and it's not always fair to write them off entirely for those mistakes. At the same time, I get it if you have a relative or friend whose life has been ruined by domestic abuse, and therefore you could never support Chapman. Don't just blindly write him off, though, talk about it with others, learn if there is something in Chapman's life that may have caused the deep-seated anger and insecurity that can sometimes lead to domestic abuse. Interact with some folks who don't share your opinion and see if you can't both leave the conversation with a fuller grasp of the issue. Just don't be glib about it.

Starting IX Franchise Roster Stats

Lineup	Yrs	G	R	H	HR	RBI	SB	BB	SO	BA	OBP	SLG	OPS+	dWAR	WAR
Pete Rose	**19**	**2722**	**1741**	3358	152	1036	146	**1210**	972	0.307	0.379	0.425	124	-4.9	**77.7**
Joe Morgan	8	1154	816	1155	152	612	406	881	410	0.288	0.415	0.470	147	4.3	57.8
Barry Larkin	**19**	2180	1329	2340	198	960	379	939	817	0.295	0.371	0.444	116	13.8	70.2
Frank Robinson	10	1502	1043	1673	324	1009	161	698	789	0.303	0.389	**0.554**	150	-2.8	63.8
Johnny Bench	17	2158	1091	2048	**389**	**1376**	68	891	1278	0.267	0.342	0.476	126	19.3	75.0
Tony Pérez	16	1948	936	1934	287	1192	39	671	**1306**	0.283	0.346	0.474	127	-2.8	45.6
Heinie Groh	9	1211	663	1323	17	408	158	513	257	0.298	0.378	0.394	130	5.2	40.6
Vada Pinson	11	1565	978	1881	186	814	221	409	831	0.297	0.341	0.469	119	-1.0	47.7
Ival Goodman	8	965	554	995	91	464	45	335	345	0.279	0.349	0.448	118	-0.9	21.4
Pitchers	Yrs	W	W%	ERA	G	CG	SHO	SV	IP	SO	ERA+	WHIP	SO/9	SO/BB	WAR
Noodles Hahn	7	127	0.580	2.52	237	209	24	0	1987.1	900	134	1.134	4.1	2.40	**45.9**
Aroldis Chapman	6	19	0.487	2.17	324	0	0	146	319.0	546	181	1.016	15.4	3.52	10.9

#7 Los Angeles Dodgers (1958-pres.); Brooklyn Dodgers (1932-1957, 1911-1912); Brooklyn Robins (1914-1931); Brooklyn Superbas (1913, 1899-1910); Brooklyn Bridegrooms (1896-1898, 1888-1890); Brooklyn Grooms (1891-1895); Brooklyn Grays (1885-1887); Brooklyn Atlantics (1884)

(Photo from Wikimedia Commons)

Team Background

Playoff appearances: 31 **Pennants: 23** **World Series titles: 6**
Collective team WAR: 541.6
Strengths: We're reversing the recent trend here: the Dodgers having a plethora of pitching…
Weaknesses: …But a few weak spots in the lineup keep them out of the truly elite group of franchise Starting IX's.
What to expect from the next 15 pages: Jackie Robinson. Vin Scully. Sandy Koufax. Clayton Kershaw. You know, just those average, run-of-the-mill, Joe Schmoe-types.

The Dodgers have one of the most storied histories in all of American sports. That should come as no surprise seeing as they have split time between the biggest city on each respective coast of the U.S. during their 130 years of existence. Their history is as well-recorded as any team (including the Yankees), due to the somewhat religious way in which the Roger Kahn-era Dodgers (1950s) are thought of throughout the sport. Kahn's *Boys of Summer* may very well be the most famous baseball book of all time, and with good reason. It is joined by an innumerable overabundance of books profiling the Dodgers during the years leading up to their move west.

This era of Dodgers lore combined an excellent team, a city full of young sports reporters, and a memorable cast of characters better than almost any other team in baseball history. But that likely sells the actual talent of the 1950s Dodgers short. The 1927 Yankees are often credited as the best offensive team in the history of baseball, but the 1953 Dodgers weren't far behind. Their typical lineup looked as such: 1) Jim Gilliam 2) Pee Wee Reese 3) Duke Snider 4) Jackie Robinson 5) Roy Campanella 6) Gil Hodges 7) Carl Furillo 8) Billy Cox

Leading off, Gilliam played second base and won Rookie of the Year, while leading the league in triples (17). He posted an incredibly impressive walk to strikeout rate of 100 to 38 and reached base over 270 times. Reese posted a .271/.374/.420 triple slash, scored 108 runs, and was actually worth more than Gilliam in terms of oWAR. Snider led the league in runs (132), slugging (.627), OPS (1.046),[353] and total bases (370), while hitting 42 home runs. His 8.7 oWAR led all of baseball. Robinson handled the switch to the outfield smoothly and had a typically-great Robinson season, posting a .329/.425/.502 triple slash with over 200 RuBIns. Campanella won the MVP out of the fifth spot in the lineup, driving in a league-leading 142 runs to go with his 41 long balls. Hodges both scored and drove in over 100 runs while posting a .302/.393/.550 triple slash. All Furillo did was win the batting title out of the seven spot. Cox was the weakest part of the lineup, but even he had a batting average (.291), on-base percentage (.363), and slugging percentage (.443) solidly above league average. The 1953 team led the league in team batting average (.285), on-base percentage (.366), slugging percentage (.474), home runs (208) and steals (90); they scored 154 more runs than any other team, the biggest difference in baseball history. According to Bill James' positional ranks in his 2001 *Baseball Abstract*, their lineup, same as above, looked like this:

1) 27th best 2B, 2) 10th best SS, 3) 6th best CF, 4) 4th best 2B, 5) 3rd best C, 6) 30th best 1B, 7) 51st best RF, 8) only position player not in his top 100.

The 1927 Yankees boasted a lineup that, again according to Bill James, looked like this:

1) 34th best CF [Earle Combs] 2) 120th best SS [Mark Koenig] 3) Best RF [Babe Ruth] 4) Best 1B [Lou Gehrig] 5) 79th best LF [Bob Meusel] 6) 19th best 2B [Tony Lazzeri] 7) 88th best 3B [Joe Dugan] 8) unranked C [Pat Collins]

Time for the arbitrarily-scored comparison! If we assign 100 points for the top ranked player at each position in James' *Abstract*, all the way down to 1 point for the 100th best (meaning Hodges receives 71 points for his 30th best first base rank, etc.), and then total up the entire lineups for the two teams, the 1953 Dodgers receive 576 points and the 1927 Yankees receive 384 points.

This is certainly a flawed system, as the difference between Ruth and Gehrig at the number one rank for their position is much bigger than the difference between, say, the 54th and 55th best second basemen of all time. It is also potentially flawed because James' ranking system takes into account their whole careers, not just the one season we are looking at.

One other way to compare the two is by the oWAR of the hitters on the team. When we add this total for the entire roster of each team, the 1927 Yankees total 43.8 oWAR (41.6 from their regular starters, 1.7 from their bench, and 0.5 from their pitchers), and the 1953 Dodgers total 39.3 oWAR (40.3 from their regulars, 0.6 from their bench, and -1.6 from their pitchers). This is a very close total, and it's even closer when looking at only the starters. The difference is mainly due to Ruth and Gehrig both having 11.0+ win seasons. In the end, the main gap between the two clubs is that, although the Yankees had two of the best 10 hitters of all time *in their prime*, the Dodgers were incredibly talented top-to-bottom, but they lacked a player on the Ruth and Gehrig level.

Transitioning out with a fun fact: the name "Dodgers" was first used for the franchise in 1911, and the term came from their fans who had to *dodge* the trolleys that traversed Brooklyn at the time.

Random cool guy associated with the franchise:

Vin Scully. Let's talk about him: Scully got his start in 1950 but rose to prominence when he became the youngest man to ever call the World Series (25 years old) after taking Red Barber's spot in the booth for the 1953 Fall Classic.

Going back four years earlier, Scully's announcing career got off to an auspicious start at his first real gig – one that he got filling in for Ernie Harwell. His first gig required Scully to call a Boston University and University of Maryland college game in Fenway Park. This may not sound bad, but, assuming he would be in a nice booth, Scully left his winter clothing back at home. When he saw a card table and a microphone set up on the roof in the bitter cold he was totally unprepared. However, Scully did his best, and when word got back to his boss, Red Barber, about how bad the setup had been at Fenway, and Barber realized that Scully hadn't complained once, Barber gained a strong respect for Scully. When Harwell left the Dodgers just a short time later, it was Scully who came to mind as the replacement.

So began the illustrious career that saw Scully active in the Dodgers play-by-play booth for 66 years. He was elected into the Hall of Fame in 1982 and, even before that, was long been regarded as the top in his field. He has announced every single one of the franchise's championships and saw three different home stadiums, 11 different managers, 20 no-hitters, and

---

[353] For comparison: Aaron Judge had an OPS of 1.049 in 2017.

three perfect games. Scully was an active part of baseball for well over half of its modern history and nearly half the sport's entire history. He was even the inspiration for the name of Gillian Anderson's character from *The X-Files*: Dana Scully.

Scully has endeared himself to his fans in numerous ways. Although Joe Buck's voice may be as smooth as "velvet mixed with peanut butter" according to Jerry Lambert,[354] Scully's voice fits better with baseball than the voice of any other man or woman to grace an MLB broadcast booth. He is a kind man who says his favorite broadcasting memory came when Hank Aaron broke Babe Ruth's hallowed home run record. In Scully's words, that call "was very important, and I don't use that word very often. After I just let the crowd roar for about a minute and a half, I collected myself and said what a great moment it was, not just for Henry and his family and the Braves, but for all of us in this country, for a black man to be honored in the deep South for breaking the record of a white icon." Scully also embraced the Spanish side of his Dodger fan base, often throwing in Spanish phrases and truly engaging his whole listening base, especially during the Fernandomania craze of 1981.

However, more than anything else, he may be most famous for his ability to make the listener (or viewer) feel as though they are truly at the stadium taking in a Dodgers game in the lovely summer air. This is not an accident. When asked about the phenomenon, Scully said, "This is very natural. One reason was that in New York, we used to have a day for the blind, and we would have hundreds and hundreds of fans brought to the ballpark who would sit in the stands and listen to the broadcast. And they loved it because they felt like they were there. They could smell the cigarette smoke, feel the roar of the crowd. They were really into it. So early on, on the radio, I got into trying to describe the surroundings, the weather, whatever it might be."

A couple of gems from Scully, both from the night of Sandy Koufax's 14-strikeout perfect game: "There are 29,000 people in the ballpark and a million butterflies." And: "So when [Koufax] wrote his name in capital letters in the record book, the 'K' stands out even more than the "O-U-F-A-X."

Scully also holds the honor of the top spot in my personal rankings of baseball men with whom I would most like to have dinner: SP) Vin Scully C) Stan Musial 1B) Jackie Robinson 2B) Bill Veeck 3B) Bill James SS) Dizzy Dean LF) Satchel Paige CF) Jack Dunn RF) Dan Quisenberry

I'll end with a brief anecdote about the newly-retired Scully, who saw as much baseball as any man or woman and did so with more aplomb than anyone else in the biz: When I was in middle school, and still a very naïve baseball fan outside of my precious Yankees, I started sleeping in the basement to stay up late watching movies and west coast baseball. On one of my first nights enjoying the freedom the basement gave me, I flipped over to a Dodgers game. I had been flipping through games with nothing really sticking, but as soon as I came to the Dodgers broadcast, I was entranced. I didn't switch the channel, even in commercials, and was curious who this man with the perfect voice was. The next morning, in all my middle school bravado, I told my father that I had discovered a really good announcer, and that he should make sure to check him out some time. My father asked what team it was, and when I responded that he was the announcer for the Dodgers, my dad simply laughed.

Starting IX

C Roy Campanella (1948-1957)

Campanella came to the Dodgers as a 26-year-old who had played nearly 10 seasons in the Negro Leagues. When he caught Don Newcombe in 1949, it was the first time there was a black battery (pitcher and catcher) in baseball history. Campanella quickly established himself as a preeminent catcher and led the Dodgers into their prime years. It was not until a car accident that left him paralyzed in 1958, that he left the game. Due to the timing of his accident, he didn't get to play a game after the Dodgers made their move to Los Angeles. However, he was present in front of what was then the largest exhibition crowd in baseball history (93,103[355]), when the masses gathered in the Los Angeles Memorial Coliseum for a benefit night to raise money for Campanella, showing just how beloved he was even in the Dodgers new city. The event was one of the most spine-tingling events in baseball history. The lights were turned off in the Coliseum, and everyone in the crowd lit a match in honor of Campy.

During his actual playing days, Campanella won three MVP awards, alternating seasons from 1951-1955. Campanella won his MVPs in an era when catchers often won the award, and players from winning teams were favored more than ever. Campanella fell into both categories, and only Barry Bonds has won more MVPs than the three that Campy won.[356] He did this despite never leading the league in WAR; in fact, his highest WAR rank in a season was seventh (1951 and 1953). Of course, WAR is a cumulative stat, making it much harder for a catcher to rank among the league leaders given the days off they need to take throughout the season.

This discussion of MVPs and their true value is not to diminish Campanella's career, but rather to make sure we

---

[354] Better known as Kevin Butler from those PS3 commercials that I swear were relevant when I first wrote that joke.
[355] With another 15,000 turned away at the gates.
[356] Several others have won three as well, and the MVP didn't exist in its current state until 1931.

don't use these awards as the be-all and end-all of comparisons.

There are ways we can combat this, however, and one such way is listed on Baseball-Reference under "Award Shares." The statistic adds up all the votes received by a player across the span of their career, unbiased by the monumental gap between first and second in a fan's memory. By this measurement, Campanella is 52nd all-time, behind eight players who never won an MVP in their whole career (Eddie Murray leads that group).

Another part of the discussion that we tend to lose track of, is that not all MVPs are created equal. Roger Peckinpaugh's MVP in 1925 was, by WAR, more than four times less valuable than Willie Mays's sixth-place finish in 1964. This is one struggle we have when trying to judge a player's career based on subjective awards.

All that being said: Campanella's 1953 season was pretty remarkable. As noted earlier, he hit 41 home runs and had 142 RBI, but what makes it incredible is that the league-average catcher that season hit *nine home runs and drove in 38 runs*. Campanella was also an excellent fielding catcher, leading all catchers in range factor/game nearly every season he played (in 1956 he finished second). He also led the league in caught stealing percentage his first five years in the league and still holds the all-time record for caught stealing percentage in a career.

Of course, with more and more metrics being created in recent years to measure the all-around impact of a catcher, (i.e. pitch-framing and game-calling, which can each be worth a couple wins in a season), those MVPs may end up having been deserved, even according to metrics like WAR. Campanella is indeed rated highly by defensive winning percentage, as Bill James pointed out in a Fox Sports post on catcher defense. The idea that Campy really had a feel for the game was almost certainly part of his MVPs, and it's cool to see metrics that begin to back that up.

1B Steve Garvey (1969-1982) vs. Gil Hodges (1943-1961)

As with most teams with a history this long, the Dodgers find themselves with two players evenly matched at a certain position. This time it is at first base, and we'll allow the breakdown to decide who takes the spot.

Contact

	BA	lgBA	Seasons ≥ .300	Career high/low	Seasons ≥ 80 SO	SO %	lgSO%	BABIP	Misc.
Garvey	.301	.262	7	.319/.269	2	10.7	13.7	.311	LL 2x H
Hodges	.274	.274	2	.304/.249	9	14.0	11.3	.279	LL 1x SO

Garvey was much more of a contact hitter than Hodges, and it shows in the numbers. Garvey was consistently a .300 hitter throughout his career; Hodges reached that magical number only twice. Garvey also struck out much less and in an era in which the league was striking out more often. This one is pretty straightforward.

EDGE: Garvey

Power

	HR	Seasons ≥ 25 HR	Career high HR	XBH	SLG%	lgSLG%	ISO	HR%	XBH%
Garvey	211	3	33	579	.459	.383	.158	3.0	8.2
Hodges	361	9	42	703	.488	.422	.214	4.6	8.9

At first glance, this appears to be pretty much the opposite of contact. Hodges had plus power, compared to Garvey, who had average power. However, it is interesting to note that the two players had similar extra-base hit percentages, and Hodges played in a much more home-run-friendly park than Garvey. The Park Factors for Ebbets Field (per Baseball-Reference) in the seven years that Hodges enjoyed his highest home run totals (1950-1956) were as follows: 103, 102, 102, 103, 104, 104. In comparison, Garvey's main seven years of power were from 1974-1980, when the Park Factors for Dodger Stadium were: 96, 95, 98, 99, 99, 99. This may not appear to be a huge difference, but according to baseball-statistics.com, the Home Run Factors for Ebbets Field in Hodges seven-year prime were well above average: 133, 120, 123, 104, 123, 122, 120. This could explain why these two have similar extra-base hit percentages but such a vast difference in home runs. Of course, there are players who simply are doubles hitters instead of home run hitters, these players rely on the gaps more than clearing the fences. So, for another comparison, Baseball-Reference's Neutralized Batting can be used. If we put both hitters in a neutral park in the NL in 2012, Hodges still leads Garvey 231 to 161 in home runs over their aforementioned seven-year stretches. So Hodges still has the advantage, and I think that this is accurate. I'm not sure the neutralized stats adjust quite enough to be honest, but since I haven't figured out a better way to adjust for park factor, the data available will have to suffice.

The fact that Garvey never had a single season with a slugging percentage over .500 during his career (a feat that

100 different players were able to achieve during Garvey's playing days, alone) supports the decision leaning towards Hodges as well.

EDGE: Hodges, although not as large as expected

Batting Eye

	BB	Seasons ≥ 70 BB	OBP	lgOBP	OPS+	BB%	SO/BB
Garvey	367	0	.337	.328	122	5.2	2.05
Hodges	925	7	.360	.345	120	11.7	1.20

Hodges. Next.

EDGE: Hodges (go figure!)

Speed

	SB	Seasons ≥ 10 SB	Career high SB	Rbaser	SB%	XBT%	GDP%
Garvey	77	3	19	-2	57	46	13
Hodges	63	1	10	-1	67	47	9

Speed was a weak spot for both players. During his career, Garvey had six 200-hit seasons. In not one of those seasons did he reach 100 runs, a fact not singularly tied to his lack of speed, but certainly affected by it. He is the only player in MLB history with such a high number of 200-hit seasons and no 100-run seasons.

The edge Garvey has in total steals is countered by Hodges' ability to steal at a more proficient rate and his lower rate of grounding into double plays. Garvey grounded into about two more double plays per year, which cancels out the difference in the less than two steals a year that Garvey has as an advantage. The smaller double play percentage, along with the fact that Hodges was caught stealing 26 fewer times in his career, gives Hodges the edge.

Slight EDGE: Hodges

Defense

	Fld%	lgFld%	dWAR	RF/9	lgRF/9	Rfield	GG	Misc.
Garvey	.996	.992	-5.8	9.95	9.99	27	4	LL 7x GP 1B, 5x PO, 4x Fld%, 2x RF/9 1B,
Hodges	.992	.990	-5.3	9.56	9.75	47	3	LL 4x GP 1B, DP 1B, 3x PO, Fld% 1B, TZR 1B, Assists, 1x RF/9 1B

Both players have a solid reputation in the field and have multiple Gold Gloves to show for it. Both men are also thought to be slightly overrated by Gold Gloves, due in part to their lack of range. Now, don't just look at their negative dWAR totals and presume that they were entirely overrated. The dWAR calculation includes the positional adjustment which kills first baseman (more than -1.0 win per season on account of playing a less-trying defensive position). This positional adjustment makes it hard for all but the truly elite first basemen to stay out of the red when it comes to dWAR, especially over the course of a career (First Base, Mets – Page 152). That being said, neither of these men were as strong as their reputation, but they were, however, absurdly close in terms of their overall defensive production. This one is too close to call.

EDGE: Draw

Health

Both players stayed quite healthy with the Dodgers, but Garvey played seven straight seasons (1976-1982) without missing a game, an impressive feat that gives him the edge. In fact, Garvey's 1,207 consecutive games played is good for fourth all time in baseball history.

EDGE: Garvey

Team Success

	W	L	T	W-L%	Seasons ≥ 90 W	Division titles	Pennants	WS	Misc.
Garvey	951	775	1	.551	6	3	4	1	1978 NLCS MVP
Hodges	1,205	794	8	.603	8	7	7	2	

Both players played for successful Dodgers teams during their career. Garvey's Dodgers won more of their regular season games, but Hodges' Dodgers had more pennants and titles, and in a time when it was harder to get to the playoffs. Both players were also successful for the Dodgers in the playoffs. As seen in the chart above, Garvey won the 1978 NLCS MVP, but he also hit over .300 in six of his eight other playoff series with the Dodgers. He also managed to collect at least four hits in every series as a Dodger, and despite the fact that three other hitters split the 1981 World Series MVP, Garvey was actually their best hitter for the series, posting a .417 average for the six games.

Hodges was no slouch in the playoffs either, sporting a .349 on-base percentage across his seven series with the club and topping a .400 OBP in three of the six series for which he was a regular. He also hit a home run in five of the six series, making him a threat to both get on base and drive in the men who reached base in front of him. The only series in which he failed to hit a home run was a 0-for-21 struggle in 1952 that we will circle back to in a bit.

Both men played on excellent Dodgers teams – in fact the two most successful eras in team's history – but the seven pennants and two titles give the slight edge to Hodges.

Slight EDGE: Hodges

Dominance

Neither player was particularly dominant in terms of normal metrics, but they shared a similar field of dominance: their ability to stay on the field. Only Garvey led in what we would consider a "classic metric,"[357] when he led the league in hits in 1978 and 1980, but both led in several fielding categories (covered in the above fielding section), with Garvey having a minor edge. Since neither player was dominant in the classic metrics, but Garvey was a little better than Hodges at "fringe metrics," we'll give him a begrudging edge here.

Slight EDGE: Garvey

Impact on the Franchise/ Popularity

Garvey and Hodges are two of the most popular players in Dodgers history. Garvey was a man who played the "right way" on the field and, for the most part, off the field, such that the writers pumped him up to be an angel. He won both the Lou Gehrig Memorial Award and the Roberto Clemente Award for his off-field work. He advocated a one-strike policy on MLB's cocaine policy stating, "I'm most concerned about influencing the next generation of fans. If we allow players to take drugs and then come back, what does that tell the kids?" Because of this, he was nicknamed "The Senator" by teammates, and the writers had only praise for him. They eventually bequeathed him the nickname "Mr. Clean." He was the first player to start in the All-Star Game as a write-in candidate, collecting more than four million votes, despite not being on the ballot. He was also one of only five former teammates who attended the funeral of Alan Wiggins when Wiggins passed away from AIDS-related illness in 1991.

However, Garvey had another side that wasn't always known to the media, which led to many writers feeling betrayed by "Mr. Clean" when they found out about this less-congenial side. When stories of Garvey's infidelity came out – they were made *very* public by his wife – the media turned on him. Some believe this cost Garvey the place he seemingly deserved in the Hall of Fame because the writers were so upset. For a man who did so much good, it is unfortunate that he wasn't able to be the perfect white knight that the writers thought he was, but it's hard to hold it against him too much. This is not at all to excuse his infidelity, but at this point it seems more difficult to find a famous male who *hasn't* had an affair (a "tradition" that certainly needs to be rooted out of our society). Considering that, outside of his propensity for the comforts of women, he was by all other accounts a great man, his blemishes shouldn't be enough to tarnish his character entirely. Instead they should merely play a part as we consider the man as a whole. The media likely started off too high on Garvey and then turned on him too quickly.

Hodges neither rose as high, nor fell off as steeply as Garvey, but he was, in his own right, a very popular Dodger. He was able to remain popular in 1952, despite his 0-for-21 performance in that year's World Series. Fans responded to his performance with cards and flowers rather than the boos and hate mail that many hitters – especially in New York – would have received. The story goes that, during the World Series, Father Herbert Redmond of St. Francis Roman Catholic Church

[357] I.e. what you might see on a baseball card.

told his parishioners: "It's far too hot for a homily. Keep the Commandments and say a prayer for Gil Hodges." This awesome story was the inspiration for the title of Thomas Oliphant's *Praying for Gil Hodges*, one of the innumerable books on the Brooklyn Dodgers, but a good read nonetheless.

Although Hodges may have never had a fall from grace like Garvey did, he also was never as important to as many people as Garvey was. In his post-playing days, Garvey lost his job with the organization as a result of standing up to the worst owners in Dodgers history, the McCourts, only solidifying this category for him. There's even a Dodgers blog called *Sons of Steve Garvey*, and his spot in Dodger lore is nearly unrivaled.

EDGE: Garvey

Hall of Fame?

Both Garvey and Hodges currently lack a bronze plaque in Cooperstown. They are both on the outside looking in, and they have two of the best cases to be in the Hall – at least on the surface. Both men stayed on the ballot for the full 15 years of eligibility, and Hodges, in particular, came excruciatingly close. Although he was not around to see it, Hodges' 1983 chance at the Hall of Fame came within 44 votes of election, the closest anyone has ever gotten to the Hall without eventually getting in. When he left the ballot, no one had ever received more cumulative votes over the years than Hodges. When he retired, Hodges was the right-handed home run king in the NL and the all-time MLB leader in grand slams, just part of his case for entrance into Cooperstown's hallowed halls.

For his part, Garvey doesn't have the gaudy numbers some others in the Hall have, but he still looks great on paper. He was a 10-time All-Star (eight times with the Dodgers), won four Gold Gloves, won an MVP and came in second in another year, and for much of his career was highly respected. However, both men are also on Jayson Stark's top five most overrated first basemen, and he's not alone. Bill James called Garvey the perfect overrated player due to primary average (empty batting average), looks, charm, etc. Since there is a lot on either side of this argument, it's time to call back the best Hall of Fame decider out there (for a narrative nihilist like myself): Hall of Stats (Second Base, Angels – Page 122). Neither Garvey nor Hodges meet the 100-point minimum necessary to be inducted to the Hall of Stats. Garvey's Hall rating of 60 doesn't come close, and Hodges' Hall rating of 76 isn't much better. So, despite the numerous arguments for these two men to make the Hall, there are definitely other "snubs" that deserve to be in there before these two. Of the two, Hodges does deserve it more, though.

EDGE: Hodges

Verdict

It doesn't get much closer than these two. In Bill James' *Abstract*, Hodges came in 37th among first basemen and Garvey at 41st. In the above categories, Hodges took five, Garvey took four, and they drew one. It certainly isn't a big difference between the two, but **Gil Hodges** gets the spot thanks to his slightly more significant numbers for a slightly more significant iteration of the franchise.

2B Jackie Robinson (1947-1956)

In as many ways as "Jackie Robinson the person" is everything that is good about baseball, much of his story is everything that is bad about baseball. So much has been written on Robinson,[358] much of it by baseball's preeminent writers, that I don't want to focus as much on what you know already, but rather take a look at the underside of some of these stories.

As was mentioned in Cap Anson's write-up, baseball never actually had a written rule against black players in the Major Leagues, just a general racist agreement that black players should not play with white players. When the matter of whether baseball should be desegregated came to a vote in 1945, the final result was a sadly unsurprising 15-to-1 tally *against*. Commissioner Happy Chandler took matters into his own hands, however, overruling them and allowing Robinson into the league.[359] So when baseball as a sport gets credit for desegregating before so many other institutions, this is not really true. It was much more the work of a few men in positions of power who had the moral fortitude to go through with what they knew was right. After Chandler's decision, he faced the expected pushback, as the St. Louis Cardinals reportedly threatened to strike when the Dodgers came to town. However, National League President Ford Frick told them that any player "directly involved in any acts of racial prejudice or disobedience would be suspended indefinitely." He also said, "I don't care if half the league strikes. This is the United States of America, and one citizen has as much right to play as

---

[358] One of the best and most original pieces coming from Bryan Curtis, entitled, "Jackie's Ghost: Roger Kahn and Jackie Robinson," on (where else) *Grantland*.

[359] Moses Fleetwood Walker was a black player in the late 1800s, and William Edward White was a black man who passed for white before Walker, but for all intents and purposes, it was Robinson who truly broke MLB's color barrier.

another." Cardinals manager Eddie Dyer denied the reports of such a strike and led his team out to a win.[360]

One problem with the way Robinson and his legacy were handled actually has to do with another man entirely: Larry Doby. Doby was the first black player to play in the AL, and he has never received nearly the attention he deserves for breaking the color barrier in AL cities. The impetus is not entirely on MLB for this, in fact it may reside more with the historians of baseball, but baseball has done very little to recognize the man who was both the second black player *and* second black manager. (Interestingly enough, he was also the first former MLB player to play professionally in Japan.)

Since Doby does get overlooked so regularly – Tris Speaker denied him a spot on Cleveland's Starting IX in this very book – and since these two men are strongly tied together, we'll give his career a brief look here. Unlike Robinson, Doby didn't have the support of any of his teammates when he first made it to Cleveland. Doby broke the color barrier in the AL just a few scant months after Robinson, and he had nearly as great an impact on the field, as well as off. Doby went on to lead the AL in home runs twice and won the respect of his teammates throughout the years. When Cleveland won the World Series in 1948, a picture of him and white pitcher Steve Gromek embracing was popularized around the country, a momentous event for America and one of the most genuinely smile-inducing photos of all time.

(Photo from Detroitathletic.com)

After his playing days, Doby continued to work in baseball and advocate for the inclusion of black men in positions of power in baseball.

Like Doby, Robinson often criticized baseball for its lack of black men in front offices and positions of power. When Frank Robinson was hired as the first black manager in MLB, Frank said his only wish was that Jackie could have been there. When Jackie Robinson first came into the league, he was quiet about such things, but once he settled into Brooklyn, Robinson was much more vocal. It was the quiet strength that Robinson had for those first few seasons that made him the perfect man to break the color barrier, and it was the powerful vocal leadership of his later years that made him a perfect ambassador for the movement of black[361] men into higher positions in baseball.

Because Robinson was so outspoken later in his career, some people criticized his teammate Roy Campanella for not being outspoken enough. Although Robinson was an excellent leader, and his ability to push for black players in the game was of extreme importance and should be lauded, it is not fair to criticize Campanella. It should not necessarily fall on the shoulders of every black player who played during this era to be a leader.

Back to the player himself: Robinson may actually be underrated as a player. He is such a symbol for the sport that often times his numbers fly under the radar. He led the league in steals two of his first three seasons, and his skills translate very well to today's advanced metrics. He drew walks, stole bases with success, was hit by pitches, played in a time of positional scarcity among second basemen, and played excellent defense. He topped 9.0 WAR twice, leading baseball in WAR both seasons, and he averaged over 6.0 WAR per season for his 10-year career. Remember, he did all of this despite the fact that he didn't have his MLB debut until he was supposedly already past his prime years (28 years old at debut).

Robinson was a leader in many senses of the word and chose to end his career a Dodger instead of being traded, a move of loyalty towards Branch Rickey and the organization that had brought him into the league. Robinson was inducted into the Hall of Fame in 1962, and as Arnold Rampersad said so well in his biography of Robinson: "In the Hall of Fame, each man was finally the same color: bronze."

---

[360] It should be noted that SABR author Bob Broeg wrote in *The National Pastime* that the Cardinals were indeed innocence in this matter.

[361] This may be a footnote that I don't have the perspective to fully comment upon, but in the use of "black" vs. "African-American," I come down on the side of using "black" because of how many black Americans don't actually hail from the continent of Africa but rather from countries throughout the world.

3B Ron Cey (1971-1982)

Cey established himself with the team in 1973 and was a consistent performer for a decade after that. Including his two brief stints in 1971 and 1972, he totaled over 225 home runs and over 1500 RuBIns with the franchise. He was very consistent in both his play and his health while with the Dodgers, as were the rest of his infield mates. In fact, the Dodgers infield of Steve Garvey, Davey Lopes, Bill Russell (no not that one), and Cey played eight and a half seasons together, a nearly-unheard-of level of continuity in the modern game.

The only season with the Dodgers in which Cey (aka "The Penguin") played less than 145 games, was the strike-shortened 1981 season; it was also the only season in which he drove in less than 77 runs. His batting average was between .241 and .288 every year, and as a regular, Cey never posted a season with a negative dWAR. In keeping with the theme of consistency, Cey never dropped below 3.5 WAR in a season in Los Angeles but was also never worth more than 6.7 wins. Along with Eddie Murray, he could easily be on the all-time "most consistent player" Starting IX. He was traded out of L.A. at the exact right time, as he never posted more than 1.8 WAR in any of his final five seasons after L.A.

Cey exemplifies the type of player who enjoys success with one team and cannot find this success elsewhere,[362] and the drop off seems more extreme than just normal aging patterns. Other examples include Carl Crawford leaving Tampa Bay, Jason Bay leaving Pittsburgh, George Foster leaving Cincinnati... really any Mets acquisition, ever. This is such a common theme that one has to wonder whether there is more to it than numbers can really evaluate. Is there something to be said for a certain player and a certain team (or manager, climate, etc.) clicking? In scientific experiments, scientists go to extreme lengths to eliminate or neutralize variables so that a true result can be found. With baseball statistics, there are so many variables that, in many ways, we have to rely on the fact that baseball has such a large sample size that it wipes out variables such as: a player sleeping on the wrong side of the bed, or getting into a tiff with his significant other before a game. However, if one of these variables – the city in which a player plays – is significant enough, it is quite reasonable to expect a large impact on the player's game. This is another case of needing a statistic that is almost certainly too invasive but would be invaluable for scouting/player development. *Minority Report 2: This Time It's About Baseball Statistics*.

SS Pee Wee Reese (1940-1958)

While "The Little Colonel" may not have had the biggest stature (160 lbs. soaking wet), his demeanor (leader in the clubhouse during one of the most volatile eras in baseball) more than made up for it. The Brooklyn Dodgers and New York Yankees played in 44 World Series games while the two franchises were in New York, and only one player on either team played in every single one of those games – Pee Wee Reese.

One tale in particular goes to show Reese's role with the team. The story goes – because no story in baseball history can truly be told without the "the story goes" caveat – that, when the Dodgers brought Jackie Robinson on board, Robinson was, sadly and unsurprisingly, given a rough time from the crowd, who could hide behind the fences with their taunts. What was really hard for Robinson was not having the support of the men he was with day-in and day-out on the Dodgers. Reese helped clear this up when he reached out to Robinson in a pre-game show of solidarity during Robinson's first year. Robinson was taking a particularly strong bout of verbal abuse from fans in Cincinnati, so Reese put his arm around Robinson while the two were out in the infield, and this moment became a key moment in baseball – and American – history, hushing the racist fans in Cincinnati and symbolically quieting racist fans across the league. The moment is honored today in the form of a bronze statue of Reese with his arm around Robinson outside the Mets' minor league affiliate's stadium. This action set the mood for the season, a season that ended with a Dodger pennant. Reese also refused to sign a petition against Rickey signing Robinson before the season, and he was an important part of the initial integration of Major League Baseball.

To think none of this would have played out the same if the Boston Red Sox had had their heads on straight, though. When he was coming into baseball, Reese was initially signed by the Red Sox. However, player/manager Joe Cronin was already the team's shortstop – and you probably see where this is going. Reese wanted out because he knew he wouldn't get playing time, given the starting shortstop was filling out the lineup card each and every day, and this ended up costing the Red Sox a Hall of Fame shortstop, not exactly a commodity that grows on trees.

This is just one example of the downside to employing a player/manager. In fact, there is very limited upside. Although the team obviously wants someone who has played in the big leagues – I know firsthand the dangers of having a boss who hasn't gone through what his/her employees are going through – the team likely needs someone a little more objective than a man whose paycheck is determined by how he plays. Can a player/manager really be objective enough about himself as a manager to bench the player version of himself if he is struggling. Can he motivate himself if he is not in the mood for baseball that day? The elimination of player/managers is one of the most logical developments in modern baseball.

To finish on Reese: the man epitomized the spirit of a baseball franchise's captain and was one of the easiest selections for captain of a Starting IX in this entire book.

---

[362] Dennis Eckersley is the captain of the antithesis to this team, where a player simply needs to find a new location to succeed.

LF Zack Wheat (1909-1926)

Probably one of the lesser-known Dodgers on the team, Wheat was never really a dominant force, but he played with the team for 18 years in the club's early days. Buck[363] was also the most popular Dodger of his time, according to Harry Grayson in *They Played the Game*. He was an excellent hitter who topped the .300 mark in 13 of his seasons with the Dodgers. He aged impressively, having his best season by WAR (6.7) at age 36 while posting .375/.428/.549 triple slashes in that 1924 season. For a 14-year span (1912-1925), he was in the top 10 in slugging percentage 11 different seasons, leading the league once. He was such a great curveball hitter that Giants manager John McGraw forbade his pitchers from throwing curves entirely when facing the 5'10" Dodgers outfielder.

Wheat's career perfectly intersected the dead ball and live ball eras, and the change in how the game was played can be seen perfectly in Wheat's statistics. Wheat broke his career high for home runs in 1921 as a 34-year-old, and he then broke that again the next season as a 35-year-old. Exactly half his career home runs (over the course of 19 seasons) came within a five-year stretch (1921-1925) that started when he was 34 years old.

Wheat was believed to be Native American, but because of the scorn he knew he would face for this, he downplayed the association. Even so, there were often quotes like this one from *Baseball Magazine*: "The lithe muscles, the panther-like motions of the Indian are his by divine right." That sort of generalization about an entire race brings to mind what is sometimes said about black athletes in modern society. Jimmy the Greek made the most infamous comments on the subject. Instead of realizing that society often only portrays successful black men as either rappers or athletes instead of the wide array of professions we tell our young white boys to chase, Jimmy the Greek and others have come to a rather inexact and unscientific conclusion.

CF Duke Snider (1947-1962)

The classic Snider cliché is that he was overlooked throughout his career because he was third in line[364] to Willie Mays and Mickey Mantle at the position of New York center fielder in the 1950s. This is true to a certain extent. Mays and Mantle were better players and are certainly more recognizable names than Snider today, but I don't think Snider owes his under-the-radar nature exclusively to these two men. I think it definitely played a role, but there were a few other factors.

For one, "The Silver Fox," despite his nickname, didn't age very well, especially after the team moved to L.A. when he supposedly could have moved out of the shadow of the other New York center fielders. Snider was worth 58.2 WAR from 1949-1957, but in the other half of his career, he wasn't even worth 10.0 WAR.

Another reason Snider never received as much recognition as he deserved was the 1955 MVP race. In all likelihood, Snider lost the MVP to teammate Roy Campanella due to a clerical error. In the final tally, Campanella received 226 points to Snider's 221. However, the only ballot that didn't have Snider had Campy listed twice, once in first and once in sixth. Most likely the voter wanted Snider in one of those two slots. If the ballot had been eliminated because of the error, Snider would have won the award. Even if Snider had been awarded the sixth-place slot, the two would have been co-MVPs, but as is, Snider never was able to claim an MVP. As mentioned previously, a lot of a player's legacy can be tied to winning an MVP. Despite three straight years of finishing in the top four of the MVP (and deserving it by WAR in 1956), Snider was never able to stake his claim to an MVP victory.

Snider very well may have been robbed of the 1955 World Series MVP, as well, a legacy-defining series in which the Dodgers finally broke through to beat the hated Yankees. Hodges far outperformed Mickey Mantle and was easily the best hitter during the series. He hit four home runs to go with eight RBI, making him the only player to hit four home runs in two different World Series (he previously knocked four out in the 1952 World Series and was the Dodgers most valuable player that World Series, as well). However, due to Johnny Podres winning Games 3 and 7 (and throwing a shutout in Game 7), Podres took home the hardware for the World Series MVP. Snider was once again overlooked, and once again, it was not due to Mays or Mantle. As is, "The Duke of Flatbush" is the all-time NL leader in home runs (11) and RBI (26) in World Series history, doing so in his 36 Fall Classic games.

All these slights – when added to the fact that he played in center field at the same time and in the same city as Mays and Mantle – mean Snider definitely didn't receive all the credit he deserved. As is, no man (Mantle and Mays included) hit more home runs in the 1950s than Snider, and Bill James has him as the sixth best center fielder of all time. Snider's struggles after leaving Brooklyn were already mentioned, so we might as well end on two positive notes on his connection to Ebbets Field, the long-time home to the Brooklyn Dodgers. First, he hit the final home run in Ebbets Field history, a fitting adieu to the historic stadium, and second, before one game, he threw a ball out of Ebbets Field – from home plate – over a 40-foot-high wall 350 feet away.

---

[363] Buck being his nickname is inconsequential except that it meant his "full nickname" was Buck Wheat. For all you Eddie Murphy *SNL* fans, that's Buckwheat of the famous "Buh-Weet Sings" and "Buckwheat Dead" skits. Buckwheat was among the best *SNL* characters of all time, and likely the jumping off point for "Ass Dan" as the modern *SNL* version of Buckwheat. "I'm'a live forever; ha HA!" RIP Ass Dan.

[364] "The zero hour, Michael. It's the end of the line. I'm the firstborn. Sick of playing second fiddle. Always third in line for everything. Tired of finishing fourth. Being the fifth wheel. There are *six* things I'm mad about, and I'm taking over."

RF Carl Furillo (1946-1960)

Nicknamed "The Reading Rifle" for his plus arm, Furillo played with the Dodgers during the post-war years, as did many others on this franchise Starting IX. As previously noted, Furillo won the 1953 batting title while batting out of the seventh spot in the lineup. I contemplated putting a few others here (namely Gary Sheffield and Raul Mondesi) who were more dominant than Furillo, but simply put: they were not in right field for the franchise long enough. Mondesi averaged nearly 4.0 wins a season but was only in L.A. for six full seasons. Sheffield, though possessing one of the three best swings of the last 25 years, was with the franchise even shorter, just three and a half seasons to be exact.

Furillo debuted at age 24 and missed a few years at the beginning of his career due to WWII. Although Furillo had not debuted by the time he left for the service in 1943, he almost certainly would have debuted earlier than as a 24-year-old in 1946, had it not been for the war.

Roger Kahn said of Furillo in his masterpiece, *Boys of Summer*, "I can imagine Reese running a Chevrolet dealership and Andy Pafko coaching high school football and Duke Snider operating a dude ranch in Nevada. But I cannot imagine Carl Furillo as anything other than a ball player. Right field in Brooklyn was his destiny." Furillo was far from the most charismatic personality on those "Boys of Summer Dodgers," however, and was eventually blackballed from the game for suing the Dodgers. Furillo sued after he was released by the club while injured. Considering that baseball often espouses its own beliefs in integrity, it's surprising that Furillo was expelled from this "Boys Club" simply because he read his contract well and went to his lawyers instead of the commissioner, thus breaking one of baseball's innumerable (and often spoofed by Grant Brisbee) unwritten rules.

Before the reader goes off feeling too bad for Furillo, a decent portion of why his relationship with the Dodgers ended so bitterly was that Furillo wasn't exactly the easiest guy with whom to get along. He didn't make too many allies in his time with Brooklyn, and when Roger Kahn met up with him well after his playing days, he sounded as bitter as they get. Somehow changing the topic of conversation to African-Americans in America, Furillo said, "What is it with the colored today? They got to get welfare? It's tough, but was it easy for the Italians? Five dollars a week in the apple orchard, was that easy? Why should the colored have it easier than anybody?"

Of course, this sort of pitting poor minorities and poor whites against each other, when the collective poor should really set their targets on the wealthy upper class who make it borderline impossible in modern society to move up the social ladder, is a story that goes all the way back to the early 20th century, if not earlier…

Back to baseball Jim, stop getting distracted.

Utility Willie Davis (1960-1973)

Willie Davis is one of three players (along with Wheat and Reese) to collect over 2,000 hits for the Dodgers. Davis was a solid player who relied on his speed and fielding to become one of the best players in Dodgers history (fifth among position players in franchise WAR). For example, in 1964, his best season by WAR, Davis' on-base percentage was a measly .316, but thanks to his 42 steals, his excellent fielding (3.4 dWAR), and the poor hitting environment in which he played, his 8.3 WAR was good for fifth in baseball, trailing only Willie Mays, Ron Santo, Dick Allen, and teammate Don Drysdale. By clearing the 8.0 wins mark with a sub-.320 on-base percentage, he joins a club consisting of just himself and Brooks Robinson (1968) as the only two to do so in baseball history. By the way, I found that stat using the Play Index tool on Baseball-Reference, and did so in under a minute… on my phone… in my bed. Play Index: The best way to spend $35 a year.

Davis finished in the top 10 in steals (NL) every year from 1961-1972 and in the top 10 in stolen base percentage (NL) 13 times in his career. Davis even helped the Dodgers when he left town, bringing in Mike Marshall via a trade with Montreal in 1974. Marshall would pitch only two and a half seasons in Los Angeles but won a Cy Young – albeit undeserved – out of the bullpen in 1974, a year in which he led the league in games (106), games finished (83), and saves (21).

Davis had a bit of a reputation as a self-absorbed man, but the statistics make it too hard to leave him off the squad.

SP Don Drysdale (1956-1969); Sandy Koufax (1955-1966); Clayton Kershaw (2008-pres.); Dazzy Vance (1922-1932; 1935)

Starting pitching in Dodgers history is as rich as any position in baseball history. The four men listed above could all easily fill the role of the club ace, so we're going to cheat a little bit and include them all. This is a treatment that could be given to a couple teams throughout the book, but none are as deserving as this quartet. With that said, let's take a look each pitcher, get a brief summary on each, and then do our best to set the rotation.

Don Drysdale: Outside of being one of the top pitchers in Dodgers history, "Big D" was remembered most for two things: he wasn't afraid to pitch inside, and he could hit as well as pitch. Drysdale used sidearm and brushback pitches to intimidate hitters. As he said, "My own little rule is two for one – if one of my teammates gets knocked down, then I knock down two on the other team." That's some next-level, Hammurabi ish. Drysdale led the league in hit batsmen five times, including four straight years (1958-1961). In 1961, his total of 20 beanballs doubled the next highest total in the league. As Orlando Cepeda said of Drysdale, "The trick against Drysdale is to hit him before he hits you." He was once ordered to intentionally walk an opposing batter. On the first pitch of the at bat he hit him instead. "Saved three pitches," was Drysdale's response.

As far as his bat is concerned, Drysdale is among the best hitting pitchers of all time. The seven home runs he hit in both the 1958 and 1965 seasons stand as the single-season record for a National League pitcher. He batted as high as sixth and was used as a pinch-hitter every once and awhile. Most impressively, he was the only Dodger with at least 100 at bats to hit .300 on the 1965 World Series Championship team. He posted an OPS+ of 140 that season, which was also highest on the team! Big D was worth 5.9 wins above *average* (WAA) as a hitter for his career, and his 1965 campaign alone was worth 2.2 WAA. Surprisingly, considering his success as a hitter, as well as the team regularly appearing in the postseason, Drysdale never collected a postseason hit, going 0-for-10 in his 12 plate appearances.

Sandy Koufax: The Dodgers most famous starter, Koufax is as well known today as almost any player in baseball history. What isn't as well known is that Koufax actually struggled a lot early in his career. His own manager said about him, "He has one pitch – high and outside." This isn't surprising considering his season walk totals of 105, 92, and 100 from 1958-1960.

His career, in many ways, is a tale of two halves. Of all pitchers to throw as many innings as Koufax from 1955-1960, only one pitcher had a higher ERA, but the Dodgers patience began to pay off around 1961. Some have surmised that Koufax's rise coincided with the team's move into their new, far more spacious, stadium. The numbers seem to back this up, as Koufax never had a full season with an ERA under 3.50 until 1962, when he rattled off five straight seasons with a total ERA under 2.00. When looking at park factors, the change is huge. According to Baseball-Reference, here are Koufax's park factors for his career, starting in 1955: 102.2, 107.4, 108.2, 100.7, 107.3, 105.6, 107.2 – moves into new Dodger Stadium – 91.5, 94.1, 92.3, 93.1, 90.8.

That's an incredible change in venue and is certainly a factor when assessing Koufax's career, but I don't think it can be said to be the only reason for Koufax's success. For one, his best seasons also came when the strike zone had its expansion at the top of the zone, going from the hitter's armpits to his shoulders between 1963 and 1969. More within his own control, Koufax also nearly cut in half the numbers of walks he was giving out starting in 1962. From 1958-1961, he averaged 98 walks per season; from 1962-1964 he averaged 56 walks. He also raised his ERA+ (a statistic which accounts for league *and park* factors) from an average of 106 from 1958-1961 to 167 from 1962-1966. He improved his stamina, topping 300.0 innings three times after 1962, never having previously topped 255.0 in a season. He threw a no-hitter each year from 1962-1965, becoming the first pitcher to throw four total – not something a simple change in ballpark could explain. However, it is important to note his HR/9 for his career: 0.43, 1.53, 1.21, 1.08, 1.35, 1.03, 0.95 – moves into new Dodger Stadium – 0.63, 0.52, 0.52, 0.70, 0.53. Those are some stark differences and certainly must have helped with Koufax's confidence, a key factor in a pitcher's approach.

Koufax's dominant reign came to an abrupt end after the 1966 season when he was only 30 years old. He had battled injuries his entire career, and he decided it was time to tap out when he began to have constant pain whenever he straightened his arm. Due in part to the timing of when Koufax walked away from the game, his reputation may be even better than deserved. He went out on top, posting one of the best four-year stretches a pitcher has ever had (Starting Pitcher, Diamondbacks – Page 54) right before his retirement. He was a legend of a man, as well. In games he pitched during his final season, the Dodgers drew 1.5 million fans. The total National League gate that season was 15 million, meaning that one in 10 tickets to games *in the entire league* were purchased to watch Sandy work his magic. In fact, the next season, the Dodgers drew nearly one million less, and the NL as a whole drew two million less.[365] In 1972, Koufax became the youngest player to be inducted into the Baseball Hall of Fame, doing so at the age 36. He is considered by many to be one of, if not *the*, best pitchers of all time, and he relied on an excellent fastball and a curveball that many, including Bill James and Rob Neyer, consider the best of all time. *Sports Illustrated* named him their favorite athlete of the 20th century, and his legacy is among the truly elite in baseball history. In the minds of many, his nickname says it all: "The Left Arm of God."

Clayton Kershaw: If Koufax is the Left Arm of God, Kershaw is the Southpaw of Allah. Meticulous, regimented, single-minded, pious, and seemingly-perfect-in-all-ways left-handed pitchers don't just grow on trees, and Kershaw is a generational rarity. If it seems like the praise is too high, consider some of the following stories and stats about Kershaw.

Kershaw broke into baseball in 2008 with a rather ho-hum 98 ERA+ in 107.2 innings. Since then, he has been anything but ho-hum. In over 1800 innings from 2009-2017, he has an ERA+ of 168 and has struck out just a hair shy of 10.0 batters per nine. Prefer your stats old school? His career ERA of 2.36 (which includes his rookie season) is the best for *any* starting pitcher with at least 300 innings since 1920. Yes, that means better than Bob Gibson… and The Big Unit… and Koufax… Better than all of them.

Kershaw has clearly been not just great, but he has been dominant over his first decade in the league, but (to date) his magnum opus was 2014. The season was so impressive that it should have demanded the bullet-point-style, amazing-stat format given to Mike Trout, Tony Gwynn, etc., throughout this book, but since Jonah Keri already penned a piece for *Grantland* entitled "Twenty-Two Jaw Dropping Factoids About Clayton Kershaw's Otherworldly Streak and Season" that would have felt like more blatant thievery than Robin Thicke ripping off Marvin Gaye. So instead we'll pick just the favorite:

---

[365] These attendance number drawn from a great article in *The National Pastime* by Lyle Spatz.

In 2014, Kershaw held all opposing hitters to an OPS of .521, which was lower than the lowest qualified hitter that season.[366]

So now we've seen a bit of the "seemingly-perfect" statistical side of Kershaw referenced, but what about all those other plaudits handed out to him at the beginning of this write-up – the "meticulous, regimented, single-minded, and pious," for the folks who care about that kind of stuff? Well, how about his humility in terms of his stardom and the wealth that comes with it? When he signed his seven-year, $215 million deal, his mother had to read it about it online, and when his family suggested they go out and celebrate, Kershaw's response was, "I don't know if money is something to really celebrate." Well then. Kershaw never curses, uses frickin instead of that other f-word when he's upset on the mound, and his girlfriend fines him $1,000 every time he swears in front of her. He even called the movie *Jackass* "Jackbutt" to a teammate when asked if he had ever seen the film. The only possible knock on Kershaw is that he has the reputation as a bit of a loner in the clubhouse, but that's likely because of his singular focus on baseball, something very common among the truly elite tier of athletes – similar to J.J. Watt in the NFL.

Kershaw also holds the honor of being (easily) the top appointment-viewing staple in baseball right now for yours truly. Part of it was that he had Vin Scully announcing his games until recently, but there's no player in all of baseball that is more likely to make me tune in to a game on a lazy summer night than Kershaw. His curveball will make me downright giddy, and if I took a shot of Jack every time I shook my head just laughing at a pitch Kershaw threw, I'd pass out before the fourth inning – the man is just so damn fun to watch. He even swings an above-average bat for a pitcher, and he has one of the best pickoff track records in baseball; the man just doesn't have flaws.

Kershaw just keeps getting better, as well. He has managed to lower his career ERA each and every season, a crazy stat from Ben Lindbergh which just goes to show how this modern legend just keeps improving in front of our eyes.

Dazzy Vance: Dazzy Vance, not Koufax or Kershaw, is actually the Dodgers all-time leader in pitcher WAR. Although Koufax and Vance both threw for 12 years, Vance was able to be worth more to the franchise thanks to his consistency. Koufax had gaudier strikeout totals, but Vance led the league in strikeouts seven times compared to only four for Koufax. Vance also won three ERA crowns, not quite as many as Koufax's five, but still more than respectable. Vance also won the 1924 MVP over Rogers Hornsby (who hit .424) by winning 28 games and losing only six, while leading the league in ERA (2.16), complete games (30), strikeouts (262), ERA+ (174), WHIP (1.022), H/9 (6.9), SO/9 (7.6), and SO/BB (3.40).

Vance's career didn't take off until he was 31[367] due to some extremely strange circumstances. Vance struggled with arm pain for much of his younger days, but it wasn't until he banged his arm on a poker table raking in his chips from a winning hand, that the arm demanded surgery. (God, I miss the ole days.) Once Vance got the surgery, he could suddenly throw hard again without pain. In a way, Vance's career is almost the inverse to Koufax in that his career improved after his freakish arm injury. Once he broke into the league for good, he did so in style, dominating like few others in league history have. In 1924, he struck out 262 hitters. Burleigh Grimes was second in the league with 135 strikeouts; in third was Dolf Luque with 86 strikeouts. Vance accounted for an incredible eight percent of the strikeouts *in the entire league* that season. In an article for *FanGraphs*, Tony Blengino measured the standard deviation of all the strikeout leaderboards throughout baseball history, and Vance had three of the top four seasons.

Vance pitched until the age of 44 and had arguably his best season as a 39-year-old (1930). That season the league ERA was 4.97, but Vance had a dazzling 2.61 ERA that translated to a 189 ERA+, both good for league bests. Vance did this while being overworked, often coming out of the bullpen on short rest because he was the club's best performer. The 1.26 gap between the ERA of Vance and the second-place Carl Hubbell set the MLB record for the biggest gap between first and second in an ERA title.

Make sure to check out Chad Dotson's piece on Vance for *The Hardball Times*, "The Improbable Career of Dazzy Vance," an excellent read with good links to other good reads on Vance, as well.

So now that we have met each member of the rotation, let's look at how it would set up.

Based on WAR with the Dodgers, it would look as such:

1) Dazzy Vance 2) Don Drysdale 3) Clayton Kershaw 4) Sandy Koufax

Based on wins (the old-school, non-WAR, Ws) it would look as such:

1) Don Drysdale 2) Dazzy Vance 3) Sandy Koufax 4) Clayton Kershaw

Based on ERA+ it would look as such:

1) Clayton Kershaw 2) Sandy Koufax 3) Dazzy Vance 4) Don Drysdale

Finally, based on one season it would look as such:

1) Sandy Koufax – 1966 2) Clayton Kershaw – 2014 3) Dazzy Vance – 1924 3) Don Drysdale – 1964

None of these are perfect, but they can help to inform the decision. I think that in many ways Koufax has become a bit overrated in the annals of history, but in this case, who else would you want to be your team's ace other than "The Left Arm of God"? In a sense, it has to do with the age-old sports argument of whether we prefer a player who showed longevity throughout his career, or a player (*saying this in the corniest way possible*) whose star shone so bright it could only last a

---

[366] Of course, we can't be too surprised by that given that he did the same thing in 2013… and 2015 – ya the man is absurd.

[367] Which is one year older than Koufax was when he retired; imagine combining those two careers.

brief time. It's Pedro Martínez vs. Warren Spahn; it's Charles Barkley vs. Karl Malone; it's Emmitt Smith vs. Barry Sanders. In many ways, longevity can be a lot harder to accomplish than the flash of brilliance, but if you have one player to choose for an imaginary Starting IX playoff, there's no way you can choose anyone other than the "flash of brilliance" player. In this case, it means Koufax will take the number one spot of the rotation.

That leaves us with three men left for the number two spot. At this point, Kershaw doesn't have enough seasons to compete with the others and is a notch below the other three. (Plus, it's a playoff, so he's definitely going to choke, right Tim?) So with Kershaw settled into the four spot, the decision is between Vance and Drysdale for the number two. If we go by the above criteria, Vance holds a small advantage in each of the advanced statistics categories. Despite that, I'm going to go with Drysdale at the two in this hypothetical rotation. I'm doing that because in many ways Koufax and Drysdale were a great yin and yang to each other, and they make the most sense as the stalwarts of the rotation. In fact, the famous incident in which Giants pitcher Juan Marichal hit Dodgers catcher John Roseboro with a bat involved Koufax, and (in a way) Drysdale.

After both pitchers tossed a few brushbacks in the early innings, when it was Koufax's turn to retaliate (for the second time in the game, mind you), he refused to hit Marichal, so Roseboro (the catcher, remember) decided to take baseball's eye-for-an-eye tactics into his own hands, whizzing the throw back to Koufax right past Marichal's head. Marichal responded infamously by clobbering the catcher in the head with his bat. Roseboro said of the incident that if Drysdale had been pitching, Big D would have responded by hitting Marichal, and Roseboro wouldn't have had to take matters into his own hands. No matter how you order them, though, the Dodgers have one hell of a rotation.

CP Éric Gagné (1999-2006)

Gagné came up with the Dodgers as a starting pitcher and struggled through his first three seasons. However, once he was moved to the bullpen the transformation was quick and extremely successful.[368] Until suffering from injuries, Gagné spent three-plus seasons as the team's closer. In that time, he went 14-7 with a 1.82 ERA, 209 games finished, 161 saves (including 84 straight), six blown saves, a 0.827 WHIP, and 13.4 SO/9.

Of course, Gagné's most famous stretch came from August 28, 2002 to July 3, 2004, when the bespectacled Canadian converted an MLB-record 84 consecutive save chances. This total easily tops any other successful save run in the history of baseball and is one of the more impressive runs any pitcher has had, ever. At the same time, with the increasing dominance of relief pitchers as a whole (Closer, Atlanta Braves – Page 212), it seems likely that, at some point, Gagné's record will fall. Still, the record deserves a closer look. No other closer has ever saved more than 54 games in a row (Tom Gordon, 1998-1999), meaning Gagné's record is 56 percent greater than any other such streak. If Joe DiMaggio's hit streak were 56 percent greater than any other hit streak, he would have gotten to 70 games. If you had a closer on your fantasy team who saved 42 straight games, you'd be borderline losing your mind. And he'd be halfway to Gagné. That's insane. Gagné gave up only eight total runs over said stretch, while striking out 139. It was a magical run, and one that deserves all the recognition it receives. (And it is the key factor in Gagné holding off Kenley Jansen for this edition – and probably only this edition – of the book.)

Gagné also holds the rather strange honor of being one of only two pitchers in this book to have undergone Tommy John surgery. Writing about Tommy John right now is a bit scary because, with the rate we are making strides in sports medicine, this entire section could be mute practically by the time it goes to press.

Just in the past two-ish years, it has gone from the assumption that a pitcher coming back from TJ is highly-damaged goods, to not being a big deal at all. However, TJ has actually always had a high success rate, and as Jon Roegele found in his piece, "An Analysis of Available Tommy John Surgery Data" for *The Hardball Times*, the 90 percent return rate from TJ has basically been the same since the surgery's inception in 1974. What *has* improved, though, is the recovery time, and the recovery time seems to be shrinking with each new case. The surgery has become so pervasive (in part thanks to just general awareness[369]), and with such a quick turnaround, that it has even become an option for high school kids. It's becoming more and more rare for pitchers *not* to undergo the procedure at some point in their career.

One thing I find interesting is that for all the #hotsportstakes surrounding Tommy John, they usually revolve around the reason why the surgery is becoming so much more prevalent ("kids playing that darned travel baseball all year 'round"), rather than where the surgery lands ethically. The surgery itself is pretty freaky-sounding and includes sewing a ligament from elsewhere in the body (or even from a corpse) into the elbow to replace the torn, or worn down, UCL (ulnar collateral ligament). For all the hoopla surrounding any supplement any player takes, throwing a random ligament into your arm seems a lot freakier and possibly performance-enhancing to me. Now I don't come down on the side of thinking that the surgery should be banned, if for no other reason than we would basically lose every fun pitcher in baseball, but it is interesting that no one is really talking about the ethics of the surgery, at least yet.

To finish up on Gagné: his time in Los Angeles represented the safest bet the team has ever had in the ninth inning, and his post-injury career was spent mostly outside of his time with the Dodgers, keeping the memory intact, among the Dodger faithful, of Gagné as a dominant force.

---

[368] This type of transformation from mediocre starter to elite reliever is something we've seen many modern organizations trying more and more often.
[369] One surgeon quoted in an excellent *SI* piece on Tommy John guessed that half of the 1927 Yankees were likely playing with torn/partially torn UCLs.

Starting IX Franchise Roster Stats

Lineup	Yrs	G	R	H	HR	RBI	SB	BB	SO	BA	OBP	SLG	OPS+	dWAR	WAR
Jackie Robinson	10	1382	947	1518	137	734	197	740	291	0.311	0.409	0.474	132	10.0	61.5
Pee Wee Reese	16	2166	**1338**	2170	126	885	232	**1210**	890	0.269	0.366	0.377	99	**25.6**	**66.4**
Duke Snider	16	1923	1199	1995	**389**	**1271**	99	893	**1123**	0.300	0.384	0.553	142	-3.8	65.8
Roy Campanella	10	1215	627	1161	242	856	25	533	501	0.276	0.360	0.500	123	5.7	34.2
Gil Hodges	16	2006	1088	1884	361	1254	63	925	1108	0.274	0.360	0.488	120	-5.3	44.4
Zack Wheat	**18**	**2322**	1255	**2804**	131	1210	203	632	567	0.317	0.367	0.452	130	-6.5	59.7
Ron Cey	12	1481	715	1378	228	842	20	765	838	0.264	0.359	0.445	125	10.5	47.5
Carl Furillo	15	1806	895	1910	192	1058	48	514	436	0.299	0.355	0.458	112	-2.1	35.2
Willie Davis	14	1952	1004	2091	154	849	335	350	815	0.279	0.312	0.413	107	11.9	54.4
Pitchers	Yrs	W	W%	ERA	G	CG	SHO	SV	IP	SO	ERA+	WHIP	SO/9	SO/BB	WAR
Clayton Kershaw	10	144	0.692	2.36	292	25	15	0	1935.0	2120	161	1.002	9.9	4.18	57.4
Sandy Koufax	12	165	0.655	2.76	397	137	40	9	2324.1	2396	131	1.106	9.3	2.93	53.2
Dazzy Vance	12	190	0.592	3.17	378	213	29	8	2757.2	1918	129	1.212	6.3	2.51	**61.6**
Don Drysdale	14	209	0.557	2.95	518	167	49	6	3432.0	2486	121	1.148	6.5	2.91	61.2
Éric Gagné	8	25	0.543	3.27	298	0	0	161	545.1	629	125	1.111	**10.4**	3.44	10.9

#6 Detroit Tigers (1901-pres.)

(Photo from Wikimedia Commons)

Team Background

Playoff appearances: 16 **Pennants: 11** **World Series titles: 4**
Collective team WAR: 754.9
Strengths: Dat outfield doe.
Weaknesses: The dying motor vehicle industry.
What to expect from the next 12 pages: You will have your Ty Cobb thoughts distorted like a trip through the "Crazed Boat Ride" in *Willy Wonka and the Chocolate Factory*. Also, the most ridiculous use of two and a half pages in the entire book. Which is saying something.

The Tigers are one of baseball's oldest franchises and are just on the other side of a bit of a team renaissance. Mike Ilitch (the founder and owner of Little Cesar's) was the team's owner from 1992 until 2017, when he passed away. Ilitch dedicated his last few years to winning, at all costs. Ever since the team's World Series loss in the 2012 season, the payroll was in the top six in baseball, and big names like Miguel Cabrera and Prince Fielder were brought to town, often at the risk of a long-term vision. That spending kept the Tigers relevant, but it never led to a title, instead leading to a future that now looks as bleak as any in baseball. They are stuck with bloated salaries and a severe lack of talent.

If history had truly been cyclical, the Tigers should have won at least one title during this time, given that each generation of Tiger fans has one title. The team's last title came in 1984, with 1968 preceding that. Prior to those two titles, the Tigers most successful run came in the 12-year period from just before WWII. The team captured two World Series titles (1935 and 1945) and two other pennants (1934 and 1940) during this time. The team also enjoyed some success in the late 'aughts, capturing three straight pennants (1907-1909) but never finishing it off with a championship. This came much to the chagrin of Ty Cobb, who was outclassed by his biggest rival, Honus Wagner, in the final of those three seasons. The team's winning percentage is just over .500 all-time at .507 – good for eighth all-time – and their 11 pennants and four World Series title are good for ninth among current franchises.

* * *

All that is good and well, but now it is time for the most absurd part of this book: the Team Name Battle Royale. The idea is simple, based on team name, which team would survive if all 30 were thrown into a "Battle Royale" style death match. With team names like Phillies and Reds there will obviously have to be some finagling, but this is far from science at this point anyway. Let's meet the players:

Inanimate objects: Red Sox, White Sox, Rockies

We're going to be generous with some of these team names, but with these three, there's just no way around it. Sorry, socks and mountains.

Logos/mascots instead of team names: Mets, Reds, Phillies

The Reds and Phillies aren't really things, but in the case of the Mets and Reds they do have mustachioed men on their logo. In the Phillies case, they have the Philly Phanatic as a mascot, a big green fuzzy dude. All three are kind of sleeper picks to be honest. Especially Mr. Red; dude looks like he could throw down in fisticuffs.

Priorities, man: Brewers, Padres, Rangers, Mariners

It just doesn't seem likely that these teams would have any skills that translate well to a Battle Royale. Cool professions, but not too useful here.

Gotta catch em to kill em: Rays, Marlins, Orioles, Blue Jays, Cardinals

The aquatic and aerial-based animals of the tournament probably wouldn't get much killing done, but they'd be mighty hard to catch. Somewhat like the buddy of yours who, when you're playing four-man Smash Bros., hangs out in the corner and lets everyone else kill each other off before joining the fray once there's only one guy left. Yeah, that guy is the worst.[370]

Useful professions: Dodgers, Athletics, Astros

Dodgers and Athletics both sound like they'd be really hard to pin down for a while during this battle and are the human equivalent to the prior group of hard-to-catch animals. If the Astros have all their astronaut equipment, they might be downright impossible to catch.

Battle-tested: Yankees, Royals, Twins, Braves, Nationals, Pirates

The Yankees and Nationals helped get this country its freedom from Great Britain, while the Braves had to battle those same groups while having their land stolen from them. Yeah, U.S. history is weird. Anyone with a twin is definitely battle-tested, as they have a natural wrestling partner through youth, as well as a natural competitive spirit to top their fellow zygote. The Royals are a little fluffy since royalty never really fight their own battles, but in many cases, the original lineage of royalty had to win their power through battle. The Pirates are definitely a sleeper pick, as they have experience on both sea and land. Plus, they are just badass as hell.

Dangerous animals: Diamondbacks, Tigers, Cubs

I would pay all 38 dollars in my savings account to watch these three battle it out on Animal Planet.

The Favorites: Giants, Angels

Giants are huge. Angels can't die. In fact, the Angels kind of seem unfair, especially if they're badass angels like in *The Golden Compass*.

Now let's turn things over to Ken Burns, noted documentarian, who will be guiding us through this PUBG-style bloodbath.

Ken Burns: "The year was 2018. America was a country as divided as ever. Politics were inescapable. They appeared everywhere (even in books that were seemingly about baseball). The country was in need of some galvanizing event. In the 1940s, the nation turned its lonely eyes to Joe DiMaggio. In 2018, the country turned its craven eyes to a MLB Team Name Battle Royale."

Ted Binkletown, Professor of American History at Yale: "The American climate was ripe for an event like the Team Name Battle Royale. There were protests and counter-protests across the country – it was only a matter of time before the country demanded to see whether a Diamondback or a Blue Jay could last longer in a survival match."

KB: "Major League Baseball and Don King announced the event would take place on July 4, 2018, seemingly aware that this event would go on to be so important in American history that, in future years, we wouldn't celebrate our nation's independence on July 4, but rather we would memorialize the coming-together Team Name Battle Royale that reunited our great nation."

Allan Lane, Professor of Sociology at Stanford, and definitely not the guy who did the voice for Ed the horse in the 1960s television program *Mister Ed*: "I remember when it was announced that they were going to clear out the entirety of Manhattan for three weeks to give the Team Name Battle Royale a location. I thought it was a bit rash at first, couldn't they have used a slightly-less populated location? But it turned out it didn't matter, as the nation came to a standstill to watch this historic event. And, I just want to get on camera that I am indeed a professor and the guy who did the voice of the horse in *Mister Ed*. Just to clarify."

KB: "The event began with the ceremonial killing off of the Red Sox (inanimate object), the White Sox (inanimate

[370] I'm looking at you, DeCap.

object), the Rockies (inanimate object), and Cleveland (racism), with the remaining 26 teams given 24 hours to disperse across the borough of Manhattan. When the initial ceremony and dispersal had occurred, Kenny G played a saxophone solo that played across speakers of Manhattan to let the participants know that the Battle Royale had begun."

Ted Binkletown: "It wasn't long before we had our first victim. The Royals, thinking that they would have servants fight for them were thoroughly mistaken. A Tiger came up and removed their faces one-by-one, netting the first kill of the match in devastating fashion."

Allan Lane: "Once the rest of the participants witnessed the face-removal of the Royals [*there were screens across the borough televising the deaths for all*] it really shook some of the mascots. The Cardinals flew straight out of the city, eliminating themselves from the competition, but saving face, quite literally. Also, I just wanted to say one more time that, while I respect the work that other Allan Lane did, I am in no way affiliated with the TV program *Misted Ed*.

KB: "Utter chaos reigned over the first 24 hours of competition. It was a blood bath in which the Giants stamped out the Dodgers, who simply couldn't live up to their name. The Athletics and Mr. Met got into a nasty beat-down, drag-out fight, that gave the Angels enough time to come over and kill them both while they were distracted. The Mariners really lucked out when they caught the Rays on their boat, but the Rays flipped the switch on the Mariners, stinging them to death before dying on the Mariners boat because they were out of the water for too long. The Yankees made an ill-fated alliance with the Twins, who, after the Yanks-Twins duo combined to take out the Phillie Phanatic, turned on the Yankees, shivving them from each side while whispering, 'This is for 2003. And 2004. And don't forget about 2009-2010. And finally, 2017 says hello.'"

Mike Rithjin, from the network: "There were actually a surprisingly high number of mascot retaliations for real-life baseball events. The Tigers must have been feeling emboldened from their face-removal of their division rival, because they made a beeline for the Giants, circling and devouring the massive Giants in the first real upset of the Battle Royale. Afterwards, they proceeded to spell out 'the true 2012 champions' on the ground in Giant blood in a real Charlie Manson-type dick move. Of course, while they were still celebrating, the Cubs snuck up and conquered the Tigers, shouting 'This is for 1935' the entire time. The Tigers were confused and commented on how long ago that was. 'People don't forget,' one Cub intoned before ripping a Tiger limb-from-limb."

KB: "Meanwhile, out on the heavy seas, the Pirates were doing some serious work. First, they snagged and killed a Marlin, before noticing that a tired-out Blue Jay had landed in their crow's nest. Since it is a crow's nest and not a Blue Jays nest, the Pirates took care of business."

Armando Christian Pérez, 48th president of the United States: "I remember being impressed with the way the Padres and Brewers were handling their business. For the first few days, they simply stayed out of the fray, the Padres quietly worshipping in a little SoHo bakery, while the Brewers tried to find the right recipe for a pumpkin spice IPA while holed out at the Stumptown Coffee Roasters on W 29th. Of course, those not-so-violent delights had violent ends, as the Padres were nabbed by a pair of Diamondbacks who smelled the bakery from miles away, and the Brewers were killed by the Angels for, in their words, 'the sake of humanity.'"

Allan Lane: "Of course, while all this was happening, the Astros were off in a quiet corner at MoMA, quietly devising the plan that would end up changing the course of U.S. history. Something I definitely wouldn't think to do if I was actually the person who voiced a horse in a classic TV show."

KB: "The next few days dragged by, with only one more elimination occurring by the end of the first week (the Rangers walked right across the Brooklyn Bridge after getting a bit too high one morning). With ten mascots remaining, we were down to the best of the best."

Mike Rithnithin, still from the network: "All that changed with the infamous Nationals fat shaming, of course."

Ted Binkletown: "There are numerous accounts of how it went down, but the story I believe goes as such: the Angels were going around minding their own business, fully aware that they were the heavy, heavy favorites to win this event – basically no one else actually had a chance. But for some reason, when they bumped into the Nationals one afternoon, the Nationals decided to say the Angels looked fat in those Halos."

Allan Lane: "I have always believed it to be because of the Nationals deep-seated insecurities stemming from a severe inability to win in the playoffs. And fine! You caught me. It is I, voice of beloved horse, Mister Ed, from the television program *Mister Ed*. Happy now?"

KB: "Whatever the cause, we all know the effect. The Angels went on a hellacious rampage. The Nats were the first to go, of course, but Mr. Red, the Braves, the Twins, and the Cubs were all wiped out in a matter of hours. The Orioles and Diamondbacks took a bit longer because of the difficulty finding them, and as we now know, those precious hours spent looking for the O's and Dbacks may have saved humanity."

Ron Dump, Associate Professor of Economics at the University of New Mexico: "What the Astros did during this time was truly remarkable. In just over a week, they managed to make what appeared to be a functioning rocket ship from only the found pieces lying around MoMA. That level of sophistication is just astounding."

KB: "Right as the Angels found the Orioles and Diamondbacks [*huddled together in the Penn Station subway stop, next to a man playing the garbage can drums who had somehow gone unnoticed during the evacuation*] and destroyed them, a sound erupted from 20 or so blocks north. The Astros, who had valiantly assembled a spaceship in hopes of escaping the Angels entirely, had failed in their mission. The spaceship had blown up, and the Angels saw the tragedy before their eyes."

Armando Christian Pérez: "It was at this exact moment that the Angels realized how senseless this whole thing was. The killing, the fighting, the bipartisanship. They found the only other team remaining, the Pirates, and offered them a peace treaty. The Pirates, because they weren't idiots, accepted. The committee running the event accepted their Peace pact, mostly out of fear of what they had created by bringing real, live Angels onto planet earth. The Angels and the Pirates stood together in front of Congress and professed a need to come together and put aside differences at this moment. They talked Nancy Pelosi and Newt Gingrich into hugging each other. They convinced Paul Ryan and Chuck Schumer to have a romantic candlelit dinner together. Whether these democrats and republicans came together out of true unity, or if they did so out of a binding fear of a 38-foot Angel walking across U.S. soil, the world may never know."

KB: "What we do know, however, is that the MLB Team Name Battle Royale will forever be remembered as the most important event in the history of the United States of America."

Allen Lane: "*Mister Ed* forever!"

Random cool things about the franchise:

- They are the only American League team to have drawn at least 1 million fans every season since 1965.
- Tom Selleck, both in real life and on *Magnum P.I.*, is a Tigers fan.
- Mark Fidrych; Ernie Harwell; Sparky Anderson.
- As their team write-up for Baseball Almanac online pointed out, the baseball team's success has somewhat mirrored the city's plight as a whole, including the recent revival of both.
- Of the teams in the inaugural 1901 American League season, only the Tigers and White Sox have never changed cities or nicknames in the century-plus since.

Starting IX

C Bill Freehan (1961; 1963-1976)

From 1963-1986, the Tigers were quite set behind the plate. Freehan held down the spot for the first 14 of those years, and Lance Parrish, another very good backstop, took over not too long after Freehan retired. The Tigers had a catcher representing them in the All-Star Game 18 of those 26 seasons, one of the best non-Yankees stretches of production for one team at the catcher position. Freehan takes the spot here thanks to the fact that he played for the Tigers his entire career, whereas, Parrish played for myriad teams. For his 15 seasons in Detroit, Freehan was worth over 40.0 WAR for the Tigers, averaging over 3.0 WAR a season if we exclude his four-game rookie debut in 1961. This average came from multiple seasons of high WAR canceled out by several low seasons, however, as Freehan was not the most consistent player during his career. Just check out his OPS by season:

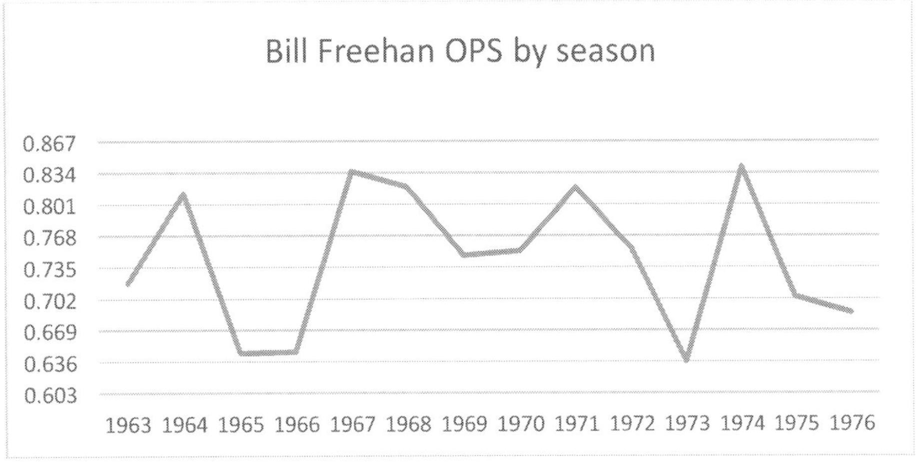

Freehan's best year was 1968, which, perhaps unsurprisingly, was the Tigers best year while he was there. Freehan didn't do anything of note in the World Series, but he was more than willing to go along for the ride with one of the strongest pitching staffs of the era. The team allowed only two runs combined in their Game 6 and 7 victories to clinch the title. Freehan's role behind the dish is something that clearly mattered to his manager, Sparky Anderson, who said, "As far as I'm concerned, the only responsibility a catcher has is to control his pitchers. He doesn't have to get a hit as long as he can do that." Most years Freehan was indeed able to be productive with his bat, but even when he wasn't, the fact that he had a positive dWAR every year except his first and last shows he was a perfect fit for Sparky.

A few more notes on Freehan's defensive abilities: in 1965, he tied the MLB record for catchers with 699 putouts.

He also retired as the all-time leader for fielding percentage among catchers (.993), a number that has since been passed numerous times, as catchers continue to fine-tune their craft. Freehan was *The Sporting News*' choice for the premier catcher in the American League for the 1960s, a well-deserved honor that, although it doesn't entirely make up for the fact that he got a bit shafted on the Hall of Fame ballot (he doesn't deserve to be in the Hall, but he deserves better than receiving only 0.5 percent of the vote and being off the ballot in just one year), can hopefully continue his legacy for future generations.

1B Hank Greenberg (1930; 1933-1946)

Greenberg was a hero to his team, his city, his religion, and the nation as a whole, in his time playing baseball. He was a Jewish hero who converted many Jewish fans from around the country to Tigers fandom. It wasn't always this way, however. In 1934, on Rosh Hashanah, Greenberg didn't want to play but was talked into it, and he subsequently hit a game-winning home run in the ninth. This was beloved by many fans, but not the Jewish ones, as many would have preferred he take the day off in honor of the Jewish holiday. However, Greenberg quickly redeemed himself on Yom Kippur of the same year. Again he faced a dilemma of whether or not to play. This time he followed his father's advice and sat out, and he won over many of the Jewish fans he had lost.

Greenberg's Judaism was a big part of his legacy as a player and as a man. He had to overcome anti-Semitic sentiments from his own teammates, including one who called him a "Goddamn Jew" during team batting practice. Lawrence Richards, writing for *The National Pastime Museum*, makes the claim that, "[Greenberg] arguably was the recipient of more obscenities and, yes, hatred than any other white ballplayer in the long history of baseball." Greenberg also played during a time when his role as a Jewish man was under the microscope. "Of course, as time went by, I came to feel that if I, as a Jew, hit a home run, I was hitting one against Hitler," Greenberg said of his playing days.

Greenberg wasn't just a hero because he was Jewish, however. He was one of the best hitters of all time, and one whose numbers were significantly hindered due to significant time lost to service for our country. In fact, his time in the war was the longest of any baseball player during WWII. This was especially impressive dedication to the war effort, because he was turned down on his first try to join the fight due to his "flat feet." He retook the physical, however, and passed the second time around. As a result, he played only 19 games in 1941, not coming back until the second half of 1945. He had quite an impact upon returning to baseball, though, posting .311/.404/.544 slash lines with 46 runs, 13 home runs, and 60 RBI in just 78 games in 1945. He also clinched the 1945 pennant with a grand slam over the St. Louis Browns in the final game of the season, and he then went on to dominate the World Series. He would have won the series MVP if the award existed, as he hit the Tigers only two home runs of the series to go with seven runs and seven RBI and a .304/.467/.696 slash line.

Before Greenberg left to serve in WWII, he was at the height of his game, making his sacrifice all the more impressive. He won the 1940 MVP with .340/.433/.670 slashes and 129 runs, 41 home runs, and 150 RBI. He finished only 12 batting points away from a Triple Crown and was second among position players in WAR (7.1), despite playing in the WAR-punished position of left field. By winning MVP while playing the year in left field, he became the first player to win MVP at two different positions, as he won the 1935 MVP while playing first base.

Greenberg is among the several players throughout the book whose career totals would look much different if he hadn't missed time in the war, so let's take a look at how Greenberg's career might have played out if Hitler wasn't born with a micropenis. (No, really, that's a thing.) If we are conservative and consider the 1941 and 1945 seasons to combine for one small season for him, we then need to give him four seasons (1942, 1943, 1944, the other half of 1941+1945) of time missed. If we take the eight years he played in the league before the war[371] and divide by two, he missed out on .326/.418/.625 slashes and 415 runs, 124 home runs, and 501 RBI. Adding those on to Greenberg's career totals as they stand today, puts Greenberg at 2,400 hits to go with nearly 1,500 runs, over 450 home runs, and nearly 1,800 RBI.

Those totals still don't do justice to just how good a player Greenberg was, however, because in addition to these totals being very conservative, his career ended early when he was barely 36 years old. A better example of his dominance is the fact that only Babe Ruth, Lou Gehrig, Jimmie Foxx, Ted Williams, and Barry Bonds have a higher slugging percentage with as many at bats as Hammerin' Hank. He's also one of only five players all-time with .300/.400/.600 career slashes, with Foxx, Gehrig, Williams, and Ruth as the other four. Greenberg was an RBI man first and foremost. This was an era of high run-scoring, and the Tigers offense was among its most potent. As such, his five best RBI seasons combined are topped by only Gehrig, Ruth, and Foxx in baseball history. However, to imply that he was simply a product of his times would be false. He is also one of only four players all-time (Ruth and Gehrig – what a surprise – joined by Rogers Hornsby this time) to have 40 doubles, 40 home runs, and 10 triples in a season, showing ability in all fields of hitting.

As a kid, Greenberg was a dedicated athlete but also great son. His dad didn't like the sawdust pile in his lawn that Hank had put down to use as a sliding pit, so he told his son to get rid of it. Instead of going against his father, Hank simply rebuilt the sawdust pile every day and cleaned it before his dad got home. All that practice paid off, however, as he would become the first major league player to get paid $100,000, making him able to buy all the sawdust piles he wanted. Interestingly enough, that six figure deal wasn't when Greenberg was in his prime, but rather at the very end of his career. Pirates owner John Galbreath became obsessed with getting Greenberg to come to Pittsburgh instead of retiring. Galbreath

[371] Which, again, is conservative considering he missed an entire season (sans 12 games) and hadn't hit his prime in his first two seasons.

was convinced that Hank would pepper the short porch in left field (brought in by 25 feet just for Greenberg's benefit), an area that was nicknamed Greenberg Gardens. Although Greenberg did not produce as much as the Pirates hoped numbers-wise, he certainly left his imprint on the club, taking a young Ralph Kiner under his wing. The two roomed together, and Greenberg was constantly giving Kiner advice. Those gardens that Galbreath had once hoped to see Greenberg peppering with long balls were instead peppered by Kiner and renamed Kiner's Korner, as such. Without Greenberg, Kiner may never have had the same success, as Kiner was on the verge of being sent to the minor leagues early in 1947.

Greenberg was a baseball lifer, becoming the first Jewish owner/general manager, as well as the first Jewish player to be elected into the Hall of Fame.

2B Charlie Gehringer (1924-1942)

Another member of the vaunted "Battalion of Death" Tigers infield[372] (along with Hank Greenberg, Billy Rogell, and Marv Owen), and a lifetime Tiger himself, Gehringer was a consistent contact hitter and a solid fielder, which is exactly what was required from the second base position in his era. A .320 career hitter, Gehringer was nicknamed the "Mechanical Man" with good reason. He frequently topped 200 hits in a season and regularly topped 100 runs and RBI. In Bill James' *Historical Baseball Abstract*, Gehringer ranks as the eighth-best second baseman all-time, and although there have been some great second baseman since that book was released, Gehringer's spot among the all-time two baggers is undeniable. He won the 1937 MVP over a Joe DiMaggio season in which DiMaggio had 151 runs, 46 home runs, and 167 RBI; and it wasn't even that egregious by WAR (DiMaggio was worth 8.2; Gehringer was worth 7.4 – that's well within the error bars for a stat like WAR). For a 14-year stretch (1927-1940), the Mechanical Man's batting average dropped below .300 only once, and that was when he hit .298 in 1932. He was like the reverse Bill Freehan.[373]

Regarding his 1932 season – the season his average dropped [*sarcasm added*] all the way down to .298 – Gehringer said, "That was the year I was going to be like Babe Ruth. I think I had eight home runs before he had any, and I began going for the fences. I wound up getting not many homers – and not many hits either." Since I am a member of the Society of American Baseball Research, I would have membership card revoked if I didn't check on this story, and unfortunately it doesn't hold much water. Gehringer did end up with 19 home runs for the season, a career-high at the time, but he only hit his eighth home run on May 30 of the 1932 season. As for Ruth, well, by May 30, he had 14 home runs. He even had four home runs in the first four games of the season.

However, this shouldn't imply that Gehringer was trying to make excuses for his 1932 season. Whenever a SABR member bursts the bubble of some historical anecdote, it can sometimes come across as accusing whoever told the story of being misleading, but really it is usually just that people's memories are inherently flawed. I actually do believe that Gehringer was swinging for the fences more that season. As Bill James inquires, "I wonder if any player in baseball history had a record of sustained improvement to equal Gehringer?... I don't know of any other player who took as many steps forward in his career. Frank White, maybe." The fact that Gehringer would try to add some power to his repertoire in his seventh full season in the big leagues seems very likely. But he didn't actually have eight home runs before Ruth had any.

Finally, Gehringer had a special relationship with the Midsummer Classic. He is the only player to appear as a starter in the first six All-Star Games, and he has the highest batting average in the All-Star Game history among hitters with at least 20 at bats. Derek Jeter is second on that list, and the Yankee legend actually makes sense as a cross-generation comp for Gehringer. The comp even works down to the fact that Gehringer was notably as graceful off the field as he was on it, and that both were bachelors for most of their careers. I'm not sure if Jeter took his mother to church every Sunday like Gehringer did, but the comparison still holds.

3B Miguel Cabrera (2008-pres.)

When I first wrote Cabrera's write-up, I started with the following pair of sentences, "This is cheating a little bit since Cabrera has played only one season at third in Detroit so far, but he played third in Miami previously. Also, considering the success the Tigers have had so far and the fact that Prince Fielder isn't going anywhere, it's fair to assume Cabrera will play there for a bit." That is no longer the case for a few reasons. Right after that sentence was written, Prince Fielder did indeed go elsewhere, as he was traded to Texas, and Cabrera moved back across the diamond to first base. However, Cabrera won both his MVPs while at third base, and unless you're dying to read about Travis Fryman, there wasn't great competition for this spot.

Plus, it's hard to deny a Starting IX spot to someone who can swing the stick as well as Cabrera can. Miggy's hitting bona fides are as impressive as any hitter of his generation, arguably culminating with his 2012 Triple Crown. Although his OPS+ was actually higher in 2010, 2011, 2013, and 2015, the Triple Crown has a (deservedly) magical effect on people. It resulted in Miggy winning his first MVP, and although some made the case for Mike Trout, it's hard to argue with only the

[372] They were also called: "Tigers Million Dollar Infield," "First Line of Defense," "Detroit's Big Guns," "The Infield of Dreams," and, easily the best, "Punch and Protection of Bounding Bengals."
[373] Which, unlike the Reverse Rick Moranis, is not a questionable sex position...

fifth Triple Crown winner to come from a first-place team; a first-place team that made it all the way to the World Series, in fact. In that World Series, the matchup between AL MVP Cabrera and NL MVP Buster Posey, was the first World Series to pit both leagues' MVPs against each other since 1988 when José Canseco's A's and Kirk Gibson's Dodgers squared off.

WAR certainly favored Trout over Cabrera in 2012 and 2013, when Cabrera won back-to-back MVPs, but with the defensive metrics as shaky as they still are, the edge isn't as blatant as many pundits made it out to be, and the injustice really wasn't too high, all things considered. Miggy was amazing those two seasons.

Cabrera made his MLB debut at the ripe age of 20, and as such, has already been fun to project career-wise to see where he may end up among the all-time greats. Whenever I go on multiple-season simulating binges in MLB The Show, I always make sure to check Cabrera's stats at the end of his career to see if he topped 762 home runs, or 2,297 RBI, or 2,295 runs, or even 4,256 hits. He wouldn't always (plus it's a videogame), but here's a fun Player A vs. Player B comp for you:

	Games	Hits	HRs	RBI	Runs	Doubles	BA	OBP	SLG	OPS+
Player A	2,279	2,792	510	1,627	1,603	484	.314	.373	.560	157
Player B	2,226	2,636	462	1,613	1,371	545	.317	.395	.553	151

Player A: Hank Aaron through his age-34 season. Player B: Miguel Cabrera through his age-34 season; an idea stolen from Jayson Stark after Cabrera's age-30 season. The comparison was updated for this spot, and almost completely holds up, despite Cabrera's less-than-usual performance in 2017. By the way, we could do another very strong comparison of Miguel Cabrera *through 2013* and Joe DiMaggio for Joltin' Joe's *entire career*.

Cabrera's three consecutive batting titles (2011-2013) were the first time an AL righty did so since the league was founded, and Nap Lajoie won the league's first four batting titles. It was the first time a right-handed batter three-peated a batting title in either league since Rogers Hornsby (1920-25). Of course, Miggy added a fourth in 2015, and he finished in the top 10 in the league in batting average every season from 2009-2016.

If Miggy were to retire right now (right now being the end of the 2017 season… I know that's not how "right now" really works, but just go with it), he would already be ahead of the following players in the following statistics for their careers: Ernie Banks (runs scored), Mickey Mantle (hits), Babe Ruth (doubles), Carl Yastrzemski (home runs), Mike Schmidt (RBI), Eddie Mathews (OPS+), and Tony Gwynn (WAR). Just amazing.

Let's end on this note reminding fans just how hard it is to compare players across generations: when Stan Musial won the MVP in 1948, he faced 52 pitchers all season; when Cabrera won his MVP in 2012, he faced 225 pitchers – all of whom have hard drives full of information on him, to boot.

SS Alan Trammell (1977-1996)

It seems wrong having Trammell here without his P.I.C. Lou Whitaker up the middle, but we'll have to forge ahead. Another lifetime Tiger,[374] Trammell was an incredible fielder and a strong hitter, who rode these talents to a borderline Hall of Fame career. I think he deservedly isn't quite in, but he is also a guy who, if the Veteran's Committee voted him in one day, I wouldn't have as much an issue with as, say, Freddie Lindstrom.

Trammell, the long-time double-play mate of a man who just missed this team (the aforementioned Whitaker) helped to form core of the Tigers throughout the 1980s. Much like Melissa McCarthy when paired with Paul Feig, Trammell and the Tigers seemed to have a symbiotic relationship in that the team's greatest success came when Trammell had his greatest success. His two best seasons by WAR (8.2 in 1987 and 6.7 in 1984) were the two times the Tigers made the playoffs while he was there. Even within the playoffs themselves, Trammell's importance can be seen. Just check out his line from the 1984 World Series team: .419 batting average, .500 on-base percentage, three home runs, seven runs, and nine RBI; versus his line from the Tigers' 1987 first-round exit: .200 BA, .238 OBP, three runs, zero homers, and two RBI.

Trammell has basically the exact same career WAR[375] as Barry Larkin (70.4 for Trammell and 70.2 for Larkin), which provides an interesting opportunity to look at their two careers in comparison. Both were shortstops who played over 2,000 games with one franchise for their entire careers. Both were excellent fielders, Trammell netting 22.0 dWAR, four Gold Gloves, and a fielding percentage significantly above league average throughout his career (.977 to .967 league average). Larkin netted 13.8 dWAR, three Gold Gloves, and a fielding percentage of .975 compared to league average of .968. Larkin started his career about a decade after Trammell so his power numbers are a little higher (13 more home runs and 29 extra slugging percentage points), but Trammell collected 25 more hits, and their OPS+ (which, again, adjusts for park and era) are very close, with Larkin leading 116 to 110. Their RuBIns are tight, with Larkin having 55 more, as well as a slight advantage in total bases. Both players won one championship and were excellent postseason performers. In fact, looking at their postseason stats, they mirror each other nearly as much as the regular seasons stats:

---

[374] If nothing else, the Tigers seem to have some of the most loyal players of any franchise Starting IX.

[375] I think Trammell's career WAR overrates him a little bit because of his position. He is 93rd all-time ahead of – by my count – 140 Hall of Famers including Tony Gwynn, Al Simmons, Ernie Banks, Ed Walsh, Willie McCovey, Jackie Robinson, Bob Feller, Yogi Berra, Harmon Killebrew, Hank Greenberg, Whitey Ford, Sandy Koufax… The list could really go on for about a chapter, and it probably shouldn't be able to.

Trammell: 10 runs, three home runs, and 11 RBI with .333/.404/.588 BA/OBP/SLG

Larkin: 11 runs, three home runs, and eight RBI with .338/.397/.465 BA/OBP/SLG

Where Larkin probably gained some favor in Hall of Fame voting[376] is his significant advantage on the base paths (143 more steals than Trammell), his MVP season (as sad as it is that the difference between Larkin's MVP year and Trammell's second place finish in 1987 is part of the difference in their legacy, it is still undeniable), and his 12 All-Star appearances to Trammell's six. Two of these are subjective – a method that the Hall of Fame has been known to use… a lot.

People think of Alex Rodriguez, Derek Jeter, Nomar Garciaparra and Miguel Tejada as ushering in the hard-hitting shortstop revolution, but really Paul Molitor, Cal Ripken Jr., and Trammell did it 15 years before that. It is interesting to note that Rob Neyer thinks that the second shortstop revolution of Jeter and his crew actually hurt Trammell's Hall of Fame case. Just as Trammell was becoming eligible for the Hall, a time in which a player's legacy is often rejuvenated through articles about whether they will join the Hall, Jeter, A-Rod, Nomar, and Tejada were completely modernizing the position and putting up numbers that no one had ever had seen from shortstops before. In comparison, Trammell's numbers would have panned, despite the obvious caveat that they were playing in completely different eras.

These are the types of things that slip under the radar, and it's why guys like Rob Neyer are so good at what they do.

LF Bobby Veach (1912-1923)

The Tigers outfield to begin the 20th century was about as strong a unit as there has been in baseball history. They boasted Bobby Veach, Harry Heilmann, Sam Crawford, and Ty Cobb. Because of this, it can be a little tricky to pick out who should represent the Tigers for their franchise's outfield. Cobb is a lock for center, but it gets a little messy after that. Veach played in left field 1,224 out of 1,291 games recorded by Baseball-Reference. Heilmann played in right field 1,525 out of 2,037 games recorded by Baseball-Reference. Finally, Crawford, the earliest of the bunch, played in right field all 81 games that Baseball-Reference has him recorded as playing in the outfield, with the information on what outfield position he played prior to that unavailable. Along with the fact that Veach joined Crawford and Cobb in 1913 – and Veach being a left fielder – this seems to be solid evidence that Crawford was the right fielder for Tigers. So, the simple solution would be to put Veach in left, Cobb in center, Crawford in right, and Heilmann at the utility spot. However, this is ignoring the fact that the Tigers have about 90 years of history outside of 1901-1925. Although there isn't a ton of talent in the outfield throughout the rest of Tigers history, there is a real stud in right field for the Tigers in the 1950s and `60s that we'll talk about in a second.

So, with center field and right field spoken for, there was a big decision between Veach, Crawford, and Heilmann for left field and utility. Since Veach was the only left fielder, at first, he was the natural lock for this position, which is why his name appears above. However, this led to a very hard decision between the other two, and it got me thinking. So here comes the first real gimmick[377] of the book: Veach isn't going to start in left. I want to give him credit, because he is the best left fielder in Tigers history, but here's the rub: Wahoo Sam and Harry Heilmann each could have been better left fielders if their team had needed them to play in left. It seems unfair to punish these players a deserved spot in team history just because of which side of Ty Cobb they lined up on. Neither was a great fielder, but Crawford was there for more of Cobb's prime so I guess we'll put him in the field and Heilmann at the utility spot.

Since we're giving the official spot to Wahoo Sam Crawford, let's turn our focus on him. Crawford is best known for being the all-time MLB leader in triples (309), which is about as safe a lock for a record to not be broken as there is in the sport. In fact, let's take a look at the most unbreakable records:

SP) Games managed: 7,755 Connie Mack – It would take 48 seasons to break this record. Considering the player/manager is dead and teams have less patience than ever, this one seems incredibly safe.

C) Career wins: 511 Cy Young – It would be beyond-shocking if we ever even get another 400-game winner, let alone 500-game winner. Count this spot for Young's career innings pitched (7356.0), games started (815), and complete games (749), as well.

1B) Grand slams in one inning: 2 Fernando Tatis – This is cheating a bit because it may well be tied again, but three grand slams in one inning? That might just end the world. Put Johnny Vander Meer's two straight no-hitters in this category, as well.

2B) Intentional walks in a season: 120 Barry Bonds – Based God.

3B) Career triples: 309 Sam Crawford – The only way this happens is if a ballpark innovator makes a funky stadium quirk, and a really fricken fast player starts and ends his career there. Also in this category, the 2,544 at bats Dave Eggler had in his career without hitting a home run, the most ever.

SS) Hit streak: 56 Joe DiMaggio – Dom Chance wrote an incredible piece on the probability of certain hit streaks by certain players. The odds of DiMaggio's hit streak? 1-in-3,394.

LF) Sacrifice hits: 512 Eddie Collins – Never bunt; hit dingers.

CF) Most All-Star Games played: 25 Hank Aaron – Here's a complete list of players in the modern era to *play* in at least 26 seasons: Nolan Ryan and, ironically, Tommy John.

---

[376] Unlike Trammell, Larkin made it into the Hall on his third try.

[377] Just look at this clock… There have been no other gimmicks in the book so far… You are getting veeerrrry sleepy…

RF) Consecutive games played: 2,632 Cal Ripken Jr. – Just doesn't seem likely with the move towards players being more well-rested.

Crawford played in a triples era, and by Bill James' calculations, if Crawford had played in Babe Ruth's era he would have hit 494 home runs and knocked in over 1,900. (It's worth noting that Baseball-Reference's Neutralized Batting metric is not nearly this generous to Crawford.) Crawford definitely had the build to push James' recalculations, though, as he was described in *Baseball Magazine* in 1916 in a very flattering light: "While we are no sculptor, we believe that if we were looking for a model for the stature of a slugger we would choose Sam Crawford for that role."

Finally, Crawford and outfield mate Ty Cobb didn't get along. It was Crawford who supplied the gem of a quote about Cobb to Lawrence Ritter in *The Glory of their Times*, "He came up from the South, you know, and he was still fighting the Civil War." Of course, not getting along with Cobb is probably as good a sign of Crawford being of high character. The two were, however, able to work together on the field mastering the double steal, and Cobb has Crawford, in part, to thank for Cobb's record 50 steals of home.

CF Ty Cobb (1905-1926)

Where to begin? Cobb is one of the most polarizing figures in baseball history, one who I would give my (potential) first born child to see play in the modern, scrutinizing "Twitter Era." Obviously, Cobb would have to be a much tamer version of the Cobb that terrorized baseball – in every sense of the word – in the beginning of the 20th century, but it would still be very intriguing. Let's start with the obvious: Cobb was a helluva player. Definitely top 10 all-time, probably top five, and you could say the best ever without being thought of as crazy (though I wouldn't agree with you). In the original Hall of Fame vote, Cobb received the most votes of anyone, yes more than even Babe Ruth. In fact, many sources say that Ruth's stature as the undisputed best player of all time is a more modern look at the two players, as Cobb was often thought of as better than Ruth in the early days of baseball history.

Cobb is the all-time leader in batting average (.366) and is second all-time in runs (2,244), hits (4,189), and triples (295). He is in the top 10 in numerous other categories, such as WAR (151.0), oWAR (150.9), OBP (.433), games played (3,034), total bases (5,854), doubles (724), RBI (1,933), stolen bases (897), and OPS+ (168). He won at least 10 batting titles (there's some Cap Anson-esque debate over a few of his batting crowns; Baseball-Reference has him at 12 BA titles) and never hit below .320 in any 100-game season; he had a 19-year stretch in which he hit .300 with an on-base percentage over .400 every year. He collected over 200 hits in a season nine times and was a speed king too, leading the league in steals six times, as well as setting the single-season stolen bases record in 1915 (96), a record that stood until Maury Wills in 1962 (104). He has the most steals of home all-time (54), and six times in his career he managed to steal his way around the bases. Yes, that includes stealing home. When he retired, he was the holder of 43 MLB records.

His abilities were not just limited to that of a contact hitter, however, and the stories of lore support it. The story goes that when Ruth supplanted him as the main star of the league, Cobb was angered and decided to prove he could hit the home runs the media seemed to want those days. The game after making this known, he hit three home runs (a feat at this time accomplished by only five men and one that Ruth himself had not yet achieved). Cobb followed that up with two more bombs the next day, before going back to his normal style of slapping the ball around with great success. This sort of story brings to mind something that Brian Kenny and Ben Lindbergh discussed in an episode of *The Ringer MLB Show* podcast. The two talked about judging players on skills that were rewarded in their day versus what skills we reward in modern baseball. Steve Garvey, for example, is a player who hit for a high batting average and drove in RBI in an era when those two stats were thought to be the be-all and end-all. Judging his low on-base percentage and saying that his RBI were a bit empty today doesn't do Garvey justice; he may well have been able to adjust his style of play in modern baseball to draw more walks and hit for more power if he had given preference to those skills. Cobb's one-series power explosion is just one example of how players throughout baseball history have adjusted to what they believe to be important, and it is something that is important to think about when judging players from a modern perspective.

One could go on for chapters about Cobb's accomplishments on the field, but here's the thing, and most of you know it's coming, one could also go on for chapters about Cobb "off the field." The story of Cobb off the field has more layers than a *Shrek* onion. The story of Cobb that many of us grew up learning was that of a virulent racist, a man who went out of his way to antagonize everyone, especially black people. The story goes that he supposedly sharpened his cleats to hurt his opponents, and he may have even committed murder. However, a large part of that legacy is due to one man: Al Stump.

Stump was Cobb's biographer and, as is coming to light now, was a self-promoting blowhard, who at best blurred the edges of Cobb's true legacy and, at worst, manipulated public opinion and wasn't afraid to falsify entire stories after Cobb's death for his own personal gain. Stump originally published Cobb's biography in 1961, just a few months after Cobb's passing, but it was his two later books – and one high-profile newspaper article after the original biography – that really shaped the Cobb-as-a-villain narrative we now think of today.

Thankfully, that's where Charles Leerhsen, as well as a couple of truth-devoted baseball writers, come into play. Leerhsen published *Ty Cobb: A Terrible Beauty* in 2015, and in it, he is able to debunk a large majority of the Cobb mythology. Leerhsen debunks the Cobb as racist narrative (yes, Cobb got into fights with black men, but he got into even more fights with white guys and was actually very supportive of desegregating the majors when Jackie Robinson joined

MLB); he disproves that Cobb ever sharpened his cleats, citing numerous teammates and contemporaries that say Cobb never did such a thing, and not one that said he did; and he disproves the "Cobb killed a man" narrative that Cobb had supposedly told Stump in his final days. In fact, Stump comes out of the book looking worse than Cobb.

An important part of Leerhsen's work is that Cobb was not, by any stretch of the imagination, a great guy. Instead, he was a troubled man, whose mother shot his father to death,[378] an incident from which he never truly recovered. He had a penchant for fighting, and he certainly wasn't the young man you'd want your daughter to show up to dinner with. However, he was also a far cry from the man many think of today. As Leerhsen himself said, "It's a warts-and-all biography. But they're warts, not tumors."

The myth of Cobb has been so entrenched, and for so many years, that Leerhsen himself has said that when he set out to write Cobb's bio, he was expecting his angle to be what a terrible man he was. I myself had the exact same surprise in research for this write-up. In fact, the first time this section was written, it included mostly the negative stories from Stump's bios and articles, and it had a section on whether Cobb was a terrible enough guy to actually ban him from a spot on the team. (The verdict: hell, no, have you seen this guy's stats?) It was only with a deeper dive that I was able to render a more accurate portrait of the man.

In a way, Cobb has gone from the easiest man to hate in baseball history to a somewhat sympathetic figure. I mean who wouldn't get into some fights after his/her mom shot his/her dad to death? Now, this sympathy may be a bridge too far, but given how far in the other direction his legacy has been tainted for the last 50 years, maybe that's fair. Plus, ask the average person on the street what they think of when they hear the name Ty Cobb, and you're going to hear "racist" and "cleat sharpener" far more often than "sympathetic figure." So, do baseball history a favor and, next time you hear Cobb's name come up a cocktail party, toss some love (or at least non-hate) Cobb's way, so we can start to swing the pendulum back towards truth.

Hopefully Cobb's legacy will one day be a man who had no fear. He was a man who would stand nearly on top of the plate when facing Walter Johnson because Johnson had told him he was scared to hit players due to the speed of his fastball. Johnson would throw a couple balls outside and then let up when down 2-0 in the count. That's when Cobb would swing. He was such a competitor that one sportswriter wrote of him, "[Cobb] would climb a mountain to punch an echo." This was a man who had his tonsils removed by a madman so that he could play in an *exhibition* game that day. Oh, and yeah, he had a violent streak and was no Stan Musial-esque man. But seriously, check out those stats again and remember to learn, and share, his full story.

RF Al Kaline (1953-1974)

The second column of the periodic table,[379] AlKaline was just a baby when he started in the league. He came into the league straight from high school, having never played in the minors. In fact, Kaline had to have the zits removed from his face on his first baseball cards because he still looked like the "Before" picture in a ProActiv commercial. Those zits didn't stop Kaline from being one of the best young players of all time, as Kaline became the youngest player ever to win the AL batting title, doing so in 1955 at the ripe age of 20. So, basically while I was drinking 40s of High Gravity bought by a friend's older brother and playing 50-60 hours of *MLB: The Show* a week, Kaline was the best hitter in baseball. Cool.

This was to be the highlight of Kaline's career, though. He never reached 200 hits again and only led the league in doubles, SLG, and OPS (once), and intentional walks (twice) in terms of black ink on his baseball card the rest of his career. This statement diminishes the rest of his career too much, though. Although his second full season may have been his best, Kaline still put together quite an impressive resume. He reached 3,000 hits with the Tigers and crossed home plate over 1,600 times, while driving in over 1,500 of his fellow Tigers. In the 1968 World Series, he hit well over .300 with two home runs and eight RBI to contribute to the Tigers World Series victory. He was the best hitter on the Tigers in the `68 Series. He was also an 18-time All-Star and only Roberto Clemente has more Total Zone Runs than Kaline in right field in the history of the game. In fact, consistency and accumulating statistics over many long, healthy seasons was Kaline's calling card. His 399 career home runs are the most ever for a player who never hit at least 30 in a single season.

Kaline was also a great team player and one of the most respected players in Tigers history. He once turned down club's first $100,000 contract, saying the club had been so fair to him that he didn't want the contract until he thought he earned it. He earned in it in his time with the club, however, finishing as the team's all-time leading home run hitter and finishing second to Cobb in numerous other categories. Kaline was one of the true Tiger legends, one who was asked to write the foreword to *The Tigers and Their Den*, a strong retelling of the franchise's history by John McCollister.

Kaline has a spot in the heart of many Tigers fans and is the all-time favorite of not just one of my best bosses of all time (Tiger fan Jim Vitanos) but also baseball writer Craig Calcaterra, who wrote an excellent piece for *The National Pastime* on Kaline being his favorite player all-time despite having never having seen him play, an affliction to which I can certainly attest. Let's call it Rose-Colored Nostalgia.[380]

---

[378] One theory on the incident was that Cobb's father believed his mother to be engaging in infidelity, so he snuck into the bedroom to catch her in the act. In shock, Cobb's mother shot him to death.

[379] This may be the most forced joke in this book of forced jokes… and I'm alright with that.

[380] I can't hear "rose-colored" and not think of one of the most amazing, and depressing, quotes from *BoJack Horseman*. When Wanda the Owl, voiced by

Utility Harry Heilmann (1914; 1916-1929)

Ask a typical baseball fan which three right-handed batters have the highest career batting averages, and many may get Rogers Hornsby. But the next two: Ed Delahanty and Harry Heilmann, are much more under-the-radar. Ty Cobb said of Heilmann, "Next to Rogers Hornsby, he was the best right-handed hitter of them all." In all fairness, Cobb was Heilmann's teammate, and it was very early in baseball history, but it does speak to how Heilmann has been lost a bit in baseball history. Heilmann hit higher than .390 four times, winning a batting title in each of those seasons. For a seven-year stretch (1921-1927), Heilmann hit a combined .380 and averaged over 200 hits a season. Of his four batting titles, he was twice offered the opportunity to sit out the final game of the season to guarantee himself a batting title, but both times he took the high road and played (a hot take I've really been banging the drum on throughout this book). Both times he was able to gather hits and still win the batting title, something we've seen has not always been the case.

Heilmann was discovered while working as biscuit company bookkeeper and was offered $10 to play in a semi-pro game by a friend he bumped into. He hit the game-winning double, and the rest is history. Said history includes quite the story that I jotted down during my research but didn't source well enough to go back and find when I wanted the complete story. Sadly, now I can't seem to find the story anywhere. It may even be better without the whole story, though, as our imaginations can take the reins. The story: Heilmann once drove his automobile down the stairs of a speakeasy. I mean we all did some dumb crap in our youth, but that would probably top the list of entertaining stories for just about all of us. Just imagine the circumstances.

Back to baseball: Heilmann had a reputation as a very good defensive outfielder but poor defensive first baseman, a strange fact given that outfield (center field in particular) is a far more challenging position than first base. The advanced metrics also show no real difference between his defense at either spot. His fielding percentage as a first baseman was five percentage points below league average in his 448 games there, while his fielding percentage in the outfield was four percentage points below league average in his 1,594 games there. In fact, when using Baseball-Reference's range factors, it looks like Heilmann was a far better first baseman actually, which makes sense given that he was so slow that his teammates called him "Slug." This only makes the fact that his defensive reputation was superior in the outfield, a position in which speed is far more necessary than first base, all the more surprising. Just goes to show how much easier it was for fallacies to be spread in baseball before we had the level of statistical sophistication that we have today. It also makes you wonder what folks will look back on one day and scoff about in sports today. Who is truly good on the offensive line in football, and the entire analysis of soccer seemed most primed.

Heilmann went on to be a beloved radio voice of the Tigers after retirement and is a solid choice for this spot, despite many middle-aged Tigers fans likely feeling that Whitaker was the better option.

SP Justin Verlander (2005-pres.)

The closest competition for Verlander was Hal Newhouser. "Prince Hal" had an interesting career, one which, on the surface, would appear to have Verlander beat for best in Tiger history. Newhouser is the only pitcher to win two straight MVPs and, for a three-year stretch, went 80-27 with an ERA under 2.00; but there's a catch. Other than that three-year stretch, he was a pretty mediocre pitcher, losing more games than he won and posting only one other season with an ERA below 3.00 (a season in which he led the league in losses). Newhouser's incredible three seasons also happen to have a bit of an asterisk next to them. The three years Newhouser dominated were 1944-1946. Any history buffs able to rack their brains and figure out what was going on at that time? That's right, WWII. Newhouser missed the draft due to a heart murmur and dominated the league during the time when Major League Baseball was missing almost all of its stars to the war effort.

Being as I love to give both sides of arguments, it should be noted that when I asked a panel of baseball historians about just how much of an asterisk should be put next to Newhouser's statistics, the group unanimously said they believed the stats to be legitimate. With all due respect to these smart minds, I have to disagree. And here's the clincher: during WWII, lifetime *hitter*, Jimmie Foxx, *pitched*, as a 37-year-old, part-time third baseman, and he threw 22.2 innings with a 1.59 ERA. Sure, Foxx was an all-timer, but if he could be dominant as a pitcher during the war years, it makes me doubt just how great Newhouser was, especially given his struggles outside of those war years. Bill James said 40 percent of MLB players during the war years were of a major league caliber. Run production also went down in part because of a different type of ball that Spalding created because rubber was needed for the war effort (Right Field, Cubs – Page 232). The evidence is just too overwhelming to cut Newhouser slack, even if he was the statistical leader in multiple pitching categories of the 1940s. (And yes, I read Chris Jaffe's excellent piece, "Prince Hal" for *The Hardball Times*, and it still didn't convince me.)

On top of all the questions about the legitimacy of Newhouser's dominance, add the fact that Justin Verlander has quite the resume himself, and it's easy to see why he gets the spot. Verlander is one of only two pitchers all-time to win Rookie of the Year, Cy Young and MVP. Don Newcombe is the other. According to *Baseball Prospectus'* deserved run average (a catch-all metric to measure what a pitcher was able to accomplish), Verlander's 2011-2012 stretch was the second-

---

the incomparable Lisa Kudrow, starts to sour on BoJack, she says, "You know, it's funny; when you look at someone through rose-colored glasses, all the red flags just look like flags." Isn't that just a punch in the tits?

most dominant two-year stretch *of the last 60 years*. Although I'm not quite buying in at that level, Verlander's 2009-2012 stretch is on par with Newhouser's most dominant run, and Verlander simply did so much more outside of that stretch and did so without the aforementioned benefits Newhouser had.

As far as how he is as a guy, Verlander always struck me as a bit standoffish and kind of a dick, but his results on the field are hard to argue with. The man seems to spit in the face of the concept that certain baseball players aren't able to step up to another level in the most important moments of a game/season. This sentiment has become more common-place after his impressive 2017 post-Tigers run with the Astros. Verlander was traded from his Starting IX affiliates a minute before the 2017 trade deadline, and he was instantly able to rev up his level of production. Pitching for a rather lackluster Tigers team, Verlander had a 3.86 ERA and 1.279 WHIP; after his move to eventual World Series winners Houston: 1.06 ERA and 0.647 WHIP. Verlander went on to win a pair of games in both the ALDS and ALCS (24.2 combined innings, just four earned runs allowed), before tossing a pair of solid, if not overwhelming starts in the World Series. Despite an 0-4 record in the World Series, Verlander was finally able to get his hands on a World Series ring, a championship he celebrated with a marriage to Kate Upton less than ten days after. Not a bad couple of weeks.

CP John Hiller (1965-1970; 1972-1980)

Hiller spent all 15 years of his career in Detroit, consistently coming out of the bullpen with solid results. After a cup of tea in 1965 and 1966, Hiller established himself in 1967 and had an ERA below 4.00 every year until 1979 (with the exception of the 1971 season, which he missed after having three [yes, three!!] heart attacks in the offseason). He had a sub-3.00 ERA eight of those years.

His best year was 1973, when he went 10-5 with a 1.44 ERA. Hiller led the league in games (65), games finished (60), and saves (38), while finishing fourth in both the Cy Young and MVP. His WAR of 8.1 is an astronomical total for a reliever in today's baseball and was even impressively high in the context of relievers of the '70s. In fact, the total is the second-highest single-season WAR total for a reliever in history, trailing only Goose Gossage in 1975 (8.2). This 1973 campaign kicked off a four-year stretch that was the best of Hiller's career. He would be a bit of an "everything man" in the pen for the Tigers during that time, compiling 41 wins with a 2.18 ERA and 462 strikeouts in 467 innings to go along with finishing 192 games for the club during that four-year prime.

Starting IX Franchise Roster Stats

Lineup	Yrs	G	R	H	HR	RBI	SB	BB	SO	BA	OBP	SLG	OPS+	dWAR	WAR
Ty Cobb	**22**	2806	**2086**	**3900**	111	**1800**	**869**	1148	653	**0.368**	**0.434**	0.516	**171**	-10.2	**144.7**
Charlie Gehringer	19	2323	1775	2839	184	1427	181	1186	372	0.320	0.404	0.480	124	10.7	80.6
Al Kaline	**22**	**2834**	1622	3007	**399**	1582	137	**1277**	1020	0.297	0.376	0.480	134	2.5	92.5
Miguel Cabrera	10	1506	922	1794	324	1090	21	743	1034	0.319	0.398	0.558	155	-11.6	50.6
Harry Heilmann	15	1990	1209	2499	164	1443	111	792	498	0.342	0.410	0.518	149	-13.9	67.6
Hank Greenberg	12	1269	975	1528	306	1200	58	748	771	0.319	0.412	**0.616**	161	-3.6	54.1
Sam Crawford	15	2114	115	2466	70	1264	318	646	450	0.309	0.362	0.448	145	-16.2	63.5
Bill Freehan	15	1774	706	1591	200	758	24	626	753	0.262	0.340	0.412	112	11.8	44.7
Alan Trammell	20	2293	1231	2365	185	1003	236	850	874	0.285	0.352	0.415	110	**22.0**	70.4
Pitchers	Yrs	W	W%	ERA	G	CG	SHO	SV	IP	SO	ERA+	WHIP	SO/9	SO/BB	WAR
Justin Verlander	13	183	0.616	3.49	380	23	7	0	2511.0	2373	123	1.191	8.5	3.10	55.0
John Hiller	15	87	0.534	2.83	**545**	13	6	125	1242.0	1036	134	1.268	7.5	1.94	31.2

#5 Oakland Athletics (1968-pres.); Kansas City Athletics (1955-1967); Philadelphia Athletics (1901-1954)

(Photo by Jim Turvey/Baseball Hall of Fame)

Team Background

Playoff appearances: 26 **Pennants: 15** **World Series titles: 9**
Collective team WAR: 556.1
Strengths: One of the more balanced lineups... A pair of studs pitching... And my undying love.
Weaknesses: They're missing that super-duper-uber star. The depth is there, but there isn't a Babe Ruth, a Hank Aaron, or even a George Brett. The few possible guys they do have in that tier never stuck around for their entire careers with the team.
What to expect from the next 12 pages: Your Al Simmons virginity will be ripped from you with reckless abandon.

If you read the inside sleeve then you will know I'll be slightly biased in my team write-up here, seeing as they were one of the teams I covered in my "illustrious" blogging career. However, even before that gig, I found the A's to be one of the most fascinating baseball franchises. The A's have a very distinct history that is easiest to look at in certain chunks of time. We'll go in reverse-chronological order just to mess with Michael Crichton.[381]

The most recent rendition of Athletics can best be referred to as, "The post-Moneyball-but-still-kind-of-Moneyball" A's. Billy Beane is still the team's GM, and he has a big say in the moves they make. However, much of the league has caught onto his tactics, meaning that the A's are no longer the only team using sabermetrics in their scouting reports. In fact, every front office has caved and brought on significant analytics departments, with most having a heavy say in the decision-making process. As such, the A's have had to stay one step ahead through finding new, unfound market inefficiencies, which, after all, was the real lesson of *Moneyball.* So maybe they're not all that different than the early 2000s, after all.

Speaking of which, the "Moneyball" A's had their most success from 1999-2006. Of course, they have been immortalized forever in Michael Lewis' catchphrase-creating book, and as such don't need too much of a delving into here. My only suggestion is to read the book, as well as seeing the movie.

Before the Moneyball-era A's, the team's last previous bout of success came in the late `80s when they reached three straight World Series (1988-1990). Tony LaRussa, Rickey Henderson, the Bash Brothers, and a solid rotation led this team into battle. The intriguing note about Henderson's appearance on the late `80s A's teams, is that he had left the A's to join the larger-market Yankees in 1985, only to come back to Oakland halfway through the 1989 season. He timed his "prodigal son" return perfectly, however, as 1989 was the one year the A's were able to win the championship. That 1989

[381] If you got this far in the book and didn't expect a weird, maybe-works-maybe-doesn't literary tactic to describe simple baseball history, that's on you.

World Series is the A's most recent title to date and was quite a memorable one. For one, the A's defeated their Bay Area Brethren (San Francisco Giants), but more notoriously, the Series is remembered for the enormous earthquake that devastated the Bay Area and nearly canceled the World Series. For an excellent oral history of the event, check out Bryan Curtis' and Patricia Lee's account on *Grantland*, "Rocked." What's a little different about the Bash Brother-era A's is that they spent money. The 1991 A's actually had highest payroll in all of baseball at just under $40 million. In case you're wondering, that does indeed mean that A-Rod made more in 2010 than most entire rosters did in the early `90s.

Before the Bash Bros. and Co., we have to go back to the A's of the early 1970s to find another successful time in franchise history. This team was one of the best dynasties in baseball history, and the squad won three straight titles (1972-1974). This made them one of two franchises (can you guess the other) to win three straight World Series titles.[382] The defining feature of these A's teams was their owner Charlie Finley.

Finley is one of the most intriguing characters in baseball's long narrative, and he had an outsize impact on the Athletics franchise. He was the Mark Cuban of his era, a young, brash owner who had lots of innovative ideas and didn't really give a crap what others thought of him.[383] Finley was the man to move the team out to Oakland after the 1967 season, an interesting change of fate given that, when Finley was first hired, he was praised by the Kansas City fans who believed that Finley had saved them from being relocated. Finley was summed up well by *L.A. Times* columnist Jim Murray: "Charles Finley is a self-made man who worships his creator." Finley could be a charmer, but he also knew how to hold a grudge and had a quick temper. He had only one manager last more than two seasons under his reign. Like Cuban, Finley was always suggesting tweaks to his sport, many of which were successful and far before their time. Among them:[384] night games in the World Series, the A's awesome green-and-gold uniforms of the `70s, and the designated hitter. However, maybe more interestingly, here are some of his unsuccessful ideas: orange baseballs, a designated runner, three balls for a walk and two strikes for a strikeout, and a mechanical rabbit that popped up to hand the umpire a new baseball when needed. Some of these were just before his time, and some of them were just kind of silly.

Finley may have been an eccentric, but he was also a smart businessman. When the owners and the newly formed MLB Players Association went into labor discussions in the early 1970s, it was Finley who pushed for any concessions necessary to avoid arbitration, even pushing for complete free agency (with no time service requirement), because it would flood the market and therefore drive down the price of all free agents. Finley realized this was simple supply and demand. However, the owners didn't listen to him, and we still have arbitration in place today, a huge win for the players and a blow to the owners that could have been avoided if they had listened to Finley, a man many of them ignored out of spite.

The A's clearly had plenty of success under Finley, and my theory is that having a crap boss that the co-workers can complain about instead of complaining about each other can actually have incredible benefits. If readers have learned one thing in this book so far, it is that I am going to force a comparison to *The Office* right now. But seriously, wouldn't Pam be more annoyed by Jim's inability to go through with anything (at least until his weird Athlead plotline) if there was no outlet of complaining about Michael/Robert California/Nelly? And I'm sure every reader has had a crap boss at some point in their life, and when you're part of a team below that crap boss, it can actually be therapeutic to take out your frustrations complaining about the crap boss instead of complaining about each other. It's a lot healthier that way.

Moving on, previous to the A's most successful period was their worst – in the words of Florence and the Machine: "It's always darkest before the dawn."[385] The club labored its way to 15 straight losing seasons, including five 100-loss seasons. For the majority of this era, the ball club was in Kansas City, and it should come as no surprise that they left considering the team's failure. Even prior to the 15 straight losing seasons, the club was struggling, posting sub-.500 records in 15 of the previous 19 seasons dating back to 1934. In fact, in 1943, the A's squad managed to lose 18 double-headers in one season – a record that easily could have appeared among the list of most unbreakable records in the last chapter. Maybe even sadder is the fact that, even without those 36 double-header losses, they would have still ended up in last place in the AL. By the way, Connie Mack was the manager for 17 of these seasons. Although Mack was one of the greatest (and longest-employed) managers of all time, he has a bit of a reputation of being the Jeff Loria of his era. But we'll get to that in a bit.

Before all this A's failure, however, from 1925-1933, the A's enjoyed one of their strongest stretches, boasting one of my personal favorite teams of all time. They reached three straight World Series (1929-1931) and won over 100 games each of those pennant-winning years – the first team to ever do so. They boasted some of the best players of all time, as well as one of the best managers of all time (Mack). Mack's roster was built on the strength of one of the strongest minor league teams of all time and scouted by arguably the best eye for talent that baseball has ever seen – Jack Dunn (Team Introduction, St. Louis Cardinals – Page 319). Back to Mack (birth name: Cornelius McGillicuddy): he was very unconventional and sold off multiple big-name players to reload several times in his managerial career. Mack was unconventional on the field, as well. During the 1929 World Series, in a very Joe Maddon-esque move, Mack had on his roster all-time legend Lefty Grove, as well as 20-game winner George Earnshaw. Naturally, for Game 1 of the series he went with Howard Ehmke who was 35 and hadn't pitched in weeks. Ehmke proved Mack's risk-taking prescient and responded with a 3-1 win, setting a new World

---

[382] It's the Yankees, who have achieved the feat on six separate occasions: 1936-1938, 1937-1939, 1949-1951, 1950-1952, 1951-1953, and 1998-2000. There's significant reason people hate them so much.

[383] It's worth noting that Cuban has a far better rapport with his coaches and staff than Finley ever had.

[384] Shout out to the useful *History of American League Baseball Since 1901* by Glenn Dickey.

[385] Or in this reverse chronological timeline – after the dawn.

Series record with 13 strikeouts along the way. In fact, Mack didn't start Grove or 18-game winner Rube Walberg all series because both were lefties, and the Cubs had eight right-handed regulars. Doesn't that sound like a Maddon thing to do? Of course, it worked, and Mack is deservedly considered one of the all-time great managers.

Prior to this bout of success, however, the A's had had another poor stretch. From 1915-1924, they finished under .500 each year, and had at least 100 losses in five of those seasons, including a heinous 228 combined losses in 1915-1916. They finished in last seven straight years, and the 1915 squad, in particular, set records for all sorts of ineptitude. The team plummeted in the standings in 1915, losing 109 games the year after they had won 99. The team finished 58 ½ games out of first and 40 games behind the next-worst team. They were so bad only one other team finished below .500 that season, and that was the Senators who were only one game below .500. The A's absorbed losses for the league like a 25-man sponge. The offense dropped by 200 runs, and the pitching gave up over 350 more runs. This isn't too surprising given that, in quick succession, the A's said goodbye to five future Hall of Famers: Eddie Collins, Home Run Baker, Chief Bender, Eddie Plank, and Herb Pennock. They left after the 1914 season because of an increase in salaries due to the renegade Federal League that was making its push to be the third professional baseball league in America, along with the AL and NL.

Finally, we get to the end of this franchise history – their origins. The A's came into existence along with the American League in 1901. Fittingly, the club's first manager was Connie Mack, meaning that the franchise had just one manager for its first 50 years of existence. The franchise found success right away, finishing over .500 each of their first seven seasons, with pennants in 1905 and 1902 (before there was a World Series). The team famously got the logo that is still in use today (the elephant), when Giants manager John McGraw said of A's owner Benjamin Shibe (for whom the stadium was named), that he had "a white elephant on his hands." Although the barb was made with contempt about the price of Shibe's team, Mack took the symbol and ran with it, and the elephant became the primary logo for the franchise. The A's finally broke through with their first World Series win in 1910, and they went on to win three of four World Series titles from 1910-1913, to go along with their 1914 and 1905 pennants. The team's success was due in large part to Mack's, "$100,000 infield," consisting of Eddie Collins, Jack Barry, Home Run Baker, and Stuffy McInnis. The 1914 edition of the infield ranks as the best single-season infield of all time, per Bill James' win shares, with the 1912 edition ranking third, and 1913 edition tied for fifth. It's no surprise then that the team experienced such great success in their earliest days as a franchise.

Back to the Future: Since the A's have always been at the forefront of baseball analytics (a tradition passed on from Connie Mack to Charlie Finley to Billy Beane), it's only fair to assume they will continue to do so in the future.

Where exactly the future of sabermetrics is headed is hard to say exactly, but there certainly seem to be some areas primed for analytical experimentation. For one, team chemistry is a field ripe for the picking. Two professors, Katerina Bezrukova, an assistant professor of group dynamics at Santa Clara University, and Rutgers associate professor Chester Spell, worked on a math solution designed to solve this very issue. The two determined that teams with overlaps in demographics (age, race, country, and salary) led to better chemistry and could help a team by as much as three wins a season (nearly $25 million on the MLB market by modern WAR/$ valuations). These links are found on teams with strong chemistry and are the reason some of those "glue guys," who put up poor statistics but still hang around a successful baseball clubhouse, make sense. Some teams are looking for ways to break down the links separating these players from different backgrounds, and the most progressive teams are experimenting with ways of doing so. Billy Beane, for what it's worth, said of chemistry, "I'm convinced that chemistry and all that are byproducts of winning." So, the debate is far from one-sided. Bill James once said, "Maybe somebody will try to figure out a way to classify personalities and quantify the impact of those, [but] I doubt that's going to happen in my career." Team chemistry is definitely one of baseball's final frontiers, and it really wouldn't surprise me if there were data for seemingly subjective characteristics of players currently being used in MLB front offices. It's not the type of thing that could go public, however, because some feelings could definitely get hurt. That said, chemistry and team composition is too huge a factor in team success for MLB front offices to be ignoring it.

The "soft" side of sabermetrics includes not just getting the team to sing from the same hymn sheet, so to speak, but also figuring out the human elements of running a baseball team. For as great as the statistical side of baseball analytics is, it often ignores the human element which separates actual Major League Baseball team from Strat-O-Matic or any other baseball simulator. As Ben Lindbergh and others pointed out after the 2014 Saber Seminar in Boston, front offices are becoming increasingly aware that the market is so flooded with "hard" analytic folks that it almost seems that no real edge can be found any more. The softer side of baseball analytics may just be the next frontier, and the baseball minds who crack those codes may become the Bill James' and Pete Palmer's of the next wave of baseball analysis.

Random cool things about the franchise:

- Their relocation from East Coast to Midwest to West Coast mirrors that of plucky mouse hero, Fievel and his journey westward in *Fievel Goes West. I suppose* it also mirrors the nation's expansion westward, as a whole.
- When they faced the Yankees in the '72 World Series, the matchup was pitted as "Hairs vs. Squares." Of course, the A's were the Hairs.
- Thanks to Finley, the A's are the only team to wear white cleats both at home and on the road.
- "Angels in the Outfield" was actually shot at the Oakland Coliseum despite centering around their division foes.
- Billy Beane's sh-t doesn't work in the playoffs.
- Instead of racing presidents at their home games, the A's race people in big blow-up suits of famous ex-Athletics.

Starting IX

C Mickey Cochrane (1925-1933)

Cochrane came up with the A's in 1925 and spent nearly a decade with the team during the exact stretch they enjoyed their greatest success. This was no coincidence, as Cochrane was a leader in the clubhouse and one of the best catchers of all time. He became the first catcher to receive 100 or more games in 10 straight seasons, and he played every single one of his games behind the plate for his first seven years. In fact, he played only one game anywhere but catcher in his entire career. Cochrane was an excellent offensive catcher, hitting over .320 six times in his time with the A's (career-high .357 in 1930). He also developed his batting eye and power stroke throughout his time in Philadelphia.

Cochrane was also a highly-regarded defensive catcher, less on the side of measurable metrics, and more on the side of how he handled the pitching staff. Noted pitching curmudgeon Lefty Grove said of Cochrane, "Before I'd even look at him, I had in my mind what I was going to pitch and I'd look up and there'd be Mickey's signal, just what I was thinking. Like he was reading my mind. That's the kind of catcher he was… he'd tell you I only shook him off about five or six times all the years he caught me." To handle Grove would have been no easy task, but to master a pitcher's plan of attack is something that the great catchers can do. It's like women's intuition, but for catchers. Cochrane, himself, had the perfect way of summing it up: "Pitchers are funny persons and must be cajoled, badgered, and conned along like babies, big bad wolves, or little sisters with injured feelings." We'll ignore the heavy gender-overtones of that sentiment, since it was a century ago.

One way we can objectively praise Cochrane is that he was able to win five AL pennants during Babe Ruth's and Lou Gehrig's prime Yankee years. Cochrane did it with two different ball clubs as well; Detroit made the leap to league champions in his first (and only) two full seasons there.

Cochrane's career ended before it had to. When in Detroit, he was hit in the head with a pitch that knocked him out and left him in a borderline coma for over a week. The injury was so bad that he could not return to baseball, despite being only 34. One more foul tip or miscommunicated pitch could have cost him his life. Head injuries are still an issue that haunts backstops in the modern game, and they have robbed the position of numerous partial or near-complete careers.

1B Jimmie Foxx (1925-1935)

Foxx came up with the Philadelphia A's as a precocious 17-year-old. He struggled to get regular time, however, since he entered the league as a catcher, and there was already a somewhat decent guy behind the plate in Philadelphia (the man about whom we just talked). Foxx spent his first four years as a backup to Cochrane, as well as a utility player, but he really burst on the scene in 1929. Finally handed the starting spot at first base, Foxx finished with 123 runs, 33 home runs, and 118 RBI, and .354/.463/.625 triple slashes, the on-base percentage leading the league. We will go more into Foxx's alleged strength in about 15 pages, but let's start with what Ted Lyons had to say about Foxx: "[Foxx] had great powerful arms, and he used to wear his sleeves cut off way up, and when he dug in and raised the bat, his muscles would bulge and ripple." Lyons was far from alone in this assessment of Foxx. The always-entertaining Lefty Gomez famously said of Foxx, "I had been having trouble with my eyes. One day my glasses fogged up while I was pitching but when I cleaned them and looked at the plate and saw Foxx clearly, it frightened me so much that I never wore them again."

Foxx hit at least 30 home runs the next 11 straight seasons (seven total coming with the A's) and was a constant RBI machine, topping 150 RBI three times in a four-year stretch (1930-1933) that included two MVPs, 173 home runs, 498 runs, 608 RBI, and two seasons with an OPS+ over 200. His 1932 campaign is one of the most impressive lines of all time (even with the high-scoring era accounted for): 151 runs, 58 home runs, and 169 RBI with .364/.469/.749 slashes.

This year is also remarkable because, as is frequently talked about in baseball books, Foxx's 58 home runs in 1932 could well have been higher. In fact, he really had a good shot to break the all-time record considering the following: two of Foxx's home runs were lost to rainouts; at least five were lost to a change in his home stadium that made the right field fence harder to hit over; Cleveland's stadium made their fences harder to clear costing him three more; and finally, an injury hindered his swing towards the end of the season. Now, some of this same logic can be applied to other player's seasons, and we could probably find evidence to boost a few of Babe Ruth's or Mickey Mantle's seasons, but someone who suffered all of those hindrances in the same season they reached the 58 home runs would be hard to find. Usually a player needs everything to go right to post a near-record breaking season.

The hefty righty followed up his legendary 1932 seasons with no slouch of a year in 1933. Foxx once again led the league in home runs (48) and RBI (163), this time adding a league-leading .356 batting average to win the Triple Crown. "This is no ordinary honey"[386] though, as Foxx won it the same year that Chuck Klein won the Triple Crown in the NL for the Philadelphia Phillies. It is the only time in baseball history that one city boasted two Triple Crowns in the same year.

Foxx was prone to big single-game outbursts, reaching nine RBI and 16 total bases in multiple games, as well as

---

386 I hate explaining references, but that *Futurama* reference is "pretty fucking obscure man." (Hey, reference within a reference and we're approaching the end of the *Kiss Kiss Bang Bang* doozies. That's some *Inception*-esque pop culture referencing right there.) [*KKBB* no. 7]

separate games in which he had six hits. He also hit for the cycle in 1933 and set the record for walks in a game with six. Before the bloated home run totals from Steroid Era, only Ruth had more home runs over their five best home run seasons than Foxx.

Foxx wasn't a perfect man, however, as he would often go to the plate with a flask in his back pocket. It must be noted, though, that he was a good enough stepfather that his stepdaughter went out of her way to write into *The National Pastime* and laud the man long after he passed. This is obviously a biased source, but the stories she tells of Foxx greeting her boyfriends in his boxers and never getting around to eating at restaurants because he was so busy accommodating his fans, paint a humble picture of this baseball legend.

One final strange, albeit impressive, note to Foxx's last days in baseball: as a 37-year-old, Foxx returned for one last season in Philadelphia in 1945, this time signing on as a free agent with the cross-town Phillies. This wouldn't be extraordinary – many late career players make brief pit stops at the end of their careers – but something stands out when looking at Foxx's age-37 season. A lifelong hitter, Foxx threw 22.2 inning for the WWII-depleted Phillies (a sinus condition kept him from being eligible to serve), and he did exceptionally well. In those 22.2 innings, Foxx gave up just four runs (all earned), good for a 1.59 ERA! He started two games and came out of the bullpen for another seven, and although he walked more batters than he struck out, this feat is pretty darn impressive. While this was previously mentioned briefly (Starting Pitcher, Tigers – Page 305), the innings Foxx threw came as part of his "doing anything to help the team" mentality and are one of the cooler footnotes in the history of baseball, so it seemed necessary to mention them again.

2B Eddie Collins (1906-1914; 1927-1930)

Fun fact: Eddie Collins is the only baseball player to play in three different centuries… Ok, that's not true, but let's just put it this way, when the world ends in a Donald Trump-Rocket Man nuclear war, the only things left remaining will be cockroaches, Twinkies, and Eddie Collins as the double play pivot man. Collins got his start with the A's in 1906, playing there nine years before moving over to the White Sox for a decade-plus. Then he came back to the A's at the end of his career, but he never played more than 100 games in any of those final four years with the franchise.

Collins hit a cool .333 for his career and made the Hall of Fame with ease after his retirement. Collins owns the 13th highest all-time WAR total (123.9), thanks to his long career, his positional scarcity, and the fact that he played at an All-Star level year-in and year-out for his teams. After his rookie year, his season batting average dropped below .300 only twice, even hitting .336 as a 40-year-old in 1927. His OPS+ was never below 100, save for his six-game 1906 campaign and his nine-game 1929 season. He is the only player in baseball history to steal six bases in a game twice in his career. His 741 steals rank eighth all-time, and his name is scattered throughout the baseball record books in nearly every significant cumulative statistic. This includes the fact that he is first all-time in sacrifice hits.

He was also a member of two of baseball's most famous teams, although both for different levels of dubious notoriety. First, he was a part of baseball's first *big splurge* as a part of the A's "$100,000 infield." Later, he was one of the innocent members of the infamous "Black Sox" team in Chicago. In terms of total seasons, Collins split his time nearly 50/50 between the two franchises (13 years in Philadelphia versus 12 in Chicago), however, in terms of total games, he played far more with Chicago, playing over 500 more games with Chicago, despite one less season there.

In Bill James' *Abstract*, he has Collins rated higher than Rogers Hornsby in one of the few times I don't see eye-to-eye with James. Now, admitting that I don't know as much baseball as Bill James' left pinkie does, let's do a little breakdown to complement the one James does in his book. This has many of the same categories as the typical longer breakdowns in this book, but without as many statistics or in-depth analysis.

Contact: SLIGHT EDGE Hornsby.

It's hard to go against either of these men in terms of ability to hit a baseball. Collins hit 60 points above the league average during his career, while Hornsby hit 76 points above the league average. That difference is just enough to give him the slight edge.

Power: EDGE Hornsby

Collins didn't rely heavily on extra-base hits; Hornsby is arguably the best power-hitting second baseman of all time, an impressive feat given some of the bloated PED-era numbers.

Batting eye: SLIGHT EDGE Collins

Hornsby led the league in walks three times compared to the one time Collins paced the league with walks, but Hornsby's walks were often the result of pitchers fearing him rather than a phenomenal eye like Collins had.

Speed: EDGE Collins

Collins' baserunning prowess was based on more than straight speed, but the fact that he finished his career with over 700 steals gives him the edge here. It's worth noting that both players have very poor stolen base percentages for the years that that statistic was kept, but that was typical across the league at this time.

Defense: SLIGHT EDGE Collins

Both men had similar career arcs in the field. Both men started their careers as very strong fielders before seeing a drop to league average for the majority of their respective careers. Hornsby was able to turn more double plays on average, while Collins made fewer mistakes. The tiebreaker comes down to Collins having slightly more range and being a second baseman in the truest sense. He spent 2,650 of his 2,701 career games at second base. Hornsby, on the other hand, spent 1,561 of his 2,164 games with a "4" next to his name in the scorebook.

Dominance: EDGE Hornsby

This is a more subjective category, but one only has to see the amount of bold scattered around Rogers Hornsby's player page at Baseball-Reference to know what an incredibly dominant hitter he was. Collins was incredibly durable, and he lasted forever, which is a talent of its own, but Hornsby was in a class of his own when he played the game.

Verdict: **Hornsby** by a hair

I have to disagree with James on this one, as Hornsby's dominance is the difference in the end. If I had to choose between their two careers, I would rather the one with the higher peak, even if Collins' durability was incredibly impressive.

3B Home Run Baker (1908-1914)

The appropriately named "Home Run" Baker was indeed one of baseball's first power hitters after the turn of the century. He led the league in home runs four straight years (1911-1914), but due to the era in which he played, the total of those four years was only 42. However, this is not where his nickname originally came from. The origin story has long been that his nickname came from the 1911 World Series. In the series, the A's faced a Giants team that sported two of the game's best pitchers (Rube Marquard and Christy Mathewson). In Game 2, Baker hit a home run off Marquard (no small feat), but Game 3 really stood out, as he hit the first-ever World Series home run off Mathewson, and the papers supposedly first gave him the name that would stick around long enough to become his official name listed in the baseball record books. However, according to SABR member Steven A. King, the nickname was actually bequeathed upon (Frank) Baker before he had even played a full season with the A's. It came from his play before the 1909 season, when he won several games in spring training with home runs. Man, SABR members just love bursting the bubbles of historical anecdotes, don't they?

Baker was more than a bat, though, as he stole 235 bases and netted his teams over 9.0 wins with his glove and positional value for his career. I am a little hesitant with fielding statistics from as long ago as Baker's era, but he does rate positively in the metrics we have available today. Baker did this despite retiring from baseball, and then returning, two separate times in his career. The first time was in 1915, when a salary dispute with Connie Mack (having to do with the Federal League, as discussed in the introductory section for this Starting IX) led to him sitting out all of 1915. After returning in 1916, he was not quite the same player, and the second year he missed (1920) was not as devastating to his career statistics. It was, however, devastating to Baker, as he sat out the season due to the loss of his wife. Bill James is on record as having said if Baker didn't miss those two seasons, he could very well be the top-rated third baseman in his positional rankings. As is, he sits fifth in James' *Abstract*. (Remember, it came out in 2001.) Personally, I have him somewhere around 12th, with his ceiling around eighth even if those hypothetical seasons happened.

Baker went on to have this successful career despite an auspicious start. He tried out for the eagle-eyed Jack Dunn but was cut from his team. Baker was one of the only mistakes Dunn ever made, as Baker went on to be one of the best hitters in baseball and a fielder who was said to have the best range of any third baseman of his day.[387]

SS Bert Campaneris (1964-1976)

Campaneris is one of the ultimate "onion players." An "onion player" is a player whose achievements need to be looked at in layers. For example, on the surface level: Campaneris is a great player. In his 13 years with the A's, he made the All-Star team five times and led the league in steals six times.

However, upon further inspection: Campaneris never hit .300 during a season; he led the league in caught stealing twice with the A's; he drew walks rarely enough that he never topped a .350 on-base percentage in a single season; he never had more than 177 hits in a season; he never scored more than 97 runs in a season; he never had more than *64* RBI in a season; he had only one season with more than eight home runs;[388] and topped an OPS+ of 100 in only four of his 13 seasons with the A's, sporting a 93 OPS+ for his whole time with the franchise.

However, upon further *further* inspection: Campaneris does well. He played in one of the toughest eras of baseball in which to hit and was a very solid fielder at an important position (his 177 hits in 1968 led the AL). He also grounded into very few double plays and often got hit by pitches (cut to Bill James diddling himself). Because of all this, his WAR totals are very strong, sporting 48.9 WAR in his 13 A's seasons, topping 4.0 six times and averaging over 3.5 WAR a year.

These onion-type players are very common during eras of either abnormally-high or abnormally-low run production, or when other extenuating circumstances play a role in the game of baseball. In Campaneris' case, he beat out a man who could have been a potential onion-type player but avoided the label with good enough all-around numbers.

Miguel Tejada played during the height of the Steroid Era, when runs were certainly not at a premium. He also played in a league that had Nomar Garciaparra, Derek Jeter, and Alex Rodriguez all at the same position as him. Regardless,

---

[387] One final note that seemed the right amount of lewd to be a footnote: one anonymous teammate of both Babe Ruth and Baker (who played for the Yankees after his A's days) said that although Ruth had the far more active "purple-headed yogurt slinger," Baker had by far the biggest, *cough*, member, *cough*, he had ever seen. Maybe the "Home Run" nickname was actually coined by a few of the ladies from cities that Baker frequented.

[388] How conspicuous would Campaneris' 22 home runs in 1970 have looked if he had played during the Steroid Era?

he won an MVP, topped 100 RBI four times, posted a positive dWAR every year after his rookie season. He was on about the same pace as Campaneris in terms of total WAR with the A's, but he played only seven years with the franchise. If he had played as many years with the A's as Campaneris had, it would have been a prime breakdown, but Tejada left for the Orioles in 2004.

Campaneris is one of the great random-fact players of his generation, and as such, has a few good anecdotes to go with his write-up. In his very first game, he made history by becoming one of five players to hit two home runs in his debut game. Later, in 1965, as part of a promotion, he played all nine positions in one game. While pitching, he threw left-handed to left-handed batters and right-handed to right-handed batters. Finally, always a bit of a fiery guy, in the 1971 American League Championship Series (a series the A's would go on to lose), "Campy" was hit by a pitch and responded by throwing his bat at the pitcher.

LF Al Simmons (1924-1932; 1940-1941; 1944)

Born Aloys Szymanski, Simmons was one of the most consistent and underrated super-stars of the 1920s and `30s. From 1924-1934, Simmons posted 11 straight seasons with .300 batting average and 100 RBI, including a three-year peak (the A's pennant-winning 1929-1931 stretch) in which he *averaged* 124 runs, 31 home runs, and 150 RBI with .378/.421/.664 triple slashes. There are a few factors that led to Simmons being a bit of a forgotten man in baseball lore.

First, he played in an era stacked with some of baseball's most famous men. At first, this would seem to benefit Simmons, but rather than be highlighted for playing in such a fun era, the others instead seem to overshadow him. Speaking of being overshadowed, Simmons was barely noticeable on his own team. The A's had so many stars at the time Simmons was playing, that he was often left in the shadows. Another factor was that, although thoroughly consistent, Simmons was never truly dominant. He did win two batting titles, but he never won an MVP,[389] nor did he ever lead the league in home runs, and it's not as if his baseball card was covered in bold. He never set any crazy records, and he wasn't as loquacious as Dizzy Dean or other notable stars of the era.

On closer inspection, however, it's even more befuddling that Simmons isn't more recognized today. Simmons played a huge role in each of the three World Series that the A's reached, blasting two home runs and hitting over .300 in each series. He even played a role in one of the most famous World Series games. In 1929, the A's trailed the Cubs 8-0 in the seventh inning, before Simmons led off with a home run. When he came to the plate again later in the seventh, the score was now 8-7, and Simmons extended the inning with a single. From the time of his first at bat of the inning to his second, the A's win probability had gone from one percent to 65 percent, and it ended the inning at 85 percent.

Simmons' 253 hits in 1925 are the most for a right-handed batter ever, and he did it in only 153 games in 1925. He got 2,000 hits in his first 1,393 career games, making him the fastest ever to that milestone. He drew the praise of his fellow colleagues, as Joe Cronin said of him, "There never was a greater left fielder in going to the line and holding a double to a single."[390] He was once called "a swashbuckling pirate of a man." His manager, no less of a baseball God than Connie Mack, said, "If I only could have coached nine players named Al Simmons." He was even purportedly clutch, as Washington Senators owner Clark Griffith said of him, "He hit 14 homers in the eighth and ninth innings and every one figured in the ballgame," in regards to Simmons' 1930 campaign.

To top it all off, he had a sweet nickname (Bucketfoot Al), the origins of which were a cool batting stance!

We'll end, as we have in the past, with a quote from Bill James. This one's a little different, however. It's not really in context, but considering I have cherry-picked a few stats in the past, I might as well cherry-pick a quote this time. So, here's a quote from Bill James *Abstract* that is quite interesting: "You could go into the [1930s] A's locker room after a game, and there'd be a dozen men running around naked except for their hats."

Seriously, how is this guy not one of the all-timers? Go out and start your local Al Simmons campaigns, everybody!

CF Rickey Henderson (1979-1984; 1989-1993; 1994-1995; 1998)

"The Man of Steal" was one of the most interesting players of his generation. A self-proclaimed showboat and hotdog, he spoke in the third person and lived for the limelight. Henderson seemed to fit more into the mold of the Michael Irvin/Deion Sanders prototype that was more common in the NFL than in the MLB in the early `90s. Because of this, Henderson was not always portrayed in a popular light by the media. He was, however, very popular with the fans, who tend to have a love-hate relationship with this type of player. Given that Henderson averaged over 5.0 WAR a year for his entire 14 years in Oakland (his 72.5 WAR are tops in A's history), it's not surprising that his relationship with Oakland was far more love than hate.

One of the most infamous stunts Henderson pulled was sliding into home plate on the home run that tied him with Ty Cobb for the all-time runs record. If you're wondering what's wrong with that, I agree. Henderson was obviously ecstatic

---

[389] Although his 122 runs, 24 home runs, and 129 RBI with .387/.419/.599 triple slashes and 6.6 WAR should have been enough to conquer Roger Peckinpaugh's 67 runs, four home runs, and 64 RBI with .294/.367/.379 triple slashes and a 2.5 WAR in 1925 – pretty egregious. Simmons just wasn't established enough, as it was just his second season in the league.

[390] This quote is why I decided to put the player you're about to read about in center field, even though he played mostly in left for the A's.

to be in the same sentence as one of baseball's all-time greats, and to be able to stake his claim to one of baseball's most impressive records. Another Henderson "stunt" is the story of how he received a $1 million bonus check from the A's and hung it on his wall without even depositing it. Hey, we bash players all the time for not managing their money and then later seeing them bankrupt on the news. If Henderson had the financial wherewithal to not need a check for a million dollars – more power to him.

There are a couple of statistical strikes against Henderson, however, that I find it harder to argue with. He is the only member of the 3,000-hit club to have more games played than hits, as he was not the most efficient player of all time. Instead, he relied on an accumulation of statistics to join the highest ranks of baseball history. Also, the year Henderson broke the all-time steals record (130), he was caught stealing 42 times. This meant all his baserunning equated to 4.5 runs (or less than half a win) according to Bill James.[391] James said of Henderson's running, "Four and a half goddamn runs, and they want to give him an MVP award for it."

However, those are only two strikes, and we all know you get three in baseball. Henderson was able to make up for both of these shortcomings, as well. Although he was not the most efficient with his hits, he has more walks than anyone in baseball history not named Barry Bonds. Because of this, Henderson has an on-base percentage over .400, good for 53rd all-time.[392] Henderson was such an on-base percentage machine that his OBP in his 40s (five seasons and 469 games at .381) was higher than Hank Aaron's career OBP (.374).

However, it wasn't just Henderson ability to get on base that jump-started his teams. Henderson finished his career with 81 leadoff home runs, by far the most in MLB history, 27 more than Alfonso Soriano in second, and more than the entire Diamondbacks, Marlins, and Rockies organizations each have in their respective histories.

When looking at his work on the basepaths, although Henderson did get caught 42 times in 1982, outside of that season, he was actually incredibly efficient on the basepaths, especially considering his volume of steals. For his career, Henderson was caught less than 20 percent of the time, well above the threshold that sabermetricians have set for a base stealer to have value. It should also be noted that of his 1,406 career steals (by far the MLB record), only 87 came when his team was either up by four runs or trailing by four runs.[393] Now, just how valuable all those steals were is a topic still being fought about, but regardless, Henderson deserves recognition for his remarkable prowess on the basepaths, as well as his undeniable place among the greatest characters the sport has ever seen.

RF Reggie Jackson (1967-1975; 1987)

One of baseball's most recognizable stars, Jackson played for the A's from their last year in Kansas City (1967) until 1975. He returned for a victory-lap season in 1987, but he is mostly remembered East of the Bay Bridge for his production during the franchise's run in the 1970s.

The A's almost didn't have the chance to enjoy the emotional roller coaster that was Jackson's career, as the Mets had the first pick in 1966, and according to Reggie's baseball coach at ASU, they would have taken Jackson except for the fact that he was black and had a white girlfriend. Instead they took Steve Chilcott, who totaled 39 career home runs… in the minor leagues. Chilcott never even made it to the majors, while Jackson went on to be one of the top players in history. Jackson's A's beat the Mets in the 1973 World Series, and wherever he went his teams continually had more success than the Mets. Who says karma doesn't exist?

Reggie was a man who was never afraid of a little attention. Baseball writer Bob Marshall once said of him, "Just as nature fills a vacuum, Reggie fills a spotlight." This was perhaps even more true once Jackson left for the big lights of New York, but it was true even in his A's days. In the words of, well, himself, "After Jackie Robinson, the most important black [man] in baseball history is Reggie Jackson." He was also once quoted as saying, "The only reason I don't like playing in the World Series is I can't watch myself play."

Well, he missed out on seeing himself play fairly regularly then. While with the A's, Jackson made the playoffs five straight seasons (1971-1975). He missed out on the 1972 World Series win due to a hamstring injury but was able to play in the 1973 and 1974 World Series victories. Jackson's postseason prowess became even more noteworthy when he moved to New York and was given the nickname, "Mr. October." The nickname was originally given to him sarcastically by teammate Thurman Munson after Jackson posted a 2-for-16 performance in his first playoff series with the team. However, Jackson would go on to prove Munson prophetic by slamming five home runs in the next series, a 1977 championship for the Yankees. This series included Jackson's famous three home runs on three pitches in Game 6, which won the Yankees the series. The fact that his nickname was originally given ironically, but went on to be legacy-defining, goes to show how quickly narratives can change in sports.

Although Jackson was often thought of as a bit of a distraction, and not the best locker room guy, Eddie Epstein and Rob Neyer challenge this notion in *Baseball's Dynasties*. They point out that if Jackson was such a toxic clubhouse guy, then how can one explain the following phenomenon: for 15 years, with four different clubs, Jackson's teams won more than half

[391] Baseball-Reference WAR had those steals worth 1.1 wins, not an insignificant difference.
[392] Strike two and a half would probably be that Henderson regularly finished seasons with a higher on-base percentage than slugging percentage.
[393] This statistic, along with the leadoff home run stat, and the OBP in comparison to Aaron, all came from the outstanding Ace of MLB Stats (@Aceballstats) on Twitter, a great follow for any baseball fan.

their games, and Mr. October captured five championships. Jackson is often lauded for his personal success in the playoffs, but it's impossible to ignore the fact that he would have never been put into the position to have that October success if his antics had derailed the team's regular season success.

One way of looking at how he affected team chemistry comes from *Baseball and Philosophy*, one in a series of interesting "(Blank) and Philosophy" books that frames baseball in a unique light. In favor of Jackson, and players of his ilk, Eric Bronson argues that although Willie Stargell's admirable "Pops" routine was great for the team chemistry of the 1979 Pirates,[394] Jackson was just as effective with Yankees. As Bronson points out, dissension was something our country's forefathers argued was essential to democracy. When everyone thinks alike, no one really thinks. Jackson was able to stir up the clubhouse wherever he went, and it's unsurprising that his teams always had success.

Outside of his grand persona, Jackson was known for his go-big or go-home style of play. During his career, he led the league in home runs four times and strikeouts five times. He is the all-time leader in strikeouts, and although the game as a whole is striking out more than ever, go and look at the all-time strikeouts leaderboard – there's not really anyone with a chance to challenge Jackson's record in the foreseeable future. Maybe Miguel Cabrera can eventually come close, but even that seems unlikely. Jackson was one of the first Three True Outcome hitters (walk, strikeout, home run), an effective strategy, and one that is becoming more and more common in the modern game. In fact, with his strong batting eye, Jackson is one of just five players all-time to be in the top-35 all-time in all three categories: walks, strikeouts, and home runs. The other four: Harmon Killebrew, Mike Schmidt, Mickey Mantle, and Jim Thome. Thome amazingly is in the top eight (!) in all Three True Outcomes.

One final note: in 1983, Jackson was voted to the All-Star Game despite hitting .214 with only 12 home runs at the break – that's a force.[395] Now I used Jackson as the example here, but this seems to happen every year. And if it isn't a washed-up veteran who doesn't deserve to be there, then it's a player from a big market who clearly just rode a big fan base to a place in the All-Star Game. Now, due to the nature of All-Star Game voting, there will always be controversy, and that can be some of the fun sometimes. However, when it becomes a joke like Jackson in 1983, it has probably gone a bit too far. The same thing can be seen in the NBA and other leagues that rely on fan voting for the All-Star Game. For instance, Yao Ming was voted the starting center his rookie year over Shaquille O'Neal, at a time when Shaq was the most dominant big man in the league. Later in his career, Yao was once again voted the starting center despite having played five games all year.

I have seen arguments that say because the All-Star Game – and the weekend that surrounds it – is more for kids and fans who will only watch a few games a season, the most famous and entertaining players should be there. I see the logic behind this reasoning, it's a fair question to ask whether the average fan really wants to see Fernando Rodney pitching to Bryan LaHair during All-Star weekend,[396] but at the same time, passing over deserving players for bigger names just doesn't seem right either.

One idea that could work would be adding a Rookies and Sophomores game to the MLB All-Star weekend like the NBA has. This could be a little different in that it would pit first-time and second-time All-Stars against each other, allowing for some of those one-year, fluke players[397] to have some time in the spotlight, as well. As far as the young guys who are going to go on to play in many All-Star Games (i.e. Mike Trout, Manny Machado, etc.) they would get to appear in the real deal in their third seasons. It would make for an interesting game because the fluke players and young stars are often the ones who take the All-Star Game seriously, and therefore the quality of play would be much higher.

The postscript to this story: Jackson made the All-Star Game again in 1984, hitting .247 with 14 home runs at the break, and it's one reason we have to be careful when counting All-Star Games as a measure of a player's worth.

Utility Sal Bando (1966-1976)

Bando began his career while the franchise played in Kansas City, but he soon moved with the franchise to Oakland. Despite playing in a hitting-depressed era, in a hitting-depressed stadium, at a hitting-depressed position, Bando put up some excellent numbers. In his 11 years with the club, Bando posted an OPS+ of 127 and netted the team over 50 wins (52.0 WAR, to be exact).

Bando often butted heads with eccentric A's owner Charlie Finley, even holding his grudge to this day. In a 2007 *Sports Illustrated* article, Bando "thanked" Finley for showing him how not to run a business, while admitting that Finley did show him that it pays to have talented people work for you. We know Finley was a tough owner to deal with, so it's hard to really blame Bando for that comment, especially when the rest of the baseball literature surrounding Bando is positive. He was Paul Molitor's mentor, and he had a good sense of humor about the Finley-run A's, as well. When asked if it was hard to leave the A's, he responded, "Was it hard leaving the Titanic?"

---

[394] As one teammate put it after receiving one of Stargell's trademark Gold Stars: "I'd been around forever, but it gave me goose bumps."
[395] Even worse, he hit .174 with just two homers after the All-Star break in 1983.
[396] This actually happened in 2012, which is slightly terrifying.
[397] And really it's one fluke half-year because the All-Star Game takes place in July.

SP Lefty Grove (1925-1933)

Robert Moses Grove came from a humble start[398] and made his A's debut on the same day as his battery mate of nine years – as well as this Starting IX – Mickey Cochrane. The two would go on to become one of, if not *the*, most successful batteries of all time. Cochrane was the stoic leader from behind the plate; Grove was the fiery competitor on the mound. He took tough losses to extremes, often pulling a Buddy Rich and flying off the handle after defeats. The story goes that when he was going for his then-record-breaking 17th straight win, he lost a game and took it particularly hard. The game was by all measures a lock to win – he was facing a much worse team, pitching against an unproven youngster and Grove was having one of the best seasons of all time. As a man who didn't take any loss well, let alone a potential record-breaker, he responded to the loss in kind. He tore his uniform, shattered bats against lockers, and broke some of the showers in the opposing locker rooms.

Stories of hyper-competitive athletes are often told in a mix of reverence and awe. Stories of Michael Jordan and Kobe Bryant, and their win-at-all-costs mentalities, are often told as if this trait is a key component of their success. For many years, the supposed lack of this trait was held against LeBron James as the reason he couldn't get over the hump. This is obviously idiotic, and since winning three titles, LeBron has proven that. Now, the hyper-competitive apologists will say that LeBron changed his mentality, and the addition of a killer instinct to his game is what brought James to the promised land. Thankfully, because baseball is much more of a team sport, this narrative is far less common. However, there is still a bit of mystique to this type of player, especially in a historical perspective.

Now a competitive spirit is certainly needed to make a good ballplayer, but when it goes to the extent described above, it simply has no positive impact. For every successful Grove or Pete Rose, there are a dozen Stan Musial, Walter Johnson, Christy Mathewson, Derek Jeter-types that play hard as hell but don't feel the need to put on a show after a loss just to show how much they care. That being said, Grove may have actually been smart about his hotheaded nature. Ted Williams said of Grove (who was a left-handed pitcher), "He was a tantrum thrower like me, but smarter. When he punched a locker, he always did it with his right hand. He was a careful tantrum thrower." Although this is an entertaining and informing quip, there is still no benefit to this behavior from a grown man. #HotSportsTakeThatIKindOfAgreeWith.

All of this being said, Grove was quite possibly the best left-handed pitcher ever, and one of the best pitchers, southpaw or not, of all time. His 103.6 WAR are the most all-time for a left-handed pitcher, despite the fact that his MLB debut was postponed until he was 25 years old.[399] While with the Baltimore Orioles minor league dynasty of the Independent League (Team Introduction, St. Louis Cardinals – Page 319), Grove totaled over 100 wins in four-plus seasons and could have easily transferred over a good chunk of those wins to his already impressive 300 wins in MLB. In fact, it would have meant that he wouldn't have had to stretch out the end of his career to make a run at 300 wins that seems to appear in more *Baseball Research Journal* pieces than any other non-Hank Aaron event in history. Grove made up for lost time by having the highest winning percentage (.680) of any of the 24 pitchers to have won 300 games. He is also one of only two pitchers (along with the Cubs Ed Reulbach) to lead the league in winning percentage three straight years, and the five times he did so in his career are most all-time. In one five-year stretch (1928-1932), Grove never finished below third in any of the pitching Triple Crown categories (wins, strikeouts, and ERA), and he won two pitching Triple Crowns straight out. Along with Rube Waddell's 1905 season, Grove's 1930 season is the only time a pitcher has won the pitching Triple Crown *and* led the league in saves.

Grove didn't just get cheap wins, however, as his nine ERA and ERA+ titles both rank best all-time. The 148 ERA+ he sports for his career trails only Mariano Rivera, Pedro Martínez (the best statistical comparison for Grove, I believe) and Jim Devlin all-time. It's obviously not a guarantee (especially since Grove posted a 98 ERA+ in his first major league season), but it's tempting to think that Grove might trail only Rivera in terms of ERA+ had a couple of Grove's minor-league Orioles seasons, in his early prime, come with the A's, instead of chasing 300 wins in Boston at the end of his career.

Grove's most impressive season was 1931, in which he posted a 2.06 ERA in a hitting-friendly era. His ERA was 2.32 runs below league average, and his 217 ERA+ was the best total for a southpaw in baseball history outside of Dutch Leonard's 1914 campaign. Grove's efforts in 1931 were rewarded with the first-ever MVP awarded by the writers. He did most of this on the strength of his fastball, and it would have been interesting to see if Pitch F/X (the current pitching-tracking technology) had existed back when Grove and Walter Johnson were pitching, whose fastball was more valuable. Westbrook Pegler of the *Chicago Daily News* said of Grove, "He could throw a lamb chop past a wolf." Grant Brisbee of *SBNation* once referred to him as "Cloud Atlas Clayton Kershaw," which is arguably the greatest four words I have ever read.

Random Stat Alert: in 1933, Grove broke the Yankees' 308-game streak of games without being shutout – I'm not sure which side of that stat is more impressive.

Grove, along with a few others on this all-franchise team, played a big part in the 1930 A's team that is my favorite team of all time. Now, this seems a bit strange seeing as I was negative 60 years old, but there's just something about this squad. In fact, this team was so awesome we're going to resort to listing their awesomeness out in bullet form:

---

[398] He was traded to Jack Dunn for a center field fence...

[399] When Grove was sold to the A's in 1924, it was for more money than Babe Ruth had been sold for just four years earlier.

* Al Simmons.
* Joining Simmons on the diamond was the most eclectic group of awesome players: Grove, Cochrane, Foxx, and even Collins for a few games, but we've already heard about them.
* Max Bishop, the team's leadoff hitter, is second all-time among qualified hitters in walk percentage, thus making him the perfect leadoff man.
* Bishop's nickname was Camera Eye due to his ability to judge the strike zone.
* Grove, George Earnshaw, and Rube Walberg, the team's three aces, all got late starts to their professional careers due to a variety of reasons. Grove's debut at the age of 25 was the youngest of the bunch.
* AL SIMMONS!
* Quite possibly the best manager of all time (Connie Mack).
* Quite possibly the coolest logo of all time (the old-school elephant).
* The team had at least one player in the top five in the league in batting average, on-base percentage, home runs, RBI, runs, slugging percentage, wins, ERA, and strikeouts.
* The lore of the 1930s baseball has got to be the best of any era.
* The team was coming off a championship, but it still had the hipster feeling of Grove not yet reaching his prime (1931). The same goes for Foxx (back-to-back MVPs in 1932-1933), and the team would always be looked at as underdogs compared to the mighty Ruth and Gehrig Yankees.
* Seriously, Aloys-effing-Szymanski!!![400]

This group is honestly approaching "I love this team so much I'm going to take it behind the Middle School and get it pregnant" Tracy Jordan-status. Now that it's clear that they are my favorite team of all time let me indulge myself in the footnotes with a Starting IX of favorite teams,[401] and we'll conclude Grove's write-up by mentioning that Bill James has him as the second-best pitcher of all time, trailing only Walter Johnson.

CP Dennis Eckersley (1987-1995)

Eckersley came to the A's in 1987 and underwent a big change in his game. The four years previous to 1987, Eckersley had hit something of a rut, posting an ERA+ of 97 and losing more games than he won. Eck began his career as a solid starting pitcher for Cleveland and later Boston, but as noted, his career had seemed to have stalled out Once Eck came to the A's, they moved him into the closer's role, and his career was completely rejuvenated. He finished 456 games in his nine seasons in Oakland, an average of over 50 a season. He led the league in saves twice, and even won a Cy Young and an MVP with his 1992 campaign.

Eck is a great example of how certain players just need a change of scenery; in this case, it was a move from starter to closer. The move allowed Eck to harness his best quality, his control, into a dominant force. Before his switch to the bullpen, Eckersley posted a 2.61 strikeout-to-walk ratio and led the league in strikeout-to-walk ratio three times. Once he became a closer, however, this skill jumped to another level. With the A's, he had a 7.15 SO/BB ratio in his nine years, topping out with an insane 18.29 SO/BB ratio from 1989-1990. During this stretch, Eckersley recorded the same number of saves (81) as walks and hits allowed *combined.*

This type of career rebuilding is not just relevant in baseball, but all walks of life. We've seen Justin Timberlake stall out a bit as a musical performer, only do a complete rebuild, changing from a pop star into a multi-faceted actor/singer/SNL hero/businessman. We've seen Ronald Reagan go from terrible actor to terrible president! Back to Eckersley now that I've successfully turned off half my readers by getting unnecessarily political: Eck is the only pitcher in baseball history to have 100 saves and 100 complete games, and he very nearly finished with 200 wins and 400 saves, missing out by three wins and 10 saves. As is, no other pitcher has reached 197 wins and 390 saves.

All that needs to be known about Eckersley's personality can be summed up perfectly by the Mike Birbiglia joke, "Roger Clemens Hates Me" off his comedy CD *My Secret Public Journal.*[402] Everyone should find the joke on their own since Birbiglia tells it far better,[403] but the gist of the joke, which is a true story – and the part that summarizes Eck perfectly – is that after Birbiglia accidentally mocked a blind man, Eck said, "Awww fuck him," about the blind dude. Just brilliant.

---

[400] I promise you I am neither a long-lost descendant of Simmons, nor is his family getting a cut of the profits for this book.

[401] SP ~~2004 Boston Red Sox~~ – jk jk jk. 1930 Philadelphia A's. C) 1996 New York Yankees – The beginning of the dynasty that I grew up loving. The "Core Four" were all just starting their illustrious careers, and they really were a lovable team led by baseball's nicest guy #nobias. 1B) 2013 Pittsburgh Pirates – Broke their playoff drought thanks to Andrew McCutchen and a lovable crew. 2B) 1948 St. Louis Cardinals – Stan the Man's best season, and only one of two seasons he overlapped with the indelible Ducky Medwick. 3B) 1927 New York Yankees – For pure entertainment reasons. SS) 1995 Seattle Mariners – Yes, they were the team to knock off the Yankees just before their 1996 season I loved so much, but if anyone could get away with that it was Junior Griffey and Edgar Martínez. LF) 2011 Boston Red Sox – Same reason as the 1927 Yankees, but a much different form of entertainment (a very schadenfreude kind). CF) 1975 Cincinnati Reds – I had to include "The Big Red Machine" on here, and although the 1976 team cruised in the playoffs, the 1975 team was their true prime. RF) 1994 Montreal Expos – Absolutely robbed.

[402] My personal favorite comedy CD of all time, by the way.

[403] For one, he doesn't give away the punch line without giving the background.

Starting IX Franchise Roster Stats

Lineup	Yrs	G	R	H	HR	RBI	SB	BB	SO	BA	OBP	SLG	OPS+	dWAR	WAR
Rickey Henderson	**14**	1704	**1270**	1768	167	648	**867**	**1227**	915	0.288	0.409	0.430	137	-0.3	**72.5**
Eddie Collins	13	1156	756	1308	16	496	373	534	263	0.337	0.423	0.437	156	5.1	57.3
Al Simmons	12	1290	969	1827	209	**1179**	65	344	413	**0.356**	0.398	0.584	147	-0.8	50.8
Jimmie Foxx	11	1256	975	1492	302	1075	48	781	644	0.339	**0.440**	**0.640**	**175**	-1.0	62.5
Reggie Jackson	10	1346	756	1228	269	776	145	633	**1226**	0.262	0.355	0.496	145	-1.5	48.0
Home Run Baker	7	899	573	1103	48	612	172	266	232	0.321	0.375	0.471	152	4.7	42.3
Mickey Cochrane	9	1167	823	1317	108	680	50	612	157	0.321	0.412	0.490	129	3.4	40.7
Sal Bando	11	1468	737	1311	192	796	60	792	702	0.255	0.359	0.418	127	6.5	52.0
Bert Campaneris	13	**1795**	983	**1882**	70	529	566	504	933	0.262	0.314	0.348	93	**17.5**	48.9
Pitchers	Yrs	W	W%	ERA	G	CG	SHO	SV	IP	SO	ERA+	WHIP	SO/9	SO/BB	WAR
Lefty Grove	9	195	**0.712**	2.88	402	179	20	50	2401.0	1523	**151**	1.250	5.7	2.06	65.2
Dennis Eckersley	9	41	0.569	2.74	**525**	0	0	**320**	637.0	658	145	**0.953**	**9.3**	**7.15**	15.9

#4 St. Louis Cardinals (1900-pres.); St. Louis Perfectos (1899); St. Louis Browns (1883-1898); St. Louis Brown Stockings (1882)

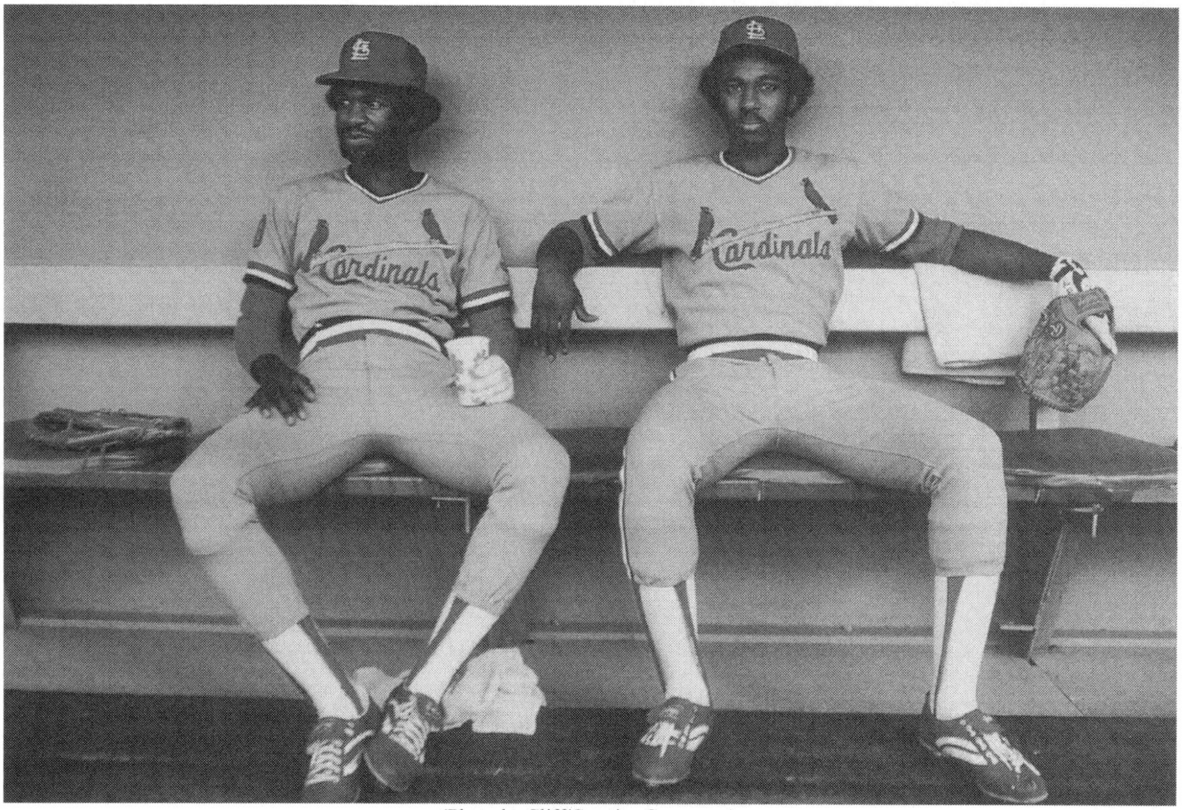

(Photo by Cliff/Creative Commons)

Team Background

Playoff appearances: 28 **Pennants: 23** **World Series titles: 11**
Collective team WAR: 724.4
Strengths: Stan. The. Effing. Man. Also, the rest of the roster is pretty elite. These rosters are starting to get pretty top-notch. Also, the team was once called THE ST. LOUIS PERFECTOS!
Weaknesses: That being said, if there are players on this Starting IX that solid baseball fans have not heard of, there are a couple teams above you.
What to expect from the next 15 pages: Pretty much what you'd expect at this point.

One of the more storied franchises in baseball history, the Cardinals are second all-time in World Series victories (11), tied for second in pennants (19), and have actually had the most players put on their jersey of any franchise in MLB history. In a way, that means making this Starting IX was the most difficult of any team in this book (Yankees players may disagree on that fact), but regardless of how it is parsed out, the Cardinals have a storied history.

Maybe the most impressive part of the Cardinals organization is that it seems like they are in contention every single year. This is not your imagination. Since 1960, the Cardinals have had consecutive losing seasons only once (1994-1995), and those seasons were both strike-shortened. No Cardinal fan born since 1902 has reached the age of 25 without having a World Series victory parade – while it's incredibly stuffy to call yourselves the Best Franchise In Baseball (BFIB), there's some definitive evidence towards the case being true.

Of course, being correct about being the BFIB only makes it more nauseating for the rest of us. So, as a punishment, the Cardinals team intro is going to be hijacked as a space for an unrelated Starting IX. The Starting IX of baseball anecdotes/tidbits/people that couldn't be woven into any other part of the book. A Best of the Rest Starting IX, if you will.

SP) Curt Flood – Like so many in baseball history, the cursory glance given to Curt Flood in this book only scratches the surface of what a curious baseball fan should know, but realize that without Flood (who refused a trade away from the Cardinals in 1969, eventually taking his case to the U.S. Supreme Court) players would have far less autonomy today, and the owners would have even more control than they still have regardless.
C) Marvin Miller – Miller is directly tied to Flood, as he was the lawyer hired as the Executive Director of the MLB Player's Association to represent Flood in his lawsuit. No less an authority than Red Barber called Miller one of the two or three most important men in baseball history.
1B) Stacy Piagno and Kelsie Whitmore – These are two female players who played the past two seasons for the Sonoma Stompers. In 2017, Piagno became the third woman since the 1950s to win an American men's professional baseball game (according to *ESPNW*). Keep trailblazing, Stacy and Kelsie. The Stompers are awesome. They were the team that had Ben Lindbergh and Sam Miller of the *Effectively Wild* podcast run the team for a year, and they had the first openly gay professional baseball player (Sean Conroy) in 2015. They even had Bill "Spaceman" Lee become the oldest pitcher to win a professional ballgame, when he did so at age 67 during the 2014 season, the club's inaugural season. The team has been around three years and has a more fascinating history than any other minor league team in existence, basically.
2B) The MLB.com error page – Seriously, go check it out. Good stuff.
3B) Jack Dunn – His name has come up a few times, and will come up a few more, but he honestly has one of the coolest histories of any of the old-timey baseball legends. The minor league Orioles dynasty he oversaw in the early 20th century has been called by some "the first real dynasty," and as noted, Dunn played a role in the discovery of Babe Ruth, Lefty Grove, and many more. He was crippled as a child, ending any possible playing career, but he channeled his love of the game into the earliest elite-level scouting the sport had seen.
SS) The Federal League – Careful readers will remember this league was the "outlaw league" that tried to join the American and National Leagues as a third major league in 1914 and 1915. I like to imagine the Federal League much like the ABA in *Semi-Pro*, but I know it was somehow even more ridiculous, just with a bit less fondue.
LF) There were more hitters with 100 strikeouts in 2012 alone than there were from 1901 to 1967 combined! And that trend has only increased in recent seasons.
CF) Eric Show, Mark Thurmond, and Dave Dravecky – These were three San Diego Padre pitchers from the 1980s whose heavy right-wing ideology (they were members of the John Birch Society) became a fascinating comparison from *The Ringer's* Bryan Curtis to the modern politicization of sports. Anyone interested in the topic should check out "Remembering Baseball's Right-wing Rotation." It's very thought-provoking for the modern age.
RF) While we're on the subject of age, it's kind of crazy to think about the fact that baseball players – in fact, athletes as a whole – hit their decline phase, either by injuries or general athleticism, at the same time most normal humans are just reaching their prime. For most folks, your 20s are a haze of failed careers, too much debt, and a couple too many hangovers. Most people have yet to really figure out anything in their lives, and it is acceptable to be a bit lost. For athletes it's the opposite, they need to be as sharp mentally as they are physically, a sooner-than-most maturity level that is lost on many fans.

Transitioning back to actually Cardinal-related material: although the team may currently be relying on Cardinals Devil Magic to turn Tommy Pham into a 6.0-WAR player and make Jedd Gyorko into an actual major leaguer, their history has seen the team rely on good old-fashioned out-smarting and out-working their opposition in order to defeat them. One of the main cogs in this history was a man (Branch Rickey) more often associated with the Dodgers, but who was with the Cardinals franchise for a far greater period of time. He was essential in making them the franchise we hate for the reasons any franchise would want to be hated (too much success, too much stability).

Random cool things about Branch Rickey:

I've said this about other baseball luminaries, and it applies once again: Rickey's career demanded entire volumes written about him, and there are such volumes, so let's just hit the main ideas, bullet-point style. This is a man known to many baseball fans only for his integration of baseball – a feat I certainly do not want to diminish – but it was far from the lone feat this man accomplished during his baseball life.

- Rickey originally got his start in law. According to him, the story of how he ended up out of law is quite an entertaining one. In his only case as a full-time practicing attorney, he went to visit his client, a man who gave Rickey one contemptuous lookover and completely dismissed him. Rickey obliged. He even left the state and ended up moving to St. Louis, where he took a job with one of the local baseball teams, the Browns not the Cardinals. Although Rickey had intended the job to be only a one-year stay, he got a raise after the year, and he had a family for which to provide.
- In terms of personality, Rickey was first and foremost a conservative man.
- He was a very religious man who once said, "The Man of Galilee lived nearly 2000 years ago. [Jesus] died at 32, just about the age when a major league pitcher should be reaching his prime. Yet he left mankind a pattern of life that has enriched millions."
- He was a fanatic against liquor and said it ruined lives (as well as costing him two pennants).

- While in St. Louis, Rickey created the Cardinal Knot Hole Gang, a club young Cardinal fans could join and gain free admission to games. All they had to do was sign a pledge to swear off smoking and profanity – classic Rickey.
- Outside of desegregating baseball, Rickey is best known for his creation of the baseball minor league farm system in the 1930s. Before Rickey tied his Cardinals to a Class-A club in Houston, minor league teams were not affiliated with major league teams. This meant that once players impressed in the minors, they were simply bought by the teams with the most money instead of having a specific minor league team affiliated with a specific big league club.
- About the creation of the farm system, Rickey said, "In St. Louis, we didn't have the capital to compete with the wealthy clubs… we decided to find a way to develop our own. It's just that quantity brings quality. We are not as smart as some of our competitors. We can compete only by outworking them." It's interesting to think about what the less-wealthy teams in baseball might do in the future to combat this issue that never really goes away.
- Quote from Rickey: "Idleness is the worst thing in this world. It's the most damnable thing that can happen to a kid – to have nothing to do."
- It was in part this belief that made Rickey a very shrewd business man. One time, when negotiating with a player, he took a fake call implying that the player would be traded to a team that was looking for a minor leaguer. The player, Bob Friend, immediately took the cheaper, guaranteed MLB deal with Rickey.
- In addition to his prior groundbreaking innovations, Rickey introduced batting cages and pitching machines. He also formed the corporation that brought the batting helmet into existence, with his team in Pittsburgh the first to wear them.
- The Starting IX of players brought into the league by Rickey, according to Bill Felber on *The National Pastime* website: SP) Don Newcombe C) Roy Campanella 1B) Gil Hodges 2B) Jackie Robinson/Bill Mazeroski 3B) Whitey Kurowski SS) Pokey Reese/Dick Groat/Marty Marion OF) Roberto Clemente, Stan Musial, and Duke Snider RP) Elroy Face. Not too shabby.

Starting IX

C Ted Simmons (1968-1980)

Simmons is one of the most underrated catchers – and players – in baseball history. Now, from the Hall of Abusing Statistics, here are some fun comparisons for Simmons: he has four times as many All-Star appearances (8) as Mickey Cochrane, as well as two more than Gabby Hartnett and one more than Thurman Munson; he scored more runs (1,074) than Gary Carter and Mike Piazza, as well as eight other Hall of Fame catchers; he has more doubles (483) than Johnny Bench, Yogi Berra, and Carlton Fisk; he has more RBI (1,389) than Bench, Pudge Rodriguez, and Piazza; he has the same batting average (.285) as Berra, and better than Bench, Carter, and Fisk; before Pudge, no catcher had more career hits than Simmons (2,472); and he has a better career on-base percentage (.348) than six Hall of Fame catchers including Bench, while once again tying with Berra.

Clearly these statistics have been cherry-picked so as to make Simmons look as good as possible, but it does show two things. First, stats can really be manipulated. Any good statistician will tell you this, but this is an extreme case. I think Simmons is underrated, probably a fringe top-ten all-time catcher (when he's usually rated around top-20), but he's certainly not in the class of Bench and Berra, and he's probably not even in Fisk or Piazza range. However, due to a long and consistent career, Simmons can outpace some of the all-time greats in cumulative statistics. His career highs for runs (84), home runs (26) and RBI (108) are not on par with the legends of the backstop position, for sure.

However, he most certainly deserves a bit more hype – even among Cardinals fans. The man wasn't even in the Cardinals Hall of Fame until 2015, for goodness sake. One possible explanation for Simmons underrated nature was that he balanced being a good offensive hitter with a strong defensive output in a way that is so rare that it has actually led to a phenomenon called Nichols' Law of Catcher Defense. The "law" states:

> "A catcher's defensive reputation is inversely proportional to their offensive abilities. Therefore, light-hitting catchers get good defensive reputations and top hitters like Ted Simmons wind up with lousy reputations. One can note that many catchers have lost a reputation for glovework once they began hitting better and that the opposite is also true, further reinforcing Nichols' Law."

Simmons' name is used in the definition, for crying out loud! When thinking back on the history of baseball, it is really only Bench, Carter, and Pudge who were able to maintain elite reputations both with the stick and the glove, but there is obviously not a direct correlation between being a good hitter and a poor fielder at the catcher position, per se. Being a good fielder may allow a below-average hitting catcher to last a bit longer (and vice versa), but there's no evidence towards not being able to do both if the skill is there.

Flashing back in his career: when Simmons came to St. Louis in 1968 as a fresh-faced 19-year-old, he came with hippy hair and hippy ideas on the war in Vietnam. He was only there for a cup of tea in 1968, but he returned in 1970 to establish himself as the Cardinals backstop for the next decade. He went on to form a particularly strong bond with the man who will act as the other half of the Cardinal battery for this Starting IX, and neither man was afraid to speak his mind.

Division rival Bruce Sutter tells the story of how one time Simmons had been riding the home plate umpire all game, so by the time Sutter, who was the closer, was in the game and pitching to Simmons, Sutter was getting any call he wanted. He got a pair of extremely outside strike calls, before accidentally grooving a splitter that he had meant to bury. Simmons got a hold of it and cleared the fence. On his way past the home plate ump, Simmons tipped his cap to the ump, who had had more than enough of Simmons and ejected him from the game. It has to be one of the only cases in which a player got ejected after hitting a home run.

One final note: when Simmons came into the big leagues it was with a (brace yourselves for this) $12,000/year salary. Just 13 years later, Simmons was able to take home $1,000,000 in free agency thanks in large part to the two men (Curt Flood and Marvin Miller) covered in the Cardinals team intro. See, it wasn't totally unrelated after all!

1B Stan Musial (1941-1963)

"Here stands baseball's perfect warrior. Here stands baseball's perfect knight."

With all fair warning, Stan the Man is my favorite player of all time. With that in mind, I felt more pressure writing his bio than any other player in the book. Where to start? The above quote from Ford Frick in regards to Musial seems to perfectly embody the Cardinal legend, but to highlight the phenomenal character of the man would undercut his incredible statistical career (Nichols' Law of Character?). Highlighting his importance to the franchise and city would then ignore how well respected he was throughout the league.

It seems to make the most sense to start with Musial the Man, though, because, although there were other players who could match Musial's statistics (although there aren't many of them), you'd be hard-pressed to find any who could match his high quality of character. Musial played baseball with a childlike love of the game; a gentleman's respect for the game; and a winner's attitude towards the game. He was a man whose batting stance was described as "a little kid peering around a corner." He played the most games in MLB history without a suspension, and he did so while taking home three MVPs, four pennants, and three World Series.

Musial built his relationship with the city of St. Louis via his outstanding character and an incredible amount of talent. He hit over .300 for 16 consecutive seasons[404] and amassed plenty of impressive numbers along the way. His best season was (no surprise) his age-27 season (1948). Musial led the league in runs (135), RBI (131), batting average (.376), on-base percentage (.450), slugging percentage (.702) OPS+ (200), hits (230), doubles (46), triples (18), total bases (429), and WAR (11.1); also known as every major offensive category except for home runs.[405] This seems appropriate, seeing as, despite Musial's incredible numbers, he still lacks a bit of the recognition he deserves. Winning the home run crown would have been the flashiest of all, and even more so, it would have completed the rare Triple Crown. Regardless, his numbers don't lie. He's the only player in MLB history to be the top 30 all-time in singles (2,253), doubles (725), triples (177), and home runs (475), but of course since he ranks "just" 30th all-time in home runs, the flashiest of the bunch.

In 1948, Musial managed four different five-hit games, tying him with Ty Cobb for the all-time single-season record. Two of these games had interesting stories attached to them. In one such game, Musial collected every hit with two strikes on him, and in another he had hurt his wrist and managed to swing the bat only five times all game, each resulting in a hit. This 1948 season was also part of a stretch of 169 games during the 1947 and 1948 seasons in which Musial hit .439, one of the best hidden seasons of all time. By hidden season, I mean 162-game stretch that is not necessarily starting and ending with the MLB calendar. Finding these hidden seasons is one of the most fun games to play, and it can lead to some incredible 162-game stretches that are lost to history due to the arbitrary beginning and end of the MLB calendar.

Musial also won the St. Louis crowd over with his loyalty to the team. In 1946, the Pasquel brothers of the Mexican Leagues tried to raid Major League Baseball and start their own league. This was similar to the attempted coups seen before in baseball history (the Federal League being the most famous case). They offered Musial a five-year contract for $125,000 with a $75,000 bonus. At the time, he was making $12,500, but he turned them down out of loyalty to the Cards (and probably in part because they were the Pasquel brothers, who I imagine to be a bit like the Savage brothers who Sean Penn enlists to help his personal detective search in *Mystic River*). One time, the St. Louis fans booed Musial during a home game – they took out an ad apologizing in the paper the next day.

Musial was also durable and had supreme longevity. In 1957, he broke the NL record for consecutive games played (895) and did so while still playing at a very productive level. In Musial's penultimate season, he became the first grandfather to hit a home run and finished the season hitting .330. Just a few years earlier, he had one of the best days a big leaguer has ever had, setting an MLB record by hitting a combined five home runs in a double header, one of which was a game-winner.

All of this came from relatively humble beginnings. When in the minor leagues, Musial was originally a pitcher, but he made the switch to left field after injuring his shoulder; what a switch it ended up being. Maybe it was from his days as a

[404] Joe Garagiola said of Musial, "He could have hit .300 with a fountain pen."
[405] He would have led the league lead in home runs had he not had one home run rained out and another incorrectly ruled a double in Shibe Park.

pitcher, but one story goes that Musial was able to memorize the speed of every pitcher in the league, and he could pick up those speeds from home plate. This seems like one of baseball's ever-so-prevalent tall tales, but who would begrudge Musial the story? The results are also hard to argue with, as only Hank Aaron has more total bases in baseball history than Musial.

Stan the Man won the respect – and fear – of everyone he played. In in his career, Willie Mays was given fair warning to Musial's supreme ability. In Mays' first game against the Cardinals, Mays' manager Leo Durocher went down the lineup giving Mays pointers on every Cardinals hitter, but he skipped the third spot on the lineup card. His logic: "[That] is Stan Musial. There is no advice I can give you about him." Preacher Roe had a different strategy on how to retire Musial: "Throw him four wide ones and try to pick him off first." Carl Erskine didn't even try that. "I just throw him my best stuff, then run over to back up third base," Erskine said of Musial. Finally, in a *Time Magazine* piece written by Ty Cobb in 1952, Stan was one of only two players Cobb said would have been a star "back in his day." Not even Cobb could dislike him!

Musial played his whole career in St. Louis, but he supposedly received his nickname from the fans in Brooklyn. When the Cardinals came to town, they would chant "here comes the man," in honor of *the man* who torched them consistently. *St. Louis Dispatch* writer Bob Broeg heard the chant, incorporated the nickname into his next story, and the rest is history. It's not too surprising that it was Dodger fans who created the nickname, as Musial did indeed massacre the Dodgers in Ebbets Field. He slashed .359/.448/.660 for his career at Ebbets, the highest OPS of any stadium in which he played during his days.

But really, any write-up about Musial should begin and end with his character. Musial was in attendance for the game in which Hank Aaron joined the 3,000-hit club. He went on the field to congratulate and welcome Aaron to the illustrious club. Although the outpouring of coverage after Musial's passing a few years back was excellent, it just showed how under-the-radar he was for so long. As William Nack pointed out for *ESPN*, "When *SI* had fans pick a 20th century All-Star team at the end of the millennium, they voted Musial 10th among *outfielders*. ESPN television failed to put him among the top 50 athletes of the 20th century. When MasterCard and professional baseball assembled their All-Century team in 1999, the voting masses virtually ignored Musial; ultimately, an 'oversight committee' slipped him onto the roster."

However, Musial's name is now a bit more prominent, and hopefully this young generation of fans can realize what a Man, Stan truly was. And while the baseball community will certainly mourn the loss of one of its true greats, as Musial himself said, "When I stopped playing, what I missed most were the sounds of the ballpark. For years after I retired, I heard those sounds in my head before I went to sleep." Something tells me he's hearing those sounds up in the Good Place today.

2B Rogers Hornsby (1915-1926; 1933)

One of the game's true greats,[406] Hornsby played his first 12 years in St. Louis and came back for one brief stint later in his career. After leaving the Cardinals, Raj had three years of success before injuries and advancing age eventually slowed him down. Those injuries took away from the form he showed in St. Louis; and man, what form that was.[407] In Ted Williams' section to come (Left Field, Red Sox – Page 340), Hornsby's best six-year stretch (1920-1925) will be shown to be among the best of all time, and as such, it should be no surprise that many consider him to be the best second baseman of all time. We touched on the best second baseman debate a bit earlier (Second Base, A's – Page 311), so let's take a look at my personal all-time 25-man roster, with a starting lineup, five-man rotation, and bullpen.

1) Honus Wagner (SS)
2) Rogers Hornsby (2B)
3) Ted Williams (LF)
4) Babe Ruth (RF)
5) Stan Musial (1B)
6) Barry Bonds (DH)
7) Willie Mays (CF)
8) Mike Schmidt (3B)
9) Johnny Bench (C)

Back-up C) Josh Gibson
Back-up 1B) Lou Gehrig
Utility Infielder) Alex Rodriguez
Team Stalwart/Pinch-hit Power Threat) Hank Aaron

---

[406] Players, not men. I'll keep this to a footnote since I put a chapter's worth on Cobb, but Bill James described Hornsby as even more of a horse's ass than Cobb. He didn't attend his own mother's funeral, was a member of the KKK, and generally had nothing going for him outside of being a great ballplayer. When asked what he did in the offseason, he replied, "Sat by the window and waited for the next baseball season to start." *
* Footnote to the footnote: Howard Green has a fascinating piece the 2001 issue of *Baseball Research Journal*, which chronicles Hornsby's life at home in the offseason. In the piece, numerous sources tell of a far-less-cold Hornsby who was actually well-liked in his hometown and is quoted as saying, "Any ballplayer that don't sign autographs for little kids ain't an American."
[407] He is the only player in MLB history to hit over .400 with at least 40 home runs in a season – again, this man was a second baseman.

Team Drinker/Highest Ceiling Award) Mickey Mantle
Team Racist/Pinch-hit Contact Guy/Pinch-runner) Ty Cobb

Starting Pitcher 1) Walter Johnson
SP2) Pete Alexander
SP3) Lefty Grove
SP4) Pedro Martínez
SP5) Warren Spahn
SP6) Clayton Kershaw
Long Relief) Cy Young
Middle Relief) Christy Mathewson
Set Up) Satchel Paige
Closer) Mariano Rivera

The missing players most likely to be disputed are probably Joe DiMaggio, Joe Morgan (behind Alex Rodriguez in particular), Jimmie Foxx, Yogi Berra, and the fact that Cy Young isn't in the starting rotation. As far as DiMaggio is concerned, he was certainly an all-time great, but unfortunately, he played the same position as two of the three best hitters of all time. Also, outfield as a whole is stacked throughout history. He also suffers from the fact that Cobb brings to the table one thing the rest of the roster is lacking, speed. If you were building a team for success, Cobb would go before DiMaggio, because Cobb's quality is less represented among the all-time greats.

Joe Morgan was a top-notch player and actually tends to be undervalued historically; however, A-Rod's dominance from a position that doesn't sport flashy offensive numbers is too much to ignore. The fact that he could play shortstop, third base, and most likely second base (he might not have the instincts there, but he would certainly have the arm for those deep plays up the middle) doesn't hurt either.

Jimmie Foxx has the problem that first base is probably the deepest of any position in league history, and although Foxx was excellent, he fell just behind the two men to make it at first. Musial is often listed as an outfielder (in particular as a right fielder; this is where Baseball-Reference lists him), but I don't really understand this. I suppose they tried to look at his prime years, but right field is the position he played the third-most games at, as he played more games at both first base *and* left field. Bill James lists his as a left fielder in his *Historical Baseball Abstract*, but I'm going to give him 1B/OF eligibility here, which only helps his case for the team.

Yogi Berra is certainly the most famous catcher of all time, and has an incredible 10 rings and 14 pennants, not to mention the honor of Bill James' best catcher, but I don't have him making the top two backstops. Bench combines great offense with great defense better than any catcher of all time. And although we know more about what Berra did, anyone who saw Gibson play said he was likely the G.O.A.T. That's good enough for me.

Finally, as for Cy Young not grabbing a starting role, even though he has the most all-time wins and the highest career WAR among pitchers, he is not deserving of a top-six starting role. His most amazing trait is that he was able to throw such a high number of innings for such a sustained amount of time. Many of the pitchers from Young's time left the game early due to the wear and tear of so many innings without the precautions and medical advancement today's pitchers have. Although Young is the all-time leader in wins and innings pitched, he never seemed as truly dominant as our starting six. He did lead the league in WAR six times, but he had only two ERA and strikeout titles, apiece. He's the perfect long relief guy.

* * *

Back to Hornsby: he was the first real power threat to come from the second base position, and his 42 home runs in 1922 are just one off the single-season record for second basemen. He did this in an era in which the home run was just blossoming, and other than the great Yankees of the 1920s, Hornsby did more for the long ball than anyone else. From 1920-1925 (his aforementioned incredible six-year stretch) Hornsby led the league in batting average, on-base percentage, slugging percentage, and OPS+ *each and every year*, while becoming the first player to snag multiple Triple Crowns (1922 and 1925).

One of the most interesting phenomena of Hornsby's time is how the home run became a staple of the sport. In 1917, Hornsby had a league-leading OPS+ of 169 but totaled only eight home runs for the season. The next few years showed the incredible growth in the presence of the long ball, however. Hornsby's home run totals went nine to 21 to 42 over the years of 1920-1922. Although part of this was the result of Hornsby blossoming into a better hitter, much of it was the result of the times. There was expansion in baseball, which led to more pitchers in the league and thus more bad pitchers whom Hornsby could hit off of. Major League Baseball also implemented rule changes to eliminate the spitball, and ballparks began to tailor themselves to hitters. There is debate as to whether Babe Ruth's popularity was a cause of this boom in home runs, or if his numbers were more the result of the changes made to the game, but either way, home runs were as in-vogue as they ever have been during the Roaring Twenties.

Hornsby was not only great in that six-year stretch, however. He led the league in OPS+ in 12 of 15 seasons from 1917-1931, meaning that, once established, he was the National League's best hitter pretty much every year until his health failed. In fact, Hornsby's ankle problems bring up one of baseball's best "What If's." What if Hornsby hadn't suffered a broken ankle during the 1930 campaign? Hornsby was a 34-year-old coming off of a decade in which his OPS+ for the 10-year stretch was 188. He was a man who didn't go to the cinema out of fear that the movies would ruin his hitting eye, and he supposedly sat around in the offseason just waiting for baseball to start back up again.

On the other hand, Hornsby was on his fourth different team in five years, and his act was beginning to wear thin around the league. He was still a great player, but at the age of 34, there were only a few more good years to be had, most likely. Hornsby could have likely helped out his cumulative statistics had he stayed healthy, but in terms of big reputation-changing injuries, Hornsby's ankle problems pale in comparison to some other baseball injuries, such as Herb Score, Kerry Wood, or even Nomar Garciaparra.

Bringing Hornsby's section to a close on a lighter note: he is the subject of one of the most fun baseball games – "Six Degrees of Rogers Hornsby." This is like "Six Degrees of Kevin Bacon," but far better because Hornsby never appeared in *R.I.P.D.* The line of thinking is the same, though. Because Hornsby had such an illustrious career, tracing any one player's "teammate lineage," to Hornsby won't take more than six players. Just how the Six Degrees of Kevin Bacon is tracked through shared movie credits, Hornsby's shared teammate list can be tracked through MLB history. All credit goes to Tom Remes for creating this brilliant game in the 1999 edition of *The National Pastime*.

3B Ken Boyer (1955-1965)

In addition to being one of the top fielding third baseman of his time, Boyer was also a solid contributor with his bat. After missing a few years at the beginning of his career due to military service, Boyer played at least 142 games in each of his 11 seasons in Cardinal Red. He averaged 90+ runs and RBI a pop, with over 20 home runs and a .293 batting average. He won the team over 10.0 games by dWAR. He is, along with Ron Santo, one of two third basemen to have seven straight seasons of 20 home runs and 90 RBI.

Ken's brother Clete was also a professional ballplayer, and the two are the only pair of brothers in MLB history to each have at least 150 home runs. The Boyer's were a baseball family, as brother Cloyd[408] was also an MLB pitcher for a brief stint.

SS Ozzie Smith (1982-1996)

At first blush, Ozzie Smith's numbers don't do much for you. He may have had almost 2,000 hits with the team, but he did so with only a .272 batting average and one season above .300. Plus, he had no power whatsoever, with only 27 home runs in 15 seasons with the team. His OPS+ was below 100 for his 15 years with the organization (93). But the Wizard of Oz had one strong suit, and one ability for the ages. He was a strong base runner – collecting over 430 stolen bases with the team – and he was an all-time great was with the glove.

He is baseball's all-time leader in dWAR (43.4) and, from 1980-1992, won 13 straight Gold Gloves (11 of them in St. Louis) at the most difficult position on the diamond. He managed to turn this slick fielding into regular All-Star appearances and over 65.0 WAR for his time with the Cardinals. He combined excellent range, strong hands, quickness, and very few mistakes to become the best fielding shortstop of his time and – by both the numbers and reputation – of all time. When he retired, Smith held the MLB records for assists (8,375), double plays (1,590), and total chances (12,905) among shortstops. He was considered so valuable that he was Major League Baseball's highest-paid player in 1988, despite being a below-average hitter (OPS+ of 98).

Smith's perceived (and calculated) value brings up an interesting note on positional defensive value. As has been noted before, up the middle defenders – catchers, second baseman, shortstops, and center fielders – have been historically valued far greater than the rest of the diamond. The numbers support this, and it is interesting that this is one idea that has been in place since baseball's origins and has been proven with the modern metrics – those are becoming less and less frequent these days.

Smith's defining move may have been his back flips on the field between innings, but his defining moment as a Cardinal came at an unlikely time – at the dish. In Game 5 of the 1985 NLCS, with the series tied at 2-2 and the game tied in the ninth, Smith proceeded to hit his first home run from the left side of the plate in his career (3,009 at bats) to walk-off and send the Cardinals on their way to the World Series. He was rewarded with the series MVP, and although they lost to their fellow Missourians (Kansas City Royals) in the World Series, that hasn't taken the historical shine off an awesome moment for Smith, as well as all Cardinals fans.

LF Lou Brock (1964-1979) vs. Joe Medwick (1932-1940; 1947-1948)

It is fitting that a franchise as steeped in history as the Cardinals should get a breakdown. (That being said if Musial had been put at left field – where he played much of his career – this wouldn't have been a contest).

---

[408] Yes, that is his real name.

Contact

	BA	lgBA	Seasons ≥ .300	Career high/low	Seasons ≥ 100 SO	SO %	lgSO%	BABIP	Misc.
Brock	.297	.261	8	.348/.272	8	14.8	14.2	.342	
Medwick	.335	.285	7	.374/.306	0	7.9	8.9	.343	LL 2x H, 1x BA

Medwick hit over .300 every full season he played in St. Louis, and although Brock was consistently right around .300, Medwick was always above it. Although hitters in Medwick's time did hit for a higher average, Medwick was a better hitter than Brock, even when compared to the rest of the league. Brock also had a much higher strikeout rate than Medwick, but when the two are compared to the league, it becomes a lot closer. Brock had the most strikeouts of any player with 3,000 hits when he reached that plateau (three have joined him since), but his strikeout totals did drop noticeably after the mound was lowered in 1969. This did not prevent him from being so concerned about his strikeout totals that he asked out of the lineup in the final game of the 1970 season to avoid reaching 100 strikeouts for the first time since 1962. On the flip side, Brock, as many fast batters do, had a high batting average on balls in play, as he was able to beat out infield hits and relied on slapping the ball to gaps. As a whole, though, Medwick was a superior contact hitter, with his victory due in part to his 1937 batting crown (.374).

EDGE: Medwick

Power

	HR	Seasons ≥ 20 HR	Career high HR	XBH	SLG%	lgSLG%	ISO	HR%	XBH%	Misc.
Brock	129	1	21	684	.414	389	.116	1.3	6.9	<10 HR final nine seasons
Medwick	152	3	31	610	.545	.404	.210	3.0	12.1	LL 3x 2B, TB, RBI, 1x HR

Medwick hit more home runs than Brock and had almost as many extra-base hits despite playing 1,073 fewer games with the franchise. His home run ratio and isolated power are about double what Brock was able to do, and he was far better in comparison to the rest of the league. It is interesting to note that before his days in St. Louis, Medwick became only the second player ever to hit a ball into the center field stands in the Polo Grounds, some 483 feet away. Medwick was a producer, as well, as he led all of baseball in RBI for the "Hidden Decades" of 1934-1943, 1935-1944, and 1936-1945. Probably not surprising that this one is not really close.

EDGE: Medwick by a lot

Batting Eye

	BB	Seasons ≥ 50 BB	OBP	lgOBP	OPS+	BB%	SO/BB
Brock	681	5	.347	.330	112	6.9	2.16
Medwick	264	0	.372	.346	142	5.2	1.51

Medwick's on-base percentage is higher than Brock's, and it is also higher in comparison to league rates, but this does not necessarily mean he had the better batting eye. Medwick's on-base percentage is boosted by his stellar batting average. When it comes to actually drawing walks, Brock was not great, but he was better than Medwick, who was about as free-swinging as they come. His walk rate was grotesquely low, and in 1934, Medwick drew only two more walks than Ted Williams did in 1953. That sounds impressive, until you realize Medwick played 149 games to get his 21 walks, while

Williams played 37 games in 1953 to get his 19 walks. I guess it's not a surprise that Medwick once said, "I never cared where the strike zone was. I wasn't looking to walk."

This is really just an embarrassing category for both, as our winner is a man who owns the worst on-base percentage in a season in which that player had at least 205 hits.

EDGE: Brock

Speed

	SB	Seasons ≥ 50 SB	Career high SB	Rbaser	SB%	XBT%	GDP%	Misc.
Brock	888	12	118	73	75	53	7	LL 8x SB, 1x 20/20
Medwick	28	0	6	0	N/A	N/A	N/A	

Lou Brock is second all-time in stolen bases (938). Brock had 888 steals with Cardinals alone, which would be good for fourth all-time. He averaged 67 steals per season over his 10-year prime and had a major league record 12 straight years with 50 or more steals. His career-high 118 steals in 1974 were a then-post-1900 single-season record and are still second all-time.

Joe Medwick grounded into four times as many double plays as he had stolen bases in his career, and his career-high for stolen bases came in 1939, when he stole six bags…

Hmmm, I guess we'll give this to Brock.

EDGE: Brock by a mile… which he would run twice as fast as Medwick

Defense

	Fld%	lgFld%	dWAR	RF/9	lgRF/9	Assists	GG	Misc.
Brock	.959	.976	-16.3	1.90	2.13	110	0	LL 7x OF E
Medwick	.976	.976	-3.1	2.23	N/A	85	N/A	LL 1x OF E, OF Fld%

Lou Brock, despite his blazing speed, was one of the worst defensive outfielders of his time. This is not as uncommon occurrence as one may think, and it truly underlines how much more there is to fielding than just sprinting to the ball. Medwick was not an exceptionally strong fielder but simply by not being as bad as Brock, he takes this category.

EDGE: Medwick

Team Success

	W	L	T	W-L%	Seasons ≥ 90 W	Division titles	Pennants	WS
Brock	1,177	1,108	4	.515	4	3	3	2
Medwick	649	553	13	.540	3	1	1	1

Both Medwick and Brock played on strong Cardinals teams over the course of their career. Both players enjoyed success in their trips to the World Series, but Brock did it in two trips, compared to one for Medwick. Brock's longer tenure with the team helps him out here, as Medwick missed three World Series wins while he was out gallivanting between his two stints in St. Louis.

EDGE: Brock

Dominance

Brock: LL: 8x SB, 2x R, 1x 2B, 3B; 6x AS
Medwick: LL: 3x TB, RBI, 2B, 2x H, 1x R, 3B, HR, BA, SLG, OPS, OPS+, WAR; 7x AS, 1x MVP

These two players led the league in entirely different ways. Brock was truly dominant as a base stealer, leading the league in steals eight times and always being near the top of the league. Medwick, on the other hand, led the league in a variety of categories but never dominated one area the way Brock did. Both players made about the same number of All-Star Games, but the tiebreaker, in this case, is that Medwick had an MVP to his name. Brock did have a second-place MVP finish, and although I have railed against this type of logic in the past, Brock never really deserved one, having never finished above eighth in WAR in a single season. It also doesn't hurt Medwick's case that he received one of baseball's greatest honors when he was once intentionally walked with the bases loaded and the Cards down four in the ninth.

EDGE: Medwick by a small margin

Nickname

Joe Medwick had two solid nicknames from his playing days: "Ducky," for his duck-like walk; and "Muscles," aptly given to one of the game's strongest hitters. However, Lou Brock had a pair of awesome nicknames himself: "The Franchise" and "The Running Redbird," making this the rare case in which a player who played later chronologically had the better nicknames.

EDGE: Brock

Great Quote

Lou Brock was a decent quote in his time, and he wasn't afraid to speak his mind on issues of race. When commenting on the nature of the intersection of sports and race in America, he made a very good point, especially for the times in which he played (although it's sadly still very true) He stated, "My contention is that sports is the only industry that has allowed the black man to come in and compete under the same rules." Given the number of black managers in baseball, and sports as a whole, that may not even be fully true.

Even though Brock's quote was far more philosophical and eye-opening, he really never had a chance against the best Medwick story. While serving in WWII, Medwick met the Pope. Was he flabbergasted and speechless? Hardly. Medwick said, "Your Holiness, I'm Joseph Medwick. I, too, used to be a Cardinal." Game. Set. Match.

If that wasn't enough, Medwick had a great quote after the 1934 World Series, as well. In Game 7 of the 1934 World Series, Medwick and the Gas House Gang Cardinals led 7-0 in the sixth inning. So, when Joe Medwick slid hard into third base, Tigers third baseman Marvin Owen took exception and stomped on Medwick's leg. Medwick retaliated with a pair of cleats to Owen's stomach, and a brawl very nearly ensued. Instead, nothing happened until the next half inning. When Medwick came out to the field he was pelted with a variety of fruits, namely apples, oranges, and grapefruits. The fans were so passionate about showing Medwick their dislike for him that the game was delayed more than a quarter of an hour before Commissioner Landis decided to throw Medwick out of the game. He could have simply told the Tigers fans they would forfeit the game if they could not stop the shenanigans, but instead he chose to punish Medwick. This decision didn't seem to make too much sense, and Medwick was unfortunate enough to have this story follow him around the rest of his career. Medwick often said that he regretted being remembered more for the 1934 incident than the rest of his career.

What does any of this have to do with a quote? Well, after the game Medwick said in response to the fruit that he was pelted with, "I know why they threw it, what I could never figure out is why they brought it to the park in the first place."

EDGE: Medwick

Better Fit

Right now, these two are quite close. Medwick probably has a small lead, but they each have their strong suits. In fact, these two are very different players, with Brock bringing a strong batting average and the ability to turn almost every single into a double by virtue of the stolen base, while Medwick's game was more based on power and run producing. So, if you were choosing a team, these men would represent much different paths to roster building.[409] In fact, I'm going to use that

[409] I feel like "roster building" is the baseball equivalent to "synergy" or "achievement gap" in other fields. It's such a buzzword right now. The fact that I still think "synergy" is still a buzzword is a good clue as to how untapped-in I am to all non-baseball fields.

as a tiebreaker in this, and only this, case. Choosing a player based on how they fit with the team may not make much sense in the historical sense, but it is kind of fun to think about these teams actually trying to mesh together. It's something that I think is important enough in how real baseball teams are made, that I want to give this thought some representation in this book. Right now, a decent lineup for this Starting IX might look like this (with spoilers for those who haven't guessed the final three spots):

1) Brock 2) Hornsby 3) Musial 4) Albert Pujols 5) Jim Edmonds 6) Boyer 7) Simmons 8) Enos Slaughter 9) Smith
OR:
1) Smith 2) Hornsby 3) Musial 4) Pujols 5) Medwick 6) Edmonds 7) Boyer 8) Simmons 9) Slaughter

To me, the first lineup looks a lot better. Brock is a solid fit for the leadoff spot (just lacking a bit of patience), where his speed can be most utilized for the team. Ozzie Smith is not nearly as good of a leadoff hitter as, despite his speed, his inability to get on base would hurt the team. Brock could also hide his below average defense surrounded by three all-time great defensive players. With Boyer and Smith in front of him, not too many balls would reach him on the ground. With Edmonds to his side in center, he'd be well covered in the air. In the end, even though the numbers may give the slightest edge to Medwick, **Lou Brock** is the better fit for this Starting IX.

CF Jim Edmonds (2000-2007)

After getting burned by Trout on the Angels Starting IX, Edmonds still finds his way into this book. Edmonds was known as an excellent fielder in his time, regularly showing up on SportsCenter's Top 10, with a few of his all-time grabs showing up whenever an MLB highlight package of the best catches ever is put together. When looking at the numbers, however, Edmonds – while certainly a solid defensively player – may have been slightly over-hyped. For all the spectacular plays he made, Edmonds was pretty much on par with the league average in terms of fielding percentage, and he only finished in the top 10 in dWAR one time in his career. (It was before his time in St. Louis.) His assists totals were above average, and his range was a tick above average, but he was usually among the league leaders in errors among center fielders.

Of course, this verdict gives a lot of weight to the stats over reputation side of defensive analysis. Edmonds' true skills were likely not quite as strong as his reputation suggested but also a bit better than the stats say. That wishy-washy, between-two-ferns approach to defensive statistics is, sadly, as good as we can get when looking back at the defensive metrics. That's why some of the newer defensive metrics, like Catch Probability, along with the rest of the Statcast defensive data, are so exciting. They are attempting to combine what real, live humans see with their eyes, as well as what the data behind each catch can tell us. Truly measuring defensive contributions has long been an incredibly difficult challenge to baseball fans and pundits alike, but once we know what to do with all the data we're collecting, it could truly be revolutionary.

As Rob Neyer said when discussing Andruw Jones in his *Big Book of Baseball Lineups*, "If you look at the raw stats, you can certainly be fooled, so a lot of people just choose to ignore them altogether. And fielding stats can be tricky even if you look at them with some sophistication. So what I look for are players with great defensive stats *and* great defensive reputations." A good analogy as to using scouting/The Eye Test, as well as statistical analysis, comes from Dayn Perry of *CBSSports* (previously of *Baseball Prospectus*), who says of the age-old "scouts or stats" question: "My answer is the same it would be if someone asked me: 'Beer or tacos?' Both, you fool."

Moving on. Edmonds was actually a little bit of an underrated hitter. Because of his glove's reputation, Edmond's ability to hit for power and average flew a bit under-the-radar.[410] Although Edmonds never finished in the top 10 in dWAR while playing for the Cardinals, Edmonds managed to crack the top 10 in oWAR four times in his eight seasons with the club. He topped 40 home runs twice and had an excellent eye. He drew over 100 walks two times, as well – in fact the same two years (2000 and 2004).

Because of this underrated hitting value, "Edmonds as a Hall of Famer" has not always been the most common of sentiments, but Jason Rosenberg of *ESPN* laid out the case after Edmond's retirement and did a pretty convincing job of showing that Edmonds might just deserve a plaque in the hallowed Halls of Cooperstown. Go check out the piece.

RF Enos Slaughter (1938-1953)

Blessed (or rather, cursed) with one of the more painful-sounding names,[411] Slaughter managed to be one of the most popular Cardinals while he played for the franchise. Nicknamed "Country," Slaughter gained popularity and notoriety on the back of his famous dash from first to home on a single in the 1946 World Series. There is even a statue in honor of the play outside Busch Stadium. The Mad Dash came in the eighth inning of Game 7 of the series, and it saw Slaughter score what would end up being the winning run.

---

[410] Another appearance for the ubiquitous Nichols' Law, this time in center field, perhaps?
[411] And tied with "Urethra Franklin" as the worst fake porn name of all time.

Slaughter was also beloved by Cardinals fans because he loved the team so dearly. "I never felt as bad when my father died as I did when I was released by the Cardinals," Slaughter once intoned. Now that's a man who feels a deep connection to his team. Possibly too deep… I imagine his father rolled over in his grave a bit after that quote.

Slaughter was one of many ball players to miss a significant chunk of time to military service, but he still collected over 2,000 hits for St. Louis. Enos was also one of those whose prime was taken from him by his service. He would have been 27 years old, and fresh off an MVP runner-up season, if he could have played in 1943. Upon his return to baseball in 1946, Slaughter had another dominant season, leading the league in RBI (130) and finishing third in the MVP. Slaughter continued to improve until 1949, which was arguably his best season as a pro. Slaughter's career faded a bit after he left St. Louis, but given his previous sentiments, that is hardly surprising.

Even though he lost three years to service time, Slaughter could have easily missed a lot more time if he had given into some of the injuries that plagued him throughout his career. He played through the disease that took his father's life. He once fractured his collarbone mid-game but stayed in the game. His next at bat, when he took a hack, the skin tore and there was some nice blood flow. He also played in the World Series with a life-risking blood clot in his elbow.

Not every Slaughter story paints a positive picture of the man, however. Slaughter allegedly tried to get other St. Louis players to boycott their first game against the Dodgers after they signed Jackie Robinson. This is a story that has long been disputed by the players of the Cardinals, especially Slaughter, and since there will be times in this book where I decry blaming alleged PED users against whom we have no hard evidence, Slaughter should be given the benefit of the doubt here, as well.

One final note on Slaughter: with 2,383 hits in 7,946 career at bats, Slaughter is listed as a .300 hitter. However, if the decimal is expanded a few significant figures, that number becomes .299899, meaning that Slaughter was technically juuuuuussssst shy of being a .300 hitter – a magical number in baseball lore. Baseball loves its hallowed numbers, whether it be 3,000 hits, 500 home runs, or a .300 batting average – these numbers have been around as long as the history of baseball. As Gavvy Cravath said, "There is a certain charm about .300. If a man hits it he is a star, if he doesn't he isn't." Let's take a look at some of the others who just missed out on some of baseball's other hallowed numbers.

Sam Rice finished his career 13 hits away from 3,000, the closest anyone has come to just missing out on 3,000. (This makes Clemente landing exactly on 3,000 hits before his untimely passing even more incredible.[412]) In terms of home runs, Al Kaline and Andres Galarraga both finished their careers with 399 home runs; Tim Salmon finished with 299; while Based God Geoff Blum finished with 99. Lefty Grove and Early Wynn finished right at 300 wins, while Bobby Mathews' 297 victories came before 300 was such a hallowed number. Possibly the most interesting aversion to finishing just shy of a round number comes via the strikeout. The closest player to 4,000 is Bert Blyleven with 3,701, and the closest to 3,000 is Jim Bunning with 2,855. For all the next generation statheads, the closest to 100 WAR is Albert Pujols with 99.4. Pujols was actually over 100.0 WAR before the 2017 season, but he is currently tracking down the all-time WAR leaderboard, as he was worth -1.8 WAR in 2017. Hopefully he can bounce back with a few more decent seasons to round out his contract and end his career with triple-digit wins above replacement. He deserves it.

So, the fair question may be: do these milestone numbers actually affect how these players are remembered? Most likely not, however, it does seem that these numbers do indeed hold a great significance to the players themselves. It can be seen in the case of Lefty Grove chasing his 300th win and numerous players (Craig Biggio comes to mind right off the bat) extending their careers to reach 3,000 hits. Often times, as fans, we assume we care way more about these silly numbers, but the players can care about them plenty, as well.

Utility Albert Pujols (2001-2011)

Pujols started his career about as well as any player in history. Just exactly where he will end up in the all-time ranks is yet to be determined, but he most likely will end up in the discussion among the top 25 players of all time. He was just outside of the 25-man roster I selected in Hornsby's section, but he very well may end up there when his career is said and done. Some impressive statistics Pujols has already achieved:

* WAR over 5.0 every year in St. Louis (his first 11 years in the league).
* OPS+ over 150 each of his first 10 seasons.
* Over 100 RBI each of his first 10 seasons. He failed to reach 100 runs only once as a Cardinal, and he had 99 that year. He also failed to reach 100 RBI in only once as a Cardinal, and he had 99 that year.
* Over 30 home runs each year as a Cardinal.
* Hit over .310 each of his first 10 years.
* Over 300 total bases each of his first 12 years.
* More walks than strikeouts every year in St. Louis, except his rookie year.

---

[412] Can you imagine if, in one of SABR's attempts to clean up the record books, a researcher somehow found out that Clemente was accidentally given a hit that he shouldn't have received, meaning he was actually just shy of his magical 3,000 career hits? I'm pretty sure no one would have the heart to actually release that revelation.

* Along with Lou Gehrig, he is one of only two players to have three seasons with 40 home runs and 40 doubles. He still has an outside chance to be the only one with four such years.
* More career home runs (614) than Edgar Martínez (309) and Rogers Hornsby (301) *combined*; more doubles (619) than Babe Ruth (506). More extra-base hits (1,249) than Lou Gehrig (1,190) and Ted Williams (1,117). More WAR (99.4) than Sandy Koufax (49.0) and Jim Rice (47.4) *combined.*
* Only player in baseball history to hit 50 doubles in both leagues; one of only two with 50 doubles on two different teams.
* .323 batting average with 19 home runs (fourth all-time) in the playoffs; has two World Series rings.

If Pujols career ended as of the time this book went to print, he'd easily have a Hall of Fame career and be considered one of the all-time greats, but he may still have a couple of years left in the tank, and possibly more than that if he can bounce back from his worst season as a professional in 2017. I certainly wouldn't write it off. Before 2017, it's not as if Pujols had been as much of a drain on the Angels as many have made him out to be. Even with the drop off, his 2016 OPS+ of 113 was higher than the career OPS+ of Astros *Hall of Famer* Craig Biggio. Same with Luke Appling. It was nine points better than Brooks freakin' Robinson. Now all three of those examples played better defense at harder positions, but it just goes to show the incredible peak that Pujols was at that his decline still leaves him a well above-average hitter (before 2017, of course).

Now, we can't complete Pujols' write-up without mentioning the unassuming Peter Parker/Tom Brady nature to Pujols' origin story: he was taken in the 13th round of the 1999 MLB draft, pick no. 402. However, it's another side of Pujols' story – what he did once he got famous – that deserves even more attention.

Dating all the way back to origins in the league, Pujols has been one of the biggest proponents for special needs awareness. This is an issue close to his heart, as his daughter, Isabella, has Down syndrome. Pujols created his own nonprofit (the Pujols Family Foundation), which "promotes awareness of special needs issues and helps kids and families living with Down syndrome both in the US and [Pujols'] native Dominican Republic." For Pujols, all the on-field accomplishments are great, but I'm sure he'd say his achievements off the field are closer to his heart.[413]

SP Bob Gibson (1959-1975)

One of the best ways to get consideration for all-time excellence is to impact the sport you play in such a severe nature that they change the rules in order to slow you down. This is partially true for Gibson. In 1968, Gibson had one of the greatest seasons of all time, going 22-9 with a record-breaking 1.12 ERA and 268 strikeouts. Gibson threw 13 shutouts and, during one four-game stretch, threw 41.0 innings as a part of four straight complete games. He threw five straight shutouts in June, part of 47.0 consecutive scoreless innings and had an even bigger stretch of 92.0 innings with only two earned runs allowed. During his magical 1968 season, and his career as a whole, Gibson relied on his nasty slider, which Rob Neyer ranks as the third-best slider of all time, and the best from a right-handed pitcher. During the entire 1968 season, Gibson was never removed from the mound once, with the only times he left games all year being for pinch-hitters. Gibson himself was actually a solid hitter, finishing his career with 24 home runs (top 10 all-time for a pitcher) and an above-the-Mendoza-line batting average (.206), as well as 7.7 oWAR.

After this sensational year, MLB changed its rules in two ways: lowering the mound five inches and moving the top of the strike zone to favor the batters. Now, to say Gibson was the sole reason for these changes would not be accurate. Although his dominance played a role,[414] the league as a whole was ready for the change. American League totals for runs scored had dropped every year since 1961, and while it was not a steady year-by-year decline for the National League, their totals were also dropping. Many pitchers had excellent seasons in 1968, with both MVPs going to pitchers – Gibson in the National League and Denny McLain in the American League. McLain is the most recent 30-game winner, doing so in 1968. There were at least 10 pitchers in each league to have an ERA below 2.50, and nine pitchers had a WHIP below 1.000. As a whole, the league realized the need for more runs to keep fans interested, as well as leveling the playing field for pitchers and batters.

Outside of his dominant 1968 season, there are a few more important things to know about Gibson: he grew up in poverty, and although he made it to college eventually, he saw a fair share of bumps in the road to the big leagues. From *Nine Innings*, Indiana University turned down Gibson's scholarship, saying "an athletic scholarship for Robert Gibson has been denied because we already have filled our quota of Negroes." Due to slights like that, Gibson carried a (deserved) chip on his shoulder throughout his career. He had an intensity that the great philosopher Ted Simmons summed up quite poetically: "Gibson sort of condensed his lifetime into each pitch."

It's maybe a bit surprising then that Gibson also seemed to have another gear, and many considered him one of the best big-game pitchers of all time. For one stretch of his career, Gibson won seven World Series starts in a row. Among those starts were two Game 7 victories: 1964 against the Yankees and 1967 against the Red Sox. In 1968, he would eventually lose

---

[413] Between the last sentences of the Musial's and Pujols' write-ups, this Cardinals Starting IX is beginning to feel a bit like the ending to a *Scrubs* episode. (Duh-Nuh, Nuh-Nuh, Nuh, Nuh, Nuhhh, Nuhhhhh).
[414] Similar to widening the lane and eliminating offensive goaltending due to Wilt Chamberlain's dominance of the sport of basketball.

a Game 7 start, just missing out on capping his amazing season. Of course, earlier that series, in Game 1, Gibson set a World Series record with 17 strikeouts.

Finally, Gibson was one of the fieriest dudes in MLB history. Of his own pitching repertoire, Gibson said, "It was said that I threw, basically five pitches – fastball, slider, curve, change-up. And knockdown. I don't believe that assessment did me justice, though. I actually used about nine pitches- two different fastballs, two sliders, a curve, a change-up, knockdown, brushback, and hit-batsman." His competitive nature was apparently not limited to baseball either. "I've played a couple of hundred games of ticktacktoe with my little daughter, and she hasn't beaten me yet," Gibson said. "I've always had to win. I've got to win." It is then surprising that, before his baseball career, he had a brief career with Harlem Globetrotters, one of the most fun-loving acts in sports. Although, given that they win every game, maybe it was a good fit.

CP Dizzy Dean (1930; 1932-1937)

One of baseball's most famous characters, Dean was in fact used out of the bullpen at times for the Cardinals during his time there. Though predominantly a starter, Dean led the league in saves in 1936, and he finished off over 10 games every year from 1932-1936.

Lists of Dean's famous stories have been filling baseball books for ages and could easily fill up the next 20 pages, but I'll try to focus on a few gems here. He, on more than one occasion, had fielders drop foul pop-ups so that he could then strike out the batter – and he usually succeeded. One such story goes that Dean bet that he would strike out Vince DiMaggio when the two played. Dean even went as far as to say he would strike him out not once, not twice, not three times, but four times. Of course, Dean got him to strike out the first three times, so when DiMaggio came up for his fourth at bat and Dean got ahead no balls and two strikes, you can imagine what happened. DiMaggio hit a pop fly in foul territory and Dean screamed for his catcher to drop it, which the backstop did, for some reason. Dean struck him out on the next pitch. Although the story itself may seem difficult to solidify, Dean did indeed strike Vince DiMaggio out four times on May 5, 1937, the first time the two met. Dean also once reportedly hit seven consecutive batters in a spring training game after giving up a big inning prior to that in the game – he didn't take losing well.

Dean was quite the showman during his time in the big leagues. In 1934, he put on quite a scene when his manager fined him for missing the team's train. Dean's response was to shred his jersey in front of his manager in a show of his anger. Not only did Dean do this for his manager, however, he also went to the trouble of shredding yet another jersey in front of the media. As a result, he was fined $36 – $18 for each jersey. Somewhere, Chris Sale smiled.

Dean once told umpire William McKinley, "Why, they shot the wrong McKinley," after disagreeing on a call with the veteran ump. Not too many ball players could get away with that, but Dean and his fourth-grade education seemed to get away with a lot.

Dizzy may well have been able to get away with running his mouth a bit because he could turn it on himself, if need be. In his own words, "The doctors X-rayed my head and found nothing." He also was able to back up what he said. In addition to the Vince DiMaggio story above, there is the story of how, before the 1934 season, Dizzy predicted he and his brother would combine for 45 wins, which would set a record for a pair of brothers. Dizzy and Paul responded with 49 combined wins that season, 30 of which came from Dizzy.

Writers undoubtedly had their fair share of pot shots about Dean (not the least of which dealt with his brains), but they also knew how to heap on the praise. Jim Murray of the *L.A. Times* said of Dean, "Someone gave him a baseball, and it was like giving Caesar a sword or Napoleon a cannon."

Late in his career, baseball's Napoleon found himself on Elba, as he suffered multiple injuries that robbed him of his once-great talent. What started off as arm injuries eventually resulted in toe injuries after he rushed back too quickly. This didn't stop Dean from sticking around the game of baseball. If we continue the Napoleon analogy, Dean had his escape from Elba in the form of announcing, but he never had to deal with the Seventh Coalition that Bonaparte did, going on to a successful post-playing career. As an announcer, Dean continued his tradition of being one of the best quotes in baseball, making up words left and right, much to the chagrin of any baseball fan in the field of education, but to the joy of everyone else.

Starting IX Franchise Roster Stats

Lineup	Yrs	G	R	H	HR	RBI	SB	BB	SO	BA	OBP	SLG	OPS+	dWAR	WAR
Lou Brock	16	2289	1427	2713	129	814	**888**	681	**1469**	0.297	0.347	0.414	112	-16.3	41.6
Rogers Hornsby	13	1580	1089	2110	193	1072	118	660	480	0.359	0.427	0.568	177	10.9	91.4
Stan Musial	**22**	**3026**	**1949**	**3630**	**475**	**1951**	78	**1599**	696	0.331	0.417	0.559	159	-9.3	**128.1**
Albert Pujols	11	1705	1291	2073	445	1329	84	975	704	0.328	0.420	0.617	170	2.7	86.4
Jim Edmonds	8	1105	690	1033	241	713	37	645	1029	0.285	0.393	0.555	143	3.7	37.8
Ken Boyer	11	1667	988	1855	255	1001	97	631	859	0.293	0.356	0.475	119	10.3	58.0
Ted Simmons	13	1564	736	1704	172	929	11	624	453	0.298	0.366	0.459	127	8.0	44.8
Enos Slaughter	13	1820	1071	2064	146	1148	64	838	429	0.305	0.384	0.463	126	-6.4	50.3
Ozzie Smith	15	1990	991	1944	27	664	433	876	423	0.272	0.350	0.344	93	**34.6**	65.6
Pitchers	Yrs	W	W%	ERA	G	CG	SHO	SV	IP	SO	ERA+	WHIP	SO/9	SO/BB	WAR
Bob Gibson	17	**251**	0.591	2.91	528	**255**	**56**	6	**3884.1**	**3117**	127	1.188	7.2	2.33	**81.9**
Dizzy Dean	7	134	0.641	2.99	273	141	23	31	1737.1	1095	132	1.204	5.7	2.69	38.5

#3 Boston Red Sox (1908- pres.); Boston Americans (1901-1908)

(Photo from Wikimedia Commons)

Team Background

Playoff appearances: 23 **Pennants: 13** **World Series titles: 8**
Collective team WAR: 614.9
Strengths: Arguments could easily be made for the best hitter in MLB history and the best pitcher in MLB history residing on this Starting IX.
Weaknesses: This high up in the rankings we're really starting to reach for weaknesses. Not having a ring for 86 years, I suppose?
What to expect from the next 20 pages: A typical Saturday night: it starts with a half-hearted apology and ends with a three-way that somehow includes Roger Clemens.

The Red Sox franchise has been in existence with their current nickname for the sixth-longest of any team in organized baseball.[415] They have eight world championships, most notably going 86 years between their 1918 and 2004 World Series wins. Between those titles, the Sawks were one measly strike away from a ring on 13 separate occasions.

In 1946, the Red Sox and Cardinals played in a Game 7 of the World Series, and the Sawks tied the game with two runs in the top of the eighth. Of course, they gave away the game in the bottom of the inning. In 1975, they got to Game 7, and even saw their win expectancy reach 90 percent in the fifth inning, before falling behind and losing to the Reds. Just 11 years later, the Sox suffered what many consider their harshest fate, when they let Game 6 slip after reaching a win

[415] Only the Phillies (1890), the Pirates (1891), the Cardinals (1900), the Tigers (1901), the White Sox (1901), and the Cubs (1903) have kept their name and location longer. Of those teams, only the Tigers and White Sox have never had a location or nickname change.

expectancy of 99 percent (!) in the tenth inning. Poor Bill Buckner. Even in the ensuing Game 7, they had an 88 percent chance of winning as late as the sixth inning. Then there's 2003, at which point Red Sox nation as a whole was catatonic. Obviously, enough has been written about the team breaking the curse so we won't go into too much detail about it here.

The Sox were able to win again in 2007 and 2013, and a city that didn't have a baseball championship for over eight decades has now become one of MLB's perennial contenders. Of course, along with that success, came droves of additional fans. Bros who thought Manny and Papi were a new Comedy Central duo, and bro-ettes in pink hats who thought The Bloody Sock was a new horror film – the dreaded bandwagon fans.

But hold on Red Sox fans, I'm not bringing this up (entirely) as a dig on your fanbase. I'm actually going to try to make the case for bandwagon fans. Or at least try to make the case that they should not be as hated as they are in the modern sports world. Which is quite hated.

The Harder Case: The Bandwagon Apologist

This is the harder of the two cases to make, so let's lead off with it. In my mind, the more common bandwagon fan these days globs onto a great player more than a great team. I know this is a baseball book, but the best example is LeBron James. Fans who liked him in Cleveland, then in Miami, and then in Cleveland again, get massacred. That's ridiculous, though. These fans are simply rooting to see greatness. By cheering for LeBron every stop of the way, they're simply cheering to witness history. By cheering for the best players, bandwagon fans aren't trying to skip the hard parts of being a fan, they're trying to be able to one day say that they saw the Greatest Of All Time. The bandwagon fan cheers for LeBron (or Alex Rodriguez or Peyton Manning) not out of ease (trust me, I'm a LeBron apologist, and I'm also the guy who turns MLB video games up a level too hard because I'd rather finish .500 than win every game 15-3), or an inability to handle losing, instead they cheer for the best because these players are simply that – the best. Being able to bear witness to greatness, and then tell the stories of that greatness to future generations, is one of the longest-standing rituals in sports. The in-moment bandwagon fan is torn apart; whereas, the historical bandwagon fan (the guy who in the present time says Bill Russell is the greatest NBA player of all time, or that Barry Bonds is no Babe Ruth) is completely accepted. In a way, the historical bandwagon fan is worse. He/she is simply stuck in his/her outdated thoughts, unwilling to accept the times. Yes, we need to pay our dues to the guys who don't appear on our TV screen every night, but don't worry, Russell and Ruth aren't going to fade from our memory anytime soon. It would be one thing if these historical bandwagon fans were promoting under-the-radar dudes like Bobby Grich or Gary Payton. But no, the typical anti-bandwagon fan is someone who honestly doesn't know enough about sports to form their own opinions, and so instead relies on their antiquated ideas of how sports should be followed via an inability to keep up with the times. [*Consider this shots fired.*]

The Slightly Easier Case: The Bandwagon Agnostic

This case is easier to make and it's also much simpler. Like, two sentences simple. Bandwagon fans – the name-mispronouncing, brand-new-t-shirt-wearing ones – by their very nature, don't invest as much into the team. Therefore, when the team eventually does win – and the fans start apparating faster than a group of Death Eaters after seeing the Dark Mark – the joy they get from the team's victory is a mere shell of the joy that the long-suffering, dedicated fan will have.

A bandwagon fan wasn't tuning into every crummy 7-3 loss during late August, a month and a half after the team got eliminated a few seasons prior. They don't know the background story of Player X, who made big Play Y, and just how much it means to that player. They didn't dedicate hours upon hours of their life each week to deep-diving into the blogosphere, reading up on every asinine theory as to why Player Z is mired in a 2-for-20 slump. As a result, they don't get nearly the same satisfaction. Life/Karma/God, whatever you want to call it, works that way. Unless you have your own personal enjoyment lowered by a bandwagon fan (which hopefully has been proven silly by this point), you, "The True Fan," will be exponentially happier than any bandwagon fan could ever be as a result of your team's success. And let's be honest. We can all spot the bandwagon fan. It's the 2005 Red Sox fan who can't pronounce Bronson Arroyo's name; it's the 2010 Yankee fan who thinks Mickey Mantle is a fast food restaurant; it's the 2012 Giants fan who doesn't know what a "McCovey Cove" is. There's simply no fun in calling them out.

Isn't the goal of sports for us to take enjoyment out of them? Who are you or I to judge how someone decides to participate in the act of following sports? Who are we to try and cut them down because of their approach? C'mon folks, it's time to give up the ghost with the whole scorn-the-bandwagon-fan thing.

Random cool things about the franchise:

- Nothing.

Starting IX

C Jason Varitek (1997-2011)

Carlton Fisk and Jason Varitek were the two main competitors for the Red Sox backstop, but Varitek takes the spot for a few reasons. First, and this has been a tenant of choosing players throughout the book, is his team loyalty. Varitek played his entire major league career with the Red Sox, while Fisk bleached his socks and headed to the South Side of Chicago in 1981.[416] The main reason, though, is that, despite the premise of this book, judging a player has more elements than just stats. In this case, Varitek was the captain of two championship teams,[417] and his two of his best playoff series were the 2004 ALCS and the 2007 World Series; two pretty important series.

Varitek is the only player ever to have played in the Little League World Series, the College World Series, the MLB World Series, the Olympics, and the World Baseball Classic – a classic all-American boy. He trails only David Ortiz in franchise postseason games played (63), and he is tied with Carlos Ruiz for the MLB record by being on the receiving end of four no-hitters. On a far more serious note (aka far less serious), he also punched A-Rod and is rumored to have slept with a certain NESN sideline reporter. Hint: it's not Gary Striewski. He embodied the very idea of both Boston and the Red Sox for his entire career, and although his statistics may trail Fisk by a decent margin (Fisk totaled over 15.0 more WAR in four fewer seasons), Varitek was a leader, and in 'MURICA we love leaders.

1B Jimmie Foxx (1936-1942)

Foxx played only six-plus seasons with the Red Sox, but he made quite an impact. This, of course, makes sense, seeing as he was one of the all-time greats. Proof that they just really don't do nicknames as well as they used to, Foxx claimed two nicknames: Beast and Double X. Either of these would rank among the best in the league now. In fact, let's look at the best nicknames of all time, Starting IX style:

C) Gary "The Kid" Carter; 1B) Jimmie "Beast," "Double X" Foxx; 2B) Luke "Old Aches and Pains" Appling; 3B) Wade "The Chicken Man" Boggs; SS) Honus "The Flying Dutchman" Wagner; LF) Stan "The Man" Musial; CF) Tris "The Grey Eagle" Speaker; RF) Babe "The Sultan of Swat," "The King of Crash," "The Colossus of Clout," "The Great Bambino!"[418] Ruth; Utility) "Shoeless Joe" Jackson; SP1) Randy "The Big Unit" Johnson; SP2) Whitey "The Chairman of the Board" Ford; SP3) Bob "The Heater from Van Meter" Feller; RP) "El Guapo"[419]

In his six full seasons with the Red Sox, Foxx put up average seasons of 117 runs, 36 home runs, and 129 RBI with .321/.431/.609 slashes. Because Foxx debuted at age 17, he is high up on many "youngest to do (blank)" lists, many of which focus on his mighty swing. Through his age-32 season, Foxx had 500 home runs. To pick that in perspective, through their respective age-32 seasons: Albert Pujols had 475 home runs, Junior Griffey had 468, Mickey Mantle had 454, Sammy Sosa had 450, Eddie Mathews had 445, Hank Aaron had 442, Babe Ruth had 416, and Willie Mays had 406. In fact, in all of baseball history, only A-Rod (518) had more long balls through his age-32 season than Foxx.

Although Foxx was productive in his time with Boston, when the Red Sox got him, he was 28 years old and fresh off four consecutive 8.0+ WAR seasons. When this is considered, the Red Sox actually probably got a little less than they had hoped for when they acquired him. Despite being just about ready to enter his prime in 1935 (age 28), Foxx went from averaging 8.0 WAR (i.e. *averaging* an MVP-level season) for the six years before the incident, to averaging 6.2 WAR the next six years and *totaling* just 4.7 WAR after those six years. His WAR/season broken down by age:

Age range	WAR/season
21-27	8.0
28-33	6.3
34-38*	1.2

* Foxx did sit out all of 1943 and most of 1944, as a 36 and 37-year-old, respectively

Whatever the reason was – and it has been speculated on throughout baseball history – Foxx wasn't able to keep healthy, or in good playing condition, in his later playing days. Sadly, his career trajectory came crashing down almost as fast as it had risen two decades before. One theory stems from an incident in a game during an offseason barnstorming session in

[416] Fisk also switched from number 27 to number 72 when switching Sox.
[417] Technically, he was named captain just after their 2004 title, but he most certainly earned that "C" in part because of the Red Sox 2004 World Series run.
[418] Oh, *Sandlot*, good memories.
[419] I refuse to admit that El Guapo has an actual name. Also, an impressive amount of Sox players on that list.

Canada, a common offseason activity for players in Foxx's generation. Foxx wasn't wearing a batting helmet and was hit in the head with a pitch. The x-ray showed nothing too serious, "just" a concussion, but based on what little was known about head injuries before even a decade ago, it's fair to surmise that Foxx's injury may have been more serious than thought at the time. It most certainly could have played a large role in the precipitous decline in Foxx's production.[420]

Those who knew Foxx said that, after his head injury, he turned to alcohol to dull the lingering pain, pain not just from his head injury, but from all the injuries he accumulated over the years. He would often drink instead of going to see a team doctor, who he believed would have him sit out of games, something he thought he couldn't afford to do. One of the great "What If's" in baseball history comes from Bill Jenkinson in the 2013 edition of *The National Pastime*: What if Foxx had been wearing a helmet that game? Would we have a different all-time home run leader? That seems like a stretch, but looking at the previously-noted home runs by age statistics, it suddenly doesn't seem as absurd. Foxx would almost certainly be higher in the pantheon of legends had he been able to accumulate stats a bit longer towards the end of his career.

Back to the positives: one man who was always impressed by Foxx was his American League counterpart, Lefty Gomez. We already saw one of Gomez's quotes on Foxx in the A's write-up, but Gomez had two other classic quotes about Foxx: "When Neil Armstrong first set foot on the moon, he and all the space scientists were puzzled by an unidentifiable white object," Gomez said. "I knew immediately what it was. That was a home run ball hit off me in 1937 by Jimmie Foxx." And even more straightforward: "[Foxx] has muscles in his hair."

These are but two of many quotes regarding Foxx's strength, not the least of which is dealt with in Bill James' *Abstract*. James breaks down the likelihood of an oft-told anecdote regarding Foxx in which he (Foxx, not James) shows off his natural strength to a baseball scout (no less than an authority than Home Run Baker) by pointing out the local baseball field by lifting up the plow he was farming with and directing the scout with the aforementioned plow. James' conclusion is that, because of Foxx's strength, this story isn't really out of the realm of possibility, but it seems too rehearsed to be real. I feel that I have done a thorough job in researching this book, but so much of baseball history is so deeply steeped in lore that it can be difficult at times to make sure of certain anecdotes. The best way to read baseball history is usually with a grain of salt. Sometimes an exaggerated tale about a player can say as much about how his teammates and the public thought of him as a true one can. This story of Foxx's strength is a prime example of the story's factuality not being as important as the fact that his raw power was so immense that it allowed this story to be believable by the general public.

2B Bobby Doerr (1937-1951)

Doerr was never a dominant force for the Red Sox, but he proved to be a steady, upper-echelon second baseman for the team in the 1940s. He is one of the most underappreciated players of all time, a man whose pedigree built as time went on and more stories about him emerged.[421] No less an authority than teammate Ted Williams called Doerr "the silent captain of the Red Sox." No less a baseball titan than Babe Ruth said, "Doerr, and not Ted Williams, is the number one player on [the Red Sox]." Ruth said that after Doerr posted a .409 batting average in a seven-game loss to the Cardinals in the 1946 World Series. This effort came one year after Doerr gave up a year of his professional baseball career to join the war effort.

Doerr was a strong fielder, leading second basemen in range factor four seasons, including 1946 when he also led the league in dWAR and probably would have won the Gold Glove had it existed. (The Gold Glove came into existence in 1957.) Doerr reminds me of Sam Jones from the Bill Russell-era Celtics. Bill Russell and Ted Williams were the faces of each Boston franchise, and no one would refer to either team as the "Sam Jones Celtics" or the "Bobby Doerr Red Sox," but both players were there, acting as the driving force behind those talented rosters. They were the ones that always seemed to step up in the clutch, and they were silent leaders in the locker room/clubhouse. This type of player has a certain allure to most hardcore fans. Anyone can root for "Teddy Ball Game" or "The Secretary of Defense," but a true fan finds the Jones' and Doerr's of the game and locks them in as their favorites.[422] Unfortunately, Doerr's career was cut short by injuries at the age of 33.

Which is why there needs to be a bit of debate for this spot. Listen: you had to know it had been far too long since a strange gimmick made its way into these pages. So, let's do this dance. When my uncle – who is a diehard Red Sox fan and probably the most-informed baseball fan who I talk to on a regular basis – read the Red Sox chapter, he had one suggestion. *You gotta have Pedroia at second base*. Now because I respect his opinion quite highly (and because it could make for a strange, yet-to-be-used literary tactic), I decided to tape record him one day when the conversation came up. Here it is:

Jim Turvey: "Give me your direct pitch for Pedroia."

Geoff Oehling: "Well, one: I'd say sports are result-driven. Those championships, those are a big thing. In the end, he had to face the same adversity that Doerr did. Because Manny, like Ted Williams for Bobby Doerr, is an issue in the clubhouse. To the media, at least. I think he's actually a great guy in the clubhouse but the media doesn't see that. So Pedroia has the same responsibilities in the clubhouse as Doerr – the grinder, the dirt dog. What's Doerr's height and weight?"

---

[420] Even in the modern era, Justin Morneau's career was never the same after his concussions.

[421] If you look at his votes received for the Hall of Fame, it is in almost perpetual increase until his induction in 1986 by the Veteran's Committee.

[422] It's the "Hipster Effect" of sports. And basically the antithesis to my Bandwagon Apologist section at the beginning of this chapter.

[*Minute to look it up*]

JT: He's 5'11" and 175 lbs. In an era of smaller players, too.

GO: Yeah, to be honest, that's one of the things that makes Pedroia one of the top Sox to ever play. Above even Williams, maybe. Williams at least looks like a man. And looks like he can hit. And he's got the military background. Pedroia, they made fun of when he showed up. And the start to his career is a shit show that somehow – if this had happened in Anaheim, people in Anaheim are not that personality. Even if he put up the same numbers, they would say *Oh he's a great player*, but does he represent Anaheim that much? But Boston, Boston is filled with short, aggressive men who think that they can hit almost .400 in a season. Somehow, he is the guy who wills himself to do shit."

So, you know I'm all about giving the readers autonomy. Geoff laid out some pretty solid points there, but I'm not going to fully accept defeat. Let's just say I wouldn't be too surprised if Pedroia takes the spot without a challenge in the second edition for myriad reasons.

3B Wade Boggs (1982-1992)

Boggs started his career with the Red Sox and played with the club for 11 seasons until signing with the New York Yankees in free agency. The Red Sox-Yankees rivalry is among the most historic in baseball and, as such, making the switch from one club to the other in free agency is a pretty rare thing. However, as of late, this rivalry has seemed a little lackluster, as the players seem more cordial than caddy, and they are chummier than ever. We see the same thing throughout most sports today,[423] and it's a trend that has been covered by many sports writers. The general feeling is that because many of today's athletes grew up playing AAU together, they no longer feel the need to be hyper-competitive when they become professionals on opposing sides. I agree with this to a certain extent, but I think part of it has to do with historical context.

When looking back at the history of rivalries, they can be compared to human evolution, in the sense that both usually have long periods of stasis punctuated by positive outbursts. I mean this to say: not every rivalry game from yesteryears included fights, or crazy walk-offs, or players truly hating each other, but a few instances created this illusion. In today's society, where everyone is able to react in a tenth of a billionth of a second, the only way we could have "true rivals" would be if Dustin Pedroia and Nick Swisher had a gladiatorial battle before each game.[424] I think the Red Sox-Yankees rivalry is just fine, it just needs another ALCS to have it showcased (my guess is 2019).

Back to Boggs: he won the American League batting title five of the first six years he was eligible, and he would have won it his rookie year if he had enough plate appearances to qualify. In fact, he set the rookie record for batting average in his freshman campaign (.349). His first year was a sign of great things to come. In his 65th career plate appearance, Boggs reached a .328 average, a career figure that he would never drop below again *for his entire career*.[425] He had seven consecutive 200-hit, 100-run seasons, the only man to do so until Ichiro Suzuki did so in his first eight seasons. In 1985, Boggs had 240 hits to go along with 96 walks. When his four hit by pitches were added, it made him one of only four players in history (along with Babe Ruth, Lou Gehrig, and Ted Williams) to reach base 340 times in a season. This is a remarkable number of times on base, especially considering that, just seven years later, no major leaguer had even 340 *total* bases.

Boggs also had a hidden .400 batting average season. From June 13, 1985 to June 8, 1986, the Red Sox played 162 games. In the 160 games that Boggs played during that stretch, he hit .400 on the dot. For his career, Boggs has some great totals, but he really made his biggest impact in his first eight years. Through this eight-year stretch to start his career, Boggs had a .352 average, which would have been good for fourth all time if he had retired then. As is, his career .328 average is the highest of any third baseman in the 20th century, and the best all-time for any player with at least 800 games at third base.

Boggs, somewhat like Ichiro, had the reputation of being a contact hitter by choice rather than a lack of power. Boggs supposedly crushed his fellow power-hitting teammates Jim Rice and Carlton Fisk in batting practice home run derby, putting on impressive displays for the fans who showed up early to watch batting practice. He may have even saved a bit of that power for a special moment, as he became the first player in MLB history to hit a home run for his 3000th hit, doing so on August 7, 1999. He also put as much (or more) fear into pitchers across the league, as his 180 career intentional walks rank higher than Mark McGwire (150), Sammy Sosa (154), Frank Thomas (168), and Jim Thome (173).

(By the way, this is too absurd for a footnote: Barry Bonds [688] easily has more than twice as many intentional walks than Albert Pujols [307] and Hank Aaron [293], who rank second and third respectively in career intentional walks – Bonds put the true fear of God into his opposition.)

Boggs had a great batting eye overall, getting plenty of walks without the help of the opposing pitcher. He notoriously very rarely took swings early in the count, and the advanced stats back it up. Data to back this up is only available back to 1988, but for his five seasons in Boston for which we have the data, his pitches per plate appearance were 4.16 compared to 3.67 league average; his swinging strike rate was 3 percent to 15 percent league average; his percent of pitches swung at was 35 percent to 46 percent league average; his contact rate was 94 percent to 80 percent league average;

---

[423] Although old schoolers like Kevin Garnett and the rest of the post-Decision Celtics' hate for the LeBron-era Heat were certainly holdouts.

[424] How great of a cage match would that be? Pedroia would absolutely go through with killing Swisher if he were able to avoid going full-on "laser show" (insane) from the playful taunts of Swisher.

[425] Another gem from the Ace of MLB Stats twitter feed (@theaceofspaeder).

and his first pitch swinging percentage was 6 percent to 31 percent league average. The difference from league average is incredible in some of these statistics, and it really shows just how disciplined Boggs was as a hitter. Just a reminder, those five years weren't even his best in a Red Sox uniform. This discipline hardly stopped during the game itself, as Boggs took batting practice at 5:17 every day, practically defining "creature-of-habit."

Boggs was not just a disciplined creature-of-habit in the batter's box, though, he ate chicken every single day as part of his diet/superstition. Boggs also had a proclivity to stay busy in another room in his house, leading to David Letterman's classic quip: "According to *The Sporting News*, over the last four years, Wade Boggs hit .800 with women in scoring position." On a different, hopefully more impressive note, Boggs reached base safely in 80 percent of his career games, a remarkable total.

Everything that has just been written about Boggs is impressive, but you all know where we're ending this – with the most impressive Boggs anecdote: supposedly, Boggs would regularly put down multiple (multiple!) cases (cases!) of Bud Light on cross-country flights during his playing days. The story came out when Jeff Nelson was asked on 710 ESPN Radio which of his teammates drank the most beer, and he said Boggs, easily. Nelson told host Steve Sandmeyer (who deserves an EGOT simply for the question that led to this revelation) that Boggs would drink 50-60 beers on cross-country flights. Sandmeyer was naturally skeptical, so they called another ex-teammate of Boggs, who, unprompted, offered the number at 70 (70!!!) beers in a single cross-country flight. Insanity.

Naturally, Boggs' most famous non-baseball moment came on a show centered around a bar. His guest appearance on *Cheers* played a role in the episode "Bar Wars" being the highest-rated episode in the show's illustrious history.

SS Nomar Garciaparra (1996-2004)

NOMAHHH! For nearly a decade, Sawks fans relished in cheering for their short stawp whose name couldn't have fit the city he played in any bettah.[426] It's pretty funny that his "nickname" – really just his name said with a Boston accent – is officially listed as "Nomah" on Baseball-Reference. Nomar was more than just a fun name, though, he won two straight batting titles (1999-2000) with a combined .365 batting average and an OPS over 1.000 each year. These two years came on the heels of his MVP runner-up in 1998 and a Rookie of the Year victory in 1997. After the 2003 season, he was regarded with Derek Jeter and Alex Rodriguez as the future of the shortstop position in baseball; bringing power, average, and a good glove to a position thought of as lacking in dominant hitters.

Nomar struggled with injuries throughout his career, however and, after the 2003 season, rumors were abound that the Red Sox front office had a big ole man crush on Alex Rodriguez, making Nomar available to the rest of the league. Adam Vaccaro of BostonSportsThenAndNow.com has an excellent piece in which he chronicles the quite interesting dismissal of Nomar, and the curse that hit the Red Sox shortstop position after Garciaparra was traded to the Cubs at the 2004 trade deadline. Vaccaro really sold me by comparing their struggles to find a replacement to the struggle to keep a Defense Against the Dark Arts professor at Hogwarts. It also got me thinking. After Nomar left there were innumerable shortstops in Boston, but the main ones were Pokey Reese, Edgar Renteria, Alex González, Julio Lugo, Nick Green, Marco Scutaro, and Stephen Drew. Mike Aviles, Orlando Cabrera, Alex Cora, and Jed Lowrie also made appearances at the accursed position, but none held the position long enough to be considered a legitimate part of the shortstop curse. So, let's play a little matching game with the seven Defense Against the Dark Arts professors and the seven Red Sox shortstops.

Quirinius Quirrell – Nick Green: A solid first half of the year for both went south rapidly in the latter stages of the year. In Quirrell's case, it was the reader empathizing with his stutter in the start of the book; for Green, it was slashing .262/.321/.434 before the All-Star break. Of course, Quirrell ended up being a vessel for Lord Voldemort, while Green slashed .206/.284/.290 after the Midsummer Classic. Not sure which was worse.

Gilderoy Lockhart – Alex González: Both were flashy on the surface (Lockhart with his books and looks, Gonzo with his defense), but they were one-trick ponies who were exposed for frauds before the end of the year.

Remus Lupin – Marco Scutaro: Both were misunderstood creatures who were probably the best of their respective bunch at the Defense Against the Dark Arts/Red Sox shortstop positions. I don't know about you, but I've never seen Scutaro play shortstop during a full moon…

Mad-Eye Moody (Bartemius Crouch Jr.) – Stephen Drew: This is the most obvious connection. Both went over to the dark side after.

Dolores Umbridge – Pokey Reese: Just unequivocally the worst.

Severus Snape – Edgar Renteria: Obviously, Renteria is nowhere near Snape's level of character depth, but he does bring to mind the "one that got away" idea with the D.A.D.A. position and Snape. Renteria came to the Sox as a 28-year-old four-time All-Star and didn't do that poorly in his year in Boston. He scored 100 runs and hit .276. However, he was traded that offseason for cash and Andy Marte, a move the Sox surely rued, as Renteria slashed .310/.374/.451 the next two seasons, while the Sox watched Alex González and Julio Lugo set a tire fire to the position of shortstop in Boston. Snape was always the perfect fit for the D.A.D.A. position, and it was one that he lusted after. Sure, Renteria had a lot of errors, and sure we all

[426] I was tempted to write this whole entry in a Boston accent, but it was just painful to read.

thought Snape was evil for a while, but as Renteria's dWAR and Snape's love for Lilly both proved, you can't judge a book by its cover.

Amycus Carrow – Julio Lugo: Yes, both of these things actually happened.

With Xander Bogaerts looking like a potential All-Star shortstop – and certainly the long-term solution at short – it looks like the Sox may have finally broken the curse, a fitting end given that J.K. Rowling noted in the epilogue of *Deathly Hallows* that the D.A.D.A. position was no longer cursed after Voldemort was vanquished.

Putting a bow on the Nomar section: in a classy move by the organization, before Nomar left the game of baseball, the Red Sox signed him to a one-day contract, allowing him to retire with the team he loved so much.

LF Ted Williams (1939-1960)

Maybe the most stacked position for any team in history, it makes it even more impressive that Williams wins here without even needing a breakdown. Sure, Carl Yastrzemski and Jim Rice[427] get some credit for their dominant play in historic Fenway left field, but when you look at the numbers, it's clear Williams gets an easy nod for the start. Williams had a *career* OPS+ of 190, a figure topped in only one season by Rice and Yaz combined (Yaz's 1967 MVP season, the last Triple Crown before Miguel Cabrera won it in 2012). That figure trails only Babe Ruth in all of baseball history. Despite missing three years of his prime,[428] Williams still ranks first in Red Sox history in home runs and only barely trails Yaz in runs and RBI, despite playing four fewer seasons. Williams won six batting titles to Yaz's three and Rice's zero; he led the league in runs six times, the other two did so three times combined; he led in home runs four times, equal to the Yaz Rice combination; Williams led in RBI four times, to three combined for YazRice. The most impressive thing might be that, barring his rookie year and his final two seasons, every year Williams qualified for the on-base percentage title, he won it. His career on-base percentage is .482, or 30 points better than any season Yaz or Rice ever had, and a figure that would be good for 43rd on the all-time *single-season* on-base percentage list. A list that, oh by the way, contains seven of Ted Williams' own seasons ahead of that .482 mark.[429] In fact, since 1901, only Babe Ruth, Mickey Mantle, Rogers Hornsby, and Barry Bonds were able to top Williams' career .482 mark in multiple seasons.

The only on-field negative to "Thumper's" career is that the Red Sox never won a World Series with Williams. They were often behind the Yankees, and with only one team making the playoffs from the American League at the time, the Sox visited the Fall Classic only once in Williams' time with the team – their 1946 World Series loss to the Cardinals. "The Splendid Splinter" hit just .200 for the seven-game series, failing to collect a single extra-base hit and tallying only three RuBIns. However, this shouldn't take away from the career of Williams. Baseball is the ultimate team sport, so being expected to carry a team to a championship is not a fair way of assessing a career.

A much more accurate way of judging a career is by an elite six-year stretch. Six years is a long enough period of dominance that the players with the best six-year stretches in their careers, are some of the all-time greats. Let's take a look at the candidates for this breakdown. Honorable Mention: Ty Cobb 1910-1915, Stan Musial 1948-1953, Mike Trout 2012-2017, Mickey Mantle 1956-1961, Albert Pujols 2004-2009, Alex Rodriguez 2000-2005, Barry Bonds 1999-2004, Joe Morgan 1972-1977, and Honus Wagner 1904-1909. Here are the finalists:

Statistics

Name	Years	G	R	H	HR	XBH	RBI	SB	BA	OBP	SLG
Hornsby	1920-25	845	711	**1296**	153	489	692	55	**.397**	.467	.666
Ruth	1919-24	839	**826**	1048	**264**	**551**	773	66	.363	.503	**.759**
Williams	1941-49	891	817	1110	211	468	**780**	10	.359	**.505**	.657
Mays	1960-65	**940**	720	1090	255	465	693	**97**	.310	.386	.598

Advanced Statistics

Name	Year	WAR	WAA	OPS+	>lgBA	>lgOBP	>lgSLG
Hornsby	1920-25	58.8	47.9	201	**.107**	.121	.264
Ruth	1919-24	**65.0**	**53.2**	**227**	.070	.143	**.354**
Williams	1941-49	58.1	48.3	208	.084	**.149**	.261
Mays	1960-65	59.6	46.3	169	.048	.061	.201

[427] And to a lesser extent (read: shorter amount of time), Manny Ramírez.

[428] Later in his career, Williams also missed basically all of 1952 and most of 1953 due to the Korean War.

[429] I feel like that sentence just ripped open a hole in the space-time continuum, *Donnie Darko*-style. Or suddenly a retired Ted Williams saw his statistics fading in his family scrapbook like Marty McFly.

League-Leading Comparison

Name	R	HR	RBI	BA	OBP	SLG	OPS+	WAR	oWAR	BB	TB	H	2B	3B	MVP
Hornsby	3	2	**4**	**6**	**6**	**6**	**6**	4	**6**	1	**5**	**4**	**4**	**1**	1
Ruth	**5**	**5**	**4**	1	5	**6**	**6**	**5**	5	4	4	X	X	X	1
Williams	**5**	4	3	5	**6**	**6**	**6**	**5**	**6**	**6**	4	X	2	X	**2**
Mays	1	3	X	X	1	2	2	**5**	3	X	2	1	X	X	1

Team/Player Postseason Success

Name	Year	R	HR	RBI	BA	OBP	SLG	Pennants	WS
Hornsby	1920-25	X	X	X	X	X	X	X	X
Ruth	1919-24	**12**	**4**	**8**	**.269**	**.420**	**.652**	**3**	**1**
Williams	1941-49	2	0	1	.200	.333	.200	1	X
Mays	1960-65	3	0	1	.250	.276	.321	1	X

One very interesting note is the limited team success any of these players had during their dominant reigns. Ruth had the most, winning three pennants, but he still won only one World Series (an especially low total given the dominance of the Yankees in the 1920s), and he didn't perform *that* well in the World Series he did reach. It just goes as further proof that baseball is truly a sport in which much more than one dominant player is needed.

Mays made the cut because of his excellent WAR totals for those six years, and if this were a measure of the most consistent over a six-year stretch, he would probably take it. But he didn't have the league domination that the other three had, barely leading the league in any of the statistical categories listed, so he's the first eliminated.

The final three players truly dominated the time in which they played. The ironic part of this is that Ruth and Hornsby had their periods of dominance at pretty much the same time. This was a time during which hitters were beginning to have more success, and these two were at the forefront at that revolution.

Of the three, Hornsby had the lowest power numbers, but he was the best hitter by average, most notably coming just three points shy of hitting .400 for the entire six year stretch.[430] This was not just a product of the times, as he won all six batting titles and finished with an average more than 100 points higher than league average during those six years. His .424 batting average in 1924 is the highest post-1900 average of all time, and only three players have been able to top that magical .400 cutoff since. One of them is the man he is going against, Ted Williams, who was the most recent, in 1941. Bill Terry also did it in 1930, and Hornsby, himself, did it again in 1925. Despite the batting average advantage, Hornsby trails Williams and Ruth by a decent margin in on-base percentage, thanks to Ruth and Williams both having reached base more than half the time they stepped into the batter's box for their respective six-year stretches – incredible. An on-base percentage over .500 sounds impressive on its own, but here's just how impressive it is: since 1900 only three men[431] outside of Ruth and Williams have had that high an on-base percentage in a single year, let alone compiled over six years. The fact that Hornsby's strongest suit was reaching base, and Ruth and Williams both topped him in doing so during their own six-year stretches, means Hornsby is eliminated.

Now it's down to Ruth and Williams, and by the numbers, Ruth seems to hold a small advantage. He has slightly better power numbers (having hit 53 more home runs, and his slugging compared to league average is insane). Plus, his WAR totals are a bit higher. Two things in Williams favor: first, Ruth had a contemporary on this list who was nearly as dominant during the same exact period of time. Hornsby was destroying the NL while Ruth destroyed the AL.[432] Williams didn't have any contemporary players on his level of dominance. The closest was Stan Musial, but his prime was slightly after Williams, and Williams' prime was better than Musial's. Although holding Hornsby against Ruth should not be a main determining factor, it does play a role when Williams and Ruth are so close. The second factor has more of an impact: Williams went to war during the middle of this stretch. He missed three full years to service, and right in his prime. The 1941 MVP race is one of the most famous of all time, and even though Williams should have won, picking Joe DiMaggio wasn't a bad choice either. The 1942 MVP award, however, is a joke. There is no way on earth Williams, winning the Triple Crown and reaching base every other time he went up to hit, should have lost to Joe Gordon, an All-Star caliber player, but no more. So basically, the two years before he left baseball, Williams was definitely the best player in the league one year, and right in the conversation the other year. He hit .400 one year, and he won a Triple Crown the other; there is no arguing he was in his prime. He then missed his age-26, 27, and 28 seasons – his exact prime.

Williams missed those years due to WWII, and he was even a standout overseas, receiving praise throughout the troops for his excellence as a pilot. He returned to win the MVP in his first year back, and as dangerous as it is to play the

---

430 And if we had used the five-year stretch from 1921-1925, his batting average would have over .400, which is the highest batting average over a five-year stretch in MLB history.

431 Barry Bonds did it four times, Mickey Mantle did it once, and fellow six-year champion Hornsby did it once.

432 Just after the Supreme Court had gotten done destroying the Federal League. BASEBALL HUMOR!

"What If" game: what if there hadn't been a war to go to? Potentially, he could have had his 1941-1946 stretch as his six years. He had a WAR over 10.0 in 1941, 1942, and 1946, and he might have been the only player ever to have six straight seasons with a WAR over 10.0. Now this is a lot of projecting and guessing, but with an all-timer like Williams, this seems a little safer than with unproven players. (See: the previous stat on winning every OBP title he ever qualified for.) In the end, Ruth has to take this award for best six-year stretch for a hitter by a hair, but this time I think it might be Ruth (and not Roger Maris or Barry Bonds) who has a tiny asterisk by his name.

Back to the years Williams missed because of the war: solid estimates for replacing the five years he missed to WWII and the Korean War place Williams with incredibly impressive "new career" numbers: .346/.482/.641 slashes with 2,395 runs, 693 home runs, and 2,425 RBI. These would make him the all-time leader in runs, RBI, extra-base hits, walks and the most, or tied for the most, times leading the league in runs, RBI, slugging percentage, and walks.[433]

Even with the time he missed due to service, Williams had one of the best careers of any baseball player. His eyesight was described by one doctor as being "one in one hundred thousand," which allowed him to pick up pitches better than almost anyone the game has seen. Williams didn't just rely on his natural ability, though, as he was also one of the premier students of the game. At the Baseball Hall of Fame, there is an exhibit with Williams' own described strike zones. It contains 77 baseballs labeled with the averages he thought he would hit if the pitch was located there, and it is my personal favorite exhibit at the Hall.

(Photos by Jim Turvey/Baseball Hall of Fame)

Speaking of the Hall of Fame, Williams used his acceptance speech to lobby for Negro Leaguers to be inducted into the Hall, and he often lobbied for Joe Jackson to earn a spot in Cooperstown. This may surprise some, as he is often portrayed as a curmudgeon, but really, enigma is a more accurate depiction.

Williams was indeed a one-of-a-kind man, a man who would zig when you thought he would zag, and vice versa. He was one of the most complex individuals to ever play the sport, and his story is one of the most interesting to tell. Because of that, two of the most fascinating baseball articles ever written focus on Williams. John Updike's, "Hub Fans Bid Kid Adieu" is the best sports article I have ever read. Full stop. It was published in *The New Yorker* in 1960, just after Updike had attended Williams last professional game. The article is the perfect unity of one of the century's most talented writers, and one the century's most interesting men. Updike grew up an admirer of Williams which makes the piece ring true on an even more innocent and childlike nature. (The prose is anything but childlike.) Though not quite on Updike's level, Richard Cramer's profile of Williams in *Esquire* in 1986 is another must-read for people who love baseball, are interested in Ted Williams, or just like a good read. It is more of a personal profile, as Cramer is actually able to meet and talk to Williams (no small feat given Williams' secluded nature when dealing with the media), and the result is just as much an enigma as one would expect. The line that is nearly universally quoted, and deservedly so, sums up Williams to a T: "He wanted fame… but he could not stand celebrity," Cramer wrote. "This is a bitch of a line to draw in America's dust."

He was a man competitive enough that, when he was sitting on a .400 batting average on the final day of the 1941 season, he decided to play instead of take the seat on the bench that his manager offered him.[434] Of course, he started both ends of the double-header, went 6-for-8, and ended season at .406. After the game, he said he didn't deserve .400 if he couldn't finish off the season. However, he was also a man too stubborn to adjust to the shifts implemented against him, insisting on hitting through the shift. For a man whose lone calling was to be considered the greatest hitter of all time, this

[433] Projections taken from *The Man Who Stole First Base.*

[434] It should be noted that the never popular (in the press) Williams would have been torn apart had he sat out that last game, and nearly every paper would have seen to it that his .400 season had an asterisk, as it had to be rounded to get there (.39955357 official average before the final game).

didn't make much sense – but nothing about Williams did.

This was a man who brought up how much he hated the press in his final game, going out of his way to say that he would like to forget those slights, but he just couldn't. At the same time, he was also an immense champion of The Jimmy Fund and helped raise millions of dollars for the cause during his lifetime. Then again, this was the man who, out of spite, refused to come out for a curtain call after hitting a homer in his last Fenway at bat. He even refused to tip his cap to the crowd because of all the slights he remembered from the Boston crowds over the years.

Speaking of those Boston fans, Williams had possibly the most intriguing relationship with his fan base of any superstar, with Mike Schmidt being his only real competition. In his *New Yorker* piece, John Updike wrote of Ted Williams's relationship with Boston: "The affair between Boston and Ted Williams has been no mere summer romance; it has been a marriage, composed of spats, mutual disappointments, and, towards the end, a mellowing hoard of shared memories." Eddie Collins said of Williams, "If he'd just tip his cap once, he could be elected Mayor of Boston in five minutes." Of course, Williams was not a man to show outward gratitude, and he certainly wasn't a man to forgive and forget, or let a grudge fade away. One night in Boston, the crowd was really getting on him. The level of vitriol towards their star had been super-charged by allegations from his ex-wife that Williams was just the sort of husband you would expect this grudge-holding perfectionist to be. After making an error, the whole crowd got on his case, and for a man who would pick out a single fan's heckling in a sea of cheers, the whole stadium riding Williams was just too much. His inner rage boiled over and he spit left, right, and just about anywhere he could, giving the fans exactly what they wanted – a classic Williams' response. Of course, the next night was Family Night, and after paying his $5,000 fine from the spitting incident, there were the Boston fans giving Williams an immense ovation – the bipolar nature of the Boston/Williams relationship could well have been the third lead in *Silver Linings Playbook*.

It wasn't just the fans. Williams was just as up and down with the writers. His relationship with the Boston media went as far as to cost him an MVP in his epic 1941 season. Williams was in such bad standing with the Boston media that one writer, *from Boston*, refused to put Williams anywhere in the top 10 on his ballot, and this was the difference in the vote (Joe DiMaggio won in his 56-game hit streak season). This animosity continued throughout his career, and when Williams hit his 400th home run, he spit towards the press box as a big "eff you" to the writers of Boston he battled with so often. Williams called the Boston sportswriters the "Knights of the Keyboard." I can taste the disdain from here.

However, to blame Williams' not-so-sweet disposition on a long battle with the media or fans of Boston would not necessarily be accurate. He was a bit of a prick – or at least very self-confident with a touch of cocky – even at a young age. In 1938 spring training (when he was a precocious 19 years of age), some of the veteran outfields were giving young Williams a hard time. His response: "I'll be back, and make more money than the three of you combined." Of course, he was correct, but the man was never a cuddly one. The media made him more grizzled in his nature – winning two Triple Crowns and going without an MVP in either season will do that to a guy – but as the saying goes: "It takes two to tango."

One criticism that Williams did not bring upon himself, and was a totally unfair one, was that he was not a clutch player. Truth sayer John Updike pointed to this very criticism in his piece in 1960 on Williams,

> "There are answers to all this, of course. The fatal weakness of the great Sox slugging teams was not-quite-good-enough pitching rather than Williams' failure to hit a home run every time he came to bat. Again, Williams' depressing effect on his teammates has never been proved. Despite ample coaching to the contrary, most insisted that they liked him. He has been generous with advice to any player who asked for it. In an increasingly combative baseball atmosphere, he continued to duck beanballs docilely. With umpires he was gracious to a fault. This courtesy itself annoyed his critics, whom there was no pleasing. And against the 10 crucial games (the seven World Series games with the St. Louis Cardinals, the 1948 playoff with Cleveland, and the two-game series with the Yankees at the end of the 1949 season, winning either one of which would have given the Red Sox the pennant) that make up the Achilles' heel of Williams' record, a mass of statistics can be set showing that day in and day out he was no slouch in the clutch. The correspondence columns of the Boston papers now and then suffer a sharp flurry of arithmetic on this score; indeed, for Williams to have distributed all his hits so they did nobody else any good would constitute a feat of placement unparalleled in the annals of selfishness."

Let's move back to Williams' feats on the diamond to wrap up: he's the only man in MLB history with 25 home runs in a season in four different decades and, as we saw above, could have been even higher up the all-time home run list if he hadn't served in multiple wars.[435]

My favorite Williams' stat: Williams would have to fail to reach base 2,000 straight times right now to drop his on-base percentage below .400. The driving force behind that crazy OBP was a batting eye rivaled by none. Williams is the only player in baseball history with 2,000 walks and fewer than 1,300 strikeouts; and fewer than 1,200 strikeouts; ditto 1,100; and yep even 1,000. In fact, in the history of baseball, when no other player with at least 2,000 walks had fewer than 1,330 strikeouts (Babe Ruth); Williams had a measly 709 career strikeouts. His career ratio of 2,021 walks to 709 strikeouts

[435] A fact that Williams said he wasn't all too pleased about in his autobiography. Williams said of having to serve in two wars, the second time in Korean, "In my heart I was bitter about it, but I made up my mind I wasn't going to bellyache."

simplifies to about 2.85 walks per strikeout. Of players with at least 5,000 plate appearances in MLB history, only 10 other players have as strong a walk to strikeout ratio. The next highest walk total is Tris Speaker, more than 600 walks away from Williams. And none of them could compete with Williams' power. Of the previously mentioned 10, none had more than 184 career home runs; Williams had 521. If the criteria are switched to players with as many plate appearances as Williams, there are only five players joining Williams with a walk to strikeout ratio of 2.85, and Williams has more home runs than *all of them combined.* He was truly one of a kind.

CF Tris Speaker (1907-1915)

Tris Speaker was a hell of a ballplayer in his own right, a vastly underrated player who ranks fifth all time in hits (3,514), and despite being in Boston for only nine years (and seven full seasons), his numbers are good enough for the start in center field. According to baseball lore, Speaker played a mean center field. He was considered a defensive revolutionary, a player who played shallow and got a good enough read on the ball to break back on it to make the play. This shallow positioning allowed him to complete unassisted double plays[436] from the outfield with more regularity than any center fielder in history. As a result, he is considered one of the best defensive outfielders of all time. He also has the most outfield assists in baseball history with 449, a total unlikely to be challenged at any point.

"The Grey Eagle"[437] was also an excellent hitter, who contributed almost 8.0 WAR every year with the team and won two World Series titles while with the Sox. When Speaker left town, it was one of the worst trades in Boston history, as Speaker was shipped out of town for a guy named "Sad Sam" and an infielder, Fred Jones, who played 44 total games in Boston. Although "Sad Sam" put up four solid seasons for the Sox, Speaker went on to collect nearly 2,000 hits and post a .444 on-base percentage with Cleveland, a lopsided trade to say the least. Maybe it should have been The Curse of the Grey Eagle.

As far as what type of a guy he was, Speaker seems to be a bit of a contradiction. He was an alleged member of the KKK, but he was also supposedly one of Larry Doby's biggest supporters when he came to Cleveland. Remember: Doby was the first black player in AL history. Also remember: usually KKK guys aren't black players' biggest supporters. The rumors may have been incorrect about the KKK, or Speaker may have been caught up in a movement that as Bill James puts it, "had a populist phase in which it toned down its racism, and drew in hundreds of thousands of men who were not racist." This is not to excuse him if he had been a member, but it might show a lot about his character that he was able to grow into a man who was able to take the first black player in the AL under his wing, as he may not have been as open to the idea in his youth.

RF Dwight Evans (1972-1990)

Dewey Evans was a Red Sock through and through. An immensely popular player for the infamous 1975 and 1986 teams, Evans provided a consistent bat and strong glove for the team for nearly two decades. He won several Gold Gloves (although the metrics didn't always agree with them), and although he was only a three-time All-Star, go up to any Red Sox fan and ask them whom they'd take as their right fielder, and dollars to (Dunkin') donuts, they'll say Dewey. Evans is not in the Hall of Fame, but Bill James has a great piece on *Grantland*[438] that breaks down his worthiness and arrives at the distinct conclusion that he is.

Evans is one of the classic trope of player who is a legend, but his fame just doesn't quite make it onto a national level, for whatever reason. These are the type of guys who will never end up in the Hall of Fame, even though they are often the lifesblood of the sport's popularity. It's a little tough to gauge who these players are from a non-diehard fan perspective, but he's a best-guess Starting IX of those type of players:

C) Carlos Ruiz, Phillies 1B) Eric Hosmer, Royals 2B) Lou Whitaker, Tigers 3B) Eric Chavez, A's SS) Johnny Pesky, Red Sox LF) Paul O'Neill, Yankees CF) Dale Murphy, Braves [Captain of the Starting IX, and the man who will cause the biggest uproar for not being on his Starting IX in this book] RF) Dwight Evans, Red Sox DH) Sean Casey, Reds SP) Fernando Valenzuela, Dodgers CP) No team's fanbase has ever liked their closer enough for him to be here

Utility Carl Yastrzemski (1961-1983)

So, here's the thing: when I began this whole process, the Red Sox utility spot was a pretty easy choice. Although David Ortiz may seem like the perfect DH for this team – with his timely hitting and immense popularity – it would have been too much of a crime against humanity to leave off Yaz. Then the Boston Marathon bombings happened, Ortiz told the nation: "This is our *fucking* city," and with that, Ortiz became inexorably linked with Boston like no other athlete and city since MJ and Chicago. Leaving Papi off the Red Sox Starting IX would seem like a near-arrest worthy offense in Boston. When I inevitably end up back in the Boston Public School system, I wouldn't be surprised if I eventually have a class of 22

---

[436] Yes, that means he would catch the ball in center field and then tag either the runner or second base before the runner got back. If you have never seen that in a game, don't worry, I've watched approximately four ex-girlfriends worth of baseball and have never seen it either.

[437] He got this nickname from his premature greying locks.

[438] By the way, reader, have you noticed I read *Grantland* just a little bit? I miss you every day, *Grantland.*

kids named David, all named in honor of the city's hero.

But here's the other thing (which was really the first thing): Yaz simply cannot be left off.

Yastrzemski played 23 major league seasons, all with the Red Sox, and he even spent his time in the minors with the team. He hit a home run in each and every one of those seasons, making him the only player in baseball history to homer in 23 straight seasons for the same team. He is the franchise leader in games (3,308), runs (1,816), hits (3,419), doubles (646), RBI (1,844), and trails only the man who beat him out for left field in home runs and All-Star Game appearances. In 1979, he reached both the 3,000-hit and 400-home run marks, making him only the fourth man to reach those marks after Willie Mays, Hank Aaron, and Stan Musial (six players have joined the ranks since). In the line of consistent longevity, Yaz also became the first player in MLB history to reach 100 hits in 20 straight seasons with the same team, when he reached that milestone in 1980. Only three men – Hank Aaron, Pete Rose, and Derek Jeter – have collected more hits than Yaz after 1950.

He had an excellent eye, and the only two times his OPS+ were below 100 was his rookie year (1961), and the (only) year he managed to play less than 100 games (1981). In the latter year, he was 42 by the end of a strike-shortened season. His numbers through his first decade with the Sox are on par with almost anyone else in the game, and although his production slipped a bit the rest of his career (of his 96.1 career WAR, 62.7 came in that first decade), he still was a perennial All-Star, and his 1975 postseason alone showed he still had it as a player (14-for-40 with 11 runs in 10 games).

Skipping back a few years: Yaz's Triple Crown[439] season of 1967 was a truly remarkable season. Time after time that season, Yaz went Greg Jennings-mode, putting the team on his back (not an easy feat for a sport like baseball), winning multiple games in the late innings for them. He hit .444 for the month of September, and in the final two weeks, he hit a staggering .523. This was not for naught, as the Sox won the pennant thanks to two late-season wins over the Twins, a team the Sox had trailed by one game before their final two games of the regular season. All Yastrzemski did in those two games: 7-for-8 with six RBI and two home runs. It's hard to imagine a better Triple Crown performance. Of Yastrzemski's 44 home runs that year, fellow Red Sock George Scott said, "Probably 43 either tied the game or put us in the lead." He was called the best clutch hitter ever by his manager Dick Williams.

Yaz didn't stop with the regular season, either. He actually topped his batting title average with a .400 average for the World Series, which would be like if J.K. Rowling finished the Harry Potter series and then when out and wrote "The Lottery" as a follow up. The Sox lost in seven, but Yastrzemski did everything short of take the mound in Game 7 to try to win them a title in 1967.

Yastrzemski's career, as a whole, is pretty impressive considering the circumstances into which he stepped in 1961. That season, after Sox legend Ted Williams retired the year before, the young Yaz had to step in to take over the left field position for Boston. These were obviously some huge shoes to fill, but Yaz did so to such a great level that Johnny Pesky said, "I'm a Ted Williams guy, but I think Yaz will go down as the best player in Red Sox history." This is even more impressive considering this is coming from a teammate of Williams. However, not all players who tried to step up and replace legends enjoyed as much success as Yaz. (Cue Starting IX music):

C) Elston Howard – Howard took over the catching role for the Yankees when they moved Yogi Berra predominantly to the outfield in 1961. The result was one of the best seasons a team has had in baseball history, as Howard posted a 5.0-win season behind the plate to go along with the rest of the dominant roster. For his first four years behind the plate, Howard totaled 19.8 WAR and was both an excellent hitter and fielder for his position. He eventually tapered off, but he was a very solid backstop for the Yankees in lieu of Berra.

1B) Allen Craig – He had two very good seasons after Albert Pujols left (receiving MVP votes in 2012 and 2013), before he crashed and burned out of St. Louis. He's already out of the league.

2B) Jim Gilliam – The Dodgers moved Jackie Robinson from his post at second base in 1953 to make way for the prized Jim Gilliam, and Gilliam responded with a Rookie of the Year campaign. However, Gilliam never really lived up to the hype, making only two All-Star Games and topping his rookie-season WAR only four times in his career. He certainly wasn't awful, but he wasn't quite all he was hyped up to be in the end.

3B) Kevin Seitzer – Tasked with the unpleasant duty of taking over third base in Kansas City after George Brett, Seitzer responded well initially, finishing second in the Rookie of the Year and collecting over 200 hits. He would be shipped out of town less than five years later, however, as he saw his oWAR drop every season in K.C.

SS) Felipe Lopez – Taking over the shortstop mantle from Barry Larkin, Lopez produced his best season and a half before being shipped out of town by the club. Sensing a theme?

LF) Carl Yastrzemski

CF) Mickey Mantle – We'll be talking plenty about him later – obviously was successful.

RF) Richie Zisk – The man chosen to replace Roberto Clemente not only in right field, but in the hearts of Pirate fans after Clemente's tragic death, Zisk may have had the hardest job of any of these players. He performed admirably, however, winning the team over 15.0 games, per WAR, before being shipped out of town for an in-his-prime Goose Gossage. Very similar production to Elston Howard.

SP) Jerry Koosman – Koosman is different from the rest of the players tasked with filling the face of the franchise role in that Koosman was already an established pitcher when Mets legend Tom Seaver left town. However, Koosman did

---

[439] Because I'm a Yankees fan – and a dick – I will point out that he only *tied* for the league lead in home runs that year.

not take well to the departure and posted a 7-30 record the season after Seaver left New York. He was later able to reestablish himself in Minnesota and pitched until the ripe age of 42.

CP) David Robertson – Closing out a game for the Yankees is a lot of pressure in and of itself, but taking over the closing role from baseball's most reliable ninth-inning man of all time (Mariano Rivera) in the biggest market in baseball, is a far-from-enviable task. Robertson handled the transition very well, however, putting in one season strong enough to make his next contract too rich for the Yankees. Of course, Robertson and the Yanks were reunited not much longer, as he came back to the squad in 2017 and is a key part of the current Super Bullpen in New York.

Yaz arguably had the best career of any of those players (Mantle is probably ahead by talent, but for longevity, Yaz is tough to beat), making his inclusion within the Red Sox Starting IX a must.

And so we're back to square one. A breakdown between Yaz and Papi would be futile as Red Sox fans would go full-on True Mother to my King Solomon judgment-to-be[440] and end up giving the utility spot to Julio Lugo to avoid having to choose between Yaz and Papi.

And so, without further ado, it's time for the first true DH spot of the book.

DH David Ortiz (2003-2016)

Although Papi's eff-bomb may have been the final straw for his inclusion on the all-franchise team, the numbers go a long way in supporting Ortiz's inclusion. When the Red Sox signed Ortiz in 2003, fresh off a release by the Minnesota Twins, there was no way they could have guessed that Ortiz would deliver nearly 500 home runs and, more importantly, three titles to their beloved Boston. Ortiz had been a .266 hitter and a .461 slugger up in Minnesota, and although that's not awful, he didn't wait long to jump to the next level in Boston. The Red Sox made the playoffs in 2003, and Ortiz tallied 31 home runs with the club. He even began to show a bit of that flair for the dramatic he would have in spades later on, hitting a pair of home runs in the 2003 Yankees ALCS matchup, but 2004 was his true breakout.

Ortiz hit 41 home runs, drove in 139 runs, and hit over .300 in the regular season, but that was just a precursor to the magical "Idiots" run in the 2004 playoffs. Ortiz ended up the ALCS MVP, and one could argue an MVP has never been more deserved. With his team down 3-0, and everyone in New York prepping themselves for a return to the World Series, Papi stepped up in a huge way in Game 4. With the Sox down 2-1 in the fifth, Ortiz gave the Sox their first lead of the game with a two-run single. Then after Mariano Rivera blew a rare playoff save opportunity, Papi made sure there was a bit more baseball to be played with a walkoff 12th inning blast into the Boston night off of Paul Quantrill, giving him four of the team's six RBI that night. With the Sox backs against the wall once again in Game 5, Ortiz got started early, giving the Sox a 1-0 lead in the bottom of the first. Then, with the Yankees six outs away from the World Series, and sporting a two-run lead, Ortiz yet again lit a fire in the team, starting the eighth inning off with a home run off Tom Gordon. The next two batters reached, and one eventually scored, meaning more extra innings in Boston. At this point it should be really freakin obvious, even to those that don't remember the games that well, that who-else-but-Ortiz would hit the walkoff in the bottom of the 14th, giving him three of the team's five RBI and putting all the pressure on New York now. Game 6 is remembered for the "Bloody Sock," and Game 7 for the complete no-show the Yankees pulled, but really the 2004 ALCS was all about Ortiz. Boston had found their God, and his name was Papi. Maybe the most impressive thing about Ortiz is looking at his playoff numbers to see just how much of a driving force he is for the Sox. In 2004, 2007, and 2013, he had his best numbers by far. It's not at all surprising that those years are now flying over Fenway. As Ortiz went, the Red Sox went. Ortiz was a natural leader and one of the game's most universally loved players.

It's only fitting to sneak in a Starting IX of best individual postseasons in Ortiz's write-up. It's hard to compare newer players to older players here, because of the fact that there are so many more playoff games in modern baseball thanks to playoff expansion. Of course, the flip side of that is that no modern player can keep up with the older player in the slash statistics because the sample sizes are so much larger these days. So, I tried to balance those two, but this Starting IX probably does skew a bit more modern simply because it's more impressive to dominate three series than one:

C) Hank Gowdy, 1914 1B) Lou Gehrig, 1928 2B) Bill Mazeroski, 1960 – Yes, this is for one swing of the bat. 3B) David Freese, 2011 SS) Derek Jeter, 2000 – I mean, he kind of has to have this spot, right? LF) Barry Bonds, 2002 CF) Carlos Beltrán, 2004 RF) Babe Ruth, 1928 – Yes, the same year as Gehrig. DH) David Ortiz, 2004 – And probably 2013, too. SP) Madison Bumgarner, 2014 RP) Mariano Rivera, Just Every Damn Year.

Now, despite the fact that Ortiz is *nearly* universally loved, there are certainly the ardent "Ortiz used steroids" crew that will forever hold that against him. Not that this type of person is not the type to be won over by logic or reason, but in case you are in that small subset that holds it against Papi but is also open to sane arguments, Ortiz has an interesting case. The lone time that Ortiz tested positive (and he says that he was tested a suspicious amount of times after) was in 2003 when Major League Baseball told players that they had to submit to an upcoming test, but the results *would not be given to the public*. Instead, the league would look at the results, see if more than five percent of the league was using, and if so, a new policy would come into play. Somehow, even though the league had told the players the test was coming, way more than five percent tested positive, among them Ortiz. Of course, this still wouldn't have been an issue, at least to the general public,

---

[440] You bet your sweet ass that's an Old Testament reference.

except for the fact that a 2009 report leaked Ortiz's name from that preliminary test, earning him the label of PED user, when he had never really done anything wrong. PED use was rampant in the league when Ortiz tested positive, and the league told the players there would be no punishment for the test on which Ortiz did test positive. The test has also had questions of legitimacy surrounding it, which was part of the reason MLB didn't want the names out in public. To lump Ortiz in with a Melky Cabrera or Alex Rodriguez or any other modern steroid user would be a false equivalency and unfair to Ortiz. And remember: this is coming from a man who almost certainly hates the Red Sox more than you do. Don't be petty in your hate for the Sox and take it out on Ortiz. The man deserves the praise he is given.

To wrap up: as far as Ortiz joining Yastrzemski in the Red Sox glory, well Yaz himself is on record as having said Ortiz is the second-best hitter in franchise history to none other than Ted Williams.

SP Roger Clemens (1984-1996) vs. Pedro Martínez (1998-2004) vs. Cy Young (1901-1908)

Time for our first three-way breakdown. Like any three-way, this might get a little messy, and two people will have their feelings hurt ~~in the morning~~ in five pages. For this breakdown, we won't pick a winner at the end of each category, but rather we'll give each pitcher a score out of 10 that will be totaled at the end to decide who should start for the Sox.

(There are a few more stats that will appear here that haven't appeared anywhere else in the book, so here's a quick primer: QS% = quality start percentage. A quality start is defined as a start in which a pitcher goes at least 6.0 innings and allows three or fewer runs; GmScA = average game score. Game score starts at 50 and points are assigned for outs, strikeouts, etc. and negative points are assigned for hits allowed, runs allowed, etc.; S/Str% = swinging strike rate. This is the percentage of pitches a pitcher gets a hitter to swing and miss on; WP = wild pitches; 1st% = percentage of first-pitch strikes.)

Advanced Statistics

	WAR	WAR (season high)	Seasons with ≥ 7.5 WAR	WAA	WaaWL%	ERA+	Seasons ≥ 200 ERA+	QS%	GmScA
Clemens	**81.3**	10.6	**6**	**56.1**	.646	144	1	65	60
Martínez	53.8	11.7	3	40.6	**.700**	**190**	**4**	**75**	**65**
Young	66.2	**12.6**	**6**	41.7	.627	147	1	XX	XX

We begin to see the different impacts on Red Sox history that each player had even in this first category. Clemens was with the team 13 years, and, therefore, his cumulative numbers will often be the highest of the three. Young and Martínez were not with the club as long, but they were there in their respective peaks. Therefore, they will often have better percentage stats. Out of Martínez and Young, Pedro has the far superior advanced numbers with an insane 190 ERA+ in his time with Boston. Reminder: this means he was 90 percent better than the average pitcher in baseball during his seven years in The Hub. If Pedro's final year in Boston (2004) is taken out of the equation (one of his weaker statistical seasons, but my guess is he wouldn't want to give that ring up), his ERA+ jumps to 212, a number topped only once *in a single season* since 2000.[441] In 2000, Pedro Martínez sported a 291 ERA+, the second-best ERA+ in *baseball history*. Only Tim Keefe (1880) topped him, and any true baseball fan knows that any stat before 1901 comes with a grain of salt, and with good reason. Keefe threw only 105 innings that season, giving Pedro a pretty good claim to the best run prevention season *ever*, given era and ballpark adjustments. Trust me, we're only getting started on the crazy Pedro stats.

For his part, Clemens' 81.3 WAR just while in Boston is a total higher than Pete Rose's entire career (79.1). Not to be outdone, Young managed to be worth 12.6 wins in 1901, tied for the seventh-highest total ever achieved in the modern era. Not a bad start for these three.

It's interesting to note that although we skipped over the surface stats (so this breakdown didn't go on for tooooo long), Roger Clemens finished his time in Boston with a record of 192-111; Cy Young? 192-112.

Clemens: 8.5; Martínez: 9.5; Young: 8

Power

	SOs	Single Season SO high	Seasons ≥ 200 SOs	SO/9	H/9	SO%	LgSO%	S/Str%
Clemens	**2,590**	291	**8**	8.4	7.6	22.8	16	17
Martínez	1,683	**313**	6	**10.9**	**6.8**	**30.6**	16.6	**22**
Young	1,314	210	2	4.4	7.7	12.9	XX	XX

[441] Ironically, it was Roger Clemens in 2005 in Houston.

Clemens and Martínez are two of baseball's most famous strikeout kings, and both posted impressive numbers while in Boston. Martínez was more in his "K-prime" with Boston, and it shows with his incredible strikeout ratios. Pedro set the MLB record for recording a strikeout in 40 straight innings in 1999. The record he broke was one of his own (33 straight innings), which also happened in 1999. Martínez struck out 13.2 hitters per nine innings in his K-licious 1999 campaign, setting the MLB record for the best strikeout per nine rate among starters with at least 200 innings in a single season. Randy Johnson would break that record two years later, but we're still looking at rarified air in which Pedro resided.

Clemens: 8.5; Martínez: 10; Young: 6

Control

	BB	Seasons ≥ 70 BBs	WP	BB/9	SO/BB	BB%	LgBB%	Str%	1st%
Clemens	856	4	72	2.8	3.03	7.5	8.7	62	58
Martínez	309	1	**30**	2.0	**5.45**	5.6	8.8	**66**	**61**
Young	**299**	**0**	35	**1.0**	4.48	**2.9**	XX	XX	XX

Clemens struggled a bit with control in his time with Boston, but comparing any pitcher's control to Pedro and Cy Young is going to make him look like Mets-era Óliver Pérez. Young was consistently one of the league's top control pitchers and, before his time in Boston, rarely relied on getting outs via the strikeout because his control was so strong. Part of his severe statistical advantage is due to the era in which Young played, but he was a control artist even in his day. Martínez, on the other hand, actually struggled a bit with his control outside of his time in Boston, but he really figured it out while with the Sawks. When he posted his 8.88 strikeout-to-walk ratio in 2000, it was the second-best since 1900, trailing only Bret Saberhagen (1994). (We're going to ignore the fact that Phil Hughes is now the single-season all-time record holder.)

Clemens: 6; Martínez: 8.5; Young: 10

Stamina

	IP	Seasons ≥ 250 IP	CGs	SHOs	IP/GS	Pit/GS
Clemens	**2,776**	6	100	**38**	7.3	117
Martínez	1,383.2	0	22	8	6.9	106
Young	2,728.1	**8**	**275**	**38**	**All the innings**	**All the pitches**

Young obviously pitched in a different era,[442] but his totals are mind-blowing nonetheless. He has greater than 1,300 more innings pitched than the second-highest innings pitched total in all of baseball history. In fact, the difference between Young (7,356.0) and the second-place Pud Galvin (6,003.1), in terms of career innings pitched, is the same as the difference between fourth-place Phil Niekro and 40th-place Jamie Moyer. He threw more innings in his career than Sandy Koufax, Mike Hampton, and Bret Saberhagen combined. Young threw over 320.0 innings in 15 consecutive seasons, and he didn't throw two consecutive "incomplete games" until he had pitched for 10 years in majors. If today's starters throw two consecutive *complete* games, it's an amazing feat.

Clemens also had good stamina and frequently went deep into games with success. Pedro, however, infamously struggled in games where his pitch count got too high. This may have been due in part to his conditioning. Pedro's conditioning was infamously bad to the point that *Sports Illustrated* once said of him, "he has the body of Bud Selig." However, when it comes down to it, Pedro threw an average of only 11 fewer pitches per start than Clemens, or about half an inning per start. This is a much smaller chasm than the difference between Clemens and Young, the latter of whom averaged a complete game each time out, for all intents and purposes.

Clemens: 8; Martínez: 6.5; Young: 10

Consistency

Clemens: Three seasons > 4.00 ERA, four seasons < 25 GS, four seasons < 3.0 WAR
Martínez: One season > 3.00 ERA, one season < 25 GS, zero seasons < 5.0 WAR
Young: One season > 3.00 ERA, zero seasons < 35 GS, one season < 7.0 WAR (2.1)

---

[442] His records may be a result of the time in which he pitched, but one number that was certainly affected negatively by the time in which Young pitched is the salary he earned. For his career, Young made somewhere in the range of $50,000-$70,000. In *Leveling the Field*, G. Scott Thomas projects that Young would have earned over a billion dollars in today's game.

Young and Martínez both had only one weak season while in Boston, but they also had less time with the Sox than Clemens. Clemens' struggles were partly due to the fact that his first two seasons adjusting to the league were spent in Boston, whereas Martínez and Young learned baseball's tricks elsewhere. That being said, three of Clemens final four years in Boston were certainly not prime-Clemens, either. (A fact many still hold against him.)

Clemens: 6.5; Martínez: 9; Young: 8.5

Dominance/Intimidation (League leader in)

Name	IP	W	K	WAR	ERA	SO/BB	SO/9	WHIP	SHO	ERA+	AS	CY	MVP
Clemens	1	2	**3**	**3**	**4**	4	2	2	**5**	**5**	**5**	**3**	**1**
Martínez	0	1	**3**	2	**4**	3	**4**	**4**	1	4	4	2	0
Young	**3**	**3**	1	0	0	**5**	0	**4**	3	1	XX	Um	XX

That's a lot to look at, but what it's showing us is that Clemens and Pedro were pretty much on even footing in terms of league dominance, but Martínez did so in about half the seasons that Rog did. Young wasn't quite as dominant, but part of that is due to the fact that Young's best abilities – control and stamina – don't have as many categories in which to lead the league. Young was certainly dominant during his 25.1 straight hitless innings in 1904. He had a perfect game mixed in there, as well as a relief appearance and the beginning of another start. It is one of the most impressive feats in baseball history. Young also probably could have pitched a while longer, but he decided to retire when he lost a 1-0 game, stating, "When you're losing to rookies it's time to go." That rookie was Pete Alexander.

But if you want to do numbers, buckle your seats, it's time for some awe-inspiring Pedro numbers from his time in Boston, thanks to Seth Mnookin's research in *Top of the Order*: in 1997, Pedro became the first right-hander since Walter Johnson to strike out 300 batters and have an ERA under 2.00. On Friday, September 10, 1999, Martínez and the Red Sox went to New York to take on the Yankees. Pedro started the game with a hit batsman in the first inning and allowed a home run in the second, but he settled down after that. Actually "settled down" really doesn't do Pedro justice – he went beast mode. He retired the final 22 batters he faced and totaled 17 strikeouts for the game (including eight of the last nine Yankees). He left to Yankee fans chanting his name, and he had David Cone – who had thrown a perfect game that season, mind you – say it was the best pitched game he'd ever seen. That 1999 season, as a whole, was pretty spectacular for Pedro. If we want to be straightforward with it, by FIP-, one of the most advanced metrics available today, it was the best season a pitcher has had since 1884 – that's not a bad place to start. Pedro didn't run through batters like a hot knife through butter, he ran through them like Excalibur through a tub of hot yogurt. Pedro went 23-4 with a 2.07 ERA and 313 strikeouts, and he ran away with the Cy Young. He won the ERA title by 1.37 runs over second place (think about that, Cone was second in the AL with a 3.44 ERA), and he took every single first place Cy Young vote.

For his encore performance in 2000, Pedro more than lived up to the hype. He posted a 1.74 ERA, which, although impressive, is even more remarkable when it is noted that the league-average ERA was 4.92. For comparison, Sandy Koufax's 1.73 ERA in 1966 was achieved when the league-average ERA was 3.61. Roger Clemens finished second in the American League in 2000 with a 3.70 ERA, in other words, higher than the average ERA Koufax's 1966 campaign. Pedro's 1.96-ERA title gap was the largest-ever difference between first and second. Pedro's 0.737 WHIP in 2000 is the best all-time, *even before accounting for league and era adjustments*. May I remind you that this was the peak of the steroid era, with the DH in the American League, and with Pedro's home games coming in one of the best hitter ballparks of the time. Pedro broke the all-time record for lowest opponent batting average (.167) in 2000 and posted an ERA *183 percent better* than league average. Pedro even managed to pitch well in losses; his ERA in his six losses (2.44) would still have led the league by a well over a run. The season was so spectacular that it triggered Ben Lindbergh's brilliant "Dear Clayton; Love Pedro" article on *Grantland* in 2014 when Clayton Kershaw was being hyped as having a historic season. The point of the article: sit down, Kershaw. Or as Matt Vasgersian would say in *MLB: The Show*, "Grab some pine, meat!"

Even though we just splooged a half-page of Pedro stats, that's not to say these other two gents weren't their own special brand of dominant. Remember when we cited Pedro having received every single first place vote in the 1999 Cy Young? Pause for a minute. Take a deep breath because this is going to blow your mind grapes. Notice anything about the award that is handed out every year to the most dominant pitcher? Yeah, it's named after our man Cy Young – that's not a coincidence. If we're talking about breaking Cy Young's all-time wins record, a pitcher could toss 17 consecutive 30-win seasons –no pitcher has won 30 games in a season since 1968 – and still come up short. They could throw 20 consecutive 25-win seasons (the most recent 25-win season was 1990), and they'd still be short. Yeah, that record isn't getting broken.

And Clemens: all he did in Boston was set, and then later tie, the MLB record with 20 strikeouts in a game, (once in 1986 and once a decade later in 1996). Only Kerry Wood has joined him in the 20-K club since.

Clemens: 7.5; Martínez: 11[443]; Young: 7

---

[443] "The numbers all go to eleven. Look right across the board, eleven, eleven, eleven..." "Does that mean it goes louder?" "Well, it's one louder isn't it?"

Team Success

Name	Team W	Team L	Team T	W/L %	Playoffs	Pennants	WS
Clemens	**1,062**	978	1	.520	**4**	1	X
Martínez	639	**494**	0	**.564**	**4**	1	**1**
Young	603	571	18	.514	1	1	**1**

Individual Postseason Numbers

Name	W	L	IP	SO	ERA	WHIP
Clemens	1	2	45.2	45	4.73	1.49
Martínez	**6**	2	**79.1**	**80**	3.40	1.12
Young	2	**1**	34.0	17	**1.85**	**1.03**

Martínez and Young both won titles, and Clemens' Red Sox were one strike away from a World Series victory on several occasions in 1986 before their infamous World Series loss. Young dominated the one World Series in which he played, and he very well may have won another title in 1904 if the World Series had not been canceled. Pedro, although not always dominant throughout every playoff series with the Red Sox (most notably his aforementioned 2003 meltdown against the Yankees that we'll get to in a second, and a 6.23 ERA in the 2004 ALCS against the Yankees), had good numbers as a whole. Clemens had a reputation for not showing up in big games, and his one win in nine postseason starts with the club speaks to that.

Of course, we can't do a postseason comparison of Pedro and Clemens without mentioning the 2003 ALCS, when the two faced off against each other for the second and third times in the playoffs. The first time they met had been in 1999, in Game 3 of an eventual Yankees series win; Pedro cruised to victory. In 1999, Clemens, then with the Yankees, lasted only two innings, and Pedro twirled seven innings of two-hit, 12-strikeout magnificence. Four years later, in the 2003 ALCS, Clemens evened the score by winning their first matchup of the series in Game 3. His victory put the Yankees up 2-1 in the series. It was a game of huge importance in which Clemens finally showed up. The two teams traded games back-and-forth until Game 7, when Clemens and Pedro met again.

Although Pedro is a historic Red Sock, he did have to suffer through what must have been an agonizingly long offseason after this 2003 ALCS. The Red Sox managed to knock Clemens out early, and Pedro looked to be cruising through six innings. However, after the sixth, Pedro told the Red Sox assistant trainer that he felt a little fatigued. He went out for the seventh, however, and labored through it, giving up a run and reaching 100 pitches. This seemed a logical time to remove the Red Sox ace, and with Ortiz's home run in the top of the eighth, the Red Sox had a comfortable three-run lead. Then stuff got weird. Pedro was brought out again for the eighth, and then in a decision that didn't need any hindsight, incorrectly left in for another 23 pitches and four hits, which allowed the Yankees to tie the game. The Yankees went on to win on Aaron Boone's home run in extra innings, and it seemed to be the ultimate example of the Yanks owning the Sox. This, in part, led to a classic quote from Pedro when, at the end of the 2004 regular season, Martínez responded to another loss to the Yankees by saying, "What can I say? I tip my hat and call the Yankees my daddy." However, Pedro was able to redeem himself in the 2004 ALCS when, although he didn't dominate the Yankees, he did get to pitch in the series-clinching Game 7 win.

Clemens: 6; Martínez: 8; Young: 8.5

Guile

Not really measurable by statistics,[444] guile is a key part of every pitcher's repertoire. Although guile should be part of any reputable pitcher's repertoire, it is usually thought of as being much more in vogue among pitchers who don't tend to overpower hitters. It makes sense then that the least powerful of these pitchers, Cy Young, is the one about whom his guile is written most often. Young was smart, and he knew teams in his era were cheap and didn't want to go through many baseballs. So, during the course of the game, he would never ask for a replacement because the balls got warped as the game went on, and they became harder to hit.

Young also owed part of his success to a photographic memory that allowed him mix pitches from at bat to at bat, for each hitter, throughout the course of a game. He also used four different motions, which is about the most guile-y thing a pitcher can do. I do think that old-time baseball writers enjoyed writing about pitcher guile more than current writers do. Plus, it was a little harder to call BS with so much less coverage in Young's time.

Having said that, it's is safe to assume that Young may have been more aware than Pedro, who once told a journalist who was interviewing him for *Sports Illustrated for Kids* (note: for kids) that his secret ambition was to make love to Sandra

[444] Although one *FanGraphs* fan writer did manage to create a "craftiness" statistic which required a low fastball velocity, low strikeout rate, and low WHIP, combined with a high left on-base percentage. Pretty solid formula.

Bullock. He most certainly did not phrase it as "making love," either. However, on the pro-guile side for Pedro, when he was growing up, his family couldn't afford baseballs, so he would practice pitching with the heads of his sister's dolls – pretty crafty. Overall, this category can be used to give a bonus point or two to Young.

Clemens: 0; Martínez: -1 (Bullock) +1 (doll head use) net 0; Young: 2

Impact on Franchise/ Relationship with Boston

When I think of a player's impact on a franchise, I think of it as a two-way street. A player can have a big impact on a franchise, but a franchise can also have a big impact on a player. In the case of these three men, the latter may be the better way to look at it. Cy Young joined the team in their inaugural season (1901), which was the AL's inaugural year, as well. He stayed with the club for eight years before leaving town. There is nothing to say he didn't enjoy his stay there, but the fact that Boston was one of five teams for which he played, along with the fact that he went back to Cleveland (his first team) after his time in Boston, would imply that Boston didn't have as much an impact on him as Cleveland did. This is backed by the fact that Young is engraved wearing his Cleveland hat in Cooperstown.

On the other hand, Pedro enjoyed a renaissance in his time with Boston, and although he did have stops before and after Boston, he never pitched like he did with the Sox. In many ways, this seems to be because both Pedro and the city of Boston are a little crazy. Don't get me wrong, it's in a good way, but they are both more than a little off their rockers.[445] This made them perfect for each other, the same way Manny was perfect for Boston until he overstayed his welcome; Pedro did the same just a few years earlier. We all know there is no bigger Boston homer than Bill Simmons, so let's turn to Simmons to give us some perspective from his piece written when Pedro was on the down side of his Boston career: "You really needed to live in New England from 1998 to 2001 to appreciate the Pedro Experience, to understand what he meant to Sox fans, to fully comprehend the thrill of watching him pitch every five days. Looking back, he was like a shooting star. That's the only way I can describe it. The man was a shooting star."

Yet another great Boston source, Peter Gammons – arguably the most well-respected man in baseball journalism – did this breakdown the favor of directly comparing Pedro to Clemens: "It was never quite the same way when Roger Clemens pitched. There was an electricity to the way he grunted and charged the mound in his halcyon Fenway days, but he didn't touch the soul of Fenway people." Pedro did. Don't believe Simmons or Gammons? How about teammate, and battery mate, Jason Varitek: "Once every five days, New England becomes Pedro's world," the Sox captain said of the electric ace. "The rest of us just work here."

Wanna know the Boston opinion of Clemens? It's perfectly summed up by a phone call I had when in the final stages of producing this book. There is an image on the next page of Pedro's Jheri curl, which I found online and wanted to get an OK to use in my book from the owner of the image. So, I called the proprietor of Supah Fans (yes, "Supah" is spelled that way on purpose) to get permission. I ended up chatting with the man who had started the t-shirt business, Kevin, an extremely nice and extremely Boston gentleman, who was not afraid to share his Red Sox opinions. When I described the premise of the book to him and told him about how Pedro was in a three-way breakdown with Cy Young and Roger Clemens, he made it clear that Pedro was the only correct choice. In fact, when I first said that he was going up against Roger Clemens, he hit me with a "Who?" I was driving in the back woods of Vermont at the time, so I repeated Clemens' name, assuming that my phone had cut out. Nope. I got another "Who?" in response, as Clemens was dead to this man. Kevin went on to rail against how Clemens had let himself go by the end of his Red Sox days, and seeing him fit and dominant in Toronto right after his Boston days only made Sox fans hate Clemens even more. This is a massively important category for any team, but for Boston in particular, they simply need to have that connection with the players. It's why my uncle went out of his way to make the case for Dustin Pedroia earlier this chapter, and it's why Roger Clemens (and really Cy Young) never had a chance in this breakdown.

Clemens: -2; Martínez: 9.5 (only Papi, Larry Bird, Tom Brady, and Bobby Orr get 10s in Boston); Young: 3

Verdict

Clemens: 49; Martínez: 71; Young: 63

Pedro Martínez takes the mound for the Sox. And honestly that feels like the right man. It seems like the baseball community has only recently become more and more in awe of what Pedro was able to accomplish in his prime, thanks in large part to progress made in the field of being able to compare across generations, a key component of this book. We've already spilled enough ink on Pedro during the course of this breakdown, so let's just leave you with this amazing picture of Pedro's next-level Jheri curl game:

---

[445] Pedro carried around a little Dominican man with him during the 2004 World Series run, a man who was often referred to as Pedro's Lucky Midget. Seems weird and vaguely offensive. And 100 percent Pedro.

That puppy is available at the aforementioned supahfans.com, by the way.

CP Jonathan Papelbon (2005-2011)

The franchise saves leader, Papelbon closed out the 2007 World Series for the Red Sox with a now infamous jig on the mound. Papelbon is an example of a player whose numbers on paper look a little better than the eye test. Maybe it was that my friends (who were Red Sox fans) and I hated him so much,[446] but Red Sox fans never really felt "Rivera-comfortable" or even "Prime K-Rod-comfortable" when Papelbon was on in the ninth.

This is where it becomes difficult to be an unbiased writer, while being a most-definitely-biased fan. Papelbon's numbers are very good for his time in Boston, and the closing role is such that even being reliable over several seasons is an impressive feat. But something about the punchable-faced righty lent to worrisome times in the ninth. (But then, what do I know? I'm a bear. I suck the heads off of fish.)[447] I guess it's good that there wasn't another great option for the closing role, because I may have been tempted to go with my gut, and not the right choice, which is almost certainly Papelbon.

Because I do hate Papelbon, however, I will use this space to discuss the final day of the 2011 season. Since it is fresh in most baseball fans' minds, only a quick refresher is needed. Going back a little over a month, the Atlanta Braves had a 10½-game lead on the St. Louis Cardinals for the NL wild card, and the Cardinals almost seemed an afterthought for the playoffs. Less than two weeks later, on September 3, the Boston Red Sox held a nine-game lead on the Tampa Bay Rays for the AL wild card, and the Sox seemed likelier to take the division from the Yankees – who were in first – than lose ground to the Rays, who were chasing them. Flash-forward three-plus weeks to September 28, the final day of the regular season, and one which will be remembered as quite possibly the best day of baseball. Ever.

Starting in the NL: the Cardinals, who had, by this point, erased the 10½-game lead and were now tied with the Braves for the wild card lead, sent Chris Carpenter to the mound against the Houston Astros. Carpenter cruised to a two-hit shutout, but all was not lost for the Braves. They looked to be in good shape to at least set up a play-in game for the wild card. They were up one run in the ninth inning and handing the ball to their lights-out closer, Craig Kimbrel. Despite an 85 percent win probability, however, the Braves blew their ninth inning lead, and lost the game – and the playoff spot – for good in the 13th inning on Hunter Pence's single off of Scott Linebrink. The Braves may well have had a two-run lead in the ninth if it wasn't for Michael Bourn breaking one of baseball main tenants and getting caught stealing third with nobody out just pitches before Dan Uggla homered in the third inning. That extra run may have been the difference between making the playoffs or not for Atlanta.

Now this would have been dramatic on its own, but the AL wasn't just about to let the NL get the ESPN lead. The Rays had erased their own hefty deficit by this point, and they also went into the night tied for the wild card spot. For most of the night, the Red Sox looked in control, however. When the rain forced a delay in Boston, the Sox players who waited to get back on the field saw their own 3-2 lead over an Orioles team with nothing to play for and heard the report that the Yankees had a 7-0 lead on the Rays, and they felt pretty good. However, by the end of the rain delay, the Rays had made their remarkable recovery[448] to take the game to extra innings. This added pressure did not bode well for the Red Sox who sent out none other than Jonathan Papelbon to close the game. Now in Papelbon's defense, the Red Sox had been 77-0 when leading

---

[446] And after his choke-job, smug-face attack on Bryce Harper late in 2015, you'd be hard-pressed to find anyone outside of the baseball Neanderthals who don't currently hate him. Also, if you think this is harsh, at least he's not Maury Wills and I'm not Bill James in his *Abstract*. AMIRIGHT?

[447] [*KKBB* no. 8] If you haven't seen *Kiss Kiss Bang Bang*, you're definitely thinking I'm off my rocker at this point. And if you have seen it you're wondering whether that was really the best time to use that quote.

[448] With definite help from Yankees manager Joe Girardi putting in the dregs of his bullpen. Who said Yanks-Sox gamesmanship was dead?

after eight innings that season so it's hard to imagine what happened next. After two strikeouts to start the ninth, Papelbon allowed a Chris Davis double to right. This was followed up by a Nolan Reimold double, and then it was capped by an incredible Robert Andino walkoff single at 12:02 am. The Orioles 8-9-1 hitters had done the unthinkable, and when Evan Longoria sealed Boston's fate a mere three minutes later with a walk-off home run over the Yankees, it was only fitting. This night had such an incredible impact that baseball immediately tried to repeat it every year by adding an extra wild card team so that each season would have a one-game playoff to get fans excited. But really nothing could top September 28, 2011.

Although that day was memorable on a small-scale enjoyment level, it is also interestingly part of a growing phenomenon in which all sports seem to have more and more epic moments than in the past. Each year seems to break some hallowed record of a collapse or comeback, regardless of the sport. This likely has to do with the increased parity in sports today. Just think about the NCAA tournament. Back in the 1980s, it used to be unreal if a mid-major team topped a team from a major conference in the tournament. It would happen once or twice, at most, in a given tournament. Now it happens five to six times in the opening weekend. Higher and higher seeds are capable of making a run to the Final Four, and Butler damn near won the thing over powerhouse Duke in 2010. A lot of this has to do with the increased talent pool available to the field of sports as a whole. It wasn't that long ago that many high school graduates had to get a job directly after high school to support their families. Then the Baby Boomer generation came along, and although they had a bit more freedom with what they did after high school graduation, they were generally a career-oriented group. Sports obsession has grown to new heights in the modern society, and as such, more and more people are finding themselves in fields of work dealing with sports. Whether it's scouting (and therefore finding more talented individuals for schools both big and small); technology; or being able to dedicate more time to training, the pool of talent for sports, as an industry, has never been higher. What does all of this have to do with Jonathan Papelbon? Nothing really, please excuse the rant, but it is great for sports fans how vast the sports talent landscape is in the modern era. There has really never been a better time to be a sports fan than the present.

Starting IX Franchise Roster Stats

Lineup	Yrs	G	R	H	HR	RBI	SB	BB	SO	BA	OBP	SLG	OPS+	dWAR	WAR
Wade Boggs	11	1625	1067	2098	85	687	16	1004	470	0.338	0.428	0.462	142	10.6	71.6
Nomar Garciaparra	9	966	709	1281	178	690	84	279	406	0.323	0.370	0.553	133	8.4	41.1
Ted Williams	19	2292	1798	2654	**521**	1839	24	**2021**	709	**0.344**	**0.482**	**0.634**	**190**	-13.3	**123.1**
Carl Yastrzemski	**23**	**3308**	**1816**	**3419**	452	**1844**	168	1845	1393	0.285	0.379	0.462	130	0.5	96.1
Jimmie Foxx	7	887	721	1051	222	788	38	624	568	0.320	0.429	0.605	156	-3.3	34.6
David Ortiz	14	1953	1204	2079	483	1530	13	1133	1411	0.290	0.386	0.570	148	-17.7	52.9
Tris Speaker	9	1065	704	1327	39	542	267	459	235	0.337	0.414	0.482	166	2.9	55.4
Bobby Doerr	14	1865	1094	2042	223	1247	54	809	608	0.288	0.362	0.461	115	13.4	51.2
Dwight Evans	19	2505	1435	2373	379	1346	76	1337	**1643**	0.272	0.369	0.473	127	-3.5	66.2
Jason Varitek	15	1546	664	1307	193	757	25	614	1216	0.256	0.341	0.435	99	8.5	24.3
Pitchers	Yrs	W	W%	ERA	G	CG	SHO	SV	IP	SO	ERA+	WHIP	SO/9	SO/BB	WAR
Pedro Martínez	7	117	**0.760**	2.52	203	22	8	0	1383.2	1683	**190**	0.978	**10.9**	**5.45**	53.8
Jonathan Papelbon	7	23	0.548	2.33	396	0	0	**219**	429.1	509	197	1.018	10.7	4.43	16.2

Tier Six: The Championship Matchup

Here we are. Just two clubs remain. The New York Yankees and the San Francisco Giants. Two teams, who were once rivals long ago, will now rekindle their rivalry in the battle for franchise supremacy. Prepare to read about a lot of really effing talented baseball players.

San Francisco Giants (1958-pres.); New York Giants (1885-1957); New York Gothams (1883-1884)
VS.
New York Yankees (1913-pres.); New York Highlanders (1903-1912)

(Photo from Wikimedia Commons)

Team Backgrounds

Playoff appearances: Yankees – 53 vs. Giants – 26
Pennants: Yankees – 40 vs. Giants – 23
World Series titles: Yankees – 27 vs. Giants – 8
Collective team WAR: Yankees – 831.0 vs. Giants – 752.4

Giants strengths vs. Yankees strengths: The Yankees all-around offensive firepower in a lineup that is so ridiculously stacked – especially in the outfield – that this doesn't even appear to be a contest at first blush vs. The Giants sneaky deep offense – and just bonkers outfield – plus a better run prevention duo than the Yanks, which makes this a lot closer than one might expect.
Yankees weaknesses vs. Giants weaknesses: In the annals of history people are going to be talking about three things: the discovery of fire, the invention of the submarine, and the ~~Flint, Michigan Megabowl~~ Starting IX Championship Matchup – there are no weaknesses here.
What to expect from the next 33 pages: The end of the journey. Well, that's like saying Odysseus was home when he reached Calypso's island. Sure, he was close, but you still got 33 pages to go, vato.

This is normally the spot where the team introduction goes. However, you're about to read a lot (and I mean a lot) about these two teams. Also, if you've made it this far in the book without losing your mind, I'm assuming you're a baseball addict, which means you probably don't need me telling you things like: "The Yankees have been very good historically," or "The Giants win the World Series every even year."

That being said, let's get a quick opening argument from each club and then get on to the action. The team vs. team breakdown won't be a series of intense breakdowns, but rather the normal player write-up, with a sentence at the end declaring a winner. There was maybe one position that could have used an actual Yankee starter vs. Giants starter breakdown, but most of the cases are clear cut. At the end, we'll look at the final tally, make some adjustments if need be, and declare a winner (with a surprise cameo from a baseball simulation website, to boot).

Yankees Opening Argument

I know I just said that I wouldn't go all "The Yankees have been really good historically" on you, but here are some pretty cool nuggets: if you just took the 1949-1964 MLB seasons, the Yankees titles (9) are topped by only the Cardinals (11) *in the entirety of baseball history*. In those same years, the Yankees pennants (14) would be topped by only the Giants (20), Cardinals (19) and Dodgers (18) in their total franchise histories. From 1923-1962, the Yankees had as many championships (20) *as the rest of the league combined*. From 1926-1964, the Yanks never finished below .500. Their 1930, 1931, and 1933 iterations of the team had eight (eight!) Hall of Famers on the roster, the only (three) times that has happened in MLB history.

Prefer more recent history? From 1995-2012, the Yankees reached the playoffs 17 of 18 years with the only year they missed out being a season in which they won 89 games. In 1995, they debuted Derek Jeter, Jorge Posada, Andy Pettitte, and Mariano Rivera, all in the same season, and all from their farm system. This "Core Four" would go on to rejuvenate the franchise to the aforementioned levels of success. Their franchise .569 winning percentage is 32 points higher than the second-place Giants. Despite eight organizations that have been around longer, they have the most home runs in history, over 1,200 more home runs than the second-place Giants. There's Ruth and Gehrig and DiMaggio and Mantle. The pinstripes,[449] the House the Ruth Built, and the interlocking NY. Simply put: the Yankees are the most famous baseball franchise for a reason. This is a franchise that puts winning on such a pedestal that, when Jeter and his cohort were in the minor leagues, they were served better food after wins then after losses – that's effed up, but that's where this organization's priorities lie.

The attention the Yankees receive may indeed be more insidious than it should be because of #EastCoastBias, and their payroll is often more bloated than Robert De Niro in *Raging Bull*, but the success the franchise has had cannot be disputed by anyone.

Giants Opening Argument

On its surface, yes, this appears to be a mismatch. Just look at the playoff success listed above and think of all the great name attached to the Yankees throughout history: Ruth, Gehrig, DiMaggio, Mantle, Jeter… Hmmm that sure seems to be a lot of hitters…

Last I remember, there's a whole nother part of the sport; something that involves a mound or something. Quick, try to guess who the Yankees are going to have as their Starting IX starting pitcher? Yeah, it's not exactly a *Murderer's Row*.

The Giants, on the other hand, have a stable of arms from which to draw. Granted, only one starting pitcher matters in this hypothetical matchup, but even there, the Giants have a huge edge. Although the theory that pitching mattering more in the postseason may not hold water, it's undeniable that in any one given game the pitcher has a huuuggee impact on the final score. Just look at how much the Vegas lines can shift from one day to the next when two teams are playing each other in a three-game series. There's almost no factor that swings a line as much as the man on the mound, and the Giants have a clear and distinct edge in this regard.

There's also the fact that they aren't exactly slouches with the sticks, either. In Barry Bonds and Willie Mays, the Giants have two of the five greatest players in baseball history standing right next to each other in the outfield. Those two

---

[449] "You know why the Yankees always win Frank?" "Cause they have Mickey Mantle?" "No, it's cause the other teams can't stop staring at those damn pinstripes."

may just be able to cancel out Ruth and Gehrig, something not too many other franchises can say. The club also doesn't have any real distinct holes, thanks to a 135-year history of being one of the more successful franchises in baseball. They have eight World Series wins and 23 pennants. They've hoisted the title of Baseball Champion as far back as 1888 and as recently as 2014 – their history is expansive. They may have been overshadowed by the Yankees when the two were in New York, but you know that sneaky hot girl/quietly cute guy who slips under-the-radar in high school because her best friend got boobs first/his buddies all had better haircuts than him? That's the Giants. They may have taken a while to get a good haircut/their boobs may have come in late, but that's the team that actually looks best when the time matters most.

Also, they have really good pitching.

Starting IX's

Catcher: Buster Posey vs. Yogi Berra

Buster Posey (2009-2017)

This spot originally went to Buck Ewing, one of the oldest players in this book, a player who played his entire career with the Giants before the turn of the 20th century. He was an innovator at the position and was among the first generation of catchers to wear chest protectors. He was the first catcher to throw out runners from his knees, showing off his excellent arm. He was a part of two championship teams, and he was the main cog on those New York Giant teams. He was such a complete player (power, speed, defense), that it is not at all surprising that Ewing was considered one of, if not the, best players before the modern era. In fact, when the Hall of Fame opened there were five pre-1900 players – Ewing tied for the most votes received among that group of players.

However, in the time it took to write this book, it became obvious that he needed to be replaced by a guy who is one of the youngest players in the book – Buster Posey. In 2012, Buster Posey joined Yogi Berra and Roy Campanella as the only catchers to win an MVP and World Series in the same year. By winning the NL MVP, Posey also became the first MVP at the catcher position since 1972. Receiving the award at the precocious age of 25, Posey became the youngest NL MVP since Ryne Sandberg in 1984. Not only did Posey win the MVP, but he also won the batting title, in the process becoming the first NL catcher to do so since Ernie Lombardi in 1942. The key to Posey's batting title was his dominance of left-handed pitching. He tore up lefties to the tune of a .433 batting average and 13 home runs. This joined him with Ryan Braun and Jeff Bagwell as the only players to reach both those numbers against lefties in a season.

Posey may well go down as one of the five or so greatest Giants in franchise history, as he is slowing no signs of slowing down. He has been worth at least 4.0 WAR each season from 2012-2017, and his career OPS+ of 135 is among the top five all-time at the catcher position. He's a pure talent we are lucky enough to be watching unfold right before our eyes.

Yogi Berra (1946-1963)

So much ink has been spilled on "Yogi the entertainer" that, as Jayson Stark points out in *The Stark Truth*, the Yankee backstop is actually underrated as "Yogi the player." The position of Yankee catcher is absolutely stacked throughout history, making Berra's selection here all the more impressive. Historically, the conversation about Berra's greatness begins and ends with his 10 championship rings. Since those rings are impossible to argue with, the conversation usually stops there. Let's delve into a few of the lesser-known stats behind this catch-phrasing catcher, though.

The first under-the-radar strength of Berra was his ability to avoid striking out. For his career, Berra struck out a measly 414 times, unthinkable in the modern era, but even impressive for Berra's time. His 1950 campaign was his most impressive in this sense. He struck out a measly 12 times all year, but was able to draw 55 walks and hit 28 home runs. This was not the only year he was able to pull off the remarkable feat of having more home runs than strikeouts. In fact, he was able to accomplish the feat four other full seasons and had the same number of home runs and strikeouts in 1957. It wasn't until nearly the end of 1957 that his career strikeout total topped his career home runs total. Imagine that, over a decade of hitting more home runs than striking out.

Now, we would be remiss to go without mentioning that while the Yankees were blessed to end up with Berra, Berra was also blessed to be with the Yankees. His next accomplishment, although impressive, is certainly owed in part to his position as catcher of the then-world-beating Yankees: he is the only player in baseball history to finish in the top four of the MVP for seven straight seasons, an achievement driven in part by his team's success, but that shouldn't take away too much from the awe that accomplishment inspires. This achievement was also driven by Berra's incredible ability to avoid missing games, despite playing behind the plate. Easily the coolest Berra-endurance stat is that, for his career, Berra caught 117 full double-headers. As in he caught Game 1, went out, strapped back on the catcher's gear, and caught Game 2 later that day – guys just don't do that anymore.

It's also fair to say that for a Catcher he embodied the letter C. He was Consistent (10 straight seasons with 20 or more home runs), Compact (his 358 home runs in a career – and 30 home runs in 1952 and 1965 – are the most ever for a player listed at 5'7"), Clutch (in the years Retrosheet has covered, he had a .307 average in high leverage situations and a .304 average in games deemed "late and close" per Baseball-Reference), and his 950 Consecutive Chances without an error set a then-record for Catchers.

Finally, we certainly couldn't go the whole write-up without giving some love to the other side of Yogi's fame – his Berra-isms. There are hundreds to choose from, but I'll go with my personal favorite: "Nobody goes there anymore, it's too crowded."

Verdict: **Yogi Berra** gets the Yankees started on the right foot, in what was a pretty easy decision. Posey could honestly get there one day, but he'd need another five or six stud seasons to have it be a conversation.

First Base: Bill Terry vs. Lou Gehrig

Bill Terry (1923-1936)

Although an older player just lost a spot on this Giants roster, Terry is here repping the early days of Giants history well. He was part of the "Hall of Fame infield" that the Giants sported in the interwar years, playing alongside a few players we'll see in a bit.

"Memphis Bill" would be much better known if it wasn't for Ted Williams. In fact, if Williams had decided to sit out that final doubleheader of 1941, or had gone 2-for-8 instead of 6-for-8, Terry would be a household name. The reason: Terry was the last player to hit .400 before Williams, (.401 in 1930). As such, he is still the most recent .400 hitter in the NL.

Bill Terry's professional career got off to a relatively late start for his day and age, due to the fact that he originally tried to make it as a pitcher in the big leagues. Obviously, that didn't work out, but he was destined for a career in baseball anyways, and "Smiling Bill" ended up one of the top hitters of all time. In the nine seasons in which he had at least 500 at bats, Terry hit at least .319 in every single one of them. He was primarily a line drive hitter of whom Dizzy Dean once said, "[Terry] once hit a ball between my legs so hard that the center fielder caught it on the fly backing up against the wall."

Terry was also a leader on the team, which allowed him to take over as player/manager part way through the 1932 season. In his first full season as manager, he brought a title to New York (the 1933 World Series), making him one of just four player/managers to win the World Series post-1930.

After the 1933 season, Terry starred in one of the best foot-in-mouth stories of all time. Shortly after the title, he was quoted as saying, "Anybody want to bet a hat that we don't win again?" He had reporters list the contenders, one of whom was a Brooklyn reporter who said, "How about Brooklyn, Bill?" Terry's response dripped with sarcasm: "Is Brooklyn still in the league?" It made for a funny quip at the time, but boy did it come back to haunt him. At the end of the 1934 season, the Giants were engaged in a close pennant race with the St. Louis Cardinals. Well, guess who came to town to try to play spoiler – the Dodgers. Brooklyn played the Giants in the last two games of the year, defeating them in both, and breaking the tie between the Cards and the Giants. This gave the Cardinals the pennant, and the next day the headlines read, "Yes, indeed, Mr. Terry, the Dodgers still are in the League."

Although there was no breakdown for this position, it should be noted that Roger Connor was also an outstanding first baseman for the Giants. In fact, his career OPS+ was higher than Terry's by a decent margin. However, the fact that Terry played his entire career with the Giants, was also a manager, led them to a championship, and played in a much more similar era to today's game, all led to his relatively easy case for first base. Connor was, however, the all-time home run leader before Babe Ruth, but that's kind of like saying Herbert Dinkletrick[450] was the best electrician before Thomas Edison.

For those of you wondering where a certain first baseman with a spot of water behind the left field fence in AT&T Park named after him is, fear not.

Lou Gehrig (1923-1939)

Gehrig is famous for so many reasons today that, similar to Berra, his worth as a baseball player is somewhat underappreciated. Depending on at what position on the diamond you put Stan Musial, Gehrig is either debatably the best first baseman of all time, or certainly the best first baseman of all time (Jimmie Foxx just didn't age well enough). One would have a very difficult time presenting a case in which Gehrig isn't one of the top 15 players of all time, but due to numerous factors, Gehrig isn't thought of in the same vein as some of the other all-time greats.

For one, Gehrig had to play in the shadow of Babe Ruth(s belly) for his entire career, a fact that was not lost on Gehrig. As Gehrig himself described it, Lou was "The fellow that follows Babe in the batting order. When Babe's turn at the bat is over… If I stood on my head at the plate, nobody would pay attention." In fact, for much of their careers, Ruth and Gehrig straight up didn't like each other. Gehrig was known to hold a grudge, and Ruth was known to do things that lent themselves to grudge-holding. However, in an interesting piece done quite a few years back in *Sports Illustrated*, Ron Fimrite notes that Gehrig's first season without the Bambino (1935) was one of Gehrig's worst, and it was not until the next year –

[450] Not a real person, for all you PolitiFact truthers.

when rookie Joe DiMaggio took the spotlight back from Gehrig – that Lou bounced back. Fimrite uses this to say that Gehrig was, "destined to be a second banana." Now from the tone of the piece, Fimrite did not at all mean that in a diminishing way to Gehrig, but with the advancements made in baseball statistics we can show that Fimrite may have been a little right and a little wrong in his analysis.

For one, the American League scored nearly 800 more runs in 1936 than 1935, meaning that Gehrig "rejuvenation" in 1936 was due at least in part to changes outside his control. There's also the fact that Gehrig's on-base percentage actually went up from 1934 to 1935, and his 1935 BABIP, although not terrible, was the worst of those three years, suggesting a bit of bad luck in 1935. The most noticeable change is the drop in power we see from Gehrig in 1935. His home run total is noticeably lower (30 home runs in 1935 compared to 49 in the surrounding seasons), and so are his total bases (312 in 1935 compared to over 400 in the surrounding seasons). This is where I happen to agree to a certain extent with Fimrite. Although the metrics say that Gehrig was actually nearly as valuable in 1935 (8.7 WAR in 1935 compared to 10.4 in 1934 and 9.1 in 1936), there's something to be said about Gehrig's approach in 1935. Although his WAR was still an incredible 8.7, he didn't really give the vibe of a man who could carry the team on his back. Without Ruth or DiMaggio behind him in the lineup, Gehrig was more than content to take pitch-after-pitch en route to an MLB-leading 132 walks. Meanwhile, Gehrig's production slipped because, although walks certainly have their place in baseball, when one is as talented as Gehrig, a few more swings of the bat may have resulted in a few more runs for the Yankees.

This is a criticism that Ted Williams (a man who played in exactly one career game against Gehrig) faced throughout his career, and Joey Votto faces today. In a sense, the statistical revolution has shown us that drawing a walk is more valuable than we previously thought, however, an all-time caliber player on a crap roster may still need to swing the bat a bit more than he might like. It's one reason the on-base percentage versus slugging percentage debate is one that is ongoing in the sabermetric community today. Gehrig was looked to as his team's leading (and slugging) man in 1935, but without a Ruth or DiMaggio, Gehrig decided to settle into the role of on-base man. There's nothing wrong with that per se, but it certainly means that Fimrite may not have been far off base with his second banana comment after all.

A few words on Gehrig's games played streak because I'm not sure how I feel about the implications that just occurred that Gehrig was anything less than one of the best players of all time. Although Ripken topped Gehrig's streak, the list of injuries Gehrig played through remains legendary. He played through multiple fractured fingers and was even knocked out cold by a pitch only to play the next day. In that game, he hit three triples in four and a half innings. He dealt with severe lower back pain, including one time when he was lucky to be on the road because that allowed Joe McCarthy to start Gehrig at shortstop and bat him in the leadoff spot. Gehrig was replaced after his first at bat, which, in typical Gehrig fashion, managed to be a hit. Maybe the most impressive part of this story? When he toughed out this start, Gehrig already had the record for consecutive games started. This was not for the fame anymore, but rather because he couldn't picture himself not in the starting lineup. Gehrig passed away 16 years to the day after he made the first start of his streak, a start that had Wally Pipp (the man he replaced at first base) regretting, as he put it, "the two most expensive aspirin in history."

Let's finish up on Gehrig with a bit more on the idea of second banana. The origin of the term goes back to the days of burlesque and vaudeville. In vaudeville acts, the straight man was often referred to as the second banana to the comedian. When you think about it, the comparison makes sense, Gehrig as the Abbott to Ruth's Costello. Sure, Gehrig won the MVP in 1927, but that was the year Ruth stole the show with his 60 home runs. Gehrig won the MVP again in 1936, but as mentioned, Ruth was gone at that point and the spotlight was shifting to DiMaggio. In the 10 years bookended by those MVPs, Gehrig averaged, let's repeat that, *averaged* .350/.457/.660 slashes with 142 runs, 39 home runs, and 153 RBI and 9.0 WAR a season – that's stupid.

It wasn't just on the field, either. Ruth was a demigod in New York city, a man bigger than life. Gehrig was a man so shy that he would get flustered when asked by women for his autograph. Gehrig was raised by his mother (his father had suffered a severe head injury that meant Lou's mom was the head of house), and he was incredibly close with her as a result. In fact, one story goes that the breaking point in Ruth and Gehrig's relationship centered around Ruth telling Gehrig's mother to stay out of the business of Ruth and his wife. Ruth appeared in commercials and lived a Hollywood life of booze and women. Gehrig once turned down an opportunity to make some extra money in a cigarette ad because he thought it would be a bad influence over his young fans.[451]

All of this is just part of the reason that June 19, 1939 – Gehrig's "Luckiest man on the face of the earth" speech – was such an amazing moment. As with almost all of Yankees history, there have been volumes of books written about this moment, but one thing that bears repeating is just how important this moment was for a man so often out-shined – and so often aware that he was out-shined. Gehrig finally managed to be on center stage. It was Gehrig who became the first player ever to have his number retired, an honor on par with any accolade. Gehrig finally had *his* moment, and no man deserved it more.

Verdict: **Lou Gehrig** gets another moment, easily trouncing Terry, and giving the Yankees a 2-0 lead.

[451] Remember, this was in a time when nearly everyone smoked, and cigarettes didn't have nearly the same stigma as they do today.

Second Base: Larry Doyle vs. TBD

Larry Doyle (1907-1916; 1918-1920)

This pick may surprise a lot of Giants fans, especially those who were fans in the early 2000s. They almost certainly remember Jeff Kent being an MVP candidate for several years, a difficult feat for a second baseman, and thus would have expected to see him here. Well, there are several factors that led to Doyle getting the spot.

For one, he played with the Giants far longer. His 1,622 games with the franchise are nearly double Kent's 900. Kent also played in a much friendlier era for hitters, and although his numbers (even by advanced metrics) are solid, so are Doyle's. Finally, and this one is much more subjective, but Kent was a dick.

Although baseball is still a team sport, the average fan doesn't hear as much about who are good teammates as say basketball or football. When on the field, the pitcher vs. batter matchup can be seen as one of the more individualized moments in sports. However, being a good teammate definitely still matters, in fact, possibly more than any other sport. Why? Because although the essential pitcher vs. batter battle is independent, in no other sport does one spend as much time with their team as baseball. The sport has the longest regular season, and it is also the only sported played basically every day when in season. Other sports have practices and travel time together, but oftentimes a baseball clubhouse is like a family. With the year-round nature of offseason workouts in the modern game, your teammates are truly your second family.

Well, if a baseball team is a family, Jeff Kent was that asshole second cousin who you really hope is adopted, because he's such a dick. Richard Justice wrote an interesting piece in *Sporting News MLB* right after Kent's retirement that paints Kent as a man who put winning before all else, including common courtesy. There are numerous anecdotes throughout the story that make Kent look like a Christmas Day Scrooge. There's the story of how Lance Berkman asked him several times: "How's it going," only to have Kent respond curtly, "What is it with you guys? You think I've got to walk around saying hello to everyone? I see you every day." His postgame interviews were must-see, cringe-worthy affairs with head-shaking and muttering more common than actual answers. Maybe nothing summed him up better than the quote, from Kent, that Justice chose to open the article: "I'd like to leave the game without a single friend." In Kent's mind, friends were the result of putting something in front of winning, a mortal sin in his eyes. When he and Bonds came to blows in the Giants dugout (right around the time both were cementing their reputation as difficult clubhouse guys), it was after Bonds stood up for a younger player whom Kent had been especially hard on. Kent was most upset by mental errors, giving his teammates a hard time, but giving himself the hardest time. As is the case with nearly all people, however, there was some good in Kent as he often would shine in the team visits to local hospitals. As a whole, however, Kent seems like a tough guy with which to work, but that's definitely not the only reason Doyle takes the spot on the Giants Starting IX.

A few words on Doyle's since it is his spot on the team: Doyle played for the Giants in 13 of his 14 professional seasons (he spent a season-plus-nine-games in the middle of his career with the Cubs). He technically was a Boston Brave for four days, but he never played a game with them, as the two trades that moved him from Chicago to Boston and then from Boston back to New York, all happened during the offseason.

He won an MVP[452] of his own in 1912, but given that he was only fifth among NL position players in WAR that season, it may have had more to do with the team's success. The season was part of a three-year stretch (1911-1913) in which the Giants won three consecutive pennants but lost all three World Series appearances. Doyle's best season came the year before he won the MVP (this often seems to be the case, as the voters are almost always a year or so behind), in which he totaled a league-leading 25 triples to along with 13 home runs, 38 steals, 102 runs, and a .397 OBP. Doyle retired at the relatively young age of 34, and although his speed and power had been diminished, he was still rather healthy (playing in 137 games his final year) and productive (a .352 on-base percentage) his final year.

Doyle was a classic old school ball player who loved to engage fans of his, especially in his later days. Two college-aged Giants fans visited him in 1970 and wrote about the visit in *The National Pastime* in 1993. According to the writer, Doyle played a board game reenactment of the 1911 World Series in which Doyle had actually played. The game took more than three times as long as normal because every action in the game would remind Doyle of an old story with which he would then regale his young visitors.

Tony Lazzeri (1926-1937) vs. Willie Randolph (1976-1988) vs. Joe Gordon (1938-1943; 1946) vs. Robinson Canó (2005-2013)

Welcome to "State Your Case," America's favorite way to determine which Yankees second baseman was the best in team history. Each participant will be given one paragraph to state his case, as well as one sentence to go on the attack and pick on one other guy, explaining why the other guy shouldn't have the spot. This is your host, A Ryan Seacrest Type. STATE. YOUR. CASE.

Joe Gordon: I held the AL record for career home runs by a second baseman until this millennium despite not

[452] Technically, the award was called the Chalmers Award and, interestingly enough, was defined as being given to the player that was the "most important and useful player to the club and to the league."

having played in six and a half decades. Plus, I beat Ted Williams out for the MVP the year in which he won the Triple Crown. Joe McCarthy even once said of me, "I'll say right now that the greatest all around player I ever saw – and I don't bar any of them – is Joe Gordon."

Fricken' Tony Lazzeri had Babe Ruth and Lou Gehrig hitting in front of him, no wonder he had such good numbers, a blind tomcat could have knocked in 100 RBI with how much those guys were on base.

Tony Lazzeri: Hey Joe, I didn't have either guy in the lineup with me in the (surprisingly deep and talented) Pacific Coast League in 1925 when I hit .355 with 60 home runs, 222 RBI and 202 runs (in 197 games)!

It took Willie Randolph six years to put up those kind of numbers.

Willie Randolph: Yeah, but you know that trendy new WAR stat all the kids are using these days, guess who is top of the heap among this group of ragtag second basemen? Yup, it's me. I played with the Yankees for 13 years, that's commitment.

Joe Gordon couldn't even commit to using the same bat twice in a row at any point in his career, he switched bats after every single time at the plate. Weird, dude.

Robinson Canó: Well, since none of you went after me, I'll have to assume you agree that I'm the best, and I can't blame you, what with my 1,649 hits in my first nine years as a Yankee being topped by only Joltin' Joe DiMaggio in franchise history. As for as you older players, sports writers love to mythologize players in their post-playing days and ignore what they have right in front of them, even if those players are truly the most deserving. Oh, and Joe Gordon, guess who now holds the record for most home runs by an AL second baseman in a career? I'll give you a hint, it rhymes with "me."

A Ryan Seacrest Type: Good point, Robby. **Robinson Canó** is our winner. Tell him what he's won, Bob.

Verdict: **Tie**. Seriously check out how close the numbers for Robinson Canó (Yankee) and Larry Doyle (Giant) are. There's just not enough of a gap to say with certainty who was the better ballplayer in his time in New York.

Third Base: Matt Williams vs. Alex Rodriguez

Matt Williams (1987-1996)

One of the more popular players of his time, Williams started his career with the Giants in 1987. He struggled with health and playing time for his first few years until his breakout 1990 performance. He led the league in RBI (122), made the All-Star Game, and finished sixth in the National League MVP. His final seven years in San Francisco would prove to be just as productive. For that stretch, he sported a 130 OPS+ and averaged 30 home runs a season. The crown jewel of his time in San Francisco was almost certainly his 1994 campaign.

The 1994 season will always be remembered for the labor strike that canceled the end of the season and the playoffs,[453] but it was almost remembered for an entirely different reason. Before the labor disputes shut down baseball, Matt Williams had hit 43 home runs through 115 games. This meant he was on pace for 61 home runs – obviously a magical number. Now, players have been on pace to break records throughout baseball history and failed to do so, but it would have made for an excellent and intriguing end to the 1994 campaign, if Williams had been given the chance. He does own a bit of baseball history, however, as over one 162-game stretch of baseball from September 3, 1993 to May 17, 1995, Williams hit 62 home runs.

When Williams was eventually traded out of San Francisco, he was able to net the Giants the man who we just discussed – Jeff Kent. This trade allowed the Giants to get an All-Star caliber second baseman, and it allowed Matt Williams to find his place in the record books once again. By homering in the World Series as a member of Cleveland in his only year there, and then homering in the Diamondbacks' 2001 World Series victory over the Yankees, Williams became the first player to hit a home run in the World Series for three different franchises (he hit his Giants World Series' home run in 1989).

In a disappointing final note on Williams: as it turns out, his home run record, had he achieved it in 1994, would have been under just as much scrutiny as McGwire's 70 and Bonds' 73, as Williams was named in the 2007 Mitchell Report as having allegedly used PEDs. (Although we know from Big Papi's write-up that the Mitchell Report leak has plenty of issues, that doesn't mean he would have avoided being dogged by these rumors if he was one of the home run record holders).

Alex Rodriguez (2004-2013; 2015-2016)

Speaking of allegedly using PEDs...

This is the third time seeing Alex Rodriguez on a Starting IX; he is the only player to accomplish such a feat.[454] This obviously speaks a lot to his skill, but it is also interesting that a player as talented as Rodriguez made so many different stops

---

[453] The 1994 strike was able to cancel the World Series, something nothing else (including those two pesky World Wars), was able to do.

[454] The two other men to hit at least 100 home runs for three different teams (Jim Thome and Reggie Jackson) appear on two Starting IX's, but neither was able to make it for all three.

in his career. Of course, I used the word "interesting" and not "surprising" because as any fan who isn't sharing an apartment with Patrick the Starfish (aka living under a rock) knows, in his playing days, A-Rod managed to make more enemies – both in the sport, as well as among fans – than almost any other player in history. As you can guess if you'd made it this far in the book, though, the story isn't as simple as "A-Rod is an A-Hole."

There are innumerable think pieces about why A-Rod drew so much ire throughout his career, and I don't use "think piece" as a pejorative here, because these are some of the most interesting articles that can be read on the interwebs.[455] They are written by some of the most creative minds in sports writing, but maybe more importantly, they are written about one of the most unique men in the history of sport. The takeaway: maybe more than any other athlete in sports, people love to project onto Rodriguez. They like to create a trope for Rodriguez and pigeonhole him into that narrative. Although people undoubtedly do this to everyone, it just never worked with Rodriguez. That really threw people off, and it is a decent chunk of why Rodriguez has taken so much heat.

Just think of the contradictions in personality we have seen from Rodriguez in his two decades in the spotlight. This was a player who, when he came to New York, gave up his natural position (shortstop) to let the Yankee Captain (Derek Jeter) stay there. A-Rod tackled a third base position he had never played before for the good of the team. If it had been Jeter who moved positions, he would have been on the cover of the Daily News for a month straight with halos over his head for the sacrifice he made to make the Yankees better. This was far from a one-time thing. When Rodriguez was voted to the All-Star Game starting lineup in Cal Ripken's final year, A-Rod gave up his spot at shortstop to Ripken. Ripken had been voted to start at third, but Cal had revolutionized the shortstop position for players like Jeter and Rodriguez, and so A-Rod deferred to him once they took the field. Can you imagine the orgy ESPN would have had with that story if it had been Jeter giving up his spot instead of A-Rod? Instead, it was a narrative that many folks may not even know about today.

Of course, at some point we have to circle back to the jab that started this write-up – A-Rod and his PED use. Rodriguez has, multiple times (!), been caught using PEDs, and he has not exactly been the most repentant every time he was caught either. A-Rod's PED use has been mentioned briefly in his past write-ups, but let's go a little more in-depth here, since it was with New York where his PED use got the most intriguing. Just a quick side note/preface before we dive in: although it can't be known if A-Rod used steroids outside of when he was caught/admitted PED use, the two times on record are 2001-03 in Texas and 2010-12 in New York.

The story of A-Rod's PED use in New York is a cluster fuck. One of the best sources on the subject is a book called *Blood Sport* by Tim Elfrink and Gus Garcia-Roberts which clarifies the confusing details that we do know. It is an interesting read, and one of the biggest takeaways I had was that the MLB's steroid policy is even more ridiculous than I had imagined. Under the current drug policy, players can apply for a "therapeutic use exemption" that allows them to take certain substances that are usually banned, but that exemption only lasts for one season. A-Rod applied for this TUE (therapeutic use exemption) in 2007 and 2008, and despite the fact that just a hair over eight percent of all players who applied for this exemption were awarded use of their requested steroid, A-Rod's request for use of testosterone – a steroid that ex-COO and current Commissioner Rob Manfred called, "the mother of all anabolic" – was granted. He was granted use of clomiphene in 2008, and as the authors of *Blood Sport* tell it, at least two of his three MVP seasons came with the help of anabolic steroids, however, his 2007 PED use *had been approved by MLB*. How confusing is that? Where it gets a little simpler is, in 2010, when Rodriguez was feeling the pressure for home run no. 600. A-Rod approached the infamous Tony Bosch looking for a synthetic edge. It was this drive to be the best ever, and shatter home run records along the way, that led Rodriguez to Bosch. Eventually, it lost Rodriguez his 2014 campaign when he served the longest-ever suspension for PED use in MLB history.

Of course, as has been noted in earlier write-ups on Rodriguez in this book, Rodriguez was an amazing player before he decided to take performance-enhancing drugs. In fact, he may well have been one of the 25 best players all-time even without any enhancers. Neil Payne of *FiveThirtyEight* penned a piece entitled, "Alex Rodriguez Would've Made The Hall Of Fame Without Steroids," which, well, is pretty self-explanatory. Payne uses a mind-blowing stat to help make his case:

"[Bill] James once developed a long-term career forecast model called Brock2 – essentially a very early progenitor of a full-fledged projection system like PECOTA – which could produce an expected career stat line for a player based on his career performance through a given age. Feed it Rodriguez's age 20-24 seasons, and it produces an absurd set of projected career totals: 3,573 hits; 668 doubles; 1,075 home runs. As mean projections for anybody, those numbers are silly."

Now, projection systems have been wrong plenty of times, but those numbers are still "kid-in-The-Matrix-bending-the-spoon" crazy, and one day, with the benefit of temporal distance, I think A-Rod will be able to be more accurately assessed. It also won't hurt his legacy that he already seems like a lock to become one of the best commentators the sport has ever seen in his post-playing days. Never underestimate people's ability to rewrite a man's narrative. Especially when it comes to Alex Rodriguez.

Verdict: **A-Rod**. By a lot.

---

[455] The best of the bunch is, unsurprisingly, Bryan Curtis' piece, "The Slugger With a Thousand Faces" on *Grantland.*

Shortstop: Travis Jackson vs. Derek Jeter

Travis Jackson (1922-1936)

Travis Jackson was the Andrelton Simmons of his time, mixing unbelievable fielding with enough pop at the plate to make him serviceable from an offensive perspective. In 1929, Jackson hit 21 home runs and was worth more than 3.0 wins with his glove and positional value, per dWAR. He was the only player to have 20+ homers and 3.0+ dWAR for the first 80+ years of baseball history (Ernie Banks joined him 30 years later). This ability to contribute on both the offensive and defensive side is what gives him the edge here over Art Fletcher, who, although he once totaled 5.1 dWAR in a single season, never totaled more than four home runs in a season. Although part of this undoubtedly has to do with Jackson playing just a few years later – in an era with many more home runs – Jackson also collected 457 more hits and 245 more walks than Fletcher in their respective time with the franchise.

Jackson was yet another member of the Giants Hall of Fame infield, but he is considered one of, if not the, weakest player in the Hall of Fame. This seems like as good a time as any to touch upon some of the Hall of Fame-level BS that the Baseball Hall of Fame has been tied to in its history (we'll touch on even more of this with the next player on this Giants franchise roster).

Don't get me wrong, the Baseball Hall of Fame, and the town of Cooperstown as a whole, is one of my favorite places of all time. In fact, given that the three times I have been to the museum I have literally stayed open to close; one could say that it might be my favorite place on this planet. I planned a friend's bachelor party for Cooperstown, for crying out loud. However, that is not to say that the museum doesn't have its flaws. For one, it struggles greatly with its subjectivity. Although baseball is a sport that relies heavily on statistics, its Hall of Fame does not have any numerical system for determining who deserves to be enshrined and who does not. I am not saying that the Hall of Fame should have a strict "you must have at least 2,500 career hits," or "you must have at least 200 wins or 500 saves," or even "you must have been worth at least 60.0 WAR." These criteria are arbitrary and would leave out Mickey Mantle, Sandy Koufax, and Yogi Berra – and who would want to go to *that* Hall of Fame?

However, the Baseball Hall of Fame sometimes seems to rely strictly on subjectivity. More popular players (among the media, mind you) are often enshrined faster and at the cost of a less popular player if the two are both on the precipice of induction. Old-timey players, whose numbers are often lacking in comparison with some of the game's new wave of players, are often favored due to ideologies such as "their historical value on the game" and the fact that "they didn't play for the numbers." When Jonah Keri tore apart the BBWAA after the 2013 debacle (no living members inducted, meaning the already-flailing Cooperstown economy had a rather slow ceremony), he used a couple of jaw-dropping quotes from BBWAA voters. Lyle Spencer, of MLB.com, wrote, "Next year, I'll use my head, weigh all the numbers. This year, I used my gut: Does this guy feel right?... I gave weight to integrity and character." News flash: the Hall of Fame isn't a social club. This isn't about the individuals who were nicest, or the ones who didn't give you a hard time when you asked for an interview. Baseball, as a whole, is undergoing such a statistical revolution, that it is seeing similar pushback to any other revolution. All the voters that don't agree with the statistically heavy approach some of the modern writers are using seem to be more stubborn than ever in their ignorance of numbers.[456] Gut checks for the Hall of Fame? In the words of Tom Jackson: "C'MON MAN."

Jackson probably isn't the worst player in the Hall of Fame,[457] but he serves as an example of why there should be some checks and balances to the Hall of Fame voting system. Maybe have a rotating exhibit on display each week that shows one of these older players who the Hall of Fame is worried will go forgotten if not included. Maybe have a wing of the museum dedicated to the Giants unrivaled infield of the 1920s. However, when Travis Jackson, Freddie Lindstrom, and Lloyd Waner all have plaques, and they *combined* for fewer Wins Above Average than Edgar Martínez,[458] who doesn't have a plaque (and will not in the foreseeable future), something is wrong with the system. This is not to mention the problem with the superiority and pettiness that the Hall of Fame exudes, which we will get to in a second.

Travis Jackson's legacy does not deserve to be *tarnished* by his place in the Hall of Fame, but it also probably doesn't deserve benefit from him being in the Hall, either. The problem with the Hall of Fame voters isn't just limited to whom they have included, however. They have pulled a lot of crap in their time. They didn't have Joe DiMaggio and Rogers Hornsby as first-ballot Hall of Famers. Lefty Grove and Jimmie Foxx each received less than 13 percent of the vote on their first ballot. In that aforementioned Jonah Keri piece, Keri made the argument that if a player deserves to be in the Hall of Fame, they should be voted for first-ballot, last-ballot, and anywhere in between. This may not make sense on the surface, because of the emphasis placed on a "First-ballot Hall of Famer" in today's mindset. However, the lingering effects of the voters not having confidence in their own voting means that Keri is right. Let me explain: Bill Conlin of the *Philadelphia Daily News* voted for Tim Raines in Raines' first year on the ballot. Now, Raines is not a typical "First-ballot Hall of Famer,"

---

[456] Kind of like how there is a run on gun sales whenever a Democratic president makes a statement on gun laws.

[457] Hallofstats.com, an excellent source for this topic, has Jackson as the 170th-ranked player in the Hall of Fame, well ahead of players such as Lloyd Waner and teammate Freddie Lindstrom, whose candidacies are slightly amusing but stand enshrined in Cooperstown's hallowed halls.

[458] Waner was actually worth negative Wins Above Average (-2.1) for his career.

but he most certainly belongs in the Hall. Once Conlin saw that less than 25 percent of his fellow writers voted for Raines, however, he changed his mind and left Raines off the ballot the next year. If everyone who believed Raines belonged in the Hall had simply voted for him that first year, it may not have caused certain voters to abandon ship the next year, thus driving down Raines' chances at Cooperstown. There's also the fact that the ballot is limited to 10 names, yet another outdated idea based on a document written in a different era (this time based on the original induction all the way back in 1936). It's a living document! The failure to modernize and adapt to the times is hardly unique to Cooperstown and the Hall of Fame process, but that doesn't make it any less annoying.

Due to all of this, at this point in time, it is unfortunately not reasonable to judge someone's career by whether they are in the Hall of Fame or not, because it is just too subjective. Baseball has a million ways to judge a player, and a plaque is not the best one.

Interestingly enough, Jackson's biggest competition for this spot was George Davis, a great player long overlooked by the Hall, eventually to the point that Bill James dedicated an entire chapter to Davis in his book questioning the Hall of Fame, *Whatever Happened to the Hall of Fame?* (Baseball Hall of Fame fretting is hardly a new phenomenon, James wrote that book in the `90s.)

Derek Jeter (1995-2014)

Outside of Stan Musial and Barry Bonds, this was one of the hardest write-ups to pen. There were just so many different angles to take. Go old school and make a Starting IX of the clutchest players in baseball history? Go new school and talk about how it's really difficult to statistically back the idea that there are players who are consistently clutch throughout their entire careers? Go Yankee Core Four homer and just jizz cool Jeter stories for two pages? Go contrarian and talk about how Jeter was actually overrated, channeling my inner Keith Olbermann and deconstructing Jeter's legacy in the process? So many possibilities. So naturally, I decided to take the wordiest path (and probably biggest cop out) and do a little bit of everything. If you thought the writing style in this book was schizophrenic before this… Just wait!

Jeter as the clutch savior: The clutch debate is both so woven into the narrative of baseball history and so difficult to disprove, that I don't see it fading away at any point in the near future. And Jeter's got quite a case. Even though postseason statistical records are skewed towards modern players (the Championship Series came into play in 1969 and the Division Series came into play in 1995), Jeter still has some crazy impressive numbers. He is the all-time leader in playoff games played (158), at bats (650), runs (111), hits (200), and total bases (302). On top of all that, his slash lines are mighty impressive, as well.

Thanks to several factors (tighter pitching rotations, days off for the bullpen, colder weather, etc.) the run-scoring environment is lower in the playoffs, typically 20 percent lower than the regular season. Here's Jeter's slash line for the regular season for his career: .310/.377/.440; here it is for the postseason: .308/.374/.465. That's not really a fluke as proven by his MLB record 158 games in the postseason – that's a full season worth of data.

And as such, here's a Starting IX of the "clutchest" players in MLB history:
SP) Bob Gibson[459] C) Yogi Berra 1B) Albert Pujols 2B) Is Daniel Murphy a prime recency bias candidate? Oh well, his homophobic ass is getting the spot. 3B) Home Run Baker SS) Derek Jeter LF) Manny Ramírez CF) Carlos Beltrán RF) Reggie Jackson DH) David Ortiz CP) Mariano Rivera

This is the perfect time to bust out a theory I have on the snowballing nature of *being clutch*. Now maybe this is something that is common sense and everyone already believes, but I haven't seen it written before, so check it: it's the "One Big Play Theory." The thinking is that once a player makes one big, clutch play, the kind that might lead off SportsCenter, every other even-halfway-clutch play becomes magnified in a snowballing effect. It's similar to when a film director bursts on to the scene with a mega-hit (M. Night Shyamalan with *The Sixth Sense*) and every subsequent film gets an inordinate amount of attention. So, because Kobe hit a couple game-winners early in his career, all the subsequent ones gets highlighted, even if the same athlete is missing five to 10 chances at a big highlight for every one highlight that he/she actually converts. Which bleeds into…

Jeter's not clutch because really no one is: This sentiment isn't anti-Jeter on the surface, but it is anti-Jeter below the surface considering how much of his legacy is tied to the idea that he is indeed Captain Clutch.

The clutch debate has been raging for years, and it's one that's bound to rage forever. It's very easy to look 25 years into the future when the statheads rule everything (one could argue we're already there), and imagine the last vestiges of the old-school types making the argument that certain players are indeed clutch. And honestly, it's not bad that we keep going back to this debate. Certain players being more clutch than others is something that on the surface seems like it would make sense, and often times Occam's Razor does prove itself correct. Take "The Hot Hand" debate in basketball. For years, the "smart" basketball writers were fond of noting that "The Hot Hand" – the idea that once a player starts making several shots in succession she/he is more likely to make her/his next shot – was a fallacy. For anyone who had ever played the sport, the idea that The Hot Hand was bunk was a hard one to wrap their mind around. And lo and behold, although The Hot Hand hasn't been strictly proven (at least as of writing this), the method behind the oft-cited study that disproved The Hot Hand has

[459] Fuck Curt Schilling.

been proven to be flawed, firing up the debate once again. The clutch debate seems like it is going to fall into this category for a long time.

Just to give you a feel for how in flux the whole debate is, in 2007 there was a piece written on *StatSpeak* called "The Final Nail in the Clutch Hitting Coffin?" Then seven years later, Russell Carlton, one of the maybe five smartest people writing about baseball, wrote an article "I Believe in Clutch Hitting," that even had numbers (real live numbers!) in support.

As such, the right answer with Jeter is likely somewhere between the "Jeter as the clutch savior" and "Jeter's not clutch because really no one is" narratives. Aren't you glad you just read the last two pages?!

Jeter as a Yankee God: You'd be hard-pressed to find a Yankee fan who would argue with this sentiment, and maybe that's the best case for this iteration of Jeter. The Jeter as a *Yankee God* narrative doesn't need to be backed up by numbers, simply opinions. That being said, it never hurts to throw some numbers out there. For starters, his 20 years playing baseball in New York are matched by only Mel Ott, who played 22 years for the Giants. Therefore, no one ever played in New York longer while donning only pinstripes in his career. Easily the Most Yankee of all Jeter numbers, though, is the one Jayson Stark rightfully used to end his "Ten Amazing Derek Jeter Numbers," article for *ESPN*, written as Jeter's career was winding down: *1*. No, that is not the number of eligible women with whom Jeter never slept, but rather it is the number of games in his entire career that Jeter had played in pinstripes while the Yankees were mathematically eliminated from the playoffs (as of when Stark wrote the piece). And although the Yankees didn't make the playoffs his final season, what did Jeter go and do the day after Stark wrote his piece, in what was his final game in Yankee Stadium? Oh, all Jeter did was hit a walkoff single, his first walkoff hit since 2007. The man has a bit of a flair for the dramatic, huh?

It's not just as a Yankee, either. Jeter is such a *Baseball God* that, as Tom Verducci pointed out in a *Sports Illustrated* feature on The Captain, even his mannerisms – most notably pulling on the brim of his cap with two hands – were well known in the baseball community. Someone like Nomar might reach that level with something crazy like his batting glove routine, but something as mundane as Jeter's cap tug? That's next level.

But how about this: it's not just in baseball. Jeter is such *God* that, in 2014, *Fortune Magazine* ranked him as the 11th-greatest leader in the world, just two spots behind the Dalai Lama. Yeah, it shouldn't be too hard to sell this next point given the absurdity of how quickly that just escalated…

Jeter as overrated: Of course, it's time to zig a bit. Personally, the case for Jeter being overrated begins and ends with the fact that he played for the Core Four Yankees. By playing for a Yankee team that enjoyed as much success as it did, every player on that team enjoyed a bit of saturation in the general public. With Jeter as the team leader, it's not even an argument to say: no player in MLB history has ever been in the public eye more. The combination of era (more games on TV, growth of internet, etc.), city, success, and looks made Jeter a megastar that past generations could never reach.[460] As such, his accomplishments were more visible than anyone else's, and the baseball viewing public was often reminded of said accomplishments. Because human nature is the way it is, this led many folks to start rolling out the "Jeter as overrated" narrative – and a lot of them had the numbers to back it up.

Keith Olbermann had the most public undressing of Jeter, one that went viral in which he opens by saying: "We begin with a correction. Contrary to what you have heard, Derek Jeter is not the greatest person in human history. He did not invent baseball. He did not discover electricity. He is not the greatest shortstop who ever lived." Olbermann's cites Jeter's lack of an MVP, lack of a batting title, and maybe most damming, the fact that Red Ruffing averaged more WAR per season as a Yankee than Jeter.[461] He also cites the now-way-too-cited defensive metric that calls him the worst defensive shortstop of the modern era (dWAR), a trope that misses a lot of context (inherent flaws in defensive metrics and the fact that he never played a game at any position other than arguably the hardest defensive spot on the diamond, to name a few) and is probably best not to parrot. However, when combined with the discussion above that Jeter simply was in the spotlight so often, I think it's entirely fair to call Jeter one of the most overrated players of all time[462] (again through no fault of his own, really). So, with that said, let's sneak in another Starting IX. The most overrated players all-time:

SP) Sandy Koufax – It kills me, but if we look at actual achievements vs. legacy, it's gotta be Koufax. Blame injuries for his spot on this Starting IX.

C) David Ross – Come at me, Cub fans.

1B) Ernie Banks – This is cheating since I'm using it to refer to Banks in his only first baseman days, when he was actually a much worse hitter than he was at shortstop. This is obviously not great considering first base is a spot where he needed to be a much better hitter to have the same value as a shortstop.

2B) Bill Mazeroski

3B) THIS COULD BE YOU: Do you play in the New York or L.A. market? Do you drive in a lot of runners in blowout games to boost your RBI totals? Did you make a really important play at a really important time of a playoff game, and are you still riding the coattails of said play? Apply at mlb.overrated.players@hotmail.com

---

[460] Of course, Jeter somehow perfected the art of flying below-the-radar with his public comments despite all of it. There are two common reasons people give: 1) he is the nicest and most genuine celebrity they have ever met, or 2) if you wronged him i.e. leaked something to the press, he was quick to freeze you out. The latter is somewhat understandable given said scrutiny.

[461] And he did it with all the charm that typically oozes out of Olbermann: zero.

[462] Plus, there's the fact that Madison Bumgarner hit more grand slams in the 2014 season alone than Jeter hit in his entire career! Just kidding, that's not a factor, but that stat is still absurd.

SS) Derek Jeter
LF) Joe Carter
CF) Lloyd Waner – Just based on the fact that he is in the Hall of Fame.
RF) Chuck Klein
DH) Dante Bichette – Yes, he was never a DH, but he posted some of the emptiest offensive numbers of all time in his time in Coors Field, hitting .316 with 201 home runs, but just 4.6 WAR in seven years.

In the end let's all just accept that Jeter was one of a kind, no matter how you view him, and then we can agree to go to *The Onion* and search his name in their online archives for the next five hours. There's no better way to honor him.

Verdict: I think we can all agree that **Derek Jeter** beats out Travis Jackson. Dear god, I hope we can agree on that.

Left Field: Barry Bonds vs. Rickey Henderson/Roy White

Barry Bonds (1993-2007)

Boy oh boy. Bonds' tenure in San Francisco may be the most well-documented time that a player has had in baseball history. As such, his story demands being broken up into vignettes to encapsulate each separate part of his legacy.

"The one where we talk about steroids"

Unfortunately with Bonds, the conversation almost always starts here. Bonds had possibly the most unfortunate timing of any baseball player. He made some poor choices, then took down one of baseball's most hallowed records right as the sports media boom was hitting, and, because of it, Bonds became the face of the Steroid Era as a whole.

Bonds' story may seem simple on the surface: a player who wanted to get ahead of the curve broke the rules of baseball to do so. However, the real story has so many more layers to it that E.L. James may as well have stolen her *Fifty Shades of Grey* title from the story of Bonds, PEDs and Major League Baseball.

First, there's the fact that the phrase "performance-enhancing drug" is one of the vaguest terms sports fans hear on such a regular basis. Some of these "drugs" can be sold over the counter. Some of them used to be banned, but now aren't. Some of them are now allowed, but they used to be banned.

Plus, to imply that Bonds, Mark McGwire, Rafael Palmeiro et al. were the first guys in baseball history to use illicit materials to gain an edge is as ignorant as it is patently incorrect. As has been noted at times during the book, numerous stars of the 1960s and `70s (notably "true home run king" Hank Aaron) have admitted amphetamine use. Amphetamines have the far cuter nickname of "greenies," but they are currently on the banned substance list in MLB and are most certainly performance-enhancing drugs. Even 60 years before those guys – and more than a century before Bonds started juicing – Pittsburgh pitcher Pud Galvin was known for doing a bit of "juicing" of his own. Before pitching, Galvin (1875-1892) would drink an elixir of "Brown-Sequard," which consisted of "essentially testosterone drained from the gonads of an animal." Folks have been at this since the legit dawn of baseball.

There's also the fact that, although Bonds may have been the scapegoat of the Steroid Era, Buster Olney has said that he believes thousands of baseball players (in both the major and minor leagues) were using some sort of performance enhancing substances during Bonds' era, and Olney is certainly not alone in this opinion.

Now I fancy myself a man of high ideals, so called,[463] and I can understand those who see these athletes as role models for the next generation of ball players. Given the devastating effect of many of these banned substances, I am fully in support of scourging the sport of them in their entirety. But here's the thing: I don't know if that's necessarily why many writers refuse to fully admit the prowess of Bonds, Roger Clemens, and the bunch…

"The one where we talk about his legacy/the dumb-ass Hall of Fame voters"

Cynical Jim thinks that maybe, just maybe, a lot of these writers covering the sport – and promoting their new book that dealt with the stars of the Steroid-Era-before-it-was-called-the-Steroid-Era – felt a bit betrayed by the narrative. A bunch of 35-year-old guys were shattering the record books, and that made the reporters look bad for not unearthing the story of the big bad home run hitters and the tainting of our national pastime earlier. The Steroid Era went on for 15 or so years without being truly reported on. If I had been covering the Giants for the local paper day-in and day-out for the better part of a decade and a half, and I missed something as big and seemingly obvious (what with its "don't ask, don't tell" policy) as Bonds using PEDs, when the whole narrative flipped I might be a bit butt hurt too. There are probably a few BBWAA writers who actually are keeping Bonds out of the Hall of Fame "For The Kids," but my guess is that there are quite a few more doing it for far pettier reasons.

And that's a shame because the Hall is hurting right now, and as much as some stuffy baseball writers refuse to admit it, inducting Bonds would be a huge boon for the Hall. It would undoubtedly draw a huge crowd, and it would give all

---

[463] If you got that reference, your next beer is on me.

the #hotsportstake Picassos plenty of time to talk about baseball. Maybe instead of the top five topics on *Around the Horn* being NFL-related, baseball could slip in there for once. The Hall could certainly use the attention – and the crowd – as in recent years it has been hemorrhaging money. Their visitation numbers are lower than ever and not electing the biggest names in the sport only amplifies these issues.

Of course, the irony of it is that the writers helped to create this monster. As Sam Miller pointed out on one of the many excellent *Effectively Wild* podcast episodes, the attention, or lack-thereof, that Bonds got for playing his not-as-flashy style of play to start his career likely played a part in his eventual steroid use. In his first four seasons, Bonds was worth 23.4 WAR – and he didn't win any MVPs. In fact, he didn't receive a single vote for MVP; heck, he didn't even make an All-Star Game! He was deserving of the accolades, but his doubles, walks, and elite defense went unnoticed by the media. Then, in 1990, he hit a career-high 33 home runs, and what happened? He won an MVP. In fact, of his first eight years in the majors, his three highest home run totals represented the three seasons in which he won the MVP award. We know correlation doesn't mean causation, but it's hard to blame him for drawing some connection, especially when, eight years later, baseball writers were bending over backwards to blow Mark McGwire and Sammy Sosa during their home run chase. Meanwhile, Bonds (8.1) was worth more than either guy by WAR in that hallowed 1998 season. Of course, Bonds finished eighth in the MVP that season. The writers made it clear that they valued home runs over anything else, and then completely eviscerated Bonds when he made some (admittedly poor) decisions to help himself hit more home runs. The hypocrisy is unreal.

Finally, we simply don't know how much Bonds' numbers are even tainted. Although many have tried, no one has been able to pin down the exact effect of PEDs on a ballplayer's numbers. Even if someone supposedly figured it out, Bonds' situation was still murkier than the waters of Lake Quinsigamond. In fact, this inability to know Bonds' true value might just be another reason some writers are choosing to leave him out of the Hall. "We don't even know his true value," they might cry. Here's the thing: we may not know his exact value, but it is undoubtedly enough to be worthy of the same lofty standards that bronzed Freddie Lindstrom and Lloyd Waner. Say we count only Bonds' numbers from his first 13 seasons. According to *Game of Shadows*, Bonds started using in 1998, so if we eliminate the entire value of the remainder of his career (which is beyond absurd, you can feed me a tub of steroids each and every day, and I promise you I'm not hitting one into McCovey Cove, but regardless) Bonds still ends up with the following numbers: 411 home runs, 2580 RuBIns, 445 steals, and 99.6 WAR. He would still be only player ever to join the 400/400 HR/SB club, and that's without his final nine years of his career. Hell, he passed Waner's total career value (by WAR) by the second month of his fifth season in the major leagues! Even if we take the 100 percent guaranteed clean version of Bonds, he is easily, EASILY, a Hall of Famer. Those 99.6 WAR would rank 32nd all-time, above so many "no brainer" Hall of Famers that it's not even worth listing them all.

In the end, leaving Bonds out of the Hall is a lose-lose for baseball and one of its best players in history. It's the same deal with Clemens and others of their like. I feel confident Bonds will be inducted one day, but the fact that he has to wait is silly.

"The one where we blow your mind with stats"

Ok, time to end on a positive note, since this has been depressing as hell so far. Time for flashy stat-bullets:

* His seven MVPs are more than twice any other player's total in MLB history.
* Even before his alleged PED use, Bonds led all of baseball in OPS+ for the 1990s and led all of baseball in WAR by more than 10.0. The next closest hitter (Ken Griffey Jr.) was more than 12.0 wins below.
* From 2001-2004 (a recurring stretch that, although possibly tainted, is still just stupid impressive), Bonds had the three best seasons by OPS+ in *baseball history*. Remember, Bonds was not the only guy juicing those days. Also, remember that OPS+ adjusts for league context.
* During that same four-year stretch, Bonds had a higher slugging percentage than the league-average OPS (on-base percentage *plus* slugging percentage).
* Bonds was walked intentionally in the first inning 95 times in his career. He was intentionally walked five times with no one on and no one out. Frank Howard is the only other player that happened to more than once in his career.

Now here are a bunch that need to be separated out because they deserve credit as all having come (along with numerous others not used here) from the same excellent episode no. 762 of *Effectively Wild*:

* Here are a couple fun 2001 nuggets: Bonds slugged 1.556 when he pulled the ball 2001. That's the first time I've ever had to think about where the decimal goes when writing a slugging percentage.
* That same year, against ground ball pitchers (as defined by B-Ref), he hit a home run every six at bats.
* Now let's move into the "from 2001-2004 Bonds" stats:
* During those four years, he got 138 plate appearances against pitchers in the *same season* they got Cy Young votes. His slash line against those aces: .327/.522/.786. Those are video game numbers.
* During that stretch, he reached base 96 percent of his games played; his longest streak without reaching base: two games, and he only did it twice.
* Over those four years, he had more intentional walks than any other *entire team*. He still has more career intentional walks

than the *entire Rays franchise*.
* He also had more intentional walks than strikeouts from 2001-04. In fact, his ability to avoid the K was a career-long ability, as he struck out more than 100 times in a season only once (102 Ks in his rookie season).
* His OPS *after an 0-2 count* during that stretch: .970, aka the OPS of Shawn Green in his 49-home run 2001 campaign.
* In fact, for his career, Bonds' OPS after an 0-1 count was .889, or the exact same as Willie McCovey's actual career OPS. You could give the pitcher a free strike every Bonds' at bat, and Bonds would still be a Hall of Famer.
* Speaking of Bonds embarrassing Hall of Famers (or in this case a future one), Bonds' career Win Probability Added *just on intentional walks* is higher than Adrián Beltré's entire career WPA.
* The most plate appearances Bonds had against a pitcher in his career without reaching base against him was six.
* Of the top 50 career OPS' against left-handed pitchers, Bonds is the only lefty on the list, and he's 14th.
* Think all he could do late in his career was hit? From 2001 on, he stole 43 bases… And was caught stealing only six times.
* Finally, and although the originator of this stat couldn't even believe it, it's one of the most amazing. Using log5 (you don't need to understand what log5 is, just know it's a way to compare these two), Sam Miller attempted to figure out peak-Bonds (2002) against peak-Pedro Martínez (2000), arguably the peak hitter all-time vs. the peak pitcher all-time. The result he got: an OPS over 1.000 for Bonds, of course.

The man was amazing, and it's time we all admit it. That means you, grumpy old man who has already skipped ahead in this chapter to find Joe DiMaggio.

Roy White (1965-1979) vs. Rickey Henderson (1985-1989)

White and Henderson offer a very interesting comparison. In one sense, the two are very similar players: speedy left fielders who worked the count to draw walks and then turn those walks into doubles via the stolen base. They were also both mediocre fielders despite this speed and, clearly, both were members of the Yankees. What is more interesting about these two, is that they actually represent two opposing prototypes that we have seen throughout the book. Henderson represents the "dominant over a shorter time frame" model whom I have given the advantage to over the "consistent but never great" player many times in the book. However, Roy White also represents the "team loyalty" player that I have rewarded over the "goes from team to team without as much significance" player.[464]

Don't worry, we won't spoil our Yankee breakdown on these two men (as you can guess, that's being saved for center field), but we can go to a mini-breakdown of which of these two types of players a GM would prefer. On the one hand, most GMs are as win-now as one can be. They often sacrifice the future for even a chance to compete (see the Red Sox trading Yoan Moncada for Chris Sale before 2017), meaning that the more dominant player would seemed to be preferred. And Henderson was certainly dominant. In his first year with the Yankees, Henderson posted 9.9 WAR with 146 runs, 24 home runs, 80 steals (only caught stealing 10 times), and a .419 on-base percentage. His 30.8 WAR over his five seasons in New York come out to an average of over 6.0 WAR a season, easily above the 5.0 WAR that Baseball-Reference has labeled as the tier for an All-Star-level player. You probably won't be surprised that Henderson is one of two men in baseball history to steal a base in four different decades,[465] so he clearly had longevity – just not within the Yankees franchise. He stayed with the Yankees for only five seasons between two long stints with the Oakland A's.

On the flip side, White was a staple of the 1960s Yankee sides that would have really crumbled without his presence in the lineup and the dugout. As is, they did bottom out a bit, but White kept it from being a disaster. As noted by Bill James, White is criminally underrated because of the legends who roamed the Yankee Stadium outfield, plus the fact that he played during the club's weakest era. In fact, in his *Baseball Abstract*, James rates White higher than Jim Rice. White was incredibly consistent as a Yankee, posting 10 straight seasons worth 3.0 or more WAR (1968-1977), and he was rewarded with two World Series rings at the end of his career. Although we noted earlier that White didn't do well by some advanced defensive metrics (-6.1 dWAR for his career), he was well above average by traditional standards. He led all left fielders in putouts every year from 1969-1977, assists in two seasons, and fielding percentage every year from 1968-1972. All of this, and he only once paced left fielders in errors.

If we look at it from strictly WAR perspective, White's totals top Henderson 46.6 to 30.8, a solid advantage. However, since White was in New York for three times as many years, that's to be expected. The real kicker, and the reason **White gets the spot**, is that, at his best, White actually managed to be nearly as dominant as Henderson. From 1968-1972, White's best five-year stretch, he totaled 27.4 WAR, basically the same as Henderson's 30.8 WAR in his five Yankee seasons. Of course, White had 10 years outside of this five-year stretch that, although not quite as productive, were still extremely valuable to the Yankee franchise. Both in terms of numbers, but also as a steadying presence with the organization.

Since we spent most of the write-up comparing the two instead of talking about Roy White's achievements, it is

---

[464] By this logic, Charlie Keller and Bob Meusel could have been brought into this discussion too, as the lesser of each of these examples. However, Meusel was never as good as White, and although Keller was such a beast that, as Lefty Gomez put it, "he wasn't scouted, he was trapped," he was more of a flash in the pan than anything substantial in Yankee history.

[465] If you can guess who the other is, I'll give you your money back for this book. It was Ted Williams. And yes, the entire SABR community is currently lined up outside my house looking for their $19.99.

only fair to end by mentioning that White was called "one of the most underrated players in baseball" by no less a source than Mickey Mantle in *Sport Magazine* in 1970. This was in response to Mantle being asked where all the Yankees star players had gone. Then, at the end of the decade, it was Reggie Jackson who called White an overlooked contributor to the Yankees, noting White's ability to avoid mistakes as a key part of his value.

Verdict: Honestly, you could add Rickey Henderson and Roy White together and I'd still take **Barry Bonds**.

Center Field: Willie Mays vs. Mickey Mantle/Joe DiMaggio

Willie Mays (1951-1952; 1954-1972)

The "Say Hey Kid" is remembered as one of, if not the, best players of all time. For my money, he is not quite at Babe Ruth's level, but one could certainly make the argument.[466] Mays will be remembered for a number of reasons, both on and off the field, and all of them positive. Most famously, Mays' 660 home runs rank fifth all-time, but this is hardly the only statistical category in which he ranks among the elite. Mays was so well-rounded, and had such a long career, that he ranks in the top 15 in nearly every single statistical category a center fielder can rank. He was the fifth-youngest player in the National League when he broke into the league (1951), and he was the second-oldest in the league upon retiring (1973).

Mays managed to play the line between showman and showboat better than any other player in baseball history. He often caught fly balls his way by tossing his hat up in the air and catching both his hat and the ball at the same time. The defensive play Mays is best-remembered for came on September 29, 1954 and is simply known today as "The Catch." Every baseball fan has seen the clip and heard the story, and with good reason. First of all, the catch came around 420 feet from home plate with Mays facing backwards and his glove turned upside down. Then, Mays' ability to turn and fire an absolute seed back to the infield – keeping the runners from tagging – made the play just like Mays: complete.

So, how did Mays stay so beloved despite playing as a black man in the notoriously stodgy 1950s-era baseball? A couple of reasons. For one, Mays was one of the most popular teammates in all baseball lore. It was said of Mays, "Willie, the Giant players will tell you, is good for what ails you. Whether he is the butt of their jokes, which is often, or working a gag of his own, he never fails to break up the clubhouse." Mays also seemed born not only to play baseball, but to be a clubhouse leader on top of that. At the age of just 23, he was dubbed the heart and soul of the team, and he continued to be so for his entire career.

Mays also won his team and league mates over by playing smart baseball. Mays has said that he would often turn down a double, settling instead for a single. Why was this smart? Because he had the wherewithal to know the pitcher would intentionally walk Willie McCovey if Mays left first base open, thus eliminating the main power threat (along with Mays) from the Giants lineup. This is a quote from Mays, so it must be taken with a grain of salt, but to even be thinking on that level is impressive. It is also worth noting that, despite playing in a spacious (and thoroughly disliked) stadium, as well as having great speed, Mays' doubles totals are consistently low for his career. He never led the league in doubles, and he finished in the top five of the NL only three times. He hit more home runs than doubles for his career. Maybe Mays really was limiting himself.

Although it may not have done as much endearing him to his teammates, Mays' off-field presence certainly helped to solidify his good guy image. When the Giants played in New York (Mays' first six seasons), either before games or during the offseason, Mays would go out into the New York City streets and play stickball with the local kids. The fact that Mays couldn't stop playing the game, even during his free time, helped mark Mays as a true baseball lover, thus endearing him to the fans who often believe they love the game even more than the players (a strange sentiment when you think about it).

Finally, although he had fun on the field, his teammates never thought that he put himself before the team. A perfect example: the story of Mays' milestone 600th home run. It came under strange circumstances, as Mays struggled after hitting home run no. 599, and it had been nine days without a home run for Mays. Clyde King, the Giants manager, started Mays off on the bench to give him a day to rest up any lingering injuries the 38-year-old Mays may have had, as well as to allow Mays to get his head on straight to make the run at 600. However, with a pennant race on the line, his manager decided that Mays was his best option off the bench, and he chose to pinch-hit Mays in the top of the seventh inning. Mays responded with his 600th homer, which ended up being the deciding factor in the game. After the game, here's what Mays had to say: "The big thing is that the homer won the ballgame." Considering Mays had just become the first right-handed hitter to ever reach 600 home runs, the team-oriented response must have been nice to hear from a teammate perspective.

All of these factors contributed to Mays being revered around the league. Leo Durocher once said, "If somebody came up and hit .450, stole 100 bases, and performed a miracle in the field every day I'd still look you in the eye and say Willie was better." Mays was one of the rare players who managed to be loved by the fans, his teammates, and even his opposition. However, even given the love-fest for Mays, he still managed to be a bit underrated at times.

His stolen base totals are impressive on their own (338 career, season-high of 40), but they are even more impressive

[466] For me, it goes: 1) Babe Ruth 2) Walter Johnson 3) Ted Williams 4) Barry Bonds 5) Willie Mays 6) Ty Cobb 7) Tom Seaver 8) Honus Wagner 9) Lefty Grove 10) Stan Musial 10a) Hank Aaron

given the era in which he played. In fact, his 179 steals in the 1950s was more than anybody else for the decade, while simultaneously being the lowest total to ever lead a decade. Then there's the matter of his two MVPs. Mays suffered from "Michael Jordan syndrome," a disease created by Bill Simmons to explain why Michael Jordan didn't win the MVP every year. It happens when MVP voters get sick of voting the same player as "most valuable" year after year. Mays led the NL in WAR *nine* times in his career, and he certainly could have expected a bit more hardware in his trophy case. In both 1960 and 1962, Mays led the league by well over 1.0 WAR but didn't take home the hardware. The season of 1964, however, takes the cake, as Mays led the NL in WAR by 2.2 wins but lost out on the MVP to Ken Boyer (who was worth a full 5.0 wins less, according to rWAR). Part of this phenomenon is also the result of Mays setting the bar too high. Many of his seasons still looked excellent, but they didn't look as good as some of his other, superior years, and as such, Mays missed out on numerous MVPs he likely deserved.

If there is any qualm with Mays, it might be that his playoff numbers are not on par with his regular season numbers. His .247 batting average and .337 slugging percentage are far cries from his regular season totals. This is almost certainly due to a depleted sample size, as anyone who saw Mays play[467] could clearly see this man had no weaknesses. It is interesting to note, however, that if Mays played in the modern era, Bill Plaschke and other #hotsportstake pundits may well have labeled Mays as a regular season player who just couldn't cut it when it really mattered, especially given his laid-back nature. In fact, just for fun, here's a mock #hotsportstake after a one-RBI, .250-BA performance from Mays in the 1962 World Series:

Mr. *Mays* has once again failed to show up in October.

Sure, he looks good during the regular season, but he has Giants fans asking, "*Willie* actually show up this time?" once the playoffs start. Right now, Mays is relying on one catch (underhanded and completely without technique, no less) to solidify his place among the greatest of all time.

I'm sorry if I'm not ready to throw my hat in the air for Mays yet, but I just don't think he's ready to graduate to the class of all timers many writers nowadays want to put him in. Sure, Mays may have won his second home run title this year, but that's not the title Giants fans want to remember in 50 years.

Call me old-fashioned, but all the glitz and glam of these new players makes me long for the days of Lou Gehrig and Hank Greenberg, players who showed up every day and led their teams to World Series victories. Maybe next year Mays can give the Bay Area the center fielder they thought they were getting in the move from the Big Apple.

Mays' defenders will point to his World Series win with the Giants in 1954, but as a brash young player with only one full season under his belt, how much credit does he really deserve? The Giants won despite the fact that he hit below .300 and didn't hit a single home run the whole series.

I think it's time we Say Hey and take a look at this Kid's stats. For his career in the regular season, he's slugging .588; in the postseason that number plummets to .281. During the regular season, Mays hits one of his beloved home runs every 16 at bats, however, despite 64 at bats in the playoffs, he's yet to leave the yard once… well except after leaving Candlestick Park with his tail between his legs after Game 7.

Mays is no spring chicken, and the clucking is only going to get louder in San Francisco if he can't bring the Giants a title on their new coast.

For a man they call a Giant, Mays sure seems small in October.

Thank God Rick Reilly wasn't yet writing in 1962.

Mickey Mantle (1951-1968) vs. Joe DiMaggio (1936-1951)

Pretty sure everyone saw this coming. Not only are Mantle and DiMaggio two of baseball's all-time best players, they are tied together for eternity by the fact that Mantle took over directly for DiMaggio in the hallowed Yankees center field position during the most glorious run in franchise history. These two men helped create the mythology of the Yankees, and they certainly created the lore that surrounds center field in Yankee Stadium. It is fitting that the two reside next to each other in Monument Park. The two men never considered themselves rivals, but they have become historical rivals because of the endless comparisons. Without a breakdown of the two, no baseball book would be complete. Well, except for all those books that don't deal with Yankees center fielders…

Contact

	BA	lgBA	Seasons ≥ .320	Career high/low	Seasons ≥ 40 SO	SO %	lgSO%	BABIP	Misc.
Mantle	.298	.256	3	.365/.237	17	17.3	13.5	.318	LL 5x SO, 1x BA
DiMaggio	.325	.276	8	.381/.263	0	4.8	9.2	.304	LL 2x BA

[467] YouTube counts!

Right of the bat, it's already a close matchup. Although DiMaggio is far superior on the surface level, Mantle is very nearly on par when taken in a historical sense. Mantle played during one of the hardest eras for hitters and still managed to top a .300 batting average in more than half his seasons. Two things tilt the scales in DiMaggio's favor, however. First, and the lesser of the two, is Joe's hit streak. DiMaggio's 56-game hit streak is written about as much as any other event in baseball history, and with good reason.

A lot of ink has been spilled specifically on the incredible odds of this streak. Odds, in this case, being both of the numerical – as well as anecdotal – sense. In one study done by Bob Brown and Peter Goodrich of SABR, a player of DiMaggio's ability could have played 18,519 years without having completed another streak of the same length. DiMaggio certainly managed to eke out a few games out here and there, with over half of the games in his streak resulting in exactly one hit for DiMaggio (only 22 multi-hit games). He also had his bat stolen partially through his streak, which actually convinced him the streak would be broken.

The streak was also not without a bit of controversy. Dan Daniel (no that is not a joke name) covered the Yankees at the time and was good friends with all the players. In fact, he would go on to pen an article for SABR entitled, "My Friend – The Yankee Clipper." Daniels doubled as the official scorer for the team, and on two occasions – games 30 and 31 of the streak – some fans went home thinking that DiMaggio's streak had ended. In both games, Luke Appling misplayed balls that at least some thought were errors, and since it was the only time DiMaggio reached base in each game, it seems as though Ringo Starr could have been channeling DiMaggio when he wrote, "I get by with a little help from my friends." Now this should not diminish from DiMaggio's accomplishment at all, as every streak of this nature needs a little help along the way. Plus, DiMaggio was robbed in the game in which he lost the streak, as we saw earlier (Third Base, Cleveland Spiders – Page 190). If either of the line drives that Ken Keltner made plays on had been hits, DiMaggio's streak would have reached 73 games (at least hypothetically), seeing as he had a 16-game hit streak right after the famous 56-game hit streak ended.

DiMaggio's hit streak has one more interesting historical connection. In the 19th game, he went 2-for-4 in a pretty famous day in-and-of its own. June 2, 1941, Day 19 of the hit streak, is better known as the day Lou Gehrig passed away, meaning that if ESPN had been around, the building would have imploded from a wealth of Yankees stories. In fact, by the end of DiMaggio's streak, Stephen A. Smith probably would have had a full-chest tattoo of the faces of every single Yankee player past and present.

However, the real reason that DiMaggio gets the nod here is his ability to avoid striking out. At the risk of sounding like a broken record, strikeouts are not as big a deal as they were once thought to be, *however*, when the difference is as vast as it is between these two men, it is clear that DiMaggio was superior in his ability to make contact, which is, after all, the name of the category. DiMaggio struck out only 13 times his entire 1941 MVP season. During his hit streak, he recorded 91 hits and had only five strikeouts. If we remove his rookie year, DiMaggio had more home runs than strikeouts (333-330) for his career. Mantle would win this category against a lot of players in history, but DiMaggio takes this way with relative ease.

EDGE: DiMaggio

Power

	HR	Seasons ≥ 40 HR	Career high HR	XBH	SLG%	lgSLG%	ISO	HR%	XBH%	Misc.
Mantle	536	4	52	952	.557	.387	.259	5.4	9.6	LL 4x SLG, HR, 3x TB, 2x AB/HR 1x 3B
DiMaggio	361	1	46	881	.579	.405	.254	4.7	11.5	LL 3x TB, 2x HR, SLG, 1x 3B, AB/HR

While "contact" may have been DiMaggio's best category, by moving into "power" we're really headed into Mantle's wheelhouse, and what a wheelhouse that was. Mantle has the longest-recorded home run of all time by many sources, a supposed 565-foot bomb in Washington's Griffith Stadium. In fact, the term "tape measure home run" was created after one of Mantle's home runs. Mantle was a switch-hitter, and he hit homers from both sides of the plate in one game 10 times in his career. The reason Mantle became a switch-hitter was that his dad and grandfather pitched to him from different sides, and as such, he learned both ways at an early age. Mantle is also one of only five men to lead the league in homers and triples in the same year, doing so in 1955.

DiMaggio was no slouch in the power realm either. He famously lost numerous home runs to the incredibly difficult dimensions of Yankee Stadium when he played there (oh the modern irony). As a right-handed batter, DiMaggio had to deal with more than 450 feet to the left-center wall, and more than 400 feet to get one out to straightaway left field. DiMaggio hit one home run in every 4.018 games on the road, which is actually better than Mantle, who hit one in every 4.4 road games. In fact, DiMaggio tops Mantle in almost every category in the chart above except for the two cumulative statistics, which makes sense since Joltin' Joe lost three years to service in WWII. Despite the nickname "Muscles" for Mantle, this category is almost too close to call. There is something to be said for both the raw power of Mantle, as well as the easy power that DiMaggio displayed throughout his career. In the end, Mantle's superior performance in comparison to the rest of the league gives him a slight edge.

EDGE: Slight Mantle

Batting eye

	BB	Seasons ≥ 90 BB	OBP	lgOBP	OPS+	BB%	SO/BB	Misc.
Mantle	1733	12	.421	.329	172	17.5	0.99	LL 8x OPS+, 5x BB, 3x OBP
DiMaggio	790	0	.398	.355	155	10.3	0.47	LL 1x OPS+

Mantle owns a near two-to-one edge on DiMaggio in career walks, and this one can't really be explained away by DiMaggio service to our country. Mantle's on-base percentage was nearly 100 points higher than league average during his career, and his batting eye was always part of his prowess at the plate.

EDGE: Mantle

Speed

	SB	Seasons ≥ 10 SB	Career high SB	Rbaser	SB%	XBT%	GDP%	Misc.
Mantle	153	6	21	49	80	54	5	LL 5x PwrSpd
DiMaggio	30	0	6	15	77	52	N/A	

Here's another category in which Mantle can stake a claim to an advantage separate from his 665-game edge over DiMaggio in games played with the Yankees during their respective careers. Mantle was one of the best power/speed threats of all time during his prime, and he could have been a near Trout-level, five-tool player if not for certain circumstances that we will come to discuss in a bit. Even with his career playing out the way it did, Mantle offered far more on the basepaths than DiMaggio.

EDGE: Mantle

Defense

	Fld%	lgFld%	dWAR	RF/9	lgRF/9	Assists	GG*	Misc.
Mantle	.982	.980	-10.1	2.41	2.27	117	1	LL 1x OF assists, OF DP, OF E, OF Fld%
DiMaggio	.978	.974	3.2	2.80	2.48	153	0	LL 1x OF PO, OF assists, OF E, OF DP, Fld%

* The Gold Glove award didn't appear until 1957, Mantle's seventh year, and obviously after DiMaggio retired.

Praise was heaped onto DiMaggio throughout his career, and one facet of his game that was as beloved as any was his defense. A cynical man might say that this makes sense, seeing as it is the one aspect of the game that can be hyperbolized more than any other – the metrics that measure defense are the least specific – but that's just a cynic. Whether or not DiMaggio is given enough credit by the advanced metrics (dWAR has him worth only 3.2 wins with the glove for his career), is a matter for another time. DiMaggio clearly holds the edge on Mantle from a defensive perspective so we don't need to debate it further.

EDGE: DiMaggio

Intangibles

As we've mentioned before, this is a relatively subjective category, but we'll use it to look at health and ability to hit in high leverage situations in this case.

DiMaggio maintained a pretty healthy career, playing less than 115 games only once and only giving way to injury at the end of his career. Mantle, on the other hand, suffered – and often played through – numerous injuries throughout his career. For Mantle, it was far more frequent to be suffering an injury than not. Despite these injuries, Mantle played less than 100 games only one season after his rookie year and played in more than 140 games in 12 of his 18 seasons. Although it's indisputable that Mantle lost a bit of performance due to these constant injuries, it is also indisputable that Mantle – even when injured – was of value in the lineup. Some players who play through injury perform admirably in the sense that they don't want to let their teammates down, but they would actually be better suited to take a seat on the bench and regain their health, because their replacement could produce more than the injured version of the player. Mantle was not at all in this category of player. Mantle had two seasons above 11.0 WAR; the only position player to have *more than* two seasons of 11.0+ WAR is Babe Ruth with six such seasons. (That's why he's the G.O.A.T.) The only position players on par with Mantle having each posted two such seasons are Barry Bonds and Willie Mays. So, although Mantle's injuries can be used against him in the sense that he could have been even greater, they certainly cannot be held against him in the sense that he hurt the Yankees by playing through them.

Another factor in intangibles is performance in high-leverage situations. These are possibly even more difficult to track than any other part of baseball because of the small sample size, and the irregularity in numbers that usually occur. Mantle, however, performs admirably in every "clutch" situation that Baseball-Reference has to offer. The following chart shows Mantle's OPS in each of the situations listed. (His career OPS was .977, for comparison.)

RISP	RISP 2 out	Late & Close	Tie Game	High Leverage	8th inning	9th inning	Extra innings
1.009	1.065	1.101	.921	1.034	1.023	1.019	1.315

In every one of those situations – except tie games – Mantle had an OPS over 1.000. Mantle's career OPS of .977 was already an incredible figure, good for 10th in baseball history – and he managed to top it in almost every single one of these "clutch" situations.

DiMaggio wasn't too far off Mantle's pace in these situations. Here's a look at his numbers in those same situations. (DiMaggio, incredibly, had the exact same .977 OPS for his career.)

RISP	RISP 2 out	Late & Close	Tie Game	High Leverage	8th inning	9th inning	Extra innings
.971	1.031	.944	1.005	1.035	.892	1.068	1.106

Although not quite at Mantle's level, DiMaggio did top a 1.000 OPS in more than half of these situations and, like Mantle, did his best work in extra-inning games. Both men consistently performed in big moments, and the fact that Mantle played through any and all injuries to still play at an elite level shows some solid *grit* and gives him the slight nod in the intangibles category.

EDGE: Slight Mantle

Team Success

	W	L	T	W-L%	Seasons ≥ 90 W	Division titles	Pennants	WS
Mantle	1376	1016	9	.575	13	12	12	7
DiMaggio	1200	619	17	.660	11	10	10	9

Both Mantle and DiMaggio played during the Golden Era of baseball in New York, and they combined to win 15 of the Yankees 27 World Series.[468] Mantle's career winning percentage is noticeably lower than DiMaggio's, but that is mostly due to the last four years Mickey spent in New York in which the club finished below .500 cumulatively. Because the two are on such even terms yet again, we need to look a little deeper by taking a look at with whom Mantle and DiMaggio played.

DiMaggio played eight seasons with Bill Dickey, four with Lou Gehrig, two with Tony Lazzeri, seven with Lefty Gomez, eight with Red Ruffing, six with Joe Gordon, eight with Charlie Keller, eight with Phil Rizzuto, six with Yogi Berra, two with Johnny Mize, one with Whitey Ford, and one with Mickey Mantle.

Mantle, on the other hand, played 13 seasons with Berra, three with Mize, six with Rizzuto, 15 with Ford, three with Johnny Sain, 13 with Elston Howard, five with Enos Slaughter, seven with Roger Maris, five with Mel Stottlemyre, one with Roy White, and, of course, one with DiMaggio.

Now this isn't an exact science because not all these players were in their primes, and it doesn't account for how good each season was by these top-notch players. Both men had excellent backstops for their whole career with Dickey, Berra, and Howard locking down the position for the time DiMaggio and Mantle roamed the outfield. Maris' few excellent years cancel out with Gehrig's few excellent years in terms of the second-best offense force in the lineup. DiMaggio played with some really solid middle infielders his whole career, one advantage he had on Mantle.

[468] I am aware that 9+7=16, but both men were present for the 1951 World Series victory over the New York Giants.

From the pitching side of things, Mantle had the advantage in that he had the best pitcher of the bunch (Ford), and he had him for well over a decade. Neither played with another *great* outfielder for any extended period of time. Keller was great but only for a few years, and he was the best of the bunch for DiMaggio. Mantle had the one incredible season (1961) with Maris, and Maris did offer another excellent outfielder, but he had only two great years. It should also be noted that much of Maris' success was due to Mantle. When Maris had Mantle batting behind him in New York, Maris had a .293 batting average with a .682 slugging percentage; without Mantle behind him, he hit .174 BA and a .365 SLG – that's a hell of a difference.

The slight edge Mantle holds in teammates surrounding him (which is actually a detriment if we're trying to see who carried a team more), combined with the fact that he got to play during expansion and thus a bit of a watered-down league for a few years, and finally the fact that DiMaggio's teams never finished below .500, gives the edge to DiMaggio.

EDGE: DiMaggio

Dominance

Mantle's Baseball-Reference page is bolder than showing up for the $50,000 Las Vegas dodgeball championship match with too few players and having to forfeit,[469] as Mantle led the league in one of the standard batting categories listed on Baseball-Reference (runs, hits, steals, etc.) an incredible 48 times. Of course, he also led the league in numerous lesser known categories throughout his career. From 1955-1962, he led the AL in oWAR every single season. That's insane. Both Mantle and DiMaggio won three MVPs, but Mantle had the right to a few more considering his five WAR titles. Despite DiMaggio's great play, he led the league in standard batting categories "only" 15 times, less than a third of the times Mantle did. Here's maybe the most impressive statement to Mantle's dominance: in Roger Maris' record-breaking 1961 season, despite 61 homers, he wasn't intentionally walked once. That's because of a certain Mick standing in the on-deck circle. This one isn't as close as it would appear on the surface.

EDGE: Mantle

Nickname

Before we get to the real big questions, let's take a look at a less important debate: "Mick" or "Joltin' Joe?" "The Commerce Comet" or "The Yankees Clipper?" Really, it's no question. "The Yankee Clipper" is one of the most iconic nicknames of all time, and the fact that Simon and Garfunkel gave him a shoutout in the brilliant "Mrs. Robinson," locks it down. Not even close.

EDGE: DiMaggio

"It" Factor

Whatever "It" is,[470] DiMaggio had *it* in spades. Mantle not as much. Here are some quotes about DiMaggio from his peers. From Phil Rizzuto: "There was an aura about [DiMaggio]. He walked like no one else walked. He did things so easily. He was immaculate in everything he did. Kings of State wanted to meet him. He carried himself so well. He could fit in any place in the world." From Ted Williams (DiMaggio's biggest rival, by the way): "It might sound corny, but he had a profound and lasting impact on the country." Even from Mantle himself: "Heroes are people who are all good with no bad in them. That's the way I always saw Joe DiMaggio."

In contrast to DiMaggio, here are some quotes from baseball historians who have long been trying to unlock the enigma that was Mickey Mantle. Victor Debs wrote in *Baseball Tidbits*, "Perhaps it was because Mantle was always hard on himself that in the end he belittled his skills and ignored the positive influence he may have been for his family, and certainly was for the public. Or was it that Mantle was impressionable, unduly influenced by the criticisms of writers and commentators who zealously point out player's faults, as if their own lives are beyond reproach?" Or this gem from a Yankee fan being quoted in a great piece in *Sport* Magazine from 1956, "They'll Always Boo Mickey Mantle." Any Yankee fan should read the whole piece, but the most interesting quote was from one typical bleacher creature in the Bronx: "Sure he hears [the booing] … and maybe it'll do him good. I know it does me good to give it to him. I just don't like the guy any more. I don't like the way he walks. I saw him on television the other night and I don't like the way he looks. He just rubs me the wrong way. He got all the breaks and what did he do with them? Nothing." This quote is basically the antithesis of what one would hear from Yankee fans about DiMaggio.

---

[469] "It's a **bold** strategy, Cotton, let's see if it pays off for them."

[470] Bill Barnwell's "The It Factor" article on *Grantland* is a great deep dive into this question, albeit in how "it" relates to football, but there's a lot of crossover in how "it" becomes a thing in any sport.

DiMaggio was a pop culture sensation. Whether it was the aforementioned "Mrs. Robinson," or dating Marilyn Monroe, DiMaggio nearly defined a generation – not of baseball, but of America. Mantle was idolized in his own way, mostly by his teammates, and DiMaggio actually had a bit of a distance from his teammates (whether or not that had to do with his Italian heritage and Italians not being fully accepted in 1930s America is a whole different matter), but in the eye of the fans and the media, it wasn't even close. Baseball's collective crush on Joe DiMaggio was half-biblical, half-homoerotic to an extent matched only by fellow Yankee, Derek Jeter. DiMaggio practically defined the "it" factor for his generation, if not for the history of the sport. There have been better players throughout baseball's history, but in terms of the indefinable "it" factor, DiMaggio could be challenged by only Derek Jeter, Roberto Clemente (post mortem), and maybe Willie Mays.

EDGE: DiMaggio

Limiting Factors

Amazingly, both players, despite their illustrious careers, could potentially have been even greater. In DiMaggio's case – similar to Ted Williams and many others of the time – he lost three years to WWII. DiMaggio left for service after the 1942 season as a 28-year-old who was just two years removed from an MVP season, and he only ended up playing to the age of 36. If DiMaggio were to have stayed in baseball and produced at the level that he did for the three seasons after he came back, he would boost his career totals up to over 2,700 hits, 445 home runs, nearly 1,900 RBI, and over 95.0 WAR, to go along with a fourth MVP. While this is not a perfect look at what DiMaggio could have produced, it is certainly more objective than trying to figure out how to calculate what Mantle missed out on.

In Mantle's case, he perpetually suffered from injuries that robbed him of a share of his natural ability. The injuries started way back in his childhood when he was kicked in the shin, and a brutal infection followed. But that was hardly all. He had shoulder issues, knee injuries and various aches and pains throughout his career. One such injury happened in a now-infamous World Series game, when, irony of ironies, DiMaggio was in center and Mantle was in right field. On a shallow fly ball to right, Mantle came flying in and caught his foot on a sprinkler (because they used to not bury those well enough, amazingly) and went down in a heap. Trying to figure out just how much this injury (along with numerous others) sapped Mantle's ability may be a futile task, but going into their background can help to flesh out Mantle's persona a bit. Mantle had multiple family members lose the battle to cancer at a young age, and as such, some have surmised that he thought he had no need to take care of his body. Mantle did indeed play – and drink – like there was no tomorrow, quite possibly because he lived in fear of death throughout his career. How much more he could have achieved by taking care of himself is a difficult question, however. The best player of all time (Ruth) treated his body like crap, and Wilt Chamberlain, one of the five best basketball players of all time, had plenty of sleepless nights thanks to his proclivity for women. The lack of care for one's body is a limit that seems as though it may be too difficult to quantify.

Mantle didn't succumb to cancer until 63, and at the time of his death, he was irrationally hard on himself as a player and as a role model. It's hard to believe the media didn't play a role in that thought process.

It's interesting to think that not only do we want these men to perform at their peak every day (who among us goes as hard as they can every day at work?), but also be friendly and chipper and a good role model for our youth when on their free time. It's great when the all-timers are able to balance all of this (Oh hi, Stan Musial), but to treat it as an expectation is a bit beyond the pale.

EDGE: Really hard to compare. Let's call this a draw out of an inability to truly determine full scope.

Impact on the Franchise

Both DiMaggio and Mantle have enormous impacts on Yankee history, and that's part of what makes this comparison such a good one. Whether Mantle or DiMaggio had a greater impact on Yankee history is essential to deciding who gets the spot here. In order to really answer the question, it requires some more in-depth sub-categories.

Inevitability

These two men are very often mentioned in the same breath, probably more than any other cross-generational duo of all time (barring possibly Barry Bonds and Babe Ruth). The impact DiMaggio's stardom had on Mantle has already been discussed, but the inevitability of these two men needs to be discussed further.

Of all the names in baseball history, *Mantle* might be the most appropriate. He took the "mantle" of next in line as a Yankee Great early in his career. In fact, when he first came to the big leagues, Mantle was given the number six because Babe Ruth had been number three, Lou Gehrig had been number four, and Joe DiMaggio had been number five. It was only natural to give the future of the Yankees the number six. This mantle was passed on to him when he was just 19 years old. He would later switch to the number seven, which feels a lot like it had something to do with Mantle never really feeling comfortable as "next in line" in Yankee lore. It is hard to blame him for this sentiment. In Carl Yastrzemski's write-up in the

Red Sox Starting IX, I gave a list of the players with the biggest shoes to fill of all time, and how they performed under that pressure. Yastrzemski and Mantle arguably did the best job of any players on those lists, but there is one main difference between the two. Yastrzemski took over the position from Ted Williams, one of the least-loved players in history, even in his hometown Boston because of his personality. Mantle had to fill in for DiMaggio, a player for whom love extended not only to the field of play, but also off the field. This was not lost on Mantle. As written in *Sport Magazine* in 1951: "But in the next inning, when the Yankees came in from the field, it was the young Mantle who carried the great man's glove in to DiMag. He did it with a reverence that raised a lump in the throat of everyone who noticed it." This was not just *Sport Magazine* getting out of hand. Mantle, himself, said of DiMaggio, "As far as I'm concerned, Joe DiMaggio was probably the greatest all-around baseball player who ever lived."

One quality that Mantle had, that may have had a role in the way these two men are remembered, was his awareness. As can be seen from the above quotes, Mickey Mantle was incredibly aware of the awe and reverence he should show the great Joe DiMaggio. This is a trait that as fans we usually laud in a player. We don't like the brash young players who come in with no sense of history, touting their own skills as far superior to any before them. However, often times, it's the over-confident young athletes who turn into the players that end up being considered greater than everybody else. It's almost as if their brash sense of personality permeates into the media's portrayal of the player, and suddenly it becomes accepted. From the other side of things, players like Mantle whose humility seems to be ideal, are often viewed in a lesser light in the long run. It's almost as if their humility comes across as self-doubt sometimes, which then permeates into the media's portrayal of their character. The balance of humility and hubris is a fine line, and that line becomes exponentially finer when the player is in the position Mantle was in – replacing a legend on a historically great team.

EDGE: Both. It's inevitable.

Why the Double Standard?

At this point, the double standard applied to these two men has been established, but it can only leave the curious baseball fan with the question as to *why* these two men were treated so differently? This question becomes even more intriguing when it becomes clear how many similarities the two men had. For instance, both men faced their fair share of criticism from the bleacher creatures in New York to start their careers. The two men handled those boo birds quite differently, however. DiMaggio was booed lustily early in his career because he held out for more money during the Great Depression. However, he was distant from others and didn't let the boo birds get to him, eventually becoming a national icon and hero. Mantle, however, grew bitter, and what fans and media took to be DiMaggio's laidback persona came across as a lack of effort from Mantle. The irony, of course, being the pain that Mantle was constantly playing through.

Another factor that may have hurt Mantle was that Willie Mays and Duke Snider were playing the same position in the same city at the same time as him. The grass is always greener, especially when it's just across the Triborough Bridge. During most of his career, DiMaggio didn't have to deal with any competition within his city to the level Mantle had to.

Yet another theory, and one that I believe holds a fair amount of water, is the historical times in which the two men played. DiMaggio played in a time unique to American history. Since this is a baseball book, and not a history book, there is no need to go too deep, but some background is necessary. When DiMaggio reached his prime, the nation was desperate for a distraction, and, as Paul Simon so eloquently put it, "our nation turned its lonely eyes to [DiMaggio]." DiMaggio responded with a hit streak[471] that enthralled the nation (1941), an MVP (1941) and then three years of service to his country (1943-1945). When Mantle was in his prime, the country was torn about by Cold War politics; he had his career-defining "moment" stolen from him by Roger Maris in 1961; and he wasn't able to serve his country because of lower body ailments. Is it really any surprise that these two legacies turned out the way they did?

EDGE: Mantle. Poor Mickey Mantle.

Versatility

When Mantle was coming up through the Yankees organization, he actually played shortstop, and he wasn't moved to the outfield until reaching the major leagues. Since this is the breakdown of all breakdowns, why not do a little "*Inception*-style" breakdown of Mantle vs. Derek Jeter if Mantle had stayed at shortstop?

---

[471] Easily the best DiMaggio hit streak story: one pitcher, Johnny Babich, said before what would eventually become DiMaggio's 40th straight game with a hit, that he was going to be the guy to stop Joltin' Joe. He walked DiMaggio on four pitches his first time up, and started the Yankee Clipper with three straight wide ones to start his second at bat. On the fourth pitch, however, DiMaggio reached outside and hit what would have been ball four back up in the box, between Babich's legs, for a base hit. According to DiMaggio, he wasn't trying to throw shade at Babich, but he did get a kick out of the fact that Babich was "white as a sheet" when DiMaggio reached first base. Kinda reminds me of when Barney first meets Marshall in *How I Met Your Mother*, and he doesn't realize Marshall is dating Lily. When Barney challenges Marshall to go pick up the super hot redhead at the bar (Lily), Marshall begrudgingly accepts and gets a nice deep kiss right then and there. Barney is convinced Marshall is a wizard and follows him around like a puppy dog for a week. DiMaggio likely could have had Babich doing his laundry for a month or so after his stunt, as he clearly left his mark on the pitcher.

Contact EDGE: Draw
Power EDGE: Mantle
Batting Eye EDGE: Mantle
Speed EDGE: Jeter
Defense (as a SS) EDGE: Hard to know definitively, but slight edge to Jeter
Intangibles EDGE: Jeter
Team Success EDGE: Draw (although Mantle's raw numbers are better, the era in which Jeter's Yankees dominated was more impressive)
Dominance EDGE: Mantle

Winner: Mantle

EDGE: Mantle

Hipster Effect

I'm not sure I consider myself a hipster. I like PBR, mustaches, and The Lumineers, but the idea of skinny jeans and black-framed glasses just aren't for me. I am, however, a bit of a contrarian, which can come across as being a "sports hipster." Basically, I do that thing that hipsters do with bands, but with teams and players in the sporting world. For example, I fell in love with the San Francisco Giants when Buster Posey and Tim Lincecum were just beginning their careers, but I abandoned them by the time of their first title because too many people liked them then. Lincecum was the perfect example of this, as I loved him when he first came up because I had "discovered" him[472] by having him on my fantasy team before anyone else, but once he won his Cy Young awards, I was nowhere to be found on the Lincecum bandwagon. Of course, once he began struggling and had Giants fans turning on him, only then did I begin to feel my Lincecum-Love revving back up. The same thing could be said of my love affair with the Oklahoma City Thunder, and it always happens on a smaller scale during March Madness. It's an affliction for which I have not found the cure but have instead decided to embrace.[473]

So what does all of that have to do with Joe DiMaggio and Mickey Mantle? Well, as I am sure the reader has surmised by this point, Mantle would certainly be the "sports hipster" pick here. Historically, any and every baseball historian has lauded DiMaggio; Mantle's praise has always come with a historical asterisk of either what could have been, or as a comparison to DiMaggio. This is a category made for Mantle.

HUGE EDGE: Mantle

Verdict

Really, you can't go wrong here. It's the most stacked position of any team in baseball history,[474] and the only thing really separating the two is opinion. For me, it comes down to two categories. One that makes sense, and one that doesn't. The first, and sensible, one is Dominance. Mantle was more dominant, and he played in more games for the Yankees. Argue DiMaggio's case all you want, but that's hard to argue with.

The not so sensible, but likely as heavily-weighted, category is The Hipster Effect. Ask any of my friends (especially the Crookston crew), I'm a devout contrarian. Whether it's taste in girls, TV shows, how to spend my free time, whatever really, I like to zig when folks zag and vice versa. One time I asked a girlfriend what she thought the one word I wanted others to think of when they thought of me, and she said *different*. (For the record, I had said empathetic – just as nauseating.)

So maybe **Mantle** gets this center field spot because he dominated the sport of baseball like DiMaggio just didn't. Or maybe DiMaggio has to settle for the utility spot because of my deep-seated need to make you remember me. Hey, it's better than going all "John Doe in *Seven*" on the world, right?

Verdict: Reallllly tempted to do a full breakdown of Mantle/Willie Mays now, but you've read enough at this point, my friends. **Willie Mays**.

---

[472] Note: It was I, and not the Giants organization, who gave him his break.

[473] To finish this editorial: I believe that my hipsterdom is the result of growing up a Yankees fan and being called a bandwagon fan so often that I had to go 180 degrees the opposite direction in my adulthood.

[474] The best of each position in baseball history: SP) Dodgers C) Yankees 1B) Cardinals 2B) Tigers 3B) Braves SS) Pirates LF) Red Sox CF) Yankees RF) Tigers.

Right Field: Mel Ott vs. Babe Ruth

Mel Ott (1926-1947)

Mel Ott has seen a bit of a drop in his historical standing lately, as some of baseball's best minds have noticed a disturbing trend in Ott's numbers. Ott has the highest percent of home runs at home of any of the members of the 500-home run club. The career-long Giant hit 323 of his 511 career home runs at the Polo Grounds; however, there are several factors that show that show this shouldn't necessarily take away from how we think of Ott.

For one, Ott's high level of home runs at home were not a mistake, or even, to a certain extent, the result of incredibly friendly confines like Chuck Klein at the Baker Bowl. The Polo Grounds did have some of the quirkiest dimensions of any baseball field in history, though. It was less than 300 feet down each line but extended to 450 feet in center field, leading to its nickname: "The Bathtub." Ott hit such a high number of home runs at his home stadium because he worked and worked on getting his swing to fit the Polo Grounds. As teammate Lefty O'Doul reveals, "We used to spend hours, just the two of us, practicing hitting the ball down the right-field foul line. We got so we could keep it fair by just a few inches." Dedication to one's game such as this should be praised instead of scorned, and Ott should be rewarded in our collective memory for dedicating himself to his surroundings.

Second, it's not as if Ott was a slouch on the road. Yes, his slugging percentage is nearly 50 points lower on the road, but it is still .510 for his career – higher than Eddie Mathews' career slugging percentage. Ott's batting average was actually 14 points higher on the road, probably as a result of not trying to pull the ball so much. Ott both drove in, and scored, nearly as many runs on the road, and his doubles and triples totals were much higher.

Finally, it's not as if all of Ott's teammates didn't have the same advantage. I mention this because Ott led the Giants in home runs 18 straight seasons. This is the longest stretch a player led his team in any of the following: stats batting average, hits, home runs, RBI or wins; the second player on that list is Warren Spahn who led his team in wins 15 straight years. And although Ott never won an MVP, no less an authority than Bill James calls him, by far, the best player to never win one. Plus, he was the first National League player to hit 500 home runs for his career.

It was a fast start to that career, as Ott made his debut at the age of just 17. He was a great player even at this precocious age, and before Bryce Harper's 2012 season, Ott's age-19 season (1928) was the best season a 19-year-old had ever turned in, according to WAR. Ott's age-20 season was no let down, as he set what would remain career highs in runs (138), home runs (42), and RBI (151). He was worth over 7.0 wins above replacement, and the ceiling seemed to be the limit for Ott. It's not that he disappointed after that, but he never really reached the next level (somewhat similar to Al Kaline), a level which would have put him in the class of Babe Ruth, Lou Gehrig, and Rogers Hornsby, who were the truly elite during Ott's playing days. Ott still led the league in home runs and walks six times apiece, and he topped the league in OPS+ five times. He led NL position players in WAR five times, two of those times leading the entire league, pitchers included. By many metrics, Ott is the third-best right fielder of all time behind Ruth and Aaron, so why is it that even in his day and age he never got the respect he deserved?

It was Ott about whom Leo Durocher said, "Nice guys finish last," during one season when the Giants were struggling. This, however, doesn't hold any water, as Ott won a World Series ring in his career and, in that series, posted an OPS of 1.222. For whatever reason, Ott has earned a spot with Al Simmons on the all-Rodney Dangerfield team of players that "don't get no respect." He's also a charter member of the short name Hall of Fame. The Starting IX of players with complete names of eight letters or less:

SP) Cy Young C) Joe Mauer 1B) Jim Thome – Screw you, Cap Anson. 2B) Rod Carew 3B) Ron Santo SS) Al Dark LF) Pete Rose CF) Ty Cobb RF) Babe Ruth Utility) Mel Ott CP) Lee Smith

I hope that makes up for folks ignoring you historically, Mr. Ott.

Babe Ruth (1920-1934)

If the last spot on the Yankees was the ultimate breakdown, this spot is just the ultimate. All discussions of the greatest player of all time typically begin and end with Ruth. He is legendary in the most literal sense of the word, having more myth surrounding his legacy than any player in any sport.

The most common myth is the "Curse of the Bambino" that supposedly dogged the Red Sox for so long. The myth has thankfully been eliminated from the baseball vernacular since 2004, but for a couple decades there it became all too pervasive. I say thankfully when talking about the elimination of the "curse" because the whole thing doesn't really add up historically. Yes, Red Sox owner Harry Frazee was a cheapskate who sold Ruth, but Frazee sold Ruth for more money than any other previous baseball player had been sold, and considering the way Ruth took care of his body – more to come on that – it seemed like at least a defensible move at the time. Of course, this move did not pan out at all for Frazee, and Ruth went on to produce at all sorts of ridiculous levels.

Entire books have been written about Ruth's records, so for this write-up, let's just look at some of the numbers that particularly stick out. We'll start with his pitching days in Boston to round out the full, historical sense of this man:

* Ruth is the only left-handed pitcher to have back-to-back 23-win seasons before the age of 23.
* He became the youngest ERA champ in AL history when he led the league with a 1.75 ERA in 1916 at the ripe age of 21.
* In 1916 and 1918, Ruth made the World Series with the Red Sox and managed to toss 29.6 consecutive scoreless innings, including the only 14-inning complete game in any round of the postseason history.
* Ruth had more wins on the mound through his age-22 season than Lefty Grove and Eddie Plank had through their age-27 seasons. Those are two pitchers who would each go on to have over 300 career wins.
* Ruth was part of the most bizarre no-hitter in MLB history, as he threw just four pitches, all balls, in a 1917 start. Ruth argued with the ump, eventually hit him with a left hook, and was thrown out of the game. Ernie Shore came on in relief; Eddie Foster, who drew the walk, was caught stealing; and Shore retired the next 26 batters in a row.
* In 1915, while still a pitcher, Ruth hit four home runs in 92 at bats, leading his entire team for the season.
* In 1917, as a pitcher (142 at bats), only Ty Cobb, George Sisler, and Tris Speaker had a better batting average in the AL.
* In 1919, while playing for the Red Sox, he hit 29 home runs with his home games coming in a pitcher's park (Fenway). His nine home runs in Fenway were three times as many as *all opposing teams* hit there *all year*.
* In 1918 and 1919, the 6' 2" goliath led baseball in home runs while throwing over 100 IP each season.
(Ruth moves to New York)
* In 1920, Ruth hit 54 home runs. No other *team* in the American League topped 50 home runs. League-wide, only the Phillies had more, and that was thanks to the Baker Bowl.
* Technically, Ruth set the MLB career home run record on each of his final 576 home runs. He broke Roger Connor's career home run record in just his third full season in the outfield. Ruth would go on to quintuple Connor's record.
* In the 1920s, Ruth averaged 47 home runs; only five others hit 40 home runs in a single season in the decade.
* Ruth was the first baseball player to hit 30 home runs in a season; and 40 in a season; and 50; and 60.
* When he hit his 600th home run, no one else had even hit 300.
* Ruth *averaged* 10.4 WAR for a 10-year stretch (1919-1928). Remember when we all lost our minds after Trout topped 10.0 WAR in one season? Yeah, Ruth averaged double-digit WAR for a decade.
* Between 1919-1928, Ruth had *more than twice as many home runs* as any other player in baseball.
* Author Bill Jenkinson makes the case that Ruth could have hit 104 home runs in 1921 if playing in modern stadiums with modern rules.
* Ruth, quite appropriately, hit the first home run in All-Star Game history.
* When Ruth retired, he owned 56 Major League records and 66 American League records including – and this is truly the greatest stat ever – the best winning percentage, among pitchers, against the New York Yankees.

What makes Ruth arguably the most famous athlete of all time was not just his legacy on the field, but his notoriety off it as well. His name has even made its way into the vernacular of the country, with Ruthian meaning a task or accomplish of greatness. He has nearly as many stories about his off-field trials and tribulations as he does about his batting records. Once again, books have been written on this, so let's just go through the highlights.

Ruth had a tough childhood, as his father worked long hours, and his mother struggled with her health. Ruth had tried beer and tobacco before the age of seven, and around this time he was declared "incorrigible" and sent to an all boy's academy. This was the best thing that could have happened to him, as he met Brother Matthias, one of the low-key, most influential people in baseball history. Matthias shaped up Ruth (at least a bit) and, more importantly in terms of a historical sense, got Ruth interested in baseball. Ruth even stole Matthias' batting style as his own. It wasn't long before Ruth mastered the game and was signed by no other than Jack Dunn (Team Introduction, Cardinals – Page 319).

It didn't take Ruth long to become a star, and possibly because of his own childhood, he immediately began setting up events for local youth, even in his time in Boston. Ruth loved children and frequently visited hospitals, promising sick children home runs, and often delivering. It was said that wherever he went there could be seen a line of kids following him. Ruth was never hesitant to sign memorabilia for any fan, especially kids. Of course, Ruth infamously came to New York when the Red Sox owner, Harry Frazee, got fed up with Ruth and his contract demands, and sold him to their rival Yankees. At the time, public opinion was actually split on the sale.

It didn't take long for Ruth to reach the next level, however. The contract negotiations didn't stop when Ruth got to New York (when Ruth was told he didn't need a pay raise because he already made more than the president, his response was, "I had a better year than he did"), but the Yankees put up with it because they had arguably the biggest star of all time. Off the field. Ruth had such a reputation that, at one point, teammates could be fined $1,000 (which went a long way in Ruth's day) if they were seen out on the town with Ruth, because it almost certainly meant trouble. The *Daily News* eventually hired one writer, full-time, 365 days a year, to write about only Ruth. Ruth is also the reason that the Yankees wear pinstripes as part of their uniform to this day. Yankees owner and New York Representative Jacob Ruppert thought they made Ruth look slimmer, so naturally he suited the club up in pinstripes. Let's be honest, though, nothing could hide Ruth's beer belly.

Ruth's antics certainly do bring to mind the question of how exactly Ruth didn't burn out given the lifestyle he lived. In fact, the argument could be made that he had one of the more blessed careers in terms of avoiding injury or becoming burnt out in the face of his recklessness off the field. As mentioned earlier, his off-field proclivities were said to be the cause of Frazee giving up on Ruth before selling him to New York.

Although these antics have distanced certain players from their home fan bases, Ruth did it in such a gregarious, fun-loving way[475] that fans loved him, and he loved them back. Although a better way of phrasing that might be that he loved the attention. Ruth once cut short a trip to Paris because he wasn't being recognized enough. In terms of his legacy, it also didn't hurt that he was great with children and was always signing autographs for them. In fact, the way he interacted with the youth of his generation had an enormous impact on the history of baseball.

One of the most remarkable things about reading *Sport Magazine* from the 1950s is that there was actually a serious concern that Ruth's lore was not being promoted enough during this time. This was the generation of writers to whom Ruth had never declined an autograph when they were kids, and now there were suddenly numerous articles worried that Ruth would soon be forgotten. At once, there began a push to educate the next generation of children all about Ruth. This push for Ruth to be considered the greatest of all time, a fact rather widely acknowledged now, didn't really exist in Ruth's own time. For example: Ty Cobb got into the Hall of Fame with more votes in the first-ever Hall of Fame ballot. Ruth was certainly admired, but his status as "Baseball G.O.A.T" didn't come around until later.

Another trend that has helped his legacy has been the home run era, and the emphasis on the long ball in today's game. With more and more players relying on home runs, and home run totals jumping up, Ruth's records became more and more impressive every year. Students of baseball began to go back and look at just how ridiculous the numbers Ruth put up were. Only time will tell if baseball scholars and statisticians will find a new way of looking at players that maybe puts Cobb (or even Willie Mays or Ted Williams) ahead of Ruth again, but for now, Ruth reigns supreme as the most dominant player who ever played the sport of baseball.

Verdict: **Babe Ruth**. Duh. That one was more lopsided than *Utility Air Regulatory Group V. Environmental Protection Agency*… AmIright, judges?![476]

Utility: Willie McCovey vs. Joe DiMaggio

Willie McCovey (1959-1973; 1977-1980)

McCovey, nicknamed "Stretch," played first base for the Giants for 19 seasons. He played his first 15 seasons with the club and, after a brief stint in San Diego and an even briefer stint in Oakland, came back to finish his career with the Giants. McCovey's career got off to an auspicious start in his very first game. McCovey and the Giants faced the Phillies and their Hall of Fame pitcher Robin Roberts. It would have been understandable had the rookie struggled in his first start against a pitcher as good as Roberts. McCovey, however, tallied four hits, including two triples, in what would be one of the best debuts a big leaguer has ever had. He continued to rampage the league for the rest of the 1959 season, sporting a 1.085 OPS, and winning Rookie of the Year despite playing in only 52 games. (For comparison's sake: Gary Sanchez's world-eating 2016 debut: 53 games with an OPS of 1.032 – McCovey was somehow better.)

Despite the eventual nickname "Stretch," and the fact that McCovey is remembered mostly as a first baseman, McCovey didn't play more than 100 games at first base until his seventh season. McCovey was a bit of a utility player (like he is here!) for those first six years because the Giants also had Orlando Cepeda playing first base. The two split time there, and McCovey dabbled in the outfield as well. During this time, McCovey built his reputation as a top slugger in baseball. He led the league in home runs in 1963; the first of three times he would do so.

It was also during this time that McCovey cemented one of his more unfortunate legacies. In 1962, the Giants won the pennant and faced the Yankees in one of the closest World Series in baseball history. The Yankees won the first game, and then the two traded games back and forth until Game 7, to be played in San Francisco. The game lived up to the hype surrounding it, and the game went into the bottom of the ninth with the Yankees holding a 1-0 lead. Matty Alou started the inning off with a bunt single, but Ralph Terry got the next two batters to strikeout. Down to their last out, Willie Mays doubled to right, bringing up McCovey with men on second and third, down one, with two outs in the ninth inning of Game 7 of the World Series – no pressure. McCovey had tripled his last time up, and early in the count, McCovey hit a ball with home run distance, but it landed foul. He kept at it, though, and responded by hitting one of the hardest balls of all time, but it was the ultimate "atom" ball. Bobby Richardson was at second base, and it was right "at him." Richardson made the catch, and the Yankees won another ring.

This unfortunate result would haunt McCovey for most of his career, despite the fact that he put together one of the best resumes of any baseball player, and no one in their right mind blamed him for the World Series loss. Still, the line drive was the only current event ever discussed in the comic strip *Peanuts*, with Charlie Brown saying, "Why couldn't [McCovey] have hit the ball three feet higher!?" In McCovey's Hall of Fame induction speech, he said he'd liked to be remembered as the man who hit the line drive over Bobby Richardson's head. It even came back up in a 2012 study by Dave Studeman of

---

[475] At least in the public eye.

[476] The extent of "research" for that "joke" was a Google search for "lopsided court decision" and clicking the first link. That's a little thing called quality book research.

The Hardball Times. Not to add insult to injury, but Studeman determined McCovey's at bat to be the most critical at bat *in the history of baseball*.

However, McCovey became an even greater hitter after this World Series, and his reputation – and legendary power – began to grow. This reputation led to McCovey being the first man to be intentionally walked 40 times in a season (1969). It was during this time that McCovey became fifth player in history to lead the league in both home runs and RBI two straight years (1968-1969). He also became the first player to hit two home runs in the same inning twice in his career, and he even had the cove behind the right field bleachers at AT&T Field named after him.

Despite playing through injuries nearly his whole career, McCovey managed to set the all-time record for most home runs by a left-handed batter in the NL, a record he held until Barry Bonds broke it in 2001. Tom Seaver once called McCovey the most intimidating hitter he ever faced, and Sparky Anderson called him, "The most awesome man I've ever seen." It is for reasons like this, and not that 1962 World Series, for which McCovey should be remembered.

Joe DiMaggio

I think it's fair to say we talked enough about DiMaggio already.

Verdict: **DiMaggio** may not have been able to topple Mantle, but he takes this one.

Starting Pitcher: Christy Mathewson vs. Whitey Ford

SP Christy Mathewson (1900-1916)

Continuing this absolute juggernaut of an all-franchise team, Christy Mathewson takes the role of starting pitcher for the Giants. One of the best pitchers of all time, Mathewson was the Greg Maddux of his time.[477] He threw with an almost incomparable precision that drove his success as a pitcher. The legend is that Mathewson honed his accuracy as a kid by throwing at a knothole in his barn; you don't see too many Tom Emanski videos for that these days. Mathewson was not without competition for this spot, however, as Juan Marichal and Carl Hubbell were both excellent pitchers with the Giants who could have started for a great number of other franchises based on their success with the team. (Marichal: 238 wins, 2.84 ERA, 62.5 WAR; Hubbell: 253 wins; 2.98 ERA; 67.8 WAR.)

Mathewson was also one of the best *men* of all time. He ushered in an era of likable ballplayers and was one of the first players to show the public that not all ball players were drunks with a penchant for fighting. Many have said no one did more to improve the public opinion of ballplayers than Mathewson, and although the public opinion of players would once again slip post-Mathewson (during the Black Sox scandal most notably), he set a precedent for later generations (like Stan Musial, Willie Mays, Ernie Banks et al.).

Mathewson's career was filled with numerous highlights on the field, too many for just one write-up, so we'll try to hit the big ones. In terms of highlighted performances, it doesn't get much better than his 1905 season. During the regular season, Mathewson won 31 games, had an ERA of 1.28, 206 strikeouts, an ERA+ of 230, and a WHIP of 0.93, all of which led the league. However, he managed to upstage all that regular season success with his World Series performance. Mathewson's 1905 World Series is probably the best a pitcher has ever had, and it's impossible to imagine anyone topping it in the future. He threw three shutouts in a five-game series (thanks to a rainout), leading the Giants to a series victory. The Giants pitchers, as a whole, had an ERA of 0.00 for the *entire series*. Their only loss was in Game 2, which was a 3-0 loss in which all three runs were unearned. Their four other wins were shutouts, which was especially impressive because their opponent, the Philadelphia A's, had led the league in runs scored during the 1905 season. Mathewson would go on to pitch in three more World Series (all losses), and post nearly as spectacular numbers, finishing his career with over 100 innings pitched in World Series play and an ERA under 1.00. That's as impressive a stat as you'll find in this entire book.

This unrivaled success makes sense seeing as he was not only one of the best pitchers of all time, but his numbers are also often thought of as slightly underrated. This is because there are multiple accounts of Mathewson easing up on opponents, either for his own entertainment or because he was a "nice guy." One such story goes that Mathewson loaded the bases with no outs one time, and his manager came out to talk to him. Mathewson's response: "Take it easy, it's more fun this way." It was indeed fun for him, as Mathewson struck out the next three to end the inning unscathed. This type of story is similar to one told about Walter Johnson, which makes sense as they were the two congenial stars of their time, a time in which a pitcher could get away with something like loading the bases for fun without as many repercussions.

Mathewson was one of the biggest winners of his time, racking up at least 22 wins every season from 1903-1914. Part of this was due to the Giants being such a strong club at this time, but much more of it was due to Mathewson. In fact, early in his career, Mathewson was a bit underrated by wins. In 1902, Mathewson finished the season 14-17, a record which might lead some fans to believe it was not a good season for him. However, he led the league in shutouts and had an ERA of 2.12. Of course, six years later, Mathewson set the NL record for wins in a season (37), a record that remains (and will

[477] Walter Johnson was, appropriately, the Randy Johnson – a flame-thrower for the early 20th century.

remain) the highest total in the modern era of the Senior Circuit. His career total of 373 wins in the NL has him tied with Pete Alexander for the most in league history. If both men were still alive (but also still really old) this could make for a great "Mr. 3000" type scenario,[478] in which the two men came out of retirement in their old age to see who could win a game first and take the crown of all-time NL wins leader. Unfortunately, Mathewson passed away before Alexander retired, and we don't have the ability to clone them. Yet. One day though.

Finally, Mathewson was one of the smartest men in baseball history, and his favorite pastime was checkers. He was an incredibly talented checkers player and defeated Newell Banks, an eight-time Checkers World Champion, when the two played.

Unfortunately, baseball lost one of its true princes at a young age when Mathewson lost his life to complications from being accidentally gassed during a WWI training exercise. He passed away at the age of 45 after battling tuberculosis for seven years. Not surprisingly, he left us with one of the best baseball quotes of all time: "You can learn little from victory. You can learn everything from defeat."

SP Whitey Ford (1950-1967)

Ford holds the honor of being the most underrated Yankee of all time. That sounds weird at first, almost like saying Piers Morgan has the most grating British accent of all time, or saying *Luck* was the worst HBO show of all time. There's still a limit to how underrated/grating/bad that Ford/Morgan/*Luck* can be[479] due to the nature of the comparison. Ford, however, is under-appreciated because of the nature of Yankee history. The Yankees, throughout their entire history, have been a team built upon hitting, with pitchers always taking a back seat. Ford was the exception to this rule, however, and his 50.0+ WAR – and incredible postseason numbers – attest to that. His run in the 1960-1961 World Series are unmatched in baseball history. Ford threw 18.0 shutout innings in 1960 and then came back and fired 14.0 more shutout innings when the Yankees broke through in 1961 for their first title since *all the way back* in 1958. In total, Ford threw 33.0 consecutive scoreless World Series innings, good for the MLB record.

It was also around this time that he was in his prime at another important factor of his game: eliminating the running game. In 1961, three runners attempted to steal on Ford all year, and all were caught stealing. That same year Ford was also able to pick off six other runners on his own. In fact, he owns the longest innings streak without allowing a steal (262.0 innings pitched), as well as a different such streak that comes in fourth (191.1 IP). On the days Ford pitched, the catcher had as much of an off-day as a catcher can have.

Ford may well have been the guy to tell his catcher that he was saving him some work, too, as the southpaw was never short on confidence. On the days that Ford pitched, he would set up a picnic in the bullpen and tell them to enjoy the day off. When he met Dizzy Dean, an established star before him, Ford said, "No wonder you won 30 games pitching in that crummy National League. I could win 40 in that league myself." Ford's brash nature was hard to hold against him. Because it was deserved. His .690 winning percentage is through the roof, higher than any other modern era starter with at least 1,000.0 innings pitched. Ford was also often moved around the Yankee rotation to face the opposing teams' aces, a fact that only underlines his career winning percentage to an even higher degree.

Ford didn't always play by the rules, however, as he was a notorious scuffer of the ball. He would often use weird substances to work the ball, and later in his career, he used a sharpened ring to knick the ball while on the mound.

However, there was never any doubt that Ford was the leader among pitchers in Yankee history. As the *New Yorker* itself said, "Ford stands on the mound like a Fifth Avenue bank president. Tight-lipped, absolutely still between pitches, all business and concentration, he personifies the big-city, emotionless perfection of his team."

Verdict: **Mathewson**. This is a big win for the Giants, even though it's just one position, it's the type of position that can swing the pendulum, especially when it's as big an edge as this one is for the Giants.

Closer: Robb Nen vs. Mariano Rivera

CP Robb Nen (1998-2002)

On a team so stacked with talented starting pitching, this position might seem to go to one of those men (i.e. Marichal or Hubbell), but Robb Nen is deserving of his spot as the closer for this team. Nen could certainly challenge for most obscure player to get two spots in this book, but he truly earned it with the Giants. He basically traded away any remaining years he had in his arm while chasing a ring with the Giants in 2002. This ended up being his final season because he wore his arm down (and then some) pitching through the arm injuries that would end his career with surgery that offseason. Ultimately, the Giants came up just short of a World Series title, but no one in the Bay Area ever questioned Nen's

[478] Yes, that is indeed multiple references to a Bernie Mac movie that has a 29 percent audience score on Rotten Tomatoes. That's a little thing called knowing your audience...

[479] Well, except for how grating Piers Morgan is. I lied. There is no limit there.

dedication, and he has a special place in their hearts to this day.

As far as his statistical presence on the team, Nen was worth over 10.0 WAR in his five years with the Giants, a surprisingly high total for a closer. He led the league in games finished twice, and saves once, averaging more than 41 saves a year in his five seasons in the Bay Area. He struck out nearly 11.0 batters per nine innings and had a strikeout to walk ratio of better than four-to-one. Although Marichal and "The Meal Ticket" Hubbell would have been more famed selections for this spot, Nen certainly earned it on the merit of his abilities as a closer, as well as his dedication to the franchise.

CP Mariano Rivera (1995-2013)

There has been a shift in recent years of baseball in which relievers are becoming more and more dominant. Whether it is managers knowing how to better use these late-inning arms, improved scouting, or simply a blip in the radar, one of my fears is that with this era of dominant relievers, the incredible career of Mariano Rivera will be somewhat diminished.

First of all, when Rivera was doing his thing – his thing being an MLB-record ERA+ of 205[480] for his career – there simply weren't other relievers doing this. Rivera led the league in saves only three times in his career, but all you need to know was that his worst season, after being moved to the bullpen, was "only" 44 percent better than league average, per ERA+. In two different seasons, he had an ERA+ of 300, which is mind-numbing (reminder: ERA+ of 100 is league average, so an ERA+ of 300 is *200 percent better* than league average). There are plenty of mind-numbing facts about Rivera.

There are the playoff stats: he has *more* than twice as many postseason saves (42) as anyone else in baseball history; he is ninth all-time in playoff innings pitched (141.0) and has more playoff innings than numerous legendary starting pitchers, including Pedro Martínez and Curt Schilling; his 0.70 postseason ERA is, naturally, best in baseball history.

There's the other-great-reliever-comparison stat: Rivera was worth more, per WAR (56.6), than Trevor Hoffman (28.0) and Billy Wagner (27.7) combined.

And there are even the aging-gracefully stats: Rivera had two post-40 seasons with at least as many saves as his age, i.e. the 44 saves he had in 2011 as a 41-year-old.[481]

Maybe you prefer a more flowery, less analytical approach to the man, though. As Lisa Miller wrote of the Yankee closer in her *New York Magazine* profile of Rivera: "A Rivera inning has thus been compared to a horror movie: The excitement is sharpened, not dulled, by the fact that everyone – the players, the ticket holders, and Rivera himself – knows exactly what's coming."[482]

Of course, to top things off, Rivera was about as beloved and respected a player as you will find in baseball history. A man who was the type to go out of his way to thank the behind-the-scenes folks at the stadium at home or on the road, Rivera is a highly faith-oriented man, who has been overly generous with the fortune that he was blessed to make during his playing days. As has been noted by many, there really wasn't a better fit than Rivera to act as the final player to hang up the historical no. 42 jersey. Rivera was the final player grandfathered in when MLB retired Jackie Robinson's legendary digits in 1997. Robinson would be proud to have a man like Rivera being the final one to bear Robinson's crest.

Verdict: Nen giving his arm in support of "the cause" is a good story, but you don't mess with **Rivera.**

Team Verdict

So now that we've gone position-by-position through these two juggernauts, is it as simple as declaring the Yankees the winner because they took seven of the 10 spots? You might, and that's fair, but I thought of going a bit further. There's a great offshoot of *Fox Sports* called "What If Sports," a website where users can, for free, build teams with any player in a specific year and simulate games between the two "Dream Teams" – nearly the exact way you would want to tackle solving which Starting IX was greater.

Of course, there are a couple of minor hiccups with this way of comparing franchises. Notably: choosing a specific year for each player listed instead of their entire output with the franchise; filling out a complete 25-man roster for each franchise which currently has just 11 players; and weighing how many years each player was with the franchise.

These were tackled as such: for the specific year issue, what I did was take each player's average WAR per season with the Yankees/Giants and find the season that was closest to that average WAR/season. That season was chosen as representative, i.e. Derek Jeter in 2002 (3.7 WAR) and Willie Mays in 1956 (7.6 WAR).

For completing 25-man roster, I simply filled out the roster using players with specific seasons on the Yankees/Giants from history when they were worth exactly 0.0 WAR. The only slight issue with this would be if the

---

[480] Of course, this career ERA+ record is a bit skewed because nearly everyone who is qualified for that list was a starting pitcher, buuuuuttt the gap between Rivera (205) and Clayton Kershaw (161) for first and second all-time in ERA+ is the same as the gap between Kershaw in second and the 165th-best ERA+ (117). A few of the legends with a 117 ERA+: Tug McGraw and Kerry Wood, soooo yeah.

[481] Several of those stats came from a great (as per usual) Jason Starks piece for *ESPN*.

[482] If you need to pour a glass of cold water on your Rivera heat right now, check out the excellent piece "The overrating of Mariano Rivera" by Jim Caple on *ESPN*. Factual while deferential at the same time.

simulator decided to lean heavily on someone like 2008 Carl Pavano out of the bullpen in certain games – you think 2000 Barry Bonds might have a bit of fun with him? Luckily, this was never an issue, as you will see in the upcoming box scores.

Finally, the hardest part: the issue of weighing seasons contributed when this is essentially a one-year snapshot of a player. What I chose to do was set the batting lineup in order of games played with the franchise. Therefore, Derek Jeter, who played the most games of any Yankees hitter, took the leadoff spot, while Matt Williams, who played the fewest games with the Giants of any Giants Starting IX member, hit last for the Giants. This method definitely wasn't fool proof, and we'll come back to it in a second.

So, what were the results of the best-of-seven style series? I think you might be quite surprised.

In Game 1, the Giants jumped out to an early series lead thanks to a 5-2 victory over the Yanks. Willie Mays was the table-setter all night, drawing four walks and stealing two bases, the first of both coming in the first inning. When added to a Bonds walk and a Travis Jackson single, this gave the Giants a 2-0 lead they would not relinquish for our opening salvo.

In Game 2, the Yankees bounced back with a 7-5 win. The men in pinstripes got out to a 5-0 lead by the bottom of the third, as three errors burned the Giants, leading to four unearned runs for the Yankees on the day. The Yankees held on, as Roy White's big day (2-for-3, home run, three RBI) was enough to see them to the finish line and tie up the series.

Game 3 was far from Whitey Ford's finest moment (remember: Ford and Mathewson are starting each and every one of these games because of the lack of a full rotation on these Starting IX's), as the Giants lit him up for eight runs over the course of 5.2 innings, with Laughing Larry Doyle doing the most damage (three runs and three RBI). The Yankees only had the offense to hang with the Giants in the early innings, as Mathewson tossed another complete game, and the Giants took their first home matchup of the series by a final score of 11-4.

Game 4 was the Christy Mathewson show, as he held the Yankees to just two runs in another complete game victory, this time holding the fearsome Yankee hitters without an extra-base hit for the entire game. Thanks to a Travis Jackson two-run single in the first and a Bill Terry RBI single in the third, the Giants had all the runs they needed in Game 4's 3-2 victory, putting them up 3-1 in the series, with a chance to clinch in Game 5.

Game 5 was the classic we were waiting for between these two teams. The Yankees went up 1-0 in the first, 2-0 in the third, and 3-0 in the fifth, but the Giants slowly battled back. First, a Babe Ruth error cut the lead to 3-1, then Travis Jackson struck again with a two-run bomb in the seventh to tie things up. Finally, in the bottom of the eighth, a Buck Ewing solo shot gave the Giants the lead and put them three outs away from a victory in the series. Here's where the simulation manager may have been a bit overconfident. Despite an incredibly well-rested Robb Nen (yet to throw an inning in the entire series…), Mathewson took the mound for the ninth with a one-run lead. And then all hell broke loose. A leadoff single from Lou Gehrig got the Yanks started, and then Yogi Berra (Yogi Berra!) hit an inside-the-park home run, quite possibly the most absurd play in Starting IX Championship history, and the Yankees took the 5-4 lead. Now the Yankees weren't afraid to go to their ninth inning man, and Rivera slammed the door, with a one-two-three inning to keep the Yanks alive and send the series back to New York.

The good vibes didn't last long for the Yanks, though, as it took less than two innings for the Giants to effectively shut the door on the series in Game 6, scoring eight runs in the first two innings off Ford, sending both Ford and the Yankees to an early shower. The Yankees tallied four runs in the latter innings, but it was not nearly enough to overcome the Giants' fast start, losing the game 11-4 and falling in the sixth game of the series.

So yeah, I guess that little issue of Ford vs. Mathewson ended up pretty important. For the six games played, Mathewson's ERA was 3.29; Ford's was 7.34. That's your series right there. Well, that and the fact that Travis Jackson transformed into the Demogorgon from *Stranger Things* for six games. Here are the combined box scores for the series for the two teams.

Giants

Year	Player	AB	R	H	RBI	BB	BA	OBP	SLG	2B	3B	HR	SB	E
1956	Willie Mays	25	5	6	2	5	0.240	0.367	0.360	0	0	1	2	0
1941	Mel Ott	25	7	8	3	5	0.320	0.433	0.560	0	0	2	0	2
2000	Barry Bonds	23	5	6	1	7	0.261	0.433	0.261	0	0	0	0	0
1933	Bill Terry	17	1	4	2	2	0.235	0.316	0.235	0	0	0	0	0
1934	Travis Jackson	28	6	12	10	1	0.429	0.448	0.714	0	1	2	0	2
1913	Larry Doyle	22	4	3	3	5	0.136	0.296	0.182	1	0	0	1	0
1996	Matt Williams	25	2	13	5	0	0.520	0.520	0.560	1	0	0	0	0
1885	Buck Ewing	24	3	9	5	1	0.375	0.400	0.583	2	0	1	0	0
1971	Willie McCovey	7	5	3	4	5	0.429	0.667	1.286	0	0	2	0	0
Year	Player	IP	H	R	ER	BB	SO	HR	ERA	WHIP				
1904	Christy Mathewson	52.0	45	23	19	28	15	2	3.29	1.40				

Yankees

Year	Player	AB	R	H	RBI	BB	BA	OBP	SLG	2B	3B	HR	SB	E
2002	Derek Jeter	22	2	2	0	6	0.091	0.286	0.091	0	0	0	0	0
1960	Mickey Mantle	17	6	5	1	3	0.294	0.400	0.353	1	0	0	0	0
1926	Lou Gehrig	23	2	9	4	4	0.391	0.481	0.478	2	0	0	0	0
1958	Yogi Berra	25	2	4	7	1	0.160	0.192	0.280	0	0	1	0	0
1928	Babe Ruth	19	3	4	1	6	0.211	0.400	0.211	0	0	0	0	1
1974	Roy White	23	3	8	5	1	0.348	0.375	0.522	1	0	1	0	0
2006	Alex Rodriguez	23	0	6	2	2	0.261	0.320	0.261	0	0	0	0	1
1941	Joe Gordon	23	2	4	0	1	0.174	0.208	0.174	0	0	0	0	0
1942	Joe DiMaggio	11	3	2	1	3	0.182	0.357	0.182	0	0	0	0	0
Year	Player	IP	H	R	ER	BB	SO	HR	ERA	WHIP				
1954	Whitey Ford	33.1	49	28	27	19	24	3	7.34	2.05				
2000	Mariano Rivera	2.1	2	1	1	0	2	1	4.29	0.95				

Of course, there are plenty of issues with this result. First of all, as is the case with the actual MLB playoffs, a seven-game series is simply not enough to determine who is truly the better team. There's also the matter of the "weighing games played" issue note above, and I definitely think that screwed the Yankees over a bit. The Yankees Starting IX combined for 19,186 games played amongst their ranks; the Giants: 17,672. I think my way of weighing games played was fair within the team itself, but it probably wasn't totally even between the two teams. Finally – and this is pretty nit-picky – but the simulation didn't have DHs for whatever reason, even when the games were in Yankee Stadium, and having Joe DiMaggio sit the bench in four of the six games was a bigger blow than the Giants missing Willie McCovey, if only by a small margin. (It certainly wouldn't make up a two-game difference, especially with DiMaggio not able to contribute with his glove and McCovey not hurting his team with his glove.)

It certainly seems that the simulator believes that the Giants edge at starting pitcher is big enough to topple the other Yankees advantages, and I have to say I agree. Being able to roll out Christy Mathewson night-after-night in this hypothetical world is massive, and maybe it points out the flaw that I only selected one pitcher per franchise (unlike Rob Neyer in his *Big Book of Lineups*, who had a full five-man rotation for each), but if you think I'm going back and adding four more players to each franchise while currently three paragraphs from finishing this beast, you've lost your gourd, man.

* * *

So there you have it. The Giants are the top Starting IX in baseball history, according to this random dude whose book you picked up by accident on the "For Sale: We Will Now Pay You to Take This Book; People Still Read Books, Right?!" table at Barnes & Noble – so congrats. Willie Mays, Barry Bonds, and the rest, you may now sleep easy.

Since I really have no idea how to end this,[483] let's just do it this way:

"Thanks for coming, please stay for the end credits, if you're wondering who the best boy is, it's somebody's nephew. Um, don't forget to validate your parking, and to all you good people in the Midwest, sorry we said fuck so much."[484]

---

[483] Other than buying a celebratory bottle of Scotch.

[484] Told you I'd get there. [*KKBB* no. 9]

Starting IX Franchise Roster Stats

Giants

Lineup	Yrs	G	R	H	HR	RBI	SB	BB	SO	BA	OBP	SLG	OPS+	dWAR	WAR
Larry Doyle	13	1622	906	1751	67	726	291	576	349	0.292	0.359	0.411	127	-1.9	42.8
Buster Posey	9	1039	505	1163	128	594	20	405	510	0.308	0.376	0.474	135	7.1	37.5
Willie Mays	21	**2857**	**2011**	**3187**	**646**	1859	336	1394	**1436**	0.304	0.385	0.564	157	18.5	**154.6**
Barry Bonds	15	1976	1555	1951	586	1440	263	1947	949	0.312	**0.477**	**0.666**	**199**	-4.1	112.3
Willie McCovey	19	2256	1113	1974	469	1388	24	1168	1351	0.274	0.377	0.524	149	-19.5	59.3
Mel Ott	**22**	2730	1859	2876	511	**1860**	89	**1708**	896	0.304	0.414	0.533	155	-6.0	107.8
Matt Williams	10	1120	594	1092	247	732	29	272	872	0.264	0.312	0.498	122	8.3	33.9
Bill Terry	14	1721	1120	2193	154	1078	56	537	449	**0.341**	0.393	0.506	136	-0.3	54.2
Travis Jackson	15	1656	833	1768	135	929	71	412	565	0.291	0.337	0.433	102	22.9	44.0
Pitchers	Yrs	W	W%	ERA	G	CG	SHO	SV	IP	SO	ERA+	WHIP	SO/9	SO/BB	WAR
Christy Mathewson	17	**372**	0.664	**2.12**	635	**434**	**79**	30	**4779.2**	**2504**	136	**1.057**	4.7	2.96	**95.6**
Robb Nen	5	24	0.490	2.43	365	0	0	**206**	378.1	453	169	1.084	10.8	4.01	10.4

Yankees

Lineup	Yrs	G	R	H	HR	RBI	SB	BB	SO	BA	OBP	SLG	OPS+	dWAR	WAR
Roy White	16	1881	964	1803	160	758	233	934	708	0.271	0.360	0.404	121	-6.1	46.7
Derek Jeter	**20**	**2747**	1923	**3465**	260	1311	**358**	1082	**1840**	0.310	0.377	0.440	115	-9.7	71.8
Babe Ruth	15	2084	**1959**	2518	**659**	1978	110	**1852**	1122	**0.349**	**0.484**	**0.711**	**209**	-1.9	**142.7**
Lou Gehrig	17	2164	1888	2721	493	**1995**	102	1508	790	0.340	0.447	0.632	179	-8.9	112.4
Joe DiMaggio	13	1736	1390	2214	361	1537	30	790	369	0.325	0.398	0.579	155	3.2	78.1
Alex Rodriguez	12	1509	1012	1580	351	1096	152	779	1292	0.283	0.378	0.523	136	0.7	54.2
Mickey Mantle	18	2401	1676	2415	536	1509	153	1733	1710	0.298	0.421	0.557	172	-10.1	109.7
Yogi Berra	18	2116	1174	2148	358	1430	30	704	411	0.285	0.348	0.483	125	8.8	59.6
Robinson Canó	9	1374	799	1649	204	822	38	350	689	0.309	0.355	0.504	126	6.2	45.3
Pitchers	Yrs	W	W%	ERA	G	CG	SHO	SV	IP	SO	ERA+	WHIP	SO/9	SO/BB	WAR
Whitey Ford	16	**236**	0.690	2.75	498	156	**45**	11	**3170.1**	1956	133	1.215	5.6	1.80	53.9
Mariano Rivera	19	82	0.577	2.21	**1115**	0	0	**652**	1283.2	1173	**205**	**1.000**	8.2	4.10	**56.6**

A final note

Hey guy. Yeah, the one who inevitably caught mistakes in this 400-page, mostly self-edited debut book. Be cool. Shoot me a message on Twitter, or send a friendly email bringing it to my attention. Or you can continue on with your life and let it slide, either way works. Just don't say, "God this guy's an idiot, what a piece of crap book, he didn't even take care to check his work." Yes, there are probably going to be a few things that slipped through the cracks. And I promise you they will burn me up more than they burn you up. I promise you I gave a lot of effs writing this, so just be cool, ok?

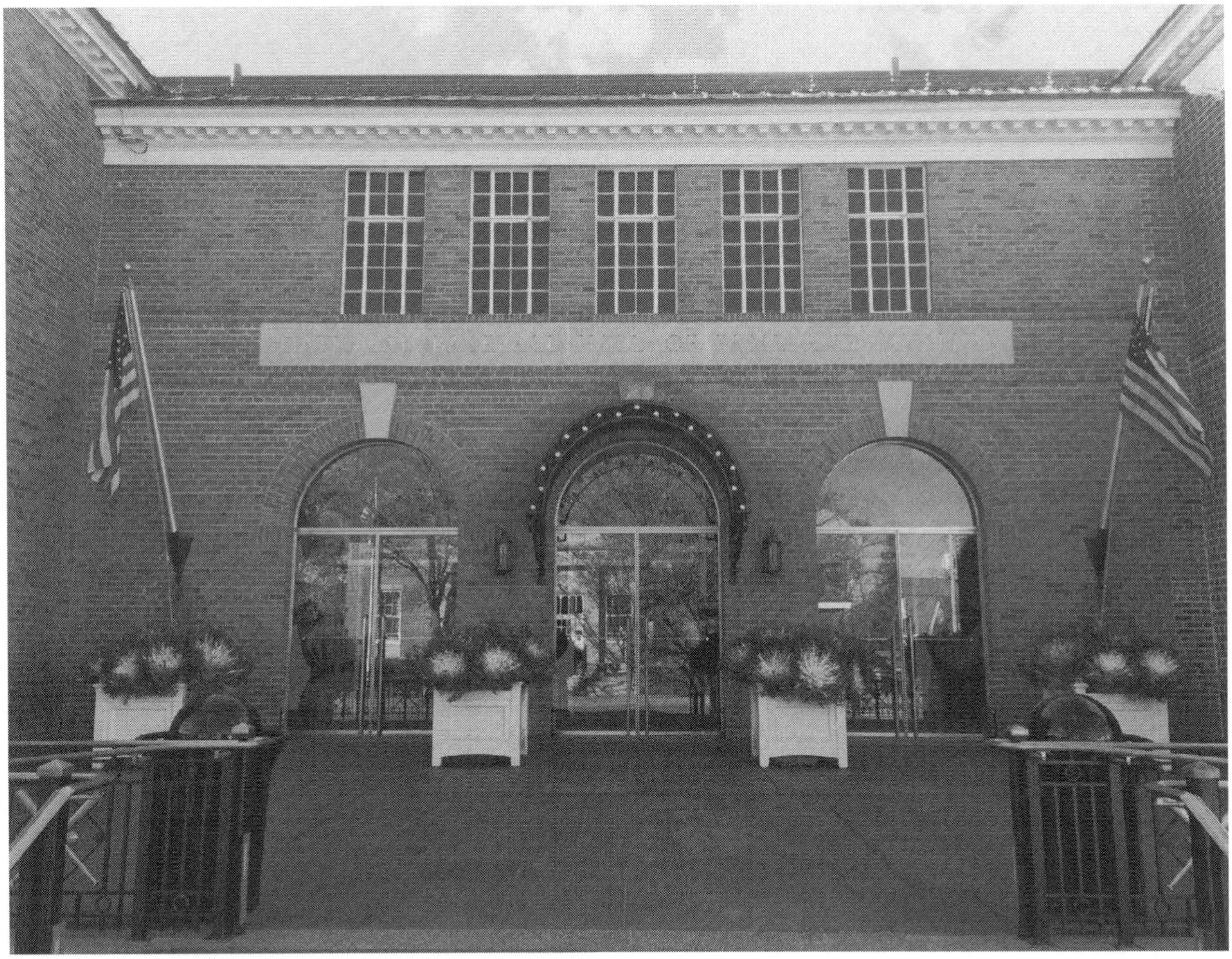

Acknowledgements

There are innumerable people that played a role in this book. I'll try to touch on everyone here, but there will undoubtedly be people that slip through the cracks. I hope that I find those people in real life and treat them to a Guinness.

First and foremost, I have to thank my family. My mother and father instilled both the love of baseball and inability to stand still for more than two minutes that played a massive role in this corny project becoming an actual book. My brother and sister were essential in its completion, between their kind messages in support of my writing, and the hours spent tinkering with the format of this book. (OK, that was more Margaret than Rick). Unthanks to Microsoft Word, which is often more confusing than a season-five episode of *Lost*.

My friends have all been incredibly supportive in the process as well. Whether it's giving my online articles clicks, or casually mentioning something from an article of mine they had clearly read, it means more than you all know. I was also fortunate enough to have several friends offer to proofread chapters of the book, because self-editing can be extremely difficult at times. Among those who read a chapter and sent back their edits: Paul Kline, Jay Flaherty, Erin Hoehl, Jess Bengtson, Corey Hanson, Carolyn Turvey, Matt Bishop, Jonathan Turvey, Lauren Lucero, Taylor Summers, Dan Dyke, Dan McGinnis, Stephanie Pearson, and Andy Cheever. (I believe that is everyone. If I forgot you, I give you 100 percent permission to give me crap for the rest of our lifetimes.)

Most people tackled one chapter, which was exceptionally kind, but I have to give a separate paragraph to Mr. Will Begley, one of the most important people in the process of this book. He not only edited about a dozen chapters, but he also contributed one of the funniest sections (Team Introduction, Toronto Blue Jays – Page 101), gave me a review for the back cover, and answered any and all grammatical questions I asked him during my final self-edit (including about a hundred different versions of "Does there need to be a comma here?").

David Dyke also gets a whole paragraph to himself for the awesome cover he created in a short turn-around right before this book was published. The cover-creation process was downright ulcer-inducing before David stepped in and took away any and all stress associated with it. Truly appreciated.

To uncles Sam and Jon (as well as my father) many thanks for the oodles of baseball cards that were gifted to me at a young age and played such a big role in my love for the statistical side of the sport.

For Tim Rose and all our text messages: dissent is the highest form of patriotism...

Geoff Oehling also contributed a section to the book (Second Base, Red Sox – Page 338), and he was a sounding board for hundreds of other ideas that ended up in this book. I have literally never walked away from a conversation with you feeling anything less than that my mind was just blown.

To Mike Christopherson: I can't thank you enough for giving me my first job in the sports writing field despite my almost certain underqualification at the time of hiring. I learned so much from you, Jess, and the newsroom crew. Plus, you and Michelle were my Minnesota parents, so that was pretty cool.

I'd also like to thank Joseph Lian for kindly gifting me his awesome and complete collection of *Baseball Research Journal* and *The National Pastime*, two invaluable sources which were used ad nauseam during the process of researching the older players in this book.

The Boston Public Library also deserves a shoutout for housing just about the most complete collection of baseball books one can imagine. I made many a trek there while living in Jamaica Plain and was never disappointed with the haul I brought back on the Orange Line.

But most of all, I'd like to thank my iPad for always being there for me with an episode of *The Office* or *How I Met Your Mother* whenever I needed one. You da real MVP.

About the Author

Jim Turvey was born in 1990, the first of three children. He is currently a sports writer who makes his actual living by tending bar (the douchey way of saying bartending). He grew up a Yankees fan in Essex, Vermont and has burned the entire month of October, 2004 out of his memory. He graduated from the University of Vermont in 2012 with a history degree before moving to Jamaica Plain to work in the Boston Public School System. After two years molding the minds of youngsters, he moved to Crookston, Minnesota to chase his sports writing dream with the *Crookston Daily Times*.

He won the Gatehouse Media Rising Star award in his first year on the job, a fact he tries to slip into far too many conversations. After a move back east, he has written for many an online MLB outlet, including: *DRays Bay* (*SBNation*), *The Cauldron*, *Beyond the Box Score*, *Baseball Prospectus Bronx*, *RotoBaller*, *Insider Baseball*, *Call to the Pen*, and *Banished to the Pen*. He has also been published in *Baseball Research Journal* and *Howler Magazine*.

He truly loves his friends and family.

Readers are encouraged to reach out to him as follows:

Email: Jim.Turvey21@gmail.com; Twitter: @BaseballTurv; or by stalking him down in real life.

Bibliography

As noted throughout the book, baseball history can be a bit funky. There are stories of lore and legend that can be difficult to source. For the most part, I relied on secondary sources, not necessarily going to the exact newspaper or periodical to which a quote was originally given, but rather relying on the incredible and innumerable excellent baseball historians to not lead me astray. If I came about a factoid or statistic from a website called The Popcorn Factory, or something like that, I would always try to find a second source before tossing it in the book. Same deal with Wikipedia. I would also go to the footnote, or do a deep dive to find another source collaborating what I read on Wikipedia.

There were a few sources that were used over and over again throughout the process of this book. First and foremost: Baseball-Reference. I probably visited that site, no joke, almost a million times in the entire process of writing this book. It's the greatest website ever, and I am so thankful for all the work Sean Forman and his crew over there do to keep the statistical history of baseball at our fingertips at all times.

I also leaned heavily on the online Baseball Almanac, and the SABR Bio archives. Both of these sources were incredibly helpful for specific players about whom I only had a paragraph or a few stats for. For both, they were used enough that to list every page on their site that I visited would be ridiculous. Instead, I wanted to shout them out first, individually.

In addition to the aforementioned online resources, I also buried my nose into each and every *Baseball Research Journal* and *National Pastime* periodical in the course of researching this book. I honest-to-God read each and every article included in those sepia-toned pages, and they were an invaluable resource. I have tried to shoutout many of them when I used a direct anecdote or theory, but in all honesty, each and every article was basically used to some extent or another in the process of researching this book.

Finally, Ryan Spaeder (@theaceofspaeder), the old Baseball-Reference Play Index Twitter handle – and now just general fun baseball statistical nugget Twitter account – gave me tons of info for this book. I tried to shoutout him out every time I directly used a stat he tweeted, but I likely missed a few. Go follow him immediately if you don't already. If you don't have a Twitter account, create one just so you can follow him.

The rest of these references are a combination of books, magazines, websites, and really anything baseball I could get my hands on for the five years I was working on this book. Thanks for reading, and thanks to all of the authors of these amazing sources for giving me the time of my life researching this book.

Here are all the rest:

Montreal Expos Attendance 1994-2004 and beyond..., mtlexpos.tripod.com/attendance_archive.htm.

Baseball in Wartime - Those Who Served A to Z, www.baseballinwartime.com/those_who_served/those_who_served_atoz.htm.

Seattle Pilots - History, Chapter 3 of 5, www.seattlepilots.com/history3.html.

TheDeadballEra.com :: Joe Cronin's Obit, www.thedeadballera.com/Obits/Obits_C/Cronin.Joe.Obit.html.

"- Rays Touch Tank." *Tampa Bay Rays*, tampabay.rays.mlb.com/tb/ballpark/information/index.jsp?content=rays_tank.

21, August. "Baseball Drug Suspensions." *Los Angeles Times*, Los Angeles Times, 21 Aug. 1997, articles.latimes.com/1997/aug/21/sports/sp-24663.

"24 Things You Might Not Know About the Kansas City Royals." *Mental Floss*, 21 Oct. 2014, mentalfloss.com/article/59620/24-things-you-might-not-know-about-kansas-city-royals.

26, 2012 Nick Cafardo Globe Staff October. "Dodgers' Carl Crawford talks fresh start, playing hurt for Red Sox fans - The Boston Globe." *BostonGlobe.com*, 26 Oct. 2012, www.bostonglobe.com/sports/2012/10/26/dodgers-carl-crawford-talks-fresh-start-playing-hurt-for-red-sox-fans/vE2qFfuEKCb9JwuR0jx87J/story.html.

"5 Fun Facts About The Kansas City Royals." *CBS New York*, 17 Oct. 2014, newyork.cbslocal.com/2014/10/17/5-fun-facts-about-the-kansas-city-royals/.

"525,600 Minutes: How Do You Measure a Player in a Year?" *FanGraphs Baseball*, www.fangraphs.com/blogs/525600-minutes-how-do-you-measure-a-player-in-a-year/.

Adomites, Paul. *The love of baseball*. Publications International, Ltd., 2007.

"Akon (Ft. Ca$h Out) – Cashin Out." *Genius*, 1 Jan. 2012, rapgenius.com/Akon-cashin-out-lyrics#note-782763.

Alipour, Sam. "Handle with care." *ESPN*, ESPN Internet Ventures, 22 Mar. 2013, www.espn.com/mlb/story/_/id/9070129/detroit-tigers-miguel-cabrera-opens-fear-people-espn-magazine.

Alvarez, Mark. *The official baseball Hall of Fame answer book*. Simon and Schuster, 1989.

Anderson, Dave. *Pennant races: baseball at its best*. Galahad Books, 1997.

Anderson, Kelli. "The Perfect Catch." *SI.com*, 13 Oct. 2015, www.si.com/vault/2006/08/07/8383281/the-perfect-catch.

"Arrested Development (TV series)." *Arrested Development (TV series) - Wikiquote*, en.wikiquote.org/wiki/Arrested_Development_(TV_series).

Aschwanden, Christie. "Your Brain Is Primed To Reach False Conclusions." *FiveThirtyEight*, FiveThirtyEight, 12 Mar. 2016, fivethirtyeight.com/features/your-brain-is-primed-to-reach-false-conclusions/.

Baker, Geoff. "Mariners' Raul Ibanez defying time." *The Seattle Times*, The Seattle Times Company, 15 July 2013, www.seattletimes.com/sports/mariners/marinersrsquo-raul-ibanez-defying-time/.

Bamberger, Michael. "HE THRIVES ON ANGER ALBERT BELLE IS ALL THE RAGE IN CLEVELAND, BECAUSE HE CAN TURN HIS FURY INTO PRODIGIOUS POWER AT THE PLATE." *SI.com*, 13 Oct. 2015, www.si.com/vault/1996/05/06/212584/he-thrives-on-anger-albert-belle-is-all-the-rage-in-cleveland-because-he-can-turn-his-fury-into-prodigious-power-at-the-plate.

Bamberger, Michael. "This Is How They Roll." *SI.com*, 13 Oct. 2015, www.si.com/vault/2007/09/10/100264144/this-is-how-they-roll.

"Baseball Integration, 1947-1986." *Baseball Integration, 1947-1986 | Society for American Baseball Research*, sabr.org/bioproj/topic/integration-1947-1986.

"Baseball Letters." *Baseball Digest*, 2012, p. 80.

"Baseball's next big competitive edge." *FOX Sports*, 11 Sept. 2014, www.foxsports.com/mlb/just-a-bit-outside/story/new-competitive-edge-in-baseball-091114.

Batard, Dan Le. "The water's edge." *ESPN*, ESPN Internet Ventures, 7 Feb. 2014, www.espn.com/mlb/story/_/id/10397352/dan-le-batard-cuban-athletes-sacrifices-espn-magazine.

Baumann, Michael J. *Philadelphia phenoms: the most amazing athletes to play in the City of Brotherly Love*. Sports Publishing, 2014.

Baumann, Michael. "The Complicated Legacy of Jimmy Rollins." *Grantland*, 16 June 2014, grantland.com/the-triangle/the-complicated-legacy-of-jimmy-rollins/.

Bellone, Jeffrey. "In Kiner's Korner." *Beyond the Box Score*, Beyond the Box Score, 7 Feb. 2014, www.beyondtheboxscore.com/2014/2/7/5387954/ralph-kiner-korner-hall-of-fame.

Berg, Ted. "15 awesome things about the Atlanta Braves." *USA Today*, Gannett Satellite Information Network, 22 Sept. 2013, ftw.usatoday.com/2013/09/atlanta-braves-clinch-awesome-nl-east-terdoslavich.

Berg, Ted. "17 awesome things about the Pittsburgh Pirates." *USA Today*, Gannett Satellite Information Network, 1 Oct. 2013, ftw.usatoday.com/2013/10/17-awesome-things-about-the-pittsburgh-pirates.

Berg, Ted. "16 awesome things about the Detroit Tigers." *USA Today*, Gannett Satellite Information Network, 26 Sept. 2013, ftw.usatoday.com/2013/09/16-awesome-things-about-the-detroit-tigers.

Berg, Ted. "9 incredible facts about Albert Pujols." *USA Today*, Gannett Satellite Information Network, 23 June 2015, ftw.usatoday.com/2014/04/albert-pujols-facts-500-home-runs-los-angeles-angels-mlb.

Berg, Ted . "Pitcher Madison Bumgarner hit more grand slams in 2014 than Derek Jeter did in his entire career." *USA Today*, Gannett Satellite Information Network, 6 Oct. 2014, ftw.usatoday.com/2014/10/madison-bumgarner-grand-slams-san-francisco-giants-derek-jeter-mlb.

"Bill James on Fielding, Part 7." *FOX Sports*, 29 Jan. 2015, www.foxsports.com/mlb/just-a-bit-outside/baseball-joe/blog/bill-james-on-fielding-part-7-012915.

"Bill Veeck: The Maverick Who Changed Baseball on the 100th Anniversary of His Birth." *Bill Veeck: The Maverick Who Changed Baseball on the 100th Anniversary of His Birth | The National Pastime Museum*, www.thenationalpastimemuseum.com/article/bill-veeck-maverick-who-changed-baseball-100th-anniversary-his-birth.

Bisher, Furman. "Has Mathews Grown Up?" *Sport*, p. 8.

Bishop, Greg. "A Star Who Jumped at the Chance to Stay." *The New York Times*, The New York Times, 13 May 2013, www.nytimes.com/2013/05/14/sports/baseball/mariners-felix-hernandez-the-star-who-stayed.html?pagewanted=all&_r=3&.

Boivin, Paola. "Ex-Diamondback Jay Bell stirs memory of million-Dollar swing." *Azcentral.com*, 10 Sept. 2011, archive.azcentral.com/sports/diamondbacks/articles/2011/09/10/20110910arizona-diamondbacks-jay-bell-swing.html?nclick_check=%5B%271%27%5D.

"Bonds steroids timeline:" *ESPN.com*, 15 Nov. 2007, espn.go.com/mlb/news/story?id=3113127.

"Bonds, Clemens denied; no one elected to Hall." *ESPN.com*, 9 Jan. 2013, espn.go.com/mlb/story/_/id/8828339/no-players-elected-baseball-hall-fame-writers.

Borden, Sam. "All-American Joe." *Men's Fitness*, Men's Fitness, 28 Mar. 2016, www.mensfitness.com/life/entertainment/all-american-joe.

Bouton, Jim, et al. *Ball four*. Collier Books, 1990.

Brenley, Bob. "The Game I'll Never Forget." *Baseball Digest*, p. 48.

Brisbee, Grant. "Jose Fernandez was pure joy." *SBNation.com*, SBNation.com, 25 Sept. 2016, www.sbnation.com/2016/9/25/13047850/jose-fernandez-was-pure-joy.

Brown, David. "Nolan Ryan chats with Robin Ventura for first time since punching him in 1993." *Yahoo! Sports*, Yahoo!, 6 Apr. 2012, sports.yahoo.com/blogs/mlb-big-league-stew/nolan-ryan-chats-robin-ventura-first-time-since-201445145.html.

Brown, David. "Rays invite 20-Foot python to clubhouse in Chinese year of the snake." *Yahoo! Sports*, Yahoo!, 15 Aug. 2013, sports.yahoo.com/blogs/mlb-big-league-stew/rays-invite-20-foot-python-clubhouse-chinese-snake-203734517.html.

Brown, Patricia Leigh. "Pine-Tar Couture." *The New York Times*, The New York Times, 17 July 1993, www.nytimes.com/1993/07/18/style/pine-tar-couture.html.

Bryant, Howard. "Spring thaw." *ESPN*, ESPN Internet Ventures, 22 Mar. 2014, www.espn.com/mlb/story/_/id/10622311/barry-bonds-returns-san-francisco-giants-spring-training-instructor-espn-magazine.

Bryant, Howard. "Going, Going, Gone." *ESPN the Mag*, 17 Feb. 2014, p. 10.

Cairns, Bob. *Pen men: baseballs greatest bullpen stories told by the men who brought the game relief.* St. Martins Press, 1993.

Calcaterra, Craig, and Ashley Varela. "Exclusive: Lance Berkman talks about persecution, tolerance and transgender people." *HardballTalk*, 10 Nov. 2015, mlb.nbcsports.com/2015/11/10/exclusive-lance-berkman-talks-about-persecution-tolerance-and-transgender-people/.

Calcaterra, Craig, and Ashley Varela. "Lance Berkman says tolerance is bad, claims he has been "persecuted"." *HardballTalk*, 5 Nov. 2015, mlb.nbcsports.com/2015/11/05/lance-berkman-says-tolerance-is-bad-claims-he-has-been-persecuted/.

Callahan, Gerry. "Mr. Generosity Diamondback Luis Gonzalez, fresh from a 30-Game hit streak, is a player who spreads around his bucks and his bingles." *SI.com*, 13 Oct. 2015, www.si.com/vault/1999/05/31/261420/mr-generosity-diamondback-luis-gonzalez-fresh-from-a-30-game-hit-streak-is-a-player-who-spreads-around-his-bucks-and-his-bingles.

Callahan, Gerry. "Leading Man BATTING FIRST AND SWIPING BASES, DECEPTIVELY LAID-BACK PIRATES CATCHER JASON KENDALL IS REDEFINING HIS POSITION." *SI.com*, 13 Oct. 2015, www.si.com/vault/1999/05/03/260056/leading-man-batting-first-and-swiping-bases-deceptively-laid-back-pirates-catcher-jason-kendall-is-redefining-his-position.

Cameron, Dave. "The Hall of Fame's Standard, and Its Biggest Problem." *FanGraphs Baseball*, www.fangraphs.com/blogs/the-hall-of-fames-standard-and-its-biggest-problem/.

Cameron, Dave. "There's always this year." *ESPN*, ESPN Internet Ventures, 23 Mar. 2013, www.espn.com/mlb/story/_/id/9070249/mlb-world-series-race-wide-open-espn-magazine.

"Caple: A pacifist approach to WAR." *ESPN.com*, 1 Feb. 2013, espn.go.com/mlb/story/_/id/8900693/call-moderation-use-wins-replacement-stat.

Carr, Jordan. "World Series: 11 Fun Facts About the Texas Rangers." *Grantland*, 19 Oct. 2011, grantland.com/the-triangle/world-series-11-fun-facts-about-the-texas-rangers/.

Chafets, Ze'ev. *Cooperstown confidential: heroes, rogues, and the inside story of the Baseball Hall of Fame*. New York, Bloomsbury USA, 2010.

"Chronicling Red Sox Shortstops Since Nomar." *Boston Sports Then & Now*, 24 Mar. 2010, boston.sportsthenandnow.com/2010/03/24/chronicling-red-sox-shortstops-since-nomar/.

Climate, Brian Bienkowski The Daily. "Valley Fever Throws Baseball a Curve." *Scientific American*, 9 May 2013, www.scientificamerican.com/article/valley-fever-throws-baseball-a-curve/.

Cohen, Rich, et al. "Looking back at Hank Aaron's record-Setting HR and the people behind it." *SI.com*, www.si.com/mlb/2014/07/16/hank-aaron-where-are-they-now.

Cohen, Rich. "Where are they now: Ernie Banks." *Sports Illustrated*, 7 July 2014, www.si.com/vault/2014/07/07/106482386/ernie-banks.

Cohen, Robert W. *A team for the ages: baseballs all-Time all-Star team*. Guilford, CT, Lyons Press, 2004.

Conn, Jordan Ritter. "Remembering José Fernández: 1992–2016." *The Ringer*, The Ringer, 26 Sept. 2016, www.theringer.com/2016/9/26/16045670/remembering-jose-fernandez-1992-2016-84fd0b0c41eb#.izrry4jgw.

Constantine, Michael. "It's Time to Forgive Ryan Braun." *Racine County Eye*, Racine County Eye, 7 May 2016, racinecountyeye.com/draft-time-forgive-ryan-braun/.

Correspondent, DAVE SEMINARA • Post-Dispatch. "Branded for life with 'The Mendoza Line'." *Stltoday.com*, 6 July 2010, www.stltoday.com/sports/baseball/professional/article_cff05af5-032e-5a29-b5a8-ecc9216b0c02.html.

Cortes, Ryan. "There's never been anyone quite like Ken Griffey Jr." *The Undefeated*, The Undefeated, 25 July 2016, theundefeated.com/features/theres-never-been-anyone-quite-like-ken-griffey-jr/.

Craig, Mary. "The myth of baseball's depoliticalization." *Beyond the Box Score*, 21 Aug. 2017, www.beyondtheboxscore.com/2017/8/21/16175984/adam-jones-carlos-delgado-racism-politics-baseball-engagement-military-flyovers-pageantry.

Cramer, Richard D. *Do Clutch Hitters Exist*, cyrilmorong.com/CramerClutch2.htm.

Cramer, Richard Ben. "What Do You Think of Ted Williams Now? by Richard Ben Cramer." *Esquire Classic*, 22 Apr. 2016, classic.esquire.com/what-do-you-think-of-ted-williams-now/.

Crasnick, Jerry. "Elvis Andrus is young and full of energy." *ESPN*, ESPN Internet Ventures, 22 Oct. 2010, www.espn.com/mlb/playoffs/2010/columns/story?columnist=crasnick_jerry&id=5712672.
Crasnick, Jerry. "Ryan Braun's reputation strikes out." *ESPN*, ESPN Internet Ventures, 22 July 2013, www.espn.com/mlb/story/_/id/9500867/ryan-braun-legacy-takes-permanent-hit.
"Crosstown Rivals: Fun Facts About the Chicago Cubs and Chicago White Sox." *The Popcorn Factory®*, 9 May 2013, blog.thepopcornfactory.com/2013/05/09/crosstown-rivals-fun-facts-about-the-chicago-cubs-and-chicago-white-sox/.
Darowski, Adam . "Hall of Stats." *Hall of Stats: Bullet Points for Bobby Grich*, www.hallofstats.com/articles/bobby-grich-hall-of-fame-case.
Davis, Al, and Elliot Horne. *The all-Lover all-Star team and 50 other improbable baseball lineups*. Morrow, 1990.
Debs, Vic. *Baseball tidbits*. Indianapolis, IN, Masters Press, 1997.
"Defending the WAR." *FOX Sports*, 23 Sept. 2014, www.foxsports.com/mlb/just-a-bit-outside/story/defending-the-war-092314.
"Derek Jeter Isn't The Greatest Player Ever - ESPN Video." *ESPN.com*, 20 Aug. 2015, espn.go.com/video/clip?id=11580820.
Derespina, Cody. "Hall of Fame debates 2013: Sammy Sosa." *Newsday*, Newsday, 2 Jan. 2013, www.newsday.com/sports/baseball/baseball-hall-of-fame-debates-2013-sammy-sosa-1.4347625.
Dickey, Glenn. *The history of National League baseball since 1876*. Stein and Day, 1979.
Dickey, Glenn. *The history of American League baseball, since 1901*. Stein and Day, 1982.
Dickson, Paul. "Playing for Laughs-Baseball's Classic Clowns." *Playing for Laughs-Baseball's Classic Clowns | The National Pastime Museum*, www.thenationalpastimemuseum.com/article/playing-laughs-baseballs-classic-clowns.
Dickson, Paul. *Baseball's Greatest Quotations*. Perennial, 1992.
Dodd, Mike. "Diamondbacks are experts at keeping heat at bay." *USA Today*, Gannett Satellite Information Network, 12 July 2011, usatoday30.usatoday.com/sports/baseball/2011-07-12-all-star-game-heat_n.htm.
Dotson, Chad. "The improbable career of Dazzy Vance." *The Hardball Times*, www.hardballtimes.com/the-improbable-career-of-dazzy-vance/.
Dow, Bill. "2012 Player of the Year." *Baseball Digest*, 2013, p. 12.
Einstein, Charles. *The Baseball reader: favorites from the Fireside books of baseball*. Bonanza Books, 1989.
Eisenberg, Matt. "Stacy Piagno earns first win in men's professional baseball league." *ESPN*, ESPN Internet Ventures, www.espn.com/espnw/culture/the-buzz/article/20079875/stacy-piagno-earns-first-win-men-professional-baseball-league.
Eisenhammer, Fred, and Jim Binkley. *Baseballs most memorable trades: superstars swapped, all-Stars copped, and megadeals that flopped*. McFarland & Co., 1997.
"Exclusive Excerpt: How MLB let A-Rod use PEDs during '07 season." *SI.com*, www.si.com/mlb/2014/07/01/bloodsport-excerpt-alex-rodriguez-new-york-yankees-steroids.
Ferraro, Michael, and John Veneziano. *Numbelievable!: the dramatic stories behind the most memorable numbers in sports history*. Triumph Books, 2007.
Fleming, Dave. "The First-Place Kansas City Royals | Articles." *BILL JAMES ONLINE*, www.billjamesonline.com/the_first-place_kansas_city_royals/.
"Frank White's still waiting ... but for what?" *FOX Sports*, 20 Oct. 2014, www.foxsports.com/mlb/just-a-bit-outside/baseball-joe/blog/frank-white-s-still-waiting-but-for-what-102014.
Friend, Tom. "Why Success Won't Change McReynolds : Baseball Is 'Just a Hobby' for the Buddy-Boy Who'd Rather Hunt and Fish." *Los Angeles Times*, 5 Apr. 1985, articles.latimes.com/1985-04-05/sports/sp-27322_1_kevin-mcreynolds/3.
Gaines, Cork. "20 Reasons Why Rays Manager Joe Maddon Is The Craziest Person In Baseball." *Business Insider*, Business Insider, 10 May 2013, www.businessinsider.com/why-joe-maddon-is-the-craziest-person-in-baseball-2013-5?op=1.
Garfien, Chuck, and Dan Hayes. "The Robin Ventura-Nolan Ryan fight story you haven't heard." *NBC Sports Chicago*, 4 Aug. 2015, www.csnchicago.com/chicago-white-sox/robin-ventura-nolan-ryan-fight-story-you-havent-heard.
Garrity, John. "Having a Monster of a Season." *Sports Illustrated*, p. 47.
"Gehrig Streak Reviewed." research.sabr.org/journals/gehrig-streak-reviewed.
Gentile, Derek, et al. *Baseballs best 101: rankings of the skills, the achievements and the performance of the greatest players of all time*. Tess Press/Black Dog & Leventhal Publishers, 2004.
Gentile, James. "Switch-Hitters, Sometimes." *Beyond the Box Score*, Beyond the Box Score, 12 July 2012, www.beyondtheboxscore.com/2012/7/12/3150099/switch-hitters-sometimes.
Goldstein, Patrick. "The Black Shadow : Satchel Paige's Legendary Showmanship Obscured the Man : DON'T LOOK BACK: Satchel Paige in the Shadows of Baseball, By Mark Ribowsky (Simon & Schuster: $23; 351 pp.)." *Los Angeles Times*, Los Angeles Times, 22 May 1994, articles.latimes.com/1994-05-22/books/bk-60560_1_satchel-paige.
"Gone forever? In search of baseball's lost treasures." *FOX Sports*, 2 Sept. 2014, www.foxsports.com/mlb/just-a-bit-outside/story/gone-forever-in-search-of-baseball-s-lost-treasures-090214.
Goodman, Irv. "Is There a Willie Mays?" *Sport*, p. 10.

Goodtimes, Johnny. "10 Phillies Facts Every Real Fan Should Know." *Philadelphia Magazine*, 27 Mar. 2012, www.phillymag.com/news/2012/03/27/10-phillies-facts-real-fan/.
Gorman, Thomas. "The BP Wayback Machine: The Arbitration Process." *Baseball Prospectus*, 18 Jan. 2012, www.baseballprospectus.com/article.php?articleid=15864#commentMessage.
Grand slam baseball: Armchair reader. West Side Publishers, 2007.
Greenberg, Steve. "SN Conversation: Josh Hamilton." *Sporting News*, 27 Sept. 2010, p. 34.
Greenspan, Sam. "11 Lamest Sports Injuries Ever." *11 Points*, www.11points.com/Sports/11_Lamest_Sports_Injuries_Ever.
Gross, Jeffrey. "In defense of Barry Bonds." *The Hardball Times*, www.hardballtimes.com/in-defense-of-barry-bonds.
Gross, Milton. "They'll Always Boo Mickey Mantle." *Sport*, p. 35.
Guilfoile, Bill, editor. *National Baseball Hall of Fame & Museum Yearbook*. 1991.
"Hammerin' Hank Greenberg." *Hammerin' Hank Greenberg | The National Pastime Museum*, www.thenationalpastimemuseum.com/article/hammerin-hank-greenberg.
"Handicapping the great -- and sometimes absurd -- team MVP debate." *FOX Sports*, 22 July 2014, www.foxsports.com/mlb/just-a-bit-outside/story/handicapping-the-great-and-sometimes-absurd-team-mvp-debate-072214.
MLBNetworkClips. "Hawk Harrelson Voices Opinion on Sabermetrics on MLB Now." *YouTube*, YouTube, 25 Apr. 2013, www.youtube.com/watch?v=hXYvc1JGcgo&feature=youtu.be.
Healy, Daniel. "Fall of the Rocket: Steroids in Baseball and the Case Against Roger Clemens." *Marquette Sports Law Review*, vol. 19, no. 1.
Hill, David. "MLB History: Cap Anson First Player with 3000 Hits." *Call to the Pen*, FanSided, 16 July 2016, calltothepen.com/2016/07/16/mlb-history-cap-anson-first-player-with-3000-hits/.
Holloman, Ray. "All-Bizarre Injury Team." *ESPN*, ESPN Internet Ventures, www.espn.com/page2/s/holloman/020307.html.
Horwich-Scholefield, Sam. "Estimating the Advantage of Switch Hitting on BB/K Splits." *Baseball Statistics and Analysis*, www.fangraphs.com/community/estimating-the-advantage-of-switch-hitting-on-bbk-splits/.
"How'd They Do That?" *Sporting News*, 22 Nov. 2010.
"Hunter Pence talks video games, Giants." *ESPN.com*, 23 Jan. 2013, espn.go.com/blog/playbook/tech/post/_/id/3886/hunter-pence-talks-video-games-giants.
"Interesting Coors Field Facts." *Examiner*, www.examiner.com/article/interesting-coors-field-facts. Last visited in 2016
Ivor-Campbell, Frederick, et al., editors. *Baseball's First Stars*. 1st ed., Society for American Baseball Research, 1996.
Jackson, Tony. "Voice of the Game." *Baseball Digest*, 2012, p. 14.
Jaffe, Chris. "10 things I didn't know about one-Hitters." *The Hardball Times*, www.hardballtimes.com/10-things-i-didnt-know-about-one-hitters/.
Jaffe, Chris . "Got the whammy, NL teams." *The Hardball Times*, www.hardballtimes.com/main/article/got-the-whamee-nl-teams/.
James, Bill. *The New Bill James Historical Baseball Abstract*. Free Press, 2003.
James, Bill, and Rob Neyer. *The Neyer/James guide to pitchers: an historical compendium of pitching, pitchers, and pitches*. Simon & Schuster, 2004.
"Jays' Wells wins Rickey Award for helping kids." *ESPN.com*, 16 Sept. 2010, sports.espn.go.com/mlb/news/story?id=5580590.
Jazayerli, Jonah Keri and Rany. "How K.C. Gets KO'd." *Grantland*, 21 May 2013, www.grantland.com/story/_/id/9295533/jonah-keri-rany-jazayerli-royals-ineptitude.
Jazayerli, Rany. "The Road Not Taken." *Grantland*, 14 Feb. 2014, grantland.com/features/alex-rodriguez-alternate-career-history-red-sox-yankees.
Jenkinson, Bill. *The year Babe Ruth hit 104 home runs: recrowning baseballs greatest slugger*. Carroll & Graf Publishers, 2007.
Jordan, Pat. "Thin Air: In The Mountains With Steve Carlton, Armed Conspiracist." *The Stacks*, Thestacks.deadspin.com, 6 May 2013, thestacks.deadspin.com/thin-air-in-the-mountains-with-steve-carlton-armed-co-478492324.
"Jose Reyes leaves game to protect title." *ESPN.com*, 28 Sept. 2011, espn.go.com/blog/sweetspot/post/_/id/16808/jose-reyes-leaves-game-to-protect-title.
Judge, Jonathan. "Prospectus Feature: DRA and Linear Weights. And Justin Verlander." *Baseball Prospectus*, 12 Oct. 2015, www.baseballprospectus.com/news/article/27663/prospectus-feature-dra-and-linear-weights-and-justin-verlander/.
Justice, Richard. "To Jeff Kent, winning was a singular pursuit." *Sporting News*, www.sportingnews.com/mlb/story/2009-01-21/to-jeff-kent-winning-was-singular-pursuit. Last visited in 2015
Kahn, Roger. *The boys of summer*. Aurum, 2013.
Kaplan, Jim. *Playing the field*. Chapel Hill, NC, Algonquin Books of Chapel Hill, 1987.
Keating, Peter. "Lost in Translation." *ESPN the Mag*, 8 July 2013.
Kelley, James. *Baseball*. DK Publishing, 2005.
Gabriel Schechter. "Ken Williams' Amazing 1922 Season." *Ken Williams' Amazing 1922 Season | The National Pastime Museum*, www.thenationalpastimemuseum.com/article/ken-williams-amazing-1922-season.

Keown, Tim. "Hunter Pence: Sign-Inspirer." *ESPN*, ESPN Internet Ventures, 4 Dec. 2014, www.espn.com/mlb/story/_/id/11972381/hunter-pence-talks-hunter-pence-signs-interview-issue.

Keown, Tim . "What Is Giancarlo Stanton Thinking?" *ESPN*, ESPN Internet Ventures, www.espn.com/espn/feature/story/_/id/12500579/giancarlo-stanton-takes-325-million-contract-play-miami-marlins.

Keri, Jonah. *Baseball between the numbers: why everything you know about the game is wrong*. BasicBooks, 2007.

Keri, Jonah. "There's Shrewd, There's Genius, Then There's Marlins Owner Jeffrey Loria." *Grantland*, 14 Nov. 2012, grantland.com/the-triangle/theres-shrewd-theres-genius-then-theres-marlins-owner-jeffrey-loria/.

Keri, Jonah. "A Baseball Hall of Fame Ballot That Sadly Won't Be Counted." *Grantland*, 29 Nov. 2012, grantland.com/the-triangle/a-baseball-hall-of-fame-ballot-that-sadly-wont-be-counted/.

Keri, Jonah. "The Value of Imperfection." *Grantland*, 27 Feb. 2013, www.grantland.com/story/_/id/8994244/jonah-keri-similarities-art-world-collecting-baseball-cards.

Keri, Jonah. "The Fallacy of the Baseball Hall of Fame." *Grantland*, 9 Jan. 2013, www.grantland.com/blog/the-triangle/post/_/id/47091/the-fallacy-of-the-baseball-hall-of-fame.

Keri, Jonah. "'Cincinnati Is a Joke to Pitch In': A Not-So-Brief Chat With Pete Rose." *Grantland*, 4 Apr. 2013, www.grantland.com/blog/the-triangle/post/_/id/57016/cincinnati-is-a-joke-to-pitch-in-a-not-so-brief-chat-with-pete-rose.

Keri, Jonah. "The Greatest Pitching Duel in Human History." *Grantland*, 9 July 2013, www.grantland.com/blog/the-triangle/post/_/id/67962/the-greatest-pitching-duel-in-human-history.

Keri, Jonah. "The BestCoolest Players I've Ever Seen: Pitchers." *Grantland*, 8 Aug. 2013, www.grantland.com/blog/the-triangle/post/_/id/70881/the-bestcoolest-players-ive-ever-seen-pitchers.

Keri, Jonah. "The BestCoolest Players I've Ever Seen: Hitters." *Grantland*, 9 Aug. 2013, www.grantland.com/blog/the-triangle/post/_/id/70992/the-bestcoolest-players-ive-ever-seen-hitters.

Keri, Jonah. "Hall Pass." *Grantland*, 18 Dec. 2013, www.grantland.com/story/_/id/10155321/breaking-baseball-hall-fame-ballot.

Keri, Jonah. "Farewell to The Kid." *Grantland*, 12 Aug. 2014, www.grantland.com/blog/the-triangle/post/_/id/17538/farewell-to-the-kid.

Keri, Jonah. "Tony Gwynn: 1960-2014." *Grantland*, 16 June 2014, grantland.com/the-triangle/tony-gwynn-1960-2014/.

Keri, Jonah. "Hall of Fame Voting Primer: My Top 10, Plus a Randy Johnson Appreciation." *Grantland*, 22 Dec. 2014, grantland.com/the-triangle/hall-of-fame-voting-primer-randy-johnson-pedro-martinez-craig-biggio/.

Keri, Jonah. "Good-Bye, Mr. November: Taking Stock of Derek Jeter's Divisive Legacy." *Grantland*, 24 Sept. 2014, grantland.com/the-triangle/derek-jeter-mr-november-legacy-new-york-yankees-retirement/.

Keri, Jonah. "Yogi Berra: 1925–2015." *Grantland*, 23 Sept. 2015, grantland.com/the-triangle/yogi-berra-1925-2015/.

Keri, Jonah. "How Bullpens Took Over Modern Baseball." *FiveThirtyEight*, FiveThirtyEight, 14 Feb. 2016, fivethirtyeight.com/features/how-bullpens-took-over-modern-baseball/.

Knight, Molly. "Investment club." *ESPN*, ESPN Internet Ventures, 11 June 2013, www.espn.com/mlb/story/_/id/9357636/houston-astros-hope-strong-farm-system-improve-club-espn-magazine.

Lewis, Michael, and Scott Brick. *Moneyball: the art of winning an unfair game*. Random House Audio, 2011.

Lindbergh, Ben. "Dear Clayton; Love, Pedro." *Grantland*, 16 Sept. 2014, grantland.com/the-triangle/pedro-martinez-letter-to-clayton-kershaw/.

Lindbergh, Ben. "No Steals for You: How Kansas City's Yordano Ventura Became the King of Controlling the Running Game." *Grantland*, 10 Sept. 2014, grantland.com/the-triangle/yordano-ventura-kansas-city-royals-controlling-running-game/.

Lindbergh, Ben. "The Leaderboard Lifer: Appreciating Matt Holliday's Underrated, Historically Bankable Excellence." *Grantland*, 26 May 2015, grantland.com/the-triangle/2015-mlb-matt-holliday-st-louis-cardinals/.

Lindbergh, Ben. "Should Ichiro Have Hit Homers?" *The Ringer*, The Ringer, 28 July 2016, www.theringer.com/2016/7/28/16041992/should-ichiro-have-hit-homers-c96633a61262#.iqx01029g.

Lindbergh, Ben. "Who Ya Got: Houston's Carlos Correa or L.A.'s Corey Seager?" *The Ringer*, The Ringer, 26 Oct. 2017, www.theringer.com/mlb/2017/10/26/16551716/carlos-correa-vs-corey-seager-who-ya-got-world-series-shortstops.

Lingo, Will. *The National Baseball Hall of Fame Almanac*. Baseball America, 2017.

Lortz, Michael . "The Rays Cowbell Conundrum." *Tampa Bay Baseball Market*, tampabaybaseballmarket.com/the-rays-cowbell-conundrum/.

Lyons, Jeffrey, and Douglas B. Lyons. *Short hops and foul tips: 1,734 wild and wacky baseball facts*. Taylor Trade Pub., 2005.

Mackin, Bob. *Off the wall baseball trivia*. Greystone, 2001.

Manning, Sean. *Top of the order: 25 writers pick their favorite baseball player*. Da Capo Press, 2010.

Margalus, Jim. "Luke Appling: From the Hall of Fame Library player files." *South Side Sox*, South Side Sox, 7 Nov. 2011, www.southsidesox.com/2011/11/7/2543747/luke-appling-from-the-hall-of-fame-library-player-files.

Margalus, Jim. "Luke Appling: From the Hall of Fame Library player files." *South Side Sox*, South Side Sox, 7 Nov. 2011, www.southsidesox.com/2011/11/7/2543747/luke-appling-from-the-hall-of-fame-library-player-files.

Margalus, Jim. "Minnie Minoso: From the Hall of Fame Library player files, Part 2." *South Side Sox*, South Side Sox, 15 Dec. 2011, www.southsidesox.com/2011/12/15/2634880/minnie-minoso-from-the-hall-of-fame-library-player-files-part-2.

Martinez, David H. *The book of baseball literacy*. Authors Choice Press, 2000.

Matz, Eddie. "The Hoss Whisperer." *ESPN the Mag*, 2 Sept. 2013.

Mays, Robert. "All Work and No Play for J.J. Watt." *Grantland*, 29 July 2014, grantland.com/features/j-j-watt-houston-texans-2014-nfl-preview/.

Mccarthy, Matt. "THE CUTTING EDGE." *SI.com*, 14 Oct. 2015, www.si.com/vault/2014/09/08/106631896/the-cutting-edge.

McGrath, Ben. "Waiting for Manny." *The New Yorker*, The New Yorker, 18 June 2017, www.newyorker.com/reporting/2007/04/23/070423fa_fact_mcgrath?currentPage=all.

McGrath, Ben. "The Professor of Baseball." *The New Yorker*, The New Yorker, 18 June 2017, www.newyorker.com/magazine/2003/07/14/the-professor-of-baseball.

Mclndoe, Sean. "New Season's Resolutions for the NHL." *Grantland*, 18 Sept. 2014, grantland.com/the-triangle/new-seasons-resolutions-for-the-nhl/.

McLendon, Kim. "Padres Salute Armed Forces With Military Appreciation Night." *Navy Home Page*, 9 Apr. 2008, www.navy.mil/submit/display.asp?story_id=36238.

McManaman, Bob. "Arizona Diamondbacks Miguel Montero sets his sights on big goals"" *The Arizona Republic*, www.azcentral.com/sports/diamondbacks/articles/2011/03/23/20110323arizona-diamondbacks-miguel-montero-sets-his-sights.html. Last visited 2014

McNear, Claire. "Chase Utley Is Still the King of Philadelphia." *The Ringer*, The Ringer, 17 Aug. 2016, www.theringer.com/2016/8/17/16037606/chase-utley-returns-dodgers-phillies-33e425f508d#.9prslhqqn.

Mellinger, Sam. "Forty years later, Royals Academy lives on in memories." *The Kansas City Star*, www.kansascity.com/sports/spt-columns-blogs/sam-mellinger/article940797.html.

"Miguel Montero Likes to Lick Baseball Bats." *Bush League Chronicle*, www.theblcblog.com/2013/07/video-miguel-montero-likes-to-lick-bats.html?utm_source=feedburner&utm_medium=feed&utm_campaign=Feed%3A BushLeagueChronicle %28Bush League Chronicle%29. Last visited in 2014

Miller, Lisa. "Saved." *NYMag.com*, nymag.com/news/features/sports/mariano-rivera-2013-6/.

Miller, Sam. "WAR is the answer." *ESPN*, ESPN Internet Ventures, 19 Feb. 2013, www.espn.com/mlb/story/_/id/8959581/why-wins-replacement-mlb-next-big-all-encompassing-stat-espn-magazine.

Miller, Sam. "The happiness project." *ESPN*, ESPN Internet Ventures, 4 Oct. 2013, www.espn.com/mlb/story/_/id/9749026/oakland-athletics-success-due-player-chemistry-not-metrics-espn-magazine.

Miller, Sam. "The Guide to Sustainable Farming." *ESPN the Mag*, 3 Mar. 2014, p. 54.

"MLB strike free ... for 10 years and prospering." *ESPN.com*, 10 Aug. 2004, sports.espn.go.com/mlb/news/story?id=1856626.

Monagan, Matt. "He does eat pizza with a fork! Hunter Pence now has a rap song about #HunterPenceSigns." *Major League Baseball*, 15 Sept. 2014, m.mlb.com/cutfour/2014/09/15/94796834/he-does-eat-pizza-with-a-fork-hunter-pence-now-has-a-rap-song-about-hunterpencesigns.

Mooney, Roger. "2012 Pitcher of the Year." *Baseball Digest*, 2013, p. 18.

Murray, Arch. "Mickey Mantle Gold-Plated Rookie." *Sport*, p. 70.

Nack, William. "Musial was 'The Man' for good reason." *ESPN.com*, 28 Aug. 2008, sports.espn.go.com/mlb/columns/story?columnist=nack_bill&id=3558127.

Nadel, Eric, and Craig R. Wright. *The man who stole first base: tales from baseballs past*. Dallas, TX, Taylor Pub. Co., 1989.

Nash, Bruce M., and Allan Zullo. *The baseball hall of shame: the best of blooperstown*. Lyons Press, 2012.

Nelson, D.L. "The Reign of Finley." *Athletics Nation*, Athletics Nation, 1 Aug. 2013, www.athleticsnation.com/2013/8/1/4576930/the-reign-of-finley.

Neyer, Rob, and Eddie Epstein. *Baseball dynasties: the greatest teams of all time*. New York, Norton, 2000.

Neyer, Rob. *Rob Neyers big book of baseball lineups: a complete guide to the best, worst, and most memorable players to ever grace the major leagues*. Fireside, 2003.

Neyer, Rob. "Crowning achievement." *ESPN.com*, 11 Nov. 2005, insider.espn.go.com/mlb/insider/columns/story?columnist=neyer_rob&id=2220999.

Neyer, Rob. *Rob Neyers big book of baseball blunders: a complete guide to the worst decisions and stupidest moments in baseball history*. Fireside/Simon & Schuster, 2006.

Neyer, Rob. "Yeah, I'm a big-Game pitcher. What about it?" *SBNation.com*, SBNation.com, 28 Jan. 2014, www.sbnation.com/2014/1/28/5353248/big-game-pitchers-roy-oswalt-all-time.

Nightengale, Bob. "The other farewell retiring tour: Paul Konerko." *USA Today*, Gannett Satellite Information Network, 18 Sept. 2014, www.usatoday.com/story/sports/mlb/2014/09/18/paul-konerko-retiring/15855943/.

"NY Mets Metsforum." *Celebrity Mets Fans In case you think... - NY Mets Metsforum*, www.facebook.com/MetsForum/posts/500384139996240.
Obojski, Robert, and Sanford Hoffman. *Baseballs strangest moments*. Sterling Pub. Co., 1988.
Okrent, Daniel, and Steve Wulf. *Baseball anecdotes*. Harper & Row, 1990.
Olney, Buster. "Clayton Kershaw abides by code." *ESPN*, ESPN Internet Ventures, www.espn.com/espn/feature/story/_/id/10619342/creative-control-clayton-kershaw-abides-strict-code.
Olney, Buster. "Thinking inside the box." *ESPN*, ESPN Internet Ventures, 19 Mar. 2013, www.espn.com/mlb/story/_/id/9067809/cincinnati-reds-hitter-joey-votto-cares-more-consistency-rbis-espn-magazine.
Oz, Mike. "Magglio Ordonez elected socialist mayor of his Venezuelan hometown." *Yahoo! Sports*, Yahoo!, 9 Dec. 2013, sports.yahoo.com/blogs/mlb-big-league-stew/magglio-ordonez-elected-socialist-mayor-venezuelan-hometown-234405966--mlb.html.
"Padres Military Outreach." *San Diego Padres*, sandiego.padres.mlb.com/sd/military/outreach.jsp.
Paine, Neil. "Alex Rodriguez Would've Made The Hall Of Fame Without Steroids." *FiveThirtyEight*, FiveThirtyEight, 26 Nov. 2014, fivethirtyeight.com/features/alex-rodriguez-wouldve-made-the-hall-of-fame-without-steroids/.
Passan, Jeff. "Ichiro's speech to All-Stars revealed." *Yahoo! Sports*, Yahoo!, 15 July 2008, sports.yahoo.com/news/ichiros-speech-stars-revealed-162200184--mlb.html.
Passan, Jeff. "How Jose Bautista Went From Baseball Vagabond To The Game's Best Slugger." *ThePostGame*, 14 June 2011, www.thepostgame.com/features/201106/number-crusher-how-blue-jays-slugger-jose-bautista-experimented-his-way-greatness.
Passan, Jeff. "Ryan Braun doped, lied and cared only for himself." *Yahoo! Sports*, Yahoo!, 23 July 2013, sports.yahoo.com/news/ryan-braun-doped--lied-and-cared-only-for-himself-050550708.html.
Patrick, Dan. "JUST MY TYPE: Mark McGwire." *SI.com*, 14 Oct. 2015, www.si.com/vault/2012/11/19/106255859/just-my-type.
Paulos, John Allen. "Does Joe DiMaggio's Streak Deserve an Asterisk?" *ABC News*, ABC News Network, 7 Oct. 2007, abcnews.go.com/Technology/WhosCounting/story?id=3694104&page=1.
Pavlidis, Harry. "Measuring MLB's best game-Callers." *ESPN*, ESPN Internet Ventures, 29 Apr. 2015, www.espn.com/mlb/story/_/id/12880518/mlb-best-game-caller-dodgers-catcher-aj-ellis.
Pearlman, Jeff. "Hot To Trot At 37, Edgar Martinez has suddenly caught fire as a home run hitter, while keeping his average well above .300." *SI.com*, 13 Oct. 2015, www.si.com/vault/2000/07/17/284709/hot-to-trot-at-37-edgar-martinez-has-suddenly-caught-fire-as-a-home-run-hitter-while-keeping-his-average-well-above-300.
Piecoro, Nick. "Former Arizona Diamondbacks slugger Luis Gonzalez wants closure." *Azcentral.com*, 16 Aug. 2012, archive.azcentral.com/arizonarepublic/sports/articles/2012/08/15/20120815former-arizona-diamondbacks-slugger-luis-gonzalez-wants-closure.html.
Posnanski, Joe, and Ashley Varela. "The remarkable career of Raul Ibanez." *HardballTalk*, 1 July 2014, hardballtalk.nbcsports.com/2014/07/01/the-remarkable-career-of-raul-ibanez/.
Pouliot, Matthew, and Ashley Varela. "Carlos Delgado: MLB's best two-Time All-Star." *HardballTalk*, 13 Apr. 2011, hardballtalk.nbcsports.com/2011/04/13/carlos-delgado-mlbs-best-two-time-all-star/.
Press, From Associated. "Otis Confesses Use of Corked Bats to Help Hit .277 as Major Leaguer." *Los Angeles Times*, Los Angeles Times, 28 Apr. 1992, articles.latimes.com/1992-04-28/sports/sp-1030_1_corked-bat.
Pressman, Stacey. "The haunting of MLB's A-List." *ESPN*, ESPN Internet Ventures, 31 May 2013, www.espn.com/mlb/story/_/id/9315544/justin-upton-more-mlb-players-spooked-milwaukee-haunted-hotel-espn-magazine.
Pressman, Stacey. "El Campeon Del Mariachi." *ESPN*, ESPN Internet Ventures, 16 Jan. 2015, www.espn.com/mlb/story/_/page/music1502027/adrian-gonzalez-mariachi-walk-king.
Rampersad, Arnold. *Jackie Robinson: a biography*. Ballantine Books, 1998.
Reidenbaugh, Lowell, et al. *Cooperstown: where the legends live forever*. Gramercy Books, 2001.
Reilly, Rick. "The Big Heart." *SI.com*, 13 Oct. 2015, www.si.com/vault/1994/08/08/131748/the-big-heart-frank-thomas-honors-the-memory-of-his-sister-by-striving-for-unprecedented-heights-with-his-bat.
Reiter, Ben. "Astro-Matic Baseball." *Sports Illustrated Longform*, www.si.com/longform/astros/index.html.
Reiter, Ben. "Second to None." *SI.com*, 14 Oct. 2015, www.si.com/vault/2012/04/09/106179454/second-to-none.
Reiter, Ben. "Birds on a Power Line." *SI.com*, 14 Oct. 2015, www.si.com/vault/2013/05/27/106326513/birds-on-a-power-line.
Richmond, Peter. "The Brief Life And Complicated Death Of Tommy Lasorda's Gay Son." *The Stacks*, Thestacks.deadspin.com, 30 Apr. 2013, thestacks.deadspin.com/the-brief-life-and-complicated-death-of-tommy-lasordas-485999366.
Roberts, Geoff. "Jason Varitek & Tim Wakefield's Boston Red Sox Legacies." *Bleacher Report*, Bleacher Report, 5 Apr. 2017, bleacherreport.com/articles/1083807-jason-varitek-tim-wakefields-boston-red-sox-legacies.

Romano, Ryan. “A "brief" history of star-Crossed players, Part I.” *Beyond the Box Score*, Beyond the Box Score, 7 Mar. 2014, www.beyondtheboxscore.com/2014/3/7/5414012/history-star-crossed-players.
Romano, Ryan. “Ben Zobrist's HOF case: The value of a peak.” *Beyond the Box Score*, Beyond the Box Score, 20 Oct. 2014, www.beyondtheboxscore.com/2014/10/20/6996235/ben-zobrist-hall-of-fame-hof-case-value-peak-war.
Rosen, Al. “They Pay off on Runs-Batted-In.” *Sport*, p. 17.
Rovell, Darren . “Lack of new star power hurting baseball Hall.” *ESPN.com*, 9 Jan. 2013, espn.go.com/blog/playbook/dollars/post/_/id/2700/lack-of-star-power-hurting-baseball-hall.
“Royals great Frank White returns to Kauffman Stadium for first time since 2011.” *The Kansas City Star*, www.kansascity.com/sports/mlb/kansas-city-royals/article2175965.html.
Rushin, Steve. “20 Frank Thomas.” *SI.com*, 13 Oct. 2015, www.si.com/vault/1995/02/09/133246/20-frank-thomas.
Rushin, Steve. “More Than Meets the Ear.” *SI.com*, 14 Oct. 2015, www.si.com/vault/2015/03/30/106752135/more-than-meets-the-ear.
Rust, Art. *"Get that nigger off the field!": a sparkling, informal history of the Black man in baseball*. Delacorte Press, 1976.
Sanchez, Robert. “'I hope they go 0-162'.” *ESPN*, ESPN Internet Ventures, 4 Mar. 2014, www.espn.com/mlb/story/_/id/10544839/ian-kinsler-intends-become-elite-second-baseman-detroit-tigers-espn-magazine.
Sanchez, Robert. “Pay This Man.” *ESPN the Mag*, 30 Mar. 2015.
Sandberg, Ryne . “The Game I’ll Never Forget.” *Baseball Digest*, p. 44.
Sargis, Joe. “Joe Morgan Sets Another Glove Mark.” *Ellensburg Daily Record*, 22 Apr. 1978.
Saunders, Patrick. “Nolan Arenado’s star power born, bred in Southern California home.” *The Denver Post*, The Denver Post, 2 Sept. 2016, www.denverpost.com/2016/07/09/nolan-arenados-star-power-born-bred-in-southern-california-home/.
Schmehl, James. “Video: Magglio Ordonez showered with boos by own fans.” *MLive.com*, 16 Mar. 2009, blog.mlive.com/cutoffman/2009/03/video_magglio_ordonez_showered.html.
Schoenfield, Dave. “All-Time top 25 players under 25.” *ESPN.com*, 23 Jan. 2013, espn.go.com/blog/sweetspot/post/_/id/32231/all-time-top-25-players-under-25.
Schoenfield, David. “The cautionary tale of Cesar Cedeno.” *ESPN.com*, 8 Aug. 2012, espn.go.com/blog/sweetspot/post/_/id/27814/the-cautionary-tale-of-cesar-cedeno.
Schoenfield, David. “Hall of Fame voting hits a new low.” *ESPN.com*, 9 Jan. 2013, espn.go.com/blog/sweetspot/post/_/id/31986/hall-of-fame-voting-hits-a-new-low.
Schoenfield, David. “Ibanez got the most out of his talent.” *ESPN.com*, 23 June 2014, espn.go.com/blog/sweetspot/post/_/id/48834/ibanez-got-the-most-out-of-his-talent.
Schwarz, Alan. “Conversation with Vernon Wells.” *ESPN.com*, 27 May 2003, sports.espn.go.com/mlb/columns/story?columnist=schwarz_alan&id=1559485.
Schwarz, Alan. *The numbers game: baseballs lifelong fascination with statistics*. Thomas Dunne Books/St. Martins Griffin, 2005.
Schwarz, Alan . “Schwarz: Conversation with Billy Wagner.” *ESPN.com*, 12 June 2003, sports.espn.go.com/mlb/columns/story?id=1566732.
Seppa, Nathan. “Baseball's resident physicist.” *The Science Life*, vol. 183, no. 6, 23 Mar. 2013, p. 32.
Several authors. “70 Years of History with Baseball Digest.” *Baseball Digest*, 2012, p. 6.
Shalin, Neil. *Yankees triviology*. Triumph Books, 2011.
Shapiro, Ari. “Toronto Blue Jays: The Legend of Tony Fernandez.” *Jays Journal*, FanSided, 6 Dec. 2016, jaysjournal.com/2016/12/06/blue-jays-legend-tony-fernandez/.
Sheehan, Joe. “Second Impressions.” *SI.com*, 14 Oct. 2015, www.si.com/vault/2013/07/22/106346381/second-impressions.
Silver, Nate. “Suspicion of Steroid Use Could Keep Bagwell and Piazza Out of Hall.” *FiveThirtyEight*, FiveThirtyEight, 15 Mar. 2014, fivethirtyeight.com/features/suspicion-of-steroid-use-could-keep-bagwell-and-piazza-out-of-hall/.
Silver, Nate. “If Hank Aaron Had Never Hit a Home Run, Would He Be a Hall of Famer?” *FiveThirtyEight*, FiveThirtyEight, 9 Apr. 2014, fivethirtyeight.com/features/if-hank-aaron-had-never-hit-a-home-run-would-he-be-a-hall-of-famer/.
Silver, Nate. “Beyond Compare?” *SI.com*, 13 Oct. 2015, www.si.com/vault/2006/08/07/8383282/beyond-compare.
Simmons, Bill . “The Sports Guy: End of the Pedro era.” *ESPN: The Worldwide Leader in Sports*, sports.espn.go.com/espn/page2/story?page=simmons%2F020402.
Simon, Tom. *Deadball stars of the National League*. Brasseys, 2004.
Smith, Ron. *Baseballs 100 greatest players: a celebration of the 20th centurys best*. Sporting News Pub. Co., 1998.
Staples, Billy, and Rich Herschlag. *Before the glory: 20 baseball heroes talk about growing up and turning hard times into home runs*. Health Communications, 2007.
Stark, Jayson. *The stark truth: the most overrated and underrated players in baseball history*. Triumph Books, 2007.
Stark, Jayson. “Thome a truly real and caring person.” *ESPN.com*, 16 Aug. 2011, espn.go.com/mlb/story/_/page/rumblings110816/jim-thome-truly-real-caring-person.

Stark, Jayson. "My (Overstuffed) Hall of Fame ballot." *ESPN.com*, 7 Jan. 2013, espn.go.com/mlb/hof13/story/_/id/8814530/jayson-stark-mlb-hall-fame-ballot.

Stark, Jayson. "Cabrera truly a magical hitter." *ESPN.com*, 15 Aug. 2013, espn.go.com/mlb/story/_/id/9568471/miguel-cabrera-truly-magical-hitter.

Stark, Jayson. "Strange But True in 2013." *ESPN.com*, 29 Dec. 2013, espn.go.com/mlb/story/_/id/10210242/mlb-strange-true-2013.

Stark, Jayson. "The greatness of Mariano Rivera." *ESPN.com*, 24 Sept. 2013, espn.go.com/mlb/story/_/id/9717908/a-21-stat-salute-mariano-rivera.

Stark, Jayson. "Tony Gwynn's incredible numbers." *ESPN.com*, 16 June 2014, espn.go.com/mlb/story/_/id/11092617/mlb-late-tony-gwynn-incredible-hitting-numbers.

Stark, Jayson. "Bud Selig's final year in office." *ESPN.com*, 27 Jan. 2014, espn.go.com/mlb/story/_/id/10349245/bud-selig-final-year-mlb-commissioner.

Stark, Jayson. "Paul Konerko's historically unique career." *ESPN.com*, 28 Sept. 2014, espn.go.com/blog/jayson-stark/post/_/id/993/paul-konerkos-historically-unique-career.

Stark, Jayson. "Remembering Ralph Kiner." *ESPN.com*, 7 Feb. 2014, espn.go.com/blog/jayson-stark/post/_/id/10/ralph-kiner-had-one-life-special-gifts-ability-laugh-himself.

Stark, Jayson. "Ten astounding Derek Jeter numbers." *ESPN.com*, 24 Sept. 2014, espn.go.com/blog/jayson-stark/post/_/id/952/ten-astounding-derek-jeter-numbers.

Studeman, Dave. "The most critical at-Bat of all time." *The Hardball Times*, www.hardballtimes.com/main/article/the-most-critical-at-bat-of-all-time/.

Sullivan, Jeff. "Pedro Martinez and Randy Johnson at Their Best, Today." *FanGraphs Baseball*, www.fangraphs.com/blogs/pedro-martinez-and-randy-johnson-at-their-best-today/.

"The History of Baseball in Pittsburgh." *Popular Pittsburgh*, 19 Mar. 2015, www.popularpittsburgh.com/baseballhistory/.

"The Nevada Daily Mail." *Google News Archive Search*, Google, news.google.com/newspapers?id=FJkfAAAAIBAJ&sjid=ZdQEAAAAIBAJ&dq=amos otis baseball&pg=3713%2C4902443.

Thomas, G. Scott. *Leveling the field: an encyclopedia of baseballs all-Time great performances as revealed through adjusted statistics*. Black Dog & Leventhal, 2002.

"Toronto Blue Jays." *Toronto Blue Jays | Team Name Origin*, teamnameorigin.com/mlb/nickname/toronto-blue-jays.

Updike, John. "Hub Fans Bid Kid Adieu." *The New Yorker*, The New Yorker, 18 June 2017, www.newyorker.com/archive/1960/10/22/1960_10_22_109_TNY_CARDS_000266305.

Verducci, Tom. "Exit Stage Center: Derek Jeter reflects on the final act of his legendary Yankees career." *Sports Illustrated Longform*, www.si.com/longform/derek_jeter/index.html.

Verducci, Tom. "Case Closed." *SI.com*, 13 Oct. 2015, www.si.com/vault/2002/05/13/323394/case-closed-with-his-intimidating-entrance-and-a-changeup-from-hell-trevor-hoffman-of-the-padres-nails-down-wins-better-than-anyone.

Verducci, Tom. "3 Seattle Mariners Aging players are moving closer to retirement than to an elusive World Series berth." *SI.com*, 13 Oct. 2015, www.si.com/vault/2003/03/31/340601/3-seattle-mariners-aging-players-are-moving-closer-to-retirement-than-to-an-elusive-world-series-berth.

Verducci, Tom. "GENERATION K." *SI.com*, 14 Oct. 2015, www.si.com/vault/2013/04/01/106303861/generation-k.

Verducci, Tom. "THE RAYS WAY." *SI.com*, 14 Oct. 2015, www.si.com/vault/2013/04/01/106303863/the-rays-way.

Verducci, Tom. "Help Needed." *Sports Illustrated*, 9 Mar. 2015.

"Wade Boggs can drink 60-70 beers on a trip from New York to Seattle!" *710 ESPN's "SMOG" - Steve Mason's Blog*, stevemasonsmog.typepad.com/710_espns_smog_steve_maso/2007/09/wade-boggs-can-.html.

Weinberg, Neil . "Positional Versatility and the Zobrist Fallacy." *The Hardball Times*, www.hardballtimes.com/positional-versatility-and-the-zobrist-fallacy/.

Weintraub, Robert. "Chipper Jones Reflects on His Mets Memories." *The New York Times*, The New York Times, 7 Sept. 2012, www.nytimes.com/2012/09/08/sports/baseball/chipper-jones-reflects-on-his-mets-memories.html?_r=0.

WERTHEIM, L. JON. "Hanley Being Hanley." *SI.com*, 14 Oct. 2015, www.si.com/vault/2010/05/31/105944008/hanley-being-hanley.

"What a ride: Pence offers reward for scooter." *ESPN.com*, 26 May 2014, espn.go.com/mlb/story/_/id/10984572/hunter-pence-san-francisco-giants-offers-reward-stolen-scooter.

"When does a franchise end?" *FOX Sports*, 23 July 2014, www.foxsports.com/mlb/just-a-bit-outside/story/orioles-yankees-american-league-franchise-history-072314.

"White Sox legend and Latin baseball pioneer Minnie Minoso will finally get his moment via a documentary to air on Channel 11." *Tribunedigital-Chicagotribune*, 7 Dec. 2012, articles.chicagotribune.com/2012-12-07/site/ct-mov-1207-minoso-documentary-20121207_1_minnie-minoso-chicago-white-sox-cuban-comet.

Wire, SI, et al. "Jose Fernandez's career will never be forgotten." *SI.com*, www.si.com/mlb/2016/09/25/jose-fernandez-miami-marlins-death.

Woodbery, Evan |. “Tigers remember Jose Fernandez as competitor with big heart.” *MLive.com*, MLive.com, 25 Sept. 2016, www.mlive.com/tigers/index.ssf/2016/09/tigers_mourn_jose_fernandez.html.

Wray, Miles. “Prospectus Review: 'That Foul Tip Had Better Have Hit Your Testicles'.” *Baseball Prospectus*, 16 Sept. 2014, www.baseballprospectus.com/article.php?articleid=24660.

Wright, Cheryl. “How Many Hits Did Cap Anson Have?” *SoSH*, 13 July 2015, sonsofsamhorn.com/baseball/ballpark-tales/how-many-hits-did-cap-anson-have.

Writer, Christina KahrlMLB Staff. “Time to reconsider Honus Wagner's and Lou Gehrig's greatness?” *ESPN*, ESPN Internet Ventures, 14 July 2016, www.espn.com/mlb/story/_/page/mlbrank100_wagnergehrig/mlbrank-exploring-greatness-honus-wagner-lou-gehrig.

“Yaz: Ortiz is second-Greatest Red Sox hitter.” *ESPN.com*, 27 July 2014, espn.go.com/boston/mlb/story/_/id/11271178/carl-yastrzemski-says-david-ortiz-boston-red-sox-second-best-hitter-ted-williams.

Young, Dick. “What About the National League and New York?” *Sport*, p. 24.

Modern Language Association 8th edition formatting by BibMe.org.

Made in the USA
Columbia, SC
05 April 2021